ENCYCLOPAEDIA OF MANIPUR

ENCYCLOPAEDIA OF MANIPUR

(In 3 Volumes)

(Volume-1)

DR. KHOMDON SINGH LISAM

KALPAZ

Encyclopaedia of Manipur

ISBN: 978-81-7835-864-2 (set)
ISBN : 978-81-7835-865-9 (Vol. 1)

Published in 2011 in India by
Kalpaz Publications
C-30, Satyawati Nagar,
Delhi-110052
E-mail: kalpaz@hotmail.com
Phone : 9212729499

Laser Type Setting by: Rudra Computer Graphics, Delhi
Printed at : Chawla Offset Printers, Delhi

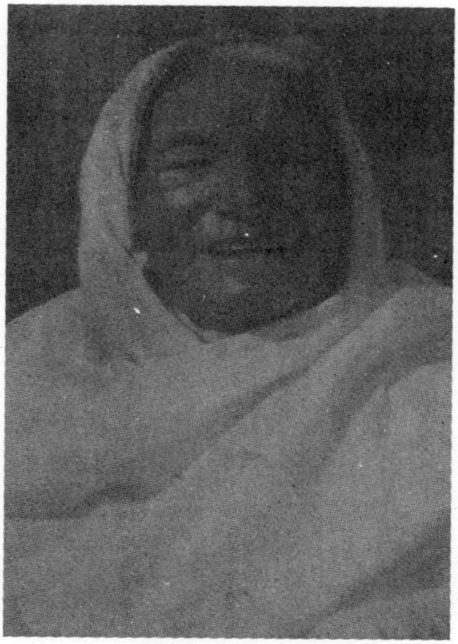

Dedicated to loving memory of my mother (Late) Lisam Ongbi Mandalini (Tondonbi) Devi (8-1 1904-30-3-1992)

Contents

Foreword xi
Preface xiii
Acknowledgements xv

1. **Introduction** 1
• Why should you visit Manipur ? • Entry Formalities / Protected Area Permit(PAP) • Inner Line Permit • Customs and Duties • How to reach Imphal • Hotel Facilities • Travel Agents • Courier Services • Health Precautions • Facts about Manipur • City Distances • Important Telephones • Places of Interest • Excursions • Shopping in Manipur

2. **Origin of Manipur and Historical Evidences** 32
• Creation of the Galaxy • Creation of Manipur: A legend • Creation of Yek and Salai • Different names of Manipur and Manipur's relations with neighbouring kingdoms • Origin of the name –Manipur • Origin of Meiteis : • Migration • Historical Evidence • Ancient Books –Chronicles or the Puyas • Stone inscriptions and Copper/Iron Plates • Coins • Historical Relevance • Account left by Europeans • Archaeological findings • Archivial sources

3. **Geography, Fauna and Flora** 55
• Climate • Boundaries of Manipur • Hill Ranges • Rivers • Lakes • Water falls • Caves • Fauna and Flora • Wildlife-a rich heritage of Manipur • Keibul Lamjao National Park • Birds,

Reptiles, common animals • Fishes • Soil • Forest • Vegetation • Wet Hill Forest • Pinus Casia Forests • Wet Temperate Forests • Sub-Alpine Forests • Teak Gurjan Forests • Semi Evergreen Forests • Trees of Manipur • Bamboo Brakes of Manipur • Cane Brakes of Manipur • Mushrooms • Rubber • Tree Bean Cultivation • Mineral resources • Flowers • Shirui Lily • Orchids • Fruits

4. **Manipur Kingdom and Kings** **118**

• Chronicle of the Manipur Kings • Great Historical Gap 1199-44 B.C. • Kingship • Lakpas • Military Service • Land Revenue • Changes in the administrative structure during various kingships • Re-organization as a result of contact with neighbouring kings • Administration of Villages • Service Relationship • Phamnaiba • Lalupkaba • Loipotkaba • Judiciary Relationship • Religious Relationship • Important Kings / Maharajas of Manipur • Tangja Leela Pakhangba • Ningthou Kangba • Koi Koi • Poireiton Khunthokpa • Luwang Punshiba • Nongda Lairen Pakhangba • Khuiyoi Tompoak • Ura Konthouba • Naothingkhong • Meidingu Ayaangba • Meidingu Yanglou Keiphaba • Meidingu Loiyumba • Meidingu Loitongba • Ningthou Khomba • Meidingu Senbi Kyaamba • Mungyamba • Khagemba • Charai Rongba • Garib Niwaj • Chit Shai • Bharat Shai • Gourshyam • Maharaja Bhagyachandra (Chingthangkhomba or Jai Singh) • Labanya Chandra and Madhuchandra • Chourajit • Marjit Singh • Hirachandra • Advance of Gambheer Singh and Signing of Treaty of Yandabo • Raja Gambheer Singh • Maharaja Chandrakirti • Maharaja Nara Singh • Maharaja Devendra Singh • Maharaja Chandrakirti • Maharaja Surchandra Singh • The Palace Revolution, 1891 • Maharaja Kulachandra • Anglo-Manipuri War of 1891 • Khongjom War • Trial and Execution of Tikendrajit and Thangal General • Jubaraj Tikendrajit • Thangal General • Maharaja Kulachandra Dhaja • Prince Angousana Senapati • Maharaja Churachand Singh • Maharaja Bodhchandra Singh • Irabot's struggle for a responsible government• Movement for a responsible Government in Manipur • Indian Independence Act of 1947 •

Situation of Manipur immediately before independence • Signing of Stand Still Agreement and Instrument of Accession • Stand Still Agreement • Instrument of Accession • Political development in Manipur after India's Independence • First Election and formation of a Ministry • Situation of Princely States immediately before Independence • Merger Agreement with other princely states • Situation of Manipur immediately before the Merger Agreement • Signing of Manipur Merger Agreement. • Maharaja Okendrajit

5. **Population and People** **294**
• The People of Manipur • Census Population • Meitei Pangan • Sikhs • Nepalese • Biharis • Marawaris • Punjabis • South Indians • Bengalis • Society and Conduct of the Manipuris • Government and Politics • Religion

6. **Meiteis** **308**
• Physical features • Meitei Clans –Salais/ Yek • Meitei Sagei and Yumnaks • Creation of Yumnak • Sagei • Apokpa Khurumba • Yum Mangba • Piba • Pibaren • Ningthou • Forms of address • Social Mores • Meitei Houses • Meitei Dress and Ornaments • Occupation • Meitei Food • Meitei Rituals • Totems • Manipuri language (Meiteilon): • Manipuri Mayek and Scriptures • Some of the common words and respectful terms of Manipuri language • Meitei Literature • Meitei Religion and Animism • The Meitei Lais • Sanamahi • The Umang Lais (Sylvan Gods) • Tree Cults of Ancient Manipur • Sacred Stones • Bamon/ Purohitism • Maibas and Maibis • Shumang Lila • Manipur Theatres • Chorus Repertory Theatre • Manipuri Cinema • Meitei Folk Songs

7. **Lois, Yaithibi and Bishnupriya** **359**
• Lois • Yaithibi • Bishnupriya

Foreword

A close reading of the work provides a wealth of information on the social organisation of muslims along "Shaqzi:(clans) kinship groups related -.by blood some difficult to trace to their *original* clans of Pangals. The reader also gets a close look at domestic life in the rural-agrarian backdrop; the education steps from maktabs to formal instruction; the skills to be mastered by a girl such as weave-phanek, khudei, pheijom; young girls trained in etiquette, court language, administration and even martial arts; customs that felicitously combined traditions of Meitei's and Muslims of Bengal. There is also considerable research on occupations and special skills, design of dwellings, cuisine and food habits, dress codes and fashions, extensive participation in agriculture and animal husbandry etc. We are also told of enrichment of vocabulary by use- of Arabic, Urdu. and-.Farsi-wordsand' phrases. The impact of Ulema and Tablighi Jamaat has been highlighted and the traditional and historical participation of Muslim women in public affairs contrasted with somewhat disappointing picture amongst the Muslims of Manipur. However, the periodic sparks of awakening are gradually merging into a more promising glow of participatory political empowerment.

The author is herself a distinguish daughter of Manipur and proudly holds the flag of equality and empowerment. By placing her researches in the public realm she has justifiably sought a place in the Sun. May she continue to be the mirror of Manipur's unique mosaic picture of little India. One can certainly place this book as part of the bonding process of India's vast and varies heritage. It makes essential reading for every person who wants to know India in its entirety.

The story of modem India is written in words and phrases contributed by many different cultures. Historians have followed differing philosophies of historiography in assessing the processes by which our composite civilization has grown. Be that as it may for different parts of India, at least for Manipur the wholesome organic assimilation theory is validated by the research that has gone into the writing of this remarkable book on the Muslims of Manipur, described variously as Pangals (derived from the word Bengal and from where the migration took place) or Meitei Pangals. Of course in Bengal itself the arrival and advent of Islam was largely the consequence of the annexation by the dynasty of Chaghatai Turks, commonly known as the Mughals. Of course as the first chapter itself shows Manipur did get targetted by a combined force of Kachari and Muslim mercenaries early in the 17th century.

Salam Irene, Professor of History at the University of Manipur has a clear ring side view of the muslim community of Manipur, almost 8 percent of the population. To many outsiders this itself would be news whilst the author takes the reader on a virtual sight seeing tour of the muslim population. Many were made prisoners and in due course settled down as a useful community, marrying Meitei women. Another significant contribution according to the author was made by the mystics or fakirs who arrived in Manipur and whose personalties had a deep impact on the population. By the beginning of the 20th century madras's began to be established, with first one at lillong.

Salman Khurshid

Preface

There are many books written by distinguished experts covering various topics like history, geography, cultures, dances, Thang Ta, sports etc. and also about the various tribes in Manipur. However there is no book which describes all the important aspects of history, geography, cultures, dances, Thang Ta, sports etc. in a single book. If any student or researcher or outsider or foreigner wants to know something of everything about Manipur, there is nothing to offer. The British Political Officers and Writers had made great contributions to Manipur by writing many books about Manipur during the 19th and beginning of 20th century. These books give useful information about Meiteis, Nagas, Kukis, their cultures and traditions etc. The people of Manipur are very grateful to them for their great contribution. However, some of these books did not reflect the true picture about the people of Manipur perhaps due to time constraints of their research and lack of adequate knowledge about the primary source. In few cases, they gave a distorted picture about Manipur to fulfill their hidden agenda and vested interest. Again, there are books written by eminent authors, which try to link Manipur with the mainstream Hindus or Sanskrit right from the beginning of Manipur history, which is a remote possibility. All these factors lead to controversies, confusions and heart burning among the youths of Manipur today. When any new Governor or bureaucrat or foreigner comes to Manipur, they come after reading these books with the result that they come with certain pre-conceived ideas and distorted view about the people of Manipur. Thus there is a wide gap between the true picture of Manipur and what the outsiders perceive.

This book will become handy to fill up this gap. The idea of writing this kind of book about Manipur obsessed me for many years. But I could not do so earlier because of my professional engagement.The main objective of this book is to present the various aspects of Manipur in a concise, easily understandable and readable form so that the young people of Manipur or any outsider or foreigner can have a better idea about the history, geography, population, cultures, ethnicity, religion etc. about Manipur.

As a part of my professional work, I had the opportunity to study the cultures of people of different countries and different states in India, which posed as a risk factor to the spread of certain diseases. The different cultures in different countries of Africa had contributed a lot to the rapid spread of HIV/AIDS. Similarly, the different ethnic groups in Europe, America or Australia have contrasting rate of HIV prevalence. I had the opportunity to study the traditions, cultures and taboos of various tribes in Manipur during the last ten years or so. When I visited the countries of South East Asia, I found similarities in our physical features, food, social habits and cultures and even thinking Moreover, there are many ongoing debates regarding the Manipur Merger Agreement, Irabot's movement for a responsible government and ongoing peace talks with the Nagas, upcoming Trans Asian Highways, Indo-Myanmar Border Trade, Investment opportunities in Manipur etc. These issues unless tackled timely will have far reaching consequences to Manipur. All these factors kindled my enthusiasm and my research work to go deeper towards a possible meaningful solution.

I hope that this small book will serve as a ready reference book about Manipur. Any young person or anybody visiting Manipur for the first time will find it useful as a ready reference material about Manipur.

Dr. Khomdon Singh Lisam

Acknowledgements

During the course of my research study, I have taken advantage of many sources from various libraries in Manipur, Delhi, Kolkata and also many internet sources and published materials. I have interviewed many eminent scholars, experts in various fields and I have discussed and consulted with them. I have visited many places, temples, historical sites, monuments and participated in many rituals. I have travelled to many villages both in the hills and valley and stayed with people to collect the relevant facts and information. I gratefully acknowledge their valuable contributions, help and support in the preparation of this publication.

I have referred to many books written by eminent scholars like Atombapu Sharma Vidyaratna, Padmashri N. Khelchandra, Singh, R.K. Sanahal Singh, L.M. Iboongohal Singh, N.K. Sanajaoba, Gangumei Kabui, Lal Dena, E. Nilakanta Singh, M. Horam, R.K. Jhalajit Singh, Sarangthem Bormani Singh, Hijam Mani Singh, Loitongbam Kalachand Singh, Pandit Ngariyambam Kulachandra Singh, Moirangthem Chandra Singh, Chongtham Iboyaima Meitei, Kh. Chandra Singh, O. Bhogeshwar Singh, Ng. Kullachandra, N. Gorachandra, Khumanlambam Yaima, Tomcha Meitei, W. Yumjao Singh,O. Kumar Singh, L. Udhob Singh, Dr. M. Kirti Singh, Dr. Smt. K. Sobita Devi, Mayanglambam Gourchandra, Dr. Saroj Nalini Parrat, S.A Ansari, Dr. S.N. Pandey, Chander Sheikher Panchani, Dr. Kh. Sarojini Devi, V.P. Sharma, B.G. Verghese, Charles Chasie, B. Dattaray, Langsun D. Mate, A.S.W. Shimray etc. I have also referred to the books written by European and other Indian writers.

I have interviewed many people on various topics like history, dances, temples, U-mang Lais. I have visited many historical and tourist sites, temples and U-mang Lais. I have also referred to many articles contributed by various writers, which appeared in E-Pao and Kanglaonline. Further I have also consulted all available books about Manipur in the State Central Library, Manipur University. I have also downloaded many resource materials from the internet.

I have interviewed many authorities on various topics like Thang Ta, Manipuri Dances, Polo, Orchids. I have also collected many information from various government departments like the Planning, Industry, Agriculture, Forestry, Horticulture, Sports etc I can not list here all the names of the persons who have given me guidance and support during the preparation of this publication. However, I humbly offer my deep gratitude to the following persons for their help, support, encouragement and contribution to make this publication a success.

I owe my gratitude and indebtedness to Shri L. Rabindra Singh, District and Sessions Judge (Retired) (Earlier Member of the Manipur Human Rights Commission), who have taken pains to read the manuscript many times and has given suggestions to improve the draft in many aspects. I am also grateful to Dr. Konsam Saratchandra Singh, Head, Department of Anthropology, Manipur University for examining the anthropological aspects of the study and Dr. Ch. Priyoranajan Singh, Professor of Economics, Manipur University for giving information on the Indo-Myanmar Border Trade. My special thanks goes to Sarangthem Bormani Singh, Padmashree N. Khelchandra Singh; Mutua Bahadur, P. Bharat Singh, IAS Commissioner (GAD and Arts and Culture), Government of Manipur, Dilip Mayengbam, Director, Jawaharlal Nehru Dance Academy, Ph. Iboton Singh, Pradhan Guru, Jawaharlal Nehru Dance Academy, Smt. Nimita Devi of Nimita Nritya Ashram, Sagolabdn Bijoygovinda, Shri Kangujam Mangi Singh, Director of Planning, Government of Manipur, Shri T. Sitlhou IAS, Director of Department of Information and Public Relations, Government of Manipur, Maisnam. Pahari Singh, Joint Director, Department of Youth Affaires and Sports, Badrinarayan Sharma, Secretary, Department of Tourism, Government of Manipur, Lisam Upendra Singh, Agriculture Officer, Thoubal, Dhanabati Laishram, Curator of Manipur State Museum for giving me materials in connection with the study. I am also grateful to M.K. Tamphasana Devi for allowing me to reproduce some of the old and rare photographs of the Manipur Royal families in this publication.

I am also grateful to Dr. Maisnam Damayanti, District Leprosy Officer, Medical Directorate, Manipur, M. Brajeswori Devi of Sagolband Babuthong, Mr. Umanand Lisam, Southern Palace Compound, Imphal, Dr. Suchitra Lisam, Programme Officer, National AIDS Control Organization, Government of India, New Delhi, Dr. Yumnam Arunkumar Singh, Under Secretary, Lok Sabha, New Delhi, Mrs. Sapam Sandhyarani Devi, Southern Palace Compound, Imphal, Mr. Dayanand Lisam, Southern Palace Compound, Imphal, Korou Lisam, Southern Palace Compound, Imphal, Hyeithoi Lisam, Southern Palace Compound, Imphal, Thokchom Seilendra Singh (Nanao), Heingang, Imphal East for their contribution during the preparation of this book.

I must make a special mention of Shri Khuraijam Krishnan Singh of Nest Advertising Agency (opposite 1st Bn. Manipur Rilfes) and his team for the cover design of the book. Photo credit should go to Mr. R.K. Budhimanta of RKCS Art Gallery, the E-pao, the Kanglaonline, Mr. Ph. Santosh of Leinong Photo Studio, Konung Mamang. Manipur State Museum, Kangla Museum and the Kangla Museum. I am very grateful to them for permitting me to use some of the rare photographs in this publication.

Last but not the least, I am grateful to Mr. Misra, Kalpaz Publications, Delhi for publishing this book.

Dr. Khomdon Singh Lisam

Volume - 1

1

Introduction

Manipur is an extraordinary place, full of charm, beauty and creativity. According to some, Manipur is "A Little Paradise on Earth", to others the "Switzerland of the East" and to many more the "Jewel of India"or "a flower on lofty heights". Really the natural beauty of Manipur has no comparison. Nature has bestowed all her treasures to decorate Manipur. The natural beauty of Manipur is very pleasing to the eyes. Enchanted by its beauty, Pandit Jawaharlal Nehru named it the "Kashmir of the East". It is a small hilly state with blue and green hills, carpets of flowers on the plains and the roof of the blue sky overhead. In the midst of all these are seen hilly falls, rivers and rivulets flowing over the entire valley. It is a "Magic Land", a "Green Paradise". It combines so many and such varied passions and beauties that one has to take a pause at least for its praise. (See Map of Manipur-Plate-1)

WHY SHOULD YOU VISIT MANIPUR ?

- It is a fascinating destination for discerning tourists. Legends say that discovery of Manipur is the result of the delight the God took in dancing. It is this remarkable bid that gives Manipur a unique identity of her own. Blessed with a salubrious climate, famous for its distinctive diverse cultures and its evergreen scenic beauty, extend the tourists a cordial invitation to visit Manipur.
- The people of Manipur are friendly, hospitable, who believe in the principle of "the Guest are the Gods"

- Manipur which literally means the "land of jewels" is a land wrapped in velvety silence. Described by Lord Irwin as the "Switzerland of India", Manipur boasts of an exotic landscape with gently undulating hills, emerald green valleys, blue lakes and dense forests, and is the gateway to the North-Eastern Region.
- The climate is very comfortable . It never goes above 36 degree.
- The modern polo game, the king of games is a gift of Manipur to the world.
- Manipur is famous for its classical and folk dances, including the graceful and soft Raas Lila, the acrobatic Pung cholom among others and the dance during the festival of God "*Lai-Haraoba*" known as "Maibi Dance". There are also various dances like Tangkhul Naga Dance, Kabui Naga Dance etc. with beautiful, exhotic dress. Manipuri dance has charmed dance-lovers from around the world. The *Raas Lila* festival has now become a national festival of Manipur. The Raas Lila dance is the outcome of king Bhagyachandra's idea of paying homage to the God, Sri Govindajee-based on *Sri Krishna's 'Lila* (play) with the Gopis. Lai-*Haraoba,* the dance festival to celebrate the reaping of new harvests in April-May is now regarded as a national festival.
- Manipur is a land of festivals.
- Keibul Lamjao, the National Park in Loktak lake is the natural habitat of the rare and endangered Brow Antlered Deer *(cervus eldi eldi)* locally known as *Sangai*. It is one of the three species of *eldi* deer in the world confined to South East Asia. Probably the most unusual natural habitat of Sangai is the floating mass of vegetation (Phumdi) on Loktak Lake, south of Imphal.
- Shirui Lily (*Lilium macklinae sealy*) is a beautiful lily found only in the upper reaches of the Shirui Hills in Manipur's Ukhrul District.
- The Indian National Army (INA), led by Netaji Subhash Chandra Bose, hoisted the Indian National Flag, Tricolour at Moirang, Manipur which was the second town liberated by the INA, the first place being Andaman and Nicobar islands. On 10th May, 1942 Japan bombed Imphal and Manipur became one of the chief arenas of fighting during the second World War. The Indian National Army (Azad Hind Forces / INA), organised by Subhash Chandra Bose, liberated a portion of Manipur from the British power.
- Manipur is also famous for its handloom industry. The handloom industry in Manipur has become a household cottage industry. Manipur

handicrafts have wide fame. Tourists cannot avoid the attractions of artifacts of bamboo and cane, table mats, embroidered bags, bedspreads and many more articles. Every house in Manipur has a handloom.

- *Rosa macrocarpa*, the beautiful species of rose, was discovered by Sir George Watt in Manipur in 1888.
- Sarit Sarak and Thang-Ta, relatively unknown and unique Manipuri Martial Art, is a very popular and impressive indigenous game of Manipur.
- Manipur is a virgin soil for any kind of anthropological research.
- Manipur has got two war cemeteries which is a living memory of those British and Japanese soldiers who sacrificed their lives for the sake of their mother land during the World War-II. There are two cemeteries maintained by the British War Graves Commission in Manipur, which are the final resting places of several Indian and allied soldiers who died here.

ENTRY FORMALITIES / PROTECTED AREA PERMIT (PAP)

Manipur is considered a sensitive border state. All foreigners intending to visit Manipur are required to obtain the **Protected** Area Permit (PAP) in addition to the valid Indian VISA.

The entire State of Manipur is under the protected area regime under the Foreigners (Protected Areas) Order, 1958. The PAP permit issued under Paragraph 3 shall be in the form specified in Schedule-II (annexed to the Order, 1958) and shall contain the following particulars: -

1. the place of entry into the protected area,
2. the place of residence, if any, in the protected area,
3. the period for which the permit shall be valid,
4. the conditions subject to which the permission is granted.

The conditions are to be specified by the issuing authority. The competent authorities to issue PAP include MHA (Ministry of Home Affaires), FRROs (Foreigners' Regional Registration Officer) at Delhi, Mumbai and Calcutta, Chief Immigration Officer, Chennai, all Indian Missions abroad and Home Commissioner, Manipur. The Resident Commissioner, Manipur Bhawan, New Delhi is also competent to issue PAP to those foreigners visiting Manipur in connection with World Bank and UN aided projects and projects sponsored by the Govt. of India or State Government. Permits are granted in pre-determined formats giving all details and DOs and DONTs for the tourists and various concerned agencies.

Open Places

At present, the following places are open to the foreigners:

- Imphal (See Map of Imphal- Plate 2)
- Loktak Lake,
- Moirang INA Memorial
- Keibul Lamjao Deer sanctuary,
- Waithou Lake and
- Khongjom War Memorial.

The following additional places are also open to foreign group tourists:

- Imphal-Bishnupur-Phubala-Moirang-Sendra- Keibul Lamjao-Imphal;
- Imphal- Moirang -Loktak Lake-Keibul Lamjao-Churachandpur-Khuga-Imphal;
- Imphal-Litan-Ukhrul- Shirui -Sangsak-Imphal;
- Imphal-Thoubal-Waithou-Lake-Khongjom-Kakching-Thongjao-Waikhong-Sugnu-Imphal;
- Imphal-Khonghampat-Kanglatongbi-Kangpokpi-Senapati-Karong-Mao Gate-Imphal;
- Imphal-Noneh-Khongsang-Nungba-Jiribam-Imphal.

The PAP is subject to the following conditions:

(a) Foreigners are permitted to visit open areas only in groups of four or more. However, in case of married couples, a group may consist of two persons;

(b) Period of stay in open places will be up to a maximum of 10 days;

(c) Foreigners associated with the Government projects are given permits for full period of work;

At present foreigners are required to travel by air from Delhi/Kolkata / Guwahati to Imphal. Foreign tourists are also allowed to enter by road along the NH-39 and NH-53.

The road circuit to be followed is :-

Dimapur-Kohima-Imphal or Silchar- Jiribam-Imphal

The State Home Department has issued a Notification dated 8th September, 2000 thereby requiring foreign nationals who are visiting Manipur to apply in the prescribed application forms to the State Home Department, Resident Commissioner, Manipur Bhawan, New Delhi, Deputy Resident

Commissioner/Kolkata and Deputy Resident Commissioner/Guwahati at least 4 (four) weeks before their proposed visit. Permission will be granted for specified tour circuits as identified with definite entry and exit points and a specified mode of transport.

You can ask your embassy to help you to speed up the process. If you are traveling in a group of four or more, you can submit the application direct to the Home Department, Government of Manipur. The process usually takes around 30 days. If you are coming on the invitation of some body from Manipur, the best option will be to ask the local men to help you in the process. There is no system of Permit on arrival .You have to mention the names of the places to be visited in your application. Furthermore, you should come to Imphal only by air and will not be permitted to travel outside the capital unless specified.

For obtaining permits, tourists may contact the following addresses:

Ministry of Home Affairs,
North Block,
Central Secretariat, New Delhi 110 001
Phones: 23092462, 23017256, 23092631, 23092361, 23092113
Fax: 23015750, 23017763

New Delhi

F. R. R. O.: Rajesh Khurana
Phone: 011 2671-1348 (Tele Fax), 23383075, 23383888 (Fax) 011-2626-2300 (R)
Email: boihq@mha.nic.infrrodelhi@hotmail.comfrrodli@nic.in
Address: In charge Foreigner's Registration (F&R) Branch East Block-VIII, Level-II, Sector-1, R.K. Puram,New Delhi - 110 066
Contact Person at AirportAFRRO (Departure/Arrival) 011 2565-2389
Contact Phone No: 011 26711-1443011 2619-5530, 2617-1944 Ext. 142/302/141011 2619-2634 Ext. 142/302/141

Mumbai

F. R. R. O.: Rajvardhan
Phone: 022 2262-1169 (O)022 2262-0721 (Fax)
Email: frromum@nic.indcpsb2.frro@indiatimes.com
Address: 3rd Floor, Special Branch Bldg.,Badruddin Tayabji Lane, Behind St. Xavier's College, Mumbai - 400 001
Contact Person at AirportAFRRO (Departure/Arrival) 022 26828098

Chennai

F. R. R. O.: Avi Prakash
Phone: 044 2345-4970 (O)044 2345-4971 (Fax)
Email: chiochn@nic.in
Address: Shastri Bhawan26 Haddows RoadChennai - 600 006
Contact Person at AirportAFRRO (Departure/Arrival) 044 2345-4977

Amritsar

F. R. R. O.: Vijay Kumar
Phone: 0183 250-8250 (O)
Email: frroasr@nic.in
Address: 123-D Ranjit Avenue,Amritsar - 143 001
Contact Person at AirportAFRRO (Departure/Arrival) 0183 259-2986

Bangalore

Commissioner of Police: 080 22260707, 22256242 Ext. 222; D.C.P. Intelligence: 080 22200920, 22256242 Ext. 291

Table -1 Entry Formalities Protected Area Permit for Foreigners

Commissioner (Home), Government of Manipur	Old Secretariat, Imphal: 795001	Telephone: 0385-2450488
Resident Commissioner, Manipur Bhawan, New Delhi	Bir Tikendrajit Marg, Chanakyapuri, New Delhi: 110021	011-26870098 011-26113150
Manipur Bhawan, New Delhi	2-Sardar Patel Marg, Chankyapuri, New Delhi-110021	011-26879846/ 47/48/49/50 26873311
Deputy Resident Commissioner Manipur Bhawan, Kolkata	26, Rowland Road Kolkata -700020	033-24747930 24742453, 247580' 24758163
Deputy Resident Commissioner Manipur Bhawan, Guwahati	Rajgarh Road, Guwahati	0361-2526707, 2540707, 2451268,2451968

Foreign Nationals who wish to visit Manipur must submit an application for Protected Area Permit (PAP) for entering Manipur in a prescribed application form which can be obtained from the following offices of the Government of Manipur on payment of Rs. 10/- (per form).

The application forms for Protected Area Permit (PAP) for entering Manipur shall be submitted or sent by posts to the offices listed above at least 4 (four) weeks before the proposed visit.

Every foreigner granted Protected Area Permit (PAP) shall be charged a fee of Rs.1500/-. Any extension of the period of the permit requires the payment of an additional fee to be decided by the state government. Grant of PAP is subject to the following conditions:·The period of stay in the place is up to 10 days

· Foreigners associated with Government projects will be given permit for full period of the work

http://travel.mapsofindia.com/travel-manipur offers online booking of hotels and tour packages to Manipur and all over India.

INNER LINE PERMIT:

If you prefer to come by road, you are required to obtain "Inner Line Permit" in addition to the Restricted Area Permit for passing through Nagaland (National Highway No-39). In 1873, in order to check the exploitation of the tribes, a traffic regulation was made for Naga Hills by the British Government (Bengal East Regulation–I, Section–V) between the hill areas and the low plain lands of the state by introducing an Inner Line Permit. According to this Act, no outsider could go without an official pass beyond Dimapur. Therefore, any one who wants to visit Manipur *via* Nagaland requires Inner Line Permit from the Union Ministry of Home Affairs (for Foreigners) or by the Deputy Resident Commissioner at Nagaland House, Delhi, Calcutta and Assistant Resident Commissioner, Shillong; Additional Deputy Commissioner, Dimapur; Deputy Commissioner, Kohima and Deputy Commissioner, Mokokchung. A permit fee of Rs. 5.00 is realised from each applicant.and from the SDO (Civil), Dimapur (Nagaland) (for any Indian).

Tourists from other Indian States except from Manipur intending to visit Manipur by road via Dimapur/Kohima require Inner Line Permit to pass through Nagaland. These are issued by the Liaison offices of the Government of Nagaland at New Delhi, Kolkata, Guwahati, Shillong and the Sub-Divisional officer (Civil), Dimapur. Deputy Commissioner, Imphal can also issue permit to tourists traveling by road from Imphal to Kohima and Dimapur to Nagaland. The said inner line permit system is still prevalent in Nagaland since 1873.

However, there is no restriction for any Indian citizen visiting Manipur by air and by way of Silchar through Cachar Road.

CUSTOMS AND DUTIES

Entering India

If you are bringing dutiable articles or unaccompanied baggage or high-value articles into India with you, these must be entered on a Tourist

Baggage Re-Export Form (TBRE). These articles must be re-exported at the time of departure. Failure to re-export anything listed on the TBRE means you'll have to pay a duty levied for each missing item.

You can bring in the following duty-free: personal effects (clothes and jewellery); cameras and up to five rolls of film; binoculars; a portable musical instrument; a radio or portable tape recorder; a tent and camping equipment; sports equipment (fishing rod, a pair of skis, two tennis rackets); 200 cigarettes or 50 cigars; 0.95 litres of liquor; and gifts not exceeding a value of Rs. 600 (about $14). You may not bring in dangerous drugs or firearms, gold coins, gold and silver bullion and silver coins not in use, Indian currency, or live plants. Depending on the attitude of the customs' official, you may or may not have to enter a portable Laptop computer on a TBRE form.

Departing India

Rupees are not allowed out of India. You must exchange them before you depart. The State Bank of India (SBI), Imphal (Mahatma Gandhi / MG Avenue) is the only bank which offer exchange facilities in Manipur. There is no exchange facility at the airport.

All animal products, souvenirs, and trophies are subject to the Wildlife (Protection) Act, 1972. The export of skins made from protected wildlife species is not allowed and India is becoming increasingly rigorous in its monitoring of such exports. Such items cannot be imported into many countries, including the United States of America. As a general rule, avoid any souvenir made of wild animal skins (except crocodile-leather goods). Ivory, unless it can be proved to be old, is also not allowed in the United States, although it is widely available for purchase. Help stop the poaching, which is reducing elephant herds: Don't buy ivory products.

Generally, items more than 100 years old cannot be exported without a permit from the Archaeological Survey of India. Reputable shops will provide you with the required permit or help you procure it. Items without permits will be detained by Indian Customs if they are believed to be over 100 years old.

HOW TO REACH IMPHAL

Imphal airport, 7 km south of Imphal town, is connected by Indian Airlines to Kolkata (5 weekly; 1 hour 5 min), Silchar (3 weekly; 35 min), Guwahati (5 weekly, 45 minutes) and Delhi (2 weekly; 3 hour 10 min). The Indian Airlines office is at the Mahatma Gandhi (MG) Avenue (0385- 2220999). However, schedules for flights may be disrupted. You have to check either in Delhi/

Kolkata/Guwahati or once you are in Imphal. Nowadays, many airlines such as Indigo, Jet Airways, Air Deccan, Kingfisher are also operating. The fares are quite reasonable and cheap

The major airlines that operate from the Imphal Airport are as follows:

Airlines and destinations

- Air Deccan (Guwahati, Kolkata, Silchar, Dimapur)
- Indian Airlines (Kolkata, Guwahati, Guwahati, Aizawl, Silchar, Dimapur)
- Indigo Airlines (Delhi, Guwahati, Agartala, Kolkata}
- Jet Airways (Kolkata, Guwahati)
- Jet Lite (Kolkata, Guwahati)
- Kingfisher Airlines from Bangalore, Guwahati, Hyderabad and Kolkata

By Air From Imphal

Table-2 Showing telephone numbers of important airlines

Name	*Designation/Place*	*Phone Number*
Air Deccan	Call Centre	1 800 425 7008
	Kolkata Office	033 25112150 / 9339393682
Indian Airlines	Station Master	245 50746
	Station In-charge	22452 0999
	Station Manager	245 0199 / 2454273
Indigo	Call Centre	99 10 38 38 38 / 1 800 180 3838
	Guwahati Office	99548 90345
Jet Airways	Hotel Nirmala	244 1547 / 244 1546
	M.G. Avenue	223 0834 / 223 0835 / 223 0836 / 244 4907
	Imphal Airport	245 8607
King Fisher	Call Center	1800 1800 101

Indian Airlines connect Imphal with cities like New Delhi, Kolkata, Guwahati, Aizwal and Silchar. It also connects with Mumbai, Bangalore and Chennai via Kolkata.

Table-3 Showing flight details of Indian Airlines

To	*Days of Operation*	*Flight No*	*Departure.*	*Arrival*
Aizawl	1,3,5	CD 7212	1210	1240
Delhi	4,7	IC 890	1425	1815
Guwahati	4,7	IC 890	1425	1515
Kolkata	1,3,5	CD 7212	1210	1405
	2,4,6	CD 7256	1215	1415
	7	IC 714	1145	1250
Silchar	2,4,6	CD 7256	1215	1245

Table-4 Showing flight timings of Indian Airlines

Sector	*Days of operation*	*Flight No.*	*Departure*	*Arrival*
Imphal-Silchar	Mon, Thurs and Sun	CD7708	1350	1425
Silchar-Imphal	Mon, Thurs and Sun	CD7707	1255	1330
Imphal-Silchar	Tue, Sat	CD7256	1215	1245
Silchar-Imphal	Tue, Sat	CD7255	1115	1145
Imphal-Aizawl	Mon,Wed and Fri	CD7212	1210	1240
Aizawl-Imphal	Mon,Wed and Fri	CD7211	1110	1140
Imphal-Guwahati	Tuesday	CD7762	1300	1400
Guwahati-Imphal	Tuesday	CD7761	1140	1240
Imphal-Guwahati	Saturday	CD7762	1120	1220
Guwahati-Imphal	Saturday	CD7761	1000	1100
Imphal-Guwahati	Wed and Sun	IC890	1415	1505
Guwahati-Imphal	Wed and Sun	IC889	1250	1340
Imphal-Kolkata	Mon, Wed and Fri	CD7212	1210	1405
Kolkata-Imphal	Mon, Wed and Fri	CD7211	945	1140
Imphal-Kolkata	Sunday	CD7218	1120	1225
Kolkata-Imphal	Sunday	CD7217	945	1050
Imphal-Kolkata	Tue and Sat	CD7256	1215	1415
Kolkata-Imphal	Tue and Sat	CD7255	945	1145
Imphal-Delhi	Wed and Sun	IC890	1415	1805
Delhi-Imphal	Wed and Sun	IC889	1000	1340

Please confirm the Airlines timing either with Indian Air Lines office or Any Travel Agency at Imphal.

By Bus to Imphal

1. From Guwahati daily on the NH- 39 via Dimapur and Kohima. Manipur State Road Transport Corporation (MSRTC) and many other private buses available.

Table-5 Showing flight timings of Jet Airways

Phone No . City Office 2230835-36.			*Airport*	*2455054/2455121*
Sector	*Days of operation*	*Flight No.*	*Departure*	*Arrival*
Imphal-Guwahati	Mon, Tue, Wed, Fri and Sat	9W616	1435	1525
Guwahati-Imphal	Mon, Tue, Wed, Fri and Sat	9W615	1250	1340
Imphal-Kolkata (via Guwahati)	Mon, Tue, Wed, Fri and Sat	9W616	1435	1710
Kolkata-Imphal (via Guwahati)	Mon, Tue, Wed, Fri and Sat	9W615	1130	1405
Guwahati-Kolkata	Daily	9W207	1205	1315
Kolkata-Guwahati	Daily	9W201	1015	1125
Guwahati-Kolkata	Thurs and Sun	9W622	1600	1710
Kolkata-Guwahati	Thurs and Sun	9W621	1105	1215
Guwahati-Kalkota	Mon, Tue, Wed, Fri and Sat	9W616	1600	1710
Kolkata-Guwahati	Mon, Tue, Wed, Fri and Sat	9W615	1105	1215
Guwahati-Delhi (via Bagdogra)	Mon, Wed and Fri	9W601	1300	1630
Delhi-Guwahati	Mon, Wed and Fri	9W601	1010	1225
Guwahati-Delhi	Tue, Thurs, Sat and Sun	9W602	1405	1630
Delhi-Guwahati (via Bagdogra)	Tue, Thurs, Sat and Sun	9W602	1010	1330

2. From Dimapur daily on the NH 39 via Kohima. Manipur State Road Transport Corporation (MSRTC) and many other private buses available.
3. From Silchar daily on the NH 53 via Jiribam. Manipur State Road Transport Corporation (MSRTC) and many other private buses available.

By Train to Imphal

There is no direct train service to Imphal. Dimapur (Nagaland), 215 kms from Imphal, is the nearest railhead. Another railhead is Jiribam, a small town 225 kms from Imphal bordering Silchar. But travellers can come up to Guwahati or Dimapur (nearest rail head from Imphal) and then rest of the journey by bus or by air to reach Imphal.

Imphal is connected by road with Guwahati (Assam) through National Highway No. 39 passing from Dimapur to Imphal and National Highway 53, passing from Silchar (Assam) to Imphal.

State buses arrive at Imphal at the Bus stand next to the North AOC and private buses at their individual offices. Bus connections with Guwahati are good but the 579-kilometre journey takes around twenty hours. Manipur Golden Travels at MG Road (Phone -221332), provides by far the best service. The 225-kilometre bus ride to Silchar with Kangleipak Tours & Travels, MG Road (Phone-222911), may look tempting, but security checkpoints along the way make it a nightmare of fourteen hours.

Auto-rickshaws and cycle rickshaws are the main means of public transport within Imphal, and taxis and rental cars can be booked through hotels. The cycle rickshaw drivers of Imphal wear water-proof straw caps, and cover their mouth and nose to keep out dust and fumes.

The telephone area STD code for Imphal is 0385.

HOTELFACILITIES

Hotel Imphal, North AOC point, Imphal -Dimapur Road, Imphal – 795001. Manipur: Tel : 2320341/2320339/2320346, Fax : 2320346, Telex: 2296202, **Location:** 7 kms from Airport., 215 Kms from Dimapur Railway Station, 225 Kms from Jiribam Railway Station., 1 Km from Downtown area., ½ Km from Allied forces World War II Cemetery. E-mail: manipur@x400.nicgw.nic.in

Accommodation:

47 Rooms,12 VIP (Air-conditioned) Suites., **Multi-Cuisine: Emoinu Restaurant.** Conference Hall and Banquet for 100 guests.

Major Hotels in Manipur

Imphal district

Table-6 Showing details of important hotels in Imphal

Sl. No.	*Name*	*Address*	*Telephone*	*No. of Rooms*
1.	Hotel Nirmala	M.G. Avenue	0385-2459014/ 2458904/ 2241112	23
2.	Imphal Hotel	Near North AOC Point, Imphal	0385-2320339, 2320346	
3.	Hotel White Palace	M.G. Avenue, Imphal	0385-2450599/ 2452322	26
4.	Hotel Apollo	Thangal Bazar,Near Kalibari	0385-2450608	25
5.	Hotel Krishtina	Pologround Road, Paona Bazar, Imphal	0385-2445255, 2242093	
6.	Hotel Prince	Thangal Bazar	0385-2453136/ 2454010/2450587	22
7.	Hotel Anand Continental	Khoyathong Bazar	0385-2453422/ 2453433	23
8.	Hotel Excellency	Airport Road	0385- 2230906/2230907	24
9.	Youths Hostel	Khuman Lampak	0385-2453422, 2453523, 2320014	12
10.	Rajasthan Guest House	Thangal Bazar, Alu Gali	0385-2230791	17
11.	Hotel Gaylord	M.G. Avenue	0385-2450720	10
12.	Hotel Nataraj	M.G. Avenue	0385-2451314	20
13.	Shri Marwari Dharmsala	Thangal Bazar	0385-2451175	28
14.	Hotel City Heart	M.G. Avenue	0385-2453371/240313	19
15.	Hotel Mayur	Assembly Road	0385-2451331	19
16.	Eastern Star Hotel	Naga Mapal	0385-2452154/ 2451042	36
17.	Mass Hotel	Assembly Road	0385-2452797/ 2444342	24
18.	Hotel Shanky	M.G. Avenue	0385-2453222/ 2452888	13
19.	Tampha Hotel	NH-39, North AOC	0385-2451486	84
20.	Hotel Pintu	NH-39, North AOC	0385-2454172	23
21.	Hotel Avenue	M.G. Avenue	0385-2241173, 2451666	8
22.	Raj Hotel	Paona Bazar	0385-2455032/ 2455032	7

(Contd.)

(Contd. Table 6)

Sl. No.	Name	Address	Telephone	No. of Rooms
23.	New Raj Hotel	Paona Bazar	0385-2459364	25
24.	Hotel Embassy	Paona Bazar	0385-2452737	16
25.	Hotel Bheigo	Wahengbam Leikai	0385-2450944, 2458904	19
26.	Eikhoigee Hotel	Paona Bazar	0385-2451056	
27.	Hotel Dinesh Delux	Thangal Bazar	0385-2450608	
28.	Hotel Grand	Thangal Bazar	0385-2450777	
29.	Hotel Irabot Tombi	North A.O.C.	0385-230044	
30.	Hotel Kangleipak	Khabam Lamkhai	0385-2422381	
31.	Hotel Langol View	Assembly Road	0385-2455507	
32.	Hotel Langol View	Kombirei Keithel, Lamphel	0385-24140679	
33.	Hotel Maharaja Executive	M.G. Avenue	0385-2459250	
34.	Hotel Shanky	M.G. Avenue	0385-2453222	
35.	Indira Hotel	Chingmeirong Khongnang Karak	0385-2422005	
36.	Kailash Hotel	Thangal Bazar	0385-2450207	
37.	Lairemsang	Waheng Leikai	0385-2459739	
38.	MBC W.D.Girls Boarding	Chingmeirong	0385-320357	
39.	Northern Hotel	Kakhulong, Paona Bazar	0385-2445691	
40.	P.C. Dutta Hotel	M.G. Avenue	0385-2458229	
41.	Park Hotel	Nagamapal Paonam Leikai	0385-2454303	
42.	Hotel Classic	-	-	

Churachandpur district

Table-7 Showing important hotels in Churachandpur

Sl. No.	Name & Address	Telephone	No. of Rooms
1.	Circuit House		3
2.	Green House		8
3.	Hotel Eden		9
4.	Thongam Babita Broadway Hotel	(03874) 33587	

Ukhrul district

Table-8 Showing important hotels in Ukhrul

Sl. No	*Name & Address*	*Telephone*	*No.of Rooms*
1.	Circuit House		3
2.	Hotel Popular		7
3.	Hotel Iceland		8

Chandel district

Table-9 Showing important hotels in Chandel district

Sl.No.	*Name & Address*	*Telephone*	*No.of Rooms*
1.	Imphal Hotel		9
2.	Hotel Eastern Palace		11
3.	Sahara Lodge		20
4.	Hotel Calgo		12
5.	Hotel Alexy, Moreh Bazar	(03873)61696	
6.	Hotel Kamal Sharma, Masjid Road, Moreh	61336	
7.	River View Hotel	61251	

Tamenglong

Table-10 Showing important hotels in Tamenglong district

Sl.No.	*Name & Address*	*Telephone*	*No.of Rooms*
1	Hotel Josh, Jadonang Road	(03877)22033	9

Tourist Information Centres

Table-11 Showing important tourist information centres

1	**Manipur Bhawan,** 2, Sardar Patel Marg, Chanakyapuri, New Delhi Tel : 011-26873311/26113150, 26873009 Fax : 011-26111803: http://manipurbhawan.nic.in/, Email:rescm-mn@hub.nic.in	2	**Manipur Information Centre,** C-7, Baba Kharak Singh Marg, New Delhi Tel. : 011-23746359 Fax : 011-23746361

(Contd.)

(Contd. Table 11)

	Kolkata		
3	**Manipur Bhawan,** 26, Rowland Road, Kolkata Tel : Phone_no: (033) 2758163/24747087/24758075/24747937/24 758163, Fax: (033) 24760310,	4	**Government of India Tourist Office** Embassy, 4, Shakespeare Sarani, Kolkata Tel : 033-22421475, 033-22423521
	Guwahati		
5	**Manipur Bhawan,** Rajgarh Road, Guwahati Tel : 2540707		
	Imphal		
	Tourist Information Centre, Directorate of Tourism, Imphal Tel : 2454603, 2450802		**Government of India Tourist Office,** Jail Road, Imphal Tel : 0385-2451131

For Bookings, Guide Services and others information.Contact: Tourist Officer, Directorate of Tourism, (Hotel Imphal Complex),Government of Manipur, Imphal, Phone no: 2450802, 2452705, 2452451, 2454635, 2454603 ,Fax: 0385-2454354 E-mail: manipur@x400.nicgw.nic.in

TRAVELAGENTS:

Table-12 Showing important Travel Agents in Imphal

Name	*Designation/Place*	*Phone Number*
Blue Hill Travels	NH-39: Near Municipality Office	0385-2456443
East India Travel Agency	Thangal Bazar	0385-2451310
Jeep Taxi Service	Rupmahal Tank	0385-2442021
Global Voyagers Travel Solution	Khuyathong Road	9436410954
Haokip Travels	M.G. Avenue	0385-2443044 / 2222772
Manipur Golden Travel	(Air Lines) / M.G. Avenue	0385-2456422
	M.G. Avenue	0385-2442777 / 2443777
	Sangaiprou	0385-2455180
Manipur Goodwill Travels	Khuyathong Road, Imphal	03852450076, 2448022 2450532 MOB 9436023322

(Contd.)

(Contd. Table 12)

Name	*Designation/Place*	*Phone Number*
Manipur Valley Travels	Kangla Park	0385-2230059
Panthoibi Tour Travel Services	B.T Road	0385-2459598
Pioneer Travels	Paona Bazar	0385-2451997

Table-13 Showing important Bus Services between Imphal and Guwahati, Shillong

Sl. No	*Names of Agency*	*Address*	*Phone Number*
1	Manipur Golden Travels	M.G. Avenue, Imphal	Tel: 0385-2451332
2.	Kangleipak Tours & Travels,	North A.O.C Imphal	Tel:. 0385-2452131.
3.	Sangai Tours & Travels,	near G.M.Hall, Imphal	Tel. 0385-2456803.
4.	Blue Hills Travels,	M.G. Avenue, Imphal	Tel :. 0385-2456443, 2454149.
5.	Zet Travels,	Imphal,	Tel : 0385-2231281
6.	Network Travels	North A.O.C. Imphal,	Tel : 0385-2330709
7.	Manipur Railway Out Agency	M.S.R.T.C. Complex, Imphal,	Tel : 0385-2450823
8.	Blue-in-Transport	North A.O.C., Imphal	Tel : 0385-451753/2458178

COURIER SERVICES

1. Blue dart, Hotel Nirmala Complex, M.G. Avenue, Imphal- 0385-2231281
2. Overnight Express, Near Pratap Talkies, Paona Bazar, Imphal- 0385-2451993
3. DTDC, Near Hotel Nirmala, M. G. Avenue, Imphal – 0385-2404057

What to bring

If you are traveling to Imphal and surrounding areas, a sky bag or a suitcase will do. Winter is quite cold but not as cold as London, Scotland or

Moscow. You can bring your suits. Overcoat may not be necessary. During June-September, you can expect rains. So a light raincoat may be necessary. Toiletries and sachets of washing powder are readily available.

Travel Insurance :

Your travel insurance in your own country may not be valid for India. Check with your insurance agent. A travel insurance policy to cover theft, loss of your laptop, video camera or any other valuable article, cancellation of trips, medical problems is a sensible and wise option.

Copies :

It is a good idea to have a photocopy of your passport and other documents like credit card, travel insurance policy, tickets etc. before you leave home. Leave a copy at home and another copy with you, separate from originals.

Customs:

You are allowed to import 200 cigarettes. There is prohibition of alcohol in Manipur.

Money :

There is only one foreign exchange facility at the State Bank of India, Mahatma Gandhi (MG) Avenue Imphal. It is better to come with sufficient amount of Indian Rupees. Credit cards are not accepted. Traveller cheques can be encashed in all nationalized banks. Hotels and shops do not accept foreign currency. Be careful of counterfeit currency notes particularly in Rs five hundred denominations. Examine large denomination currency notes if given to you . There are ATM (Automated Teller Machines) facilities available at the State Bank of India Branch at the Manipur Secretariat, Imphal (opposite Chief Minister's Secretariat), Manipur University and few other places.

Mobile Phones

The mobile phones working in other Indian cities do not work in Manipur without re-setting Aircell, Airtel, Vodafone, Tata Indicom, Reliance Mobile and BSNL (MTNL) phones with post paid facility may work in Manipur. The mobile telephone service is not up to the standard.

E-mail

Hotels do not have internet facility as in other countries . However, cyber cafe with internet facility are available in the city on payment of nominal rates.

HEALTH PRECAUTIONS

Food, not water is the most common source of gut troubles. Diarrhoea, Dysentery, Hepatitis, Tuberculosis, Typhoid, Viral Fever may be common among travellers. Personal hygiene is also important. Mineral water is available in Imphal and other important towns. The tape water is not fit for drinking. HIV infection is common among commercial sex workers (11.2%), Men having sex with men (11.6%) and injecting drug users (19.4%) in Manipur. Having sufficient number of good quality latex condoms may be a good idea. It is good if you bring some first aid medicines for fever, headache, stomach pains etc. Manipur is an insurgency prone area. There are many insurgency groups fighting mainly for the independence of Manipur. But they do not attack the foreigners.

FACTS ABOUT MANIPUR

Table -14 Showing important facts about Manipur

Neighbours:	Nagaland	North
	Mizoram & Burma (Myanmar)	South
	Assam	West
	Burma (Myanmar)	East
State Symbols:	Kangla Sha	State Emblem
	Sangai (*Cervus Eldi Eldi*)	State Animal
	Nongyeen (*Syrmitacus huminae humina*)	State Bird
	Shirui lily (*Lilium macklinae sealy*)	State Flower
	Uningthou (Phoecha Hainensiana)	State Tree
	State Fish	Pengba (Osteobrama belangeril)
	State Game	Polo
Language	Official State Language	Manipuri
Language Script	Official Script of the Manipuri Language	Manipuri Script (Meitei Mayek)
Important Facts	Number of districts	9
	Number of Sub-divisions	37
	Number of Towns	33
	Literacy Rate	68.87%
	Sex Ratio	978
	Minimum mean temperature	0.0°C

(Contd.)

(Contd. Table 14)

Weather:	Maximum mean temperature	36.0°C
	Average annual Rainfall	1467.5 mm
Representation in the Indian Union:	Lok Sabha (Lower House)	2
	Rajya Sabha (Upper House)	1
Assembly Constituencies	Hill	20
	Valley	40
Districts Headquarters:	Imphal East	Porompat
	Imphal West	Lamphelpat
	Thoubal	Thoubal
	Bishnupur	Bishnupur
	Churachandpur	Churachandpur
	Ukhrul	Ukhrul
	Senapati	Senapati
	Tamenglong	Tamenglong
	Chandel	Chandel
General Information:	Highest Rainfall Area	High Hill areas in Tamenglong
	Lowest Rainfall Area	Churachandpur
	Warmest Area	Jiribam area
	Coldest month	January
	Warmest month	September
	Largest agricultural product	Rice
	Largest exported Agriculture Product	Maize
	Largest Fruit product	Pineapple
	Largest Mineral product	Limestone
	Hill Area	89.99 %
	Valley Area	10.01 %
	Biggest Fresh Water Lake (Also biggest in NE India)	Loktak Lake
	Important Dance Forms	Raas Lila Lai Haraoba Maibi Dance Khamba-Thoibi Dance Nupi Pala Pung Cholom Kabui Naga Dance Mao Naga Dance Tangkhul Naga Dance Kuki Bamboo Dance Thadou Kuki Dance Tarao War Dance etc.

CITY DISTANCES

Table-15 Showing Distances of Imphal from other cities in India

City	*Distance in km*	*City*	*Distance in km*	*City*	*Distance in km*
Agartala	538	Agra	2240	Ahmedabad	2907
Aizawl	361	Ajmer	2576	Akola	2643
Aligarh	2260	Allahabad	1788	Ambala	2583
Amritsar	2838	Asansol	1505	Aurangabad	2871
Bangalore	3416	Barauni	1326	Bareilly	2189
Bellary	3221	Bhagalpur	1416	Belgaum	3381
Bhavnagar	3094	Bhopal	2339	Bikaner	2793
Bilaspur	2426	Chandigarh	2629	Chennai	3202
Coimbatore	3693	Cuttack	1942	Dehra Dun	2528
Delhi	2443	Dhanbad	1523	Dibrugarh	502
Dimapur	215	Durgapur	1504	Ganganagar	2824
Gangtok	1073	Gaya	1492	Ghaziabad	2372
Ghazipur	1659	Gorakhpur	1706	Guntur	2806
Gurgaon	2409	Guwahati	579	Gwalior	2250
Haldia	1681	Hubli	3317	Hyderabad	2854
Indore	2636	Jabalpur	2103	Jaipur	2445
Jaisalmer	3015	Jalandhar	2755	Jammu	2974
Jamshedpur	1687	Jhansi	2174	Jodhpur	2776
Jorhat	366	Kakinada	2554	Kandla	3283
Kanyakumari	3885	Kanpur	1983	Kochi	3886
Kohima	145	Kolhapur	3278	Kurnool	3064
Krishnagiri	3464	Lucknow	1963	Ludhiana	2696
Madurai	3646	Mangalore	3754	Meerut	2388
Moradabad	2285	Mumbai	3230	Muzaffarnagar	2448
Muzaffarpur	1420	Mysore	3546	Nagpur	2367
Nashik	3045	Panaji	3504	Pathankot	2867
Patna	1428	Pondicherry	3367	Porbandar	3301
Pune	3247	Purulia	1602	Raipur	2347
Rajkot	3123	Rameswaram	3794	Ranchi	1690
Raurkela	1912	Rohtak	2487	Sagar	2233
Saharanpur	2510	Salem	3528	Sambalpur	2085
Shahjahanpur	2114	Siliguri	959	Shillong	447
Shimla	2734	Silchar	245	Solapur	3031

(Contd.)

(Contd. Table 15)

City	Distance in km	City	Distance in km	City	Distance in km
Srinagar	3267	Surat	3115	Thane	3187
Thiruvananthapuram	3910	Thrissur	3807	Tiruchchirappalli	3518
Tirupati	3160	Tuticorin	3781	Udaipur	2783
Vadodara	2959	Varanasi	1663	Vellore	3210
Vijayawada	2774	Vishakhapatnam	2392	Warangal	2817

IMPORTANT TELEPHONES

Table-16 Showing Important telephone numbers to have while in Imphal

Bus and Tata Sumo services:	Golden Travels	0385-2453491
	Network Travels	0385-2455182
	Network Travels North AOC	0385-2244285
	Blue Hills Travels	0385-2456443
	Blue Hills Travels North AOC	0385-2454149
Public utility service:	Fire station	0385-2450101
	Imphal City Police Station	0385-2458515
	Singjamei Police Station	0385-2450316
	Lamlong Police Station	0385-310616
	Nambol Police Station	0385-933/235
	Imphal East –Police Hq	0385-2441404
	Lamphel Police station	0385-2414616
	Imphal West Police Hq.	0385-2450002
	RIMS Casualty	0385-2414728
	J.N. Hospital Casualty	0385-2453516/ 2450385
	Shija Hospital, Langol, Imphal	0385-2310522
	Imphal Hospital, RIMS Road	03852410333, 2411353
	Langol View Clinic, Imphal	0385-2310679, 2454027
	MSRTC & Railway out agency	0385-2450823
	Postal Enquiry	2450146
	Speed Post Enquiry	2450146
	Flood control	2450319
electricity complaint:	Imphal	2450169
	Lamphel	2414730
	Khuman Lampak	24502S3

PLACES OF INTEREST

- *Shri Govindajee Temple*: This temple, adjoining the Manipur Palace of the former rulers of Manipur, is a historic centre for the Hindus.
- *Khwairamband Keithel or Sanakeithel* : The market is very special because there is Ima (Mother) market exclusively manned by women.
- *Manipur State Museum* : This interesting museum near the Polo Ground has a fairly good display of Manipur's tribal heritage and a collection of portraits of Manipur's former rulers. Open - 1000 to 1630 hours. Closed on Sundays and Holidays. Entrance : Adult- Rs. 5, Child-00.50.
- *The Kangla* : In the heart of the town, there are interesting ruins of an old fortress wall and a palace. Visitors are permitted to see the Kangla.
- *War Cemeteries* : The British and Indian Army Cemeteries commemorating those who died in the second World War are serene and well-maintained with little stone markers and bronze plaques recording their anguish and sacrifice.
- *Manipur Zoological Garden* : About 6 kms off Imphal, towards the west, is this zoological garden at Iroishemba on the Imphal-Kangchup road.
- *Khonghampat Orchidarium* : The Orchid Yard of the Forest Department, on National Highway No. 39, about 7 kms from Imphal, is another place of interest. Peak blooming season is April-May.
- *Saheed Minar* : The Minar at Bir Tikendrajit Park in the heart of Imphal town commemorates the indomitable spirit of Manipur martyrs who sacrificed their lives while fighting against the British in 1891.
- *Langthabal* : 8 km down the Indo-Burma road lies this small hill feature with the relics of an old historic palace.

EXCURSIONS

- *Loktak Lake* (45 kms) : (See plate- 4) The largest fresh water lake in the North-Eastern India. Its vast expanse of water with both resident and migratory birds offers scope for shooting, fishing and boating. The importance of Loktak Lake is the little Islands Thanga and Karang in the centre of the lake, labyrinth of boat routes amidst the floating marshes.
- *Sendra* (48 kms): An islet in the middle of Loktak Lake is a view point overlooking the lake and its surroundings. A telescope is to be installed here to watch the animals in their natural habits in Keibul Lamjao National

Park. Accommodation : Tourist Home. Rs. 25 (S), 50 (D). Reservation: Deputy Director of Tourism, Govt. of Manipur, Imphal, Tel. 220802.

- *Keibul Lamjao National Park* (53 kms): Inside the famous Loktak Lake, the only floating National Park of its kind in India. It is the natural habitat of the rare Brow antlered deer found nowhere else.
- *Bishnupur* (27 kms): There is a single-celled, conical roofed temple of Lord Vishnu.
- *Phubala* (40 kms): To the south of Imphal on the western fringes of Loktak Lake lies this charming resort. Accommodation : Tourist Home. Rs. 25 (S), 50 (D). Reservation.: Director of Tourism, Govt. of Manipur, Imphal, Tel. 2454603, 2450802.
- *Moirang* (45 kms): From Imphal to the south, is one of the ancient villages of Manipur contributing much to Manipur culture. Traditional "Moirang Lai Haraoba" is celebrated sometime in the month of May every year from the olden days. During the festival, men and women in hundreds dance and sing in honour of Lord Thangjing. During the Second World War, Moirang was the head quarters of the Azad Hind Fauz (INA) where Netaji Subhas Chandra Bose hoisted for the first time the flag of I.N.A. in Manipur. There is one I.N.A. memorial with the Statue of Netaji Subhas Chandra Bose.
- *Churachandpur* (59 kms): District H. Q. of Manipur south and an advanced tribal (Kuki) town where local handicrafts are available in the market. Accommodation : Tourist Bunglow. Reservation. : Director of Tourism, Govt. of Manipur, Imphal, Tel. 2454603, 2450802; Hotel Rajdoot, Hotel International, Green Hotel, Hotel Eden.
- *Kangchup* (16 kms): At an altitude of 921 metres above MSL and a distance of 16 km from Imphal in the west is a health resort on the hills over-looking Manipur valley. It is also a mountain pass on the road to Tamenglong. Accommodation : There is one Inspection Bungalow.
- *Koubru hill* (50 kms): 8404 feet high Koubru Hill is a pilgrim centre.
- *Mao* (106 kms): 1757 metres high Mao is a hill station half-way between Dimapur and Imphal on National Highway -39. The place is rich in Mao Naga culture.
- *Ukhrul* (83 kms): To the east of Imphal, the district headquarters of Ukhrul district is the highest hill station of Manipur. Accommodation : Circuit House. Reservation. : D.C. Ukhrul; Hotel Iceland, Hotel Rebekah, Hotel Soso.

- *Kaina* (29 kms): A beautiful hillock, can be reached by bus via Thoubal. Accommodation : Kaina Tourist Home. Reservation. : Director of Tourism, Govt. of Manipur, Imphal, Tel. 2454603, 2450802.
- *Waithou lake* (16 kms): On Indo-Burma road by the side of the lake is a picturesque village famous for its pineapples. Accommodation : Waithou Tourist Home: Reservation : Director of Tourism, Govt. of Manipur, Tel. 2454603.
- *Khongjom* (36 kms): On Indo-Burma road it is a place of great historic importance. Here Major Paona Brajabashi, one of the great warriors of Manipur, proved his valour against the invading British Army in 1891. The hillock at the foot of which he laid down his life in defence of his motherland. A war memorial on the top of this hill feature adds charm to this historic site. Khongjom Day is celebrated as a state function every year on April 23. Accommodation.: Khongjom Tourist Home. Reservation. : Director of Tourism, Govt. of Manipur, Imphal, Tel.: 2454603.
- *Tengnoupal* (69 kms): Highest point of the Imphal-Burma road and from here one can have a full view of the valley of Manipur.
- *Moreh* (110 KM.): The border town of India on the Indo-Burma road. Accommodation. : Forest Bunglow. Rs.20/bed. Reservation : Principal Chief Conservator of Forest, Forest Department, Imphal. P.W.D. Inspection Bunglow. Rs. 25/bed. Reservation : Executive Engineer P.W.D., Khuyathong Bazar, Imphal. Hotel Eastern Palace, Rachna Hotel, River View, Hotel Imphal.

SHOPPING IN MANIPUR

The people of Manipur are traditional craftsmen. The skilled Manipuri people make exquisite handicrafts and handlooms, which make shopping in Manipur a pleasant experience. Be it in the hills or in the valley, the Manipuris seem to have a genuine flair for crafting outstanding artifacts. No wonder if you find a loom in almost every household in Manipur, and the womenfolk weaving out enchanting variety of fabric and embroidery in distinctive shade and design. Not only that, artifacts made of bamboo, peppier mache, cane and wood, crafted out by the Manipuris make for prized items for shopping in Manipur.

Picking up some worth-buying souvenir, while taking a stroll in the local market (Keithel), from the artisans is not a hassle at all. Check out, while shopping in Manipur:

- Manipuri bed covers of Moirangphi
- Hand-woven and embroidered textiles
- Manipuri dance doll
- Cane and bamboo work and wood carvings
- Mats made of Kouna (water reed)
- Shawls and blankets

It is also not unusual to find a general assortment of specialty handicrafts from neighbouring northeastern states. There are a number of Governments Emporia and also some private outlets for shopping in Manipur. Khwairamband Keithel (market) is the largest exclusive women's market in the country, where a visit is a must.

Imported goods from the smallest of sun-flower seeds to the big home theaters are all available at the markets but the best one is situated at the India-Myanmar border by the name of Moreh (Indian side) and Namphalong (Myanmar side). Imported goods are also available at the Paona Bazar (Keisampat Junction). Shoppers can buy the exotic shawl (Haophee), the Tangkhul scarf, the various wood craft items and the most popular Moirangphi (a thin cloth) for their own. In Imphal, buying is quite easy as the markets are placed together but people have to travel three hours for Moreh market. What makes Moreh stand out is the picturesque journey and the cheap imported goods available.

Popular Shopping Outlets for local handicrafts in Imphal :

- Handloom House, Paona Bazar, Tel 0385-2450340
- Manipur Handlooms and Handicrafts Development Corporation, Paona Bazar, Tel 0385-2451495
- Eastern Handlooms and Handicrafts, Paona Bazar
- Manipur Development Society, Uripok, Tel -0385-2452968
- Ningthibi Collections, Naga Mapal, Imphal
- Kangla Emporium (MDS), Uripok, Imphal
- Crafts Centre, Sagolband Cachar Road, Imphal
- Emoinu Cooperative, Uripok, Imphal
- IMA Market, Khwaramband Bazar, Imphal
- Keisampat Junction, Paona Bazar (for foreign goods), Imphal

It is because of these that you would like to return to Manipur again and again.

Manipur State Tourism Policy

Objectives: The objectives of the Manipur State Tourism Policy are as follows:-

1. To create self sustainable employment and self employment opportunities for the local youths of the State.
2. To create a business climate which will attract outside investments.
3. To project an image of care and hospitality to the world at large and make the State one of the best tourist destinations of the country.
4. To encourage traditional artisans, weavers and handicrafts sector.

The Government's role:-

The state Government is trying to make Manipur a tourist-friendly state. The Government role is restricted to :-

1. Providing support facilities and facilitation services to private enterprises along with appropriate incentives.
2. Planning tourism development as a part of the other overall and development strategy.
3. Providing efficient transport and communication services.

References

Allen, B.C., 1905: Naga Hills and Manipur, Socio-Economic History, Gyan Publishing House, Delhi-7.

André Béteille, 1987. *The Idea of Natural Inequality and Other Essays,* Oxford University Press, New Delhi.

Dr. A. Lalit Singh, Journal of the Geographical Society of Manipur, (July-Dec. 1997).

Grierson, Sir G.A. and Konow, S. Eds. 1903-28. *Linguistics Survey of India.* Volume III, Parts 1-3, *Tibeto-Burman Family.* Reprinted 1967 by Motilal Banarsidass (Delhi, Varanasi, Patna).

K.C. Tensuba, An Approach to the History of Meiteis and Thais, (1993).

Manipur Today, January, 1989.

Manipur Today, August, 1989.

Manipur Tourism, Government of Manipur, India.

Manipur Tourism Department Bulletins.

M. Horam and S.H.M. Rizvi, People of India, Manipur, (1998).

http://stedt.berkeley.edu/html/STfamily.html

http://www.ethnologue.com/

http://culturalpursuits.com/state_entry_formalities.htm

http://kaladan.com/390/inner-line-permit-ilp-issue-causes-furore-in-northeast/

http://manipur.nic.in

http://manipur.nic.in/GOM.htm
http://imphalwest.nic.in/iwfront.htm
http://investinmanipur.nic.in/tourism.htm
http://www.yatra.com/travel/india-tourism/manipur-tourism.html
http://www.c-nes.org/manipur

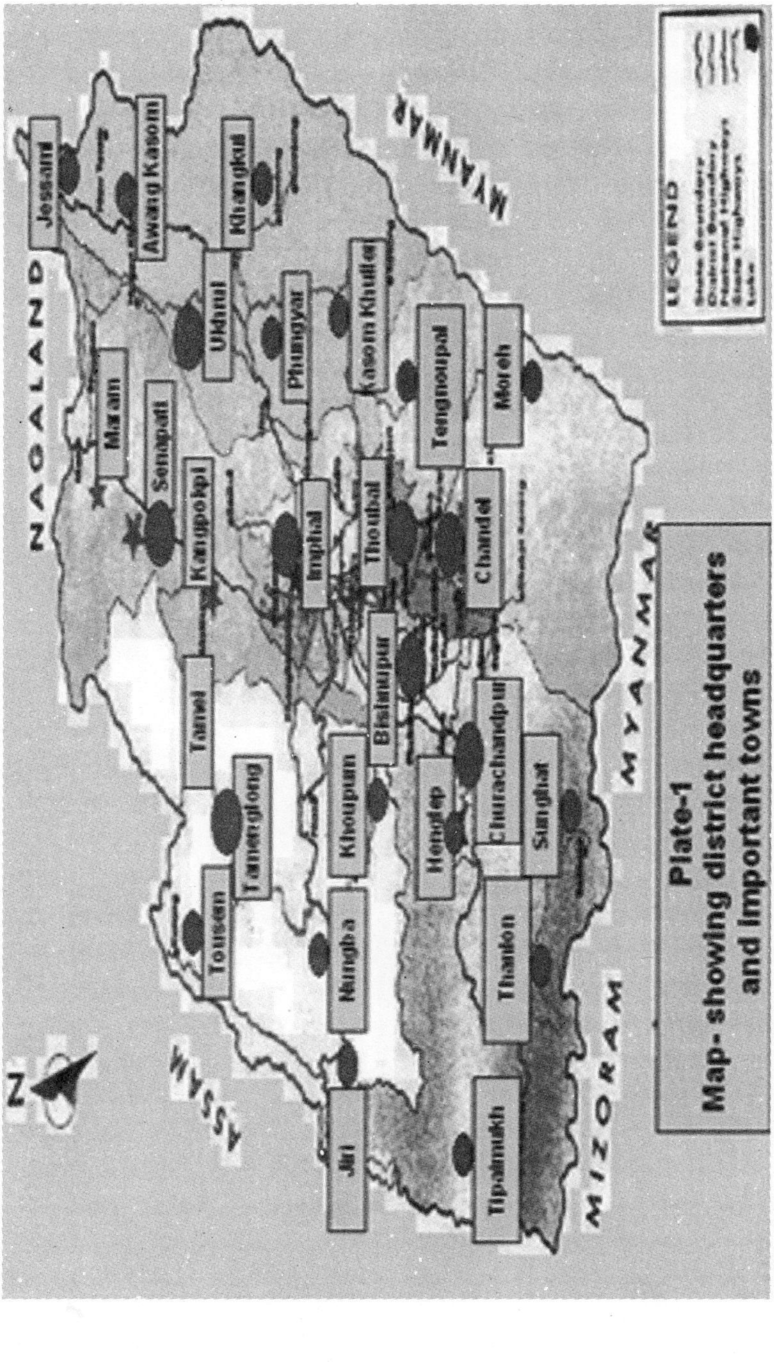

Plate-1
Map- showing district headquarters and important towns

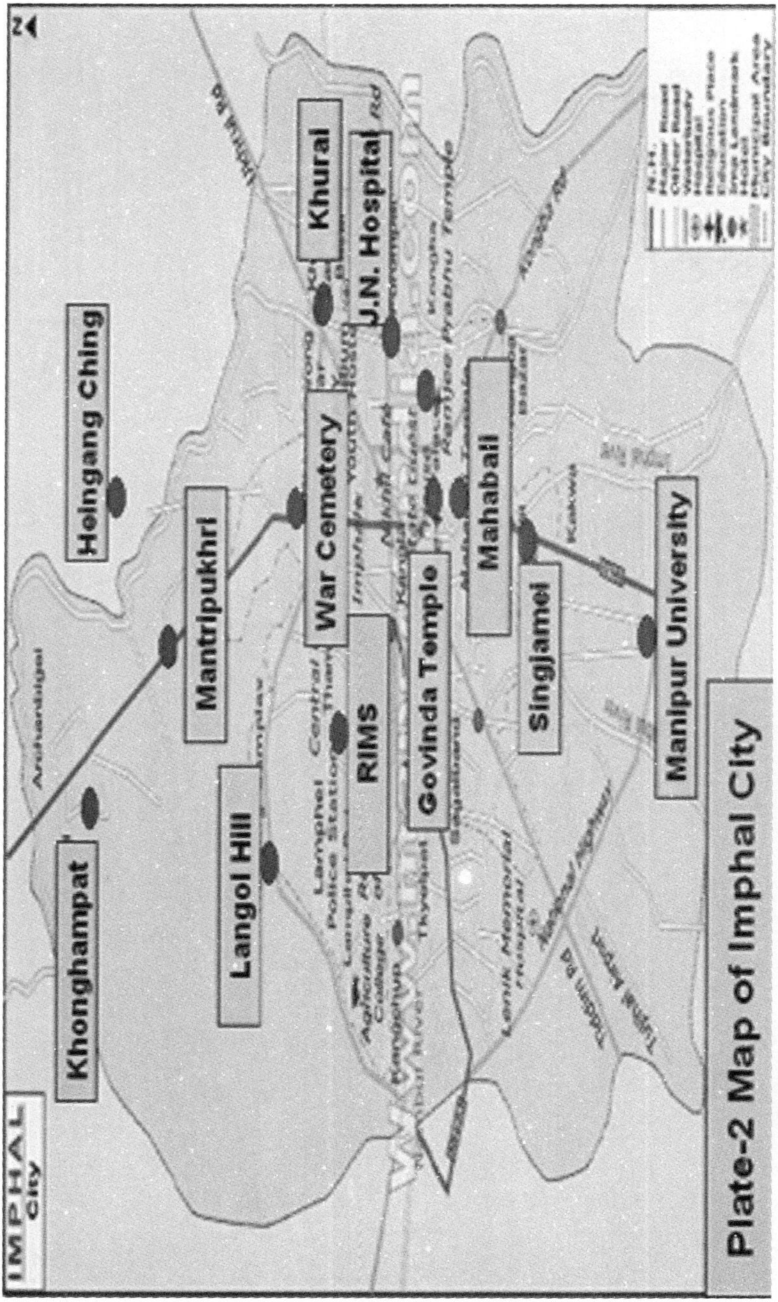

Plate-2 Map of Imphal City

Plate-3 :A rainbow in the Imphal valley

Plate-4 : Loktak Lake

2

Origin of Manipur and Historical Evidences

CREATION OF THE GALAXY

According to the Meitei beliefs, there were two great times orders–the Hanko and the Chak. The Hangko age is the age of Gods having four divisions–Ko, Thoi, Poi and Tayo, each division with countless number of years. After the Hanko age, comes the Chak or the human age–the emergence of the human world. Chak has four divisions – Hayi, Haya, Khunung and Langba (Konna). In the beginning of the Hayi Chak, the Gods and human beings were living together. At the end of the Langba Chak, the universe is dissolved. All the manifested deities and the primal elements were consumed by the fire of Langba. Nothing remains except Atingkok (Formless, boundless expanse) and Amamba (darkness). From this state of nothingness, the will of Atiya Kuru Sidaba brings forth new creation.

According to Manipuri legend, in the beginning there was no galaxy, no earth and no sun or moon. When there was nothing in this universe, it was known as "Ting-Ka-Kok" or "total emptiness" in the ancient Meitei version. It was only space. Atiya Kuru (Guru) Sidaba (Lord of the space and sky) stood in the space and he made the wind and water collided in the space giving rise to a lot of vapour. This vapour in course of time contracted more and more till it exploded giving rise to innumerable fire balls. These fire balls became the suns and stars. There were two suns but one was destroyed and only one remained. The sun again exploded giving rise to the earth. In the beginning, the earth was also a mass of fire. It exploded again and one smaller mass was kept hanging a little distance from the earth but still attached to it. This became the moon. In course of time, the earth cools down and solidifies.

Having created the earth, the sun and the galaxy, Atiya Kuru Sidaba thought of creating human beings.

CREATION OF MANIPUR AND HUMAN BEINGS : A LEGEND :

According to the "Leithak Leikharol" Puya, Manipur was a bowl-shaped lake surrounded by magnificent green hills on all sides. Atiya Kuru Sidaba wished to have a beautiful plateau for human habitations. He instructed the Seven Lainuras to create the land of Manipur by throwing earth into the water. He, then directed Kodin to establish some mortal beings on the soil. Kodin obeyed the instruction and created seven monkeys and seven frogs but these creatures were rejected as they had limited intelligence. Kodin accordingly created a new shape exactly like the image of Kuru and produced it before the Kuru as human being. The Kuru put life into the image (Mee) and thus the first man (Mee) appeared on the earth. The monkeys were sent to the hills, the frogs to the water and the man was retained in the valley. Then were created the Sun in human form, *Kojintu-Thokpa,* and the Moon, in human form, *Ashiva,* by the Kuru. After the creation of the world, the Kuru disappeared. (Chander Sheikher Panchani, Manipur, Religiom, Culture and Society, Konark Publishers Pvt. Ltd.)

Creation of Clans and Yek Salai

One day, the Kuru wanted to test the faithfulness and devotion of his two sons, Kuptreng (Sanamahi/Asiba) and Sentreng (Pakhangba/Apanba). He appeared in the guise of a dead cow flowed along the Vijaya river (Imphal river). Sentreng on seeing the moving tail of the dead cow immediately recognized it to be their father. He told Kuptreng to join him in dragging the dead cow towards the river bank. The Kuru then appeared in the original form and blessed his sons. He said to Sentreng "So, you have recognised your father. Henceforth, you would be known as Pakhangba"–meaning the one who recognized his father. Kuptreng was given the complexion of hot gold and hence he was known as "Sanamahi". The *Cheitharol Kumbaba* mentioned that Pakhangba was a man, the unifier of the people who was connected explicitly with the Ningthouja clan. According to this account, Pakhangba arrived in Manipur during the period of successive migrations associated with the name of Poireiton. The *Ningthourol Lambuba* describes Pakhangba as "God by day but man by night". Another aspect of Pakhangba is in the form of a snake.

Atiya Kuru Sidaba asked his elder son Sanamahi (the liquid of life spreading in all direction like the rays of the Sun, so also the Sun God) to create all the life forms on earth. After Sanamahi created the living beings, Atiya Kuru Sidaba, the god-father wanted to appoint a leader to protect the living and to lead a happy life on earth.

One day, the Kuru told his two sons Kuptreng (Sanamahi) and Sentreng (Pakhangba) "I have decided to give the throne to one of you, who would be able to report to me first after going round the earth seven times". On hearing this, Sanamahi went round the earth riding a tiger. The younger brother, Pakhangba following the advice of his mother Ima Leimarel Sidabi just moved around the seat of the Kuru seven times and reported first to his father, the Kuru. The Kuru was very happy that his son Pakhangba knew that moving around the seat of the Kuru was the same as that of going around the earth. But Sanamahi became furious to know that Pakhangba did not travel round the earth. In view of the imminent fight between the brothers, the Kuru decided that each of them would rule Manipur 12 years at a time in rotation. While Pakhangba ascended the throne, Sanamahi would be worshipped in every house as a deity. Thus peace was restored.

Accordingly he sent his son Pakhangba to earth to sustain and propagate life there In course of time, Pakhangba became the protector, the king, and was represented by the symbol of a Dragon God. The Kuru then disappeared leaving his two sons under the care of Taobaia, the Snake God.

Table-17 Showing names of seven clans / Yeks of Meiteis

Sl. No	*Names of seven Goddesses*	*Names of the Clans*
1	Pithet Leima	Angom
2	Pukshi Khombi	Mangang/ Ningthouja
3	Huimu Leima	Luwang
4	Thongai Lembi	Khuman
5	Khoujao Tonbi	Moirang
6	Tali Leima	Khaba Nganba
7	Nonghainu (Lili Leima)	Chenglei (Sarang Leishangthem)

The Kuru appeared again accompanied by seven Lainuras (goddesses). The Kuru had given the seven Lainuras to his son Pakhangba in marriage and from their union, each goddess seven different clans were established:- Angom, Mangang (Ningthouja), Luwang, Khuman, Moirang, Khaba Nganba and Chenglei (Sarang Leishangthem). People trace their origin to these families. (Sarangthem Bormani, "Meiteigi Laining Laishol, Chander Sheikher Panchani, Manipur, Religion, Culture and Society, Konark Publishers Pvt.Ltd). Thus the clan system of seven Salais started.

He then instructed his son not to allow marriages among the members of the same clan and in that case, he/ she would become the enemy of the clan (Yek thokpa).

After creation of the human beings (Mee), the descendants Pakhangba distributed (yennaba) the body of the Kuru. The human body is called "Sa". There was one original head (Lai) for every group of human beings –hence called "Salai". Out of the heart of the Kuru, Mee came forth with brightness and henceforth called Nganpa. Out of the long tongue came forth with great length and was henceforth called Leisangthem; out of the Leiyeng came forth with mixed colour and was henceforth called Sarangthem. Out of the brain came forth Luwang. From the right hand emerged Khuman. From the neck came forth Angom. From the right eye emerged Ningthem. Out of the Sinung came forth Moirang. The body of the Kuru was then dispersed. Sarang Leisangthem took the thop(Brain), Nganpa, the "Tong" (flesh), Luwang, the Uri, Angom the Kok (head), Ningthoucha, the Sinnung; Khuman the Machum, Moirang the Singli (nerve) or blood vessels. From the term "Yennaba" comes the "Yek". Hence called Yek Salai. (Dr. Kh. Ratan Kumar, Lai Haraoba of Manipur, 2001)

DIFFERENT NAMES OF MANIPUR AND MANIPUR'S RELATIONS WITH NEIGHBOURING KINGDOMS

The early name of Manipur was– "Tilli Koktong" during the time of King Kangba (1405-1359 BC).Then it was known as "Tai-Pong-Pan." during the reign of Chingkhong Poireiton (34-18 BC). Manipur was known by different names by different neighbouring people in ancient and medieval times. It was known as "Kathes" or "Ponnas" to the Burmese, Hsiao Po-lo-mein to the Chinese. Sir G. A. Grieorson (1903) said "The people (Manipuris) are known to the Burmese as Ponnas (Lingustic Survey of India, Part III, Vol. III). To quote W. McCulloch (1859), "the country inhabited by the Muneepoorees (Manipuris) is named by the people of Cachar, Moglai ; by those of Assam,

Mekhlee and by the Shans or those who inhabit the country east of Ningthee or Khyendwen river it is known as Cassay or Kasse of which term the Burmese word Kathe is a corruption." The narrative of Symes and the maps of that period gave the name "Cassay" to this country. In Rennell's Memoir and maps of India, it is mentioned as "Meklee." The name "Mekhele" is found in the treaty of King Bhagyachandra and the British East India Company in 1762 A.D. Other popular names by which it is known are Manipur, "Meitrabak" or "Meitei Leibak" (Land of Meiteis), "Sanaleibak" and "Kangleipak". Manipur was known to the Arabic, Persian, Greek, Roman, Chinese, Burmese, Shan and other historians as the international trade route of the past (comprising the Middle East, Europe, Asia and Oriental countries) passed through the inter mountainous tracts of the region. Manipur was featured in Ptolemy's Atlas.

Manipur's relations with its neighbouring kingdoms are available from written records like *Cheitharol Kumbaba*, *Ningthourol Lambuba,* etc. (starting from the 12th century). Parallel records are found in *Buronji* of the Ahoms (Assam) and *Rajmala* of the Tripuris. Tripura was known to the Manipuris as Takhel. There were wars between Tripura and Manipur in 1533, 1634 and 1696. In 1534, a canal called Takhel Khong was dug in Manipur to commemorate the victory of Manipur over the Tripuris. The canal served as a useful boat-way and a water reservoir. Manipur's contacts with the Mughals traced to the time of Jahangir (1605–1622). Bengali migration to Manipur took place through Tripura. Assam was known to the Manipuris as Tekhao. It was the Dikhou river that runs near Sibsagar from which name of "Tekhao." was derived. There were diplomatic and trade relations between the two kingdoms of Assam and Manipur. Subsequently, the road to Assam was improved in 1536. The Chinese were known to the Manipuris as "Khagi". King Khagemba got his name, which etymologically means "conqueror of the Chinese" after he captured a Chinese town in 1631, as recorded in *Ningthourol Lambuba*. Burma (Myanmar) was known as Kabow and the Burmese were known as "Ava". Tobacco plants and tobacco smoking spread in Manipur in 1610 from Bengal, which was a part of the Mughal empire. The first *hookah* (smoking pipe) imported was called *mangalphu* (Mughal pot). Chilies spread to Manipur through Mughal empire during the reign of Khagemba (1597–1652). Royal chronicles further recorded that two Mughal brick makers arrived in Manipur in 1671. King Garib Niwaj, considered the greatest of the Manipuri kings, had the largest number of war engaged with China and Burma. During his 39 years of reign, 64 wars were fought.

ORIGIN OF THE NAME–MANIPUR

The name "Manipur" for "Meitrabak" or "Sana Leibak" came to existence in 1774 AD during the time of Maharaja Bhagyachandra. Warren Hastings was the Governor General of India during those days.There are some legends regarding ancestral connection of Meiteis to the Hindus of mainland India, which appear to have been developed after the Meiteis were converted to Hinduism. However, majority of the people of Manipur rejected these legends.

ORIGIN OF MEITEIS :

The Meiteis are the majority population groups in Manipur. There are many theories about the origin of the Meiteis in Manipur. Some of the theories of origin of Meiteis are as follows :-

1. Tartar descendant theory:

R.B. Pemberton (The Eastern Frontier of India, 1835, Mittal Publications, New Delhi) in his book concluded that the Manipuris are "the descendents of a Tartar colony, which emigrated from the north west border of China during the sanguinary conflicts for supremacy. "However, this theory does not fit in the recorded history of Manipur and is liable to be rejected.

2. Tibeto-Burman origin theory:

Some writers are of the opinion that the Meiteis originated from "those of the Tibeto-Burman races". T.C Hodson (1908) says that the Meiteis are Tibeto-Burman Language speakers while the Tais are of Siamese-Chinese linguistic family. Sir G. A. Grierson, E.T. Dalton and T. C. Hudson holds that the Meiteis and their language is affiliated to Kuki chin group of Tibeto-Burman family. Sir G.A. Grierson (1903) put forward the theory that the Tibeto Burman and other Mongolian ethnic groups inhabited the upper courses of the Yangtza and the Hung-Ho rivers in China in pre-historic times. Their kinsmen migrated southwards and settled in the Hukwang Valley of the present land of the Catnips in upper Burma before they moved further down to Manipur valley.

3. Hindu descendant theory

There are many legends to suggest that the Meiteis are the descendants of the Hindus from the time of Mahabharatas. Chatterjee (1950) identified the Meiteis and the other tribes with the "Kiratas" of the Vedic literature. However, majority of the people of Manipur rejected this theory of Hindu origin of the

Meiteis because Hinduism came to Manipur only recently (16th century) and also the physical features, cultures and traditions of the Manipuris do not in any way resemble the Hindus of mainland India.

4. Descendent of surrounding hill tribes Theory:

T.C. Hodson (1908) opined in his book "The Meitheis" that "the Munniporees (Manipuris) meaning the Meiteis are the descendants of the surrounding hill tribes". T.C. Hodson stated "the origin of the Munniporees from the surrounding hill tribes is the proper and only conclusion to be arrived at. I think it probable that when only a small part of the valley skirting the hills was capable of cultivation, the hill men bordering it used to descend and cultivate the little land there then was, returning to their homes in the hills after reaping their harvests: as however land increased, some of them settled permanently in the plain, gradually increasing in numbers. The various tribes thus settling in different parts of the valley would in time come into contact, and after a struggle for supremacy, amalgamate." (T.C. Hudson, The Meitheis, 1908, Low Price Publications, Delhi-110052)

5. Naga-origin Theory:

There are many legends to suggest that the Meiteis and the Nagas originated from a common ancestor. Col. James Johnstone (1877-1886) is quoted, "There can be little doubt that some time or other the Naga tribes to the North made one of their chiefs Raja of Manipur" who even after "adopting the civilization of the country, retain some of their old customs".

6. Manipuris- aboriginal settlers :

There are enough archaeological evidences to establish the existence of prehistoric population, at least in the hills, and later on in historic times in the valley as well. It was believed that the entire valley of Manipur was submerged under water. Initially the inhabitation of human beings started in the hills as the valley was under water. The caves and rock in the hills were once inhabited by prehistoric people as evident from the findings of the explorations at Khangkhui caves, Tharon caves, Sangbu (Chandel District), Machi Khul, Sekta Mound, Irengbam, Phunan, Panjao Phallum Ching, Khurai Lamlong Bazar, Nongpok Keithelmanbi (Senapati District), Mongjam (Imphal District) and Napaching (Wangoo) by the state Archaeological Department. Some antiquities found by them are classified as Palaeolithic tools (early phase of stone age-2.5 million years), Neolithic (later part of stone age, 4th to

8th millennium BC) tools like edged tools and grindstones; hand made pottery with potsherds available in plain wares, stamped pottery, incised pottery, cord marked pottery, and with circular lead to the proof of existence of human inhabitation during the prehistoric period. The Palaeolithic man lived in caves while the Neolithic lived in open -air sites. Neolithic man reached the Manipur Valley not later than 2000 B.C.

The caves gave the evidence that there were signs of human settlement even during the stone age around 32,000 years back in Manipur. The cord marked potsherds, from the excavation of Napachik dates back to 1450 B.C. Further, the discovery of fossils of Cuttle marine fish during excavation of earth at the time of road construction at Koubru Ching in the Tamenglong road at a height of 6000 feet above sea level supported the theory that Manipur was once submerged under water. It was proved scientifically that the Cuttle marine fish existed about 4 million years ago. These archeological findings suggest that the Meiteis together with the hill tribes have been in existence since time immemorial. Further many legends and folklores of almost all the ethnic groups in Manipur suggest their origin from caves.

The legends and folklores of the Meiteis also suggest that the Meiteis have been existing in Manipur since time immemorial. The word "Meitei" means "Men of mixed blood". There are many folktales which indicated that Meiteis is the name given to those people who were born out of wedlock between different tribes of Manipur.

7. Different Ethnic Groups Merging in to a single people, the Meiteis :

The land of Manipur was formerly divided into small territories occupied by different clans of people, namely, the Khumans, the Moirangs, the Angoms, the Luwangs, the Ningthoujas, etc. The territories were named after the names of the respective clans and they lived side by side in Manipur for centuries. The Khumans were the most powerful and after them the Moirangs. The different tribes came from different quarters. In course of time, they intermarried themselves and merged into a single people. The ethnonym "Meiteis" was originally applied to the "Ningthouja Salai" (clan-dynasty), which was one of the seven "Salais" who ruled seven independent principalities in the valley in the early part of the recorded history. Later on, the Ningthouja Salai overruled other principalities thereby absorbing the different social groups thereof to form the "Meiteis". They called themselves the "Meiteis". The Meiteis occupied all the territories towards 15th century AD and established a sovereign kingdom known as "Meitei –Leipak" or "Meitrabak" (the land of Meiteis)". Ultimately the Meiteis subdued all remaining tribes and form them into a single people." (Assam District Gazetteer, Part -IX by V.C Elen, page 11).

The Meiteis of today are of Tibeto-Burman Mongoloid ethnic group.This racial blending is intimately hooked to the evolution of a distinct civilization in Manipur valley. Again, Mc Culloch (1859), R. Brown (1874) and T.C. Hodson (1908) subscribed to the theory of the Naga origin of the Meiteis. This ethnic homogeneity facilitated the absorption of many tribes into the Meitei social groups.

Besides, oriental Mongolians consisting of Shans Burmese and Chinese etc. who settled in the valley either as war captives or peaceful immigrants were also absorbed into the Meitei society. The settlement of people from the east continued since the time of king Naothingkhong (663-763 A.D) till the time of King Maramba / Gourshyam (1753-1759) and (1762-1763 A.D).

Absorption of people from the rest of India was rather late. The settlement of these people probably started since the time of king Thangbi Lanthaba (1302-1324 A.D). The absorption of the new entrants into the Meitei society was effected by conferring them appropriate "Sageis" (surnames) and "Salai" (clans). This "Meiteisation" of different migrants gave the Meiteis, not only numerical advantage but also helped in enriching their culture and literature and ultimately evolving into a settled civilization with pristine national heritage of its own long before the Aryans came.

8. Meitei and Tangkhuls Ties :

The oral history of the Tangkhuls says that the Meiteis and Tangkhuls were brothers being descendants of the same ancestors in the distant past. The theory that Tangkhuls and Meiteis emerged from the same one ancestor is found in the Sana Puya, the royal chronicles of the Meitei Raja. According to Sana Puya, Ningthou Kangba (1405-1359 B.C) had three sons – Thangal, Hungbum (Hundung), and Meitei. Thangal found their settlement in the present Thangal area, the Hundung Awunga (Village Chief) and his brother Meitei proceeded as far as Hundung village and from there they separated. Hundung is a big Tangkhul village in Ukhrul district. The chief of the Hundung village and the king of Manipur were brothers. The younger brother, who had been fascinated by the fortune of the valley lost contact with the elder brother. Fearing that he might be in danger of the enemies and ferocious animals, the elder brother went in search of him and at last found him in the valley. But the younger brother refused to accept food and drinks offered by his elder brother because he feared that any acceptance of food would amount to surrendering himself to his elder brother's wishes. The young brother conveyed his decision to settle down in the valley. The elder brother agreed but said that the mutual relationship between brothers should be maintained and there should be exchange of gifts every year as a sign of brother hood. The elder brother performed some rituals, offered some sacrifices for the peace, prosperity and success of his younger brother. The younger brother requested his elder brother to give him some cult so that he might be able to perform the rituals and ceremonies, worship the deity, carry out cultivation without any problem. Accordingly, the elder brother took out a leather in which the Tangkhul scripts were written, copied it into a bamboo pulp and gave it to his younger brother. He told his brother that the deity he had to worship was called goddess *"Sam Sangba"* and advised his brother to mark the beginning and close of the year by performing certain rituals. The end of the year might be marked by celebrating a ritual known as *"Yu Hongba"* After the harvest and the beginning of year can be marked by invoking sylvan god *"Umang Lai"*. The elder brother asked his younger brother as to "how could he knew that his younger brother is safe and sound" The younger brother replied that every year starting from the full moon day of "Mera", he would display a lamp on the top of a bamboo pole from his house for one month (*Mera Thangmei thanba)* so that his elder brother could easily see it from the top of the hill at any time of the month." If you could see the lamp, please take it for granted that I am safe and sound. So saying, the elder brother departed. The younger brother formed a new clan known as *"Songvai"* meaning the one who has become or formed a clan.

The Meiteis continued to perform the *Umang Lai-Haraoba* and *Mera Thangmei thanba* even to this day every year. In this Umang Lai Haraoba, a number of war dances like Thang hainaba, Ta–khousaba (dancing with Tangkhul swords and spear), Ten Kappa (archery or arrow shooting) were performed and displayed, which were the folk art of the Tankhuls. Umang Lai Haraoba illustrates the intimate connection between Tankhuls and Meiteis. The Meitei enact Tangkhul customs and Tangkhul Saba (Imitating Tankhul), which means acting like a Tangkhul or representing a Tangkhul. The actors and actresses have to appear in Tangkhul costume and act the Tangkhul way of talking and living. Without Tangkhul costume, the Lai Haraoba is never complete. The Meiteis believed that failure to perform that rituals will bring disease, disaster to the village and its people.

At the time of coronation of the Manipuri Kings and Queens, they had to appear in Tangkhul costume to validate the ceremony. Once in a year, the kings and queens were required to sit on the throne in Tangkhul costume even for a short while. In early days, they were escorted by two or three Meitei armed guards in Tangkhul war dress and weapons. This practice was continued even after conversion of the Meiteis into Hinduism. The younger brother used to send his due share of "Loipot" (Tribute) to his elder brother, the Chief of Hundung village Awunga (Khullakpa)

The inhabitation must have shown gradual shift from the hills towards the valley by the gradual shrinking of the lake, increase in the size of the valley, better prospects for human habitation and better chances for cultivation.

There are many historical and archaeological evidences to the growth and development of civilization in Manipur.

MIGRATION

The accounts of earlier settlement in this land are given in the ancient books/puyas like Sagok Lamlem, Thangchat etc.Further information of the people who migrated and settled in Manipur are found in books like Poireiton Khuntokpa (34-18 B.C.), Nongpok Haram, Nongchup Haram, Kumbilon, Mayang Khunthok, etc.

HISTORICAL EVIDENCE

1. ANCIENT BOOKS-CHRONICLES OR THE PUYAS :

The ancient books and chronicles points to the evolution of Manipuris, creation of clans, development of kingdoms and activities of the kings. Some of the ancients books, chronicles are :-

1.1. *Cheitharol Kumbaba –a royal chronicle*

1.2. *Chakpa Khunda Khunthok*

1.3. *Pakhangba Laihui*

1.4. *Panthoibi Khongul*

1.5. *Khaba Sokchromba*

1.6. *Leithak Laikharol* – It gives an account or the theory of evolution, human affairs, sports of different feats of strength, merry-making of gods and goddess, songs and dances

1.7. *Phundin*–It is also almost the same as the Leithak Leikharol.

1.8. *Chekhong Nongkhrang*–It is a book written about the origin of the Salais (Clans) and Yumnaks (Surnames).

1.9. *Langthabal Ḷon*–It is a book which describes the origin of Salais and Yumnaks.

1.10. *Sanggai Phamang*–A similar book, which describes the origin of the Yumnaks and seven Salais.

1.11. *Khagemba Yumlep*–It is a book, which describes how men was created after the image of the Kuru. The meaning of Meitei Yumnak and the origin of the different genealogy of Yumnaks are also described in this book.

1.12. *Ningthourol Lambuba*–It narrates the activities of the Meitei kings, their victory and title.

1.13. *Moirang Ningthourol Lambuba*-Chronology of the Moirang Kings who ruled in and around the Loktak Lake to the South West of Manipur.

1.14. *Chengleirol*–It is a historical account of the kings of the Chenglei dynasty who later on merged into Sarang Leisangthem Salai and ruled in some parts of Manipur in the past.

1.15. *Chakparol*–It is the history of Chakpas (Lois) of Manipur; they are believed to be aborigines who settled before the Christian era.

1.16. *Khuman Kanglairol*–It is an account of Khuman rulers who maintained an independent principality in the southern part of Manipur. The history records how the dominion of Khuman clan was merged to the region of Meitei King Kongyamba (1324-1335 A.D.).

1.17. *"Ningthou Kangbalon"* by one Maichou (Meitei scholar) named *Thongak Kurumba*

1.18. *Sagok Lamlen*

1.19. *Thangchat*

1.20. *Nongpok Haram*

1.21. *Nongchup Haram*

1.22. *Kumbilon*

2. STONE INSCRIPTIONS AND COPPER/ IRON PLATES

2.1. Stone inscription of King Kyaamba: The stone was erected in 15th century A.D. at Khoibu Maring village in Tengnoupal district of Manipur. It was written in old Meitei (Manipuri) script.

2.2. Stone inscriptions of Charairongba of 17th century: This stone is in the compound of Kongthoujam Lairembi in Imphal West district and the inscription is in the old Manipuri script.

2.3. Stone inscription at Ngaprum Chingjeng: It is also inscribed in old Manipuri script recorded on Sunday, the 17th day of the Manipuri month Hiyangei 1684 S.E. now in Senapati District. This stone inscription is now in the State Museum.

2.4. Stone inscriptions at Haochong was erected in 1764 S.E. and other in 1766 S.E.

2.5. Stone inscription at Wangoi, Leisangkhong. The stone was erected on the occasion of the opening of Mayang Ngamba Keithel (Bazar) to commemorate the victory of Maharaja Marjit (1813-1819 A.D) over the king of Mayang (Cachar).

2.6. A stone inscription at Andro village at eastern foot of Nongmaijing hill, Imphal East.

2.7. Stone inscription of Maharaja Gambheer Singh (1825-1834 A.D) at Kohima was a landmark and now preserved at Nagaland Museum.

2.8. Phayeng copper plates prepared by King Khongtekcha during 763-773 A.D.

2.9. Iron plate of Maharaja Bhagyachandra (1763-1798 A.D) at Chothe village in Manipur Churachandpur District. It was written in Bengali script.

2.10. A copper plate of the time of Maharaja Gambheer Singh (1825-1834 A.D) is now in Andro. It is preserved by the Khullakpa of Andro.

2.11. A copper plate issued by Maharaja Chandra Kirti Singh (1850-1886 A.D) is now at the Manipur State Museum.

2.12. There is also one copper plate at Kharam Pallel village near the new Cachar road in Tamenglong district. This was recorded during the time of Maharaja Chandra Kirti Singh (1850-1886). It signified that the Maharaja allowed the hill people to settle there. (Laimayum Bishwanath Sharma, Guide Book, Mutua Museum, Cultural Heritage Complex, Mutua Museum, 2006).

3. COINS

Coins in Archaic Meitei (Manipuri) Script

3.1.1. Coins of King Ura Konthouba (568-658 A.D): The characteristics of the coins issued by him are: (a) material -bell metal; (b) form-Square; (c) Size–2 sq. cms. The most important feature of his coins is that "WU" initial letter of the king's name is found depicted in archaic Manipuri on the obverse side of the coins when the reverse is found blank. Denomination value of coin is one Sheljao.

3.1.2. Coins of King Ayangba (821-910 A.D): After the death of King Yaraba, Ayangba ascended the throne in 821 A.D and ruled for 89 years. Coins issued by him were of bell-metal. The other characteristics of the coins are: (a) shape –Circular, (b) size–0.9 cm. (diameter). Initial letter "A" is written on the obverse side of the coins in archaic Manipuri in order to represent the name of the king. The reverse side is found blank and flat.

3.1.3. Coins of King Lairenba (1394-99 A.D) : After the death of King Tabungba in 1394. A.D. Lairenba reigned for 5 years. The coins issued by him were of bell-metal. Other characteristics of his coins are found similar with those of King Ura Konthouba. However, initial letter "LA" is found depicted on the obverse side of the coins in archaic Manipuri in order to symbolize the name of the king. The denomination of the coin is Seljao.

3.1.4. Coins of King Khagemba /Mayangamba (1597-1652 A.D) : King Khagemba issued coins. The features of his coins are : (a) shape-circular (b) size – 1 cm. in diameter. The word "MA" in archaic Manipuri is found depicted in his coins, connoting his name Mayangamba.

3.1.5. Coins of King Paikhomba (1666-1697 A.D) : Paikhomba issued coins of bell-metal. It is square in shape. The word "PA" is found depicted in the coin in archaic Manipuri script.

3.2. Coins of Deva Nagari scripts

3.2.1 King Garib Niwaj (1709-1748 A.D) issued coins of both Deva Nagari and Bengali scripts. His coins of Deva Nagari script are square in shape and bear different legends. The legends of the coins are :

- The first type coins of King Garib Niwaj are found depicting the legend in Deva Nagari script as *je shri garibniwaja mekhaieshwar gomati rani se* (meaning Je Shri Garibniwaja King of Makhale Gomati the Queen). These coins are of bell-metal.
- The second type of coins of the king are found depicting the legend *cheitra sudhi tarsha vadda 2 samvada 1646.*(1724 A.D) These are bell-metal coins.
- The third type of coins of the king are found depicting *cheitra suchi tarshavada 1646* (1724 A.D). These coins are bell-metal coins. It is of Feikak denomination, which is between Seljao and Selmakhai denomination.
- The fourth type of coins of the king are also of bell-metal. The legend *je shri garibniwaja* is found depicted on the coins.
- The fifth type of coins of the king bear the legend "JE SHRI RAM". It is also of bell-metal.
- The sixth type of coins of King Garib Niwaj were also of bell-metal. The legend *jayaram* is depicted on these coins.

The seventh type of coins also bear the depiction "*ram*". It is also of bell-metal.

3.2.2. Coins of King Chit Sai (1748-1752 A.D): King Chit Sai issued bell-metal coins during his time. Characteristics of his coins are: (a) shape-circular; (b) size – 1 cm. in diameter. The word "CHA" in Deva Nagari script is found depicted on the coins.

3.2.3. Coins of King Bhagyachandra / Jai Singh (1763-1798 A.D): Jai Singh issued gold coins of two different legends. One is found depicted as *shriman manipureshwara shri jaia simha nripabarasy sake 1691* on the obverse side while *shrimad radha govinda padravinda makaranda madhukarasya* is on the reverse side. Another is also found depicted as *"shri shri jaya simha nripabarasya saka 1694* on the obverse side while *shri shri govinda pada suman madhukarasya* is on the reverse side. Further, these coins are of one mohur denomination shape of the coins is circular for first one while is square for the later.

King Jai Singh not only issued gold coins but also issued silver coins. In this coin *shri jaya simhasya* is found depicted on the obverse side while *shri govinda deva* is found depicted on the reverse side. Another square-shaped coins depicting Deva Nagari script "JA" of bell-metal were also issued by the king.

3.2.4. Coins of King Labanyachandra (1798-1801 A.D): Labanyachandra issued gold coins of one mohur denomination. It is circular in shape having 8.66 mm. in diameter. In the obverse side of the coins the legend *shriman manipurshwara shri harshchandra nritavarasy sake 1721* is found depicted while *shrimad radha govinda padaravinda makaranda madhukarasya* is on the reverse side.

3.2.5. Coins of King Chourajit (1803-1813 A.D) : King Chourajit issued gold and silver coins depicted in Deva Nagari script. Gold coins issued by King Chourajit Singh was of one mohur denomination. It was square in shape. Legend *shriman manipureshwara shri chourajit simha nripavarasya saka* 1731 was depicted on the obverse side of the coin, while *shrimad radha govinda padaravinda makaranda mano madhukarasya* was on the reverse side.

Silver coins issued by the king were of three types. These coins were all square in shape. The coins issued by the king of one denomination is found the same legend depicted in gold coin. But *"saka 1734"* is found depicted on gold coins. Similarly, silver coins of half mohur denomination were found to depict *shri chaurajita simha nripavarasya saka 1726* on the obverse side while *shri shri radha govinda apada sevaka* on the reverse side. Silver coins of quarter mohur denomination are found depicted as *shri chourajita simha nripavarasya saka 1729* on the obverse side while *shri radha govinda padabaja imano madhukarasya* is on the reverse side.

3.2.6. Coins of King Marjit Singh (1813-1819 A.D): Amongst the coins issued by King Marjit gold and silver coins were also included. His gold coins were of two types according to the legends depicted thereon. The gold coins of depicted legend *hidambajita shri marjit manipureshwara shri simha nripasya saka 1741* on the obverse side was square in shape but on the reverse side was found depicted *shri shri radha govinda padarabinda mano madhukarasya.* However, the most illustrious depiction of his coins was image of Lord Govinda standing in tribhanga pose, playing a flute. Another gold coins issued by the king were also circular in shape. It is also found the legend *shriman manipureshwara shri marjita simha nripavaprasya saka 1741* depicted on the obverse side while *shriman manipureshwara shri marjita simha nripavarasya* is on the reverse side.

3.2.7. Coins of King Jai Singh II (1822 A.D): King Jai Singh–II during seven years devastation period of Manipur, reigned Manipur for only one month in 1822 A.D. During this very short period, he also issued one type of gold coins of one mohur denomination. The coins were of circular in shape having a diameter of 33.8 mm. The legend *shri shriman shri jaya simha nripavarasya saka 1753* is found depicted on the obverse side, while Shri Radha Govinda in tribhanga pose on the reverse side.

3.2.8. Coins of King Gambheer Singh (1825-1834 A.D) : Among the coins issued by the King, bell-metal coins was one of them. It is circular in shape having a diameter of 1cm. "GA" initial letter of King's name is found depicted in the coins.

3.2.9. Coins of King Nara Singh (1844-1850 A.D): Nara Singh issued gold coins of one mohur denomination. The coins are circular in shape having a diameter of 18.9 mm. On the obverse side of the coins, it is found depicted as *shriman manipureshwara shri nara simha nripavarasya saka 1763;* while Radha and Govinda standing in tribhanga pose is found depicted on the reverse side.

3.2.10 Coins of King Kulachandra (1890-1891 A.D): King Kulachandra, last king of independent Manipur issued bell-metal coins. The coins are circular in shape having a diameter of 9 mm. The initial letter "KU" of the king's name is found depicted on the coins in Deva Nagari script.

3.3. Coins of Bengali Scripts

The Manipuri kings also issued coins in Bengali scripts :-

3.3.1. Coins of King Garib Niwaj (1709-1748 A.D): King Garib Niwaj not only issued coins of bell-metal of Deva Nagari script but issued of Bengali script also. One of the coins issued by the king bears the legend SHRI RAMA on the obverse side of the coins. It is circular in shape having a diameter of 1cm.

3.3.2. Coins of King Bhagyachandra / Jai Singh (1759-1762 A.D): King Jai Singh above all his gold and silver coins also issued bell-metal coins. It is circular in shape having a diameter of 2 cm. The coins bear the initial letter "JA" of Bengali script.

3.3.3. Coins of King Labanyachandra (1798-1801 A.D): Bell-metal coins issued by King Labanyachandra consist of the legend "LA", the initial letter of King's name. This type of coin is of circular in shape having a diameter of 1 cm. each.

3.3.4. Coins of King Gambheer Singh (1825-1834 A.D): King Gambheer Singh has been regarded as the only king who issued gold coins of Assamese-Bengali script in the coinage history of Manipur. These coins were of square in shape of one mohur denomination. On the obverse side of the coins *Shri radha govinda charana sevakasya* is found depicted, while *Shri gambheera sinha nripavarasya chandrabda* 1043 is on the reverse side.

3.3.5. Coins of King Surchandra (1886-1890 A.D) : King Surchandra during his period of about 4 years issued bell-metal coins of Bengali script. His coins are circular in shape having a diameter of 1 cm. The initial letter "SA" of the king's name in Bengali script is found depicted on the obverse side of the coin.

3.3.6. Coins of King Kulachandra (1890-1891 A.D): Kulachandra, last king of independent Manipur issued bell-metal coins of Bengali script. They are circular in shape having a diameter of 8 mm. initial letter "KU" of the King's name is found depicted in his coins.

3.3.7. In the coinage history of Manipur King Maramba alias Gourashyam (1753-1759 A.D. and 1762-1763) has been regarded as the first king who introduced gold and silver coins. The coins issued by the king were square in shape and found depicted the name of the king and the year of coinage but coins of quarter mohur denomination was undated. Unfortunately, these coins issued by King Maramba alias Gourashyam could not be included under any of the above three categories because of lack of information on the legend and the script. (P. Gunindra Singh, Manipuri Numismatics, Mutua Museum, 1983).

HISTORICALRELEVANCE

Certain observations of historical relevance may be inferred from the study of the above coins as follows :-

Firstly, many authors claim that Manipur had many names as called by the people of different regions. In other words, it means that this land of Manipur was familiar with other countries. The coins of King Garib Niwaj (1709-1748 A.D) depicted *"Jeshri Garibaniwaja Mekhleshwar Gomati Ranise"* which clearly means Gariba Niwaj was the King of Mekhele.

Secondly: It has clearly revealed that the Manipuri script had been practiced during the time of Ura Konthouba during 568–658 A.D. because his coins depicted the initial letter of the king's name "WU" in archaic Manipuri script.

Thirdly, The coins of King Garib Niwaj were of Deva Nagari and Bengali scripts and found 'depicted' Rama in his coins. It appears that the later kings after Garib Niwaj were the devotees of Lord Krishna/ Govindajee. This is confirmed by the coins of later kings invariably inscribing 'Govinda' in their coinage. Further, it also suggested that Bengali and Deva Nagari scripts became quite popular during those days.

Fourthly, history of Manipur records that during King Maramba / Gourashyam (1753-1759 and 1762-1763), he paid 500 Manipuri gold rupees to be valued at twelve British Indian rupees to the British as a part of the Treaty. Thus, the above statement confirms, that gold coins of Manipur were used as a medium of transaction with other countries.

Fifthly, in few cases, the coins revealed the second names of certain kings. For example, the coins of Labanyachandra (gold coins) reveal his another name as Harshachandra which is not found in any literary book. Similarly, gold coins of King Marjit indicate his another title as Hodambahjit. This name was given to him for his victory over Cachar (Hedamba-Cachar).

Sixthly, It is worth mentioning that the system of Lunar Calendar was recorded in the gold coins of King Gambheer Singh (1825-1834). This is clearly proved by the legend 'Chandrabda' depicted in his coins.

4. ACCOUNT LEFT BY EUROPEANS

Some Europeans wrote account about Manipur of 18th and 19th centuries A.D. Many of them were genuinely interested in the development of Manipur. They had given immense contribution to the society of Manipur. These writings furnish useful sources about the history and development of Manipur.

- Capt.R. Boileau, Pemberton., Report on the Eastern Frontier of British India, Government of Assam (1835)
- W. Mc. Culloch. Publications of G.H. Damat, An Account of the valley of Manipur and the hill tribes, 1859.
- Sir James Johnstone., My Experience in Manipur and 'Naga Hill' (1896)
- T.C. Hodson, The Meitheis (1908)
- T.C. Hodson, The Naga Tribes of Manipur, MacMillan & Co., London 1911.
- B.C. Allen, E.A. Gait, C.G.H. Allen, H.F. Howard, Gazetteer of Bengal and North East India,
- B.C. Allen, Gazetteer of Naga Hills and Manipur (1905)
- B.C. Allen, Assam District Gazetteer-Naga Hills and Manipur, Volume-IX, Part-II, Calcutta Baptist Mission Press, 1905,
- R. Brown, Statistical Account of the native state of Manipur and the hill territory under its rule, 1874
- Alexander Mackenzie, North East Frontier of India (1884)
- Alexander Mackenzie, History of Relations of the Government with the Hill Tribes of the North East Frontier of Bengal, Calcutta, Home Press, 1884
- Grim wood, St. Ethel, My three years in Manipur (1892)
- Capt. Dun E.W, Gazetteer of Manipur by, Delhi, (First Edn.1886)
- Harvey G.E, History of Burma (1925)
- L.W. Shakespeare, History of Manipur Rifles (1929)
- Sir Robert Reid (Governor of Assam, History of Frontier Areas bordering on Assam, 1937-42)
- Administration Report of the Manipur Political Agency, 1873-74,1875-76, 1877-78, 1878-79, 1891-95, 1904-05
- Administration Report of the Manipur State, 1913-14, 1934-35,1939-40,1940-41,
- Dorothy Woodman,The Making of Burma (1962)
- Sir G. A. Grieorson, Linguistic Survey of India, Part III, Vol. III). by 1967 (1st Edn- 1903)
- Julian Jacobs, The Nagas, Hill People of Northeast India, 1990

5. ARCHAEOLOGICAL FINDINGS

Excavations at historical sites were made by the late W. Yumjao Singh, a research scholar at historical sites. Among others, 13 cannons were excavated from the bed of the Imphal river near Sanjenthong bridge in 1935 A.D. Some of them are at the Manipur Museum.

- In 1937 "a coffin of about 12 feet in length was found at Moirang with some pieces of human bones, potteries of a peculiar nature, 12 beads and a piece of silver bangle."
- On 25th February, 1967 while digging a pipe-line in Kangla area (old Palace of Manipur a gold peacock of five tolas, a crèche of cowries, were found inside a bell-metal vessel. This is now at the Manipur State Museum.
- Recently, while digging a spot on the top of "Lamboiching" a hillock in the Chingmeirong area a skull decorated with ornaments, was found and it is now in possession of the Archaeological Department of the Government of Manipur. These findings will also provide some sources of the history of Manipur.

6. ARCHIVAL SOURCES

Important historical records of Manipur of the 18th and 19th centuries are available in the National Archives of India. New Delhi, West Bengal State Archives, Kolkata, Assam State Records Room, Dispur, Maharastra Archives, Bombay, Asiatic Society Library, Bombay, etc. Many historical documents are also available in the British Museum, London and India Office Library, London. Photos, paintings of historical importance of Manipur are now available in Mansell Collection, London. Recently, in March 1982 Manipur State Archives was established and official Records, files, etc. of historical importance have since been collected. The Archives unit of the Manipur State Kala Academy is also collecting old records in respect of the history and culture of Manipur.

References

Administration Report of the Manipur Political Agency, 1873-74,1875-76, 1877-78, 1878-79, 1891-95, 1904-05.

Administration Report of the Manipur State, 1913-14, 1934-35,1939-40,1940-41.

Allen, B.C., 1905: Naga Hills and Manipur, Socio-Economic History, Gyan Publishing House, Delhi-110002.

Alexander Mackenzie, North East Frontier of India (1884).

Alexander Mackenzie, History of Relationssss of the Government with the Hill Tribes of the North East Frontier of Bengal, Calcutta, Home Press, 1884Angou Luwang, N., 1976.

A.S.W. Shimray, "History of Tangkhul Nagas", Akansha Publishing House, New Delhi, 2001.

Atombapu Sharma, Manipur Itihas, pp. 238-269.

B.C. Allen, E.A. Gait, C.G.H. Allen, H.F. Howard, Gazetteer of Bengal and North East India.

Bhogeswor, O., Ninghthourol Lambuba, 1967.

Bhogeswor, O., 1967: Ninghourol Sereng, 1967.

Brown, R., The Statistical Account of Manipur, 1873.

Byasa Deva's Mahabharata (*Sloks* 9 -13, chapter 211, Adiparva), Bengali scripts.

Bidhan Singha,Cultural Heritage of North-East India, Guwahati, 1999.

Bhimsen Singha - Let History and Facts speak about Manipuris, Silchar 1984.

Col. James Johnston, - My Experience in Manipur and Naga Hills, 1896.

Col Geini quoted by L Ibungohal Singh, Introduction to Manipur, pp 9-10.

Dinesh Chandra Sen : Brihod Banga, Page 32, Kolkata 35).

Dr. Anuradha Banarjee : Assam Khanda, Page 42.

Dr. Lal Dena (1826-1946),History of Modern Manipur,1990.

Dun E.W, Gazetteer of Manipur by, Delhi, Vivek Publishing House, 1975 (First Edn.1886)

Dr. Dinesh Chandra Sen - Brihod Bongo, 1935.

Dr. R. Brown - Imperial Gazetteer of India, 1908, Vol. xvii.

D. G.E. Hall, History of South East Asia, p. 121.

Dr. K.P. Sinha - The Bishnupriya Manipuri Language, 1984

Dr. M. Kirti Singh - Religious developments in Manipur in the 18th and 19th century, 1980.

Dr. M. Kirti Singh - Religion and Culture of Manipur, 1988.

G.E. Harvey, History of Burma, p. 9, 1925.

Grim wood, St. Ethel, My three years in Manipur (1892).

Hodson T.C. : The Meitheis.

Ibungohal L., Cheitharol Kumbaba, 1967.

Julon Mutua, Bijoy Panchalee (History of Manipur), 1936.

James Johnstone, 1896, 1971, 1983: Manipur and Naga Hills.

K.C. Tensuba, A Brief History of Meiteis and Thais,1993.

Khelchandra N, Padmashree, and Lairenjam Iboongohal Singh, Cheitharol Kumbaba, 1989.

Krishnamohon Dhar : Purbabango O Assam, 1909.

Laimayum Bishwanath Sharma, Guide Book, Mutua Museum, Cultural Heritage Complex, Mutua Museum, 2006.

L Ibunghal Singh - Introduction to Manipur, 1987.

L. Mani Singh and Shri Mangi Singh, Bijoy Panchali Part II.

L.W. Shakespeare, History of Manipur Rifles (1929).

Nagendranath Basu : Biswakosh (Encyclopedia Indica, vol. XIII, 1309, Bangla).

Naorem Sanajaoba "Manipur Treaties and Documents (1110-1971), Mittal Publications, New Delhi, 1993.

Nongthonbammacha Angou Luwang "Ningthou Kangbalon (Christagi managgi Ningthousing), P.S. Printers and Stationery, Imphal, 2002.

NBMM - The Mahasabha review, 1970.

NBMSS - Movement for safeguard of ethnic, cultural and linguistic identity, 1993.

Prof. Jyotirmoy Roy - History of Manipur 1973.

Mohendra Kumar Singha - Prachin Manopurer Itihas.

Mukundalal Chowdhury- Manipurer Itihas.

Ochchutcharan Chaudhury - Srihotter Itibritta, 1905.

P. Gunindra "Manipuri Numismatics, Mutua Museum, 1983.

Prof. Gangmumei Kabui, History of Manipur -1990.

R.C. Majumdar, Expansion of Aryan Culture in eastern India, pp. 12,15.

R.K. Jhalajit Singh, Manipur from 1508-1709, 1999, p. 6.

R.K. Jhalajit Singh, Padmashree, "A short history of Manipur (33 A.D to the present time), O.K. Store, Imphal, 1965.

R. Brown, Statistical Account of the native state of Manipur and the hill territory under its rule, Mittal Publications, 1874.

Roy, Jyotimor, History of Manipur, (1958,) (2nd edition 1973) -.

1835), 2000.

R.K. Sanahal Singh, Glimpse of Manipur, p. 3.

R.M. Nath -, The Background of Assamese Culture 2nd edn, 1978.

Sarangthem Bormani Singh, Sahitya Bhusan, "Meitei Ningthourol", Rajesh Book Store, Imphal, 2000.

Sena Singha- Prachinadhunik Somkhipta monipurer Itiha

Sir A. Phyre, History of Burma, p. 3.

Sir G. A. Grieorson - Linguistic Survey of India, Part III, vol. III.

S. Janaki - Unfolding Truth, 1992.

T.C.Hudson, The Meitheis, 1908, Low Price Publications, Delhi-110052.

T.C. Hodson, "The Naga Tribes of Manipur", MacMillan & Co., London 1911.

W. Mc. Culloch. Publications of G.H. Damat, An Account of the valley of Manipur and the hill tribes, 1859.

W. Yumjao Singh - An Early History of Manipur, 1966.

W. Yumjao Singh- Report on Archaeological studies in Manipur, p. 5.

W. Ibohal Singh, The History of Manipur.

Yule and Burnell, A Glossary of Anglo Indian Words, p. 597.

3

Geography, Fauna and Flora

Manipur (see plate-1) state has an area of 22,347 sq. km (8628 sq. miles) with a population of 2,388,634 (2001-Census) situated in the north easterns corner of India. It is situated between the parallels (23°50′N) -(25°41′N) and the meridians (92°59′E)- (94°45′E). It comprises of 2238 sq. km of flat plateau of alluvial valley and 20109 sq. km of hill territory and forms a part of the Himalayan mountain system which carries this cup-shaped valley inside its series of hill ranges. The plain or the valley is approximately 10% of the total area. It has a border of 854 km of which 398 km is international border with Myanmar (Burma) on the East. The remaining 456 km long border separates her from the neighbouring states of Nagaland on the North, Assam on the West and Mizoram on the So uth and the South West. The valley is oval shaped with a gentle slope towards the South measuring an altitude of 798 metres above MSL at the extreme North and 746 metres above MSL at the Southern end. The Imphal city (see plate-2) stands at an altitude of 790 metres above MSL.

CLIMATE

The climate of Manipur is cool and pleasant. The temperature never goes above 36 degree centigrade. At the hottest seasons, the night and morning are always cool. In the winter, there are sharp frost at night and heavy fogs often hang over the valley till the day is well advanced. The annual rainfall is about 70 inches in the hills and 100 inches in the valley. The valley gets the reflection of the heat of the summer and the cold of the winter from the neighbouring hills. The months of November, December, January and February remain dry and the remaining eight months are more or less rainy. January is very cold in winter and May-June are the hottest in summer.

There are six seasons in Manipur :-

- Yenningtha : Spring (February-March)
- Olangtha : Summer (April-May)
- Nongjutha: Rainy Season (June-July)
- Napungtha : Leafy (August-September)
- Louroktha : Autumn (October-November)
- Ningthamtha : Winter (December-Januray)

BOUNDARIES OF MANIPUR

Manipur is bounded by the Indian states of Nagaland in the north, Mizoram in the south and Assam in the west. it also borders the country of Myanmar to the east. Capt. R.B. Pemberton (1835) remarked that the territories of Manipur have fluctuated at various times with the fortunes of the princes, frequently extending for three or four days journey east beyond Chindwin river Ningthee, and west to the plains of Cachar "(Capt. R.B. Pemberton, Eastern Frontier of British India by, 1885, pp. 20). Sir James Johnstone, the political agent (1877–1886) also gave similar opinion. In 1885, indeed the forest between Manipur and the Doyeng and Dhunsiri was declared to be the boundary between Manipur and Assam. (Alexander Mackenzie. The North East Frontier of Bengal by, 1884, pp. 102). According to old chronicles, the boundary of Manipur extended upto Kale in Burma during the time of Ura Konthouba (639 A.D). During the time of Kyaamba (1467-1508 A.D), the boundary extended upto the whole of the Noajeeree hills running between the Moo and Chindwin (Ningthee) rivers on the east, upto Malugram of Cachar on the west.

HILL RANGES

The hills around the cup-shaped valley add to the natural beauty of Manipur. The hills are part of the Himalayas and are termed as Sub-Himalayan ranges. They are spread into ranges with irregular serrated ridges with tapering cliffs. There are several names given to these ranges. (See Plate-8)

The hill ranges on the west are :-

- Nunjaibong

- Kalanaga
- Chakka-Nungba
- Kaupum (a spur from the Laimatol)
- Kopru-Laimatol.

The hill ranges on the north are :-

- The Khunho spurs
- Thumion-Mayang-Khang
- Laisom
- Sirohifara.

The hill ranges on the east are

- Ching-angauba or Surameti
- Somrah
- Kassom
- Nupitel or Mapithel
- Yomadoung.
- Shirui Frar

The hill ranges on the south is Haobi. And other ranges

Among these Ching angauba or Surameti peak is the highest with 12,557ft.

The greatest altitude is attained in the extreme north, where Mao thana is overhung by a peak nearly 10,000 feet above the level of the sea. The hills between Cachar and Manipur are covered with dense evergreen forests and bamboo jungle. Pine tress are abundant in the western part, in the eastern part and along the Imphal- Mao road.

A traveller who enters Manipur by the Cachar road (Jiribam-Imphal) obtains a magnificent view of the valley from the summit of the Laimatol hill. The eastern face of the hill is covered with short grass. The valley lies before him like a map. At the northern end, some twenty miles away, are the dark-green groves that conceal the town of Imphal. Elsewhere are level rice fields, and land covered with grass, about which are dotted the clumps of trees that mark the villages. Low ridges of hills stand up above the soil and sheets of water gleam in the shallow depressions on the plain. To the south, the Loktak Lake sparkles in the sun, and on every side the view is bounded by hills.

The terrain, mostly jungle, is on a high plateau, about 2,600 ft (790 m) above sea level. The Manipur Hills have peaks rising to 8,500 ft (2,590 m) and are mainly covered with jungle.

RIVERS

The principal rivers in the Manipur valley are Imphal river, Barak river, Iril river, Irang, Thoubal river, Nambool river. The Imphal river originate from the Bolen Pat in Kangpokpi areas, flows through the valley and falls into the Chindwin river (Ningthi River) in Myanmar (Burma). The Iril river originates from Lakhamai of Purul block about 15 miles east of Maram, flows through the eastern part of the valley and falls into the Imphal river at Lilong. The Nambool river originates from Kounu range, Ablok and flows to the west of Imphal, where the Naga river joins at Imphal city near Maharani thong and falls into the Loktak lake. (see Plate-9 and 10).

The Nambool emerges from the Loktak Lake under the name Khordak. This river eventually joins the Imphal river and their united waters, which are known as Manipur river finally falls into Kendat (Chingnunghut) and thus into the Chindwin river. (Ningthi River). In the hills these rivers are bright and sparkling streams, flowing along over their rocky beds but in the valley they are muddy. The rivers in the valley are navigable by dug out canoes at all seasons of the year. During winter, the water in these rivers are very shallow. During the rainy season, they rise to a considerable height with considerable depth of water and sometimes overtop their banks leading to floods. The valley had many experiences of flooding in the past. The Thoubal river originates from the Ukhrul district and falls to the Imphal river near Irong Chesaba near Mayang Imphal.

The principal rivers in the hills are the Barak, Jiri, Makru, Irang, Lengba and Leimatak. The Jiri which forms the boundary between Assam and Manipur is about 40 yards wide where it is crossed by the Government road and is fordable in the dry season. The Makru which runs parallel to Jiri has a very clear stream and is also fordable in the dry season. In the eastern hills, there are numerous small streams which drain into the Yu and thence into the Chindwin. (Ningthi River). They flow through deep valleys, and are liable to sudden floods which render them difficult to cross, but only one of them, the Maklang, has any depth of water in the winter.

The principal rivers in the western hills are the Barak (Gwai river) and its tributary, the Irang. The Barak (Gwai) is the largest and most important river in Manipur hill territory. It originates from the Karong Mao area and falls into the Brahmaputra river. It receives the Makru river, the Irang, the Tipai which flows north from Mizoram and finally the Jiri. It is navigable for canoes above its junction with the Tipai. The Barak rises about ten miles east of Mao thana, and flows a westerly course as far as Kairong, where it crosses the Imphal -Kohima road. Here it takes a bend towards the north, and then turns westward, till it reaches the north-west corner of the State. The river then curves away towards the south, and flows the whole way to Tipaimukh near the tri-junction point of Manipur, Cachar (Assam) and the Lushai Hills (Mizoram) along the eastern side of the last main range of hills which separates Mizoram from Manipur. At Tipaimukh, the Barak turns sharply to the north, and as far as Jirighat, flows almost parallel with, though in the opposite direction to, the section of the river that lies between Kalanaga and Tipaimukh. In this portion of its course, it forms the boundary between Cachar and Manipur, but at Jirighat it turns again to the west, and, after a tortuous course through the districts of Cachar and Sylhet, falls into the old bed of the Brahmaputra near Bhairab Bazar. The principal tributary of the Barak is the Irang, which rises a little to the west of Kairong, and falls into it about 20 miles north of Tipaimukh. The Barak at Kairong contains a few inches of water only in the cold weather. The Irang river originates from the Langka Chongjan area of Kangpokpi and falls into the Barak river.

Two other rivers of some importance are the Jiri and the Makru. In the rains they are liable to sudden freshets, and, though there is no very great depth of water in the river, the current is extremely swift and strong.

LAKES *(IN MANIPURI, PAT MEANS LAKE)*

It was believed that the Manipur valley originally consisted of a large lake basin which gradually contracted in size until nothing remains but the Loktak Lake. According to R.B. Pemberton, this hypothesis is not correct (R.B. Pemberton, The Eastern Frontier of India", Mittal Publications, New Delhi-page 613). However subsequent discoveryof fossils of Cuttle marine fish at Koubru Ching at a height of 6000 fett above sea level supported the theory that Manipur was once submerged under water.

The Loktak Lake is a natural lake of 36 metres depth at Moirang in Bishnupur district. It is 8 miles long from north-west to south-east and 5 miles broad at its greatest breadth from the east to west. The dark green Eichornia (phumdi/water Hyacinth), reed and other aquatic plants floats on its surface abundantly. (see Plate- 4)

Dotted about the valley are numerous small lakes (Pats/ jhils) which only differ from the Loktak in point of size and depth. Many of them dry up completely in winter, or only contain a few pools in the lowest levels.The Lamphel Pat,Takyel Pats (lakes), Porompat, Kakwa Pat near Imphal are now becoming valuable as grazing grounds. The Waithou Shorien, the Waithou Phoomnaw, the Ekope, Kajipat, and Poomlen Pats were sold for considerable sums of money as fisheries.These, however, are but a few of the most important marshes in the valley, and, during the rainy season, there are probably between sixty and seventy small lakes in the valley of Manipur. Some other lakes are Kharung Pat, Sana Pat, Loukoi Pat, Ishok Pat, Lousi pat, Utra Pat, Heingang pat, Kachouphung Lake, Zailad Lake etc.

WATERFALLS

Important waterfalls are :-

- Barak waterfall
- Sadu Chiru waterfall
- Leimram waterfall
- Dilily waterfall
- Khayang waterfall

CAVES

Important caves are :-

- Khangkhui cave (Ukhrul)
- Tharon cave (Tamenglong)
- Tonglon cave (Churachandpur)
- Hundung Mangva (Ukhrul)
- Sangboo (Chandel)
- Khukse (Churachandpur)

FAUNA AND FLORA

Blessed with an amazing variety of flora and fauna, 68% of the geographical area of Manipur is hill tract covered with forests. Depending on the altitude of hill ranges, the climatic condition varies from tropical to sub-alpine. The wet forests and the pine forests occur between 900-2700 metres above MSL and they together sustain a host of rare and endemic plant and animal life.

WILDLIFE - A RICH NATURAL HERITAGE OF MANIPUR

Manipur has a rich heritage of wild life. (see plates 11-20) The common animals found in Manipur are as follows:-

Table-18 Showing varieties of wild life in Manipur

Sl. No.	*English Name*	*Manipuri Name*	*Scientific Name*
1.	Bison/ Mithun	Sandang	Bos Frontalis
2.	Duck, Spot bills, etc	Nganu Thangong, Pirrel	
3.	Wild Goose	Lamkanga	
4.	Snipe	Nganu Thoidingnam	
5.	Ducks	Uthum, Ura	
6.	Turtle Dove	Lamkhunu	Streptopelia Orientalis
7.	Brown Owl	Ching Maku	Strix Indranee
8.	Blyth's Tragopan	Lamyen	Tragopan Belythi
9.	Pheasant	Nongin	Syrmitacus huminae humina
10.	Ducks (Quail)	Wainu Laisagol (Soibol)	Grus grus litfordi
11.	Partridge (Grey & Black)	Urembi	
12.	Deer	Shaji	Muntiacus Muntjak
13.	Deer (Spotted)	Shaji Arangba	Axis Axis
14.	Monkey	Yong	Macaca Assaminesis
15.	Slow Loris	Yong Ekaithibi	Necticebus Coucang
16.	Hoolock Gibbon	Yongmu	Hylobates hoolock hoolock
17.	Black Bear	Sawom	Selenarectos Thebetanus
18.	Civet Cat	Moirang Sathibi	Viverra Spp
19.	Leopard Cat	Keijenglang	Felis Bengalensis
20.	Serow	Sabeng	Capricornis sumatrensis
21.	Porcupine	Sabou	Hystrix Indica
22.	Hog Deer	Kharsa	Axis Proxinus
23.		Umu	Porphyrio Porphyrio
24.	Brow antlered deer	Sangai	Cervus Eldi Eldi
25.	Deer (Sambar)	Shajan	Cervus Unicolor
26.	Tiger	Keijao	Panthera Tigris
27.	Leopard	Kabokei	Panthera Pardus
	Python	Lairen	Python Molurus

In-situ conservation sites:

Table-19 Showing In-situ Consrvation sites in Manipur

Conservation site	*Location (District)*	*Area in sq. km*
Keibul Lamjao National Park	Bishnupur	40.00
Yangoupokpi Lokchao Wildlife Sanctury	Chandel	184.80
Bunning Wildlife Sanctury	Tamenglong	115.80
Zeliad Wildlife Sanctury	Tamenglong	21.00
Keilam Wildlife Sanctury	Churachandpur	187.50
Jiri-Makru Wildlife Sanctury	Tamenglong	198.00
Shirui Hill National Park	Ukhrul	41.00

Ex-situ conservation sites

Table-20 Showing Ex-situ Consrvation sites in Manipur

Conservation sites	*Location (District)*	*Area in sq.km*
Manipur Zoological Garden (including second home of Sangai)	Imphal (Iroisemba)	0.68
Orchid Preservation Centre	Imphal (Khonghampat)	0.50

Manipur is exceedingly rich in natural resources with a vast and varied fauna heritage. Many of the species of animals found in Manipur are endemic, foremost among them being the Sangai or the Brow Antlered Deer (Cervus Eldi Eldi), which in its unique wetland ecosystem is restricted to Manipur only. The other two related species have been reported from Myanmar and Thailand. The Manipuri Sangai stand at about 45 inches at the shoulder, and are fawn-coloured in summer and of a darker hue in winter. The height and weight of a fully grown stag may be approximately 115-125 cm. and 95 to 110 kg. respectively. Males are higher and heavier than female. The horns have an extremely long curved brow-antler, joining the beam in such a manner that the two form one continuous curve at right angles to the pedicel. The beam is un-branched for a considerable distance, generally more than half the length, and curved backwards, then outwards, and lastly forwards; towards the end it bears a number of small points. These deers are no longer common, and are generally found in swampy ground. The related species of cervus eldi are found in Burma, the Malay Peninsula, Cambodia, and Hainan.

KEIBUL LAMJAO NATIONAL PARK

The Keibul Lamjao was declared as a national park on 28 March, 1977. The extent of area is 40 sq.km. It is a moist semi–evergreen type of forest. It has a combination of aquatic wetland and terrestrial eco-system.

Once believed to be extinct, this rare most *Cervus Eldi Eldi* was rediscovered in the year 1953. The unique habitat of this most threatened Cervus Eldi in the world constitute mostly of floating mass of vegetation (known locally as phum/phumdi) on Loktak Lake. Though not a spectacular increase, the population from about 14 heads in 1974, has grown to 180 individuals in 2003. In this fragile eco-system, this endemic deer still faces the danger of extinction. All efforts are being made by the Wildlife Wing of the Forest Department of Manipur with the active co-operation of local people to save this race of deer.

Many vertebrates faunas like Fishes, Amphibian, Reptiles-such as Tortoise, Viper, Krait, Cobra, python, Common Lizard, Mammals-Sangai, hog deer, Wild boar, Large Indian Civet Cat, Common Otter etc. are available at Keibul Lamjao. The only ape found in India, the Hoolock Gibbon locally known as *Yongmu,* commonly occurs in all the five hill districts of Manipur. Similarly, the Slow Loris, the Stump Tailed Macaque, the Pig-Tailed Macaque are the other rare primates that occur in the forests of Manipur.

Amongst the carnivores, the Clouded Leopard and the Golden Cat are the rare nocturnal animals found in Manipur. Tigers and leopards are found in the interior parts of the state. The leopards are more common, whereas tigers are seldom reported now. The elephant, makes seasonal migration into the State in the Indo-Myanmar border areas, along the Taret river course and also in the western parts from Assam.

The Himalayan Black Bear (Selenarctos thibetanus) is commonly found all over the hills of Manipur. The rare and elusive Malayan Sun Bear (Helarctos Malyanus) is restricted to the forests in the Indo-Myanmar border areas and inhabits the Yangoupokpi Lokchao Wildlife Sanctuary of Manipur.

If one were to take a tour of New Samtal, a small town in the Indo-Myanmar border areas, specially during the night, one can see herds of Bison, as well as of Sambhar along the road. The Barking Deer, the commonest Cervus in Manipur prefers the hilly areas while the Hog Deer, another deer found in the North-East India can be sighted at Keibul Lamjao National Park in Manipur. Serow *(Sabeng)* (Capricornis sumatraensis) is another rarity in the wilderness of Manipur. The animal chooses to live in the most inhospitable area for man, but finds itself at ease on the steep slopes of rocky mountains in Tamenglong and Senapati districts and Keilam hill ranges of Churachandpur district. The true badgers are not found in Asia. However, the Hog badgers and Ferret Badgers are the rarest South East Asian representatives. They are widely distributed in the hills of Manipur. Of the two, the Hog Badgers known as *Nungok* are more common in Manipur. The Ferret Badgers have nocturnal mode of life and are seldom sighted and the population is small. The Pangolins, Bear Cats, Spotted Linsangs are declining in numbers. The Spotted Linsang and Himalayan Yellow Throated Marten are quite beautiful and found in the Barak watershed. The Pangolins are encountered in the Indo-Myanmar border areas and the Binturongs or Bear Cats are found in the forests of Senapati district.

The Javan Rhinoceros was seen roaming along the Khuga river valley in Churachandpur district as late as the beginning of 20th century, but now it is extinct from Manipur and hence from India. The wild Ox of Myanmar (Bantering) known as *'Santhou'* in Manipuri was last seen thirty years ago. In all probability these animals have vanished from the Manipur soil forever. The Hoolock Gibbon, Stump Tailed macaques, Slow Loris, Clouded Leopard, Golden Cat, Marbled Cat, Banturong, Spotted Linsang, Malayan Sun Bear, Smooth Indian Otter, Hog Badger, Malayan Gaint Squirrel, the Serow (Sabeng) and most other denizens of forest are making a precarious existence in the forests of Manipur, and all of them are on the verge of extinction: (source–Forest Department of Manipur).

The common aquatic floras in Keibuil Lamjao are Zizania latifolia *(Ishing kambong),* Saccharum munja *(Khoimom)*, Saccharum bengalensis, Eiranthus procerus *(Singnang),* Dioschoria bulbifera (*Phum),*Cynodon dactylon *(Tingthou),* Alpinia galanga *(Pullei),* Eichornia crossipes *(Kabokang),* Hedychium coronarium *(Loklei),* Nelumbo nucifera *(Thambal),*Phragmites karka *(Tou)* and 100 other species:(source–Forest Department of Manipur)

BIRDS, REPTILES, COMMON ANIMALS

Among the birds, the White Wood Duck, Pink Headed Duck, Grey-Leg Goose, Mallard, Brahminy Duck, Clucking-teal, Plover, Hooded Crane, Brown

Headed gull, Avocat White ibis, Glossy Ibis, Indian Shag, Open Bill stork, Black Necked Stork, and a host of others have become extremely rare, and many of them are probably extinct from the State.

Nongin was recorded originally in Manipur, Patkai Naga and Mizo hills. Heavy bodied, walk and run well. Food habit - Omnivorous but seeds and berries are the staple diet. Cannot fly for long distances. Believed to be monogamous, the breeding season is mainly April to June. Eggs 6-11, cream to rosy white, incubation period 27 days. Colourful, head, neck and rump bright burnt sienna with three prominent white areas on each side. Female largely reddish brown, streaked with black and has shorter tail. Have soft plumage and the males have a more brilliant colouring than females.

Manipur should be proud of her rich avi-fauna. All the members of phasinidae are colourful but Mrs. Hume's barred back Pheasant (Syrmitacus huminae) and Blyth's Tragopan found in Manipur are spectacular and stand out from the rest of the group.

The Khaleej Pheasant found in Manipur is a rich mixture of steely black and white and is definitely quite elegant. The Burmese pea fowls and jungle fowls are the other long feathered pheasants found in Manipur. The important birds found in Manipur are : Hume's pleasant (phasianus humix), peacock pheasant (polyplectrum), ordinary Kalij pheasant, jungle fowl (gallus ferrugineus), Wood cock, Jungle fowl (gallus ferrugineus). (source–Forest department of Manipur).

FISHES : The fishes commonly found in Manipur are as follows :

Table-21 Showing variesties of indigenous fishes available in Manipur

Sl.No	*Local Name*	*Scientific Name*
1.	Khajing	Machrobrachium rossenbergii
2.	Ukabi	Anabas testudineus
3.	Pengba (see plate -58)	Osteobrama belangeril
4.	Meitei Sareng	Wallago attee
5.	Nunga	Tor putitora
6.	Nunga	Tor progenies
7.	Nunga	Acrossoceilus hexagonolepis
8.	Nunga	Acrossoceilus manipurensis
9.	Nunga	Balitora brucei
10.	Nunga	Pseudochensis sulcatus
11.	Ngakijou	Lepidocephalchthys berdmorei
12.	Ngaten	Ompok bimaculatus
13.	Ngaten	Ompok pabada
14.	Ngaten	Ompok pabo

(Contd.)

(Contd. Table 21)

Sl.No	Local Name	Scientific Name
15.	Ngaten	Danio acuticephala
16.	Ngaren	Danio devaria
17.	Ngaren	Bagarius bagaius
18.	Ngasang	Gudusia chapra
19.	Ngasang	Esomus denricus
20.	Ngasang	Esomus manipurensis
21.	Ngasang	Dani acquipinnatus
22.	Ngasang	Danio manipurensis
23.	Ngasang	Danio naganensis
24.	Ngasang	Rasbora rasbora
25.	Ngasang	Rasbora elanga
26.	Ngaton/Khabak	Cirrhinus reba
27	Ngaton	Labeo angra
28.	Ngamu	Channa spp
29.	Ngapai	Notopierus chitala
30.	Nganap	Lepidocephalus guntea
31.	Ngasep	Mystus bleekeri
32.	Ngasep	Mystus tengra
33.	Ngasep	Mystus carvasius
34.	Ngachik	Heteropneusleas fossilis
35.	Ngapang	Glyptothorax pectinopterus
36.	Ngapang	Glyptothorax pectinatus
37.	Ngapang	Glyptothorax telchita
38.	Ngapang	Glyptothorax lonah
39.	Ngapang	Glyptothorax cavia
40.	Ngapang	Glyptothorax manipurensis
41.	Ngapang	Glyptothorax trilineatus
42.	Ngaril	Macrognatus alboguttatus
43.	Ngaril Leina	Anguilla bengalensis
44.	Phabounga	Puntius Chola
45.	Phabounga	Puntius clavatus clavatus
46.	Phabounga	Puntius clavatus burtoni
47.	Phabounga	Puntius saphore
48.	Phabounga	Puntius Chola
49.	Phabounga	Puntius clavatus clavatus
50.	Phabounga	Puntius clavatus burtoni
51.	Phabounga	Puntius saphore
52.	Nganoi	Puntius sarana
53.	Nganoi	Puntius sarana orphoides
54.	Ngakha	Punitius ticto
55.	Ngakra	Clarias batrachus
56.	Sarengkhoibi	Botia hymenophysa
57.	Sarengkhoibi	Botia berdmorei

Fish coming from outside

Table-22 Showing variestioes of fishes imported from outside

Sl. No	*Local Name*	*Scientific Name*
1.	Rou/Rohu	Labeo rohita
2.	Catla	Catla Catla
3.	Kuri	Labeo Gonius
4.	Mirgal	Cirrhinus mrigala
5.	Silver Carp	Hypopthalmichthys molitrix
6.	Puklaobi	Cyprimus carpio var specularis
7.	Puklaobi	Cyprimus carpio var communis
8.	Puklaobi	Cyprimus carpio var nudus
9.	Napi chabi (Grass Carp)	Ctneopharyngodon idella

Fish is an important item of food for the people of Manipur. The state can produce about 18600 metric tons of fish every year against the requirement of about 25600 metric tons of fish. There are 113 fisheries under the State Revenue Department covering about 40,000 hectares. (Source Fishery Department, Government of Manipur, 2008)

SOIL

The soil is considered fit for all kinds of grain crops, vegetables and fruits. The soil of the Manipur valley is an alluvial clay washed down from the surrounding hills. The mountains to the north are largely composed of pre tertiary slates and sandstones with upper tertiary deposits on the higher ridges and on the hills overhanging the Chindwin valley. The natural vegetation occupies an area of nearly 67% of the total geographical area of the state. It is blessed with amazing varieties of fauna and flora. Depending on the altitude of the hill ranges, the forest ranges from tropical to sub-alpine. The wet forests, the temperate forests and the pine forests occur between 900-2700 m above sea level and they together sustain hosts of rare and endemic plant and animal life. In Manipur natural habitat grows in soil or on trees and shrubs, spreading their beauty and colour, stunning the eye that is not used to seeing them in such profusion.

FOREST

Forests are the natural treasure trove of biological and genetic diversity. It is a self-supporting and self-sustained biological system and forms the fresh and livable habitat for living beings including human. Manipur has 78.92 percent of its total geographical area covered by forests according to the ground survey report of the Forest Survey of India in 1995. This accounts for an area of 17,621 sq. km. under forest cover. The coverage of dense or true forests is estimated as 719.3 sq. km. only, which merely constitutes 3.2 % of the total geographical area of the state.

It has been reported that Manipur is one of the regions having very large area of forests under Jhum cultivation (Shifting Cultivation) in India as 83,526 families are reportedly practicing it. In 1976, the total area under jhuming has been 1,832 sq. km. but the area has gradually increased 1.9 and 2.6 times by 1983 and 1990 respectively. Now, the total area under Jhum is estimated at 4,905 sq. km (8% of total jhum land of India) and the largest area cleared for the practice is 1,400 sq km in Senapat district, followed successively by 1200, 710 and 675 sq km at Churachandpur, Ukhrul and Tamenglong districts respectively.

Massive burning practiced during the "slash and burn" process of jhum is the major cause of the depletion of the important tree species like pine, teak, phoebe (Uningthou), Juglans (Heijuga) etc. Besides, a number of important shrubs, bamboos, canes, aromatic and medicinal plants (some of which are endemic in the State) are also vanishing from the forest. Another important consequence of the rapid depletion of forest in Manipur is the gradual decrease of fuel wood production from 70,264 cu m in 1986 to 24,958 cu m in 1990 (Govt. of Manipur, 1991). The reduction of fuel wood over the span of 5 years is –estimated at 11,300 cu m annually. The per capita availability of fuel wood in the state is also substantially reduced from 0.03 cu m in 1981 to 0.013 cu m by 1991. When this figure is compared to the per capita availability of fuel wood for India during 1980-1990 (0.02 cu m) a very acute shortage in fuel wood availability is evident in the state.

VEGETATION

The natural vegetation occupies an area of about 14,365 sq. km. which is nearly 64% of the total geographical area of the State. The vegetation consists of a large variety of plants ranging from short and tall grasses, reeds and bamboos to trees of various species.

Area covered by different forest types under Tree Forest and Open Forest in Manipur, 1976

Table-23 Showing types of forests in Manipur

Types of Forest	*Tree Forest*		*Open Forest*	
	Area (sq.km.)	*P.C. to Total Forest Area*	*Area (sq.km.)*	*P.C. to Total Forest Area*
Wet Hill Forest	3,918.20	25.86	2672.09	17.63
Pinus-casia Forest	1,519.40	10.03	923.37	6.09
Wet Temperate Forest	1,284.90	8.48	166.11	1.10
Teak Gurjan Forest	459.24	3.03	151.45	1.00
Semi-Evergreen Forest	439.70	2.90	205.19	1.35
Total Forest	7,621.44	50.29	4,118.51	27.18

Source : Statistical Bulletin of Forest Department, 1999-2000, Govt. of Manipur.

WET HILL FORESTS

A Saurauja-Belis chmiedia-phoebe association is found to cover the upper slopes upto the top of the medium elevations. The dominant species found are, *Saouraja nepalensis, S. panduana, S. roxburhiana, Phoebe lanceolata, P. paniculata, Beilscmiedia assamica, B. rosburghiana, Schima wallichii, Quercus sp. Nyssa sessiliflora, Cinnamom cecidodaphne, C. pauciflora, Eriobotrya bengalensis, Echinocarpus dasycarpus, Morus laevigata, Litsea panamonja, L. sebifera, Cryptocarea andersoni, Machilus odoratissima, M. parviflora, M. bombycina, Ostodes paniculata, Lithocarpus spicatus, Engelhadtia sp., Vaecinium dominianum, Castanopsis sp.* These forests are found extensively in Manipur covering an area of 3918.20 sq. km. of Tree forests and 2,672.09 sq.km. of open forests that may account for 43.49% of the total forest area of the state. (source–Forest Department, Government of Manipur)

PINUS CASIA FORESTS

Pine forests are found in the sub-mountain zones of the north-eastern and southern hills of Manipur. These form 10.03% of the tree forests and 6.09% of the open forests. Associated dominant species are, *Quercus sp., Pasania sp, Castanopsis sp.* etc.

Pines (Uchan) are mostly large trees with a straight trunk with whorls of smaller lateral branches, but they have a wide range of habits varying from tall narrow trees to small bushy trees to prostrate shrubs. They are generally long-lived, usually over 100 years in suitable environments. All pine species are evergreen, i.e., they keep their leaves for at least two growing seasons (and up to about 30 years in the case of P. longaeva). (see plate-23)

Pines are evergreen and resinous. The bark of most pines is thick and scaly, but some species have thin, flaking bark. The branches are produced in regular "pseudowhorls", actually a very tight spiral but appearing like a ring of branches arising from the same point. Many pines are *uninodal*, producing just one such whorl of branches each year, from buds at the tip of the year's new shoot, but others are *multinodal*, producing two or more whorls of branches per year. The spiral growth of branches, needles and cone scales are arranged in Fibonacci number ratios. The new spring shoots are sometimes called "candles"; they are light-coloured and point upward at first, then later darken and spread outward. These "candles" offer foresters a means to evaluate fertility of the soil and vigour of the trees.

Table-24 Showing Forest Area According to Vegetation Types in Manipur, 1976

Vegetation Type	*Area in sq.km.*	*P.C. to total forest area*	*P.C. to total land area*
Tree Forests	7,621.44	50.29	34.14
Open Forests	4,118.51	27.18	18.45
Bamboo brakes	3,268.00	21.57	14.64
Grass brakes	146.00	0.96	0.65
Total	**15,153.95**	**100.00**	**67.87**

Source: Statistical Bulletin of Forest Department, 1995-96, Govt. of Manipur.

WET TEMPERATE FORESTS

Extensive luxuriant primary forests can be seen between the altitudes 1800-2700 m. the area covered is predominantly by the Tree forest i.e. 8.48% while disturbed open forests account for only 1.10% of total forest area. A vegetation of Quercus Manolia-Acer association is found in these forests. The dominant species are *Quercus iliate, Q. iliate, Q. glauca, Pasania xylocarpa, P.pachyphylla, P.iliate, Michelia lanugiosa, M. Campbell, Phoeba paniculata, Schima khasiana, Alseodaphane dumicola, Castanopsis tribuloides, Evodia fraxinifolia, Acer campbelli, Betula alnodes, Prunus cerasoides, Pyrus pashia, Osa gigantia, Mohima manipurensis, Manglietia insignis, Illicium griffithii, Bucklandia pupulanea, Michlia manipurensis* etc. The high altitude dwarf bamboo, Arundinaria malines is also found in these forests.

SUB-ALPINE FORESTS

Not many ranges reach a height beyond 2700 metres in Manipur. A sub-alpine vegetation is observed on sporadic hill tops with characteristic species comprising *Prunus sp, Pyrus sp, Taxus sp.Ilex sp, Ternstroemia sp., Bucklandia populanea, Acer campbelli, Magnolia campbelli, Castanopsis aribuloides, Rhododendron madinii, R. johnstoneaum, R. manipurensis, R. Wattii, R. elliottii, Primula sp.* etc.

The name *Eucalyptus* means "well-covered"; it describes the bud cap (technically called an operculum). The most readily recognisable characteristics of *Eucalyptus* species are the distinctive flowers and fruits. This cap forms from modified petals and falls off as the flower opens. Thus flowers have no petals, decorating themselves instead with many showy stamens. The woody fruits are roughly cone-shaped and have valves at the end which open to release the seeds. (see plate -24)

Nearly all eucalypts are evergreen but some tropical species lose their leaves at the end of the dry season. An essential oil extracted from eucalypt leaves contains compounds that are powerful natural disinfectants and which can be toxic in large quantities.

Eucalypts have many uses which have made them economically important trees. They provide many desirable characteristics for use as ornament, timber, firewood and pulpwood. Fast growth also makes eucalypts suitable as windbreaks. Eucalypts draw a tremendous amount of water from the soil through the process of transpiration. They have been planted (or re-planted) in some places to lower the water table and reduce soil salination. Eucalypts have also been used as a way of reducing malaria by draining the soil. Drainage removes swamps which provide a habitat for mosquito larvae.

The Eucalyptus cinerea grows to an average of 20 to 30 feet tall. Young leaves are round, grey-green, and about 1 inch in diameter and grow opposite each other on the stem. They become longer, more oval shaped with pointed ends as they get older. The flowers are a creamy white and grow in 1 inch clusters. The bark is reddish-brown and fibrous.

Doctors and herbalists around the world use Eucalyptus in medicines to treat many sicknesses such as: infections, colds, flu, sore throats, bronchitis, pneumonia, aching, stiffness, neuralgia and even some skin infections.

TEAK GURJAN FORESTS

These forests are found along the eastern longitudinal strip of Indo-Burma border at low altitude under a tropical climate constituting 4.03% of total forest area. The dominant species of Teak available in this belt are *Tectona grandis, Dipterocarpus tuburculatus, D. tearbinatus, Melanorrahoea usitata, Dillenia sp, Xylia sp, Langestroemias, Terminalia sp, Gmelina sp, Bombax sp*, etc. (see plate-25)

Money doesn't grow on trees. But money can grow on Teaks. Teak timber fetches very high price because of its grain, colour and strength. It is said that furniture made of teak last about 200 years without any problem. Hence teak plantations have been raised for industrial purposes since long. Teak prefers moist, warm tropical climate. It can withstand extremes of temperature, but maximum and minimum shade temperatures of 39- 44°C and 13–17°C respectively are the most favourable for its growth.

At 20 years of age the height growth was 23.1 metres and diameter was 28.7 cm. The first quality teak at 20 years of age will attain the average diameter is 27.2 cm and average height of 23.2 m. The number of trees per acre is 102. The total yield of stem timber is 28.04 m^3; that means on an average a tree on first quality site at 20 years of age under natural conditions of growth will yield around 0.283 cubic metres of timber on good sites. At the best, we may expect a tree to produce a maximum of 0.60 m^3 of timber in 20 years under best conditions of intensive management and there could be a maximum of 100 trees per acre. Manipur soil is very good for growing teak. Teak grows very welll in the valley. But the Forest department of Manipur is not taking up any systematic and long term plan to grow teak while most of hills are lying barren. Teak is a big, precious tree. The Forest Department, Government of Manipur need to do a lot of hard work to popularize and plant teak trees in the valley and hill districts of Manipur

Children's Story

The Teak Tree

"My grandchildren, my brothers and sisters, my sons and daughters, it is morning now. Shall we go for a walk? Look at this dense teak forest. The government of Sri Lanka grows thousands of these teak trees. Do you know why they grow this particular tree? Because its wood is quite valuable, and they can sell it to other countries. It is very beautiful, useful, light, and durable. Because teak is easier to work with than the wood of any other tree, it can be used for many purposes. Carpenters can make beds, tables, and

chairs out of this wood, and builders can use the seasoned planks for houses and roofs. To gain the greatest benefit from the teak tree, however, you should wait at least twenty to thirty years before cutting it down. Only then will its oil develop and its color darken. The oil in the seasoned wood is so bitter and poisonous that insects will not attack it. But when the tree is young, the oil is mixed with water, and the quality of the wood is poor. It can still be sold as teak, but it is not as beautiful or durable as it will be later. Only after it reaches a mature state will it attain its full value and last for two to three hundred years, long after other woods have rotted. Its planks will be firm, and the buildings and furniture made from it will remain strong and beautiful. If you polish it, you can make it shine like a mirror, and from generation to generation, it will need only occasional cleaning and reconditioning.

My grandchildren, look at that tree over there. It seems to be mature enough for cutting. It is probably about forty or fifty years old. Most of the other trees here are only two or three years old. Look how small they are, measuring less than a foot in circumference. If their branches are pruned regularly, they will grow straight, and in twenty years they will be ready for cutting. However, because the government is impatient to use them for building, they often chop down the young trees while the wood is still white. But these trees are not strong and should not be used so soon. The rain and wind will rot the wood within a year.

My love to you, my grandchildren. Man is like the teak tree. Even though he may be called a human being, he will not develop his full value until he reaches maturity. Before then, no matter how learned he may be, no matter how many arts and sciences he has studied, he will be like the young teak tree, of no use to himself or anyone else. If he is cut down before his time, he will not be of any use at all in this birth. The immature man will be destroyed.(Courtesy- **M. R. Bawa Muhaiyaddeen-** *Come to the Secret Garden: Sufi Tales of Wisdom)*

SEMI EVERGREEN FORESTS

These forests are found in the western part of Manipur adjoining Cachar district of Assam. The forests of this type comprise a vegetation of Laurus-Melia Bauhinia association. Family Lauraceae is represented by *Phoebe lanceolata, Cinnamom cecidodaphne, C.abtusifolium, Actinodaphne sikkimensis, A.aboyata, Machilus macrantha, M. parviflora, Litsaea salicifolia, Lindera merlastomaea, Meliceae includes, Amoora rohituka, A.*

wallichii, Toona iliate, Cedrela febrifusa, Dysoxlum binectariferum and D. hamiltonii.Jhum fields.

TREES OF MANIPUR

Many hills in Manipur are covered with luxuriant growth of forests with nageswar, jurul, India-rubber, tan, oak, ash, teak, palm (in eastern slopes). Pinus Longifolia is found in Somrah basin and in northern portion. (Gazetteer by Captain Dun and B.C. Allen Gazetteer of Naga Hills and Manipur). Uningthou, Uningthou manbi, Pine, Teak, Khew Oak, Khangra, Leihao, Tairen, Nageswar., Tolhao, Bamboo, Cane, etc. are important forest resources growing in plenty in Manipur.

The following trees are the main forest resources of the state.

Table-25 Showing names of Trees of Manipur

Sl.No	*Manipur Name*	*English Name*	*Botanical Name*
1.	Chingsu	Teak	Tectona grandis
2.	Uningthou		Phocbe hainensiana bradic
3.	Tera	Silk Cotton Tree	Bambax malabaricum D.C
4.	Khuman Tera		Bambox insigni
5.	Uchan	Pine	Pinus insularia Endl
6.	Leihao	Chanpac	Michelia champaka. Linn
7.	Khewu	Burmese Lacquer Tree	Melanorrhoea usitata wall
8.	Nageshor	Iron wood	Mesua ferrea Linn
9.	Khangra	English Gurjun Tree	Diptoriocarpus tuberculatus Roxb
10.	Thangji		Castanopsis hystrix Miers MMiersMiers
11.	Tairel	Red Cedar	Cedrela toona Roxb
12.	Ching tairel	Wild cedar	Cedrella serrata
13.	Taimareng	Chittagong wood	Chukrassia tabularis A. Juss
14.	Wang	Malay bush beech	Gmelina arborea Linn
15.	Heijuga	Walnut	Juglans regia Linn
16.	Jarol	Queen's flora	Lagerstroemia flos raginal
17.	Usoi	Needle wood	Schima wallichii (Dc) Koth
18.	Misi	Trumpet flower	Stereospermum personatum (H) D chelonoides
19.	Tolhao		Terminalia myriocarpa
20.	Ushingsha	Cinnamon	Cinnamomum zeylanicum Breyn

(Contd.)

(Contd. Table 25)

Sl.No	Manipur Name	English Name	Botanical Name
21.	Mekruk	East India Copal	Canarium bengalense Roxb
22.	Khal		Albizzia procera Benth
23.	Ueel	Siris	Albizzia lebbeck Becth
24.	Pareng		Alnus nepalesis D. Don
25.	Manahi	Yellow myrobalan	Terminalia chebula Retz
26.	Wangphop		Trewia nudiflora Linn
27.	Heirangoi		Amoora rohituka W & Arn
28.	Keli Kodom		Anthocepalus cadamba
29.	Theibong	Jack fruit Tree	Artocarpus intergrifolia
30.	Uthum Naraobi	Bishop Weed	Bischofia javanica Blume
31.	Tal		Duabanga grandiflora ® Walp sonneratioides
32.	Heikru	Indian Goose berry	Phyllanthus Emblica Linn
33.	Jam	Java Plum	Eugenia jambalana Lamk
34.	Cham		Artocarpus chaplasha
35.	Chahui	Gold Shower (Indian labournum)	Cassia fistula Linn
36.	Nanap		Gynometra polyandra
37.	Yangou	English gurjan	Dipterocarpus tuberculantus Roxb
38.	Khabi		Kydia calycina Roxb
39.	Tumitla		Litseaea potyantha Juss
40.	Lakoi		Macaranga denticulate M. Arg
41.	Heinou	Mango Tree	Mangifera indica Linn
42.	Heibi		Meyna Robyns taxiflora
43.	Heiri Khagok	Bael Tree	Aegle marmelos
44.	Yongchak	Tree Bean	Perkia roxburghii G. Don
45.	Chingthrao Angouba	White Bauhinia	Bauhinia acuminata
46.	Chningthrao Angangba	Red Bauhinia	Bauhinia variegatta
47.	Ureirom	Anatto	Bixa orellana
48.	Tomal Pambi		Garcinia Morella Desr.
49.	Sahi Pambi		Castonopsis tribuloides A. Dc.
50.	Rubber Pambi		Ficus elastica Roxb.
51.	U-thambal	Southern Magnolia	Magnolia grandiflora
52.	Heikreng		Celtis australis Linn
53.	Kabuliya	Silver Oak	Gravillea robusta
55.	Boroi	Ber tree	Zyzyfus jujuba
56.	Khok	Albizza stipulata	Albizia chinensis (o) Merr
57.	Karpur	Camphor	Cinnamomum Camphora
58.	Tejpat	Indian cassia	Cinnamomum tamala
59.	Mangge	Tamarind	Tamarindus indica
66.	Aagar	Eagle wood	Aqui;avia ,elaccensis lamk
67.	Heibong	Fig	Ficus carica Linn

(Contd.)

(Contd. Table 25)

Sl. No	*Manipur Name*	*English Name*	*Botanical Name*
68.	Heiba	Eve's apron	Ficus auriculata lour
69.	Heibung		Garcinia anomala planch
70.	Heiyen	Big nay	Antidesma bunius (L) Spreng
71.	Heitroi	Puneala plum	Flacourtia jangoomas (L) Rouch
72.	Heimang	Varnich tree	Rhus semialata Murr.

Uningthou: (Phoebe ssp.) Phoebe hainensiana

Uningthou means "the King of Trees". This is a dominant evergreen and timberable tree with bark thick and dark grey colour, attaining a height upto 150 ft. and 20 ft. girth with clean bole with rounded crown. It yield yellow wood excellent for use of furniture. It is found more in wet mixed and evergreen type of forests of south, west and eastern part of Manipur. Seed time is September-October and the best time for collection of seed is the end of October. Dormancy period of seed is over two months. Germination percentage is about 80%. This is a very popular tree in Manipur. (see plate-22)

BAMBOO BRAKES OF MANIPUR

There are different varieties of bamboos all over Manipur. The bamboo brakes cover an area of 3268.00 sq. km. which is 14.64% of the total geographical area of the state or 21.51% of the total forest area. (see plate-21)

Table-26 Showing varieties of bamboos available in Manipur

Sl. No.	*Local Names*	*Technical Names*
1.	Tenwa	Arundinaria callosa
2.	Watang khoi	Bambusa vulgaris
3.	Saneibi	Bambusa balcoa / Bambusa arundinacea
4.	Khok –wa.(Male bamboo)	Dendrocalamus strictus (Roxb) Nees.
5.	Utang	Bambusa pallida / Bambusa tulda
6.		Bambusa. kingiana,
7.		Bambusa. arundinacea,
8.	Pokshang	Cepholostachyum
9.		Cephalostachyum fuchsianum,
10.		Cephalostachyum pogracil
11.	Unan	Dendrocalamus strictus

(Contd.)

(Contd. Table 26)

Sl. No	*Local Names*	*Technical Names*
12.	Uei	Dendrocalamus sericeous
13.	Longnga	Dendrocalamus flagellifer
14.	Wanap/unap/pecha	Dendrocalamus hamiltonii /
15.	Meirabob	Dendrocalamus giganteus
16.	Muli	Melocanna baccifera
17.	Moubi	Melocanna bambusoides
18.		Melocanna humilis
19.	Raat	Teinostachyum wightii
20.	Dulu	Teinostachya dulooa
21.	Khok	

The Forest Department, Government of Manipur has carried out a survey of bamboo stock and growing stock of bamboo to determine the average yield per annum, as given below:

Table-27 Showing varieties of bamboos available in Manipur

Sl. No.	*Name of Block*	*Geographical area (sq. kms.)*	*Total Bamboo area (sq. kms.)*	*Qty. of bamboo in lakh tonnes*	*Annual yield calculated on growing stick (in lakh tonnes)*
1.	Thanlon	1238.40	387.00	10.14	1.69
2.	Henglep	637.26	206.08	4.63	0.77
3.	Nungba	1465.44	278.14	13.89	2.28
4.	Tipaimukh	789.48	278.64	7.92	1.32
5.	Jiribam	309.60	36.12	0.70	0.12
6.	Tamenglong	1083.60	283.80	5.09	0.85
	Total:	5523.78	1470.28	42.37	7.03

CANE BRAKES OF MANIPUR

In the shady, wet ill-drained humus-rich clay soils found particularly in the western hills of Manipur under tropical climates, impenetrable thorny thickets of various species of canes grow along with palm trees such as *Livistoinia*, *Lionia*, sp. etc. and Duloo bamboos. Important cane species are *Calamus tenuis RV, C. leptospadix RV, C. florivundus R, C. latifolium R, C. flagellum Rare and V. vulnerable RV, C. erectus Rare and V. vulnerable RV, Daemonorops jenkinisianus Rare and V. vulnerable RV.*

MUSHROOMS

Manipur is having favourable climatic conditions for growing mushrooms. Wild varieties of mushrooms grow abundantly and some of such mushrooms are edible. Pleurotus and Agaricus mushroom varieties can be grown throughout the year in the State. Similarly other varieties such as, Auricularia Auricula *(Uchina),* Schizphyllum commune *(Kanglayen),* Letimula edodes (*Thngjiyen),* Volvariella SPP *(Charuyen),* etc. can also be cultivated. Substrate for cultivation of mushrooms are available locally except few chemicals that are to be procured from other states.

Table-28 Showing Mushroom Varieties available in Manipur

Sl. No	*Type of Mushroom*	*Season*
1.	Agaricus bisporus (Button Mushrooms)	December - March
2.	Agaricus bitorquis	February - April/August-October
3.	Pleurotus Flabellatus	April - July
4.	Pleurotus Sajor - Caju	August - November
5.	Pleurotus Ostreatus	December - March.

The following varieties of mushrooms are found in Manipur

The Shrubs found in Manipur are-*Rhododendron elliotii, E, R. formosum, R, R. macabeanum, R,R.manipurense, R, R. triflorum, R,R. wattii E, R. johnstoneanum * E, Lilium mackliniae, RV, Lilium chitrangadae, Rare and V vulnerable.*

Food and cash crops occupy the main vegetation cover in the valley. Paddy occupies about 86% of the total valley area. Other important crops include maize, sugarcane, potato, tobacco, mustard and pulses. Horticultural trees and plants like pineapple, banana, lemon, pears, peach, etc. constitute other vegetation cover.

In addition, rubber, tea, coffee, orange, cardamom, etc. are also, grown in hill areas. The forests offer avenue of livelihood and employment to large section of the hill population.

RUBBER

Rubber Plantation under Forest Department, Manipur was started in 1977-78 in Jiribam area covering about 938 Hectares.

A total of 15,000 nos. of Rubber trees are put under tapping under half spiral alternate daily system (1/2 s d/2 system). All the mature areas are not put under tapping because of many factors such as non-availability of mature and tappable trees at regular spacing. The production of raw rubber is maximum during the dry season in Jiribam (Sept. to January).

Rubber trees required deep and well drained soil of lateritic type. It also requires humid, equable climate (21 to 35°C) and fairly well distributed annual rainfall of 200 cm for optimum growth.

Jiribam area is, in fact, a non-traditional area for the Rubber Crop. However, due to prevalence of optimum climate, edaphic conditions required for successful growth of the crop, Jiribam has got good potential for undertaking plantation of rubber in a large commercial scale. Besides, there is a good transport facility to connect the area with good markets of Rubber Crop.

There is quite a good scope for cultivation of rubber in Jiribam area. In general, rubber trees can be put under tapping after 7 years of plantation and the financial returns would outpace the investment once tapping/production of raw rubber commences. As per Rubber Board Index expenditure norm, around Rs. 40,000/- per hectare. is the expenditure upto 7th Year of plantation and taking an average yield of 1000 kg of raw rubber per hectare and market price (conservative figure) of Rs. 40/-per kg, the return would be to the tune of Rs. 40,000/- per hectare In other words, the investment made during the first 6-7 years may be said to have been recovered in the first year of tapping and production. Since rubber trees can be put under effective tapping for 25-30 years, the total return per hectare would be quite high.

Minor Products

Various forms of animal produce, Bamboo and Cane, Fodder and Fuel wood, Grass and reeds, Incense and Perfume and Medicinal plants form the minor forest products which account for a total value of 21 lakhs of annual revenue of the state. This is to the tune of about 40% of total annual forest revenue. Agarwood, Dalchini and Smilax form significant groups among these.

TREE BEAN CULTIVATION

Tree bean (*Parkia roxburghii*) locally known as *Yongchak,* belongs to the family mimosacae and produces long tender beans which are the most delicious, popular favourite vegetable of Manipur. It is taken in different forms of preparations, either fresh or cooked. *Yongchak Ironba* and *Yongchak Singju* are favourites of the Manipuris. According to the consumers' preference, the tree bean pods are consumed at different stages of maturity. The pod contains 15.6 to 18.0% Protein. This tree enjoys the status of an economic crop in Manipur. A tree bean when it starts bearing bean pods after 5-6 years of plantation, can fetch an income of Rs.10,000-20,000/-per annum at farm gate price.

MINERAL RESOURCES

The Manipuris started using iron, limestone, gold, silver copper and brass for nearly 4000 years before and gold was discovered in Kanglei Irel, Kongba Meirombi, Kasom, silver was discovered in Aru Ching, Lakkhong, iron was discovered in Kakching, Copper was discovered in Sibong, precious stones were discovered in Mombi (Tamenglong) and limestone were discovered in Laimaton, Ukhrul, Heiyailok, Khongnangpal etc as early as 154 A.D.

However, since the knowledge of geology of the state is still too incomplete, mineral-exploration remains awaited. Poor communication facilities, inaccessibility and inclement climate have been the constraints in mineral explorations. However, the first attempt of systematic geological survey in Ukhrul District in the recent years have located quite a number of minerals whose mining potential needs be assessed after a detailed study. As it is clear from the Mineral Map, more occurrences of the minerals of whatever indication it is, are met with in the eastern longitudinal half of the state where the rocks are comparatively of older Disang formations. A part of the 220 km long ophiolite belt running north-south is also extended into the eastern border areas. These metamorphose rocks have more possibilities to undergo greater mineralisation. Investigations have revealed the occurrence of the following minerals.

Limestone

A substantial deposit of good quality limestone suitable for use in the manufacture of cement has been located during the recent years by the Geological Survey of India near Ukhrul. Limestone has also been located at a number of other areas e.g. Hundung, Phungyar, Meiring, Mova, Khonggoi, Lambui and Paoyi. In the Ukhrul area, limestone occurs in two bands. A reserve of 579 million tonnes has been proved by drilling to a depth of 105 meters. Other deposits are 0.26 million tonnes at Khonggoi and 1.88 million tonnes at Hundung. A reserve of 6.35 million tonnes of cement grade limestones have been estimated for Phungyar limestone. Meiring limestone reserve may provide an estimated 5.76 million tonnes of limestone.

All these deposits taken together are expected to be able to feed a cement plant of modest capacity of 200 tonnes per day for about 45 years. But the present installed capacity is only 50 TPD (tonne per day).

Evaporities

Evaporities are the mineralised salt sediments from the evaporation of saline water specially the seawater. These are used in fertilizer, chemical, drug and building industries. Minor occurrences of magnesium and other salts in Kongai area of Chingai sub-division of Ukhrul District have been located.

Mineral Water

A number of brine wells occur at Chingai, Challao, Nameri, Luchai-Khullen, Mariem and Kharawam in Ukhrul District and at Ningel and Chandrakhong village in Thoubal District. The spring water is locally used in making salt cakes.

Chromite

Chromite deposits containing partly metallurgical grade ore have been located at Kwatha and Khudengthabi in Chandel District and near Shirui Peak in Ukhrul District. Open cast mining has been operated by M/s Orissa Industries Pvt. Ltd., Rourkela. Possibilities of locating bigger deposits are indicated. Production of Chromite in 1993-94, 1994-95, 1995-96, 1996-97 were 643 metric tonnes, 784 metric tonnes, 470 metric tonnes and 62 metric tonnes respectively. 28 locations have so far been identified as Chromium reserve areas.

Ferrous Alloy Metals

Nickeliferous magnetite's, copper and cobalt have been located at Kwatha, Khudengthabi and Namphesha along the ultramaphic expositions near Moreh. The ore grade and size of deposit need further assessment with investigations extended into the northern strips of the ultramaphic belt. The possibility of locating platinum in this ophiolite belt has been observed (NEC).

Asbestos

Minor occurrences of these minerals have been reported from the ultramaphic suites of rocks particularly in the Ukhrul and Moreh areas.

Semi Precious Stones

Jadeite, a semi-precious mineral occurs in the Indo-Burma borders. While Burma and China have abundant resource of these minerals, Indian occurrences are very poor. Other compact coloured minerals include the surpentinites found in the same belt.

FLOWERS

The common varieties of flowers in Manipur (see plates-29-56) are as follows :-

Table-29 Showing common variesties of flowers available in Manipur

Sl.No	*Manipuri Name*	*English Name*	*Scientific Name*
1.	Shirui Lily	Shirui Lily	Lilium Macklinae sealy
2.	Nageshwar	Iron wood	Mesua Ferrea Linn
3.	Leihao	Champak	Michelia Chanpaka Linn
4.	Chigonglei	Babul Acasia	Acacia Arabica Wild
5.	Kundo	Star Jasmine	Jasmini Multiflorum (BF) ·Andr
6.	Malika	Wild Jasmine	Jasmini Angustifolium Vahl
7.	Modolei	Spider lily	Hymenocallis littoralis
8.	Leibaklei		Kaemferia Galanga Linn
9.	Ketuki	Screw Pine	Pandanus Odoratissimus L.F.
10.	Petruklei	Globe Amaranth	Gomphrena Globosa Linn
11.	Chandramukhi	Chrysanthemum	Chrysinthemum coronarium
12.	Kundalei	Tube Rose	Polyanthus Tuberosa Linn
13.	Khagi Leihao	Pagoda Tree	Plumeria Aeutifolia Poir
14.	Numitlei	Sunflower	Helianthus Anus Linn
15.	Thambal 108	Sacred Lotus	Nelumbo Nucifera Gaertn
16.	Singarei	Night Jasmine	Nyitrys arborlristris(L)
17.	Chini Champra		Arbotrys hexpetalus (LT)
18.	Kombirei	Iris	Iris Bakery Wall
19.	Kaboklei	Cape Jasmine	Gardenia Florida Linn
20.	Sanarei Angangba	Stripped Marigold	Tegetes Tenuifolia Cav
21.	Sanarei	French Marigold	Tegetes Pitula Linn
22.	Tharo Angangba	Red Water Lily	Nymphaea Rubra ® ex salisb
23.	Tharo Angouba	White Water Lily	Nymphaea alba linn
24.	Aprajita	Clitoria	Clitoria Turnatea Linn
25.	Madhumati	Japanese honey sickle	Lonicera Japonica thub
26.	Madhabi		Hiptage Bengalensis keor
27.	Malati		Jasminium Flexile Vehl
28.	Mukaklei	4 Oclock	Mirabilis jalapa linn
29.	Parijat	Rangoon Creeper	Quiscualis Indica Linn
30.	Leisang		Lycopodiumcernuum
31.	Jubakusum	China Rose	Hibiscus Mutabilis
32.	Radhika Nachom	Passion Flower	Passiflora Edulis Sims
33.	Nachomlei		Ascocentrum ampullacum

(Contd.)

(Contd. Table 29)

Sl.No	*Manipuri Name*	*English Name*	*Scientific Name*
34.	U-Takhellei		Thunia marshalliana Reich
35.	Poppy	Opium Poppy	Papaver Somniferum Linn
36.	Ador Gulap	Damask Rose	Rose damascena Mill
37.	Ador Gulap		Rose Indica H.f.non.L
38.	Gulap	White cabbage rose	Rosa alba linn
39.	Gulapjam	Rose apple	Syzygium jumbos (l) Alston
40.	Dzuko Lily	Dzuko lily	Lilium Chitrangadivikram
41.	Chingthrao Angouba	White Bauhinia	Bauhinia acuminate Linn
42.	Chingthrao Arangba	Variegated Bauhinia	Bauhinia variegate Linn
43.	Chingthrao Pink	Pink Bauhinia	Bauhinia purpurea Linn
44.	Warak Kundo	Angel winged jasmine	Jasminium nitidum
45.	U-Thambal	Southern magnifolia	Magnolia grandiflora
46.	Thariktha	Blue water lily	Nymphaea Stellata Willd
47.	Takhellei	Ginger Lily	Hedichium Spicatum Buch Ham
48.	Naton Chabi	Wild Rose	Rosa multiflora Thunb
49.	Khujang	Balsum	Impatiens balsamina Linn
50.	Kusumlei	Safflower	Carthamus tinetoriuss Linn
51.	Kangphal Ikaithabi	Sensitive plant	Mimosa pudica Linn
52.	Kamini Kusum	Orange Jasmine	Murraya exotica Linn
53.	Kaberei	Indian Oleander	Nerium indicum Mill
54.	Kaberei Angangba	Oleander	Nerium Oleander Linn
55.	Jati Kuppi	Jasmine	Jasmium humile Linn
56.	Hao Sanarei	Cock's comb	Celosis cristata Linn
57.	Cherei	Bougain Villea	Bougain Villea spectabilis Willd
58.	Bokul	Spanish cherry	Mimusops elangi Linn
59.	Gulmohor	Jacaranda	Jacaranda mimosifolia D.Don

SHIRUI LILY

Shirui Lily (Lilium Macklinae sealy) discovered by Mr. Frank Kingdon Ward in 1948. is endemic to Manipur and in Ukhrul district it is confined to Shirui peak. Shirui peak is known as "Shirui Kashung" to the Tangkhuls. The name is called so, as the creation of the mount is so high among many mounts in Tangkhuls ("*Varena phungpha mida mashonshei eina shongmihaiya*"). The peak lies at an elevation of 2500 metres. In fine weather specially in the month of April and October the peak offers a magnificent view of Myanmar (Burma) and Imphal valley. Shirui hill has beautiful grassland on top and thick forest at the foothills. (see plate-29 and 30)

Shirui Kashung has three peaks. The highest peak is called "*Shongrei*" – where lily grows, the middle one is called "*Sarum kateng*"–here lies a spring where all the wild animal comes for a drink. A hole is also there which is believed to reach "*Ongshim ngayi*" in Pushing village. The lowest one is called *shongrã*. Further apart from *shongrei*, there is a small peak called *shongshangh*. The sides are steep like precipice. This is a home for many Blythii trapogon, one of the most threatened pheasant species.

It is believed that if hailstone falls on *shongrei* by January or February noblemen get good harvest. If the hailstone falls on *shongrã,* the common men get good harvest. If the hailstone falls on both *shongrei* and *shongrã* both the noble men and common men get good harvest. According to myth, the Shirui peak fairy *"Shirui Kashung philava"* is the greatest among all fairies. The big lions are her dogs; all the wild boars are her pigs; stag and deer are her cows and buffaloes. All the birds are her chicken. Thus all the wild animals are her domestic animals. The saying goes on, as the hunters who are pleased with philava will kill the animals. Few years back the lily is found growing and blooming in "*Chingchui matha*" a hill in Chingjaroi village. It is believed that the *"Shirui Kashung philava"* marry the fairy of "*Chingchui matha*" and so the philava take the lily along with her and bloom there.

ORCHIDS

Some of the most coveted, most beautiful orchids with exotic blooms are found in Manipur their natural habitat growing in soil or on trees.There are 500 varieties of orchids which grow in Manipur of which 472 have been identified. Some of the common indigenous orchids of Manipur (see plates-31-44) are as follows :

Table-30 Showing common variesties of orchids available in Manipu

Sl.No	*Manipuri Name*	*Scientific Name*	*Season of flower*
1.	Kongyamba lei	Arundina bambusifolia Lindl	
2.	Nachom lei	Ascocentrum ampullaceum	
3.	Nachomlei var	Ascocentrum empulacum	
4.	Kwaklei angouba	Aerides Vandarum	
5.	Samjirei tangjaobi	Aerides odoratum	June
6.	Samjirei manbi	Aerides multiflorum	
7.	White	Aerides vandarum	March
8.		Aerides Rosea	
9.		Bletilla striata	February

(Contd.)

(Contd. Table 30)

Sl.No	*Manipuri Name*	*Scientific Name*	*Season of flower*
10.		Bulbophyllum Dixoni	
11.		Cymbidium mostershi	November
12.		Cymbidium giganteum	October
13.		Cymbidium Mostershi	
14.		Cymbidium devonianum	Jume
15.		Cymbidium Mostershi	
16.	Khongban takhellei	Costus speciosus (k) sm	
17.	Mitmubi	Dendrobium fimbriatum Hook (variety-Oculatum)	
18.	Melei/Mityaodabi	Dendrobium fimbriatum Lindi	
19.	Melei leishna	Dendrobium densiflorum	April
20.	Melei leishna anouba	Dendrobium thyrsiflorum	April
21.	Mera leikham	Dendrobium chrysanthum Wall	April
22.	Yerum lei	Dendrobium nobile Lindl	April
23.	Tengthou lei	Dendrobium faleoneri	May
24.	Khongumelei	Dendrobium chrysotoxum Lindl	April
25.		Dendrobium clavatum	April
26.	Sempak lei	Dendrobium parisii Rei,	
27.	Thengu lei (Macha)	Dendrobium genkinsii	
28.	Thengu lei (Achouba)	Dendrobium aggregatum Roxb.	March
29.		Dendrobium transparens	May
30.	Urei rani	Dendrobium devonianum Paxt	April
31.		Dendrobium crepidatum	March
32.	Mera leikham	Dendrobium chrysanthum	October
33.		Dendrobium devonianum	July
34.		Dendrobium heterocarpum	December
35.	Eyong lei	Dendrobium williamsoii	April
36.	Yerumlei	Dendrobium noble Lindl	April
37.	Sahilei	Dendrobium lituiflorum Lindl.	
38.	Ingellei	Dendrobium moschatum Wall	
39.	Nongmai mani sanamachu	Phaius Waliichii	
40.	Nongmai mani	Phaius tankervillial (variety- Minor)	June
41.	Kwaklei hangampal	Renathera imschootiana	May
42.	Shamjirei	Rhynchostylis gigantean Ridl. (variety – Retusa)	
43.	Shamjirei	Rhynchostylis retusa	April
44.	Kwaklei angangba	Remanthera gmschootiana	April
45.	U –takhellei	Thunia marshallana Reich	

(Contd.)

(Contd. Table 30)

Sl.No	Manipuri Name	Scientific Name	Season of flower
47.		Venda amesiana	February
48.	Kwaklei	Venda coerulea Griff	April
49.	Kwaklei pink	Venda coerulea	November
50.	Kwaklei amuba	Venda coerulea (a variety)	October
51.		Venda Coeruleseence	
52.	Wainulei	Vanila pilifera	

FRUITS

Some of the fruits commonly available in Manipur are as follows:-

Table-31 Showing common varieties of fruits available in Manipur

Sl.No	Manipuri Name	English Name	Scientific Name
1.	Kihom	Pineapple	Ananas Comosus
2.	Komla	Sweet Orange	Citrus Sinensis
3.	Komla	Sour Orange	Citrus aurantium
4.	Champra	Lemon	Citrus Limon
5.	Chorphon	Olive	Elaeocarpus Floribundus
6.	Chumbrei	Peach	Prunus Persica
7.	Heikha	Plum	Prunus Domestica
8.	Malhei	Wild Himalayan Cherry	Prunus Puddam
9.	Heitup	Indian Crab apple	Pyrus Indica
10.	Heithum	Grape Fruit	Citrus Pardisi
11.	Nobab	Mandarin	Citrus Reticulata
12.	Heikhagok	Bael Tree	Aegle Marmelos
13.	Heikru	Indian gooseberry	Phylanthus Emblica
14.	Heibung		Garcinia Anomala
15.	Heiyai		Elaegnus Umbellata
16.	Heimang		Rhus Semialata
17.	Heinoujom	Carambola	Averrhoea Carambola
18.	Heirangoi		Amieera Rohituka
19.	Heiri		Calamus Tenuis
20.	Heirit		Ficus Cunia
21.	Naspati	Pear	Pyrus Communis
22.	Heiyen	Big Nay	Antidesma Bunius

(Contd.)

(Contd. Table 31)

Sl.No	*Manipuri Name*	*English Name*	*Scientific Name*
23.	Ataphon	Custard Apple	Annona Reticulata
24.	Sitaphon	Sugar Apple	Annona Squamosa
25.	Gihori	Phyllanthus Acidus	
26.	Heijang		Citrus Medica
27.	Heining	Hog Plum	Spondia Pinnata
28.	Heirabob		Citrus Macroptera
29.	Mongjam Hei		Tetrastigma Banjus
30.	Pungdon	Guava	Psidium Guajava
31.	Thangtup	Date Palm	Phoenix Dactylifera
32.	Boroi		Zyzyphus jujuba

References

Singh, S.S. The Economic plants of Manipur and their uses, September, 2006, pp. 1-87.

Singh U. Lisam, Thesis, Intercroppisnmg Crops, M.P. Agricultural Univerversity (MS), 1987, pp. 50-70.

Piper, C.S., 1966 Soil and plant analysis, Indian Edition, Hanks Publisher, Mumbai.

Anonymous, 1985-Annual Report on Research accomplishment, Agricultural Research and Education, New Delhi, pp. 15-59.

Capt. R.B. Pemberton, Eastern Frontier of British India by, 1885, pp. 20). Sir James Johnstone.

Dobelis, Inge. (1996) The Magic and Medicine of Plants. Pleasantville, NY: Readers Digest Inc.Chevallier, Andrew. (1996) The Encyclopedia of Medicinal Plants. New York, NY: The DK Publishing Company.

Forest Department of Manipur- publications, annual reports, bulletins etc.

Statistical Bulletin of Forest Department, 1999-2000, Govt. of Manipur.

M. R. Bawa Muhaiyaddeen- *Come to the Secret Garden: Sufi Tales of Wisdom.*

Plate-5: Dzuko Valley

Plate-6 : Manipur Valley

Plate-7 : Dzuko Lily

Plate--8 : Hill Ranges

Plate- 9 : Imphal River at Serou

Plate-10 : Barak River (Gwai River)

Plate-11 : Sangai

Plate-12 : Slow Loris

Plate-13 : Hoolock gibbon (*Hylobates hoolock hoolock*)

Plate-14 : Leopard Cat (*Felis Bengalensis)*

Plate -15 : SEROW
(Capricornis sumantraensis)

Plate-16 : Flying Squirrel (Petaurista petaurista)

Plate-17 : Nongin: (Syrmaticus huminae huminae)

Plate-18 : Migratory Bird

Plate -19 : Nganu Thanggong

Plate-20 : Ngarakpi (Kinghfisher)

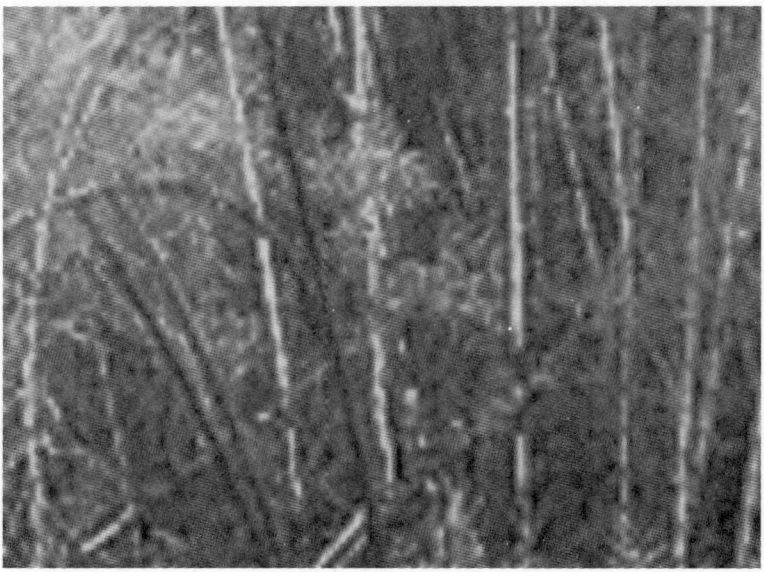

Plate -21 : Wapal (Bamboo Forest)

Plate -22 : Uningthou Tree

Plate-23 : Uchan (Pine Trees)

Plate-24 : Eucalyptus Trees

Plate-25 : Chingsu (Teak Trees)

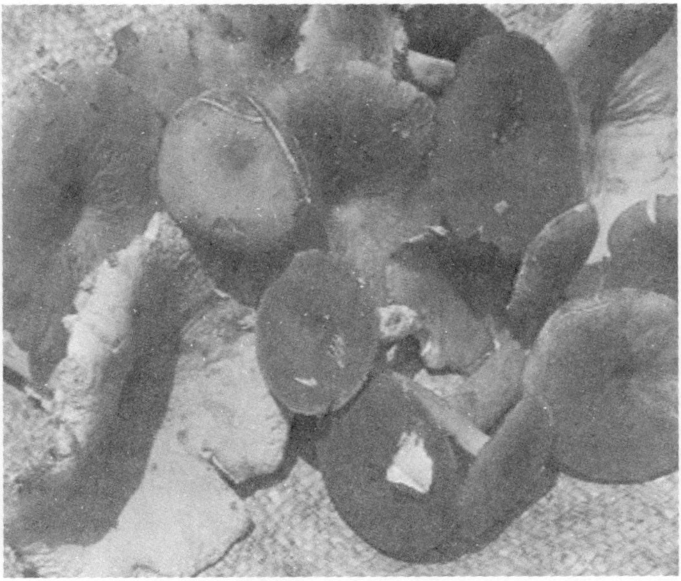

Plate-26 : Chenggum (Mushroom)

Plate -27 : Yongchak (Tree Bean)

Plate -28 : U- morok (King Chilli)

Plate -29 : Shirui Lily

Plate =30: Shirui Lily

Plate -31: A variety of orchid

Plate -32: Dendrobium

Plate -33: Dendrobium Chrysnthum

Plate -34 : Rhynchostylis retusa

Plate -35:*Tingthou- Lei*

Plate -36: ***Nachomlei***

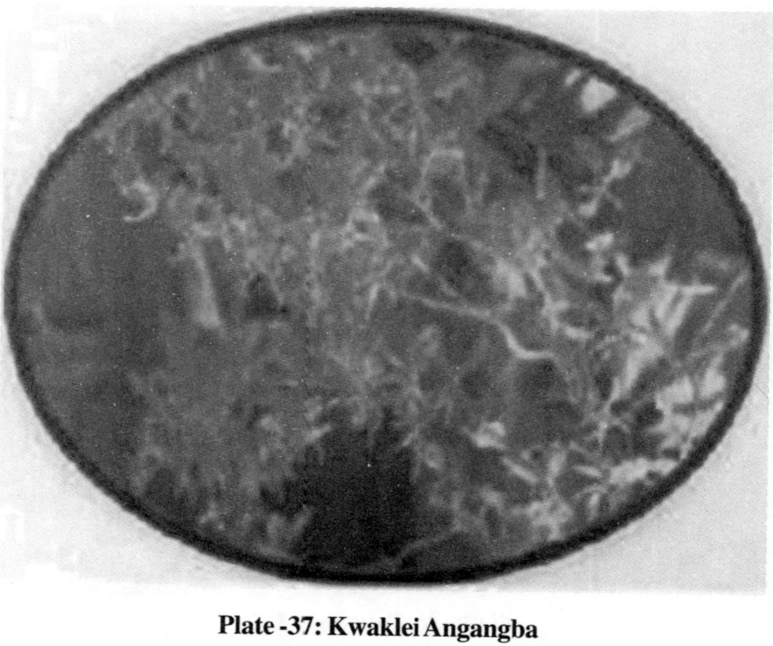

Plate -37: Kwaklei Angangba

Plate-38 Khongumelei

Plate -39: Cheiteklei

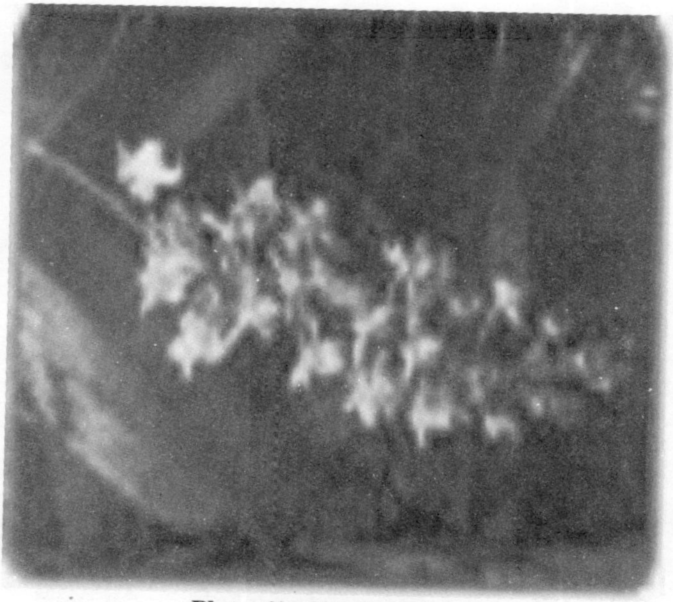

Plate -40: Samjirei Manbi

Plate -41: A variety of Orchid

Plate -42 Dendrobium Noble Lindl

Plate -43: Orchid

Plate -44: Yerumlei

Plate -45: Kombirei

Plate -46: U-Thambal

Plate -47: Red Rose

Plate -48: Lotus Lake at Khonghampat

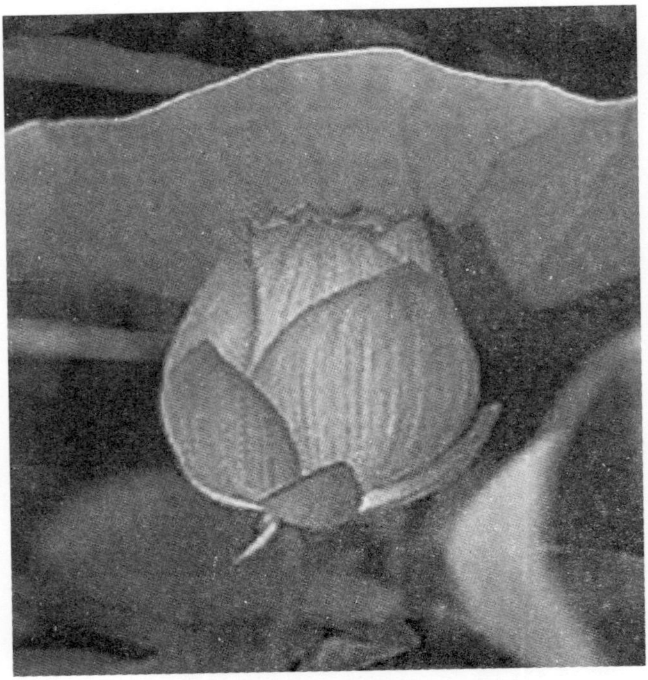

Plate -49 : Thambal Angnagba Red Lotus

Plate -50 : Juba Khusum China Rose

Plate -51: Utonglei (Yellow Oleander

Plate -52: Aprajita (Clitoria)

Plate -53: Khagi Leihao (Pagoda Tree)

Plate -54: Tharo Angangba(Red water lily)

Plate -55 : Thangjing

Plate -56 : Leihao

Plate - 57: Chumbrei

Plate - 58: Pengba

Plate -59 : Heiyai

4

Manipur Kingdom and Kings

The kingdom of Manipur existed since 1445 B. C, had all the basic requirements of a kingdom such as kingship, a capital or seat of power, an administrative set-up, a territory with well defined boundary including regional principalities, rules, regulations and laws of the land which guide governance, courts of justice, revenue and administrative division of the kingdom in the form of provinces, districts, countries, boroughs etc., hierarchy of nobles and officials, an army to defend the kingdom or to attack neighbouring countries for annexation, coinage for trade and commerce, literature, script and culture indicating civilization, a recorded history for future generations and so on.

CHRONICLE OF THE MANIPUR KINGS

Table-32 Showing chronology of Kings of Manipur before 33 A. D.

Sl. No.	*Names of Kings*	*Period of reign*	*Number of years*
1.	Taangja Leelaa Paakhangba	1445-1405 B.C	40
2.	Ningthou Kangba	1405-1359 B.C.	46
3.	Koi Koi / Maria Fambaalchaa	1359-1329 B.C.	30
4.	Ningthou Kaksuba	1329-1297 B.C.	32
5.	Ningthou Tonkonba	1297-1276 B.C.	21

(Contd.)

(Contd. Table 32)

Sl. No.	*Names of Kings*	*Period of reign*	*Number of years*
6.	Ningthou Pottingkoi	1276-1251 B.C.	25
7.	Ningthou Lanbicha	1251-1229 B.C.	22
8.	Ningthou Sopaiba	1251-1229 B.C.	
9.	Ningthou Puthiba	1209-1199 B.C.	10
10.	Great Historical Gap		1155
11.	Samlunghphaa	44-34 B.C.	10
12.	Poireiton Khunthokpa	34-18 B.C.	16
13.	Singtabung	18-8 B.C.	10
14.	Paangminnaba	8-1 B.C.	7
15.	Luwang Khunthiba	1B.C.-5 A.D.	6
16.	Luwang Punshiba	5-33 A.D.	28

Table-33 Showing chronology of Kings of Manipur after 33 A. D.

Sl. No.	*Names of Kings*	*Period of reign A.D.*	*Number of years*
1.	Nongda Lairen Pakhangba	33-154	121
2.	Khuiyoi Tompok	154-264	110
3.	Taothingmang	264-364	100
4.	Khui Ningonba	364-379	15
5.	Pengsiba	379-394	15
6.	Kaokhangba	394-411	17
7.	Naokhamba	411-428	17
8.	Naophangba	428-518	90
9.	Sameirang	518-568	50
10.	Ura konthouba	568-658	90
11.	Naothingkhong	663-763	100
12.	Khongtekcha	763-773	10
13.	Keirencha	784-799	15
14.	Yaraba	799-821	22
15,	Ayaangba	821-910	89
16.	Ningthoucheng	910-949	39
17.	Chenglie-Ipan-Lanthaba	949-969	20
18.	Keiphaba Yanglon	969-984	15
19.	Irengba	984-1074	90
20.	Loiyumba	1074-1112	48
21.	Loitongba	1122-1150	28
22.	Atom Yoiremba	1150-1163	13
23.	Iwanthaba	1163-1195	32

(Contd.)

(Contd. Table 33)

Sl. No.	Names of Kings	Period of reign A.D.	Number of years
24.	Thawanthaba	1195-1231	36
25.	Chingthang Lanthaba	1231-1242	11
26.	Thingbai Shelhongba	1242-1247	5
27.	Puranthaba	1247-1263	16
28.	Khumomba	1263-1278	15
29.	Moiramba	1278-1302	24
30.	Thangbi Lanthaba	1302-1324	22
31.	Kongyamba	1324-1335	11
32.	Telheiba	1335-1355	20
33.	Tonaba	1355-1359	4
34.	Tabungba	1359-1394	35
35.	Lairenba	1394-1399	5
	No king	1399-1404	5
36.	Punsiba	1404-1432	28
37.	Ningthoukhomba	1432-1467	35
38.	Kyaamba	1467-1508	41
39.	Koiremba	1508-1512	4
40.	Lamkhyamba	1512-1523	11
41.	Nonginphaba	1523-1524	1
42.	Kabomba	1524-1542	18
43.	Tangjamba	1542-1545	3
44.	Chalamba	1545-1562	17
45.	Mungyamba	1562-1597	35
46.	Khagemba	1597-1652	55
47.	Khunjaoba	1652-1666	14
48.	Paikhomba	1666-1697	31
49.	Charairongba	1697-1709	12
50.	Garib Niwaj	1709-1748	39
51.	Chitshai	1748-1752	4
52.	Bharatsai	1752-1753	1
53.	Maramba / Gourshyam	1753-1759	6
54.	Chingthangkhomba / Bhagyachandra /Jai Singh	1759-1762	3
55.	Maramba / Gourshyam	1762-1763	1
56.	Chingthangkhomba / Bhagyachandra / Jai Singh	1763-1798	35
57.	Labanyachandra	1798-1801	3
58.	Madhuchandra	1801-1803	2
59.	Chourajit Singh	1803-1813	10
60.	Marjit Singh	1813-1819	6
61.	Hirachandra (Takooningthou)	1819	1
62.	Yumjaotaba	1820	1

(Contd.)

(Contd. Table 33)

Sl. No.	*Names of Kings*	*Period of reign A.D.*	*Number of years*
63.	Gambheer Singh	1821	6 months
64.	Jai Singh	1822	1
65.	Jadu Singh (Nongpok Chinglenkhomba)	1823	1
66.	Raghab Singh	1823-1824	1
67.	Nongchup Lamgaingamba (Bhadrasingh)	1824	1
68.	Gambheer Singh (Chinglen Nongdrenkhomba)	1825-1834	9
69.	Chandrakirti (Ningthempishak)	1834-1844	10
70.	Nara Singh	1844-1850	6
71.	Debendra Singh	1850-	3 months
72.	Chandrakirti (K.C.S.I.)	1850-1886	36
73.	Surchandra	1886-1890	4
74.	Kulachandra	1890-1891	1
75.	Churachand Singh (KCSI, CBE)	1891-1941	50
76.	Bodhchandra Singh	1941-1955	14
77.	Okendro Singh	1955-1972	17

GREAT HISTORICAL GAP 1199-44 B. C.

Table-34 Showing the Great Historical Gap 1199-44 BC

1.	Khoiyum Ingouba	
2.	Khing Khing Laangba	
3.	Ngaangjeng Leitakpa	
4.	Khing Khing Ngaangba	
5.	Sana Manik	
6.	Toukai Ngamba	
7.	Tingkoi Ngamba	
8.	Korou Nongdren Paakhangba	
9.	Sentreng (and Kuptreng the elder)	
10.	Machi Sanaa	
11.	Khuman Lalheiba	
12.	Ahong Ningthou Haanba	
13.	Ningthou Kaangba	
14.	Lamyaingamba etc. etc. etc	

C. 1990 A. D. = M. F. 3388 = Buddha Era 2534 = Aijepi Sag (P. S.) 2534.

(K. C. Tensuba, Genesis of Indian Tribes : An Approach to the Meiteis and Thais,1993).

KINGSHIP

The kingship in Manipur was organized and administered in a very systematic way. It comprised of the following offices :

1. Cheirap–Civil Court.
2. Dolaipaba Loisang–Office to arrange the Dolai (Palanquin.)
3. Feida Loisang–Office to contact the king at night when he is with his family members.
4. Fourungba–Office to deal with paddy.
5. Garot–Military Court.
6. Haomacha Loisang–Office to teach respectful language, respectful behaviour, etiquette, etc.
7. Hira Hinao–Office to manage the boat race.
8. Hao Panaba–Office to look after hao (tribals).
9. Huiroi–Office to arrange hunting for the king.
10. Keirungba Yairekshang–Godown and Treasury's guard.
11. Lanmee Yairekshang–Office of the army for night duty.
12. Maiba Sanglen–Office of the literati and local priests.
13. Mongalsang–Court of the Mohammedan.
14. Ningthousenba Yairekshang–Bodyguard of the King.
15. Paja/Pacha–Women's Court.
16. Potsangba Sanglen–Office to arrange different necessary articles during any contingent occasion.
17. Talyeiba Loisang–Office to maintain the time, calendar and so on. This office had four sections, namely,
    - 17.1. Pandit Loisang (literati's Office).
    - 17.2 Pena Loisang (musician's Office).
    - 17.3. Maiba Loisang (office of the priest)
    - 17.4. Maibi Loisang (office of the priestesses).
18. Sengoi-Senba–Office to serve the king while he is with his family members.
19. Leima Senba–Office of the personal assistants of the princess.
20. Ningthouja Yek-Salai-Chief of Potsangba–Office to dye clothes and to supply dress.
21. Leikai Sangsaroi–Office to construct roads, bridges, etc.

22. Hidakphu Fanba Ningthourei – Office to keep contact with the sons of the king.
23. Lourungba–Office to deal with paddy fields.
24. Thumjaorungba–Office to deal with salt and other alkali.
25. Thangjapanaba–Office to deal with iron implements.
26. Paijasaba–Office to deal with the things made of wood.
27. Arangba–Office for arranging and preparing articles of worship,
28. Lanmee–Office of the Army.
29. Kangla–Office to arrange rice during haochongba, that is, a ceremony performed by the tribals in the palace.
30. Samu Sang–Office of the overseers of elephants.
31. Sagol Sang–Office of the overseers of horses.
32. Kon Sang–Office to supply brass pots.
33. Khutheiba–Artisan's office.
34. Ayekpa–Painter's office.
35. Sangom Sang–Office to supply milk.
36. Tengkhal–Gardener's office.
37. Furungba–Office to supply earthen pots.
38. Ametpa–Physicians' Office.
39. Sanglingba–Office of the executioner.
40. Hidaksungba–Office to supply firewood.
41. Sinnai–Office to supply baskets.

The head of every office is known as "Hanjaba" and his deputy is known as "Hidang". Some of these are cited below:

1. Sagol Senba Hanjaba–Head of the Office of the overseer of horses,
2. Sangoiba Hanjaba–Head instructor.
3. Sangoiba Hidang–Assistant instructor.
4. Potsangba Hanjaba–Head store keeper
5. Potsangba Hidang–Assistant store keeper.
6. Samu Hanjaba–Head of overseers of the elephants.
7. Ametpa Hanjaba–Head Medicine Man.
8. Hinao Hanjaba–Head of the Office that manage boat race.
9. Pacha Hanjaba–President of the Pacha / Paja, that is, womens' court.

This principle may not apply in some cases. Angom Ningthou was traditionally the president of Cheirap, which was a civil court. Senapati was the president of Garot, which was a Military court. Kaji was the head of Mongalsang, which was court of the Mohammedan. Pana Hajari was the head of Lanmee, which was the office of sepoys. (Ranajit Kumar Saha, Valley Society of Manipur, Punthi –Pustak, Calcutta, 1994)

LAKPAS

Lakpas were the communication agents. Specific designation may be given for the specific task. Khunthong Lakpa was the communication agent for the village; Leikai Lakpa, was the communication agent for the local area (Leikai). Yaiskul Lakpa was the communication agent for the Yaiskul Pana. Thus there were Khwai Lakpa, Khabam Lakpa, Laipham Lakpa, Ahallup Lakpa and Naharup Lakpa. The communication agent for outside Manipur is known as Lamlai Lakpa. The communication agent for the servants and for different offices were Naishu Lakpa and Sanglen Lakpa respectively. The Laichol Lakpa acted as chowkidar. The Lakpas used to keep contact with their respective areas for various types of information and other communications. The designation of those who used to arrange different articles in different occasions were Khanba. For example, Khudong Khanba served by arranging the hookah. Besides, persons who were given a particular job to perform were designated as chingba. For example, the Lalup chingbas were given the duty of causing attendance of Lalup Kabas. Lalup Kaba was performing free service for the king for ten days in every forty days. (Ranajit Kumar. Saha, Valley Society of Manipur, Punthi–Pustak, Calcutta, 1994)

MILITARY SERVICE

There was no fixed military regiment under the king till the time of Gambheer Singh (1825-1834). The soldiers of Manipur were called Lanmees. All the common people were treated as Lanmee except the king's family and other officials who served the king. If there was no war, then their duties were civil. The military officers were called Pana Hazari and Hazari. Gambheer Singh was the first king to introduce organized military service. During his time, there were eight Tulis (Army regiments) of more than 5000 men, namely:-

1. The Tulihan
2. Tuli Yaima
3. Tulinaha
4. Bhitna
5. Bishnu Seinya Ahal,
6. Bishnu Naha
7. Top Tuli and
8. Aya-Purel Tuli.

Some regiments of less importance were Kang Tuli, Kang Nao Tuli, Oinamlong Tuli and Nawa. Each of these Tulis was composed of different companies. Each of the regular Tuli was commanded by a Major or a Poila. One Havildar Major and two Kuts were attached to it. In a company there were one Subadar, one Jamandar, one Agari Holder, one Havildar and one Amandar (L. I. Singh 1963:36-37).

LAND REVENUE

According to R. Brown (1874), "The whole land system of the valley starts with the assumption that all the land belongs to the Raja, and he can give away or retain as he pleases". An officer under him, named "Phunan Selungba" superintended all matters connected with land cultivation. He looked after the measurement, received the rent in kind and transacted all the matters connected with land on behalf of Raja. One third of the total land was under the direct control of the king. More than a third was in the possession of the ruling family, Brahmins and Sepoys. The rest of the land was in the hands of the headman, officials, and so on, who held it by favour from the Raja (R. Brown, Statistical Account of the native state of Manipur and the hill territory under its rule, Mittal Publications, 1874)

The land was divided into villages and their surroundings. The headman of each village looked after the cultivation and was responsible for the realization of the tax payable in kind by each cultivator. The headman was merely an agent of the Raja. He held no interest in the land. The land under the direct control of the King was cultivated by the Lalup Kabas. Those who were liable for Lalup were entitled to cultivate for their support one pari (2. 5 acres) of land subject to the payment of tax in kind. Grants of land were given to officials and favourites, sometimes for their own lives only or for a specified time, sometimes for themselves and descendants and the relatives of the Raja. But they had to pay tax in kind on any increase of land cultivated beyond the fixed proportion (Dr. R. Brown-1874)

According to R. Brown (1874), "the tax, although fixed varied from two baskets to thirteen baskets per Pari of land. Two baskets of paddy were realized from the favourites only but for others it could be as high as twelve baskets yearly. This may be exceeded in rare emergencies as in war etc. This was applicable to the land cultivated for the Raja or held by those subject to the Lalup. It was also as high as twentyfour baskets in case of the land held by officials, etc., as a middleman".

CHANGES IN THE ADMINISTRATIVE STRUCTURE DURING VARIOUS KINGSHIPS

Pandit Moirangthem Chandra Singh produced from his records that certain kings added certain posts and offices during their period of reign.

King Loiyumba (1074–1112) added the following posts:

- Kongbamluk–Cashier
- Thanjaluk–Labour officer,
- Angomluk–Communication officer for the Angom,
- Luplunluk–Engineer,
- Lokhubaluk–Body guards,
- Khurailuk–Communication officer for Khurai.

King Kyaamba (1467–1508) introduced two institutions namely Ahallup Sanglup and Naharup Sanglup, which served as dormitory for the boys between ten and thirteen years of age.

King Garib Niwaz (1709-1748) added the following designations :

- Jubaraj – Crown Prince,
- Mantri – Minister,
- Senapati – Commanding Officer-in-Charge of the Army.
- Katoal – Functions not known.

King Bhagyachandra (1763-1798) added the following designations:

1. Hajari–Function is not known,
2. Kaji–Officer-in-Charge of the Mohammedan,
3. Lourungba Purel–Officer in change of the settlement of land,
4. Selung Purel–Overseer of cows
5. Shatoal–Idol maker of Ravana.
6. Thumjao Purel–Overseer of salt,
7. Thangsaba Purel–Overseer of iron implements,
8. Urung Purel–Overseer of wooden furniture and implements etc.

The traditional Kingship organization existed in full swing upto Anglo-Manipuri war of 1891. In 1835, the first political Agent was appointed for friendly intercourse as medium of communication and the king had to obey the treaty made from time to time with the British. In 1891, the British exerted its complete political control over the territory. In 1892 Major Maxwell, the Political Agent announced the abolition of Lalup system. In place of Lalup he imposed a Land revenue of Rs. 5/- at a uniform rate per Pari of land. A special house tax of Rs. 2/- was also levied (J. Singh 1965: 297-298). Roy (1973;137). In 1908 a "Darbar" was constituted under the Presidentship of the Maharaja Churachand to help the administration. A British I. C. S. officer, was the Vice-

President of the "Darbar". In addition to the I. C. S. Officer, there were six Manipuri members. The regular military organization was also constituted under the sponsorship of the British. The pothang (a system of forced labour) was abolished on June 9th 1913 (Report of Manipur Administration. 1913-1914). In 1916 Raja retained only the supervisory control and was assisted by the "Darbar". Thereafter the President of the "Darbar" selected by the Governor of Assam, usually was a member of the Indian Civil Service. There were at least three Manipuri members of the "Darbar" (Roy 1973:137). (Ranajit Kumar. Saha, Valley Society of Manipur, Punthi –Pustak, Calcutta, 1994)

Re-organization as a Result of Contact with Neighbouring Kings

In due course of time, the the Manipuri King came in contact with the kings of Ahom (Assam), Cachar and Tripura. (Roy 1973, Saha,1981, R. K. Jhalajit Singh, 1965). As a result of this contact, the Kings were exposed to the administrative procedures of other kingdoms. The Manipuri Kings tried to bring about administaruive changes to gain more power and control over his people as that of the surrounding kingdoms. The following changes occurred.

Administration of Villages

The villages were very systematically organized in relation to the Kingship. For every village, a village headman is appointed. The hedaman had to keep contact with the communicating Agent for the village, that is, the Khunthong Lakpa in the palace. Whenever the king used to visit any village, prior information was given to its headman through the respective Khunthong Lakpas. It was the responsibility of the village headman to arrange all the necessary services and other requirements for the king. The village headman had to take note of the Lalup Kabas and report their attendance to the Lalup Chingba in the palace. The absentees either were allowed to offer substitute or paid the fixed amount charged for the substitute. The link between the king and the people was of three categories, namely:-

1. Service relationship
2. Judicial relationship
3. Religious relationship.

1. Service relationship

The king developed a system of services to the King to strengthen the the relationship of the people with the king. This system comprised of three types of services, namely, Phamnaiba, Lalupkaba and Loipotkaba.

All people in the valley served the king in relation to the type of services under the provisions allowed to them. These services can be classified into three categories, namely:-

- Phamnaiba (prestigious)
- Lalupkaba (essential) and
- Loipotkaba (dishonourable).

Phamnaiba

The Phamnaibas were the nobles, the aristocratic section of the society. They include the high officials in the judiciary, administrative and military services and the customary laws. The Vaishnavite kings added the ritual service of the Brahmin to it. The King used to select high officials in the customary laws, judiciary, administrative and military services from amongst his relatives and also from his favourites. They comprised of the aristocratic section.

The Phamnaibas enjoyed many privileges and facilities. McColloch (1859:12) mentioned that, "The appointment to the office exempts the holder's immediate family from the performance of any heavy duty, and, if above certain rank, entitled his heirs to the distinction of bearing silver spears and being horsemen in attendance on the Raja. Some officers are entitled to 'Loin sil', that is to be a follower or followers, who perform any work they may be set to". He also mentioned that some officers were given the privilege of "Yim tinaba", that is, some families or "tribes" were given to them by the Raja to serve them. Whenever these officers build any house all members of the "tribe" assisted him. Whenever the wives of these officers went "abroad" the wives of the members of whole of the "tribe" attended. This system, however, was abolished by Maharaja Debendra Singh in 1850 (McColloch (1859), R. Brown (1874, 85-86) pointed out that these officers were given a certain amount of tax free land. These officers enjoyed the most fertile land in the valley. They were also provided with the facility of a system known as "Pothang". Under this system whenever those officials used to go on tour, they forced the villagers to carry their luggages free of cost. Even the princesses were given in marriage to persons belonging to this class of people.

Privileges and facilities were also given to the Brahmins. The religious services were assigned to the Brahmins. They worshipped the idol of Govindajee and performed all the religious and other ceremonies. McColloch (1859:12) pointed out that they also had their Lalup, that is, they had to cook for the Raja and for the idol of Govindajee. R. Brown (1874) mentioned that they were also given a certain amount of tax free land. The kings used to grant lands to their relatives as "Khorpos" lands and to the Brahmins as "Lugoon Lous" (lands).

Lalupkaba

Lalup Kaba means performing certain compulsory essential services for the Raja by every common Meitei between the age of sixteen and sixty for ten days out of every forty days. The members of the four Panas of the Meitei, namely, Khabam, Laipham, Ahallup and Naharup used to perform Lalup in rotation. There was no payment for this work either in cash or in kind. Each individual who performed Lalup was entitled to cultivate one Part of land for his sustenance but on the condition that he would make the payment of regular tax in kind (R. Brown 1874). The village headman and the Pana heads were responsible for taking into account the Lalupkabas. McColloch (1859) mentioned that the individuals entrusted with lalup could remain at home by paying their chief officers for it. He also mentioned that even the sick people had to pay if they missed the Lalup. (Ranajit Kumar. Saha, Valley Society of Manipur, Punthi–Pustak, Calcutta, 1994)

According to McColloch (1859:12), the head of each "family" or "tribe" was responsible to furnish the proper persons for different Lalup services. Based on these different services, there is a sort of hierarchy amongst the Lalup Kabas. For example, the Pibas would act as "Ningthou Selba" or personal attendant of the king. He, as the seniormost head of the clan was not to perform any heavy duty. However, other clan members had to perform the Lalup in the "Leikai". The families of the third and fourth in "seniority" had to perform the duty as "Lanmee" that is, soldiers and "Sungsa roi", that is civil services. Their main duty was to build houses and bridges and collect materials for the purpose of building houses and bridges. The duties of the families after the fourth position were not fixed. Some were "Khoot naiba" or artisans such as goldsmith, blacksmith, carpenters, workers in brass and bell metal and so on. They had to perform any work in their respective lines as assigned. The rest of the families performed the other duities as required. Some attended the Raja's elephants, some to his ponies, horses, etc.

R. Brown (1874) mentioned twenty seven functional groups along with the nature of their employment as follows:

1. Ningthou Senba–Raja's body guard and house servants.
2. Leima Senba–Rani's bodyguard and house servents,
3. Maiba Sanglel–Medical practitioners and Kabiraj,
4. Pacha–Court of justice for women,

5. Pena Khongba–Musicians and Singers,
6. Sagol Sang–Overseers of the royal stables,
7. Samoo Sang–Overseers of the elephants,
8. Arangba–Butlers, look after the food,
9. Thangja Panaba–Overseers of blacksmiths,
10. Baladeo Seina–Overseers of firewood,
11. Fourungba–Overseers of rice,
12. Thumjaorungba–Overseers of salt,
13. Poogai–Charge of money – chest,
14. Maiba tul–Strikers of gongs,
15. Doolai Paba–Champrassies or messangers,
16. Apalba–Mounted troops,
17. Doolairoi Sang–Carry Dollaies (Palanquins),
18. Sebuk Thang-Sooba–Raja's sword-bearers,
19. U-Suba–Carpenters,
20. Lou roongba–Cultivators,
21. Thang-Saba–Blacksmiths,
22. Kon-Saba–Jewellers and workers in brass,
23. Koodumba–Bone-setters,
24. Aheiba–Metal-casters,
25. Sanglei–Cutcherry Work,
26. Sangooba–Cutcherry Work,
27. Laikai–House builders.

Loipotkaba

Loipotkaba means paying tribute to the king and also performing the heavy duties for the king. The Loi/Chakpa, Bishnupriya and the Yaithibi, who were considered as degraded class performed these Loipot services. They need not perform Lalup but they should pay tribute to the king. The Lois were considered to be of low status. They had certain assigned occupations, some of these were heavy in nature like smelting of iron, manufacturing of silk, distillery of spirits, making of earthen pots, manufacturing salt, fishery, cutting grass for the Raja's ponies, cutting of beams, posts and making of canoes etc. The tribute was paid in kind. The "Lois" who produced salt had to manufacture for the Raja "a certain quantity" of salt monthly (McColloch -1859). R. Brown (1874) mentioned that the proportion that went to the Raja was thirty percent of the quantity manufactured. Dun (1886) mentioned that the "Mayangs"

(Bishnupriyas) supplied grass for the royal stable and ponies. The tribute could also be paid in coins. Those "Lois" who used to pay tribute in "Sel" that is, the coin of the country. (McColloch 1859). As for example the "Lois" who were engaged in fishing had to pay a tax of Rs. 2/- to Rs. 4/- monthly (R. Brown 1874).

Thus the king had a clear economic policy which was differentially applied to his favourites and disfavourites. The job opportunities for the degraded were limited and closed and for the commoner unlimited and open. Ithing and Thanga used to fish in the Loktak, Ningel used to make salt, Sugnu prepared lime, Kakching smelted iron, Chairel used to make earthen pots and so on. None of these degraded groups had any other choice than to do the work specified to them. Because of the pattern of distribution of the ethnic groups along with their occupations, the king could have a firm control over the surplus. The king could get all the surplus products of the degraded in the form of tribute. The commoner could cultivate a fixed amount of land for their survival on paying regular tax in kind. The rest of the land were cultivated by the commoner in the form of Lalup service and the products were under the control of the king. The aristocrat could enjoy a specific amount of land free of tax but had to pay certain amount of tax in kind for any increase of land under their control. The king accumulated all the surplus in the traditional way. (Ranajit Kumar Saha, Valley Society of Manipur, Punthi –Pustak, Calcutta, 1994)

2. Judiciary relationship

Every village had a village head, who was an agent of the king. He had to keep in contact with the villagers and report anything significant in the matter of law and order, social and religious significance to the officer concerned in the palace. Breach of social and religious taboos was severly dealt with and the accused was punished by ex-communication. Without the permission of the king, the villagers had no right to use either the particular colour anywhere on any occasion or the particular dress that the king used. Those who violated this restriction were punished.

There were four courts, namely, Cheirap (civil and criminal court), Garot (military court), Paja / Pacha (women's court) and Mongalsang (Court of Mohammedan) to deal with judicial matters.

Dun (1886) mentioned that the Cheirap was composed of 13 senior members appointed by the Raja. Garot was composed of eight senior army officers, namely, majors and some other officers in the army. Paja/Pacha was composed of six members appointed by the Raja. The Presidents of Cheirap Garot, Paja/Pacha were Angom Ningthou, Senapati, and Pajahanba/Pachahanba respectively. McColloch (1859) mentioned that the "Paja" was formerly consisted of the hereditary president "Paja Hanba" and other twelve hereditary members. Cheirap had formerly 60 to 80 hereditary members. He also mentioned that at the time of his stay in Manipur the posts were also obtained by means of money. The will of the ruling princes was the law. He mentioned that treason was the highest crime. Murder was next. Murder committed by a Brahmin or by a woman was not awarded capital punishment. The utmost punishment of a Brahmin was expulsion from the country and in case of a woman she had to be exposed in the market with shaved head with someone announcing the crime she had committed in public. Excommunication or exile was another form of punishment. Some guilty persons were also forced to do hard and dishonourable jobs.

Alexander Mackenize (1884) referred to one case and said that in the month of May, 1882 the fourth son of Maharaja Chandrakirty killed one servant. The offender was tried for that act. As a punishment, he was exiled to Thanga, an isolated, lonely island in Loktak lake. He also mentioned another case that occurred on 23rd June, 1881. At that time the political Agent was absent on leave. A man named Irengba claimed descent from one of the former kings. He declared that in dream he got the divine message to become king. Soon he collected some followers. He selected 18 persons as his ministers and chief of the army. He proceeded towards the capital with about 300 followers. But they were put down by the Maharaja's troops. The 18 ring leaders were tried and executed. Some of the followers were compelled to manufacture salt. This kind of punishment locally known as "Loithaba" was prevalent. As a result, many high status Meitei were degraded to low status. Some villages were populated by such excommunicated people. All these cases proved that the king successfully maintained his control over the economic surplus through judicial power. (Ranajit Kumar Saha, Valley Society of Manipur, Punthi–Pustak, Calcutta, 1994)

3. Religious Relationship

The king and his people practiced the indigenous religion, Sanamahi before the arrival of Hinduism. During those days, the religious institution called Maiba Sanglen was divided into three elements–the Maiba and Maibi Loisang (the institution of the priest and priestess) the Maichou Loisang (the council of the literati) and the Pena Loisang (the institution of the musicians).

Maichous (Scholars) later on known as Pandits are the repositories of all sorts of Puyas. They could give guidance to the Maiba and the Maibi and also to the masses. The king used to take advice of the Pandits in every sphere of activity. The King and the people abided by the advice of the Pandits. At the time of worship of Umang Lai, the Maibas and Maibis are sent from the Maiba and the Maibi Loisang. of the palace. The writing up of the genealogy of every lineage up-to-date in the sacred book Yum-Changba Puya was done by the Pandits. Adoption to a lineage was done under the guidance of the Pandits. All sorts of disputes with regard to religion, worship, lineage, clan, marriage of any forbidden category and so on, was settled by the Palace Pandits. Another main duty of the Pandits was the maintenance of a daily diary. They used to record all the happenings in it. People believed that they maintained the Chronicle, called Cheitharol Kumbaba (Ranajit Kumar. Saha, Valley Society of Manipur, Punthi –Pustak, Calcutta, 1994)

IMPORTANT KINGS / MAHARAJAS OF MANIPUR : TANGJA LEELA PANKHANBA (1445-1404 B.C.)

Tangja Leela Pankhanba was the king of Manipur during 1445-1404 B. C. He married Sinbee Leima, daughter of Lei-Hou Chief and established his kingdom around 1445 BC. The ancient chronicle *Ningthourol Lambuba* describes a Manipuri folk song relatd to the migration of Tangja Leela Pakhangba :-

Leenwai yi maru
Tangja Leela Pakhangba waichatlam
Hanggoi konthing nurabi waikoilam
Haorei Laina pangbalam
Leenwai yi maru
Phatlou lai makol
Lwai kharangpok
Kaklen seenang sangkon
Mee ra pong thoklam
Ouri samei thang
Lamlen konbira (Ningthourol Lambuba, page-6)
(K. C. Tensuba, "Meitrabak, Heeri Konba Lup", Manipur, 2008)

NINGTHOU KANGBA (1405-1359 BC):

Kangba, son of Tangja Leela Pakhangba ascended the throne after his father's death. He named his kingdom– "Tilli Koktong" and constructed a

Lai-Yum (a temple) for Sanamahi God at Waroiching. There was no clan system during his time. Dead bodies were thrown in the open, neither buried nor cremated. The religious belief was "Atreppa – meaning to know HIM". (Dr. Kh. Ratan Kumar, Lai Haraoba of Manipur, 2001) He ruled over his kingdom for 46 years. He had his capital at "Kangngamong" or "Kangamung" or "Kangapung". His wife was Leima Taritnu, daughter of Nongpok Ningthou at the eastern hills of present day Imphal. At that time Manipur valley did not exist. King Kangba gave the name "Loktak" (Lok=water or stream in hillocks; Tak=vast or the end) for the vast water body covering the valley. They used dug out boats to communicate between them. King Kangba and Leima Taritnu gave birth to a son- Koikoi at a place which later on named as Kangpokpi. He was very fond of Mukna, Khong Kangjei and Sagol Kangjei (Polo). It was recorded in the chronicles that King Kangba introduced "Sagol Kang-jei", the modern Polo. Hence the name "Kang-jei" for the stick and "Kang-droom" for the round ball, "Kangjeibung" for the Pologround after his name. He entrusted the making of Kangjei Kanghu to one particular family clan which later on known as "Kanghujam". He was credited for digging out the Maklang river. According to Sakok Lamlen Ahanba, the deity worshipped during the time of Kangba was Sanamahi. (Dr. Kh. Ratan Kumar, Lai Haraoba, 2001) The story of Ningthou Kangba, his father and his descendants were written down for the first time in the Meitei script "Ningthou Kangbalon" by one Maichou (Meitei scholar) named *Thongak Kurumba* from Thursday, the 3rd of Kalen (May) onwards during the time of Khu-Yoi Tompok (2nd Century AD), the son of Nongda Lairen Pakhangba. (which was transliterated into Bengali script by Nongthombamcha Angou Luwang and published by Thokchomba Ibotombi in 1976)

KOI-KOI, also Known as MARIYA FAMBAL-CHA (1359 BC-1329 BC)

Koikoi, son of Ningthou Kangba ascended the throne at the age of 39 years. From this day, the dating of Meitei Calendar (Cheiraoba) known as Mari-Fam (MF) was introduced. Taking the birthday of Koikoi as 00 MF, 1359 BC will be 39 MF, 1 A. D will be 1398 MF and 2000 AD will be 3398 MF according to Meitei Calendar. The surnames Koijam, Keirambam, etc. were started from this time. Mariya Fambal-Cha (Koikoi) and his wife, Lee-oi Nungoibee had two sons. His first son, Pong left his parents early to start his own kingdom, so his second son, Kaksu Tonkonba (Born on 3rd November, Meitei Hiyangei month, 1355 BC) became Meidingu (Ningthou or King) around 1329 BC. Meidigu Tonkonba was born prematurely at 8 months, hence the nickname Kaksu (for dwarf or not matured) was given when he was a child. Urum Khou-Chonbi was his Queen. He developed a place called "Kakwa". Clan system was not yet formed. Burial of dead bodies were introduced during his time. Soraren Achiba was the deity worshipped. The religious belief was to realize the soul, to know the truth. (Dr. Kh. Ratan Kumar, Lai Haraoba, 2001)

POIREITON KHUNTHOKPA (34-18 BC)

Poireiton Khunthokpa was the ruler of Tai-Pong-Pan (Manipur) during 34-18 B.C. Tai-Pong-Pan was the name of the present Manipur during those days. Poireiton migrated from the region of Kham situated between Burma, Tibet and China. For more than 700 years, there was no ruler in Tai-Pong-Pan.

So some people of Tai-Pong-Pan invited Thongarel of Kham-Nung Saowa, the great man of the Nung tribe, to rule over Tai-Pong-Pan. But, Thongarel was very old. He asked his younger brother Chingkhong Poireiton to go to Tai-Pong-Pan and rule over the region. Poireiton had already lost his wife after having four sons and two daughters. Thongarel offered his second wife Leima Leinaotabi to accompany Poireiton who also accepted the offer. Poreiton was the leader of the group comprising of men, women and children. They were armed with axes, swords, spears, bows and arrows. Poreiton himself carried an iron stick. They carried burning husk filled in an earthen pot wherever they went. They crossed the narrow Chaukan pass from the region of Kham and sojourned in the Hukawng valley and followed the course of Chindwin (Ningthi) river and then trickled through the northern region of the present day Ukhrul district of Manipur to reach the source of Iril river. Poireiton settled somewhere near northern Kanglatongbi from where a vast water extent and swampy areas could be seen stretched towards the south. Poireiton worked hard for the unification of the people inhabiting along the Koubru hill range. In his journey from Kham, Poireiton was accompanied by tribes of Chakpa, Nung, Kham, Mon, Khu, Nga, etc. who were all neo-Tibetans. During his reign, the kingdom was named as Poirei-lam (the land of Poireiton) and the people were called Poirei-Meetei. The coming of Poreiton with his followers exerted a great influence on the life and culture of Manipuris. It is said that the Manipuri Calendar comprising of 12 months, of which the second, third, fourth, sixth and seventh months were named after the activities of Poreiton. Poreiton brough a kind of sweet smelling, black rice which the future generations named "Chakhao Poreiton". The accounts of Poireiton and his migration were recorded in a manuscript called "Poireiton Khunthokpa" in a perfect prose.

LUWANG PUNSHIBA (5-33 A. D.)

Luwang king Hongnem Luwang Punshiba was credited to have introduced boat for the first time after seeing a locust crossing the Singda river with a piece of dry grass and a mouse supported by a Khikloi (a plant). He asked his two brothers Luwang Wamitkhu and Wangmanao Silheiba to bring a big tree for making the boat. The two brothers brought a big Uningthou tree from Kouba Ingen Ching and a boat was made according to the design given by the king. The king put the head of a Sangai Chiren Tompokpa at the head of the boat. At the tail end of the boat, a human skull is also mounted.

NONGDA LAIREN PAKHANGBA (33-153 AD or 1431-1551 MF)

Nongda Lairen Pakhangba ruled Manipur from 33 to 153 A. D. He was from the Ningthouja clan, the royal clan of Manipur. He was connected with the snake cult. Only the Ningthouja clan has got this connection with the snake cult.

Nongda Lairen Pakhangba was the son of Leinung Yabirok (mother). He married Laisna, a younger sister of Poireiton. Nongda Lairen Pakhangba ascended the throne with Laisna as his queen in 33 AD on one Monday at "Kangleipungmayol", the name of his capital, after making bards sing "Ougree" a song sung in praise of the god for prosperity of the King and his people. Ougri was believed to be a song of peculiar charm having the power to destroy the place of the enemy where it was sung. Meidingu Pakhangba was an able descendant of Ningthou Kangba and Tangja Leela Pakhangba but the accounts of his father has yet to be traced although Tupu Likleng alias Luwang Langmaiba was suggested to be his father in "The History of Manipur" by W. Ibohal Singh. He started expanding his kingdom toward the low lying areas after the water in the valley started draining slowly at Ching-Nung-Hut in South-West Manipur. He named his palace Kangla [dry land] because this place was the first dry land discovered after draining out the vast water in the valley. From him, the Mangang clan (Ningthouja) originated. When he was a young boy, he used to catch fish at the source of Iril river. One day he came across Kouba Angang-nga who tried to invade his father's kingdom. He stopped the approach of the enemy. He was a great devotee of Sanamahi. During his long life, Meidingu Pakhangba was known as Leinung Lonja Pakhangba and Lolaang Pakhangba and attained the status of a Lai-Ningthou (God King). Cheitharol Kumbaba chronicle started the chronology of kings from Nongda Lairen Pakhangba.

KHUIYOI TOMPOK (154-264 A. D.)

Khuiyol Tompok ruled Manipur during 154-264 A. D. Khamen Chatpa and Ningkham Samjin were introduced during his time. (Dr. K. Sobita, Traditional Dress of the Meiteis, Bhubon Publishing House, Imphal, 1998). He experimented making drums using deer-skin and tiger-skin but the sound was not satisfactory. Later on, he experimented with neat-skin which gives the pleasing sound. Thus neat skin has been used in making Manipuri drums till today. A copper plate inscription credits King Khuiyoi Tompok with the introduction of drums and cymbals into Manipuri dance.

URA KONTHOUBA (568-658 A. D.)

Ura Konthouba ruled Manipur during 568-658 A.D. He was a great warrior. He was the first king of Manipur to have issued coins and this gives much material evidence of history. He issued a bell metal coin of more or less the same texture with initial letter of king's name "WU". During his time, a great person named Poireiton entered Manipur and started their function as religious Kurus. He happened to face hostilities from the neighbouring Nagas, Angoms who used to create disturbances in the valley.

NAOTHINGKHONG (663-763)

King Naothingkhong ruled Manipur during 663-763A.D. He was known as Hongnem Yoi Khunjao. He ran away from home for fear of wrath of his father at a very young age. He lived with the Sheilloy Langmai in Nongmaijing Hills and married a Langmai girl named Petangnga. When he became the king at Kangla, Petangnga came to see him. She was shocked to find a Khuman princess, daughter of Punshi Yumoiba sitting at the seat of the queen. She died of shock and disappointment. After her death, she was worshipped as "Yumjao Lairembi" by the royal family. King Naothingkhong used to worship Mangang Kuru, Luwang Kuru and Khuman Kuru.

Early Relations of Manipur with Burma

In the year 777 A. D, the king of Pong Murgnow died leaving two sons called Sookampha and Samlongpha. The eldest son Sookampha ascended the throne of Pong. The king sent his brother Samlongpha as the head of a powerful force to subdue first the countries to the east including probably the principality of Bhamo, which extends from the left bank of the Irrawady river to the frontiers of Yunnan. This expedition was successful. Samlongpha leaving the capital Mogaung arrived at the western country of Basa king, which probably means Banga, the ancient capital of Cachar. He received submission of Cachar king and also the king of Tripura. From Tripura, he crossed the hills and came to Manipur valley near Moirang, a village on the western bank of Loktak Lake. Samlongpha, in consideration of the extreme poverty of Manipur remitted all tributes but appeared to have directed the Manipuris for adoption of certain observances in dress and diet, calculated to improve the habits and manners of the people who were evidently in the lowest stage of civilization. (R. B. Pemberton-The Eastern Frontier of India", Mittal Publications, New Delhi, 1835, pp. 109-110)

MEIDINGU AYAANGBA (821-910 A. D.)

Ayaangba ruled Manipur during 821-910 A. D. He is known for his road construction which still exists after him as "Ayangpalli" in the Imphal East District. He issued coins which are characterized by their circular shapes and carry the initial name "A" in archaic Manipuri script on the obverse side of the coin with a diameter of 0. 9 cm.

MEIDINGU YANGLOU KEIPHABA (965-983 AD or 2363-2381 MF)

Khamlang Atonba, the son of Meidingu Chenglei Lanthaba, ascended the throne after his father in 965 AD. One day he went for hunting to a place called Yanglou Louchipan and caught six tigers alive. Henceforth, he became to be known as Yanglou Keiphaba (Kei-tiger; phaba-to capture). He married Lairenjam Chanu Mubisu, the daughter of Louthog-pak Chief. She was a great Sinbee, a master of weaving and embroidery. She invented the Khoi-Mayek style of Meitei Phanek Mayek Naibi (Manipur women's dress). Still today this design is a favourite for Meitei women. (Dr. K. Sobita, Traditional Dress of the Meiteis, Bhubon Publishing House, Imphal, 1998)

MEIDINGU LOIYUMBA (1074-1112 A. D.)

Loiyumba ruled Manipur during 1074-1112 A. D. Loiyumba Shilyen is an important historical document of his time, which deals with the social distribution, administrative and religious functions proclaimed by the king. It gives details about the number of traditional deities worshipped during his time. The book specifies the duties of Sageis to look after the maintenance of the deities. For example, Sorokhaibam was given the assignment to look after Phou-oi-bi, Irom –Khamlangba, Heisnam–Panthoibi, Khoisnam–Petangnga, Konthoujam-Huimureima, Moirangthem-Puthiba, Ningthoujam–Chinga–Leima etc. The Maibas were also given different duties of healing the sick, performing rites, offering sacrifices, preparation for birth and death ceremonies. He also introduced certain administrative changes (Dr. Kh. Ratan Kumar, Lai Haroba of Manipur, Smt. Ph. Pratima Devi, Mayang Imphal, 2001)

MEIDINGU LOITONGBA (1121-1149 AD or 2519-2547 MF)

When king Loiyumba, Loitongba's father, ascended the throne, his mother Sum-Leima was pregnant with Loitongba; hence, the name Loitongba; who ascended the throne together with his parents. He was a man of games and sports. It is mentioned that he invented the game of "Kang-Sanaba" of Meiteis. Some scholars argued that Kang-Sanaba had already existed and Loitongba was a master of the game. His son Atom Yoiremba ascended the throne (1149-1162 AD) but his brother Hemtou Iwan -Thaba invaded him and drove him out of the Kingdom.

NINGTHOU KHOMBA (1432-1467 A. D.)

Ninghtou Khomba ruled during 1432-1467 A. D. During his time, the Burmese invaded Manipur on the eastern border and the king went to fight the war at the Kabow valley and captured Akala. The Tangkhuls from Tuishem village, taking advantage of the king's absence from the capital came down to Imphal and created problems in the valley. But his queen Linthoi Ngambi organised her forces with other women, put on the royal noble's dress and fought the invading Tangkhuls in the guise of a king and his army. Queen Linthoingambi succeeded in capturing the Tangkhul Chief Hempuringba and in driving away the Tangkhuls from the valley. During his reign, four persons from Kabow valley married Manipuri women and their descendants merged in the Manipuri population. Ningthou Khomba died in 1467 leaving a consolidated Manipuri kingdom.

MEIDINGU SENBI KYAAMBA (1467-1508 AD)

Meidingu Senbi Kyaamba, the son of Ningthou Khomba and Leima Linthoingambi, became the king at the age of 24 in 1467 AD. His original name was Thangwai Ningthouba. He was given the title of Kyaamba after conquering Kyaang, a Shan kingdom in the Kabow Valley. Kyaang or Kyaang Khambaat was a Shan kingdom in the Kabow valley. Kyaamba captured and brought the king of Kyaang, Chao Seng along with their family members. In the third year of his reign, Thangwai Ningthouba and his ally Choupha Khek Khomba, the king of Pong attacked Kyaang. They destroyed Kyaang with an army of only 100 Manipuri cavalry. They celebrated their victory with great pomp-by eating and drinking from the vessels of gold (Li). Thangwai Ningthouba was then Kyaamba, the conqueror of Kyaang.

The relation between Choupha Khek Khomba and Kyaamba was very cordial. Choupha Khek Khomba requested the help of Kyaamba in his war against Kyaang-Khumbat (Khumpat: khum for gold and Pat for lake) to which the Manipur king agreed to support the cause of the king of Pong. Thus the joint forces of the two kings raided Kyaang-Khumbat and subdued its chief named Chao Seng and Kyaamba was offered one princess and another girl, the daughter of one Haoroksu. The cause of the joint expedition against the Khumbat Raja arose from the fact that two princesses of Khekkhomba were given in marriage-one to each of the chiefs of Samjok (Thangdaud) and of Kuambat who were tributary chiefs of Khek khomba. When the two princesses reached Samjok, the one who had to proceed upto Khumbat, did not like the separation and therefore requested their father to review the negotiation. The king agreed and she was allowed to stay at Samjok. At this the Raja of Khumbat felt offended. The Khumbat Raja demanded that the dowry he was to have received with the princess should be still paid and a remission of tribute be granted to him for three years. The latter request only was complied with. The Khumbat Raja was angry at the treatment, built a strong fort and prepared to throw off his allegiance to the king of Pong. In this state of affairs, the King of Pong sent an embassy headed by a Shan nobleman called Chow Lang Hiee to Thangwai Ningthouba, the king of Manipur requesting for a daughter in marriage. Thangwai Ningthouba agreed and sent his younger sister since he did not have any daughter princess of marriageable age at that time. In 1475, the Manipuri princess left Manipur for Pong escorted by Chow Lang Hiee. On reaching the Sekmoo hill, the cavalcade was attacked and the Manipuri princess was carried off by the Raja of Khumbat. The Shan nobleman made his escape and reported the disaster of the capture of the princess to the king of Pong. The king of Pong immediately took measures to avenge the gross insult. He crossed the Ningthee or Chindwin river with a considerable force, entered the valley where he was joined by the Manipur king. They besieged Khumbat and the Khumbat Raja made his escape to the southward on a spotted elephant.

The two kings exchanged gifts and also concluded their friendly treaty by fixing the common boundary between Manipur and the kingdom of Pong. According to the treaty, the eastern limit of the Kingdom of Manipur was the whole of the Noajeeree hills running between the Moo and Chindwin (Ningthee) rivers, which was then established as the boundary between

Manipur and Pong. Southward, the boundary extended to the Meeyatoung or Meeya hills and to the north to a very celebrated mango tree near Moongkhum where the two kings separated and returned to their respective capitals. This tract of land is known as Kabow valley. (R. B. Pemberton- "The Eastern Frontier of India", Mittal Publications, New Delhi, 1835, pp. 112-113). Chindwin river (Ningthee) is the western branch of the Irrawady river (Ayeyarwady), which is known to the Shans by the name of Numpurong, to the Burmese Kyendwen or Thanlawattee and to the Manipuris–Ningthee, which means "beautiful river". Between the Kabow valley and Ningthee river, there is an uninhabited range of hills called "Ungoching" across which there were several passes from Manipur to the Ningthee river. The valley itself is divided into three principalities–Samjok (Thangdaud), Khumbat and Kule. Khumbat never regain its prosperity after its destruction by the united forces of Pong and Manipur. The Kabow valley when viewed from above, presents a vast expanse of dark primeval Saul (Teak) forest, in the very heart of which cleared spaces are discerned, varying from two to eight miles in circumference as the spot happens to be the site of a village or town. (R. B. Pemberton-The Eastern Frontier of India, Mittal Publications, New Delhi, 1835, pp. 122, 117).

In 1474, the King of Pong visited Manipur and presented Kyaamba a golden box made of 80 mohurs of gold containing a stone idol, known as "PHEIYA" (Almighty), having the power of God and a sacred spear to guard the stone. It is said that the Pheiya appeared in the dream of Choupha Khek Khomba, King of Pong and told him that "He is Bishnu and asked him to present the stone idol to Kyaamba, king of Manipur so that he may be cured of his illness." The King of Pong narrated the stories to Kyaamba. At that time, the people of Manipur did not know about the worship of God in the form of a sacred stone. The King of Pong also presented the guava trees and guava fruits for treatment of dysentery which occurred in epidemic proportions in Manipur in those days. The guava is hence called Pongdon (Pungdon) by the Meiteis. The King of Pong also brought a kind of pulses, which later on known as "Pong Hawai".

King Kyaamba once fell sick and no physician could diagnose his sickness. The oracles were consulted and advice was received through Maibis or Amaibis (Priestess) that the King could be cured if worship was offered to Lord Bishnu. Some Brahmins who were well acquainted with puja (ritual) of Lord Bishnu were available in Manipur in those days.

In 1475, King Kyaamba in respect of the King of Pong built a brick temple at Lamangdong, 27 km south of Imphal. Later, two Brahmins namely

Banamali and Haribidyasur, migrated from Cachar understood "PHEIYA" as the Hindu God, Bishnu. They announced that rice boiled in cow milk (Sangom Ksheer) should be offered to the deity in order to bring good fortune to the King and the people of his kingdom. Accordingly, Meidingu Kyaamba appointed the Brahmins in the service of the deity. Afterwards, the followers of the Brahmin were known as Bishnupriya and the place was named Bishnupur. Thus, the worship of Bishnu was started in Manipur during the reign of King Kyaamba. From the Burmese words "Pheiya", the temple in which Bishnu was wroshipped was known as "Phura" in Manipuri. The descendants of the Brahmin who worshipped at the Phura became known as Phurailatpam.

In 1485 AD, King Kyaamba introduced the system of CHEITHABA in which a man would declare before the king and nobles the last day of the year and that he would bear all the misfortunes which might befall the kingdom in the coming year. The man then becomes "Cheithaba" – and the year was named after him. But the Cheithaba was not banished or allowed to escape in wilderness like a scapegoat. He continued to remain in the country like any other subject. He was exempted from onerous duties of the State. After making the announcement before the king and the nobles, he was given a reward of some clothes and some baskets of salt. Hiyang Loi Namoi Chaoba was the first person whose name was used as the first Cheithaba, which meant he would volunteer to bear the burden and sufferings of the kingdom, which might befall during that particular year. Earlier, it was known as Cheiraoba-someone with a Khok bamboo pole (Chei) fixed with a bell would run around on horseback and declare (Laoba) the end of the year. This system was in vague from the time of Naophangba (428-518).

Kyaamba was a powerful and an able king. During his time, the kingdom expanded to the distant hills. The area from Moran in the northern hills upto Lushai hills in the southern part was under him. For administrative convenience, he divided Manipur into four administrative Panas-Ahallup, Naharup, Khabam and Laipham. He constructed huge store house to store grains at a place, which later on known as "Kyaamgei" (Store house of Kyaamba). He also introduced a design of jewellery known as "Kyaam Likfang" for women. He encouraged polo game and boat race in the country. He effected a reform in maintaining the royal chronicle, Cheitharol Kumbaba.

During Kyaamba's time, many Brahmins came from Sylhet, Assam, Gujarat, Kanpur, Nandagram. Kharadah. They were allowed to settle in Manipur and marry Manipuri women and they became Manipuris. The ancestors of Lairikyengbams and Brahmins with surnames like Sija Gurumayum,

Leihaothabam, Takhenchangbam, Phurailatpam, Adhikarimayum came during Kyaamba's time. Similary, there was an influx of Shan during his time, they were also absorbed in the Manipuri society. Kyaamba reigned for 40 years and died in 1508 at the age of 64 years.

MUNGYAMBA (1562-1597)

Mungyamba succeeded his father Chalaamba in 1562. His earlier name was Thangwai Ningthou Kyaamba. He had two wives-Chabongbi and Thokchom Chanu. Chabongbi gave birth to three sons- Khagemba (Ningthou Lanba), Khurailakpa Chingsomba, Sanongba whereas Thokchom Chanu gave birth to only one son- Pukhramba. In 1566, he subdued Mungyang, a principality near Kabow valley and he assumed the tile of Mungyamba, conqueror of Mungyang. He captured Mungkhong Mungyai, Akala and Mangsha and brought a number of prisoners and horses. In 1563, he captured Khamaran in the Kabow valley. In 1571, he attacked Samjok (Thangdaud) and brought some prisoners of war. In 1580, he quelled the rising of Moyons, a hill people living the southern extremity of Manipur. In 1585, he again attacked Samjok. In 1591, he again attacked and devastated Samjok (Thangdaud). Mungyamba constructed a large store house for storing grains and paddy and this place was later known as "Mungshangei" (Store house of Mungyamba). Mungyamba died in 1597 after a successful reign of 35 years.

KHAGEMBA (1597-1652)

After Mungyamba, his son Sana Hihonba Poirei Ningthouhanba ascended the throne at the age of 21 years in 1597. Khagemba means conqueror of the "Khagi". Khagi means "Chinese" in Manipuri and Ngamba means "Kill or conquer". He defeated the Chinese. Khagi was the place on the eastern part of the Chindwin river (Ningthee river) near Yunnan province of the present day China. In 1602, he invaded Khagi and captured its king, Choupha Hongdei. However, according to Hudson, the war with Khagi (China) was in the year 1630. Khagemba ruled Manipur during 1597-1652 A. D. During this time, Kyaang again revolted against the king. Khagemba invaded Kyaang and brought 177 prisoners of war. In 1607, he invaded Samjok and also captured Chakpa situated in the Ungo Ching (hill) range. He gave in marriage one of his daughters Chanu Toksennu to the king of Cachar in 1602 and in 1604, he made a treaty of trade relations with the king of Cachar. He also gave in marriage one of his daughter Chanu Sanahekpi to the king of Burma (Anaukhpetlun ?/1605-1628). Khagemba had two younger brothers. One brother was Sanongba. He was about 10 years younger and held the office of Yaiskullakpa. But due to some misunderstanding, he revolted against his brother, the king Khagemba. He was defeated. He fled to Cachar, raised a big army under the patronage of Cachar King Sapadram including a large number of Muslims under the leadership of Yakharek, Bhim Bon, equipped with firearms and invaded Manipur in 1606. It was during the palmy days of the Mughal Empire with Jahangir as the Emperor. The king went in person with a sufficiently strong army with able leaders like Pala Koireng, Yumnam Kiyamba, Haobam Aroy, Elangbam Khubam Lairikyengbam Dhananjoy to repel the invaders. After some fighting, the king won a decisive battle. The battle was concluded on 17th Inga, 1606 with the surrender of 1007 army, 30 elephants, 1000 muskets. But some of the sepoys who escaped collected a large number of cows for transportation to Cachar. Having heard the news, the king captured these sepoys and they were brought to the capital by binding them with a long rope dragging them towards the capital. This place was later known as "Mayang Lanching". The surrendered army included a large number of Muslims and Bishnupriyas. Many of the captured persons were blacksmiths, utensil makers, artisans, musicians, washermen, grooms, elephant tenders. All the captured persons were allowed to settle in Manipur by giving free lands and Manipuri women. These surrendered sepoys spoke Bangali and there they were called "Bangal", later on "Pangan". They were given Meitei surnames. A new office was opened for administering justice to them according to Mohammedan customary laws. On 10th Lamda, 1631, (Wednesday), he shifted his palace to Kangla and worshipped his ancestral Gods with hundreds of buffaloes, cows, sheep, lambs, dogs, pigs etc. He introduced boat race, *Hiyang Tanaba* in the month of Hiyangei, 1635 A. D. as a part of the celebration of the old traditional ritual known as "Hiyangei Kumjanba".

In 1645, Charaikong, Maram Chief invaded the kingdom. There was a battle at Charai field in which Charaikong along with a number of his men were taken prionser. After some time, Charaikong was put to death at Sugnoo.

Development Works

He introduced the system of awarding gold and silver decorations for distinguished service in 1605. He established ten new Keithels (bazaars) in different parts of Manipur in 1614 A. D. Smoking of tobacco was introduced and tobacco was cultivated as a new luxury. Regular playing of Polo was done in 1620 A. D. The people started extracting salt from salt springs He also defeated the king of Tripura in 1634 A. D. Three tigers were caught at Chinga hill in 1644 A. D.

The use of firearms started from his time. The Manipuris started learning manufacture of heavy artillery (Top guns). Boring of muskets was successful in 1628. Special areas or Leikais like Singjamei Top Sapam Leikai, Keisamthong Top Leirak were earmarked for manufacture of heavy artillery, Top guns. Nongmeikappam family were expert in manufacture of guns. These heavy artillery were drawn by carriages and tested and this area became known as "Top Chingtha". Artillery fire was used to signal the message of war or attack by ferocious animals. A special mound was created to station the artillery gun and this became known as "Nongmeipung". Earlier, only drum was used to declare the message of war to the people and that place was known as "Lanlao pung". Khagemba encouraged people to manufacture guns and artillery.

Khagemba constructed many roads and bridges. Khagempalli was developed during his time. He constructed a brick wall at the palace gate at Kangla in 1632. He planted a new variety of rice known as "Taothabi". He introduced several administrative reforms like the system of measuring lands and weighing goods. Khagemba was an ardent follower of Sanamahi religion. A contemporary text *"Khagemba Langjel"* is the expression of the supremacy of Sanamahi as the universal God of the Meiteis. It is believed that belief in Sanamahi would bring peace and prosperity to the king and the country. This religion flourished to a new height during the time of Khagemba. According to *"Thiren Layat"*, a contemporary treatise on Meitei religion, three types of worship were mentioned–Charat (human sacrifice), Karat (animal sacrifice) and Marat (offering of flower,fruit and fish). All types of animals like buffaloes, shandang (Mithun), cats, puppies were sacrificed. During his time, many eminent Meitei scholars like Konok Thengra, Lanngol Lukhoi, Apoimacha, Salam Sana, Yumnam Tomba were in his durbar. The Lai haraoba festival flourished to a great extent during the reign of Khagemba. During his time, the hills and valley were united into a strong kingdom. Khagemba further improved the manner of keeping and maintaining the old chronicle, Cheitharol Kumbaba.

He introduced some reforms in the Polo Game. He reformed that each team of Polo should be of seven players, each player having a specific designation. He redesigned the "Kokyet" of each player to make it more lovely and convenient. During his time, many books in Meitei mayek (Meitei script) were written and published.

He divided the kingdom into eight divisions. He also introduced "Lalup" or compulsory free labour for the state. He defeated Mayangs and therefore he was also given the name "Mayang Ngamba". He issued coins with his name "Ma" which was depicted in archaic Manipuri script on the obverse side of the coin. His coins were circular in shape with 1 cm diameter. The arrival of Brahmins continued as before and they were given Manipuri surnames like Aribam Bishnulatpam, Aribam Sagolailatpam, Aribam Tampallailatpam, Samurailatpam, Sanglakpam,Thongratabam Kongbrailatpam, Hidangmayum. Some wandering pilgrims arrived in Manipur and they were given Manipur women and allowed to settle in Manipur.

The long reign of Khagemba for 55 years was peaceful and prosperous. He died on Sunday, Ingel, 1652 A. D. at the age of 76 years.

CHARAI RONGBA (1697-1709)

Meidingu Charai Rongba ascended the throne in 1697 A. D. In 1701 A. D, Loyumba and his group of people waged a war against Charairongba. Charairongba subdued the revolt and killed Loyumba and 30 others. He was the first Manipuri king to be formally initiated to Vaisnavism. King Charairongba and his family were initiated first into Nimandi sect of Vaisnavism. The Brahmins continued to arrive and they were allowed to settle in Manipur after giving Manipuri surnames like Guru Aribam, Laimayum, Laipubam, Hangoibam, Hazarimayum, Manoharmayum, Laimayum Anoubam, Choudhurimayaum. Brahmins from Nabadwip, Krishnanagar, Kanchan Nagar of Bengal adorned the courts of Charairongba (1697-1709 A. D). In 1703 A. D. A Brahman preacher named Krishnacharya alias Rai Vanamali from Shweta Ganga, Puri arrived in Manipur. He was accompanied by his wife, Krishnamayi, two Shudras and a Brahmin named Balabhadra Brahmachari. On Wednesday, the 5th Sajibu (April), 1704, Krishnacharya formally initiated the king into Nirmandi cult of Vaisnavism. Under this cult, Shri Krishna is regarded as the full incarnation of Vishnu. Charai Rongba built a brick temple of Shri Krishna at Brahmapur Guru Aribam Leikai. He gave to this guru a village, a hill and 100 hectares of paddy field as Guru Dakshina. He built a nine room brick house for his Guru. But it was destroyed by the Burmese during the First Devastation (Khuntak Ahanba, 1755-1759) of Manipur. In 1704, Charairongba declared Vaisnavism as the State Religion. (Chander Sheikher Panchani, Manipur, Religiom, Culture and Society, Konark Publishers Pvt. Ltd.) Since Krishnacharya was the guru of the king, his descendants came to be known as the Guru Aribams or the family of the old Guru. The Guru Aribams were highly respected Brahmins and they were given a special seat of honour in festivals and ceremonies held in the king's palace and other places. Next year about 36 Hindu monks, including a preceptor of the king of Assam arrived. There were arrivals of many Brahmins during his time.

There was trade relations with Burma. The import of elephants from Burma continued as before. A Burmese mission arrived in 1702 to ask for the hand of some Manipuri princes for the king of Burma. (R. K. Jhalajit Singh, "A Short History of Manipur", 1965, O. K. Store, Imphal). He gave his daughter, Chakpa Makhaongambi in marriage to the king of Burma, Sane (1698-1714). Chakpa Makhaongambi was made the queen only to be demoted after some years. Charairongba was very upset with this disgraceful news. Burmese architects and dancers visited Manipur in 1706. He diverted the Imphal river from Singjamei to Lilong. He used the army from Tekhao (Tripura) in the excavation work and that place was known as "Tekhao Pat". He erected a stone edict inscribing the government and administration of justice in 1698. During his time, the punishment for theft was death. In 1705, the king awarded death sentences to eight thieves by way of drowning them in Imphal river below Sugnoo. (R. K. Jhalajit Singh, "A Short History of Manipur", 1965,O. K. Store, Imphal). Crimes were very few. Two Kali temples were constructed in 1706 and 1707 probably under supervision of a Burmese architect. He used to invite the hill chiefs to his palace and asked his nobles to develop personal friendships with them.

Charai Rongba, warned by prophecy that he would be slain by his son, wanted abortion of his child in the womb. But the mother of Pamheiba (Garib Niwaz), Noongthil Chaibee refused and smuggled the child away to a village–Makeng Thangal where he was brought up by Thangal tribesmen. The boy's grandfather escaped with him to the village of Thangal in the hills to the north occupied by Quiron tribe of Nagas. Pamheiba was brought to the king's palace at the age of 11 years after the death of Noongthil Chaibi. In 1702, the Tusuk Kukis rose in rebellion against the king. Expeditions were sent to subdue the rebellion. But they could not achieve their goal. In 1709, Charairongba himself went to Tusuk village to subdue the rebellion there. The chief of Tusuk was killed in the battle. Fifteen Tusk Kukis were brought as prisoners. After subduing the rebellion, he came back. On his onward journey, he took rest just below a Pipal tree and at this time, lightening struck him. At this juncture, Pamheiba speared him to death. He died on Sunday, the 7th of Ingen (July) 1709 in his 37th birthday. Before his death, he called his son Pamheiba to his side and charged him to invade Burma to avenge the neglect of his daughter by her husband, the king of Burma. (R. K. Jhalajit Singh, "A Short History of Manipur", 1965, O. K. Store, Imphal). He also cursed Pamheiba that he also would also be killed by his own son.

GARIB NIWAZ (PAMHEIBA) (1709- 1748)

Pamheiba more popularly known as Garib Niwaz (see plate -60), ascended the throne on Wednesday, the 23rd Thawan (August), 1709 at the age of 19 years under the reign name Mayaamba. Pamheiba was born on 22nd Poinu, 1690 (Saturday) when his father Charai Rongba was a prince. Garib Niwaj's mother was Nungthil Chaibi of Sapam family from Uchiwa village.

In 1710 (Inga /June), the king and his queen distributed clothes to the weak and disabled. In Ingen, 1714, he sat on a slab of stone before the gate of the palace and distributed paddy liberally to the weak and disabled. The name Garib Niwaz means "Shelter to the poor".

In 1715, on 23rd Langban (September),he delegated the work of judicial administration to his nobles. In the winter of 1715, the king went for hunting elephants to Yairipok and 28 elephants were caught.

In 1716 on 10th Wakching, messengers arrived from Ava with a fresh proposal for marrying Tamphasana, the daughter of Garib Niwaz to the King of Ava (Taninganway,1714-1733). (Sarangthem Bormani, Meitei Ningthourol, 2000). Garib Niwaz saw it as an opportunity not to be missed. He directed the Burmese messengers to tell the king to make preparations to receive the princess at the confluence of the Chindwin (Ningthee) river on an appointed day.

King Garib Niwaj gave away one of his daughters in marriage to Wahengbam Khelei Nungnang Telheiba, the king of Moirang and took the latter with him during the Burmese campaign. Khelei Nugnang Telheiba proved his mettle by his exemplary courage and skill.

In 1717, the king Garib Niwaz got himself initiated into Vaishnavism in Mera (Sept/Oct) by appointing Gopal Dass as his Guru. The king became very conscious about following the Hindu traditions.

In 1718, the Burmese king at Ava (Inwa),Taninganway (1714-1733) invaded Manipur after crossing Ningthee river. Garib Niwaj fought the battle at Wangjing and drive away the Burmese. He also fought wars during 1720, 1722 at Samjok near Irrawadi river (Ayeyarwady) and maintained peace at Kabow valley. Ava (Inwa) was founded as the royal capital in 1364 on the Ayeyarwady river by the Shan king Thadominbya and remained a royal capital for most the time until Amarapura was founded in 1782.

Garib Niwaj started a series of conquests. He was described as a "a thorn in the side of the upper Burma" by the Burmese king. Manipur was famous for its ponies and in those days, every man however humble rank possessed two or three ponies. Polo played forty a side was universal in

Manipur and made the Manipuri expert horsemen. (G. E. Harvey, History of Burma, 1925).

In 1723, he faced two wars–one from Takhel (Tripura) and another from Burma. In 1723, the Burmese king, Taninganway again sent an army to invade Manipur. Garib Niwaj sent a big army under the command of Kopeng Keirunghanba, Gaiviram Huidromba, with 4000 Naga army, 5000 Meitei army and an Arambai division of 300 soldiers. The Burmese army was headed by Kengtu Ngamba. They had battle at Kakching. The Manipuri army first retreated upto Wangjing and then it was reinforced by a bigger army comprising of the Maharaja himself. The Manipur army surrounded the Burmese army from three directions and defeated the Burmese. They brought a large number of prisoners including one of their leader named Chouthap. After winning the Burmese war, Garib Niwaj turned his attention to the Takhel war which he defeated and brought many prisoners.

In 1723, Sanamahism was abolished. In 1724 A. D. the king exhumed the bones of his ancestors and had them cremated on the banks of the Chindwin (Ningthee) river. It was from this time that cremation became the customary method of disposal of the dead for the Manipuri Hindus. Sati, the self–immolation of widows on their husband's funeral pyre, was uncommon and entirely voluntary. It was forbidden to keep unclean animals like pigs and hen in the house. Those who did not obey were sent to the rural areas.

According to Burmese chronicles, Garib Niwaz came riding upper Burma upto Sagaing opposite Ava. In 1724, the Manipuris came by saying that they would present another girl to the king of Burma (Taninganwe) to provide company for the one presented in 1704. But when three hundred lords, ladies and attendants from the Ava court came to receive her at the mouth of the Yu river in the upper Chindwin district, they were not met by tame princes but by wild horsemen who carried them all away into Manipur. The following year, the Burmese sent an expedition in revenge but it was ambushed in the swamps near Heirok, south of Thoubal and losing heavily retreated in haste. It is said that Garib Niwaz repulsed an army of 30,000 men and captured entire three divisions. He brought many Burmese captives including men and women and they were settled in the area known as Kabo Leikai. (G. E Harvey, History of Burma, 1925).

In 1725, Garib Niwaj fought with a huge Burmese army of around 30,000 who invaded the Kabow valley. The war continued till 1726 and ultimately Garib Niwaj won the war.

In 1726, he got collected all the Umang Lais and buried them at the Mongba Hanba Umang (Mahabali Umang). In 1726, he excavated a huge pond called "Ningthem Pukhri at Wangkhei Leikai and also some other ponds at some other places for the benefit of the people. The King himself supervised the digging of ther pond by sitting in the palanquin.

In 1727, he invaded Takhel (Tripura) and got the submission of the king of Takhel. By 1734, he subdued most parts of Takhel.

During 1728 A. D. Santi Das Gosai (see plate-61), a Hindu preacher from Sylhet, arrived in Manipur and started his mission to preach Ramandi cult of Vaishnavism. Some subjects followed Santi Das but the king was not happy. Some people were also punished for following the new sect of Santi Das. However later on, the king himself became a follower of Santi Das.

In 1729, the king took the sacred thread for the second time on full moon day in the month of Wakching (Dec. /Jan). On Wednesday the king and the Guru (Santi Das) dipped themselves and performed the Nongkhrang Iruppa (Nungkhrang Luppa) in the Lilong river at about 7 A. M. From that day, the tradition of planting Brinda Tulshi at the shumang (courtyard) in place of Ram Tulshi was started.

During the time of King Garib Niwaj (1709-48), Vaishnavism became a state religion and it was practically forced on the people. At the instance of the King and his Brahmin Gurus, the people were forced to adopt the Bengali alphabets. The Manipuri versions of the Indian epics, specially of Krittibas Ramayan and Kashidas Mahabharata appeared.

In 1729 A. D. the sacred Mongba Hanba Umang had been converted into Mahabali Umang and a large image of Hanuman was installed in the temple at the Mongba Hanba Umang (Mahabali Umang) on the bank of Imphal River. The king also worshipped Hanuman.

Hiyangthang Lairembi had been converted into Kamakhya (Durga), Mondum had been converted to Mahadeva, Kaina had been converted into Hindu place, Nongpok Ningthou had been converted to Shiva Mahadeva Baruni. The festival of "Ahong Khongjingba" had been converted into Ratha Yatra, "Ireng Papalon Luklen" had been converted into "Tarpan Katpa", Wakhambung Chingnung Nongombi was substituted by "Kwaktanba" of Durga Puja. The Meiteis were allotted Gotras for the seven Salais namely Sandilya for Ningthouja, Kaushik for Angoms, Bhardwaj for Chenglei, Kashyap for Luwang, Madhukalya for Khuman, Atreya for Moirang and Gautam for Phantek.

And his Mayang Gurus forcibly offered to drink choronamrita (Choron mean feet, amrita means nectar) which was actually their Khongbi Machum (the water after sinking the big toe) to Meiteis in the name of purification and conversion into Hinduism. Garib Niwaz tortured the Pibas of Seven Salais who disobeyed to drink his Mayang Gurus' Khongbi Machum for purifying for the conversion into Hinduism.

In 1732, on the 17th Mera (Sunday), all the sacred Puyas of Meiteis written by Maichous (Scholars/Prophets/Sagei Pibas) were got collected and burnt down to ashes. This episode was known as "Puya Meithaba" (Burning of Meitei scriptures). About 125 old puyas, records, scriptures, books were burnt down (Puya Meithaba or Meitei Lairik Manghanba) at the instigation of Santi Das. Pamheiba and his Guru Santi Das substituted Meitei script with Bengali script and changed the original or personal name of Meitei into a Hindu's name. For example, the Meitei name of "Pamheiba" was changed into a Hindu name" Garib Niwaj" The tradition of Meidingu or Ningthou has been changed into "Maharaja" and the queen known as "Maharani". Thus he was known as Maharaja Garib Niwaj and his queen Gomti Maharani. Some people said that when Garib Niwaj married Wahengbam chanu, Irom ongbi Gomti, she was called "Thambal" and was already pregnant living with her husband at Chinga Makha. Her husband came to the king to lodge a complaint and he was speared to death at the palace gate. Gomti exacted a promise from the king that her unborn child would be made the king of Manipur, which Garib Niwaj promised to keep. In due course of time, Chit Shai was born.

Garib Niwaj tortured and punished those who disobeyed conversion into Hinduism with death penalty to many people including eminent persons of Meiteis of that era like Chingngu Khongnangthaba, Moirang Lalhanba etc. There were five famous Maichous (Pandits) in the court of Garib Niwaj. They were Chingu Khongnagthaba, Langol Lukhoi, Ningombam Akong, Yambem Foubak, Moirang Lanhamba. These five Maichous (scholars) had predicted that there would be conflicts among the descendants of the king Garib Niwaj. They would kill each other for the sake of the throne.

In course of time, Santi Das was striken by a terrible disease. The disease never got cured in spite of treatment by many physicians. In disgust, the Guru retired in a lonely hut at Wakha village and could not even comb his beard which became bushy and people made currency of a satirical song "Wakhataba Koijomba, Nakoi fat thadatke" (O, Setler of Wakha with a long beard, we will plug your beard). Finding no hope of cure, he reluctantly asked the advice Chingngu Khongnagthaba. Chingngu Khongnagthaba, told him that "you had incurred the wrath of Lainingthou Sanamahi by destroying the Sanamahi Kollu. Now you have no choice but surrender youself to Lainingthou

Sanamahi. Worship Sanamahi from the corner of your heart and your disease would be cured "Santi Das carried out the instruction faithfully, prayed to Lainingthou Sanamahi and ultimately he was completely cured of the disease. The news spread far and wide and from that day onwards, the Brahmains also started worshipping Lainingthou Sanamahi. On 1st of Thawan, 1733 (Monday), Garib Niwaj worshipped Lainingthou Sanamahi and Leimarel Sidabi at Tollong Ingkhol (present 1st Manipur Rifles). At Leisangkhong, a shrine dedicated to Laiwa Haiba was inaugurated and the image of Laiwa Haiba was installed. The worship of traditional deities was given royal permission and revived once again.

In 1734, the two princes of Pong called Mongpo and Kyathon fled to Raja Garib Niwaz of Manipur and solicited his protection against the Burmese King. Garib Niwaz attacked and destroyed the town of Meeto and establishing the two princes at Moongkhong in the month of May, bestowed his daughter Yenjeejoyaee in marriage to the eldest. From Moongkhong, they returned in August to Mongmaorong, the ancient capital of Pong.

In 1735, Garib Niwaz crossed Ningthee river attacked and destroyed the town of Myedu in Swebo district on the bank of Moo river and carried off 7000 Burmese, 700 head of cavalry and 20 elephants (G. E. Harvey, History of Burma, 1925). Mahadhammaraza Dipadi was the king of Burma (1733-1752) during those days.

In 1737, he subsequently defeated two Burmese armies of 7000 foot soldiers, 700 horses and 20 elephants and devastated the whole country from the banks of Khodoung Khyoung to Debayen. He killed two thirds of a royal levy sent to oppose them, including the commander, who was drunk and swept down to Tabayin in Swebo district, burning everything they met. (G. E. Harvey, History of Burma, 1925)

In 1737, in the month of Hiyangei (Oct. /Nov.) on the full moon day, on Thursday, Santi Das initiated the King along with 300 important persons into his Hindu religion. This way the King took the sacred thread of the Hindus for the third time. This event marked the beginning of Ramandi cult in Manipur. The images of Rama with Sita, Lakshman, Bharat and Shatrughan were installed in the temples. The temple of Ramji Prabhu was located at the Nigthem Pukhri mapal.

The military might of Pamheiba became the strongest one in the region, particularly of the cavalry force who consisted of very well trained fighters equipped with the then most feared special weapons of poisoned arrows known as "Arambais". It was because of the great might of the Manipuri cavalry force and also of the great ability and courage of the generals, particularly of one most able and courageous general, named Thangjaba Chakrapani that Pamheiba came out always victorious in all the wars and made the neighboring kingdoms and enemies feel his unchallengeable skills and prowess by forcing his sway very deep into their areas.

The first instance of Sati burning was reported in the year 1725 when a prince Murari died, his two wives volunteered to be burnt along with their husband. The second instance was in 1733 when one Khurailakpa of Sapam family died at Chinga and his wife died along with him. A Brahmin's two wives committed Sati in the same year. Most of the Sati burning happened during the reign of Garib Niwaz.

In 1738, when the Burmese king garrisoned Myedu and Tabayin in Shwebo district and Mingin in the Upper Chindwin district against the Manipuris, they simply cantered past, camped at Thalunbyu, west of Sagaing, burnt every house and monastery upto the walls of Ava and stormed the stockade built to protect the Kaunghmudaw Paya (Pagoda) in Sagaing near Mandalay killing the commandant, a minister of Hluttaw Council. The old door-leaves of the Pagoda's eastern gateway show a gash made by the sword of Gharib Niwaj when he was forcing his entrance. (G. E Harvey, History of Burma, 1925). The Kaunghmudaw Paya (see plate-62) was constructed in honor of a buxom Burmese queen. Sagaing, was the former capital which lies on the right bank of the Ayeyarwady river. Sagaing, founded by Athinkhaya Sawyun, a Shan chieftain, in 1315, was the Shan capital until 1364, when Ava was founded. Sagaing was the capital from 1315 to 1364 and again from 1760 to 1764

In 1738, he again crossed the Chindwin (Ningthee) river, raided Mutseng, Dibayan, Meydoo and Saigaing and set fire to a number of houses and granaries and disbursed a Burmese army of 15000 foot soldiers, 3000 horses and 30 elephants.

In 1739, the Burmese king oppressed the Chief of Samjok who was a vassal of Manipur. Garib Niwaj again invaded Burma and devastated the country upto Sagaing. (R. K. Jhalajit, A short history of Manipur, 1965)

According to Burmese history, "one reason why the Manipuris raided Burma was that they had just been converted into Hinduism by preachers who said that if they bathed in the Irrawady river at Sagaing, all blessedness would attend them. Indeed their chief Brahmin insisted on coming to Ava himself in 1744 in order to convert the Golden Palace but he fell ill and died after staying a month and his group of lesser Brahmins then returned home." (G. E. Harvey, History of Burma, 1925).

The Manipuris raided Burma again in 1740 but in 1741 they sent an envoy with a jacket for the Raja's kinswomen who had been presented to the Ava harem in 1704, he also brought complimentary presents for the king whose orders were that his presents should be sent in at once and then he should be kept waiting a month before being granted an audience or seeing the princess.

In 1749, Garib Niwaz, on his last raid with an army of 20,000 men and 3000 horses, encamped near the confluence of the Chindwin and Irrawady rivers waiting for a favourable opportunity to cross the river and attack the capital of Burma, thinking : "If there is an opportunity to fight, I will fight and if there is not, I will present my daughter" Mahadammayaza Dipati was the Burmese king (1733-1752). On reaching Ava, he found the Burmese forces so numerous that they stretched from Shwekyetyet to Londawpauk, moreover during the night his standard was blown down, a terrible potent always celebrated for his royal wisdom, he now perceived that this was not the occasion to fight and instead he presented his twelve year old daughter who accompanied him. (G. E. Harvey, History of Burma, 1925, page 209). The Burmese historians added that "The Manipuris were occasionally troubled by Burmese levies but usually did as they liked. Living in an obscure valley, knowing nothing of the outer world, they thought themselves heroes, able to take their pleasure of Burma when they willed. They did not realize that Burma was several times the size of their country and that they were laying up for themselves a frightful vengeance and the only reason for vengeance never seemed to come was Burma happened to be under an incapable king". (G. E. Harvey, History of Burma, 1925, page 209).

On his return journey, he was attacked by the Koees, a fierce tribe inhabiting Myedoo near the Moo river. But he quickly subdued and resuming his journey reached the Maglung river, the Yoo Khyoung.

On his return, he was upbraided with unsuccessful termination of his expedition and with having tendered homage to the king of Ava by the presentation of his daughter. This produced a strong feeling of dissatisfaction among the troops, most of whom deserted him except 500 men. With this 500 men, he resided for a short time at Tseengain and gave a daughter to the Toungngoo Raja under whose protection, he remained until Ava was destroyed by the Peguers.

Garib Niwaj had 10 queens

4. Chingakham Chanu Apambi–Shyam Shai

5. Gomti – Chit Shai, Nanda Shai, Tanga Shai, Sabat Shai, Bharat Shai, Shatrughana Shai (Tolentomba)
6. Arambam Chanu–Tamphasana, Naha
7. Haobam Chanu Khagi Keithel Thanbi–no issue
8. Ngangbam Chanu Pangga Keithel Thanbi- Muwari
9. Lairikyengbam Chanu Haripriya–Ananta Shai
10. Maibam Chanu Charoi Ngambi–Ngoubram Shai, Hari Priya
11. Yaikhom Chanu Herangambi-Hari Shai
12. Moirangthem Chanu-Keshor Shai
13. Chingkham Chanu–Gadadhar Shai, Haricharan, Dulav Shai.

Garib Niwaj abdicated his throne in favour of his son, Chit Shai in 1748 as part of fulfilment of his promise to his favourite queen, Gomti. As Chit Shai ascended the throne in 1748, he expelled his father Garib Niwaj from the capital. Garib Niwaj led his life miserably first in the old capital of Angoms and then at Thanga, a hilly island in Loktak Lake and in 1751 on 29 Hiyanggei (Friday) he was exiled to Burma. But Burma was also in turmoil and therefore he had to return to Manipur. Chit Shai, the reigning king sent an emissary to receive the ex-king with a secret instruction to kill him. The two parties met each other near Ningthee river and Garib Niwaz was cruelly murdered at Tonfang Hiden on Wednesday, 26th Poinu (December) 1748 by the emissaries of Chit Shai together with his eldest son Shyam Shai and all principal men of the court.

CHIT SHAI (1748-1752)

Chit Shai became the king on 10th of Kalen (Wednesday), 1748. But the secrecy surrounding assassination of Garib Niwaj came to light in 1752. There was widespread dissatisfaction against the reigning King, Chit Shai. He was expelled by his brother Bharat shai in Kalen (May), 1752. Chitshai went to Tripura (Takhel) and then to Chittagong. He approached the British East India Company to help him to regain the throne (1752 AD). However, he did not get their help. He went to Jaintia and died there. This was the first contact of Meiteis with the British.

BHARAT SHAI (1752-1753)

Bharat Shai ascended the throne on the full moon day (Saturday) of Kalen, 1752. As soon as he became king, he exiled Devashai, son of Chit Shai, his borther Senapati, Menkhomba and Tolentomba and also started plotting to kill all possible claimants to the throne. Fearing attack from Bharat Shai,

Chakha Loikhombi, mother of Gourshyam and Bhagyachandra went to hiding along her sons at Tonghu village. The Chief of Tonghu village shifted their hide out to an interior place. There was a fight between Bharat Shai's men and Gourshyam. But the villagers of Tonghu killed all the attackers. After this, the Chief of Tonghu handed over Gourshyam and Bhagyachandra to the Maring Chief. After some time, Khellei Nongnang Telheiba, king of Moirang came to their rescue and brought them to Moirang for a safe custody. Khelei Nongnang Telheiba was preparing for a war against Bharai Shai. Seeing his own unpopularity among his subjects and fearing an attack from Moirang, he surrendered to Alaungpaya, king of Burma with a request to restore him to the throne of Manipur. He died without leaving any issue in 1753.

GOUR SHYAM (MARAMBA) (1763-1759)

Gourshyam, the eldest son of Shyam Shai became King in 1753. He was a crippled because of his leg injury when he fell down from the horse while retreating from Burma. He, therefore associated his younger brother Jai Singh (Bhagyachandra/ Jai Singh) in the administration of the country. The two brothers agreed between themselves that each should reign for five years in turn.

In 1755, Alaungpaya(1752-1760), King of Burma, belonging to the celebrated Koubaung dynasty sent an expedition to "instil respect" into the Manipuris. The Manipuris found the Burmese on this occasion using firearms for the first time, their weapons like those of the Manipuris having previously been only swords, spears, bows and arrows. Alaungpaya had been harbouring grudges against the Manipur kings for their repeated attacks to Burma during 1692 to 1738. Many times, he had seen the cruel Manipuris cantered past his home at Swebo during his childhood.

In 1758-59 again, Alaungpaya personally led an expedition against Manipur. Alaungpaya proceeded up the Chindwin devastating the villages of the Manipur. He crossed the hills by the Khumbat route and entered the Manipur valley. At Pallel in the Aimol Pass, they gave him battle. After a stubborn battle, the Manipuris fled. The King and all the people fled to the hills. Alaungpaya entered Imphal only to find it empty for the inhabitants were hiding in the woods. He halted at Imphal for thirteen days, set up a stone inscription, took what loot there was, threw into the river two canons of a cubit caliber as they were too heavy to move and returned home leaving garrisons in permanent stockades at Tamu and Thaugdut. He massacred more than four thousand Manipuri prisoners because they stubbornly refused to march way into captivity. The invasion of Alaungpaya from 1755-1759 is described as the "First Devastation" of Manipur (Khuntak Lansi Ahanba) in the history of Burma. (G. E. Harvey, History of Burma, 1925, page-228) Alaungpaya died in 1760 at the age of 46. (see Chapter- 15, Historical Landmarks)

In 1759, Gour Shyam abdicated the throne in favour of his younger brother, Jai Singh. Jai Singh ascended the throne on 7th of Sajubu (Thursday), 1759. However, he abdicated his throne in favour of his elder brother, Gourshyam due to murder of a Brahmin by his servant at Tangkham village. He again ascended the throne on 29th Thawan, (Tuesday), 1763 after the death of his elder brother.

Jai Singh knew that Manipur needed firearms and supply for troops to fight with the Burmese for which he needed to negotiate a treaty with the British. On 14th September, 1762, the British and Manipur signed a treaty known as the Treaty of Chittagong (signed by Harry Das Gussein acting on behalf of Jai Singh and Mr. Harry Verelst, Chief of Chittagong Factory on behalf of British), which spells that British and Manipur would encourage trade and commerce. The British would give necessary help to protect the kingdom of Manipur from outside invaders and Manipur would provide a piece of land in Manipur for the East India Company posting.

In pursuance of the treaty, a detachment of English troops with Mr. Verelst as the head left Chittagong for Manipur in January, 1763 and reached Cachar in April, 1763. In the meantime, Gourshyam had again come to the throne for the second time. The English troops were called back to Chittagong due to a war between Mir Kasim, the Nawab of Bengal and the British. In October, 1763, Gourshyam sent three accredited agents to Mr. Verelst at Chittagong to reconfirm the terms of the treaty by offering 500 Manipuri gold coins at a value of twelve British Indian rupees per Manipuri Gold Coin. Gourshyam died without any male issue in 1763.

MAHARAJA BHAGYACHANDRA (CHING-THANG KHOMBA OR JAI SINGH)= (1759-1762 and 1763-1798 AD or 3157-3160 and 3161-3196 MF.)

Maharaja Bhagyachandra or Ningthou Ching-Thang Khomba or Jai Singh or Karta (see plate-63) was the son of Shyam Shai Khurai-Lakpa (the eldest son of Garib Niwaj). Ching-Thang Khomba was born in 1748 at Yaiskul. His birth place was later known as Janmasthan.

In 1763 AD, after the death of Gour Shyam, Ching-Thang Khomba ascended the throne for the second time. In 1763, Ching-Thang Khomba along with his followers performed the "Nongkhrang Iruppa" by dipping themselves at the Nungjeng Pukhri of Kangla and took the oath to follow the Vaisnavism. (Lal Dena-History of Modern Manipur, Orbit Publishers–Distributors, New Delhi,1991)

Wahengbam Khelei Nungnang Telheiba (Khelemba), King of Moirang who was the maternal uncle of Ching-Thang Khomba conspired against him. He presented his daughter Sija Samjamani to Hsinbyushin (1763-76) the second son of Alaungpaya, king of Burma and requested him to invade Manipur and make him the King of Manipur.

In December, 1764, the Burmese king, Hsinbyushin himself raided Manipur carrying away its people into captivity for he wished to increase the population of the new capital, Ava into which he moved in April, 1765. Ching-Thang Khomba fled to Cachar. Khelei Nungnang Telheiba was set on the throne of Manipur. Hsinbyushin had taken a large number of captives to populate his capital city of Ava. According to Burmese historians, "the Manipuris were famous for their skill in handicraft and the Burmese valued them highly, settling them in the capital in the riverine villages of Sagaing district and at Amarapura. They served as boatmen and silversmiths, as silkworkers they introduced the "*Acheik pattern*", women's dress, they gave the Burmese army its best cavalry (the Cassey cavalry) and they supplied the bulk of the court astrologers, who at levees stood robed in white, intoning benedictions as the king took seat on the throne". (G. E. Harvey, History of Burma, 1925, page-239). The various wards of Ava were allotted on racial lines, thus Indian traders lived in one, the Chinese in another, the Christians in another and in others were the Siamese and Manipur captives. Hsinbyushin died in 1776. He was succeeded by his son Singu Min (1776-82).

In 1765, the Burmese under the command of Shembegwen gave a crushing defeat to the Manipuris and ravaged the country. The people left their hearth and home for dear life and remained holed up in the deep forests and ravines. They passed terrrible days sleeping under the trees and tangled creepers.

Ching-Thang Khomba sought the help of the Ahom King (King of Tekhao) Swarga Deva Rajeswar Singh (1751-1769) to drive out the Burmese from Manipur. The name Jai Singh was given to him by the Ahom king, Swarga Deva after he captured a wild elephant.

The King of Ahom Swarga Deva had heard of King Bhagyachandra's virtues and was pleased to receive him. They became close friends and Swarga Deva arranged for Bhagyachandra to stay in the vicinity of the royal palace.

But Bhagyachandra's crafty uncle Khelei Nungnang Telheiba wrote a letter to the King saying that the person taking refuge at his court was an imposter, not the great Bhagyachandra. The uncle advised the King of Ahom to destroy him. The message seems to have influenced King Swarga Deva. Though not entirely convinced, he began treating Bhagyachandra with coolness and suspicion. The real Bhagyachandra was said to have supernatural powers. So finally, on the advice of senior ministers, King Swarga Deva reluctantly devised a plan to test the wisdom of Bhagyachandra and to test him unarmed in a public arena to catch and tame a wild elephant.

The night before Bhagyachandra's trial, Lord Govindajee appeared to him in a dream. Confronted with this humanly impossible task, King Bhagyachandra prayed to Lord Krishna for guidance. Lord Govindajee appeared in his dream in the most beautiful and special dress more suitable for the softest dances. The Lord was in his Natabar besh, anklets, bracelets, adorned with golden clothes and a flute in his hand and a top-knot (Chura) of peacock feathers on his head. The union (jugal murti) of Lord Krishna and Srimati Radhika was seen in his dream. The Lord advised him to enter the arena with a garland and japa beads in hand. Victory, Lord Krishna told him, was assured. In the future, the Lord said, Bhagyachandra would be the sole king of Manipur. Upon regaining the kingdom, he should install a Krishna Deity. The Deity, Govindajee, should be carved from a certain old jackfruit tree growing on the slopes of a hill known as Kaina, and the physical features of the Deity should match those the king was seeing then. After installing the Deity, the Lord said, the king should arrange for the performance of a Raas Lila, in which the Deity should be worshipped with songs and dances. The Lord enabled Bhagyachandra to envision in detail the kinds of dress the dancers should wear and the manner in which the songs and dances should be composed. He woke up from sleep with full of happiness and surprise. He narrated his dream to his follower Wangkhei Angom Gopiram Patchachanba.

The next morning, thousands of people gathered at the arena where the wild elephant was let loose and Chingthangkhomba was asked to fight with the wild elephant. Crowds waited on rooftops and treetops to see the fate of the supposed King of Manipur.

Chingthangkhomba remembered the image of Govindajee in his heart and with confidence, he approached the wild elephant holding the garland and japa beads chanting the holy name of Lord Krishna. The wild elephant started running towards Chingthangkhomba as if to kill him on the spot but as soon as he reached the spot where Chingthangkhomba was standing, the elephant stooped down and prostrated before him with the trunks tucked to the ground. According to some accounts, the elephant seemed as though struck repeatedly by some unseen enemy. King Bhagyachandra alone could see Lord Govinda sitting atop the elephant's head like a mahout. And to that Lord, the King offered the garland from his hand. The king then mounted the elephant and rode triumphantly through the cheering crowds.

All the people shouted in praise of Chingthangkhomba. The people of Assam hailed him as an incarnation of God and conferred him the title of "Jai Singh". From that day, he was known as Jai Singh. Jai Singh gave his elder brother Gourshyam's daughter Kuranganayani in marriage to Swarga Deva Rajeswar Singh. She was made the queen of Assam King Swarga Deva Rajeswar Singh gave a touching farewell to Bhagyachandra with a strong force of Ahom army. As they had to make their way through inhospitable forest routes by cutting latticed creepers, the expedition is recorded in the history of Assam as "Lata Kata Ran". Two thirds of the armed men perished on the way as the Naga tribes ambushed them and seized their provision while some fell victim to malaria, dysentery, snake bites and spider bites. Jai Singh reached Manipur and disposed the usurper, Khelei Nungnang Telheiba whose life was spared. In 1768, Jai Singh having obtained assistance from Swarga Deva Rajeswar Singh, the Ahom King, drove away the Burmese and resumed the throne of Manipur.

In 1769, the Burmese attacked Manipur again at the invitation of one Haobam Keibiram. Khelei Nungnang Telheiba was killed in an ambush by Khumbong Chandramani and Nandalal while he was returning home from Burma.

In January, 1770, Mahathihathura, the commander –in chief of king Hsinbyushin came to Manipur to have a fresh harvest of slaves and cattle to appease the King. Here again Kokilananda, the younger brother of Jai Singh was responsible to bring the Burmese to Manipur. The Burmese forces advanced in two divisions – one of which proceeding by water devastated the villages on the western bank of the Ningthee river while the other penetrating through the valley of Kabow, entered Manipur valley and fought a battle near Langthabal which lasted for three days. The King Bhagyachandra fled to Assam. The Burmese raised their own nominee, Kokilananda, younger brother of Jai Singh to the throne and returned taking with them such of the population as were not hiding in the woods. But when Jai Singh returned from Cachar, Kokilananda abdicated the throne in favour of his elder brother Jai Singh. In 1772, again, Maan Senaba, son of Khelei Nungnanag Telheiba invited the Burmese to invade Manipur as a revenge for the death of his father. When the Burmese came, Jai Singh and all other people fled to Cachar. One Wangkhei Pukhrambam Binodram volunteered to be the king of Manipur, subordinate to Burma. So he was set on the throne and the Burmese had returned home.

At last, in 1773 AD, Manipur was taken back. Maharaja Bhagyachandra adopted the name "MANIPUR" in place of "Meklee" or "Meitrabak" or "Sana-Leipak" in 1774 AD on the advice of his Guru when Warren Hastings was the Governor General of India. Mr. Rendel assigned the name, Manipur and the kingdom extended from Ningthee in the east to Chittagong in the South and up to Brahmaputra area in the North and Cachar in the West.

In Phairen, 1775, Bhagyachandra returned from Tekhao (Assam) and established his capital at Lamangdong (Bishnupur). He again moved his capital to Langthabal (Canchipur) on 3rd of Kalen, (Tuesday) 1779. When he moved his capital, he made the image of Govindajee from a Jackfruit tree growing in the Kaina hill.

Bringing of Jack fruit tree from Kaina and coronation of Govindajee

One Pangambam Uma alias Muni Singh of Poiroukhongjin village developed a beautiful park and orchard in Kaina Hill. There were many kinds of trees and flowers growing in his orchard. There were also two fully grown two jack fruit trees (Artocarpus heterophylus) in his orchard. One day, he came to the royal palace and reported to the King that one old tribal widow was trespassing his orchard and she was offering food to a young handsome boy everyday near the Jackfruit tree of his orchard. "Nobody knew where the boy came from. On the repeated query of the tribal woman, the boy told his identity to her but the woman refused to disclose it to me". The King became inquisitive. He ordered ten men to accompany Pangambam Uma and bring the old tribal woman. Uma went with the ten men to the house of the tribal widow and told her to come to the palace as commanded by the King. But she refused to comply with their request. Again, the King sent Uma with 50 men. The King said "Bring her with respect in the palanquin. Do not show any discourtesy or force to her" The old woman was brought in the palanquin. On questioning by the King about the identity of the boy, she answered "When I was carrying food for my sons working in the field, the boy appeared from nowhere, accosted me and begged me for food. He said that he had been starving for the last many days. He also asked me to take him as one of her sons. I was completely moved. When I said that how can I give you food, you are a Meitei by caste and I am a tribal. But he continued begging me food.

When I gave him food, he was very happy and he danced so well in font of me. I was completely charmed. I can not stop giving him food everyday. He came to me everyday. He looked very charming" The king asked her "who was the boy ?". The woman said that she did not know much. But the boy said that he saved the life of a King when he was in Takhao but the King had completely forgotten him. The king started trembling with ecstasy. He asked the woman "How did he look like ?". The woman said "Oh the boy looked so charming with anklets, adorned with golden clothes and a flute in his hand". Bhagyachndra iommediately remembered his dream at Tekhao. Bhagyachandra cried with tears in his eyes and he said "Oh mother, you are so lucky. please tell me how can I address him.. what was his name". The woman refused to narrate further. She said "the boy told me not to disclose his name to anybody otherwise he would not come again. I was just a poor destitute widow. Now after meeting the boy, I was quite well off. "Then Bhagyachanbdra bowed down to her and begged her to speak up the name of the boy. The woman said "Oh king of Manipur, let me devote my life to you. The boy said, his mother was Yashoda. He said his mother lovingly called him Kanhai, Govinda and the Gopis called him Gopal. On hearing this the king fainted. When he came to senses, he wept bitterly. He cursed himself for having forgotten his divine dreams at Tekhao. He immediately told his servants to go to Kaina in search of the jackfruit tree. At this moment, Pangambam Uma told the king about the two jackfruit trees in his orchard where the woman gave food everyday to the boy. The King consulted his Pandits about the manner in which the tree should be felled. It was decided to cut the tree after perfoming a puja. Khumbong Chandramani gave the auspicious hour to Pangambam Uma for felling the tree. After praying to God, Pangambam Uma applied his axe. But to everyone's surprise, blood oozed out of the tree. Immediately Uma stopped cutting the tree. The matter was reported to the king. The King sent for Langol Lukhoi. The King asked Lukhoi about the cause of bleeding. Lukhoi said that the jack fruit tree was possessed by Pakhangba and he advised the king to wrap up the wounded portion of the tree with his turban and to ask for his forgiveness. The King prayed to the Lord Pakhangba to forgive him for the wrong he did and the bleeding of the tree stopped. Lukhoi then advised the King to uproot the tree. Accordingly, the tree was uprooted and brought along Lisam Lok of Angtha hill slope and then through Khoirita / Khoirpok. It was decided to float the tree down the Iril river upto Langthabal. At Tronglaobi, the tree was floated down the river. The King's officials and the general public arranged for bringing the tree via Iril river upto Langthabal. The King left for

Langthabal on horseback. After the king left the place, the tree sank into water at a place called Naokhal Irel at the foot of Phunal Hill. All attempts by expert divers to rope in the tree inside water failed. The matter was again reported to the King. The King came back and with the help of Langol Lukhoi, Guru Bhaskar peformed pujas. At the end of the puja, the tree floated again on the surface. *Arati* was offered to the tree with beating of drums, beating of of cymbals and blowing of conches. The place where the tree sank is known as "Urup" and the place where the *Arati* was performed is known as "Arapti". The tree reached the confluence of the Iril river and the Imphal river and from there it continued its journey along the Imphal river to reach Langthabal and from there it was pulled above the Langthabal Hill. The tree was kept inside a hut built for the purpose at a sacred site known as Heijingkhang (opposite the present Manipur Univrsity Gate). The King's officials performed *"Arati"* with lamp and incense to the tree everyday while the king left for his residence at Lamangdong (Bishnupur). It was about eight months from 22nd of Lamda (Wednesday), 1775 to 12th of Hiyangei, 1776 that the tree was kept at Langthabal for drying. When the tree was completely dry, the king asked Angom Gopiram to begin sculpting the image of the Lord Govindajee. Angom Gopiram entrusted the work to master sculptor Sapam Lokhon.

Making of Images

After performing a puja, Sapam Lokhon applied his tools on the second log and started making the image. When it was finished, the king was not quite happy as it slightly lacks in resemblance to the Lord he had seen in his dream. This had become the image of Bijoy Govinda. (P. Bharat Singh, The Sacred Jack Tree of Kaina, 2007). His uncle Ananta Shai and his descendents were made responsible for Sri Bijoy Govinda and the annual festival of Heikru Hitongba (boat racing) held on the 11th of Langban (September) every year.

Another image was made and this time the king was fully satisfied. Thus the image of Lord Govindajee was completed. The height of Govindajee was 3 feet 10 inches. The commencement of making the image was Friday, the 12th Hiyanggei, 1776 and its coronation was 11th Hiyanggei, 1779 (Friday) It took 3 years to complete the image. (P. Bharat Singh, The Sacred Jack Tree of Kaina, 2007)

The installation of the image of Gopinathjee was done on 8th of Hiyanggei, 1781 and Shri Kirtidhwaja, son of the King by his wife Kesari was entrusted with the task of worshipping it at Ningthoukhong. (P. Bharat Singh, The Sacred Jack Tree of Kaina, 2007)

The making of the image of Shree Nityainanda Prabhu /Arambam Nityananda was started on the fullmoon day of Lamda (Thursday), 1794 out of the fourth log. It was coronated on 13th day of Wakching, 1795. It took ten months to complete it. When Premabati, the king's daughter was married to Arambam Tamradhaja Singh, she requested her father to allow her and her husband to worship Shree Nityainanda at her husband's place at Khwai Lamabam Leikai. The king agreed and the deity was shifted to Khwai Lamabam Leikai and the deity is worshipped by the Arambam family. (P. Bharat Singh, The Sacred Jack Tree of Kaina, 2007)

The image of Madanmohon was the fifth image to be made out of the fifth log. At the request of prince Labanyachandra, the King allowed his son to worship Shree Madanmohon. (P. Bharat Singh, The Sacred Jack Tree of Kaina, 2007)

Shree Anuprabhu is the sixth image made out of the tree. The coronation was done on the full moon day of Phairen, 1795 (Thursday) at 10 a. m. Princess Bimbabati (Sija Lairoibi) worshipped the image at Nabadwip, Nadia in West Bengal. The present site at Nabadwip is believed to have been donated by Raja Krishnanagar, Raja Girischandra and Smt Amla Devi, sister of Deshbandhu Chittaranjan Das. (P. Bharat Singh, The Sacred Jack Tree of Kaina, 2007)

The image of Shree Abdeitya Prabhu of Lamangdong was the seventh image curved out of the root of jack tree from Kaina The image was coronated on 7th day of Lamda, 1793. The King gave his daughter Dharmeswari Shija in marriage to a devout Brahmin priest Gurumayum Jatiswar Sharma and entrusted him the duties of worshipping the deity. (A. Chitraswor Sharma, Meitei Nongaron", April, 1988).

It is also believed that the two idols of Bangshibadan at Khangabok and Gourangaprabhu at Keisampat were also made from the branches of Jack fruit tree of Kaina. (P. Bharat Singh, The Sacred Jack Tree of Kaina, 2007)

First Raas Lila and Coronation of the Shree Shree Govindajee

The first Raas Lila of Radha Krishna was performed at Langthabal on the day of coronation of the image of Govindajee on 11th day of Hiyanggei (November), 1779 on the full moon night in the most enthusiastic mood of the religious people of Manipur. Raas Lila was played for five days continuousely in the open ground of Raas Mandal Pukhri at Langthabal to commomorate the coronation. At that time there was no deity of the Lord's consort, Srimati Radharani. Who then would play her role? For the pleasure of Lord Govindajee, the King selected his own daughter, the young and beautiful princess Bimbabati. (see plate-64) The King himself became one of the mridanga drummers (Pung) for the satisfaction of the Lord. By all accounts it was a splendid performance. Over the years, the rendering of Raas Lila through dance and devotional song developed into a highly refined art, and even today it is celebrated as a sacred tradition in Manipur. Whenever it is performed, a prayer is made to Govindajee on behalf of King Bhagyachandra. Princess Bimbabati herself was so overwhelmed that she renounced the world and spent the rest of her life serving Lord Krishna and singing His holy names. She became famous as 'Sija Lairoibi', meaning 'the princess who owned the Lord'. The golden deity of Radharani at the Govindaji temple was later made in her likeness.

The King left a great legacy, the legend of Rajarshi Bhagyachandra. He had his dream to make true and with this inspiration he resolved to worship Lord Shri Krishna performing the Raas-Lila-dances which he had seen in his dream. After this the Rajarshi tried his dream of the Raas Lila to be a living legend and taking essence of Shrimad Bhagavatam Darshan which are known as the Raspanchadhyaya. He trained many artists for the different kinds of Raas Lila of Radha-Krishna.

King Bhagyachandra was an ardent follower of Srila Narottama Das Thakur, an exponent of GaudiyaVaisnavism. He was initiated by Srila Ganga Narayana Chakravarti, a disciple of Srila Narottama Das Thakur, who visited Manipur to spread the Bhagavata Culture.

The Sati burning was no longer popular during the time of Bhagyachandra. In 1777 on Friday (2nd of Wakching), Yaishkullapa died and his wife ran away as she failed to die along with him. She was exiled to Sugnu. A poor and innocent wife was penalised because she could not commit Sati burning.

During his reign Chaitanya sect of Vaisnavism was established. Yaosang, the great festival of Meiteis, was invented by Bhagyachandra on the full moon day of Lamda (March).

Between 1764 and 1782, Jai Singh had made no less than four attempts to regain his throne but he was expelled by fresh Burmese forces and on each occasion was compelled to fled to Cachar where he obtained a temporary refuge.

During his time, the tradition of "Wari Liba" and "Lairik Thiba" were introduced.

In 1784 in the month of Mera, one Brahmin priest Bhaskar was speared to death by Madhuchandra (son of Bhagyachandra) and Chourajit. On 25th Sajibu, 1796 AD (Monday) his capital was moved from Langthabal (Canchipur) to Konthoujam Yumpham (present Raj Bhawan).

During his reign, he brought Manipur on a distinct cultural footing. He gained the title of Rajarshi Bhagyachandra after constructing the Govindajee temple. His daughter Sija Lairoibi (Bimbabati) became the lifelong devotee of Lord Govinda and attained a high order of spiritual charisma. She was also an accomplished dancer of Raas Lila and she used to perform the dance before Govindajee playing the part of Rasheswari. She was a combination of spirituality and aestheticism before the Lord. She composed several devotional songs in praise of the Lord.

During the time of Bhagyachandra, many Brahmins came from West Bengal, Lahore, Vrindavan, Assam and settled in Manipur. They were given surnames like Adhikarimayum, Anoubam, Warilibam, Brajabasimayum, Dhyandasmayum etc.

In 1791, Gournath Singh, the Ahom ruler frantically sought the help of Bhagyachandra to subdue the revolt of Mao Marias, which posed an immediate danger to his throne. King Bhagyachandra immediately responded and set out for Assam accompanied by his son Madhuchandra. King Bhagyachandra subdued the revolt with exemplary courage in which 700 Manipuris lost their lives.

In January, 1797, he left his eldest surviving son Labanya Chandra in charge of administration. He did not abdicate, he retained some of the royal insigna with him.

In 1798, after ruling for 39 years, King Bhagyachandra set out for pilgrimage to Murshidabad (West Bengal), the birthplace of Srila Narottama Das Thakur on 20th Wakching (January), 1798 with a large retinue comprising of his queens, four sons, three daughters, and a number of nobles and attendants. Following the course of the Barak river, he reached Cachar where the king of Cachar presented with a big amount of silver coins. He reached Sylhet through Jaintia and Surma, where the Englishman administering Sylhet provided him with one elephant to carry his luggage to Agartala and two armed sepoys to escort. He gave his daughter Hariseswari in marriage to Rajdhan Manik, King of Tripura. From Agartala, he proceeded towards Krinanagar in Nadia district of West Bengal. The pilgrims went in a fleet of 67 boats. After reaching the old channel of Ganga, he proceeded towards Krishnanagar while sending the boats to Nabadwip. After some days, he arrived at Nabadwip and from there, he proceeded on the Ganga by boat towards Vrindaban. But he died at Shri Bat Kshetra, near Bhagavangola in Murshidabad on the bank of Ganges on his way to Vrindaban on 3rd of Langban, (Friday), 1798. His body was cremated there, near the tomb of Srila Narottama Das Thakur, of whom many devotees in those times believed him an incarnation. The Brahmanas of those days gave him the title 'Rajarshi' meaning "a sage in the form of a King". According to the King's will, a portion of his ashes was bought back to Manipur and buried at the royal cremation ground, while another portion was brought to Nabadwip, the abode of Sri Chaitanya Mahaprabhu.

Bhagyachandra had 92 queens. 84 of the queens did not have any child.

1. Akham Chanu Liklangkhombi–Sanahal Nabananda, Labyanachandra (born in 1763), Sanatomba
2. Ngangbam Chanu Harimati–Madhuchandra born in 1763.
3. Khumbongmayum Chanu Bhagyabati–Biswanath (Khong-jaingamba), Gambheer Singh
4. Soraisam Chanu Priya–Lomokanta
5. Chingakham Chanu Devahuti (Sokpaongambi) – Hemchandra, Chourajit born in 1776
6. Akham Chanu Chandramukhi-Tuljit
7. Pukhrambam Chanu Kesari-Kirti Dhaja Kalaraj
8. Sapam Chanu Nungthil Chaibi–Marjit born in 1776

LABANYA CHANDRA (1798-1800) AND MADHU CHANDRA (1801-1803)

Labanya Chandra ascended the throne on 10th of Wakching, 1798 (Wednesday). But he was murdered by two brothers, Khumbong Chandramani and Nandalal during a Polo match in 1800. After hearing the news, Madhuchandra, younger brother of Labanya Chandra was crowned hurriedly as the King of Manipur by Ananta Shai, grand father of Madhuchandra. Thus, Moadhuchandra ascended the throne on 27th Hiyangei, 1800 (Saturday) on the day Labanya Chandra died making his brother Chourajit, the Crown Prince and Marjit, the Senapatti. However, he was again coronated by observing all the formalities on 17th Kalen, 1801. The two brothers Khumbong Chandramani and Nadala were killed on a plot devised by Ananta Shai as a revenge for killing King Labanya Chandra. At this time, Chourajit Singh, the Crown Prince went to Cachar on 5th of Langban, 1802 (Saturday) on the pretext of going to Vrindaban. However, he gathered a large force in Cachar and invaded Manipur. On hearing the news, Modhuchandra drove out Chingakhambi Sokpaongambi, mother of Chourajit from the palace. At this time, Marjit, the Senapati was camping at Sangaithen to fight with Chourajit. Marjit was brought up under the loving care of Chingakhambi Sokpaongambi when the mother of Marjit died at a young age. Chingakhambi Sokpaongambi came to Marjit and narrated the incident and persuaded him to join Chourajit to defeat Madhuchandra. Thus Chourajit was helped by Marjit Singh, the Senapati. Madhuchandra was defeated in the battle at Sangaithen and fled to Cachar.

CHOURAJIT (1803-1813)

Chourajit ascended the throne on 9th Phairen, 1803 (Sunday) at the age of 27 years. He made Marjit, the Crown Prince and the Chief of the Army. While in Cachar, Madhuchandra gave his daughter Indu Prabha in marriage to the Cachar King, Krishna Chandra and with his help invaded Manipur with 700 soldiers headed by Aagya Khongnang to claim the throne. However, Madhuchandra was killed along with 100 followers in the battle at Samupal in 1806.

In the mean time, his brother Marjit revolted against him. In 1808, they decided to settle the issue of succession to the throne by a single combat in the Polo field located within the precinct of the palace. (see plate-306). Chourajit opted for sword and Marjit chose the spear. They fought on horse back fiercely. Marjit was defeated. He fled to Tamu and requested for assistance from the King of Ava, Badawpaya (1782-1819). Badawpaya negotiated a settlement between the brothers through his emissaries. Marjit was pardoned by Chourajit Singh but again he rebelled against his brother. He was defeated and fled to Cachar. He sought the help of Govindachandra, the King of Cachar. But Govindachandra hatched a plan to revenge the death of Madhuchandra. So he fled to Ava through Arakan and surrendered to Badawpaya. He remained in Burma at Amarapura for six or seven years and in 1812, he succeeded in inducing the King of Ava, Badawpaya to take up his cause and to place him on the throne of Manipur for which he agreed to renounce the claim on the Kabow valley and to acknowledge his dependence on the King of Burma. Amarapura was founded as a royal capital by King Bodawpaya in 1782 and was such until 1823.

In the cold weather of 1812, a very considerable army marched to establish Marjit on the throne. Two divisions were formed–one Burmese division accompanied by Marjit Singh entered Manipur from the Aimol Pass and debouched in the valley near Kakching Khulel. the second under Samjok Raja approached through Machi route and encamped near Heirok. This division was completely routed and its leader killed by Petumber Singh, a nephew of the Raja Chourajit Singh, who with the main army advanced to Kakching. A conflict which lasted for five days terminated in his discomfiture. Raja Chourajit Singh fled to Cachar with a few of his followers-leaving the yoke of Manipur to Marjit Singh. At the expiration of ten days, Marjit Singh dismissed his Burmese friends and continued for five years in undisturbed possession of Manipur.

MARJIT SINGH (1813-1819)

In 1813, the Burmese had set Marjit Singh on the throne of Manipur and the Burmese were rewarded with the cession of the Kabow valley (G. E Harvey, the History of Burma, 1925, page- 283). Marjit Singh murdered many of Chourajit's followers and attempted murder of many of his nephews. That is why the people of Manipur were not happy with his rule. In 1818, he invaded Cachar with a large force which penetrated the hills in three divisions. At that time, Govindachandra was the King of Cachar. Govindachandra ascended the throne in 1813 after the death of his brother Raja Kishenchandra, descendant of Bhim, the original founder of their family. The eastern portion of Cachar was already overran by Marjit Singh. On hearing the news, his brother Chourajit Singh came to the rescue of Govindrachandra. Marjit Singh made a quick retreat. From this period to the commencement of the year 1823, Cachar was the arena on which three Manipuri princes-Chourajit, Marjit and Gambheer Singh contended for supremacy with the result that a very considerable portion of the inhabitants fled to the adjacent districts of Sylhet, Jaintia and Tripura. At the commencement of the year 1823, Gambheer Singh had secured the possession of southern Cachar with the exception of Hailakandi, which was held by his brother Marjit.

Chahi Taret Khuntakpa

According to Burmese historians, Marjit Singh and his nobles having lived at the Burmese court introduced luxurious habits and affected greatly with the natural simplicity of Manipur. The Burmese King, Bagyidaw (1819-37) felt that he had to be rebuked for cutting timbers in the Kabow valley and for building a guilded palace which the Burmese allowed to no king but their own.

Marjit Singh showed disloyally to Bagyidaw. He failed to appear at Bagyidaw's coronation. The coronation ceremony was celebrated with an unusual degree of splendour and all the tributaries princes, as was the customary on such occasions, were summoned personally to do homage to the new sovereign. Bayidaw wanted to punish Marjit Singh.

In 1819, the Burmese forces overran Manipur with 30,000 soldiers using guns procured from the Portugese under an able general called Mingimala Bandulla. This was the beginning of the "Seven Years Devastation". (Chahi Taret Khuntakpa). Manipuris faced the invasion fiercely with only 7000 soldiers for seven days. It is said that about 3000 Manipur soldiers and 7000 Burmese soldiers died in the battle. The battle was terminated by the retreat of Marjit Singh. Majit Singh fled to Cachar and met his brothers Chourajit Singh and Gambheer Singh. Marjit Singh became reconciled to his brothers. They re-entered Manipur in overwhelming strength. But they were defeated by the Burmese and the people fled to different places in the West. Most of the people from Manipur fled to Cachar and other neighbouring areas. Those who could not flee to far places, took shelter in the hills. The Burmese occupied and stayed in Manipur from 1819 to 1826, which is known as "Seven Years Devastation". (Chahi Taret Khuntakpa) to the Manipuris. (see Chapter-15: Historical Landmarks). During this anarchy, Burmese destroyed Manipur very badly. The palace was leveled to the ground. Inummerable houses and temples were destroyed and looted. The population of the valley was reduced to about 10,000. Thousands of Manipuris were captuired and forcibly taken to Burma.

HIRACHANDRA (1819)

Hirachandra was the grandson of King Bhagyachandra. He was the son of King Labyanachandra and his queen Akoijam Chanu Apambi. He was born on 5th Kalen, 1798. In 1813 when Marjit became the King of Manipur with the support of the Burmese, Marjit murdered many of Chourajit's followers and attempted murder of many of his nephews. Hirachandra also fled and took shelter in a Khongjai village in the hills. In the beginning of seven years devastation in 1819, he was only 21 years old. He was a tall, fair complexion and handsome boy with pleasing personality with burning patriotism in his blood. He knew the might and superior power of Burmese forces in terms of numerical strength and better equipment. When Hirachandra saw the oppressions, he mobilized people to fight the Burmese in his own capacity. He formed the "Takoo Forces", who were ready to lay down their lives for the sake of motherland. He was also known as "Takoo Ningthou" to the Burmese because of his guarrilla warfare. He became King of Manipur in 1819. He adopted guarrilla tactics to fight with the superior Burmses forces. When the news of Hirachandra Takoo Forces reached the Burmese stockades, they were afraid to go out and they were seldom safe outside the stoackades. The Burmese suffered ghastly ambushes at the hands of Hirachandra and could get nothing to eat. On 5th of Kalen, 1820, when about 500 Burmese forces tried to collect rice and vegetables from Moirang, Hirachandra killed 200 of Burmese forces. He was assisted in this task by five of his followers namely Akoijam Khamba, Angom Subunath Mani, Elangbam Amu, Mayengba Shyam, Moirangthem Labanga. He was having 800 followers, 50 horses and 12 guns after this battle.

Hearing that Sana Yumjaotaba had returned from Cachar on 12th of Kalen 1820, Hirachandra and Huidrom Subol went to Maklang and welcomed Sana Yumjaotaba. Sana Yumjaotaba was the son of Maharaja Modhuchandra (1801-1803). It was decided that Yumajaotaba would surrender to the Burmese commander and try to get more horse and guns. He got two horses, three guns and five daggers from Hirachandra to accomplish the mission. He met the Burmese commander Kaleun on 17th Kalen, 1820. After five days, the Burmese commander asked him to bring rice from Sekami with 100 soldiers. The mission was accomplished successfully. Having gained the confidence of the Burmese commander, the Burmese commander sent Yumajaotaba to capture Hirachandra with 200 soldiers, 40 horses, 20 guns. Hirachandra's Takoo forces had battle with the Burmese forces at Hayel Hangoon, near Uchiwa and killed 20 Burmese soldiers. Yumjaotaba had built his stockade at Khomidok and Hirachandra built his stockade at Moirangkhom. Yumjaotaba's life was spared and they decided to fight jointly with the Burmese. On 4th of Ingen, Hirachandra's Takoo forces killed many Burmese soldiers who made their stockade at Kakching. He also killed many Burmese soldiers who fled from the battle field towards the Manipur palace at Chaopok Chingjin. After these three successful expeditions, Hirachandra came out openly and established his stockade at Singjamei. On 7th of Thawan, he attacked the Burmese stoackades and killed many Burmese soldiers. His follower Moirangthem Labanga killed the Burmese leader Amulapa and 10 soldieres were captured alive and 30 guns were seized. After hearing the ghastly ambushes taken up by Hirachandra, the Burmese King Bagyidaw sent about 10,000 Burmese soldiers as reinforcement in the month of Hiyangei, 1820 under the leadership of Pakhaun. They arrived at Kakching and proceeded towards Thoubal. Hirachandra's forces gave battle at Thoubal but they could not resist the advance of the superior Burmese forces and they fled to Cachar. The newly invading Burmese army set one Huidrom Subol on the throne of Manipur in Phairen 1820. They stayed for about two months and when they returned to Burma, they had taken about 30,000 Manipuris as captives. (R. K. Jhalajit, A Short History of Manipur). Since Huidrom Subol did not belong to the royal family, he had no ally. There were disagreement among the followers and there was chaos. After the departure of Burmese forces, Hirachandra came back and invaded against Huidrom Subol. However, Huidrom Subol surrendered and they together decided to fight the Burmese.

Hirachandra made Sana Yumjaotaba the king of Manipur in the month of Lamda 1820. As soon as Yumjaotaba became king, he started plots to kill Hirachandra at the instigation of some of his followers. Hirachandra left the palace disgusted. After this incident nothing was known about Hirachandra. There are different versions about his disappearance. Some said that he was killed in action in the battle with the Burmese at Kakching towards Pallel. Others said that he was still fighting the Burmese forces along wirth Gambheer Singh and Nar Singh at Lokchao in 1825. Another version said that he was murdered by Gambheer Singh by submerging him in water in Ngabong Khao.

In the mean time, Marjit Singh proved to be not a mere fugitive. He proceeded to drive out Govindachandra, King of Cachar, Govindachandra appealed to both the British and the Burmese to assist him to regain his kingdom. Refugees from Cachar fled into adjoining Jaintia. The British became alarmed that the trouble might spread to Bengal itself. The Raja of Cachar, Govindachandra brought in the Burmese in 1824. The British took swift action and declared both Cachar and Jaintia to be protectorates. The Burmese would not recognize this declaration as legal and continued to chase the rebel refugees. When the Governor General, Lord Amherst demanded that the frontier be clearly demarcated and sent two officers to inspect, the Burmese arrested them. British troops then occupied an island in the river but the Burmese attacked and overcame them.

The rival Manipuri princes in Cachar fell out this time over a polo pony. One of them applied to the English for help and so did the rightful Raja of Cachar.

Advance of Gambheer Singh and Signing of Treaty of Yandabo

The relationship the British with Burma during this was going from bad to worse. In 1823 the British Government opened communication with

Gambheer Singh 500 Manipuris under the command of Gambheer Singh were taken into the pay of the British Government. It was denominated as the "Manipur Levy" and was paid, accounted and supplied with ammunition by the British Government. Gambheer Singh cooperated with the British in driving out Burmese out of Cachar.

In January, 1824, the Burmese troops again marched into Cachar and on the 5th March, 1824, the British declared war against the Burmese, known as the First Anglo- Burmese War. Maha Bandula, the Burmese Commander-in-chief with headquarters in Assam decided on a two pronged attack, one from Assam and Manipur through Cachar and the other from Arakan, the two armies meeting in Bengal and together attacking Calcutta. Maha Bandula himself led the army from Arakan. Bandula used a combination of guerrilla tactics and frontal attacks. Burmese canons only fired balls whereas the British canons fired exploding shells. The Burmese lost about a hundred men whilst six Sipahi were killed on the British side. This was the first skirmish in the First Anglo-Burmese War. The British thought of penetrating Burma through Manipur as a part of their strategy for the First Anglo-Burmese War.

The Governor-General-in-Council at Fort William decided upon the detachment of a large body of regular force under the direct command of Brigadier-General Shuldham instead of sending Gambheer Singh's levy in advance and also postponed the granting of the amount of rupees one lakh to Gambheer Singh for meeting the expenses of increasing his infantry. On 24 February, 1825, the British forces under Shuldham arrived at Bashkandi. On 11 March, 1825, Shuldham reported that "the state of the road is such that it is quite impossible to send supplies on to the advance, either on camels, bullocks, elephants or men". The unusual rains also made the march much more hopeless. There remained Manipur Brigadier General Shuldham,commanding Eastern frontier, abandoned his first attempt of transport and the beginning of the monsoon made it imposible.

Gambheer Singh and his 500 men then decided to take up the task which was considered impossible by Brigadier General Shuldham and left Sylhet on 17 May, 1825, accompanied by a British officer Lieutenant R. B. Pemberton. They arrived at Bashkandi on 23 May, 1825. despite bad weather, inadequate supplies and innumerable hardships, they managed to reach the western limit of the valley of Manipur on 10 June, 1825. The Burmese forces had already evacuated most part of Manipur and encamped themselves at Andro, a place situated on the eastern side of Imphal. Gambheer Singh and his men occupied imphal without much difficulty. Emboldened with these successes, Gambheer Singh further moved on to Andro but found it evacuated. The Manipuri forces did not meet any serious opposition from the Burmese army.

Gambheer Singh resumed his second campaign on 18 December, 1825. This time, he was accompanied by Captain Grant. During his six month's stay at Sylhet, Gambheer Singh could mobilize fresh reinforcements (1500 muskets and requisite number of men). On arrival at Manipur, Gambheer Singh found that there were still 300 or 400 Burmese soldiers in the Kabow valley. After a few days, Gambheer Singh was again informed of the withdrawal of the Burmese soldiers from the valley to Tamu, a border town in Burma. The valley was left under the protection of 500 local people. Meanwhile, the Sumjok Raja mobilised about 200 men in and around Tamu to counter the Manipuri forces. It was here that the Manipuris whom Gambheer had sent early in January could hardly make any penetration into the enemy's camp. Realising the seriousness of the situation, Gambheer Singh and Captain Grant lost no time to rush to the assistance of the advance forces and joined them in the fight on 18 January 1826.

On 19 January, 1826, the combined forces assaulted the Burmese positions, and though the latter made several spirited sorties to check the mounting attacks from Manipuri soldiers, they were resisted with greater spirit. By the night of 22 January, 1826, the Burmese began their retreat and completely evacuated the stockade. Captain Grant gave his eye-witness account thus: "... the activity, judgement and skill he (Gambheer Singh) has displayed on this occasion, have proved the justice of the opinion previously entertained on his merits. The steady gallantry which, without the usual aid of cannon, could force a brave enemy to evacuate a strongly fortified position is a very satisfactory illustration of the character of his followers...".

In 1825, Manipuris led by Gambheer Singh attacked Burmese occupation and drove them beyond Ningthee (Chindwin) river and reached Yandabo.

Treaty of Yandabo

The Treaty of Yandabo was signed on 24 February 1826. The war had lasted two years. At the conclusion of the Yandabo Peace Treaty, after the end of Anglo-Burmese war in February 1826, Gambheer Singh was recognized as the Raja of Manipur. According to article 2 of the treaty of Yandaboo concluded on 24 February, 1826, the King of Burma recognized Gambheer Singh as the Raja of Manipur. Obviously, the desire of the British officials in India that Manipur should be treated as an independent kingdom was fulfilled. Kabow valley was restored to Manipur.

RAJA GAMBHEER SINGH (CHINGLEN NONGDRENKHOMBA) (1825-1834)

On 26th Inga (June), 1825, Gambheer Singh declared himself as the King of Manipur. He constructed his palace (Konung) at the top of Bishnupur hill in April, 1826 AD. Later, he shifted his capital to Langthabal. (see plate-65)

When Gambheer Singh declared himself as the king of Manipur, the population in the valley was hardly 10,000. The valley was like a grass jungle, interspersed with marshes. Rice fields became shallow swamps. There were ruins of the prosperous villages. The condition in the hills was not better. Slowly, the area under cultivation increased and some of the people who had fled to other places returned.

The Raja Gambheer Singh issued coins in gold and bell metal. The intial letter of his name "Ga" is depicted in the Deva Nagri script. He built a new palace on the hillock of Langthabal.

Spiritual Life and Introduction of Festivals

The image of Govindajee was brought back from Cachar and worshiped at Langthabal. Marjit Singh took it with him in his flight to Cachar. The spiritual life of the people had been re-established. There was migration of Brahmins from Tripura, Vrindaban, Dacca and they were given surnames like Anoubam, Brajabashimayum, Acharyamayum. In 1830, the Maharaja sent Nongmaithem Nongthonba to erect a temple at Vrindaban. In 1831, Nongthonba completed the temple and came back to Manipur.

In 1832, one Panda from Jagannath Kshetra arrived and curved out the image of Lord Jagannath and the festival of Ratha Yatra was started. He also introduced "Gostha Asthami" and "Sansenba" depicting the heroic activities of boy Krishna and boy Balaram and killing many demons while tending cows.

Relations with the British

At the request of the British Government by Governor General, Mr. Scott, Maharaja Gambheer Singh went to Khasi hills to help the British who were unable to fight the Khasis. Gambheer Singh went there and subdued the Khasis and he was given the title of "Khasi Ngamba".

Relations with Nagas of Naga Hills

Maharaja Gambheer Singh subdued the recalcitrant Nagas and occupied Thibomei (Kohima) in 1832. To commemorate the event, he left footprints engraved on a slab of stone. A festive ceremony was performed in which the Naga villages contributed one buffalo, two goats and one hundred pigs. Later 600 heads of cattle were presented to Maharaja Gambheer Singh as a tribute.

Opening of Trade Route between Manipur and Assam through Naga Hills

Gambheer Singh embarked upon opening of a route from Imphal to Nowgong in Assam across the extensive hills and deep gorges. The British supported his plan. In January, 1832, Captain Jenkins and Lieutenant Pemberton escorted by 700 Manipuri troops forced a passage through the Naga Hills to find out a practicable route to Assam. In the cold season (1832-33) again, Raja Gambheer Singh accompanied by Manipur Levy under Lieutenant Gordon again marched through Naga Hills to Assam by a route a few miles to the east of Jenkins' tract. On both these occasions, the Manipuris had to fight every foot of their journey with the Nagas. The Nagas particularly the Angamese equipped with spears, muskets and stone boulders made unprovoked attacks resulting in the death of many workers. This route was the first route connecting Imphal with Assam. Much valuable information were collected in these two expeditions. The passage was of course constructed after the death of Gambheer Singh connecting Manipur with the Brahmaputra valley via the Naga Hills and by the early 20th century, this passage had become the lifeline of not only for Manipur but also for the Naga Hills (now called the National Highway no. 39). Gambheer Singh also improved the main route connecting Manipur with Cachar and Sylhet encouraging trade between Manipur and Assam.

The Manipur territory extended right upto Chindwin river.

Loss of Kabow Valley to Burma

In 1830, the new Governor General Lord William Cavendish Bentinck sent Major Burney as the first resident envoy to Ava. Bagyidaw was the king of Burma (1819-37). Major Burney also gained friendship of the king's younger brother, the Prince of Tharrawaddy.

The Burmese had never given up their hopes of modifications in the Treaty of Yandabo. When Major Burney arrived in Ava as Resident, the king believed that he could now reopen the question of Kabow valley. The documents relating to Kabow valley were examined with laborious care by Major Burney, Captain Grant and Captain R. B. Pemberton. The right of the Manipuris to Kabow valley had been formally acknowledged. The Burmese ministers provided their historical records to claim that the kingdom of Pong was conquered and became tributary to Ava 33 years before the Kabow valley was handed over to Manipur. They claimed that the Kabow valley distinct from Manipur had been for a long series of years considered as part of the empire of Ava. and that it was in the uninterrupted possession of Ava.

Manipur occupied Kabow valley only in 1475. In September, 1830, the Burmese Court selected two men to go to Calcutta with the following objectives :-

1. the return of Kabow Valley
2. the Burmese claimed that part of the Martaban district which lay to the east of the Salween, the dividing line between British and Burmese territory.
3. the abrogration of the article -7 of the Treaty of Yandabo which provided for the exchange of residents and
4. the return of Arakan and Tenasserim as an act of friendship.

The two Burmese envoys, accompanied with Captain George Burney, younger brother of Major Burney left Ava by water on 9 October, 1830. The Burmese mission numbered eighty four including wives, daughters, attendants, male and female interpreters, draftsmen and a physician. They were in no hurry to get to Calcutta and made the most of their grand tour. They stopped at every pagoda on their route down the river, made offerings and aked for a safe return. When they arrived in Calcutta, the Governor General Lord Bentinck was in the north and they needed permission to meet him. This took ten months. Major Burney, embittered by his experience in Ava where he not only waited for audience with the king but also had to take off his shoes off in king's presence, advised the authorities in Calcutta to make the Burmese envoys wait as long as possible before being honoured with the audience of the Governor General. Finally the Governor General arrived near Agra on 18 November, 1832 and they were granted interview on 23rd November, 1832. The Governor General was presented with two ruby rings of great value, two saphire rings of great value, 10 pieces of Burmese silk cloth of from 31 to 19 stripes, 30 pieces of Burmese silk, plain, 37 Burmese lacquered boxes of all kinds and sizes, 1000 cut rubies and polished, 1000 rubies rough and unpolished. After a great deal of ceremonial, the envoys presented their letter. It was already two years since the mission left Ava.

The Burmese King had always considered it a humiliation to concede Kabow valley to Gambheer Singh. Gambheer Singh was considered as a protégé of the British and Article -2 of the Treaty of Yandabo stipulating that "should he return to Manipur, the King should recognize him as Raja" was a source of great irritation to Ava. Major Burney knew that the Kabow valley was so important not from economic point of view but it was considered to be a humiliation to lose it to Gambheer Singh. It was so much a matter of prestige for the Ava court that Burmese would risk another war rather than see the British puppet Gambheer Singh in possession of it. When the actual conference took place at Calcutta, the Governor General was persuaded of the wisdom of returning the Kabow valley to Ava. The Government's reply to the King's letter was given to the envoys on 16 March, 1832 announcing the return of the Kabow valley. The Governor General presented the envoys with gifts for the Burmese king–Rees Encyclopaedia-45 volumes, two pieces plum-coloured velvet, two rolls red velvet, 12 pieces fine English handkerchief, 2 rolls gold brocade, one roll blue velvet, one roll green velvet, two pieces fine gold flowered muslin, one fine large looking glass, two English carpets, two cubits square, one fine guilded chair. They were presented with a large image of Buddha made of black marble. The most important achievement of the mission was the successful return of Kabow valley. This happened in 1832 when, in a treaty signed by the British High Commissioners, Major Grant and Major Pemberton on 9th January. At one time, Gambheer Singh and the British Government made a verbal agreement that Kabow valley would be leased to Burma for cultivation and Maharaja of Manipur would receive a sum of Rs. 6000/- per annum as a tribute. This story was recorded in the Cheitharol Kumbaba by Meiteis. The British thought that they would avert another war with the Burmese by transferring the Kabow valley to the Burmese. Gambheer Singh could sense the possibility of transfer of Kabow valley to Burma.

Two treaties were concluded with the Manipur Raja in 1833 and again in 1834. By the Treaty of 1834, the Kabow valley was transferred from Manipur to Burma and a money compensation was awarded to the Raja by the British Government in the shape of a monthly stipend of Rs. 500. The treaty was formally signed on 25th January, 1834. between Major F. J. Grant and Captain R. Boileu Pemberton.

Acquisition of Jiribam

By the treaty of 1833, signed 18th April, 1833, the British Government agreed to give to the Raja of Manipur the line of the Jiri river and western bank of Barak river as the boundary, the Raja in return agreeing to the following conditions :-

1. The Raja will remove his Thana from Chundrapore and establish it on the eastern bank of Jiri.
2. The Raja will in no way obstruct the trade carried on between the two countries by Bengali or Manipuri merchants ; he will not excact heavy duties and he will make a monopoly of no article of merchandise whatsoever.
3. The Raja will not prevent the Nagas inhabiting the Kalanaga and Noonjai ranges of hills from selling or bartering ginger, cotton, pepper and every other article, the produce of their country in the plains of Cachar, at the Baskandi and Oodharbun bazars as has been their custom
4. With regard to road commencing from eastern bank of the Jiri and continued via Kalanaga and Kowpoom as far as the valley of Manipur, after the road has been finished, the Raja will keep it in repairs so as to enable laden bullocks to pass the cold and dry seasons. Further, at the making of the road, if British Officers be sent to examine or superintend the same, the Raja will agree to everything these officers may suggest.
5. With reference to the intercourse already existing between the territories of the British Government and those of the Raja, if the intercourse be further extended, it will be well in every respect and it will be highly advantageous to both the Raja and his country. In order therefore, that this may speedily take place, the Raja at the requisition of the British Government will furnish a quota of Nagas to assist at the construction of the road.
6. In the event of war with the Burmese, if troops be sent to Manipur, either to protect that country or to advance beyond Ningthee, the Raja, at the requisition of the British Government will provide hill porters to assist in transporting the ammunition and baggage of such troops
7. In the event of anything happening on the Eastern Frontier of the British Territories, the Raja will, when required assist the British Government with a portion of his troops.
8. The Raja will be answerable for all the ammunition he receives from the British Government and will, for the information of the British Government, give in every month a statement of expenditure to the British Officer attached to the levy. (Alexander Mckenzie, North East Frontier of India, Mittal Publications, 1884, Page-101).

Maharaja Gambheer Singh heard about the news of transfer of Kabow valley to Burma. He felt being betrayed as he was not consulted before. He was totally dejected. He developed heart ailments. He did not live long to hear news of the actual transfer of Kabow valley to Burma. He died of heart attack at Langthabal on 9th January, 1834. The actual agreement for transfer of Kabow valley to Burma was signed on 25th January,1834 A. D. by British Political Agents, Major F. J. Grant, Captain R. Boileu Pemberton.

Maharaja Gambheer Singh had 11 queens.

Langmaithem Chanu Tulshipriya –Maharani

Laishom Chanu Meghamala –Apanbi Ahal

Maisnam Chanu Kumudini- Apanbi Naha –Chandrakirti

Narengbam Chanu Dhanabati

Phijam Chanu Rupeshwari

Potsangbam Chanu Devajani

Maibam Chanu Thaba –Sanahal Manaraj Singh

Maibam Chanu Tuteshwari

Yumlembam Chanu Rashbati

Angom Chanu Tulali

Out of eleven, nine queens did not have a son. The monument erected at the time of his death can be seen at Lanthabal on the western side of the National Highway–39.

MAHARAJA CHANDRAKIRTI (NINGTHEMPISHAK) (1834-1844 AD or 3232-3242 MF)

The only son of Maharaja Gambheer Singh and Maisnam Chanu Kumudini (Ponglen-Khombi) Chandrakirti ascended the throne on 9th January, 1834 (Thursday) at the age of 2 years with his uncle Nara Singh as regent.

Political Agency opened for the first time in Manipur

Lord Bentinct, the Governor General of India decided to keep a British Agent in Manipur. The Officer should be in the character of "Political Agent". The primary objective was." the preservation of friendly relation between Manipur and British and as a medium of communication with the Manipur Government and as occasion may require, with the Burmese authorities on that frontier and more specially to prevent border feuds between Manipuris and Burmese ". In 1835, Lt. Gordon (1835-1844) was appointed by, as the first Political Agent in Manipur on a consolidated salary of Rs. 1000/- per mensum and he held this post till his death in December, 1844. Thus the compensation money for the loss of the entire Kabow valley was just half of the Political Agent's salary. Lt. Gordon was popular for introducing English fruits and vegetables in Manipur

The establishment of the office of the British Political Agent in Manipur in the year 1835 marked the beginning of the consolidation of the British control over Manipur. In the beginning, the Political Agent is dependent on the wish and pleasure of Maharaja for everything. His every movement is known to the Maharaj. He is in fact a British officer under the Manipur surveillance. If the Maharaja is not pleased with the Political Agent he cannot get anything, But with the establishment of Chief Commissioner's province in Assam in 1874, the Political Agent in Manipur was placed under the Chief Commissioner of Assam. After this, the office of the Political Agent became more and more powerful because of the internecine quarrel among the princes of Manipur which gave an opportunity to the Political Agent to interfere directly or indirectly in every domestic affairs of the state. Under these circumstances the position of the Political Agent was something like that of a de-facto administrator of the state. (Lal Dena, History of Modern Manipur, 1825-1948, Orbit Publishers, New Delhi, 1991).

Construction of Imphal-Cachar Road

The construction of the Imphal-Cachar Road began in 1837 at the joint expense of the Government of India and the Government of Manipur. The construction was completed in 1844.

Attempts to Dethrone Chandrakirti

In 1835, Sana Tarangkhomba, son of Labanyachandra along with Kekru Taba tried to seize the throne. They were defeated at a battle at Maklang. On 23rd Kalen 1841, (Thursday), Sana Tribhuvan along with his brother Ram Singh, two sons of Chourajit tried to usurp the throne. But they were killed. Another attempt was made by Jogindra Singh, son of Marjit. But Jogindra Singh and his son were killed in the hills on their way from Cachar to Imphal. After defeating these repeated attempts to usurp the throne, the popularity and power of Nar Singh, the regent increased.

Attempts on the Life of Nara Singh, the Regent

The dowager Queen Kumudini feared that the regent would finally usurp the throne. She finally hatched a conspiracy to kill Nara Singh, the regent through one Nobin Singh. But the plot misfired and Nobin Singh was killed in action. Then Kumudini along with Chandrakirti fled to Cachar on Jan 27, 1844 AD, when Maharaja was 12 years old. But according to R. Brown, "Nobin Singh acted solely on his own initiative because of an old grudge.

Kumudini thought that Nara Singh had been killed and she fled to Cachar escorted by Thangal on horse back fearing that there was nobody to protect the minor King". After reaching Cachar, Kumudini placed herself and her son under protection of the British. The British authorities provided a guard of some sepoys for their protection and a small allowance of Rs. 100 per month from the Kabow valley compensation money for their maintenance.

NARA SINGH (1844-1850)

Nar Singh (see plate-66) ascended the throne on 19th Phairel, 1844 at the age of 51 years with Haobam Chanu Liklai Pokpi as his queen and he was recognised as a Raja in September, 1844. He moved the capital from Langthabal to Kangla on 19th of Kalen (15th April), 1844 AD. Melei Khomba and his brother, descendants of Charai Rongba invaded Manipur from Cachar to dethrone Nara Singh. But Nara Singh's forces defeated them. Melei Khomba was taken prisoner. He was put into a sack, the mouth of the sack was securely tied and thrown into the river. During his time, Jalakelli was introduced.

Immigration of Kukis

A large number of Kukis migrated to Manipur and with great efforts through Col. Mc Culloch, the Political Agent, they were settled in various parts of Manipur. Nara Singh died of Cholera on April 10, 1850 AD. He had three sons–Bhubon Singh, Setu Singh and Sana Borajaoba.

DEVENDRA SINGH

Nar Singh was succeeded by his younger brother Devendra Singh. McCulloch, Political Agent (1844-1862) recommended Devendra Singh to the Government of India and requested them to recognise him as the King of Manipur. Accordingly, the British authorities at Fort William accepted the recommendation and recognised Devendra Singh as the King of Manipur in June, 1850. Devendra ruled for three months and during this time, he married 96 wives. By the time Devendra ascended the throne, Chandrakirti was about 18 years of age and he was ready to fight for the throne. The people of Manipur remembered him fondly as a king, called "Ningthem Pishak (Baby King)". Three sons of Nara Singh supported him. Chandrakriti was making preparation to advance to Manipur. The British authorities tried to resist the advance of Chandrakirti. They increased the number of guards on Chandrakriti. But Chandrakriti Singh escaped from his place with eighteen men on 10 June 1850 causing a great concern to the British authorities. The British authorities sent 60 soldiers of Sylhet Light Infantry immediately to chase after him. McCulloch also asked the British authorities in Cachar to resist Chandrakriti before his entry into Manipur. But Chandrakriti and his followers could cross the Jiri river, reached Kala Naga Hills on 24 June, 1850. A large number of people from both Cachar and Sylhet also began to join him. When he reached Manipur valley, a large number of people came to his side and hence Chandrakriti Singh rapidly gained strength. McCulloch and King Devendra Singh could not resist the force of Chandrakriti. A large number of Manipuri soldiers joined with Chandrakriti. The British were fully aware of the popularity of Chandrakriti among the people of Manipur. On 12 July, 1850, McCulloch said "Devendra Singh had only three hundred men and majority of the population were in favour of Chandrakriti." On that very day, King Devendra Singh fought against the army of Chandrakriti. In the battle that followed, Devendra Singh was defeated and fled from Manipur at night. (Lal Dena, History of Modern Manipur, 1826-1949, Orbit Publishers, New Delhi, 1991).

MAHARAJA CHANDRAKIRTI (1850-1886)

Chandrakirti (see plate-67) ascended the throne on 4th Ingel (13th July), 1850 (Saturday) at the age of 19 years. On 15th July, 1850, (Monday), he went to Major Mc Culloch and informed him that he had become the King of Manipur (here the protocol is reversed)

Attempts to dethrone Chandrakirti

Within a fortnight, one of Devendra's brother in alliance with Nara Singh's son and 600 followers attempted to seize the throne but they were defeated. After about two months from his flight, Devendra invaded Manipur but he was defeated again. Devendra had to retreat to Cachar again. Devendra again tried to invade Manipur. But the Government of India began to take action to stop this practice of using Cachar as a spring board for invading Manipur. Devendra was arrested and he was put in Dacca jail. He was known as "Dacca taba ningthou". He died in Dacca jail in 1871.

The payment of compensation money of Kabow valley was delayed due to non-ecognition of Chandrakirti as the King of Manipur for some months. The Government of Manipur openly said that they would occupy the Kabow valley if the compensation money was not paid. About December, 1850, the Government of Manipur supplied arms and men to a group of Nagas, who were hostile to the British. But the Political Agent came to know of this plot and he rebuked the king saying that "Manipur existed only because of the sufferance of the Government of India". In February, 1851, the Government of India publicly avowed that they would guranttee the Raja to Chandrakirti and his descendants and any attempot to dislodge him would be prevented.

In 1852. Naol Singh, son of Madhuchandra made an attempt to dethrone Chandrakirti. One Keipha was tried but convicted under section 125 of the Indian Penal Code for waging war against the King. Kanhai Singh, son of Marjit made an attempt and also another attempt in 1864. He was tried and convicted under section 125 of the Indian Penal Code and convicted to seven years imprisonment. Maipak Singh, a descendant of Garib Niwaj made two attempts in 1859 and 1862. Gokul Singh son of Devendra made another attempt in 1866. All these attempts failed. After 1866, there was no more attempt.

Subdue of Lushais

In 1853, the Lushais attacked on southern frontier of Manipur. Chandrakirti sent a large army and captured Beijing Raja, the leader of Lushai along with five persons. In 1854, the Lushais attacked again. But Chandrakirti was able to subdue them with the help of Superintendent of Cachar.

In 1855, the Beithob of Sri Sri Govindajee of Kangla was built by Maharaja Chandrakirti.

Sepoy Mutiny and Manipur

In December, 1857 AD, Sepoys of the 34th Native Infantry at Chittagong mutinied against British, and the news was spread in Manipur by the British Government that Hindu sepoys will invade Europeans and take over Manipur. When the news of the "Sepoy Mutiny" came to Manipur. Chandrakriti immediately went to McCulloch (1844-1862) and expressed his desire to extend his support to the British. McCulloch requested Chandrakriti to send the Manipuri soldiers to the frontier areas to prevent the mutineers from entering Manipur. Chandrakriti sent about 600 soldiers led by Nameirakpam Menjor and subdued the Sepoy mutiny. A number of sepoys were arrested and handed over to the British. The British government was very grateful to Chandrakriti for his valuable help. On the recommendation of McCulloch, the British Government presented a dress of honour, a sword and a belt to Chandrakriti. Besides, the government also honoured eight Manipuri officers for their services. (Lal Dena, History of Modern Manipur, 1826-1949, Orbit Publishers, New Delhi, 1991)

In 1857, Maharaja Chandrajirti went in person to Akam Hao to subdue a rebellion with 1500 sepoys. However, the army retreated leaving the

Maharaja with only 20 guards. The Maharaja was saved by Naol Singh (Paona Brajabashi) and for which he was made Subedar with six Paris of paddy field, Jaypattra flag by the King.

In February, 1861, Sir Richard Temple proposed the abolition of Political Agency in Manipur. He said that the Political Agent would no longer be required considering the good relationship between Burmese and British. Further government would be able to save Rs. 14,000/- annually if the Political Agency is abolished. Sir Richard proposed to transfer the duties of the Political Agent to the Superintendent of Cachar to maintain the existing relationship between Manipur and British. McCulloch with the support of Maharaja Chandrakirti strongly emphasised the importance of this office of the Political Agency for the maintenance of law and order situation of the state.

Murder of Sana Chappando

During 1861 one unhappy incident occurred. There was one Sana Chappando, belonging to Rajkumar clan; who was very popular among the people. He was very expert in "Thang-ta" (spear and sword). People believed that he could protect himself from any attack of spear and sword. Not only that he could also manufacture guns including artillery and ammunitions. Seeing his rising popularity and skill, Chandrakirti at the instigation of his mother Kumudini got him killed by submerging him in water in "Ngabong Khao" at Lilong Turel along with three of his followers. Two persons Chongtha Hajari and Sorokhaiba Hajari were terminated from service. Three persons namely Maisnam Subedar, Nepra Jamadra, and Keisa Satawal were exiled to Cachar. From this time onward, nobody wanted to show off any skill in any field for fear of the King.

In 1863, Chandrakirti sent for one Punjabi martial art expert from Lahore, to teach Thang –ta to his sons. But the Punjabi expert was defeated by Paona Brajabashi.

For the first time in 1868 A. D. photography was introduced in Manipur. Durga Puja was introduced during the time of Chandrakirti.

In 1869, the Govindajee temple of Kangla was rebuilt by Chandrakirti Maharaja. In 1872, Maharaja entered into a treaty with Lushai to extend full cooperation for the development of trade relationship and to establish harmonious relationships between Manipur and Lushai.

On 13th Dec, 1873 AD, re-demarcation of Manipur's boundary (present day map) was done again with R. Brown (FRCSE) and Thangal General as leaders from both sides.

In 1873, there were 5737 houses in Imphal (Khwai, Yaiskul, Khurai and Wangkhei). In 1873, R. Brown estimated the population of Manipur at 74,000 hill men and 65,000 Meiteis making a total of 139,000. The first Census operation was conducted in 1881. The population of the valley was around 120,000 and the hill around 100,000.

Zila Durbar at Cachar

In the meantime, Lord Northbrook, the Viceroy of India (see Plate-69) had to visit some places of the eastern region. Taking advantage of this visit, R. Brown, (1867-1875) the Political Agent made an arrangement for a meeting between the Maharaja of Manipur and the Viceroy at Cachar in August 1874. Chandrakirti started for Cachar on 17th Ingel, 1874 (Friday) along with his two sons, several nobles to attend the Zila Durbar (durbar held in Cachar) with Lord North Brook, the Viceroy of India (see plate-71). An advance party of 500 sepoys under Thangal Major was sent to clear the way for the King. About 1000 sepoys including eight elephants, a number of cavalry accompanied the King as body guards. The durbar was held on 30th July, 1874 on board the Viceroy's yacht on the Barak river (Gwai river). On 31st July, 1874, an exhibition Polo match was displayed at Sichar in honour of Lord Northbrook, the Governor General and Viceroy of India. Chandrakirti made his return journey on 14th August, 1874.

R. Brown (1867-1875) published the Meitei script for the first time for the Asiatic Society of Bengal. The then Bengal Government donated a few books and started teaching Bengali script and English.

Polo Teams to Calcutta

In 1875, Chandrakirti sent two Polo teams to Calcutta to play before His Royal Highness, the Prince of Wales (afterward King Edward-VII) during his visit to India. (see plate-307) He also dedicated two bells to Shree Govindajee in 1875. The circumference of the bell was 8 feet 8 inches and the height was 3 feet 4 inches. It weighted 16 maunds.

Arrival of James Johnstone

On 18th August, 1876, R. Brown died. In 1877, Col. James Johnstone was appointed as the Political Agent of Manipur. He arrived together with his wife, a nurse and two tiny sons after covering hazardous hill tracks and crossing precariously suspended rope and cane bridges on the hill torrents over the Barak river (Gwai river) and the Makru river.

Immigration of Kukis

During 1876-77, about 2000 Kukis migrated to Manipur being driven northwards by more powerful groups. They were tall with good physique. They brought a large number of muskets and ammunition. The Maharaja allowed them to settle near Moirang in the south western corner of the valley. In the early part of 1877 a group of Kukis attacked the border area of Manipur and killed a large number of Manipuris. (R. K. Jhalajit : A Short History of Manipur, 1965).

Repair of Imphal-Cachar Road

The repairing of Imphal-Cachar road was undertaken with the help of Johnstone, the Political Agent (1877-1886). The export–import business was streamlined. Agriculture was given much importance. Wheat was introduced on experimental basis. Opium was found cultivated in Muslim areas.

In 1879, at the instigation of the Samjok Raja, Tongu the leader of the Chasad Kuki declared that they were no longer under the control of the king of Manipur. It again flared up in 1880 but was subdued in time.

Development of State Administration

Legal and judiciary system was streamlined. Rebellion against the King was punishable with death. The punishment for murder was death. At the suggestion of Johnstone, decapitation was introduced as the sole mode of execution.. Political offences and stealing of fire-arms was a serious offence punishable with imprisonment without specifying the terms. The lowest civil and criminal court at the village level is the Shinglup (meaning firewood association). It tried petty civil and criminal cases. It's another non-judicial function is procurement of firewood for cremation of anyone dying within its jurisdiction. Pacha is a special court to try cases connected with women – adultery, wife beating etc. Cheirap is the court for ordinary civil and criminal cases. The King was the highest civil and criminal court.

Exposure of women in the hot sun at the market place for a specified number of days or Khongoinanba was the only punishment for women. Brahmins were never awarded death punishment. Maximum punishment for a Brahmin was banishment or transportation for life.

Kohima Expedition

Towards the end of October, 1877 the Angamis of Khonomah village along with a few people from Chukha village attacked Gwelnong, a Naga village of Manipur. In the meantime, another group of Angami tribe tried to collect levy from a Naga village of Manipur near the border areas. They were arrested by the Manipuri Army and all the captives were brought before the Political Agent, Sir James Johnstone (1877-1886). Later on, they were released by the Political Agent. In Naga Hills again the Angami tribes of Mozemorah village attacked the post of British army. On hearing this news of this outrage Johnstone immediately rushed to the Naga Hills along with the Balaram Singh, a principal minister of the Maharaja of Manipur with an army of 100 soldiers, to help the Political Agent of Naga Hills.

Before reaching there Johnstone received an information about the attack on the border outpost of Manipur at Kongal by the army of the Raja of Samjok. They killed eight men. Johnstone took it very seriously and he returned to Imphal very soon leaving a large number of soldiers in Naga Hills to support the British.

But gradually the problems created by the Angami tribe became very serious. In 1879, the Angami Nagas were prepared for an armed uprising against British.

On 4 October, 1879, Dr. G. H. Damant, the Political Agent of Naga Hills and 50 British soldiers were murdered and many British women and children were detained at Naga Hills. Lt. Col. James Jonstone, the Political Agent in Manipur (1877-1886) made a desperate appeal to Maharaja Chandrakirti for immediate help. Chandrakirti prompty dispatched his own sons Surchandra, Tikendrajit along and Thangal General along with 2000 Manipuri sepoys. They were accompanied by 35 sepoys of Bengal Infantry and 50 men of Cachar Police. In no time, the rebelling Nagas were subdued and peace was restored. This expedition was known as Kohima Expedition. (see plate-68) The Britsh women and children were saved in time. The timely action saved the fall of Kohima to the hands of the Angamese. The Chief Commissioner of Assam Sir Steuart Bayley came to Manipur in February,1880 and Maharaja Chandrakirti was awarded the title of K. C. S. I. in a meeting of the Durbar by the British Government for his timely help and friendship to the British.

Border Dispute with Burma

In December 1877, the Burmese forces attacked the Kongal Thana within the territory of Manipur and killed the guards who were posted there. Johnstone went to Kongal Thana with a large force and he also reported the matter to the Government of India. The matter was also brought to the knowledge of the Burmese courts and to the Council of the Governor General. In order to bring up an amicable solution, the Council of the Governor-General asked the British Commissioner of Burma to give a detail report about the border problem. Soon Government of India set up a Border Commission and Sir James Johnstone was made the Commissioner to avoid all the border problems. They also sought help and co-operation from the Burmese Government and requested them to send a Commissioner. But Burmese Government did not send their officers to the Commission. At the wishes of the British authorities, Johnstone finally prepared a new boundary line between Manipur and Burma. He erected stone pillars on both sides of the Nanmiya river which runs near the Kongal Thana. In 1884, the Burmese Government threatened to destroy the Kongal Thana and the stone pillars. At this juncture the Third Anglo-Burmese war broke out and the settlement of boundary disputes between the two countries was kept in abeyance for sometime.

Cholera Epidemic

In 1880, a terrible Cholera epidemic broke out in Manipur. The river banks were lined with funeral pyres. The Durbar could not be held due to absence of members. Cholera and small pox were the two most dreaded diseases in those days. There was two severe earthquakes in 1869 and again in 1880, which destroyed the palace buildings at Langthabal.

Bhadra Singh, Painter

There was a renown classical painter named Ningthoujam Bhadra Singh (1861-1927) (see plate- 91). He was a child prodigy in his time. He was born in 1861. He was appointed as a royal painter in 1881. His paintings used to decorate the royal palaces, courts and even common households. Some of his famous paintings are – Keiphaba, Kaophaba, Loikaba, Zila darbar, Hiyang tannaba, Jhulon leela, Gour Lila, Radha Krishna, Nouka bilas, Pancha tattva etc. He learnt paintings from Mangsatabam Angangmacha. His followers were Mangsatabam Kalachand, Koijam Bharat Singh, Maibam Yaima Singh, Huirem Aton Singh. Contemporary to Bhadra was Rajkumar Yumjaosana Singh (1870-1954) (father of famous painter RKCS). Bhadra was a court painter till the end of his life. He painted more than 32 paintings for Cheirap court and 22 paintings for Panchai court.

Construction of Imphal-Mao road

The construction of Imphal-Mao road was completed under supervision of Lieutenant Raban R. E in January, 1881. During this time, Chandrakirti introduced efficient postal services. He issued coins of bell metel which are circular in shape. His other name is "Naochinglen Nongdrenkhomba". Therefore, the initial name "NA" in Bengali script was depicted on the obverse side of the coin.

Start of English Education in Manipur

The British considered the Meiteis very illiterate who did not want to be educated. In 1872, Major General W. F. Nuthall, the Political Agent initiated for establishment of an English school. The Government of Bengal donated books, maps and other materials valued Rs. 400-500. But the attendance was poor. By 1873, only 50-60 students including two girls attended the school.

In 1885, Sir James Johnstone, the Political Agent,with the approval of the Maharaja, established an English school. He took every possible means for the development of this school. The establishment of an English school was, indeed, a great contribution of Johnstone in the field of education. The school is still functioning in Imphal in the name of Johnstone Higher Secondary School.

The 3rd Anglo-Burmese War and Manipur

The Third Anglo Burmese War (Last Burmese War) broke out in 1885. On 17 December, 1885, Johnstone received a letter from A. J. Morgan, the Chief Agent of the Bombay Burma Corporation at Kendat (Burma) in which he was informed that the Secretary of the Queen of Burma killed three British employees of the Corporation and others were kept under arrest. Johnstone proceeded to Burma with 50 sepoys of the Bengal Infantry and 900 troops of Manipur under the command of Balaram, who was incharge of Burmese Affairs. On reaching Kabow valley, Johnstone realized that the situation was quite difficult. He therefore wrote to the Maharaja to send another 1000 troops under Thangal Major to lay in wait for events at Moreh and another 500 troops to reach him in Burma. Maharaja sent 3,000 soldiers under the command of Thangal to Kendat. With the help and support of Manipuri troops, Johnstone was able to occupy Kendat Province of Burma. Within 20 days of declartion of war, Mandalay fell and the whole of Burma was annexed to the British Empire. Mandalay was founded in 1857 by King Mindon. Mandalay was the last capital (1860–1885) of the last independent Burmese Kingdom before annexation by the British after the Third Anglo-Burmese War in 1885. Mandalay was set up in an empty area at the foot of 236 meter Mandalay Hill. According to a prophecy made by the Buddha that in that exact place a great city, a metropolis of Buddhism, would come into existence on the occasion of the 2,400th jubilee of Buddhism. King Mindon decided to fulfil the prophecy and during his reign in the Kingdom of Amarapura he issued a royal proclamation on 13 January 1857 to establish a new kingdom. The Ceremony of ascending the Throne was celebrated in July, 1858 and the former royal city of Amarapura was dismantled and moved by elephants to the new location at the foot of Mandalay Hill. With the Ground-breaking ceremony, King Mindon laid the foundation of Mandalay on the 6th waning day of Kason (1857). The fall of Burma also marked the end of border disputes between Burma and Manipur.

Sir James Johnstone left Imphal on 19 March, 1886 after retirement on health grounds. The British officials were not able to find a suitable person for this post. Finally, they appointed Major Trotter as the next Political Agent in Manipur. But he did not live long in Manipur. He died six months after his appointment in Manipur. But in 1888 this post was filled up by Frank St. Clair Grimwood, a Junior Officer of Sylhet. He was in Manipur for 11 months and after that he was transferred to Shillong. He was succeeded by A. E. Heath who died within a few days after his arrival at Imphal. After his death, the Government of India appointed Frank St. Clair Grimwood again as the next Political Agent in Manipur.

Chandrakirti Maharaja was considered as a congenial ruler from 1850 to 1886, more perhaps for his loyalty to the British during the mutiny than his enlightenment although he was considered more progressive than most of his contemporaries. (Lawrence James, RAJ, the Making of British India, ABACUS Page- 327)

Chandrakirti died on 17th Kalen (May),1886 AD at the age of 54 at Kangla in Yumpham (Imphal) after reigning 36 years as the Maharaja of Manipur.

Chandrakirti had eight queens and ten sons.

Principal Queen, Angom Chanu Lokeshwari-Surchandra, Pakasana, Kesorijit (alias Thambousana) and Gopalsana

Second Rani–Chongtham Chanu Lokeshwari-Kullachandra and Gandhar Singh

Third Rani-Chongtham Chanu Kouseswari–Tikendrajit

Fourth Rani: Oinam Chanu Thourani- Pheijaosana (Jhalakirti) and Sanayaima. Jhalakirti died at the age of 30 years.

Fifth Rani: Haobam Chanu Rupabati – Angousana

Sixth Rani–Akoijam Chanu Khandalekhi–Zilangamba and two daughters–Sanatombi and Wangonsana.

MAHARAJA SURCHANDRA SINGH (1886-1890 AD or 3284-3288 MF.)

Maharaja Surchandra, (see plate-72) the eldest son of Chandrakirti ascended the throne on 17th Kalen, 1886 at the age of 35 years with 50 gun salutes after the death of his father. Kulachandra was made the Jubraj or crowned Prince, Pheijaosana was the Senapati – Commander of Armed Forces. Pheijaosana died within one month and therefore Tikendrajit became the Senapati. Pakasana was the Sagol Hanjaba–Commander of Royal Horses, Kesarijit was the Samu Hanjaba, Gopalsana was the Dolai Hanjaba. Surchandra ruled for five years. (see plate-73)

Revolt of Sana Borajaoba

Sana Borajaoba, Yaiskullakpa, son of Nara Singh in collusion with his younger brother Megazine Singh, Paonam Naol (Paona Brajabashi) and Chongtha Mia with the help of 200 followers planned to enter the western gate of the palace in the early morning. Sensing some danger. Thangal Major ringed the bell of Shri Govindajee before time. All the people were awakened by the bell. Sana Borajaoba instructed his followers to withdraw the attack in spite of objection by his followers. But the secret plot came to light. In the subsequent battles, Sana Borajaoba, Paonam Naol Singh were captured and imprisoned. Chongtha Mia was defeated in the battle.

Arrival of Mr. Frank St. Clair Grimwood

In December, 1887, Frank St. Clair Grimwood arrived accomapined by his wife, Ethel St. Clair Grim Wood and he was received by Col. Maisnam Shamu Singh with 11 elephants at Bishnupur. Mr. Frank St. Clair Grimwood (1888-1891) was the Political Agent during 1887-1889 and again from December 1889 to 24 March, 1891.

Gathering storm at the Palace

Maharaj Surchandra appointed Dinachandra, grand son of Labyanachandra as Wangkheirakpa. Dinachandra was a clever man carrying out all the duties assigned by the Maharaja with all sincerity. Dinachandra by dint of his hard work became increasing influential in the palace, which Thangal Major did not like. He hatched a plan to oust Dinachandra and to incite one brother against another so that he might continue to enjoy the influential position in the palace. On 25th Langban, 1887, Dinachnadra organized a "Tarpan Utshop" by inviting a large number of his relatives and friends. Thangal Major informed the Maharaja that Dinachandra was not hosting

"Tarpan Utshop" but he was hatching a plan to revolt against the King. Believing Thangal's words, Surchandra ordered artillery fire towards his house. A battle was ensued in which Dinachandra and some of his followers were killed. When Pakasana was playing "Choubor" at the highway near Sanjenthong bridge, all the people gathered around to see the Choubor Game–blocking the passage. When one of Tikendrajit's servant Samphaba came to report the matter to Tikendrajit, he found Tikendrajit sitting with Thangal major. Thangal said "Pakasana is acting and speaking in whatever way he likes as if he is the only real brother of Maharaja. He may become dangerous if you do not take timely action". This inflamed the ego of Tikendrajit. Tikendrajit came in person along with Samphaba to stop Pakasana from playing Choubor. There was a quarrel between Tikendrajit and Pakasana. Pakasana stroked Tikendrajit with the wooden Choubor on his forehead and ran away. Tikendrajit followed him. From a distance, he could see Pakasana entering the King's chamber. Tikendrajit was furious. He came to the King and asked the wheeaboiuts of Pakasana. The King feigned ignorance. Tikendrajit felt offended.

By 1887, Manipur palace had become a divided house. The ten sons of the late Maharaja by his eight queens were divided into two groups-one led by Surchandra Singh and the other by Tikendrajit Singh. Tikendrajit Singh was the most popular prince. He was the idol of the masses and most capable prince. There were a chain of rebellions among the groups.

THE PALACE REVOLUTION, 1891

The gathering storm burst on the night of 21st September in 1890. Prince Zilangamba and Angousana with a handful of followers scaled the wall leading to the Maharaja's apartment and opened fire into the windows. Kulachandra, the then Yubaraja, was away from Imphal as he did not like the conflict between brothers.

They fired into the private chamber of the King. Surchandra was woken up by the firing. He tried to wear his turban and at that moment, his turban was shot by a bullet. Surchandra fled by the back door towards the Residency to seek asylum. He was accompanied by Keirungba and other servants. At Sanjenthong, he was met by his brother Pakasana with about 80 soldiers. Pakasana pleaded with Surchandra to return to the palace. But he refused. Tikendrajit Senapati lost no time to join the revolt. He immediately released all the priosoners and asked them to join the revolt. They occupied all the important places in the palace. Mr. Grimwood, the Political Agent was woken up at about 2. 10 a. m. and narrated all the incidents. All the people accompanying the King were disarmed by the Political Agent. On the next day, Surchandra wrote a letter to Tikendrajit that he wanted to proceed to Vrindaban. He also mentioned that Tikendrajit could take over the King's Kokyet and his personal sword and to send Rs. 10,000 to meet the expenditure for his travel to Vrindaban. Tikendrajit sent Rs. 1000 saying that the remaining money would be sent as soon as he reached Vrindaban. Surchndra informed the Political Agent that he abdicated the throne and wished to go to Vrindaban.

Surchandra abdicated the throne

After thirty six hours of sanctuary in the Residency the King formally abdicated, nominating the Jubraj, Kula Chandra, as his successor according to Manipuri custom, and declaring his intention of making a pilgrimage to Vrindaban.

The Political Agent thereupon made arrangements for an escort of Gurkhas to take the ex-Maharaja and his three full brothers, Pakasana, Kesarjit and Gopalsana together with followers to Cachar and wrote out a safe conduct for them accordingly. Maharaja Surchandra accompanied by Pakasana and two other brothers and attendants –in all about 60 persons left Manipur in the evening of 23rd September at about 7. 30 p. m. under an escort of 35 rifles of 44th Gurkha Light Infantry who saw the party safely to Cachar. On 3rd October, 1890, he reached Cachar and immediately he sent a telegram to Shillong saying that the Political Agent had misunderstood him and he had no intention of abdicationg the throne.

On reaching Calcutta, Surchandra applied to the Viceroy on 14th November, 1890, to restore him to the throne.

MAHARAJA KULACHANDRA (1890-1891)

Kulachandra (see plate-74) ascended the throne on 23 September, 1890 (Tuesday) at 3 P. M. according to Manipuri customs.

Although Frank St. Clair Grimwood did his best to reinstate Surchandra, he realized that he was a weak ruler and that his main advisor, Paka Sana, was both unpopular and trouble some. According to Mr. Grimwood, Tikendrajt Senapati was the real man, the real Governor and it was considered a beneficial thing for Manipur that there should be a change in which the Senapati should be the moving spirit. He was the man of great ability and the greatest force of character among the ruling family of Manipur. He was a man who was extremely popular among the people, who had a reputation of having impoverished himself by his generosity.

The Government of India was inclined to restore Surchandra but Mr. Grimwood and Mr. J. W. Quinton, the Chief Commissioner of Assam were opposed to this idea. They pressed for recognition of Kulachandra who ascended the throne. The Government of India doubted very much whether this would be the wise course.

Decision of the Viceroy of India

After much discussion and correpondence, the Viceroy, Lord Landsdowne (see plate -78) (10 December 1988 to 11 October, 1894) took the following decisions as conveyed in their letter letter no. 360-E dated 21st February1891:-

1. That the Yubraj (Kulachandra) should be recognized as the Maharaja and that the Ex-Maharaja should not be restored.
2. That the Senapati (Tekendrajit) should be removed from Manipur.
3. The Chief Commissioner of Assam should go to Manipur and announce the decision on the spot.

Quinton's attempt to implement the decision

Having decided to implement the decision to confirm Kulachandra as Maharaja and to expel Tikendrajit, the Government of India conveyed these decisions to J. W. Quinton (see plate-83), the Chief Commissioner of Assam with orders to carry them out in whatever way he felt fit.

On 13th Wakching (December), a "Lai" appear in the pond near the palace court. On 19th Wakching, the God Brindabanchandra turned away his face. On 22nd Wakching, there was sound of stamping in the temple of Brindabanchandra where the royal brothers and the Maharaja worshipped.

On 21st February, 1891, Mr. Frank St. Clair Grimwood (see plate-86) received a telegram from the Chief Commissioner of Assam informing him that Mr. J. W. Quinton, Chief Commissioner of Assam would visit Manipur shortly and all preparations should be made for his visit.

On the 7th March, 1891, Mr. J. W. Quinton left Golaghat for Manipur. with an escort of 400 men of the 42nd and 44th Gorkha Rifles under the command of Col. Charles MCD Donald Skene (see plate-84), DSO of 42nd Gurkha Regiment. The Chief Commissioner, Quinton left Kohima on 18th March,1891 with his escort of Gurkhas under the command of Col. Charles MacDonald Skene. He was received by Thangal General and a number of highest officials along wioth 700 sepoys at Mao. On Saturday, the 21st March, 1891 the party halted at Sekmai, the last stage before Imphal. At Sekmai, Quinton was received by the Senapati, Angou Sana with his own personal escort of some fifty soldiers. At about 10 a. m. on the 22nd of March, 1891 the Chief Commissioner was welcomed outside Imphal by Yubaraj Tikendrajit and then they proceeded into the city along a route lined with 500 Manipuri sepoys. Elaborate preparation had been made, banana and sugar canes plants had been specially planted along the way, and lamps were burning at every corner of the city. Mr. J. W. Quinton planned to summon a durbar at the Residency at midday on the following morning, soon after his arrival. Mr. Quinton planned to arrest Tikendrajit in the durbar, which had been scheduled at the Residency at 12 noon.

Quinton's attempt to capture Tikendrajit at the Durbar failed

The Maharaja and his three brothers including Tikendrajit (see plate-79), Angou Sana, Zilangamba, together with several of the nobles including Thangal General (see plate-76), Colonel Maisnam Samu Singh (Luwang Nigthou/ Plate-82), Giridhari Singh (Angom Ningthou), had arrived at the appointed time at outer gate of the Residency compound. They were escorted by about a hundred men, armed with a variety of rifles. Some of the King's escort managed to gain access to the Residency grounds, and noticed the unusual military precautions and the British officers and Gurkha soldiers under arms. Troops were kept in readiness round Reisidency where durbar was held in case of resistance. This information was conveyed to the Maharaja and Tikendrajit,who were still waiting on horseback at the gate. The indignity of being kept waiting in the sun (about which Kulachandra was later to complain in writing) was exacerbated by a message that the durbar had been delayed because the Chief Commissioner had not yet taken breakfast. Actually the delay was due to undue delay in getting the proclamation translated into Manipuri by Rassiklal Kundu, head clerk and others, who were conversant with Manipuri language. Rassiklal Kundu was the head clerk of the Political Agent.

The waiting was more than one hour. Later on, Tikendrajit left the gate complaining that he was feeling ill. He had indeed been unwell for some time, suffering from gall stones. He along with Angou Sana, the Senapati returned to the palace. Maharaja remained along with Prince Zilangamba, Thangal General, and several other nobles. All hope of arresting the Jubraj without incident had gone in vain. After a lapse of three hours, Mr. Quinton postponed the Durbar as he came to know the absence of Tikendarjit and sheduled it again for the next day (the 23rd of March) at 8 am. On 22nd March, 1890 at about 6 p. m. Mr. Grimwood along with Lt. Simpson and Rassik Lal Kundu went ot see the condition of the Jubaraj, Tikendrajit Singh. But the Jubaraj sent words to say that he was too ill to come out. On 23rd March, 1891 (Monday) at about 6 a. m, the Political Agent along with Rassik lal Kundu went to see the Jubaraj but they were refused interview. No one turned up at the Darbar at 8 a. m. Again at about 9 a. m, the Political Agent sent his head clerk Rassik Lal Kundu to see the Jubaraj without any effect.

On 23rd March,1891 at about 4. 30 p. m, Mr. Grimwood along with Lt. W. H. Simpson (see plate-85) (43rd Gurkha Rifles) came to the Durbar Hall and handed the King the Government of India's letter containing the decisions to recognize him as the king of Manipur but to deport his brother Tikendrajit outside Manipur. After consulting his advisors, the Maharaja responded that it was not in his power to surrender his brother and the Manipuri Durbar did not wish him to do so. Mr. Grimwood returned from the palace and announced that his mission had failed.

British attack at the Kangla Fort to capture Tikendrajit

On the night of 23rd March, a Raas Lila was organized in honour of Mr. Quinton. After the conclusion of the Raas Lila performance, the Chief Commissioner after consulting with Col Skene and Mr. Grimwood arrived at a decision to enforce the order of the Government of India. On 24th March, 1891, a contingent of 150 troops launched the attack at the Kangla Fort to capture Tikendrajit. On the 24th of March 1891 at 3 a. m., the British army entered the palace, and obtained possession of Tikendrajit's house. When Butcher's men gained control of the Jubraj's compound it become clear that the Yubaraj Tikendrajit was not there. The British army committed atrocities on men,women and children. Pukhramba Tanko had a hand to hand fight with a British Officer (probably Lt. Brackenbury) and died together. Seven sepoys of the British crossed Minuthong bridge, entered the house of one Muslim Sardar and killed three women. One Brahmin and two Tangkhuls were also killed. They also killed women, boys and girls, male and female servants, attacked the temple, stole the jewels of the idol. They burnt houses at Usham Leikai, Yambem Leikai, Saikhom Leikai. One Yambem Tolenkhomba was also killed.

Then the full fire power of the Manipuri force was turned upon the Residency. Severe fighting continued for the whole day. Many British army personnel were killed. Mr. Quinton decided that the only alternative open to them was to seek a truce and parley with the Manipur Maharaja. Accordingly, as darkness began to fall, at around seven in the evening, the British buglers were ordered sound the cease fire. Mr. J. W. Quinton, Mr. Grimwood and four other British Officers entered Kangla at night to seek the terms and conditions of truce.

Execution of Quinton and other British officers

A Durbar was held in front of the Durbar room of the palace. Yubaraj Tikendrajit, Thangal General, Colonel Maisnam Samu, Angom Ningthou, Haobam Dewan, Chongtha Mia and many were present on the Manipuri side. There was a great crowd shouting for justice for the violence and atrocities the British had committed in the previous night. At the durbar that followed, Tikendrajit protested against Quinton's aggressive action in attacking the capital without provocation thus starting the war by himself and demanded the surrender of arms as a guarantee for safe conduct of the British. Quinton refused to surrender the arms by saying that "we cannot surrender the arms. They belonged to the Government". Although the Durbar lasted for about an hour, the talks failed. After that the officers were escorted to the gate and Tikendrajit returned to the Top Guard. Grimwood then approached the Angom Ningthou and asked him to see the Chief Commissioner's party safely to the gate. Angom Ningthou asked the Jubraj who had begun to walk away towards the Top Guard, if he should do so and was told "Certainly, see them out". The Angom Ningthou and the five Europeans together with the bugler then began to move slowly toward the Lion Gate (Kangla Sha). They were followed closely by the mob, who threatened to press upon them.

This sudden action seemed to have sparked off latent hostility of the crowd. A great noise of shouting broke out from the Manipuri sepoys and onlookers, and cries of "kill them" could be heard above the din. The crowd now become an uncontrollable mob. The British found themselves hemmed in from all sides, pushed and jostled, and then struck with the butts of rifles, sticks and flying stones. Manipuris armed with swords and spears joined in the attack and thrust their weapons at the British officers.

The Angom Ningthou and Chongtha Mia Major at first tried to calm the mob, but when they realized that it could not be restrained they began to fight their way back towards the relative safety of the Durbar room, closely followed by Quinton and the others. In the melee, the Chief Commissioner had been struck in the arm, and Simpson had received a severe sword cut to the side of his head and another on the arm. All had been hit with sticks and stones. Mr. Grimwood was the last to reach the steps up to the Durbar Room just as he did so he was pushed violently by a Manipuri, one Neprakot and as he tried to defend himself received a spear thrust from a sepoy, Kajao Pukhramba Phingang. As he collapsed beneath the steps, he cried out for water and Chongtha Mia Major brought some water to him where he lay. Only three Europeans and the bugler had reached the safety of the room. The Angom Ningthou went down again and found Simpson and Grimwood beneath the steps, and he and Yubraj managed to held the wounded lieutenant into the room Tikendrajit then ordered the Angom Ningthou to guard the British well and turned back in the direction of the Top Guard. Beneath the steps of the Durbar Room Political Agent Grimwood lay dead. Thangal General said "Sahibloki machil thupchillo"- shut the mouths of the sahibs. When Tikendrajit was informed what Thangal had said, he replied "Did the old man really give such an order ? Do not do such a thing; they are not to be harmed in any way. Wait, I am coming" Usurba returned immediately to the Top Guard and reported to Thangal General what the Yubraj had said.

All three later testified that when the Yubraj entered the Top Guard he said to Thangal ; "Ipu { grandfather} why did you order the sahibs to be killed ?. These Shahibs should not be harmed in any way". Thangal replied that there was then no way they could remain on friendly terms with the British and then added "You are only a boy. I have served here for many years ; we shall drive the Sirkar's people into the sea". Tikendrajit looked very ill and tired and lay down near Thangal. He replied, "It cannot be done". and said that they must consult the Maharaja next morning. The Yubraj said "I am tired and I am going to sleep". The Yubraj was still sleeping in the same room at the time Thangal asked the Lalupchingba why he had not yet carried out the Jubraj's order that the British should be executed and ordered him to do so. Yenkoiba returned to the Durbar Room and told one of the sentries outside that the Thangal General had commanded that the sahibs be handed over to the executioner. The sentries then brought out Quinton, Cossins, Skene and the bugler Gunna Ram, but Simpson was so weak from loss of blood that he had to be supported by one of the soldiers. They were taken the distance of twenty yards through the Lion Gate to the stone Lions (Kangla Sha). A crowd had gathered there, but the people made no noise. One by one the five were handed over to the executioner, Sagolsem Dhana Singh (son of Anandaram) of Waikhom Babaji Leikai (present Waikhom Leikai) near Khongnang Feidekpi, and beheaded, standing and facing towards the west. They were executed one by one on 24th March, 1891.

1. Mr. J. W. Quinton. C. S. I I. E. Chief Commissioner of Assam.
2. Lt. Col. E. MCD Skene, D. S. O. 42nd Gurkha Rifles.

3. W. H. Cossino, I. C. S. Assistant Secretary to the commission.
4. Lt. W. H. Simpson, 43rd Gurkha Rifles and
5. A Gurkha Bugler

ANGLO-MANIPURI WAR OF 1891

The machinery of retribution was soon put in action. The British Government declared war against Manipur on 31st of March 1891. Within a fortnight, British forces mainly Gurkhas were converging on Manipur. By the first week of April, 1891, the following columns were ordered to invade Manipur from three directions :

1. *Kohima Column*

   No. 8 (Bengal) Mountain Battery (two guns)
   13th Regiment of Bengal Infantry
   36th (Sikh) Regiment of Bengal Infantry

2. *Silchar Column*

   No. 8 (Bengal) of Bengal Infantry
   19th Regiment of Bengal Infantry (Six Companies)
   1st Battalion, 2nd Gurkha Regiment

3. *Tamu Column*

   No. 2 Mountain Battery, Royal Artillery (Four Guns)
   2nd Battalion, Oxfordshire Light Infantry (200 men)
   The 4th Battalion King's Royal Rifle Corps (half battalion)
   2nd Battalion, 4th Gurkha Regiment
   12th Regiment (2nd Burma Battalion) of Madras Infantry

Tamu Column	=	4 guns and 1800 rifles
Kohima Column	=	3 guns and 1200 rifles
Silchar Column	=	2 guns and 1700 rifles
Total	=	9 guns and 4700 rifles

Each column consisted of 1000 soldiers. The Maharaja sent 800 soldiers under Khwairakpa, Maisnam Samu, Laisramba Jambhuban Major, Heigrujam Poila and Maibeya Tamra Singh Subedar to the north to defend against the British column coming from Kohima. One thousand soldiers were sent to the west under the command of Rajkumar Kala Singh, Sagol Hanjaba, Sana Ngamba, Lourung Purel, Yenkhoiba Poila, and Longjamba Poila to oppose the British Silchar column from Cachar. Seven Hundred sepoys were sent under Maipak Sana alias Lokendra Birjit Singh, Wankheirakpa and Rudra Singh Yenkhoiba

Major to meet the British column from Tamu (Burma). Yengkhoiba Major first made his camp at Tengnoupal. As the British forces advanced, he retreated and made his camp at Lamabam Ingkhol at Thoubal Athokpam with reinforcement of 300 sepoys under command of Chongtham Nilamani Ava Purel Major. When the Manipuri forces could resist the advances of the British forces, the Maharaja sent Yaiskullakpa with his son Senggoisana and 300 sepoys equipped with Top guns and accompanied with Top gun expert Maisnam Keirungba and Narengba Poila. They encamped at the western side of Thoubal keithel. The British forces made their camp at Sagolsem Ingkhol at Thoubal Athokpam. The Manipuri forces shifted their camp to Thoubal Tomjing hillock. In the fighting that followed Yaiskullalkpa and his son Senggoisana died together. Later on the British forces retreated to Pallel. Later on Maharaja after Consultation with Tikendrajit and Thangal General sent Maipaksana Wangkheilakpa Major with 700 sepoys to Thoubal. In the mean time, the Maharaja received a letter from Yengkhoiba and Chongtha Aya Purel Major requesting for reinforcement. The Maharaja could not think of any capable leader who can lead the Manipur forces against the British. At this juncture, Thangal General mentioned the name of Paonam Naol Singh, who at one time revolted against Maharaja Surchandra in favour of his friend Sana Borajaoba in collusion with Chongtha Mia. Both Paonam Naol Singh and Chongtha Mia were imprisoned for some years and they were released from the prision only recently. Paonam Naol Singh spent a long time at Vrindaban and therefore he was also known as Paona Brajabashi (see plate- 76). Both Paonam Naol Singh and Chongtha Mia were called up from their residences. They were given the post of Major with all the royal entitlement and they were given the task of defending the country against the agrressors. Thus Paona started his journey from his residence at Keisamthong on 10th April, 1891. His wive Hemlata dedicated 108 burning sticks to Lord Govindajee but it was suddenly extinguished without any reason. He together with Chongtha Mia and 400 sepoys started the journey for war. At Nityaipat Chithek, they were joined by Chinglensana and Heingang Khongja, the disciples of Paona Brajabashi. Chinglensana's mother requested Paona to hand over her son again to her after the war. They proceeded towards Kakching.

KHONGJOM WAR

The last war was fought at Khongjom, about 21 miles from Imphal. Maharaja Kulachandra made an appeal to the people to volunteer as soldiers in the fight against the British who had committed aggression against Manipur.

The Manipuris fought with determined efforts under the leadership of Major Paona Brajabashi (see Plate-75). But ultimately, Paona Major was killed by Takhellambam Rashman Subedar from Cachar on 23rd April, 1891 (Thursday) along with 131 soldiers. It is said that about 400 Manipuri heroes were killed in the Khongjom war. On the British side, Lt Grant reported 2 men killed, 13 wounded includng himself and three other British Officers. Grant admitted that they fought as hard as they could and the Manipuris fought till the last. After winning the Khongjom war, they had an easy walk over on all fronts and marched towards Imphal.

Before the fall of the Government, Kulachandra, Tikendrajit and other leaders left the Palace on 26 April, 1891 and went underground. General Collet entered the Palace on 27 April, 1891 and announced the occupation of Manipur by the British and ordered the people of Manipur to surrender all arms and ammunition to the British. Captain Allen destroyed the Kangla sha in front of Kangla by artillery fire. The British Government issued a proclamation offering rewards for the capturing of the following persons :

1. Manipur Maharaja - Rs. 5000
2. Tikendrajit Rs. 5000
3. Dolai Hanjaba Rs. 2000
4. Zilangamba Rs. 2000
5. Thangal General Rs. 2000

(see Chapter- 15: Historical Landmarks)

TRIAL AND EXECUTION OF TIKENDRAJIT AND THANGAL GENERAL

Niranjan Subedar was arrested on 2nd May, 1891. Thangal General surrendered on 7th May, 1891. Maharaja Kulachandra was captured on 9th May and Angousana on 18th May, 1891. Tikendrajit was arrested (see plate-79 and 81) in the evening of Saturday 23rd May, 1891 from the house of Thokchom Dewan of Singjamei Mathak after a severe struggle by Subedar Khelendra Singh from Cachar. A special court comprising of Lt. Col St. John Fancourt Mitchell, Assistant Adjutant General as president, Major Richard Kirly Ridgeway V. C, Commandant 44th Gurkha Rifles as member, A. W. Davis Esq, Civil Service, Deputy Commissioner, Naga Hills as member, which commenced on 11th May 1891. The trial of Tikendrajit lasted from 1st June to 10th June, 1891. The court found Tikendarjit, Kulachandra and Thangal General guilty of waging war against the Queen Empress and murder of British Officers and passed death sentences on all of them.

The Governor General confirmed the death sentence passed on Tikendarjit and Thangal General. The order was announced on 13th of August 1891. The two gallows were completed at Pheida Pung by mid-day on 13th August, 1981 and from early morning a crowd of Manipuris commenced to assemble and continued to increase till the time fixed for the execution when it must have aggregated over eight thousand persons, who kept up a wail of lament throughout the whole proceedings. On arrival at the gallows, the prisoners were again informed of the order of their execution and mounted the scaffold. The drop fell and the death was instantaneous. The hanging took place at 5 p. m. in presence of Chief Political Officer, H. Maxwell, Senior Medical Officer A. Coleman. After hanging for one hour, the senior Surgeon A. Coleman examined the bodies and pronounced life to be extinct. Tikendarjit and Thangal General were hanged at the spot where the present Saheed Minar (see Plate-186) is standing.

People who were tried by the British for waging war against the Queen Empress were :-

Kajao Pukhramba Phingarg was also hanged unto death on 25th May, 1891 at Central Jail, Imphal for spearing to death Mr. Grimwood. Chirai Thangal alias Chirai Naga was hanged on 13th October, 1891 for killing two Britishers including the Superintendent of Telephone Department. Niranjan Subedar was hanged on 8th June, 1891. (Lawrence James, RAJ, the Making of British India, ABACUS, Page- 332) Kulachandra Dhaja Singh, Angou Sana, the third prince were tried and convicted of waging war against the queen Empress of India and sentenced to death, which sentence by the exercise of the prerogative mercy, the Government of India commuted to a sentence of transportation Uru Singh, Usaba, Mongjao Singh, Yengkhoiba, Chowbi Hida Machahal, for life to Andaman and Nicober Islands with for feiture of all property.

Ghun Singh Kangdra, Kumbea Singh Laisraba, Dhaja Singh Myemba, Noni Singh, Nepra Machahal, Trilok Singh, Nongthoiba Satwal and Sagolsem Dhana Singh, Sagal Senba were tried and convicted of the murder of British Officers and were sentenced to death sentence, which had been commuted to transportation for life during the pleasure of the Governor General in Council and the subjects of Manipur state were enjoined to take warning by the punishment inflicted on the above named persons found guilty of rebellion and murder. (Naorem Sanajaoba, Manipur Treaties and Documents, 1110-1971, Volume one, page-11)

Thus, the British conquered Manipur on 27th April, 1891 AD. Manipur lost its independence. (Lawrence James, RAJ, the Making of British India, ABACUS, Page- 332)

Names of the people who were tried and punished for waing war against the Queen Empress were :-

1. Yubraj Tikendrajit (32 years)-hanged on 13th August, 1891 at Pheida Pung (Mapal Kangjeibung)
2. Thangal General (85 years)–hanged on 13th August, 1891 at Pheida Pung (Mapal Kangjeibung.)
3. Kulachandra Maharaja (35 years, 5 feet 8 inches tall)–transported for life with forfeiture of property to Port Blair, Andaman and Nicober (Kalapani) –died on 26th January, 1934 at Radhakund.
4. Prince Angousana Senapati (28 years)-transported for life to Port Blair, Andaman and Nicober (Kalapani)
5. Chongtha Mia Major-transported for life to Port Blair, Andaman and Nicober (Kalapani)-died at Radhakund.
6. Chongtham Nilamani, Ava Purel-transported for life to Port Blaire (Kalipani) with forfeiture of property–died at Vrindaban in 1897.
7. Lokendra Birjit Singh (Wangkheirakpa) transported for life with forfeiture of property to Port Blair, Andaman and Nicober (Kalapani)
8. Colonel Maisnam Samu Singh alias Luwang Ningthou-transported for life to Port Blair, Andaman and Nicober (Kalapani)
9. Uru Singh Usuba- transported for life to Port Blair, Andaman and Nicober (Kalapani)
10. Chaoba Hida Machahal-transported for life to Port Blair, Andaman and Nicober (Kalapani)
11. Kumba Singh Laishraba-transported for life to Port Blair, Andaman and Nicober (Kalapani)
12. Dhaja Singh Mayengba-transported for life to Port Blair, Andaman and Nicober (Kalapani)
13. Nani Singh Nepra Machahal-transported for life to Port Blair, Andaman and Nicober (Kalapani)
14. Trilok Singh Nongthonba-transported for life to Port Blair, Andaman and Nicober (Kalapani)
15. Dhana Singh Sagolsemba-transported for life. to Port Blair, Andaman and Nicober (Kalapani)
16. Ghuna Singh Indujamba Jamadar-transported for life to Port Blair, Andaman and Nicober (Kalapani)
17. Ningthaoba Singh, Chingsuba Jamadar-transported for life to Port Blair, Andaman and Nicober (Kalapani)

18. Thaoba Singh, Phanjao Jamadar-transported for life to Port Blair, Andaman and Nicober (Kalapani)
19. Tonjao Singh, Mangshataba Jamadar-transported for life. to Port Blair, Andaman and Nicober (Kalapani)
20. Chaobaton Singh Heigrujamba Subedar-transported for life to Port Blair, Andaman and Nicober (Kalapani)
21. Poradhumba Singh, Ashangba Khut-transported for life to Port Blair, Andaman and Nicober (Kalapani)
22. Chowkami Naga of Mayangkhang-transported for life to Port Blair, Andaman and Nicober (Kalapani)
23. Gowho Naga of Mayangkhang-transported for life to Port Blair, Andaman and Nicober (Kalapani)
24. Chirai Naga alias Chirai Thangal-hanged on 13th October, 1891 at Central Jail, Imphal for murder of Mr. Melville, Superintendent of Telegraph Department.
25. Kajao Pukhramba Phingang–hanged on 25th May, 1891 at Central Jail, Imphal for spearing to death Mr. Grimwood.
26. Niranjan Subedar–hanged on 8th June, 1891 at Central Jail
27. Ghuna Singh Khongdram- transported for life to Port Blair, Andaman and Nicober (Kalapani)

JUBRAJ TIKENDRAJIT (1858-1891)

Jubraj Tikendrajit Singh, the hero of the Manipur revolution of 1891, was born on 29th December, 1856. He was the son of Maharaja Chandrakirti Singh and his mother's name was Chongtham Chanu Kouseswari Devi.

During the reign of his father (Maharaja Chandrakirti), he was Kotwal, Senapati (during the period of Surchandra) and Yubraj (during the period of Kulachandra). In his individual capacity, he deposed Surchandra, the reigning King in the year 1890 and installed Kulachandra as the King of Manipur. The rise of such a powerful prince in the eastern most corner of India was considered as a threat to the British Supremacy and the British decided to "chopping the tall poppy". Lord Landsdowne regarded this act of indiscretion on the part of Tikendrajit as a great offence. It also gave an opportunity to the British to interfere in the internal affairs of Manipur. Mr. J. W. Quinton arrived in Manipur on 22nd March, 1891and he asked the Maharaja to hand over Tikendrajit to him as desired by the Governor General of India. The British launched an undeclared war against the Manipur and massacred many people and burnt many houses, which angered the masses. The mob fury led to the death of Mr. Grimwood, the Political Agent. In course of the skirmish, which took place in the palace campus, Quinton himself and a number of British officers were put to death. On receipt of this news the British Government decaled war against Mnipur and sent three columns of troops to Manipur from Kohima, Silchar and Tamu. To save their motherland, the Manipuris fought very bravely under the direction of Tikendrajit. But it was all in vain against the superior might and arms of the British. On 27th April, 1891 the British occupied Manipur. Tikendrajit was arrested and after a farcical trial by a general court-martial, he was publicly hanged at Pheida Pung presently Bir Tikendrajit Park (B. T. Park) on 13th August 1891. Eyewitness accounts said that thousands of crying women rushed in to stop the execution. His family members were sent to Sylhet as internees for 10 years.

THANGAL GENERAL : General Thangal was one of the most prominent heroes of the Anglo-Manipur war 1891. Some of the Naga tribes of Manipur claimed that he was originally a Naga converted to Hindu and absorbed into the Meitei Community. Meitei Scholars asserted that Thangal was a Meitei. His real name was Kangabam Chitananda Singh. He was born in the Ningthouja clan. His father's name was Kangabam Kshetri Singh, and his mother's name was Thokchom Chanu Puinu of Wangkhei Angom Leikai. He was born in 1806. He had been introduced at the Court of Gambheer Singh at an early age. Once he accompanied the Maharaja in an expedition against the Thangal village inhabited by Naga Tribes. He was given the name in memory of the event. (Rajkumar Sanahal Singh, Thangal General, 1979). Thangal General served under four kings- Maharaja Gambheer Singh, Maharaja Chandrakirti, Maharaja Sucrchandra and Maharaja Kulachandra. He became popular since the period of Maharaja Gambheer Singh. During the period of Chandrakirti Maharaja, Thangal Major was the most powerful member of the Durbar. He was very loyal to Maharaja Chandrakirti and his sons. The posts held by him were Hajari, Apanba Sanglakpa, Laiphamlakpa, Nunehanjaba, Commandant of the Tuli Naha Regiment of the Manipur Army with the rank of Menjor (Major), the highest military rank, the Avapurel, Minister in charge of Burmese affairs, a Minister of the Durbar and later a General etc. He was both feared and respected by successive British Political Agents in Manipur. The Political Agents respected him for his wit, intelligence and wisdom. He was about 85 years of age when he was hanged.

However, things changed after the death of Chandrakirti Maharaja in 1886. In the palace revolt of 1890. Yubraj Tikendrajit and Thangal drove out

Surchandra, the reigning King and installed Kulachandra as a new ruler of Manipur. This gave an opportunity to the British to intervene in the affairs of Manipur administration. The Government of India deputed Quinton and his associates, who were executed under the order of Thangal General. The British declared war against Manipur. The British defeated Manipur in the Anglo-Manipuri war of 1891.

Thangal General surrendered to the British on 7th May 1891. A special court sentenced him to death for waging war against the Queen and abetment of the murder of British officers. On the evening of 13th August, 1891, he was hanged with Tikendrajit. The bravery of General Thangal at the moment of his hanging was vividly described by one British officer Lt. Col. Alban Wilson in the following words: - "Thangal pretends to be too ill to walk up the gallows, and he was carried up in a chair and placed beneath the noose...A sergeant of gunners, who was executioner tapped the Thangal General on the shoulder and said, "Now then, old man, stand up or I can't hang you".

Thangal gazed at him blankly, and then at the interpreter who translated the remark, on which the old fellow shook his head and roared with laughter. The interpreter said, "Sir, he will not rise". The Sergeant said, most persuasively "just tell the old gentleman I'm not going to hurt him." This too, was translated but Thangal would not budge. Then ensued a most ghastly pause, whilst a man climbed up to the top of gallows to lengthen the rope, and when it was adjusted, both criminals were loosened off." He was a man of undaunted courage, unwavering conviction and unflinching faith. The patriotism and heroism of Thangal General is still remembered by the people of Manipur.

MAHARAJA KULACHANDRA DHAJA

Maharaja Kulachandra Dhaja, was the second son of Maharaja Chandrakirti and Chongtham Chanu Naha Lukeswari. He accompanied Chandrakirti Maharaja in the Zila Durbar in August, 1874 when Lord North Brook, the Viceroy and Governor General held a durbar on board the Viceroy's yatch at Cachar. Tikendrajit and General Thangal rebelled against the reigning King Surchandra who had abdicated in favour of his half-brother Kulachandra Dhaja. Kulachandra ascended the throne of Manipur on 23rd Sept. 1890. By temparament he was a man of noble and mild manners. According to Meitei Puya "Kulachandra Singh always tried to adjust his brothers with one another. He promised to his father before his death that he would always be amicable with his brothers. When he became the King of Manipur, he tried to distribute the land to the landless people." But unfortunately with the coming of Mr. Quinton to Manipur, war broke out.

After the war of Independence 1891, Maharaja Kulachandra was arrested on 8th May, 1891, and was tried before a special commission under the presidency of Lt. Col. St. John Mitchell on charge of waging war against the Queen Empress and transported for life with forfiture of property. He was deported to Port Blair in 1891 and was released from there in 1895 and was residing at Hazaribagh. On release from Hazaribagh, he spent the rest of his life at Radhakund (Vrindaban) and he died on 26 January,1934 at Radhakund.

PRINCE ANGOUSANA SENAPATI

Prince Angousana Senapati (see Plate-80) aged 25 years son of Maharaja Chandrakirti Singh and Queen Haobam Chanu. During the period of Maharaja Surchandra he was Dolairoi Hanjaba. According to the statement of Angou Senapati "I have been Senapati since October 1890, i. e. about one month after Kulachandra became Maharaja". Angou Senapati fought against the British on 24th March, 1891. He was arrested on 18th May, 1891, by the British.

A Special court comprising

1. Lieutenant Colonel St. John Fancourt Mitchell, Asst. Adjutant General as president,
2. Major Richard Kirly Ridgeway V. C. Commandant 44th Gurkha Rifles as member and
3. A. W. Davis Esq. Indian Civil Service Deputy Commissioner, Naga Hills as member

was constituted for trying the Manipur Princes. Angousana, Senapati was tried by the Special Court from 17th to 22nd June 1891 and found him guilty of waging war against Queen Empress of India and abetment of murder of Mr. Quinton, Colonel Skene, Lieutenant Simpson, Mr. Cossins and he was sentenced to death but his sentence was later commuted to transportation for life with forfeiture of property. He was deported to Port Blair in 1891 and was released from there in 1896-97 and was detained as a political detenue at Hazaribagh on pension. (Administrative Report of Manipur, Political Agency for 1896-97).

Kajao Pukhramba Phingang

Kajao alias Pukhramba Phingang, son of Chaoba Singh of Langoljam Leikai of Kangamong village aged 35 years (born in 1855). He dressed himself in red colour as his favourite colour. That is why people called him "Puhramba Phingang". He joined Borachaoba Singh son of Maharaja Nara Singh in the rebellion against Maharaja Surchandra on 20 May, 1886 and was in the jail. He was released by Jubraj Tikendrajit from jail in September 1890 and appointed as a Jamadar. After the Durbar in the palace on the night of 24 April 1891 he speared to death Mr. Grimwood, the Political Agent on the steps leading to the Durbar House as he did not want the Sahibs to interfere in the administration of Manipur. He did not have any enimity with any particular Sahib. During the trial on19 May, 1891, he said : "..... we were all excited and the crowd was shouting kill...kill kill. I raised my spear and speared a Sahib at the foot of the steps leading to the Durbar House. I cannot say what Sahib this was". He was tried by the Chief Political Officer Manipur Field Force. He was sentenced to death. He was hanged on 25th May, 1891 at 7 a. m. 1891 at the Central Jail. He was 35 years of age when he was hanged.

Niranjan Subedar

Niranjan Subedar, aged 39 years was the son of Daria Singh Chetri of village Tikuamoh. He was an ex-army (Shiphai) of the 34th Native Infantry. He left the Britishers and joined the native force of Manipur and later appointed as Subedar by the Tikendrajit Yubraj. He was tried by the Chief Political Officer, Manipur Field Force and was sentenced to be hanged by the neck for assisting the Manipuris against the British. The sentence was confirmed by the officer Commanding Manipur Field Force and the Government of India. He was hanged on 8th June, 1891at the Central Jail.

Lokendra Birjit Singh, Wangkheirakpa

Lokendra Birjit Singh, Wangkheirakpa, son of Singh Dhaja Senapati of Kangjeibung Mapal, aged 43 was a prominent man. He fought against the British on 24th March 1891 and attacked the western face of British Residency and also subsequently fought against the British troop at Thoubal. He was arrested on 9th July 1891 and tried by the Chief Political Officer, Manipur Field Force. He was transported for life to Port Blair in 1891 with forfeiture of property and was released from there in 1896-97 and died shortly after his arrival at Nuddeca (Vide No. 1690 E. from Deputy Secretary to Government of India, to General Officer Commanding, Manipur Field Force, dated the 20th August 1891 and Administrative Report of Manipur, Political Agency for 1896-97).

Colonel Maisnam Samu Singh

Colonel Maisnam Samu Singh, alias Luwang Ningthou of Arambam Nityainanda Leikai, aged 60 years was one of the prominent officers of the Maharaja. He was the son of Maisnam Gourshyam Singh and younger brother of Kumudini Maharani. During the reign of Chandrakirti, he was the Selungbahal (Senior Selungba) and on 1st January, 1870, he was appointed as Major and later as Colonel in the Manipuri Army. He and Wahengbam Major caught 29 elkephants at Leimatak. In 1874, he caught one elephant from Konyang Lok. During the reign of Maharaja Surchandra, he was awarded with three Paris (hectare) of land and nine Phirans (flags). On 7th October, 1886, he was appointed as Luwang Ningthou, which gave him magisterial power throughout the valley. He was one of the members of the Manipur State Durbar. In December, 1887, he was sent to receive Frank St. Clair Grimwood along with his wife with 11 elephants at Bishnupur. On 20th March, 1891, he accompanied Angou Sana to receive Mr. J. W. Quinton at Sekami. On 22nd March, he accompanied the Maharaja to attend the Durbar at the residency. When the infuriated crowd began to throw stones and spears at the British officers, he called out the people to desist and Giridhari Singh and Angom Ningthou placed themselves in front of the British officers to save them. On 24th March 1891 when fighting went on between the British troops and armed forces of Manipur State, he was in command of the guard at the firing point of Southern Gate of the fort. He was tried by the Chief Political Officer, Manipur Field Force and was sentenced t death on the charge of Waging War against Queen Empress of India and abetment of murder of British Officers. The Governor General in Council commuted the capital punishment and he was transported for life to Port Blair, Andaman and Nicober (Kalapani) with forfeiture of property in 1891 and was released from there in 1896-97 and lived the rest of his life at Vrindaban. (Administrative Report of Manipur, Political Agency for 1896-97)

Chongtha Mia Singh Major

Chongtha Mia Singh, Major was son of Badrian of Lalambung, aged 50. He fought against the British troops on 24th and 25th March 1891 when the British troops attacked the Palace to arrest Tikendrajit Senapati and later at Thoubal as a leader of Manipur Force. He commanded Manipuri troops at Khongjom and resisted the advance of Tamu column on 25th April 1891. He was arrested at Thoubal. He was later tried by the Chief Political Officer, Manipur Field Force from 5th May to 12th May 1891 and sentenced to death for waging war against the Queen Empress. The order was confirmed by H. Collett, Major General Commanding, and Manipur Field Force on 12th May, 1891. But the sentence of death was commuted to one of transportation for life by order of Government of India. But he was released from Penal settlement of Port Blair, Andaman, in the year 1897. In the year 1898 on 28th October he applied to the British Government requesting for grant of Rs. 100/- (Rupees one hundred) for his maintenance. At that time he was at Radhakund, The Government of India agreed to his prayer regarding the grant of Rs. 100/- (Rupees one hundred) for his maintenance also ordered to reside anywhere in India except in Manipur. Accordingly Chongtha Mia Singh resided at Radhakund and after some time, he left Radhakund for Tripura and died there.

Chongtham Nilamani Singh, Ava Purel

Chongtham Nilamani Singh, Ava Purel Major, son of Kala Singh of Nongthonbam Leikai, aged 55 years was in charge of Burmese affairs (External affairs) and was in command of the Maharaja's bodyguard and of the citadel, after the conquest of Manipur by the British. He was arrested on 9th May, 1891. He was tried by the Chief Political Officer, Manipur Field Force and sentenced to death but subsequently transportation for life to Port Blair, Andaman and Nicober Islands (Kalapani) with forfeiture of property. He died at Vrindaban in the year 1897.

Uru Singh Usurba

Uru Singh, Usurba, son of Churamani Singh of Kabo Leikai. Lalup Chingba was attached to the Top Guard. He was one of the sentries who marched Mr. Quinton, Chief Commissioner of Assam and other British Officers on the night of 24th March, 1891 to the scene of their execution. He was tried by the Chief Political Officer, Manipur Field Force in May, 1891 and convicted of transportation during the pleasure of the Government of India. He was deported in 1891. He was released from the Andamans in July, 1906 and was allowed to settle in the district of Darang. (Vide Secretary to Government of India's No. 1653 E. dated the 18th August 1891, to General Officer Commanding Manipur Field).

Chaoba Hida Machahal

Chaoba Hida Machahal, son of Guna Singh of village Ningombam was one of the sentries who marched the Chief Commissioner of Assam and other British Officers to the scene of their execution on the night of 24th March, 1891. He was tried by the Chief Political Officer, Manipur Field Force and sentenced to death on the charge of murder of British Officers, but commuted to transportation during the pleasure of Government of India vide Vide Secretary to the Government of India's No. 1653 E, dated the 18th August 1891 to the General Officer Commanding, Manipur Field Force. He was deported in 1891. He was released from the Andamans in July, 1906 and was allowed to settle in the district of Darang.

Ghuna Singh Khongdram

Ghuna Singh Khongdram, Lalupchingba son of Lilaiba of Wangkhei, aged 50 years was at the Top-Guard and he was one of the eight Sentries who marched Mr. J. W. Quinton, Chief Commissioner of Assam and other British Officers viz. Colonel Skene, Lieutenant Simpson, Mr. Cossins to the scene of their execution on the night of 24th March, 1891. He was tried by the Chief Political Officer and sentenced him to death on 6th July 1891. But the order was later commuted to transportation during the pleasure of the Government of India. He was deported in 1891. He was released from the Andamans in July, 1896 and was allowed to settle in the district of Darang.

Kumba Singh, Laishraba

Kumba Singh, Laishram, son of Kajao of Yumnam Leikai, aged 27 years was a Sipahi and one of the sentries who marched the British Officers viz. Mr. J. W. Quinton, Chief Commissioner of Assam, Col. Skene, Lieutenant Simpson Mr. Cossins to the scene of their execution. He was tried before the Chief Political officer, Manipur Field Force and sentenced him to death. But the order was commuted to transportment for life. He was deported in 1891. He died at Port Blair on 17th December, 1894.

Dhaja Singh Mayengba

Dhaja Singh, Mayengba son of Dharma Singh of Mayengbam Leikai, 33 years of age was a Sipahi and one of the sentries who marched the four British Officers including Chief Commissioner of Assam on the night of 24th March 1891 to the scene of their execution. He was tried by Major Maxwell, the Chief Political officer, Manipur field Force, and sentenced him to death. The order was commuted to transportation during the pleasure of Government of India. He was deported in 1891. He was released from the Andamans in July, 1906 and was allowed to settle in the district of Darang (vide Administration Report of the Political Agency, Manipur for 1906-1907).

Nani Singh, Nepra Machahal

Nani Singh, Nepra Machahal, son of Kumba Singh of Yambem Leikai, aged 28 years was one of the sentries who marched the four British officers on the night of 24th March, 1891 from the Durbar Hall to the scene of their execution. He was tried along with other sentries by the Chief Political Officer, Manipur Field Force and sentenced him to death for the murder of British Officers. The order of capital punishment was commuted to transportation for life during the pleasure of Government of India (Vide Secretary to the Government of India's No. 1653 E. dated the 18th August, 1891 to the General Officer Commanding, Manipur Field Force). He was deported in 1891. He was released from the Andamans in July, 1906 and was allowed to settle in the district of Darang.

Trilok Singh

Trilok Singh, Nongthonba Satwal, son of Kala Singh of Kabo Leikai, aged 60 years was Satwal or Head of Lanmees who carry out executions. He was tried by the Chief Political Officer, Manipur Field Force and passed order on 6th July 1891 for putting to death four British Officers viz, Mr. J. W. Quinton. Chief Commissioner of Assam, Colonel Skene, Liutenant Simpson and Mr. Cossins. The sentence was commuted to transportation during the pleasure of the Governor General in Council (Vide Telegram to 1609 E. dated Simla the 11th August 1891 from the Secretary to the Government of India. Foreign Department to the Secretary to the Chief Commissioner of Assam). He was deported in 1891.

Dhana Singh Sagolsemba

Dhana Singh, Sagolsem, son of Anandram of Waikhom Babaji Liekai, Khongang Pheidekpi, aged 50 years was the man who actually beheaded the Chief Commissioner of Assam and other British Officers. Detail of the actual execution are now available in the Manipur State Archives. Two public executioners namely Wokramba and Leisangthemba came to call him. Sagolsem Dhana Singh used a "TENDONG THANG"- a long handled, heavy bladed sword for the execution. He stood in front of the two Kangla Sha facing north while the Britishers were brought out one by one. The Britisher was in a standing position in front of the Kangla Sha facing west while Sagolsem Dhana faced North. Two of the Britishers was beheaded in one blow of the sword, while two Britishers needed two blows of the sword to decapitate their heads. He was tried by the Chief Political Officer, Manipur Field Force and convicted of the death which sentence had been commuted to transportation during the pleasure of the Governor General in council.

Ningthouba Singh

Ningthouba Singh, Chingsuba Jamadar, son of Bir Singh of Kabo Leikai, aged 41 years was dispatched up the Kohima Road after fighting began on 24th March, 1891 between British troops and Manipuris to reinforce the Manipuris outposts. He was present when the last volley was fired into the Chief Political Officer. Manipur Field Force and was sentenced to transportation for life on 6th September, 1891 on the charge of (1) Waging war against the Queen and (2) Murder of Signaller O'Brien of Telegraph Department. He was deported in 1891. He was released from the Andamans and was permitted to live in the state in 1901-1902 (vide Administration Report of the Political Agency, Manipur for 1906-1907)

Thaoba Singh Phanjao Jamadar

Thaoba Singh Phanjao Jamadar son of Angao Singh of Kabo Leikai, aged 40 years was in Mayangkhang when Mr. O'Brien Signaller of the Telegraph Department was killed. He was tried and sentenced to transportation for life on the charge of (1) waging War against the Queen and (2) Murder of Signaller O'Brien on 25-3-1891. He was deported in 1891. He was released from the Andamans and was permitted to live in the state in 1901-1902 (vide Administration Report of the Political Agency, Manipur for 1906-1907).

Tonjao Singh Mangsataba Jamadar

Tonjao Singh, Mangsataba Jamadar son of Chaotol Singh of Kabo Leikai was tried and charged with waging war against the Queen and for the murder of Messrs Melville and O'Brien sentenced to transportation for life. He was deported in 1891. He was released from the Andamans and was permitted to live in the state in 1901-1902 (vide Administration Report of the Political Agency, Manipur for 1906-1907).

Chaobatol Singh, Heigrujamba Subedar

Chaobatol Singh, Heigrujamba Subedar, son of Pangandong of Kongmapan, aged 62 years was in command of the party of Manipuri troops sent up the Kohima road on 24th March, 1891. He was charged with waging war against the Queen and for the murder of Messrs Melville and O'Brien of Telegraph Department at Mayangkhang and sentenced to death on 6th September, 1891 which sentence was commuted to transportation for life. He was deported in 1891. He was released from the Andamans and was permitted to live in the state in 1901-1902 (vide Administration Report of the Political Agency, Manipur for 1906-1907).

Paradhumba Singh Ashangba Khut

Paradhumba Singh, Ashangba Khut, son of Tonjaoba Singh of Wangkhei was a Havildar of Mayangkhang outpost and was on duty on 24th, 25th and 26th March, 1891. On receipt of orders from the Maharaja of Manipur to arrest British subjects and if they resist to kill them. He collected Nagas from Mayangkhang village to carry out the orders before the arrival of the Jamadars and Subedars. He was tried before the court of the Chief Political officer, Manipur Field Force and sentenced to transportation for life on the charge of murder of Signaller O'Brien of Telegraph Department. He was deported in 1891. He was released from the Andamans and was permitted to live in the state in 1901-1902 (vide Administration Report of the Political Agency, Manipur for 1906-1907).

Chowkami Naga of Mayangkhang

Chowkami Naga was present during the attack on Mayangkhang Bunglow when the Sinaller O'Brien was killed. He was also with Chirai Naga when the latter killed Mr. Melville, the Superintendent of the Telegraph Department. He was tried and sentenced to transportation for life on 7th March, 1892 on the charge of (1) murder of Signaller O'Brien and (2) abetment of murder of Mr. Melville. He was deported in 1891. He was released from the Andamans and was permitted to live in the state in 1901-1902 (vide Administration Report of the Political Agency, Manipur for 1906-1907) (Vide Secretary to the Chief Commissioner's No. 1822 dated 23rd April, 1892).

Gowho Naga of Mayangkhang

Gowho Naga was present during the attack on Mayangkhang Bunglow when the Signaller O'Brien was killed. He was also with Chirai Naga when latter killed Mr. Melville, the Superintendent of the Telegraph Department. He was tried and sentenced to transportation for life on 7th March, 1892 on the charge of (1) murder of Signaller O'Brien and (2) abetment of Murder of Mr. Melville. He was deported in 1891. He was released from the Andamans and was permitted to live in the state in 1901-1902 (vide Administration Report of the Political Agency, Manipur for 1906-1907).

Chirai Naga alias Chirai Thangal

Chirai Naga / Chirai Thangal son of Chunba Naga of Mayangkhang aged 30 years was put to trial by the Chief Political Officers, Manipur Field force for the attack and murder of the Telegraph officers at Mayangkhang viz

W. B. Melville and O'Brien. On 25th April 1891 after the execution of the five Britisher at Kangla a column of Manipuri troops under the leadership of– Ashangba Khut, Poila came to Mayangkhang. When the Manipuri troops reached Mayangkhang, the villagers told that two British Offficers of the Telegraph Deptt. were staying in the Mayangkhang Dak Bunglow. When the Manipuris fired volleys of shots, Mr. O'Brien was instantly killed but W. B. Melville escaped with his rifle under cover of darkness. A big search was mounted in the nearby jungle. Chirai Naga found W. B. Melville near a stream wounded. He was killed and his head cut off by Chirai Naga and brought to the village as a Trophy.

Chirai Naga was arrested and tried by the Political Officer of the Manipur field Force from 3rd August, 1891 to 6th September, 1891 and hanged on 13th Oct. 1891, inside the jail.

Ghuna Singh Indujamba Jamadar

Ghuna Singh Indujamba Jamadar, son of Sajouba Singh of Sagolband aged 42 years was present when the last volleys were fired by Nagas and Manipuris into the Mayangkhang Dak Bunglow where Mr. O'Brien was killed. He was tried by the Chief Political Officer, Manipur Field Force and the court was of the opinion that he must have been present from the very beginning. Under these circumstances he was transported for life for waging war against the Queen and murder of Signaller O'Brien of Telegraph Department (vide No. 2093 E. dated the 22nd October, 1891, from the Under Secretary to the Government of India, to the Chief Political Officer, Manipur). (Source: Manipur Who is Who 1891, published by Manipur State Archives in 1990)

MAHARAJA CHURACHAND SINGH (1891-1941 AD or 3289-3339 MF)

On 19th April, 1891, Mr. H. M. Durand, the Secretary to the Government of India conveyed the proclamation of Her Majesty, the Queen Empress of India that "the authority of Kulachandra Singh was declared to an end and the administration of the state was assumed by the General Officer Commanding Her Majesty's Forces in Manipur territory and that the Governor General in Council will make known hereafter the name of the person selected to rule the state and the conditions under which he will be invested with power". After the British conquered Manipur on 27th April, 1891 AD, there was no King.

As soon as the British troops occupied Manipur, the officer commanding the field force issued an order of disarming the whole population of Manipur. The British authorities collected about 400 firearms. When the

British occupied Manipur, Major Maxwell was, under instruction from Government of India looking after the administration of the state as the Superintendent.

Slavery persisted in Manipur until 1891. Major Maxwell (see plate 87) counted 1331 slaves of the King excluding the slave population in the individual households. The Maharaja of Manipur possessed several thousand slaves, some of whom he occasionally gave as presents to his favourites and his subjects were permitted to buy and sell them.

The British wanted to put somebody who would be loyal to the British on the throne of Manipur. They wanted a king who would acquiesce to their colonial administration, so they denied the Kulachandra's or Surchandra's family the right to the throne. The Britsh selected a young boy as a king from the descendants of Raja Nar Singh. After studying the genealogy of the Kings of Manipur, Major Maxwell asked Pandit Sarangthem Jugol Singh about the details of the descendants of Raja Nar Singh. He sent Angom Ningthou to bring the four sons of Moirangthem Chanu Latamanjuri–Drumba Singh, Dimbon Singh, Chandrahas and Churachand along with their horoscopes. Moirangthem Chanu Latamanjuri was the wife of late Chowbiyaima, grandson of Nar Singh. Their horoscopes were consulted and compared by the astrologers. Major Maxwell saw some qualities and courage in the youngest son Churachand, a boy of eight years, who was sitting without any sign of timidity or fear on seeing the British Officers. His date of birth was 12th May, 1883. Churachand was declared as the King of Manipur on 12th Langban, 1891(September). His grand father Moirangthem Ramanand was made Moirang Ningthou. On hearing this news, Thangjam Chanu Chitrabati (Numitsija), the second wife of Chowbiyama brought her only son Digendrajit to Major Maxwel along with the horoscope. Seeing the good qualities of Digendrajit, Major Maxwell decided to send Churachand and Digendrajit for education outside Manipur. Digendrajit was only some months older than Churachand.

Articles of the Sanad

Mr. H. M. Durand, the Secretary to the Government of India conveyed the Sanad vide Government of India, Foreign Department Notification No. 1862 E, dated Simla, the 18 September 1891 of the Governor General in Council as under :-

- Churachand was granted the title of Raja of Manipur and a salute of 11 guns "The Chiefship of Manipur, the title and salute will be hereditary in his family and will descend in the direct line by primogeniture provided that in each case the succession is approved by the Government of India".

He and his successor would pay an annual tribute to the British Government.

"The permanence of the grant conveyed by this Sanad will depend upon the ready fulfilment of all orders given by the British Government with regard to the administration of the territory, the control of hill tribes dependent upon Manipur, the composition of armed forces of the state and any other matter in which the British Government might be pleased to intervene". "So long as his house was loyal to the Crown and faithful to the conditions of this Sanad, he and his successor would enjoy the favour and protection of the British Government".

Investiture ceremony and abolition of slavery and Lallup

The investiture ceremony was held on 29th April, 1892 (Friday) at 4. 30 P. M. in presence of about 8000 people with the 43rd Gurkhas presenting the guard of honour and 11 gun salute. All the Chiefs from hills and valley were required to give their allegiance to the Raja. On this day, Major Maxwell announced abolition of slavery that "all persons present in slavery to private individuls shall cease to be slaves in five years from 29th April, 1892 or any previous date on repayment of the purchase money". Lalup was a compulsory or forced labour rendered by all adult subjects to the King for ten days out of every 40 days. The service might be in the form of military duties or developmental or economic work like contstruction of road, working in King's estate etc. Those who rendered Lalup service need not pay revenue. The Lalup system was introduced by King Loiyumba in 1110A. D. King Loiyumba, in his edicts known as "Loiyumba Shilyen" divided Manipur into six adinistrative units known as Lup (Pana). Each Lup sent a team of workers who were to work for the state. Each team was called Lalup (Lalup means war organization, lal= war, lup= organisation). Women were exempted from Lalup. Similarly, the blacksmiths, goldsmiths, carpenters were exempted. The Poltical Agent declared on 29 April, 1892. that this Lalup system was abolished. Instead of Lalup, an uniform house tax of Rs. 2 per year was levied. A land revenue of Rs. 5 per Pari was levied. In the hills, a house tax of Rs. 3 per year was levied. Major Maxwell appointed one Chowkidar for every 100 houses on a remuneration of two Sangams of paddy field (half of one Hectare) to each Chowkidar. Each Chowkidar was given a belt with identification sign, which would give him the power to exercise his authority in the villages. He appointed four Lakpas and four Muhori–to be in charge of collecting taxes from each Panna. Each Lakpa was given 25 Paris (Pari=Hectare) of land and each Muhori was given four Paris of land. In the hill areas, Lambus were appointed giving them proper identification signs. Major Maxwell also appointed 400 men as police personnel to help him in the maintenance of law and order. He also established Cheirap (Criminal court) and Panchai (Civil Court) by appointment of five members in each court. Each member of the Cheirap was given 50 Paris of land and each member of the Panchai was given 25 Paris of land.

Construction of a new palace (see plate-89) and Govindajee temple were started at the vacant land of "Leisangthem Ingkhol" previously occupied by Avapuren Major, Chongtham Nilamani. On the 14th Mera, 1892, Sanatombi, daughter of Maharaja Surchandra by Sapam Chanu Jasomati eloped with Major Maxwell, the Political Agent and stayed at the Residency as his wife leaving her husband Nongmaithem Manikchand. Since the Meiteis have not yet recovered from the trauma of defeat and subsequent subjugation, this incident was looked upon as disgusting and shameful by the Meiteis. Her mother destroyed all the Chaphu-Uyan (earthen pots) saying that her daughter had died.

The place where Churachand was born was named as "Sana Janmasthan". When Churachand attained 11 years, the Political Agent, under instruction from the Government of India, sent Churachand and Digendrajit to Ajmer on 23rd Ingel (Monday), 1895 for formal education. The aim of education was "to make Churachand a practical ruler contented with his position and surrounding and willing to spend his life in the management of his state". Churachand and Digendrajit came back to Manipur after five years of education. A Durbar was held with Churachand as the head of the state where all the Cheirap and Panchai members were present. Major Maxwell took Churachand for a Durbar to Delhi along with 13 Polo players.

In 1901, Lord Curzon, the Governor General of India visited Manipur. On 27th July, 1904, a Raas Lila was played with Sanatombi as "Makokchingbi" by erecting a mandop in the courtyard of the Bungalow of the Political Agent. Many people resented that playing the Raas Lila at the courtyard of a British Agent violated the traditional sanctity of the Raas Lila.

Churachand Maharaja married Ngangbam Ningol Ibemcha, daughter of Ngangbam Jugol Singh at the Rajbari on 17th March, 1905(Administrative Report of the Political Agency, 1904-1905). In course of time, queen Ibemcha became famous as Ngangbi Maharani.

Handing over of administration

The administration of Manipur was handed over to Raja Churachand on 15 May, 1907 at the age of 22 years. (see plates-93. 94. 95). He was asssisted in his administration by a State Durbar comprising of eight Durbar members. He was the president of the Durbar. The Vice President was a British ICS Officer from Eastern Bengal and Assam cadre. Besides them, there were six Manipuri members. On the occasion of the Raja's formal installation, Sir Lancelot Hare, Lt. Governor of Eastern Bengal and Assam read out the *kharita* from His Excellency, the Governor General. Raja Churachand occupied the new palace on the 21st of Wakching (Wednesday), 1908. On the same day, the statues of Gonvindajee, which was lying at Khongman was again enshrined in the Govindajee temple. In 1916, One British ICS Officer was made the President of the Durbar.

Administration of Hill areas

The day to day administration of the entire hill areas was entrusted to a member of the Durbar, the Vice President. The objective is the effective control of hill tribes. This was done to facilitate the day to day administration of hill areas and not to undermine the power of the King. According to clause 14 of the Rules for management of the state of Manipur, it was written "The hill tribes are administered by the President assisted by one or more of officers on the Highness's behalf in accordance with the rules approved by the Government of Assam". Here some section of the people claimed that the hills were not under the King quoting this example. That is not true. The claim of some section of the people is therefore misleading and deceitful. The only communication between the tribal population and the Vice President was the Manipuri Lambus who were something like peons or messengers The British recognized the tribal chiefs who enjoyed considerable powers and privileges within their chiefdom.

The main objective of the British was to collect house taxes and exact forced labour (Pothang) through the tribal chiefs. The second hidden objective of the British was to make mass conversion of the hill people into Christianity. The Pothang was of two types–Pothang Bekari and Pothang Senkhai. According to Pothang Bekari, the people were under obligation to carry goods or baggage for the officers touring the hill areas without any payment or to make bridges or roads and build new bunglows without any payment. According to the Pothang Senkhai, each household was to subscribe money, chicken, eggs or other domestic animals to feed the touring officials free of cost. The chiefs assumed two important judicial roles – first as an interpreter of customary laws and secondly as judges whithin their respective chiefdom.

First World War

The outbreak of the First World War in Europe was a turning point in the history of Manipur. On 1st August, 1914, Germany declared war at 1910 hours against Russia. On 4th August Britain declared war against Germany as the Germans rejected their ultimatum requesting their troops to leave the Belgian soil. The First World War had been described as a "war to end all wars" Raja Churachand gave whole hearted support to the British during the war. The Maharaja had donated Rs. 134,000 as a war loan to the British authorities. He donated an aeroplane and two amubances. In addition to this, he raised the Manipur Labour Corps with 2000 Nagas and Kukis and they were sent to France in May, 1917 much against their will to dig tunnels. The Raja again proposed to recruit another labour corps compring of mainly the Meiteies and the Kukis for service in Egypt. This has led to the outbreak of Kuki Uprising (1917-1919) (see Chapter-15, Historical Landmarks).

Award of C. B. E

In recognition of his service during the First World War, Raja Churachand was conferred the title of C. B. E in December, 1917 "(Sir Robert Reid, History of Fromtier Areas Bordering Assam") and later on given the title of "Maharaja" in 1918.

Cholera Epidemic

Cholera epidemic known as Pukchatpa or Anaba Achouba occurred three times during the reign of Churachand. The 1894 epidemic killed 6054 people including the wife of Capt. Cole, Political Agent. The 1908 epidemic killed 12491 people and the 1924 epidemic killed 7327 people.

Visit of Governor General to Manipur -1931

Lord Irwin, the Governor General of India visited Manipur in 1931. He was given a rousing reception by erecting gates with specially decorated arch. Ovewhelmed by the scenic beauty of Manipur, Lord Irwin was pleased to name Manipur as "Switzerland of India".

Award of K. C. S. I

On the 1st January, 1934, Maharaja Churachand was awarded K. C. S. I. (Sir Robert Reid, History of Frontier Areas Bordering Assam)

Misunderstandin between Churachand and his son, Bodhchandra

In the month of Sajibu,1934 Bodhchandra, son of Churachand Maharaja went to worship Lord Thangjing and Ayangleima at Moirang along with Chinglen Keirungba, Sanajaoba, Amudon and others when Maharaja Churachand was on pilgrimage at Nabadwip. On his return journey, he went to the Umanglai "Oknarel Thangnarel". One Pungfai Maibi predicted that Bodhchandra would become the Maharaja of Manipur after his father. All the people were very happy. On the next day, Bodhchandra organized a "Sankritana procession" on the streets of Ningthoukhong with a large number of people. All the people were very happy and they used fireworks to celebrate the occasion. Somebody misinformed the Maharaja Churachand on his return from pilgrimage that Bodhchandra was collecting people to revolt against the King. Maharaja Churachand suspected him for attempting to ascend the throne through invocation of a sylvan deity when he was away on pilgrimage to Nabadwip.

All the people who joined the procession were called up by the Maharaja and they were beaten by the sepoys on the order of the Maharaja. All the ring leaders were detained as a punishment at the palace for three days. On the third day, a case was filed in the Manipur State Durbar to punish them. The case was tried by the Political Agent. The statement of all the people were taken. When the truth came out that they were just celebrating Sankritana procession without any evil intension, they were all released by the Political Agent However the Maharaja Churachand was not happy with the decision. Seeing the moods of his father, Bodhchandra went to Kashi (Benaras) as "Self Exile" along with his wife Ram Piyari from Orissa. After spending for about three years in Kashi, he came back to Manipur in the month of Mera in 1937. However, Ram Piyari continued to stay at Kashi. After some years she died at Kashi.

Some developmental Works of Maharaja Churachand

- One hydro-electric plant was commissioned at Imphal.
- One water supply plant was commissioned in 1920.
- Three more High schools – Churachand, Tombisana and Tamphasana (1939) were established.
- The Johnstone school was upgraded into a high school.
- More roads were constructed and metalled.
- Treatment of diseases and control of epidemics were brought into scientific lines. Manipuris were sent for training in medical science.

- The first Manipuri doctor appeared in 1924. His name was Dr. Thokchom Gobardhon Singh.
- Donated two bells—each weighing about six mounds to the Govindajee temple.
- Donated gold plates to cover the two domes of the Govindajee temple.
- Opening of police stations in various parts of the state.
- In 1924, students from Manipur can appear at the Matriculation examination under the Calcutta university with Manipuri language.
- Meiteilon was introduced in the Nata Sankirtana.

The Government of India Act-1935.

The Government of India Act, 1935 was one of the most important events in the history of India. The provincial part of the Act, which went into effect automatically, basically followed the recommendations of the Simon Commission. As a result of several previous Government of India Acts and Round Table Conferences, the Government of India Act 1935 was finally introduced. It changed the Federation of India in the aspects of the structure of government, legislation, and so on. It granted Indian provinces autonomy and provided for establishment of India Federation. Direct elections were introduced and the right to vote was increased. The Government of India Act, 1935 established a foothold toward modern India. The Government of India Act, 1935 is important because it is one of the foundation stones of the current Republic of India.

The Government of India Act 1858 was the first Act to be introduced. It was an Act of the Parliament of the United Kingdom. After the Sepoy Mutiny in 1857, the British Government took over administrative powers from the British East India Company. The British East India Company had to transfer its function because of the provisions of the liquidation. As a result, India became a formal crown colony. The Government of India Act 1909 is generally known as the Morley-Minto Reforms. The Act of 1909 was important because it allowed the election of Indians to the various legislative councils for the first time. It laid the groundwork for the parliamentary system. The Government of India Act 1919 incorporated the dual form of Government, referred to as a diarchy. The Government of India Act 1919 lasted for 10 years, from 1919 to 1929.

Through the three Round Table Conferences, British India and the Princely States could be integrated into the federated Dominion of India. However, Congress and the Muslims had different opinions on the structure of this federation. "This lack of agreement left the British Government free to draft legislative proposals (the white paper) in line with its own views. The British Government let the Joint Committee under the Chairmanship of Lord Linlithgow, to formulate the new Act of India. The Committee comprised of both members of the House of Commons and House of Lords and representatives from British India and the princely states. The Committee came out with the draft Bill on February 5, 1935 and the House of Commons reviewed it. Finally, the Government of India Act 1935 was proclaimed in July, 1935.

Burma was separated from India and enacted a separate constitution as a result of the Act The Government of India Act 1935 was closely related to a Dominion Constitution. The Act provided that the Indian Federation would include Princely States. This scheme came close to success, but was abandoned in 1939 as a result of the outbreak of the Second World War. By 1939, the Congress' official stance was that the princely states must enter independent India, on the same terms and with the same autonomy as the provinces of British India, and with their people granted responsible government. As a result, it insisted on the incorporation of the princely states into India in its negotiations with Mountbatten. Thus the question of merger of princely states was decided as early as 1935 under this Act. But seeing the trend of events that followed in Manipur, it appeared that this act was not discussed in Manipur during Churachand Maharaja's time.

Political Consciousness :

The political consciousness of the people started in 1930 with the formation of the Nikhil Hindu Manipuri Mahasabha. Later on the word "Hindu" was dropped. Hijam Irabot (see plate-98) was elected as the President of the Nikhil Manipuri Mahasabha in its fourth annual session held at Chinga. The Mahasabha demanded :-

- a full responsible government of Manipur
- administration of hill and valley of Manipur
- release of Rani Gaidinliu
- abolition of feudal levies.

Hijam Irabot demanded abolition of the Manipur State Durbar which was composed of nominees of the King. Manipuir State Durbar declared the Mahasabha as a political party and directed all the Government servants who were associated with the Mahasabha to resign. Hijam Irabot also resigned from the government service.

Several movements led by Hijam Irabot sprang up in the demand for self rule of Manipur against the British Government. Hijam Irabot was born on Wednesday, the 30th September, 1896 in a poor family at Pishum Oinam Leikai, Imphal His father had died while he was in the cradle and his mother also died while he was still very young. He was brought up by his paternal aunt. He was educated at the Johnstone School. In 1922, he edited the first Manipuri journal named "Meitei Chanu". He married Khominsana, daughter of Chandrahas Singh, elder brother of Maharaj Churachand Singh. He was appointed as a judge of the Sadar Panchayat and given all the feudal privileges of a noble.

In 1938, about 356 leading citizens of Manipur submitted a petition to the Maharaja requesting him to establish a Legislative Council and also to nominate the members of the Durbar from among the members of the Legislative Council. In 1939, the Nikhil Manipuri Mahasabha submitted another petition requesting the Maharaja to establish a Unicameral Legislature of 100 members, 80 to be elected and another 20 to be nominated by the Maharaja.

On 12th December, 1939, the Nupi Lal was started. Hijam Irabot converted the Nupi Lal (Women's Agitation) into a political movement aimed at the end of British rule in Manipur. On 7 January, 1940, he was arrested and sentenced to three years imprisonment for giving a public speech. Inside the Imphal jail, he agitated for improving the living conditions of the prisoners. Although, the authrorities brought about some reforms, he was transferred to Sylhet jail where he was influenced by Marxist ideology. He became a communist while in jail and through one Biresh Mishra, he came in contact with the Communist Party of India.

Pangka Dharma

During the reign of Churachand Maharaja, the Brahma Sabha, who enjoyed the support and backing of the King imposed many rules and regulations on the ignorant Meiteis.

1. Since the arrival of Hindusim, the seven Yeks of the Meiteis were categorized into seven Gotras of Hindusim like Shandilya, Kashyap, Gautam, Atreya, Bharadwaj(Naimis), Madhugalya and Vathistha.
2. Utmost respect should be given to the Brahmins. The Meiteis should prostrate before the Brahmins wherever and whenever they met.
3. The Meiteis cannot marry Brahmin girls whereas the Brahmins can marry Meitei girls.
4. A Brahmin cannot take food prepared by Meiteis whereas Meiteis can take food prepared by Brahmins.

5. In the marriage ceremony, the Brahmin Purohit should be first adorned with clothes and wealth to beg his blessings. In case the Brahmin purohit is not available, one of his sons or descedants should be offered the position.
6. The Brahmins are not allowed to plough the field, to work as blacksmith or goldsmith or carpenter etc.
7. All the collections of offering from Saradha (death ritual) or any other ceremonial offering to the deities should be offered to the Brahmin.
8. The Brahmins should be respected. Even if a Brahimin commit murder, he should not be given capital punishment. He should be banished from the kingdom in other words, he should be allowed to return to his orginal home.
9. The dead body of the child below 24 months should not be burnt but should be buried. The dead bodies of any person above 24 months should be burnt and Saradha ceremony should be performed on the 14th day from the day of death.
10. The Saradha ceremony should be perfomed by the Brahmin Purohit and all the worldly requirements such as utensils, clothes, furniture etc should be offered to the Brahmin Purohit so that the soul may go to heaven.
11. The Meiteis were not allowed to speak in the Brahma Sabha. They should hire some Brahmin to speak on their behalf in the Brahma Sabha.

The treatment meted out to the Meiteis by the Brahmins were discriminatory and unacceptable. The Meiteis tolerated only for fear of the King. But the kings was always in favour of Brahmins. At this juncture, Thongbam Yumjao introduced the Pangka Dharma to save the Meiteis from the onslaught of the Brahmins particularly at the time of death rituals. He was popularly known as Thongbia because of his surname. He was living in the Thongbam Ingkhol (present Chief Minister's residence) at Babupara. He shifted his house to Thongju at the age of around 45 years due to acquisition of his land by the British Government.

He did not preach for a separate religion. He remained a Hindu but he advised his followers to perform initiation for the outgoing soul at the time of death irrespective of young and old into Beiragya Dharma or Sannyas order, that means "Dharma of a renounced monk" or "Lamboiba" at the very moment of departure of the soul. Then the soul is beyond the bindings of the Veda or Brahmanical religion. The soul is free from all worldly ties, no desire for anything. Hence, for the Saradha ceremony of the renounced monk's departed soul, no offering of material property and no rules and regulations are required. He argued that for satisfaction of those who attended the funeral and the family members, simple ceremony like hearing of holy book and simple religious songs can be performed with least expenditure. For those who want to perform the Saradha ceremony on the 14th day, they can do so to satisfy their ego but no purohit is required. He divided his groups in various smaller groups known as Pangkas (Leikais). But the Brahmins called them "Pangkots" means "fools". The popularity of the Pangka system increased day by day. People were happy with the new found religious freedom. One day a young boy of about 13 years named Kendrosana son of Thongbam Ningol Ningthemcha ongbi Pachasija died due to drowning at the Pechu Pukhri. Thongbia had given Beiragya Dharma to the young boy. Taking advantage of this, some Brahmins reported the matter to Brahma Sabha. Mayambunghal, elder brother of Churachand summoned Thongbia to the Brahma Sabha. The Brahma Sabha was held on 8th day of Langban (Friday), 1923 under the Presidentship of Mayambunghal in presence of hundreds of Brahmins. Thongbia hired one Brahmin named Sirigurumayum Madhop Sharma to speak in the Brahma Sabha as he was not allowed to speak in the Brahma Sabha. The main question asked to Thongbia was "How and why the Beiragya Dharma was given to a child ignoring the Vedic principles". Thongbia replied that Dhruba and Pralhad realised God in their early childhood and then why not others?

No Brahmin member in the Brahma Sabha could raise argument against this point. The President asked the Brahma Sabha again and again to raise argument against this point of Thongbia yet no one could raise their head. Mayambungahal remarked "What were prevalent before should be followed". This remark was interpreted in both ways. The Brahmins claimed that they had won the case whereas Thongbia claimed that he had won the case. Thongbia continued his activities as before. News reached Churachand Maharaja. Thongbia organized Jatrawali (Shumang Lila) to propagate the message of Beiragya Dharma and also Kajilila, Gourlila, Udhukhon etc. The Pangka group of Hindus therefore, enjoyed the freedom of religion, freedom of faith, freedom of social status without fear for anybody. The King was helpless and he could not suppress the popularity of Pangka sect of religion. (K. C. Tensuba Sannyas and Thongbia, All Meditators Association, 2002)

Mangba –Sengba Culture of Maharaja Churachand

However, Maharaja Churachand was notorious for his Mangba–Sengba culture which was the root cause of division between the Meiteis and the hill people. This culture has ruined not only the relationship between the valley people and hill people but also ruined social status of the Meiteis.

During 1913-1941, many hill tribes came to the Manipur palace with a request to allow them to convert to Meitei Hindu. But they were required to pay Rs. eightyfour, three sikees, one anna and six pai as a tax to the Maharaja, which was a lot of money for the common people in those days. Thus this Mangba –Sengba culture was a cause of irritation to both the Meiteis and hill people. It was not only the hill people who suffered but also the Meiteis at the hands of the Maharaja on account of Mangba –Sengba.

There was one highly powerful Brahma Sabha. The Brahma Sabha encouraged and supported the Maharaja to sustain this Mangba –Sengba culture. This Brahma Sabha or the King can label anybody whom the King did not like for no fault of his as untouchable (Mangba). If someone had been declared as "Mangba", he and his family are forbidden to mix with their relatives, neighbours or community members. If anybody is found to be mixed with him, again the person will be labeled as "Mangba". This was a gross social injustice and most severe punishment. Again such "Mangba" men can be cleansed by paying a fine of Rs. 80 one Sikee and one Pai to the King. If he can not pay, he had to remain as "Mangba" for the whole life. That was the ugliest part of the Mangba culture. Like this, he made it compulsory for everybody to put Chandal paste (Chandal thinba) on his or her forehead after paying certain fees. Those who could not pay the fees were not allowed to put the Chandal paste on his / her forehead. People who could not pay the fees to the King could be easily identified during social functions as he / she did not put the Chandal paste on his or her forehead. He also made it compulsory for some people including tribal to carry the palanquin of the king and his nobles. Sometime people carrying the palanquin were beaten or kicked for going too fast or too slow. Like this, he introduced some oppressive measures like Pach Napet, Yarek Santri, compulsory provision of food for Amins and Peons by the people etc.

One can visualize why Maharaja Churachand adopted such evil practices. One theory was that almost all his powers have been snatched away by the Political Agent and he was almost without any work. He did not like to be regarded as a powerless King in the eyes of his people. So he adopted such evil practices to show to the people that he still had the power to punish the people. Moreover, it gave him some revenue. During his days, the Mangba–Sengba was so strict that many people committed suicide. Such kind of "Mangba–Sengba" culture did not disturb the usual normal administration of the country. So, the Political Agent did not interfere

One of the the pitfalls of Maharaja Churachand was that he appeared like a stooge in the hands of the British. He was not as powerful as any other king in the past. He served largely as a cultural symbol rather than an administrator.

There were widespread dissatisfaction among the people during the reign of Churachand Maharaja as eveident from the two Nupi Lals revolting openly against the State administration (1904 and 1939), outbreak of Kuki Uprising during 1917-1919 and also Zeliangrong Movement under leadership of Jadonang and Rani Gaidinliu during 1930-1949 (see Chapter-15: Historical Landmarks), repeated occurance of Cholera epidemics and Mangba–Sengba Culture. Naoria Phullo from Cachar also came out strongly to revive the Sanamahi religion.

Murder of Digendrajit

Immediately after the Nupi Lal, on 22nd March, 1940, Digendrajit, Mayambung macha was murdered at about 11 A. M. when he was supervising digging of a pond in his homestead at Rajbari. Digendrajit was a Panchai member at the time of his death. He was sent to Ajmer along with Churachand for education. One Heisnam Gopal came to Digendrajit very often in Ngabong phi with a request to help him in a criminal case for about three months. On this fateful day, Digendrajit was sitting in a relaxed position talking with one Gurumayum Lalabi Sharma. Heisnam Gopal arrived as usual, he took out a sword from inside his "Ngabong phi" and beheaded Gurumayum Lalabi and then stabbed Digendrajit several times. He then ran towards the palace. He was pursued by Khuraijam Tombimacha Sija, wife of Digendrajit shouting to arrest the murderer all the time. When they were nearing the Manipur palace, Heisnam Gopal turned and tried to stab Tombimacha Sija. Hearing the voice of Tombimacha Sija, Panchami Jamadar came out from the Manipur palace. In trying to rescue Tombimacha Sija, he got stab wounds from Heisnam Gopal. He was immedtaley arrested and put him to prison. (Sarangthem Bormani Singh, Meitei Ningthourol, 2000). Inside the prison, he shouted to everyone that he was just carrying out the King's order. Although the Nupilal had subsided, the Manipuri women were still very active at that time. They had fond memories about Digendrajit, who had provided them plenty of rice during the scarcity of rice on the eve of Nupilal. The women demanded that the murderer of Digendrajit should be immediately executed in public. People were asking the question "Why did Gopal, the murderer was running towards the palace after commiting the murder and why he was saying that he was just carrying out the King's order". It is said that the women gathered at night, took out a procession and shouted "Utilmanba Ningthou .... Meehatpa Ningthou" around the Manipur palace. In order to subside the increasing tension, the King ordered that the murderer should be paraded in and around the market place. He was thus put in some sort of guillotine on bullock cart and paraded him in the market place. His throat was reportedly tied with a rope so that he could not speak out anything. Immediately after parading him, he was hanged to death. There was however, a widespread rumour that Digendrajit might have been murdered at the instigation of Maharaja Churachand as the King saw Digendrajit as a constant threat to his throne. The descendants of Digendrajit claimed that he was due to become King very soon and only the decision was to be announced within 4-5 days. Probably, there might be tension between the Maharaja Churachand and the Political Agent, Mr. Christopher Gimson, who saw the increasing unpopularity of Churachand Maharaja.

Churachand Maharaja was much troubled by the failing relationship with the Political Agent. In 1941, one day, the Maharaja suddenly started his journey in his private car for Nabadwip with a determination not to come back to Manipur along with few of his family members without informing the Political agent. When they were halting for the night at Mao Dak Bunglow, the Political Agent, Mr. Christopher Gimson catched up with him at Mao and had a long discussion. On his way to Nabadwip, he spent some days at Shillong and then proceeded to Nabadwip. He decided to spend the rest of his life at Nabadwip. However, he did not abdicate his throne. Maharaj Churachand died on 17th Hiyangei (16th November, Thursday) 1941 at 9. 20 P. M. at Nabadwip. (Sarangthem Bormani Singh, Meitei Ningthourol, 2000)

According to tradition, a Manipuri King can have five queens. The title of these five queens were :

1. Leimaren (Maharani).
2. Apambi Ahal (Rani).
3. Leimakhubi Ahal (Rani).
4. Apambi Naha (Rani).
5. Leimakhubi Naha (Rani).

(M. K. Binodini, Churachand Maharj gi Imung, 2008)

Maharaja Churachand had ten queens. Two queens namely Chongtham Chanu Chetanmanjuri Tampak and Angom Chanù did not have any issue. He had six sons and eleven daughters (M. K. Binodini, Chuarachand Maharaja gi Imung, 2008):-

Leimaren (Maharani) Ngangbam Chanu Ibemcha Ngangbi Maharani (Dhanamanjuri) - four daughters- Tamphasana, Angousana, Sanatombi, Binodini (see plate-103)

Rani Chingakham Chanu Shyamasakhi (Apambi Ahal) – Bodhachandra, Priyobarta, Khedasana

Rani Ngangbam Ningol Priyosakhi (Leimakhubi Ahal) - Joy Singh, daughters Chamusana and Radhasana

Chongtham Chanu Ibemma Chetanmanjuri Tampak (Apambi Naha) – she died on 7th June, 1959 (Thursday) at the age of 63 years without leaving any issue.

Haobam Chanu Ilabati (Leimakhubi Naha)–Lokendra and daughter Bhabinisana.

Ngangbam Chanu Sakhitombi –Maisnam Chanu Subadani – Maipaksana, daughter Sanatombi.

Chingakham Chanu Apanbi – Kamanding.

MAHARAJA BODHCHANDRA SINGH (1941-1955 AD or 3339-3353 MF):

After the death of Maharaja Churachand, his eldest son Bodhchandra became the King of Manipur with Ishori Devi, the eldest daughter of Ramraj, Yubaraj of Ramnagar (Champram) as Leima or Maharani on 18th Hiyangei, 1941 (Friday) (21 November, 1941). He married Ishori Devi on Thursday, the 18th June, 1941 at Calcutta. He had inherited all the political and social problems which were started during Churachand Maharaja's time.

Second World War and Manipur

The first bombing of Imphal by the Japanese Tojo during the Second World war took place on Sunday, 10 May 1942 at about 11 A. M at various localities, namely, Nungyungbi, Khuyathong, Menjorkhul, Thangmeiband, Chingmeirong, Mantripukhri, Koirengei airstrip, etc. The afternoon of 10 May, 1942 wore a ghostly look of Imphal as people left their homesteads for the countryside in search of safety and shelter. In the south, the Pallel/Kakching airstrips were also bombarded. However, the British and their Indian engineers repaired the damages quickly every time. On 16 May (Saturday), Keisampat, Wahengbam Leikai were bombarded and many people were killed and wounded. On 10 April, 1943, Khurai Tellipati, Khomidok were bombarded. More than 100 people were killed and many houses were burnt due to bombing when people were enjoying Utshop at the Khurai Chingangbam Mandop.

Martial Law was promulgated in Manipur and the King's powers were forfeited during the war. The World War II started on 1st September, 1939 when a German force of 53 divisions supported by 1600 aircraft invaded Poland.

The Japanese army attacked Imphal continuously, and the British and its Allies resisted fiercely. When the Japanese crossed over to Burma from Siam (Thailand) in March, 1842, lakhs of Indians, Burmese and Europeans fled from Burma and transit refugee camps were organized at Koirengei.

The prices of essential commodities inceased more than ten times the original price. The small Leimram village was attacked and bombarded by the Royal Airforce planes on suspicion that some Japanese soldiers had taken shelter there. The bombing of Imphal and Manipur valley continued for almost two years. Imphal inhabitants had run away to different villages, which is still remembered as "Japan Lanchenba" or running away from the Japan war. At first, the Japanese made rapid advance but their supply of essential items were cut off and this forced them to beg for food from villagers. One Bheigya Singh of Irengbam village help Mr. Simoda, a Japanese soldier of 33rd Mountain Gun Regimen during such a crtical time. He survived the war and after four decades, he came all the way from Japan to pay homage to those who died in Manipur. He visited Irengbam village and happened to meet the same Bheigya Singh. Simoda embraced Bheigya Singh in gratitude and wept like a child.

According to oral history narrated by war veterans, two Japanese soldiers disguised themselves as local workers (the British employed a large number of local inhabitants as labourers and housekeepers) and stole an aircraft from the Pallel airstrip. The Indian National Army (INA) used aeroplanes to drop leaflets informing the people that the Japanese and the INA were in fact friends of India and that they were trying to free India from Britain. They had to show the picture of Netaji Subash Bose with Mahatma Gandhi. By that time Manipur already had a large number of followers of Gandhiji's Indian National Congress and they knew about Netaji Subash Bose's earlier role in the Congress Party. Finally, several locals joined INA, and underground movements started. The British army immediately collected all leaflets by offering large sums of money to those who were loyal and would bring it to them. The theatre of the second world war took place at Maibam Lokpa Ching, near Nambol keithel. In August, 1945, both the Japanese and the Allied Forces were locked in deadly combat using tanks, field guns and mortars. The Japanese were outnumbered in terms of men and machine. Instead of surrendering, they sacrificed their lives. Incidentally, the wife of the Japanese soldiers gave birth to a son on the day her husband died. The child now fully grown came to Manipur and offered flowers at the site where his father and compatriots died. He took away a lump of earth from this sacred spot.

Several members of the Manipur Mahasabha and leaders from the hills and plains were rounded up at the Langthabal military camp. Thus, INA led by Netaji Subash Chandra Bose for the first time on 14 April 1944 hoisted the Indian National (tricolor) flag at Moirang, 45 km south of Imphal at Tiddim road. (see Chapter- 15: Histprical Landmarks)

Remission of the annual tribute of Rs. 50,000

The people of Manipur provided their full support and cooperation to the British in fighting and driving away the Japanese during Woprld War-II. In recognition of the service rendered by the Maharaja Bodhchandra Singh and the people of Manipur, the annual tribute of Rs. 50,000 payable to the British Government was remitted in perpetuity in 1945 by His Majesty, King Emperor George.

IRABOT'S STRUGGLE FOR A RESPONSIBLE GOVERNMENT

After his release from jail in 1943, Hijam Irabot came upto Mao but he was not allowed to enter Manipur Hijam Irabot (see Plate- 100) went to Cachar and lived there for three years. He was suspected of having colluded with Netaji Subhas Chandra Bose to wage war against the British. He was again arrested under the Defence of India Rule in 1944 and put him in Silchar jail for eight months. After his release from jail, he contested election from Silchar constituency to the Assam Provincial Legislative Assembly as a CPI (Communist Party of India) candidate. He was defeated by a narrow margin.

In 1946, Irabot returned to Manipur. Irabot wanted an independent Manipur with full responsible government elected by the people with the King remaining as a constitutional head. He also wanted establishment of Gram Panchayat in every village, one school in every village, free compulsory primary education, one dispensary for every village, post office in the villages, payment of war compensation etc. On 12 and 14 May, 1947, the Hindustan Standard of Calcutta published a news item that U Aungsan, the Vice President of the Burmese Interim Government and father of modern Burma might visit Manipur and that Manipur wanted to merge with Burma. The Manipur State Congress alleged that Communist Irabot had connived with the Burmese. Irabot was in contact with the Manipuris in Mandalay and some of the Burmese Communists. It is said that the British Government had already given their green signal in the year 1935 to Maharaja Sir Churachand Singh for the State of Manipur to join with the Dominion of Burma (now Myanmar) when it was being carved out by separating it from the British India.

Irabot wanted to preserve the integrity of Manipur. In November, 1947, he convened a meeting of all political parties in hills and valley. Many organizations such as Tangkhul Long, Kuki National Assembly, Kabui Association, Khul Union, Mizo Union, Manipur Praja Sabha, Manipuir Krishak Sabha, Meitei Marup and Nongpok Apunba Marup attended the meeting. The meeting demanded for a full responsible government. In the mean time, the Government of India took precautionary measures to suppress any communist uprising in Manipur. On 12 September, 1948, a shooting incident happened at Pungdongbam in which a police officer was killed. The incident happened during a scuffle between the police and the party workers of Irabot when the workers were coming for a public meeting at Imphal against the proposed creation of Purbanchal. The Interim Government issued a warrant to arrest Irabot. The Government banned Praja Sabha, Krishak Sabha, Mahila Sanmelini and Communist Party. All party workers went underground. Irabot also went underground. However, he continued to publish his weekly "Anouba Jug" and issued press notes and memoranda to the government from underground. The Government announced a reward of Rs. 10,000 for his arrest. (N. Joykumar, Towards Freedom and Integration, 1938-1949). In 1950, Irabot organized the peasant revolution but all his prominent party workers like Thokchom Boro Singh, Mohendro Singh, Benoy Singh, M. Megha and others were arrested and put in jail. The police atrocities were very strong. People believed that Irabot went to Burma to seek the help of the Burmes Communist for starting a revolution for an independent Socialist Republic in Manipur. Irabot organized a conference for the three quarreling communist parties of Burma namely the Communist Party of Burma, Burma Communist Party, Peoples Comrade Party, which decided to form a united front against the Burmese Government. The conference agreed to give back the Kabow valley and Ungo Ching on the west of Chindwin river to Manipur. It is said that Irabot started regular administration over some areas of Kabow valley. However, after three years of self exile, he died at Tangbo village in the Kabow valley on 26 September, 1951. Nowadays, people are asking the question- why did Hijam Irabot ran away fearing for a mere police arrest if he were a true leader? Why did he not return to Manipur till his death if he loved Manipur ? Why did he not face the hardship and atrocities of the police for the sake of the country if he were a true leader?

Here one may remember the biography of Simon Bolivar, the liberator of Bolivia Simon Bolivar was expelled five times from the South American soil and he fled five times during 1812 -1816. He was literally ridiculed, defeated and alone but was determined to return home. He returned five times and won his first victory at Boyaca in August, 1819. Bolivar led the independence movements of several Latin American countries, notably in what was known as Gran Colombia, which includes the modern nations of Colombia, Venezuela and Ecuador. Bolivar had a dream of forming a sort of United States of South America, which never came to pass. Venezuela declared its independence from Spain July 5, 1811, beginning its wars against that country. In 1812, Spanish forces defeated the Venezuelan revolutionary army, ending the first phase of the revolutionary war. After his defeat in the Venezuelan War of Independence in 1812, revolutionary leader Simón Bolívar fled to New Granada. He later returned with a new army, and the war entered an increasingly violent phase. Bolívar's forces invaded Venezuela from New Granada in 1813, waging a campaign with a ferocity captured perfectly by their motto, "war to the death". Bolívar's forces defeated the royalist army in a series of battles and entered Caracas on August 6, 1813. With loyalists displaying the same passion and violence, the rebels achieved only short-lived victories. In 1814, royalist forces reinforced by new *llanero* (cowboy) recruits and led by José Tomás Boves lost a series of battles to Bolívar's forces but then decisively defeated Bolivar at La Puerta on June 15, 1814 and again defeated Bolívar's army at Aragua in August 18, 1814. Bolívar and other leaders then fled to New Granada.

A large military expedition sent by the Spanish forces in that year reconquered Venezuela and most of New Granada. Yet another invasion led by Bolívar in 1816 fails miserably. Bolívar returned to Venezuela in December 1816, again leading a largely unsuccessful insurrection against Spain in 1816-18. In 1819, Bolívar's forces from Venezuela crossed the Andes into New Granada in June-July 1819. At Boyacá August 7, his army of 2,000 defeated a Spanish and colonial force of 3,000. On August 10, 1819 Bolívar's republican forces took Bogotá. The Congress of Angostura then elected him the first president of the Republic of [Gran] Colombia. Bolívar returned to Venezuela in April 1821, leading an army of 7,000 from New Granada. At Carabobo, June 24, his forces decisively defeated Spanish and colonial forces, winning Venezuelan independence. Bolívar was now president of Gran Colombia and Peru. Only a small section of the continent in Upper Peru was still defended by royalist forces. The liberation of this region fell to Antonio de Sucre, and, in April

1825, he reported that the task had been completed. The new nation chose to be called Bolivia after the name of the Bolivar, the Liberator.

MOVEMENT FOR A RESPONSIBLE GOVERNMENT IN MANIPUR

The growth of political consciousness in Manipur started late. Before 1938, there was no political organization in Manipur. There was only one organsiation called the "Nikhil Hindu Manipuri Mahasabha" established in 1934 under the chief patronage of the Maharaja of Manipur. The Nikhil Hindu Manipuri Mahasabha in its fourth session on 29 and 30 December, 1938 changed the name to "Nikhil Manipuri Mahasabha" and the Maharaja declared it to be a political party. The request for the introducing reforms in Manipur had been made in 1938. In 1939, Hijam Irabot established a new party called Praja Samelani, which had become involved in the second Nupilal for which Hijam Irabot was imprisoned. In the mean time, the Nikhil Manipuri Mahasabha headed by Lalita Madhop Sharma started working in collaboration with the king and British authorities.

The popular vigour of this movement was heightened by the "Nupi Lal" which began on 12th December 1939.

The people led by Nikhil Manipur Mahashabha demanded a responsible government in 1939 defying prohibitory laws with full vigour.

In 1945, a new party named Praja Sangha Party was established with the following objectives :-

- achievemnent of independence of Manipur
- abolition of feudal rule
- establishment of a responsible government
- introduction of adult universal franchise based on democracy
- introduction of a classless society.
- integration of people lving in hills and valley.

At this time, there was a peasant society known as "Krishi Samelan" to look after the grievanves of the peasants.

In 1945, Irabot demanded a responsible form of government. He regenerated political organization like Praja Samelani, Praja Sangha, Mahilla Samelan, etc. Their main objectives were :-

- abolition of the colonial and feudal rules,
- establishment of a responsible Government,
- achievement of independence,
- introduction of adult universal franchise in Manipur.

On 16 May, 1946, this society was converted into a political organsation and the name had been changed to "Manipur Krishak Sabha". This was the only peasant-based political oirganisation in Manipur. On 4 October, 1946, the Nikhil Manipuri Mahasabha had been converted into Manipur State Congress Party at a meeting held at the Aryan Theatre, Imphal. Later on, this party had become an unit of the All India Congress Committee. All the members of the Nikhil Manipur Mahasabha became members of the Manipur State Congress Party. Many members from Praja Sangha, Krishik Sabha also joined the Manipur State Congress Party. Later on, the Praja Sangha Party became the Manipur State Communist Party. All former INA members also became members of the Manipur State Congress Party. The main objectives of the Manipur State Congress party was as follows:-

1. establishment of a responsible government
2. abolition of social injustices of the feudal rule

Later on, the members of the Manipur State Congress Party started fighting among themselves for their selfish ends. Maharaj Bodhchandra abolished "Pothang or Forced Labour", removed the traditions of "Mangba –Senga", allowed the Yaithibis to attend the court. In the mean time, the Congress members were all busy thinking about how to get the handing over the king's power to them. They were greatly influenced by the stories of Gandhi's struggle for India's freedom, non-violence and civil disobedience movement. They are looking for every opportunity to go to hartal. All the educated and rich people were attracted to the Manipur State Congress Party. Even the followers of Hijam Irabot who did not believe in Communism joined the Manipur State Congress Party. India's national flag, Khadi dhoti and Gandhi Cap became very popular. The Congress members proudly displayed their Khadi dhoti and Gandhi cap in every occasion. They were working in collusion and under supervision of the Indian National Congress and the State People's Conference, which is the Congress Party of Princely States. They boasted that they are the only elite, educated group in Manipur who knew the Manipur Politics very well and therefore tried to poke their nose in every matter.

When the Britishers were preparing to leave after India achieved independence, Maharaj Bodhchandra wanted to establish a separate administrative unit of his own.

On 21 September, 1946, he asked the British Authorities to allow him to make a royal proclamation regarding the new administrave reforms of his state. Mr. Gimson, the political agent requested the Maharaja ro supply a draft copy of the proclamation. On 30 October, 1946, the Maharaja explicitly expressed his desire to establish a democratic system of government with an elected Advisory Assembly constituted by the representatives of both hills and valley. However, instead of accepting the demands of the political parties for establishment of a responsible government, the Maharaja provided some "Administrative Rules" explaining the relationship between the state Durbar and the Maharaja and the powers of the individual members of the State Council.

On 1 November 1946, the Congress Party submitted a memorandum to the Maharaja and urged him to make a royal proclamation for establishment of a legislative assembly based on the democratic principles in Manipur. The Maharaja could sense the increasing influence of democratic movement in India and the mood of the people.

On 12 December, 1946, the Maharaja constituted a "Constitution Making Committee" to draft a constitution for governance of the state. The Constitution Making Committee under the chairmanship of the President of the Manipur State Durbar comprised of -

1. three members from the Durbar nominated by the President of the Manipur State Durbar
2. One member from the Palace nominated by the Maharaja
3. One representative deputed by each Tahshil circles from the three Tehshils in the valley
4. One representative each from Ukhrul, Mao, Tamenglong, Churachandpur and South East Areas.

Every political party was given opportunity to take part in the preparation of the Constitution of the state.

On 21 January, 1947, the Election Committee was formed with S. Somorendro Singh, Jail member of the Durbar as chairman and 14 other members. On 12 and 14 May, the Hindustan Standard of Calcutta carried a news item that U. Aungsan, the Vice President of the Burmese Interim Government and father of modern Burma might visit Manipur and Manipur wanted to merge with Burma. This news item created a lot of political controversy in Manipur and the Congress Party alleged that Irabot Singh, who used to visit Burma quite often might have connived with the Burmese. The Communist Party of India of which Hijam Irabot is also a member supported the merger of Manipur with Indian Union. However, Irabot was strongly against merger with India. It was reported that the reason why Irabot Singh went to Burma was to seek help of the Burmese Communists in staging a revolution for an independent Socialist Republic in Manipur. The Indian National Congress did not directly participate in the politics of a princely state of Manipur. However, the Manipur State Congress was connected with the All India State Peoples Conference, which wanted Manipur to be merged with India.

On 1 July,1947, the Manipur State Durbar which was established in 1907 was abolished and it was named as Manipur State Council. All former Council members were re-designated as ministers. The President of the Council was redesignated as Chief Minister. On 15 July, 1947, Mr. Pearson, ICS President of the Manipur State Durbar became the Bodchandra of Manipur. He was soon replaced by the Maharaja Bodhchandra. (N. Joykumar Singh, History of Modern Manipur edited by Lal Dena page-152)

During the first half of July, 1947, Krishna Mohon and Dwijamani had given their names to the Chief Minister for inclusion of their names as ministers. This episode was strongly objected by some members of the Congress including Salam Tombi Singh, Dr. Ningthujam Leiren, Thokchom Achou, Tompok Singh, Laishram Achou etc. The move was supported by Lalita Madhop Sharma, Dwijamani Sharam, Jugeswar Singh, Krishnamohon Singh etc. The decision of the meeting had led to the split of the Manipuir State Congress–one Congress Party head by Bhubonsana, another part headed by Tompok Singh.

On 27 July, 1947 the draft constitution was submitted to the Maharaja. However, the Maharaja, instead of implementing the demands of the political parties, founded an interim government in Manipur.

On 15 June, 1947, the Indian National Congress adopted a resolution that they could not admit the right of any state in India to declare its independence and to live in isolation from the rest of India. As a first step, they asked the Maharaja of Manipur to sign the Instrument of Accession and the Stand Still Agreement under which only the responsibilities of Defence, Communication and External affairs were to be looked after by the Government of India. The Agreement was signed on 11 August, 1947.

INDIAN INDEPENDENCE ACT OF 1947

The Indian Independence Act 1947 was the legislation (10 and 11 Geo VI, c. 30) designed by the Prime Minister Clement Attlee, passed and enacted by the British Parliament that officially announced the Independence of India and the partition of India. The Act received royal assent on July 18, 1947.

The legislation was formulated by the British Government of Prime Minister Clement Attlee, after representatives of the Indian National Congress, the Muslim League, and the Sikh community came to an agreement with the Viceroy of India, Louis Mountbatten, on what has come to be known as the *3 June Plan* or *Mountbatten Plan.*

Indian independence Act was passed in June 1947, which specified the follows:

1. The British rule of India should be over on the midnight of August 15,1947.
2. An independent dominion of India shall be created out of the United Provinces, Central Provinces, Bombay Presidency, Madras Presidency, the Carnatic, East Punjab, West Bengal, Assam and the Northeast Frontier Agency. The territories of the Andaman and Nicobar Islands, and the Lakshadweep Islands are also turned over to the Indian Dominion.
3. Subject to the provisions of subsection (3) (4) of this section, the territories of India shall be the territories under the sovereignty of His Majesty which, immediately before the appointed day, were included in British India except the territories which, under subsection (2) of this section, are to be the territories of Pakistan.
3. An independent dominion of Pakistan shall be created out of the provinces of West Punjab, North West Frontier Province,Sindh and East Bengal.
4. The all Princely states that were officially related to British Empire were made free from all the treaties and relationships and they could decide which dominion to join or to remain independent. Lord Mountbatten thought that if the princely state remained independent within the dominion that may lead to chaos and thus made their accession a necessity of the Indian Independence Act.
5. Both the Indian and Pakistan Dominions would be members of the British Commonwealth and was allowed to leave whenever they pleased.
6. Both Dominions of India and Pakistan were completely self-governing in their internal affairs, foreign affairs and national security but the British monarch will continue to be their head of state, represented by the Governor-General of India and a new Governor-General of Pakistan. Both Dominions shall convene their Constituent Assemblies and write their respective constitutions.
7. The British monarch shall be permitted to remove the title of Emperor of India from the Royal Style and Titles. King George VI subsequently removed the tit!e by Order in council on June 22, 1948.

Lord Louis Mountbatten was the last Viceroy of India under British rules and became the Governor General of Independent India. Jawaharlal Nehru became the Prime Minister of India, Dr. Rajendra Prasad was the President and Sardar Vallabhbhai Patel was the Deputy Prime Minister of India.

Whereas the Indian Independence Act, 1947 provides that as from the fifteenth day of August, 1947, there shall be set up an Independent Dominion known as India, and that the Government of India Act, 1935 be applicable to the Dominion of India. The Government of India Act 1935, as adopted in the Indian Independence Act, 1947, provided, "An Indian State shall be deemed to have acceded to the Dominion if the Governor General has signified the acceptance of an Instrument of Accession executed by the Ruler thereof."

A few British leaders, particularly Lord Mountbatten were also uncomfortable with breaking links between independent India and the princely states. Mountbatten was also persuaded by the argument of Indian leaders such as V. P. Menon that the integration of the princely states into independent India would to some extent assuage the wounds of partition. The result was that Mountbatten personally favoured and worked towards the accession of princely states to India following the transfer of power, as proposed by the Congress.

Mountbatten believed that securing the princely states' accession to India was crucial to reaching a negotiated settlement with the Congress for the transfer of power. Mountbatten used his influence with the princes to push them towards accession. He declared that the British Government would not grant dominion status to any of the princely states, nor would it accept them into the British Commonwealth, which meant that the states would sever all connections with the British crown unless they joined either India or Pakistan. He pointed out that the Indian subcontinent was one economic entity, and that the states would suffer most if the link were broken. He also pointed to the difficulties that princes would face maintaining order in the face of threats such as the rise of communal violence and communist movements. According to the Indian Independence Act of 1947 passed by the British on 18th July, 1949, the dominion of India came in the shoes of the British crown. The Congress' stated position was that the princely states were not sovereign entities, and as such could not opt to be independent notwithstanding the end of paramountcy.

SITUATION OF MANIPUR IMMEDIATELY BEFORE INDEPENDENCE:

On 14th August, 1947, the State Council of Manipur was abolished and an interim council was established with Shri M. K. Priyobarta as the Chief

Minister (see plate-99) (Sarangthem Bormani Singh, Meitei Ningthourol, Rajesh Book Store, 2000) The other ministers were :-

Sinam Krishnamohon	-	Finance
Rajkumar Bhubon	-	Revenue
Konjengbam Gouro	-	Education and Local Self Government
T. C. Tiangkham	-	Forest and Agriculture
Major R. Khathing	-	Hill Administration and Manipour Rifles
M. Basiruddin Ahmed	-	Medical and PWD

On the night of 15th August, 1947 at 12 P. M., Mr. Gerald Pakenham Stewart, the Political Agent informed Maharaja Bodhchandra that the paramountcy of British rule in India had come to an end and he handed over the reigns of Manipur administration to Maharaja Budhchandra Singh. On 29th Thawan, 1947 (Friday), Maharaja Bodhchandra and Maharani Ishwori Devi entered Kangla and hoisted the National Flag of Manipur bearing the Pakhangba Flag in presence of all senior Officers and a large number of people Top-guns were fired 18 times by Ahongsangbam Bidhu, Top Major in honour of the transfer of power from the British Crown to the Maharaja Bodhchandra and declaration of independence of Manipur.

SIGNING OF STANDSTILL AGREEMENT AND THE INSTRUMENT OF ACCESSION

Maharaja Bodhchandra signed Standstill Agreement and the Instrument of Accession on 11th August, 1947. With the signing of these two documents, Manipur had gone one step further towards merger with the dominion of India.

STANDSTILL AGREEMENT

The Standstill Agreement confirmed that the agreements and administrative practices that existed as between the princely state in question and the British would be continued by the dominion of independent India.

Standstill Agreement is an agreement whereby two or more parties agree not to deal with other parties in a particular matter for a period of time. For example, in negotiations for a merger or acquisition, the target and the purchaser may enter into an agreement where they each agree not to solicit or embark on acquisitions from or of other parties. This allows the parties to invest more heavily into the negotiation, due diligence, and details of a potential acquisition. (see Appendix- 3)

INSTRUMENT OF ACCESSION

The Instrument of Accession was the legal document designed to provide the legal basis for future relations. It was executed by the government of India on the one hand with the rulers of each of the princely states, individually, on the other hand, who were both to be signatories. (see Appendix-2)

According to the basic tenets of the treaty:

- The Government of India would basically control only foreign affairs, defence and communications, leaving all internal issues to be administered by the states.
- The monarchs of the states that would join would be allowed to retain their property, titles and estates. They would be equal citizens of India, and fully eligible to run for public office.
- As a compensation for the loss of income, the monarchs would be compensated with a privy purse, which would be guaranteed in the future Constitution of India.

On accession by a princely state, its territories and administrations be merged into the Union of India. The rulers of the princely states were allowed to retain their hereditary titles and official residences. Depending upon their size, importance and revenue they were also allowed to retain additional properties and given privy purses (in compensation of the state's revenue which now would go to the new Union)

From June to August 15th, 1947, 562 of the 565 India-linked states signed the instrument of accession, largely due to the personal appeals and direct diplomacy of Sardar Patel, V. P. Menon and with the help of Lord Mountbatten and Jawaharlal Nehru.

On accession by a princely state, its territories and administrations merged into the Union of India. The rulers of the princely states were allowed to retain their hereditary titles and official residences.

Thus it is clear that after signing the Instrument of Accession and the Standstill Agreement, the merger of Manipur to India is already imminient, only the formalities are left. But the political leaders and the people of Manipur of that time were probably not aware of these developments as evident from the subsequent events.

POLITICAL DEVELOPMENT IN MANIPUR AFTER INDIA'S INDEPENDENCE:

On 15th September, 1947, when Rajkumar Surendra, teacher of Gurukul School, Thangmeiband was prevented from entering the Govindajee temple with Indian National Flag and Gandhi Cap, the Manipur Congress made it a big issue. They charged the Maharaja with not respecting the Indian Flag and Gandhi Cap. They violated the Maharaja's rules concerning the Gondindajee Temple and the Manipur Palace wearing Gandhi cap and hoisting Indian National flag. They shouted slogans against the King. Sougaijam Somorendra was the leader of this "Flag and Cap Satyagrahah". Anticipating that the King would be powerless, they started showing disrespect to the king. The Flag Satyagaraha was started on 19th September, 1947. When the King declared that he did not have any intention to disregard the Indian National Flag and Gandhi Cap, the Satyagarha was closed on 24th September, 1947. (Rajkumar Maipaksana, Manipur da Ihan Hanba Satyagraha Andolon, 1996)

On 4 October, 1947, the Manipur State Congress Party adopted a resolution for establishment of a responsible government based on adult franchise before 1st April, 1948.

The Manipur State Conress Party under Elangbam Tompok started a Satyagraha on 6th November 1947. Actually it was a civil disobedient movement and it made Manipur unstable. Sougaijam Somorendra, Bankabihari Sharma, Chandrahas etc. were the leaders of the Satygraha movement. The demands were :-

- to establish an interin Government by abolition of the existing Council
- to request the Maharaja to declare the establishment of a responsible government from 1st April, 1948
- to establish a constituent assembly comprising of people's representatives, elected by the people for running the responsible government

In order to fulfil the demands, they had decided to organise non-coperation movement as follows:-

- not to cooperate with the Maharaja's State Council and its governace.
- to request the employees under the State Government to resign from their posts.
- to organise hartals to stop the functioning of schools, colleges, offices, courts, shops and markets, entertainment places, motor vehicles, bullock carts etc.
- to wilfully violate all rules and regulations of the State which are not liked by the people.
- to stop paying taxes to the state
- to establish a parallel government –by establishing a Satyagraha Panchayat in every Tehsil / Subdivision and to collect teaxes from the people.

These lines of action were approved by senior members like Elangbam Tompk, Irom Chandrahas, Kwarirakpam Giri Singh and the civil disobedient movement was started on 6 November, 1947. They established 20 different braches in different parts of the valley to carry out the movement. They shouted slogans like "Manipur Raja Gunda Hai-Bhulo Mat-Bhulo Mat". They even sent one Chandrakumar to meet Gandhi and take his blessings. Chandrakumar was directed to meet Sardar Patel, the Home Minister.

The Chief Minister of the Interim Government, M. K. Priyobarta Singh declared on 23rd November, 1947 that a responsible Government would be introduced in Manipur within six months. The civil disobedience movement was called off on 26th November, 1947.

THE FIRST ELECTION AND FORMATION OF A MINISTRY

The Manipur State Council constituted a "Francise Sub-committee" comprising of nine members with L. Ibungohal Singh as the chairman. As per rule of the Francise Sub-committee, the Manipur valley is divided into 29 constituencies and hill into 18 constituencies. Anybody who had attained an age of 21 years was eligible to cast vote and anybody who had attained an age of 25 years was eligible to contest election. Mr. R. K. Bhaskar was the chairman of the Election Tribunal and Mr. P. C. Deb was appointed as the Returning Officer on 3rd April, 1948. The first election in Manipur was held on 11 June, 1948. The Manipur State Congress, inspite of having acquired the the single largest majority could not form a ministry and a coalition ministry was formed with M. K. Priobarta Singh as the Chief Minister.

The party-wise position was as follows :

1.	Manipur State Congress	-	14
2.	Manipur Krishak Sabha	-	5
3.	Socialist Party	-	3
4.	Hill (Imndependents)	-	15
5.	Independents (Praja Shanti)	-	12
6.	Nomination		1
	Total	-	53

The Government of India deputed one Dominion Agent in place of the Political Agent. Mr. Debeshwar Sharma, the then Chief Whip of the Assam Congress Legislative Party came as the Dominion Agent. Mr. Akbar Hydari, Governor of Assam asked the Maharaja of Manipur to appoint a Dewan in place of the Dominion Agent. Major General Rewal Amar Singh was appointed as the Dewan of Manipur on 10th April, 1948. The Dominion Agent have all the powers in all relevant matters which was agreed upon between the Government of India and Manipur. Thus the Dominion Agent could play an important role in the internal politics of Manipur. If Manipur wanted to choose to remain independent, they should have resisted the appointment of Dominion Agent or the Dewan.

On 11 and 18 June, 1948, election were held in the valley areas and on 26 and 27th July, elections were held in the hill areas to elect people's representatives. The Manipur State Congress Party, inspite of having the single largest majority could not form a ministry and a coalition government was formed with Maharajkumar Priyobarta Singh (see Plate-99), younger brother of Bodhchandra as the Chief Minister. The first session of the Assembly was held on 18 October, 1948. (N. Joykumar Singh, History of Modern Manipur edited by Lal Dena–page-150-173)

The ministry had the following ministers :-

Dr. Ningthoujam, Leiren	–	Minister in charge of Education and PWD
Ayekpam Gourbidhu	-	Commerce and Industry
Arambam Ibotomba	-	Finance
Major R. Khathing	-	Minister in charge of Hills
Mr. Tebkilo	-	Forest and Agriculture
Md. Alimmuddin	-	Jail and Medical

Sougaijam Somorendro was the Opposition Leader. Immediately after defeat in the election, the Manipur State Congress party took up the cause of forming a separate province called "Purbanchal" comprising of Manipur, Cachar, Lushai Hills and Tripura, which was the game plan of Sardar Patel. They established relationships with the All India Congress Party. They invited one Dr. Prafulla Chandra Ghose, an eminent Congress Leader of Bengal to Manipur. Dr. Prafulla Chandra Ghose delivered a speech supporting the proposal of the Manipur State Congress for formation of Purbanchal Pradesh.

On 3rd July, 1949, (Sunday) the Manipur State Congress led by Jugeshwar, General Secretary of the Manipur State Congress, Salam Tombi and Loitam Yaima and their followers organized a meeting at Thoubal and advocated for abolision of kingship and merging Manipur with India. On 6 July, 1949, (Wednesday) a large meeting was organized at the playground of Wangjing L. P. School by the people of Khangabok, Tentha, Sangai Yumpham, Lamding, Wangjing, Heirok, Kairenbikhok and adopted a resolution not to abolish the kingship and not to destroy the integrity of Manipur.

On 3rd August, 1949, a resolution was taken in a big meeting opposing the movement for merger of Manipur with India and a copy of the resolution was sent to Pandit Jawaharlal Nehru, Prime Minister of India. On 25 August, 1949, the Praja Santi Political party sent a copy of the resolution opposing the proposal for merger of Manipir with India to Sardar Patel, the Deputy Prime Minister of India. On 18th September, 1949, all the leaders of hills and valley strongly opposed the proposal for formation of the Purbanchal Pradesh. Thus the idea of formation of Purbanchal Pradesh was nibbed in the bud. Later on, the Manipur State Congress Party was able to get recognititon from the All India Congress Committee and finally, it became a political unit of the All India Congress Committee.

In the mean time, the Government of India instructed the Government of Assam to complete the negotiation for merger of Manipur into India by 20th September, 1948.

SITUATION OF PRINCELY STATES IMMEDIATELY BEFORE INDEPENDENCE

The British Government announced in the Indian Independence Act 1947 that with the transfer of power on August 15th, 1947, all of these states would be freed of their obligations to the British Empire, and free to join either India or Pakistan, or choose to become independent. According to the Indian Independence Act, the territories of India shall be the territories under the sovereignty of His Majesty which, immediately before the appointed day, were included in British India.

There were approximately 565 princely states which enjoyed a special recognition and relationship with the British Raj. The princely states formed more than half of the territory of modern India, and one fifth of its population. It was clear to one and all at the time that without these states, or without even one state, India would be incomplete, fragmented and susceptible to political and social conflicts. The nation would not be united or secure, and thus independence would be tenuous at best. Lord Mountbatten thought that if the princely state remained independent within the dominion that may lead to chaos and thus made their accession a necessity of the Indian Independence Act. Moreover, on 15th June, 1947, the Indian National Congress adopted a resolution that "they could not admit the right of any state in India to declare its independence and to live in isolation from the rest of India".

Sardar Vallabhbhai Patel as Minister for Home and States Affairs had the responsibility of welding the British Indian provinces and the princely states into an united India.

By far the most significant factor that led to the princes' decision to accede to India was the policy of the Congress and, in particular, of the two key figures in the States Department, Sardar Vallabhbhai Patel and V. P. Menon.

The rulers of the princely states were not uniformly enthusiastic about integrating their domains into independent India. Some, such as the Kings of Bikaner and Jawhar, were motivated to join India out of ideological and patriotic considerations, but others insisted that they had the right to join either India or Pakistan, to remain independent, or form a union of their own. Bhopal, Travancore and Hyderabad announced that they did not intend to join either dominion. Hyderabad went as far as to appoint trade representatives in European countries and commencing negotiations with the Portuguese to lease or buy Goa to give it access to the sea, and Travancore pointed to the strategic importance to western countries of its thorium reserves while asking for recognition. Some states proposed a subcontinent-wide confederation of princely states, as a third entity in addition to India and Pakistan. Bhopal attempted to build an alliance between the princely states and the Muslim League to counter the pressure being put on rulers by the Congress. A number of factors contributed to the collapse of this initial resistance and to nearly all princely states agreeing to accede to India. An important factor was the lack of unity among the princes. The smaller states did not trust the larger states to protect their interests, and many Hindu rulers did not trust Muslim princes,.

The Congress' stated position was that the princely states were not sovereign entities, and as such could not opt to be independent notwithstanding the end of paramountcy. The princely states, it declared, must therefore accede to either India or Pakistan. In July 1946, Nehru pointedly observed that no princely state could prevail militarily against the army of independent India. In January 1947, he said that independent India would not accept the Divine Right of Kings, and in May 1947, he declared that any princely state which refused to join the Constituent Assembly would be treated as an enemy state. Other Congress leaders, such as C. Rajagopalachari, argued that as paramountcy "came into being as a fact and not by agreement", it would necessarily pass to the government of independent India, as the successors of the British.

Many princes were also pressured by popular sentiment favouring merger with India, which meant their plans for independence had little support from their subjects. The King of Travancore, for example, definitively abandoned his plans for independence after the attempted assassination of his Dewan, Sir C.P. Ramaswamy Aiyar. In a few states, the chief ministers or dewans played a significant role in convincing the princes to accede to India. The key factors that led the states to accept integration into India were, however, the efforts of Lord Mountbatten, the last Viceroy of British India, and Vallabhbhai Patel and V.P. Menon, who were respectively the political and administrative heads of the Indian Government's States Department, which was in charge of relations with the princely states.

Sardar Patel and Menon backed up their diplomatic efforts by producing treaties that were designed to be attractive to the rulers of princely states. Two key documents were produced. The first was the Standstill Agreement, which confirmed that the agreements and administrative practices that existed as between the princely state in question and the British would be continued by India. The second was the Instrument of Accession, by which the ruler of the princely state in question agreed to the accession of his kingdom to independent India, and to granting India to control over specified subject matters. The nature of the subject matters varied depending on the acceding state. The states which had internal autonomy under the British signed an Instrument of Accession which only ceded three subjects to the government of India—defence, external affairs, and communications, each defined in accordance with List 1 to Schedule VII of the Government of India Act 1935.

Sardar Patel and V. P. Menon came up with a formula to propose to the Indian monarchs. Considering that the princes had to sign away the sovereignty of states where their families had reigned for hundreds of years, and that a secure union and free nation were impossible if even one state refused to sign on. Patel and Menon were of the opinion that this was the best deal that could be put to the princes without jeopardizing India's unity and security. While negotiating with the states, Patel and Menon also worked two un-official but important points:

- The monarchs who signed willingly would be retained as constitutional heads of state
- The power would be handed over to an elected government formed by the state's people.

The accession was to be chosen by its ruling Prince, not by the population, akin to the 16th century European principle of *cuius regio eius religio*. Most acceded peacefully, except for four: Junagadh, Hyderabad, Jammu and Kashmir and Tripura.

Once signed, the state would be merged as a distinct province in India, and represented in the Constituent Assembly of India, thus becoming an active participant in the process of framing the new Constitution of India.

Five hundred and sixty two princely states were annexed with India, among which Junagadh and Hyderabad were taken over after military action. After the British announced their imminent exit from India, it became necessary to place the future relations between these states and the government of free India on a regularized legal footing.

MERGER AGREEMENT WITH OTHER PRINCELY STATES

The Merger Agreements required rulers to cede "full and exclusive jurisdiction and powers for and in relation to governance" of their state to the Dominion of India. In return for their agreement to entirely cede their states, it gave princes a large number of guarantees. Princes would receive an annual payment from the Indian government in the form of a privy purse as compensation for the surrender of their powers and the dissolution of their states. While state property would be taken over, their private property would be protected, as would all personal privileges, dignities and titles. Succession was also guaranteed according to custom. In addition, the provincial administration was obliged to take on the staff of the princely states with guarantees of equal pay and treatment.

Although the Merger Agreements were principally intended for smaller, non-viable states, they were also applied to a few larger states. Kutch in western India, and Tripura and Manipur in North-East India, all of which lay along international borders, were also asked to sign Merger Agreements, despite being larger states, following which they became Chief Commissioners' Provinces. Bhopal, whose ruler was proud of the efficiency of his administration and feared that it would lose its identity if merged with the Maratha states that were its neighbours, also became a directly administered Chief Commissioner's Province, as did Bilaspur.

Five hundred and sixty two princely states were annexed with India, among which Junagadh and Hyderabad were tatken over after military action. After the British announced their imminent exit from India, it became necessary to place the future relations between these states and the government of free India on a regularized legal footing.

SITUATION OF MANIPUR IMMEDIATELY BEFORE THE MERGER AGREEMENT

Immediately before merger, Manipur was plagued by so many political controversies and uncertainties :-

1. Sardar Patel, Home Minister of India proposed creation of a new Purbanchal Pradesh comprising of Manipur, Cachar, Tripura, Lushai Hills.
2. The Manipur State Congress which was connected with the All India State Peoples Conference wanted Manipur to merge with the Indian Union. They launched a movement for abolition of kingship and integration of Manipur with India. At that time, Congress was the single largest majority.
3. The Naga National Council under Phizo wanted to curve out an independent Nagaland comprising of Naga inhabited areas of Naga Hills and surrounding areas.
4. There was a rising influence of communism under Hijam Irabot, who was deeply influenced by Maxism revolutionary theories. After departure of the British, Irabot wanted an independent Manipur with a full responsible Government elected by the people with the king remaining as the constitutional head. Irabot was strongly against megrger with India. It was reported that the reason why Irabot Singh went to Burma was to seek help from the Burmese Communists in staging a revolution for an independent Socialist Republic in Manipur.
5. There was a controversy about merger of Manipur with Burma. On 12 and 14th May, 1947, the Hindustan Standard of Calcutta carried a news item that U. Aungsan, the Vice President of the Burmese Interim Government might visit Manipur and Manipur wanted to merge with Burma. The State Congress alleged that Hijam Irabot had connived with the Burmese.
6. Maharaja Bodhchandra wanted to establish a separate administrative unit of his own. On 21 Sepetember, 1946, he asked the British Authorities to allow him to make a royal proclamation regarding the new administrave reforms of his state.
7. At this juncture, the Indian Independence Act - 1947 was passed. On 11 August, 1947, Maharaja Bodhchandra signed the Standstill Agreement and the Instrument of Accession.
8. The Interim Government of Manipur issued warrant to arrest Irabot in connection with the killing of one police officer, Shri Keisam Naran Singh, Officer- in-Charge of Imphal P. S at Pungdongbam 21 October, 1948 (History of Manipur Police)
9. The election was held on 11th June, 1948. The Manipur State Congress has got the 14 out of 53 seats and a coalition government was formed

with Maharajkumar Priyobarta Singh, younger brother of Maharaja Bodhchandra (see plate -97) as the Chief Minister. The maiden session of the Assembly was held on 18 October, 1948. In the mean time, pressure was exerted on Manipur through the Maniour State Congress to merge with the Indian Union.

10. There was some sort of civil disobedience movement in the valley. Maharaja Bodhchandra knew that the people openly opposed the monarchy. He could remember people organizing Satyagraha movement all over the valley –taking out processions around his palace and shouting slogans like "Ningthousaba Bodhchandra" "Manipur Raja Gunda hai, bhulo mat, bhulo mat" against him. The Satyagrahis even openly performed organised looting of his farms at Top Khoingnang, Warok at Ngarian Ching, Lamlongei Forest Reserve, Lamlai Yaingang Inkhol by cutting bamboos and trees and catching fish from his fish farms.. (Rjkumar Maipaksana, Manipurda Ihan hanba Satyagaraha Aandolon, 1996). There was no unity among the politicians and also between the politicians and the Maharaja.
11. The issue of return of Kabow valley was raised again.
12. There was strong pressure both from the Indian National Congress as well as from the Government of India on Manipur through the Manipur State Congress to merge Manipur with India.

    The Manipur State Congress Party mentioned that

    - the Government of Manipur was not able to maintain law and order situation of the country.
    - there was an apprehension of taking over the country by the Communist revolution in Burma.
    - the integration of Manipur with India would have peace and development.

Now the Government of India and the Indian National Congress got an opportunity to interfere in the internal affairs of Manipur with blessings and support from the Manipur State Congress. Maharaja Bodhchandra wanted Manipur as an autonomous unit of India enjoying responsible government with his highness as the constitutional head.

SIGNING OF MANIPUR MERGER AGREEMENT

The Government of India asked the Maharaja of Manipur to establish a close relationship with the Government of India As a first step, they asked the Maharaja of Manipur to sign the Stand Still Agreement and the Instrument of Accession under which only the responsibilities of Defence, Communication and External affairs were to be looked after by the Government of India. The Maharaja had already signed the Stand Still Agreement and the Instrument of Accession on 11 August, 1947.

The Standstill Agreement confirmed that the agreements and administrative practices that existed as between the princely state in question and the British would be continued by the Domion of independent India. That means the Dominion of India simply replaces the British India and they came into the shoes of British India. Indirectly, Manipur had already expressed its desire to merge with Dominion of India.

Again, some of the important provisions of the Instrument of Accession were as follows :-

"And whereas the Government of India Act-1935 as so adopted by the Governor General provides that an Indian State may accede to the Dominion of India by an Instrument of Accession executed by the Ruler thereof ......

Now therefore, I Bodhchandra Singh, Ruler of Manipur State in excercise of my sovereignty in and over my state do hereby execute this my instrument of Accession and ....

I, hereby declare that I accede to the Domion of India —— but subject always to the terms thereof ......" (Mayengbam Anandamohon, Shillong, 1949)

By signing the Instrument of Accession, Manipur had agreed to be acceded to the Domion of India.

Under the Instrument of Accession, the Government of India would be responsible for defence, communication and external affaires. Probably, the King and the political leaders were not fully aware of the the Government of India Act-1935, the Indian Independce Act -1947 and also the implications of the Standstill Agreement and the Instrument of Accession. Otherwise, they could have voiced their concerns and they could have avoided signing the Standstill Agreement and the Instrument of Accession.

On 1st January, 1949, Sardar Patel came to Shillong for a meeting with Mr. Akbar Hydari, the Governor of Assam about the possible merger of Manipur. Later on, Akbar Hydari, the Governor of Assam asked the Maharaja of Manipur to appoint a Dewan in place of Dominion Agent. The Maharaja wanted to know the administrative power of the Dewan. The Governor came in person to Manipur along with Rustomji on 23 June, 1948 and proposed for appointment of Mr. M. K. Priyobarta Singh as the Dewan of Manipur. Mr. Akbar Hyder Ali, the Governor of Assam died of heart attack in Manipur while going for a trip for shooting ducks to Waikhong near the Waikhong Salt Spring. Mr. Akbar Hydari was succeeded by Mr. Prakash from Bihar.

Mr. Prakash came to Manipur on 21-24 March, 1949 to assess the situation between Manipur and Burma. He simply said that the appointment of the Dewan would strengthen the relation between Manipur and India. It is said that Maharaj Bodhchandra was not in favour of appointing his brother Mr. M. K. Priyobarta Singh as the Dewan of Manipur. Major General Rewal Amar Singh was appointed as the Dewan of Manipur on 14th April, 1949. According to the letter addressed to the Maharaja on 14th April, the the Dewan would held the direct charge of the portfolio of Law and Order, administration of Hill Tracts, State Forces and relation with the Government of India. The administration of the Manipur State shall be carried out under the general superintendence, guidance and control of the Dewan. The Dewan would be assisted by Major Khating of Manipur. Mr. Prakash also informed the Maharaja that the Government of India did not recognize the Manipur State Council and also the Manipur State Assembly.

In the mean time, the Government of India instructed the Government of Assam to complete the negotiation for merger of Manipur into India by 20th September, 1949. However, the Government of India wished to accomplish the merging of all the Princely States, which remains Independent. By the Second week of September 1949, only Manipur was left out.

Maharaja Bodhchandra Singh was invited to come to Shillong for a discussion with Mr. Prakash, the Governor of Assam. The news of his going to Shillong was published in the newspaper called "Bhagyabati Pratika" of dated 13th September, 1949. On hearing the news, Mr. T. C. Tiyankham, Speaker of the Manipur Assembly sent a letter to the Private Secretary of the Maharaja requesting the Maharaja to discuss the issues in the Manipur Assembly before proceeding to Shillong (Pan Manipur Youth League, Bharat ki Loilam Manipur, 1993). But the Maharaja did not find time to give a reply to this important matter. On 14th September, he did open one Manipur State Judicial Council. He was busy in arranging things for going to Shillong. The Maharaja left Imphal on 15th September along with his private secretary, Sanasam Gourahari and his ADC Mr. Mayengbam Anandamohon Singh and eight security personnel from the Manipur Rifles to meet the Governor of Assam to discuss administrative problems of Manipur. The Maharaja reached his private Bunglow at the Red Lands Rajbari, Shillong on the 17th September, 1949.

The meeting with Governor Mr. Prakash on the first day, 18 September, 1949 ended abruptly, as the Maharaja got emotionally upset, when Nari

Rustomji, Advisor to the Governorof Assam unceremoniously and abruptly produced the Manipur Merger Agreement for signature.

On 18 September in the evening, Maharaja Bodhchandra wrote to Mr. Prakash, the Governor of Assam "Now that the sovereignty of the State has been vested in the people, it would be in the fitness of things to hear the people's voice and learn their sentiments so that the time of action may not in any case be unconstitutional". He also said ".... Should the administration of Manipur State be taken over by the Centre, I shall be entitled to a sum of Rs. two lakhs and twentyfive thousand per year as my privy purse for my life time but as I have no personal property worth mentioning it, it would be more graceful for the Government of India if it is raised to the extent of Rs. four lakhs. .... your Excellency will kindly enable me to expedite the matter by returning to Imphal tomorrow since I do not wish to lose time". He did not get a reply to this letter.

On 19 September, again he wrote "If I am compelled to work independently of my people, my action will be quite unjustifiable ...It seems to me that the best course would be to allow me to go back to Imphal and arrange to bring about a very speedy solution of the matter. Mr. Prakash replied on 19 September, "Your Highness may rest assured that the Government of India will take complete responsibility in the matter of meeting whatever objections may be raised by the people of the State. Your Highness need, therefore have no apprenhension regarding the reaction of the people to the negotiations that are now in progress. Your Highness will be afforded every protection by the Government of India and will continue to enjoy the same personal rights, privileges, dignities and titles that Your Highness has been enjoying hitherto. It is because the Government of India are desirous of having Your Highness' cooperation rather than take ex-parte decisions that might be prejudicial to the interest of Your Highness. I should make ample provision to ensure that Your Highness may be able to maintain Your Highness's dignity and status as befits the Ruler of a State of such glorious tradition and history as the State of Manipur".

On the second day, 19 September, 1949 despite an appointment, the Maharaja did not go to meet the Governor. On the contrary, His Highness informed Mr. Prakash of his intention to go back to Manipur. A series of exchange of letters took place between Governor and the Maharaja. By evening the Maharaja gave up his plan of returning to Imphal and agreed to meet the Governor on the next day, the 20th September, 1949 as proposed.

In the evening of 19 September, 1949 one Mr. Das Gupta, who was earlier Superintendent of Police of Manipur, called on the Maharaja. He was at that point of time, the Superintendent of Police (S. P.) (CID) at Shillong. Mr. Das Gupta might have mentioned to the Maharaja the articles of the Sanad (vide Government of India, Foreign Department Notification No. 1862 E, dated Simla, the 18 September 1891 of the Governor General in Council, 1891).

The articles of the Sanad said that "the permanence of the grant conveyed by this Sanad will depend upon the ready fulfilment of all orders given by the British Government with regard to the administration of the territory, the control of hill tribes dependent upon Manipur, the composition of armed forces of the state, and any other matter in which the British Government might be pleased to intervene". "So long as his house was loyal to the Crown and faithful to the conditions of this Sanad, he and his successor would enjoy the favour and protection of the British Government". Mr. Das Gupta politely informed the Maharaja that if he did not agree to sign the Merger Agreement, the Dominion Government of India could and would make someone else as Maharaja, who would sign the Merger Agreement. So, the loss would be that of Bodhchandra in person. It was said that Das Gupta told his story with tears in his eyes. The Maharaja believed what Mr. Das Gupta said. The Maharaja agreed to examine articles of the Merger Agreement in detail. The articles were again drafted and redrafted several times. Though the Maharaja did not commit anything, the meeting ended in a cordial atmosphere. (Lt. Col. Bhubon-Annexation(?) of Manipur)

Mr. Prakash, the Governor of Assam had known the Maharaja Bodhchandra since August 1934, when Bodhachandra was a young prince. Bodhchandra was once banished by his father for his alleged attempt to ascend the throne through invocation of a sylvan deity, when his father was away on pilgrimage to Nabadwip. Prince Bodhchandra spent about three years in self-exile under the patronage of Mr. Prakash. The Maharaja Bodhchandra addressed Mr. Prakash as "Baba".

Though Mr. Prakash sent a note to the Maharaja that he would come around 5 pm, he came much earlier without any escort and personal staff. When the Governor arrived at Red Lands Rajbari, the Maharaja was enjoying his afternoon nap. The Governor told the servants not to wake up the Maharaja. He waited in the drawing room. When Bodhchandra came in, His Excellency stood up and lovingly said, "Hai, Bodhchandra:", not "Your Highness". The Maharaja replied, "Haa, Baba". Sri Prakasa continued "I have come as your Baba, not as the Governor". (Lt. Col. Bhubon- Annexation (?) of Manipur)

Then, Mr. Prakash requested the Maharaja to send all his officers out of the room so that he could have a heart to heart talk. He told the Maharaja that New Delhi would not permit any delay. It may be presumed that Mr. Prakash might have briefed the Maharaja about the provision of the Indian Independence Act, the Government of India Act, the articles of the Sanad of the Governor General in Council, the implications of the Standstill Agreement and the Instrument of Accession under which there is no option for Manipur to be a separate sovereign country.

The strong argument that the Maharaja put up initially was that since the sovereignty of the State has already been vested in the people and he remains only as the nominal head of the state at that time it would be in the fitness of things to hear people's voice and learn their sentiment and obtain their due opinions and "acceptance" so that the line of action may not in any case be unconstitutional. But according to the instrument of Accession which the Maharaha signed on11 Augsut, 1949, only the consent of the ruler is required, not of the population.

Mr. Prakash told the Maharaja that he was prepared to resign from his Governorship, but a new Governor would forcibly effect the merger under terms and conditions more harmful to Manipur and to the Maharaja. The Governor said, "Mein bhig mangne aya hung (I have come to beg)". Then the Maharaja negotiated for the increase of the privy purses which was subsequently allowed. Ultimately Maharaja Bodhchnadra agreed to sign the Merger Agreement. (Lt. Col. Bhubon- Annexation (?) of Manipur)

Thus the Manipur Merger Agreement was signed on the next day, 21 September 1949. (see plate-96). They stood up and embraced each other and Manipur got officially merged into India on 15 October 1949. The signatories were Maharaja Bodhachandra Singh, V.P. Menon, Advisor to Government of India (Ministry of States) and Sri Prakash, Governor of Assam. Article 1 of the Agreement says, "His Highness the Maharaja of Manipur hereby cedes to the dominion Government full and exclusive authority, jurisdiction and powers for and in relation to the government of the state and agrees to transfer the state to the Dominion Government on the fifteenth day of October, 1949..." Manipur was first accorded the Part C State status (1949-56), then a Union Territory (1957-71) and finally the Statehood (1972 onwards).

After a careful study of the Government of India Act-1935, the Indian Independence Act-1947 and the circumstances under which Maharaja Bodhachandra had signed the Standstill Agreement and the Instrucment of Accession on 11 August, 1947 and also considering the political situation prevailing at that point of time and strategic location of Manipur just near Burma and China, one may conclude that what Maharaja Bodhachandra did was a wise step and that he had signed the Merger Agreement willingly and voluntarily.

This can be verified from the numerous letters exchanged between Maharaja Bodhchandra and Mr. Prakash, the Governor of Assam. On the first day itself, the Maharaja pleaded to increase the privy purse. One the second day, the Governor said that the Government of India would take complete responsibility about objections that may be raised by the people of Manipur. He also indicated that he was willing to consider the increase of privy purse. Maharaja gave up his plan of going back to Manipur. Then the relationships developed which led to complete understanding between the two parties. Maharaja understood the prevailing anti- monarchy activities in Manipur and increasing tension between the people and monarchy very well. He could sense that the time of monarchy had come to an end. The Manipur State Congress Party was demanding integration of Manipur with India in connivance with the Indian National Congress. There was no unity between the Maharaja and the political leaders. That was probably the reason why he was interested in negotiating for the privy purse. Nobody raised a single voice against the Merger Agreement during the life time of Maharaja Bodhchandra and even for decades after the death of Maharaja Bodhchandra. One historian observed, "if you fight with the past, there will be no future".

This fact was also evident from the sequence of events that followed after the Merger Agreement. There was no public protest of any kind against the Merger. The people in general were happy with the merger of Manipur with India. The Manipur State Congress Party took out a procession with band party to celebrate the occasion. They expressed their happiness by throwing up their congress caps into the sky in the pologround. People were busy in trying to get a foothold in the new Government.

After the merger of Manipur with the Indian dominion, Bodhchandra accompanied by Sanasam Gourahari Singh paid a visit to Delhi and was warmly welcomed by C. Raja Gopalchari, the last Governor General of India on 28 November, 1949. The Maharaja presented a Kaosel, a Manipuri decorative vessel made of polished brass to the Governor General.

When Jawaharlal Nehru came to Manipur with his daughter Indira Gandhi on 28 March, 1953, he was received warmly by Maharaja Bodhachandra in Hiyang dress. U-Nu, Prime Minister of Burma arrived on the next day at Imphal. (see plates- 97 and 98) Nehru had discontinued payment of Kabow valley compensation. There was no public outcry. Nehru was served with 108 dishes in typical Manipuri style. Nobody raised any objection to the discontinuation of payment of Kabow valley compensation or about the Merger Agreement during that crucial hour. People were immensely happy when Nehru said that "Manipur is a Jewel of India". A number of dances and festivals were performed to satisfy Nehru. Sanasam Gourahari who was very fond of writing books did not consider it worthwhile to record the proceedings of the Merger Agreement in writing. Probably, he took it as a closed chapter. Similarly Mayengbam Anandamohon did not think it worthwhile for writing a book about Merger Agreement for almost 54 years. But the book entitled "Shillong 1949" written by Mayengbam Anandamohon in 2004 gave a vivid picture of what transpired during the negotiation process of Merger Agreement. He narrated the sequence of events very clearly. He did not suggest that the Maharaj was forced to sign the Merger Agreement. Again Mayengbam Anandamohon squarely blamed the so called educated politicians of those days. (Mayengbam Anadamohon, Shillong 1949, page 54). He used the word "Rajnitiwala Saba" (Fake politicians ?).

Strength and weaknesses of Merger Agreement

1. Maharaja Bodhchandra signed Standstill Agreement and the Instrument of Accession on 11th August, 1947. But this was probably not discussed in the Manipur Constituent Assembly. The Manipur Constituent Assembly had not ratified the Instrument of Accession.
2. On 29th Thawan, 1947 (Friday), Maharaja Bodhchandra declared independence of Manipur. That means, the Maharaja had decided to opt for independence. But the Manipur Constituent Assembly had never adopted a resolution in this regard.
3. The Manipur Merger Agreement was signed on September 1949. Manipur was having a democratically elected Manipur Constituent Assembly when the Merger Agreement was signed. The Manipur Constituent Assembly had not ratified the Agreement.
4. On 18 October, 1948, the first session of the Constituent Assembly was held. The State got officially merged with India on 15 October 1949. The State Assembly did not pass any resolution either favouring or opposing the Merger Agreement. Why did the Manipur Constituent Assembly not discussed such an important issue like signing of Instrument of Accession or the Merger Agreement ? The time available was almost one year.

5. The Manipur Merger Agreement and the Instrument of Accession was never ratified by the then existing Manipur Constituent Assembly or by the Manipur State Assembly till date. In case of Kashmir, the Instrument of Accession signed by Maharaja Hari Singh on 26 October, 1947 was ratified by the Constituent Assembly of Jammu and Kashmir and they adopted a resolution for perpetual merger with the Union of India. This did not happen with Maniour
6. . Does the non-ratification of the signing of Instrument of Accession or the Merger Agreement provide any room for negotiation with the Government of India.
7. The State Constituent Assembly was still existing when Maharaja Bodhchandra returned after signing the Merger Agreement. If Maharaja Bodhchandra were forcibly asked to sign the Merger Agreement, he would have asked the State Assembly to adopt a resolution opposing the Merger of Manipur with India.
8. Mr. Rawal Amar Singh, Chief Commissioner of Manipur issued an order notification no. 219-P in the Gazette of India dated 15 October, 1949 that "the Ministers of Manipur State shall cease to function and the legislature shall stand dissolved from the midday of Saturday, the 15 October, 1949 and all the portfolios are taken over by the Chief Commissioner". It is questionalble whether the Chief Commissioner has got the authority and power to abolish such a democratically elected legislature. Why not democratic India did respect a democratically elected legislature of Manipur.

It appears that the educated politicians of those days did not discuss the relevant Acts and Rules including the Government of India Act-1935, the Indian Independence Act-1947, the implications of the Standstill Agreement and the Instrument of Accession before signing the Standstill Agreement, the Instrument of Accession and the Merger Agreement. Even after signing the Standstill Agreement and the Instrument of Accession, they could have discussed this in the Manipur Constituent Assembly. If they sign the Instrument of Accession with all honesty and sincereity, the merger of Manipur to Union of India is already imminent and all the exercise of civil disobedience movement, movement for responsible government, forming of constitution making committee, the general election and subsequent forming of the Assembly, the Manipur Constitution Act became useless exercise. This shows complete ignorance about the prevailing Acts, rules and regulations, lack of political maturity and lack of foresight on the part of the educated politicians of those days. Probably the band of newly educated elites of those days were intoxicated with the Gandhian theory of "Satyagraha". Similarly, Hijam Irabot was intoxicated with his newly found theory of Marxism and all sections of politicians were busy trying to dislodge the King without studying the implications and without knowing the consequences.

But Maharaja Bodhchandra might have been briefed about all these Acts and rules. After studying the sequence of events and other elevant facts, it is very difficult to believe that our Maharaja would succumb to threats of any kind in Shillong.

On October 15, 1949, Maharaja declared handing over the reigns of Manipur Government to the Government of India at the Polo ground and Major General Rawal Amar Singh as the first Chief Commissioner of Manipur. However Major General Rawal Amar Singh hurriedly left Manipur on 18th October, 1949 due to some misunderstanding between himself and Maharaja Bodhchandra Singh. Manipur's status was lowered to a Part C Territory under the Indian rule. In 1956, the States Reorganization Act reorganised the former British provinces and princely states on the basis of language Simultaneously, the Seventh Amendment to the Constitution renamed the Part C States as "Union Territories".

Maharaja Bodhchandra died on Friday, 26th of Hiyangei, 1955. (November) at 9 a. m. He was cremated at the Manglen, Kangla Fort with 11 gun salute. (Sarangthem Bormani Singh, Meitei Ningthourol, 2000). After the death of the Maharaja Bodhchadra, Maharanbi Ishwori Devi was made in charge of Manipur till the next King is appointed by the Government of India.

The first Rani was Ram Pryari Devi whom Maharaja Bodhchandra Singh married in 1929 when he was the Yubraj. She was the daughter of Raja of Bodo Khimdi in Ganjam district of the erstwhile Madras Presidency. She was divorced in 1941 to a "point of no return" due to strained relationship between Maharaja Churachand Singh and the Raja of Bodo Khimdi on the issue of "royal dowry" (Damodar Waikhom - Merger of Manipur With The Dominion Of India).

Maharaja Bodhchandra had nine wives with five sons and one daughter :-

Ram Pyari

Maharani Ishwori Devi, Princess of Rasmnagar

Waikhom Ningol Kamlabati Devi (Apambi/Sangai-see plates-101 and 105)–Tamphasana (see plate-106), Okendrajit and Kebisana

Khumallambam (Ningombam) Kamini of Keisampat - Sanatombi
Khwairakpam Chanu Rashi (Nambol)–Sanayaima alias Sarat
Nongthombam Chanu Prava of Kongba-Sivananda
Elangbam Chanu Khedani.
Hijam Chanu Khedi Rani Tombi (Thangmeiband Rani)-
Khumanthem Chanu Ibempishak–Sanayaima

On the death of Maharaja Bodhchandra, the people recited the words *"Chatloko hey athouba, pukphaba, dharmachenba, Eningthou, nahakna chatkhibadi khunai asigi aroiba nummit takhibanido"* (Englsih translation-'Hey noble and religious and courageous king of Manipur. We all bid 'adieu' to you on your great soul's departure for the journey to heaven. Your departure from us do mark, indeed, the setting of the last monarchical sun of this hoary land) (Damudor Waikhom-Merger of Manipur With The Dominion of India)

MAHARAJA OKENDRAJIT (1955-1972)

Okendrajit was the last Maharaja of Manipur. Okendrajit (see plates-102 and 104) was recognized by the President of India as the Maharaja of Manipur on the 9th December, 1955. He was only four years old when he became King. M. K. Priyobarta was appointed as the regent of the king. Another name of Okendrajit was Pareihanba. With the abolition of Privy Purses in 1972 during Indira Gandhi's time, all the priviledges,privy purses and titles (financial grants) to the Maharaja were withdrawan by the Government of India.

On 23 April,1992, Okendrajit Sana declared that "I open the Lubak Tabu and abandon Hinduism as state religion and recognition is hereby withdrawn by the Royal Customary Law of the Country, instead the Royal Customary Law revives the Lainingthouism as the state religion and do hereby give recognition as state religion". He lived as a common man. He died on 5th August, 1996 at the Manipur Palace. The next day he was cremated at the Manglen at the Kangla Fort according to Hindu rites.

References

Administration Report of the Manipur Political Agency, 1873-74,1875-76, 1877-78, 1878-79, 1891-95, 1904-05.

Administration Report of the Manipur State, 1913-14, 1934-35,1939-40,1940-41.

Allen, B.C., 1905: Naga Hills and Manipur, Socio-Economic History, Gian Publication, Delhi-7.

Alexander Mackenzie, North East Frontier of India (1884).

Alexander Mackenzie, History of Relationssss of the Government with the Hill Tribes of the North East Frontier of Bengal, Calcutta, Home Press, 1884.

Angou Luwang, N., 1976: Ningthou Kaangbalon. Archaeology of Manipur, 1988.

Ashton, S.R. (1982), *British Policy towards the Indian States, 1905–1938*, London Studies on South Asia no. 2, London: Curzon Press, ISBN 0-700-70146-X

Anglo-Manipur Conflict of 1891", Har-Anand Publications, 1992.

Asoso Yonou, Naga Struggle against British Rule under Jadonnang and Rani Gaidiuluiu, 1982.

B.C. Allen, Assam District Gazetteer-Naga Hills and Manipur, Volume-IX, Part-II, Calcutta Baptist Mission Press, 1905.

B.C. Allen, E.A. Gait, C.G.H. Allen, H.F. Howard,Gazetteer of Bengal and North East India.

Bhogeswor, O. : Ninghthourol Lambuba, 1967.

Capt. R. Boileau. Pemberton, Report on the Eastern Frontier of British India, Government of Assam (1835).

Copland, Ian (1993), "Lord Mountbatten and the Integration of the Indian States: A Reappraisal", *The Journal of Imperial and Commonwealth History* 21 (2): 385–408.

Copland, Ian (1997), *The Princes of India in the Endgame of Empire, 1917–1947*, Cambridge, England: Cambridge University Press, ISBN 0-521-57179-0.

Damudor Waikhom -Merger Of Manipur With The Dominion of India

Dorothy Woodman,The Making of Burma (1962).

Dr. Lal Dena (1826-1946),History of Modern Manipur,1990.

Dun E. W., Gazetteer of Manipur by, Delhi, Vivek Publishing House, 1975 (First Edn. 1886).

E. Nilakanta Singh, "Fragments of Manipuri Culture", Omson Publications, New Delhi, 1993.

Fifield, Russell H. (1952), "New States in the Indian Realm", *The American Journal of International Law* 46 (3): 450–463.

Fisher, Michael H. (1984), "Indirect Rule in the British Empire: The Foundations of the Residency System in India (1764–1858)", *Modern Asian Studies* 18 (3): 393–428.

Furber, Holden (1951), "The Unification of India, 1947–1951", *Pacific Affairs* 24 (4): 352–371.

Grim wood, St. Ethel, My three years in Manipur (1892).

Harvey G.E., History of Burma (1925).

Hodson T.C. : The Meiteis.

Hardgrave, Robert L. (1983), "The Northeast, the Punjab, and the Regionalization of Indian Politics", *Asian Survey* 23 (11): 1171–1181.

Ibungohal L., Cheitharol Kumbaba, 1967.

Ibohal W. : The History of Manipur.

Julon Mutua, Bijoy Panchalee (History of Manipur), 1936.

James Johnstone, 1896, 1971, 1983: Manipur and Naga Hills.

John G. Martin It Began at Imphal: The Combat Cargo Story, 1988.

John Parratt, Saroj Parratt" Queen Empress Vs Tikendrajit, Prince of Manipur-the

Karan, Pradyumna P. (1960), "A Free Access to Colonial Enclaves", *Annals of the Association of American Geographers* 50 (2): 188–190.

Keith, Arthur Berriedale (1969), *A Constitutional History of India, 1600–1935* (2nd ed.), London: Methuen.

Karam Manimohan Singh, History of Christianity in Manipur - 1991.

K.C. Tensuba, A Brief History of Meiteis and Thais, 1993.

K.C. Tensuba, Genesis of Indian Tribes : An Approach to the Meiteis and Thais, 1993.

Kosambi D.D. : Myth and Reality.

Kumar Ph. : Kege Moirang.

Keertichand T., Dhammapada (Translation), 1983.

Khelchandra N., Padmashree, and Lairenjam Iboongohal Singh, Cheitharol Kumbaba, 1989.

Lal Dena, History of Modern Manipur, 1825-1948, Orbit Publishers, New Delhi, 1991.

Lt. Col. Bhubon- Annexation (?) of Manipur.

L.W. Shakespeare,History of Manipur Rifles (1929).

Lumby, E.W.R. (1954), *The Transfer of Power in India, 1945–1947*, London: George Allen and Unwin.

Mayengbam Anandamohon, Shillong, 1949, Lamyanba Printers, Konung Lampak

Maipaksana "Manipurda Ihan hanba Satyagraha Aandolon", Padma Printers, 1996.

Manipur Today, January, 1989.

Manipur Today, August, 1989.

Maung Htin Aung "A history of Burma", Columbia University Press, New York and London, 1967.

Menon, V.P. (1956), *The Story of the Integration of the Indian States*, New York: Macmillan.

M.K. Binodini Devi, M.K. : Borsaheb Ongbi Sanatombi, 1979, Lamyanba Printers, Konung Lampak.

M.K. Binodini Devi, Churachand Maharaj gi Imung Manung, 2008, Lamyanba Printers, Konung Lampak.

Mosley, Leonard (1961), *The last days of the British Raj*, London: Weidenfield and Nicolson.

Mutua Bahadur, Traditional Textiles of Manipur,Mutua Museum Imphal, 1997.

Mutua Bahadur, Cane and Bamboo Crafts of Manipur,Mutua Museum Imphal, 1994.

Mutua Bahadur, Research work on Manipuri Art.

Mutua Tombi "Imphal- Vol. 1," 1975.

N. Khelchandra,War Prisoners Deported from Manipur, 100 years (1891-1991) Manipur's Last War iof Independence, DIPR, 1991.

N. Khelchandra,Dramatis Personae of 1891 War, 100 years (1891-1991) Manipur's Last War iof Independence, DIPR, 1991.

Naorem Sanajaoba "Manipur Treaties and Documents (1110-1971)", Mittal Publications, New Delhi, 1993.

Nongthonbammacha Angou Luwang "Ningthou Kangbalon (Christagi managgi Ningthousing)", P.S. Printers and Stationery, Imphal, 2002.

N. Tombi Singh, "Manipur and The Mainstream", 1975.

Phadnis, Urmila (1968), *Towards the Integration of the Indian States, 1919–1947*, London: Asia Publishing House.

Paonam Pholendrajit Singh "Paona Brajabashi, 100 years (1891-1991) Manipur's Last War of Independence", DIPR, 1991.

Paonam Pholendrajit Singh "Paona Brajabashi Amasung Khongjom Day, 1998".

Prof. Gangmumei Kabui, History of Manipur -1990.

Rajkumar Sanahakl "Thangal General", 1979.

Ramusack, Barbara N. (1978), *The Princes of India in the Twilight of Empire: Dissolution of a patron-client system, 1914–1939*, Colombus, Ohio: Ohio State University Press, ISBN 0-814-20272-1

Ramusack, Barbara N. (1988), "Congress and the People's Movement in Princely India": Ramusack, Barbara N. (2004), *The Indian Princes and Their States*, The New Cambridge History of India III. 6, Cambridge, England: Cambridge University Press, ISBN 0-521-26727-7

Ranajit Kumar. Saha, Valley Society of Manipur, Punthi –Pustak, Calcutta, 1994 R.K. Jhalajit Singh, Padmashree, "A short history of Manipur (33 A.D. to the present time)" O.K. Store, Imphal, 1965.

R.B. Pemberton "The Eastern Frontier of India", Mittal; Publications, (First published –1835), reprinted -2000.

R. Brown,Statistical Account of the native state of Manipur and the hill territory under its rule ",Mittal Publications, 1874.

Roy, Jyotimor, History of Manipur, (1958,) (2nd edition 1973) -1835), 2000.

Sarangthem Bormani Singh, Sahitya Bhusan, "Meitei Ningthourol", Rajesh Book Store, Imphal, 2000.

Singh, B.P. (1987), "North-East India: Demography, Culture and Identity Crisis", *Modern Asian Studies* **21** (2): 257–282.

Sir Edward Gatt "A history of Assam", Khagendra Narayan Dutta Baruah, Guwahati, (First published -1905), 1997.

Sir James Johnstone, My Experience in Manipur and 'Naga Hill' by (1896)

Sir Robert Reid (Governor of Assam, History of Frontier Areas bordering on Assam, 1937-42).

T.C. Hodson, The Meitheis (1908).

T.C. Hodson, "The Naga Tribes of Manipur", MacMillan & Co, London 1911

Wainwright, A. M. (1994), *Inheritance of Empire: Britain, India and the Balance of Power in Asia, 1938–55*, Westport: Praeger, ISBN 0-275-94733-5.

Warner, Sir William Lee (1910), *The Native States of India* (2nd ed.), London: Macmillan.

Wood, John (1985), "Dividing the Jewel: Mountbatten and the Transfer of Power to India and Pakistan", *Pacific Affairs* 58 (4): 653–662.

W. Ibohal Singh, The History of Manipur.

Wahengbam Inaomacha "Meiteigi Phamthol chataret yangkhei" Eureka Printing Press, Imphal, 1992.

W. Mc. Culloch. Publications of G.H. Damat, An Account of the valley of Manipur and the hill tribes,1859.

Plate -60: King Garib Niwaj

Plate -61: Santidas Gosai

Plate-62 : Kaunghmudaw Pagoda in Sagaing, Burma – 1738 which Garib Niwaj attacked in 1738.

Plate -63:King Bhagyachandra (1763-1798)

Plate -64: Bimbabati , Sija Laioibi
Courtesy – RKCS Gallery

Plate -65: King Gambheer Singh
(1825-1834)

Plate -66: Maharaja Nara Singh
(1844-1850)

Plate -67 : Maharaja Chandrakirti
(1850-1886)

Plate :68 Kohima Expedition(1879)
Courtesy –RKCS Art Gallery

Plate -69:Lord Northbrook-1874

Plate- 70 National Flag of Manipur (1834-44, 1850-1886)

Plate-71: Zila Durbar(1874)
Courtesy- RKCS Art Gallery

Plate-72: Maharaja Surchandra (1886-1890).

Plate-73: Maharaja Surchandra with his brothers and noblemen

Plate- 74: Maharaja Kulachandra (1890-1891)

Plate- 75: Paona Major (1833-1891)

Plate-76; Thangal General (1806-1891)

Plate-77: Maharaja Kulachandra Thangal General and Chongtham Ava Puren Major

Plate-78: Lord Landsdowne, Viceroy of India-1894

Plate -79: Bir Tikendrajit (1858-1891)

Plate-80 : Angousana Senapati (1891)

Plate-81 : Left Middle = Tikendrajit, Right Middle – Kulachndra (1891) Courtesy-E-pao

Plate-82: Col. Samu alias Luwang Ningthou

Plate -83: J.W. Quinton-1891

Plate -84: Col. E.MCD Skene 1891

Plate-85:Lt. W.H. Simpson (1891)

Plate-86 :Frank St. Clair Grimwood (1891)

Plate-87: Major Maxwell (1891)

Plate- 88: Kala Singh Sagolhanjaba

Plate-89: Maj. Rudra Yengkhoiba

Plate-90: Maibeya Tamra Singh

Plate-91: British Residency-1891

Plate-92 : Durbar Hall -1891 (X is the spot where Grimwood fell)

Plate-93 Coronation of Maharaja Churachand (15 May, 1907)
Courtesy-RKCS Art Gallery

Plate -94: Manipur Palace

Plate – 95 : Maharaja Churachand (1891-1941)

Plate-96: Signing of Merger Agreement (21 September 1949.)

Plate-97: Maharaja Bodhchandra, Jawaharlal Nehru , U –Nu (28 March, 1953) : RKCS Art Gallery

Plate-98: Maharaja Bodhachandra, Jawaharlal Nehru, Indira Gandhi and Maharani Ishwari

Plate-99 : M.K. Priyobarta

Plate-100: Irabot

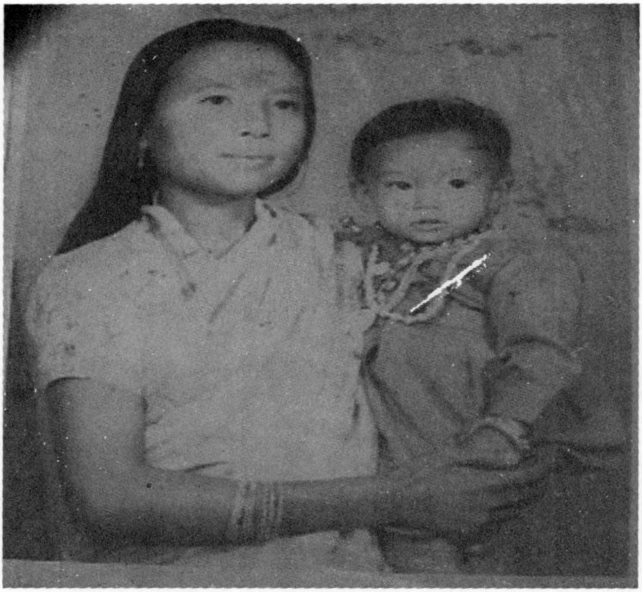

Plate-101:Sangai Maharani with baby Okendro

Plate- 102 Okendro Maharaja after coronation-1955

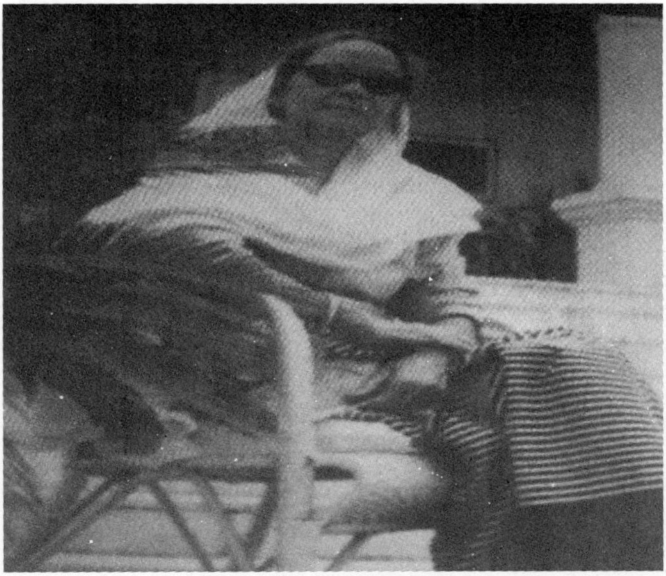

Plate-103 : M.K. Binodini

Plate- 104: Okendro Maharaja in Kwak Tanba

Plate- 105: Sangai Maharani with Y.V. Chavan

Plate-106:M.K. Tamphasana

5

Population and People

THE PEOPLE OF MANIPUR

The Meiteis, the Nagas, the Kuki-Chin are the predominant groups in Manipur. They belong to the Mongoloid race and have very close similarities in their physical features, culture and traditional habits. The legend of all tribes claimed that they originated somewhere in the north from a cave. In the later part of the history, the Meiteis were converted to the Hindu Vaishnavism and the hill tribes became Christians. Traditional semantic rituals resembled very closely. Rice is the staple food for all the ethnic groups of Manipur and fish and seasonal vegetables are their favourites. Meiteis prefer fish and elders usually do not take meat. The hill tribes take rice beer and meat. The original Meitei communities of Chakpas (Loi) make Yu (Rice Beer) and eat meat. The Meiteis believed in curing illness by freeing a chicken away in the woods just as the Maos and other tribes. Meitei men wore long hair similar to the Kuki-Chin group in earlier days and still some Meitei Marups, Sanamahi worshippers used to keep long hairs. In the Meitei martial arts "Thang-Ta, the Ta (spear) is primarily a Naga weapon although Meiteis developed and perfected their own war techniques and skills in using them. All practiced head hunting at one time of their history. (see Chapter-6:Meiteis)

At present, the Meiteis perform rituals and ceremonies according to the Hindu customs, while the hill tribes perform according to Christian faith. Among the Meiteis themselves, there were Chakpas (Lois) and Yaithibis, who were driven out of the Meitei community to far off villages as untouchables

Table-35 Showing the population of Manipur -2001

State/Districts	Total Population Persons	Males	Females	Sex Ratio (females per 1000 males)	Density (per sq. km)	Decadal growth in % (1991-2001)
Manipur	2,388,634	1,297,338	1,181,296	978	107	30.02
Imphal East	3,93,780	197,710	196,070	992	555	19.16
Imphal West	4,39,532	218,947	220,585	1,007	847	15.42
Thoubal	3,66,341	183,338	183,003	998	713	24.62
Bishnupur	2,05,907	102,772	103,135	1,004	415	13.90
Churachanpur	2,28,707	114,740	113,967	993	50	29.81
Ukhrul	1,40,946	73,413	67,533	920	31	28.98
Senapati	3,79,214	196,646	1,82,568	928	116	81.96
Tamenglong	1,11,496	57,994	53,499	922	25	29.23
Chandel	1,22,714	61,778	60,936	986	37	72.80

Source- Census of Manipur-2001

by the Maharaja, for they did not accept Hinduism. (See chapter-7:Lois, Yaithibis and Bishnupriya)

Among the Naga tribes of Manipur, the Tangkhuls were the first to receive Christianity; (see Chapter-15: Historical Landmarks). Therefore, they were more educated and better adapted to the modern and western cultures than other tribes. Naturally, they became leaders and helped to establish schools and churches not only in Manipur hills but also in Kohima, Makokchung, and Dimapur in Nagaland state. (See Chapter no–9: Nagas, Chaptr-10: Tangkhuls)

The Kuki-Chin tribes were of comparatively late migrators to Manipur from the Chin state of Burma during 18th and 19th century. The Manipur Maharaja allowed them to settle in different parts of the hills, which were not inhabited at that time. The population of Manipur was very sparse in those days. Therefore, Thadous and other Kuki groups live in many districts of Manipur but the Naga tribes have their own territories marked clearly. (See Chapter-8: Scheduled Castes and Tribes, Chapter-11: Kukis and Hmars).

All tribes have their own distinct dialects but in conversing with others they speak Manipuri language (Meiteilon). In addition, Sikhs, Punjabis, Nepali, Bengali, Marwari and other Indian communities have also settled in Manipur.

CENSUS POPULATION

The first census of Manipur in 1881 reported a total population of 2,21,070, of which 1,17,108 were Meiteis, 85,288 hill tribes, 105 foreigners, and

Muslims, Loi, Kei and Mayang counted for 18, 569 (Dun:,E.W. Gazetteer of Manipur, 1886). The figures for 1891 census are not available as the records were destroyed in the Anglo-Manipur War, 1891. The population in 1901 was 284,465 giving a density of 34 persons per square mile. Women exceeded men in numbers probably due to frequent wars with Burma. Of the population in 1901, 60% were Hindus and 36 % were aboriginal tribes. The Nagas constituted 21% and Kukis 14% and Muslims 4% of the population. The state contains one town and 467 villages. According to the 1991 census report, the total population of Manipur was 18.26 lakhs but in the 2001 census, the population is 2.39 millions. The sex ratio was 978 females for every 1000 males. The Hindus constitute 58% followed by the Christians (34.11%) and the Muslims (7.26%). There are 44 tribes in the state speaking different dialects. Thirty two such tribes have now become the constitutional categories under the label "Scheduled Tribes "The non Hindu, Meiteilon speaking population have been placed under the "Scheduled Caste" category. The Meitei Hindus constitute the largest ethnic group of the state. The population escalation during the last three decades has been helped by the insidious infiltration of illegal foreigners from Nepal, Bangladesh, Burma and influx of emigrant workers from other states.

MEITEI PANGAN (MANIPURI MUSLIMS)

In certain historical events, Manipur Rajas used to take sojourn to Sylhet or Cachar of Assam. The Muslims used to serve them and on the return journey, they (Rajas) would take Muslims along as servants. It is said that a large number of Muslims entered Manipur along with Sanongba, the younger brother of King Khagemba as sepoys to fight against the King. They were defeated but allowed to settle, provided free lands and given Manipur women. Some Muslims from U.P. and Bihar also migrated in search of employment. There were a few Muslim families which came from Afghanistan. R. Brown (1874) mentioned that the Pangan, the Manipuri Muslims (Mussalmans) were almost entirely the emigrant Bengalis, chiefly from the districts of Sylhet and Cachar. They were a mixed population. Khan (1972) mentioned that the Mohammedan came from the land of "Bangla". Probably, the word Pangan had been derived from "Bangla. Johnston (1896) mentioned that formerly they had to prostrate themselves before the Raja like other subjects. After they had made a representation to the King, Chandrakirti that this was against their religion Chandrakirti (1850–1886) excused them from doing that and allowed them to offer "Salam" (salute) instead. R. Brown (1874) mentioned that they chiefly followed the trades of gardening, turning, carpentry and pottery and they also served as sepoys. He also mentioned that nearly all the buglers and drummers attached to the Raja's army were Mussalmans. Further he said that these Pangans had the reputation of being hardworking. They performed Lalup like other Manipuris. McColloch (1859) wrote that the Mussalman are divided into four classes-sepoys, gardeners, turners and potters. The Kazi was appointed by the Raja to look after the Mussalman on account of the service he might have done for the Raja as manual servant. The Muslims from Cachar were employed as labourers in the agricultural fields. Some of them started their own cultivation. At present the Manipuri Pangans (Muslims) (see plates-119, 120) are living in several villages at Lilong, Mayang Imphal, Yairipok, Thoubal, Kwakta, Kshetrigao etc. Their main occupation is agriculture. Many educated ones now are doing official jobs in the State and Central government services. They have mixed characters of Mongoloid and Aryan in their features. They follow the norms of the Muslim Society. The marriage and divorce is strictly on the basis of Islamic codes. The structure of the house is not in any detail different from a Meitei house. In villages the houses are constructed with bamboo or wood and roofs thatched with grass. Some affluent Muslims also construct their houses with bricks and use cement and concrete material, the roof is covered with CGI sheets. They rear buffaloes and goats; the cattle sheds are arranged separately. They know the art of milking. The poultry is popular among the Muslims and tribal. Muslims are the best in poultry and they have got monopoly in fowl breeding.

Following the Nong Shamei Puya (an old manuscript) Khan mentioned that some of the contributions of the Manipuri Mussalman to the valley are transplanting of paddy plant, carrying of dolai (a sort of palanquin), hidak thakpa (smoking tobacco), paper making and so on. The Pangans speak Manipuiri (Meiteilon) as their mother tongue.(See Chapter-15, Historical Landmarks).

SIKHS

There is a saying that "Sikhs and Potatoes are found everywhere in the world". Manipur is not an exception. All Sikhs settled in Manipur are of Punjab origin but in earlier times, most of them have come from Burma where they had gone from Punjab. Some of them entered Manipur after the Second World War and some others after the Burmese government refused them the citizenship. They have Gurudwaras at Imphal and Moreh.

Sikh is the name given to the followrs of Sikhism. The term has its origin in the Sanskrit term *[icya*, meaning "disciple, learner" or *[ikca*, meaning "instruction".

According to Article I of the "Rehat Maryada" (the Sikh code of conduct and conventions), a Sikh is defined as "any human being who faithfully believes in One Immortal Being; ten Gurus, from Guru Nanak Dev to Sri Guru Gobind Singh; the Sri Guru Granth Sahib; the utterances and teachings of the ten Gurus and the baptism bequeathed by the tenth Guru; and who does not owe allegiance to any other religion". The most common symbol of all Sikhs, because of its simplicity, is uncut hair (including beards for men) and turbans.

It is important to understand that all the symbols that make a fully baptized Sikh's appearance so distinctive are optional to "slow-adopter" (sahajdhari) Sikhs. These individuals believe in the principles of Sikhism and identify as Sikh but have not yet decided they are ready to make the commitment to become baptized. Some Sikhs may never make this decision in their lifetimes. While some slow-adopter Sikhs will display some of the most overt signs, such as uncut hair, and consequently turbans and beards on males, this is not necessarily the case.

The core philosophy of the Sikh religion can be understood in the beginning hymn of the holy Guru Granth Sahib,

"There is one supreme eternal reality; the truth; immanent in all things; creator of all things; immanent in creation. Without fear and without hatred; not subject to time; beyond birth and death; self-revealing. Known by the Guru's grace"

Guru Nanak, the founder of the faith, summed up the basis of Sikh lifestyle in three requirements: Naam Japo, Kirat Karni and Wand kay Shako, which means meditate on the holy name (Waheguru), work diligently and honestly and share one's fruits.

The Sikhs revere Guru Granth Sahib as their supreme teacher, as it is a literal transcript of the teachings of the Sikh Gurus.The tenth Guru appointed Guru Granth Sahib as his successor. Compiled by the Sikh Gurus, and maintained in its original form, Sikhs revere Guru Granth Sahib as their supreme guide. Non-Sikhs can partake fully in Sikh prayer meetings and social functions. Their daily prayers include the well being of all of mankind.

The martyrdom of the 9th Guru for trying to protect Hindus from religious persecution, in Delhi on 11 November 1675 AD is an example to be followed.

Sikhs are required not to renounce the world and aspire to live a modest life. Seva (service) is an integral part of Sikh worship, very easily observed in the Gurdwara. Visitors of any religious or socio-economic background are welcomed, where langar, (food for all) is always served.

The Sikhs also revere *Bhaktas* or Saints belonging to different social backgrounds. The work of these Bhagats is collected in Guru Granth Sahib, and is known as Bhagat-Bani (sacred word of bhagat) as against work of Sikh Gurus being known as Gur-Bani (sacred word of guru).

The Five Ks, or *panj kakaar/kakke*, are five articles of faith that all *baptized Sikhs* (also called Khalsa Sikhs) are typically obliged (but not forced) to wear at all times, as commanded by the tenth Sikh Guru, who so ordered on the day of Baisakhi Amrit Sanskar in 1699. The symbols are worn for identification and representation of the ideals of Sikhism, such as honesty, equality, fidelity, meditating on God, and never bowing to tyranny.

The five symbols are:-

- Kesh (uncut hair)
- Kanga (wooden comb)
- Kachchhera (undergarment to wear)
- Kara (iron bracelet)
- Kirpan (strapped sword).

Before breathing his last, Guru Gobind Singh, the 10th Sikh Guru bestowed Guruship to Guru Granth Sahib. He also conferred a similar status to the Khalsa Panth (collective wisdom of baptized Sikhs). Hence the authority now lies both on Guru Granth Sahib as well as on the collective wisdom of Khalsa Panth.

A Guru for Sikhs is the guide to the religious path. Shri Guru Gobind Singh Ji was the tenth and the last Guru. In Sikh religion, therefore, no one else can be of the status of the Guru except those from first to tenth Gurus mentioned in the Granth Sahib. The greatest secular value of the Adi Granth is that it contains the writings and ideas, thoughts, religious experiences etc. of different personalities compiled to form the Holy Granth Sahib. In the Adi Granth there are the hymns of Farid (12th Century), Sadhana (13th Century), Tribocana (13th Century), Namdev (13th Century), Ramananda (1360-1450), Saini (1390-1440), Ravidas (15th Century), Pipa (15th Century), Kabir (1440-1518), Dhana (early 16th Century), Bhikkon (16th Century), Surdas (16th Century) and Parmananda (15th Century). These hymns and gospels of Gurus are sweet words arranged in Divine love and reverence. The intimate spirit touching expression in realization of God brings the mind under a mystical spell when you carefully listen to the verses of the Granth Sahib. Guru Nanak traveled in all directions to remote places in India to create awakening and devotion towards God among men and women and to make them involved in nation-building. He preached equality and brotherhood amongst the masses. He tried hard for the Hindu-Muslim unity. The Guru himself considered that he was a kind of saint who is guru of Hindus and pir for Muslims (Guru Nanak

Shah Fakir; Hindu ka Guru Musalman ka Pir). He was also against the useless customs which were prevailing among the Hindus and the Muslims.

The Akal Takht in Amritsar is the highest temporal seat of the Sikhs and its Jathedar holds the highest position. He along with the Jathedars of other four takhats holds an authoritative position among Sikhs. The Golden Temple in Amritswar is one of the oldest Sikh Gurudwara and houses Akal Takht

All Sikhs in Manipur are businessmen dealing in transport, cloths, and contracts etc. They are pioneer transporters in Manipur. They speak Punjabi among themselves but are also fluent in Manipuri (Meiteilon) and even tribal dialects. The Sikhs of Moreh also speak Burmese fluently. They are an adaptable society; no doubt, they keep their Punjabi culture but manage to get along with all groups of society. The Sikhs are very particular about their faith and the ritualistic performances in the Gurudwaras and their homes. *"Sat Sri Akal, Vahe Guru Di Fateh"* is the sentence which is recited by every Sikh or anybody who attends the Gurudwara, after the prayers in the temple. The words when recited create a rhythm with sounds appealing to the spirit. Sat Sri Akal (Sat-truth, Sri-salutation, Akal-God) means the salutation to the real God Almighty, which is timeless and a reality in existence from times immemorial.

NEPALESE

Nepalese means people of Nepal origin speaking Nepalese language. Nepalese started coming to Manipur from the British period as sepoys. Most of the Nepalese entered Manipur as servants and labourers and settled here. At the same time there had been influx of Nepalese into Manipur and they went into the interiors of the hills and found a suitable climate for cultivating land. Some started cultivation of the tribal chief's land as tenants with sufficient share of the crops. They were known for cattle rearing. In the interiors of Manipur, there is no dearth of pastures, so most of the settlers started dairies along with their agriculture. Nepalese are settled in Mao, Maram, Karong and Kangpokpi areas. There is a huge concentration of Nepalese in the Tamei-Tamenglong and also between Tamei and Kangpokpi. On Churachandpur-Sugnu road via hills, one finds several small valleys scattered between the hill ridges. These were uninhabited areas but Nepalese have made them granaries. Similarly on Churachandpur-Tiddim route they have settled in the hill ranges. The main reason for their existence on these forbidden hills is their courage to resist the tribal and the vagaries of nature. They are quick to adapt to the new environment and prompt to convert the habitat. How they changed habitat is the main point to understand. The Nepalese will penetrate into the most interior of the forest and make the land productive and fertile for agriculture The greatest contribution of the Nepalese is to transform the habitat to their advantage. They can till the land, grow crops, establish dairies, poultry farming, rearing of pigs, fowls etc. They organise Durga Puja and other Hindu festivals.

BIHARIS

Bihari are an Indo-Aryan ethnic group originating from the state of Bihar. Biharis speak Bihari languages such as Magahi, Bhojpuri, Maithili, amongst other local dialects, as well as Hindi or Urdu. Bihar was called "Magadha" in ancient times. From Magadha arose two traditions, Jainism and Buddhism. The first Indian empire, the Maurya empire, originated from Magadha, with its capital at Patliputra (modern Patna) in 325 BC. The Mauryan Emperor, Ashoka, is believed to be one of the greatest rulers in the history of India. After seeing all the carnage that war caused, he was placed on the path of Lord Buddha by his spiritual guide Manjushri. The Gupta Empire, which again originated from Magadha in 240 AD, is referred to as the Golden Age of India in science, mathematics, astronomy, religion and Indian philosophy. The peace and prosperity created under leadership of Guptas enabled the pursuit of scientific and artistic endeavours.The capital of Gupta empire was Pataliputra, present day Patna. The Vikramshila and Nalanda Universities, were among the oldest and best centres of education in ancient India. Some writers believe the period between the 400 AD and 1000 AD saw gains by Hinduism at the expense of Buddhism.

The Biharis constitute the labour class people in Manipur. To earn their bread they have come to Manipur. Because of Manipur's comfortable climate, classless society and easy opportunity for earning money, they do not want to go back. They worked as manual labourer, hair dresser, cleaner, coolies, cobbler, masons, rickshaw driver, small time businessmen. Some people from Bihar also run very good business. The Bihari shops and Bihari boys are a common sight in any small town in Manipur. They are fluent in Manipuri language (Meiteilon) as well as in Tribal dialects. They have established themselves throughout the valley on all routes. This linguistic exchange is a great social advantage to both sides. They eat rice, vegetables, chapatti, dal and fish. Some of them take meat as well. Basically hard working and spending very little of their income, the major portion of it goes to their home in Bihar. They are all Hindus, some are from upper castes and some from Scheduled Castes. Some Bihari Muslims have also migrated from Bihar in search of jobs or to run shops in Manipur. The curious character of Biharis is that they get adapted to any society. Many Biharis have settled here with their families. There are several cases of their getting married to Meitei or tribal women. There is no restriction in Manipur on a women marrying a Mayang (outsider) provided she is respectfully owned and kept by the man. There are some big businessmen also who belong to Bihar. They have a good hold on business. The Biharis in general help each other. They are known for their unity.

MARWARIS

Marwaris constitute the main business community in Manipur.In Manipur they are established as a business class. They deal in big business and wholesale trade.Therefore, their concentrations are only in the established old towns and business centres like Imphal, Churachandpur and Moreh. They have entered Manipur in the late nineteenth and early twentieth century. About 90 percent of wholesale business of Manipur is in their hands. They migrated from Rajasthan. Their religion is Hinduism, some observe Jainism and some Sanatan Dharma. Some have adopted Vaishnavite sect also. They are expert in business but they are self-centred community. They marry within their own community. Generally they live as joint family. Their food habits are very simple, generally they are vegetarian and refrain from eating fish, meat, egg, chicken and alcoholic drinks. Some, especially the youth, however, do take non-vegetarian food Their dress is unique white Kurta, Pajama without turban or with white turban. Their women wear sari and choli. During Hindu festivals their women are dressed in costly saris. Their marriage parties are the occasions to display their rich clothes they wear. Their greatest contribution to Manipuri society is business mobilization in Manipur. The stabilization of trade between Manipur and other parts of the country was difficult, but they have created a vital business link between Moreh, Imphal, Dimapur and other cities outside Manipur. The Marwari community at Guwahati or Dimapur shares the business activities of their counterparts at Imphal and Moreh. This trade link has facilitated the Manipuri goods outflow from the state to the markets outside and also the inflow of articles in the state. Today Imphal is a city where varieties of articles are available. Their religious processions in Imphal town are worth witnessing on occasions of Jain festivals. There is a Jain temple in the town.

PUNJABIS

The Punjabi people are the natives of Punjab, speaking Punjabi language and following Punjabi culture and traditions. The non-Sikh Punjabi traders from Punjab and some from Myanmar are also settled at Imphal. Their contribution to Punjabi culture is worth mentioning. Punjabi Culture is the culture of the Punjab region. Punjabi Cuisine has an immense range of dishes and are very tasty. They stick to their food habits, the chapatti, fried vegetables, the curd curries, fried rice and parauthas. Their meat preparations are good. Bhangra is one of the many Punjabi musical art forms and is becoming a mainstream favourite.They retain their habit of speaking Punjabi amongst themselves.

Punjabi Dances are normally performed at times of celebration the most prominent being at Punjabi weddings, where the elation is usually particularly intense. Punjabi wedding traditions and ceremonies are traditionally conducted in Punjabi and are a strong reflection of Punjabi culture. A Punjabi feels at ease whenever he finds a Punjabi-speaking person to talk to him. They speak in a hilarious and jubilant mood. Their women wear salwar-kurta, sari and are very fond of cosmetics. They believe in decent living and eating. The Punjabi community in Manipur is a business community.

SOUTH INDIANS

South Indians are people coming from of Tamil Nadu, Kerala, Andhra Pradesh, Karnataka, Pondicherry and Maharastra. There are a lot of South Indians–mostly Tamils and Keralites in Manipur. They live mostly in Imphal, Moreh and other big towns. Moreh town of Manipur is the real settlement of the Tamils and the Keralites. Most of them are refugees from Burma. In all big towns–Imphal, Churachandpur, Ukhrul and Chandel, one can find these people either in government jobs or in business. They have introduced Idli and Dosa, the famous snack dishes of South Indians in Manipur. The South Indians are mostly rice eaters. A meal cannot go without Sambar. Both times the rice is taken with Sambar and vegetables. The men dress in lungi and shirt. However, office-goers wear pants and shirts also. The women wear sari and blouse. They are mostly Hindus and some are Christians. Moreh Tamils are all Hindus and have established several temples of Kali, Durga and Shiva in the town. They also celebrate their festivals with great pomp and show. They have mastered their tongue in all dialects Hindi is a common language for them. In Moreh, South Indians speak Burmese also very fluently, that goes to their credit to transact business successfully with their Myanmar counterparts at the border town at Tamu in Myanmar (Burma).

BENGALIS

The Bengalis are people speaking Bengali language and coming from the states of West Bengal, Tripura, Assam or Bangladesh.

Lord Sri Krishna Chaitanya (born on full moon day of 18 February, 1486) who has pleased His devotees by giving them the priceless gifts of Bhakti and Prem and who has manifested all the qualities of God completely to allay the sorrows and ignorance of His devotees and who has crushed the false pride of the non-believers with the thunder-like great roar of Sri Harinâm-sankirtan belongs to West Bengal. Sri Ramakrishna Paramahamsa (18 February, 1836–16 August, 1886), Swami Vivekananda (12 January, 1863–4 July, 1902) belong to West Benagl. West Bengal also produced many freedom fighters. The prominent freedom fighters were Chittaranjan Das, Surendranath Banerjea, Netaji Subhash Chandra Bose, Prafulla Chaki, Bagha Jatin, Khudiram Bose, Surya Sen, Binoy-Badal-Dinesh, Sarojini Naidu, Aurobindo Ghosh, Rashbehari Bose and many more. Three Nobel Prize Winners -Rabindranath Tagore (1861 -1941/Nobel Prize for Literature-1913), Mother Teresa (1910–1997/Nobel Prize for peace -1979), Dr. Amartya Sen (Nobel Prize for Economics-1998) are from West Bengal.

The Bengal Renaissance refers to a social reform movement during the nineteenth and early twentieth centuries in the region of Bengal in undivided India during the period of British rule. The Bengal renaissance can be said to have started with Raja Ram Mohan Roy (1775-1833) and ended with Rabindranath Tagore (1861-1941. Nineteenth century Bengal was a unique blend of religious and social reformers, scholars, literary giants, journalists, patriotic orators and scientists, all merging to form the image of a renaissance, and marked the transition from the 'medieval' to the 'modern'.

The Bengalis came to Manipur with the arrival of Hinduism during the time of King Kyaamba (1467-1508). The religious transformation in the valley is the result of the Bengal impact. There was large scale migration of Bengalis and many of them have been absorbed in the Manipuri society as Brahmins, who performed religious rituals for the Hindu Meiteis. They were accepted as Gurus of the kings. They influenced the religious and other social practices to a great extent. They have effected a socio-religious change in Manipur. Many Bengal immigrants have been absorbed into the Meitei society during the Raja's time. They have made a profound impact on Manipuri literature. They worked as interpreters, clerks of the Maharajas during the British period. Bengali dress of the men is dhoti, kurta, shawl and turban. The women wear sari and blouse.. The Manipuris adopted the Bengali style of dress-dhoti, kurta, shawl and turban during the Rajas's time. Bengalis are also rice-eaters and fish is the main dish at every evening meal. The Manipuris also adopted the Bengali style of cooking. At one time, Bengali language was the official language of Manipur. After the "Puya Meithaba", Bengali script was adopted as the Manipuri script. The Bengalis supported and popularized the Raas Lila and other Manipuri dances all over the country. They take keen interest in celebrations of Hindu festivals. The processions on Durga Puja, Saraswati Puja and Kali Puja are worth attending. They have maintained their Bengali culture with its finest heritage. They worked as clerks and other government employees during the time of political agents. Shri Rashiklal Kundu was a Bengali Head Clerk of Mr. Grimwood, Political Agent before the Anglo-Manipuri war of 1891.He married a Manipuri woman called Tharo of Takhellabam family from Lallampung. Their descendants are still living in Thangmeiband. Nowadays, Bengalese are found in almost every office, in teaching professions and in business. Some of them have married Meitei women. There are several families in Manipur, who trace their origin to Bengal on the father's side.

SOCIETY AND CONDUCT OF THE MANIPURIS

There are some social conduct which one has to follow in Manipur:-

1. Address people in respectful terms
2. Removal of shoes before entering a house. If you are entering the house without removing the shoes, the house owner may not say anything but he will consider you as somebody not cultured and who does not respect the social etiquette.The same tradition is followed in Japan, Myanmar, Thailand and other South East Asian countries also. The mainland India do not have such traditions. This is a good and scientific tradition.
3. Speaking frankly
4. Smiling- A smile does not always mean happiness.
5. Do not touch the head and the body :
6. Do not shake hands with females unless initiated by the female.
7. Do not speak against the religion.
8. Tobacco diplomacy.
9. Avoid discussion of the insurgency problem in public :

It is considered polite to offer a cigarette when meeting somebody at least in male to male relationship. However, one is under no obligation to smoke. If you are given a cigarette, you can politely refuse with a smile or just by a wave of the hand. If you are offering the cigarette, you are supposed to open the pack with a cigarette protruding from it. Do not remove a single cigarette from pack and hand it over. Foreign brand cigarette like 555 or Marlboro or a famous Indian brand will be highly appreciated. Offer your cigarettes to the guest before smoking through. But cigarette smoking is dangerous to health and smoking in public places is prohibited by law.

GOVERNMENT AND POLITICS

The Manipur State Government is a democratic form of Government established under the Indian Constitution. The Manipur State Government is headed by a Chief Minister. The Chief Minister is a political leader from a political party who enjoyed majority in the last Manipur State Assembly Election. There are seven important political parties-The Indian National Congress(INC), the Bharata Janata Party (BJP), the Manipur Peoples Party (MPP), the Samajwadi Party, the Communist Party of India(CPI), NCP, RJD, There is a Governor who is the constitutional head of the Government. There are 60 Members of the Manipur Legislative Assembly of which only 12% are allowed to become Ministers.The Government is run through 32 Government departments–like Home, Agriculture, Finance, Medical and Health care, Rural Development, Planning, Industry, Education, Law and Legislative Affairs.

RELIGION

Manipur has a population of 23.88 lakhs (2001 Census). Of the total population, 58.9% live in the valley and the remaining 41.1% live in the hills. In Manipur, the Hindus constitute 57.67% followed by the Christians (34.11%) and the Muslims (7.27%), Sikhs (0.07), Jains (0.07), Buddhists (0.04) and others (0.07). About 235,000-250,000 Manipuri Hindus identified themselves as followers of Sanamahi religion. Around 99% of the hill people (tribal) are Christians.

References

Administration Report of the Manipur Political Agency, 1873-74,1875-76, 1877-78, 1878- 1891-95, 1904-05.

Administration Report of the Manipur State, 1934-35,1939-40,1940-41, 79.

Alexander Mackenzie, North East Frontier of India,1884.

B.C. Allen, Gazetteer of Naga Hills and Manipur, 1905.

B.C. Allen, E.A. Gait, C.G.H. Allen, H.F. Howard, Gazetteer of Bengal and North East Census of India, Manipur, 2001.

Chandrika Singh, Naga Politics - A Critical Account - Mittal Publications - 2004.

Dun, E.W. Gazetteer of Manipur, 1886.

G.A. Grieorson, Linguistic Survey of India, Part III, Vol. III).

G.E Harvey, History of Burma 1925.

Grimwood, St. Ethel, My three years in Manipur 1892.

H.M. Bareh Encyclopaedia of North East India - Mittal Publications - 2001.

Julian Jacobs, The Nagas, Hill People of Northeast India, 1990.

Kuhoi K. Zhimomi, Politics and Militancy in Nagaland - Deep and Deep Publications Private Ltd. New Delhi -110027 - 2004.

L.W. Shakespeare, History of Manipur Rifles,1929.

Khan

N.K. Das, Ethnic Identity Ethnicity and Social Stratification in North East India - Inter - India Publications, New Delhi -1989.

N. Lokendra Singh, Unquiet Valley - Mittal Publications - 1998.

N. Sanajaoba, Manipur - A British Anthology Vol. I - Akansha Publishing House - 2003.

Phanjoubam Tarapot, Bleeding Manipur - Har Anand Publication, New Delhi, 2003.

P.S. Dutta, Autonomy Movement in Assam - Documents - Omsons Publications - 1992.

Contesting Marginality by Sajal Nag - Manohar - 2002. R. Brown, Statistical Account of Manipur, 1874.

Sir James Johnstone., "My Experience in Manipur and Naga Hill" by (1896).

R.M.Nath, The Background of Assamese Culture, Guwahati, 1978, p. 90.

S.C. Sharma, Insurgency or Ethnic Conflict - Magnum -2000.

Sir James Johnstone, My Experience in Manipur and 'Naga Hill' by, 1896.

S.K. Khanna, Encyclopaedia of Northeast - Indian Publishers -1999.

T.C. Hodson, The Meitheis, 1908.

T.C. Hodson,The Naga Tribes of Manipur.

W. Mc. Culloch. Publications of G.H. Damat, An Account of the valley of Manipur and the hill tribes, 1859.

Web Sites: www.satp.org, www.ploughshares.ca/content/ACR00 - IndiaNortheast.html,

6

Meiteis

The Meiteis are the majority and dominant group in Manipur with definite customs, traditions, culture, religious beliefs of their own. They constitute about 60% of the whole population of Manipur.They inhabit mainly the valley of Manipur. They speak "Meiteilon", which is known as Manipuri language.

The old puya 'Leithak Leikharol' describes about the history of the Meitei society, their culture, customs, traditions, religious beliefs, art, and literature. (see Chapter-2:Origin of Manipur and Historical Evidences)

Among the Meiteis, the Hindu Meiteis are the majority whereas those who follow Sanamahi faith and the Brahmins (Bamons), the Chakpas (previously called Lois) and Thoubal Khunous (previously called Yaithibis) are the minority

PHYSICAL FEATURES

The Meiteis are of Mongoloid race with small eyes, fair complexion, rudimentary beards. Majority of the males usually do not exceed 5′7" in height whereas the females are on an average about 4" shorter than males. Men are muscular and stout with well developed chest and hard limbs. They possess enormous stamina and muscular power. Hair are generally coarse and black.Very few grow beard and moustache is not in fashion.The women are beautiful with improved Mongoloid features like slightly sharp facial features.Meitei women can be easily distinguished from hill women. The complexion are usually fair but in general the woman are either fair wheatish or dark. The hair growth of the women is luxuriant. Some unmarried girls prefer to bob their hair and across the forehead cut in circle. Some others keep long hair, parted at the centre and combed backward. (see plate-107, 108 and 109)

MEITEI CLANS- SALAIS/ YEK

Meiteis are divided into seven clans or Salais. "Sa" means body, "Lai" means God (head of the clan). They used to worship their ancestors. It is the unique style of respecting and identifying their forefathers. The "Salais" means a large group of families who originate from the same ancestor. The seven Salais are-Angom, Ningthouja, Luwang, Khuman, Moirang, Khaba Nganba, Chenglei (Sarang Leisangthem).

In the ancient custom, Meeteis used to call their names along with the name of their particular SALAI (clan) e.g. Moirang Thoibi, Khuman Khamba and Angom Nongban etc. (Thokchom Angouyaima, Doren)

After the conversion into Hinduism, these Salais or clans had been given Gotras.

MEITEI SAGEI AND YUMNAKS:

The descendants of a Yumnak has become members of a particular Yumnak. All the members of a particular Yumnak living or dead, can be traced in a genealogy starting from the ancestor. But the Yumnak members maintain their "Yumchangba puya" or "Paripuri", which can trace their genealogy. The Paripuri is written by the literati. It is sacred to them. Normally it is not shown to any person other than the member of the particular Yumnak.

In early days before the arrival of Hindu Vaishnavism, all the members of a particular Yumnak used to gather in the house of Pibaren, the eldest living man in the line, at the intervals ranging between five to ten years. They would ask their literati to read out the whole Paripuri normally during "Apokpa Khurumjaba" (worship of Apokpa / forefathers). At the end of all the recitals, the names of new members added either by birth or by adoption were written in the Paripuri. The girls born to Yumnak were excluded from its Paripuri, but the girls married by the members of any Yumnak become female members of the husband's Yumnak. Nowadays, people observe the Apokpa Khurumjaba but the Paripuri is not given much importance.

Some Manipuri scholars have written books on the topic. They have collected materials from Puyas. N.K. Singh (1969) mentioned the name of the Puyas which are the sources of these materials. L.K. Singh (1965) mentioned the names of the persons from whom the Yumnak originated. By consulting Puya dealing with the Yumnak and the royal chronology it is possible to know the period of a King when a particular Yumnak was created. But this is possible only in the case of the Ningthouja Yek-Salai because the Ningthouja are the

Table-36 Showing Salais with corresponding Gotras of Meiteis

Sl. No	*Salai*	*Colour Insignia*	*Number of Yumnaks or Surnames*	*Gotra*
1.	Angom	White	74	Gautam
2.	Ningthouja	Red	131	Shandillya
3.	Luwang	Blue	69	Kashyap
4.	Khuman	Black	111	Madhugalya
5.	Moirang	Redish Yellow	80	Attreya- Angiras
6.	Khaba Nganba	Green	23	Bharadwaj (Naimis)
7.	Sarang-Leisangthem (Chinglei)	Grey	50	Vasthistha
	Total		538	

descendants of the Kings from time of creation of some Yumnaks. N.K. Singh (1969) mentioned that each of these Yumnaks had its respective occupation. (Loiyumba Silyen-Wayen Pathap written during the period of king Loiyumba /1074-1112). Nowadays, only a limited number of Yumnaks pursue their Yumnak occupations, as for example, the Thangjam manufactured iron implements, the Aheibam produced brass pots, Kangabams and Tourangbams are goldsmiths.

CREATION OF A YUMNAK

King Loiyumba (Meitei khutthek thapalon-1074 A.D) reorganized the seven Salais into "Yumnaks" (family names or surname). H.M. Singh (1968) mentioned how the names for the Yumnaks were derived. According to him, the Yumnaks were named after any of the following characteristics:

- occupation performed by a Yumnak member
- the title given by the King to the creator of a Yumnak
- the service rendered to the King by the Yumnak members
- the service allotted to the creator by the King
- any peculiar behaviour or charactaristics of the creator
- the name of the creator
- the residence of the creator and
- the nature of the creator of the Yumnak.

For example, Ayekpam of the Angom clan is so called because they are painters (ayekpa = painting).Khwairakpam (Ningthouja) is the name of a village level officer. Loitongbam (Ningthouja) is so called because they used to wash the head of the King (luton=upper portion of the head, chamba=to wash).

Mayanglambam (Ningthouja) is so called because the creator was the officer-in-charge of the Mayangs (mayangs=of the Mayang, lanba=officer-in-charge). Huidrom (Ningthouja) is the name of a person,who created the Yumnak. Kongbam (Ningthouja) is taken from the place name, Kongba where the creator settled. The nature of the creator of Naoroitam (Luwang) was that he used to look after the children (nauroi=to look after the child) everywhere.

The literati and the commoners believe in early days that every Yumnak had its respective yelhen (totem) which was not eaten or touched by their Yumnak members. These totems were mostly plants and were not originally treated as such. Certain plants were later on accepted as totem when they were unexpectedly associated with some accidents met with by the members of a particular Yumnak. For instance, when a member of a Yumnak died either by falling down from a tree or by drowning, the very plant or water was treated as Yelhen. They thought that the death was caused by either of those aforesaid agents. So these were not touched or taken. But as no one could live without water, the elders of the Yumnak to which the deceased person belonged held a meeting to choose a plant instead of water as the totem. This decision taken was then communicated to all the members. Nowdays they do not observe the totemic restrictions. Most of these have been forgotten.

The Yumnak members believe that they have descended from a certain person of a particular clan. The genealogies covering every Yumnak under a Yek-Salai constitute a clan. Thus the relationship between members of different Yumnaks under the same Yek-Salai can be traced through genealogy.Yumnaks, may thus be descirbed as a lineage in accordance with the definition by Evans–Pritchard (1940). The segment of a Yumnak is known as Sagei. Every Yumnak is divided into a number of Sageis.

Konsam Manikchand claims the total number of Sageis to be 645, while W. Ibohal puts the figure as 712 and L.Iboongohal Singh put it 446. (W. Ibohal, The history of Manipur; L. Iboongohal Singh, Introduction to Manipur)

SAGEI

Sagei is a segment of a Yumnak. When the Yumnak becomes very large and spread over a vast area creating difficulties in communication or regular contact, then a particular Yumnak may be divided into segments called Sageis. They will retain the same Yumnak but they will have a new Piba or head of the Yumnak. The Meiteis used to inform its Yumnak members at the time of birth and death rituals. They will observe "Yum Mangba" (ritual pollution). They will destroy the Chaphu-Uyan (earthen cooking pots) or clean the metal cooking pots as a mark of observance of the Yum Mangba. When the Yumnak becomes very large, troubles arose regarding the communication of the news of birth and death to fellow Yumnak members for observing the ritual Mangba This is one of the reasons for dividing some of the Yumnaks into appropriate segments called Sageis. Or when a large number of the same Yumnak members go to some distant place or foreign country, they can also form their own Sagei there. These are called "Phukainaba" (Phu-pitcher, kainaba-to break). Sometimes Sageis are developed out of factional rivalry within a Yumnak.

As a rule, the newly created Sagei group should follow certain principles to be qualified as a Sagei. They should follow all the functions, which were performed by the original Yumnak. They should establish a separate Apokpa Laipham (shrine of the clan ancestor). They will bring some earth from the original Apokpa Laipham and keep it at a certain place where they want to establish Apokpa Laipham. Then they should perform Apokpa Khurumjaba. They will search and find out the eldest living person in the line amongst their group members and select him as the *Piba* of the newly segmented Sagei. He will be introduced to all the sagei members. Every Sagei preserve their Paripuri (genealogy) written by the Pandit just like the original Yumnak. The Paripuri should be kept with the Piba and also a copy with the Pandit. The Paripuri is considered to be sacred and as such, one cannot touch it without taking bath. It is also kept secret and normally not disclosed to any outsider.

Sometime, a man can change his affiliation to a particular Sagei within the same Yumnak. The reason may be due to difference of opinion with the Piba or dissatisfaction with Piba or the Sagei members. Under such circumstances, he can approaches the Piba of another Sagei. The Piba then consults other elderly persons and also the Pandit. If every thing is agreeable then the man has to perform the *"Lathaba"* ceremony. In this ceremony Apokpa is worshipped and then the "sagai chakchaba" (a feast enjoyed by all the members together) is performed. During this feast the Piba introduces the new comer to all and then declares that from then on he belongs to their own Sagei. A man of any Sagei may adopt a child of any other Sagei also. But to ensure the membership in the Sagei he is to perform *"Lathaba"* ceremony.

In olden days, people coming from outside Manipur were allowed to settle in Maniur. They were allowed to marry Manipuri women and they were given new Yumnaks under one Yek Salai. Many outsiders including all the Brahmins were given a particular Yumnak or Sagei by the King. But now, they have been so integrated within the Meitei society that it is hardly possible to trace them out without going into details of their family history. Many a time, the Pandits used to manipulate the Paripuri to include the non-Manipuri into the Meitei Yumnak.

If a particular Sagei member wants to trace his genealogy, there may be difficulty due to change of membership from one Sagei to another and he will be required to trace it from the point which they believe to be the starting point of the Yumnak.

Yumnak and sagei are synonymous to the common people for all purposes. If someboy ask, what is your Yumnak or Sagei, the answer will be the same. The only difference is that a particular member belongs to a particular segment of a Yumnak and not necessariy to the original Yumnak. The Sagei members will also perform the same religious and ritual functions as that of the original Yumnak. That is why the Yumnak and the Sagei have become synonymous to the common people. But the difference is that Sagei is a smaller group and it is recognized through their respective Piba and by the observance of Yum Mangba.

APOKPA KHURUMBA

The members of a Sagei worship Apokpa (ancestors) and performed "Apokpa Khurumjaba" (worship of ancestors). There are two important functions of the Apokpa Khurumjaba. One of them is the *"Saren chanba"*, that is, the offering of the Sareng fish *(Wallago attee)* to the Apokpa. The consecrated food is only taken by elders of the Sagei. The Piba takes it first. The other important function is the *SageiChakchaba or* the grand feast. Besides ceremonial functions, the Sagei members observe certain regular activities.

YUM MANGBA

In early days the Yumnak members had to observe *"Yum Mangba"* (birth and death pollution). If any one of a particular Sagei dies all its members are informed. All the families in the Sagei as a sign of mourning break and change their cooking earthern pots, clean and washed the metal pots. They observe death pollution (yummangba) for 7 days in case of a child, 12 days in case of adult of both the sexes and 14 days in case of lamboiba (monk). They observe birth pollution also for 12 days. After 12 days, the house is made sacred by performing a cleansing ceremony and chanting of hymes by the Brahmin called *" Yum Sengba"*.

PIBA

Piba is simply structural head of the Sagei. He is given certain amount of power to exert upon the Sagei members usually limited to certain social and religious functions. Piba should inaugurate Apokpa Khurumjaba. A marriage is only recognized when Piba accepts the food offered by the couple for the Sagei. In early days when the Ningthou (Yek-Salai head) ruled over them, Piba had control on the economic aspects of the Sagei members and he had also some amount of judicial power. They said that Piba used to make the service and the products available to the Ningthou from amongst the Sagei members. The Piba had the power to punish any one who breached the social and religious taboos. Piba is exmpted from Lalup. He should attend to the service of the King.

PIBAREN

Pibaren is the head of all Pibas. When the Yumnak is very big, there may be many Sageis and many Pibas. The eldest living person in the line of a particular Yumnak is called *"Pibaren"*. Pibaren is the head of a Yumnak. If the family history of every Yumnak is followed through, the Pibaren can be traced. The office of the Pibaren is now defunct. When the offices of both the Piba and the Pibaren were in vogue, more power was vested on Pibaren than on the Piba. The Pandits say that the Pibaren used to organize the Sagei members through the Piba in offering the service and products to the Ningthou, the Yek-Salai head. The Pibaren also had more judicial authority than the Piba. The Pibaren used to contact people through the Piba. The Paripuri used to be kept with the Pibaren. It was re-written and new members added to it under the sponsorship of the Pibaren.

NINGTHOU

The tradition of Ningthou (Yek-Salai head) does not exist now. Even if it exist, it does not enjoy the power and prestige. In earlier days, Ningthou used to have even the powers of a magistrate just like Luwang Ningthou during Maharaja Chandrakirti's time. Usually Ningthou is slected by the King from among the seniormost living persons of the Yek-Salai according to the genealogical tree. Ningthou is the Chief of the Clan to which he belonged. It was believed that the ancestor of Ningthou came to this earth earlier than the ancestor of other lineages. That is why he is given the seniormost position and all the lineage members are obliged to recognize this position. Ningthou will organize the functions of the clan such as Lai Haraoba, Saren chanba, Sagei lathaba, Apokpa Khurumjaba etc. through the Pibaren and the Piba. This kind of tradition ensures some sort of social control among the lineage members. This also gives the Ningthou prestige and power within the clan.

FORM OF ADDRESS

Meeteis used to call their names along with the name of their particular "Yumnak" or "Sagei" e.g. Paona Brajabashi, Hijam Irabot, Potsangbam Mani, Lourembam Khongnangthaba, Maisnam Kumudini, Pukhramba Phingang etc.

With the adoption of Hinduism in Manipur, the Meitei were given the suffix "Singh" in case of males, "Devi" in case of females and "Sharma" in case of Brahmins after their personal names as an imitation of the outsiders e.g. Gambheer Singh,Jai Singh, Marjit Singh, Nara Singh etc. Then the descendents of the Kings were given the pre-fix "R.K" or "M.K" meaning Rajkumar or Maharaj Kumar as they didn't possess any Yumnak-Sagei. Meeteis who are residing out side Manipur (Assam, Bangladesh and Tripura etc.) are still using the word "Singha" or "Singh" to call their names for both gender without any name of Salais, Sageis and Yumnaks because of the fact that they fled from Manipur at the time of "First devastation" (Khuntak Ahanba,1755-1759) and "Seven years devastations" (i.e. Chahi Taret Khuntakpa-1819 to 1826) when Singha or Singh was a fashion just like Tarpan Singha, Anita Singha, Bimala Singha etc.

SOCIAL MORES:

There is no caste system in Manipur. Everybody is equal in the eyes of the society. The existence of the seven Salais (clans) was exogamous and not endogamous as in the case of Hindu caste system. Women enjoyed an equal status with men folk before the advent of Hinduism. "Sati" and "Pardah" systems were unknown. At present, families are patriarchal.

MEITEI HOUSES

The traditional Meitei houses are well adapted to the climatic conditions of Manipur. The roofs are normally two sloped..It is made of the wooden posts and beams covered with thatched roof or corrugated tin sheets.The walls of both types are of reeds plastered with a mixture of earth, stems of paddy and cow dung covered with thatched roof. All dwelling houses face eastward in which direction they have a large open Mangon (front verandah).

A standard Meitei house is known as *"Yumjao ka manga"* means five room house. The doors and windows are made of wood. The rooms are airy, spacious, and very clean. Every family has a fairly spacious house divided into different compartments and a separate cowshed for those who have cows and a separate latrine. The main big house is divided into many compartments – Mangon (Front verandah), Ningolka (Room for unmarried daughters), Mayaika (Middle Room), Funga (Fire Place), Sanamahi Ka (Room for Sanamahi) and Chakhum (Kitchen). Mangon is the verandah that is the front side of the house which is used as drawing room. The right side of the Mangon is alloted for the seniormost member (father or grand father) of the house. A *kouna fak* (mat) is always spread over there. Excepting the seniormost member, no outsider is allowed to sit on this mat. The first compartment of the house is Ningolka. This is the bedroom of the unmarried daughter of the house. It may be divided into further small compartments. The second compartment in the big room known as Mayaika, the middle part of the house, is the best part of the house and is used as bedroom by the married members of the house. The rear part is the kitchen which is also used as dining room. However, some families have separate kitchen. Four alcoves, namely, Funga, Fungalairu, Sanamahi kachin and a place for the goddess Laimarel are preserved as the abodes of the gods and goddesses in every Meitei house. Funga (Fire place) is a sacred fire place in the centre of the most important part of the house. Fire is always preserved in this fire place with the husks and other materials. Just to the west and close to Funga there hole known as Fungalairu. This is much respected and also feared because this is considered to be the abode of the goddess of prosperity called "Immoinu". The place for the goddess Laimaren is allotted near the wall just to the north of the Funga. The south-west corner of the house is given for the god Sanamahi. This spot is known as Sanamahi Kachin. Sanamahi and Laimaren are worshipped everyday in their alcoves. In every house there is a sumang (courtyard) in front of the big house. A tulsi (Ocimum sanctum) plant which symbolizes the goddess Brindadevi (a feature of Vaishnava Hinduism) is on the middle of the courtyard of the Meitei Hindu house. It is known as tulsibong. This tulsibong to to be washed and cleansed every early morning by the daughter in law of the house. A place, named, Khangenpham is ear -marked on the extreme south eastern portion of the courtyard. Immediately after the death of an inmate a temporary hut (shang khanba) to keep the dead body is constructed with bamboo and straw at the place called khangenpham. The dead body is shifted to this newly constructed hut which is called khangen-sang. It is considered to be a bad omen to cross the Khangenpham when one is out for a good job. Besides, every house has an attached kitchen garden where various kinds of vegetables are grown.

Nowadays, some affluent people have redesigned the houses and replaced these old types with concrete materials with steel, cement and brick. In towns, the modern type of house construction is common. In villages, there are clusters of traditional type of houses in pockets distributed throughout the valley.

MEITEI DRESS AND ORNAMENTS

The traditional dress of a man is Pheijom (white dhoti), Pungyat (Kurta) and Kokyet (turban). Their dresses are distinct and specific for particular ceremonial occasions. The woollen or endi or silk shawl is wrapped round the body over the white Kurta and dhoti. No other dress is allowed on ceremonial occasions like Luhongba (marriage) or Swaradha ceremony (death ritual). Young people and office goers used to wear pants, shirts and coats. The women dress themselves with a peculiar skirt called *"Phanek"*, which is wrapped around the waist up to the ankles and Furit (Blouse) and Innafi (chadder) to cover the upper portion of the body. Under Phanek no portion of legs is kept bare. It is tied at the waist by simply adjusting the knot by arranging the wrapping ends of the cloth. It is not adjusted with the help of a belt. The knot can be untied easily at any time to adjust the Phanek properly. Another old style of wearing the Phanek is that the cloth is wrapped round the body, at bust and on their back and it goes under the armpits over the breast keeping their portion of body upward the neck bare, it is kept in position by a knot at the side of the body. The common Phanek is Phanek Mayek naibi. The floral designs of the Phanek Mayek Naibi may be Hija Mayek, Hija Mayek Higok Langhou, Khoi-Mayek, Chinglei Mayek Naibi, Kumjenglei Mayek Naibi, Phige Phijol, Phige Kumjengbi etc. On certain religious or ceremonial occasions, a light pink coloured Phanek called *"Pumngou Phanek"* and a white Innafi (chadar) are worn. The craze for imported western skirt is very common among unmarried young girls. They wear knee-long modern skirts. These skirts do not serve the purpose of covering the cylindrical calves as is done with the Phanek. Unmarried girls wear Phanek below the navel whereas the married women wear Phanek covering the breast.

Women are fond of gold ornaments. (see plate-108) The possession of gold is considered as a status symbol and a sign of richness. The most common ornaments for the women is the gold ornaments such as necklaces, bangles (Khuji Popchaobi), ear rings (Angot Lei, Kokhor), arm ring (Pambom phabi) and sometimes nasika (nose ring). Some of the designs of neklaces are:-Kiyam Likphang, Ngangoi Pareng, Heigru Pareng, Kondum Pareng, Tharoi Maning Pareng, Heibi Mapal, Angot Pareng, Liklee Pareng, Sanabung Ngangoi Pareng, Marei Pareng, Likyan Sanarembi Pareng, Sandrembi Pareng, Thambal Mana Pareng. For finger rings, Lairen makhoi, Hambru mapal, Khoi mahum, Charie Khudop were popular. There are hundreds of designs of bangles, necklaces and ear rings. Platinum (white gold) and diamond are becoming popular nowadays. Tattooing is not common among the Meiteis.

OCCUPATION

Agriculture is the main occupation of the Meiteis. Therefore some rituals are concerned with it. The rice goddess is called *"Phouoibi"*. The ploughing must commence on the Panchami festival. The goddess is invoked by the 'Maiba'. The rice and flowers are mixed and wrapped in a Planta in leaf.

It is then taken to the paddy field and the mixture is sprinkled on all four sides. The goddess is also worshipped after the harvest. *'Phou-Kouba'* ceremony is observed by offering *"Sareng"* fish cooked with herb without spices and offered to the goddess with rice. They also carry out some rain rituals on the occasion of heavy rains or when there is severe drought. Kirtans and Bhajans are arranged in temples. In rural areas their main occupation is cultivation and fishing. Weaving and basket making are the main interests of the Meitei women. In every house, there is a loom. Women weave the cloth not only to meet the requirement of the family but also to earn money to sustain the family. The women are expert in the art of weaving. In agriculture Meiteis are much more advanced and self-sufficient in food grains right from the historical times. Fishing is taken as a hobby as well as a profession. The educated people seek official jobs and some people engage themselves in different kinds of business. Some of them run big textile shops, some are retailers, grocers etc.

MEITEI FOOD

Rice and fish are the common and most preferred articles of diet. The Meitei elders usually do not take meat like chicken or mutton or pork or beef. Non-vegetarian food is not prepared in any Meitei house. People do not take chappatti (Tal). People who take chapatti are considered to be very poor. Breakfast is called *"Charawanba"*.

Meitei cuisine is a unique experience in itself. *Chak Chanaba* (Community feast) and Utsav are occasions where more than 200-1000 people use to have a feast together. It will have at least 20-25 different items. (see plate-112) In exceptional cases, more than 108 different items are served. Common items of food are Nga Thongba (Fish curry), Kobi thongba (cabbage or cauli flower), Hanggam Thongba (vegetable mustard), Hawai Thongba (Dal curry), Iromba (kind of chutney), Hawaijar (fermented soyabeans)chagempomba, Champhut (boiled vegetables). Iromba may be of various types of which yongchak iromba tree beans), Soibum (bamboo shoots) and Laphu iromba (plantain stem) are common. Nowadays, young people take all kinds of food including chicken, mutton, pork and sometimes beef. In the early days, Meiteis used to brew and drink alcohol. But they have given up this practice after they became Hindus. Other vegetarian delicacies are– Sanggom Sana thongaba, Madhur Jhan (sweet made of milk, sugar and gram flour), Maroi Morok Thongba, Uti Thongba. Uti Thongba may be of various types- mangal uti, chagem Uti, Hawaijar Uiti etc. Chakhao is another delicacy.

It is a kind of sweet smelling rice, deep violet in colour and is taken combined with milk, sugar, coconut or dry fruits or Sanggom Ksheer. Sanggon Ksheer is another dessert served just before the end of the feast.

The new bamboo shoot known as Ushoi is used as a food by the Meiteis. The Ushoi is finely sliced and prepared as curry mixing with pulses. Another variety of food obtained from the bamboo is the Shoibum or fermented sliced bamboo shoots. The tender shoots of a very small variety of bamboo are chopped into pieces and then fermented to provide a food called Shoidon.This is again one of the popular dishes of the Meiteis. The hottest chilli is the *U-morok*

Utong Chak is another delicacy. In earlier time, Kings and queens used to go out to eat Utong chak. Utong chak is the rice cooked in bamboo tubes. Bamboo tubes, about 60 cm long, cut from a small variety of bamboo are stuffed with cleaned rice and after providing a lid on the open end of the tube, it is grilled in fire. The burnt or charred outer layer is first remoived completely. Thereafter, the cooked rice contained within the tube is eaten by peeling off the pulpy layer of the bamboo.The best variety of bambbo for preparing Utong chak is the Pokshang (Cephalostachyum pergracile) variety.

MEITEI RITUALS

1. Marriage

All the Salai members think that they are related to each other by blood. So they normally follow the exogamous rules of marriage. According to the Meitei custom, marriage within the same Salai is strictly prohibited. Marriage within the same Salai is known as "YEK-THOKPA" ('Yek' means enemy and 'Thokpa' means 'to become' i.e., "to become enemy"). It means; if the bride and groom are from the same Salai, they become enemy to each other (Yek-thokpa) for the purpose of marriage. Marriages are performed in accordance with the Hindu customs but in the typical Meitei style. Before the marriage, the parents of the boy go to meet parents of the girl. This starting approach is termed *'Hainaba'* (engagement). The horoscopes of the boy and the girl are consulted and if both the parents agree, then the next date for the next meeting is fixed. On the next meeting, called *"Yathang Thanaba"*, the consent is given by the girl's parents. The next stage is *"Waroipot puba"* and the groom's family members bring food, fruits and other materials and the contract is considered as finally sealed. Finally the engagement is declared amongst the friends and relatives, this is called *"Heijingpot Puba"*. Friends and relatives from the boy's side go to the girl's parents with food, fruits and presents. The girl's parents also invite their friends and relatives to the occasion. The marriage *(Luhongba)* is fixed by the parents through consultation with the horoscope. The men will come for the marriage in dhoti and kurta with a shawl wrapped around and women in Phanek Mayek naiba and beautiful shawl or innaphi (chader)

At the time of marriage ceremony, the arrangement for sitting is made around the Tulsiboung (Tulsi rostrum). In each Meitei house the Tulsi plant is grown over a raised rostrum. All ceremonies are conducted around this Tulsi plant.

The bride groom will arrive at the appointed hour with a huge following in a grand way with a big band party. The bride goom is received by the women relatives of the bride at the gate with a ritual of *"dyuti okpa*". A separate sitting arrangement is made for the bridegroom and his party. The bride-groom's dress is white dhoti, kurta, Chader and turban. He is attended all the time by a *"Bor sennaba"* who is an elderly person expert in handling such affairs.

The bridal dress (see plate-110) is unique. It is obligatory for the bride to wear the Raas Lila dress called the Potloi.This was introduced by Major Maxwell (1891-1896). She can also choose to wear Phanek in the typical Meitei style if she prefers. The Sankritan is started as soon as the arrival of bridegroom's party is announced. Kirtans and Shehnai music is started. After some time, the bridegroom enters the centre stage of the Sankritan with the sounding of the band party. Before the appearance of the bride, the father of the bride performed the *"Kanyadan"* under the guidance of the Brahmin amidst chanting of hymes. Then the bride is brought out by the mother and other female relatives of the bride. The bride is made to sit near the bridegroom. (see plate-110, 111).The bride makes seven rounds around the bridegroom. At the completion of each round, she will pour flowers on the head of the bridegroom. The bride follows the steps in rhythmic styles in tune with the kirtan music. After completion of the seven rounds, the bridegroom and the bride were made to sit together and exchange *"Kundo garlands"* (Jasmini Multiflorum). No other flower is allowed for the garland in Manipuri marriages except Kundo (Star Jasmine / a white beautiful small flower). The tail ends of their clothes are then tied together and they are asked to enter the house of the bride. Inside the Immung, they are made to sit togther and they exchange *"Kwa Lannaba"* (betel nuts). The sweets are distributed after the marriage ceremony. The guests are given Dakshina. After the end of the religious ceremony, the bride accompanied with the relatives and friends go the house of the bridegroom where the bride is received by the mother in law and other family relatives. The ceremony is never complete until the bride is blessed for a prosperous future by the maternal uncle of the bride. Dowry does not constitute an essential feature in marriages. The dowry is not a compulsion but voluntary. The dowry consists of only essential items for her use such as utensils, beds, almirahs, cupboards,dressing mirror, etc. Nobody talks of dowry in the Meitei marriage.

Polygamy was common in the past due to scarcity of male members because of repeated wars with Burma, devastation of the male population. In the present day the trend is mostly to have only one wedded wife but polygamy is still tolerated. Child marriage is completely absent. Widow remarriage is socially permitted but not within the clan. There is no polyandry system and there is no system of widow inheritance. Divorce is very uncommon.

2. Births

Among the Meiteis, the pregnant woman is not restricted to any kind of food. Ṣwasti Puja or Birth Ritual is performed on the sixth day of the birth of the child. On the sixth day relatives and friends from the parental home of the mother visit the house bringing all sorts of food, fruits and jewellery for the new born child. They come in a procession. This procession is a unique one. The women wear Phanek mayek naiba (special fanek with special design) and beautiful Innafi (chader) and woollen endi or white silk shawl.They bring presents in numerous Firuks (round baskets), Lukmais (flate baskets) in which Kabok (Muri Laddoos), Lalloo, betel leaves, betel nuts, coconut, dried fish and new garments, vegetables of all kinds, fruits of all kinds etc. for the child and the mother are placed. The procession is arranged in a single file. The women are followed by the men. When they reach the house, they keep the gifts in Tulsiboung (Shumang / Courtyard) around the Tulsi plant. Kirtans are arranged. Gifts to the new born child in the form of cash are given one by one by the relatives and friends. One of the maternal uncles will shoot arrows in the four directions and also towards the sky and towards the ground with the idea of driving away the evil spirits. The young maternal uncle is handsomely rewarded with an appropriate *Dakshina* for driving away the evil spirits. Then elaborate food is shared among relatives, friends and invitees. Some families organized various kinds of entertainment programmes for the guests.

3. Chawumba :

The Chawumba is first feeding of the new born child with solid food. The solid food is usually in the form of Sanggom ksheer –soft rice cooked with milk and sugar. It may be usually on completion of the sixth month after birth. The ceremony is performed with a lot of gaiety. A grand luncheon or dinner is arranged by the parents of the child. As a part of the ceremony, various items like paddy, books, pen, money and other materials are placed in front of the baby and the baby is allowed to touch anyone of them. It is believed that if the child touches books first, then he or she will be highy educated. If the child touches money, then he or she will be very rich. Like this, the type of matrerials the baby touches will reflect the future of the child then a nice Sanggom Ksheer, is given to the child. Then all those who are coming are served with delicious foods. Sometimes, dances and musics are also arranged according to the wish of the parents.

4. Naa Hutpa

Naa Hutpa is the ear-piecing ceremony of the child. Every Meitei boy or girl will have a small hole in the earlobes of the ear. It is not a fashion. It is a tradition according to Hindu rites. During childhood, gold or silver ear rings are inserted into the holes. When the boy passed puberty, the ear ring is removed. When the girl passed puberty, the small ear ring is changed into a bigger ear ring made of gold. This ceremony is performed with much fanfare with friends and relatives with a grand feast to celebrate. People do not accept gifts for this occasion. The child's head is clean shaven and goes through a ritual of cleansing. A very beautiful sight. This is a lovely ceremony.

5. Lugoon Thangba or Sacred Thread Ceremony

The Lugoon Thangba ceremony is exclusively for boys. Every Meitei Hindu boy wears the Lugoon or the holy thread at least on this occasion. Of course they keep it hidden. They wear it during the customary one month after the ceremony and then keep it somewhere in a safe place. Manipuri Brahmins are supposed to wear it at all times throughout their lives. The Lugoon of common people consists of only seven threads whereas the Lugoon of Brahmins consists of nine threads The Lugoon Thangba cremony is done anytime after a male child reaches the age of 15. As a part of this ceremony, the boy has to act as if he is going away as a brahmachari (unmarried monk) imitating the way Chaitanya Mahaprabhu had done it centuries ago and his mother and other relatives and friends would stop the boy from going away as a monk. The boy's head will be clean shaven. The boy will wear safrone dhoti and saffron cloth with an umbrella made of bamboo just like a Hindu monk. The boy will go around like a monk with a bowl begging alms from the relatives around there. The relatives will fill the jhola (special bag) with rice, pulses, money, gold and silver. The boy will practice brahmacharihood for 7 days after which the boy is eligible to get married. Without this Lugoon Thangba ceremony, no Meitei Hindu boy is supposed to get married.

6. Yum Sengba

Yum Sengba is the cleansing ceremony of the household. This is the ritual to make the house where the birth had taken place clean by sprinkling water and incantations of mantras. This is ususally done on the fourteenth day of the birth of the child.

7. Yum Sanggaba

This is the inauguration or house warming ceremony of a new house. The house owner of the new house will invite his relatives and friends. They will perform some Puja or house warming ritual with the worship of Ganesh and then a grand feast is hosted. All the people, relatives and friends enjoy the feast. They will come with different kinds of gifts like bed cover, pillow cover, cash and any kind of gift for the house owner.

8. Death Ritual of Meiteis

The dying person is taken out of the house to the mangon (front verandah) and then to the Khangenpham (Shumang/Courtyard). The dead body is given bath and dressed in white clothes before it is cremated. In many cases, the dead body is dressed like a Hindu monk and given a special name of a devotee of the God, Krishna or Radha so that the soul can easily surrender to God in heaven. The dead bodies are cremated according to Hindu rites. The cremation is done on the bank of a river or lake. The fire is taken from the deceased's house. The dead body is placed in a wooden coffin hastily constructed for the purpose.In the mean time, few able bodied men will go to the grave yard (Cremation ground) and make the necessary preparations for the cremation of the dead body. They will dug a shallow pit and then place fire woods across it and thus the funeral pyre is prepared. Four bamboo poles with cotton strings to fasten the Thakkan about 10-15 feet above the funeral pyre is erected. The dead body is carried by four people in the coffin amidst kirtans with cymbals and Pung. The dead body is followed by a procession of relatives and friends. The dead body is placed on the pyre. A son or nearest relative of the deceased with a pitcher-full of water on his shoulder and a burning wooden stick in his hand –followed by the near relatives of the deceased will circle the funeral pyre five times and then the funeral pyre is lighted by the eldest son. The Brahmin does incantations during the rounds. The males stay back till the body is consumed by fire. The female members go back after lighting the funeral pyre. The persons who attend the funeral do not go home direct. They are allowed to enter the house only after taking bath. Then they must walk across a small fire before they enter the house. This is done to ward off the evil spirits. The deceased person's bedding and personal clothing are burnt. It takes from 4-5 hours to complete the cremation. Some burnt bones of the deceased are collected from the ashes. The ashes or piece of bone collected is kept buried at the grave yard. After the completion of the burning, the particular spot of funeral pyre is swept neat and clean with water. On the sixth day, the "Asthi Sanchaya" is performed where the relatives and friends will come, collect the ashes or piece of bone, which is carried by the son or near relative of the deceased. On the 14th day, the Swaradha ceremony is performed where Kirtans are held with singing of hymns and incantations by the Brahmins. All the males will come only in dhoti, kurta, chader and the women in Pungou Fanek and white innafi as a sign of mourning. All the people coming are given food to eat (Fola or Tal or chak or kshechri) and Dakshina. The Swaradha ceremony is considered to be a sacred ritual and everybody is supposed to come after taking bath at home with a chandal (sandal paste) on the forehead. Thes ashes or piece of bone collected is placed in abamboo tube and after a few months, it is taken to holy places like Vrindaban or Nabadwip or Sangam and immersed in a sacred river like the Ganges at Sangam or at Vrindavan or Nabadwip.

TOTEMS

Totems in the form of tall bamboo poles decorated with three to nine circular bamboo rings, draped with cloth cut in geometrical designs are a marked feature of the Meitei society. The bamboo poles have to be straight ones and of the biggest variety. The rings are of uneven sizes, the smallest one adorning the tip of the poles and the biggest ring comes the last. These totems are known as "Shattra". They are a must for various rituals and ceremonies. Shattras are offered and used as a sacred item for festivals honouring the sylvan deities (Umang Lais). These totems are used in rituals connected with inauguration of Pukhris (ponds), death ceremonies and first death anniversary of the Meiteis. On festive occasion of Hari-oo-than, Meitei Hindus erect tall, straight bamboo poles on which circular rings are fixed. In the villages, young girls prepare garlands of marigold flowers with which they decorate the rings on the bamboo poles, thus presenting lovely flower totems to appease or to honour Wangbren of the Meiteis.

In a village called Karang on the Loktak lake, people put up tall, straight bamboo poles with a lovely cluster of small branches and leaves at the tip in their courtyard to declare the engagement of their daughters to their future husbands.

The Maring tribes also put up several bamboo totems in their courtyard on the occasion of the *Yaakiyo* ceremony. These totems are erected to inform the people about the ceremony being observed. On the tip of these totems are hung replicas of birds and animals made of bamboo and wood. An elevated balcony of bamboo is constructed all around the courtyard. This serves as the seats for the people who play drums, gongs etc on the occasion.

MANIPURI LANGUAGE (MEITEILON): AND MANIPURI SCRIPT (MEITEIMAYEK)

The Manipuri language (Meiteilon) is the official language of Manipur. It has a long past history. Manipuri Language and literature has been offered as a subject of study upto M.A. level. It is also taught in many universities in India. Manipur has its own script called Meitei Mayek (Manipuri Script) which has been in use since the ancient times. Though it had been stopped to be in use for certain period, now it is revived and become increasingly popular. It is the link language among all different tribes and people inhibiting Manipur The Meiteilon or Manipuri language is included in the Schedule-VIII to the Indian Constitution and is the lingua franca of all tribes in Manipur.

MANIPURI MAYEK AND SCRIPTURES

Meiteis have their own script, literature and scriptures.The Manipuri script is so much meaningful that in the explanation of the alphabets all the philosophies of the ancient religion and thoughts of the Meiteis are found in significant meanings of the composition of the alphabet. For example, Kok (K in English) is composed of seven lines representing the seven Yumphams (Chakras) denoting the seven colours of the sun light, or, the seven Salais (Clans) of the Meiteis, or, the Lainura taret (seven women mother goddesses), or, the seven layers of the heaven, etc. Thus all the alphabet have their own highly philosophical meanings. The scriptures - *Wakoklen Thilel Salai Amailon Pukok, Sakok Lamlen Ahanba, Leithak Leikharol, Pakhangba Yangbi, Pakhangba Phambal, Indri Sekning, Pombi Lang, Khangoi Yangoi Sekning,* and many others discuss the soul and its existence in human body, the soul of all creatures, the secret state of life and death, the origin of this universe and so on.The most specific feature of the scriptures is the place of the male and female deities in the religious practices of the Meiteis. The scriptures give the highest place of the Lainuras: Panthoibi and Ima Leimarel Sidabi, the supreme mother and its incarnations as the mother of all kinds of living beings and as the mother of the origin of the Universe: the sun, the planets, the stars, the moon, the earth, etc. After studying these scriptures, the Sanamahi religion may be called the Pakhangba Laining.

Atiyadagi Thokpa Khonthok Mayek

Table-37Showing the Manipuri Script Meitei

Meitei Mayek	*Bengali*	*Meitei Mayek Key Stroke*
ꯑꯥ	আ	A a
ꯑꯦ	এ	A e
ꯑꯩ	ঐ	A E
ꯑꯣ	ও	A o
ꯑꯧ	ঔ	A O
ꯑꯪ	অং	A q

Mapum Mayekki Khonthok

ꯀ- Kok	ক	k
ꯁ- Sam	স	s
ꯂ- Lai	ল	l
ꯃ- Mit	ম	m
ꯄ- Pa	প	p
ꯅ- Na	ন	n
ꯆ- Chin	চ	c
ꯇ- Tin	ত	t
ꯈ- Khou	খ	K
ꯉ- Ngou	ঙ	Ng
ꯊ- Thou	থ	Th
ꯋ- Wai	ৱ	W

(Contd.)

(Contd. Table-37)

ꯋ - Wai	ৱ	W
ꯌ - Yang	য়	Y
ꯍ - Huk	হ	H
ꯎ - Un	উ	U
ꯏ - Ee	ই	I
ꯐ - Fam	ফ	F
ꯑ - Atiya	অ	A
ꯒ - Gok	গ	G
ꯓ - Jham	ঝ	Jh
ꯔ - Rai	র	R
ꯕ - Baa	ব	B
ꯖ - Jil	জ	J
ꯗ - Dil	দ	D
ꯘ - Ghou	ঘ	Gh
ꯙ - Dhou	ধ	Dh
ꯚ - Bham	ভ	bh

Cheitap Mayekki Khonthok

ꯥ - Aatap	া	a
ꯦ - Yetnap	ে	e
ꯨ - Unap	ু	u
ꯤ - Enap	ি	i
ꯩ - Cheinap	ৈ	E
ꯣ - Otnap	ো	o
ꯧ - Sounap	ৌ	O
ꯪ - Nung	ং	q

(Contd.)

(Contd. Table-37)

Mashing Mayek

꯱- Ama	১	**1**
꯲- Ani	২	**2**
꯳- Ahum	৩	**3**
꯴- Mari	৪	**4**
꯵- Manga	৫	**5**
꯶- Taruk	৬	**6**
꯷- Taret	৭	**7**
꯸- Nipal	৮	**8**
꯹- Mapal	৯	**9**
꯱꯰- Tara	১০	10

Lonsum Mayek

Mayek	*Key Stroke*
ꯛ- Kok Lonsum	Q
ꯜ- Lai Lonsum	L
ꯝ- Mit Lonsum	M
Mayek	*Key Stroke*
ꯞ- Pa Lonsum	P
ꯟ- Na Lonsum	N
ꯠ- Tin Lonsum	T
ꯡ- Ngou Lonsum	Ng
ꯢ- Ee Lonsum	I

Khudam Mayek

Mayek	*Key Stroke*
꯫- Cheikhei	|
꯭- Apun	_
꯬- Lum	.

SOME OF THE COMMON WORDS AND RESPECTFUL TERMS OF MANIPURI LANGUAGE (MEITEILON) ARE AS FOLLOWS :-

Table-38 Showing common terms in English-Manipuri

Sl.No	*English*	*Common Manipuri language*	*Respectful terms in Manipuri language*	*More respectful terms in Manipuri language*
1.	Father	Paji/ Ipa	Pabung	Pabung Sanakhya
2.	Elder Brother	Tada /Ibung	Tamo/Ibung	Yambung/Ibung
3.	Wife	Nupi / Matu	Loinabi / Moi mama	Taloi
4.	Husband	Nupa/ Mawa	Ma-bungo /Moi pabung	Ma-bungo
5.	Younger Brother	Inao	Inao Ibungo	Inao Ibungo
6.	Elder Sister	Iche	Ichebemma	Ichebemma
7.	Younger Sister	Ichal	Ichal Ibemma	Ichal Ibemma
8.	Sister-in –law	Iteima	Iteibemma	Iteibemma
9.	Uncle	Khura	Khuraibungo	Itonibungo
10.	Maternal Uncle	Mama	Maibungo	Maibungo
11.	My son	Icha Nupa	Ichaibungo	Icha Ibungo
12.	My daughter	Icha Nupi	Ichaibemma	Icha Ibemma
13.	His /Her son	Machanupa	Machaibungo	Majaibungo
14.	His /Her daughter	Machanupi	Machaibemma	Majaibemma
15.	Drink	Thakpa	Fanba	Fanba
16.	Meal	Chak	Luk	Luk
17.	Eating	Chaba	Haba	Haba
18.	Eating Rice	Chakl Chaba	Luk Haba	Luk Haba
19.	Have you taken meal	Chak charabra	Luk habirabra	Luk Katpirabra
20.	Please take your meal	Chak chabiro	Luk habiro	Luk Katpiro
21.	Please come in	Changbirak-u	Lengsinbirak-u	Lengsinbiraksi
22.	Please go	Chatpiro	Lengbiro	Sana khonglengbirasi

(Contd.)

(Contd. Table-38)

Sl.No	English	Common Manipuri language	Respectful terms in Manipuri language	More respectful terms in Manipuri language
23.	I am going	Ei chatle	Ei chtachare	Nanai Ei chatcharage
24.	I am telling you	Eina hairi	Eina haiajari	Nanai eina hangatchari
25.	Where is your home?	Yum kadaidano ?	Sangai Kadaidano ?	Sana Sangai Kadaidano
26.	Illness	naba	Hakchang eeba	Sana hakchang eeba
27.	Your body	Nahaki hakchang	Nahaki hakchang	Sana hakchang
28.	Legs	Khong	Khong	Sana Khong
29.	Are you sleeping ?	Tumbirabra ?	Cheppirabra ?	Cheppirabra
30.	Giving Birth	Macha pokpa	Angang Unaba	Soinaiba
31.	Seat	Phambam	Khuda	Khuda
32.	Taking bath	Irujaba	Chaithaba	Chaithaba
33.	Walking	Chatpa	Khongdoi hunba	Khongdoi hunba
34.	To serve	Seba touba	Thougal touba	Thougal touba
35.	Attendant	Seba touba Mee	Thougal Macha	Thougal Macha
36.	Governess	Yokchabi	Yokchabi	Sana Mapi
37.	Dressing	Phi setpa	Phi thonba	Phi thonba
38.	Turban	Kokyet	Kokyet	Khokthon
39.	Good Morning	Kamdouri, Nungairibra	Kamdoubiri, Nungaibiribra	Kamdoubiri, Nungaibiribra
40.	Good Night	Phare Kainarasi	Phare Kainarasi	Phare Kainarasiko
41.	Can I get a Taxi	Taxi fanggadra	Taxi Fangbigadra	Taxi Fangbigadra
42.	Can I get a Hotel Tariff	Hotel gi tariff ama piyu	Hotel gi tariff ama pibiyu	Hotel gi tariff ama pibigadra
43.	Can you give some discount	Discount khara piyudana	Discount khara pibiyu	Discount khara pibigadra
44.	Kill	hatpa	Angang olhanba	Angang olhanba
45.	Bury	Fumjinba	Leiron chanba	Leiron chanba
46.	Mind	Pukning	Paima Pukning	Paima Pukning
47.	Death	Shiba	Nongaba, Amang yaithong kumba	Nonggaba, Amang yaithong kumba
48.	Yours faithfully	Nahakki sebada	Adomgi sebada	Nanai Ei , Tollaba Nanai Ei
49.	Yes	Hoi	Ahoi	Ahoi
50.	No	yade	yajadre	Yajadre
51.	Bye bye	Kainarasi	Kainarasiko	Kainarasiko

MEITEI LITERATURE

Literature is like a mirror reflecting the stage of development of a society.The Meitei literature may be divided into three periods; the ancient period (from the early periods to the seventh century) the medieval period (from the eighth century to the first quarter of the twentieth century) and the modern period, from the end of the first quarter of twentieth century onward.

Ancient Literaure

The ancient period literature is valuable in tracing the history of civilization. The classical volumes in the ancient Meitei literature are:

- *Ougri*: It is composed in beautiful verses about the creation of the universe. It is said that it was recited at the coronation of Nongda Lairen Pakhangba, the king of Manipur, thereafter it became the custom to recite it on coronations.
- *Khencho* is an ancient composition, it is sung in chorus at Lai-Haraoba festival.
- *Sana Lamok* is another composition in archaic Manipuri. It is sung to evoke the spirit of Pakhangba.
- *Numit Kappa*, the shooting of the sun has been described in it.
- *Panthoibi Khongul*: about the female beauty, the description is from her childhood to her becoming the Divine Mother.
- *Hijan Hirac* is a composition about the nature around. It is in verse form.
- *Poireiton Khun Thokpa* is the account of migration of Poireiton from the east and establishment of Pouirei Meitei Lam.He is said to be present during the coronation of King Pakhangba, whose queen was Laisna, a younger sister of Poireiton.
- *Cheitharol Kumbaba* is in archaic Meitei language and is considered to be the earliest recorded chronicle starting from the reign of King Pakhangba in 33 A.D.
- *Nongdam Ponbi Luwaoba* is the story about heroeship of Ponbi. The hero wins over the agents of the death and saves his wife.
- *Khongjomnubi Nonggarol* is a work giving a legend about six girls.
- *Leithak Leikharol* gives the story of the creation of the world.

Medieval Literature :

In the medieval period, there was a tremendous growth in literary activities. The period was also a period of social intercourse with Indian mainland, their societies, cultures and religions. The Renaissance was introduced by Bhagyachandra. Manipuri poets contributed to the work Dharmi Sanhita in Bengali. Bengali language continued till 1924. Ramayana, Mahabharata, Chaitanya Charitamrita were written in Bengali. The devotional Kirtan in 'Panchali' and Brata-Katha were also composed in Bengali. Samjok Ngamba, Takhel Ngamba, Ava Ngamba, Khagi Ngamba and romantic tales in Chotha Thangwai Pakhangba and Sanamanik. Khomba Gangachitra giving the account of Maharaja Bhagyachandra's pilgrimage to Nabadwip were written in Manipuri. Angom Gopi translated Ramayana and Mahabharata in Manipuri. On the whole the medieval period in Manipuri literature proved to be a period of assimilation and germination of new ideas.

Modern Literature

After the first quarter of the twentieth century, Manipur had seen advent of modern literature in the form of Manipuri dramas, short stories, lyrics, novels, poems and prose written by various writers. Kwarakpam Chaoba (1895-1950) was a famous Manipuri poet. Dr. Kamal Singh's novel Madhavi and Lei Pareng touched the heart of Manipuri people. Hijam Anganghal Singh wrote an epic Khamba Thoibi Sheireng, and a narrative poem of love Shingen Indu. He was a successful novelist as well. His novel "Jahera" depicts the story of love between a Hindu young man and a Muslim young girl. Dorendra Singh authored "Kangsha Bodha". Kapal Kundala of Bankim Chandra was translated by Mutum Shyamsunder Singh and Abhijnana Shakuntalam was translated by Vasudev Sharma. There was further development of Meitei literature after World War II. The following are some of the famous authors and their masterworks during the period.

- A. Minaketan - Meitei Upanyash
- A.C. Singh - Achaiba Lei and Sahitya Neinaba Wareng
- Braja Bihari Sharma translated Kalidas.
- Ch. Manihar Singh - Liklam.
- Dr. Komol- Madhabi, Leipareng
- E. Nila Kanta - "Chatlasine" Kadaidano Ibani, Manipuri Kavitagi Chhanda
- Hijam Guno Singh -"Khudol" "Laman", and "Aroiba Paodam"
- Hijam Anganghal Singh – Jahera, Khamba Thoibi Seireng
- Ibohal Singh - "Edi Oktabini"
- Kala Chand Shastri translated Mahabharata in more than 33 volumes. He was a Padmashri award winner as a writer.

- Khwairakpam Chaoba – Labanga Lata
- L. Premchand- Imagee Phanek Machet
- Late Panditraj Atombapu Sharma translated from Sanskrit to Manipuri, Chanakya Niti, Chaitanya Charitamrita, Gita and Alhorba Veda.
- Longjam Parshuram – Langoi Shagol Thaba
- L. Somorendra Singh - "Wa Amatta Haige Telanga,"
- M.K. Binodini- Bor Saheb Ongbi Sanatombi, Churachand Maharaj's Immung and many other stories.
- N. Biren- "Tollaba Sha Adugi Wakhal"
- N. Khelachandra Singh -Manipur Shahityagi Ariba Itihas
- Nilabir - "Ithak Ipom".
- N. Kunjamohon- Elisha Amagi Mahao
- O. Bogeseshor – Numit Kappa
- Pacha Meitei -"Na Tathiba Ahal Ama", "Haji and Hayad Begum"
- Prof. Nandlal Sharma has contributed in the field of Manipuri Philosophy.
- R.K. Surendra-Chhand Veena
- R.K. Shitaljit's - novels Ima, Rohini and Thadokpa
- T. Thoibi Devi -Radha, Nugshi Echel, Chingda Shatpi Ingellei
- Prakash, Nilabir, Biren, Chitreshwar, Dinamani, Tejamani, M.K. Binodini are also famous writers.
- R.K. Madhubir, R.K. Surendra, E. Rajanikanta, T. Thoibi Devi, B. Jayanta Kumar Sharma and Kh. Prakash are most valuable in enriching the Manipuri literature.

MEITEI RELIGION AND ANIMISM

In the initial stages the aboriginal tribal society followed the animistic way of religious life. Animism made religion of all mysteries and started worshipping the unknown spirit. Any thing which threatened them and caused death was most powerful for them. They believed that the spirit is the root cause behind death. This belief led them to propitiate the spirit. Later it became the ritual. They also believed that the animals they take as food can be offered to please the spirit so that they themselves are not harmed. Thus started the concept of animal sacrifice. They smeared the objects of their faith with blood as they felt blood was something important for life. Mysteries confused their minds. Superstitions became part and parcel of their faith.They followed curious customs for social life and also followed strongly the cult of the death.

To find out the good or bad omens or to cure the patients or to get the effect of the evil spirit removed, an egg is broken and its yolk is examined by the animist priest. On examining the egg he tells about the type of the spirit which had cast spell upon the patient or any other members of the family. Depending upon the intensity of the effect of the spirit or the type of the spirit, animal sacrifice is suggested. If the effect is not very serious then a hen is sacrificed, otherwise a pig or dog is sacrificed. In case if it is very severe then the sacrifice of buffalo or mithun may also be suggested. The meat of the sacrificed animal is given to the patient. The blood is smeared on the deity and some pieces of the meat are offered to the deity or the spirit. They believe in ancestor worship and that the spirit of the death assumes the form of ghost. Some offerings are occasionally made to the dead.

THE MEITEI LAIS

The number of deities worshipped by the Manipuri Meiteis, is computed to be three hundred and sixty four in addition to the three members of trinity, i.e, Atiya Kuru Sidaba or Sidaba Mapu, Pakhangba, Sanamahi, Leimaren Sidabi, Panthoibi, Nongpok Ningthou.The supreme god is Atiya Kuru Sidaba or Sidaba Mapu.For purpose of the worship the deities can be divided into several groups, viz, Lam Lai-gods of countryside; Umang Lai -forest deities; Imung Lai-the tutelary deity of each house and Apokpa-the ancestors of each clan.

SANAMAHI

The Meiteis had their own system of religion which had its own myths and legends, gods and goddesses, priests and priestesses, rituals and festivals, etc. though it was more or less akin to the animism. The Meiteis used to worship the forces of nature like fire, water, mountain etc. ancestor worship (Apokpa), Lamlai, Yumlai, Ningthoulai and Umanglai.

Sanamahi religion is one of the oldest religions of South-East Asia. There is reference to the worship of Sanamahi by King Kangba during 1405-1359 B.C in Hayi age. Thus Sanamahi was the religion of the Manipuris from 1405 B.C till abolition of Sanamahism in 1723 by Maharaja Garib Niwaj. It originated in Manipur and mainly worshipped by the Meiteis, Kabuis and Zeliangrong and few other communities who inhabit in Manipur, Assam, Tripura, U.P, Myanmar, Bangladesh.

The ancient Kings and people of Manipur worshipped Sanamahi before the arrival of Hinduism. The study of Sanamahi religion may be termed as "Sanamahism" and the followers as Sanamahists". They worship "Atiya Kuru

Sidaba or Sidaba Mapu" or the immortal one–the immortal God. They worship Sanamahi, Leimarel Sidabi, Panthoibi, Nongpok Ningthou. During the reign of Nongda Lairen Pakhangba, Pakhangba Laining became popular. Pakhangba Laining means "know Him, to know the soul, to know the Lord, to know father and mother–to be honest". Worship of Umanglai was a part and parcel of Sanamahism. Pakhangba was the King of Kangla (cult of the ruling dynasty) and Sanamahi was the ruler in every house (cult of masses). Some of the salient features and aspects of Sanamahism are like "in Sanamahism there is the belief in one God underlying many gods and goddesses". It also include worship of forces of nature like fire, water, mountain etc. Ancestor worship (Apokpa), Lamlai, Yumlai, Ningthoulai and Umanglai. Atiya Shidaba, Apanba and Asheeba are the three manifestations or incarnations of God as the creator, the preserver and the annihilator of this universe respectively. Pakhangba, Sannamahi and Nongpok Ningthou are the incarnations who play the role of the male deities of the Meiteis whereas Leimarel Shidabi and Panthoibi, the role of female deities. Panthoibi is the Mother of the Universe and Nongpok Ningthou is her mate. Besides these, three hundred and sixty four deities with their consorts are the most important deities worshipped by the Meiteis.

According to the last census, about eleven percent of Manipur belong to Sanamahism. This represents a significant increase over the previous census. The revivalism of Sanamahism is recognized by the census records of the government of India due to the praise worthy efforts of late R.K. Birendro Singh, I.A.S. The story of Sanamahi faith of Meiteis has been briefly desribed under creation of Clans and Yek salai. (See Chapter-2:Origin of Manipur and Historical Evidences).

The Sanamahi Laishon became an everyday life of Meiteis with verbal chantings and singings and was common to all people. When Pakhangba became King, the Pakhangba Laining became very popular. Pakhangba Laining (mediation) is the art of looking into the self by the self for the self, which was coined as "Hee-ree Kon-ba". No verbal chanting was allowed in Pakhangba Laining and required deep concentration and meditation. It was performed by Kings, nobles and maichous (scholars) to enlighten self and to be able to live conscientiously. (K.C. Tensuba-Heeree Konba, 1994)

After the conversion to Hinduism, the exactions of the Brahmins on the common people had made their life quite miserable. Such a feeling was first expressed by a young Meitei from Cachar named Naoria Phullo.He was born in 1889 in a peasant family. He passed Matriculation Examination, entered the Police service and resigned from the post of Sub-Inspector of Railway Police.

While he was in the school, he was insulted by his fellow Bengali students that Manipuris did not have any script of their own but borrowed the Bengali Scripts. Such insults had made young Phullo to think about his self identity, racial consciousness of the Meitei nation. He founded the Apokpa Marup at Laishram Leikai in Cachar in 1930 at the age of 41 years to do research on the ancient religion, Sanamahi and also cultures of Manipur. This Apokpa Marup or society became very powerful in due course of time.

He also wrote many books on on different subjects of Meitei culture, traditions, beliefs and practices. Many of his books contains poems, hymns and philosophy. An extract from one of his poems in the book named Tengbanba amasung Lainingthou Laipao reads as follows :-

Houro Houro Parikhoi
Mapugi paobu lakle ibungosing
Houro Houro Parikhoi
Poklen Pokpa Ya-olle
Tungna Mang oirakle
Pangdharuba singli Hourakle

His love for his motherland is expressed in the following poem:-

Koubru Chingna Lemphuni
Kanglanadi Khoidouni
Loktak sana tengotni'
Meetei thawai oibani

Meiteilonna sak-chage, Meitei lonna son-jage
Eswar haiba mingkheibu apokpani haijage

Phaarabasu Imani, thirabasu imani
Imatabu nungsini, imatabu thougalni

Once the Maharaja Sir Churachand Singh and his Raj Pandit had an encounter with Naoria Phullo in 1936. The news about the activities of Phullo reached Manipur in late 1930s. His movement took the anti-Brahmin, anti-Bengali and later on anti-Hindu forms. He had established contacts with friends in Manipur, among them were Pukhrambam Surachand, Pukhrambam Ibomcha, Takhellambam Bokul. Naoria Phullo after a decade of vigorous religious and scholarly life died on 30th June, 1941. He had re-discovered the Meitei script, wrote religious hymns and treatises to be used by his followers.

However in Manipur, the Sanamahi movement took a definite shape when the Meitei Phurup was established at Thambalkhong, Imphal on 14th

May, 1945 with Pukhramba Surachand as the President. On the day of formation of the Meitei Phurup, they hoisted the "Seven Colour Flag" as the symbol of unity of the seven Ye-Salais of the Meiteis.The meeting passed 28 resolutions which among other things decided to revive the cultural heritage of the Meitei people, to do research in the ancient history and other literature, to revive the Meitei script, to worship and chant religious hymns in the mother tongue. Takhellambam Bokul who appears to be the theoretician of the Meieti Phurup took pains in explaining that they were not anti Hindus, what they wanted to, according to him was the substitution of Meiteis names for Hindu gods. Though the movement was not anti-Hindu in the late 1940s, but it was definitely anti-Brahmin. Those who took the leading part were those who were persecuted by the Brahma Samaj. The Brahma Samaj reacted violently against the Marup and there were allegations made against the Brahma Samaj. What is the fundamental basis of Sanamahi movement? It is to revive the Sanamahi cult, the indigenous religion of the Meiteis. They believe in Atiya Guru Sidaba, the Supreme God, Pakhangba, Leimaren, Sanamahi, and host of Umanglais (forest gods or local deities). Sanamahi is a household god which in Manipur, every family Hindu or Meitei, even Manipur Brahmin worships.

The fact that they were anti-Brahmin is indicated by the religious debates between Sanamahi protogonists and the Brahmins. They devoted themselves to discovery of the ancient manuscripts, or puya, popularisation of Meitei script. They have been making attempt to de-sanskritise Manipuri history. They opposed the theories of Manipur connected with Mahabharatta or the Aryans. Their efforts have produced tremendous effects; the myth of the Aryan origin of the Meiteis has now been exploded. There are many societies or marups in villages scattered all over the valley. The central council is the Meitei Phurup. There are a lot of literature published by these societies.They claim that their population is more than 88,000 now. The Sanamahi movement gives strong emphasis on the national identity of the Meitei; and there is a tendency to turn towards a political movement. The support to this movement came from the farmers and some businessmen; but less support from the Govt. employees. There is a popular support from the young students though their religious attachments is not deep. This Sanamahi movement's popularity depends on the anti-Brahmin propaganda and racial self-consciousness of Meiteis.

The revivalist movement of the Sanamahism moves faster for the re-vitalization of the ancient religion and culture of Meiteis. Nowadays, there is a revivalism of the Sanamahi religion and Meitei Mayek scripts in Manipur since 1944.The impact of Sanamahism became more and more embedded in the hearts and mind of the people at large. As a result, it gave a new hope and dimension in the process of the revivalist's movement of Sanamahism. Due to increasing education and consciousness among the people, Sanamahism has gained a strong foothold now. Moreover in the census of 1981, 2001, Sanamahi religion was recorded as one of the recognized religion of Manipur.

On April 23 1992, the then Maharaja of Manipur, Okendrajit Sana declared that "I open the Lubak Tabu and abandon Hinduism as state religion and recognition is hereby withdrawn by the Royal Customary Law of the Country, instead the Royal Customary Law revives the Lainingthouism as the state religion and do hereby give recognition as state religion".

The festival of Sanamahi religion has become more popular and is being observed by more and more people in the recent times. Sajibu Cheiraouba is being observed to welcome the New Year (Sajibu Nongma Panba). Meitei mayek is formally included in the school curriculum. Many images of Lord Sanamahi from its Brahmin Pujari from many place like Keisamthong Moirang Ningthou Leirak Imphal, Kongmaroo, Mongba Hanba Forest, Hiyangthang Lairembi and the sacred place Nongmaijing Nongpok Ningthou. Many books on how to conduct religious ceremonies with rites and rituals are being published. With the establishment of many religious organizations devoted to Sanamahism, the old religion is gaining popularity among the educated and uneducated alike.

THE UMANG LAIS (SYLVAN GODS)

The term "Umang Lai" is used generally to cover all the categories of Manipuri gods, although it has a narrower meaning when it applied specifically with Sacred groves. Etymologically the term Umang Lai means Forest or Wood deity (Umang=forest, Lai=god), but in many cases deities termed Umang Lais have no connection with trees whatsoever. Umang Lais can be classified broadly into four categories-

- *Ancestral Gods* : Ancestors or Gods that were believed to have had a human existence in the past. Examples are Pakhangba, Nongpok Panthoibi etc.
- *Gods associated with yek's* : Gods associated with particular yek's or Salai. For example, Thangjing is the god of the Moirangs, Oknarel as for the Khumans etc.
- *Domestic Deities* : The Yumjao Lai's or clan gods associated with particular clan or family groups (Sagei). Traditionaly there are 565 Sagei's,

each of which has its own Lai's. Household deities like Sanamahi, Leimaren and Phungga fells into this category.

Tutelary Deities : Guardian spirit connected with particular place or areas. For example, Marjing is the guardian of North-East, Khana Chaoba is the guardian of the south.

Some the popular Umang Lais are Moirang Thangjing, Konthoujam Lairembi, Khorifaba, Khamlangba, Ibudhou Irum Ningthou, Khana Chaoba Wangbaren, Tampha Lairembi, Hiyangthang Lairembi, Panthoibi, Phaoibi, Kounu Lairembi, Yumjao Lairembi, etc.

TREE CULTS OF ANCIENT MANIPUR

Trees are worshipped or given very high magico-religious value by the Meiteis as an integral part of the Manipuri tradition of nature worship. There are many references in the Cheitharol Kumbaba which shows that tree reverence was very common during the pre-Hindu periods. Worship of the Tree consist of bowing and sometimes offering of fruits and flowers. The religious significance of plants like tairel is seen during rituals like Lai Haraoba and Yumsengba. Some of the sacred trees are :-

Table-39 Showing the plants worshipped by the Meiteis

Sl. No	*Plants Worshipped*	*Plants given magical-religious importance*
1.	Ficu Religiosa (Peepal) –Sana Khongnang	Toona Ciliata (Australian Red Cedar)
2.	Ficus Bengalensis (Banyan) – Khongnang	Dactyloctenum Aegypticum (Crowfoot Grass)
3.	Hydnocarpus Kurjii Karpoor	Blumea Balsamifera (Camphor)
4.	Mangifera Indica (Mango)-Heinou	Mangifera Indica
5.	Ocimum Sanctum (Sacred Balsii)-Tulsi	Ocimum Sanctum
6.	Terminalla Arjuna	Cynodon Dactylon (Bermuda or Durva Grass, Aegle marmalos (Wood Apple) Xylosoma Longifolia, Oroxylum Indicum, Piectranthus Ternifolius,
7.	Cedrela toona Roxb – Tairel	Red Cedar

Some plants like mango, wood apple, Bermuda or 'durva' grass, and sacred basil (Ocimum sanctum) are either worshipped or used in religious rituals by the Hindus all over India. It is, therefore, obvious that these plants were included by the Meeteis under the Hindu Vaishnavite influence. Plants taboo on specific days or periods, or to a particular clan is still preserved by orthodox Manipuris. It is a custom for the Maiba-Maibi (priest and priestess) of Manipur to always ask forgiveness of a tree whenever it is cut for some purpose. Some plant taboos observed are-

- Bamboo is not harvested on Tuesday, Thursday, and Saturday, and on new moon days,
- Banana not harvested on Saturday,
- Hatoda Vasica not harvested on Sunday because Sunday is the birthday of this plant,
- Water dropwort or water parsley not consumed during August-September because violator will have worms in stomach,
- Luffa cylindrica not consumed by the Ningthouja clan.

SACRED STONES

There are evidences that sacred stones are worshipped by the Manipuris in the early days. The cultic significance of stones among the early Meeteis was remarkable. The Moirang cultic hero 'Yaosurakpa' said to be transformed himself into a stone. Two sacred stones are situated at Thangjing where annual Lai-Haraoba is held. A funeral in Kangla also marked by a stone.

In the manuscript called "Shagokshading", there is a list of such sacred stones which have cultic significances. Several of the stones claimed to have supernatural powers whatsoever.

BAMON/PUROHITISM

After the spread of Hinduism in Manipur, a new class of Purohits and Pandits have emerged. They are commonly known as Brahmans or Bamons. In the Hindu society the Purohits are from the Brahmin caste. They have the monopoly over ritualistic performances in temples and houses of Hindus. The Brahmins are completely amalgamated with the society of Meiteis and the priests have got a complete hold over the society and the religious institutions. They are no longer considered as Mayang (outsiders). The major factor for this has been the matrimonial relations. The migrated Brahmins married the local Manipuri women. This overcame the local resentment for their continuance as priests.The descendants of the Brahmin priests, who married the Meitei women, inherited the priesthood. In ancient times, the Brahims came to Manipuir without women. They were given free land and allowed to marry Manipuri women. It is said that no Meitei women was willing to marry the Brahmins who were outsiders. Those women who were willing were considered as very courageous. In Manipur language, courage means "Thouna". So those women who married the Brahmins were given the title of "Thourani". The white dhoti, kurta and white turban is the common dress of the Manipuri Brahmin priest.The Lugoon (Sacred thread) is an essential garment of a Brahmin priest. It arches from the left shoulder down to the right hip on each side from back and front. The forehead is distinctively marked with the sandal paste. He is supposed to possess a thorough knowledge of Sanskrit. He utters Sanskrit slokas from the holy books (Bhagavat Gita) while performing worship in the temples or performing the religious rituals in the households.. Since Hinduism was a religion patronized by the Kings, the Brahmin Purohits command respect and recognition in the society. The Brahmins do not take food prepared by the Meiteis whereas Meiteis take food prepared by Brahmins. Some Brahmin families prohibit marriage of their Brahmin daughters to the Meiteis whereas the Meiteis do not have such prohibitions. This is quite ridiculours due to the fact that almost all the Brahmins in Manipur had married Meitei women in the early part of their history.

MAIBAS AND MAIBIS

The traditional priests of Manipur are called the 'Maibas'. Maibaism is related to the traditional Manipuri animistic faith. The Maiba and Maibis (priestesses) are from Manipuri Hindus. There are two types of Maibas and Maibis. One type of Maibas perform religious rituals and the others are traditional healers like Vaids.The Maibis are females who play a vital role in performances of rituals in Umang Lai temples and in the society. The Maibis dress themselves very distinctively. It is all white. A white Phanek (skirt) over which is worn an additional waist wrapper reaching the hips, a white blouse mostly with full sleeves, a white Innafi (shawl) is also worn. The male Maiba is also dressed in all white, a white dhoti, long jacket, white sash around the waist and a white turban on the head. Both Maiba and Maibi have got certain restrictions in social life. They cannot take food which is not clean or prepared in the house where child birth has taken place or a food prepared by a woman in her menstruation period. They have to be above the common people as they are the men and women closely connected with Lai (spirits). It is believed that a Lai (spirit) possesses the female Maibi. Maibi is generally possessed by a goddess. In that case a woman becomes hysterical while dancing and performing dance in wild frenzy and gets into a state of trance. In the state of trance she will utter different words, which will forecast the future of somebody or reflect the wishes of the spirit. The female can be possessed by the Lai directly. In that case the female at the initial stage will show an abnormal behaviour by singing songs, pulling her hair, shouting, trembling and speaking in an unusual tongue. The choice on the part of the Lai may fall upon a female of any age. The girl at the age of seven may become a Maibi and a woman of forty or fifty also can be chosen as Maibi by the Lai. Both married and unmarried are acceptable. It is believed that a Maibi from the tender age becomes a successful Maibi. If a Maibi is married then she sleeps on the left side of the bed with her husband. The Lai (spirit) may visit the Maibi during the nights on some fixed dates of the month. On these particular days she sleeps alone. The Lai may appear in the form of a human being and the Maibi experience the sensation of copulation. It is said that it is more satisfying when the Lai appear in the human form. The Lai also visits the Maibi during her menstruation but no copulation sensation is felt by the Maibi during this period. In case of the married Maibi the husband sometimes feels the presence of the Lai with his wife. Therefore he leaves her alone to be comfortable with the Lai. The Lai is said to be never happy if Maibi bears a child. The Maibi herself will not develop natural affection for the child or may ill-treat or ignore the child.

The Maibas and Maibis play a very important role in Meitei rituals, Lai haraoba and Umang Lai temples. In several social traditions for ritualistic performances, the presence of Maiba or Maibi is considered essential and the ceremony is not considered complete without his or her presence. Their services are also taken in getting the evil spirits driven away from the house. They are also invited to cure the patients. Some cure their patients by their traditional excorcism and others do it through nature cure. It is believed that they communicate and speak with the Lais and the dead persons and thus also convey their messages to the living human beings.

Meitei Singers :

Famous Singers are Sagolsem Kalidamon, Khangembam Gulapi Singh (plate – 118), Laisram Tolpishak, Laisram Ibohal Macha, Thangjam Chaoba, Elangbam Anganghal, Nityaibi, Lakpati, Kesho. Femous female Singers are Kshetri Tombi, Lourembam Tombi, Yaiskul Gambhini, Manimacha, Tampakleima, Lairentombi, Thanga Ashangbi.

SHUMANG LILA

Shumang Lila means "Courtyard Performance", Shumang mean courtyard, Lila means play or performance. The other name of Shumang Lila is Jatra or jatrawali, derived from Assamese or Bengalese culture. The play is usually performed in an open space of around 12 x 12 sq. feet in the centre of any open space - courtyard or open playground or mandap (pavilion) or bank of a river.

Common people particularly the women and children are very fond of Shumang Lila. It is performed in a very simple way. Only one small table, two chairs and sometimes one Kouna Phak (one mat) is required. No raised plateform., no curtain or no enclosure is required. Shumang Lila is often described as the theatre of the masses. Shumang Lila is performed by a touring band of 12-15 professional artistes on invitation basis. These troupes may be either exclusively males (Nupa Shumang lila) or exclusively females (Nupi Shumang Lila). In case of Nupi Shumang Lila, the male characters are enacted by the female artistes in the case of the Nupa Shumang lila the female roles are played by the male artistes or nupishabis whom we call male actresses. They are feminine par excellence in their looks, bodily gestures and facial expressions. These male actresses are very popular and they are the main attraction of any Shumang lila play.

Probably, the first Shumang lila was "Phagee Lila" (farce), performed during the reign of Maharaja Chandrakirti (1850-1886), though the traces of it were already present in the episode of Tangkhul-Nurabi Loutaba of Lai haraoba festival. Phagee lila was out and out comedy, adducing and cooking up of absurd stories on the spot, caricaturing of the King and the nobles, making funny physical contortions etc.

The main aim of Shumang lila is to entertain people, making them forget their day-to-day worries and anxieties. But it also carries a heavy responsibility to educate people on various social issues-both local and international.

Then it was succeeded by such plays as Ramlila, Sabha parba, Kabul lila etc. But the real Shumang lila with various rasas (sentiments) was ushered in with the epic play Harishchandra (1918). Then it was followed by others such as Sabitri Satyavan, Meiraba charan,Thok lila etc. One of the most successful plays of this era was Moirang parba (an epic play based on the legendary lovers-Khamba and Thoibi of Moirang). The big leap came in 1950 when scripts were introduced with the plays like "Puranmeithaba" and "B.A. Mapa Lamboiba". It was a boost for literature loving people of Manipur and also it brought in professionalism in Shumang Lila. Second major change came in 1970s with the introduction of Eshei lila with the introduction of its background music, sound system and playback singing. Some of them were Krishna bal lila (1975), Thadoi (976) and Chakthekpi (1977).

Today we have only Eshei lila genre with its ever expanding wings. The competitive zeal of the troupes is kept burning by the annual Shumang lila festival which started in 1972.

Acting in Shumang lila is particularly difficult for the whole body of the actor has to act as he/she cannot hide anything in the middle of an over looming audience. Once he/she is in the performance space, he/she is left to himself/herself and is quite vulnerable also since no prompting will save him/her from stammering. The actor is now completely at the mercy of the audience.

Today, the most popular plays are Kunti (4 series), Love-2000, Keisamthong Thoibi. The Shumang lila play 'World Trade Centre', showcases the agony of the loss of basic human relationship in the aftermath of 11 September 2001 attack of Twin Towers. The Shumang Lila parties are also engaged to spread the message of HIV/AIDS prevention, Leprosy prevention, family planning etc. Some of the very popular plays are-Ngasigi Nonglei, Matamgi khoimu etc. The author had introduced Shumang Lila in tribal dilects – like Tangkhul, Kabui and Kuki during 2000-2002. Surprisingly, these tribal Shumang Lila were very popular and they could not survive long due to lack of support from the State Government.

The famous Shumang Lila Script Writers are Chana Lukhoi, Manaobi M.M. The popular Shumang Lila Artists are – Narendra Ningombam, Robindro, Keirao Rajen, Dhanabir, Sanaton etc. In additon to Shuman Lila, we have "Nokfadey", " Ipom", which make the people laugh. The three famous Ipon artistes were-Mayang Imphal Tombi (Yongchak Laitharoi Lan soknabagi wari), Chaoba, Babu.

Nowadays, the National School of Drama, New Delhi has started taking keen interest in the Shumang Lila of Manipur.

MANIPURI THEATRES:

The modern theatre movement descended on Manipuri theatre culture with the performance of Pravas Milan (1902) under the enthusiastic patronage of Sir Churachand Maharaja (1891-1941). Manipur had its first permanent theatre house in the first decade of 20th century called the Manipur Friends Dramatic Union (1930). During this era plays were mainly Manipuri adaptation of Bangali plays. But 1925 saw the beginning of truly Manipuri plays with "Nara Singh". The pace of theatrical movement was geared up with the institution of various groups such as Manipur Dramatic Union (MDU) (1930), Aryan Theatre (1935), Chitrangada Natya Mandir (1936), Society Theatre (1937), Rupmahal (1942), Cosmopolitan Dramatic Union (1968), the Chorus Repertory Theatre of Ratan Thiyam (1976), Panthoibi Natya Mandir etc. These groups started experimenting with various types of plays apart from historical and pauranic ones. As a result theatre started disseminating to other parts of Manipur such as Nambol, Kakching to encourage people to take active part in developing this art form.

Then social dramas came in which were the depictions of various socio-politico-economic issues of Manipuri society. They may be daily social happenings, family affairs, state administration, corruption, unemployment problems, insurgency problems, complaints of the disgruntled youths etc. The themes can be anything, ranging from heaven to hell since both the genres cannot be bound within certain space and time.

CHORUS REPERTORY THEATRE

The auditorium of the Chorus Repertory theatre is situated on the out-skirts of Imphal and the campus stretches for about 2 acres (8,100 m^2). It has housing and working quarters to accommodate a self-sufficiency of life. The theatre association has churned out internationally acclaimed plays like *Chakravyuha* and *Uttarpriyadashi*. Its' 25 years of existence in theatre had disciplined its performers to a world of excellence. *Chakravyuha* taken from the Mahabharat epic had won Fringe Firsts Award, 1987 at the Edinburgh International Theatre Festival. *Chakravyuha* deals with the story of Abhimanyu (son of Arjun) of his last battle and approaching death whereas *Uttarpriyadashi* is an 80-minute exposition of Emperor Ashoka's redemption.

On the other hand Ratan Thiyam, an internationally renown dramatist and Padmashri awardee has been using the red colour as depiction of futility of the war and the comfort of peace through his various plays such as Chakravyuha (1984), Hiroshima (1996), Uttarapriyadarshi (1996) etc. This way both the theatres are working as 'infotainment'. Whether they are seriously received or not depends on the analytical capability of the audience.

Manipuri plays, both Shumang lila and stage Lila, have been a regular feature in the annual festival of National School of Drama, New Delhi. It is not a mean success for Manipur and for the North East States as a whole.

MANIPURI CINEMA:

Cinema show was started in Manipur in the Year 1920 A.D. The first licence holder for conducting Cinema shows was Aagya Gunamani Sharma during the reign of Maharaja Churachand. It is said that even Ngangbi Maharani contributed money for purchase of cinema equipment for aagya Gunamani. (M.K. Binodini, Churachand Maharaj gio Imung, 2008). But full fledged Cinema halls were established after the second World War. Manipur's pioneer film making organisation was Shree Govindajee Film Company (established in 1946-47). Its first attempted feature film was Mainu Pemcha (1948). Film Society, Manipur was established in 1966. The Manipur Film Development Council was established in 1980 and it became Manipur Film Development Corporation in 1987 (MFDC). Today, MFDC, an autonomous body, located at Palace Compound, Imphal is organizing various activities for promotion of film industry in Manipur including national film festivals.

The first feature film Matam-gi Manipur (35 mm, black and white) was screened on 9th April, 1972 at Usha Cinema, Friends Talkies in Imphal and Azad Cinema in Kakching. With the establishment of Film Society in 1966, Imphal Cine Club in 1979 and Manipur Film Developement Council in 1980, the Manipuri Cinema got the required momentum to come upto the national level. So far 9 Manipuri films have got National Awards. Manipur started producing colour films from 1984 onwards. The first colour film was "Langlen Thadoi" (1984-directed by Kh. Pramodini Devi) followed by "Brojendrogi Luhongba". The first Manipuri producer was Karam Manmohon Singh (K.T. Films).The first Manipuri Director was S.N. Chand. The first Manipuri Film actor was Robindro Sharma, the first Manipuri Film actress was Rashi Devi.The best child actor of indian films for the year 1982 was child artist Leikhendra Singh (at 8 years of age).

The first Manipuri direct 35 mm colour film was Madhabi (directed by L. Banka Sharma) The first Manipuri Film to receive the best documentary film award was "Sanaleibak Manipur" (1980) directed by Shyam Sharma. The first Manipuri documentary film was "Maipak-son of Manipur" (1970) -directed by Debkumar Bose.

The following Manipuri films were shown in Film Festivals at : International level.

1. IMAGEE NINGTHEM
2. PAOKHUM AMA
3. ISHANOU
4. SANABI
5. SANA KEITHEL
6. SAMBAL WANGMA
7. KHONTHANG

The first Indian film to get the grand prix at the Nante International Film Festival was Manipur's film "Imagee Ningthem"–(1982) (my child my prestige) [script by M.K. Binodini and directed by a Shyam Sharma]. The documentary film "Sangai" directed by Shyam Sharma won five merit awards in the 12th International Film Festival of Wild Life in USA in 1989. "Sangai was also declared as an outstanding film at the London Film Festival in 1989. A short documentary film "Pebet" directed by H. Kanhailal won both national and international awards. "Eshanou" won international awards. "Sana Keithel", "Sanabi" and "Chatledo Eidi" won a national awards.

With the advent of digital films and after banning of Hindi Films in Manipur, the Manipuri Films is gaining popularity among the masses. Many film companies have sprung up and many digital films are produced. This is because the population of Manipur is very small and the market for Manipuri film is very limited. Production of 35 mm films is usually a great economic loss to the producer.

The popular films actresses are Saikhom Kamala, Mayachowdhuri, Binita, the popular film actors are Keiku, Sadananda, Olen (Ta-Tomba).

MEITEI FOLK SONGS

Ougri

Ougri is an ancient Meitei folk song sung usually in praise of Sun, Moon, Kings etc. and mostly sung during Lai haraoba festival.

Khullang Ishei or Khunung Ishei

This typical Manipuri folk song commonly sung by the Meiteis in villages at the time of harvesting, collecting firewood, hunting or fishing. There is no set system of words and sentences. The theme is love. The singer adjusts his words and stanzas of verses of his own to the tune. This folk song is sung without musical instrument and the theme is usually related to love and romance.

Khongjom Parva

This is a musical narration of the heroic struggle and sacrifice of Paona Brajabashi and other Manipuri heroes during the Khongjom war of 1891 with the help of Dhulok (a kind of drum) in a sitting position. It is believed that Dhobi Leinou started singing Khongjom Parva by thumping his hands on his knees and sometimes on an empty tin. Dhobi Leinou happened to be an eye witness of the bloody battle fought between the Manipuris and the British forces at Khongjom. He married Mongjam Ningol Amubi and had five childre –Lala, Thambou, Tonsija, Dhabali and Gandhar. Dhobi Leinou earned his livelihood by washing the clothes of Mr. Grimwood, the Political Agent of Manipur and other British officers. He lived at Dhobi Leikai (present PWD Office). He was the son of Samjetsabam Chaoton. When Mrs. Grimwood fled away to Cachar along with 200 Gorkha slodiers, they arrested 50 Manipuris to be deployed as porters for their journey. Dhobi Leinou was one of them. Leinou was again taken to Tamu and re-entered Manipur along with the British troops as the flag bearer. The British employed Dhobi Leinou as a route guide to lead them towards Manipur by paying a large sum of money. It is said that Dhobi Leinou had seen the water of the Khongjom river turned into crimson red with the blood of the dead and wounded Manipuris and that the bank of the river remained slimy for months with the putrid flesh of the deceased. The dead bodies remain putrified days as no body came up to claim the body and there was no arrangement to cremate the dead body. The sight was unbearable agony for him. At the age of 50 years, he began to sing the reminiscing the heroic fight of the Manipuris whenever he was alone on the roadside, under the tree. He left many disciples – Khumanthem Chaoba (Wangkhei), Leimapokpam Herachandra (Nganappi Thong), Laishram Tona Siongh (Thouda Bhavok Leikai) and Kalijao alia Chaoba (Hiyangthang). (see plate-113). Thanga Mangoljao and Ibeni are very famous Khongjom Parva Artistes.

Nowadays, Khongjom Parva include any kind of stories from Khamba and Thoibi, Ramayana, Mahabharata etc.

Pena Ishei

The song is accompanied with the music produced through Pena. A Pena is a musical instrument, to the round dry shell of coconut is attached a slender bamboo rod. The shell is cut out to make a circular opening which is covered with a thin hide covering to make a drum. A string of horse tail is fastened from the end of the bamboo rod over the drum. The adjusting pieces are attached to make the string lose or tight on the bamboo rod. Another string is fastened to the curved iron rod is held in the right hand, the string on the bamboo is rubbed with that on the curved iron rod producing a sweet musical sound. The theme of the song is usually the love story of Khamba-Thoibi. (see plates–114, 115). Pena Ishei is also sung at the time of invocation of Umang Lai (Yakairol).

Lai Haraoba Ishei

These songs are full of erotic mysticism but the real meaning is veiled by the use of innocent sounding words. The rhythm of the tune is its quality. It is sung on the ceremonial occasions at Lai Haraoba.

Dhob: It is sung with a large cymbal known as Jhal. The song is accompanied with the Manipuri style of beating of the drum.

Manohar Sai are the songs named after Manohar Sai who came to Manipur in nineteenth century. The songs are accompanied with small cymbals called Ramkartal and drum called Khol. The songs are devotional.

Nupi Pala is a devotional song sung by women. The small cymbal called Mandila is used during this song.

Khubak Ishei

During the summer month of June-July, the Manipuris observe Rath Jatra (Drawing of Chariot of Lord Jagannath) on the model of Puri festival. According to Manipuri tradition every Hindu temple in every place will observe it with great supports of peoples who contributes their funds and materials to its success. It has a 9-day programme of devotional music and dances followed by the free distribution of Kshechri, a dish made of rice, dal mixed with turmeric served with Hawai mangal Utti (Pea nut mixed with bamboo shoots). Khubak Ishei and Jaya Deva are the gifts of Rath Jatra in Manipuri culture. The significant events for the daily service during the nine days, apart from the above are listening to sacred texts explained by a specialist in the day, the recitation and singing of Dasa Avtar Slokas and the performance of Khubak Ishei by the male or female artists. Khubak Ishei is a type of Clapping song mainly performed by the female singers with a male drummer. This form of singing was initiated during the reign of King Churachand Maharaja. They sing the song of Radha's pangs of separation after Krishna left her and the Gopis and went to Mathura on a chariot to join Kamsa's Yajna. (see plate–116)

Moibung Ishei

The conch music is quite peculiar, distinct, entertaining, extraordinary and soothing. The artist usually played two conches simultaneously. This is played uaully just signaling starting of a function and in between including religious ceremonoies like Swaradha. For swaradha ceremonies, it is compulsory to include conch music. Nowadays, it is used in the opening ceremonies of any big event. (see plate-117)

Wari Liba

Wari Liba was introduced during the time of Maharaja Bhagyachandra (Ching-Thang Khomba or Jai Singh- 1763-1798 AD). This is an art form of story-telling.The theme may be from Mahabharata or Ramayana.

Indigenous Games of the Meiteis -See chaper no–17: Games and Sports

Festivals of Meiteis–see Chapter no-13: Festivals of Manipur

Dances of Meiteis –See Chapter no-16: Manipuri Dances

Handicrafts-See Chapter no-19 : Handlooms and Handicrafts

Polo - See Chapter no. 18 : Polo

References

Asok K. Ghosh, Kumar Suresh Singh, S. B. Roy, *People of India.*

Atombapu Sharma Vidyaratna "Meiteigi Meihourol", Churachand Printing Works, 1955.

Atombapu Sharma Vidyaratna "Manipur Itihas" (1st part), Churachand Printing Works, Imphal.

Atombapu Sharma, Religion and Cultuiral Integration of India, 1967.

Bhogeshwor, Ningthourol Lambuba, 1967.

Brenda Davidson Shaddox, Naga Festival, SST Tourism Co.Ltd, Yangon, 2002

Chander Sheikher Panchani, Manipur Religion, Culture and Society, Konark Publishing Pvt. Ltd, New Delhi, 1987.

Chongtham Iboyaima, Meitei Yek Taret Salai Mapan Leisemlon, Swaraj Press, 1960.

Ch Manihar Singh, *A History of Manipuri Literature,* p. 82.

Directorate of Census Operations, Government of India, 2001 Census.

Gangumei Kabui, Glimpses of land and people of Ancient Manipur, Manipur Past and Present, Delhi, 1988.

Dr. M. Kirti Singh, Religious Developments in Manipur in the 18th and 19th Centuries, 1982.

Dr. Saroj Nalini Parrat, the Religion of Manipur, 1980.

Dr. S.N. Pandey Sources of History of Manipur and the adjoining Areas, Manipur University, Imphjal, National Publishing House, New Delhi, 1985.

Dr. Smt. K. Sobita Devi, Traditional Dress of the Meioteis, Bhubon Publishing House, Imphal, 1998.

E. Nilakanta, Fragments of Manipuri Culture, Onmson Publications, New Delhi-1993.

E. Nilakanta Singh, Aspects of Indian Culture, 1982.

G.E Gerini, Researches on Ptolemy's Geograpohy, London, 1909.

Hijam Mani Singh "Meihouron Salai Sakok Puiya Amasung Salai Taret Makki Yumnak

I. Bhogeshwor, Numit Kappa, 1977.

I. Bhogeshwor, Ningthourol Sheireng, 1967.

Khumanlambam Yaima, Pakhangba Phambal, 1967.

Khumanlambam Yaima, Meihourol Pukok, 1972.

Khumanlambam Yaima, Poireiton Khunthok, 1972.

Kh. Chandra Singh, Loiyumba Shilyen, 1975.

Lenkum Bekhigya, Leithak Leikharol, 1967.

L.I. and N.K. Singh "Chetharol Kumbaba", Manipur Sahitya Parisad, Imphal, 1967.

L.K. Singh (1965).

L.M. Iboongohal Singh, Meaning of Mayang, Imphal Cooperative Publihing Society Ltd.

Lairenmayum Iboongohal Singh, Introduction to Manipur, Imphal Friends Union Press, 1963.

Loitongbam Kalachand Singh, Sagei Salai Lon, O.K. Store, 1965.

L. Udhob Singh, A Brief History of Agricultural Development in Manipur, 1946-1983 1989.

Madhab and Khelchandra, Khunung Lichat Sajat, 1970.

Mayanglambam Gourchandra, Ariba Meiteigi Sahitya –Sanamahi Thounirol, 1981.

Modhu Maiba, Apokpa Khurumba, 1967.

Mahendrakumar Singh, Manipurer Prachin Itihas, Silchar Cachar Press, 1952.

Manjusri Chaki-Sircar, P. 62, *Feminism in a traditional society.*

Moirangthem Chandra Singh, Manipuri Muslim, The Tribal Meitei Cooperative Printing Works, 1973.

Moirangthem Chandra Singh, Panthoibi Khongkul, Sucheta Printing Works, Imphal, 1863.

Namingthon Puiya, Imphal Press, 1968.

N. Amuyaima, Chengleilon, 1979.

N. Ibochouba, Thiren Layai, 1981.

N. Gorachandra, Nongkhan, 1980.

N. Khelchandra Singh, Ariba Manipuri Sahityagi Itihas, 1966.

N.K. Singh (1969).

Ng. Kullachandra, Apokpa Thounirokl, Leimarel Nayam, 1969.

O. Bhogeshwar Singh, Loina Shillon, 1967.

O.K. Singh, Archeological Research in Manipur vide T.C. Sharma and D.N. Majumdar, Eastern Himalayas, Gauhati University, 1980.

O.K. Singh and T.C. Sharma, Discovery of Stone Age Relics from Manipur –Jr/ Assam Sc.Sec X, 1969.

O.. Bhogeshwar Singh, Sanamahi Laikan, 1972.

O.. Bhogeshwar Singh, Khagemnba Langjei, 1968.

O.K. Singh, The Antiquities of Manipur, Bull, Manipur State Museum No.1, 1972.

O.K. Singh, A Report of the State Archeological Deptt, Govt. of Manipur, 1983.

Pandit Ngariyambam Kulachandra Singh, Apokpa Thounirol, 1967.

R.K. Jhalajit Singh, A Short Historyt of Manipur, Imphal, O.K. Store, 1965.

R.K. Sanahal, Manipur Itihas, 1947.

S.A Ansari, Manipur : Tribal Demography and Socio Economic Development, Daya Publishing House, 1991.

Sarangthenm Bormani " Moirang Saiown, 2003.

S.S. Shashi, *Encyclopaedia of Indian Tribes,* p. 204.

T. Bokul, Manipuri Muslim Kouba Lairikki Maramda, Imphal Meitei Marup, 1974.

Tomcha Meitei, Yek Salai, 1970.

W. Yumjao Singh, A Report on Archeological Studies in Manispour, 1935.

W. Yumjao Singh, An Early History of Manipur, 1966.

Y. Bhagya, Leithak Leikharol, Manipur Sahitya Parisad, 1967.

http://themanipurpage.tripod.com/history/puwarimeitei.html.

Plate-107: Meitei Couple in traditional dress

Plate-108: A Meitei woman wearing Marei Preng

Plate -109 :Meitei women

Plate -110: Manipuri Bride

Plate-111: Meitei Luhongba

Plate-112: Meitei Chakluk

Plate -113: Khongjom Parba
Courtesy-Santos

Plate -114: Pena Ishei Courtesy-Santos

Plate -115: Pena Ishei
Courtesy-Santos

Plate -116: Khubak Ishei

Plate-117: Playing Moibung Ishei

Plate- 118 Guru Khangembam Gulapi Singh

7

Lois, Yaithibi and Bishnupriya

LOIS

There are many theories regarding the origin of the Lois. The term Loi means "dependent or subdued". They are also known as Chakpas. According to R. Brown (1874) "The Lois appear to be original tribes which formerly occupied Moirang, the valley to the south of Manipur. They were formerly independent, but were subdued by the Meiteis, hence the name Loi or subdued". The Lois consider themselves as the oldest indigenous people of Manipur. According to another theory, Lois are the original Meiteis in custom, habits and behaviour before conversion to Hinduism. When the Meitei became more and more inclined towards Hinduism, the Lois still preserved their Sanamahi religion and their indigenous customs and traditions. The Lois are also regarded by the Meitei as a tributary group who used to pay tribute (Loipot) to the Meitei Kings during their rule. Capt. Dun E.W (1886) identified the Lois as the people of the five villages situated in the west and north-west of the valley close to the hills who were engaged in "silk culture". They are settled in Sekmai, Khurkhul, Phayeng, Andro and Chairel. All of them speak Meitielon but the accent is a bit different.

The Lois complained that formally they were not allowed to accept Vaishnavism because of their habit of taking meat and liquor etc. A great social distance was created between the Lois and the Meiteis with the arrival of Hinduism and the latter's adoption of Vaishnavism. The Lois were not allowed to participate in community feasts along with the Meiteis. They adhered to their own indigenous faith which was not substantially different from the indigenous Meitei religion. They have their own ritual specialists, but any one can directly pray to their gods and goddesses. They try to emulate the Meitei customs and manners but were not at par with the latter. They take wine and meat. According to the Meiteis, their dialect is marked by "defective pronunciation" and "bad quality". They do not use respectful terms for seniors though of late, emulating the Meiteis, they have begun using respectful terms of address.

Like the Meiteis, they use Sagei (lineage) name as their forename. They have also allotted sacred spots for Phunga, Sanamahi and Laimaren. Their house god Sanamahi and the goddess Laimaren are worshipped in the same way as the Meiteis do, though not regularly.

Physical Features of Lois

Lois are of Mongoloid people with sharp features. Their noses in both sexes are very sharp. The cheek bones, eyes sockets and thickness of lips show progression towards sharpness. It may be possible that their group was originally of Mongoloid but it got the chance of mixing and produced a group with mixed characters in their body features.

Religion

The religion of Lois resembles animism. The Lois sacrifice pigs and goats to their deities. They worship fire. There is a fire at Andro village which is believed to be burning since time of Poireiton Khunthokpa (34-18 B.C.)

Rituals and Festivals

Their life cycle rituals are more or less the same as those of the Meiteis without Vaishnava elements. Their rituals are not marked by Sankritana. They rather sing folk songs and play their traditional musical instrument called Pena instead of pung (drum) and kartal (cymbals.) It may also be mentioned here that the Meiteis also sing folk songs, accompanied by Pena when they participate in their non-Vaishnava indigenous festivals. The cycle of annual festivals of both the Lois and the Meitei is more or less the same.

Like the Meiteis, the Lois observe Cheiraoba (worship of the God Sanamahi on the first day of the year) in the month of Sajibu (March-April); Khunthonglatpa (worshipping evil spirits to appease them at the main,entrance of the village) in the months of Lamda (February-March)and Kalen (April-May); Phoukouba (worshipping God Puthiba for bumper crop) in the month of Hiyanggei (October-November); and Lai Haraoba festival (worship of the village God Umang Lai). The Lois practice sha tanba (hunting ceremony) in the month of Phairen (January-February) and Khoi katpa (gathering ceremony, that is, collecting larvae of bees and honey and offering those to Umanglai god) in the month of Mera (September-October). These hunting and fathering ceremonies are not practiced by the Meitei. (Ranajit Kumar Saha, Valley of Manipur, Punthi-Pustak, Calcutta, 1994)

According to oral tradition, Atiya Kuru Sidaba, after creation of the earth, brought from Korou (heaven) two groups of seven Salais (clans) consisting of fourteen brothers. One group was known as Haleng and another group known as Hanjok. They arrived at Meiteng Ngu's keithel, from where they got some fishes for their meal. They prepared their meal at Wangkhei. Haleng prepared Ngakha and ate it The Hanjok brothers prepared Khajing (prawns). The Haleng groups had already started their journey asking their younger brothers to follow their sword marks which they would leave on trees. The Hanjok brother could not complete the cooking of the Khajing. When they resumed the journey, they could not find any sword mark of their Haleng brothers and therefore returned. For this they became known as Handro i.e. those who returned. The Haleng were divided into five groups and settled at different locations; the first called Hori and settled at Andro, the second called Hero settled at South Sekmai, the third called Yawa settled at North Sekmai, the fourth called Kosang settled at Phayeng Koudruk, the fifth called Kamu settled at Thambalkhong. The main deities worshipped by Lois (Chakpa) are Nongpok Ningthou or Panam Ningthou and Pureilomba at Andro, Koubru and Loyarakpa at Phayeng and Sekmai.

They celebrate Lai-Haraoba according to their own customs which only differ with the Meiteis in minor details. Besides the general Laiharaoba festival, they observe a special Laiharaoba festival when no outsider is allowed to witness the same. It may be concluded that the Lois practice the Meitei culture although with a distinct ethnic accent of their own. Their cultural life is similar to that of the Meities. In dress and food habit there is practically no difference with that of the Meities.

Deities of Lois (Chakpas) :

The main deities worshipped by the Lois (Chakpas) of Andro are Panam Ningthou (see plate-122) and Pureilomba. The celebration of Panam Ningthou is held in the month of Lamda (February-March) for nine days and that of Pureilomba in the month of Kalen (April-May) from nine to thirteen days. Other deities like Chingsomba (of Sarungbam), Sanahongba (of Phanjoubam), Korouhanba (ofThokchom), Chaningleima (of Yumkhaibam), Thongbulakpa (of Chingakham), Sanglenlakpa (of Chingakham), Soraren (of Heikrujam), Peng-khu-lai (of Sagolsem), Meira-thanbi (of Ningthoujam), Uran lakpa (of Puthem), and Penakhongba (of Salam) are also worshipped in Andro. A hut is erected for adults (Haleng) and this is known as Ahallup Sang and the leader is known as Khullakpa. One hut for youngsters (Hanjok) and this is known as Naharup Sang. Another hut is jointly erected by both Haleng and Hanjok and this is known as Sanglen (main hut) and Khunjahanba is made its leader. A hut is erected by the Halengs for boys and girls and this is called Ahallup Kosho and the person in charge is known as Pakhanglakpa. Another hut is erected by Hanjok for boys and girls to live in and this is known as Naharup Kosho and the person in charge is known as Naharakpa. Another hut is erected for Pureiromba and the person in charge of the hut is called Laipu Yupanba. There are two kinds of Panam Ningthou Haraoba. The first kind known as Sang Kaba Haraoba is celebrated for five days. The second one known as Chaoren Haraoba is celebrated for nine days. Both kinds of Haraoba are performed in the month of Lamda (February-March). No outsider or stranger is permitted to witness the celebration of Panam Ningthou Haraoba. It is believed that observation of the festival by the outsider will bring harm and destruction of the people of the village.

The term "Lois" has a derogatory connotation and implies low status. Brahmins did not serve them. The Meitei King assigned certain specific occupations for the Lois such as poultry farming, distillation, cultivation of mulberry and rearing of silk worms, pottery and so on. (G.A. Grierson Linguistic Survey of India, Part III, Vol III. 1967 1st Edition- 1903) with the help of the vocabulary of the Lois published by McColloch shows that Lois vocabulary apparently has some connections with the Naga dialects especially with those of eastern sub-group. Dr. Brown mentioned that "The Manipuris are frequently degraded to Lois as a punishment. The punishment may be remitted after some time. If there is no remission, then the punishment descends to the wife and family of the culprit who becomes Lois". When there was some infighting between the ruling Meitei King and others, when they were defeated, they were exiled and driven out towards the foothills and become Lois. By this derogatory act of being defeated, they were designated as Lois and later on they formed a separate ethnic group, Lois.

Four important features of the Loi identity have been mentioned-(1) they emerged from a tribal group, (2) they are tributary group, (3) they have fixed assigned occupations, and (4) they share the same segmentary system as that of the Meiteis.

The "Lois"of Andro wanted to erase the stigma of "Lois" identity and sought the Meitei identity. So they adopted Vaisnavism and settled at a particular portion of Andro village. But still they failed to acquire Meitei identity. Some of the "Lois" of Phayeng and of other villages also wanted to remove their "Lois" identity. So they call themselves Chakpa. But they have not been successful in erasing the "Lois" identity. (Ranajit Kumar Saha, Valley of Manipur, Punthi-Pustak, Calcutta, 1994)

The Chairel is a village and the villagers who live here are termed Chairels. They were forced to settle in that fixed village site by the King. In such a condition finding no other means of livelihood they accepted the occupation of making earthen pots considered to be a "derogatory" occupation. Some of the Chairels tried to come out of their low position. They left their village and settled in Taothong village near the Lamsang Keithel and left their traditional calling. Some of them follow the Hindu Vaisnavite and a few follow the Sanamahi religion. Other people do not dare to call them Chairels. In common parlance they are called Taothong but they are now identified as Meiteis. (Ranajit Kumar Saha, Valley of Manipur, Punthi-Pustak, Calcutta, 1994)

Occupation

The Lois are expert in agriculture and hold monopoly in the silk, iron smelting and other craft work. Now they have been given scheduled caste status and the state government is taking keen interest in their social upliftment Lois are the victim of political de-recognition from the past. They are not given recognition so as to avoid their political rising The Lois are not much involved in social activities and political affairs.

There is no caste system in Manipur. Nowadays, nobody dare to call them Lois and they are treated as at par with the Meiteis.

YAITHIBI

The Yaithibis were originally pure Meiteis. The social and cultural patterns of the Yaithibi and the Meitei are the same. The Meiteis do not call the Yaithibis as Meiteis because they were exiled and treated as socially outcaste people on account of their grave offence such as marrying near relatives like sisters, step-mothers and other near relatives. The Yaithibis also agreed that they are the outcastes but they do not accept the Meitei's version of the reasons of their ex-communication. They mentioned that their fore fathers were King's once favourites. They were compelled to accept their present low position because of bad luck. In fact the literal meaning of the term Yaithibi is 'bad luck' (Yai=luck, thibi=bad). The Yaithibi are a part and parcel of the Meitei indigenous culture and society. (Ranajit Kumar Saha, Valley of Manipur, Punthi-Pustak, Calcutta, 1994)

They usually narrate three stories to support their claim. :-

1. According to one version, once during the period of a King (they did not remember the name of the King and his time) a few Meiteis were in good book of the King. They were so favoured and faithful that they had access even to the interior part of the palace where the queen resided. A few other people could not tolerate this favoritism. So they conspired to punish the former. They were trying to create ill feeling between the favoured people and the King. At last they complained to the King against them and said that those people had illicit relations with some queens. The King became very angry to hear that. He did not try to enquire how far it was correct.

Instead, he sentenced the people to death. The wives of those men begged the King to pardon the lives of their husbands. Then those people were not killed but were exiled along with their wives and children to a remote place near Waithou close to the hills. This was done in pursuance of the custom then in vogue. The King announced that if any person would try to maintain any social communication with those people he would also be exiled from the Meitei society. Thus they being the ill fated people, were called Yaithibi. And they were treated as "untouchables" when Vaishnavism was introduced in Manipur.

2 During the reign of a King, probably Garib Niwaz (1709–1749) there was a beautiful maidservant by name Laisram Ningol Thambal Nganbi in the palace. Her father and brother also worked in the palace. She was described as a girl of incomparable beauty. The then prince Chit Shai fell in love with her. He approached his father to permit him to marry the girl. One day she was called inside the palace. But as soon as the King saw the girl, he was very much charmed by her beauty. He forgot that the girl was betrothed to his own son. The King arranged a picnic at Thoubal lake along with the girl. The King and the girl were in a boat in the lake. The lake was full of lily. They took out the stems of lily and ate them. The King enjoyed the picnic very much although the girl did not like it. She used to remind the King that being father of the

prince, to whom she was betrothed, he should not behave like that. But the King did not give any attention. When the news reached the prince, he was very unhappy. He was thinking to fight with his father, the King.One day, he came along with his soldiers upto the Ushoipokpi bridge to fight with the King. The Lourembam Khongnangthaba, the palace Maichou (Pandit) knew it and he ran to the spot. On the eve of starting the fight, Lourembam Khongnangthaba reached the spot and stood in the middle of the two parties. He realized the imminent danger and consequently he tried to stop the fight. Neither the father nor the son dared to kill Lourembam Khongnangthaba. So they stopped their intended fight. The son was, however, very much dissatisfied with the behaviour of his father and the girl. He did not try to understand the helpless condition of the girl. After the lapse of several years the King died and the prince became the King. After he became the King, he punished the girl on the plea that she had illicit relations with his father. As a punishment, he exiled her along with family members and her relatives. The descendants of the girl became Yaithibis.

3. Another story says that during the reign of various Kings, the Cheirap (Highest court) gave verdict of capital punishment for those who committed grave offences. In such cases their lives could only be saved by the wife of Sugnoo Hanjaba, that is, headman of the Sugnoo village. Sugnoo is a village where criminals were executioned during the native rule. This was then an isolated village. The man who was to be executioned had to reach the village by a boat along the river. Sugnoo was the last village. Each headman en route the villages used to tie one small paya (split bamboo strip) on the hand of the man when he reached these villages. If the wife of the Sugnoo Hanjaba did not allow her husband to tie the bamboo string by some traditional method the life of the man was saved. But on such occasions those people were not allowed to live in the society. They had to live at a distance in isolation. Later on they were termed as Yaithibi and treated as "untouchables".

During the native rule, the Yaithibi were treated as "untouchables". They were not allowed to move freely on all roads and streets. Even their shadows were not to be touched by the Meitei. When they used to come out of their houses they had to wear "Higok machu Phi" (blue coloured cloth) and higok machu turban so that people could easily identify them from a distance. It is said that they were then employed as sweepers in the palace. R. Brown (1874) mentions that the Yaithibi are the exiled people and they used to perform the scavenger's job in the palace only for the Raja and his family.

Like the Meiteis, their title is Singh and they use their Sagei name as their forename. There is no significant difference between the Meiteis and the

Yaithibi. But the Meiteis said that the Yaithibis were not "neat and clean" and their language was "crude". According to the Meiteis, the Yaithibi do not use any respectful term for their elders. But in actual practice, they are now using respectful terms for their elders copying the Meiteis. The Meiteis say that the Yaithibi had no religion. As they lived in isolation and in state of social degradation, they were perhaps not following the elaborate rituals of the Meiteis. Now some of them have accepted Vaishnavism, some follow Christianity and some others cling to Sanamahi religion. Like the Meiteis, the Yaithibi have also sacred places in their houses. The Vaisnavite Yaithibi employ Brahmins to propitiate the Vaishnava gods and goddesses, and to conduct their life cycle rituals and annual festivals which are not different from those of the Vaisnavite Meiteis. Similarly the Sanamahi Yaithibi follows the Sanamahi Meiteis in their daily activities, life cycle rituals, and other annual festivals. The Christian Yaithibi adhere to Christian festivals and life cycle rituals.

Many of the Yaithibi wanted to change the stigmatised and derogatory name "Yaithibi" They left their original village and settled in another new village and named it Waithou Mapal. But this was taken as having the sense as that of the Yaithibi. They changed the village again Their new village was named Thoubal Khunou. In common practice they try to identify themselves as Meitei but officially they identify themselves as Thoubal Khunou not to lose the scheduled caste benefits. The people living in surrounding village, however, have not forgotten that they are the traditional Yaithibi, because they resettled within the same area where their traditional village was located.

Nowadays, the Yaithis are considered as at par with the original Meiteis. There is no discrimination or stigmatization of Yaithibis. Rather, they got all the benefits of a scheduled caste. (Ranajit Kumar Saha, Valley of Manipur, Punthi-Pustak, Calcutta, 1994)

BISHNUPRIYA

In 1474, Meidingu Kyaamba started worshipping Vishnu and built a brick temple (Phura) at Lamangdong, 27 km south of Imphal. Later, two Brahmins namely, Banamali and Haribidyasur, migrated from Cachar announced that rice boiled in cow milk (Sanggom Ksheer) should be offered to the deity in order to bring good fortune to the King and the people of his kingdom. Accordingly, Meidingu Kyaamba appointed the Brahmins in the service of the deity. Afterwards, the followers of the Brahmin were known as Bishnupriya and the place was named Bishnupur. A sizable population of Ningthoukhong, Heirok, Khangabok identify themselves as Bishnupriyas. However, they are classified and taken as Meiteis for all practical purposes.

In 1729, Maharaja Garib Niwaj took the sacred thread for the second time on full moon in the month of Wakching (Dec./Jan, Wednesday). Santi Das Gosai and the King submerged themselves and performed the Nongkhrang Iruppa (Nungkhrang Luppa) in the Lilong river with a number of followers at about 7 A.M. A section of people led by Khuman Ningthou went to complain against the Nungkhrang Luppa. Santi Das Gosai said to the Khuman King "Why is your Majesty opposed to the ceremony?" The Khuman King said, "Goswami, all the people of Manipur are not tribal. There is a good number of clans like Khuman and Luwang etc. initiated to Nama since their forefathers' time. They are opposed to such odd practices. They may therefore, be exempted". King Garib Niwaj nodded his head and said "Yes, Gosai ! It is correct". Santi Das Gosai then turned to the Khuman Ninthou and said "O king, my cult is Rama-worship, so you too please accept the Ramandi religion". The Khuman King replied "My forefathers were devoted to Bishnu. We are not ready to give up the deva of our ancestors". Hearing this, Santi Das Gosai replied, "O King, I see you are very much attached to Bishnu. So You will be given the name Bishnupriya on account of your untagged love to Bishnu."

The Bishnupriyas say that when the Meitei King accepted Vaishnavism, he invited the Bushnupriyas to teach the Meitei the Hindu way of living. Thus they claim to be the carriers of a superior culture. (Navadbip Singh, Tripura). The Meitei King at first mistook the Bishnupriya as a "culturally superior" group. But when it was detected that the culture of the Bishnupriya was of 'inferior' quality, they were allotted the work of supplying forage for the royal stable.

In 1606, Sanongba, the younger brother of Khagemba revolted and invaded Manipur from outside. The battle was concluded on 17th Inga, 1606 with the surrender of 1007 army, 30 elephants, 1000 muskets. The surrendered army included a large number of Muslims and Bishnupriyas. Many of the captured persons were blacksmiths, utensil makers, artisans, musicians, washer men, grooms, elephant tenders. All the captured persons were allowed to settle in Manipur by giving lands and Manipuri women. They were allowed to settle at Chotheyangbi and Pangal Siphai along with Muslims. But due to serious conflict between Bishnupriyas and Muslims, the Bishnupriyas were shifted to Lamangdong (Bishnupur) and Ningthoukhong and the Muslims were settled at Lilong, and other places. Later on, the Bishnupriyas fled to Cachar during the seven years devastation (1819-1826), only 188 remained in Manipur. These 188 became absorbed in Meitei society.

Some writers are of the view that the Bishnupriya originally, belonged to different "Gotras" which are not of indigenous origin. Their original God

Bishnu is not an indigenous God. The Meiteis consider them as "outsiders" who came to Manipur from the west. "Mayang" is the word used by the Meitei to denote these "westerners" or " outsiders" who came to the valley specially through Cachar. In support of their view, they quote M. Singh (1952: 81-82), a Bishnupriya writer, who holds that the Bishnupriyas are the descendants of Arjun and other "Kshetriya Bansas" of western India. M. Singh (1952:82) mentions that the Bishnupriyas mainly belong to "Chandra Bansa". The orthodox Bishnupriyas hold the view that that Bishnupriyas were carried over to Manipur by some immigrants from Dwaraka and Hastinapur just after Kurukshetra War during Mahabharata era (1500 BC). It is further said that these people were led by Vabhrubahana, the son of Arjun and Chitrangada, who also brought a Bishnu image from Hastinapura and installed it in Bishnupur of Manipur. But majority of the Meiteis do not accept this theory.

According to Sir G. A. Grierson (Linguistic Survey of India, Part III, Vol III) by, 1967 1st Edition-1903), it was mentioned that "there is also a degraded class called Kalachaiya or Bishnupriya, which consists of the descendants of the dooms (fishermen) and other Bengalis of low caste. Their occupation was originally that of supplying grass for the royal stables. They speak a language which is different from that of the true Manipuris and is in fact closely allied to vulgar Bengali". G.A. Grierson (1967 : 20) comes to the conclusion that the Bishnupriyas came into Manipur from the Aryan speaking locality. Gait mentions (Grierson 1967 : 20) that the degraded class "Kalachaiya" or Bishnupriyas consist of descendants of the Doom and other Bengalis of low caste. Dun E.W (Gazetteer of Manipur, Vivek Publishing House, Delhi,1975 / First Edn.1886) mentions that the "Mayangs" (Bishnupriyas) are the descendants of the "Hindus" who immigrated from the west. He also mentions that the Chief of the "Mayang" was called "Kalaraj" or "Mayang Ningthou" (Western Chief). The Meitei sometimes call them as "Kalisha Macha" McColloch (1895:14) designates them as the "grass cutters".

However, the main contentions of the Bishnupriya that they are the authochthon kshetriyas of the valley. They claim to be the descendents of Vabhruvahana of the Mahabharata. The Bishnupriya also claim that they are the first settlers in the valley as worshipper of God Vishnu. Later the Meitei King acquired stronger power and drove them out of the country. They however, came back again and settled there. However, this theory can not fit in to the long recorded history of Manipur.

Bishnupriya Culture: Customs and Traditions

The Bishnupriya Manipuris are mainly divided into two sections, viz. the Brahmins and the kshetriyas. There are no Vaishyas and Sudras in this community. Again the society is subdivided into five lokeis or clans; (1) Kshumal; (2) Moirang; (3) Angom; (4) Luwang, and (5) Mangang. They are collectively known as the Pancha-Bishnupriyas inhabiting the five main region of Manipur Valley. Besides, there are nearly 70 Lokeis or clans of which Raja Lokei (Nighthou-Khongiya) or members of Royal family), Lempa Lokei (*Thokchom*) and Moirang Lokei (*Moirang-them*) are the dominating groups. Each of the groups have their distinct ethnic identity or *Gotras*.

The essential elements of Bishnupriya Manipuri culture are identical with those of Meitei culture. religious performances, fine arts, festivals, marriage, dress, ornaments - all these are common to both Bishnupriyas and Meiteis.

Sanamahi and Leimarel are worshiped in every house of the Meiteis. The other gods and the three hundred and sixty four deities are worshipped in the "Umang Lai Laisangs" (temple of gods in the reserved woods with spacious grounds) in the villages. These performances are absent in Bishnupriya Culture. Tulsibong and Githanipung are worshiped in every house of the Bishnupriyas and the "Kartika -festival" and "Pali", which are performed gorgeously by the Bishnupriyas has little relevance to the Meitei culture.

Festivals

To the Bishnupriya Manipuris festivals are the symbols of their cultural, social and religious aspirations which, besides removing the monotony of life by providing physical diversions, mental recreation and emotional outlet, help them lead a better and fuller life. Bishu, Rath Yatra or Kang-Festival, Kartika festival, Maharas Purnima, Phaguwa or Holi festival, Lai-Harouba, Thabol Chongba etc. are major Bishnupriya Manipuri festivals.

Marriage

Marriage in Bishnupriya Manipuri society is based on the Hindu pattern and mostly Aryan and non-Aryan elements having certain traditional customs. Out of the eight forms of marriage as referred in the Manu Samhita only Brahma and Kanyadan or Prajapatya are prevalent in the Society. There is the practice of Gandharva (secret union) system. Marriage is restricted within the sub-clans or Gotras in Bishnupriya Manipuri community.

Dress and Ornaments

The dresses and garments used by the Manipuri Bishnupriya's and Meiteis are identical. The traditional dress used by the Bishnupriya males is called Pachhati - about five feet long cloth manufactured by themselves which is worn round the waist. Females usually wear blouses with traditional Lashing/ Phanek/Chakshabi (a coarse cloth with length wise stripes and embroidered on both sides length wise) with an Innaphi (Single or multicolor coarse cloth with laces on both ends) and an Angei or blouse. The beauty of women dress is the design of Moirangphi, a special and artistic design invented by weavers of Moirang.

Deities

The deities worshipped by Bishnupriyas are :-

1. *Apokpa:* The most important deity is the Apokpa, the ancestor clan god worshipped in every Manipuri Bishnupriya house, as a form of family god, called as Goror-Dou or Apokpa.
2. *Soraren*-Soraren came to be identified with Atiya Kuru Sidaba of Manipuri Meiteis. Soraren (Sora-sky and ren-the chief or the highest) may originally been a family god. The most renowned ancient folk songs of Bishnupriya Manipuri refers a lot about Soraren. The Rain-Invoking Songs (1450-1700) and also Madoi-Soraren songs(1500-1600), mentioned Soraren as the King of all gods.
3. *Githanipung*: Another household deity is Githanipung, very much identical with Leimaren Sidabi of Meiteis. A pot containing water needs to be filled up with new water every Tuesday.
4. *Pahangpa:* Identical with Pakhangba of Meiteis. The offering of chapals (Chapal Katkorani/ Latkorani) for satisfying negative and evil spirit related with worshipping of Pahangpa.
5. *Phunka:* The phunka or phungga Lairu, consists of a small hole, situated on the west of fire hearth in which there is an earthen pot, the hollow usually covered with a clay roof.
6. *Lamor Dou*: The worshipping of the tutelary deity by offering foods.

References

Atombapu Sharma, Meiteigi Meihourol, Churachand Printing Works, Imphal, 1955

A. Grierson (Linguistic Survey of India, Part III, Vol III) by, 1967 1st Edn- 1903)

Barun Kumar Sinha. Emerging Pattern of the Bisnupriya Manipuri Society- A Study in Cultural Identity, an essay. Dept. Of English, S.S. College, Hailakandi.

B.C. Allen, E.A. Gait, C.G.H. Allen, H.F. Howard, Gazetteer of Bengal and North East India.

B.C. Allen, Gazetteer of Naga Hills and Manipur by (1905).

B.C. Allen, Assam District Gazetteer-Naga Hills and Manipur, Volume-IX, Part-II, Calcutta Baptist Mission Press, 1905.

Bidhan Sinha. Cultural Heritage of North-East India, Assam. 1999.

Capt. R. Boileau. Pemberton., Report on the Eastern Frontier of British India, Government of Assam (1835).

Dun E.W, Gazetteer of Manipur, 1885, by, Delhi, Vivek Publishing House, 1975 (First Edn.1886).

Edgar C. Polome. Language, Society, and Pa.

G.K. Ghose. Tribals and Their Culture in Manipur and Nagaland, 1982.

Ranajit Kumar Saha, Valley of Manipur, Punthi-Pustak, Calcutta, 1994.

K.P. Sinha. Bhasatatvar Ruprekha. 1977.

K.P. Sinha. An Anthological Dictionary of Bishnupriya Manipuri. 1982.

McColloch (1895:14).

M. Kirti Singh. Religious Developments in Manipur in the 18th and 19th Century. 1980.

R. Brown, Statistical Account of the native state of Manipur and the hill territory under its rule", Mittal Publications, 1874.

R.K. Jhalajit Singh "A Short History of Manipur", O.K. Store, 1965.

Singh, L.M. Iboongohal "Meaning of Mayangh", Manipur Cooperative Publishing Society Ltd.

Singh Ningthoujam Khelchandra "Ariva Manipuri Shitwagee Itihas", Churachand Printing Works, Imphal, 1969.

Singh Ngariyambam Kulachandra, Apokpa Thounirol, Imphal, 1967.

Singh Hijam Mani, Meihouron Salai Sabok Puiya Amasung Salai Taret Makki Yumnak Namingthon Puiya, the Imphal Press, 1968.

Singha, Jagat Mohan & Singha, Birendra. The Bishnupriya Manipuris & Their Language. Silchar, 1976.

Singha, Mahendra Kumar. Prachin Manipurer Itihas, 1965.

S.K. Chatterjee. Language and Literature of India, 1963.

Sir G. A. Grieorson, Linguistic Survey of India, Part III, Vol III) by, 1967 (1st Edn-1903).

Sir G. A. Grierson. Linguistic Survey of India, Vol-5. 1903.

Sir G. A. Grierson. Linguistic Survey of India, Vol-3. 1904.

Sri Sena Singha/Prachinadhunik Samkhipta Manipurer Itihas.

T.C. Hodson, The Meitheis (1908).

T.C. Hodson, The Naga Tribes of Manipur Status, MacMillan & Co, London 1911.

Vidyavinode, P. Gaits History of Assam. 1908.

W. Mc. Culloch. Publications of G.H. Damat, An Account of the valley of Manipur and the hill tribes, 1859.

Plate-119 : Manipuri Pangal (Muslim) Couple

Plate -120: Oldest Masjid at Porompat

Plate -121 : Phayeng Lai Fagi
Courtesy -Santosh

Plate - 122: Chakpa Panam Ningthou Meihoupirol Sanglen

ENCYCLOPAEDIA OF MANIPUR

ENCYCLOPAEDIA OF MANIPUR

(In 3 Volumes)

(Volume-2)

DR. KHOMDON SINGH LISAM

KALPAZ

Encyclopaedia of Manipur

ISBN: 978-81-7835-864-2 (set)
ISBN : 978-81-7835-866-6 (Vol. 2)

Published in 2011 in India by
Kalpaz Publications
C-30, Satyawati Nagar,
Delhi-110052
E-mail: kalpaz@hotmail.com
Phone : 9212729499

Laser Type Setting by: Rudra Computer Graphics, Delhi
Printed at : Chawla Offset Printers, Delhi

Contents

8. **Scheduled Castes and Scheduled Tribes :** 377
• Scheduled Castes • Scheduled Tribes • Aimol • Anal • Chiru • Chothe • Gangte • Kacha Naga • Koirao • Koireng • Kom • Lamgang • Mao • Maram • Maring • Mate • Mizo • Lai/ Pawih • Monsang • Moyon • Paite • Poumai Naga • Purum • Salhte(Soktes) • Tarao • Thadou • Vaiphei • Zeliangrong • Zou

9. **The Naga Tribes** 428
• Origin of the term Naga • How many Naga Tribes are there? • Origin and Migration of Nagas : • Physical Features • Head Taking • Occupation • Houses • Food • Religion • Social Life and Village Organisation • Oath Taking : • Dress and Ornaments • Handicraft • Design of clothes • The Morung • Economic Activities • Marriage • Child Birth • Inheritance • Death Ritual • Tattooing • Feasts of Merit • Early Relations with the British • Naga National Movement • Govt. of India Act-1919 • Simon Commission-1929 • Govt. of India Act-1935 • Visit of Cabinet Mission • The 9-Point Agreement • Declaration of Naga Independence-August 14, 1947 • Naga Voluntary Plebiscite of 1951• Proclamation of the Federal Government • Naga People's Convention • Birth of State of Nagaland • Earlier Indo-Naga Peace Talks • Shillong Accord

• Birth of NSCN • Split of NSCN • NSCN-IM • Linkages of NSCN-IM • NSCN-K • Rivalry between NSCN-IM and NSCN-K • Peace Process • The Manipur Factor and the Peace Process • Weakness of NSCN's demands for Greater Nagaland • Possible solutions

10. **Tangkhuls** 515

• Origin of the word "Tangkhul" • Migration of Tangkhuls • Origin of Tangkhuls • Tangkhul and Meitei Ties • Physical appearance of Tangkhuls • Tangkhul House • Occupation • Hairstyle (Coiffure) • Tattooing • Ornaments • Weapons • Tangkhul Language • Religion • Longshim (Bachelors Dormitory) • Ngalalong : (Girls Dormitory) • Awunga • Hangva • Marriage • Disposal of dead • Log Drum • War : Head Taking • Swearing and Oath Taking : • Economy • Tangkhul festivals • Music and Dances • Art and Culture • Textiles and Clothes • Maran Kasa (Feast of Merit)

11. **Kukis and Hmars** 552

• Kukis: origin of Kukis • Physical Features • Dress and Ornaments • Settlement area (Kho) • Villages of Kukis • Houses of Kukis • Family • Marriage • Divorce • Cultivation • Village administration • Land and mode of inheritance • Death Ritual • Food • Som Inn (Bachelors Dormitory • Musical instruments • Dances • Games and sports • Economic life • Hmars • Origin and Migration • Hmar Clans • Houses • Marriage • Family and Inheritances of Hmars • Traditional Political system of Hmars • Busung Sadar • Thiempu • The Village Crier • Siehmang Upas (Councillors) • Youth Dormitory (Buonzawl) • Val –Upsa • Courtship • Religion • Dances of Hmars • Musical Instruments • Textiles of Hmars • Handicrafts of Hmrars • Decorative Arts

12. **Prominent Tourist Spots** 576

• Imphal City • Kangla fort, -the ancient Manipur Palace • Khwairamband Keithel (Sana Keithel) • IMA Keithel or Mothers Market . • Saheed Minar • Shree Govindajee Temple

• Temple of Thangal General • Manipur State Museum : • Manipur Zoological Garden : • War Cemeteries • Khonghampat Orchidarium • Heecham Yaicham Pat • Kaina • Andro - the ancient village : • Langthabal • Khongjom • Moirang • Loktak Lake and Sendra Island • Keibul Lamjao National Park • Phubala • Sekta Kei Mound -Archeological Living Museum • Waithou Lake • Singda • Tamenglong • Ukhrul • Shirui Lily • Moreh • Churachandpur

13. **Festivals of Manipur** 608
• Festival of Meiteis • Cheiraoba - The Meitei NewYear • Ningol Chakouba - the social festival of Meiteis • Yaoshang - The premier festival of the Meiteis • Baruni • Kang Chingba or Ratha Yatra • Krishna Janmashtami • Durga Puja • Diwali • Heikru Hitongba • Mera Houchongba : • Lai Haraoba : "'Frolic of the gods" • The festival of Christians - Christmas • Festival of Tangkhuls • Festival of Zeliangrong Nagas • Festival of Poumai Nagas • Festival of Kukis • Festival of Muslims

14. **Temples and Monuments** 655
• Vishnu Temple of Bishnupur • Lord Krishna Temple of Brahmapur Leikai • Shri Hanuman Thakur Temple of Mahabali Umang • Shri Govindajee Temple of Old Palace Kangla • Thangal General Temple of Wangkhei • Leimapokpam Keirungba Temple • Shri Govindajee Temple of New Palace • Shri Radha Raman Temple of Langthabal . • Lord Krishnachandra Temple of Kakching • Nara Singh Temple of Kakching • Abdeitya Temple of Lamangdong (Bishnupur) • Gopinath Temple of Ningthoukhong • Radha Madhav Temple of Ningthoukhong • Ramji Prabhu Temple of Ningthem Pukhri Mapal • Bijoy Govinda Temple of Sagolband • Nara Singh Thakur of Naorem Leikai • Nityainanda of RIMS Road • Madan Mohan Temple of Kongba • Sri Sri Radha Krishna Manimandir of ISKON • Gopinath Temple of Sanakhyahal • Hiyangthang Lairembi (Kamakhya) Temple • Thongam Mondum • Lord Sanamahi Temple, Imphal • Ibudhou Thangjing Temple of Moirang • Konthoujam Lairembi • Khamlangba of Kakching • Samadhi of Maharaja Gambheer

Singh • Samadhi of Maharaja Nongchup Lamgaingamba (Bhadra Singh) • Samadhi of Luwang Ningthou

15. **Historical Landmarks** 701

• Chronology of important historical landmarks • Arrival of Muslims • Arrival of Hinduism • First Devastation "(Khuntak Ahanba-1755) • Seven Years Devastation (Chahi Taret Khuntakpa) • The Anglo-Manipuri war of 1891 (Khongjom War) • The Palace Revolution-1891 • Khongjom War-1891 • Paona Brajabashi • Chinglensana Phunganai Sanglakpa • Trial and death of Tikendrajit and Thangal General • Arrival of Christianity • First Nupi Lal (First Women's Agitation - 1904) • Kuki Uprising -1917-1919 • Zeliangrong Movement - 1930-1949 • Jadonang : • Rani Gaidinliu : • Second Nupi Lal – (Second Women's Agitation -1939) • Manipur and World War -II

16. **Manipuri Dances** 794

• Manipur Classical Dance Forms • Manipur Raas Lila • Vasanta Raas • Characteristics of Manipuri Dance • Techniques of Manipuri Dance • Raas Lila Musical Instruments • Raas Dance Costumes • Early Period of Manipuri Dance • Maniprui Dance in Modern Times • Gostha Lila • Khamba Thoibi Dance • Maibi Dance • Pung Cholom • Nupa Pala • Famous Maniprui Dance Gurus

Volume - 2

8

Scheduled Castes and Scheduled Tribes

The Scheduled Castes and Scheduled Tribes of Manipur were listed in the President's Schedule Castes and Scheduled Tribes List (Modification) order of the Government of India -1956. The order came into force from 29th October, 1956.

1. Schedule Castes :

1. Lois (See Chapeter-7) 2. Yaithibi (See Chapter-7) 3. Dhupi or Dhobi 4. Muchi or Ravidas 5. Namsudra 6. Pati 7. Sutradhar

2. Schedule Tribes :

1. Aimol 2. Anal 3. Angami 4. Chiru 5. Chothe 6. Gangte 7. Hmar 8. Kabui 9. Kacha Naga 10. Kharam 11. Koirao 12. Koireng 3. Kom 14. Lamgang 15. Any Mizo or Lushai Tribe 16. Maram 17. Maring 18. Mao 19. Monsang 20. Moyon 21. Paite 22. Poumai 23. Purum 24. Ralte 25. Sema 26. Mimite 27. Sahte (Soktes) 28. Thadou 29. Tangkhul 30. Tarao 31. Vaiphei 32. Zou 33. Any other Kuki Tribe

The Lois and Yaithibis have been described in a separate chapter (see chapter-7:Lois, Yaithibis and Bishnupriyas).

The scheduled tribes inhabit mainly in all districts.

Churachandpur district:-Hmar, Paite and Thadou are the major groups. Mizo.Vaiphei, Gangte, Simte, Ralte, Anal, Kabui, Kom, Zou, Aimol, Sukte also settle there.

Ukrhul district:Tangkhuls are the major group. Thadou, Taraos and other Kuki groups are also settle there.

Senapati district:-Mao, Maram, Poumai, Thadou Kuki are the major groups and Tangkhuls, Maring, Chiru, Kom, Voireng, Vaiphei, Kacha Naga, Sema, Keirao, are also living in this district as minor groups.

Tamenglong district:- The main ethnic group is the Zeliangrong, which is a composite group of three related groups-Rongmei (Kabuis), Liangmei and Zemei (also called Kacha Nagas). Kabuis are living in large number in all districts of Manipur. Kuki tribes also settle in large numbers in this district.

Chandel district:-Anal, Maring, Thadou are the major groups in this district whereas Lamgang, Gangte, Moyon, Monsang, Aimol, Chothe, Purum, Mizo, Tangkhul and Kom are the minor groups.

Aimol

The Aimols are settled at Aimol Khullen at Unapal, Satu, Kumiei, Chingnunghut, Aimol Tampak, Khodamphai, Ngarong Aimol, Chandonpokpi, Soibong (Khudengthabi) at the Chandel District and Kha-Aimol, Luichungbum village at the Churachandpur district. It is also believed that some of them have migrated from Mizoram and Tripura. The existence of Aimols were recorded as early as 1723 A.D. The word Aimol means "mountain of crabs" (ai=crab; mol=mountain). Thus, their legend believes that they came out of mountain like the mountain crabs. According to the 2001 census, they number about 2643 individuals.

Clans

The tribe is divided into five clans-Chongom (with 3 sub-clans), Laita (3 sub-clans), Lanu (4 sub-clans), Chaithu (no sub-clan) and Chongthu (2 sub-clans).

Houses and Occupations

The traditional house of the Aimol people resembles like those of the Meiteis and Purums. The houses are basically made of wood, bamboo and mud with thatched roofing. Granary storehouse, cattle shed, and pig stall are situated near the house. The direction of houses is always towards the east, facing the rising sun. Their main occupation is agriculture and allied activities including domestication of cattle, pig and fowl. Cultivation of paddy is carried out by both sexes. Weaving and livestock rearing gives a good income to the family. They practice both wet and Jhum (shifting) paddy cultivation in the hill.

Village administration

The chief of the village is called *"Tamsakoi"*, which is the hereditary post. He is head of the village council known as *"Parakaret"*, which consists of eight councilors.The subordinate council i.e. *"Thoukanai"* also consist of the same number of posts. Tamsakoi remains the exclusive right for the eldest Chongom clan member.

Marriage

The clans are exogamous and so also the sub clans. A person should find his or her spouse from other clans than his or her clan.

Traditional deities

Aimols believe in many deities and spirits. They believe in the existence of the village deity (Kho-Pathia) and the house deity (In-Pathian). They worshipped Sailing and Bonglei, protector of village; Chahou (Pathian of agriculture and paddy) Miso for prosperity and peace. Arkun Pathian (goddess of Human fertility) is worshipped particularly by pregnant women. To ward off diseases and for curing illness, Randoi and Song Kot are worshipped with rituals. Likewise, success or failure in war and hunting is ascribed to the action of Chuwan Pathian. A goat or a hen is sacrificed at the time of worship.

Most of the Aimols are now converted to Christianity and identify with the Nagas although they are related to the Chin-Kuki group.

Textiles

The textiles of Aimols are Shekili, Hulike Chu, Laijiak, Punthal, Shorte, Panchai, Shuiboh, Puante, Puandum for males and Khamtang, Kuwapaam, Shenchil, Aitang, Reinuam, Khongkhihmor and Saipikhup for females.

Anal

More than 94% of the Anals are settled in the Chandel district. They are known as Pakan among themselves. During migration, they were splitted to Anal, Lamkang, Moyon, and Monsang tribes. Anal is considered to be one of the oldest Chin-Kuki tribes of Manipur and belong to the Tibeto-Burman family of tribes. They fluently speak Manipuri while talking to other tribes. They now identify themselves as one of the Naga tribes. In 2001, their population was 13,853 living in 45 villages. A pregnant woman in the Anal community do not work hard and the husband is taboo from planting banana or bamboo plants. She may not eat double bananas or any creepy plants that bear fruits. Their cultural life is rich and preserved in traditional folklores and folksongs.

The festivals include "Akam" performed to invoke divine blessings. Kamdon dance is performed during the Akam festival both by man and woman. (see plate-123)

Angamese

The Angamese numbering about 650 (2001-Census) are very small tribe in Manipur inhabiting areas which are contiguous with Nagaland.

Chiru

Their numbers are about 5487 persons (2001 Census). Dollang Chiru in Tamenglong district is the largest Chiru Village where nearly 26% live. The Chirus are concentrated in Tamenglong, Senapati and Bishnupur districts of Manipur. Their manners, customs, and language appear to identify with Kuki origin but their physique, habits, hairstyle, and bachelors' quarters are Naga way of life. The word Chiru means the seed of a plant. Women play an important role in agricultural work, collection of firewood, and fetching water for drinking and household uses. They practice both Jhum (shifting)and wet cultivation. Fruits like banana, orange, lemon, and papaya are grown for family consumption and market trading. The main cottage industries are basket and cane works, weaving, carpentry and manufacture of musical instruments. (see plate-131)

Chothe

More than 85% are settled in 10 villages in Chandel district and their number was approximately 2675 (Census- 2001). Agriculture is the main occupation, and they grow cash crops which are sold in Pallel, Tengnoupal, Kakching and Imphal. The main festival of the Chothe is harvesting festival (Sasuhang) along with Christmas, New Year, Good Friday, etc. Dance and Music are their cultural life both in religious and recreational events. Inter-marriage with neighboring Nagas have made good alliances with them and they identify themselves with the Nagas. (see plate-130)

Gangte

The Gangtes are colourful tribe numbering about 15,100 (Census-2001). The Paite, Vaiphei and Thadou call them Gangte but Mizos call them Rangte. Their origin is traced in a cave called *khul* somewhere in the extreme north. More than 68.6% inhabit in Churachandpur district. Appeasement of the village deity was an annual feature before they were converted to Christianity. They share folksongs, folktales and dances with other communities like Paite, Zou, Thadou, Vaiphei and vice versa.

Gangte Village

According to Rev. G.S. Gangte (Gangte Chronicle), "the village constitutes the bedrock of social, economic and administrative complex of the Gangtes". The location of their jhum sites solely determines the situation of their settlements. The Gangtes built their villages on hill-tops in consideration of defence against wild animals and enemies. Khawmuol is the gateway that leads to the village. The villagers erect a wooden post here upon which they hang the heads of enemies taken after tribal wars. Dignitaries from outside or other tribes are welcomed and received here. Magical incantations to cast off wild spirit are done here.

Gangte village chief is all powerful.exacting unquestioning obedience and loyalty from the subjects. Disobedience of the Chief merits expulsion from the village, and neither could outsiders immigrate without his assent. The chief usually decides the distribution of and access to wealth of the land. The Chief is not only the ruler over his villagers; he is also their protector in times of adversity like famines and tribal wars. If a villager migrate without proper consent of the chief, his property and belonging are detained by the Chief. The Gangte Chief is entitled to certain tributes from his subjects viz, Changseu, Salieng and Khuotha.

Changseu

This is a tribute paid to the chief out of reverence and loyalty. Practised till now, Changseu is a form of tribal taxation system, customarily paid in paddy produce. It varies from two, three or five tins of rice grain. The Chief can exempt certain class of villagers who are needy and poor from paying Changseu. This exempted lot are anticipated to offer either chicken or tribal brew to the Chief on the day of Changseu collection.

Salieng

Salieng means shoulder blade of animals gifted to the Chief by anyone who caught wild animals in gratitude to his permission to hunt within the boundary of his Chiefdom. If someone plays truancy, then he is punishied and punishment entails slaying of a mithun or payment of rupees forty.

Khuotha

Khuotha means collective labour force of all household in the village that a chief can call for if the need arises. Even the villagers are entitled to invite Khuotha but they must provide lunch for the village labour corps on the day of social work. Further, the Chief can make a trade for Khuotha in lieu of Changseu but is not obliged to provide meal on the day he asks for the labour force.

Siehmang Upa

Siehmang Upa are selected members of the village council who assist the Chief in the administration of the village. Siehmang Upa are men of impeccable integrity and excellence in all walks of life. They are exempted from all kinds of tributes and taxes. The number of Siehmang Upa is relative of the size of the village.

Tangsam:

Tangsam is village crier and official spokesmen of the village. He is given the duty to inform the Siehmang Upa members when and where the village council is to meet, and also to apprise the villagers of the outcome of the council's deliberations. He is given a tin of paddy per household annually.

Thiempu is the village priest, who is also the doctor of the village. There are certain areas of jurisdiction where his decision is the law. Priesthood is the only office that can challenge and curb the tyranny of the Chief. Priesthood is hereditary. The nuances of healing and enigma of medicine are well-kept secrets, The passage of tricks of the trade is only between the priest and his sons or grandsons. One has to spend considerable amount of time to learn the secrets of healing. The priest also conducts divine sessions with the spirit and prays for productivity of the land. Hunters returning from a successful safari are welcome by the priest at the Khawmuol with drums and chants for which the priest is entitled with a bulk of the meat of the hunted. The priest does not charge any consultation fee from the villagers. But the villagers pay for his service in the form of of paddy or other items.

Thiksek: Thiksek is the blacksmith of the village. In fact, every village has its blacksmith to manufacture swords, spears, daggers, guns, gun powders, knives, spades, saws and other instruments for daily work in the fields. No village can exist without a blacksmith. The villagers will give a tin of paddy per household annually to the blacksmith. Should any villager be successful in their hunting expeditions, they are bonded by custom to gift a chunk of the catch to the blacksmith as Thiksek-sa.

Suok/Slaves:

Chroniclers like John Shakepeare were the first to highlight the existence of slavery in the CHIKIM society. In his work, "The Lushai Kuki Clans "(1912), he put forth a detailed view on tribal slavery. On the whole, slavery among the tribals vastly differs from that of the West or New World. Tribal slavery is not under duress, it is almost voluntary. Close observation gives the impression that in most cases, slavery seemed to be the only option for survival. Among the Gangtes three variants of slavery were practiced. *Inpi Suok :* Inpi Suok are mostly orphans, the incapacitated who cannot look after themselves and the poor in abject poverty or misery. The Inpi Suok are conventionally treated as members of the Chief's family but they must work and toil harder than genuine members. The chief, being their guardian, is fully responsible for the welfare and security of the Inpi Suok. *Chemsan Suok*–means "Slavery due to stained sword." This class of slaves are the murderers, criminals or insolvents who took refuge to the Chief. for them slavery is the salvation. Once they give in to the chief, they are saved and it is against the law to harm them. Harming them would tantamount to making a mockery of the Chief's chair and the penalty would also be grave. The chief is entitled to the dowry of any Chemsan Suok's daughter. L.B.Thanga (the Mizos, 1979) says that till 1928, Chemsan Suok can buy freedom by compensating the Chief, his master, with a mithun or forty rupees in cash. *Tuklut Suok* - Tuklut Suok are slaves as a consequence of village wars and they usually belong to the losing side in the battle. For safety, the losing party give themselves to the victorious one and hence, the label Tuklut, meaning give in?.Tuklut Suok can build shelter in the victorious village as and when they can handover a healthy mithun to the Chief and if the Tuklut Suok are of small family, even a mithun can buy their freedom.

Hmar- **see Chapter -11: Kukis and Hmars Kacha Naga**

Kacha Nagas are the people belonging to the Naga ethnicity and are scattered over states of Manipur and Nagaland. Their population was 17138 as given in the Government of Manipur census report of 1981.

Origin

Kacha Naga is formed by Liangmei and Zeme tribes. The word Kacha Naga is probably derived from the Angami word 'Ketsa' meaning thick forest. They are fair complexioned, long headed, slim but of medium height. Legend says that their forefathers had emerged from Ramting Kabin (Ram=land, ting=sky, Kabin=narrow passage), which is a narrow passage between the earth and sky, which ultimately leads to a cave. The cave is located in the Mao-Maram area of the Senapati district of Manipur. From this cave, they moved and settled in and around Chawang Phungning later on known as Makuilongdi. The Kacha Nagas live in dwelling houses with thatched roofs.

Traditions and beliefs

The Kacha Naga does not live long in one village. As the population increases, they leave to form newer villages where one of them becomes the chief. A temporary gate would first be constructed for their entry into the new village. After the village gate, Kareng, was constructed facing the direction from where the people came.There is also a necklace called Talui Tiuriang which is an essential item for the new settlement ritual. Loss of the necklace by theft, force or any cause is supposed to bring calamity to the village and its people and hence, it is preserved in the safe custody of the Chief.

The first sacrifice in the village was made at a particular place somewhere in the central part of the village. This place becomes the village shrine and is called the *Sangbam*. For a newly established village, fire is not brought from outside but is made by rubbing a dry bamboo piece against a particular piece of wood called Magang and the fire so produced is distributed to every household.

All the grown up boys come and stay together at a dormitory called *Khangchiu.* Here they are imparted moral discipline and other necessary training in the art of handicraft like basket making, wooden craft etc. There is also a dormitory for girls called *Liuchiu.* They look after the welfare of the village by contributing the voluntary services in the form of collecting firewood and water for the poor and deserted widows. They are also trained in the trades like spinning, weaving etc.

Village administration

The village Chief carries out the village administration, which is a hereditary post and its council known as the *Apaiki.* Age and seniority in the clan is the main criteria for membership. Next to the chief is *Nangpen* who assists the chief. The village council decides village disputes by imposing penalty to the wrong doers. Time for all religious functions are fixed by another body called *Khangkiang Phoum* whose nominal head is *Tingku*, who is also the village crier.

Cultures and Taboos

At the beginning of each year, the chief performs a community offering to the spirit of the corns asking for abundant harvest. This day is tabooed for the villagers to cross outside the village and the chief also is abstained from sexual relation with his wife. Celebrations are held when big game or valuable articles are brought in the village. The head of the enemy is accorded with highest celebration for five days. The second highest honour is the killing of python. Killing of bear, killing of wild pigs etc, are the third grade of valour. Celebration of these occasions restricts males to go out of the village. With the advent of Christianity, these traditional ways of life are fast getting neglected and forgotten.

Koirao:

Koirao population was just 1200 (Census-2001). They accept themselves by the name Thangal. The Koirao or the Thangal inhabit in nine hill villages of Sadar Hill areas of the Senapati District. The villages are: Mapao Thangal, Thangal Surung, Makeng Thangal, Tumnou Pokpi, Yaikongpou, Tikhulen, Ningthoubam, Mayangkhong and Gailongde. (see plate-148)

Legends and Clans

The people believe that they come from the northern direction emerging from a cave. Their legend says that there were three brothers whose parents were not known. The eldest brother was the originator of the present tribe while the second and youngest brothers became originators of Tangkhul and Meitei respectively. From this folktale, their first settlement site was at the Kaipong range to the east of Maram in Manipur. It is said that Maharaja Pamheiba of Manipur (Garib Niwaz) was a Thangal boy or was brought up within the tribe.

In the Koirao society, there are 17 clans of which Kadei Keimei, Payei Naomei, Syong Duimi, Payot Naomei and Deibung Naomi are the oldest ones from which other clans were separated. They believe that children are a gift of God and the village Maibi will pronounce the birth of a child by saying *Haiguiye* while holding a dagger in her hand. In earlier days, they bartered their agricultural products, baskets and black smithy with Meiteis for food, with Tangkhuls for earthen pots and with Kukis for beaded necklaces.

Village administration

Khullakpa is the chief of the village council known as *katammi*. The traditional village authority was fully vested in a council, led by a hereditary office of Khullakpa. The council consists of: Khullakpa (chief), Luplakpa, Kangpara or Ganpara and two Tans. Khullakpa is the chief and restricted to the Kaduikeimi lineage only.

Marriage and Inheritence

The Koirao is a monogamous society. Marrying a cousin from the maternal side through engagement is the usual type of marriage. This goes through a number of stages. The present frequently reported type is elopement. Bride price may or may not be given depending on the wish of the bride's party. The Koirao inheritance rule is patri-lineal.

Festivals and Social Events

The festivals in pre Christian Thangal society were as many as the number of the months. The majority of these festivals were related with their socio-religious belief associated with agriculture.

The full moon (Hadet) plays a vital role in fixing days of festivals. In the month of *Kaphala* (May), the first Thangal month, they observe two-day festival of Kapha worshipping Keirong-raiba for good health and prosperous society. In *Jangheiha* month (May-June) there are festivals of Imphoi Imphoi Dangnit, prayers to protect the seed-grain from pests etc., and Janghei, a two day festival to drive out evil spirit, Saraikagai. The dance of this festival is Kakhoi Yagathou. In the month of *Tundeiha* (June-July) a ritual, Malangathou, is observed to call the soul spirit of paddy. In the month of *Noudanda* (July-August), the selected performer cuts the grass at main gate indicating the cutting of bad grass to give way for the good ones. On this day, people cook chicken and refrain from doing work. From the next day, they start cultivation. In the month of *Mathala* (Aug-Sept), Malangathou is observed. This involves praying to the deity for prosperity and growth of village. Naogagathou genna is celebrated for the welfare of children praying the household deity Khumdung in Ganha (Sept-Oct). Worship of granary deity, Phouraiba by offering a cock of single colour and wine takes place in Torotakha (Dec- Jan). During the month of *Taha* (Jan-Feb) a ritual offering to the departed souls during the proceeding year is observed on an auspicious day. Giphiyotangatha, care of weapon and sharpening them, is held on the first or second day after the full moon of Giphiyoha (Feb-March). On the 24th day of Keithakha (March-April) the ritual of linhut Dangsit for seed sowing is performed. Favourite festival is *Linhut tangnit* (Seed sowing festival), along with Christian festivals. Females are engaged in various cottage industries, weaving in particular. The agricultural implements are more or less similar with other foothill dwellers or plain inhabitants and include plough and yoke, adze, sickle, axe, dao etc. The women, in social gatherings, use Mik Keap thoi, a skirt and shawl Tang Kol maphi while men use Khom'nei as loin cloth and a piece of cloth called Chak'rei across the chest.

Koireng:

The word Koireng is derived from Kouiren (Kol-east and ren-men). The Koirengs believe that they originated from a cave. Pathian is believed to be their supreme God before Christianity. According to 1981 census, the Koireng population in Manipur was 603. Their number is small, only 1056 (Census-2001), 80% inhabiting in Senapati district. The present geographical distribution of the Koirengs include Longa Koireng, Sadu Koireng, Awang Koireng, Utonglog and Kamu Koireng in Senapati District; Tarung and Koireng Colony in Imphal West district. Imphal river, Iril, and Maklang rivers run through their villages. (see plate-143)

Their literacy rates are low compared to the surrounding tribes. From the linguistic point of view, they belong to the Kuki chin group of Tibeto Burmese Language.

Physical features

The males are commonly 5' to 5'-6" tall whereas female is 4'-6" to 5'-3". They have dark brown skin; slim looking but sturdily built body. Their hair is usually black and straight. An oval shaped face; non prominent cheek bones, small eyes with absence of epicanthic folds; mesorine nose with its root high, piercing of ear lobes and slight prognathous of Chin are also distinctive features.

Status of women

The status of women is relatively high due to their taking part in economic activities. A woman member is also represented in the village council. They cultivate paddy, maize, sesame, potato, arum and ginger and trade with the Meiteis.

Clans

The two Clans-Songthu and Yeite are divided into a number of subclans. The Songthu Clan is divided into two groups; Chungnung (upper) and Noineng (lower). Chungnung is sub-divided into Rengphamak and Rengkhumak while the Noineng clan is divided into Rangsokhet, Rongkhotinson, Ranglisek, Rongleisong, Toltung and Thaiba. The Yeite clan is divided into Norsel, Barreng, Ranglihon, Leisel, Wanbe, Tente, Tumtin, Lunqlai, Maite.

Amongst the clans, there is the exogamous rule for marriages but amongst the sub clans certain groups are allowed to inter marriage while certain groups are restricted to intermarriage.

Houses, dress, ornaments, and customs

They lived in thatched houses with earthen plinth and a verandah. Their important dress and customs are -(i) for males- onthal (especially for males), Puonwon, Murkisen thaite (turban) and (ii) for females-Puonhem (ascribing higher status for being adorn with it), Ponsel, Saipikhup. Lungum Puonkokhoi, Ponlang, Koram (the latter two clothes are waist belts). The Koireng women use ornaments with Har (armlet), Yakseir (armlet) - all made of bead and Rikarui (necklace of red beads). The Koireng men use feathers of hen and fur of goat to decorate along with turban. Musical instruments they use to rejoice with are Khung (drum) Rushem (Bagpipe), Sekhi (horn), Sum (gong), Serangdar (violin like instrument) etc.

They used implements like spear, fishing basket, carrying baskets, hoe, plough yoke etc. The supreme God is Pathian and next to Him is In-Pathian (House-god). An individual's life is entwined in a series of rituals – from nailuwoi (naming ceremony) on the third day of a birth; Theikal, ceremony to strengthen limbs of the child who are 15 day old; Mason, ceremony performed to recognize the child as human being and allowed to wear earrings; marriage that prevails as noiruoi (engagement) or Tan (elopement) or Keitout (capture) to death ceremony. They also believe in the rebirth of soul. Their material items includes those from the cultural, social and economic spheres.

The social events and festivals are as follows :-

Bedal: It is the genna in the month of *Tolbol* (Jan-Feb) before which the growing of crop is forbidden. Offerings are made to the goddess-who was the daughter of Miriem, taken by Lord Thangjing as his wife when she was a sacred virgin- near a pool/ rivulet.

Palchoi: It is a religious service to liberate them from disasters. At the village gate, the Khullakpa worship with wine and creepers of costus ap and after the completion he is brought on the back of a Changloi.

Kangrai Mindai: It is a three day festival in the month of *Phurpa* (May-June). On the first day, village elders worship (Yupanthaba) Pathian at the gate with wine along with pig, hen and a dog, which the anterior portion is feasted after the rite. Lomnur (leader of boys) and Tamsai (leader of girls) are selected on the second day, they consume cooked remaining meat of the previous day and entertain by cutting jokes and singing song, but there is no dancing. On the third day, youngster fetch flower, firewood and a bundle of firewood is kept in front of each house. In the evening, a tug of war, won compulsorily by Khulenlom is arranged between Khumlon (upper group) and Khulenton (lower group). Afterwards, there is Meiomlam dancing and singing.

Chaonlei: This is celebrated in the month of *Inga* for prosperous growing of crops combined with Charaikhei ritual for healthy growing of crops.

Tuikuong Khuor: This is the worshipping of the water spirit in the month of *Jingpi* (Aug-Sep) at a water hole and waterways are cleared. In addition, use of fishing net on this day is tabooed.

Lamkir Lei: Megalith erected areas are cleared and there Yupanthaba is carried out.

Chamer Sier: On the first day of these two days festival, village elders ritualistically offer wine, dog, pig and hen at the village gate and enjoy the flavour of the meat. On this day, village elders throw torches (Meihun) in between houses so as to exorcise evil spirits from the village. On the last day, nisolam dance is performed by 4-5 men holding spears in gala dress and Kalamchei dance by the assistants of newly installed noblemen is held. On this day, a bamboo post is erected by each family.

Lamthel Lei: This is a road/village cleaning festival at Panthong. The village elders string the gate with creepers and folk song telling the tales of mythical hero Neisong is sung. Khullakpa and a newly installed officer are brought back on the backs of Changlois.

Chathar Lei: This is the festival of Koirengs enoying the first taste of harvested rice celebrated in the month of *Thapal* (Nov-Dec).

Lengwai: This is celebrated on the very next day of Chathar Lei. On this day, sisters' sons are given feast by maternal uncles.

Chalam Kei: This is a divine service that includes offering of harvested rice by the Khullakpa in month of *Birip* (Dec-Jan). The village is genna that day and nobody is allowed to go out of the village.

The Koireng economy persists mainly on agriculture which they carry on by both Jhum (shifting) and wet cultivation method. Paddy, potato, ginger, arum etc, are main products. Gathering economy and basket products for commercial goods form trade and market. People of younger generation are nominally Christians, but old indeginous practices linger on and only non-Christian elders enjoy privileges for Chieftainship. Traditionally rules to impose fine to wrong doers exists in each village which might be different from village to village.

Kom: The Koms population was 15467 in 2001 census in 22 villages. Most of the villages are scattered in the Churachandpur, Chandel and Senapati districts and also in valley districts. They speak a dialect that has affinities with old Kukis under Tibeto-Burman language.Their language is recognised by the Aimol, Koireng and Chiru. They also have close relationship with the Hmar. The Koms are easily identified by their way of dressing. They wear a black shawl embroidered in the border. Koms believe in Pathen, the supreme god and goddess, Lengjai. The literacy rate is quite high and they actively participate in political activities of the state. (see plate-125, 132)

Origin and Legends

According to the legends of their origin, their forefathers are believed to have come out through a Cave which led them to the Fort of Manipur from another world. A tiger used to lay in wait to kill them. Karongpa who came out wearing a stripped cloth made friends with the tiger as his cloth resembled its skin and therefore his descendents were refrained from eating or killing a tiger. Salchapa came out and killed the tiger. Leivonpa cut out the tiger's tongue and wrapped it up on his waist. But according to another version, Pu Songthu, the leader of the party killed a big snake and a tiger for obstructing their way. Then, they were free of danger and rejoiced at the house of Telenpa. In the subsequent generations they became the head of the various Kom clans namely Karong, Saiche, Leivon, Tellein, Hmangte, Serto and Lupheng.

Miration

According to Kom researchers, between 100 B.C. and 100 A.D., they entered Burma and sometime in 200 A.D. they had moved toward Arakan Hills and Bay of Bengal. Then the Kom people entered Tripura and from there they entered Manipur as they were ousted by the Soktes.Their typical house is thatch roofed one.

Dress and Ornaments

The art of weaving, believed to have been followed from Chongnu who fell in love with a Python-God, still continues in loin looms. Before she joined him in the realm of immorality, she copied the markings of her lover's body in her loom.The ordinary dress of a man is a dhoti fastened round the waist while a man of distinction wears pasppan, the cloth bearing the skin mark of Python-god.The womenfolk, who are the designated weavers of the tribe, wear Saipikhup, Khamtlang, Ponlak etc. that bear remarkable designs on the borders as bodice or skirt.They also use wrist bands. They wear necklace made of semi-precious stones and cowries.

They use weapons such as axe, dao, spear, bow and arrow etc.

The Koms are self-sufficient in their economy. They depend on agriculture for their substinence. They practise both Jhum (shifting) and wet cultivation. They cultivate paddy and grow potatoes which had been imported by Rev.William Pettigrew, the first missionary who came to Manipur.They also cultivate millet and yam. Domesticated animals include pigs, fowls, goats, cows, buffaloes, mithun etc.

Clans and Inheritence

Their society is divided into social groups which are again sub divided into smaller groups. The Clan is the biggest social group and reflects in ascertaining at final relationship. These clans are exogamous in nature and include Karong, Saicha, Leivon, Tellein, Such, Lupheng and Hmangte. Descent is traced exclusively through the male line. The youngest male issue of the family inherits the property.

Marriage

The marriage of the son is to be arranged by the parents. For a male member, his mother's brother's daughter was the mate prescribed by the society. The marrying groom had to serve at his father-in-law's house for three years. This custom was known as Numhei-hle. The alternate form of acquiring bride was to pay bride price or mangkat three times. At times this creates a havoc because of its excessiveness. At present, bride is secured by mutual consent.

Deities

Non Christian Koms believe in two deities - Pathen,(the supreme one) and Lungjei. Pathen is creator of all living being and the Universe in consultation with his brother Lungjei, They also worship Inroi as their household god. They also believe in the existence of soul after death and heaven and hell are abodes of these souls.

Festivals

They do observe a number of festivals both social and religion in nature.

These festivals are:

Seling - Erection of wood

Belaro - Erection of bamboo on the top of which is placed a bird to be targeted for arrow shooting thereby testing skills.

Table-40 Showing the festivals of Kom tribes

Festivals	*Month*	
	Kom	*English*
Seling, Belaro, Lukasun Lhungphung, Khongnangkhong	Matai	March
Cheiraoba	Martum	April
Kasalai	Karani	September
Lamkut	Eartha	October

Lukasun- Offering last rite to deceased persons.

Lhungphung- Erection of mega stone.

Khongnanghong- Performance of festival for a big banyan tree in his name so as to retain his name after death.

Cheiraoba-New Year Festival.

Hlodei- Wedding rite.

Lamkut-At dusk, song and dance (Lamkut lam) are held in every house, accompanied by feast to sanctify them and to keep their houses as sacred places through out the current year. Its period continues for one month.

Lamgang:

The population was about 4524 according to 2001 census, mainly inhabiting in Chandel district of Manipur near Chakpikarong, Kakching Khunou and scatter in 24 villages. The Lamgang dialect is quite similar to Anal, Moyon and Monsang of the Kuki-Chin group of languages of the Tibeto-Burman family. They speak fluent Manipuri (Meiteilon) while talking to others. They address themselves as Kasen. Hiroi Lamgang was a Meitei name used to address them for they made boat (hi) for the Meitei Kings. They still lag behind literacy as compared to Moyon, Monsang and other tribes. (see plate-133)

Mao:

Their population was 80568 as per 2001 census, 98.5% of them the Mao hill ranges to the extreme north of Manipur on Highway 39 under Senapati district. The Mao as such is the name of the village or place and the people are Maomei or Imemei. The Angamis of Kohima call them as Shipfumei. The literacy rate among tribes in the Mao area are high. They actively participate in state politics and several professionals, doctors and engineers come out of this tribe. Majority are agriculturists and cultivate terraced paddyfields.

They rear cows, buffalos, pigs, fowls, etc. At present the regional potato farm is located at Mao and it assists the nearby villages in growing more potato through modern techniques. Mao is also a commercial centre and station for Tourist buses, and commercial trucks plying through the Imphal-Dimapur road.The Mao areas are electrified and have better communication facilities. (see plate-124, 134)

Maram:

They numbered about 10510 in 2001 scattered in 28 villages in the Senapati District but 99% of them live in Maram village of Senapati district. They call themselves Maram-mei (people of Maram). The Barak river runs through their territory. They have close similarity with the Maos, Angami and Koireng and use the same designs and color combinations of shawls.

The average height of Men is about 165.25 cm while female statute is about 153.75 cm.

Legends

According to legend, the God (Paramhaba) created heaven and earth joined together at the horizon. He created creatures one after another naming them tiger, bear and so on. The exhausted God went to a place and stood by catching hold of a tree and bending over it. He thought for a while and spat in his right fingers with a murmur and picked up an Nchet (a stem borer insect) out of the tree (mandung bang) and threw it on the ground. A man in his likeness stood up. The God was overjoyed and named him Madiingkasii. After a while he spat with murmur in his fingers fetching water from the pond and he created sam ongpui. Again he murmured and threw it down over ground and there stood up a women. He gave her the name of Samotingdungpui. By the union of these first Man and woman, they begot three sons Karambungsa, the eldest, Makikangba and Kela Sanglang, the youngest. The three brothers depart from Meikhel. The eldest brother is considered progenitor of the Marams and his four sons became 4 clans of Maram Khullel.

Marriage

The community is exogamous and marriage within the clan was not allowed. They intermarry with the Mao, Angami, Zeliangrong, Paomai, Thangal and other Naga groups. Engagement is the ideal form of marriage.

Occupation

Wet cultivation is adopted by the Marams whose staple food is rice and whose main occupation is cultivation. The women folk do ~~most~~ of the house hold chores. Thus fetching water and firewood, cooking and looking after children are responsibilities of women. The men folk cut trees for firewood and indulge in the harvesting and cultivation. But womenfolk also help in digging the field for sowing and harvesting.

The Marams of Senapati villages do not speak the same dialect. Though understandable, the totality and mode of expression are quite different. They are constructing a common language based on the spoken language of Maram Khullel.

The descendant and inheritance of Marams follow Patrilineal lines. Their village is divided into 'Sadung' or 'Khel'. Each Khel draws its own name from a common ancestor for instance, Rangnamei means descendants of Rang. In other word, Khel is based on consanguine relatives. The Maram Society is divided into 3 exogamous social groups, which are again subdivided into lineages and sub lineages.

Clans

The three groups (Clans) according to Maram Khullen dialect are: Ng'kukui (makha or lower section), DikaKuina (Khullakpa or chief's group) and Rangbung raiyinamai (mathak or upper section). Each lineages in Maram Khullen has its own sagong but they are subject to the sagong of Lamkhana (or Dikakhuina/khullakpa Sagei) in matter of cult and morals and referred to as the Great Chief.

Sagong was the de-facto and de-jure head of the village. Every Khel has its own gate and dormitories. Boys' dormitory is called Rehangki whereas that of the girls' is Rulaki.

According to Maram custom, when a child is born, the child remains inside the house.for ten days according to regulation of genna But naming ceremony is done after five days or a week by turning the child towards the sun. The child is blessed by the father after searching a crab within ten days by the father of the child. To be a full fledged member of the society, a ritual of Purification is also carried out.

Textiles

The Maram man wears a black cotton kilt embellished by three or four rows of white cowries which at present are replaced by buttons. The ladies wear an inner loin cloth usually just like the Kilt of men without cowries. They also use a white rug like cloth. Now-a-days this piece of cloth is replaced by shawls which is a mixture of black and white colour.

Deities

The people are pantheon worshippers. Their deities are Paranba (Supreme God), Akrkot (House deity), Sara Kachinu (mentioned in oath taking) and powmungba (wind deity).

Houses

Types of houses are :-

- Sbaki (Simplest form without ritual)
- Ratsangki (roofing with thatch reaches the ground)
- Karatki
- Akikah
- Kinaboi (adorn with horns)
- Ziileki (several gennas are associated to construct it)
- Rafiiki (roof with plank) and
- Pungtaki (highest form of house).

Their houses also determine the social status of a person. The Marams refrains from taking the pork.

Festivals

They perform three main festivals - Ponghi, Kanghi and Rakakkou. During festivals, they dance with no segregation of sexes. But their songs are sung by one person or two or group according to their norm.

Maring:

The Marings had a population of 17361 (2001 census), more than 80% of them live in hilly villages in the Tengnoupal subdivision in Chandel district bordering Myanmar. It is said that they had close relationship with the Meitei Kings and their name is said to have derived from mei (fire) and ring (start or produce). Meitei Kings depended on them during wars with Burma. There are three mains groups of Marings who identify themselves with different colours in their clothing: Black, Red, and Red and Black on the border. The village of Machi is regarded as their original place, which is the centre of the Black Marings. Their language is closer to the Kuki-Chin branch of Tibeto-Burman family although they are affiliated to the Nagas. They also have many Meitei words used by them. At one time, Haobam Marak of Imphal was considered to be the settlement of the Marings. The infrastructure in Maring villages are rudimentary, and are economically weak. However, they are educational enthusiasts. They participate actively in the State politics. If provided adequate road connectivity and communication infrastructure, they will be a very progressive group of tribes. (see plate-127, 136).

Mate Tribe

The four clans of Mate Tribe namely Langsun, Sheilai, Chningthat, Haolim inhabit the Tuisomjang village of Senapati district.They pay great respect to the first progenitor "Songza", who once lived at Nawigam.Villagers under one chief can not migrate to another village without the permission of the chief otherwise the chief will confiscate all the property and standing crop.The God is called "Tung-Pasian". They worship –Daw-In (household God), Dawi-Gam (God of the jungle), Kho-Dawi (village deity for prosperity and wellbeing of the village, Dongpi- Dawi (deity worshipped when the village was founded).

The man wears long hair and combed back in a knot on the nap of the neck (Tuk). Woman dress consist of a kilt shaped piece of cloth reaching from the navel to half way down the thigh called *"Nik"* over the breast another cloth is worn reaching above the knee called " *Pounve*". They wear large silver ring called "Bilba" and "Tau" (copper disc), "Khiba" necklaces. Man wear Khingoo, Saha (animal tooth).

A Mate village is administered by the *Housa* (Chief) whose position is strictly hereditary. His assisted by Mantri and *Taangsam* (village crier). All disputes must be appealed to the Housa through the *Semang* with jar of Ju.

When the boys and girls attain puberty, they are admitted into the village dormitory called "Sawm buk". When a child is born, the umbilical cord is cut with a bamboo blade and the umbilical cord and placenta are buried under the threshold of the main door. The wife's family members bring cooked rice and meat for her. The birth of a male child is preferred. The baby is given a name on the first day itself. The baby is considered impure for the first seven days and the father is not allowed to touch the baby. On the seventh day, a feast called *"nao juneh or nao dop an"* is performed. The eldest son inherit all the parental property. If the family has got daughters only, the nearest male relative will inherit the property and the daughter receives nothing.

Monogamy is the rule in Mate society. Polygamy is not permitted. If the husband dies, the wife can marry the younger brother of the husband. Widow remarriage is allowed.

The bride price of a Mate girl is 10 mithuns (Bisons), two necklaces, two Mate Poundum (Mate type traditional cloth) and two gongs. Bride price is never paid in full at the time of wedding for the reason that no one has enough money and payment of balance installments gives a chance to both the parties a kind of social contract which binds them together. A mithun generally may cost Rs.2000-5000 and therefore full bride price may come to Rs. 20000–Rs.50,000.

When somebody dies, the male relatives stamps on the floor, hammers on the wall and shot firegun to declare death and clear his way to heaven. The village *Tanglawi* (Chowkidar) rings the bell of death in a slow rhythm lasting for aboput 20 minutes. They make *Sanglai* (like an arm chair made of bamboo or wooden planks) to keep the dead body. The dead body is given bath, new clothes are worn and placed in the Sanglai. They put some meat and Ju near the Sanglai. In case of females, the presence of her father or brothers is essential and no burial ceremony can be performed without their presence. The son –in –laws of the deceased will dug the pit for burial of the dead body. The body is slid down into the pit on its back with the head pointing towards the east where the sun rises. The male relatives place the belongings of the deceased like bow, arrow, spear etc. by the side of the dead body. The relatives will sing the clan song and the gun is fired. A man with a spear comes forward to clear the way towards heaven and to prevent the evil spirits to divert the way towards hell. Then the pit is closed by filling it with earth and a small mound is raised over it. If hunter, animal figures are carved on a post planted in the middle of the grave. In case of female, the post is carved with the figures of basket, hoe or winnowing fan signifying her status symbol. The death ceremony is performed on the eight day. (Langsun D.Mate, "the Mate Tribe of Manipur", Omsons Publications, 107 Rajouri Garden, New Delhi, 2000).

Mizo

The Mizo means hill people (mi-people, zo-hill).Though the term Mizo is often used to name a Tribe, it is just an umbrella term used to denote the various tribes who share distinctive similarities. The term Mizo was coined only recently and it does not have a language as such which can be particularised as Mizo. A number of languages are spoken under the generic umbrella of Mizo; they are Hmar, Paite, Kuki, Lushai (a dialect of the Duliens/ Duhlians; a Hmar sub-clan like the Thieks who still speak their own language), Mara to name a few. Their languages (of which the largest is Dulien/Duhlian) belong to the Tibeto-Burman, and are closely related to those of the Chin in the adjacent Chin State of Myanmar, as well as those of the Nagas, Kukis and others. The Lushai people were the first clan to have an external exposure and hence the people are initially known as the Lushai people. The demand for a distinct political territory for the people of Lushai Hills resulted in the creation of a separate Union Territory and afterwards the State of Mizoram. The spread of education by Christian missionaries led to the high percentage of literacy (95% as per national sample survey). (see plate-137)

The Mizos numbering about 10520 (Census-2001) inhabit all the districts of Manipur except Tamenglong although there is main concentration in the Churachandpur district.

Lai/ Pawih

With the promulgation of the constitution as a Sovereign Democratic Republic in 1950, the Lai, a semi-nomadic migratory community has been given constitutional safeguards by granting them an autonomous Lai Regional Council under the sixth schedule of the Indian constitution.

Monsang:

The name Monsang is derived from the name of the village called Monsang by the Meiteis and others whereas they themselves called *sirti* or southerners. They live mostly in the Chandel District in five villages namely Liwachaning, Heibunglok, Liwa Sarei, Japhou, and Monsang Pantha. They speak a similar language with the Anals. They use Meiteilon while conversing with Tangkhul, Maring, Thadou and other communities. The Monsangs come in regular contact with other communities through economic activities mainly at Pallel, Kakching, and Chandel and Imphal. Monsang parents attach great importance to education.Their population was about 1635 (Census-2001). In 1920, they joined Christianity. 98% of them live in the Chandel district. (see plate-138)

Moyon:

The Moyon themselves are known as Bujuur. Their legend indicates that they originated from a cave located at Sijjur. They live in 14 villages in Chandel district and their name derives from one of the villages called Moyon Khullen. Their name is found in the royal Chronicles as far as 1580 A.D during King Mungyamba's time. The Meitei King defeated the Moyon Chiefs and he was known as Moyon Ngamba or Mungyamba. Their population was 1710 (Census-2001) and 95% of them live in Chandel distrrict. Marriage is by negotiation (luhong) or elopement (itaen).Their seed sowing festival is known as *Sachii ichii and* harvest festival is *Buren Iimpeh.* They also believe that they originated from a cave, known as Khur or Khul. The Moyons attach considerable importance to education and every village has at least one primary school. They converse and read Meiteilon (Manipuri) very well.

Paite:

The word "Paite" means "a group of people marching" (pai-march; te-"plural maker"). They live in Churachandpur district in Southern Manipur. Their population was 44861 (Census-2001) spreading over 125 villages. Paites are one of the most educationally advanced ethnic group in India. They believed in supreme god Pathian and believed to have originated from a cave or Khul. Jhum cultivation is their main occupation on the slopes near the villages. Folksongs and folktales related to everyday life and culture of the people are orally passed through generations. (see plate-135, 139)

Almost all ethnic Paites follows Christianity, mostly Protestant denominations like Baptists, Lutherans, Penticostal, Church of Christ though there are a good percentage of Roman Catholics as well. They adopted Christianity in the 19th century with the intervention of British missionaries. The Paites are mainly shy, introvert people who are sincerely devoted in whatsoever they perform. They take active part in State politics.

Poumai Naga

The Poumai Naga villages are geographically located in Senapati District, Manipur. According to Hill House Tax in 2000, the total population of Poumai tribe is 1,67,034. (including the Poumai in Nagaland). About 96.1% of the total population of Poumai inhabits in Senapati District, Manipur. The percentage of Poumai Naga to the total population of Senapati District is 42.3% in 2001. The Poumai is one of the oldest and major Naga tribe. Their *Pouli* (Pottery) and *Poutai* (Pou salt) production was well known to the entire tribal areas in Manipur in ancient time. The main occupation of Poumai Naga is agriculture. Shifting cultivation is hardly practiced now in Poumai villages. (see plate-126)

Festivals

Laoniis is one of the important festival of the Poumi Nagas. Laonii is celebrated in Poumai villages after the rice transplantation. In olden days, the young men and women who sleep in the *Kheloukizii* or *Reipeiki* (Dormitory) celebrated this festival with full of enthusiasm and excitement. In this festival, pork is the main meat. It is usually celebrated every year in the first week of July.

The first day of the festival is known as *Kikhaiyou*. On this day, all the Yaosomai take two small branch of Mousii (a kind of small tree) and insert to the side of the wall of the house as a part of their custom.

The second day of the festival is called *Sepoyou* and third day is called *Murasouyou or Ranaiyou.* On the third day, the cattle are not taken out for grazing in the open space. Fodders are brought and fed the cattle in the shed.

The fourth day of the festival is called *Loutouyou*. The newly born sons are given birth rituals. A cock is sacrificed on this day in honour of the boy. On this day, all the male folk above 10 years have separate kitchen. They are restricted to partake food with the female folk. The fire is obtained through ignition from a smooth stick after long rubbing with a split small bamboo rope and due to friction fire comes out.

The fifth day is called *Niidu*, which means the main day of the feast. Lots of meats are cut and smoked in the kitchen for use in the next four days.

The sixth day is called *Sepaoyou,* which means sending off the visitors/ guests. Meat and rice beer are given to all their relatives/guests on their departure day. The women married to other villages, friends and relatives who came from other villages to join the Laonii festival are sent off to their villages on this day. On this day, it is the customary of the Poumai to give *Sousha* (some piece of meat) to their younger sisters-who are married to other village. It is a sign and symbol of blessing, love and remembrance.The aunts and nieces are also given Sousha. Giving Sousha indicates the bond of love and remembrance.

On the seventh day all the males have separate kitchen like on the fourth day. A cock is killed on this day and have together all the males in the family.

The eight day is called *Hahpayou,* which means the cultivators can go to their paddy field to work. The young men and women go to paddy field for weeding in groups on this day.

On the ninth day, the last day of the Laonii Festival, as the custom of Poumai Naga tribe, the head of the family takes child beyond the village gate and kills a chicken. The chicken is cut into two pieces and one piece is thrown to the right and other to the left. It is their belief that through this religious rites and rituals their sins are forgiven and God will protect them from all kinds of diseases.

In olden days, the young men and women who sleep in the Kheloukizii or Reipeiki (Dormitory) celebrated this festival with joy and excitement. The young men usually presented the pork to the females in their dormitory and in return they gave rice beer and other vegetables. A day is fixed and the boys visited the girls' dormitory to celebrate together the feast.

Folk songs competition between the boys and girls was performed on this special day. Romantic folksongs are also sung and enjoyed together. It was a big and important festival for the young boys and girls. All the Poumai boys and girls celebrate the festival together.

Purum

The Purums are an "old Kuki" tribe of Manipur. According to the 1931 Census of India, the Purums numbered 145 men and 158 women, all practising their ancestral tribal religion; in 1936 they numbered 303 individuals but in the 1951 census they numbered only 43 individuals. According to 2001 Census report, they number only about 503 distributed in small villages in Senapati district. The Purums are divided into five siblings, namely, Marrim, Makan, Kheyang, Thao and Parpa. (see plate-140)

Their marriage system is the subject of ethnographical studies.Buchler said that "they are perhaps the most over-analyzed society in anthropology" Purums marry only in one or more selected siblings fixed by the traditional customs.

Ralte

Ralte tribe numbering about 110 (Census-2001) is an extremely small tribe-mostly in Churachandpur district.

Sema

Sema numbering about 25 (Census-2001) people are in all districts but the number is small.

Simte

Simte numbering about 7150 (Census -2001) are in all districts but more than 90% are in Churachandpur district.

Salhte (Soktes) :

'Sok' means 'to go down' or 'below' and 'te' means persons and hence the name Sokte implies those who went south or below the parent village to settle. (see plate-141)

Population

According to the 2001 census report, their number is 311 (2001 Census). The geographical dstribution of Soktes includes 16 villages viz, Moreh in

Chandel district, New Lamka-G, Simbuk, Tanglon (T), Tonglon (P),Rakwal, Sumcheavum,Tangnuam, Pangzawl, Lanva, Singhat, Suangdai, Behiang, Behiang (T), Suangphuk and Tingkangphai in Churachandpur district. According to the official record of 1981 census, there were only 5 Salhtes. The president of the Chin Youth Association, Churachandpur says that they have strength of about 3,500 individuals. Molbem to the south of Chin Nwe was the original capital of the Sokte (Sukte) tribe (B.S. Carey and H.N. Tuck in the Chin Hills Vol. I, p. 118). Soktes arrived at Manipur in 1906 (according to K. Hatzo, Haosa Tonglon (T) village, Churachandpur.

Marriage and Divorce

Marriage with cousin or marriage with the maternal uncle's daughter is preferred. For their institution, the parents engage before reaching the marriage partners' puberty and assurance is endowed as *Yuthol* in the Sokte literature. When they attain puberty, it is remained and confirmed by another gift or Yu from the boy's side to the girl's residence and it is known as Moupiching. However, the spouse is not allowed to have physical relationship and for this the girl sleeps with a girl friend during this period.

After the completion of one month the Sempu takes off the restriction ritualistically. The husband can initiate a divorce on the ground of barrenness, otherwise; he has to give a mithun to the divorced woman.

Village administration

Their village level administration is carried on by *Housa*, a hereditary post and a council of *Upa*, which are nominated officials from *Beh* (leaders) of lineages. There are 36 lineages of the Soktes. Publicity is done by one so-called *Tangkou* (village crier). In the olden days, in every Sokte village there used to be a blacksmith or *Sikek* as he is called. There is also a village medicant known as *Sempu.* After the site for jhum cultivation is selected by the authority, the land allocation is done by the council.

The Sokte wear Puondun, Tangching (men's cloth), Puonlaisan (for men); Nikphei (skirt), Zounik (skirt), Khepheu (for women) etc. Their economy mainly depends on agriculture. They live in houses made on raised platform.

The *Housa* is given a foreleg for each animal killed by members of the village.

Inheritence and Culture

The eldest son is the rightful heir to the ancestral property. When the daughter comes back as a divorcee or widow, she has obligation to him and stays in his house. When a child is one year old, naming ceremony is solemnized. For this the child's mother's brother brings a jar of rice beer. Sempu gives the first extraction of the beer (machin) to the mother. The chicken meat is served and the child is given using the last letter of the grandparents as its initial letter.

Death Rituals

The dead are kept in jungle or at a particular place to decay into skeleton. Then the bones, except the skull are buried. The dead are given food at regular intervals. These involvements are however predominantly a pre-Christian custom.

Festivals

The pre-Christians Soktes also performed many festivals. *Khobol* is the festival of seed sowing and prayer for rainfall in the month of Dota (April-May). *Khodou* is observed for 5-7 days in Vulkha (Oct.) and it is the harvest festival. The Soktes at Tiddim Chin grew maize and so, it is held in October even though Soktes of Manipur grew rice and it falls before harvesting. *Saai* is the festival hosted by a good hunter.The man who has a yield of good crop that year hosts *Tangai* in the name of his wife. *Galai* is the confirmatory festival hosted by men to achieve higher status. After conversion to Christianity, none of the pre-Christian festivals except for Khobol and Khodou are performed.

Tangkhul: - See Chapter-10: Tangkhuls

Tarao:

They are a minor community in the Chandel district and Thawai village of Uklhrul district. They speak Taraotrong but speak Manipuri well with others. The Taraos were also referred to as Kuki in earlier ethnographic studies but now they identify themselves with the Nagas. It is said that Maharaja Chingthang Khomba had an orchard at a place near Pallel and his orange trees were looked after by the Taraos at Komlathabi. They are concentrated at four villages.They are involved in planting fruits like banana, lemon, pineapple, papaya, etc. Their land is considered to be the driest place in Manipur

Thadou:

The Thadou are classified as an Old Kuki group by the anthropologists. Their communities are dispersed in several districts of Manipur. According to the 2001 census, their population was 115,045 and formed about 4.81 percent of the total population of Manipur. The history of this community is found in oral traditions including folklore and folktales. Their origin, like other tribes of Manipur traces to a cave located at the origin of Gun river (Imphal river). They can be identified by the traditional design of the shawls, which are marked in black with a few stripes of red. The design is simple and devoid of any geometrical figures.They speak Thadou dialects and converse in chaste Manipuri language with others. The Thadous are non-vegetarians and fond of drinking *zu* made from rice or maize. However, Christianity has prevented them from taking liquor and gradually replaced with tea. The price of a bride is taken in the form of Mithun, gongs, beads and necklaces, though not practiced anymore. Marriage is through negotiation known as *Neila*. The groom arrives at the brides residence along with his associates, followed by a feast. Basketry, poultry, weaving, and cane work are the traditional crafts of the Thadous. Although agriculture is the main occupation of many Thadous, the younger generation have taken up jobs in professional fields in the Government services, teaching, etc. They participate actively in local and state politics. Several Ministerial positions are held from this tribe in the Government of Manipur. (see plate-128)

Vaiphei

The Vaipheis claimed that they are the descendants of **Vaiphei,** son of Za Hong/Nuai Mangpa. According to a legend, Song Za and Za Hong once lived together in the sub-terranian world. Their progenitor Za Hong decided to come out to the above world. But the door of the Khul (Cave) was closed by a great serpent. Zahong cut the serpent into three pieces with his sword, Vangalpa removed the stone enclosing the cave and thus Zahong, Khupngam and Vangalpa came out of the Khul. Many other people followed and came out after him. It was because he opened the door of the Khul for many that, he was called Za Hong (Za - Many, or hundred, Hong-open, open for many people). Za Hong led the people and finally settled down at Ciimnuai and ruled there as its chief. He beget Vai Phei and Vai Phei beget Hong Lian. Ciimnuai soon became overcrowded. Hong Lian then along with many other people left Ciimnuai and founded a settlement 'Khaw Vaiphei' named after his father 'Vaiphei'. According to some of the Vaiphei older generations, both Vaiphei and Thadou are descended from Zahong. And Vaiphei had one son Honglian, from whom are descended the three brothers- Phulum, Lianlum/ Lianlut and Lunglum. (see plate-145)

Migration

It is said that when the Thibom dynasty of Mandalay became powerful and began to subjugate smaller communities, the Vaipheis left their settlement site in fear. They moved to a place near the Ningthee river called Kalemeyo and then to Saijang. From Saijang they moved to Chimniy and Khosak respectively. From Khosak they move to Ngatam lui and there they were divided into Sijang and Vaiphei. Vaiphei group from there went towards the Chin Hills and settled at Phaiza. This group further moved themseleves to Kamhou and from there they began to enter the south eastern hilly regions of Manipur around 1891 A.D.

Their population was recorded as 27791 in 2001 census report of the Government of India. At present, the Vaipheis are mainly concentrated in the Churachandpur district, Senapati district and Chandel district of Manipur. Their dialect is Vaiphei and slightly different from Gangte, Zou and Paite. Their speech is closer to Gangte but spell similar to Paite. They use Roman scripts. They have one of the highest literacy rates in Manipur

Clans and Culture

The Vaiphei society is patriarchal.The family is often a joint family. In olden days, although the father is the head of the family, both the husband and wife never mention each other's name as a sign of respect. The children also never mention their parents' name even after they grow up as a sign of respect. Parents are usually addressed by the name of their eldest child, suffixed with 'pa' (father) and 'ma' (mother). The tribe is divided into a number of clans and sub clans.

The clans are endogamous though inter clan marriage is not uncommon. Marriage is by engagement or negotiation. Traditionally the prescribed mate for a boy was the daughter of his maternal uncle called Neinu. Pre-marital sex is considered a disgraceful act and if the boy after 'polluting' the girl refuses to marry her, he is imposed a fine of one mithun and one pig. An individual born in the Vaiphei society was welcomed through a function called *Naoyuneck,* when the pregnant mother is about seven or eight months due. The birth ceremony of a child was held on the seventh day of the child by its father entertaining the villagers with a feast. Children whether male or female, get their earlobes pierced with a tough hair of Saku (porcupine) and black and red thread.

Death ceremony of a child under six months is not necessary. Otherwise the dead is buried with the head facing eastwards. Cooked spleen of cattle, considered to be the food of the deceased, is also buried along with the corpse.

Many Vaipheis are confused about the exact number of their clan. Each clan has its head called 'Upa'. The eldest son inherits his father's property.

Occupation

Their main occupation, agriculture, is practiced through both types of cultivation – Jhum (shifting) and wet cultivation. The major economic source is the jhum cultivation for paddy and depend on forest products. Among them, there exists a system of community and social obligations under the term and conditions of Tawmngaihna and Kihutuana which means the services rendered to others in times of need or in other words, solidarity of the village in every moments of joy, sorrow or calamity.

Village administration

Every Vaiphei village has a legitimate traditional chief called *Khaw Hausa,* whose position is hereditary and the entire land belonged to him. He is assisted by a members of elders known as *Siamang Upa* (Ministers, nobles or elders). *Pachawng* is incharge of tax collections. *Taangsampu* is the village crier, informing the entire village in any matter. *Thiik-Seekpu* (Blacksmith), *Tunpu* (hunting commander) also command respect from the villagers. Every dispute is tried in the *Innpi-Vaihawmna* (village court) by the Chief and the nobles.

Religion

The traditional religion of the Vaipheis was a combination of ancestor worship and animism. Amorphous deities and spirits are responsible for benevolent and malevolent effects. The supreme deity is *Pathian* (God). They also believed in manna-like powers, which in their dialect is known as *Bulung* and possesson of it enables him to have a good harvest. They also have a family deity known as *Dawibawm.* From around 1907 A.D. under the Welsh Missionaries, the Vaipheis were converted to Christianity. (Lungpau and Thangkai were the first persons who were converted to Christianity.) which eventually led them to ignore or neglect many traditional practices and customs incompatible with the Christian faith.

Festivals

The most important traditional festivals include Thazinglap chawn (a dead festival), Sa-ai (hunting), gallu-ai (head hunting), Oa ai (fishing), Bu-ai (harvest). Sawm zu (Boys' dormitory) and lawm zu (Friends' organization) are important institutions. Sometimes a rich person can perform the 'feast of merit' involving combined celebration of Sa-ai and Bu-ai lasting for at least a week.

The Vaiphei Puandum, Khiangkawi and Thansua puan are the three important traditional cloth of the Vaipheis.

Zeliangrong:

The Zeliangrong is a composite group of three related tribes inhabiting in the Tamenglong district of Western Manipur. The three groups are Rongmei (Kabuis) (see plate- 129, 142), Liangmei and Zemei (also called Kacha Nagas). Many Kabui villages are also found in the plains of Manipur, Assam and few settlements in Nagaland. According to 2001 Census, they numbered about 62,216. Their legend believe that they came out of a cave, which was blocked by a big stone and later removed by a mithun. The word, "Kabui" is considered to be a corruption of *Apui* meaning mother, which they worship as goddess, *Leimaren.* They speak Meitei language well and had close interactions with the Meiteis. The Kabui is divided into four exogamous clans: Kammei, Gangmei, Langmei and Ganmei. The main occupation is cultivation and practice Jhum cultivation in the hills and wet cultivation in the plains. Some of their crops are maize, soyabean, pumpkin, gourd, ginger, tomato chili and groundnut. Carpentry, weaving, basketry are cottage industries. They are considered to be one of the most skill crafts men of Manipur. The plain Kabuis received considerable influence of the Vaishnavite tradition and Meitei culture. Facilities of education, medical care, and employment programmes have reach them well and their population consists of scholars, administrators, teachers, doctors, nurses, entrepreneurs, etc. They are also actively involved in the political scene in Manipur. After the formation of the Zeliangrong community of the North East India, they constitute a powerful lobbying community. They prefer to be called as Zeliangrong than Kabui or Kacha Naga.

The Zemi (Zemei) and Liangmei are separated by rivers and mountain barriers and their dialects are different from one another. Meiteilon is the *lingua franca* of the people and they use Roman scripts. According to their belief, the supreme god (*Charawang*) created the universe and gave human beings shelter in the caves. *Pokrei* (a male) and *Dichalu* (a female) gave birth to four sons. Their sons and descendents form the Liangmei, Anpuimei, Zemei, Maram, Rongmei, Tangkhul and Meitei. The history of Manipur reveals that the Zeliangrongs had a close relationship with the Meiteis. During the Burmese invasion, the Meiteis of the Imphal valley left their homes and took shelter in Zeliangrong areas. Politically they are active and the "Zeliangrong movement of the 1927-32" led by Jadonang and Rani Gaidinliu is well celebrated in Manipur. Road communication to Tamenglong, their headquarter is very poor. The villagers plant oranges, potato, ginger, pineapple etc. and cane and bamboo works are their main crafts. (see plate-146)

Zou:

The Zou/Zo tribe is concentrated in Churachandpur and Chandel districts of Manipur.. Zous live close to the Paites and have close similarities. They share many oral traditions, folklore, dance and music with Paites. They also claim to have originated from a cave or *khul* somewhere in the extreme north. Their number is about 19,112 in 2001. The village administration is at the hands of the village chief. (see plate-147)

The Zou/Zo language is one of the prescribed Major Indian Languages in the high schools and higher secondary schools of Manipur state. The Zou/Zo community has a script of its own known as "Zolai". Zou youngsters learn their script as a piece of curiosity; but the Roman script is the official script.

Origin

Oral tradition maintains that the Zomis hailed from the first three Zomi brothers - Songthu alias Chongthu, Songza and Zahong. The Zou tribe traces their origin to a Cave variously known as "Khul" or "Chhinlung", "Sinlung" or Khur, near a village called Saizang in the Chin State in North Western part of Burma, where the descendants of Songthu became Thawmte tribe. Official statistics for the year 1893 showed that the Zou tribe consisted of nineteen villages and 630 households, inhabiting a tract lying between 60 and 90 miles north and north-west of Fort White. The tribe had the second largest number of villages in Northern Chin Hills, next only to the Thadou tribe

The term Zo is an indigenous usage that dates back to antiquity, or (at least) pre-modern history. Dr. Vumkhohau, a Zo scholar and diplomat from Burma, in his profile of the 'Burmese Frontier Man' has affirmed that "we called ourselves Zomi from time immemorial". There are different theories regarding the etymology of the root word Zo. In the year 862 AD, a Chinese historian, Fan Ch'o Hao in his book already used the word Zo to call a peculiar ethnic group of people. Another scholar, a Catholic Father Vincent, in his book published in 1783 mentioned a group of people known as Zo. Sir Henry

Yule's narrative of the Mission to the court of Ava in 1885 showed the Chindwin plains and the area west of Chindwin River as Zo district. FK Lehman, a renowned Social Anthropologist in his book 'Structure of the Chin Society' reiterated the fact that the so called Kuki-Chin linguistic groups have a special term for themselves variously spelt as Zo, Yo etc.

Kuki Uprising and Zou Tribe

The Zou tribe joined the so-called "Kuki Uprising" in Manipur against the British from 7 March, 1917 to 20 May 1919. Hiengtam and Gotengkot Forts were two main centres of resistance among the Zous. Pu Do Ngul Taithul was the chief of Gotengkot, which was a fairly big and fortified Zou village. Captain Steadman was the man responsible for suppressing Gotengkot with considerable casualties on both sides. The Zou tribe was a non-Thadou tribe to have participated in this abortive, yet bold attempt to oust the white imperialist from Manipur, even as a local folk song composed on the occasion of the revolt runs in the Zou dialect as follows:

Tuizum Mangkang kîl bang hing khang/
Zota kuolsung zil bang lîng e/
Pienna ka gamlei hie! phal si'ng e!/
Ka nâmtem hiem a, i Zogam lei lâl ka naw/
Sansi'n zîl e!/
Ngalliem vontawi ka lâulou lâi e.

English translation

The seafaring White Imperialist springs up like the fast growing cactus plant,
The Zo land shakes like the earthquake,
Tis the land of my birth: I shall not part with it !
My sharp sword is stained with blood, I faced enemies,
Being brave son of my father i shall not fear

There stands a dilapidated, tin-roofed hall called "Zogal Memorial Hall" at Zoveng, Churachandpur built in honour of the Zomis who fought against British colonizers. The anti-colonial legacy of the Zou is a tribute to the multi-ethnnic people of Manipur itself. However, the dilapidated condition of Zogal Memorial Hall reflects the lack of official patronage for its shared history and collective memory.

The Zou people resisted the British imperialism and its colonial culture, including Christian conversion. A missionary called Watkin Roberts arrived at Senvon village in the southern hills of Manipur in 1910. While their neighbouring communities converted to Christianity, the Zous clung on to their traditional religion called *Sakhua*. The experience of many young Zomis as a labour corps in World War-I made them more open to Western education. The NEIG Mission Compound at Old Churachandpur (Suangpi) became the centre of literate culture in southern Manipur since 1930. By 1947, many literate Zous were convinced about the power of Western education and medicine.

Some intelligent Zou youngsters organised on 20 Feb. 1954 the first Zou Conference at Daizang village. This historic conference accelerated mass conversion to Christian faith into an irreversible social movement within the Zou community.

Occupation

According to the 2001 Census of India, around 60% of the Zou population were engaged in agricultural labour. The Zous had taken to Jhum (shifting) cultivation ever since the beginning of their recorded history in the 19th century. They used iron tools (e.g. iron axe, hoe and dao) to cultivate a variety of rice through a rather primitive method - sometimes described as "slash and burn" technique. They procured their iron tools through barter trade from Manipur and Burma. In the absence of cash economy, mithun or gayal (*bos frontalis*) and rice grain served as the chief forms of wealth.

The jhum method was ecologically sustainable as long as population increase was minimal and cultivable land was plentiful. But even favourable population-land ratio did not guarantee against periodic famines called *mautam*. Such famines are associated with the flowering of bamboos whose seeds led to the multiplication of rats and other pests.

Their customary laws related to marriage practices have been institutionalized by the church. Their tribal musical instrument (*khuang* made of wood and animal skin) is an integral part of church music. The Bible translations and hymnals preserve the best part of their traditional vacabulary harnessed to a different purpose.

References

Aung-Thwin, Michael (1996) "The Myth of the 'Three Shan brothers' and the Ava period in Burmese history", *Journal of Asian Studies*, Vol. 55, No. 4, pp. 881-901.

Braghin, Cecilia (1998) "The Archaeological Investigation into Ancient Chinese Beads"

Braghin, Cecilia (1998) "An Archaeological Investigation into Ancient Chinese Beads" pp. 273-293, Lidia D. Sciama & Joanne B. Eicher, (eds.) *Beads and Bead Makers*, Oxford & New York: Berg.

Buchler, I. R. (1969). *Game theory in the behavioural sciences*. Pittsburgh University Press.

B.S.Carey and H.N.Tuck in the Chin Hills Vol. I, p. 118.

Carey, Bertram S. and Tuck, H.N. (1896) *The Chin Hills: A History of the people, our dealings with them, their customs and manners, and a Gazetteer of their country* (Reprinted by Delhi, Cultural Publishing House, 1983).

Chaube, S.K. 1999. Hill Politics in North-east India. Patna: Orient Longman.

Dr. A. Lalit Singh, Journal of the Geographical Society of Manipur, 1997.

Manipur Tourism Department Bulletins.

Fowler, E.O. (1924) Letter to Howchinkhup, General Department, No. 3432/7M-11, office of the Commissioner, North West Border Division, 25 march 1924, in Acts and Achievements of Hau Chin Khup, KMS, Chief of the Kamhau clan, Chin Hills, Tiddim (Ratnadipan Pitika Press, Mandalay, 1927) p. 17.

John and Saroj Arambam Parrat, Queen Empress vs. Tikendrajit Prince of Manipur, 1992.

K.C. Tensuba, An Approach to the History of Meiteis and Thais, 1993.

Khai, Sing Khaw (1995) *Zo People and their Culture; A historical, cultural study and critical analysis of Zo and its ethnic tribes* (Published by Khampu Hatzaw, Churachandpur, Manipur.

Go, Khup Za (1996) *A Critical Historical Study of Bible Translations among the Zo people in Northeast India*, Churachandpur: Chin Baptist Literature Board

Hsu Cho-yun & Linduff, K.M. (1988) *Western Zhou Civilization*, New Haven and London: Yale University Press.

Lalnithanga, P. 1997. Mizoram. New Delhi: Ministry of Information and Broadcasting. Govt. of India. Patiala House.

National Archives of India (NAI) New Delhi (hereafter NAI), Foreign Department, Extl. A, October 1893, Nos. 33 – 34, dated Camp Falam, 28 September 1892

National Archives of India (NAI) New Delhi, Foreign Dept. Sept 1893, Nos. 80 –88

Parry, N.E. 1988. Lushai custom; A monograph on Lushai customs and ceremonies. Aizwal: Tribal Research Institute.

Sangermano, Father (1833) *A Description of the Burmese Empire: Compiled chiefly from Burmese Documents*, (Translated by William Tandy and reprinted by Susil Gupta, London, 1966.

Shakespear, J. 1988. The Lushai Kuki Clans. Aizwal : Tribal Research Unit.

Tribal Research Institute. 1994. The Tribes of Mizoram. (A Dissertation) Aizwal: Tribal Research Institute, Directorate of Art and Culture.

The Socio-Economics Of Linguistic Identity A Case Study In The Lushai Hills. Satarupa Dattamajumdar, Ph.D

Tedim Thu Kizakna Lai (Tedim Journal), July 1937, p. 4.

"Yao people of Yunnan (China)".; also Yao - Chinese Ethnic Groups (1998)

Zou, David Vumlallian (2005). "Raiding the dread past: Representations of headhunting and human sacrifice in north-east India", *Contributions to Indian Sociology* (n.s.) Vol. 39, No. 1, pp. 75-105 [This article refers to Kuki Uprising & Zou folk song, See pp. 88-89].

MELC Archives, Zomi Colony (Churachandpur), *JCA Minute Book* (20 February 1954 – 24 January 1958)

Lalnunmawi, E (1996) *Impact of Christianity on the Zou women* (Unpublised Dissertation) Banglalore: South Asia Institute of Advanced Christian Studies (SAIACS)

Downs, Frederick S. (1996) *The Christian Impact on the Status of Women in North East Inda*, Shillong: NEHU Publications

Ralte, Lalrinawmi (2004) *Bible Women-te Nghilhlohnan* (In Memory of Bible Women), Bangalore: Shalom Publications

M. Horam and S.H.M. Rizvi, People of India, Manipur, 1998

Mutua Bahadur, Cane and Bamboo Crafts of Manipur, 1994

Mutua Bahadur, Traditional Textiles Of Manipur, 1997

H Lienzamang Gangte –The gangtes, contributes to e-pao.net regularly. The writer can be contacted at glienza (at) sify (dot)com. This socio-political abstract of Gangtes is contributed by the author and webcasted here on 3rd September 2003.

Manindra Konsam from Sanathong wrote this article.

Needham, R. (1958). "A structural analysis of Purum society". *American Anthropologist* 60: 75-101.

White, H. C. (1963). *An anatomy of kinship*. Prentice= Hall.

Needham 1958

R.B. Thohe Pou, a Ph.D. Research Scholar at the University of Pune, is doing Research on Poumai Naga tribe.

External links

http://dsal.uchicago.edu/dictionaries/lorrain Mizo Dictionary

http://www.zogam.org, http://www.zogam.com, http://www.zogam.net

http://www.zogamonline.com

http://video.google.com/videoplay?docid=7798938964281962092&q=paite

http://mizoram.nic.in/, Zo Peoples' Online,http://www.sinlung.com

http://www.worldscriptures.org/pages/paite.html

http://www.cic.nic.in/cicmanipur/html/c_syll_paite.asp

http://www.ethnologue.com/show_language.asp?code=pck http://en.wiki pedia.org/wiki/Zou_people_(India)"

"http://en.wikipedia.org/wiki/Paite"

Plate - 123: Anal Couple

Plate -124: Mao Woman

Plate-125 :Kom Girl

Plate-126: Poumai Couple

Plate-127: Maring Girl

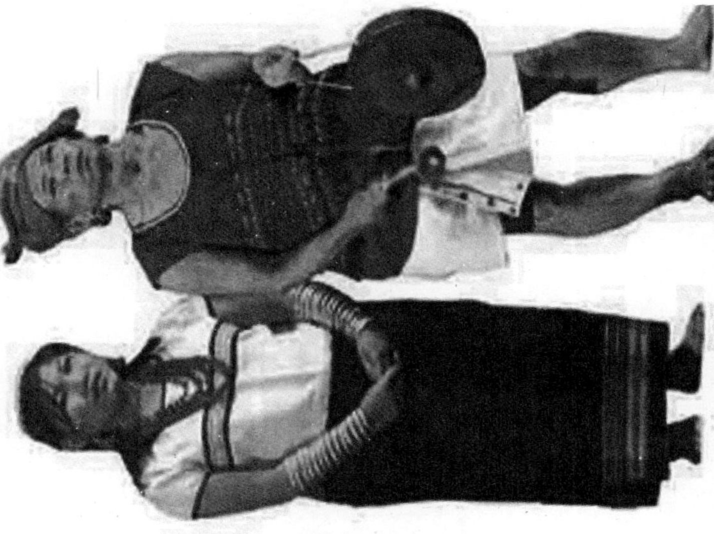

Plate-128: Thadou Couple

Plate-129: Kabui Couple

Plate-130: Chothe Couple

Plate-131:Chiru Couple

Plate-132: Kom Couple

Plate-133: Lamgang Couple

Plate-134: : Mao Couple

Plate-135: Paite Girl

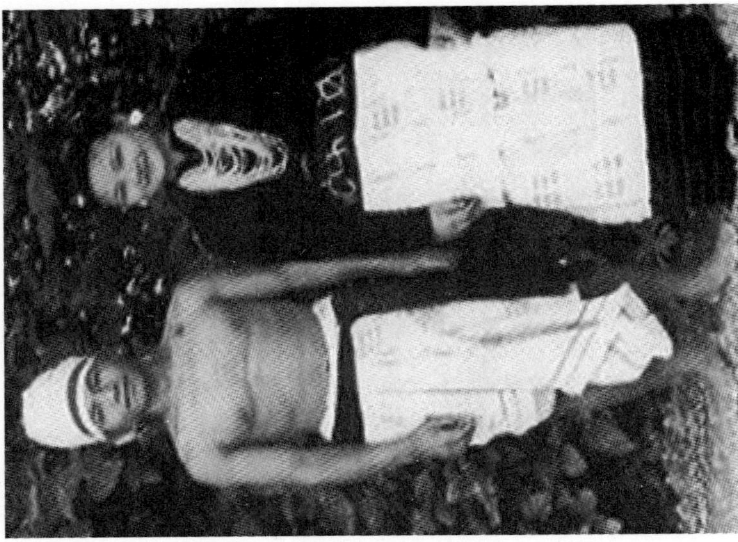

Plate-136: Maring Couple

Plate-137: Mizo Couple

Plate-138: Monsang Couple

Plate -139: Paite Couple

Plate -140: Purum Couple

Plate-141: Sukte Couple

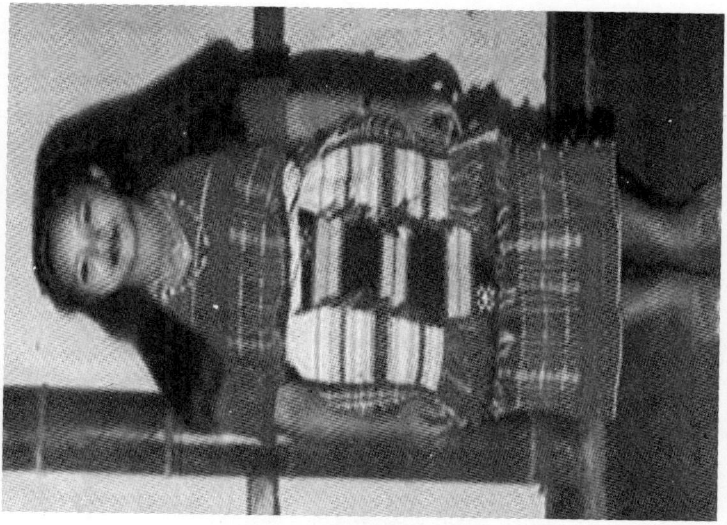

Plate-142: Kabui Girl (Rongmei)

Plate-143: Koireng Couple

Plate-144: Tangkhul Couple

Plate-145: Vaiphei Couple

Plate-146: Zeliangrong Couple

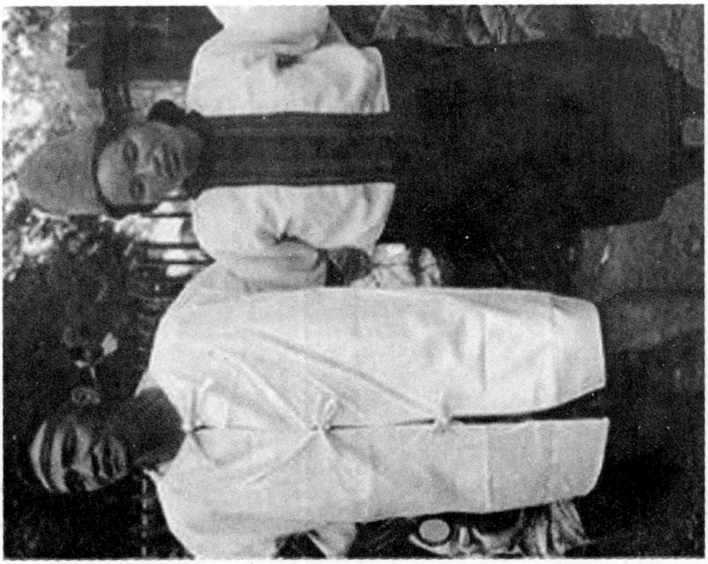

Plate-147: Zou Couple

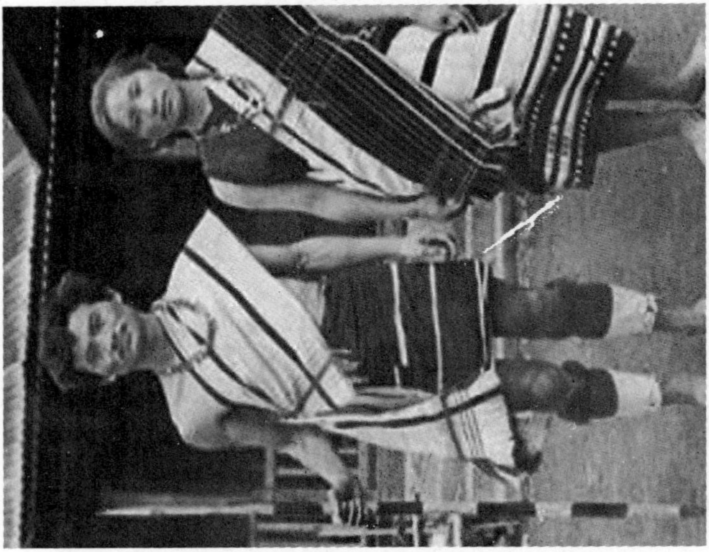

Plate -148: Koirao Couple

Plate -149: Hmar Couple

9

The Naga Tribes

The beauty of the Nagas lies in their cultures and traditions.

Origin of the term Naga

There are many legends regarding the origin of the term Naga. Naga itself is a name used by the plain people rather than by the people of the hills themselves. The term Naga comes from "Nangga", which means "Naked" given by the Assamese to a number of different tribes –the Angamese, Ao, Lhotas and other tribes living in the hills with scanty clothes. Another theory says that the word "Naga" comes from Sanskrit "Nag" means snake but the Nagas are not snake worshippers. Another theory says that the word "Naga comes from the Burmese word "Naka", which means people with pierced earlobes. Most of the Naga tribes migrated to India from Burma and therefore the name Naka or Naga was given to them even before they reached India. (ASW, History of the Tangkhul Nagas, Akansha Publishing House, New Delhi-2001)

The Nagas had no written records of their own. But they have very rich folktale, songs folklore and legends, which suggest their origin and their migration. The Nagas had political and commercial relations with the Ahom kings for a long time. The Nagas were granted lands in the valleys, fought in the Ahom armies and sheltered Ahom princes fleeing from court conflicts. The Nagas nearest the plains acted as a buffer between the Nagas of the interior and the valley population.

How many Naga Tribes are there?

How many Naga tribes are there? One early British military explorer in 1879 suggested 18. Seventeen years later, a survey listed nine. In 1921,

Table-41 Showing the Naga Tribes inhabiting India and Myanmar

1	Anal	2	Angami	3	Ao	4	Chakhesang
5	Chang	6	Cheril (M)	7	Chirr (M)	8	Chiru
9	Chothe	10	Helmi (M)	11	Hewa	12	Htangan (M)
13	Inpui	14	Konyak	15	Khiamniungam	16	Kharam Khaklak (M)
17	Koireng /Moyon	18	Kayo (M)	19	Khaklak (M)	20	Kengu (M)
21	Lamkang	22	Liangmai	23	Laihe (M)	24	Lainung (M)
25	Lohta	26	Maram	27	Mao	28	Maring
29	Moyon	30	Monsang	31	Malang (M)	32	Macharay (M)
33	Nokle (M)	34	Nokho (M)	35	Nolang (M)	36	Namshik (M)
37	Pakang (M)	38	Pheillongri (M)	39	Phom	40	Pochuri
41	Phango (M)	42	Phangkem (M)	43	Pangmi (M)	44	Pangu (M)
45	Para (M)	46	Poumai	47	Rangpan (M)	48	Rasti (M)
49	Rekho (M)	50	Rengma	51	Rongmei	52	Sangtam
53	Saplo	54	Shangphuri(M)	55	Singpho.	56	Sira (M)
57	Somi (M)	58	Sema	59	Tarao	60	Tangkhul
61	Thangal	62	Tangsa	63	Tikhir	64	Wanchao
65	Yimchunger	66	Zemi				
			M=Myanmar (29)				

Hutton listed 14 as did Edwin in 1961, in the 1970 Horam gave 30 and Yonuo 38.Both these include some groups living in Burma, and a number of groups who would probably not have counted themselves as Nagas fifty years ago, but who for various reasons find it appropriate or advantageous to do so today" (Julian Jacobs, The Nagas, Hill Peoples of North east India Thames and Hudson Ltd, London–1998, page-20).The names of different Naga tribes are as follows:-

The important Naga Groups of Manipur are Tangkhul, Poumai, Mao, Maram, Kabui, Koireng, Chiru and Maring. The Angami, Ao, Konyak, Lhota, Rengma, Liangmai, Zemi and Sema are important Nagas of Nagaland. They have very few population in Manipur. The Nagas occupy the northern, north-eastern, and north-western hills of Manipur.

There are several stories about the origin of different groups of Nagas. It is believed that Nagas and Meiteis have common ancestors.

Origin and Migration of Nagas

It is believed that the Nagas migrated from mainland of China by following route along the Salween river to Myanmar to reach the southern seas of Moulmein sea coast (Myanmar) where they settled for generations. That is why Nagas are very fond of marine shells like cowries and conches for decorating their dresses (Kilt). These marine shells are not found in the hills. They also lived in Irrawaddy (Ayeyarwadi) and Chindwin valley in the periphery of Salween river. Following through the confluence of the three rivers along the Chindwin river, they finally reached the Naga Hills. Some more powerful aboriginal settlers in Irrawaddy valley might have pressed the Nagas to the Hills where they are occupying now.

ASW Shimray (2001) mentioned that the custom and tradition of Nagas have more resemblance to those of the Tribes of Indonesia, Thailand, Myanmar, Philippines. Headhunting in Naga Hills virtually ceased soon after the British started administrative control of Naga villages, though it continued in Tuensang district for some time. The last known case of head hunting in Naga Hills was reported and recorded in 1958, 1963 and 1969. (ASW Shimray, History of Tangkhul Nagas, Akansa Publishing House, New Delhi, 2001), (Prakash Singh, Kohima to Kashmir on the Terrorist Trail, Rupa & Co, New Delhi, 2001)

According to S.K. Chatterjee, the presence of the Nagas in the Naga Hills was felt by the 8th century B.C.

The Meiteis themselves were originally a Hill community who overran the valley and settled there. The Meitei king, on his coronation, traditionally wore a costume very like that of the neighbouring Nagas. (Horam-1988). Some items of Naga material culture indicate a long history of contact between Plains and Hills of Manipur. The elephant cloth; for instance with complex animal motif has its origin in the wish of the ruler of Manipur in the mid-seventeenth century to present his Naga allies with a special cloth. (Julian Jacobs, The Nagas, Hill Peoples of North East India, Thames and Hudson Ltd. London-1998). Similarly Thang –ta were used by the Nagas, perfected by the Meiteis.

Physical Features

The Nagas belong to mongoloid race. They are medium sized and sturdy. The men are muscular and sturdy and full of stamina. Marings are tall and well built. The Tangkhuls, Mao-Maram Nagas are generally fairer as compared to the other tribe. The nose is flattened at the nostrils but the Tangkhuls show some marked sharp features.

The women are short but stout. Their eyes are deep set with bulged eye sockets. The nose is slightly flattened at the nostrils and its length is also comparatively short. The lips are thick but some Tangkhul women like their men folk having sharpness in their nose and other features. Women are generally fair in complexion especially Tangkhul women.

The Nagas are cheerful and friendly in times of peace and musically inclined. As they march along the roads, they keep time to a chant, which is varied to suit the gradient and the length of step and they sing as they reap their rice. (See Plate-162)

Head Taking

Head taking is one important aspect of Naga life. Head taking is considered to be central to the fertility complex of the Nagas. It is a pre-requisite for marriage also. Youths have to gain a head to qualify themselves to be eligible marriage partners.

The heads gained played a central role in all kinds of Naga rituals. In 1946, W.G. Archer asked the Sangtam Nagas why do they need a head every time they bring a log-gong into their village. Log gong is a huge gong made out of a single tree trunk. They said that the log drum must not be beaten until a human head is offered If a stranger happens to pass by the village, he is immediately beheaded but this is very rare since all the neighbouring villagers are on the alert. Therefore, they have to wait for the opportunity for a long time and have to go to far off places to gain a head. In the process, they may lose their own man. When Sangsomo brought a new log drum in 1917 they had to wait for one year before they took a head from the Sema village of Komongsu and in doing so they themselves lost one man but not his head.When the news of head-taking reached the Sangsomo village, all the young men went down to the Tizu River with food and rice beer to meet the party and bring in the head. Young men {not yet warriors} touched the head with their daos. They put the head in the hollow groove and then everyone joined in beating the log drum. Then the warriors who had shared in the killing gave animals for a village feasts and there was a general dance. By evening they took the head from the drum and went to the *magutung* {head tree}. Then the head taker cuts a bamboo by slicing upwards. An old man will bore a hole in the head and the head is tied to the top of the bamboo. The bamboo is then placed leaning against the tree. Taking a head is considered to be a sign of potency and manifestation of fertility both for the head taker as well as for the whole village. (Julian Jacobs,The Nagas, Hill Peoples of North east India, Thames and Hudson Ltd. London -1998).

Why head taking?

The Nagas were very clear why head taking was important. Since "head- taking was stopped, Wanching village has got smaller. Earlier when illness swept through the village, we took a head, offered it and the sickness stopped. Nowadays we cannot offer heads and the sickness goes on and on. Man after man falls ill and dies, and there is nothing we can do. The fields too have gone off and we do not get the crops we did. In short when the village had heads, the people were healthier and the crops were better Another Konyak put it thus: "If we do not get a head every year, the crops will be bad, the pigs and cattle will not increase, our children will get ill"

Head-taking consist of a three-stage ritual. For the Semas, the process started with the inauguration of hostilities called "*agjuch*". An offering is made to the stone containing spirit, which lie near the chief s house. The warriors observe a genna. Then the head – taking attack is the carried out against an enemy village. Those who took part in head taking were re- incorporated into society after observing the *aghupfu* ritual. The men were symbolically set apart from the rest of the community. They entered temporary huts where they wore only white clothes, with no black thread, ate food cooked only by men, and remained chaste for a period of time. (Julian Jacobs, The Nagas, Hill Peoples of North east India, Thames and Hudson Ltd, London -1998).

Women in head hunting

Heads are required for good crops. It is a tangible proof of valour for the head taker. Women are partly responsible for head taking. Women encourage men to undertake head- taking as a pre- requisite to marriage. Women and children were prized targets of attack.

Fire-making

In olden days, fire-stick method is usually adopted for making fire for everyday use and for ceremonial purposes. After splitting a stick half–way down, a small stone is inserted to keep it open. A notch was cut in the underside of the split end, in which a thong of bamboo fibre can be placed. Tinder was placed around the end of the stick. When the bamboo thong is drawn rapidly to and fro, the friction lights the tinder. The other main method of making fire was by striking a flint stone with a piece of iron.

Occupation

The main occupation of the Nagas is agriculture. The main crop is rice. They usually adopted Jhooming cultivation, where forest is felled and the site used for two years only. The soil becomes infertile quickly. After being worked for two years, a new site needs to be chosen. They also practiced terrace cultivation. If there is good rainfall with fertile soil this system can provide an annual surplus of rice. They used hoe, spade, dao, sickle, rake, winnowing fan for cultivation and harvesting. All males keep Dao. It is made of iron blade, set in a wooden handle. It is very useful and is kept always by men. It is used for clearing the way in thick forest. In the slash-and-burn method of agriculture the Dao plays an important role. The Nagas decorate their Dao very beautifully. They are also very fond of hunting and fishing. But fishing is prohibited during cultivating seasons. They are expert in bow fight, spear throwing and in the use of Dao. The arrows are poisoned with the help of a herb extract called Aconite. These are used only on war or in hunting of big animals. Buffalo hide of oblong, round shapes are used for making shields for use during hunting and wars.

Basket making and other kind of bamboo work is done in every house.

Houses

The Naga village is always situated at a convenient place near a ridge in the hills where water is available nearby. The houses are made of wooden poles and bamboo. The walls are made of spilt bamboo. The roof is thatched with grass and on each side given a slope, the eves of which are kept slightly above the ground. Their houses are well suited for the climatic conditions. They also construct granaries for storing grains at a certain distance from house to protect them from fire.The granary is raised from the ground and its walls are stronger than the ordinary house. The house of the Naga chiefs in a village will be distinct by the size and strength of the material used. The horns of the animals are displayed in front of the house. Every house has a loom for weaving. The thread used for making cloth is cotton or synthetics. (see plates-150, 161)

Food

Rice is the staple food for the Nagas. It is cooked in earthen or metal pots or in bamboo tubes. The young bamboo shoots are collected during the summer season and then peeled off, sliced, dried and then used with rice. Dried fish is eaten by all groups. They eat fish and all kinds of domestic animals except the cat. They also eat locusts, dog, all kinds of birds. Their common drink is 'Zu', the rice beer. On all ceremonial occasions it is served to the guests.

Religion

Traditionally Nagas were described as animists.They believed in the existence of spiritual beings. There are three types of spirits in each Naga group: a High God or Gods, a God or spirit who lives in the sky, and earth spirits.

All Naga groups believe in a close link between the living and the dead, who at one time inhabited the same world. They regarded the land of the dead to be in the sky or underground. They believed in the life after death, which resembles the life on earth. The dead persons have to fight the slain enemy again in the land of the dead. But the land of the dead is not the only destination for the soul after death. They also believed that one of the several souls is likely to return to earth as an insect or other animal. The living and the dead are brought together in dreams. They tried to interpret the meaning of dreams. Dreams can influence agricultural activities, ritual practice.

They also believe that there is a close connection between human beings and the tiger. The myths of Naga origin say that the spirit, man, and the tiger were the three sons of the same woman, and it is common to find a genna period for the killing of a tiger.

Social life and village organization

The basis of the Naga society is the village organization. Among the Thendu group, the village Chiefs called Great Angs are very powerful. They married strictly within other Great Ang clans. They could exercise sexual rights over the women of commoner {Ben}clans. Their houses were the largest in the village, outshining the morungs in wealth or carvings. They were entitled to the first share of meat, typically the leg They and their family members were entitled to particular ornaments : in Longkhai. The wives of Great Angs were entitled to carry a specially carved spear.

However, the situation of a Ang chief was not secure. He was responsible for the village's prosperity. If the village did not prosper, the Ang might be blamed. If the crops failed and he was unable to give the feasts that symbolized his power, his power would be at stake. Equally, if land was unavailable for expanding his domain, his power could be questioned. The Nagas have distinct customs, laws, traditions and social life. Every village is an independent unit in the tribe. They practiced animism before conversion to Christianity. They retain their traditional laws and customs and village organization even after conversion to Christianity. (Julian Jacobs, The Nagas, Hill Peoples of North east India, Thames and Hudson Ltd, London-1998).

Games

"Kang" is the popular game among the Nagas. It is played with the round seed of creeper which is like horse-chestnut. Another game they play is "Tiger and the Men". Wrestling, long jump, spear throwing and stone lifting are commonly played in villages.

Oath Taking

The Nagas take oath taking as a very serious matter. Disputes are settled by the village elders. It may be in the form of self-ordeals like plunging into the water pool and staying longest there or biting tiger's teeth, touching tiger's teeth by Dao or taking some verbal oath.

Dress and Ornaments

The Naga dress is very simple.The dress of the Angamese is effective and colourful. They decorate their spears and daos with goat's hair. (see plate–160). The Aos too have a nice dress. (B.C. Allen, E.A Gait, H.F Howard, C.G, Allen, Gazetteer of Bengal and North East India, Mittal Publications, Page 473)

Men used a piece of cloth wrapped round the waist, its ends are allowed to hang down. The cloth is made of cotton or synthetic fibre. Horizontal stripes are given to the piece of cloth in red or white linings. A piece of cloth is also kept around the shoulders to cover the upper portion of the body. However, their ceremonial dress is more elaborate and colourful. Leggings with bands of colours are used around the calves. The waist cloth is also colourful with matching stripes. Two pieces of scarf with a colourful linings of horizontal bands are thrown round the shoulders to hang down on the back and on the chest in such a way that the loose ends of the scarves cross each other on either side.

Woman wear a piece of cloth wrapped around the waist. It may reach up to the knee or up to mid-calves. They wrap cloth round the waist without the use of belt. The pattern of the cloth is artistic with horizontal colourful lines and geometrical blocks The breasts are covered with choli type garment or by wrapping a simple piece of cloth. Some women also wrap their bodies with a long piece of cloth which covers the body from the bust down to the thighs. It is simply rolled round the body below the armpits, making its edges over the bosoms and tucked generally on the right side of the breast.

Both men and women are very fond of ornaments. They wear a wide range of ornaments. During childhood, the ear lobes are pierced to make holes. The ear-rings are also very big in size. Coiled wire rings and spiral rings of big size are inserted into the holes of the earlobes. They also wear armlets of brass or other metals. Men wear typical and strong metal ornaments for self defence. Cane or brass rings are also worn below the knees to provide strength in climbing hills. Men wear necklaces with red stone and any kind of glass or precious stones, beads, metals and cowries. Women wear necklace of polished hexagonal cornelian beads. They wear small ear-rings. Brass and metal armlets are common ornaments of woman. Some wear collarets of blue beads. Wealthy woman wear ivory armlets, bead necklaces are also preferred. Necklace made of red pebbles is worn only by wealthy gentry. (see plates - 151,157,158) Many woman adorn their upper calves with cane rings and upper arm with a brass ornament made of a thick wire finished into a bell-shaped mouth at both the extremities. The ornaments are worn round tightly crossing the hinder portion of the bell over each other. Tattooing is customary only in remote areas in the North and the East.

Children, like adults, show their status through ornaments.Thus, an Ao boy at three months starts wearing earring of goat's hair, which is only discarded when he is admitted to the morung. At puberty Rengma girls wear particular skirts and ornament indicating their unmarried status, and their heads are shaved until marriage. Their dress may also indicate the status of their fathers and grandfathers. Eastern Angami girls don a particular type of dress at puberty which is then worn for the rest their adult lives.

Some old men keep their hair long and arranged in tangled knots, but in the present day the fashion is to wear hair up to the ears only. Women grow hair but some prefer bob cuts. The bobbed hair makes the young Naga girl look more beautiful with her ruddy face.

Handicrafts

The Nagas are expert in weaving, basketry, simpler forms of wood carvings, spinning and pottery, metalwork etc. As in agriculture, there is a gender division of labour, but it is not uniform between the different groups. The Naga handicrafts and Naga dress is famous for it's beauty, colourful motifs and designs.

Designs of Clothes :

The designs of textiles of the Nagas reflect minute identification of social organization and social status. The designs and colours of clothes symbolize ascribed status such as village, clan, and morung membership, and achieved prestige status arising from head- taking and feasting. Perhaps the most developed system of cloth design as indication of status, is found amongst the Aos, who have a wide variety of significant colours and designs, each meaning something very specific. The Ao cloth *aosu* is worn by a man who has done the mithun sacrifice at least once, but is also worn by his sons, his daughters, and his sons' sons- that is, his lineage descendants. (see plates-152-155)

The Morung

The Mornung is the youth's dormitory. This is a big building covering about 50 feet x 30 feet, decorated with hornbill, tiger, mithun {bison} and human heads.This is a sleeping place for the young unmarried men. In the earlier head hunting days, it served as a guard –house for the warriors. It is also a school where the young people learn about social practices and belief from their elders. This is an all-male institution.There is also a dormitory for girls.

A Naga village is typically divided into two or more geographical areas called *Khels.* Each khel has one or more morungs. Each khel and its morung will contain members of one or more clans. Every three years, a group of boys about 12 years old is initiated into a morung. This marks the transition from childhood to adolescence. When a new age-group is being initiated, the initiation action may involve symbolic representation of head taking. Among the Konyak, this includes throwing of miniature spears into a tree just outside the village. Membership of a morung may decide choice of marriage partner. It is usually forbidden to marry within the morung, and reciprocal relations are therefore built up with other morungs, from whom a marriage partner is chosen. Such reciprocal relations would also involve helping with rebuilding the morung. Soon after puberty. boys and girls from different morungs or clans may begin to meet,and in most groups young people are free to make love. Adulthood is indicated by the initiation into the morung, which is followed by a head–taking ritual setting–foot in enemy territory is considered adequate for symbolic representation of head taking. In olden days, some Naga communities would obtain and kill a slave for this purpose.

At this stage the boy and girl may exchange customary love-tokens or small gifts {the boy giving bamboo comb or ear-plugs and receiving an embroidered loin cloth.} subsequently, the girl may ask the boy to work with her in her father's fields the next day, where they might share food from the same dish {something forbidden to members of the same morung}.

The morung and its surrounding areas is a social centre for the khel, and also a centre for important rituals, especially where it is strongly associated with a log-gong. Morungs are more or less autonomous and are managed by a council of morung elders, even conducting their own political relations with other villages' morungs. This might include the morung {not the village} receiving tribute from subjugated villages nearby. The elders would adjudicate disputes, determine the choice of fields to cultivate, and proclaim village ritual days These morung elders would then meet together to form a village council.

Economic Activities :

By the 1930s the Nagas become involved in economic activities quite outside their traditional patterns. Naga started working in the railways, in the coal mines or in tea gardens and tea plantation sites. This gave them adequate opportunity to mix up with outsiders creating new opportunities. This also led them to addiction to opium. The Government sought to control the opium trade through granting licenses to traders and through allocating passes allowing set amounts of the drug to known addicts. Nowadays Nagas are engaged in any kind of economic activity.

Marriage

Among the Nagas, young women marry at between 15 and 20; young men between 20 and 25. The marriage partner must be from outside the clan or morung which have built up a reciprocal relationship. There is a preference for marriage with woman who come into the category of "mother's brother's daughter". A man's mother's brother's daughter is therefore a fairly close relation, not too close, she is not from the same lineage as himself {which would be a forbidden marriage}. A girl on the other hand will see it as a situation in which she is likely to marry a man in the category of "father's sister's son". The Nagas feel that marriage is a bond and it has to be performed in the right way. They believe that marriage confers a woman the right to enter the clan of her husband.

Among the Rengma, there is a myth that the first man tricked his brother tiger resulting in their permanent hostility. Before parting, the tiger warned man to keep clear of him, but also had three pieces of brotherly advice. Two of these concerned agricultural practices and the third was, 'never marry a women of your own clan'.

The man pays a "bride price" to the family of the bride. The bride-price will be paid in installments over a long period of time. Presenting a spearhead to the bride' family – a gift of a spear is a universal-Naga symbol of tribute between groups. Payments of bride price involve exchanges of objects of material and ceremonial value. But the man receives gifts in return, and gift exchange continues between the two groups for the whole of their lives. When the man goes hunting, he shares hind leg with his wife's parents. His wife's brothers give him presents of rice and rice- beer at feasts, and he reciprocates. The woman never ceases to belong to her own clan, and a husband who mistreats his wife will find her clan brothers lining up behind her. When his wife dies, he must give her family a field, but his children will receive gifts from their mother's brothers. A man will do "bride-service", working for his father-in law for some years.

The Thendu husband and wife call each other by their personal names, while in Thenkoh, they call each other 'mother of / father of so- and –so'.

Child Birth

The Naga women are hard working. They worked upto the full term of pregnancy. The pregnant women can take any type of food except taboo animals. They are helped in the process of delivery by their female relatives. Sometimes, the women may start labour while working in the field and she may give birth to a child in the field. Such a birth is considered to be auspicious because of the analogy between human and agricultural fertility among the Rengma Nagas. The Liengmai Nagas put up a small stone monument on the path leading to the fields to every child born in this way.

When the birth takes place at home, the father is asked to remain in an outer room during the delivery. He will be later called on to cut the umbilical cord and to bury the placenta. A child is born not only into a household but also into a clan.

Among the Aos, the ear of the child is pierced on the second day and a tuft of hair is cut off by the father indicating formal recognition by the father that the child is his and is therefore a member of his clan. In the Zemi Naga community, a baby is also claimed by one or other of the morungs of the khel, as well as by a clan; shortly after birth. The old men or women of different morungs "compete" to be the first to tie a thread around the baby's wrist, signifying his or her life-long morung membership.

The "social paternity" of a child is considered to be more important than biological paternity'. On divorce, the child once weaned would be raised by the father's family; the mother having no more connection with the child once she has been paid a compensatory 'milk price'. There is no restriction on remarriage of widows. The widow may marry the deceased husband's brother but it is not a rule. Divorce is not common. Polyandry is not a custom.

Inheritance

The wealth of household will be affected by the inheritance laws of each community. The Nagas are patrilineal that is decent and inheritance go through males. Generally, each brother receives a similar amount of property from the father. Among Angamis, the youngest son get most of the property whereas in case of the Konyaks the eldest son gets all the property. Movable property can be inherited by sons and daughters.

Death Rituals :

The Nagas have different kinds of death rituals. The Ang and Ben had different funeral practices. In the Thendu village of Wangla, the heads of Ang corpses were placed in stone pots, while those of Ben corpses were placed in clay pots. The Angamis bury their dead bodies in stone-lined graves; the Lhota do likewise. Sometimes, they used a canoe-shaped coffin; the Konyak practice exposure of the corpse after first removing the head. The head is placed in a pot or stone cist. It is then fed during agricultural festivals in the subsequent years. During the next harvest, the skull is painted in geometric designs turning the face outwards. The Nagas believed that there is a definite relationship between death and fertility i.e. harvest. Fertility is taken out during harvest whereas fertility is returned to the earth at the time of death. The corpse is often buried with implements, which he may require in the next birth along with a dog or chicken to keep company. Often stone edifice is erected at the burial site indicating the status of the deceased.

In the village of Laruri and in the Kalyo Kengyu area, the corpse is smoked in the house to dry, put into a canoe–shaped coffin and hung up under the eaves of the house. It remains there until the first day of the new year's sowing genna. Little houses are built on stilts for the soul to rest along with miniature implements. When the sowing genna comes, the corpse is taken out of the coffin, the bones are separated and put it into a covered pot. Then it is placed in the family granary. The flesh and wrappings of the corpse is put back into the coffin and then the whole thing is placed on a cliff. When the harvest is collected, a small portion of the grain is given to the miniature house. Then the little house is dismantled and the deceased is no longer considered. (Julian Jacobs, The Nagas, Hill Peoples of North east India, Thames and Hudson Ltd. London-1998).

Tattooing

Thendu men tattoo their faces as a sign of head–taking and wear their heir long, while Thenkoh men do not practice face-tattooing and keep their hair short.

Feasts of Merit

Feast-giving is usually connected with setting up of monolith indicating large scale collective act enhancing prestige of the feast giver.

Each monolith represents a certain amount of wealth expended. A great feast is given for setting up the monolith for 3-5 days. The feast giver have to engage a large number of young people to drag the big stone into the village and set it up at a suitable spot. The feast including food and drinks has to be given continuously till the work is completed. This will serve two purposes-it will enhance the prestige of the feast giver and perpetuate his own memory.

Feast also should be given while erecting Y-shaped posts or adding a carved house horns or sacrificing a mithun. The Feasts of Merit may be repeated, if the individual can afford to do it twice. These ceremonies both mark and create distinctions in social status. The Feast converts material wealth into social rank. A man who has enough wealth to give a Feast would at the same time obviously be a man possessing 'fertility': his wealth is a sign of this. The Feast is therefore a recognition of his ritual status, and a mechanism for spreading his 'fertility' among his follow villagers.

In this respect two things are important. First, the Feasts of merit tend to take place at the same time as significant agricultural-cycle rituals, and second, the Y-posts that are erected are said to be basically sexual in shape. The Sema forked Y posts are symbols of the female sex, and the Angami erect two stones together- a male and a female. It is through their planting in the earth that the Feasts-giver transmits his fertility into the common land of the village.

The celebration of particular "Feasts of Merit" is vividly commemorated not only in the stones and posts erected, but also in the special clothes worn by the feast giver–and also by his wife, daughter, son and grandson. The clothes do not merely mark status, but also promote competitiveness.

Early Relations with the British

The story of early British relation with the Naga tribes were of perpetual conflict.

The first British expedition into Naga territory took place in January, 1832. Maharaja Gambheer Singh embarked upon opening of a route from Imphal to Nowgong in Assam across the extensive hills and deep gorges. He set out with three British officers Capt. Jenkin, Capt. Pemberton and Capt. Gordon in January, 1832. Altogether 700 foot soldiers and 800 coolies were pressed into service for this gigantic work. But the Nagas particularly the Angamese equipped with spears, muskets and stone boulders made unprovoked attacks resulting in the death of many workers. This route was the first route connecting between Imphal with Assam. This route was known as "Manipur Road" for a long time. Now this route is named as National Highway No.-39.

Maharaja Gambheer Singh thought of subduing the recalcitrant Nagas and occupied Thibomei (Kohima) in 1832. To commemorate the event, he left footprints engraved on a slab of stone. A festive ceremony was performed in which the Naga villages contributed one buffalo, two goats and one hundred pigs. Later 600 heads of cattle were presented to Maharaja Gambheer Singh as a tribute.

During 1839 to 1935, ten military expeditions were led into the Naga hills, the majority of which were dispatched to punish raids. After the last of these, in which the village of Kekrima which had challenged British troops to a hand to hand fight lost 100 men, the Government of India decided upon a complete withdrawal and an abstention from all interference with the hill tribes.

In 1851, the troops were recalled. But before the end of that year, 22 Naga raids had taken place in which 55 persons were killed, 10 wounded and 113 taken captive.

During 1853 to 1865, 19 raids were committed in which 233 British subjects were killed, wounded or captured. The Government accordingly agreed to the formation of a new district in 1866 with the headquarters at Samuguting. In 1869, Captain Butler was appointed to take this charge. He did much to consolidate British power in the Naga hills and exploration and survey work were diligently pushed forward. These advances were however resented by the Nagas. In February, 1875, Lieutenant Holcombe who was in charge of one of the survey party was killed with 80 of his followers. Butler himself was three times attacked and was mortally wounded on the following Christmas Day by the Lhota Nagas of Pangti. Two years later, his successor Mr. Carnegy was accidentally shot by a sentry when occupying the village of Mozema which had refused to give up the persons guilty of a raid into North Cachar.

In 1875, a subdivision was opened at Wokha to exercise control over the Lhota Nagas. Fourteen years later, it was found possible to withdraw the European Officer stationed there and a subdivision was opened at Mokokchung in the Ao territory.

In 1878, it was decided to transfer the headquarters of the district from Samuguting to Kohima, in the heart of Angamese territory.

In January, 1879, the troubles again flared up. The Political Officer, Mr. Damant determined to visit the villages of Jotsoma, Khonoma and Mozema before starting the cold season. On reaching Khonoma, he found the gates of the village closed and as he stood before the gate, he was shot dead. The Nagas then poured a volley of bullets into his escort who turned and fled with a loss of 35 killed and 19 wounded. A campaign against the Nagas ensued which lasted till March, 1880. The most notable event in this campaign was a daring raid upon the Baladhan tea garden in Cachar where they killed the Tea Garden Manager, and 16 coolies and burnt down everything in the place. This raid was carried out by a party of Khonoma men at the very time when their village was in the occupation of the British troops. Within a short space of five years, four European officers while engaged in civil duties had come to a violent end. But the Nagas had learnt their lessons and under the able administration of Mr. McCabe the district was reduced to a condition of peace and order.

In the Naga battle of 1879, the relief of Kohima was effected by the troops of the King of Manipur. In return for his service, King Chandrakirti was created KCSI. The Raja Churachand was formally installed in 1908. During the World War-I, the Raja Churachand placed all his resources at the disposal of the British Government and his valuable services were recognized by the bestowal of the hereditary title of Maharaja. He raised a corps of 2000 labourers for France but his endeavour to raise a second corps led to a rising among the Kukis (Kuki Rebellion), which was only suppressed with the direct intervention by Raja Churachand with a large force of Assam Rifles and Burma Military Police. (Sir Edward Gait, A History of Assam –page- 331)

In 1898, the Mikir and Rengma hills with the valley of Dhansiri which formed the northernmost part of the district as originally constituted was transferred to Nowgong and then to Sibsagar in 1889 in order to protect the Ao Nagas from aggression of the tribe that live in the east of Dikho river.

At the census of 1901, only 1.3 percent of the Nagas were reported as literate. There were one secondary, 22 primary and two special schools in the district in 1903-04 and 76 female students.

The official policy towards the Nagas was the traditional one adopted for backward and isolated animists : gradual conversion to more settled civilized habits. (Lawrence James, Raj: The Making of British India, Abacus, A division of Little, Brown and Company (UK), Brettenham House, Lancaster Place, London, WC2E 7 EN, 1977, Page 414)

As late as 1926-28, Political Officers accompanied by small parties of troops were travelling from village to village freeing slaves and extracting promises from chiefs to abandon sacrifices of children. Each chief bit a tiger's tooth and declared that if he broke his vow, she would be eaten by a tiger. The senior Political Agent H.E. Mitchell altered the ceremony by substituting a bullet after having given the oath taker and his warriors a demonstration of Lewis machine gun fire. It was a valuable eye opener for people whose only firearms were flintlock muskets. In one village, a priest who sacrificed children was encountered and told that he might be clever enough to play on the imagination of his ignorant, opium–sodden villagers but he could not succeed with the Government. Coaxing and coercing in this manner had some effect, for in 1928, only two human sacrifices were reported. Lord Salisbury observed "a barbarous mountain population exists by the side of a civilized population dwelling in the plains". (Lawrence James, Raj: The Making of British India, Abacus, A division of Little, Brown and Company (UK), Brettenham House, Lancaster Place, London, WC2E 7 EN, 1977, Page 415)

Naga National Movement

The First World War show the seed of Naga National movement. During 1914-1919 the Naga National movement began during the First World War when a Labor Corps of about 4,000 Nagas, were sent to France, where they saw great civilized nations fighting for their ends and interests while Nagas were condemned as barbarous for their head hunting ways (Yunuo, 1974: 125; cited in Eaton, 1997: 256).

In 1918, after returning from France, twenty Nagas including few government officials and leading Naga chiefs formed an organisation known as the "Naga Club" at Kohima for promoting the interests of the Nagas. The Club was informally supported by local British administrators mainly Mr. Charles Pawsay, the then Deputy Commissioner. When Indian Independence was imminent, this same Naga Club transformed itself into Naga National Council (NNC) in 1946, at the behest of Mr. Charles Pawsay. Pawsay was rewarded and became Sir Charles Pawsay. Thus, a mere club became a National Council or Parliament. This club provided a common platform for leaders of different tribes of Nagas. In the absence of any other organisation, the Naga Club turned into an effective political forum for the Naga tribes. The first stirrings of Naga nationalism were prompted or at least encouraged by certain British Colonial Officers, who felt that the *"distinctiveness of Naga culture"* would be at risk in an united India. It will be recalled that the crystallization of the "tribes, Nagas" were itself aided, if not created, by British administrators and anthropologists. The other factor in the development of Naga national consciousness was Christianity–specifically that of the American Baptist Church. The Nagas called "Nagaland for Christ" with a view to win the Christian world on their side. The first American Baptist missionaries were invited into the Naga Hills by early British explorers such as Major Jenkins in the 1830s, but it was not until the 1870s that really significant missionary activity developed. The first settled mission was in the Ao country, at Deka Haimong {Molungyimchen}, in 1876.

The Government of India Act 1919

According to the Government of India Act 1919 the "Naga Hills District" was declared as a "Backward Tract" and it was made clear in the above Act that no Acts passed by the Indian Legislature were to apply to this "Backward Tract".

Simon Commission -1929

Simon Commission formed in 1927 by the British Government was boycotted as an "All White Commission". In disapproval against the Commission, a widespread demonstration was held in Calcutta on 19 February, 1928, the day of Simon's arrival to the city. In 1929, when the Simon Commission visited Naga Hills in 1929. The Naga representatives submitted a memorandum to the Simon Commission signed by 20 Nagas. This visit and submission of memorandum were arranged through the kind courtesy of Mr. J.H. Hutton, the then Deputy Commissioner of Naga Hills District of Assam.The signatories claimed to represent all those tribes-Angamis, Katcha Nagas, Kukis, Semas, Lothas and Rangmas (Simon Memorandum, 1999: 166). The memorandum submitted on 10th January, 1929 said :-

"We, the undersigned Nagas of the Club at Kohima, who are the only persons at present who can voice for our people, our hills may be withdrawn from the Reformed Scheme and placed outside the reforms but directly under the British Government ..... Our country within the administered area consist of more than eight tribe quite different from one another with quite different languages which can't be understood by each other, and there are more tribes outside the administered area which are known at present. We have no unity amongst us and it is only the British that is holding us together now... The occupation of our country by the British Government being so recent as 1880, ... We are looked down upon by one for our beef and the other for our pork and by both for want of education ... we have not yet got one who is able to represent all our different tribes or master our languages much less one to represent us in any council of a province.... We claim to represent all those tribes to which we belong : Angamis, Kacha Nagas, Kukis, Semas, Lothas and Rengmas. "(Charles Chasie" The Naga Imbrogio- A Personal Perspective), Standard Printers and Publishers, Kohima, 1999)

The memorandum asked Government that the Nagas not to be included in any reform scheme because they were not unified as a group, educational levels were poor, and because given their small numbers, in any electoral system based on numbers their interests were sure to be overwhelmed. The memorandum interpreted the pre-colonial past of the Nagas as that of an unvanquished people. "Before the British Government conquered our country in 1879-80", said the memorandum, "we were living in a state of intermittent warfare with Assamese of the Assam valley to the North and West of our country and the Manipuris to the South. They never conquered us, nor were we ever subjected to their rule" (Simon Memorandum, 1999: 165-166). Thus the Nagas were demanding that the Naga hills be excluded from the proposed reform scheme and kept under direct British rule.

Government of India Act 1935

Under the Government of India Act 1935 which was passed on the recommendations of the Simon Commission, the "Naga Hills District" (Backward Tract according to Act of 1919) was declared to be treated as "Excluded Area" on March 3, 1935. Declared as an "Excluded Area" they continued to be administered by the Government of Assam. Separate tribal councils were subsequently formed, the first two being a Lhota council {1923} and an Ao council {1928}. These councils were nurtured by the British.

The World Wars had a tremendous impact on the Nagas. During World War I the Naga members of the Labour Corps brought money and dresses, but World War II was fought in Nagaland itself. The Nagas were introduced to modern guerilla fighting which was natural to them. The War brought a greater degree of unity among the Nagas. The dumps of arms and ammunition left by the retreating Japanese Army provided ready material to be used against the security forces later.

Politically the most important development of the war years was the emergence of a British Government plan for Naga independence. The British had already offered India the propend of independence in return for loyalty during the war; also on the table was a plan for a Crown Colony for the Nagas and other hill peoples.

Satisfied with the participation of the "hill tribes" in the war and their loyalty to the Government, some British officers abroad suggested new plans for the hill areas of Northeast India.(NE). Before the British left India in 1947, they had a plan to create a "Crown Colony" comprising of the entire north eastern region.This was to separate the entire northeast region from India. The region was to be formed into an independent political authority separate from both India and Burma, turning into a special colony directly under the British crown. The man behind the proposal was R. Coup Land, who came to India as Secretary to Strafford Cripps. The British Political Officers like Robert Reid and others supported the proposal. The north eastern region was considered to be a territory distinct from India and Burma.The scheme of a "Crown Colony could not gain ground due to the peculiar political and constitutional situation facing India on the eve of Indian Independence." (R. Coup land, Future of India-London 1944, p-160).

In April 1945, after the second world war, at the initiative of C.R. Pawsey, then British Deputy Commissioner of Naga Hills District, the "Naga Hills Districts Tribal Council" was formed to help the relief and rehabilitation work. The main objective was to unify the Nagas on modern lines. In April, 1946, it was converted into "Naga National Council" (NNC) at Wokha with the aim to carry out social and political upliftment of the Nagas. It was organized as a federation of several tribal councils and brought out a small newspaper called the "Naga Nation". In the beginning, the political objective of the Naga National Council was solidarity of all Nagas, including those of the un-administered areas and the inclusion of their hills within the province of Assam in a free India, with local autonomy and adequate safeguards for the interest of the Nagas. This demand of the Nagas was well received in the circle of the Indian National Congress.

Visit of Cabinet Mission -1946

The British Government sent a Cabinet Mission to India to study the political situation in the country in April 1946. The Naga National Council submitted a memorandum to the Cabinet Mission on April 9,1946 that the Naga future will not be bound by any arbitrary decision of the British Government, and that no recommendation will be accepted without consultation. In the beginning, the political objective of the Naga National Council was local autonomy for Naga Hills within the province of Assam. But with the arrival of Angami Zapu Phizo (see plate-163) from Burma, the whole scenario had changed. In May, 1947,the Constituent Assembly Sub Committee visited Kohima but NNC still refused to join the Indian Union. In June, 1947, the NNC declared that the Naga Hills would cease to be a part of India with the departure of the British. The NNC. turned down the offer of autonomy envisaged in the sixth Schedule of the Constituent Assembly

The 9-Point Agreement:

On 27 June, 1947, an attempt was made to resolve the deadlock with the coming of Sir, Akbar Hydari, the Governor of Assam to Kohima. Theyiechuthie Sakhrie or T. Sakhrie demanded "In fairness, justice and equality, Naga lands should be restored to the Nagas. During the three days of Sir, Akbar Hydari's stay (27-29 June), a nine point agreement was signed between NNC and the Government of India.It was mentioned in the agreement that "The Governor of Assam will have a special responsibility for a period of ten years to ensure due observance of this agreement ; at the end of this period, the Naga National Council will be asked whether they require the above agreement to be extended for a further period, a new agreement regarding the future of the Naga people arrived at". Within three days, the Naga public rejected Sir Hydari's agreement.Sir Hydari threatened the Nagas with military might in presence of Sir Pawsey and others.

In 1947, both Gandhi and Nehru had reportedly said "they were sympathetic to the Nagas and would not support forced unions".

On 18 July, 1947, the British Parliament passed the Indian Independence Act 1947.

Declaration of Naga Independence - August 14, 1947

On 14th August, 1947, A.Z. Phizo had declared Naga Independence and informed the U.N. Headquarters in New York. On 15th August, 1947, India declared Independence.

Follow up of thc 9-Point Agreement

Naga delegation met His Excellency the Governor of Assam Sir Akbar Hydari, in Shillong on May 9, 1948. The purpose of the delegation was to ascertain the position of the 9-Point Agreement of June, 1947. The Governor said that the agreement would be incorporated in the Sixth Scheduled of the Constitution of India, although the 9-Point Agreement made no reference to the Constitution of India.

Further assurance for the 10-Year Agreement's (9-Point Agreement) implementation was given to the NNC by N.K. Rustomji, Adviser to the Governor of Assam vide his Memo No. 490/C Dated 11th June, 1948. The letter reads: "I am desired by His Excellency, the Governor of Assam to state that the machinery necessary to that end is already in motion. There was never, nor shall be, any question of non-implementation of the terms of the Agreement". The final assurance for implementation of the 10-Year Agreement was made in a signed statement to the Naga National Council by both Sir Akbar Hydari, Governor of Assam and Shri Gopinath Bordoloi the Premier of Assam under Memo No. 88-C/47-570-72 dated June 22, 1948.

In order to extract a clear statement about the actual fate of the 10-Year Agreement (9-Point Agreement) a 3-man Delegation of the Naga National Council (NNC) met the representatives of the Government of India in Shillong on November 3, 1949. The Naga delegation was bluntly told that there was no agreement called "Nine point Akbar Hydari Agreement made with the Nagas". Shri Gopinath Bordoloi, the Premier of Assam himself sorrowfully admitted to the Nagas in the Government House in Shillong on November 9, 1949 that the Agreement was no longer considered to exist by the Indian Government. The Nagas took it as a betrayal of their cause. The Naga National Council said "It was a direct insult to the Nagas. It hurt the Naga sentiments greatly"

In 1949, Phizo was arrested and imprisoned but he was released later on compassionate grounds following the death of his son in a motor cycle accident.

On 11 December, 1950, Angami Zapu Phizo was elected as the president of NNC, which has led to a plebiscite in May 1951, boycott of General Elections of 1952, establishment of a parallel government in 1956 and showed the seed of insurgency movement in the Naga Hills.

The Naga Voluntary Plebiscite of 1951

Early in 1951, the Naga National Council (NNC) launched a voluntary plebiscite. On 16 May, 1951, the plebiscite on the question of Naga Independence was inaugurated. About six thousand people attended the inaugural function. All Naga adult males and females above the age of 15 years were included in the plebiscite. The overall conduct of the Naga plebiscite took over six months to complete. Tuensang district was not included in the plebiscite because Tuensang was under a different administrative set up at that time. 99% vote for Independence was declared.

On 29 December, 1951, Phizo informed Jawaharlal Nehru about the verdict of the Plebiscite. In 1951 Pandit Nehru reportedly told a Naga delegation "...it is impossible to consider even for a moment such an absurd demand for independence of the Nagas. I am doubtful whether the Nagas realise the consequences of what they are asking for. their present demand would ruin them." (Dinesh Kotwal, The Naga Insurgency: The Past And The Future)

In March 1952, Pandit Nehru reportedly told a Naga delegation "...even if the heavens fell or India went to pieces and the blood runs red in the country, I do not care. Whether I am here or for that matter any other body comes, I do not care, Nagas will never be allowed to become independent" (M. Horam, Naga Insurgency, Cosmo Publications, 1988, page-50). Phizo reaffirms his earlier political stance that "Nagas are not Indians and Naga areas are not part of India. Historically Naga lands had neither political nor legal relations with India."

On 7th August, 1952, Jawaharlal Nehru declared in the Indian Parliament that "We want no forced marriages or forced unions. This great republic of

India is a free, voluntary, friendly and affectionate union of the States of India".

Tension between India and Nagas grew as the Government of India was determined to do away with the aspirations of the Nagas. The leaders and members of the Naga National Council (NNC) became the first target of arrest and torture. On 18 October, 1952, while NNC was taking a peaceful procession, Mr. Zasibito Nagi of Zotsoma village, a member of NNC was shot dead by the police on the main road at Kohima. He was the first Naga to be shot.

On March 30, 1953, Jawaharlal Nehru visited Kohima along with the Burmese Prime Minister U.Nu and was greeted with derision as the Nagas were not allowed to speak to Nehru. This was followed by an even more impressive "walk out" protest by ten thousand Nagas from a meeting convened and addressed by Prime Ministers Nehru and U Nu. A civil disobedience campaign was launched. In the same year, nine police out–posts were opened in the Naga Hills. Action against the NNC. members was intensified. Different Acts, including the "Assam Disturbed Areas Act 1955" were imposed to enable the armed forces personnel to carry out their difficult task. In 1956, army units were deployed in important towns like Kohima and Mokokchung.

By October, 1955, the war began. To quote B.N. Mullik, Personal secretary to Nehru "Troops moved into Tuensang and the war with Naga started then". (B.N. Mullik : My years with Nehru, Caxton Press Private Limited, Delhi-1972, page -308) Mullik wrote "Now there were two Naga demands before the Government, the first by the NNC for complete independence and the second by the NPC for statehood within the Indian Union. To do anything lesser would be against the expressed desire of the entire Naga people.

Tension into Direct Confrontations

The Indian Government launched large scale operations in Naga territory branding the Nagas as 'hostiles', 'insurgents', 'misguided elements' 'extremists', 'miscreants', 'terrorists', 'treacherously blood-thirsty' and the like.

The Web site of the NSCN describes untold suffering of the Nagas at the hands of the Indian Army like murder, rape, burning of houses, collectives fines for the villagers, sexual harassment, human right violations.

The following is the brief description found in the NSCN Web site.

"Villagers were flushed out and gathered at open places days and nights together. Unbearable restrictions and curfews were imposed upon them and shoot-at-sight at the suspect was standing order everywhere. Some villages were burnt down more than twenty times. Besides, a large number of villages were uprooted from one place to another causing sufferings beyond words.Granaries were burnt to ashes without exception. Standing crops were destroyed. Schools and Churches were razed to the ground". It was also alleged that on 15 November, 1954, Indian Armed Forces raided the village of Yangpang and killed 60 men, women and children. Yangpang village was attacked on the morning of Monday 15 November by Indian troops from Noklak camp. The killing lasted for two hours from 5 till 7, led by a political officer and his assistant. All the victims were beheaded, some alive, some after being shot and their heads were taken back to Noklak to be photographed.

"On 27 Nov, 1954 a battalion of the Indian Armed Forces destroyed the village of Chingmei by bombardment causing an unknown number of deaths. In Chemong village, two persons, Chenemong and Shemshimong were crucified after torturing for several hours. Time and again almost the whole population was driven into jungles where they live on roots and leaves without food and medical care. They were hunted down daily. Thousands died of starvation and diseases. They used all unimaginable methods in their attempt to liquidate Nagas. It clearly amounted to genocide. The whole population underwent untold sufferings since 1954. As a result of such inhuman carnage, starvations, diseases and deprivation of other necessities of life more than a hundred thousand died within 1954-1964."

"By 1956 the strength of the regular Indian Armed Forces had already reached one hundred thousands in Nagas Hills and Tuensang areas. All hopes of negotiated settlement of the issue frittered away. In view of this imposing challenge Nagas promptly took decisive decision and solemnly declared the "Naga Federal Republic" on the 22nd March 1956. An army organisation known as "Naga Home Guard" was set up to help the government and defend the country which was later changed into Naga Army. Nagas were, thus, driven to take up arms."

Proclamation of the Federal Government of Nagas (FGN)

On 22 March, 1956, the NNC. set up its government– "Naga Central Government" replacing the earlier "Sovereign Republic of Nagaland "set up in September, 1954 and hoisted the republic's flag at Phesinyu, a Rengma village. An elaborate ceremony was organized with the singing of their National Anthem :

God bless my Nagaland
Land that I love,
Stand beside her and guide her,
Through the night with the light from above
From the mountains and the valleys
And the hill-tops where I roam,
God bless my Nagaland
My home, sweet home,

This song was probably borrowed from the American patriotic song originally written by Irving Berlin in 1918 "God bless America", which runs as follows :-

God Bless America,
Land that I love.
Stand beside her, and guide her
Thru the night with a light from above.
From the mountains, to the prairies,
To the oceans, white with foam
God bless America, My home sweet home.

Irving Berlin originally wrote the song in 1918 while serving in the U.S. Army at Camp Upton in Yaphank, New York. The song was popularised by singer Kate Smith who introduced the revised version during her radio broadcast on Armistice Day, 1938. "God Bless America" is a quintessentially American song. This anthem, with its history, is meaningful for Americans, but how does it resonate with the Nagas ?

In 1956, T. Sakhrie, the General Secretary of the NNC fell out with Phizo on ideological grounds. Sakhrie was accused of being an Indian agent. One day while he was on his way to his Angami girl friend's village, he was arrested by his Naga friends, who tortured him, bound him to a tree and killed him brutally leaving a note behind "This is the man who betrayed the Nagas". Official circles blamed Phizo responsible for Sakhrie's murder and a case is still pending against him on a charge of murder under the Indian Penal Code.

In November 1957 Phizo left for East Pakistan (now Bangladesh) to seek aids from friendly countries. From Dacca, he proceeded to Karachi and flew onwards to London via Zurich. Eventually, he became a citizen of United Kingdom. In 1959, the Federal Government of Nagaland (FGN) was created (Charles Chasie, The Naga Imbroglio, Standard Printers & Publishers, Kohima, 1999). Within two months, it raised a standing army called "Naga Safe

Guards". The NNC. activists also formed the Naga Home Guard (NHG). There is a Parliament called Tatar which consists of two houses called Kimhao (Upper House) and Tatar Hoho (Assembly of Representatives) represented by a region having a population of 15,000. There is also a cabinet comprising of six Kilonsers (ministers).This was strongly supported by the Burmese Communist Party. It shot down an Indian Air Force transport aircraft on a supply dropping mission and the crew were held hostage for many years. Soon large–scale violence erupted throughout Naga Hills.

The exit of Phizo to England weakened the role of Angamese in the underground setup. By 1960, Kukhato Shukhai Sema became the Prime Minister of the Federal Government of Nagaland and by 1961 he made his brother in law Scate Swu the President replacing Khrisanisa Angami. Kaito Sema, brother in law of Sukhai had been promoted to the post of Defence Minister from the post of Commander in Chief of the Federal Army. Issac Swu and Kehovi Sema were appointed Foreign Minister and Information Minister respectively. Practically all the important offices in the Federal setup were in the hands of the Sema tribe.

On April 11, 1962, the President of India issued the Nagaland Security Regulation, 1962, for the suppression of subversive activities, maintenance of essential supplies and services and control of military requirements.

Naga People's Convention (NPC)

In 1957, the first Naga People's Convention (NPC) was held from August 22-26 to act as a mediator between the Government of India and the underground Nagas. A nine men delegation led by Dr. Imkongliba Ao was sent by the Convention to Delhi on 27 September, 1957 to meet the Prime Minister, Pandit Nehru. On 1 December, 1957, the Naga People's Convention desired a new administrative unit known as "Naga Hills Tuensang Area "to be formed and placed under the ministry of external affaires. The second NPC convention was held on 21 May, 1958 in the Ao village of Ungma. They prepared a 16–point memorandum which was discussed and endorsed by the Third NPC held at Makokchung in the Ao area from October 22-26, 1959. There was some opposition to the 16 –point memorandum but the member delegation were determined to go ahead. They took a chartered flight from Jorhat Airport (Assam) and made a dash to New Delhi and presented the 16–point memorandum to the Prime Minister Pandit Nehru. The memorandum was accepted in principle and the Prime minister announced the outcome of the meeting "Our policy has always been to give the fullest autonomy and opportunity of self government to the Naga people without interfering in any way in their internal affairs or way of life"

Birth of State of Nagaland

In August 1962, Nehru moved in Parliament the Bills for the 13th amendment of the Constitution and for the creation of the state of Nagaland. The Bill was given assent by the President on September 4, 1962.

In 1962, the Constitution (Thirteenth Amendment) Act passed lays down that :-

No Act of Parliament in respect of -

(a) Religious or social practices of the Nagas

(b) Naga customary law and procedure

(c) Administration of civil and criminal justice involving decisions according to Naga customary law

(d) Ownership and transfer of land and its resources

shall apply to the State of Nagaland unless the Legislative Assembly of Nagaland by a resolution so decides. It is tantamount to freedom of Nagas. (Prakash Singh, Kohima to Kashmir on the Terrorist Trail, Rupa & Co, New Delhi, 2001)

On December 1, 1963, President Radhakrishnan inaugurated the State of Nagaland comprising the areas earlier known as Naga Hills–Tuensang area at Kohima. Mr. P. Shilly Ao became the Chief Minister and declared the occasion "a day of rejoicing" and "the day to redeem our pledge".

Earlier Indo-Naga peace talks

On the 6th September 1964, the Cease-Fire Agreement was signed between the Indian Government and the Federal Government of Nagaland through the initiative of the Nagaland Baptist Church Council. The Naga Peace Mission was formed consisting of Rev. Micheal Scott, Mr. Chaliha and Jaya Prakash Narayan. Michael Scott played host to Phizo when he fled to England. He had "heart to heart talk" with the Naga underground leaders whereas they refused to meet other two members. While the Cease-fire Draft was in the making, the Prime Minister Pandit Nehru passed away on 27 May, 1964. However, the Suspension of Operation Agreement was signed by both parties on 15 August, 1964 which was officially christened as Cease–fire, which came into effect from 6 September, 1964. A part of the Cease –fire Agreement read as follows:-

"The Government of India welcome the steps intended to bring about peace in Nagaland and with this object in view as already stated, they will depute representatives with whom will be associated the representatives of the Government of Nagaland, to take part in talks with leaders of the Underground. To facilitate these talks and taking note of the letter of 10 August, 1964, referred to above, it has been ordered that with effect from 6 September, 1964 and for a period thereafter of one month at present, the security forces will not undertake :-

(a) jungle operations
(b) raiding of camps of the Underground
(c) patrolling beyond one thousand yards of security posts
(d) searching of villages
(e) aerial action
(f) arrests and
(g) imposition of labour by way of punishment

The Underground Nagas also agreed that during this period, they will refrain from :-

(a) sniping and ambushing
(b) imposition of fines
(c) kidnapping and recruiting
(d) sabotage activities
(e) raiding and firing on security posts, towns and administrative centres and
(f) moving with arms or in uniform in towns, villages and administrative centrers,

wherever there are security posts and approaching within one thousand yards of security posts.

On the 23 September 1964, the first session of the Naga Peace Mission was held at the peace camp, Chedema near Kohima. During the talks Indian representatives tried to treat the problem as "Law and order", whereas the Federal government's representatives took a firm stand that it was political one. Hence, the talks came to a stalemate.

On 20 December, 1964 Naga Peace Mission made proposal that the leaders of Federal Government should advise the people to agree to join the Union of India "on their own volition". Thereupon, the talks were taken up at the Prime Minister level. The talks took place in New Delhi for six rounds.

On 18 February, 1966, the first round of Ministerial talks was held between Indira Gandhi, Prime Minister and Naga leaders led by Kukhato Ato

Kilonser. The other leaders were Imkongmaren, Vice President of NNC, Isaac Swu, Foreign Minister, Z. Ramyo, Minister and a few others. The second round of talks was held on 11-12 April, 1966, where Indira Gandhi "was willing to consider to grant maximum possible autonomy to the Nagas within the framework of Indian Constitution".

Even before the Naga delegates returned to Nagaland, there was a violent explosion in the Assam Mail near Tinsukia killing as many as 37 persons and injuring 52. Hardly had the Naga delegates returned to Nagaland when another serious bomb explosion took place at Lamding Railway station killing 40 passengers on the spot and injuring 120. Five other persons died on the way to hospital and nine succumbed to injuries later totaling 54 deaths. Three days after the Lamding incident, another bomb explosion killed 54 persons and 120 injured at Diphu. It is said that the underground army wing reportedly tried to sabotage the talks. The Indian press came out very strongly blaming the Underground Nagas and Rev. Michael Scott. On 3 May, 1966, Rev. Michael Scott was served with an order to leave the country immediately. The acts of sabotage by the Underground Nagas also sabotage the Indo-Naga peace talks. On 4 May, 1966, B.P. Chaliha announced his resignation and recommended for dissolution of the Peace Mission. The third round of talks was held on 10-11 August, 1966 in New Delhi. The fourth round of talks was held on 27-29 October, 1966 where Kukhato presented 14 point statement.The Prime Minister Mrs. Indira Gandhi assured the Naga delegation maximum autonomy within the Indian Union but reiterated that there could be no question of Nagaland seceding from India. The fifth round of talks was held on 25 January, 1967. On his way back, Mr. Kukhato Sukhai declared in Calcutta that "the Nagas would never surrender their sovereignty and accept any settlement within the Indian Union". This statement of Sukhai to the press in Calcutta caused serious setback in the progress of the talks. The sixth round of talks was held on 5 October, 1967, which lasted only 40 minutes which ended in a dubious and pessimistic note. After two days of their return to Nagaland, Mr. Imkongmaren, Vice President of NNC issued a statement "So far as the talks are concerned, they are finished".

There were as many as six rounds of Ministerial talks between February, 1966 to October, 1967.

Soon after the 1967 peace talks both the Federal Government President Kukhato Sukhai and Prime Minister Scato Swu were forced to leave their posts. Kukhato was charged of accepting bribes from the Indian Government. Their exit resulted in the birth of the Revolutionary Group.

On 8 August, 1972, an assassination attempt was made on the life of the Chief Minister, Hokishe Sema while returning from Shillong with his daughter. The car showed 57 bullet holes and damaged beyond repair. However, the Chief Minister miraculously escaped while the driver and two of his body guards were killed. In the wake of the electrifying effect of the assassination attempt, the Indian Government declared the NNC, Federal Government of Nagaland and its army "unlawful associations" under the Unlawful Activities (Prevention) Act, 1967 on August 31, 1972. (M. Horam, Naga Insurgency Cosmo Publications, New Delhi, 1988)

In the mean time, the atrocities in Nagaland continued as before :-

On 9th December 1970, mass rape was allegedly committed by Indian troops against women residents of Cheswezy village where 18 unmarried girls, nine married women were raped and 53 women molested.

In March, 1974, Miss Ngaithingla, girl of 24 years from Grihang village, was brought in a near-dying condition by the villagers, she had been allegedly tortured and raped for three days from 3 to 5 March, by a group of 95 BSF personnel under the command of Major Prakash. On the third day she was dragged to the school building where the other villagers had been rounded up. She was dragged by her hair to the class room, kicked and beaten and stripped. Sticks were inserted into her private parts causing profuse bleeding.

On 6 March, 1974, at about 6.30 p.m. Mrs. Paothingla, Miss. Shiningla were taken by two constable under the order of Major Dhram Prakash. One of the constable took Mrs. Paothingla into the jungle from the main road. All her garments were forcibly taken off at gun point and she was severely beaten and raped. Another constable took Miss Shiningla and repeatedly raped her.

Shillong Accord

By September 1975, the Naga underground leaders were agreeable for the first time "not to insist on independence as a precondition". A six member underground delegation led by Kevi Yallya (Phizo's brother) met L.P. Singh, Governor of Assam on 10 November, 1975 at Raj Bhavan, Shillong, which led to the signing of the "Shillong Accord". On November 11, 1975, the "Shillong Accord" was signed between the Government of India and the NNC. Under this agreement, the NNC had agreed (1) to accept the solution of the Naga problem within the framework of the Indian Constitution, (2) abjure violence, bring out the armed men (3) to surrender weapons and resolve the residual problems through discussions.

However, the National Assembly summoned by Th. Muivah Gen. Secretary NNC on 15th to 17th August, 1976 at Suphao, condemned outright the "Shillong Accord" as the work of the sole traitors.It also condemned the Zashei Huire for the high treason. The condemnation paper was signed by Messrs Isak Chishi Swu and Th. Muivah in their respective capacities as the Vice-President and the General Secretary NNC.The Assembly elected Mr. Isak Chishi Swu to the Vice-Presidency. Phizo intentionally refused to condemn it right up to the time he breathed his last in 1990. Instead he went on welcoming the "traitors" including his own younger brother, Kevi Yalley, the architect of the Shillong Accord at his London residence.

In June, 1977 Phizo met Morarji Desai, Prime Minister of India in London and the talk was a failure.

Phizo's men overpowered both the NNC and Federal government at home on ground of condemning the Shillong Accord which Phizo himself did not, and joined forces with the "traitors" to crush the "patriots" starting the point of sanguinary war between the "traitors" and the "patriots".

Birth of NSCN

On January 31, 1980, several underground Naga members, who had strongly opposed the Shillong Accord, led by Isak Chishi Swu and Thuingaleng Muivah (see Plates-164,165) ultimately founded the "National Socialist Council of Nagaland" (NSCN) with Isak Chishi Swu as the Chairman, S.S Khaplang, a Hemis Naga of upper Myanmar, as Vice–President and Thuingaleng Muivah, a Tangkhul Naga of Manipur's Ukhrul district, as the General Secretary. The initial strength of the outfit was approximately 150 cadres and rose to 3,000 with Konyaks and Tangkhuls forming the main recruits. Other tribes in lesser numbers include, Semas, Yumchungus, and Maos. With a large array of sophisticated weapons procured through robberies, Kachin. Independent Army (KIA), and international markets, the NSCN, soon developed and turned out to be one of the most powerful underground organisation in Nagaland. Several Kilonsers (ministers) were appointed and areas divided into different regions with a senior underground member in charge of each regional unit.

Split of NSCN

The NSCN split when Khaplang suspected Isak and Muivah of secretly initiating talks with the Indian Government. Differences surfaced within the NSCN outfit over the issue of commencing a dialogue process with the Indian

Government. On April 30, 1988, an attempt to assassinate Muivah and Tangkhul cadre in the NSCN set–up was executed in which a large number of undergrounds were killed. Mr. Khaplang alleged that "Chairman Isak, General Secretary Muivah and Kilonser Hanong are ready to surrender to India by accepting uncle Suisa's proposal and that they were prepared to seize all the arms to surrender them to India. They are ready to eliminate all the Konyak and the Pangmi National Workers". However, Muivah escaped and as a result, NSCN was vertically split into two factions namely NSCN led by Isak and Muivah (NSCN-IM) and NSCN led by S.S. Khaplang.(NSCN-K) It was the bloodiest internal clash in the history of Naga insurgency. The Konyaks formed the NSCN-K under the leadership of Khole Konyak and S S Khaplang. The Tangkhul faction, the NSCN-IM (Isak-Muivah) was led by Isak Chisi Swu and Th. Muivah. (Sanjay Kumar)

NSCN-IM

The NSCN-IM is led by Isak Chisi Swu and Thuingaleng Muivah. (see plates-164, 165) The outfit aims to establish a "Greater Nagaland" ('Nagalim' or the People's Republic of Nagaland) based on Mao Tse Tung's ideology. The outfit has also established a government-in-exile called the Government of the People's Republic of Nagaland (GPRN). The GPRN sends emissaries abroad to garner support and raise funds for the Naga cause. It has an estimated 4,500 strong cadre base. It is supported by a section of Aos, Semas, Zeilangs, Anals, Maos and Manipur-based Tangkhul Nagas. The NSCN (IM) has been passing its annual budget to the tune of Rs 200 million to Rs. 250 million each year. It is alleged that drug trafficking from Myanmar is reported to be a major source of income for the NSCN-IM, and it also reportedly engages in extortion, bank robberies and other criminal pursuits to obtain finance. NSCN-IM uses money earned through narcotics trade to buy arms and also pay for training of their cadres. http://www.satp.org/satporgtp/countries/india/states/nagaland/terrorist_outfits/Nscn_im.htm)

Linkages of NSCN-IM

Insurgents of the National Socialist Council of Nagaland (Isak-Muivah group) are reportedly being trained at two camps in Pakistan.The NSCN-IM has linkages with the Naga groups operating in Myanmar. The outfit also runs camps for training other militant outfits on a purely mercenary basis. They have established reliable contacts for arms procurement in Thailand and other South East Asian nations, and have very well established links for transportation through Bangladesh and Myanmar. With the funds generated through its various financial operations, as well as from aid provided by the ISI, the NSCN-IM has purchased large stocks of Chinese AK rifles, machine guns, mortars and explosives from black markets in South East Asian and Bangladesh.

Prior to his arrest by Thai authorities in January 2000, Muivah was spotted in Karachi and was believed to have visited some other places as well in Pakistan, besides having met various people there. He was arrested at Bangkok on arrival on a flight from Karachi for travelling on a fake South Korean passport.

A top-NSCN-IM functionary was reportedly dispatched to strike a deal with Chinese officials in the Kunming province to provide them with a 'major arms consignment'; and the NSCN-IM was pleading with the Chinese to use their good offices to secure a passage for the consignment through the territory controlled by the Kachin rebels. Reports of February 2000 indicated that the NSCN-IM have a "full-fledged liaison office" in territories in China across the border with Arunachal Pradesh.

The outfit has also opened up contacts with international organisations like the UN Human Rights Organisation in Geneva, Unrepresented Nations People's Organisation (UNPO) at the Hague and the UN Working Group on Indigenous People (UNWGIP)

The NSCN (IM) has a group of its strong supporters in Thailand. Most of them operate front companies–mainly in travel and tourism, real estate and toy manufacture. The NSCN (IM) also has a large number of bank accounts in Thailand, Bangladesh and Burma. NSCN-IM's weapons are smuggled from the Thai-Cambodian border. Reports indicate that Pakistani embassy officials in Thailand provide assistance to the NSCN-IM and other North-Eastern insurgent groups in procuring weapons.

The NSCN (IM), as part of its strategy of insurgency, is playing the role behind the formation of several ethnic insurgent organisations among the different ethnic groups in the region. NSCN (IM), had masterminded A'Chik Liberation Matgrik Army (ALMA), a Garo insurgent organization. The sole motive behind floating this organisation was to make a quick fortune at gunpoint. It seems that the Garo youths having little experience of underground life, joined the ALMA only due to the lure of easy money. They were then trained by NSCN- (IM) activists. During its three year existence, a series of bank robberies were jointly undertaken by ALMA and NSCN (IM) in the Garo Hills. It is learnt that 70 per cent of the booty collected from such joint operations used to go to NSCN (IM) as charges for its services and for arms and ammunitions, while the remaining 30 per cent was left with the ALMA as a reward for its local cover. NSCN (IM) had similar links with Dimasa National Volunteers (DNV) of North Cachar Hills (Assam) as well as Hmar People's Convention (HPC) (Mizoram) (Dinesh Kotwal, The Naga Insurgency: The Past And The Future)

NSCN (IM) has also brought outfits like People's United Liberation Front (PULF), Muslim United Liberation Tigers of Assam (MULTA), and Zomi Revolutionary Army (ZRA), under its fold.. Floating of such smaller ethnic insurgent groups serve two broad purposes for NSCN (IM). First, it opens up multiple fronts for the counter–insurgency agencies like police, army, intelligence, etc., and keeps them busy elsewhere rather than concentrating in the strongholds of the core insurgent group. Second, it helps the core insurgent group to mobilise additional resources from areas beyond its sphere of influence as well as provides the necessary cover–ups for its operations in an altogether different ethno–social milieu. Further, the act of engineering insurgent movements among the different ethnic groups also fits into the NSCN (IM) strategy to turn its own war with the Indian State into a war of the nationalities of the region. The NSCN (IM) has resolved to form a United Front by coordinating the activities of the other ethnic insurgent groups. The formation of United Liberation Front of the Seven Sisters (ULFSS) in 1993 under the leadership of NSCN (IM), is a pointer in this regard. (Dinesh Kotwal, The Naga Insurgency: The Past and The Future)

National Socialist Council of Nagaland (Khaplang) (NSCN-K)

The National Socialist Council of Nagaland–Khaplang (NSCN-K) was formed on April 30, 1988 following an assassination attempt on the General Secretary of what emerged as the rival outfit–NSCN (IM)–Thuingaleng Muivah. Clannish divisions among the Nagas (Konyaks and Tangkhuls) were the primary reason behind the split of the NSCN in 1988. The Konyaks formed the NSCN-K (Khaplang) under the leadership of Khole Konyak and S S Khaplang. The Tangkhul faction, the NSCN-IM (Isak-Muivah), was led by Isak Chisi Swu and T. Muivah. Mr. S S Khaplang is the Chairman of the NSCN(K). N Kitovi Zhimomi acts as the General Secretary and Akaho Asumi is the Publicity Secretary. The primary objective of the NSCN-K is the establishment of a "Greater Nagaland" comprising of the Naga dominated areas of the neighbouring States within India, and contiguous areas in Myanmar. The NSCN-K runs a government-in-exile called the Government of the People's

Republic of Nagaland (GPRN, NSCN-K.) The General Head Quarters (GHQ) of the GPRN,NSCN-K is located in Eastern Nagaland (Myanmar). Kitovi Zhimomi is the self-styled "Prime minister of the Government of the People's Republic of Nagaland". For generation of finance, the group reportedly indulges in kidnapping, extortion and other terrorist activities. The NSCN-K accounted for 62 civilian and 26 security forces' fatalities during the period 1992 to 2000, and lost 245 of its men over this period. The NSCN (K) also runs trainings for other North East insurgent groups such as PREPAK, United Liberation Front of Assam (ULFA) and United National Liberation Front (UNLF). The group is reported to have training camps and its headquarters in Myanmar. "The NSCN (K) Headquarters along with some mobile camps are located in remote areas of northwestern Burma, bordering with India. Mr S.S Khaplang said "he continues to stick to the demand for Naga sovereignty and his organization will take up the issue of Naga-inhabited areas in Burma with the Burmese Government only after it sorted out the problem of Naga areas in India.

In April, 1990, A.Z. Phizo died in London after living in self exile in London since 1957. Some of his supporters called a meeting and passed on the mantle of NNC leadership to his daughter, Adino–leading to formation of their own parallel NNC.

Rivalry between two NSCN(IM) and NSCN(K) and Unification Attempts :

The two warring factions are engaged in a bitter fratricidal war for territorial supremacy with at least 200 cadres killed during the past several years. Hundreds of police and paramilitary troopers were deployed in Nagaland (Tuesday, 17 April, 2007) after six people were killed in clashes between rival tribal separatist groups. On 12 September, 2007 the Nagaland Baptist Church Council (NBCC), National Socialist Women Organization of Nagalim (NSWON) and Western Sumi Totimi Hoho (WSTH) have condemned the killings of five NSCN (IM) activists that also included Chaplain P.K Stone and his wife Maireila, whose bodies were recovered near Jotsoma village, Kohima on September 9.The five NSCN (IM) activists were killed after abduction while they were coming to Dimapur from Ukhrul in a Bolero.

Tangkhuls are the backbone of NSCN-IM military outfit. They are considered most ruthless and also more numerous. They, it is feared, would outnumber most of the 16 major Naga communities of Nagaland and would be in a position to control the state not only politically but also would be disturbing peace in the state. They say that Tangkhuls in Manipur are not Nagas and should not be integrated into Naga society of Nagaland. The Nagas in

Nagaland, Aaos, Angamis, Phom and even NSCN (Khaplang) recently opposed the move of Manipur Tangkhuls to allow them to be a part of Nagaland Board of Secondary Education. They have burnt Manipuri language textbooks and demanding separation from Manipur to join Nagaland Board of Secondary Education. The Nephu Rio government at one stage had almost acquiesced to their demand but had to backtrack because of severe protest from almost all the major 16 Naga tribes from Nagaland.

The Nephu Rio ministry is perceived to have won the elections with forceful support of the NSCN (IM). It is alleged that the NSCN (IM) group with every passing day has been treating the Naga people in a ruthless manner. A number of Nagaland University students talking on condition of anonymity said that they wanted the settlement to be made at a wider level and not restricted to the NSCN(IM)group. Some of them said that the NSCN (IM)group had been torturing Naga people to extort money and other favours. Recently women in Mokokchung alleged that the NSCN (IM) activists not only demanding money and chicken but they also raped some of the Ao girls. In the recent past. NSCN (IM) men were involved in raping girls in the Chakasang area.

The younger generation feels that if any understanding is reached with NSCN(IM) it would be an injustice to most of the Nagas and lead to bloodbath.

The NSCN (K) issued "Quit Nagaland Notice" to Tangkhul Nagas. Sometime back NSCN-IM had given such quit notices to Kukis, who are a major strength for the Khaplang group. The NSCN (K) Chairman felt that the activities of the Tangkhul members in the NSCN (IM) "might necessitate" the NSCN (K) Council of *kilonsers* (ministers) to take the drastic decision of branding all the community members a partner in "criminalisation". Khaplang also said the community was a victim of its "own terrorism" and called upon all the right-minded citizens of the tribe to raise their voice against such forms of terrorism.

Most Nagas now do not consider the faction of Muivah as representing cause of Nagas. They said that Muivah does not have the right to speak on behalf of Nagas. Muivah in fact is not even considered a "Naga". He is considered as a Manipuri by the influential Angamis and Ao Nagas as he is from the Tangkhul community of Manipur. Isak is a Sema but Semas now have started feeling that Isak is only playing a second fiddle to Muivah.

Muivah has not ruled out a one to one interaction with the Khaplang faction for the greater cause of "Naga unity". A section of Naga insurgents led by Azheto Chophy of the NSCN (IM) and C. Singson of the NSCN (K) signed a "Joint Declaration" at Niuland near Dimapur, which claimed that the two warring factions are being united. The new group, reportedly stationed at Vihokhu near Dimapur town, seeks to unite all Naga insurgent groups for the common cause. In its view, Muivah has been an obstacle to the unification of Nagas. Mr. S.S. Khaplang has said that he was not averse to unification between the two NSCN factions, provided NSCN (IM) leaders Isak Chishi Swu and Thuingaleng Muivah wrote to him directly. Khaplang also wants the NSCN (IM) leadership to "withdraw their charter of demands which has been submitted to New Delhi for federal relationship between the India and Nagalim". Senior *kilonsers* Kughalu Mulatonu and A.Z. Jamir and Kitovi Zhimomi want unification, but minus the Tangkhuls, who are dominant force in the NSCN (IM) hierarchy.

Both the NSCN factions are operating a ceasefire with New Delhi - the NSCN-(IM) is holding peace talks after the group entered into a truce in 1997. The NSCN-(K) is yet to begin formal talks with New Delhi although the group signed a ceasefire pact with the Central Government in 2001. Even as peace talks in Nagaland are progressing, there are serious apprehensions that the state is heading for a bloodbath. The talk of an interim government to be headed by the NSCN-(IM), instead of happiness, has caused serious concern to the Naga society. Nobody seems to trust the course of the talks. "The talks have been in vain and will achieve nothing even in 100 years unless all the Nagas stand united," (A brief history of Naga Insurgency, retrieved from http://en.wikipedia.org/wiki/National_Socialist_Council_of_Nagaland).

Peace Process

Prime Minister P.V. Narasimha Rao set the ball rolling by meeting with Isak Chishi Swu and T. Muivah in Paris on June 15, 1995. During the talks Mr. Rao underlined the Government's stand: "We must solve the problem through political talks and dialogue".

Prime Minister H.D. Deve Gowda went as far as sending the former Union Minister for State, Rajesh Pilot in November 1996 on a trip to Bangkok for bringing the NSCN (IM) to the path of negotiation. Mr. Deve Gowda and NSCN (IM) leaders met on February 3, 1997, in Zurich, Switzerland. The ceasefire with NSCN (IM) came into force in August 1997.

The ceasefire has been in force since then with several rounds of talks taking place first with Swaraj Kaushal as the interlocutor and then with the former Home Secretary, K. Padmanabhiah. Swaraj Kaushal, who made an irresponsible statement "wherever they are, we observe cease-fire, even abroad... it covers Delhi and even Paris," (Shantanu Nandan Sharma,The Naga Question:Violence and the Peace Process). This shows his complete ignorance of the complexities of the Naga insurgency problem. G.K. Pillai, the then Joint Secretary (North East) in the Ministry of Home Affairs (MHA) later clarified that "the cease-fire area is limited only to the State of Nagaland." This was done on the protest by Manipur.

However, the peace process entered a crucial phase with the NSCN (Khaplang) faction formally announcing its unilateral cease–fire decision on April 9, 2000 and indicating that it is willing to hold peace talks with the Centre.

The Nagaland Chief Minister, Mr. S.C. Jamir met both the Prime Minister and the Union Home Minister and urged them to include the NSCN (K) in the process.

The Nagaland Chief Minister, who escaped a major attempt on his life on November 29, 1999 reportedly wanted Muivah in captivity. Mr. S.C.Jamir suspected that an attempt on his life might be the handiwork of NSCN (IM).

The Government of India found out that Muivah was in Pakistan during the peace negotiations. It was alleged that he might be plotting against India with the help of the ISI by organising the transport of weapons from Thailand to the Northeast through Myanmar. It was estimated that more than 250 NSCN cadres had completed their training in the past while they engaged the Union Government in peace talks. It also maintained that the NSCN had violated the truce conditions. It was also apprehensive that the NSCN (IM) was using the ceasefire period for stockpiling of weapons.

(1) In the first place, the Isak–Muivah leadership has shown no flexible attitude for a negotiated settlement.

(2) Another major hindrance to carry on the process for peace in Nagaland is the existence of more than one organisation, each claiming to be representative of Naga people. The announcement by the Government of India to involve the NSCN (K) faction in the peace process met with a veritable wave of protests launched by the powerful Naga Hoho and the Nagaland People's Council (NPC).

(3) The demand of the NSCN, which would involve slicing off parts of three neighbouring states of Manipur, Assam and Arunachal Pradesh is strongly opposed by the Government of India and three neighbouring states of Manipur, Assam and Arunachal Pradesh.

No authority at the Centre can afford to bypass the State Governments as these demands direct affect them and also the law and order is a state subject. On 13 September, 2007, United Nations General Assembly has adopted the Declaration on the Rights of Indigenous Peoples which has immensely boosted the morale of the NSCN-IM. In a statement issued on 15 September, 2007, the NSCN-IM said that Article 3 of the UN Declaration has added a new dimension to the Indo-Naga issue. The Article 3 of the UN Declaration says "Indigenous peoples have the right of self-determination. By virtue of that they freely determine their political status and freely pursue their economic, social and cultural development. (Dinesh Kotwal, The Naga Insurgency: The Past And The Future)

The British Role –

The British Crown allowed Christian missionaries to proselytize among the tribal population. The Land of the Nagas was identified as "virgin soil" for planting Christianity. "*Among* a people so thoroughly primitive, and so independent of religious profession, we might reasonably expect missionary zeal would be most successful," stated the 1875 document, as quoted in the "Descriptive Account of Assam," by William Robinson and Angus Hamilton. *Missionaries* were also encouraged to open government-aided schools in the Naga Hills. Between 1891 and 1901, the number of native Christians increased by 128%.

Phizo left Nagaland hiding in a coffin. He then showed up in 1963 in Britain, holding a Peruvian passport. It is strongly suspected that the British Baptist Church, which is very powerful in Nagaland, is the contact between British intelligence and the Naga undergrounds operating on the ground at that time.

Once Phizo arrived in Britain, Lord Bertrand Russell courted Phizo, and became his new friend. Russell was deeply impressed with Phizo's "earnestness" for a peaceful settlement. What, perhaps, impressed Russell the most is that Phizo had control over the militant Nagas, who had launched a movement under the Naga National Council (NNC) to secede from the Indian Republic. In a letter dated Feb. 12, 1963, Sir Bertrand Russell told Indian Prime Minister Jawaharlal Nehru, "I find it hard to understand the difficulty of coming to an agreement which would put an end to the very painful occurrences incidental to the present policy of India."

It is believed in some circles that New Delhi's 1964 ceasefire with the Nagas might have been influenced by the letter from Russell that was handed to Nehru by Rev. Michael Scott. Rev. Michael Scott later went to Nagaland as part of a peace mission, along with B.P. Chaliha and Jaya Prakash Naraya.

While Lord Bertrand Russell was pushing Nehru to make the Nagas an independent country through peaceful negotiations, British involvement in direct conflict continued. On Jan. 30, 1992, soldiers of the Assam Rifles arrested two British nationals along the Nagaland-Burma border. David Ward and Stephen Hill posed as members of BBC-TV, and were travelling in jeeps with Naga rebels carrying arms. Subsequent interrogation revealed that both were operatives of Naga Vigil, a U.K.-based group. Both Ward and Hill claimed that they started the organization while in jail, influenced by Phizo's niece, Rano Soriza. Both have served six-year prison terms for various crimes in Britain. Naga Vigil petitioned for their release in the Guwahti High Court. Phizo's niece took up the issue with then-Nagaland Chief Minister Vamuzo. **(Ramtanu Maitra,** *The Indian North East,Next week: "Baluchistan and FATA in Pakistan."* *(*http://wondersofpakistan.wordpress.com/2009/04/23/south-asian-terrorism-all-roads-lead-to-the-british-empire/*)*

The role of British is mainly –information sharing, guiding, encouraging, supporting the Naga National movement from the time of formation of the Naga Club in 1918, visit of Simon Commission in 1929 and Cabinet Mission in 1946 as has been mentioned above. The British helped the Nagas to internationalise the Naga issues using the Church and Christian network as early as 1964 from the time of Rev. Michael Scott. and 1970 from the time of Mr. Raymond Hutchinson.

The US Role

Till the beginning of 1971, the USA continued to be the patron of the insurgents, though the actual supplies of arms and ammunitions from this source were not always steady. Bangkok became the Operational Headquarters of the C.I.A. Arms flowed from Bangkok liberally to any group that wanted to embark on adventure. Besides, Pakistan provided the insurgents with transit camps, training centrers and a route to Bangkok and Peking. Dacca–Bangkok–London–Pindi–Peking channel was used to operate on the common ground of "hatred towards India".

As early as 1950s, the C.I.A. had extended its activities into Nagaland and was financing the underground movement in Nagaland. "American spies handed the tribal leaders several million rupees, weapons and secret instructions prepared in Washington". A journalist Dhruva Mazumdar, the author of 'Confession of a Journalist', states that he was paid by the C.I.A. to file reports from Northeastern India on movements of the Indian Army and "barrack room gossip". Again, it was before Bangladesh was liberated that the U.S.A. and some other western powers hatched a conspiracy to create an "Independent Bengal" comprising East Pakistan, West Bengal, Assam, Nagaland, Manipur, Tripura, Sikkim and Bhutan. The "Blueprint of this design was spelt out in a Dacca datelined dispatch circulated by Agencies International De Presa (International Press Agency) on December 7, 1963". The separatist leaders are said to have accepted the plot of independent Bengal with its capital in Calcutta. It promised the Nagas and Mizos of 'Greater Nagaland' and 'Greater Mizoram' as autonomous units within the framework of 'Great Bengal'. (Dinesh Kotwal, The Naga Insurgency: The Past And The Future)

The Chinese Role

There has always been a permanent representative of the Federal Government of Nagaland (FGN)in Beijing. The Beijing leadership took batches of Naga youths to different places in China in order to give them training. In 1996, the first batch of Naga army led by Muivah and Thinusellie returned from China with huge quantities of arms and ammunitions. But it was mainly from 1972 that Beijing stepped up its help to the Naga insurgents. On 19 June, 1968, the Indian External Affairs Ministry summoned the Chinese Charge 'd Affair and officially charged the Chinese Government with aiding and abetting the Naga insurgents. The Taiwanese Foreign Minister, De Wei Tao–Ming accused the Chinese Government on 22 October, 1969 of helping and training hundreds of Naga guerrillas in the Yunnan province and sending them back to fight the Indian Government. (M. Horam, Naga Insurgency, Cosmo Publications, New Delhi, 1988). Mr. Kukhato Sema, Fedral Prime Minister reportedly told the Chinese Prime Minister Mr. Chou En Lai that Nagaland would give full support to his country if China attacked India through Nagaland".

Batches of Naga insurgents went to China where they were welcomed as "brothers". In early 1975, a strong contingent of underground Nagas led by Muivah and Isaac went to China. However, Muivah could not penetrate back into Nagaland and Manipur. So, they established the Beijing backed camp in the Sahpa village in northeastern Myanmar where a large number of undergrounds lived. Since then this area has become a meeting point and training centre of the insurgent organisations of Northeastern India. It was reported that the leadership of the Burmese camp of the Nagas signed an agreement of "mutual–co–operation" and "assistance" with the Communist Party of China instead of with the Government.

In 1987, there was a report in the newspapers that the Chinese had withdrawn the support to the insurgents. (Dinesh Kotwal, The Naga Insurgency: The Past And The Future)

The Role of Pakistan and Bangladesh

In early 1962, Kaito Sema, the commander–in–chief of the Naga home guards went to Pakistan for training and to acquire arms for terrorist activities in India. On May 20, 1962, Phizo visited Karachi to oversee the training of the Naga underground men. Phizo, in a thankful mood towards Pakistan said in London on May 8, 1963, that in case of a plebiscite, Nagas would also have the choice to join Pakistan. Between 1962 and 1968, ten Naga groups visited Pakistan to procure monetary help and weaponry from Pakistan. By 1963, the first batch of 173 trained underground Army men returned to Nagaland from East Pakistan (now Bangladesh) and they brought 12 two-inch mortars, 16 light machine guns, 30 stenguns, 20 pistols, 100 rifles, 190 hand grenades and 74 strim grenades and other ammunitions and explosives. By October, 1963, the second batch of 202 Nagas left for East Pakistan via Burma for seeking arms and training and they returned with huge quantities of arms and ammunitions. The third party of 150 Nagas returned in June, 1964 via Burma with various kinds of arms and ammunitions. The erstwhile East Pakistan had trained some 2,500 Naga underground men and had supplied a large amount of money and arms. Recently, Muivah was in Karachi before flying to Bangkok on January 19, 2000, where he was arrested by the Thai police on charges of travelling on a forged passport and subsequently for jumping bail.

(http://www.satp.org/satporgtp/countries/india/states/nagaland/terrorist_outfits/Nscn_im.htm)

What had led Britain, USA, China, Bangladesh, and Pakistan to extend support is not their genuine love for the people of Nagaland or the Northeast India. The support is not for the real liberation of these people who have grievances. Their main purpose was probably to destabilize and weaken India. (Dinesh Kotwal, The Naga Insurgency: The Past and The Future). However, recently Bangladesh has promised not to give shelter to any insurgent groups from the north eastern India.

Linkage with Burmese Insurgents

The Naga underground groups are taking shelter and having close links with the Burmese insurgent groups like Karen National Defence Organisation, who are fighting for an independent Karen Country as late as

1960. They are also working with the Kachin Independent Army who are demanding for Independent Kachinland. They are having a close liaison with the Shan United Army, Zomi Liberation Front in the Chin Hills, the Arakan Independent Army etc.

Linkages with International Organisations

The NSCN (I–M) has extended its activities even abroad linking up with such international organizations like the UN Human Rights Organisation in Geneva, the Unrepresented Nations People's Organisation (UNPO) at the Hague and the UN Working Group on Indigenous People to further its campaign of self–determination.

On April 24, 1998 the Chairman of the NSCN addressed the United Nations Commission on Human Rights at Geneva. He described the Nagas as a "distinct people" and nation of about three million people, occupying an area of one hundred thousand square km that is, as alleged, "under occupation by the Indian and Burmese armed forces."

Linkage with Local Insurgent Groups :

The NSCN is the oldest and one of the most experienced, well trained insurgent group in the North East India. The NSCN (IM) provided logistic support to various ethnic insurgent groups in the region like the ULFA, NDFB, NLFT, PLA, etc., and its approval of the terrorism in Punjab as well as militancy in Jammu and Kashmir. It has got links with many insurgent groups like Dimasa National Volunteers (DNV) of North Cachar Hills (Assam), Hmar People's Convention (HPC) (Mizoram), Hynniewtrep National Liberation Council (HNLC), A'chik National Volunteers Council (ANVC) of Meghalaya, National Democratic Front of Bodoland of Assam,National Liberation Front of Tripura (NLFT), Muslim United Liberation Tigers of Assam (MULTA), and Zomi Revolutionary Army (ZRA), People's United Liberation Front (PULF). (Dinesh Kotwal, The Naga Insurgency: The Past And The Future)

These organisations have been involved in killings, kidnappings and extortions. Some of the underground organizations have their bases in Jiribam in the Imphal East district of Manipur.

NSCN's communal card of discrimination, Oppression, Slavery, exploitation of Nagas by the Meiteis

Why is Muivah playing the communal cared against the Meiteis? The sovereignty or independence of NagaI and is out of question. His vision of

Greater Nagaland or Nagalim is very dim. He set an unilateral agenda to create a greater Nagaland or Nagalim by slicing four districts from Manipur, some parts of Assam and Arunachal Pradesh. The Government of India has repeatedly told Muivah that the settlement of Naga issues may be within the Indian Constitution but the boundaries of other states will not disturbed. He is getting old and he wants a settlement which is honourable to him in person. He is reportedly not in good health. He is very desperate to fulfill his dream ofNagalim in his life time. Assam did not react because imposing the same kind of economic blockade in Assam will lead to starvation in Nagaland. So Assam do not consider this as an important issue. Similarly, Arunachal can not touched be by Nagaland in any respect. But Manipur is highly vulnerable as the life line NH-39 passes through Nagaland and Naga inhabited areas of Senapati district. He has quoted examples from the Manipur history during the Maharaja's time to justify his statement and inflame the innocent minds of the common Nagss.

That is why T. Muivah played a communal card against the Meiteis to achieve his objective to create enmity and hatred between the Nagas and the Meiteis.

NSCN (1M) adopted four main strategies

1. Imposition of frequent economic blockade in National Highway no39 and NH-53 at their own sweet will
2. Spreading the rumour of discrimination, oppression, ill-treatment, exploitation of Nagas by the Meiteis.
3. Imposition of illegal tax by the NSCN (IM) raging from Rs. 5000-15,000 per truck per trip, which will earn croes of Rupees every month forNSCN(lM).
4. The Naga areas are left under-developed by the Meiteis.

Impsition of economic blaockade by the Nagas is the easiest and most effective way of oppressing the majority Meiteis.{In 2010, the ANSAM (7AH Naga Students AssociatioikL-Manipur), UNC (United Naga Council) Naga Hoho which are considered as the over ground wing of NSCN(IM) imposed an economic blockade on NH-39 and NH-53 with effect from II April, 2010 protesting against the Manipur Government's refusal to Muivah to come to his home village, Somdal and holding of Autonomous District Council election in Manipur. The Naga Students Federation of Nagai and jumped into the fray and banned all Manipur bound vehicles passing through Nagaland followed by burning of trucks and intimidation and abduction of drivers. Later on the frustrated Neiphew Rio, Chief Minister of Nagaland openly supported the illegal movement of the Naga Orgnizations and also the economic blockade. On 5 May, 201 Oz.-there was a stand-off between NSCN(lM) and the Government of Manipur on the issue of T. Muivah's visit to his ancestral home village. The Home Ministry of Government of India sent a copy of the tour programme of T. Muivah to the Manipur State Government.His tour programme included addressing a series of public meetings in Naga inhabited areas of Ukhrul and Senapati district. The hidden agenda of T.Muivah was to spread the venom of communal hatred against the Meiteis in order to win the Nagas over the issue of Greater Nagaland or NagalilTf2,. Knowing the gravity of the situation and to avert any possible communal riot in Manipurf_the State Government of Manipur refused entry of Muivah to Manipur, which was endOrsed and appreciated by all non- Nagas in Manipur. Eventually the Government of India asked T. Muivah to leave Vishwema where he had been camping since 5 May, 2010. The economic blockade was lifted on 18, June, 2010.

Is it true that Nagas are discriminated, oppressed, ill-treated and exploited by the Meiteis, The Nagas gave the examples from the history of Manipur during the 18th century to beginning of 20th century when the Nagas were used as labourers, slaves and treated as untouchables.

The history of the world from 18th to middle of 20th century was full of instances of such discrimination, oppressiorf', ill-treatmenC, exploitation of minority groups by the majority all over the world. Manipur is notan exception Alexander, the Great (Alexander III of Macedon 1356-323 Be) tried to conquer the world because he believed that only the Greeks were chosen by God to rule the world. The root cause of second world war was Hitler's belief that the inequality of races is inevitable and only the Nazis are the best race (volkJ6-who should rule the worldrMein Kampf ('My Struggle') published in 1923, http://academic.sun. ac.zalforlanglberghlan/reallholocaustlholo8.htm)

Discrimination - The worst form of discrimination in India was the "untouchability" which is the social exclusion of people because of the population they are born into -used to be common in Europe, India, Bangladesh, Burma, Japan, Korea, Nepal, Nigeria, Pakistan, Sri Lanka, Yemen and elsewhere.

In India, untouchability system is the longest surviving system of hereditary inequality in the world. In the Indian Hindu society, there are four castes -the Brahmins are the learned, the Kshatriyas are the warriors, the Vaishyas are the traders, and the Sudras perform menial tasks and physical labour. Brahmins are on the highest rung of the social hierarchy, and Sudras are on the lowest. The Sudras were denied the rights of participation in religious activities and even to read the sacred texts. The 'untouchables (Harijans/ Dalits) are outside the caste system, and placed even lower than the Sudras in society. The untouchable included people whose occupations or habits of life involved activities considered to be polluting, such as taking life for a living (e.g., fishermen); killing or disposing of dead cattle or working with their hides; coming into contact with human waste (e.g., sweepers); and eating flesh of cattle, pigs, or chickens. The 'untouchables were not only barred from the temples, but also from the roads leading to the temple. They lived outside the city, and not only the touch, but even the sight of them was considered impure. An 'untouchable' had to carry an earthen pot around his neck so that his spittle may not pollute the earth. In Maharashtra, an 'untouchable' wore a black thread either in his neck or on his wrist for ready identification, while in Gujarat a horn had to be worn for identification. Intermarriage between castes and eating with a member of another caste is strictly forbidden even today by Hindu caste society. (http://american - almanac.tripod.com/untouch.htmhttp:/ /american - almanac.tripod.com/un touch.htm)

The untouchables were not allowed to wear decent clothes, ride on a horse during marriage processions, draw water from the village well or remain seated while an upper caste person was standing. Many untouchables converted to other religions such as Buddhism and Christianity to escape discrimination.

During the initial days of the British rule, caste system was encouraged. The British policies of "divide and rule" as well as enumeration of the population into rigid categories during the 10 year census contributed towards the hardening of caste system in India. Mahatma Gandhi launched the war against untouchability with the "epic fast" of Sept. 20-26, 1932. Gandhi was arrested by the British and was imprisoned in the Yervada jail near Pune. Gandhi had warned as early as Sept. 13, 1932 that he would undertake the fast in protest against the "Communal A ward" of the British Government. Under the "divide-and-conquer" tactics. the British were to establish a separate electorate for the untouchables, and the British had succeeded in winning over lower caste leaders to the idea. Despite Gandhi's threats, the British executed the Communal Award, in the name of "democracy". The 'untouchables' constitute 15% of the total population of the Indian sub-continent and have been referred to as Depressed Classes, Scheduled Castes and Scheduled Tribes. In 1947, untouchability was banned by the Indian constitution established after independence from the British. More than 60 years after Independence, untouchability is still alive and thriving in

India's hinterlands. (http://timesofindia.indiatimes.com/indial After-60-yrs-of-Independence-untouchabi I ity-alive-and-kicking-in-Indialarticleshow/4850136.cms). Even in Radhanagar in Hooghly district, the birthplace of social reformer Raja Ram Mohan Roy, there are separate crematoria for Brahmins and non-Brahmins. And in a bizarre case in Waganagere village in Gulbarga district of Karnataka, 120 Dalit households were forced to draw water from their well even after a dog fell in and died. During festivities, not only are they served food separately, but they have to bring their own plates and tumblers. (http://www.iheu.org/node/1814). In UP, almost every village has a chamar toli, a place segregated for them. Dalit children are made to sit separately in schools. In Malasa village in Kanpur Dehat, though the post of gram pradhan was reserved for scheduled castes, it has been lying vacant as no Dalit has the courage to contest the election, fearing backlash from the dominant Thakurs. And when they do so, as two Dalits did last year, their candidature was rejected because no one, not even Dalits, seconded them during the filing of nomination papers. In Rajpur tehsil, 60 km from Kanpur, Thakurs withdrew their children from a primary school after a Dalit cook was employed to prepare mid-day meals. Caste system is also prevalent among Christians. Christians in Kerala are divided into several communities, including Syrian Christians and the so-called "Latin" or "New Rite" Christians. The "New Rite "Christians were among the scheduled castes in the coastal belt of Kerala, where fishing was the primary occupation. They were actively converted by missionaries in the 16th and 19th centuries. Syrian Christians, especially Knanaya Christians are not allowed to intermarry with other Christian castes.

Discrimination is still prevalent in the modern times in many parts of the world. The mass demonstrations and riots against African students in Nanjing, China, lasted from December 1988 to January 1989. (Black Africa Leaves China In Quandary. The New York Times. December 30, 1988). Bar owners in central Beijing had been forced "not to serve black people or Mongolians" during the 2008 Summer Olympics. (Fears of a 'no-fun' Olympics in Beijing. The Age July 19, 2008) (http://en.wikipedia.org/wiki/Racism). Some 70,000 black African Mauritanians were expelled from Mauritania in the late 1980s. (Mauritania Fair elections haunted by racial imbalance. IRIN Africa. March 5, 2007.) In the Sudan, black African captives in the civil war were often enslaved, and female prisoners were often used sexually (Arab militia use 'rape camps' for ethnic cleansing of Sudan. Telegraph May 30, 2004.). According to Herbert Bix, Racial discrimination against other Asians was habitual in Imperial Japan. (Herbert Bix, *Hirohito and the Making of Modern Japan*, 2001, p. 280)

During the Congo Civil War (1998–2003), Pygmies were hunted down like game animals and eaten. Both sides of the war regarded them as "subhuman" and some say their flesh can confer magical powers. ("Dr.Congo Pygmies appeal to UN". BBC News. 2003-05-23. http://news.bbc.co.uk/2/hi/africa/2933524.stm. Retrieved 2010-05-23.)

The Pan-German League (*Alldeutscher Verband*), created in 1891, promoted German imperialism, "racial hygiene" thus justifying ethnic cleansing in order to achieve "racial purity" and also to achieve ethnic homogeneity in the nation-state.

On April 1, 1933, the Nazi boycott of Jewish businesses was observed throughout Germany. Only six days later, the Law for the Restoration of the Professional Civil Service was passed, banning Jews from government jobs. In May 1935, Jews were forbidden to join the *Wehrmacht* (the army). On 25 August 1933, the Nazis even signed the Haavara Agreement with Zionists to allow German Jews to emigrate to Palestine. On September 15, 1935 the "Law for the Protection of German Blood and Honor" was passed, preventing marriage between any Jew and non-Jews. At the same time, the "Reich Citizenship Law" was passed, which deprived the Jews of basic citizens' rights, e.g., the right to vote. In 1936, Jews were banned from all professional jobs, effectively preventing them from having any influence in education, politics, higher education, and industry.

Approximately six million European Jews (of two-thirds of the population of nine million Jews) were exterminated during World War II (1-9-1939- 2-9-1945) through a programme of systematic state-sponsored extermination by Nazi Germany. (Niewyk, Donald L. *The Columbia Guide to the Holocaust*, Columbia University Press, 2000, p. 45) (Brian Levin, Director, Center for the Study of Hate and Extremism, California State University:" Huffingtonpost.com. http://www.huffingtonpost.com/brian-levin-jd/stone-cold-jew-baiting_b_659335.html. Retrieved 2010-07-31). The persecution and genocide were carried out in stages. Legislation to remove the Jews from civil society was enacted years before the outbreak of World War II. Concentration camps were established in which inmates were used as slave labour until they died of exhaustion or disease. Where the Third Reich conquered new territory in eastern Europe, specialized units called Einsatzgruppen murdered Jews and political opponents in mass shootings. Jews and Romani were confined in overcrowded ghettos before being transported by freight train to extermination camps where, if they survived the journey, the majority of them were systematically killed in gas chambers. Every arm of Nazi Germany's bureaucracy was involved in the logistics of the mass murder, turning the country into what one Holocaust scholar has called "a genocidal state". (Berenbaum, Michael. *The World Must Know", United States Holocaust Museum*, 2006, p. 103.)

Slavery

Slavery existed in all societies throughout the world in all ages, in which one human being is legally the property of another, can be bought or sold, is not allowed to escape and must work for the owner without any choice involved.

Slavery and Christianity : Slavery in different forms existed within Christianity for over 18 centuries. The Bible uses the Hebrew term *ebed* to refer to slavery. (*Jewish Encyclopedia* (1901), article on *Slaves and Slavery).* The Bible does not regard slavery as an abomination, and regulates its practice, and occasionally compels the enslavement of others. (Deuteronomy 21:10-11, http://en.wikipedia.org/wiki/Christianity_and_ slavery) For many centuries, the Church was part of a slave-holding society. The Church accepted slavery as a social institution even into the Medieval period. Christianity rarely criticised the actual *institution* of slavery. No pope or council ever made a sweeping condemnation of slavery as such. The popes themselves held slaves, including at times hundreds of Muslim captives to man their galleys. American Catholic Church continued to support slaveholding interests until the abolition of slavery. No Father or Doctor of the Church advocated for abolition of slavery. (Avery Dulles, http://en.wikipedia.org/wiki/Christianity_and_ slavery)

Slavery in India : Slavery existed in India since ancient times. Most extensive records of the Mughal Badsha's interest in the slave trade is available for Shah Jahan (1630 C.E. - 1658 C.E). (Badshah Nama, Abdul Hamid Lahori). Abd Allah Khan Firuz Jang, governor of Kalpi and Kher and, in the process of subjugating the local rebels, "beheaded the leaders and enslaved their women, daughters and children, who were more than 200,000 in number". (Francisco Pelsaert, A Dutch Chronicle of Mughal India, translated and edited by Brij Narain and Sri Ram Sharma (Lahore, 1978), p. 48). When Shah Shuja was appointed as governor of Kabul he carried on a ruthless war in the Hindu territory beyond Indus, in which the captured women were distributed among Muslim Mansabdars. (Niccolao Manucci, Storia do Mogor, or Mogul India 1653-1708, 4 vols, translated by W. Irvine London, 1907-8). Under Shah Jahan, peasants were compelled to sell their women and children. The peasants were carried off to various markets and fairs to be sold with their poor unhappy wives carrying their small children crying and lamenting. Shah Jahan had decreed that they should be sold to Muslim lords. (Badshah Nama, Qazinivi, Badshah Nama, Abdul Hamid Lahori)

Slavery was practiced throughout colonial India in various manifestations. In reality, the movement of Indians and Afghans to the Bukharan slave markets did not cease and Indian slaves continued to be sold in the markets of Bukhara well into the nineteenth century..According to Sir Henry Bartle Frere (who sat on the Viceroy's Council), there were an estimated 8,000,000 or 9,000,000 slaves in India in 1841. In Malabar, about 15% of the population were slaves. Slavery was abolished in both Hindu and Muslim India by the Indian Slavery Act V. of 1843. Provisions of the Indian Penal Code of 1861 formally tried to abolish slavery in India by making the enslavement of human beings a criminal offense. However slavery appeared to survive as late as 1873. In Sylhet district (now part of Bangladesh) polygamy was widely practised, and wives, sisters and daughters were sometimes surrendered to a rich man or a debtor to be a slave for life.(Female slavery in India, The New York Times, Published: August 21, 1873. Vinod Patel 2008 Copyright © The New York Times)

Slavery in other cuntries :Britain played a prominent role in the Atlantic slave trade which began arounc the mid-fifteenth century. Romans inherited the institution of slavery from the Greeks (Slavery" The Encyclopedia Americana, 1981, page 19). Some 50,000 British convicts were sent to colonial America, representing perhaps one-quarter of all British emigrants during the eighteenth century (James Davie Butler, "British Convicts Shipped to American Colonies," *American Historical Review,* Vol. 2, No. 1 (Oct., 1896), pp. 12–33 in JSTOR)

The Arab slave trade lasted more than a millennium.. The Arab or Middle Eastern slave trade continued into the early 1900s, The Arab or Middle Eastern slave trade continued even to this day. As recently as the 1950s, Saudi Arabia had an estimated 450,000 slaves, 20% of the population

Slaves were slain and offered in sacrifice to the spirit of the owner when dead, or by him to his ancestors: sometimes given as a substitute to suffer the death penalty incurred by his owner or in fulfillment of a vow. Nearly all prostitutes are slaves. Some people sell their slaves girls to men wanting a wife for themselves or for a son of theirs. (William Mesny. (13 May 1905). *Mesny's Miscellany*, Vol. IV, p. 399.)

In Mauritania, it is estimated that up to 600,000 men, women and children, or 20% of the population, are currently enslaved, many of them used as bonded labour. Slavery in Mauritania was criminalized only in August 2007.

Slavery in North America : America was notorious for slavery. On October 12, 1492 (the first day Christopher Columbus e encountered the native people of the Americas), he wrote "The natives would make fine servants. With fifty men we could subjugate them and make them do whatever we want". The problem with dehumanizing people in order to take their land is that the next step is to take their lives also". These captives were later paraded through the streets of Barcelona and Seville when Columbus returned to Spain (Bourne, pp. 111-112; Page 18 of Hanke, L. (1949). *The Spanish struggle for justice in the conquest of America*. Philadelphia, PA: University of Pennsylvania Press,. http://www. nytimes.com/1989/11/04/opinion/l-slavery-and-colonialism-make-up-the-true-legacy-of-columbus-866089.html). Perhaps the most prominent and notable form of American racism began with the institution of slavery, during which Africans were enslaved and treated as property. After the institution of slavery, the status of Africans was stigmatized, and this stigma persisted up unto the late 20th century. According to the 1860 U.S. census, there were about 385,000 slave owners out of approximately 1.5 million white families. Slaves were used as a labour force in agricultural production, shipyards, docks, and as domestic servants By the 1860 United States Census, the slave population in the United States had grown to four million (Introduction – Social Aspects of the Civil War, National Park Service)

Approximately, there are 27 million slaves in the world today, more than at any point in history and more than twice as many as all African slaves who survived being taken to the Americas in the Atlantic slave trade (Bales, Kevin (1999). "1". *Disposable People: New Slavery in the Global Economy*. University of California Press. p. 9. ISBN 0-520-21797-7.)

The first African slaves arrived in Jamestown, Virginia in 1619, (David Brion Davis, *Inhuman Bondage: The Rise and Fall of Slavery in the New World*. Oxford University Press, 2006, p. 124). Native Americans, who have lived on the North American continent for at least 20,000 years faced wars, massacres, forced displacement (such as in the Trail of Tears), and the imposition of treaties. The territories of Native Americans, were forcibly taken and once their territories were incorporated into the United States, surviving Native Americans were denied equality before the law. The first two years of the "California Gold Rush" saw the deaths of thousands of Native Americans. Under Mexican rule in California, Indians were subjected to *de facto* enslavement under a system of peonage. Nonwhites were prohibited from testifying against whites, a prohibition extended to the Chinese. From 1981 to 1997, the United States Department of Agriculture discriminated against tens of thousands of African American farmers, denying loans provided to white farmers in similar circumstances. The discrimination was the subject of the Pigford v. Glickman lawsuit brought by members of the National Black Farmers Association, which resulted in two settlement agreements of $1.25 billion in 1999 and of $1.15 billion in 2009.

The truth is that slavery, discrimination, oppression, exploitation still exists in virtually every country of this world, according to human rights organisations, scholars and journalists. In fact, legal slavery did end. Slavery is illegal in every country of the world. However, there are more slaves today than ever before: 27 million, twice as many as the number of Africans enslaved during the four centuries of transatlantic slave trade.

Slavery used to be a practiced among the Nagas also. Among the Rengmas, the slaves were known by the names *menugetenyu* and *itsakesa.*

In Manipur, Vaishnavism became a state religion during the time of King Garib Niwaz (1709-48), and it was practically forced on the people.. Under the instruction from their Mayang Gurus, the Manipur kings practiced segregation or untouchability and discrimination between the Meiteis and Haos (Hill people); between Meitei Hindus and Lois and between Meitei Hindus and Yaithibis who eat beef, pog and chicken. But the untouchability and discrimination practiced in Manipur was not as severe as that of mainland India or other parts of thw world. Maharaja Churachand was notorious for his Mangba –Sengba culture (untouchability) which was the root cause of division between the Meiteis and the hill people. But it was not only the hill people who suffered but also the Meiteis at the hands of the Maharaja on account of Mangba –Sengba. The British encouraged the king to practice untouchability because that will help in conversion of non-Hindus into Christianity. For the first time, a Christian Missionary, William Pettigrew was allowed by the British Political Agent to work in Ukhrul among Tangkhuls on 10 February, 1897. The untouchability reached its zenith during the time of Maharaja Churachand. During 1891-1941. The spread of Christianity in Manipur also reached its zenith during 1891-1941.

It was not only the Nagas but also the Meiteis, who were equally suffering during the days of kings and Maharajas

1. Meiteis who refused to adopt Hinduism were treated as "outcasts and untouchables". They were sent to distant places as Lois. They were assigned to do some derogatory works like pottery, black smithy, rearing of silk worms etc.
2. Ordinary Meiteis people were assigned to do a specific work for the king. (see Chapter-4)

3. Ordinary Meiteis people were subjected Lallup Kaba (see Chapter-4)
4. Some of the Meiteis people were subjected Loipot Kaba (see Chapter-4)
5. Ordinary Meiteis people were subjected to Mangba –Sengba culture (see Chapter-4) Untouchability was practiced not only among the Nagas and Meiteis but also among the lois, Yaithibis and ordinary people.
6. Brahmin was considered as the highest class – all Meities were expected to prostrate before a Brahmin.

Slavery was prevalent in Manipur during the days of Kings and Maharajas although the nature and type of slavery was different. This is a part of the history. If we look at the history of Europe or America or mainland India, the discrimination, exploitation, oppression, ill-treatment of some minority groups by the majority community is everywhere. This is a history of the past.

What is more important is the history of today. Today, there is no caste system, no untouchability , no slavery, no discrimination, no oppression or no exploitation of Nagas or Kukis or any other population group by the Meiteis in Manipur.

Let us see who exploits whom from the following facts :-

1. Nagas in spite of their big territory can legally acquire land and settle in the small heartland of Meiteis (valley) whereas Meteis can not legally acquire land and settle in the Naga inhabited areas of the Hills. Presently, there are more than 20,000 elite Nagas, permanently settled in the valley with buildings
2. The Nagas are getting plumb post in the IAS, IPS and other All India services out of the reserved quota for "Schedule Tribes" whereas Meteies with much higher percentage of marks and higher population are denied this privilege.
3. The NSCN (IM) conducted ethnic cleansing operations from May 1992 to November 1995, in which more than 575 innocent Kuki civilians were shot or hacked to death by Naga militants in Manipur alone, whereas about 121 Kukis were liquidated in Nagaland, without counting the heads of missing persons. Altogether 230 Kuki hamlets and villages were burnt down and scores of Kuki villages were deserted out of sheer terror, taking the number of Kuki refugees to over 50,000. (Donn Morgan Kipgen, Kuki International Forum /USA, www.kukiforum.com). This shows that violence and oppressions are created by the Nagas not by the majority Meiteis.

4. The NSCN(IM) are extorting illegal tax ranging from 5000-25,000 per truck per trip to each commercial vehicle passing through Naga inhabited areas of Manipur, which runs into crores of Rupees every month.
5. The Meiteis passing through Naga inhabited areas of Manipur are often looted, harassed, bullied, beaten, even killed by the Nagas for no fault of theirs.
6. Meitei Truck drivers passing through NH-39 and NH-53 importing goods from outside the state are subjected to extortion, humiliation, beating and thrashed inhumanly by the Nagas as if it their birth right to do so. A number of truck drivers have been killed, some have gone missing and untraceable till date.
7. Meiteis have no choice but to buy the same goods at exorbitant prices in the valley.

Muivah claims that Meiteis are responsible for under development of Naga areas. First and foremost is the question of who are responsible for development of the Naga inhabited areas. Rishang Keishing, in spite of his belonging ness to minority Naga community was the Chief Minister of Manipur for three times (November, 1980- March, 1988). Shri Yangmasho Shaiza, another Naga was the Chief Minister of Manipur two times (July-December, 1974 and 1977-1979). Tribal development Minister was always a tribal- not a Meitei. Moreover, most of the key responsible post the rank of IAS officers are the tribal –not the Meiteis. Has any one of them done any worthwhile and tangible tribal development work till date ?

The fact is that most of the Naga politicians and bureaucrats do not want to go back to their native village. When a particular Naga MLA is elected, his first priority is to acquire a land and construct a house in Imphal. Their secnd priority is to purchase a flat in Delhi or other metropolitan cities. They constructed palatial buildings at Imphal, amassed huge sums of money and live like a king at Imphal. They need not pay income tax and nobody can question the source of their illegal money One particular D.C. of Tamenglong District was accused by his own people, the Nagas of having misappropriated huge sums of development fund. He has reportedly constructed a huge palatial building at Imphal and acquired many hectares of land in Imphal. Many a time, Naga MLAs in connivance with the transport contractors has misappropriated their own people's rice quota and other also other quota like CGI sheet, cement, fertilizers etc. The Naga political leaders wants to keep the Naga inhabited areas underdeveloped so as to enable them to blame th Meiteis. In the name of minority, they are exploiting the majority Meities.

North East and Muivah

North East India is like a sleeping giant. If the North States become united and tried to unify among themselves, that may become a deadly blow to India. India knows it very well about the unique identity of North East India in terms of physical features, culture, traditions, language etc. Moreover India do not forget the theory of a "Crown Colony" comprising of all states of North East. The North East India can exist itself independently as a sovereign country. It has got all the resources like petrol, diesel, gas and very rich in agricultural and forest products. North East (212186 sq.km) is bigger than more than 112 countries of the world. It is bigger than Bangladesh (144000 sq.km), Nepal(147,181 sq.km), Greece (131,057 sq.km), Cambodia (181,055 sq.km), South Korea (98480 sq.km)), Cuba (110860 sq.km), Sri Lanka (65,010 sq.km). If the "Chicken neck "comprising of about 25 km near Garo Hills and Siliguri is cut off, the Indian Army may not be able to penetrate North East. Moreover, Manipur was recognized as a nation state through various international treaties. Manipur is located in a strategic position. The Government of India since the time of Pandit Nehru wants to maintain Manipur as a buffer state, isolated and underdeveloped. They are more interested to keep Manipur in a perpetual conflict situation.

The North East India has got talented human resources who are fit to become Prime Ministers, Presidents, Ambassadors, Governors. But under the peculiar Indian democratic system, the prospect of any indigenous person from North East becoming Prime Minister or President of India is very remote. The political leaders and top bureaucrats of India are trying to keep North East always in a conflict situation and in turmoil by continuing the British policy of "Divide and Rule". Mr. T. Muivah becomes very handy in this game plan of Government of India and he become a willing puppet to achieve this goal. He can not see beyond the Nagas. He wants to fight with Manipur, Assam, Arunachal Pradesh to achieve his dream of integrating all Naga inhabited areas. With his advancing age, his frustrations is also mounting. Muivah will lose face and have a threat on his life if he returns empty handed with no take-home presents. He is in a big dilemma. The violence perpetuated by the UNC, ANSAM and other Naga Orgnaisations in the name of democracy shows their frustrations and rationality.

The Manipur Factor and the Peace Process

The Manipur factor is a very recent phenomenon in the Naga national movement. Today the Manipur factor poses the most formidable obstacle to the peace process of the Nagas because of the following factors :-

1. Manipur was a sovereign Kingdom with more than 2000 years of history with its own Kingdom, laws, rules, regulations, scripts, language etc. The Manipur language is included in the Schedule-VIII to the Indian Constitution. All the hill districts including Ukhrul, Senapati, Tamenglong and Chandel and all the tribes were under the Manipur King from time immemorial. The Tangkhuls, Maos, Marams, Kabuis and other Nagas were protecting the territorial integrity of Manipur for thousands of years. Four days before India's independence on 15 August 1947, the King of Manipur had signed the Standstill Agreement and the Instrument of Accession entrusting defence, communication and foreign affairs to the Government of India. Manipur then adopted a new state Constitution under which democratic elections to a State Assembly were held and Manipur had a democratically elected Government. The Manipur Maharaja Bodhchandra signed the Merger Agreement with the Government of India on 21st September, 1949. The Government of India and the Nagas can't afford to ignore the 2000-year old history of Manipur.
2. The Meiteis always supported the Nagas in their political aspirations. Two Tangkhul politicians, Yangmasho Shaiza and Rishang Keishang, in spite of their small size, have been Chief Ministers of Manipur with the strong support of the majority Meiteis. There is no love lost between Meiteis and the Nagas.
3. The Meiteis and Nagas have very close historical and cultural ties. Many Meiteis have been converted into Nagas and they have settled down in the hills. Similarly many Nagas have been converted into Meiteis and absorbed into the Meitei society. Presently around one hundred thousand Nagas are permanently settled in the valley and thousands of Naga women are part and parcel of the Meitei families. This ties can not be severed even with a major blood shed and civil war.
4. Christianity came to Manipur through the liberal outlook and generosity of the Manipur Maharaja. In fact, the first Christian convert was a Meitei from Imphal. Now, there are thousands of Meitei Christians working hand to hand with the Nagas in Churches.
5. In 1994 when the Nagaland Assembly called for the unification of all Naga areas, the Manipur State Assembly unanimously adopted a resolution to uphold the territorial integrity of Manipur, whole heartedly supported by the Chief Minister of Manipur, Rishang Keising, a Tangkhul Naga.

6. The possible effect of destroying the territorial integrity of Manipur can be gauged from the past few events in Manipur. Manipuri street protests against the cease-fire began as soon as the present ceasefire came to effect on 1 August 1997. On 4 August 1997, hundreds of thousands of people (more than 3 Lakhs people) participated in a protest rally in Imphal and the Manipur Legislative Assembly passed a resolution protesting the extension of the ceasefire. This was probably the biggest rally so far in India.

The mood that animated the spectacular protest in Manipur after the June 2001 announcement of the ceasefire having "no territorial limits" is best captured in the words of a Manipuri activist. "The people of Manipur naturally felt that their apprehension was now coming true. Feeling deeply betrayed, they rose in protest against the Central Government's decision. When the news of the signing of the 14 June agreement in Bangkok reached Manipur there was a general disbelief. Gloom was writ large on the people's faces. The initial general disbelief and gloom soon turned to an unprecedented demonstration of strong, powerful protests".

The Great June Uprising (18 June, 2001, see plate- 166) need no introduction. People came out to streets in hundreds of thousands (more than half a million) without any word all over the valley. The protest included general strikes, social boycott of all political parties, burnings of the Indian National flag and of effigies of Indian political leaders, attack on leading political leaders irrespective of party, burning of Manipur State Legislative Assembly, demolition of some MLAs' quarters, disarming of the Manipur police etc. This happened in spite of curfew imposed by the Manipur State Government. The worst disaster happened on 18 June, 2001 when there was a police firing leading to 18 deaths and hundreds of injuries. But people's tempo never died down. But not a single Manipuri Nagas was attacked –not even slapped. But fearing violence due to the tense situation, some educated Manipuri Nagas fled to Dimapur and gave false news to the national TV channels like NDTV that they were attacked. Since NDTV itself was more interested in creating a controversy and in giving sensational news, people lost faith in the NDTV. But since the reality was otherwise, it did not give any impact. The protests died down only after India's Home Minister announced on 27 July 2001 that the three words "without territorial limits" would be dropped from the agreement signed with the NSCN-IM regarding the scope of the cease-fire. This is nothing but lack of political maturity and lack of understanding about the complexities of the insurgency problem in the north eastern India on the part of the Government of India. Now Manipur is demanding for an amendment of the Indian Constitution to guarantee the inviolability of Manipur's borders. Since it had a definite historical international boundary at the time of the merger with India, the Government of India should not destroy these boundaries. No alien force nor internal contradictions can break the territorial integrity of Manipur (AMCTA, 2001: 38, 48). Nagaland should learn to respect the 2000 years old historical boundary of Manipur if they expect other people to respect their distinct identity.

Weakness of NSCN's demands for Greater Nagaland

The history of Naga National movement is a long and tragic history. Mr. A.Z. Phizo was a great and charismatic leader of not only the Nagas but of the North East. He was a far sighted, visionary man. The Nagas have suffered to the extreme and have made great sacrifice to achieve Independence.

In view of the changing world political scenario, it is now time to rethink their strategy and goals. Vision and ambition is one thing, practicality is another thing. The general views of the majority of the people of Manipur are in favour of non-territory solution to the Naga movement. They may think in terms of tangible results. It is their great wisdom to have dropped their earlier demand of Independence from India. By September, 1975 (Shillong Accord), the Naga underground leaders have agreed not to insist on independence. Now their demand is Greater Nagaland or Nagalim or Southern Nagaland. It is a great achievement for them to have raised from "a village republic" to Statehood. The following are some of the historical facts and the general views of the common people of Manipur.

1. The unique history of the Nagas is that they do not have any written history.. Nagas did not have a Raja or a King. Nagas did not have a well defined kingdom or territory. Even the term Naga was given by outsiders. Every village of every tribe was an independent republic in its own right. No tribe had ever ruled over any other tribe or any village over any other village. Naga society was literally the village. (Charles Chasie, The Naga Imbroglio - A personal perspective, United Publishers, Guwahati, 1999). Moreover, there are many tribes in the north eastern India having such similar history.

2. In the pamphlet entitled Bedrock of Naga Society published by the Nagaland State Congress Party (Chief minister S.C. Jamir /NPCC, 2000), they raised the question "is it really true that Nagas have been a separate independent entity from time immemorial ? The same pamphlet gave the answer as follows -

"The stark and inescapable truth is that neither did we have a definite and unified political structure and nor did we exist as a nation. We were actually a group of heterogeneous, primitive and diverse tribes living in far-flung villages that had very little in common and negligible contact with each other. Each village was practically an entity in itself. The main contact between villages was through the savage practice of headhunting. Mutual suspicion and distrust was rife. Internecine warfare was the order of the day. There was no trust or interaction between different tribes. In these circumstances, the question of a unified Naga nation did not arise (NPCC, 2000).

In this version of Naga history, the idea of Naga nationhood gained momentum in the 1950s. The plebiscite of 1951 when volunteers of the Naga National Council went to far-flung villages to collect thumb prints of every Naga to announce that 99.9% of the Nagas want independence emotionally integrated the various Naga tribes. The 16 points agreement was the result of an impasse. It had become evident that under no circumstances the Indian Government would have conceded the Naga demand for sovereignty and the Naga movement had reached a dead end. Some Nagas took stock of the situation, and resolved that 'even if Independence was not possible, the land, identity and individuality of the Naga people should never be compromised. The result was the agreement that led to the creation of Nagaland in 1963, which 'gave the Nagas worth and significance in the eyes of the world. (NPCC, 2000)"

3. Some Nagas claimed that prior to 1947, Nagaland was largely a sovereign country. This is not correct. In olden days, Naga Hills and Tuensang areas ills Hill were simply a congregation of villages with no definite boundary, no rule of law and no system of administration with the practice of head hunting. Each village was independent and there was fighting among the villages. No village rule another village. The British brought some sort of control only in the nineteenth century. There was no treaty between the Nagas and the British relating to annexation or surrender. The fact is that prior to 1947, there was no Nagaland. In 1950, the Naga Hills district was put under the sixth schedule of the Indian Constitution as an autonomous district under Part-I–within the state of Assam. In 1957, under the Naga Hills Tuensang Areas Act, 1957, the Tuensang Frontier Division of NEFA was added to the territory of Naga Hills. It was only Naga Hills administered under Assam. The Ahom kings and the British did not want to interfere in their internal feuds and head hunting wars. Since every village is independent, there was no question of treaty. The objective was limited to protecting the valley from the

incursions of the Nagas. In 1866, the Angami country was taken possession with headquarters at Samagutting, which was later shifted to Kohima. In 1875, the country of Lotha Nagas was annexed and one British Officer was posted at Wokha in 1889. After the foundation of the new district, the Angamis gave no trouble until 1877. (Sir Edward Gatt, A history of Assam, 1905, page- 300)

4. In the letter to the then Prime Minister Jawaharala Nehru dated 30 June, 1956, the Federal Authority of Government of Nagaland said that Naga territory is not and has never been a part of Indian territory. And we cannot give our country. This is the actual position". This statement automatically excludes the Naga inhabited districts of Manipur. Because, the Tangkhul and other Naga groups in Manipur have been under the Manipur kings and subsequently under the Manipur and Indian Government for almost 2000 years.

5. There are 'nearly 40 major tribes sub-tribes among the Nagas living inside and outside India, each of which speaks a different language and many of whom have unrelenting histories of internecine conflict. (Gill, 2001). They speak as many as thirty different dialects. There is no common language. The official language is English which is understood by few. They sing the National Anthem –borrowed from America in English. Their only unifying force is Christianity. There is enmity between Angamis, Koyaks, Lhotas, Tangkuls as evidenced from recent violence and killings in Nagaland. There can be no Naga integration without unity.

6. Many of the so called Nagas so far identified recently belonged to Kukis of comparatively small population groups and they have agreed to be categorised as Nagas fearing violence from the Naga underground elements. The Nagas believed that this will increase Naga population and enlarge the Naga territory.

7. The demographic realities does not support at all the Naga Cease Fire Extension and demand for Greater Nagaland.

- Senapati district is a pro-ceasefire and pro-NSCN area where apart from Nagas, there are Thadous (23060), Vaipheis (3057), Paites (202), Mizo (298), Kom (2602), Koireng (762), Koirao (918), Kabui (3702), Hmar (138), Gangte (347), Chiru (2064) and Aimol (86) , who have openly protested against the extension of ceasefire to Manipur and vehemently opposed the idea of Greater Nagaland. Thus about 56% of the district population do not support the claim for Greater Nagaland.
- In Tamenglong district also, the population group of Thadous and other categories vehemently opposed the extension of ceasefire to Manipur and the idea of Greater Nagaland.

Ukhrul district is the birthplace of Th. Muivah, General Secretary of NSCN(IM). He has recruited a large number of Tangkhul youths to the NSCN cadres. But not all Tangkhuls are followers of Th. Muivah. Shri Rishang Keising and Youngmasho Shaiza were two prominent and popular Tangkhul leaders who, in spite of small size of Tangkhul population ruled Manipur as Chief Ministers of Manipur for more than 12 years and in whose time many resolutions opposing the demands of Greater Nagaland were passed unanimously by the State Legislative Assembly. This shows the lack of unanimity of the demand for Greater Nagaland even among the Tangkhul Nagas.

8. The Kukis claim to hold about 50% of the land in these hill districts, which the NSCN (IM) wishes to be made part of a Greater Nagaland. The Kukis vehemently objected to the idea of integrating Naga areas of Manipur, which ultimately led to "Quit Notice" and "Ethnic Cleaning" perpetrated by the NSCN leading a serious communal clash between the Nagas and Kukis in 1992-1994 where more than 900 innocent people were killed. In the Zoupi (Tamenglong) in the massacre of 13 September, 1993, about 90 Kuki men were hacked to death with machetes. On 13 September, 1993, 13 infants were butchered to death in front of their mothers. On 7 June, 1993 at Khatong, Sadar Hills, 8 women were raped and then killed along with three men and three children. On 8 October, 1992, at Moultuh in Chandel district, three women were killed after being raped. Two men and one two month old child was also killed. On 19 November, 1994 at Thingsan in Chandel district, NSCN-IM cadres dressed in Indian Security Forces uniforms killed 25 Kuki men (P.S. Haokip, Zale'n-Gam, the Kuki Nation, Kuki National Organisation, 1998 – page- 530)

9. The NSCN (IM)'s territorial claims to Kuki inhabited areas in Manipur and Assam is pregnant with the seeds of a bloody ethnic conflict. Kukis, who co-inhabit the hill districts of Senapati, Chandel, Tamenglong and Ukhrul in Manipur with the various Naga tribes, are averse to the concept of a Greater Nagaland or Nagalim or Southern Nagaland.

10. On 12 December, 1964, the Nagaland Assembly passed a resolution for integration of Naga areas adjoining the state of Nagaland. On 5 December, 1967, the Nagaland Baptist Church adopted a resolution to move the Government of India to integrate immediately all the contiguous Naga areas of Manipur, Assam and NEFA. The same resolution was again adopted by the Nagaland Assembly in 1970. The Government of India ignored the unreasonable demand and passed the North East Reorganization Act-1971 and Manipur became a full fledged state. Nagaland is becoming a dangerous and bad

neighbour working against the Christian spirit. However, the Indian Prime Ministers including Prime Minister Indira Gandhi had assured that "the interest of Manipur will not be subordinated to the interest of any other part of the country.

11. In 1994, the Nagaland Assembly again reiterated the earlier resolution of integrating the Naga areas adjoining Nagaland. In response to this anti-Manipuri activities of Nagaland Assembly, the Manipur State Assembly vehemently condemned the resolution of the Nagaland State Assembly and to stop all demands of Homeland on 24 March, 1995 The resolution was taken when Rishang Keising, a Tangkhul Naga Leader from Ukhrul was the Chief Minister of Manipur. This was a great loss to the credibility of Naga unity On 14 March, 1997, the Manipur State Legislative Assembly commits to protect and safeguard the territorial integrity of Manipur The same resolution was adopted again on 22 March, 2002 and again on 12 June, 2002.

12. Phizo's prolonged absence from 1957 to 1990 plunged the Naga morale into the abyss of despair. It is reported that a good number of his followers surrendered to the Indian Government in protest against his escape to England. He was enjoying life in England in comforts whereas many Nagas were suffering. He has many children and none of them joined the underground movement whereas many poor villagers have sacrificed their lives. His own daughter (Tutu) was married to a Indian Army Officer. His niece Mrs. Rano Saiza contested an Assembly election seat in spite of public protest.

13. The Naga movement became paralysed with internal disorders and disunity as early as 1956 with the murder of T. Sakhrie, the then Secretary General of NNC – showing the seed of discord. Mr. Scato Swu Sema, the erstwhile President of the Federal Government of Nagaland who surrendered as an Underground leader on 16 August, 1973 and became a Member of Parliament in the Rajya Sabha once commented "even if we get independence, Nagas would not be able to live together. We will fight among ourselves as there is a lot of tribal politics."

14. The Naga guerrillas did not try to get the support of the masses. On the slightest pretext, the boys in arms tortured the villagers, collected funds forcibly, killed suspects (M. Horam, Naga Insurgency, Cosmo Publications, New Delhi, 1988)

15. The ethnic cleansing perpetrated by the NSCN (IM) on the Kuki inhabitants of these districts between the summer of 1992 and winter of 1995 was perhaps intended to evict the Kukis from the so called Naga Territory or force them to identify themselves as Naga but the land belong to the Kukis

for many centuries. Thus the NSCN has earned the image of "perpetrators of genocide"

16. The NSCN (IM) openly indulged in terrorist activities like kidnapping, extortion, illegal drug trafficking, imposing compulsory tax to commercial vehicles running in the national highways. This is an open secret.

17. The NSCN imposed a tax on every commercial vehicle, charging Rs. 3000-5,000 per trip. Receipts for such collections are openly issued in the name of the Government of the People's Republic of Nagaland. In 1996, the first public protest against the NSCN(IM)'s extortion on the national highway—the sole supply line running through the Naga hill areas into the Manipur valley—was led by the Manipur Truck Drivers Association. The Meitei public supported this strike even though it led to a severe shortage of essential commodities and inflation. Despite such protests, the practice continues, and the current rate is reported to be Rs. 10,000. During such lengthy blockade of the National Highway sponsored by the NSCN(IM), there was a great scarcity of food in the valley and food have to be transported by air by the Government of India from neighbouring states. This weakened the claims of the NSCN(IM).

18. It is clear that the Naga insurgency movement had been initiated by the British when the Nagas came back brainwashed after the First World War. The hidden agenda of the British was to convert the Manipuri and Nagaland tribal into Christianity. That is why the British adopted the policy of "Divide and Rule" between the Meiteis and Nagas. The British sought the assistance of the Manipur Maharaja whenever they were in trouble in Naga Hills. When the Manipuri forces adopted the same strategy to subdue the Nagas, the British said "it was impossible to get Manipur to carry out honestly the orders of the Government (Mackenzie, 2001: 108)". After two such expeditions to the Angami Naga country, Lieutenant Vincent reported in 1850 that in every Angami village, there were two parties, one attached to the interests of Manipur and the other to the British, but each only working for an alliance to get aid in crushing the opposite faction (Mackenzie, 2001: 112). Further the British laid down a boundary between the Naga Hills territory and Manipur in 1842 and reasserted it in 1867 just to avoid annexation of Naga Hills by the Manipur Forces, but it was little regarded by Manipuri (Mackenzie, 2001: 122).

19. The Nagas were inspired by Christian Missionaries for more than one century. Their spokesmen were often British or Americans. The presence of foreign nationals like Rev. Michael Scott, a British citizen was one of the

few examples. When Scott was compelled to leave India on 3 May, 1966, the Nagas felt that the expulsion of Scott spelt general defeat of the Nagas and the wind was taken out of the sails of Naga underground movement. Christianity was a strong unifying force. among the Nagas. The British gave them advance information and guided them at every step steering formation of Naga Club, submission of memorandum to the Simon Commission. The movement was sustained and supported by the British, the USA, Pakistan, Bangladesh and China. But nowadays, every country has faced the brunt of terrorism specially after the 11 September incident where the twin World Trade Towers were destroyed by the Terrorist Groups. So any country would hesitate to come forward openly to help the NSCN or any other insurgent organization. In the absence of international support, the power and popularity of NSCN are bound to decline.

20. While the NSCN(IM) claims to represent the Nagas, this is contradicted by a press statement issued by its rival faction, the NSCN (K), on 27 June 2002, cautioning against using the term 'Nagas' in place of NSCN(IM). In another press release dated 11 July 2002, the NSCN (K) went to the extent of declaring Th. Muivah a non-Naga, stating that Tangkhuls are not Naga citizens and had only ten years of association with the Nagas.

21. The NSCN began to be internally riven with the Muivah group (NACN-IM), locked in a bitter fight with the Khaplang group (NSCN-K), dominated by the Konyak (the largest Naga tribe in Nagaland) and Hemi Nagas (who live in contiguous areas of Burma).

22.The past decade has seen some of the bloodiest fighting between the NSCN(IM) and NSCN(K) groups resulting in the loss of innocent civilian lives caught in the crossfire, and deepening the divide between the twelve major Naga tribes. While all Nagas acknowledge the armed might and organisational superiority of the NSCN(I-M), and its crucial role in any settlement with the Government of India, many powerful Naga tribes are unwilling to accept the NSCN(IM) as the sole arbiter of the Naga destiny. But since they are fighting for a common cause, they is no need to fight among themselves.

23. The Nags claimed that they are peace-long people. They do not want the Manipur police, IRBs, police commandos to be posted in Naga areas and they want to be left alone. They even pleaded that every trial should be conducted according to their customary laws and the CRPCs and IPCs should be not be operative in Naga inhabited areas. In other words, they want to revert o the head-hunting days in the 21st century. A glaring example is the

murder of an idealistic Meitei officer named Dr. Kishan, SDO of Kasom Kullen. Dr. Kishan attempted to do something good for the common people for development of Kasom Kullen subdivision under Ukhrul district. He was murdered mercilessly by the NSCN without warning and prevented him from doing any development work. The NSCN want undoubtedly the Government funds flowing freely into their hands. They are not interested to improve the plight of the Nagas.

24. It is alleged that most of the underground organizations can't tolerate "Freedom of Press". They threaten and intimidate the press and journalists for expressing free opinions in the press. The NSCN is not an exception. There have been many protests from the press in the North East India in the last decade. The question that can legitimately be asked is how such organisations can claim to speak on behalf of an entire people in negotiations with the federal government and in international fora, when they silence the public back home at gunpoint and ruthlessly stamp out dissent. This may be an allegation. But both the NSCN-IM and NSDCN-K should try to project themselves as the champion of Naga cause sticking to respect for universal declaration of human rights.

25. Many government servants pay up to 25 per cent of their salaries as 'tax' to insurgent groups which is efficiently 'deducted at source' by routine collections from the office cash box. In the villages, each household in Nagaland is forced to pay an annual tax of INR 400, apart from providing services as and when demanded, such as porterage and hospitality to 'national workers'. For cash-starved Naga villagers with no money to pay for the health and education needs of their children (the government schools and health services are in shambles), such taxes for the 'N.ga cause' are a huge burden.

26. The ordinary rural people are not interested in this kind of politics. They are already fed up with this kind of perpetual violence. They are in fact not supporting any underground movement of any kind. But they can't express their opinion simply for fear of violence. In rural, interior Nagaland, villagers have no time to waste on dreams, so intense is their preoccupation with daily survival and the need to provide meaningful opportunities for their children. This is the handy work of so called politicians and elite group including underground leaders who dictate their strategies from the cosy apartments of London, Amsterdam, Bangkok, Beijing to the innocent poor Nagas fighting for their life in the jungles.

27. In Manipur, where the NSCN runs underground operations, several times over the past six years, the Meiteis have come together to protest, against both the Meitei organisations and against the NSCN(IM).

28. Now the people of Heirok and Chajing are demanding for supply of guns to protect themselves and their villages from underground elements. This shows the sentiments of the common people against the underground outfits. This is time for the underground organizations to respond to this wake-up call.

29. In Manipur a porous border with Burma has facilitated a massive inflow of heroin from the Golden Triangle, en route to the international market. While the heroin drug trade supported the insurgent groups in their quest for arms and easy money at least in the earlier phase, it was destroying the youth and the future generation of Manipur and Nagaland.

30. The Naga Hoho, a powerful consortium of Naga tribal organisations, has sought to provide an answer to Nagas who ask what the fight has been all about. The Naga Hoho is trying to involve civil society in a dialogue with the different rival groups in an effort to make the latter accountable to the public. This is important because many tribes view the NSCN's "muscle flexing" as the continuing attempt by the Tangkhuls and their allies to assert their supremacy in the region. Some Naga intellectuals say that the recent Meitei riots, in the aftermath of the extension of the Naga ceasefire to Manipur and Assam, augured a "paradigm shift".

31. The moderate Naga group (the NPC) was co-operating with the Indian Government under an agreement signed in 1961 by which Nagaland has become an autonomous State within the Indian Union. The new State of Nagaland comprises of the former Naga Hills and Tuensang areas.

32. The NSCN allegedly used child soldiers of about 15 years, 17 years and sometimes 13 years because they are easy to brainwash and easily expendable items, which constitute abuse of child rights and abuse of human rights of people.

33. Many Naga leaders used to say "Let us first achieve our independence, then we will deal with the problems of corruption, alcohol and drugs, and the divisions between Naga tribes". But history shows that redrawing of boundaries has never solved the problems of the common people, and in this age of globalization such smallness of vision cannot sustain their own people.

34. The NSCN (IM) views Mr. S.C. Jamir, the then Chief minister of the democratically elected Government of Nagaland and the underground group NSCN (K) under Khaplang as anti–Nagas. Therefore, any attempt to find a way out of the present imbroglio would require an impartial stand on the part of the Government of India. The Government cannot afford to be seen as

favouring one or the other faction. For any meaningful outcome, all factions of the undergrounds including over grounds, shall have to be involved, otherwise piecemeal peace/dialogue will not bring any satisfactory political solution.

35. The State Government of Nagaland must be involved and must have a say in any peace initiative. The State Government of Assam, Arunachal Pradesh and Manipur who are affected by the NSCN demands must be allowed to participate in the peace process. The state Government of Manipur, the people of Manipur and Meitei insurgents in Manipur are vehemently opposed to any change in the 2000 years old geographical integrity and history of Manipur.

36. Further, solving the problems of NSCN-IM and NSCN-K alone will not solve the problem of insurgency problem either in Nagaland or in the North East India. The Government of India should therefore adopt an open door policy and an uniform strategy and uniform policy for all main insurgency groups in Manipur and Nagaland.

37. Nagaland as a sovereign country will not be economically viable, considering the poor resources. They do not produce, petrol coal, gas, iron or any other mineral. They are depending entirely on the Government of India's fund for subsistence. Their area is land-locked. They have to depend on neighbouring states for their own survival. They can't live now as their forefathers did centuries ago. They do not have enough muscles and strengths to defend themselves.

38. The Naga peace process should not be left to the senior bureaucrats under the Government of India, who have no background knowledge about the history, cultures, traditions of the people of North East India. Many a time, their irresponsible statements created serious problems among the various ethnic groups in the north eastern India.

Why the Government of India and NSCN are fighting shy of inviting the political and other leaders from Manipur, Assam or Arunachal Pradesh to hasten the peace process ? The Manipur Government and the Manipur people should be allowed to participate in the peace process otherwise there will not be any long lasting solution. Mutual jealousy and mutual suspicion will only delay and ruin the peace process. Since the talk is revolving round the issue of slicing some part of Manipur, no solution will be possible and practicable without involving the Manipur Government. One question which common people often raised is - "why is the NSCN not involving the people of Manipur in discussing historical facts and in finding a solution ?"

The Government of India is well aware that any settlement with the NSCN (IM) ignoring the complex ethnic relations of the North East India is likely to fuel rather than douse the flames of discord in the region. So, they will not take any hasty decision. The NSCN should therefore revise their strategy. They should not stick to their ambition to disturb the geographical boundaries of other neighbouring states of Manipur, Assam and Arunachal Pradesh. It is unfortunate that some Nagas are trying to portray a distorted picture of history to the Naga people just to satisfy their vested interest and to mislead the people.

Possible solutions

The Nagas should insist on non-territorial solutions without disturbing the boundary of other states. Religion and culture is not the only unifying force. Why the Muslims are fighting against the Muslims in Iraq ? How can the Nagas guarantee love and unity among the odd 40 Naga tribes and sub-tribes, speaking more than 30 dialects ? A lasting solution lies in genuine economic development, human resource development, accelerated infrastructural development, creation of job opportunities, opening of new international trade routes, foreign investment, more autonomy to the state of Nagaland, more Central funds and a little bit of pressure on militant groups to accept the peace proposal based on non-territorial solutions. Sincerity on the part of political and insurgent leadership and unity among the Nagas alone can bring 'peace to the land of the exhilarating Nagas. Lasting solution lies in love and unity among the Nagas and other tribes of north eastern India.

Nagaland can see the wisdom of peaceful co-existence and live like a good neighbour in the spirit of a true Christian and insist on non-territorial solutions. They can demand for an Upper House, demand for a more strength in the Nagaland State Assembly, more representation in Indian Parliament, demand for more autonomy. They can adopt a policy to invite other Nagas from other states or countries who would like to come and settle in Nagaland giving them free land, citizenship encouraging economic investment. This will increase their population. This will be a more effective instrument to measure Naga solidarity than Plebiscite. They can demand more share in education, employment in central services, army, central police forces, railways and All India Services. This will benefit thousands of educated youths from Nagaland. They can demand for exploration of mineral and forest resources, development of tourism, hydro-electricity, Information Technology, Industries, foreign investment, removal of Inner Line Permit or Restricted Area Permit, etc.

These measure will definitely uplift the economic condition of the masses. They can demand for speedy completion of the Asian Trans Highway passing through Nagaland and Manipur via Myanmar to Bangkok or Chiangmai and open up the international trade routes. They can demand for a bigger financial package from the Government of India in addition to plan money every year for another twenty years to create infrastructure, employment generation, industrialization and boost the economy. The NSCN leaders are great, charismatic and patriotic leaders. They should be given an honourabe position in the Central and state politics and state administration of Nagaland. The Prime Minister may be persuaded to give ministerial positions in the Central Cabinet for the leaders of NSCN. The present politicians of Nagaland should sacrifice their positions as Chief Minister and offer the top positions to the T. Muivah and Khaplang. Other leaders from other organizations may be accommodated in the ministerial posts but they have to face the election in due course of time as per Indian Constitution. When they come to power, let them achieve their vision and mission. The people of Nagaland perhaps would like to see them as Chief Ministers before they are too old.

What the Manipur Government should do

1. The Manipur Government may consider constituting a "Think Tank" comprising of civil society representatives including UCM, AMUCO, prominent citizens of Manipur. Appointing a politician as Advisor to CM may not serve the purpose.
2. The State Government may plead with the Government of India to change the nomenclature of "Indo-Naga Peace Talk to" Naga Peace Talk: since the talk is between an Underground Organization and the Government of India.
3. The Manipur Government may take a resolution in the Manipur State Legislative Assembly to plead with the Government of India to include Manipur representative in the Naga peace talk since Manipur is adversely affected by the onging peace talk irrespective of the outcome.
4. The Manipur Government may take a resolution in the Manipur State Legislative Assembly to plead with the Government of India to amend the Indian Constitution so that historical boundary of Manipur may not be violated at any cost.
5. The State Government may compile all the crimes committed by the NSCN(IM) and file FIR for all cases. Every instance of looting, extortion, beating, murder, imposition of blockade, ethnic cleansing constitute a

crime. Taking into consideration all the crimes, NSCN (IM) might have committed more than 10,000 crimes. Recently the State Government has decided to institute FIR of only 324 cases. This is grossly under-estimated and under-reported.

6. The Manipur Government may take a resolution in the Manipur State Legislative Assembly to declare Muivah as a "Wanted Terrorist "and they should ask the Government of India to hand over Muivah to the Manipur State Government for trial for committing crimes in Manipur. The Government is asking Pakistan to hand over those suspected militants of masterminding a single Mumbai blast killing persons. Then why not Government of India hand over Muivah for committing thousands of such crimes including ethnic cleansing and killing of more than 900 Kukis in Manipur.
7. The Manipur Government may take a resolution in the Manipur State Legislative Assembly to plead with the Government of India to allow Manipur to do full time business with Myanmar by removing the "restricted items" and by opening passport office and VISA office, foreign exchange facility and credit cards system so that all the essential commodities of Manipur can be procured from Myanmar. This will remove the dependency on the NH-39 and NH-53.
8. The State Government may consider launching of a national TV network and having a linkage with the national media channels so that the state Government may project the true picture of what is happening in Manipur to the outside world. NSCN IM) with all its money and muscle power can buy and influence the national TV channels very easily as evident from recent experiences
9. The State Government may register the complaints from the drivers and transporters through NH-39 and NH-53 and ask for re-imbursement of these illegal taxes since the NSCN(IM) who is having a peace talk with Government of India is imposing the illegal tax under the very nose of Indian security forces.
10. The State Government should not allow open display of weapons by the NSCN cadres in public places and open support of these activities by the Assam Rifles, BSF and other central forces.
11. The State Government should not allow functioning of any NSCN(IM) camps inside Manipur.
12. The State Government may station companies of Manipur Rifles and Police Commandos with adequate fire-power in sensitive areas like

Mao, Senati, Noney, Moreh so that the two highways may not be disturbed by NSCN(IM) or any other underground organizatin.

13. The State Government may consider extension of MLR Act in the hill districts.
14. The State Government may ensure that the Assam-Manipur railway network comes upto Imphal (not Tupul) and completed speedily to overcome the problems of frequent economic blockade along NH-53. and NH-39
15. The State Government may ensure that the Trans-Asia Highway be started without further delay and completed in time to overcome the problems of frequent economic blockade along NH-39 and NH-53.

References

A. Hamilton "In Abor Jungles of North east India, Mittal Publications, New Delhi, 1997.

AMCTA (All Manipur College Teachers Association), 2001. Manipur Fact File 2001.Imphal, Manipur: All Manipur College Teachers Association.

Aly, Gotz, Susanne Heim. *Architects of Annihilation: Auschwitz and the Logic of Destruction*, London, Weidenfeld & Nicolson, 2002, 514 pp, ISBN 2978427819.

Angami, Sakhrie, Azeto Sumi, N. Chakhesang, Moa Ao and Sekhosie, 2002. 'Genesis of Nagalimí in http://www.kuknalim.net/focus/2002/focusApr2002item1.html (2 November 2002).

Alexander Mackenzie, The North East Frontier of India Mittal Publications, New Delhi, 1884.

Ao Tajenyuba; British Occupation of Naga Country, (Mokokchung: Naga Literature Society, 1995), p. 280. Back 1.

Aram, M" Peace in Nagaland : Eight Years Story", 1964-72, Arnold-Heinemann, New Delhi, 1974). Gandhi asked the Nagas to shun the path of violence means.

ASW Shimray, History of Tangkhul Nagas, Akansa Publishing House, New Delhi, 2001.

B.C. Allen, E.A. Gait, H.F. Howard, C.G H. Allen "Gazeteer of Bengal and North East India ", A Mittal Publication, 2001.

B.G Verghese, "India's Northeast Resurgent, Ethnicity, Insurgency, Governance, development, Konark Publishers Pvt. Ltd,, 1996.

B.N. Mullik : My years with Nehru, Caxton Press Private Limited, Delhi-1972, page 308.

Bauer, Yehuda. *A History Of The Holocaust*, New York : F. Watts, 1982 ISBN 0-531-09862-1.

Browning, Christopher. *The Origins of the Final Solution: The Evolution of Nazi Jewish Policy*, University of Nebraska Press, 2004, 616pp, ISBN 0803213271.

Burleigh, Michael & Wippermann, Wolfgang. *The Racial State : Germany 1933-1945*, Cambridge : Cambridge University Press, 1991 ISBN 0-521-39114-8.

Ehrenreich, Eric. *The Nazi Ancestral Proof: Genealogy, Racial Science, and the Final Solution*. Bloomington, IN: Indiana University Press, 2007. ISBN 978-0-253-34945-3R.R. Shimray (1985), Origin and Culture of Nagas, New Delhi: Somsok Publications, p. 18.

Assam Tribune, 2000. 'Extend Ceasefire, Nagaland Congress Urges Centre, NSCN Factions, The Assam Tribune (Guwahati) 21 July.

B. Rahmatulla, Evolution of National Socialist Council of Nagaland: The Renewal of Insurgency, Kohima: Platform, February 25–March 4, 1982, Vol. 5, No. 40), pp. 3–4.

B. Pakem, Insurgency In North–East India, (New Delhi: OMSONS Publications), p. 190. Back.

Baruah, Sanjib, 2003. 'Citizens and Denizens: Ethnicity, Homelands and the Crisis of Displacement in Northeast Indiaí, Journal of Refugee Studies 16(1): 00-00.

Baruah, Sanjib, 1997. 'Cutting States to Sizeí, Seminar (New Delhi) November, 459: 27-30.

Bose, Manilal, ed., 1979. Historical and Constitutional Documents of Northeast India, 1824-1973. Delhi: Concept Publishing Company.

Burling, Robbins, 0000. 'The Tibeto-Burman Languages of Northeastern Indiaí, in Graham Thurgood and Randy LaPolla, eds, The Sino-Tibetan Languages. London: Curzon Press (000-000).

Chakravarti, The Evolution of India's Northern Borders, (Bombay: Asia Publishing House, 1971), pp. 39–40. Back.

Chassie, Charles, 1999. The Naga Imbroglio: A Personal Perspective. Kohima, Nagaland: Standard Printers and Publishers.

David C., "Unreached Peoples" 81 –Cook Publishing Co.

Dinesh Kotwal, The Naga Insurgency: The Past And The Future

Dr M. Aram, Peace in Nagaland, (New Delhi: Arnold–Heinemann, 1974), p. 54. Back.

Dr Verrier Elwin, Nagaland, (Shillong: 1961), p. 51–54. Back.

D.R. Mankekar, On The Slippery Slopes Of Nagaland, (Bombay: Maniktala, 1967), p. 39. Back.

Dr. S.K. Chatterjee, Kirata–Jana–Kirti, (Calcutta: Asiatic Society, 1951), p. 167.

David Galula, Counter Insurgency Warfare–Theory & Practice, (New Delhi: Sagar Publication), p.4. Back.

Eaton, Richard M., 1997. 'Comparative History as World History: Religious Conversion in Modern Indiaí, Journal of World History 8(2): 243-271.

Elwin Verrier 1961, Nagaland, Shillong: Published by P.Dutta for the research Dept. Adviser's Secretariat Page –12.

Elwin Verrier 1961, Nagaland, Shillong: Published by P.Dutta for the research Dept. Adviser's Secretariat Page –8.

Friedländer, Saul. *Nazi Germany and the Jews Volume 1 The Years of Persecution, 1933-1939*, New York : HarperCollins, 1997 ISBN 0-06-019042-6.

Fürer-Haimendorf, Christoph von, 1976. Return to The Naked Nagas, New Delhi: Vikas Publishing House.

Galanter, Marc, 1984. Competing Equalities. Berkeley, CA: University of California Press.

Gill, K.P.S., 2001. "Managing Northeast: More Foresight Needed" The Pioneer (New Delhi) 30 June.

Hazarika, Sanjoy, 2002. 'Of the Nagas, Regionalism and Power, The Statesman. (New Delhi) 27 April.

H.K. Sareen, Insurgency in North–East India, (New Delhi: Sterling Publishers Pvt. Ltd., 1980), p. 30. Back.

Hutton, J.H., 1921. The Angami Nagas, with Some Notes on Neighbouring Tribes. London: Macmillan and Company.

Hutton, J.H., 1922. 'Introductioní, in James Philip Mills, The Lhota Nagas. London: Macmillan and Company.

Jacobs, Julian; Alan MacFarlane, Sarah Harrison & Anita Herle, 1990. The Nagas: The Hill People of Northeast India: Society, Culture and the Colonial Encounter, Thames and Hudson Ltd, London -1998.

Johnstone, James, 1971 [1896]. Manipur and the Naga Hills. Delhi: Vivek Publishing House (Original title: My Experiences in Manipur and the Naga Hills. London: S. Low, Marston & Company).

Julian Jacobs, The Nagas, Hill Peoples of North east India, Thames and Hudson Ltd, London -1998.

Kaka D. Iralu "Nagaland and India , a historical account of the fifty two years Indo-Naga war and the story of yhose who were never allopwed to tell it", 2000.

Karmakar, Rahul, 2000. 'Words Replace Guns in Nagaland Againí, The Hindustan Times (New Delhi) 1 November.

Kühl, Stefan. *The Nazi Connection: Eugenics, American Racism, and German National Socialism*, Oxford University Press, 2002 ISBN 0195149785.

Licklider, Roy, 1995. 'The Consequences of Negotiated Settlements in Civil Wars, 1945ó1993í, American Political Science Review 89(3): 681ó690.

Lawrence James, Raj: The Making of British India, Abacus, A division of Little, Brown and Company (UK), Brettenham House, Lancaster Place, London, WC2E 7 EN, 1977, Page 414.

Mackenzie, Alexander, 2001 [1884]. The North East Frontier of India. New Delhi: Mittal Publications (Original title: History of the Relations of the Government with the Hill Tribes of the North-East Frontier of Bengal. Calcutta: Home Department Press).

M. Horam, Naga Insurgency, (New Delhi: Cosmo Publication, 1988), page. 253.

M. Horam, Naga Insurgency, Cosmo Publications, 1988, page-50.

N.K. Das, The Emergence And Role Of Naga Elite In Independent India, p. 265: in The Emergence And Role Of Middle Class In North–East India, by B. P Roy, (New Delhi: Uppal Publishing House, 1983). Back.

NPCC (Nagaland Pradesh Congress Committee), 2000. Bedrock of Naga Society.

http://www.nenanews.com/ng10.htm (2 November 2002).

NSCM-IM (Naga National Socialist Council faction led by Isaak Chisi Swu and Thuingaleh Muivah), 2002. Website. http://www.angelfire.com/mo/Nagaland/Background.html (2 November 2002).

Prakash Singh, Nagaland, (New Delhi: National Book Trust of India, 1972), pp. 211–214. Back..

Prakash Singh "Kohima to Kashmir on the Terrorist Trail, Rupa & Co, New Delhi, 2001.

Peukert, Detlev. *Inside Nazi Germany : conformity, opposition and racism in everyday life* London : Batsford, 1987 ISBN 0-7134-5217-X.

Ratan, Khumajam, 2001. 'A Retrospective on June 18 Uprisingí, in The Book of Selfless Sacrifice: A Tribute to the Martyrs of Manipurís Territorial Integrity Movement. Imphal, Manipur: Publication Committee, Manipur Territorial Integrity Movement (1-5).

R.B. Pemberton, "the Eastern Frontier of India", Mittal Publications, New Delhi, 1835.

R.B. Thohe Pou, a Ph.D. Research Scholar, contributes regularly to e-pao.net. (thohepou@rediffmail.com), 19th April 2006.

R. Coup land, Future of India-London 1944, p-160.

Singh, R.K. Ranjit, 1990. 'Emergent Ethnic Processes in Manipur: A Reappraisalí, in B. Pakem, ed., Nationality, Ethnicity and Cultural Identity in North-East India. New Delhi: Omsons Publications (233-251).

Sahadevan, P., 2000. Coping with Disorder: Strategies to End Internal Wars in South Asia, Colombo, Sri Lanka: Regional Centre for Strategic Studies, Colombo Policy Studies Paper 17. http://www.rcss.org/publications/POLICY/ps-17-5.html (2 November 2002).

Scott, James C., 2000. 'Hill and Valley in Southeast Asia.... or Why the State is the Enemy of the People who Move Around... or... Why Civilizations Canít Climb Hillsí in http://www.artsci.wustl.edu/~symp2000/jscott.PDF (2 November 2002).

Shantanu Nandan Sharma,The Naga Question:Violence and the Peace Process Simon Memorandum, 1999: 165-166.

Shimray, U.A., 2001. 'Ethnicity and Socio-Political Assertioní, Economic and Political Weekly 36(39): 3674-3677.

Shimray R.R.1985 Origin and Culture of Nagas, New Delhi, Somsok Publications.

Simon Memorandum, 1999 [1929]. 'Memorandum of the Naga Hills to the Statutory Commission on Constitutional Reforms (Simon Commission),í 10 January 1929, Appendix A in Chassie, 1999: 165-67.

Sir Edward Gait, KCSI, CIE "A History of Assam", Lawyers Book Stall, Guwahati, Assam, 1905.

Suny, Ronald Grigor, 2001. 'Constructing Primordialism: Old Histories for New Nationsí, in http://www.dartmouth.edu/~crn/crn_papers/Suny3.pdf (2 November 2002).

Taylor, Charles, 1994. 'The Politics of Recognitioní, in Amu Gutman ed., Multiculturalism: Examining the Politics of Recognition. Princeton, NJ: Princeton University Press (25-73).

The Observer of Business and Politics, "Unquiet hills of the north–east" November 17, 1997. Back.

The North East Sun, "NSCM views at Geneva", May 1–14, 1998, p. 7. Back.

The North–East Sun, "Good Beginning doubtful Ending" October 15–31, 1999. Back.

The Assam Tribune, "Naga Talks In Jeopardy" February 4, 2000. Back.

The Outlook, "Ceasefire Under Fire" December 13, 1999. Back.

The Hindustan Times, "Muviha arrest brings to fore another intelligence failure" January 29, 2000. Back.

The NSCN (I–M) has expressed that it did not regard either the Khaplang group or the N.N.C. as freedom fighters. According to them, the day N.N.C. sold out Naga interest through the Shilong Accord, they have ceased to be freedom fighters. Regarding the Khaplang faction, the view of the I–M faction is that it is a creation of the Government of India, so they were never the real freedom fighters. Back.

The Indian Express, "Jamir Lucky As Rebels ambush Convoy", November 30, 1999. Back.

The Asian Age, "Muviha's in Manipur torn between Hoho and polls" February 5, 2000. Back.

The Telegraph, "Nagas in Manipur torn between Hoho and polls" September 28, 1999. Back.

The North East Sun, "Picking Up the Peace(s)", July 1–14, 1996, p. 6. Back.

The North East Sun, "Ultras Give Shillong the Shudders", July 15–31, 1999, p. 16. Back.

The Sentinel, Guwahati, April 22, 2000. Back.

The Sentinel, Guwahati, April 25, 2000. Back.

The North East Sun, "Valley Insurgents New Front", March 15–31, 1999, p. 5. Back.

The North East Sun, March 15–31, 1999, p. 5. These Manipur based insurgent outfits have formed a new front called the Manipur Peoples Liberation Front (MPLF) on March 1, 1999 with declaration to jointly carry out the operations against the security forces.

Times of India, 2001. 'Nagas Invite N-E Expert to Broker Peaceí, Times of India (New Delhi) 20 June.

Tully, James, 1995. Strange Multiplicity: Constitutionalism in an Age of Diversity. Cambridge: Cambridge University Press.

Vashum R., (2000), Nagas' Right to Self Determination-An Anthropological Historical Perspective, Delhi: Mittal Publications, pp-22 (cf. Raising et al 1994:1) 3. Op. Cit. Shimray, pp-24.

V.I.K. Sarim, India's North–East In Flames, (New Delhi: Vikas Publishing House, 1980), p. 94. Back.

V.K. Anand, Conflict In Nagaland,(Delhi: Chanakya Publications, 1980), p. 55. Back.

Walzer, Michael, 1995 [1992]. 'The New Tribalism: Notes on a Difficult Problemí in Omar Dahbour and Micheline R. Ishay eds., The Nationalism Reader. Atlantic Highlands, N.J.: Humanities Press (322-332) (Originally published in Dissent (Spring): 164-171). Winichakul, Thongchai, 1994. Siam Mapped: A History of the Geo-Body of a Nation. Honolulu: University of Hawaii Press.

Weindling, Paul. *Health, Race and German Politics between National Unification and Nazism, 1870-1945*. Cambridge University Press, 1989. ISBN 0-521-42397-X.

Y.D. Gundevia, War & Peace In Nagaland, (New Delhi: Palit, 1975), p. 42.-The Conversion commenced with the arrival of American Baptist Mission in 1872. Back. Nari Rustomji, Imperilled Frontiers; India's North–Eastern Borderlands, (Delhi: Oxford University Press, 1983), p, 85. Back.

Yunuo, Asoso, 1974. The Rising Nagas: A Historical and Political Study. Delhi: Vivek Publishing House.

http://www.nscnonline.org.

http://nscn.livejournal.com/2007/09/10/.

http://www.satp.org/satporgtp/countries/india/states/nagaland/terrorist_outfits/Nscn_im.htm.

http://timesofindia.indiatimes.com/india.

India/articleshow/4850136.cms.

http://american_almanac.tripod.com/untouch.htm .

http://www.answers.com/topic/untouchable.

http://en.wikipedia.org/wiki/Dalit.

http://www.iheyo.org/node/842.

http://www.aigenom.com/.

http://en.wikipedia.org/wiki/Christianity_and_slavery.

Plate -150: Traditional Naga House

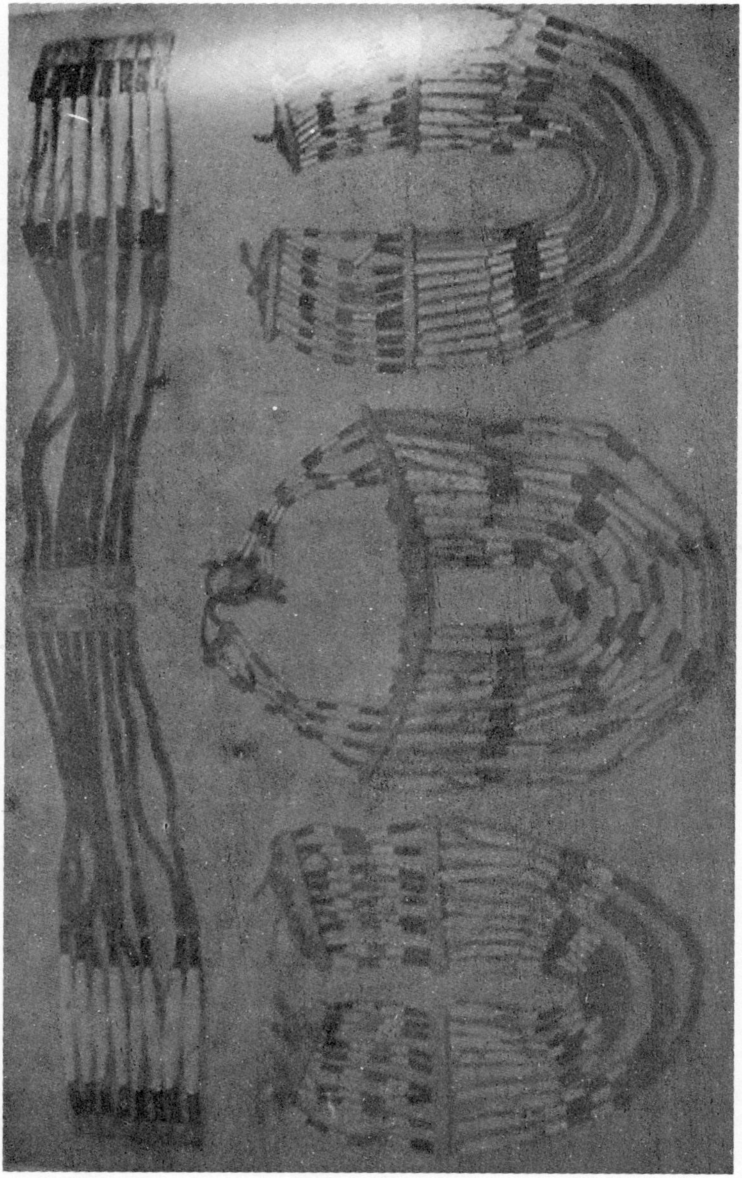

Plate -151: Ornaments of Nagas

Plate-152: Naga Shawl

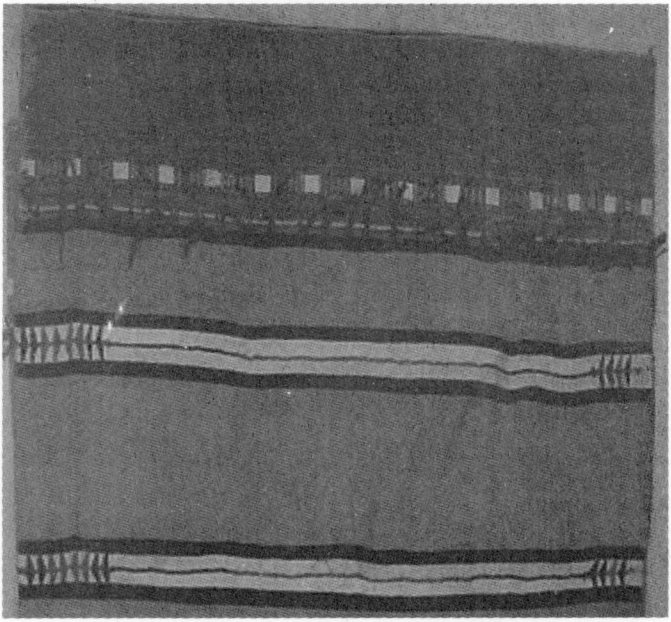

Plate-153: Naga Shawl

Plate-154: Naga Shawl

Plate-155: Naga Shawl

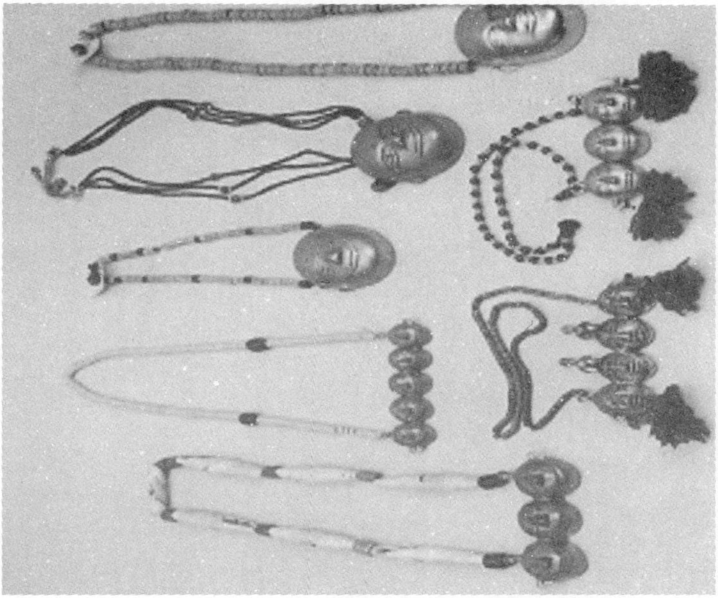

Plate -157:Ornaments of Nagas

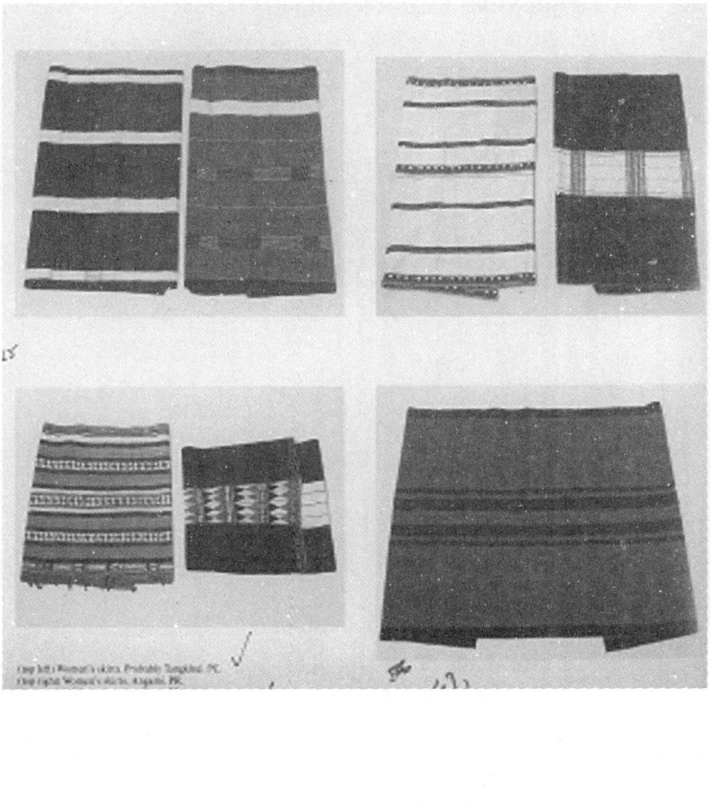

Plate – 156: Naga Shawls

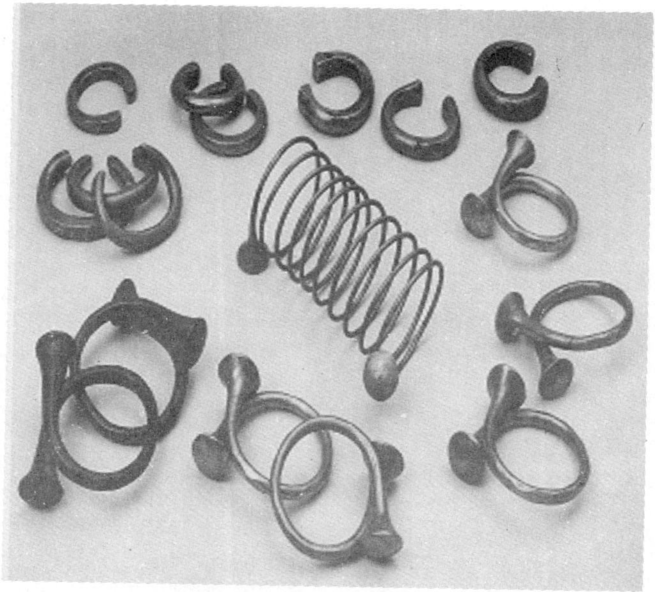

Plate -158: Brass Ornaments

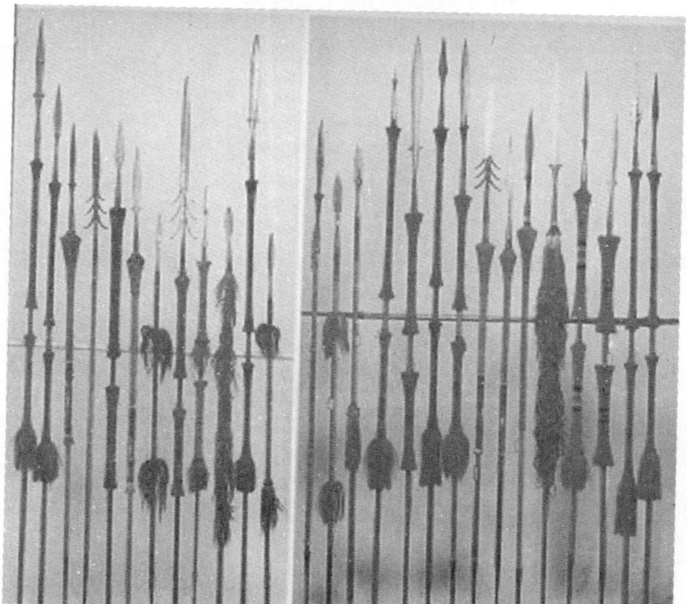

Plate -159: Naga Spears

Plate -160: Decorated Daos

Plate -161: Maram House

Plate -162: Maram

Plate-163: A.Z. Phizo

Plate -164: Thuingaleng Muivah and Colleague

Plate -165: Thuingaleng Muivah

Plate- 166: A part of the Great June Uprising in Manipur, 2001

10

Tangkhuls

The Tangkhuls, numbering 112,944 in (Census-2001) constitute about 4.8 percent of the total population of Manipur. Ukhrul district is the home of the Tangkhuls since time immemorial. They live in eight territorial areas in the Ukhrul district and their sub-tribes have distinct dialects. (See plate-141). Since the Ukhrul was chosen by the first Christian Missionary in Manipur in 1896 for conversion, the people of Ukhrul town dominates other Tangkhuls and Naga groups.

The Tangkhuls are the largest community after the majority Meitei community in Manipur. The northern Tangkhuls were also called the Luhupas. Tangkhuls spread over 12 villages at the time of boundary demarcation in 1880, resulting to transfer some of these 12 villages to Burma.The Gazetteer of Manipur by E.W. Dun showed the 1881 Census figures of Tangkhul population as follows: Luhupas-28552; Tangkhuls-4490 : Total=32,852. Luhupas are Tangkhuls who used to wear helmets on certain occasions. The name has disappeared long back and no longer spoken of even among the Manipuris now. The population growth rate in Ukhrul district is 32% which is considered normal.

They are the most educated tribe of Manipur. Several Chief Ministers and Ministers in Manipur State had belonged to Tangkhuls. They have produced many Indian Administrative Services (IAS) officers, Doctors, Engineers, Professors and leaders in all walks of life. Next to the Meiteis, the

Tangkhuls have the highest number of professionals in Manipur.They are also leaders in Baptist Church Activities of Manipur.

Shirui Kashong famous for Shirui Lily and Khangkhui cave are in the Ukhrul district. During the world war II, the Japanese occupied the Tangkhul areas in the invasion of Imphal. At present, a large number Tangkhuls have settled at Imphal mostly from the rich and influential upper class group. (See Chapter-10, Tangkhuls).

Origin of the word "Tangkhul"

The name Tangkhul was given to them by the Meiteis. There are many legends regarding the origin of the word Tangkhul.

1. The word Tangkhul is believed to have emerged from name of a person named "Tangkhu" who was well expert in war dance, had excellent skills in war tactics including use of swords, spears etc. According to legend, "Thang" (swords) and "Ta" (Spear) are inseparable items of Tangkhul life. Hence Tangkhul means "village of the people of "Thang –ta" (sword and spear).
2. Tangkhuls are very generous and full of hospitality who provided food and drinks to their guests. Therefore, the Meiteis called them "Atangba Khul" Antangba means precious of very high value, khul means village. In other words, there is no village as hospitable, liberal and generous as the Tangkhuls.
3. According to another legend, Iron is everything for Tangkhul life. In Burmese language, "Than" means iron. The Tangkhuls used iron (than) for making swords, spears, agricultural implements and even for paying bride price or purchasing land. The Avas made the iron available to the Tangkhuls according to their needs. At one time, there is increasing demand of iron from the Tangkhul community so much so that the Avas or Burmese called them "Thanpi, which means "Iron people".
4. According to another legend, there was a time when the Samjok king was so weak that the Meitei King attacked Samjok and subdued it. The Burmese called the Nagas "Thanpi". The Meitei called the village "Than-khul" meaning "Than–village" or Thankhul.

Migration of Tangkhuls

The original Tangkhul population is believed to have migrated from somewhere in Yunnan province of China. There was a cruel and oppressive rule of Yin and Shan dynasties in China around 3000 B.C. People migrated in different directions in order to escape the cruel rule. (Gao-Daxian). According to some historians, the earliest home of the Tangkhuls was the upper reaches of Huang Heo and Yangtze rivers which lies in the Zinjiang province of China. The people dispersed from this place to different directions. One group moved towards east and southeast to become known as Chinese, another group moved southward to become the tribes of Tibeto-Burman which includes the Tangkhuls and other tribes. That was between 10,000 B.C. to 8000 B.C.

A group of men and women escaped to Hainam island and landed at the Five Finger Mountain. One of them called Li went out for hunting and chased a doe. When Li pointed his arrow and ready to shoot, the doe turned into a beautiful girl. They got married and in due course of time, they had five sons- Meifu –Li, Ziao-Li, Oi-Li, Detou-Li and Local-Li. From these five brothers emerges the five tribes which have been still living in Hainam Island, South West Chinese provinces and Indo China countries. According to Kachin legend, Meifu-Li had a son called Jingpo. His nephew Lengdo (a descendant of Xiao-Li) came back to the Yunnan Province and lived in the territory between Salwin and Mekong rivers for some time. At last they settled at the mountain region of Phaungchuang, east of the Hmaikha river in the Kachin state in Myanmar. While Jingpo was living in Phaungchuang, he married a local girl and had two sons. When the two sons grew up and become quite strong and adventurous. Lengdo and elder son of Jingpo discovered a vast area of valley between the Chindwin and Irrawady rivers during their hunting expedition. They were extremely happy to have discovered such a fertile valley. During this period, Jingpo and his younger son became anxious and restless. They tried to locate Jingpo and Legdo. They have to trace the direction and footprints of Lengdo and the elder son. But they could not leave Phuangchuang immediately because of the aged condition of the mother. The young son, realizing that his mother was an obstacle to his plan to follow his elder brother killed his mother. After some days, Jingpo and his younger son started to trace the footprints of Lengdo and his elder son. When they found any new footprint, they shouted to each other "Khang, Khang" meaning footprint, footprint. Since then, the descendants of Jingpo's elder son are known as "Akhang" by the Shans and Burmese. Today, the Shans and Burmese called the Nagas "Akhang". Jingpo and his second son continued to live in Phuangchuang. Jingpo's elder son and Lengdo left in search of a new fertile land. They came and settled down at Zibyu-Tuang which was a very fertile land. In course of time, the descendants of Jingpo's elder son increased and they occupied Chindwin river valley and Patkoi ranges under leadership of Kabo Khari and Chaphang. They established their homes at Hongkha Muja. It is believed that the tradition of Tangkhul Awunga was established during their stay at Zibyu–Tuang and Chindwin valley. After some time, they looked for a more suitable place in the plain area and came to Kongkhan Thana. The original name of Kongkhan Thana was "Phaipa" meaning "Vast valley". When Kabo Khari become a powerful ruler, his dominion was known as "Kabow valley". King Kabo Khari established his palace and called it Samjok. Originally, this place was known as Songshuingreng meaning land of mass settlement. In due course of time, Samjok became a great political, social and commercial centre, which attracted the jealousy of the neighbouring states. Moguong, King of Shans attacked Samjok. The Burmese King of Pagan attacked Samjok (Thuangdut) and occupied it. These frequent attacks led to the dispersal of Tangkhuls from Samjok to other safer places. The Tangkhul began to disperse from Samjok after the invasion of Ko-lo-feng and his successor I-mau-shun, the King of Nan-chao (Yunnan province) in the closing part of the 8th century A.D. and beginning of the 9th century A.D. They were further driven towards the north west of Myanmar by the Shan people. Thus, the Tangkhuls have travelled from China to Myanmar and from there finally they came into their present land. According to W.I. Singh, in his "The History of Manipur", the Tangkhuls settled in Samjok (Thuangdut) area in Myanmar. They belong to "Yakkha" tribe in China. The Tangkhuls were first noticed in Manipur by Poireiton (34-18 B.C.) one of the earliest Kings of Manipur.

There is a Tangkhul folk song, which shows the migration of Tangkhuls from Samjok :-

Oh whence cometh thou originally ?
Oh we originate from Samsok in Burma
We call and gather all our kindred at Shokvao
We make fire at Meichailung
We distribute at Ru-Ngatak
Oh Hungphun Chief, the eldest,
Oh Ronra Shimray your tributes are everywhere
Au ....Oh

Origin of Tangkhuls :

The ancient Tangkhul history is an unrecorded past. However, Tankhuls have got very rich folklores, folktales and legends. Some historians are of the opinion that the Tangkhuls came from the Hao city (now called Xian in China) and they had been called Hao. Meifu–li who belonged to the Hao tribe of China was the progenitor of the Tangkhuls and the Tangkhuls carried this tribal name Hao.The Tangkhuls called themselves Hao. Now Tangkhuls call themselves "Wu". Their traditional dresses, songs and day to day items were known by Hao names. Thus, Hao –la means Hao-song, Hao- coiffure means Hao hairstyle, Hao –Kuiret, Hao-Kachon etc.In fact, Hao was the earliest name ever used to the Tangkhuls although the Meiteis used this terminology to all tribal including all Nagas, Kukis of Tibeto- Burman origin. Hao is not a derogatory term.

The Tangkhuls entered the present habitat in waves following one after another and in some cases in close succession. It is considered that the Tangkhuls came together with the Maos, Poumeis, Marams and Thangals because all of them have references to their dispersal from Makhel, a Mao village in Senapati district.They had also erected megaliths at Makhel in memory of their having dispersed from there to various directions.

The Tangkhuls believed that their forefathers had migrated from the seashore. Most of the ornaments of the Tangkhuls such as Kongsang, Huishon, etc. were made of sea shells, Cowries and Conch shells, which are prominent features of the people who live on the sea shore. By 2nd century A.D. the Tangkhuls were living in Samjok (Thuangdut) in Myanmar. Ptolemy, a Greek astronomer and geographer of Alexandria in his Geography of Further India.140 A.D. referred to the Tangkhul (Nangalogue) at Triglypton (Thuangdut).

The History of Tangkhuls became more enlightened by the beginning of the 13th century owing to the cultural, trade and sometimes turbulent relations which had grown up with the people of the valley of Manipur. We find a reference to the Tangkhuls as early as the 13th century during the reign of Thawanthaba (1195-1231AD) of Ningthouja Meitei dynasty. The chronicles refer to the frequent raids in many tribal villages. Thawanthaba raided Chingshong Tangkhul village which was defeated.

There has always been relationship between the Tangkhuls and the Meiteis in terms of political alliance and trade relation. There is a long history of contact between the plain and hills. The "Elephant Cloth" (Leirungphi), for instance, resplendent with complex animal designs, worn by the Nagas of Manipur, has its origin in the wish of the ruler of Manipur in the mid-seventeenth century to present his Naga allies with a special cloth. The popular Tangkhul shawl "Changkhom" is also known as "Karaophi" in Manipur. The Tangkhul dance (pheichak) was known as "Chingkheirol" in

Manipuri., from the fact that it came from "Chingkhei" (North East of Imphal), the direction of Tangkhuls.

During the reign of the most powerful Meitei King Pamheiba or Garib Niwaz (1709-1748), the heartland area of the Tangkhul territory was brought under the suzerainty of Manipur. In 1716, the King's forces invaded the great Tangkhul village of Hundung and sixty eight prisoners were captured. In 1733, the King sent a military expedition to Ukhrul and conquered. The outcome of the expeditions incurred heavy casualty on the King's forces; the royal chronicles record the death of seventy Meitei soldiers. The defeat of these two big villages situated in the heart of Tangkhul territory was landmark in the establishment of the Meitei political regime over the Tangkhul hills which started feeling the brunt of the Meitei power. The Ningek inscription of King Garib Niwaz refers to the Khullakpa of Ukhrul. Ukhrul was the headquarters of the Tangkhul Long (Tangkhul Assembly), as well as the Tangkhul annual fair locally known as "Leh Khangapha" used to be held at Somsai in Ukhrul. Hence the fall of Ukhrul in 1733 in the hands of the Meitei Maharaja heralded the entry of the Tangkhul territory into the administration.

The next significant relationship between the hills and the valley took place during the reign of Bhagyachandra (1759-1762 and 1763-1798).In 1779 king Bhagyachandra established a new capital at Langthabal about seven kilometers south east of Imphal. For the next 17 years Langthabal remained as the capital. Many Tangkhuls and Kabuis joined in the digging of moats around the new capital of Langthabal. Of the many Tangkhul Khullakpas, Khullakpa of Hundung and Ukhrul made friendship with the King. The Tangkhul Khullakpas of Ukhrul, Hundung and Huining came to pay respect to the King. King Bhagyachandra allocated land to the Tangkhuls for settlement of a Tangkhul village in the valley at a place called Puru pat. (*Ramnganing Muivah I.A.S. An Introduction to Ukhrul in "Tangkhul Baptist Long (TBL) Centenary-96" page 16-18, 1996).*

The origin of Tangkhuls is reflected in their folklores, folktales and songs. This song is very popular among the present generation and is sung during festivals and other ceremonial functions.

Bungpa Mathingkung, Bungpa Mathingkung, aprongye
Sungza prongma leiyang saying leihaosa
Sungza prongmaya, sungza prongmaya
Khungkhuleing Sachingna Ching
Leiyang Sayang leihaosa
Sachingna chingye, Sachingna chingye

Khungkhuiteng rachong khaleo
Rachong Khaleoya, Mathingza Khinigchang?
Leiyang saying leihaosa
Khiningchang leida, khining les, Mathingza ?
Sungzato rung, leiyang saying leihaosa,
Sungzato rungya, Sungzato rungya
Aungkhungla, Khining phaning ?
Leiyang Sayang leihaosa.

(A.S. W Shimray, History of the Tangkhul Nagas, Akansha Publishing House, New Delhi 110059)

Tangkhul and Meitei Ties

1. The relationship between the Tangkhuls and the Meiteis during the mediaeval period was very much on trade, commerce and social contact. They carried on regular trade and commerce. The Tangkhul supplied cotton to the valley. They also came and do business in the Sanakeithel (Khwairamband Keithel) which was the principal market in Imphal. The Tangkhuls used Manipuri coin of bell-metal locally called 'sel' as a medium of exchange which was introduced during the reign of Khagemba (1597-1652).

2. The boundary of Manipur and Burma (Myanmar) was laid down by an agreement signed between the British authorities (East India Company) and Burma on 9th January, 1834 on the river bank of Nighthee (Chindwin). The transfers of Kabow Valley in 1834 and the 12 Somra villages in 1880 to Burma were glaring instances of gross injustice knowingly committed by the British against Manipur and against the Tangkhuls. As a result of this boundary demarcation, many Tangkhul village situated in Somrah hills were transferred to Burma.

3. The oral history of the Tangkhuls say that the Meiteis and Tangkhuls were brothers being descendants of the same ancestors in the distant past. The theory that Tangkhuls and Meitei emerged from the same ancestor is found in the Sana Puya, the royal chronicles of the Meitei Raja. (See Chapter-2: Origin of Manipur). Tangkhul was the elder brother and the Meitei the younger brother. The younger brother used to send his due share of tribute (Loipot) to his elder brother, the chief of Hundung village.

Maharaj Churachand, King of Manipur re-established the relationship between Meitei and Hundung Awunga. In honour of this historic event, he erected a memorial stone in front of the house of Hundung Awunga on which his footprints were engraved. Maharaja Bodhchandra, son of Maharaja

Churachand also visited and erected a memorial stone on 11th November, 1945 by the side of the first one. His successor, Maharaja Okendrajit or Pareihanba meaning "revival –revival" celebrated Mera Hou chongba at Imphal in 1992. Maharaja Okendrajit (or Pareihanba) with a dance troupe of 300 strong and a number of people proceeded to Hundung Thawaijao village where A.S. Wungnaoyo Zimik, Awunga of Hundung village offered a warm welcome. The same Pareihanba celebration was performed with erection of a memorial stone of the Meitei Tangkhul oneness. Maharaja Okendrajit Singh presented a female buffalo to Hundung Awungwa and there was exchange of gifts between the two brothers. Thousands of people joined the celebration.

4. The Meiteis emerged from the Hundung Awunga. T.C Hodson said "the origin of Manipuris from the surrounding hill tribes is the proper and only conclusion to be arrived at".

5. During the protracted war between Burma and Manipur, many Meitei families fled to Ukhrul Hills and took shelter in Tangkhul villages to escape from the oppressions and atrocities in the hands of Burmese soldiers. Some families returned to the valley while many others got themselves absorbed in Tangkhul society.

6. Some valley people, driven out from the Valley by the Ningthoujas, fled to the Tangkhul Hills merged among the Kabuis and the Tangkhuls carrying with their original Salais of Meiteis. This happened in the first century A.D.

7. The Burmese tried to subdue the Tangkhul and a force of 700 Burmese soldiers were entirely annihilated. The 1891 Census has identified at least nine headmen of Tangkhul Villages of Ukhrul District, bearing Meitei names such as Thawaijao, Sajaoba, etc.

Physical appearance of Tangkhuls

The Tangkhuls belong to the Mongolian race. The Tangkhuls are generally tall, fair in complexion, handsome and more akin to the Mongolians in facial appearance and stature. Tangkhul women are quite beautiful. There is a Manipuri song "Ukhrul da eigi thawai leihoure "capturing the beauty of Tangkhul girls. (see plate 144, 177)

Tangkhul House

The typical Tangkhul house is known as Phen Sam, which is made of wood and bamboo. The upper roof of the house is covered with thatch and the plank of wood is used for walls and floor of the house. The front side is a bit higher than the backside. There is a cross sign at the top of the front side of the house. The approximate size of the house is 11.10 metres in length and 4.50 metres in width. The front wall is made of wood. There are wood carvings of different shapes, sizes and forms such as human heads, dancing performances, tiger's stripes and paintings etc. on the face of the front wall. By reading these carvings and paintings, one can tell the history of the community. The Tangkhul house structure is more or less similar for all the villages, but the carvings on the posts and blinks vary from village to village and area to area. To display the splendour and wealth of the rich and noble families, tree trunks– "Tarung" are erected in front of the house. Some even erect monoliths in the courtyards or at some prominent sites in the village area. Construction of all these entails strict ritualistic procedures and norms. (see plate-167)

Occupation :

Like most other communities in Manipur, most Tangkhuls are also primarily agriculturists. Rice is the staple food. Other crops and vegetables are cotton, millet, maize, arum, chili, sesame, ginger, tomato, pumpkin, cucumber, beans, etc.

Hairstyle (Coiffure)

In olden days, the Tangkhul men used to wear a distinctive hair style called' "Coiffure". They cut the hair closely at the edges, leaving a broad crest, which varies from two to five inches down the middle of the skull. From the point of the skull, the crest narrows to the nape of the neck where the hair, which they allow to grow long and is tied in a loop (T.C. Hudson-The Naga Tribes of Manipur, page-27) Small boys have their hair shaved off with a round patch left on the point of the skull. The Tangkhuls do not wear a beard or moustache because the women regard those with beard or moustache as disfigurement. Very young girls have their heads shaved but on reaching the marriageable age, they allow the hair to grow long and wear a fringe combed over the forehead and parted down the middle like the married girls among the Meteis.

Tattooing

Tattooing was common among the Tangkhul women. They used tattooing to identify their women. Tattooing starts as three lines of about three –eighths of an inch in width starts from the point of the chin round the neck right up to the navel. The upper arm might be tattooed in a similar pattern with lines in diagonal fashion making two crosses, which are generally kept separate. The breast were not tattooed. They learnt this art from the Shans. Tattooing was done in installments always in the cold weather. Lampblack and the juice of wild indigo were used as colouring matter. An old women who was acquainted with the skills pierced the skin with a sharp bamboo splinter.

Ornaments

Both Tangkhul men and women loved to wear ornaments. The men have their ears pierced at an early age and gradually distend the holes in the ear lobes until they are large enough to receive rolls of cotton of considerable size or bamboo ornaments.

Brass cylindrical ornaments or empty cartridge case were often inserted as a personal decoration. The ear lobe is frequently pierced with many holes into which blue or black cotton rolls were inserted. They wore costly necklaces of beads and as a mark of distinction a collar of red and yellow cane work with geometrical pattern was hanging down the back. One peculiar ornament is a loose collar of brass about six inches wide in front of the neck and tapering gradually to the back where it is fastened.

The Tangkhuls also wear heavy armlets on the forearm and sometimes coiled wire rings. They also wear cane or brass rings coiled below the knee which are believed to give support while climbing hills.The ornaments worn by the women are necklaces of the polished hexagonal cornelian beads, the number and value of which affects the price. They have the ears pierced and wear similar but smaller ornaments. Young girls wear metal armlets on the upper arm, which are made of white metal nut. (see plate-168, 173, 176).

Weapons

The Tangkhuls used spear, dao, bow and arrow and fire arms as weapons. The spear may be of great length and is used for thrusting. The dao is a steel blade about eighteen inches long narrow at the shaft and square and broad at the tip, pointless and sharpened on one side only. It may be decorated with Goat's hair (see plate-172) The blade is set in a handle of wood, a bamboo root is considered the best. The fighting dao is differently shaped, this is a long, pointless sword set in a wooden handle or ebony. It is very heavy and a blow of almost incredible power can be given by one of these weapons. The dao is the bread winner for the Tangkhuls. With this, he cuts his jhoom, builds his house, fashions the women's weaving tools, defends himself from attacks of wild animals. The southern Tangkhuls were said to be using poisoned bows and arrows. The bow is strong and the arrow head barbed. The arrows are poisoned with vegetable extract, which is dark brown, gummy –looking extract soluble in water. Two types of shields are used. A long, oblong shield sometimes curved at the top and the round buckler, the efficacy of which is really due to the skill and agility of the man behind it. The oblong shield is about four feet long and two feet six inches wide at the top narrowing to two feet at the bottom. It is made of buffalo hide or closely plaited cane and is strong enough to turn a spear. It is held by two loops inside and decorated with plumes of toucan's feathers and pendent tassels of cock's feathers. Often it is embellished by a leopard's skin or by black cloth with a broad stripe of red in the middle. The round buckler is also made of buffalo hide.

Traditional tools / implements ornaments : The following are the traditional tools and implements :-

Table-42 Showing traditional tools / implements of Tangkhuls

Man's	*Woman's*	*Man's*	*Woman's*
Varao Kazei	Zeithing	Mayong pasi	Huishon
Kazei	Vakui	Khommasing	
Malah	Mayongcha	Haar Kazao	
Khairei	Pheimakhei	Nakhui	
Kuisikhai	Kangra	Mani	
Ngalasop			
Ngalsop Kasai			
Khaiva	Yotpak	Kazao	
Khainao/shori	Kiantin	Charei	
Changkui	Changphar	Kongsang	
Raikhai	Lingriham	Narengthei	
Ngaha	Kasai	. Cha	

Tangkhul Language

Tangkhuls have several dialects but the Ukhrul dialect serves as the medium of communication among the Tangkhuls and it is called the Tangkhul language. They do not have written script of their own. They used Roman script as medium for writing. The Tangkhul dialect belong to the Sino-Tibetan family and within that family to the sub-family Tibeto-Burman. They converse well in chaste Manipuri language with others.

Religion

The Tangkhul Religion, known to some as Hao Religion, is a monotheistic religion with a little blend of animism. They believed in the existence of a Supreme God whom they call by different names such as "*Kasa Akhava*" (Creator or Master of Creation)", "*Varivara*" (Source of peace), *Kazingpa* (dweller of heaven) and *Reisang Chonmi.* They believe in the existence of heaven (*Kazigram*) and Hell *(Kazeiram).* The God is situated in the heaven or the sky above whereas the hell is situated in the heart of the earth, an underground world. The souls of those who committed sins and crimes go to *Kazeiram* and *Kokto*, the King of dead rules over them.

They also believed in the existence of spirits who are capable of creating harms such as diseases and sickness, calamities and causing death. They call these spirits *Chipee, Kameo.* The evil spirits are called *"Rai Kaphung".*

This religious background makes them receptive to Christian Faith, and hence it's ready acceptance. Ukhrul is the birthplace of Christianity and western education in Manipur State, brought as early as 1896 by a Baptist Missionary called Rev. Pettigrew. Now, almost 95 % of the population have embraced Christianity. The main Christian sects are: Baptist Church, Catholic Church, Seventh Dav Adventist Church, Church of Christ etc. There are also some small groups of Hindus, Muslims, and others who settled in Ukhrul.

Longshim (Bachelors Dormitory)

Longshim is one of the most important institution of Tangkhul village. "Long" means association or collection of people. "Shim" means house or club or chamber or dormitory. Every Thangkhul village has one Longshim or more where unmarried boys and girls sleep in their separate sleeping Longshims. Longshim plays an important role in the cultural, religious, social, economic, military and political life of Tangkhuls. It is also called "Morung". Longshim is also a cultural, entertainment and educational centre where young people are trained in various arts and crafts, dance and music, morality, discipline, as well as in the arts of defence and offence. Discipline is strictly enforced.

Ngalalong : (Girls Dormitory)

Ngalalong is the dormitory for the girls. Ngala means maiden and Long means group or association. In most cases, separate quarters are provided attached to the house of a clan head or a rich man who act as a patron of Ngalalong. The running of Ngalalong including admission, training and functions are all the same as that of Longshim. All unmarried girls who have attained puberty should take membership of Ngalalong and sleep there till marriage. The senior members taught the girls weaving, spinning, stitching, embroidery and imparted moral lessons and behaviours towards opposite sex. In this way, the character of a Tangkhul girl is moulded to enable them to maintain a safe, healthy and responsible behaviour and to take the responsibilities of motherhood.

Awunga

The Chief of the Tangkhul village is called Awunga. The post is hereditary and continues in the family by succession of the eldest male according to the principles of primogeniture. It can't be disputed nor purchased or sold. The Tangkhul villages are independent of each other. Awunga is not the sole owner of the village land. The land belongs to the whole village community. Awunga was maker of the law called *Mayonrin* on the basis of democracy. Most of the laws are derived from custom, tradition, culture and religious principles. Awunga has to exercise his power prescribed by the customary law. Customary laws has religious sanction. Awunga has secular function as the head of the village. At the same time, he has religious functions also. In his religious function, he is assisted by the village priest (Sherra). The secular functions include protection of his subjects, defending the village from enemies, peace, prosperity of the village, erection of village gates. He summons the village council, *Hangva* and presides over it. Every visitor should report to him regarding the nature and purpose of visit. It is his duty to ensure that no visitor is maltreated. There is no class division in the Tangkhul society. Slavery is unknown He is assisted in his work by the chiefs of the clans residing in the village. These Clan Chiefs are known as *Wungnaos*. As a part of his religious duties, he has to ensure that social and religious functions are held with performance of rituals and sacrifices. He has to observe strict religious discipline, taboos. In all functions, he occupies the most prominent seat of honour, gets the best portion of wine and meat. He gets a portion of animals killed in the village and from all hunted games. He is entitled to get a portion of the harvest from the villagers.

Hangva

Hangva is the village authority with the village chief as the head and the Clan Chiefs as members. If the clan is very big, more membership may be accepted. If representation of some influential people will be beneficial, then they can be taken as members of the Hangva. Hangva has got executive, administrative and judiciary functions. *Riyan* is the unwritten constitution of the Tangkhuls. Culture, traditions, customs and conventions serve as the foundations of Riyan. Hangva carries out the day to day administration of the village. The collective wisdom of this Hangva governs the village administration. The decisions of the Hangva is based on consensus unanimity.

Marriage

The marriages according to Tangkhul custom are a happy blend of tradition and love and affection. The marriage is usually an arranged marriage but nowadays love marriage is also becoming popular. But the boys and girls must secure the consent of their parents before marriage. Similarly, if the parents want to get married, they must seek and secure the consent of their children. An unmarried bachelor has no place in the Tangkhul society Marriage within the same clan is a taboo and forbidden. Marriage against the customary laws like co-sanguinary marriage, incest resulted in expulsion from the village and their children will have the stigma. Cross cousin marriages is also forbidden by the customary laws of Tangkhuls. A person can marry the daughter of his mother's brother and not vice versa and under no circumstances, such marriages should not be denied. If either party failed to fulfill this term, heavy fine can be imposed on the defaulter. Monogamy is universally prevalent in the Tangkhul society. There is no dowry system and there is no bride price. The Tangkhul couples can not divorce whatever hardship may come in their lives. Adultery or infertility of the women may constitute ground for divorce. Widow marriage is sanctioned by the custom of the Tangkhuls either to the brother of the deceased or any other person provided the marriage is based on the principle of exogamy.

Disposal of dead

The Tangkhuls bury their dead outside their houses to the depth of the length of the corpse plus a margin for top dressing of stones. Every household has its own grave in which all dead bodies from the ancestors are buried. Where there are no family graves near the house, other graves can be opened if there has been no burial during the past year. But before doing so, a sort of ceremony has to be performed with the bones of the departed. One man of the village is usually set apart to do this kind of job. On opening the family grave, the bone are collected, cleaned with water and then wrapped in a large cloth, new or old and put on the side of the grave. When a great number of bones are collected, and there is no sufficient room for a fresh corpse, they are taken out of the tomb and when the fresh corpse has been buried and covered to the depth of a few feet, the bones are thrown in to help fill up the graves. The bottom of the grave is made circular to hold the corpse and the things buried in it. The Tangkhuls bury the dead body with the used, old cloths for the use of the dead man and along new cloth as a present for the deity of Heaven (Kokto). Tobacco and a pipe are laid near at hand. In case of females, food and drinks are given along with cooking pots, digging sticks and brow hands which she used to carry loads from the fields during her life time. If a man dies of tiger bite, they put a bugle in his grave to scare away the tigers on the road to heaven. Sometimes, they provide spear and kill a dog to keep him company on his long journey to heaven. Over the body they play the bugle before burial. On the day of burial, the rich kill a buffalo, others manage a cow or a pig. The animals are killed before starting digging of the grave and left whole until the grave is finished. It is then cut up, the relations take half and grave diggers the other half of intestine. The head is given to the nearest male relative, the right hind leg given to the eldest daughter, the left hind leg to the next daughter. The forelegs are given to other distant relatives. The heart, liver, kidneys, spleen, lungs etc., are handed over to the village priest (Sherra). The Sherra will divide the meat into portions–six portions for a male and five potions for a female and takes them to the next door neighbour's house and cook the same. He then brings them to the deceased's house and places them on the top of rice and vegetables which the relatives have brought in the morning. He then offers the food to the Kameo (evil spirit) by reciting "*Thisan yamsanrava, shaiphung shap phungda thulu*" and calls up the dead to eat this offering, take the special portion on a plate of his own and throws them away in the compound. Beer is also offered. After this ceremony of the priest, the rest of the meat and rice is divided among all and eaten before the burial. One of the relatives of the deceased takes a pine torch from a house nearby and descends into the grave and twirling it round beseeches the ancestors of the dead to come down and meet him on the way to Kazeiram by saying the prayer "*O awo ayi ! ishava rarali ungngaroklu*". The hands of the corpse are washed with water. Then the body is placed in the grave with all the gifts. After filling the grave with earth, the Sherra placed a pole above the mound while others placed six prongs of wood around a small hole made in the mound wherein placed a pine torch. On lighting the pine torch, all leave the grave and enter the home. On entering, fresh fire is brought from another house nearby and the people sit around the fire. Next morning and evening, the pine torch on the grave is again lighted. This is continued for three days The spirit, after meeting with the Kokto and after handing over the gifts he had brought to the ancestors is supposed to return on the following day after burial. For this reason, family keeps all doors open from morning to night and from that day until the final disposal of the spirit from the village at the great feast of *"Kathi Kasham"* the family prepares with their own meals a similar one for the spirit. It is then put into a plate used when alive by the deceased and put on his or her own seat twice a day. If the deceased is a warrior, then his nearest relation takes a spear and wounds the corpse by a blow with it on the head so that on his arrival in the next world, he may be known and received with distinction.

However, if any death occurs due to war or accident outside the village, the dead body is buried outside the village gate. Whenever a death occurs in a village, a public solemn is declared and engagement in work is prohibited. An animal is killed in honour of the dead whether big or small according to the ability of the family and the meat is shared among the family members of the dead and those who were engaged in the burial of the dead. A special portion of the meat goes to the village priest (Sharra) for performing sacrificial rites. A portion of the belongings of the dead are buried along. It is believed that these belongings will be used by the soul of the dead in "Kazeiram" and that the comfort of the life after death partly depends on the preparation of the family for the dead.

The Tangkhuls believe in life after death.Those who live a righteous life on this earth will go to heaven after death and live with God with bliss and happiness. Tangkhuls believed that their dead go to heaven by a path over the crest of Sirohifurar. This is the realm of the Diety "Kok-thi-yong" "Kok–thi-makha" "Kok-thu" or Kokto. This place is called "Kazeiram". They also believed that the spirits of the dead appear at a distance from the village in a faint moonlight wending their way slowly over the hills and driving before them the victims they may have slain or the cattle stolen during their life time. The procession disappears amidst the wails of the villagers. Unless the village priest is well fed, it is said that this appearance will not take place.

Log Drum

The log drum is constructed out of a single giant tree about fifty to sixty feet long and ten feet in diameter. The trunk is made hollow all along with a slit in its upper side. When it is beaten with drum sticks, it produces mighty sounds reaching about hundred miles distance. The log drum is an essential item in the life of Tangkhuls, who used it at time of war and peace. The occurrence of war, death, victory in war, advent of festivals etc are signaled by beating the log drum in various styles conveying specific sounds appropriate for the occasion. The people would respond to the sound of the drum according to the message conveyed. In the earlier days, the log drum was used to announce the arrival of enemies from the neighbouring village so that people could take defensive position in time against the raid and attack the enemy.

War : Head Taking

The Tangkhuls are fierce war like people and continuously occupied with head taking. How can the community know that a warrior has killed the enemy without the head of the enemy being produced by him? How can he boast about the fact that his enemy has been killed by him without producing the proof? Therefore bringing of the heads of the enemy killed in the war was a must for a Tangkhul warrior to testify his achievement of killing the enemy in war.

Head taking is associated with blood feuds. Once started, they indulged in head taking till the tally of heads is numerically equal. No young man could find a wife until he has taken a head. In 1891 David observed that the desire for head taking was more the fault of the woman than of the man. Success in head taking was essential to marriage. Head taking was regarded at least as a token of having passed from adolescence to maturity. In Tangkhul villages, there are heaps of stones which are considered as places of great sanctity where the heads taken in the raid are placed for five days during which the warriors were subjected to a process of social or religious restrictions. The Meiteis called these places "Laipham" means places of God. An oath taken on these stones is regarded as "most binding".

The Tangkhuls have refined customary laws and principles of war that guide their participation in warfare. According to Tangkhul custom, it is forbidden for a Tangkhul warrior to touch a woman immediately before or after the war for a certain length of time even for months when he is observing divination except for chopping of heads. This shows high standard of morality of the Tangkhul war. It is believed that possession of human head brings fertility of women, soil, social prestige and happiness after death, the soul of the victim being the servant of the soul of the victor in the land of "Kazeiram". War is inevitable when there is violation of inter-village boundary, laws, divorce of woman without reasonable cause or murder without sufficient reason by one party.

No price is too costly for the Tangkhuls for defending their village or the people. Before going to war, the warrior had to abstain from having conjugal relationship with his wife or touch anything which belongs to women. He should perform rites and sacrifices and consult the meaning of dreams and divinations. When he found positive responses from the spirit, then only he could go to war equipped with dao, spear, shield, helmet and sometimes bow and arrow. The declaration of war is made to the enemy village through a war messenger. If the security of the messenger is in question, then the message is sent through a neutral village. The two parties met either at the appointed battle field or the aggressive party could make surprise attacks to the enemy village using their tactics. Each village has its own defence system with well secured village gate with heavy solid beam surrounded by stone boulders, ditch and sharp–pointed bamboo spikes. The war may continue for days, weeks months, or years even for generations. Agricultural season is however honoured. Sometimes, the warring parties chose the best warriors to fight on behalf of the whole village. The warriors so chosen will come forward with war dance and war cry and measured footsteps. They displayed their war tactics and met each other. Each of them tried to step on the spear of the opponent and pressed it hard on the ground. Then immediately the one who was in a better position demanded his opponent to lay down arms and surrender. The one who has surrendered should not be killed and his head should not be taken under any circumstances. The village of the one who win the battle was declared winner of the war. The village Awunga of Tangkhuls do not permit to fight inter clan war within the village. The victorious party coming back home with heads as a war trophy yelled and howled with war cry as a sign of their victorious return. Then people at home come out with burning torch at the village gate and welcomed their war heroes. On the night of their return, they beat a log drum for victory and spent the night singing and dancing with war weapons. Lavish food, drink and meat were served. Then the head is deposited at Longshim. Women should not participate in the war rites and ceremonies. They could not touch the meat. Those who killed the enemies and brought the heads are entitled to wear a shawl embroidered in a special way. This type of Shawl could also be worn by the "Awunga" and those who performed Feats of Merit. They had the privilege to decorate their dresses and war weapons with human hair. But surprisingly, those who killed women and children are more honourable than those who killed a warrior in the belief that during those period of war, women and children were kept in the most secured places and only those who are strong and courageous enough could penetrate through and take their head.

Peace could be initiated by either party through the service of Pukreila, usually a woman married to a man of the enemy village. She is called Ambassador of Peace, who can not be harmed. She has to hold a branch of green leaves as a sign of peace. Peace could also be brought about by the intervention of a neutral village. When peace was established, there was exchange of food and drink to signify peaceful settlement

Swearing and Oath Taking

To the Tangkhuls, swearing and oath taking is a life and death question not only to the swearer but also the family and even to the village. The Tangkhuls never take it lightly. They swear only in extremely serious cases when he is convinced that he is right and the opponent is wrong. They believed that if they swear in the name of almighty, the God may punish them and their lives and the lives of the family members may be in perpetual danger. Oath may take different forms. Tiger's tooth is frequently used in oath taking. The man who swears bites the tiger's tooth saying that if he falsely swears he will be eaten by the tiger. People also swear in the name of thunder saying that if he swears falsely, he will be hit and killed by the thunder. In case of land dispute, the earth of the disputed land is taken into the mouth and swallowed to testify that he is the actual owner of the land. They believed that "the result of the swear or oath taking is bound to them in course of time and no one can escape from the words he utters in the name of God". Sometimes ordeals are made in case of trials. They are asked to bite burning charcoal and the one who is innocent will escape the burn of the charcoal unharmed. One form of ordeal is diving into the water pond. The one who stays longer is declared the winner of the case. This form of ordeal is usually used to decide cases involving women. Another form of ordeal is to fight out justice by combat. But it has to be sanctioned by the village court (Hangva). The village court makes two clubs or daos or swords of equal size-length, breadth and weight, which are kept in safe custody for one or two days. If the parties still insisted on the combat, then it is allowed by the court. The one who strike or hit the opponent first was declared the winner and ultimately the case was settled.

Economy

The Tangkhuls were self-reliant and self-sufficient. But with the advent of modern civilization, their requirements increased. The people could maintain and afford to meet their requirements for their day to day subsistence and livelihood. Their requirements were small and minimal. The main sources of income of the people are agriculture, industries, forest wealth, riverine wealth and animal husbandry.

Tangkhul Festivals

The ancestors of Tangkhuls were agriculturists and the year cycle festivals are associated with the year-round seasonal agricultural activities. All these festivals associated with sacred religious rituals and there were strict codes of conduct for all these festivals. The major year cycle festivals are :

1. Luira Phanit

This is the New Year festival of Tangkhuls. This is also known as seed sowing festival which falls during the month of January to March. It is usually celebrated in the full moon of February–March of the year lasting about 10-15 days. There is an elaborate arrangement for food, drinks and clothing well in advance. The Awunga of the village fix the date and period of the festival where the village crier announces the date and period of the Luira Phanit to the entire community. On the first day, a number of animals such as cattle and pigs are sacrificed. First, the village Awunga will eat and test the meat and blesses the people.Then the villages are allowed to start eating. The village gate is closed for a few days to stop entering of outsiders or the villagers leaving the village. These first few days are considered to be solemn days where no work is to be performed except singing and dancing throughout the day and night to relieve the people from their daily monotonous daily routine work. At the end of the first few days of solemn period, the Awunga and his wife go the field with a chicken and perform ceremonial rite, offer prayers for protection of crops and bumper harvest of the year. The blood of the chicken on a clean handful of paddy are sprayed on the prepared ground as a symbolic sowing. Thus the sowing season is inaugurated and the villagers are allowed to start cultivation. If anybody violates the rules and sows ahead of the Awunga, heavy punishment is meted out to the violator because it is considered that such violation will bring famine to the village. After the few days, the relatives and outsiders are invited and welcome to the village and they are lavishly entertained.This feast is celebrated with great fervour at Longpi and Hundung. Longpi, befitting their generosity, entertain their guests with lavish eats and drinks, whilst in Hundung one can see the maiden virgin dance performance.

2. Yarra

This is festival celebrated before starting cultivation and it falls during the months of April and May. Though it is celebrated by all, it is essentially a youth festival.

3. Mangkhap

This is a festival of Tangkhuls usually performed at the end of June or beginning of July every year when the hard work of seed sowing or shifting cultivation is over. This is a post-transplantation festival. It usually last for three or four days spending time in singing and feasting or by burning lamps or torch of pine resin. During this festival, the people pray for luxurious growth of the crops after thanksgiving prayer for the timely rain.

4. Darreo

This is a pre-harvest festival. Darreo means the plucking of the new crop. On this day the first crops, fishes, live-stocks and other items are brought out for sale in the village market. It is fete day for the village. This day is specially observed in Hundung village.

5. Darshat Phanit

Dharshat Phanit is the harvest festival of the Tangkhuls. The Awunga of the village will go to the field one day ahead of his people and bring a basketful of paddy. He performs rituals, ceremonies and offers prayers for the rich harvest of the whole village. On the next day, the villages are allowed to pluck the new crop. They will also perform the same rituals and offer prayers to their domestic household deities so that there may be enough food throughout the year. The day is dedicated to prayer and no other form of work is done.

6. Chumphut Phanit

Chumphut Phanit is a new rice eating festival celebrated by women or housewives after the harvest is over. It falls during the months of November and December.This is a festival of thanksgiving for rich harvest, now gathered in the granary.The mother performs special offerings to the God of harvest and the keeper of the granary. During this festival, the male members of the village are required to stay outside the village gate so that they might not see the performance of their women at night. If they happen to see their wives performing the Chumphut Phanit, it is believed that ill-luck would strike the home and there would be shortage of food grains for the house before the next season. While the mother performs her rituals all males are not allowed to enter the house, hence they are outside the house for the night with lavish supplies of eats and drinks. While performing this festival, the village ponds are cleaned, the existing water of the pond is thoroughly drained off, new rice is cooked with fresh water. A village virgin whose character is above reproach has to draw the water first then she is followed by other women. During this festival, working at home and outside is strictly prohibited. The festival may last for three or four days. Blowing bugles is allowed till the commencement of the Thisham Phanit festival. When the villagers test the newly cooked rice, they say "Rice is bitter, rice is bitter" so that the evil spirit will not enter the house where the rice is bitter. Because of the nature of its celebration, it is sometimes known as the Feast of the mother or the Feast of the granary.

7. Longra Khamang

The family which had a rich harvest celebrates this festival inviting the group of the son's or daughter's friends who had worked in groups during the cultivation and harvesting. This is a festival for giving special treatments to the sons and daughters.

8. Thisham Phanit

The Thisam Phanit marks the end of the Tangkhul year, which is held sometime in December-January every year. Thisham is a festival in commemoration of the dead. The Thisham Phanit is performed with a special arrangement of food and drinks to send off the soul to "Kazeiram" where Kokto, the King of dead rules. It is on this occasion that the dance of the Dead is performed. This is the final ritual performed by the family for the dead. The festival is meant for families where death has occurred but the whole village celebrates it together and it last for about ten days. Animals are sacrificed and prepare food and other articles for the dead. They engage the service of the village priest. The priest invokes the Kokto and the soul of the dead by singing, dancing and chanting. First, he pleads the Kokto to welcome the soul of the dead and not to bring death to the family any more. The priest also ask the soul to depart in peace with offerings made by the family for his journey to Kazeiram and for use in the land of dead. The priest donned the cloths and articles of the dead and threw them off outside the village gate never to be picked up again and bade farewell to the departed soul.

The relatives of the dead take a procession at night singing and dancing howling war cry and march outside the village gate. Some of them stay awake throughout the night.

9. Kathi Kasham :

The festival is meant to expel the dead from the village. Kathi means "dead", Kasham means "expulsion". According to Tangkhul belief, the soul of the dead remains in the house enjoying food and drinks before it goes to "Kazeiram", the land of death.

1st day : The ropes for binding animals for sacrifice and the poles for hanging cloths are procured from the jungles.

2nd day : The males tested the ropes whether it will withstand the strain by the animals being sacrificed. The women are busy collecting and staking woods.

3rd day : This is the day for sacrificing the animals, buffaloes and cows. It is considered quite a sight and crowds gather to see the horrible sight. Then animals are cut into pieces and distributed in the same way as performed on the death of the person. Then the village priest offer it to "Kameo". (evil spirits)

4th day : They collect huge quantities of wood for fire and there is a lot of singing and dancing during the feast.The representative of the dead *(Thila Kapo)* collect the "Khamuina" a kind of broad plantain leaf used for the unleavened bread made the next day.

5th day: Pigs and dogs are killed and cut into small pieces, cooked and offered to Kameo (evil spirits) and distributed with a small cake of bread wrapped in the Khamuina leaves among the mourners. On this day, cloths of all varieties and qualities are attached to long poles and erected outside each house of the dead. The more cloths displayed the greater one is thought of.

6th day: Rice beer which has been fermenting for some days in prepared in large cask and any other work left unfinished is completed.

7th day:Before arrival of guests and relatives, the females offer prayer and gifts to *"Kameo"* and then the village priest (Sherra) made offerings of slices of pork to *Kameo* by placing it on the platform of the "Wonyai thing". Then the relatives and guests from surrounding village start arriving. After arrival of the villagers, each family of the dead calls for the *Thila Kapo,* representative of the dead. The *Thila Kapo* is decked with bright head gear, necklaces, armlets and leglets. He performs a dance outside and then on entering introduced to the seat of the dead. From this point till the end of the feast, he is looked upon as the dead person in life and he is treated as somebody, near and dear one with no prospect of seeing him again. He is presented with all the food cooked and given all the hospitality. The cloths hung upon poles after having been seen and admired by the villagers are taken down and brought into the house to be given to the representative of dead later on.

8th day : The representative of the dead, *Thila Kapo* gives to the villagers, who are already dressed up for the occasion, a specimen of dancing powers in the large space called "*Laingapha Kayang*". The village priest cut up a portion of the skins of the pigs killed on the fifth day and offer to *Kameo*. The remaining portion is cooked. After the exhibition by the "*Thila Kapo*", the cooked food is taken and fed by the female members. Then the representative of the dead collects the clothes going from house to house. By the time, he finished visiting, he has already collected a good pile of cloths and he takes the first opportunity to sell all he does not require for himself.

9th day : This is a great day of feast. The family procures the plantain leaves to cover the pine torches which are made extra large for use at sunset. Pig's meat and rice are cooked and placed on large plates with salt and fish and brought on the village compound. The relatives and friends gather at the lowest point of the village where a death has occurred, each carrying his or her load of meat, ginger, rice, beer and cloths. These are placed on mats in a row. Empty plates and pots are also placed near and are then filled up. Everybody is dressed up for the occasion. When everybody is ready, the village priest gives a great shout "*He, hiaina tatang taranga*" and everybody takes hold of the plates and pots and holding them above their heads take all to the "*Thila kapos*". They may have another meal here. When the sunset come, there is a great procession headed by pine torch bearers followed by a crowd of elders in their war garb and lastly the *Thila Kapos* with lot of lamenting and grief. The procession proceeds slowly towards "*Zaiphar*" a spot at the north end of the village overshadowed by a large tree. The idea is that the spirit need to be led in the gathering twilight to show them the way to their place of abode "*Kazeiram*" and warriors are also needed as a guard to protect them from all harms on their way. The spirit is supposed to enter into the lighted pine torches as soon as they are thrown down at *Zaiphar.* By the time, these torches reach this place, the *Thila Kapo* have reached the limit of the village boundary. The headgear is broken up on the spot. The villagers return to the village while the torch bearers returned to the village taking another route. Before entering their house the "*wonyai thing*" structure erected outside is dismantled. A torch is placed on a stone lighted just inside the house at the front door not to allow the spirits of the living to go off with the spirits of the dead.

10th day : This is a day of rest. It is believed that the embodied spirit in "Kazeiram" cut all their hair off on the tenth day and have a sort of wash and brush up to remove all connection with the mother earth. On this day, nobody is supposed to take bath or touch water.

Apart from these major festivals, there are some event-occasioned festivals like; Kashong Kahao Zakhalat, a sacred ritual for dispelling pests and germs; Maa Khungkashat, acknowledgement of the rich crop. Ears of corn are plucked and placed at a post set apart for this sacred ritual in the house; Mawonzai, a feast to invoke the graceful blessings of God to human labour; Khana Kasa, a purification and naming feast; Ming Kaphok, this is a title endowment feast; Chumsin Sa Kashai, this is the ordaining feast of the daughter-in-low to priestess-hood, thereby endowing her with all the rights and duties of a family mother. Prior to this, she is not allowed to enter into the granary; Shimsak Kasa, this is the royal or noble house construction feast; Maran-sak and Tarung Khangkasang, stone or tree trunks erection feast to display the wealth and power of the noble.

Musical Instruments

The stringed musical instruments like Pena, Ollobii Kada, Tingtila, Saringda, solid instruments like Gong, Cymbal, small Cymbals (locally known as mandila) and Upum (Hollow wood) are used. Different kinds of drums for different festivals and ceremonies are also used. The wind instruments like Tharaochi, Conch, all made of bamboo are also used.

Some of the musical instruments are: 1. Tingteila (Violin), 2. Tala (Trumpet), 3. Phung (Drum), 4. Mazo (Woman's mouth-piece), 5. Sipa (Flute), 6. Kaha Ngashingkhon (Bamboo pipe) etc.

Music and Dances

Tangkhuls are music lovers and their songs are soft and melodious. Apart from encoding into the music the varied seasonal and cultural ideas and philosophies, music is a medium wherein historical events are also related in the lyrics. In as much as religious fervour is incorporated and composed in the songs, the romantic nature of the people also finds its expressions in the music. There are various varieties of songs, some are mood special, some are festival/seasonal specials. These folksongs and folklores can be taught and sung by anybody, anytime, but there are also some specific musical expressive melodies of every region or area.

These folksongs and folklores can be played or accompanied by musical instruments. Corresponding to the rhythmic composition of the songs, the dances of the Tangkhuls are also rhythmic and these are eventful and vigorous. Thrilling as they are, there are also some special occasional dances, like the Kathi Mahon - dance for the dead, Tangkhul war dance (see plate-167) Laa Khanganui - virgin dance during Luira Festival, Rain Pheichak -war Dance etc.

Laa Khanganui (Virgin Dance)

The Laa Khanganui is truly the most colourful and grandeour, most exciting music or song competition, where all the unmarried girls who have attained puberty must take part and where the most beautiful girl of the village is to be selected from among the virgins. Any girl who refused to participate at the Laa Khanganui is suspected of being pregnant and heavy punishment is meted out to her.The competitors are allowed to wear well designed and embroidered traditional short skirt exposing the calves and the upper portion of the body from the waist. Their heads are decorated with headgears, the hands with armlets, bangles and kongsang for the lone covering of their breasts. The participants will move on the ground being surrounded by spectators. As they move in, they can rock their bodies, perform slow movement or dance with the tune of the music. The spectators are the judges and they will decide the fate of the virgin who become the most beautiful virgin. If the girl missed uniform footsteps, falls down on the ground or one of her ornaments falls off her body, it is considered that the morality of the girl is not above reproach. Heavy fine is imposed on such a girl by the village as well as by the Ngalalong where she belongs to. This kind of ritual encourage the Tangkhul girls to remain virgin and maintain high moral standard till they marry and live with their husbands.

Art and Culture

The life and art of the Tangkhul are attractive and captivating. Their different costumes and wears, utensils, architecture, monumental erections and memorial set-ups depict their dexterity in art, which also speak of their sense of beauty and fineness. Though there are common costumes and wears, both for male and female, there are also some costumes and wears exclusively meant for male and female.

Textiles and Clothes

Some of the traditional clothes and clothes/shawls are as follows:- (man's and women's) (see plates-166-168)

Table-43 Showing Varieties of Traditional Clothes of Tangkhuls

Man's	*Woman's*	*Both for Man and Women*
1. Haora (Man's mostly)	1. Malao	1. Phangyai
2. Chonkhom (Women's mostly)	2. Laokha	2. Kahang Kashan
3. Thangkang (for man and woman)	3. Kahang Malao	3. Seichang Kashan
4. Luirim (man's mostly)	4. Thangkang	4. Thangkang Kashan
5. Raivat Kachon (Common)	5. Khuilang Kashan	
6. Khuilang Kachon (woman's mostly)	6. Kongrah Kashan	
7. Phingui Kachon (common)	7. Shanphaila	
8. Phaphir (common)	8 Kuiying Muka (upper cover)	
9. Phorei Kachon (man's mostly)	9. Zingtai Kashan	
10. Luingamla Kashan		

Maran Kasa (Feast of Merit)

Maran Kasa means feast of merit. This is a feast offered by rich or capable and generous people to provide food and drinks to the village community particularly poor people, widows and orphans. It was purely a social and philanthropic service that he shared his wealth with people in the community. After performing two or three times of *Maran Kasa,* the donor is entitled to wear a special type of embroidered cloth and erect a "*Tarung*" (a tree) in front of his house or to raise house horn called *"Lenchangkui"* at the facade of his house.

The one who intends to perform Maran Kasa should observe certain rituals. He should refrain from having conjugal relationship with his wife and consult with the village priest about the possible good or bad impact of the Maran Kansa he is likely to perform. If the result is positive, he makes a public declaration about the Maran Kasa. Preparations for the Maran Kasa may begin months ahead of the date of the Maran Kasa. When the actual day of

Maran kasa comes, the selected tree of the Tarung is felled down and carved into its design. Then the able male population of the village drag it home with the music of "Ho-Ho" cry filling the air. There should be uninterrupted supply of food and drinks in the course of dragging the Tarung. It may take days or even weeks to bring the Tarung home. While erecting the Tarung, a large number of buffaloes, cows, pigs etc were sacrificed and the blood of the animals sacrificed are smeared to the post erected in front of the house (Tarung). The Awunga is invited to this ceremony and given the most prominent seat and served the best choice of meat and wine. The entire village is invited and the feast continued for days even for weeks until all the domestic animals are killed and eaten. Then the whole village blessed the one who perform the feast and offer prayers that they may enjoy happy an prosperous life.

References

Alexander Mackenzie, The North East Frontier of India Mittal Publications, New Delhi, 1884

A.S. W Shimray, History of the Tangkhul Nagas, Akansha Publishing House, New Delhi 110059, 2001

Atombapu Sharma, Manipur Itihas, Part 2

B.C. Allen, E.A. Gait, H.F. Howard, C.G H. Allen "Gazeteer of Bengal and North East India", A Mittal Publication, 2001.

Brown, R., 1873: The Statistical Account of Manipur.

Charles Chasle "The Naga Imbroglio (A personal perspective", United Publishers, Guwahati, 1999.

Columbia: B.C.S and T. Edward Gaide, 1963: A History of Assam.

Eaton, Richard M., 1997. 'Comparative History as World History: Religious Conversion in Modern India, Journal of World History 8(2): 243-271.

Dr. Lal Dena, History of Modern Manipur (1826-1946) edited,1990

Dr. M. Kirti Singha, Religious developments in Manipur in the 18th and 19th century, 1980

Dr. M. Kirti Singha,Religion and Culture of Manipur 1988

Gangmumei Kabui, History of Manipur - 1990

Hodson T.C. : "The Naga Tribes of Manipur", Low Price Publications, Delhi, 1996 (First Published – 1911)

Hodson T.C. : The Meitheis.

Ibungohal L., 1967: Cheitharol Kumbaba.

Ibohal W.: The History of Manipur.

James Johnstone, My Experience in Manipur and Naga Hills by 1896

Johnstone, James, 1971 [1896]. Manipur and the Naga Hills. Delhi: Vivek Publishing House (Original title

Johnstone, James, My Experiences in Manipur and the Naga Hills. London: S. Low, Marston & Company).

Jacobs, Julian; Alan MacFarlane, Sarah Harrison & Anita Herle, 1990. The Nagas: The Hill People of Northeast India: Society, Culture and the Colonial Encounter, Thames and Hudson Ltd, London -1998.

Jyotimor Roy,History of Manipur -1958, 2nd edition 1973.

Julian Jacobs "The Nagas", Hill People of Northeast India, Thames and Hudson Ltd, London, 1990.

Karam Manimohan Singh, History of Christianity in Manipur - 1991.

L Ibunghal Singh, Introduction to Manipur 1987.

M. Horam "Naga Insurgency", Rani Kapoor (Mrs), Cosmo Publications, New Delhi, 1988.

Ramnganing Muivah I.A.S. An Introduction to Ukhrul in "Tangkhul Baptist Long (TBL) Centenary-96" page 16-18, 1996.

R.B. Pemberton, "the Eastern Frontier of India", Mittal Publications, New Delhi, 1835

R.K. Jhalajit Singh, 1987. *A Short History of Manipur*, 2nd ed., Imphal.

R.R. Shimray (1985), Origin and Culture of Nagas, New Delhi: Somsok Publications.

Saroj Nalini Parratt,The Religion of Manipur, Calcutta 1980.

Shimray R.R.1985 Origin and Culture of Nagas, New Delhi, Somsok Publications.

Sir Edward Gait, KCSI, CIE "A History of Assam", Lawyers Book Stall, Guwahati, Assam, 1905.

W. Yamjao Singh, An Early History of Manipur, 1966.

Mutua Bahadur" Tribal Hand Woven fabrics of Manipur, Mutua Museum, 2000.

Mutua Bahadur, Ms. Y. Santabai, Tribal Art of Manipur, Mutua Museum, 1996.

Laimayum Bishwanath, Guidebook, Mutua Museum, Cultural Heritage complex, Mutua Museum, 2006.

M. Horam, Naga Polity.

M. Horam, Social and Cultural Life of Nagas, Page-76.

Verriel Edwin, The Nagas of Nineteenth Century, Page-42.

Sir James Jiohnstoine, Manipur and Naga Hills, Manipur State Administrative Report of Lt.Col.H. St.P. Maxwell, Political Agent in Manipur and Superintendent of the State, 1891-1895. S.C. Sardeshpande, The Patkoi Nagas, Page-25.

William Pettigrew, 40 years in Manipur, Assam, page-6.

G.A. Grierson, Linguistic Survey of India, Vol-III, Part-1, Page-72.

Sanyu Visier, Nagas in History, Nagas, 90.

T.C. Hudson, The Naga Tribes of Manipur.

Sipra Sen, Tribes and Castes of Manipur, page-20.

R.R. Shimray, Origin and Culture of Nagas.

Jyotir Roy, History of Manipur.

T.C. Hodson, Asstt. Political Agent and Superintendent of the State, Low Price Publications, A Division of the D.K. Publishers Distributors (P) Ltd., Delhi-110052, 1996.

Plate - 167 Traditional Tangkhul House

Plate - 168: Bead and shell necklace of Tangkhuls

Plate - 170: Body cloth- Tangkhul

Plate - 169:Women's skirts-Tangkhul

Plate- 171: Body cloth-=Tangkhul

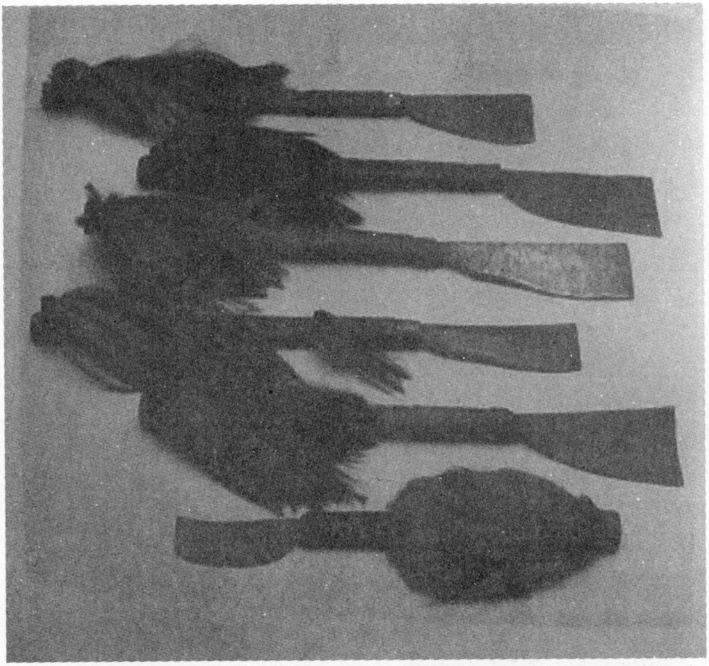

Plate- 172: Decorated Dao

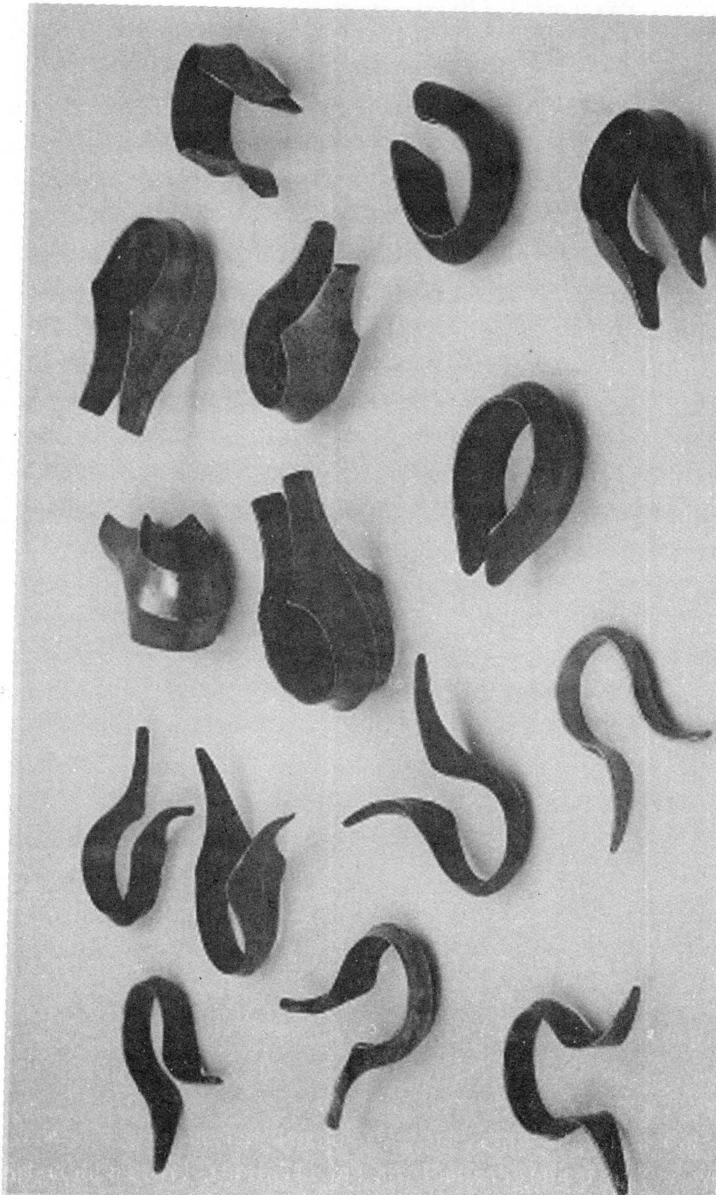

Plate 173 : Slid brass ornaments of Tangkhuls

Plate- 174: Tangkhul youth roasting a killed animal

Courtesy-RKCS Gallery

Plate- 175: Tangkhul War Dance

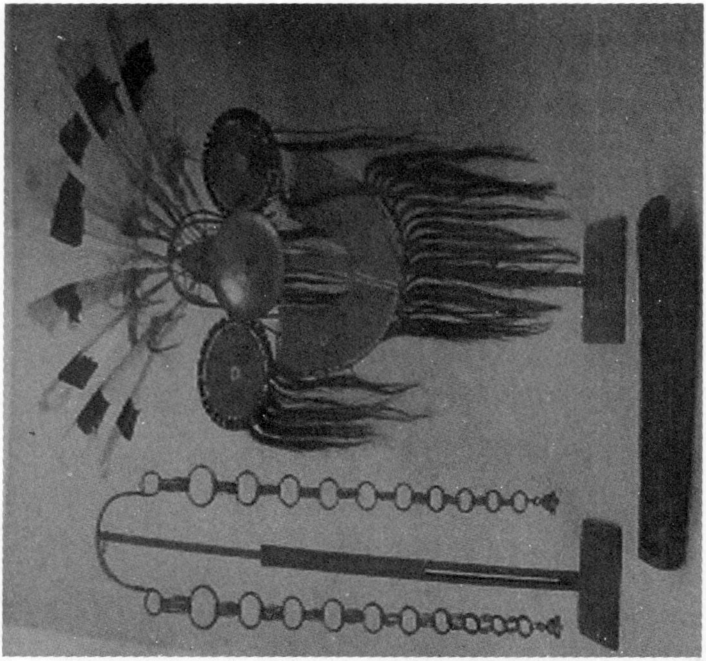

Plate - 176: Male headdress of hornbill feathers of Tangkhul

Plate-177 : Tangkhul Girl

11

Kukis and Hmars

The Kukis are also called as Khongjais.They are distributed widely in Manipur, occupying the south-western, southern and south-eastern hills covering about 4,000 sq. miles of area which spread in the districts of Churachandpur, Chandel and Sadar Hills in the Senapati, Ukhrul and the valley districts of Manipur.

Origin of Kukis

There are different beliefs about the origin of Kukis. Some of the Kukis believe their origin is in the North at a place called Makhel where the parents of three brothers resided. A stone is erected there to mark the emergence of their common ancestors from that place. According to Col. McCulloch (1859) although the Kukis occupy the hills to the south of Manipur, their traditions do not give the southern hills as the place of their origin. Some traces their links with Zomi who migrated from China. The term Zomi is an ancient and historical name of the Zo ethnic groups. The Kukis who came to Manipur during 1830 and 1840 were nomadic race coming from Burma. There are different groups of Kukis. Those who migrated from Mizoram are called Mizos. Another group of Kukis who migrated from Burma in 1830 are mostly Paites.

McCulloch (1859) refers to one legend about their origin. The Kukis were living in the bowel of the earth. One day the younger brother of their King went for hunting hedgehogs, with his dog. The dog entered the cave.

The prince also followed the dog expecting a good game inside but could not get any animal. They went on and at last found themselves on the surface of the earth. The prince was amazed to see the new world with curious flora and fauna all around, the brooks down the hills, the rivers flowing on the even surface of the valley and lakes and marshes, all enchanting. He decided to establish his brother's royal authority over this wonderland. He narrated the entire story to his brother King. The next day the King, the queen and the subjects marched towards the cave. They entered the cave led by the dog and the prince. After covering a certain distance inside the cave they came across a big python. They kill the python with great difficulty. Then they moved further and again caught sight of a strange thing, a bird carrying a big-sized stone hung in its leg and a big wooden plate full of meat. The King and the queen were rather scared of the sight and were hesitant to move ahead but the prince along with his dog moved on. Some subjects also followed the prince leaving the King and the queen behind. Nemnik the King's wife cursed her brother-in-law and those who followed him. The bird threw the stone over the King and the queen and they died there. The prince, his dog and some subjects reached the surface of the earth. All were happy to see the new land. They saw a bird near the bank of a lake. They also reached the bank of the lake, where they prepared their meals.

After the meals the prince went hunting into the jungle where he mistakenly hit a local boy who died on the spot. The prince felt some pain and returned to his place. He was resting there with a severe pain and his faithful dog seeing his master in helpless condition, started licking his hands but the prince got extremely enraged and hit the dog with his dao. Some blood spurting from its throat fell on prince's throat. His pain was no more there. Since then for throat pain the Kukis sacrifice dog and apply its blood to the throat. Similarly they felt that the effect of the curse of queen Nemnik was still on them and whenever she was unhappy then something bad would come to them. So they propitiate her by sacrificing a fowl or a pig or a mithun.

The prince who came to the surface of the earth became the King of the land. He had three sons. Once they were playing together, their father asked them to catch a rat. Because of confusion of language they were unable to carry out the task. The eldest spoke Lamyang, the second the Thadou and the third the Vaiphei. The Thadou group consider themselves as superior clan as compared to others. In Manipur they are mostly inhabiting the hills between Churachandpur and Tipaimukh. Thadous are divided into larger clans like Thadou, Shingsol, Chongloi, Hangseen, Keepgen and Hankeep. Also connected are other clans which they consider slightly inferior. These are Chongfoot, Telnok, Helting, Mangnoong and Voongtung.

Physical Features

Kukis have Mongoloid features like Nagas and Meiteis. Comparatively their Mongoloid features are more distinct and prominent. The men are short as well as medium sized. Their face is broad and round, the cheek-bones prominently bulged with bulged eye sockets. Men are physically smart and thickly fleshy. The skin colour is generally wheatish, but one finds fair complexion also in both males and females in the hills of Churachandpur. Some groups in south-east develop a slightly dark colour. The hair is dark and rarely turn grey by age. Kukis prefer long hair. The women too have prominent Mongoloid features. They are generally of short stature. The face is round but full. The almond shaped deep set eyes are arranged in prominent bulged eye sockets. The nose is short and particularly flattened at the nostrils. They look smart with their stout body. The skin colour is white and wheatish in general but some women of the south-east hills are slightly darkish. Their lips are prominently thick. Their hair is luxuriant and puffy and coloured deep dark. Those who keep long hair, part it at the centre and plait at the sides; the long plaits are then coiled round over the head. The long hair is tied in a knot at the nape, which was called *Tuhcha.* But most young and modern women prefer bob cuts. The male children's earlobe were pierced at birth and in each ear a cornelian bead was inserted fastened by a cotton string.

Dress and Ornaments

The men generally wear a loin cloth *(Champai)* round the waist and cover the body above with a coarse sheet. They used a sort of shoulder bag *(Paipeh),* woven from bamboo or cane for carrying food items and tobacco. They wear a type of neckwear called *Sa-O,* which carry a tiger's tooth and a rooster's feather. They also wear a sleepless shirt called *Boitong,* usually white in colour like the modern waistcoat. A ceremonial dress is more colourful. A geometrically designed scarf type broad piece of cloth is thrown round one of the shoulders and the ends allowed to hang down from one side. A turban *(Diel Kop)* of cotton or silk cloth is also worn; the feather plumes are also adjusted to one side.

Bare footed like the men, the Kuki women wear a knee-length *Ponve,* a type of lungi or wrap around. McCulloch (1859) describes a Kuki woman's dress: "Wrap a scanty strip of cloth round their persons, sufficient to prevent them from being called naked, over their shoulders they throw a sheet or if young, wrap it round their bodies under armpits." A home-made piece of long cloth with artistic borders is wrapped round the body from the bust down to the knees, making it pass below the armpits, and over the breasts and tucked on the left side or may be adjusted by means of a piece of another cloth by giving knot to it one side. The piece of cloth is also wrapped round the waist down to below the knees. The knot, to keep it fixed, is given on one side, the ends are not sewn together so the vertical flap of the cloth from waist downward is free except for its being tied at the knot. It thus offers a free movement to the legs, while walking. The above garment is a choli type garment. Nowadays the young and also married women prefer knee-long synthetic imported skirts and blouses. This western fashion has also entered the villages. One finds women in skirts and blouses with their bare calves moving about in the villages as well.

Kuki men are not as much fond of ornaments as their Naga counterparts: at least the present generation does not show any liking for ornaments. The women are, no doubt, very much fond of ornaments. The necklaces called *Khi* were made of red and blue beads. The brass armlets are fantastically strong and raised into a long chain of rings in spiral order. It also serves them in self-defence. The ear-rings are of varied types. The ear-rings of brass and other metal, with flat globulous, wired and long circular shapes are common favourites. Precious beads and glass bead necklaces are also liked by them. Nostrils in any case were not seen pierced or ornamented with any kind of ornament. The modern girls wear a variety of ear-rings, bangles or rings generally available in shops.

Settlement area (Kho)

The Kukis are nomadic tribes. They were in search of more productive land. For selecting a village site the eldest would first slept one night at the proposed site by taking with them a cock. If the cock did not crow before down, the site would be considered not suitable. On abandoning the old village, the old hearth would be doused with water so that none of the misfortunes and curse of the abandoned village should follow them.

Villages of Kukis

The villages of Kukis are established on the hill ridge especially on the passes which connect the two faces of a hill range. The availability of water in the vicinity is kept in mind. A cluster of houses are found amongst the woods. Due to the social pressure some original inhabitants in south and south-east were forced to migrate. For a certain period they continued to shift from one place to another along with their belongings of cattle, household and valuables. That is the reason one finds a Kuki establishment considerably more distributed.

Houses of Kukis

The typical Kuki house is known as *Malai Kuki Inn*, which is about 11.10 metre in length and 4.80 metres in width. The houses of Kukis are raised about 4-5 feet high from the ground. The floor is made of split bamboo and if wood is available, then of wooden planks. The walls are made of split bamboo and the roof with thatching of grass or tree or banana or fan plant leaves. Except the main door, they do not have any windows or ventilations. The house of a Thadou Chief is large as compared with other houses in the village. In Churachandpur, Thanlon, Parbung and Tipaimukh, there are several village chiefs who are appointed as Extra Departmental Postmasters. The chief is in fact the owner of the land and the forest of a certain area in that locality. It is not possible for him to cultivate the entire land by himself; the land is divided amongst the willing tillers. They have to give him certain portion of paddy as tax. If the forest produce is utilized by any villager in his area then the user will have to pay the tax. There are certain obligatory gifts and services for the chief; a basket of rice and other produce after the harvest, one each of the litter of pigs and brood of fowls. The service to the chief is rendered by preparing ground of Jhum field, service during chief 's house construction, free service during ceremonies in chief 's house etc.

Family

Family occupies the most important and prominent place in the history of the Kukis. Their family is a nuclear family which ultimately become a joint family. In the Kuki family, the father exercise all supreme authority over matters pertaining to the family and the women folk have no significant roles in decision making. Traditionally the wife is a subordinate to the husband in the household management. A wife never called her husband by his name. But when a son or daughter is born she addressed him as the father of the child. On the death of a father the eldest son is all responsible who like the father exercise the same nature of power.

Marriage

The form of marriage of the Kukis right from its inception was a marriage by purchase. They pay bride price. The price of a bride varies from clan to clan. However, if both the two parties mutually agreed the price may not be required at all. A bride's price is determined in terms of '*Sel*' or Mithun. The bride price is based upon the brides beauty, dowry value and the clan she belongs to. The bride price of a Chief's daughter used to be ten mithuns. The bride's parents kill two pigs or cows. The boy's parents come with a mug of rice beer to settle the bride price.

There are also some clans who charged up to ten mithuns. The price can also be paid in certain articles or goods which were equivalent to mithun. It is also customary for a man to marry his mother's brother's daughter (cousin) which in local term is called *'Neite'*. But today this practice is hardly seen and parents prefer marriage outside the family.

There is a marriage by arrangement, marriage by mutual love. Inter clan marriage was never allowed in the past. But, in the present day such practices have been observed without any nullification. There is also no restriction with regard to marriage between different linguistic groups of tribe.

Usually marriage involves a series of three visits by the groom's party to the bride's party at the end of which marriage ceremony is performed. These visits and marriage are possible only if the bride's parents have consented. Other than the Church the marriage is not bound by any court or authority to register.

Kukis observe exogamy as regards the family and endogamy as regard the clan. Marriage is permitted between the two exogamous clans namely Chanang (Musum) and Kori (Mulchal) only and marriage of the same exogamous clan is forbidden. The parents of the boy go to the parents of a girl and the engagement is settled. The side which breaks the engagement is fined with one mithun. In the Kuki society polygamy is not a system. It is only the Chief who used to have more than one wife. Widow remarriage solely depends upon the will of the widow. Adultery is punishable and rape is regarded as a crime.

Divorce

Divorce may not be common but easy to settle if the couple is not in a position to continue their married life together under certain circumstances. There are certain recognised reasons under which divorce can be claimed such as adultery, issueless, imperforated vagina etc. A mithun is given to the wife if divorce is due to the husband breach of marriage vows. If the divorce is caused by the wife, the bride price is returned to the husband.

Cultivation

Cultivation is done by the method of slash-and-burn, Jhum cultivation. The terrain where the Kukis live is so uneven and hilly that it can not be developed into terraced fields. The existing system of agriculture is simple and rain water serves for natural irrigation. Animal traction is also not introduced anywhere. Rice, maize, millet, potato, tomato, radish, pumpkin, onion, chilies, ginger, garlic, pulses etc. are grown by Kukis in the hills.

Village Administration

The Kuki village Chiefs are called Haosas. The traditional form of governance may consist of 1. Upa Innpi or Bulpite Vaipohna (Upper House) 2. Haosa Innpi or Kho Haosa Vaipohna (Lower House). The Council of ministers called Semang and Pachong assisted the Chief in the day to day administration. Changloi (Assistant), Lhangsam (Village Crier), Thiempu (Priest), Lawm Upa (in charge of youth), Thihpu (Blacksmith) comprise of essential elements of village administration.

Every village has its own Chief who in theory is despot within his jurisdiction. His words are law in his own village. All disputes and cases have to be decided by him. He is also assisted by his Council of Advisors. He imposed customary punishment to the erring subjects. In the modern administration, justice is carried out by the village authority with Chief as the Chairman. Dispute which could not be settled by the village authority are usually referred to the area court (Area Kuki Inpi). If the Area Court fails to settle the disputes, it is then referred to Kuki Inpi (apex body) for final settlement.

Land and mode of inheritance

Land can be owned by an individual if it is in the area where the MLR and LR Act 1960 is extended. But in the hill areas where the said Act does not extend it belongs to the Chief. Transfer of land in the hill areas is not possible as it entirely belongs to the Chief. But land where MLR and LR Act of 1960 was extended can be transferred and inherited by the eldest son on the death of the father. The mode of inheritance among the Kukis is counted in the male line. It is their custom and tradition that all the parental properties are inherited by the eldest son of the family. In the absence of male heir, the nearest kin inherit the deceased's properties. However, this depends entirely upon the final will of the father. It is rare that woman inherits property but there are certain cases where women have inherited father's property.

Death Ritual

McCulloch (1859) has quoted Lt. Steward, "The bodies of wealthy men or of Chief are dried over a slow fire until the flesh gets smoked and hardened to the bone, they are then dressed and laid out and kept in this way for a month or two before being finally deposited in the earth. During the whole period the hospitality in the house of mourning is unbounded, mithuns, cows, buffaloes, horses, pigs, goats, and dogs are killed in numbers to feast the guests, portions of the flesh being likewise sent to distant villages where any friend of the family may reside. The heads of the slain animals together with those of enemies are placed under the body as property of the deceased in the other world."

Food

Rice is the staple food. It is taken with boiled vegetables, fish or mutton. They eat mithun, buffaloes, cows, pigs, goats and birds. They have certain restrictions in eating animal flesh. The intoxicating drink is rice beer, both men and women enjoy it. It is served to the guests on all ceremonial occasions. Smoking is common among men and women. The women smoke tobacco through a water pipe. A metal or earthen bowl serves as the container of water; the bowl is attached to the vertical pipe which holds the tobacco cup; to the bowl is also attached a thin pipe obliquely, through which the smoke is sucked in, the nicotine under sucking pressure is sucked down from the tobacco cup, it impregnates the water in the bowl and then after filtration the smoke comes to the mouth. The water in the bowl, now the nicotine water, is collected and is used by men. They carry it along with them on journeys and sip the juice at intervals. Dr. Brown (1874) makes his statement on this tobacco juice. "I may add that I have been informed that the juice acts as a tonic, and I have traveled with Kukis who are nothing all day but kept their strength up by constant sips of this juice, which they retained in the mouth not more than three minutes at a time. Its odour is very pungent and penetrating."

Som Inn (Bachelors Dormitory)

Som inn or the bachelors' dormitory is one of the institution of the Kukis which fosters and nurtures the youths into a responsible and matured person in the society. The bachelors choose a leader from amongst them and it is customary for the inmates to obey their chosen leader. The dormitory leader mobilize the youth and render free and compulsory services to the society. All the male youths of the village who had attained the age of puberty are made to sleep in the dormitory in the night. The village dormitory serves as a sleeping place, recreational centre for unmarried. It is also used for imparting and training the young boys. It also served as an inn for a man from another village.

Musical instruments

Kukis have been using musical instruments since time immemorial. They had different kinds of musical instruments. To name a few their instruments include *Khuongcha* or small drum, *Goshem* (bamboo pipe) which is made of dry gourd and dry bamboo pipe, '*Dahpi*' (big gong), *Pengkul* (Trumpet) and '*Dah Cha*' (Small gong), '*Selki*' (mithun's horn), *Theiphit* (Whistle) '*Theile*' (Flute) which is made of dry bamboo pipe, Harps, cymbals, *Lhemlhei* etc.

Dances

By nature the Kukis love social bustles, singing, dancing and drinking, blended forming a common feature of life. They have various types of dances which have their own uniqueness. The dances are generally performed by both men and women with elegancy and affinity. Their music and songs are classical melancholic and sentimental. Most of the songs are sung with the accompaniment of drums and music.

Games and sports

The Kukis are sport loving and competitive minded people. One of their common games is wrestling. This game was occasionally done in the bachelors' dormitory as a routine exercise. Visitors to a village were usually challenged by the local youth and a fair competition was fought till one become the winner. Weight lifting was another popular game. In the early days in every village of the Kukis, there would be one or two stone used for weight lifting. Young men competed among themselves either in the morning or in the evening. There are different games played by man, women and children.

Economic life

In the early period, Jhuming constituted the main basis of the economy of the Kukis and it still remains. The people could manage themselves with the kind of food they produced from the Jhum. They had limited wants and were contented with their economic life. Their staple food was rice. Besides paddy, maize, millet, yams, sweet potatoes etc. were also grown. Buying and selling were most counted much, business was transacted through barter system. Cottons were grown and yearned into thread. They knew how to dye their clothes by using a species of dwarf indigo grown in their village. Goats, cows, buffaloes, dogs, pigs, mithuns etc. were domesticated by them. Mithun occupied a key role in the social as well as in the economic life of their early life. They kept them for trading and for festival purpose. Rice beer was very common and no ceremony was complete without rice beer. Nevertheless young men and women hardly drank as drinking in the presence of elders by young men and women was considered unseemly. (Sominthang Doungel, Structure of Chin-Kuki-Mizo's social institutions, April, 2006)

HMARS

According to 2001 census, the Hmars (see plate-149) had a population of 42690, 88% of which are settled in 35 villages in Tipaimukh and Churachandpur areas of Manipur. They speak Hmar language and converse well in Manipuri (Meiteilon). They also have populations in Cachar, North Cachar and Aizwal district of Mizoram. They are one of the highly educated Christian communities of Manipur. They enjoy zu, home brewed rice beer. Earlier Hmars worshiped spirits, the mountains, the rocks and rivers. (See Chapter-15: Historical Landmarks)

Origin and Migration

There are various legends regarding the origin and migration of Hmars. The meaning of the term Hmar means "northeners". The Hmar oral tradition suggest that the term Hmar was derived from "Hmarh", which means "tying of one's hair in a knot on the nape of the head "The Hmar folk song used to suggest that they came from "Sinlung", which is located near the Yulung river in Szechuan province of China.

My motherland, famous Sinlung,
Home of my ancestors,
Out of Sinlung,
I jumped out like a mithun,
Innumerable were our encounters,
The chidren of men.
My ancestors' footsteps werebetter,
Sinung's footsteps were indeed better

From Sinung, they moved southward following the Yunlung river and settled at Yunlung Shan for some centuries. Later on crossing over the Mekong river and Salween river, they lived among the Mishmi tribes for over a generation. From Mishmiland, they moved westward and settled at Kachin state in Burma. From Kachin, they followed the Chindwin river and settled at Kawlphai for several centuries. The tradition of Hmar clans and chieftainship evolved during their settlement in the Kabow valley. They might have been forced to leave Kabow valley by the powerful Shans and entered Mizoram. (Lal Dena, In search of identity: Hmars of North–East India", Akansa Publishing House, New Delhi-110002, 2008). Hmars might have entered Manipur during 1844-50 during the reign of Nara Singh and 1876-77 during the reign of Chandrakirti Maharaja. Many of them also migrated from Mizoram also.

Hmar Clans

Hmar have got 24 clans, which is further subdivided into 180 subclans. Each of these clans resides in a particular area or village and many of the villages are named after the name of the clan occupying it.

1. Ngurte 2. Khawbung 3. Lawitang 4. Zote 5. Theik 6. Lungtau 7. Hrangate 8. Darngawn 9. Pakhuong 10. Faihriem 11. Leiri 12. Chawnthei 13. Vangsie 14. Khuolhring / Khawlring 15. Khiengte 16. Biete 17. Pautu 18. Rawite 19. Chawthe 20. Hrangkhawl/ Hrangate 21. Chawrai 22. Hrmarlusei 23. Darlong 24. Sakum.

Houses

Hmars construct their house on the cliff with wood for floor and bamboo mats for walls plastered with mud. The Chief's head is distinctly decorated with mithun's head.

Marriage

Among the Hmars, marriage can take place between male and female who are not related to each other for three ascending generations. One can marry almost anybody except one's own sister, aunt or mother or grand mother.

One's maternal cross cousin is the preferred choice. One can marry first cousin from the maternal side. The boy marrying a maternal cross cousin called *"Pu Tuinnei"* is considered to be lucky and will get fowls in abundance. Marriages are decided by the parents. Marriage negotiation is started by the boy's side through a messenger called *Palai.* The Palai may be some kinsmen(*Laibung*) or the boy's sister's husband (Makpas). The Palai will approach the girl's parents and invite them for a drink of rice beer "Zu". If the girls parents accepted of the invitation, it symbolizes the acceptance of the marriage proposal. The Palai will carry with him a cloth, *Thidam,* i.e. a hoe and a pot of Zu which he leaves behind at the bride's place. During the drinks session, the other negotiations like the bride price are finalized. The bride price (*Nuhmei man*) usually consists of 3-7 mithun according to the clan of the bride. The bride price is usually paid in installments over a period of twenty years. The first installment is given on the wedding day. The bride price is divided into three parts (1) *Manpui* (received in kind- mithun, gong etc.). Manpui is paid to the bride's father. (2) *Mansiper*-Mansiper is divided into three parts – Pangthak, Nisum and sangdon. Pangsak is divided among the friends of the bride's father. Nisum is exclusively the bride's paternal aunt's share. After receiving the Nisum, the aunt will invite the newly wed couple to a dinner. The Sangdon is distributed among the younger sisters of the bride and (3) *Pusum*-The Pusum is paid to the bride's mother's father. After getting Pusum, the man will give a feast of pig to the bride and give her Sadar: full leg upto shoulder of a pig as a gift. When the first installment is distributed as described above, the groom's family will arrange a feast at the bride's residence by killing mithun, cows and pigs. When the feast is over, the friends (*zawl*) of the groom will escort the bride to the groom's residence where the actual wedding ceremony is solemnized. If the boy and the girl decided to marry in the teeth of opposition from parents, it is called *"Pathien samsui".* There is also another practice of elopement of bride which is also acceptable to the Hmras. This is called "*Sumhrui satan"* where any boy can elope a girl before marriage. If a boy has eloped a girl under "Sumhruisatan", then he must marry the girl otherwise he will give a fine of Rs. 40 to the bride's family. Divorce is not much of a problem. A girl seeking divorce simply has to persuade her parents to agree to refund the bride price they have received. This is called "*Suminsuo".* If the boy wants divorce, the has to give Sekhat i.e. Rs. 40 to the girl, he takes her to her parent's house. This payment by the boy is called *"Makman".* If the two have separated by mutual consent and wish to remarry, they can do so. In case of remarriage, the boy making the advances has to make up the overdue of the payment. However, if the woman makes the advances for the remarriages, the boy has nothing to pay.

Family and Inheritance of Hmars

Among the Hmars, father is the head of the family and his decision is regarded as final in all matters. Children look upon their parents with great respect and do not call them by name. The general rule of inheritance of the property, the youngest son inherit all the properties. Adoption is allowed if the couples are barren with the permission of the village Chief after a small ceremony. In case of death of the head of the family, the adopted son is entitled to inherit all the property. Women are not allowed to inherit any property.

Traditional Political system of Hmars

The traditional Hmar political system consists of the Chief (*Lal*), the Councillors (*Siehmang Upas*), the priest (*Thiempu*) and Youth Commanders (*Val Upas*). The Hmar leaders who can build new villages or conquer new territories become the Chief of that village. As the Hmars become more stable with the Jhoom cultivation as the mode of production, the position of the village Chiefs become much more deep rooted to the society. The Chief is the sole owner of the entire village land. It is believed that Hmars were once organized under a King called *"Cheonhmang"* who had finally migrated to Tripura. The Chief was dependent on the labour of the people. The chief used to receive the following services :-

Busung Sadar

Every household cultivating the village land has to give six baskets of paddy after harvest Whenever a wild animal is killed in hunting, the right front leg is given to the Chief. Anyone who is getting salt from the salt spring has to give on tenth of to the Chief as tax. The Chief gets a share in fishing expedition also. The wild food gatherer is to bring the collection to the chief who would keep his share and return the rest to them. The whole village contributes to free labour in construction and reconstruction of Hmar Chief's house.

The Chief works for the welfare of the villagers. He, supported by his councillors is the administrator of the village. He hears cases of theft, adultery, rape, seduction, murder and dispenses justice. His verdict is final and binding to both parties. It is his duty to distribute cultivable land to each and very family. A villager under one Chief would not migrate to another village without the permission of the village chief otherwise he can confiscate half of the paddy and house they left. The house of the Chief is the harbour of refuge. A criminal taking shelter in the house of the Chief can't be harmed and was protected till the case is heard. In case of death of the chief, the next one will be nominated from his own clan. The Chiefs are usually from a particular clan known as Ngurte clan. For his service, the chief used to receive a day's labour from every family in the village.

Thiempu

The *Thiempu* or the priest is next to the chief of the village in the hierarchical power structure. The source of his authority lies from the assumption that the priest could control certain natural phenomena like epidemics, draughts, famines etc. The *Thiempu* is the supreme authority so far as the religious functions are concerned. He acted as a mediator between the God (*Pathiem*) and the people. He offers prayers for the prosperity of crops. He could decide cases which the village council could not decide. The chief used to nominate a head priest (*Lalthiempu*).

The Village Crier

Every village has a village crier who announces or proclaims the decisions and orders of the village council to the villagers. He is also responsible for supervising the public works in the village.

Siehmang Upas (Councillors)

Selection of councillors depends upon the village Chief. Councillors are selected from among the village elders with some economic status in the village. The number of councilors are not fixed. The Councillors are expected to help the Chief in the smooth and proper running of the village administration. In recognition of their service, they are provided with good fertile land for agriculture.

Youth Dormitory (*Buonzawl)*

The Youth dormitory is called *"Buonzawl"*. Every village has a specially designed big house called "Buonzawl". The whole village contributes to the construction of the Buonzawl. It has a definite shape and size. It is constructed in an open place, at some distance from the village proper. The building is a closed house with a single access made by a platform of rough wood. A large place is constructed to keep the fire burning. There is sleeping arrangement on three sides of the Buonzawl leaving one side in front, which is used for wrestling matches and dances. The Buonzawl is meant only for the unmarried Hmar male youth.

Val Upsa

The Chief of Buonzawl is called *Val Upas.* One of the function of the Val Upsa is the protection of land and property of the village against any possible aggression from other tribal groups and to educate the young people about the customs, mores, legends and for settled and undisturbed social life which enables all the members of the society to engage in their daily pursuits. The youngsters in the village is divided into two categories – adolescents and boys. The duties of the boys is to work as apprentices whose job is to supply the Buonzawl with fire wood, bamboos, stones etc., wash the cloths and carry out any other tasks as assigned to them from time to time. The boys are changed every week. Monitors are appointed to control and supervise the boys. There is a roll call everyday after 7 P.M. to find out whether the boys have actually carried out the tasks assigned to them. Discipline is strictly enforced. The Val Upas arranges the tasks to be taken by the inmates of the Buonzawl. It includes helping the villagers in preparation of Jhoom field, pounding paddy, arrangement for hunting, carrying sick people to medicine men, preventing incest and any other work that may be necessary. Theft from Buonzawl is considered as disgraceful and punishment is Sekhat i.e. Rs. 40 regardless of the value of articles stolen which should be returned. Only the Chief can take action on the inmates of the Buonzawl in consultation with the Val Upas.

Courtship

Among the Hmars, courtship is an institution. There is a tradition called "*Inlenghai*" which regulates the courtship between opposite sexes. All the inmates of the Buonzawl gather round the fire after dinner before sunset. Then they decide to call on the girls in the village for gossip, smoking and singing. The boys approach the girls of their choice along with pouches of tobacco which is handed over to the girl. Then the boys take up household chores like cutting firewood, pounding paddy while the girl starts rolling cigarettes. They wait for the message of love expressed by the girl in the form of coloured threads used as cigarette band. The message of love or rejection is expressed by different colours of bands. Blue and green express reciprocal love and acceptance while red indicates rejection. The neutral attitude is expressed by white bands. Blue and Green are intoxicating colours for the Hmar youth. They may keep visiting the girl till they get blue or green colours.

Religion

The Hmars believed in the existence of a Supreme God called *Pathien* and also in the existence of various spirits like (1) *Khawchom* (which used to kill domestic animals), (2) *Khuovang* (guardian spirit) (3) *Zasam* (a dreadful beast which lived in the forest), (4) *Phung or Khawhring* (which caused illnesses) (5) *Lasi* (good female spirit who blessed the hunters and often married them). They also believed in the life after death. They believed in the existence of heaven called *Pielral* (abode of bliss) and Hell called *Mithikhuo* which is situated underground. The priest (*Thiempu*) will perform dead-departing rite (*Thitin*) accompanied with feast, colourful clothes so that the spirit of the deceased called *Thlahrang* may enter *Mithikhuo.* The soul of *Thangsuo,* who performed heroic deeds or publicly honoured with a special head gear called *Tonlairang* and *Puondum* or organized feast or killing mithuns will directly go to Pielral. The soul of wicked people can not enter Pielral.

The first Christian missionary to the Southern Manipur, Watkin Roberts of Wales arrived and established Church at Senvon, a Hmar village in 1912 and conversion of Hmars started. Today 82.4% of the Hmars are converted into Christianity. (see Chapter-15: Historical Landmarks)

Dances of Hmars

Lam Lam (Gateway Dance)

Lam Lam or Gateway dance is a dance performed while entering the dancing floor. The dancers, symmetrically arranged in two rows are led by a boy and a girl into the ground singing and dancing. This dance is the start of the main dance. The dancers advance two steps, the right leg leading the step bending their knees down in attentive position and then retreat a step, the left leg leading the retreating step and advance the step rapidly and enter the ground singing and dancing.

Chawng Lam (Chawng dance)

Chawn festival is the name of a sacrifice or ceremony of three days feast and dancing given by a single individual or a family over things as a good rice harvest or a bumper crop of a hundred red pumpkins etc. and also his success in life. Chawng Lam is the celebrating dance of this. This is performed in an open air on occasion of Chawng festival usually held at the end of every harvest season to celebrate the good crop. The person playing host to the villagers kills animals for feast.

Pheiphit Lam (Pheiphit Dance)

Pheiphit Lam is the hunting dance. Upon very successful raid or hunting, feasts are held to celebrate the success and the dance is performed. The girls prepare a beautiful plait of red and black cotton and the long tail of drongo and tied them on the warrior's head gear– a mark of bravery and distinction. Led by the warrior who has taken the head, wearing his best clothes and the villages would dance around the heads of animals which are hung in the street in front of the warrior's house. In his right hand, he holds either a gun or a ceremonial dao. Behind him follows his friends, also dressed in finest clothes. Musicians stand in groups beating the drum, gong and playing music. Pheiphit Lam is the dance celebrating this.

Dar Lam (Dar dance)

When a wealthy or an important man in the society dies, a dance is performed on the funeral occasion and at other times to show their last respect to the departed soul. The funeral procession is led by a dancing party followed by a bier carried by kinsfolk of the bereaved family and the people. Drums and large Burmese gongs, bungles and small gongs specially a set of three different sizes, each producing a different tone form the funeral band.

Hrang Lam (Hrang Dance)

Hrang Lam is another type of dance to celebrate the successful raid or hunting. They erect "Puiro" which is a very high bamboo pole, on the one end of which an animal's head is hung up. They sing along with dancing for the whole day and night. The dances of the warrior or the hunter is the same with Pheilphit Dance. Hrang Lam is also known as *"Salu Ram"* (Head Dance) because Hmars were head hunters till they were converted to Christianity.

Tinna Hla (Parting Dance)

This type of dance is a parting dance. The movements and the song proceed in unison. With the sound of the drum the dancers begin to sing and the two leaders lead the party out of the dancing ground.

Musical Instruments

Hmars are very fond of music and songs. Music is used in war, hunting expeditions, during feasts and festivals, at the time of sowing, harvesting, love making and other activities. Music has also played an important role in social cohesion and integration. Music is also used in sending messages.

They have musical instruments like *Darkhuong*. This is a large Burmese gong with the boss at the centre with 27" in diameter and 17" diameter of the boss in the centre and 3.5" projection above the surface. This is beaten with the help of a club –shaped with a bamboo handle. The beating of the gong is called *"Dharkhuang –Tum"* The boss at the centre is called *"Dharkhuangtum pawn"*. The death of the village Chief is announced by beating the gong continuously till all tribesmen assembled to participate for the Chief's funeral. The dances and songs are backed by this gong.

Gongs and Bells of Brass

Darbu

This is a Burmese gong made of brass in three different size, fitted to each other with a boss in the centre. Each of these gongs has a different tone and is used to produce harmonious tunes during dances and singing. The largest is of 10.5" diameter, the second 10" diameter and third 8" diameter. It produces melodious tunes.

Darmang

This small brass gong produces plenty of melodious sounds and is used at the time of tiger hunting or while carrying big stones or wooden logs. This is a plane disc type gong with 11" diameter without a boss. This is played with the help of wooden stick. The beating of this gong is called "Darmang Tum".

Khuong

This is a big drum like "Dhol". This is a cylinder shaped drum hollowed out block of wood with a cow hide cover on both sides. It is sounded with a club like a stick. It is slung from the shoulders of the drummer or used by keeping it at a height at a fixed place to produce the drum beat during dances. Both sides of the membrane plates are attached by strings to give the desired tension for production of the sound.

Tuithei-Khuong

This is a 1.5 feet long bamboo piece hollowed from one side and the other side remains closed. It is usually a device for carrying water from river. The women folk while carrying water use one piece of this water carrier as musical instrument. They play it with the help of a small bamboo stick and sing songs to it's beat. This production of music by this Khuong helps them avoid harassment during water carrying. The Hmar women produces beautiful sounds on it accompanied by their folk songs.

Raw Khuong

This is a string instrument, made of one inter-node piece. The internode is hollowed in such a manner that the upper surface i.e. the cover of the bamboo remains and the inside materials are taken out with the help of a sharp knife. Then this leafy portion is turned like a round string. Two bamboo jewels are put at both ends to lift the string and give tension to it. There are three strings of this type with various thickness. It is arranged in such a fashion that the left string being thick produces the base for sound and the remaining two which are thinner strings produces fine tunes. It is played by fingers along with singing.

Tingtang

This is also a string instrument. It is made with the help of a gourd and bamboo stick. The gourd is hollowed and a bamboo stick is inserted. Three strings are fixed to the base of the bamboo with a key for its tightening. The strings are made up of Tungzai (a kind of creeper oil plant).

Pheiphit

This is a xylophone. This is made of a special kind of bamboo piece which produces distinct sounds. Three such pieces are selected to produce three different tunes. Three persons are required to play it at one time. Each player plays one tune one piece followed by another two persons with different tunes on different pieces. The enchanting music produced by these three pieces of instrument by three different persons reflect their expertise and correlation. They play the tunes as accompanied to songs and dances.

Hnamut

The Hmars are real music lovers. Whenever they move empty handed without any musical instrument they just pluck a leaf from any tree and roll it to produce music. Then they play it with amazing expertise like an instrument.

Textiles of Hmars

The Hmars prepares fabric from cotton fibre which they grow in their Jhooms. Weaving is reserved only for females and no male is allowed to touch the loom. They produce the cloths to meet the requirement of the family. The girl must know the art of weaving and acquire the necessary skills otherwise it is considered a disqualification for marriage. A Hmar girl learns weaving by observing and participating in weaving since her early childhood from her mother. By the age of five, she is provided with a toy loom called *"Tatebem"* by her mother on which she learns the process of weaving. The males are responsible for preparing and supplying them the required materials. A Hmar girl must learn how to prepare *"Puonri Puonri"*, a blanket made out of unspun cotton and cotton threads of about 78" x 50". If a bride does not bring a "Puonri Puonri "to the groom's family at the time of marriage, it is considered very disgraceful. Weaving of cloth is done on indigenous handloom called *"Loinloom"*.

Thangsuo Puon

This is a dress worn by those heroes who have killed 100 dreaded animals or enemies in hunt and war and their wives. The Hmras had a system of honoruing the community leaders by bestowing such leaders the title of "*Thangsuo*". Thangsuo Puon is a special design shawl with geometric designs.

Nemrangpuon

This is a kind of shawl measuring 5feet 6 inches in length and 3 feet 6 inches wide, made of by joining two pieces together lengthwise in the middle. This is made of cotton white or saffron colour. The Hmar women used to wear this on special occasions. The wearing of this design is called *"Tlandunguel"*. This covers from the breast part of the body below the armpit upto the knee.

Puonlaisen

This is a distinctive dress of Hmar women used on ceremonial occasions. This is 53 inches in length and divided into three parts on the basis of designs. The two pieces are heavily decorated with geometric designs and the middle portion has simple straps. This is a highly decorative design which reflects the imagination and attraction of weaver towards artistic expressions.

Zakulaisen

This is a woman's blouse or upper garment bearing a significant taboo not to touch.

Samlukhim

This is a head gear made of wool having six strands of red and black colour and white wool work.

Handicrafts of Hmars

Basketery

The Hmars are experts in the art of making baskets.

Paikawing

This is used in carrying paddy and other articles from Jhoom fields. It is available in various sizes but the most common basket size is one foot eight inches in height and six inches diameter at the bottom and 1.5 feet at the top opening. This is slung from the middle of the head resting vertically on the back with the help of a string made up of cane fibres called Hnam.

Leider

This is a Beatle leaf like structure, a bamboo tray. This is available in standard sizes of 2 feet in length 1 foot 10 inches diameter in the middle and one foot 7 inches diameter in the upper portion and 8 inches in the front portion. The weaving of this basket is called *"Leider –Ta"*. This is used to separate the husked rice from the unhusked and broken rice.

Leikhor

This is a small basket used specially for taking out or measuring cleaned rice for cooking. This is also used for holding halls of thread while preparing the wrap of weaving. It has a standard size of 11 "with a base opening of 14 inches diameter and six inches height or depth.

Kawngvar

This is an open work basket used for carrying firewood from forests and water pots which are made of bamboos only. The Hmar village is always settled on the high hills, therefore, the womenfolk carry water from river flowing down the hills. The carrying process is the same as *Pail awn.* i.e. with the help of strap string.

Dawrawn

This is a closely woven basket tapering downwards used specially for carrying unhusked rice and for measuring the same. These are of different sizes. A large Dawrawn, full of grain generally weighs about a mound. It is 31 inches in height with 6 inches diameter at the bottom and 40 inches diameter at the top opening.

Tlam

This is a big container used by males to carry paddy from Jhoom fields to the threshing ground. The size is usually 22 inches high, 24 inches diameter at the opening and 11 inches diameter at the base. It rests on four legs. It is carried with strap strings.

Bemkhuong

This is a small basket with a lid available in various sizes, used by women for keeping balls of thread.

Tieng

This is a big bamboo made sieve, square in shape, available in 3 feet x 3 feet in diameter with small and big holes, used for separating unwanted grains from rice.

Bahuk:

This is a mat like structure of 3 feet x 3 feet without holes used for spreading paddy / rice for drying, kept near the fire place or in the sun.

Rel

This is a prestigious basket, having a diameter of 30 inches, 25 inches high and 12 inches square at the bottom used for preserving valuable materials. This is closed with a lid having locking arrangement. Rels are considered as bride's property. A bride must bring a *"Rel"* to the groom's house. If she fails to do so, then it is considered to be disgraceful. If the parents provides the Rel later on, then her bride price will be reduced by Rs. 20 for Rel. The Rel is used for keeping valuables and ornaments by her.

Decorative Arts

The Hmar males used different materials which are useful, functional and decorative. Such things are *Singtur Dumbel*, the male smoking pipe, *Funki*, the Mithun's horn used for keeping Gun Powder, *Meitawk*, fire lighter made of two pieces of ivory box which carry cotton, stones and iron pieces to produce fire on friction. The male covers his head with a cloth and decorate it by inserting a number of decorated bars which represent the number of kills by the *Thangsuo.* The tail hair of wild cliff goat represents the efficiency of hunter who has killed two animals at a time. He puts this Thangsuon on the head gear. They also used long tail feathers of *Vakul* (Dissermrus Paradiscus). A plum made of this feather is worn as a head dress by a man who has given a community feast. Without killing a Vakul, a Thangsuon is not considered a perfect hunter. Expertise in hunting is accepted as perfect when he kills a

Vakul which is fast running bird. Gun is also considered as a functional as well as a decorative weapon which they put on their shoulders. The females have limited decorative items.The concept and practice of tattooing is absent among Hmars. The females use necklaces made of amber beads which are brought from Burma. This is made of 8-9 cylindrical beads with red or pink threads. This is known as *Thihna.* Another decorative piece is the ear ring made of brass from Burma. *Samkhim* is a term for types of hairdo. This is an identifying mark of Hmar women.

References

Alexander Mackenzie, North East Frontier of India, Mittal Publications, Delhi, 1994.

B.C. Allen, Assam District Gazetteer-Naga Hills and Manipur, Volume-IX, Part-II, Calcutta Baptist Mission Press, 1905.

C.A. Soppit, A Short Account of Kuki-:ushai Tribes of North East Frontier with an outline grammar, Shillong, 1887.

Col. MacCulloch (1859) - Publications or G.H. Damat, An Account of the Valley of Manipur and hill tribes, 1859.

Dr. Brown (1874) Statistical Account of native state of Manipur and the hill territory under its rule, 1874.

Darliensang, The Hmars, Churachandpur, Manipur, 1988.

Dr. Thangkim Haolai, Kukis of North Cachar Hills, Guwahati, 2006.

E.B. Elly, Military Report on the Chin-Lushai Country, Firma KLM (P) Ltd, Calcutta, 1893.

ETD, Lambert, Lampart Report, dated 25 October, 1944, Note on the Kuki situation in Manipur state as a result of Japanese Invasion (File No. XLI, Cabin No. 29, Japanese War), Secretarial Library, Imphal, Manipur, 1944.

J. Shakespear, The Lushai-Kuki Clan, MacMillan & Co., London, 1912.

G.A. Grierson, Tibeto-Burman Family: Specimens of the Kuki-Chin and Burma Groups, Government Printing Press, Calcutta, 1904.

Gangumei Kabui, Vol. III, Mittal Publications, Delhi.

G.R. Gereni, Researches on Ptolemy Geography of Eastern Asia, Royal Geographical Society, London, 1909.

Lal Dena "In search of identify : Hmars of North East India, Akansa Publishing House, New Delhi-110002, 2008.

Lhungdim Ngulkhohao, History of Manipur.

Louis L. Keivom, Hmar Pi le Pu Dan (Hmar Customary Laws), Good Will Press, Imphal, 1982, Oral Traditions of the Hmar People. Rochunga Pudaite, TheEducation of the Hmar People, Sielmat, Churachandpur, 1972.

Vijay Prakash Sharma, The Hmars of Manipur- an Anthropological Exploration, Anmol Publications, 1992.

12

Prominent Tourist Spots

IMPHAL CITY

Imphal is the capital of Manipur, nestled in the lap of an oval shaped valley intersected by the 24'N latitude and 94'E longitude, and it is 2,619 feet above sea level. The foundation of Imphal can be traced back to the first century AD making it one of the oldest state capitals of India. (see plate-2)

The name Imphal is derived from the word 'Yumphal' meaning a "collection of houses". Geographically Imphal is situated in the centre of the oval–shaped Manipur valley and Kangla, the palace of the kings, is situated on the western bank of the Imphal river. Other rivers which flow through Imphal are the Nambool river, Naga river and the Iril river.

What Sir James Johnstone, the Political Agent during the time of Maharaja Sir Chandrakriti Singh (1850- 1886) wrote about Imphal : "The capital Imphal as it existed formerly was a large mass of villages looking like a forest from the neighbouring heights and covering about 15 square miles". "On the northern side it touches on some low hills called Chingmeirong and running westward is bounded by a shallow lake (Lamphelpat) which is partly surrounded by a continuation of hills, here called Langol, on which is grown a celebrated cane used for polo sticks. Then running south, it is intersected by several roads, notably the road to Silchar, which enters the capital at a place called Kwak keithel (Crow Bazar). Here it is bounded by rich cultivation.

Going further south, and sweeping round in an easternly direction, it is bounded by the plain of Langthabal, at the extremity of which lies the old capital, here two rivers intersect (Lilong). And going further east, it is bounded by the lower slopes of a hill rising 2,500 feet above the valley (Nongmaching). Then turning to north and crossing two rivers, we come again to the place from which we started". Captain E.W. Dun in his Gazetteer of Manipur, 1886, estimated that the size of Imphal was 6 miles long from north to south $4^{1/2}$ miles broad from east to west".

But so much change have occurred in Imphal, which is now becoming a city. Imphal can be easily approached by road from Guwahti, Silchar (Assam), Dimapur (Nagaland) and by air direct from Delhi, Mumbai, Bangalore, Kolkata or Guwahati.

Imphal City has got a population of around 250,000. Any Indian visiting Imphal for the first time thinks that he has arrived at a foreign land. In fact, Imphal looks like any other city in the South East Asia. The mongoloid features of the Manipuris, the distinctive dress of Manipuri women, the peculiar Manipuri language, the distinctive chandal in the forehead of Manipuri women, the peculiar customs and traditions which are quite different from the mainland India –all these give the impression of a foreign land.

The city's Polo Ground dominates the area. It was in this pologround that the game of Sagol Kangjei (Polo) originated and spread to the rest of the world as modern Polo. The Kangla Fort, Khwaramband Keithel, Shaheed Minar, Manipur State Museum, Pologround, War Cemetery, Govindajee Temple, Hanuman Mandir, Kali Mandir are some of the interesting places in Imphal town.

The distance of important towns from Imphal are give below :

Table-44 Showing distances of important towns from Imphal

Destination	*Distance in Kilometer*	*Destination*	*Distance in Kilometer*
Andro	27	Khongjom	36
Bishnupur	27	Koubru Hill	50
Chandel	64		
Churachandpur	59	Khonghampat Orchidarium	7
Dimapur	215	Mao	106
Langthabal	8	Moirang	45

(Contd.)

(Contd. Table 44)

Destination	Distance in Kilometer	Destination	Distance in Kilometer
Kaina	29	Moreh	110
Sekta	18	Phubala	40
Sendra	48	Singda	16
Jiribam	225	Tamenglong	156
Kakching		Tengnoupal	69
Keibul Lamjao	59	Ukhrul	84
Litan		Waithou	16
Loktak	45	Zoological Garden	6
Kaina	35	Kangchup	16

KANGLA FORT,-THE ANCIENT MANIPUR PALACE

'Kangla' was the ancient Manipur royal Palace (see plates-178, 179,180,181,187) since the reign of Nongda Lairen Pakhangba in 33 A.D. down to the year 1891 A.D. Pakhangba and his queen Laisra were coronated at Kangla in 33 A.D. It is also considered to be a holy place for religious worship and ceremonies. It is located in the heart of the Imphal city on the western bank of the Imphal River.

There are a number of ancient treaties/manuscripts especially "*Sakoklamlen*" "*Chinglon Laihui*", "*Nunglon*" etc., which lay down the rules for the construction, worship, ceremonies relating to 'Kangla'.

The rules for the construction of the King's palace and temples in the Kangla were written into a treatise called *"Kangla Houba"/ "Kanglalon"* (construction of the Kangla) by Ashangbam Laiba in the fifth century A.D. during the reign of Naophangba (428-518 A.D.). Naophangba was credited with the construction of a seven storied palatial building at Kangla. This work records that in the court of the King, there was a Pandit who most probably came from Bengal. This Pandit wanted to introduce a lot of changes and according to his advice, the construction of the Kangla was planned. The materials used were wood, bamboo, thatch and cane. But a 13 – year old Maichow (Philosopher) named Asangbam Laiba objected to the plan of the Pandit. At that time, blood gushed out of the holes of the pillars. Laiba told the King that the blood gushed out because the pillar holes struck on the body of the snake -god Taoroinai. Accordingly, he was asked by the King to prepare the correct layout of the Kangla. Laiba ordered all the pillar posts be thrown into the Loktak lake in the southern part of Manipur valley. He instructed the royal artisans to collect construction materials like wood, bamboo, and thatch from Koubru, Chingkhei, Pishum, Wangbren Langjing, Hoibok, Khobu-Karong, Nongmeijing. Thangjing and Langol Hills. Laiba brought a boar, which licked up the blood out of the holes of the pillar post and the construction of the Kangla was completed. Laiba's treatise was followed from 5th century A.D. onwards.

During the reign of King Mungyamba (1562-1597), the digging of the "Thangapat" (Moat) had begun and it was continued upto the reign of Khagemba (1597-1652). The royal chronicle, Cheitharol Kumbaba records that Uttra Sanggai (Coronation hall) was constructed for the first time during the reign of King Khagemba in 1629. In 1632 A.D., King Khagemba constructed a brick wall at the western gate of 'Kangla Fort'. It appears that the art of brick making was acquired from the Chinese prisoners who were captured during the Chinese invasion of the eastern frontier of Manipur. The huge mud wall enclosure of the entire fort which had a perimeter of about four miles had begun during the reign of Khagemba. (N. Khelchandra Singh et al, Kangla, the Ancient Capital of Manipur, State Archaeology, 2006)

The work continued during the time of Khunjaoba (1652-66) and completed during the period of King Paikhomba(1666-1697). Khunjaoba excavated a moat (Thangapat) in front of the gateway. Paikhomba engaged 503 personnel for three months in moulding bricks and constructed many buildings. Paikhomba (1666-1697) constructed the Lainingthou Sanamahi temple and Lai Kasha in 1678. The palatial building and Yumjao were constructed in 1697. Charairongba (1697-1707) was credited with the casting of the bronze statues of Panthoibi and Sanamahi. Garib Niwaj (1709-1748) excavated the outer moat and constructed the brick wall all around the moat and erection of fencing on the other side of the moat in 1735. He constructed Kalika temple in 1717 and Krishna temple in 1722 at Kangla. He also constructed one five storied palatial building. The Fort was further improved and enlarged by King Garib Niwaj and after him by successive Kings of Manipur. (N. Khelchandra Singh et al, Kangla, the Ancient Capital of Manipur, State Archaeology, 2006)

King Chourajit (1803-1813) constructed two huge statues of Kangla Sha or Lion in front of Uttra and Navaratna temple in 1804.These two statues were destroyed by the Burmese during Chahi Taret Khuntakpa (1819-1826). King Chourajit also constructed the Govindajee temple and a religious hall with 84 pillars known as "Chourasi Khamba" in 1805 A.D. During his time, Laktong, the gate in between the two Kangla Sha became an important gate. Nara Singh Maharaja again constructed the two Kangla Shas during June-July, 1844. Again the two statues were blown off by the British on 20 July, 1891. Nara Singh laid the foundation stone of Top Garod (Top Guard/ military headquarter) at Kangla on 29 April, 1844.

Marjit (1813-1819 A.D.) developed the Mapal Kangjeibung. He also constructed a royal residence with teak wood from Kabow valley. The structure was roofed with planks which was guilded. He also constructed Uttra, Nongkham Shang, Iru Shang, Yumjao which were roofed with wooden planks and guilded. Chandrakirti (1850-1886) constructed a five storied building at Kangla in 1852. He also constructed the Citadel, the innermost fort around the palace in 1873. The Uttra Shanglen was again constructed. During his time, Kangla became a well fortified palace.

Kangla was destroyed and deserted several times during the Burmese invasion. Many of the structures were destroyed by the Burmese during the Seven Years Devastation (1819-26). During the reign of Nara Singh, the capital was shifted back from Langthabal to 'Kangla' in 1844. During the Anglo-Manipur War of 1891, the British forces, under orders from Mr. J.W. Quinton, the Chief Commissioner of Assam, attacked on 'Kangla', in the early hours of 24th March, 1891. They conquered 'Kangla Fort' on the 27th April, 1891 (see plate-173) Yubaraj Tikendrajit and Thangal General etc., were publicly executed by the British. After the defeat of the Manipuris in the Anglo-Manipuri War of 1891, the British entered and occupied the Kangla Fort on the 27th April 1891. During the colonial rule of the British Empire many buildings were destroyed except some of the religious shrines or temples. The British Government stationed the Assam Rifles Battalion at the Kangla Fort in 1891. The same condition prevailed even after India achieved independence (1947) and Manipur became a full fledged state (1972). The people of Manipur have been demanding that the Kangla Fort should be handed to the people of Manipur and it should not be occupied by the security forces. Ultimately, the Prime Minister of India, Dr. Manamohan Singh handed over the Kangla to the Chief Minister of Manipur. Shri O. Ibobi Singh on the 20th November, 2004. (see plates-175, 176)

It is believed that Lord Pakhangba resides under 'Kangla and ruled the Kingdom of Manipur and the Universe. It is also believed that there are 360 important holy/sacred places in 'Kangla'. Some of the important holy places in 'Kangla' are:-

1. **Nungjeng Pukhri** and other ponds : This is a sacred pond believed to be the abode of Lord Pakhangba. It is located to the north-west of the "Uttra". Religious rituals are performed here. Besides this, there are other holy ponds like "*Chingkhei Nungjeng*", "*Manung Nungjeng*" and "*Lai Pukhri*" etc. (see plate183)

2. **Nunggoibi** : The site is a sacred place of worship of the Goddess of War. The "*Huyein Lalu Chanba*" ritual was performed here, whenever a King of Manipur emerged victorious in battle.

3. **Manglen** :It is the cremation site of the Kings of Manipur. The "*Manglen*" is believed to have been developed by Maharaj Garib Niwaj in 1738 A.D. According to the royal chronicle, the "*Cheitharol Kumbaba*", Nara Singh Maharaj (1844-50 A.D.) was cremated here at the "*Manglen*". Bodhchandra and Okendrajit Maharajas were also cremated here. .

4.**Kangla Men Surung** :This is a sacred place where the kings of Manipur performed their coronation ceremony. It is believed that the King will be able to tell whether he will be able to rule the state or not according to the results of the puja.

5. **Site of Lord Wangbaren** : This is located to the southeastern corner of 'Kangla' where pujas were performed in connection with flood and natural calamities.

6. **Site for Lord Koubru** : It is located to the northwestern corner of 'Kangla' and is worshipped mainly for good rainfall etc.

Besides these, there are "*Paotak Pung*", "*Pakhangba Pung*", "*Pakhangba Khuda*", "*Nata Pung*", "*Yaorei Khukal Tetnou Yotli Khingba Ching*", "*Yaoreibi*" "*Yaichampat*", Yumjao, "*Lukhrapat*", the sites of "*Mangang Guru*", "*Shumshang*", "*Yumjaolairenbi*", *Mayaipung, Mahouchanalok, Maring Khunbirok, Sana Thengru Ching, Sana Khong, Sana Sangai, Nungjeng Macha,* "*Lai-Nongshaba*", etc.

7. Monuments and Archaeological sites in Kangla' Fort

7.1. **Ruins of the Citadel (Royal Enclosure)**: "Cheitharol Kumbaba", the royal chronicle, records the construction of the Citadel in the year 1611 A.D., that is, during the reign of Maharaj Khagemba (1597-1652 A.D.).Twenty feet high, the Citadel is built of well-burnt bricks. A number of sacred places, including the coronation site of Pakhangba, were located within the enclosure of the citadel. The citadel enclosure had three entrances, two on the western side and one on the southern side. The entrance on the left end of the western face was opposite to the coronation hall and the entrance to the right end of the same wall faced the Durbar Hall. The southern entrance was connected with the passage leading to the Shree Shree Govindajee Temple. (see plate - 183)

7.2. **Ruins of the Uttra** : The "*Uttra*" is the ancestral coronation hall of the Manipur Kings. The installation ceremonies took place here. The building housing the coronation hall was destroyed in air raids during the Second World War. The flight of the steps and the ruins of the foundation are the only remains of the "*Uttra*".

7.3. **Site of the two 'Kangla Sha' (Dragon)** : Two huge '*Kangla Sha*' King Chourajit (1803-1813) constructed two huge statues of Kangla Sha or Lion in front of Uttra in 1804.These two statues were destroyed by the Burmese during Chahi Taret Khuntakpa (1819-1826). Nara Singh Maharaja again constructed the two Kangla Shas during June-July, 1844. Two huge Kangla Shas (Lion Statues) made of brick used to stand in front of the "*Uttra*" on either side of the path leading to the "Uttra". (see plate- 183). The site is remembered historically as the place where the Chief Commissioner of Assam and other three senior officers were beheaded by the Manipuri soldiers. On seeing the stain of blood in the mouth of the Kangla Sha, (the gigantic sculpture of two Kangla Sha / dragons of about 18 ft high) (see plate-180) which was believed to be the blood of the British officers beheaded before the altar by the Manipuris before the advent of the war, the British blasted the two giant statues of Kangla Sha into pieces on 20 July, 1891. Mr. T.C. Hudson wrote in his book "The Meitheis", that the Kangla Sha was the National Emblem of the Meiteis. According to Sir James Johnstone, these Kangla Shas were originally erected with the help of the Chinese war captives.

7.4.**Temple of Shree, Shree Govindajee** : The temple of Shree Shree Govindajee was originally built in 1846 A.D., that is, during the reign of Maharaja Nara Singh (1844-1850 A.D). It was severely damaged in the great earthquake of 1868 A.D. The idols of Radha Govinda was damaged when parts of the temple collapsed in the earthquake (*Cheitharol Kumbaba, p.375*). Maharaj Chandrakriti (1850-1886 A.D) reconstructed the temple in its original form. The temple is dedicated to Lord Govindajee and His consort Radha. (see plate-182).The Brindabanchandra Temple of Yubaraj Tikendrajit is also located here (see plate-184) (see Chapter-14: Temples)

7.5. **Stone Inscription** : There is a stone inscription belonging to the period of Maharaja Marjit (1813-1819) (See Chapter-2)

8. Important structures of the British/Post Independence period: There are many important historical and architectural buildings/structures which belong to the British and post-independence period viz.:

8.1 Field Marshal General Slim's Cottage - the famous General of Second World War.

8.2 Sir Akbar Hydari's tomb - the Governor of Assam.

8.3 Residence/Bungalows of the British Officers

8.4 Samadhi of Maharaj Bodhachandra of Manipur / Okendrajit (last Maharaja of Manipur) etc.

8.5 Memorial Stone at Kekrupat, which was erected in memory of those who sacrificed their lives during the historic event of the Great June Uprising, June 18, 2002.

KHWAIRAMBAND KEITHEL (SANA KEITHEL)

This is the biggest market in Manipur. Khwairamband Keithel is sandwiched between the Kangla Fort on the east and Nambool river on the west. The Keithel (Bazar) has got three streets–Paona Bazar, Thangal Bazar and Bir Tikendrajit Road. There are rows of shops selling varieties of items on both side of the street. There is one large of statue of King Bhagyachandra capturing elephant in the middle of the market at the junction of the Paona Bazar and the Thangal Bazar. The Ima Keithel (Mothers Market) is also located here. Across the road, the other half of the market sells local fish and vegetables, along with basic provisions, while smaller markets nearby include one dedicated to cane and wicker. Vegetables, fishes, household utensils and implements and fruits are sold on one side and colourful handloom shawls, phaneks, khudeis, bed sheets on the other side. Not far from here, is a street where beautiful cane baskets and furniture are sold. Fixed-price shops include Manipur Development Society, Sangai Handloom and Handicrafts near Gandhi Memorial Hall (G.M Hall), and the Clock Tower, and the Handloom House in Paona Bazaar.

Other smaller markets are Singjamei Keithel, Kongba Keithel, Lamlong Keithel Kwakeithel, Heirangkhoithong, Terakeithel, Naoremthong etc.

IMA KEITHEL OR MOTHERS MARKET

A great number of markets were established during the period of Meidingu Senbi Khagemba (1592-1652) in different places by observing suitable conditions of business transactions relating to respective areas. All the marketing of the country was conducted by women in the open air and the markets were held in the morning. Of course the situation is different at present and the market is opened from morning till night. The women's market *Ima - Keithel* of Manipur is one of the biggest market in Asia controlled and run by women. The Ima keithel is one of India's oldest and largest women's markets. One of its two sections is devoted to textiles, selling shawls and fabrics including the Moirangphi, the traditional Meitei dress. This distinctive striped skirt comes in two pieces; for a small fee, women with sewing machines will stitch them together with amazing speed.

In the market, all selling and buying are done by women. The women who are involved in this trade mostly belong to age group of 45-70 years. The shops are built by the Government and the shopkeeper is to pay tax for it. The women are so emotionally attached to their market that even one has commented "if I had to stop my shop, it will be like stopping my breadth."

SAHEED MINAR

This tall Minar at the Bir Tikendrajit Park in the heart of the capital commemorates the indomitable spirit of Manipur martyrs who sacrificed their lives while fighting against the British in 1891. The Shaheed Minar was erected in memory of Tikendrajit and Thangal General who were publicly hanged on 13th August, 1891 for waging war against the British Empire. The granite stone inscription at the entrance gate of the Shaheed Minar reads :-

"After the defeat of Manipur by the British in 1891, Yubaraj Tikendrajit Singh and Thanagal General were hanged at this site on 13 August, 1891 in front of 8000 white clothed women in order to subjugate Manipuri defiance and pride. The attempted humiliation failed when Thangal General laughed aloud before being hanged in a gesture of radiant defiance against oppression." (see plate -188)

SHREE SHREE GOVINDAJEE TEMPLE

This is the biggest and most sacred temple in Manipur.This temple, adjoining the palace of the former rulers of Manipur, is a historic centre for the valley people of Manipur. It is a simple and beautiful structure with domes, a paved court and a large raised congregation hall. The presiding deity Radha Govinda in the center is flanked by idols of Balaram and Krishna on one side and Jagannath, Balabhadra and Subhadra on the other. Priests come down the steps to accept offering from devotees standing on the paved courtyard.(see plate- 189) (see Chapter-14: Temples)

TEMPLE OF THANGAL GENERAL

The temple is attributed to Kangabam Chitananda Singh popularly known as Thangal General in Manipur history.He is son of Kangabam Kshetri

Singh of Wangkhei Angom Leikai. Thangal General was a prominent figure in the court of Maharaj Kulachandra (1890-91A.D) and he was hanged to death on 13th August, 1891 along with Bir Tikendrajit. He was in the royal court since the time of Maharaja Gambheer Singh. The Thangal Tribes. claim that he belonged to them. The protected area of the temple is 650 sq. metres (see plate-245) (see Chapter-14: Temples)

MANIPUR STATE MUSEUM

Inaugurated by the then Prime Minister Indira Gandhi on September 23, 1969, the Manipur State Museum located at the heart of Imphal city has been expanded into a full-fledged multipurpose museum with many different sections, including the ethnological gallery. The renovated Ethnological Gallery was formally reopened by Manipur Governor Ved Marwah on Jan. 20, 2001. (see plate-191)

The fascinating exhibits in the museum include tribal ornaments, headgears, agricultural implements, domestic implements, hunting kits, smoking pipes and lighters, earthen pottery, indigenous games of Manipur, gold and silver utensils, polo saddlery, traditional hookahs, Manipuri textiles, Meitei ornaments, time measuring equipment, Buddhist relics including gold mask, caskets, rider less horse, arms and armoury, basketry, tribal costumes besides, the statues and dioramas depicting the hill and valley environments of Manipur. The colourful designs of the tribal textile and basketry too are testimony of the gifted skills of the tribal people living in the hills of Manipur through the ages. These being the articles of use in their everyday life, they speak of Manipur's "impeccable tastes of artistic creations". Besides, the time measuring implement "*tanyei pung*" and "*tanyei chei*" show the well-maintained knowledge system of a civilized nation state. The costumes are important exhibits to be studied for understanding Manipur's social structure. (Bit Irom, Ethnological Gallery : Exhibits Manipur's Multi Ethnic Identities).The Museum is opened from 10 A.M. to 4.30 P.M. everyday except Sundays and holidays

MANIPUR ZOOLOGICAL GARDEN

The Manipur Zoological Garden is situated at Iroisemba (Imphal-Kangchup Road), about 6 km. from Imphal towards the west. Here you can see the graceful brow-antlered deer, "Sangai" in sylvan surroundings. A trip to this garden at the foot of the pine-growing hillocks in the westernmost corner of Lamphelpat is really enjoyable. You can see various kinds of animals. The garden was established on 2nd October, 1976. It covers an area of 68 hectares of land. They accept visitors all the year round

WAR CEMETERIES

You can feel peace and tranquility when you visit the British and the Indian Army Cemeteries, just about 2 km from the Khwairamband Keithel (Bazar), the heart of Imphal City. The Imphal cemetery has 1300 British Burials, 10 Canadians, 5 Australians, 220 Indian, 40 East Africans, 10 West Africans and 10 Burmese. "When you go home tell them of us and say for your tomorrow we gave our today". The two war cemeteries are dedicated to commemorate the soldiers who died in the Second World War, far away from home. These are well-maintained with little stone markers and bronze plaques recording the anguish and great sacrifice of the soldiers. These graves are maintained by the Commonwealth War Graves Commission. (see plate-195)

KHONGHAMPAT ORCHIDARIUM

Khonghampat Orchidarium is an Orchid Yard of the Forest Department situated at about 12 km from Imphal city along the Imphal-Dimapur road (National Highway No. 39). Here you can see more than 150 varieties of Orchids, including several rare species. It was established in 1976 and covers an area of 50 hectares. Peak flowering season is April- July.

Some important Orchid species preserved are :- Ascocentrum ampullaceum (Nachom Lei), Dendrobium chrysotoxum, Dendrobium chrysanthum (Mera Leikham), Dendrobium moschatum (Engalei), Dendrobium pendulum (Tangkaklei), Dendrobium wardivanum (Yerum Lei Tangjoubi), Kalimpongia narajiti, Rhynchostylis retusa (Samjirei), Vanda coerolea (Kwaklei)

HEECHAM YAICHAM PAT

Heecham Yaicham Pat is the spot where Yubaraj Tikendrajit was cremated on 13 August, 1891 after he was hanged by the British. The Government of Manipur has constructed a memorial at this site. The stone inscription gives a brief life history of Yubaraj Tikendrajit . About the Heecham Yaicham Pat, the inscription says "At this south-eastern corner of a bend in the Imphal river, a lake existed. It was traditionally considered to be an abode for deities who neutralize negative energies. Many reptiles, caterpillars and insects unearthed from the Kongba Leithong Phatpa rituals were dropped at the lake after prayers by the Maibas for the welfare of the state.. When the residential palace of the king was profaned by the accidental entries of serpents, owls, pythons, waterhens or termites, these creatures were released at the lake to neutralize their evil influences and energies".

KAINA

Kaina is situated on a beautiful hillock, around 35 kms to the east of Imphal on the Imphal-Yairipok road. It is a sacred place for Hindus. According to legend, Shree Govindajee appeared to His devotee King Bhagyachandra (1763,1798) in his dream and asked him to build a temple enshrined with His image carved out of a jackfruit tree which was then growing at Kaina. On 3rd of Poinu, 1775, the jackfruit tree was cut and the cut tree was taken along the Iril river but a few distance from Lilong, it got submerged under water. It was not possible to pull up the tree out of water even with the help of elephants. The place is known as "Urup". But when the Maharaja joined himself in pulling out the tree, it got floated again. People performed "Aarti" in praise of Govindajee and the place where Aarti was performed is known as "Arapti ". On 12th of Hiyangei (Friday), 1776, Rajarshri Bhagyachandra, established the Govindajee Temple and inaugurated the divine idol of Govindajee, Radha Krishna and began to worship the Lord in the Royal Palace. The sculpture of image of Shri Govindajee was made by an artisan named Sapam Lokhon and it took 11 months to complete it. The images of Gopinath, Bijoy Govinda, Abdeitya, Nityainanda were also sculptured from the remaining portion of the jackfruit tree. Bhagyachandra moved his capital from Bishnupur to Langthabal (Canchipur) on 3rd of Kalen, (Tuesday), 1779. On 11th Hiyanggei, 1779 A.D.(Friday, Hari-uthan), Raas Lila (Manipuri dance) was played for five days continuously in the open grounds of Raas Mandal Pukhri at Langthabal to commemorate the coronation of Shree Radha Govinda.

Kaina therefore assumed importance as the place where the image of the Lord Govindajee originated and consequently became an important religious and historical place for Meitei Hindus. A new temple of Shree shree Govindajee was inaugurated on 7 June, 2009. But there is no idol. (see plate-190) Only a picture of Govindajee is placed for worship. The total area covered is 22 X 18.40 sq.m. (Reservation: Director of Tourism, Govt. of Manipur, Imphal. Telephone: 0385-2450802)

ANDRO - THE ANCIENT VILLAGE

Andro, a pottery-making village is about 27 km towards east of Imphal city. This is a village where the pre-Hindu Manipuris live. They worship fire, believed to be burning from the time of Poireiton Khunthokpa (34-18 B.C.) and also a big Pung (drum). They worship Chakpa Panam Ningthou Meihoupirol. They are categorized as "Scheduled Caste" according to the Indian Constitution. There is one Cultural Complex known as Mutua Museum. The

Mutua Museum tried to present the cultural practices of various tribes in Manipur and consists of fabrics, textiles, paintings, wood carvings, drums, potteries of the North Eastern India and also a "Doll-House "where dolls of 29 recognized tribes of Manipur (both male and female) are displayed. In Andro, brewery of alcohol is practiced as a costume and people used to take local made alcohol known as "Andro". Andro is also famous for different kinds of pottery.

LANGTHABAL

Langthabal is the place where the old historic Manipur Palace is situated. It is about 8 km. from Imphal city along the Indo-Burma Road. The old historic palace comprised of relics of the palace, well-planned temples and ceremonial houses amidst pine and jackfruit trees planted symmetrically on the top of the Langthabal Hill. Overlooking the Manipur University, Canchipur and surrounding villages, it offers a pleasant view of the surroundings.

KHONGJOM

Khongjom is famous for the Anglo-Manipur war of 1891. It is about 36 km. from Imphal, situated on the Imphal-Moreh (Indo-Burma) Road. This is a place of greatest historic importance to the Manipuris. It is here that Major Paona Brajabashi, one of the great warriors of Manipur and hundreds of his followers proved their valour against the superior force of the invading British Army and sacrificed their lives for the sake of their mother land in 1891. Paona Brajabashi laid down his life in defence of his motherland at the foot of the Kheba Ching (Khongjom). A war memorial on the top of the hill adds charm to this heroic site. Khongjom day is celebrated as a State Holiday on the 23rd April, every year. Free transport is available around 6 A.M. at Imphal in front of the 1st Battalion Manipur Rifles, Imphal for the people for going to Khongjom on this particular day. (see plates 194, 265, -268)

MOIRANG : INA MUSEUM

Moirang is famous for mainly five things (1) the pre-Hindu deity, Lord Thangjing (2) the Indian National Army (INA) Museum including the statue of Netaji Subhas Chandra Bose. (3) Loktak Pat (4) Sendra Island (5) Folk Tales regarding the immortal love stories of Khamba and Thoibi, Kadeng Thangjahanba and Tonu Laijinglembi, Khuyon Haoba and Yaithing Konu, Ura Naha Khongjomba and Pidonnu, Henjunaha and Thongnang Lairoulembi. Moirang is situated about 45 km. from Imphal along the Imphal-Churachandpur road. Moirang was once the capital of Moirang Clan with a series of 52 Kings. Later on, they were defeated by the Ningthouja Clan and merged into Kangleipung. Moirang was divided into two divisions- Kege and Ngangngoi. It was subdivided to eight *Leikais*- Ngangkha, Khoyon, Nganglou, Khambi, Higa, Okchin, Chenglei, Yaoshu. There were nine markets – Khoyon, Ngangkha, Nganglou, Khambi, Higa, Khori, Chenglei, Yaoshu, Okchin. The Thangjing Lai Haraoba is a very popular festival in Moirang. In the month of April-May every year, all kinds of people men, women and children in gorgeous traditional costumes, sing and dance in honour of the Lord Thangjing here at Moirang. It was from the village of Moirang, that the graceful Khamba-Thoibi dance originated.

The temple of IbudhouThangjing is situated just near the bank of the Loktak Lake. Again, it was at Moirang that the flag of the Indian National Army (INA) was first hoisted here on April 14, 1944 under instruction from Netaji Subhas Chandra Bose. There is one INA Museum exhibiting letters, photographs, badges of ranks and other articles associated with this INA movement. There is also a bronze statue of Netaji in uniform. There are frequent buses which operate from Waheng Leikai junction of Imphal to Moirang from 8 a.m. to 6 p.m. Journey time is around 1 hour.

LOKTAK PAT (LAKE) AND SENDRA ISLAND

Loktak Pat (Lake) is situated 48 km. from Imphal. The Loktak Lake is a natural lake of 36 metres depth at Moirang in Bishnupur district. It is 8 miles long from north-west to south-east and 5 miles broad at its greatest breadth from the east to west.The dark green Eichornia (phumdi/water Hyacinth), reed and other aquatic plants floats on its surface abundantly. A huge and beautiful stretch of water, this lake is like a miniature inland sea. From the Tourist Bungalow, set atop Sendra Island, visitors can get a bird's eye view of the lake and the life on it, (see plates 4, 197)

The fisherman and their families who live in neat huts on its shores and who make full use of their watery environment. They cast their nets on it, rear fish farms in it using nets as floating walls, harvest it for the water chestnut known as Heikak, and even build their houses on the islands of floating weed that dart around the lake. There are buses and cycle rickshaws to cover the last 3 km. to Sendra. The Tourist Home charges Rs. 10 per bed.

KEIBUL LAMJAO NATIONAL PARK

It covers an area of 40 sq km. This is the only floating sanctuary in India. A small population of Sangai,(brow-antlered deer), hog deer, panther, fishing cat, wild boar and water birds are the most interesting wild animals and birds seen here. The Sangai (*Cervus Eldi Eldi*) is one of the most endangered species of deer in the world. (see plate -11)

The Keibul Lamjao was declared as a National Park on 28 March, 1977. The forest type is moist semi-evergreen forest with a combination of aquatic wetland and terrestrial eco-system.(see Chapter-3 : Geography, Fauna and Flora) It is situated at an altitude of 767 metres above sea level and between latitude - 24°27'N-24°31'N , longitude-93°53'E-93°55'E. The Sangai (*Cervus Eldi Eldi*) population in Keibul Lamjao is as follows:-

Table-45 Showing Sangai Population in Manipur

Year	*Type of Survey*	*Stag*	*Hind*	*Fawn*	*Total*
1990	Aerial census	29	35	12	76
1991	Ground census	37	51	16	104
1992	Aerial census	21	32	9	62
1993	Aerial census	38	48	12	98
1994	Ground census	36	65	16	137
1995	Ground census	58	69	25	152
1996	Ground census	57	65	21	143
1997	Ground census	58	72	17	147
1998	Ground census	56	62	28	146
1999	Ground census	63	61	25	149
2000	Ground census	54	76	32	162
2003	Ground census	65	74	41	180

PHUBALA

Phubala is a charming resort on the western fringe of Loktak Lake, about 40 km. from Imphal along the Imphal-Churachandpur road. Here you can enjoy the beautiful scenery of the Loktak Lake.(Bungalow Reservation: Director of Tourism, Govt. of Manipur, Imphal.Telephone: 0385-220802)

SEKTA KEI MOUND-ARCHAEOLOGICAL LIVING MUSEUM

Sekta Kei Mound locally known as the "Sekta Kei" is a protected Archaeological Site. The site is located at Sekta village, about 18 km. from Imphal on the Imphal-Ukhrul Road on the bank of the Iril river and around 4 kms north of Lamlai.It is a site where practice of secondary burial was discovered. The site was jointly excavated by the Archaeological Survey of India and the State Archaeology, Manipur and is preserved as a Living Museum. There are reportedly six well demarked burial areas in village Sekta. However only one burial mound was located, excavated and protected by the State Archeology. The total area under protection is 0.35 acre. The excavation at the Sekta burial site revealed important information of the burial customs of the Sekta people and their social and economic life. This has helped archeologist and historians to reassess the historical process of the people of Manipur.

WAITHOU LAKE

Situated at 16 km on the Indo-Myanmar Road, this idyllic spot is famous for its pineapple slopes. There is also a tourist lodge, at the fringe of the lake. (Reservation: Director of Tourism, Govt. of Manipur, Imphal. Telephone: 0385-220802)

SINGDA

Singda is situated at a distance of 16 km to the west from Imphal along the Imphal- Jiribam road at an altitude of 921 metres. It is a hill resort on the hills overlooking Manipur Valley. The scenery is very enchanting. It is also a mountain pass on the road to Tamenglong. There is an inspection Bungalow here. There is a nice artificial lake called Singda Dam. It is now a multipurpose project. (Reservation: Director of Tourism, Govt. of Manipur, Imphal. Telephone: 0385-220802) (see plate-196)

TAMENGLONG

It is 156 km from Imphal and is the District Headquarters of the Tamenglong District. This region is known for its exotic orchids. The Tharon Cave, Booning Meadow, Zeliad Lake,Barak Waterfalls are some of the places of tourist interest. (See Chapter-20 : All Districts)

UKHRUL

Located at 83 kms to the east of Imphal, this district headquarters of Manipur. Ukhrul district is one of the highest hill stations of Manipur. A centre of the colourful warrior tribe Tangkhui Nagas, it is well developed, and renowned for a peculiar type of lily - the Shirui, grown on the Shirui Hills. Shirui Hills and Khangkhui Lime Caves are interesting places for tourists. (See Chapter-20:All Districts)

SHIRUI LILY : THE JEWEL OF THE NORTHEAST INDIA

"Shirui Lily" flower (Lilium Macklinae sealy) (see plates – 29, 30) is one of the rarest and one of the most famous flowers in the world. Shirui Lily can't be grown and transplanted in any other place in spite of maximum care except the Shirui Kashung Hill of Ukhrul district. Nobody can explain why this flower doesn't grow in other place in spite of the maximum care. Shirui Lily is found growing and blooming in Shirui Kashung Hill in Ukhrul district of Manipur. Shirui is the name of the village, located about 15 km in the east of Ukhrul. town Shirui Lily has been growing and blooming from time immemorial. In 1946 Mr. Kingdon Ward who came to Manipur Hills for botanical collection on behalf of the New York Botanical Society collected the Shirui Lily and displayed it at the Royal Horticultural Society Flower Show in London in 1948 and he bagged the prestigious merit prize of the year,1948. That is how Shirui Lily has become world famous. "Lilium Macklinae Sealy" is the botanical name of Shirui Lily named after the maiden name of the wife, Jean Macklin discoverer Kingdon Frank Ward. Shirui Lily flower is a seasonal flower. Its best blooming season is in the month of May and June. The peak season of its bloom is between 15th May to 5th June. The height of the plant is between 1 to 3 ft. or 30 to 90 cms and 1 to 7 flowers per plant. In early years one could see even up to 11 / 12 flowers per plant, which is very rare now. Shirui Lily is native to Manipur and the species belongs to the liliane family distributed in the damped alpine areas of Shirui peak. The flower is light pinkish in colour. Its beauty lies in its bell shaped petals in bowing position like a modest girl. (Source- www.angelfire.com/az3/shiruilily)

MOREH:

Moreh is a border town adjacent to Tamu town in Burma (Maynmar) the distance of Moreh is about 110 km. from Imphal along the Indo-Burma road. There are a number of buses, Tata Sumo vehicles and Taxis going to Moreh everyday. Moreh is becoming an important business centre where Indo-Myanmar trade is carried on everyday. This commercial town is attracting a large number of people from Manipur and other neighbouring places. Tamu is hardly 5 km. from Moreh. There is a gate manned by security personnel from India as well as from Myanmar. You have to hand over your identity card like passport or driving licence or voter ID and can proceed towards Tamu and collect the ID card on your return from Tamu. There is no fee for entering Tamu. You can go upto about 5 km inside Myanmar. However, nowadays, organized trips to Mandalay or Kalewa or Kalemyo are also arranged. There is a checkpost at pallel on the way to Moreh. In Moreh, you can see Myanmar women coming and doing small time business in their national attire with sandal (chandal) pasted on the cheeks. After entering Tamu, you will see an entirely different environment with different people speaking Myanmarese language, wearing their typical national dress. Here you can enjoy Myanmar food at a comparatively low price. The food is delicious. In Moreh, you can buy electronic goods, Chinese or Thai garments, wooden furniture, wooden carving wooden images of various gods and animals. Moreh is a notorious smuggling centre, indulged in smuggling of Heroin No-4 (China White), methamphetamine, Myanmar jades, precious stones etc. There is illegal transaction of huge money in this smuggling business That is why some people say "MOREH" stands for "Millions of Rupees Enter Here". In Tamu, you can see a different architecture of buildings and Pagodas. The road from Tamu to Kalymyo (about 83 km) is constructed and maintained by the Government of India as a courtesy of goodwill to Myanmar government. The road is very good. (see plates -192, 198)

CHURACHANDPUR

Located at 59 km from Imphal District headquarters of Manipur South, Churachandpur is mainly inhabited by the Kuki, Hmar and Paite tribes.An ideal place for sightseeing and holidaying, it is also an advanced tribal town where local handicrafts are available in the market. (See Chapter-20: All Districts)

References

Pangambam Bharat Singh, IAS, "Kangla, the National Heritage of Manipur", 2008.

N. Khlechandra Singh, Sapam Bheigya, S. Rupoban Singh, Kangla, the ancient capital of Manipur, State Archaeological Department, 2006.

DIPR, One hundred years of Manipur's last war of independence (1891-1991).

Sarangthem Bormani, Meitei Ningthourol, 2000.

Dr. Nalini Thakur, The concept development plan of Kangla, 2003.

Kh. Sorojini, the British Political Agency (1835-1947), 2005.

Prof. Sairem Nilbir, "Laining Nat amasung Puwarigi Meetyengda Kangla", 2007.

Plate -178: Prime Minister Man Mohan handing over of Kangla to O. Ibobi , C.M. on 20th Nov, 2004

Plate -179: Kangla at the Southern boundary

Plate -180: Kangla Sha (1891)

Plate -181: Western Gate of Kangla 1891

Plate-182: Govindajee Temple at Kangla dedicated by Maharaja Chandrakirti

Plate -183: Old Southern part of Citadel at Kangla

Plate -184: Brindabanchandra Temple of Jubraj Tikendrajit

Plate -185:Kangla Museum

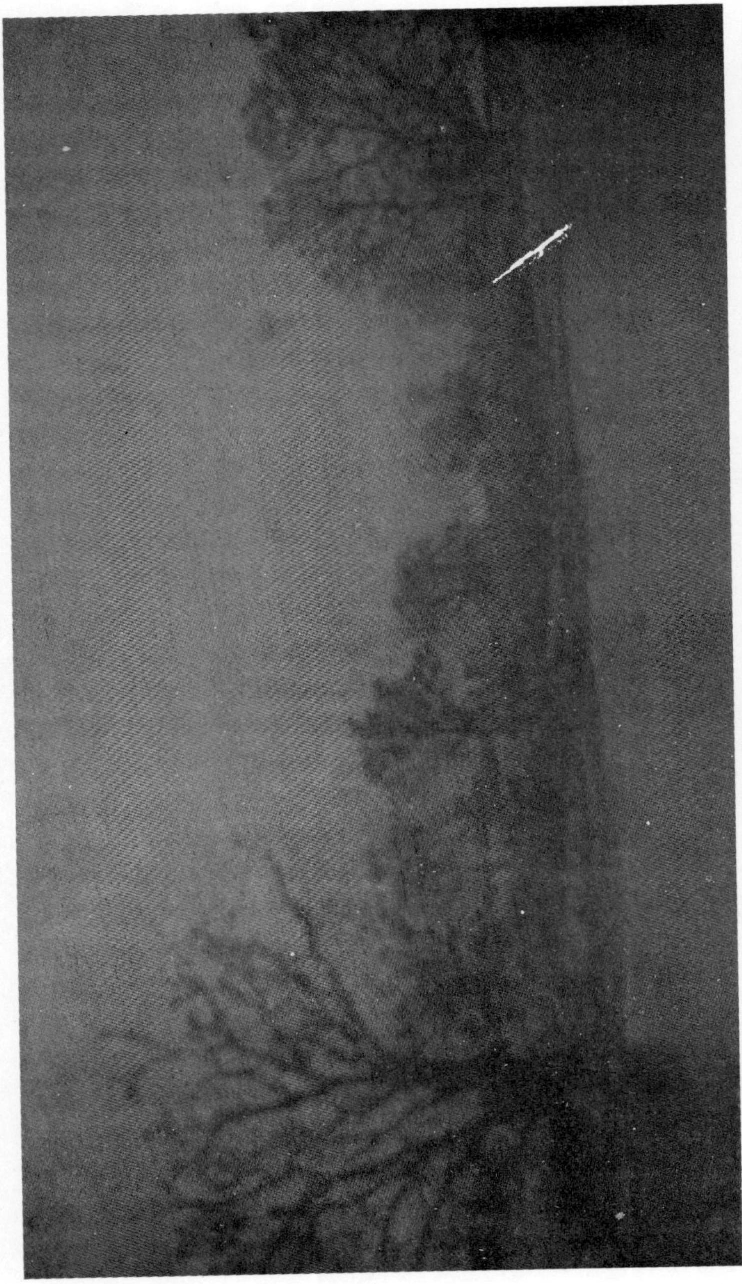

Plate-186: Nungjeng Pukhri Achouba

Plate -187: Present Gate of Kangla

Plate -188: Shahid Minar

Plate -189: Govindajee Temple

Plate -190: Govindajee Temple at Kaina

Plate-191: Manipur State Museum

Plate -192: Moreh Bridge at Myanmar border

Plate -193: Nupilal Memorial at Imphal

Plate -194: Paona Memorial at Khongjom

Plate -195: War Cemetery at Imphal

Plate -196: Singda Dam

Plate -197: Fishing at Loktak Lake

Plate -198: Myanmar women at Moreh

13

Festivals of Manipur

Manipur is a land of festivals, merriments and mirth all the year round. A year in Manipur presents a cycle of festivals. Hardly a month passes without a festival or two. To the Manipuris, festivals are the symbols of their cultural, social and religious aspirations which, besides removing the monotony of life by providing physical diversions, mental recreation and emotional outlet, help them lead a better and fuller life.

FESTIVAL OF MEITEIS

CHEIRAOBA-THE MEITEI NEWYEAR

Cheiraoba' is the new year festival of Meiteis. It is celebrated on the first day of the month of Sajibu (April). Sajibu is the first month of the Meitei Calendar. Preliminary works such as cleaning up of the house, utensils, furniture, washing of clothes and shopping for new clothes are done one or two days ahead of the festival. In the early morning, women of every house will prepare *Athelpot* containing rice, raw vegetables, fruits, flowers and offered to Lainingthou Sanamahi and Ima Leimarel Sidabi (household deity). It is believed that Lainingthou Sanamahi stays sitting on the altar (Sanamahi kachin) of the house waiting for the offering from the devotees (family members). The family members pray together at the Sanamahi kachin for the welfare of the family in the coming years and seek the blessings of Lainingthou Sanamahi, Ima Leimarel Sidabi, Imoinu Ima. After some time, the offered food stuffs are prepared and cooked by making different varieties of dishes. A nice plantain leave is cut round called *chakluk tangga* and some items of the prepared foods are placed on the *chakluk tannga* and the *donna* and offered to at the gate of the house where the God spirits *Hanu Kokchao* and *Hanu Leikham* resides with a prayer not to disturb the happiness of the family and to protect the family from any misfortune or difficulties during the whole coming years. (see plate-199) A kind of flower known as *Kombirei* is offered as an essential item as a part of the ritual. But nowadays, this flower is not available. After completion of this ritual, the family members dine together in a jolly and pleasing mood. People also exchange varieties of dishes to get different tastes of different families. After some time, people, young and old will climb the nearby hillock known as *"Cheirao Ching Kaba"* (see plate-200) in the belief that it will enable them to rise to greater heights in their worldly life.

The domestic deity, *Sanamahi,* is worshipped in each house. An annual festival is also arranged in the temple of Sanamahi. People wear new clothes and buy new utensils. The festival is also related with the *"Cheithaba"* (the name given to coming year). In olden days, "Cheithaba" was also selected on this day. The "Cheithaba" was the man who gave his name to the year, who bears all the sins of the people for the year, and whose luck, good or ill, influenced the luck of the whole community. The custom was instituted by the king Kyaamba in the year 1485. The first Cheithaba appointed was Hiyang Loi Namoi Chaoba. Chahitaba was nominated by "Maibas" after comparing the horoscope.

According to T.C. Hodson, "Chahi (year) or Chei (stick), and Thaba means to count, to count by sticks. Others derived it from Chahi, a year, and taba, to fall, because the fall of one year implies the commencement of a new year. According to another opinion, Chahi, bears the meaning of a year and Taba is connected with the root 'Takpa', to show or indicate, to point out – thus making the phrase to mean the person who indicates or means the year.

NINGOL CHAKOUBA - THE SOCIAL FESTIVAL OF MEITEIS

It is a very important social festival of the Meiteis. It is celebrated on the second day of Hiyangei (October-November) every year. In earlier days, the married sisters used to invite the brothers for a feast. But from the time of Maharaja Chandrakirti, the brothers invited the sisters for a feast. This may be for the sake of convenience or safety and security of the brothers. The festival signifies the good meaning of love and attachment between brothers and sisters of the family Married women of the family who were married to near or distant places come to the parental house along with their children and enjoy sumptuous feast. It is a form of family rejoin to revive family ties and familial affection. After the feast, the married women "Ningol" and her children were given some gifts and the women blessed their parents, brothers and sisters in return. The festival is also observed by the Pangans (Manipuri Muslims) to a certain extent. Nowadays, the Meiteis and some Meitei Organizations invites sisters of other ethnic groups like Tangkhuls, Kukis, Kabuis, Pangans etc and dine together to create love and understanding between the communities. This is very important to instill the idea of mutual love, affection and understanding and for creating peace and harmony among the people.

YAOSANG-THE PREMIER FESTIVAL OF THE MEITEIS

In early days, the Meiteis had been observing "Loipan", which was a festival for merri-making of Gods and Goddesses. During the reign of King Bhagyachandra, with the introduction of Chaitanya sect of Vaisnavism this Loipan festival has been renamed as "Yaosang" on the full moon day of Lamda (March) to coincide with the Holi festival of the Hindus and the birthday of Chaitanya Mahaprabhu.

Lamda is very important month of the Meiteis. The extreme cold season is almost over. Beautiful flowers start blooming. Fruits start ripening on beautiful branches. The birds start making their small nests. Leipaklei flower starts protruding in full bloom from under the earth with its violet colour by breaking open the hard soil. The wind is breezing slowly energizing the people. The scenery looks beautiful. Naturally, hearts and minds of the people become soft and tender. People wear new clothes. Everybody is in jubilant and festive mood.

'Yaosang', the Holi festival is celebrated on the full moon of Lamda (March). It lasts for six days. The young boys and girls take active part in this festival. Bamboo hut called 'Yaosang', is erected (see plate-201) and an idol of Lord Chaitanya is placed in the hut by a Brahmin. Puja is offered to the idol. Kirtans and recitations from the holy books are chanted. These are rituals in the morning. By evening, the idol is removed from the hut and the hut is set on fire. The shouts of 'Hari-Bola' and 'He Hari' are exchanged while the hut is burning. The burnt embers are considered to be very auspicious. Therefore, the ash is collected and used to mark the foreheads of the worshippers and the entrance of the houses. After this young children in groups go round in the locality from house to house begging for money by saying "*Nakathengba*

Lakliye". This may continue till next morning.The entire valley reflects a festive look during the days of Holi.

The real festive show of Holi is celebrated in Govindajee temple near the Manipur Palace. In the Mandapa, hundreds of *Holi Pala* will come and sing songs in praise of the Lord Chaitanya.(see plate-202). On the day of Halankar, holi water mixed with aaber (red powder) will be sprayed to all the devotees. Men and women visit the temple, Mandapa and play Holi. The music is also played. Songs are sung in praise of Lord Krishna. If you go to any part of the valley during Holi festival, you will find in each street, village and temple, the boys and girls celebrating the festival, dancing and spraying colour on each other.

If you are enroute in vehicle or on foot the young Manipuri girls will stop your vehicle by blocking the road with the help of a rope barrier. The vehicle will be surrounded in front by making a semi-circular ring by the girls. (see plate- 203) The girls will come forward, spray colour on you and stand on smiling. They will not allow your vehicle to move till you donate some money. Nowadays, sports festival is performed in every locality during the Yaosang festival.

People also observed one traditional ritual known as Saroi khangba. People believed that all the evil spirits used to gather on Saturdays at night on the crossings of streets and discussed the destinies of people in the locality. They also decided "who is going to die in the coming year". This is called *"Lai khundinnaba"*. So the family members prepared "Athelpot" of rice, vegetables, fruits and offered to Sanamahi and Ima Leimarel Sidabi and prayed to protect them from the dangers and death of any member of the family in the coming year. So Saroikhangba is performed on the crossings of streets by elderly women on the first and second Saturdays of the month of Lamda. The ritual is performed in the morning offering uncooked rice, vegetables, fruits, chilies, salt, coins with a prayer to protect the people in the locality from any danger or death during the coming year.

Thabal Chongba

The most beautiful and seductive dance of the Manipuri Meiteis is "Thabal Chongba" dance performed at night during Yaoshang festival. (see plate- 204). Thabal Chongba literally means "Jumping in moon light". The youth of the village flock together in hundreds. As soon as the moon rises over the hills the flute, the drums and the cymbals starts pouring out music. The boys and girls in a circle clutch each others hands with rhythms of music slow and fast, high and low, up and down. If the number is great they may form two or three circles so that everybody and anybody can participate in the dance. They dance together holding hand in hand with the feet jumping in a rhythm in consonant with the music of the band party. They wear no make-up and special costumes. In olden days, the Thabal Chongba was very simple. The dance was performed with a small "Dhulok" and a "Kartal" in the moonlight. At the most, they used to have one or two lanterns. The young people used to recite *"Haribola – He Hari, Ngasina Lairel Nongjada"* and people will sing in chorus. The Dholok beating provided the tempo and rhythms of the dancers. Nowadays, the Dholok beating is replaced by big band party with mike with lots of electric lighting and decorations. The dance usually starts at dusk and may continue for four or five hours at a stretch.

BARUNI

The Baruni festival is celebrated on the thirteenth day of the later half of Lamda (March). It is devoted to worship of Lord Shiva. It was introduced by Maharaj Chandrakirti (1834-1844 AD). On this day the devotee boys, girls and elders make a pilgrimage to *Nongmaijing* Hill on the eastern part of the valley. It is a tradition to take ritual dip in the *Chinggoi* stream. After taking the bath they climb the hill at night by the northward route and follow the opposite side route for descending. The phallic stone in the Shiva shrine on the mountain is worshiped. The pilgrims present their offerings to the Shivalinga. Kirtans are also arranged in the temple. The crowd is massive and provides a festive look on this isolated spot.

KANG CHINGBA OR RATHA YATRA

This festival was started from the time of Raja Gambheer Singh in 1832. One Panda from Jagannath Kshetra, Puri (Orissa) arrived and curved out the image of Lord Jagannatha, Balabhadra and Subhadra and started the Kang Chingba or Rath Yatra festival on the 2nd Ingen (Saturday) 1832. The image of Lord Jagannatha was curved out from the mango tree in Heibok Ching.

Ratha Yatra locally known as "Kang Chingba", is held on the second day after new moon of Inga (June-July) until the tenth day. In each temple the Ratha (Chariot) is constructed. It is provided with four wheels. The structure is covered with a white cloth and contains a canopy. Some pictures of Hindu deities like Hanuman, Vishnu, Krishna, Ravana stealing Sita etc. are displayed on the sides of the Chariot. The deities of Lord Krishna, Balabhadra and Subhadra are decorated with rich clothes (see plate -205) and brought out of the temple in special chair carriers. The devotees will perform Nupa Pala Sankritana before the idols are taken to the chariot (see plate- 207) The idols are carried up to the place where the magnificent chariot (Ratha) is stationed. The idols are removed from the chair carriers and placed on the Ratha. The Ratha is pulled with the help of ropes by the devotees along the road where people will offer all kinds of fruits and prayers known as Kang Heiruk Okpa (see plate -206). The women wear special dress for the occasion, the light pink coloured 'Fanek' and white 'chader'. Man wear white dhoti and kurta. Some old people also wear white Kokyet (turban). On the tenth day of the month, the Ratha is brought back to the temple again in a public procession. During the Rath Yatra the procession follows the music party with a 'Pung' (drum), Jhal (large cymbals), gongs, bells and conch. The devotees sing devotional songs and dance.

The offerings of Barti (short sticks having cotton fibre wrapping around, soaked in ghee), flowers and fruits are made by devotees at different places in the locality. The Kirtan, called 'Khubakishei', is performed by the devotees.

In the evening, devotional songs known as *Jayadev Chongba* were held and various plays connected with the festival were performed and a special kind of food known as Kshechri – yellow rice (rice cooked with pulses, spices, turmeric, salt and ghee) with Uti (Peas, pieces of bamboo shoots with salt and soda) and Laphu Ironba (boiled plantain trunk mixed with chili and salt) were served to the devotees in the Mandapas of temples. The rich families of the locality contribute to the nine day festival in cash or in kind. But every household used to offer something to Lord Jagannatha.

KRISHNA JANMASHTAMI

In Manipur Lord Krishna's birthday called Janmashtami is celebrated on the eight day of the new moon in the month of Thawan (July-Aug) since the installation of the Shree Govindajee by Rajarshi Bhagyachandra (1763-1798 AD) It is celebrated by the Manipuris with great enthusiasm and devotion. (see plate–211, 212) The devotees keep fast on this day and visit temples. People of all ages flock to the Hanuman Temple at Mahabali Umang for prayer. Various food stalls are opened near the temples and children enjoy the festival very much. The devotees also offered eatables like banana, chana to the monkeys, who are seen playing enjoying themselves. The monkeys may not allow you to go without offering something to them. After going to the Mahabali Temple, people will go to Shree Govindajee temple for a prayer. A kind of festival is arranged there. In other temples also the priests recite stories of the birth and life of Lord Krishna.The devotees participate at the "Abhishekam" at midnight at the Govindajee temple and also at ISKON temple.The devotees are offered "prasadam". On the next day, Nanda Utsav, a grand feast is arranged at the temples.

DURGA PUJA

The Durga Puja festival was started from the time of Maharaja Chandrakirti (1850-1886). Durga Puja is celebrated in Mera Tha (October month). (see plate- 208)

Shree Durga has got ten arms having powers to do anything in all directions. Lion is used as her vehicle. She accompanies Lakhsmi (Goddess of wealth), Saraswati (Goddess of Education), Ganesh and Kartik. This festival is observed for five days at different places of the valley. Every household and every locality used to hold Durga Puja five days during this time. However, the main centre of worship of Durga Puja is at the Kalimai Temple of Imphal town and Hiyangthang Lairembi at the hillock of Hiyangthang, about 10 km from Imphal. The images of Goddess Durga are made of clay and worshipped at several places in Mandapas and in public places in the entire valley of Manipur. Durga is the main deity of the Bengalis. They used to organize Durga Puja in a grand scale. According to their philosophy, Gods should be worshipped in the form of "Mother". The Mandapas are decorated during these days and Puja is held in praise of the Goddess. The Brahmins recite stories of Puranas, Krishna, Radha and Chaitanya. The second day of the festival is observed as Bornumit (Boons Day). Thousands of people will come and assemble from the early morning to seek boons and blessings from Hiyangthang Lairembi at the Hiyangthang Lairembi Mandir. (see plate-258, see Chapter- 14: Temples). The last day of the festival is observed as Kwak Tanba or Kwak yatra (driving away the crow) similar to killing of Ravana. It represents the victory of righteousness over evil. At a selected place, temporary sheds are erected for the King and nobles. The King will arrive in a beautifully decorated (Shembang Mahum) elephant and nobles used to arrive on horses and palanquins while coming to enjoy the festival. Thang –ta or swords and spear plays are performed in front of the King. A selected messenger will bring the news of killing of Ravana and informs the King on which part of the Ravana's body was pierced by the arrow and according the good or bad omen for the coming year will be announced by the priest. At night, the light festivity for immersing the Durga image at Thangapat (moat) alongside the Manipur Palace known as *Nouka Khela* is performed. In other places, the idol of Goddess is carried in a procession on the last day and immersed in the river.

DIWALI

The Diwali festival or festival of lights is celebrated with great enthusiasm. The houses are cleaned and decorated. The temples, temple yards, houses, shops and public places are illuminated with divas, candles and electric lights. The Goddess of wealth, the Lakshmi, is worshipped in temples and houses. Children enjoy playing with fireworks. Sweets are offered to the Goddess Lakhsmi. It is believed that the Goddess of wealth will visit and bless your home or shop during the festival.

HEIKRU HITONGBA

Heikru Hitongba is an annual ceremony performed in the form of worship and boat race to commemorate the victory of our heroic fore-fathers over foreign aggressors through the blessings of the Lord Govindajee and the unity of the country. It is celebrated on the eleventh day of Langban month (September) of Meitei Calendar at the Thangapat (moat) of Shree Bijoy Govindajee, Sagolband, Imphal. (see plates- 209, 210)

It was believed that Heikru Hitongba was introduced during the time of Meidingu Irengba (984-1074) for the welfare of the people.The earliest reference to Heikru Hitongba is found in the chronicles in 1508 A.D. In 1779 AD, Ananta Shai, uncle of Bhagyachabndra and his descendents were made responsible for Shree Bijoy Govinda and the annual festival of Heikru Hitongba (boat race) held on the 11th of Langban (September) every year.

It is performed with the offering of Heikru (Amalaki) fruit to the Lord accompanied with an exciting contest of 'Hiyang Tanaba' (Boat race) in the sacred Thangapat Moat of Sagolband, Bijoy Govinda). Heigru Hitongba puja is dedicated only to Lord Bijoy Govinda under the sole management of the descendants of the pious ancient Mantri in co-operation with the local citizens. Ananta Shai also dug up one big pond known as "Mantri Pukhri" and planted many banyan trees. One such banyan tree called "Mantri Khongnag" is still existing.

Heikru Hitongba comprises of the following activities:-

One day before the festival, the Maibas (priest) cleanses and purify the boat with chanting of mantras and throw Konyai (offering of gold and silver coins) on the boat and pray to Pakhangba.Sanakonyai (Gold Coins), Lupa Konyai (Silver coins) and a Langthrei Pareng (garland) are also offered. Those who are to stand on Tengmai (deck of the boat) should also offer gold and silver coins by putting together in Nganthak Awumba (earth bowl of hookah) to Shree Bijoy Govinda on the late hours of the day one day ahead of the boat race. They will also offer Athelpot of rice, vegetables, fruits to Shree Govinda.

On the day of boat race, two boats are joined together, known as Hi-Khabak Lakpa.

Taking out the sacred image/idol of the Lord Govinda out of the sacred temple (Mani Mandir) to the sacred boat (Khunet-hi) in the early part of the day. On 12th Hiyangei, 1779, the Lord Govinda is actually taken out and put on the boat to celebrate the Heikru Hitongba.

Offering of the Heikru Pareng (Heikru Garland) made of 108 Heigrus with an alternate bud of Hup (grass) and also a garland of Cheng Machang made of 108 pieces of choicest rice to the Lord in the most solemn and devoted manner by the priests for the peace and welfare of the country and especially for the emancipation of the worshippers or devotees.

The King used to offer Konyai for the prosperity of the country. Two temporary camps of the two Tengmai Leppa are erected on the southern and northern sides of Thangapat that runs east to west. There are Hirois (rowers) and Khongban Chenba (who will run along the bank of the moat to prevent any accident or cheer the rowers to row faster) Boat race will be staged off with the musical sounding of Moibung. Tengmai leppas, the Hirois and Khongban Chenba are well dressed up with coloured turbans, special shirts and dhotis. The Tengmai Leppa will wear Ningkham Samjin, Khadangchet Lakpa. Graceful boat journey of the Lord continues throughout the length of the moat to receive offerings from hundreds of thousands of spectators lining on both the banks of the moat. The 'Thakurs' will bless them with showers of flowers and fruits. Boat race between two well recognized teams, red and yellow and entertainments of teams and distinguished spectators are part of the Heikru Hitongba festival. The first winner Tengmai Leppa will raise high his Nou (oar) to indicate that he has won the race and will prostrate before the Shree Bijoy Govinda and Rasheswari.Then the boat race will resume for the second time.

The Pandit will decide good or bad omen for the year to come.

Retreat of the Lord into the Mani-Mandir after the boat race in the midst of singing of devotional songs.

MERA HOUCHONGBA

This is a festival organized by the King of Manipur on the 15th day of Mera to strengthen the cordial ties and relationship between the Meiteis and hill tribes. (see plate- 213, 214)

In this event, the Village Chiefs of hills were invited and welcomed by the King and nobles, exchanged gifts and they dined and danced together to celebrate the occasion. All the Village Chiefs of hill tribes used to come down and pay whatever products available to the King as tributes. The hill tribes dressed up with their beautiful traditional dresses and decorated their heads with amazing headwear. Captain E.W. Dun mentioned about Mera Houchongba thus "This festival in October last for only one day. It is a great gathering of the hill tribes under the Manipuri Government, and is a curious sight on account of the number of different tribes assembled, with their curious dress and weapons, differing from each other in feature and language but all unanimous in one particular, to get drunk as speedily and remain so long, as possible. The Hillman indulge in feats of strength before the Raja such as carrying heavy weights etc. They also indulged in war dance and sham fights. The sports of the day conclude with a feast" (Captain E.W. Dun, Gazeteer of Manipur, Calcutta, 1886)

The King gifted Shammi Lanmi Phi as rewards to the successful tribal hunters and warriors. This cloth has got attractive animal motifs in the centre of the shawl having a pair of elephants in between the horses. (see plate- 335) The motifs immediately below and above the elephants are fishes and are bordered by a motif of the moon. Below it is the peacock motif flanked by Numeet mayek symbolizing the radiating sun. This kind of shawl was initially introduced by Meidingu Loiyumba and crafted by the Khoisnam family clan. The king also gifted red blankets to the Chiefs of villages as a mark of respect for the loyalty to the King. The arrangement of the festival such as accommodation, food was done by the Hao Macha Loisang (Office of Tribal Affairs) in consultation with the Lambus (Messengers for the hill areas). Each village Chief is supposed to introduce himself by indicating his name, name of the tribe, and names of articles he had given as tribute to the King last year. This festival was discontinued or ignored for a long time. But nowadays the festival is revived and many organizations come forward to organize Mera Houchongba on a grand scale. This festival seeks to create love, understating, unity, peace and harmony among the valley people and the hill people.

LAI HARAOBA : "FROLIC OF THE GODS"

Lai Haraoba, the 'frolic of the gods' is a festival of the Meiteis dedicated to the deities called Umanglais (Sylvan Gods) performed by the Maibis (priestess) and Maibas (priest) who are specially chosen by the Gods to honour them. The Lai Haraoba is a ritualistic dance depicting the Creation of universe. The Lai Haraoba is still an important living tradition in Manipur. (see plate-216-220)

Types of Lai Haraoba

There are six major types of Lai Haraoba:

1. Kanglei (Imphal) Haraoba,
2. Chakpa Haraoba,
3. Andro Haraoba,
4. Sekmai Haraoba,
5. Moirang / Thangjing Lai Haraoba and
6. Kakching Haraoba.

Chakpa Haraoba is performed at Andro, Sekmai, Khurkhul, Leimaram, Tairenpokpi and Koutruk. The inner significance and the gist of all six types are the same. It is believed that the Gods held the first Lai Haraoba on the Koubru hill, so that their descendants should imitate them and perform the same to remind them the sacred story of the creation of this universe and the cycle of birth and death on this earth.

Process of Lai Haraoba

The decision of Lai Haraoba of a particular Umang Lai is taken by a group of elders known as *"Lai Selungba"*. There are also other groups known as Choubon, Pakhanglakpa, Ningolakpa etc. The Choubon will inform Maibas and Maibis and Penakhongba about the date and other details of the festival in advance.

First of all, the *Laibung or Haraobung* (festival ground) is properly cleaned with water and all items for the festival are placed at the Laibung. Then the dressing and decoration of the deities called Lai Phi Setpa is done and the deities are placed on the respective thrones inside the Laibung. This ritual is called *"Phamdengba"*.

Separate sitting arrangement is done for the King, the Knights, the warrior chiefs, the ladies, the village elders and the youths and the girls. The audience thus sit around the festival ground on the three sides of the Laibung opposite the *Yathokshang* (temporary temple of the deity for the festival).

The festival continues from one day to 10-15 days and even up to thirty days.

The first step for Lai haraoba is *Lei Langba*, plucking of flowers representing the God and Goddess with the collection of many other kinds of flowers for offering in the festival. The most important character of Lei Langba is the keeping of celibacy of the Leiroihanjaba (the one in charge of Lei Langba) with his attendants. All the participants: the maiba-maibis (priest and priestesses), the dolairengba (the bearers of the palanquin), the pena khongba (the player of an indigenous string instrument, Pena), the chong paibas (the special umbrella bearers), the sword and spear (Thang-Ta) bearers, Kwagok-Sengok pubas (the bearers of the ornamented vessels for betel nuts, flower and money for donations and awards to the top participants) and all the other members should strictly follow the discipline of keeping celibacy during the festival.

The actual ritual starts with the calling up of the spirit from water (a pond or a river) known as *"Lai Ikouba"*. Two persons are selected as *Laipuba* to carry the deity on the *Ishaiphus* (earthern pitchers) which contain *Leiyum.* The Maibi wraps up Ishaiphu containing hiri (a thread) in a higaophi (a kind of shawl) and tie them around the neck of the Laipuba. The Maibi then begins the opening dance Laihou Jagoi to the tune of Pena (a musical instrument) along with Maibas and Pena singers lead the procession to the pond or river. The Maibi performs the ritual Konyai Hunba by chanting *Konthabol.* Gold and silver coins representing the sky were thrown into the water. After this, the Maibas and Maibis performs *Khayom Lakpa. The Khayom of Lainingthou is known as Nongthak Khayom* (heaven) and the Khayom of Lairembi is known as *Leikha Khayom* (earth). This is known as *Leithak–Leikha Lakpa* (binding of heaven and earth together). When the chanting is over, both the Khayoms are thrown into the water at the same time. Then the Maibi takes the two Ikouphus from the Laipuba holding the Lainingthou Ikouphus on the right hand and the Lairembi Ikopuphu on the left hand and started dancing known as Chuk Pharon Jagoi to please the lords of four directions -Thangjing, Marjing, Wangbren and Koubru. After the dance, the Ikouphus are returned to the Lapubas. Now the whole procession enter the Laibung and the Maiba and the Maibi hold the Hiri of the Ikouphus. The Maiba holding the Hiri touches the navel of the Lainingthou and the Maibi holding the Hiri touches the navel of the Mairembi-thus the spirits are transmitted into the deities. This is known as Thawai Happa. The Maibas performs the purification rite known as *Anam Aha* Kokpa and the Pena singers sing Karakpa song in praise of the virtues and chivalries of the deities. The Maibi delivers the oracle *(Laipao chenba).* She will then perform *Saroi Khangba* (appeasement of the evil spirits) to guard off any dangers or hurdles during the festival.

The second day starts with the singing of Pena to awaken the deity known as "Yakaiba" followed by Laipao Taba or delivery of oracle by the Maibi. The complete festival begins in the day time of the second day. *Laiboula Thaba* is the most important part of the beginning of *Laibou Shaba* (creation of the Universe and the synthesis of the human body). A plantain leaf on the specific place represents the unseen God manifesting the world.

In the evening, the Maibi will perform *Laihou Jagoi* followed by Lei Langba and offering of flowers to Leiroi Hanjaba. The Maibi with all the participants who also join in the *Lai Ikouba* and *Lei Langba* should move around the plantain leaf three times symbolising the manifestations of Mangang Kuru Sidaba, Luwang Kuru Sidaba, and Khuman Kuru Sidaba (clan deities). After this the Maiba-Maibis stand erect before the deity and pray for the beginning of the *Laibou.* At this time, no one should move, speak or change his/her position. No one could come in or out of the Laibung during this item, *Hoirou Haya Laoba.* The Maibi begins to move in the form of the *Khayom Jagoi* (a dance with hands at the level of the navel) with the *Hoirou Haya* hymn. When the Maibi sings *"Hayingeina noibadi meina waina noiye; he tangna shamna noiye"*, after some of his/her hymns, all the participants begin to move their footsteps without dancing their hands and body.

In *Laibou Shaba*, the Maibi narrates with hymns and dances the creation of this universe; the sun, the stars, the planets, the moon, the earth, air, water, etc. After making this earth inhabitable, the dances shows the creation of all beings including man. The last part of the dance confines with the song, *Paosha Ishei*, for the welfare of all the individuals, the control of lust, keeping strict discipline of celibacy and control of the mind are very clearly and forcefully sung to remind all the participants the importance and the value of life in this human birth.

Then comes the *Hoi Lauba* shouting by the Maiba followed by *Laibou Jagoi* and singing of *Anoirol or Naheirol.* There are individual or group dances where anybody can take part. Laibou dance is an important step revealing the birth of the child, construction of house, plantation of cotton, weaving of clothes and offering of finished product to the deity.The *Laibou Jagoi consists* of 364 khut –theks (hand movements) known as *Laibou Khut thek.* Laibou Khut thek demonstrates the development of human embryo known as *Hakchang Saba. Yumsarol Khut thek* depicts the various stages of house construction starting from site selection, levelling of ground, laying the foundation, construction of the house and dedication to the deity. This is followed by *Panthoibi Jagoi* which is a duet dance portraying the romantic affairs between Nongpok Ningthou and Panthoibi. This is followed by *Pam yanba* portraying cultivation of land, planting of cotton seeds, plucking the cotton, weaving of clothes and dedication to the deity. Nowadays, Panthoibi jagoi is replaced by Khamba Thoibi Dance.

The next important dance is the *Lairel Mathek* (dance depicting the never ending cosmic creation in serpentine pattern). A Maiba has to lead the dance in procession as it involves technical movement of hands and foot starting from south west encircling each of the pillars of the Mandop representing the four directions. The procession moves in such a way that it looks like moving of a snake, that is why is it is called *Lairel Mathek Chatpa* (moving like a snake). Lairen Mathek and *Chongkhong Litpa* are played to represent the continuity of human life.

Kanglei-thokpa is a ritual in which the Maibi covering her face with a veil and holding a polo stick goes round looking for a suitable girl known as *Lai Nupi Thiba* (searching for a consort for the deity) and ultimately hooks a girl from among the crowd. The girl so chosen has to come out and dance in public with the Maibi. Nowadays, this item has been dropped as it affects the psychology of the girl child. *Lai-Lam-Thokpa* is a play of the festival performed outside the Laibung, in any place suitable for assembling greater number of participants. Lairoi (the end of haraoba) is very important and it includes performances. *Thang ta khousaba, Tangkhul Thokpa* (appearanace of Tangkhul) are performed. *Ougri Hangen* (the song of the control of mind), *Khencho* (the concept of the third birth or the next birth or the human birth), *Hijan Hirao* (the song of cutting big trees for two big boats: one for the male deity, the other for the female deity and with which boat race is held) are sung. *Mukna* (Meitei wrestling), *Kangjei* (Meitei hockey), *Sagol Kangjei* or polo and races are held and prizes are given to those who win in the competitions of sports and games. Then various rituals like *Thawai Mi Kouba,* (calling the soul and spirit), *Hithi –Yenthi Yeppa, Sharit Litpa, Lai Nong Gaba* (retreat of the deity to heaven) and Lai Tin Thaba (appeasement of the deity) and *Saroi Khangba* are performed. With this, the Lai Haraoba festival is concluded. The different kinds of Lai Haraoba have different kinds of special programmes and items.

Thus, Lai Haraoba is the cultural activity in which social, philosophical and religious life of the Meiteis are depicted very deeply and carefully.

The Lai-Haraoba of Moirang is celebrated during April/May. This is the biggest and most popular Lai Haraoba festival in Manipur.

THE FESTIVAL OF CHRISTIANS

CHRISTMAS

The Christmas is the festival celebrated on the birthday of Jesus Christ. This is the greatest festival of all the Christians of Manipur, observed for two days on December 24 and 25. Prayers, reading of Gospels, eating, singing of hymns, lectures on Christ, sports etc., form the major part of the festival. In some villages where the inhabitants are well-off, the celebration continues till January 1 on which the New Years day is also observed.

Mothers and dad, who take their children to Church never get into trouble. Christian life consists of faith and charity. Christianity has given clear-cut answers to the demands of the human soul. The Christian life is not only knowing or hearing but doing the will of Christ. To raise society to a higher level is the chief business of the Church. To overcome evil with good is the genius of Christianity.

FESTIVAL OF TANGKHULS

CHUMPHA

The Chumpha festival is a great festival of the Tangkhul Nagas celebrated for seven days in the month of December. The festival is held after harvest. The last three days are devoted to social gatherings and rejoicing. Unlike other festivals, women play a special role in this festival. The concluding part of the festival ends with a procession within the village. (See Chapter-10, Tanghuls)

LUI–NGAI–NI

Lui–Ngai–Ni is a Naga seed sowing festival celebrated during spring. The word Lui –Ngai –Ni is derived from three Naga words- Tangkhul, Rongmei and Poumai /Mao. Lui is a Tangkhul word derived from Luira/ Luita, which means seed sowing festival. Ngai is a Rongmei word derived from Gan Ngai, which means festival. Ni is a Poumai / Mao word, which means festival. Lui–Ngai–Ni is listed as one of the tourist festivals of India by the Ministry of Tourism, Government of India. The Government of Manipur declared public holiday for this festival.

During this festival, the Gods of crops are invoked to shower their blessings on the seeds sown so that they bear abundant fruits for bumper harvest and thus the gener͏ ! well-being of the people may be ensured. The people sought the blessings of the supreme deity through dances, songs and rituals. This festival is observed by all Naga tribes simultaneously. This festival is a part of the rich and colourful Naga cultural heritage. (see plate- 227, 228) (see Chapter-10: Tangkhuls)

FESTIVAL OF ZELIANGRONG NAGAS

GAAN-NGAI

Gaan-Ngai is the greatest festival of the Zeliangrong Nagas. It is a festival of light symbolizing victory over evils. It is celebrated for five days in the month of Wakching (December/January). Gaan Ngai is a state holiday in Manipur. (see plate-221)

Gaan-Ngai literally means the festival of winter season (Gaan or Ganh means winter or dry season and Ngai means festival).

The Gaan-Ngai is a post harvest festival. This is a festival heralding the New Year. Every tribal New Year festival is marked by the production of new fire either by friction of wood and bamboos or friction of the flint. The Gaan-Ngai performs the production of fire, Mairapmei.

The Gaan-Ngai is a festival during which those who died in the previous year are given ritual farewell or departure; their graves are beautified, dances are performed and feast is given to the community in honour of the dead.

Gaan-Shanmei - Gaan-Shanmei is heralding of the winter season or the Gaan-Ngai festival. The village elders will announce the coming of the festival by blowing the Gaan-Ngai. There is blowing of the horn of the buffalo or the mithun informing the community to make the necessary arrangement for the festival.

The first day of the festival is called *Ngai-Gangmei* (Starting or coming of the festival). The village elder will offer egg and ginger to the village deity (Shong or Bambu) outside at the village gate.

Sacrifice to Tingkao Ragwang: The whole village elders, men, youth will gather at the respective boys' dormitory (*Khangchu*) and the girls' dormitory (Luchu). An animal either a pig or a mithun will be sacrificed as offering to the Supreme God, Tingkao Ragwang. This will be preceded by a competitive catching of the pig or the mithun. After the sacrifice of the pig, the spleen will be examined to find out the omen for the future. There will be community feast at the dormitories.

Hoigammei (Hoi procession)

In the afternoon, there is the Hoigammei procession. Every male, the elder, married male, youth and even child putting on the best ceremonial dresses, holding spears, participate in the Hoigammei procession. Competition in stone throwing, long jump and wresting are carried out in the presence of the whole community.

Mairapmei (making of new fire)

The procession goes to the boys' dormitory where the new fire is produced by the wood and bamboos friction and the fire will be distributed to every household or several team of youth visit the individual families to produce the new fire. The evening will be spent in merry making, drinking and eating and singing in the dormitories.

Ngaidai (The great festival)

The second day is called *'Ngai-dai'* (the great festival). The senior members of the boys' dormitory and family members of both the boys and girls will present the Tamcha (gift in the form of food, drinks, meat, vegetables and rice) to their respective dormitories The parents of the dead members give the Tamcha in remembrance of their deceased near and dear ones. There will be feasts in the respective dormitories.

Tamchan Laam Dance

In the evening, girls will perform a dance in the selected families. This dance is known as 'Tamchan Laam' (Tam means chutney of vegetables; chan means request; Laam means dance, dance requesting for Tam). Because of the performance of the Tamchan dance; the day is also known as Tamchan Ngai.

Tuna Gaan-Ngai

The third day is known as the *Tuna-Gaan-Ngai* (Festival of the youth).

The Thei-Kadi-Laam (Dance in honour of the death) will be performed at the selected families where death occurred in the previous year. The family will prepare the graves of the death to which offering in the form of food and drink will be made. The dead will be given a ritual farewell. The performance of the dance in honour of the dead is performed if the deceased happens to be a member of the dormitory.

Rangteng pammei (Ritual of reaffirmation)

On the third day or on the eve of the Long ruimei (Hill trekking) when there is no dancing, a ceremony known as the *Rangteng pammei* is performed. This is a ceremony to strengthen and confirm the village against the elements and forces inimical to the village. Rangtang pammei literally means "embracing" the village gates.

Khunnummei (offering at the hole of the village gate)

In the afternoon, the Chief of the village (Nampou) will go to the village gates and will dig holes in which he offers an egg and iron pieces with the chanting of hymns

Two warriors dressed in ceremonial warrior dress, holding dao and spear cut the village gate pole (Rangteng Khumei). It is followed by the Ho-Hoing of the gathering to scare away the wild beasts and evil elements followed by a complete silence. The two warriors report to the elder, "Our village is protected and safe it will be prosperous" The people will respond "gaiye, gaiye, gaiye" (meaning good four times). The gathering proceeds shouting Hoi to the village jumping ground.

On this day, the dance, merry making, songs of the Zeliangrong are performed.

Longkumei: Hill Trekking

The fourth day is called *Long Kumei or Long ruimei* (Hill Trekking) performed by the boys, girls and members of the dormitories in a nearby mountain range.

Napchanmei

The fifth day is called *Napchanme*i, offering of pig and fowls to God for good harvest and prosperity followed by the feasting at the dormitories. Individual families may perform this ceremony. A pig is sacrificed at the boys' dormitory to the God and a fowl is also offered.

There will be feasting with the invocation of God by Ho-Hoing, after the feast, there will be song competition between the boys and girls and merry making. There will be Kairong Lonmei (Guarding of the village with youth singing village guarding songs). Those who participate are entertained by the individual families.

Rangpatmei

Rangpatmei is the offering of sacrifice to the deities of the pantheon of Gods worshipped by the villagers. A sacrifice known as *Ralen-loumei* will be performed. The village priest and the elders will perform this sacrifice with offerings of fowls, egg, ginger and water. A complete genna or *neihmei* is observed in the village during the period of the sacrifice. The elder will eat the chicken cooked at the ritual place.

This is the last day of the festival. In the early morning, there will be a ponnimmei, exchange of gifts in form of money, necklace, bangles among the members of the boys and girls dormitories as a mark of farewell, marking the end of the happy Gaan-Ngai.

Bukaomei (Calling of the Soul)

The elders will return to the village Pei (office of the village council) and perform another ceremony known as the *Bukaomei* (calling of the souls) invoking Tingkao Ragwang, the Supreme God to extend protection to the people of the village from death and danger and provide welfare to the village and its people. The cock, sacrificed will be cooked and eaten by the elders and pieces of the meat will be distributed to every household. Gaan-Ngai is a great festival and an institution through which the community sustains their cultural heritage and way of life. Gaan-Ngai is the essence of the Zeliangrong culture.

FESTIVAL OF POUMAI NAGAS

LAONII

Laonii is one of the important festival of the Poumai Nagas, which constitute about 42.3% of the total population of Senapati District. It is usually celebrated every year in the first week of July. Laonii is celebrated in Poumai villages after the rice transplantation. In olden days, the young men and women who sleep in the *Kheloukizii or Reipeiki* (Dormitory) celebrated this festival with full of joy and excitement. In this festival, pork is the main meat, which is cut for the people. In Lepaona circle, it is celebrated for nine days and five days in Paomata circle. As a custom of the *Yaosomai* (traditional religion believers) no villager is allowed rice transplantation after the Laonii Festival. (see plate- 234)

This festival is the time to enjoy with full of joy after successful rice transplantation and to rejuvenate their mind and health after hard work in rice transplantation. In olden days, the young men and women prepared lots of rice beer and enjoy together in groups.

The First day of the festival is known as *Kikhaiyou*. On this day, all the Yaosomai take two small branches of Mousii (a kind of small tree) and insert to the side of the wall of the house as a part of their custom.

The Second day of the festival is called *Sepoyou* and Third day is called as *Murasouyou or Ranaiyou.* On the third day, the cattle are not taken out for grazing in the open space. Fodders are brought and fed the cattle in the shed.

The Fourth day is called as *Loutouyou.* The newly born sons are given birth ceremonial celebration. A cock is sacrificed on this day in honour of him as a sign of a boy. On this day, all the male folk above 10 years old have separate kitchen. They are restricted to partake food with the female folk.

The fire is ignited from a smooth stick after long scouring (rubbing) with a split small bamboo rope and due to friction fire comes out.

The Fifth day is called Niidu, which means the main day of the feast. Lots of meats are cut on this day and meats are smoked in the kitchen for use in the next four days.

The Sixth day is called *Sepaoyou,* which means sending off the visitors/ guests. Meats and rice beer also given to all their relatives/guests on their departure day. The women married to other villages, friends and relatives who came from other villages to join the Laonii festival are sent off to their villages on this day.

On this day, it is the customary of the Poumai to give *Sousha* (some piece of meat) to their younger sisters - who are married to other village. It is a sign and symbol of blessing and remembrance. Sometimes, aunts and nieces are also given Sousha. Giving Sousha reflects the bond of love and remembrance even though they are married to other village. Thus the bond of love and relationship is still kept with the women married to other villages through such kind of festival.

On the Seventh day all the males have separate kitchen like on the Fourth day. A cock is sacrificed on this day and had together all the males in the family.

The Eight Day is called *Hahpayou,* which means that the cultivators can go to their paddy field to work. The young men and women go to paddy field for weeding in groups on this day.

On the Ninth Day, the last day of the Laonii Festival, as the custom of Poumai Naga tribe, the head of the family takes children beyond the village gate and sacrifice a chicken. The chicken is cut into two pieces and throws one piece to the right and other to the left. It is their belief that through this religious rites and rituals their sins are forgiven and God will protect them from all kinds of diseases. (R.B. Thohe Pou,-thohepou@rediffmail.com)

FESTIVAL OF KUKIS

CHAVANG KUT FESTIVAL

Chavang Kut is an autumn festival of the different tribes of Kuki-Chin-Mizo groups of Manipur observed every year on 1st November. The festival has been variously described at different places amongst different tribes as Chavang-Kut or Khodou etc. It is a happy occasion for the villagers whose food stock is bountiful after a year of hard labour.

The festival is a thanks giving feasts with songs and dances in merriment and joviality for all, in honour of the giver of an abundant harvest. This is observed with the arrival of new crops or after harvesting. It is a time for the farmers to be happy and relaxed. The granaries are full and the farmers have peaceful time for respite and recreation.

Some of the Kut festivals celebrated by the Kuki-Chin-Mizo groups are as follows :-

1. Mim Kut
2. Chang Kut
3. Pawl Kut
4. Thai Lop

Kut is a time for praying, feasting, merry making, singing, dancing and sporting Kut has now become a unifying force, a valued cultural tradition among the Kuki-Chin-Mizo groups and also an instrument of socialization process across other ethnic groups. Kut is declared a state holiday in Manipur. Kut festival is joined by the Meiteis in large numbers. (see plate- 222, 233)

Kuki Bamboo Dance

The Kukis of Churachandpur perform a beautiful dance called Bamboo dance. It is a group dance performed by girls. Similar kind of dance is also performed in Philippines and by Chins of Burma, by Mizos, Rongmeis and Liangmeis of Manipur. The costume of the dancer is colourful. The performers wear skirt of a colourful combination of horizontal and vertical stripes, geometric designs of varied colours. The skirt is tied at the waist and goes down to cover the thighs and legs upto the feet. The upper body is covered with blouse. The head-dress is unique, a ribbon of bamboo strip encircles round the head with plumes adjusted around, at the back of the head the ribbon carries a horizontal rod with strings hanging down. The dancers perform the dance by lightly jumping over the bamboo sticks. The bamboo sticks are placed horizontally in parallel spacing, over the vertically placed bamboo sticks to form criss-cross. Two women, each sitting on one side, strike the horizontal bamboo sticks over the vertically placed bamboo sticks on the ground, with the rhythm of the music. The striking of the sticks also produces the music. The dancers adjust rhythmic hops of their feet according to the music and according to the spacing available for them, a light miscalculation in following the rhythmic sequence may hurt the delicate legs of the dancers by the striking impact of bamboo sticks. (see plate-233). The same dance form is also observed in Philippines. But in case of Philippines, it is presented in the form of a story– a prince trying to woo a beautiful girl and the girl trying to escape and running around by jumping. Ultimately the prince also joins the dance and they dance together.

The dance forms of other ethnic groups have been described in the relevant chapters. (see Chapte-8: Scheduled Castes and Tribes, Chapter-10: Tangkhuls)

Apart from these, there are many festivals for various tribes of people like the Aimol, Anal, Monsang, Karam, Kabuis, Thadous etc. They also celebrate many festivals. Some of their dance forms are shown at plates 223- 238.

FESTIVAL OF MUSLIMS

RAMAZAN–ID-UL-FITR

Id-Ul-Fitr literally means feast of breaking the fast. Id-ul-Fitr is a festival that is celebrated on the first day after Ramazan by having festive meals, wearing new clothes and giving gifts to charity. It is also called the feast of Ramazan or the feast of Alms. It is celebrated on the first day of the month of shawwal (see plate- 239, Marifat)

Ramazan Id is the most popular festival of the Manipuri Muslims (Meitei Pangan) in Manipur and is observed in the usual spirits of joy and festivities as in other Muslim countries. Ramazan is the ninth month of Hijri year since the time of prophet Muhammed and during this month the Muslims practice fasting by avoiding any food, drink and smoke from pre-dawn till sunset. During this month, the days are spent in prayers. After the month on the second day of shawwal, when the new moon is visible they break the fast and this fast-breaking day is called Id-ul-Fitre. On this day, they go to the mosques to offer prayers and take delicious dishes, exchange greetings and call on friends and relatives. But before going to the place of prayer, the Sadaqa or propitiatory offering are made to the poor in the name of God. People assemble at the principal mosque or proceed to the Idgah, which is the special place for worship during festivals. The worship commences with the prayer for remission of sins, recovery of the sick, increase of rain, abundance of corns, protection from misfortune, freedom from debt. The people in the congregation will say "Ameen" at the end of prayer. At the end of the service, the members of the congregation will salute and embrace each other, offer mutual congratulations and then return to their homes. They spend the rest of the day in feasting and merry making.

References

Chander Sheikher Panchani "Manipur : Religion, Culture and Society" Konark Publishers Pvt. Ltd., 1987.

Dr. S.C. Joshi, Manipur, the Jewel of India, Akansa Publishing House, New Delhi-110059, 2002.

Dr. Kh. Ratan Kumar, Lai Haraoba of Manipur

Government of Manipur, "Manipur Tourism", 2008.

Khullem Chandrasekhor Singh, Inatki Harao Kumei.

Laishram Subhakumar, Wangjing "Meiteigi Harao Kumaei Makhal Khara.

Latest Whos Who, 2009 Edition, Ramesh Publishing House, New Delhi.

N. Ibochouba Pandit, "Tharol".

N. Mangi Devi (Manjaridevidasi), "Festivals of Manipur" Monica Printers, Keisamthong Keithel, Imphal, 2008.

R. Gupta's Popular "Manipur General Knowledge", (with Current Affaiers and Publishers Pvt. Ltd. New Delhi, 1987.

W. Yumjao, An early history of Manipur.

Sunil Kumar Chatterjee, Kirata- Jana Kirata, the Asiatic Society, 1974.

Yumnam Gourmani Singh, Ancient Cult and Culture of Manipur.

Plate-199: Cheiraoba

Plate -200: Cheirao Ching Kaba

Plate -201: Yaoshang

Plate -202: Yaoshang

Plate-203: Yaoshang Sel Munba

Plate-204: Yaoshang Thabal Chongba

Plate-205: Jagannath, Balabhadra and Subhadra on Rath Yatra

Plate-206 : Kang Heiruk Okpa

Plate-207 : Nupa pala Kang at Govidajee Mandop

Plate -208: Durga Puja

Plate-209: Govinda being worshipped for Heikru Hitongba

Plate -210: Hiyang Tannaba on Heikru Hitongba

Plate-211:: Brahmins reciting vedic hymes from Gita on Krihna Janma

Plate-212: Traditional dolls being sold on Krishna Janma

Plate-213: Mera Houchongba at Manipur Palace

Plate-214: Mera Houchongba at Manipur Palace

Plate-215: Sansenba

Plates-216, 217: Lai Haroba Haraoba

Plates-218 : Lai Haroba Haraoba

Plate -219: Moirang Thangjing Haraoba

Plate -220: Lai Lam Thokpa

Plate -221: Gaan Ngai

Plate -222: Kut Festival

Plate-223: An Aimol musical troup
Courtesy:Santos

Plate -224: An Aimol lady playing a musical instrument by the mouth
Courtesy:Santos

Plate -225: Aimol Musical Group

Plate -226: Aimol playing traditional music

Plate - 227: Lui-Ngai-Ni (Naga seed sowing festival) at Chandel

Plate-228: Lui-Ngai-Ni Dance at Chandel

Plate-229: Anal Dance

Plate - 230 : Kabui Naga dance

Plate - 231 : Kabui Naga dance

Plate -232 : Naga Dance

Plate - 233: Kuki Bamboo Dance

Plate-234: Poumai Naga dance

Plate -235: Mongsang Tribe in Traditional Attire.
Courtesy: The Sangai Express.

Plate -236: Karam traditional Dance

Plate-237: Thadou Dance

Plate-238: Governor Ved Marwah participating in a traditional Komrem dance during the platinum Jublee Celebration of the Komrem Student's Union on Friday the 13th December 2002 at BOAT Imphal

Plate -239:Manipuri Muslims(Pangal) prsenting Marifat

14

Temples and Monuments

There is no record of construction of Hindu temples in Manipur before 1507 A.D although there are numerous temples for the sylvan Gods (U-mang Lais). However, after 1507 A.D, there was a proliferation of Hindu temples and all kings patronized temples. Today, there are many Hindu temples in the Manipur valley. In fact, every leikai or locality has got a temple. There are also many U-mang Lai temples in the valley. Only the most significant ones are described here.

VISHNU TEMPLE OF BISHNUPUR

The Vishnu temple is situated near the Bishnupur Police Station about 1 km from Bishnupur keithel. (see plate-240) The old name of the town was Lamlangdong, later on Lamangdong and now called Bishnupur, once the capital of King Kyaamba (1467-1508 A.D). History recorded the facts of its origin. As soon as Kyaamba ascended throne of Manipur in 1467 A.D he conquered Kyaang, which was a Shan kingdom in the Kabow Valley at the age of 27 years in alliance with the Pong king, Chaopha Khek Khomba. Then he assumed the name of Kyaamba which means the conqueror of Kyaang. There always had been a good relation between the Pongs and the Meities. Actually it was the good foreign policy of King Kyaamba that he was able to have a good relation with the neighbouring countries. It is said that an image of Vishnu was given by the Pong King Chaopha Khek Khomba along with the fruit Pongdon – don means "hei" (fruits of Pong /guava) and the Pong hawai (a kind of pulses). Kyaamba kept the given "Vishnu" image at Lamangdong which came to be known as Bishnupur i.e. abode of Vishnu. It was during the reign of Kyaamba that Vishnu worship started in Manipur. King Kyaamba requisitioned the service of Brahmins and began the regular worship of Vishnu at Bishnupur. The temple is now standing as a symbol of the remains of ancient times

The temple was built by the King during 1507 A.D. It is the oldest temple of Manipur. It is not in use now. The monument had been declared to be of national importance under the Ancient Monuments and Archaeological Sites and Remains Act, 1958: 24 of 1958).

The entire structure of the temple is made of good quality brick and mud plaster. It reflects the Burmese architectural influence. The pedestal consists of a series of five brick layers in concentric arrangement. The lowest layer starts on one foot and two inches high platform.The brick layers at corners towards the portico and the staircases have been oriented to make a parallel turn in such a manner that these form a nice coherency of brick layers in niches.The temple body over its pedestal is in two storey, the lower sanctum cube, lower Jangha, and the upper sanctum Cube, the upper Jangha. The porch in front reaches up to the cornice in its height. The cornice forms a beam of five layers of bricks stepping out in ascending order from the point of the vertical alignment, and, similarly five brick layers stepping back in descending order again to the point of the vertical alignment, between the upper and the lower sanctum. All three walls of the east, the north and the west, have corbelled arch. Below each corbelled arch is a window made to form three slits by placing two bricks longitudinally at a parallel distance. The façade is facing south. Above the cornice is the four walled upper sanctum cube. There are two false windows on each side; however, on the southern wall there is a single long rectangular and half-way perforated window. The solidity of the interior walls blocks the holes; therefore, the holes do not serve the purpose of providing light to the sanctum hall. The roof above the upper Jangha is constructed in parabolic style and formed into a dome-like structure by semicircular arches which converge at the base of the protuberance on the top. The artistic display is in brick work in its stepping in corbelled, juxtaposition, perpendicular and parallel concentric layers. (Chander Sheikher Panchani "Manipur : Religion, Culture and Society", Konark Publishers Pvt. Ltd., New Delhi, 1987, Mutua Museum," Manipur Temple Architecture, Bulletin No-3, August, 1983, Keisampat, Imphal) Recently some researchers opined that the Vishnu temple might have not been built during the reign of Kyaamba but it needs further verification and research.

LORD KRISHNA TEMPLE OF BRAHMAPUR LEIKAI

The Lord Krishna Temple is situated in Imphal at Brahmapur Guru Aribam Leikai, on the bank of the Imphal river near Thumbuthong. (see plate -241) The temple was built in 1704 A.D by King, Charairongba and patronized by the King as a gift to his guru, Krishnacharya alias Rai Vanamali from Shweta Ganga, Puri. He gave to this guru a village, a hill and 100 hectares of rice field as Guru Dakshina. He built a nine room brick house for his Guru. Brahmapur Leikai is the locality of the Brahmins, who migrated from Jagannathpuri to Manipur during the reign of King Charairongba (1697-1709 A.D.) The temple is still in use, maintained by the descendants of Guru Aribam.

The temple is built in bricks. It is believed that these bricks were made by Chinese artisans. The pedestal is raised in three layers of bricks. The height of the pedestal is three feet and ten inches. A sound panel of flying staircases in the south facing façade matches the sturdy structure of the temple base. The sanctum cube and the porch walls separately support the dome-like hemispherical roof. The porch dome is shorter in height. The surface of the dome is decorated with the floral motifs. Above the floral motifs, it is shaped into a short neck to rest the circular crown. The crown further carries two Kalasas placed one above the other; the pinnacle above the top vase also carries a Nilachakra.

There are different idols of Lord Krishna depicting different events from his childhood to adult stage. The modulation of the idols is done in a very artistic manner. The temple was the second oldest temple in Manipur. (Chander Sheikher Panchani "Manipur : Religion, Culture and Society", Konark Publishers Pvt. Ltd., New Delhi, 1987) ("Mutua Museum," Manipur Temple Architecture, Bulletin No-3, August, 1983, Keisampat, Imphal)

SHRI HANUMAN THAKUR TEMPLE OF MAHABALI UMANG

Shri Hanuman Thakur temple is situated in Imphal on the bank of Imphal river amongst the groves, Mongba Hanba (Mahabali Forest). (see plate -242) It was built by King Garib Niwaj (1709-48 A.D.) in the year of 1725 A.D. The temple was built in bricks and later a cement coating was given to the entire structure. A Mandap has been constructed recently in front of the temple, which has overshadowed the structure of the main temple. The pedestal of the temple is not visible from outside and it looks as if the sanctum cube is raised right from the ground level. But from inside, we find a rectangular base for the sanctum cube and the porch. The sanctum cube and the porch walls are raised as a rectangular structure up to the roof. The eastern and western walls have got a triangular window having nine slits. The sanctum cube hall is covered with a dome-shaped hemispherical roof. The arches converge at the base of the crown, they are distinctively visible through their raised ridges on the surface of the roof from above. The top of the roof carries a double lotus crown in a criss-cross pattern. The *Kalasas* are rested over the crown, the uppermost vase carries the pinnacle with *Nilachakra.* The roof of the porch hall is not dome-shaped but barrel vaulted type.

According to the royal chronicle Cheitharol Kumbaba, the sculpture of Hanumanjee was carved out of a big slab of stone at Khwairamband Keithel in 1729 and then enshrined in the Mahabali temple.The sculpture of Hanuman has been shown in human form in full size in dancing posture, wearing a dhoti in a typical Hindu priest style. The head is shown with tangled knot of hair, with sparkling eyes, distinct tilak and aura around in white background. Around the neck, there are three *Rudraksha Malas* (Garlands) and in right hand, the *Gadah* handle. The tail shown is quite long which touches the upper border of the *Mehrab.* The Mehrab itself looks like a temple door and is decently designed with floral motifs. The colour applied seems to be of rich quality as even today we observe sufficient shine. The colour scheme is also fantastic in combinations. It is the only temple which was built during the period of Garib Niwaj. The temple is an important monumental evidence of the religious history of Manipur. The people used to go for worship to this temple every Tuesday and also on *Krishnajanma* and *Radha Janma* festivals. (Chander Sheikher Panchani "Manipur : Religion, Culture and Society", Konark Publishers Pvt. Ltd., New Delhi, 1987) ("Mutua Museum," Manipur Temple Architecture, Bulletin No. 3, August, 1983, Keisampat, Imphal)

SHREE GOVINDAJEE TEMPLE OF OLD PALACE KANGLA

The temple is situated in the old Kangla fort. It was constructed during the time of King Nara Singh in 1845 A.D with bricks brought from Langthabal (see plate- 243). The Bethab was dedicated to Lord Govindajee by Maharaja Chandrakirti in July, 1855 but the structure collapsed in March, 1868 due to an earthquake. The temple was reconstructed in 1869 by Maharaja Chandrakirti Singh. The Britishers removed the marble slabs and gold leaf of the dome on 21 Hiyangei, 1897 after the Anglo-Manipuri War of 18191 and sold them in public auction. The temple is not in use now as the deity, Shree Govindajee has been shifted to the new Govindajee temple near the Manipur palace. At present the Pakhangba deity, which is connected with the royal family of Ningthouja clan is in this temple.

The temple is made of bricks. The temple can be divided into five distinct sections- (1) the pedestal on which the whole structure stands (2) the wall of the temple upto the cornice (3) the lower railing with small shrines at the four corners (4) the upper railing which is the replica of the lower (5) the dome portion.

The pedestal measures 61′-9" x 47′-4". It is two celled structure facing east. The façade carries a verandah with a sturdy system of pillars which support the beam of brick–made cornice. Above the cornice is the first railing just above the verandah, having mini-shrines, Salas, one each of the corner. The railing covers the terrace above the verandah. The outer jacket wall on all sides is raised up to the cornice and then the second railing having Salas one each at the corner and two arch doors openings in the railing connects the verandah and *Prahiksana* Patha terrace. The sanctum cube wall is raised right up to the cornice and then the third railings is made which is the replica of the first and second railings. It also contains Salas, one each at the corner. From the base of the railings, starts the dome, the arches of which converge at the base of the rectangular flat corner on the top.

The sanctum hall is rectangular. There are three holes in the hall floor which are believed to be the caves: on the northern side with 5½" diameter, is called the Luang cave: on the southern side with 6" diameter, is called the Mangang cave; and that on the southern side of the western wall with 3½" diameter, is called the Khuman cave. It is believed that the deity Pakhangba in the snake form appears through these caves. The *Prahiksana* Patha is on all three sides of south, west and north, between the sanctum cube wall and the outer jacket wall, and opens to the verandah through north and south doors. The temple has a rectangular base and on the top it culminates with a rectangular crown over the dome. The artistic designs are available as floral motifs on the walls which are now worn out. (Chander Sheikher Panchani "Manipur : Religion, Culture and Society", Konark Publishers Pvt. Ltd, New Delhi, 1987) ("Mutua Museum," Manipur Temple Architecture, Bulletin No. 3, August, 1983, Keisampat, Imphal).

THANGAL GENERAL TEMPLE OF WANGKHEI

The temple was dedicated by Thangal General in 1879 A.D. The temple is situated in Wangkhei near the All India Radio office. (see plate-245)

The temple structure has a distinct platform with the square pedestal measuring 32′-8" x 32′-8". The sanctum cube of the internal sanctum and the outer jacket is raised straight up from the base up to the moulding cornice. The outer jacket wall on each side opens out with a rectangular opening to lead in front into four flying steps of staircases. This facilitates the approach to the circumambulatory path or the *Prahiksana* patha from any side. The cornice is achieved by stepping outward a few courses of brick layers to make a projection and then making a slant to the projection. Thereafter the first railing starts, having four Salas or mini-shrines, one on each corner. The railing is made by alternate spacing and brick wall and finally giving a horizontal brick layer on colonnades gripping the corner Salas. The first railing perfectly covers the terrace above the *Prahiksana* patha.

The sanctum cube of the sanctum hall is raised further till it reaches the second cornice built with the same pattern of brick work as mentioned above. Then the second railing is the replica of the lower railing. The octagonal dome is after the second railing. The arches converge at the base of the inverted *Kalasa* placed at the top of the dome. Each arch line can be seen having its ridge line on the dome surface from above. On the ground at all four corners, there is one temple replica of Bengal hut type on each corner. (Chander Sheikher Panchani "Manipur: Religion, Culture and Society", Konark Publishers Pvt. Ltd, New Delhi, 1987) ("Mutua Museum," Manipur Temple Architecture, Bulletin No-3, August, 1983, Keisampat, Imphal)

The entire structure is in brick, the mastery of brick masonry is of high order.

LEIMAPOKPAM KEIRUNGBA TEMPLE

The Leimapokpam Keirungba temple is situated in Imphal town, in the compound of the erstwhile Manipur State Road Transport Corporation (MSRTC). It is donated by Leimapokpam Keirungba (Sajou) in 1875 A.D. It is not in use now. The transport authorities were using it for dumping the diesel drums and automobile spare part junks. The smoke and the rubbish of the nearby workshop had applied its own colour to this monument. Peepal trees, *Khongnangs*, are growing from the walls of the temple. All these factors are ruining the monument.

The whole structure of the temple is made of bricks. It is a square cube and appears just rising from the ground level. In fact its pedestal is not raised sufficiently above the ground. It is facing south. The façade wall is decorated and in front there is a semicircular arch supported by three pillars on each side, pillar 4′-8" in diameter, connected by the arch, the archivolt of which is formed by a series of curves. The arch towards its outer extremity is thickened with additional brick layers having hexagonal holes. On either side of the arch stands the replica of shrine with Stupi. The cornice is achieved by giving different layers of bricks by making their courses outward and then giving a slant to the projection with the help of flat bricks. Above the cornice is the railing. The outer jacket cube has got a row of arcades in its eastern and southern walls. There are no arcades in the western wall, a staircase is, however, provided to it on a raised rostrum with 5′-10" height having flying steps from both sides and then it leads into the thirteen spiral staircases ending above to open to the terrace of the building.

It is Nagara type of temple, a square temple with a square shikhar. It has no superstructure above, the temple ends in a single storey. The capitals over pillars are decorated with leaves. The floral motifs on the façade wall, below the cornice and in the railing show an advancement in art expression. The arrangement of pillars, the archivolt with multifold curves, the geometric modulation of arch holes, the foil arrangement inside arcades etc. show an architectural improvement as compared to that of the eighteenth century and the first half of the nineteenth century temple construction. (Chander Sheikher Panchani "Manipur : Religion, Culture and Society", Konark Publishers Pvt. Ltd., New Delhi, 1987) ("Mutua Museum," Manipur Temple Architecture, Bulletin No. 3, August, 1983, Keisampat, Imphal)

SHREE GOVINDAJEE TEMPLE OF NEW PALACE

This is the most magnificent, biggest and most popular temple of Manipur. It enshrines the royal deity, Shree Shree Govindajee. The temple is situated just near the present Manipur palace. The image of Lord Govindajee is 3 feet 10 inches high. (see plate-246). The commencement of making the image was on Friday, the 12th Hiyanggei, 1776 and its coronation was 11th Hiyanggei, 1779 (Friday). From the 11th day of Hiyanggei (November), 1779 to the full-moon day, the Raas-Lila of Radha Krishna was performed with the most enthusiastic mood of the religious people of Manipur. Raas Lila (Manipuri dance) was played for five days continuously in the open grounds of Raas Mandal Pukhri at Langthabal to commemorate the coronation.

Maharaja Churachand occupied the new palace on the 21st of Wakching (Wednesday), 1908. On the same day, the statues of Govindajee, which was lying in Khongman was again enshrined in the present Govindajee temple. The royal deities were shifted from the old Govindajee temple of Kangla Fort to Khongman during the 1891 war and it remained there till 1908.The surroundings of the Govindajee temple is very beautiful. There is a beautiful temple garden, a small lake and a big ground with lofty trees in the periphery.

The temple structure has been constructed in a palatial form raised on a square and on sufficiently high pedestal. It has got internal sanctum and outer jacket with Pradakshana path. The internal cell is further partitioned by two septica walls. The outer cube and the portico cube are constructed in the form of massive pillars raised at intervals in the arcade system. Above the arch the wall goes up to the cornice, above the cornice is the first railing, covering the terrace above the circumambulatory path. The first railing is having mini-shrines, the Salas, one each at the corner. There is no other superstructure over the portico roof after the first railing. The sanctum cube walls are raised up to the terrace of the first railing, right up to the cornice, then the second railing which surrounds the two domes. Externally the sanctum wall does not show any partition but internally the partition walls divide it into three chambers. Then the two multi-arched domes are raised from the cornice level. The arches of each dome converge at the base of the crown. The crown carries the Amalika-Sila and then the Kalasa with long pinnacle with the white temple flag. Both the dome surfaces from above are covered with gold-plated sheets. The façade is to the east.

The main deity of Govindajee, with Radha is placed in the central chamber; Jagannath, Subhadra and Balabhadra in the extreme northern chamber; and Balabhadra and Krishna in the extreme southern chamber. The chambers are nicely maintained. The front arcades are provided with curtains.

The idol of Lord Govindajee and Radha are made of the special wood and from the left out wood were made the idols of Jagannath, Subhadra and Balabhadra. The idols are decorated with Muktas on special occasions. Krishna and Balarama idols are made of plaster and given charming combination of colours.

The temple is the centre of religious activities of Manipur. It is now controlled by a committee in which some important priests and persons of the town are members. The morning and evening prayers are punctually performed in strict discipline and in ritualistic manner. A music party is permanently engaged to perform music during the prayers. Several special festivals like Halangkar (Holi festival), are celebrated in this temple with particular display of Manipuri dances. This temple has a socio-religious force and helps maintain the social order in Manipur Valley.

The Mandapa of Govindajee temple shows the palatial majesty of its structure. It is a separate structure just in front of the eastern façade of the temple having the common compound with the main temple body. Its front façade facing the temple, carries two double storeyed structures having a roof gallery over the first storey in between, which is supported with a solid line of railing. The cornice near the projected roof of the side building shows the supporting projection of a row of elephant heads carrying the sloping roof plates. At the roof slab of each side building there is a minaret in the form of a mini temple.There is a free entrance to the Mandapa hall. The entire structure is raised on several rows of pillars. On two sides, east and south, a concentric seating arrangement has been made for the colourful cultural and religious programmes performed in the temple. The roof is broken in two portions with slants to both sides in each portion. The corrugated cement sheets serve as the material for roof cover. On the western side of the temple there is another Mandapa called Natyasala. The structure is raised on the pillars with arcades and on the roof it has Salas, each one at the corner.

The worship ritual is impressive. The bell tower began to ring loudly, the conch men blew on their conches and the huge doors of the main building opened, revealing several large and ornate statues. The devotees will lined up in rows, men on one side, women on the other, each holding a brass plate or bell.

There's a strict dress code for visiting the Govindajee temple. Devotees are to wear white shirt and dhoti or a light-coloured kurta, Pungou phanek and Innafi, salwar-kameez or sari. Photography of the idols of the deities is prohibited. Janmastami (Aug) and Kang (Rathajatra, Jun-Jul) draw great crowds. The temple is an important venue for Raas lila performances, which can last all night, and are particularly famous during Basanta Purnima (Feb) and Kartik Purnima (October). (Chander Sheikher Panchani "Manipur : Religion, Culture and Society", Konark Publishers Pvt. Ltd., New Delhi, 1987) ("Mutua Museum," Manipur Temple Architecture, Bulletin No.-3, August, 1983, Keisampat, Imphal)

The temple is managed by the Govindajee Temple Board.

SHREE RADHA RAMAN TEMPLE OF LANGTHABAL

Radha Raman is another name of Lord Krishna. It was a temple of the royal family. It had royal patronage. The temple is situated at the old Langthabal palace, on hill ridge, near the present Manipur University campus. It was dedicated by Maharaj Churachand in the year 1917 A.D. It is not in use now.

It is said that the idol of Radha Raman was installed on the inauguration day with great pomp and show.

The temple structure is raised on a square pedestal, 4′ high above the ground level. It is facing south. In front, there are five steps of staircases, having steps from three sides. The temple is two celled. Its outer base measures 23′-6" x 23′-6" and then internal sanctum externally measure 12′-6" x 12′-6" and internally 9′x9′. The *Prahiksana* Patha is approachable by front staircases from the south and from three flying steps from the west. The outer jacket is arranged in columns with arcades. The sanctum cube of the outer jacket is raised to the cornice above which is a mini-temple, the Sala. The first railing covers the terrace above the *Prahiksana* Patha. The internal sanctum cube ends at the terrace level and then the octagonal structure with eight walls is raised. It appears as the octagonal core on the terrace of the temple. It carries second railing with arches. The eight pillars, one each at the corner of the railing, support the dome arches which converge at the base of the crown at the top. The parabolic ridges of the dome are distinctively visible on the surface of the dome from above.

The Garbha Griha opens in front with a 4′-6" and towards east by 3′-2" broad doors. Towards the east is a window with arch. Internally the octagonal structure is seen raised on the four walls of the sanctum cube. The structure with eight walls is also clearly visible with its dome's parabolic walls in the roof. The northern wall, internally has got a raised rostrum, probably for the installation of the deity.

The whole structure is made of brick with cement coating. Some designs are seen drawn on the walls but now there are only traces of these. It is based on Nagra style but ends with octagonal core exclusively constructed on the square walls of the sanctum. The decoration of walls with floral motifs is a further advancement shown in expressing the temple art. The whole structure is made of brick and thereafter given a cement coating. Some designs are seen drawn on the walls. The structure was designed in a very artistic way with architectural impact. The temple is the example of the proliferation of the Vaishnavite cult. Today, the structure is in ruins and the site is occupied by the army and nobody is allowed to visit the temple. (Chander Sheikher Panchani "Manipur: Religion, Culture and Society", Konark Publishers Pvt. Ltd, New Delhi,1987) ("Mutua Museum," Manipur Temple Architecture, Bulletin No.-3, August, 1983, Keisampat, Imphal)

LORD KRISHNACHANDRA TEMPLE OF KAKCHING

The Lord Krishnachandra Temple is situated just near the Kakching Keithel on Budhiraj road.(see plate-250) The temple consists of Lord Krishna,

Radha, Jagannath, Balabhadra and Subhadra. The temple was originally located on the western side of the Sekmai river and subsequently it was brought to the eastern side of the river inside the Kakching Khullen village. One Mayanglambam, Chaoba donated the present temple building. Every year, Raas Lilas are performed on the Mera Purnima and Hiyanggei Purnima in honour of the deity. Jalakelli is also performed on the Kalen Purnima every year.

When Meidingu Charairongba (1697-1709) came to visit the Sikhong Ningel Salt spring near Thoubal, he came across with one Langsai man. Langsoi is the pointed instrument made of either wood or iron which was used by the people of Khamlangba tribe for locating iron ore. Langsai is the name of the village where the Langsoi used to live. The man immediately plucked three leaves of grass and presented to the king. On enquiry, he said "you are the King. You are God. My meeting with you is unexpected. I am supposed to present something to you according to our custom. But I do not have anything now. That is why I am presenting these grasses". Satisfied with his reply, the King said "You are very intelligent. So you are given the title of Budhiraj" (Intelligent) and you should be the King of your village. Later on in 1740, he settled in Kakching near the bank of Sekmai river and became the King of Kakching. The title of Budhiraj was given to all subsequent kings of Kakching. That is why the name of the road is also given as Budhiraj road.

When the dowager Queen Kumudini along with King Chandrakirti fled to Cachar on 27 January, 1844 AD, one Moirangthem Gourshyam from Kakching along with many others accompanied them. Moirangthem Gourshyam served the King with all devotion and dedication. Chandrakirti ascended the throne on 4th Ingel (13th July), 1850 (Saturday) at the age of 19 years after returning from Cachar. In 1855, Moirangthem Gourshyam was made the King of Kaching. Chandrakirti asked him "Is there anything else which you want me to do". Gourshyam politely requested the Maharaja Chandrakirti to "establish Radha Govinda Temple at Kakching". The king simply said "With the divine blessing of Radha Govinda, your wish could be fulfilled".

After some time, Radha Govinda appeared in the dream of Raja Chandrakirti and told him "I am Krishna, you can ask the people in the villages of three Ks to worship me and you will be blessed". The King consulted with his nobles. He went in person to Bishnupur to find out suitable trees for making the idol of Krishna Chandra. Ultimately the tree was found, it was uprooted and brought to the Palace. One sculptor Chungkham Lala (Lokhon) Hajari was engaged to make the idol. In due course of time, the idols were completed. The King was very happy to see the idols and he named the idol Krishnachandra. He had decided to give it for worship to the people inhabiting in Kakching Khullen, Kakching Khunou and Kakching Wairi, the villages with three Ks. The King also remembered what he told to Gourshyam. So one day he called Gourshyam and asked him to select any idol of his choice. Gourshyam selected the idol of Krishnachandra. Thus on 5th of Sajibu, 1852, the idol of Krishnachandra was coronated at Kakching in presence of Maharaja Chandrakirti, his nobles and queens. One Gotimayum Tolen Sharma, cook of Ayapuren Major was asked to go to Kaching and serve the Lord as the Brahmin. The descendants of Gotimayum Tolen Sharma are still worshipping Krishnachndra of Kakching till date. Presently Kshetrimayum Ibotombi Singh is the Rajdhari of Lord Krishnachandra. (Naorem Amuyaima, Pandit Achouba, "Shri Shri Jangannath Nirupon, Govinda Nirupon and Krishnachandra Nirupon", Kakching, Mayanglamabam Gourchandra "Meitrabakki Puyarida Kakching", People's Museum, Kakching, 2002.)

NARA SINGH TEMPLE OF KAKCHING

The Nara Singh temple of Kaching is situated at the Paji Leikai of Kakching Kullen (see plate- 251). The temple was named after the name of King Nara Singh of Manipur. The temple consist of Nara Singh Saligram, the idols of Krishna, Radha, Jagannath, Balabhadhra and Subhadra. The present temple was donated by one Mayanglambam, Chaoba.

In 1467, when Kyaamba was the King of Manipur, there was a terrible cholera epidemic. One day while King Kyaamba was praying to God, three stone images in the form of Saligram appeared. One look like an elephant named it Samulai , the second one looked like a horse named it Sagollai and the third one looked like oyster with corrugated surface named it Konggreng Lai. King Kyaamba worshipped the three Saligrams and in due course of time, the epidemic subsided. He retained the Samulai and he had given the Sagollai to the prince and the Konggrenglai to Angom Ningthou.

After a long time, Nara Singh (1844-1850) came in possession of the Sagollai. When Nara Singh came and stayed at Naopipat, Kakching on the bank of Sekmai river, he also brought the Sagollai. He established military camps at Kakching to protect Manipur from any possible invasion from Burma. During these hectic activities, the Saligram Sagollai was lost. After a long time, one Yengkhom Subha Mendo had come across one shining pebble near the Thumkhong Lokmang near the forest and it was identified to be the missing Sagollai. The Sagollai was brought to its original place. By this time, Nara

Singh had already returned to the palace. The people of Kakching decided to return the Saligram Sagollai to Nara Singh. They took the Saligram and handed over to Nara Singh in his palace at Kangla. After a few days, the party returned to Kakching. But when they returned to Kakching, they found the same Saligram in its original place at Kakching. The matter was reported to Nara Singh, who kindly ordered that the Saligram would be worshipped by the people of Kakching. One Chandradas Babaji, a monk from Charangpat was in the service of the Saligram.

During the time of Raja Chandrakirti, when Krishnachandra was coronated, Gotimayum Tolen Sharma was asked to look after both the Krishnachandra as well as Nara Singh Temple. Now the descendants of Gotimayum Tolen Sharma are looking after the Nara Singh temple.

ABDEITYA TEMPLE OF LAMANGDONG (BISHNUPUR)

Abdeitya Temple of Lamangdong (see plate-248) is one the oldest temples of Manipur. Abdeitya was the seventh image curved out of the root of jackfruit tree from Kaina. (P. Bharat Singh, The Sacred Jack Tree of Kaina, 2007). The idols of Radha, Krishna, Ram, Jagannath, Balabhadra, Subhadra and also small idols of Sita and Hanuman are in the temple. The image was coronated on 7th day of Lamda, 1793. It is believed that four Shaktis (powers) namely Gokulnath, Basudeva, Dwarkanath and Radhika were merged into one called Abdeitya. Originally the temple was situated in the "Konung at Lamangdong" where the present C.I., College is situated.

Shyamjai Khurailakpa, son of Garib Niwaj developed an orchard and garden in this place. Later on Bhagyachandra made it his capital before shifting to Langthabal. King Bhagyachandra gave his daughter Dharmeswari Shija in marriage to a devout Brahmin priest Gurumayum Jatiswar Sharma and entrusted him the duties of worshipping the deity (A. Chitraswor Sharma, Meitei Nongaron", April, 1988). Now the descendants of Gurumayum Jatiswar Sharma are looking after the temple. Presently the three brothers Gurumayum Nilamani Sharma., Krishnatri Sharma, Viswanath Sharma are looking after the temple. They have four hectares of paddy field in the name of the temple. The temple is in its present site since 1941. The existing temple was donated in 1972 by one old woman named Tolangou from Uripok, Imphal and the Mandapa was donated by Ngangbam Meghachandra Singh of Chingamakhong, Imphal.

GOPINATH TEMPLE OF NINGTHOUKHONG

Gopinath Temple of Ningthoukhong is a small beautiful temple located in a peaceful surrounding, surrounded by very old Bokul trees. (see plate-247)

King Bhagyachandra came to Chiru village during the war with Khelhei Nungnang Telheiba of Moirang. He was roaming just like a commoner immediately after returning from Tekhao (Assam). One old woman said to him "you look so tired. You look like our king". Bhagyachandra disclosed his identity to the old woman. The old woman took him to her house at Ningthoukhong and asked her grand daughter Pukhrambam Kesari to look after the King. Kesari was the daughter of Dushraj, who was the head of the Bishnupriya clan. Bhagyachandra took Kesari as his wife.Later on, a son was born in 1768 and he was named Kirti Dhaja Kalaraj. Bhagyachandra gave the idol of Gopinath to his wife Kesari and entrusted his son Kirti Dhaja Kalaraj with the task of worshipping it. The installation of the image of Gopinathjee was done at 9 A.M. on 8th of Hiyanggei, 1781. (Rajkumar Sanahal Guneshwar, Yaiskul "Manipur Govinda Nirupon, 1980). The original brick temple was destroyed by bombing during the second world war. The new temple was constructed in 1963 and the Mandapa in 2002. Presently R.K. Jilasana, a descendant of Kirti Dhaja Kalaraj is looking after the temple. The temple has got about one hectare of plot land and 14 hectares of paddy field in the name of the temple.

RADHA MADHAV TEMPLE OF NINGTHOUKHONG

Radha Madhav temple at Ningthoukhong is a small beautiful temple located at about 250 metres from the Ningthoukhong Keithel on the eastern side of the State Highway. This is one of the oldest temple in Manipur (see plate-249)

It has got three doors. The middle chamber consists of Lord Krishna and Radha, the northern chamber consists of Ram Krishna. The southern chamber consist of Jagannath, Balabhadra and Subhadra. The whole complex comprises of about 41,140 sq, feet. It has got a huge mandapa covering about 1000 sq. feet and a big tank.

Ram Krishna idols were given by King Chourajit to Krishnachandra, the first Khuman King. At the time of coronation of King Chourajit, the representatives of the seven Yek Salais have to pour water on the king. One Madhamu Laishraba, a Phamnaiba from Ningthoukhong produced the two brothers Krishnachandra and Kabichandra as the true representatives of the Khuman Yek. The King made Krishnachandra as the Khuman king It is said that the Krishnachandra poured water on Maharaja Chourjit at the time of his coronation in 1803. He was given the idols of Ram Krishna along with two Paris of land. Later Kumudini Maharani gave the idols of Radha Madha along with six Paris of land. Now the temple is managed by a committee under the care and supervision of the descendants of the Krishnachandra.

RAMJI PRABHU TEMPLE OF NINGTHEM PUKHRI MAPAL

Ramji Prabhu temple of Ningthem Pukhri Mapal, Imphal consists of Ram, Lakshsman, and Hanuman It also worship Jagannath, Cheiteinya Mahaprabhu. The temple also worship the idols of Garib Niwaj Maharaja and Santi Das Gosai. The temple belongs to the Angom Ningthou Clan. (see plate-254, 259)

Ramji Prabhu is an old temple, existing since the time of Garib Niwaj (1709-1748). The images of Rama with Sita, Lakshman, Bharat and Shatrughan were installed in the temples in 1737. The King used to entrust anybody who was near and dear to the King to worship Ramji Prabhu. Angom Ningthou was very powerful during the time of Maharajas. Angom Ningthou was the president of Cheirap (Civil and criminal court). He used to hear cases pertaining to disputes regarding Sylvan gods. During the time of Maharaja Bodhachandra, Nongmaithem Jugolchandra of Wanghei Pukhrambam Leikai was appointed as Angom Ningthou. His wife Anubisana got the title of Khuraileima. It is said that the Temple of Ramji Prabhu was given to Khuraileima as a dowry by King Bodhachandra along with the land, five hectares of paddy field and a stipend. Every year, Ramnabami, which is the 9th of Sajibu is celebrated to commemorate the coronation of Shree Ram to the throne of Ayodhya and the 9th day of Kalen is celebrated as the Sita Nabami. On these auspicious occasions, Raas Lila was performed and the King and the Angom Ningthou used to give rewards to the people in the form of Khamen Chatpa, Tal etc.

On the Kwak Jatra festivals, the idols of Ram, Lakshman and Hanuman were taken out and the actual ritual of Kwak Jatra was started only after arrival of the idols at the particular spot.

Once the idols of Shri Ram went missing during the Burmese war. Therefore a new idol of Shri Ram was sculptured and installed during the time of Nara Singh Maharaja. After a long time, the idol was found in the thick jungles and it was subsequently restored to it original place. Nowadays, the descendants of the Angom Ningthou is worshipping the Ramji Prabhu in its original place.

BIJOY GOVINDA TEMPLE OF SAGOLBAND

The Bijoy Govinda temple is situated at Sagolband. (see plate -252) After performing a puja, Sapam Lokhon applied his tools on the second log of the Jackfruit tree from Kaina and started making the images of Govindajee. When it was finished, King Bhagyachandra was not quite happy as it slightly lacks in resemblance to the Lord he had seen in his dream. This had become the image of Bijoy Govinda. (P. Bharat Singh, The Sacred Jack Tree of Kaina, 2007). In 1779, Bhagyachandra's uncle Ananta Shai and his descendants were made responsible for Sri Bijoy Govinda and the annual festival of Heikru Hitongba (Boat Race) held on the 11th day of Langban (September) every year. Heikru Hitongba (see Chapter-13: Festivals of Manipur) is celebrated on the eleventh day of Langban month (September) of Meitei Calendar at the Thangapat (moat) of Shri Bijoy Govindajee, Sagolband, Imphal. It is performed with the offering of Heikru (Amalaki) fruit to the Lord accompanied with an exciting contest of 'Hiyang Tanaba' (Boat race) in the sacred Thangapat Moat of Sagolband, Bijoy Govinda). Heigru Hitongba puja is dedicated only to Lord Bijoy Govinda under the sole management of the descendants of the pious ancient Mantri in collaboration with the local people.

The temple is now managed by the descendants of Ananta Shai

NARA SINGH THAKUR OF NAOREM LEIKAI

The Lord Nar Singh Thakur Temple is situated at Naorem Leikai, Imphal. (see plate- 256) The Lord Nar Singh Thakur Temple came into existence immediately after the Khongjom war. Naorem Tharakchao was a prominent Maiba of the royal family during the reign of Kulachandra. When the royal family was in turmoil and in utter confusion due to Khongjom war, Maharja Kulachandra blessed his faithful Maiba with the work of worshipping the Lord Narasingh. He had also given five hectares of paddy field in the name of the Lord Narasingh. He asked one Brahmin from Thangmeiband to take the image of Lord Narasingh to the place of Naorem Tharakchao. Tharakchao with the help of the Brahmin took away the image from the royal palace by crossing the Imphal river near the Mahaballi Umang and started worshipping it in his Ingkhol at Naorem Leikai. The image remained there for more than ten years. His son Naorem Menjor was a Pena Khongba of the royal palace. After some years, Shanglakpam clan started looking after the image. But one unfortunate event took place where Brahmin Laphoichaba, the main Purohit died by drowning. After that Sijagurumayum clan started worshipping it. Presently, Sijagurumayum Bimola Devi is looking after the deity. The temple has now many deities -Nara Singh, Hiranyakoushikpu, Laxmi, Pralhada, Krishna, Radha, Jagannath, Nityainanda, Gopal Deva, Chaitanya Mahaprabhu. It is believed that "if you pray and worship Narasingh, your wishes will be fulfilled." If somebody has done some harm to you and "if you pray to Nara Singh, your enemy would be punished". Nara Singh Janma is held on the 14th of Kalen every year where people in thousands will come and pray to Lord Nara Singh.

The present temple was constructed by Okram Chaoba Singh, Special Class Contractor of Khongman Okram Chithek in 1965. The renovation work was done by Shri Thounaojam Ranbir Singh and Thounaojam Ongbi Malini Devi of Thangmeiband Hijam Dewan Leikai.

TEMPLE OF NITYAINANDA PRABHU OF RIMS ROAD

The temple of Shree Nityainanda Prabhu /Arambam Nityananda is situated at RIMS Road, Lamphel, Imphal. The making of the image of Shree Nityainanda Prabhu /Arambam Nityananda was started on the full moon day of Lamda (Thursday), 1794 out of the fourth log of the sacred jackfruit tree from Kaina. The sculptor was Sapam Lokhon Singh. It was coronated on 13th day of Wakching, 1795. It took ten months to complete it. When Premabati, the King's daughter was married to Arambam Tamradhwaja, she requested her father to allow her and her husband to worship Shri Shri Nityananda at her husband's place at Khwai Lamabam Leikai. The King agreed and the deity was shifted to Khwai Lamabam Leikai and the deity is worshipped by the Arambam family. (P. Bharat Singh, The Sacred Jack Tree of Kaina, 2007)

MADAN MOHAN TEMPLE OF KONGBA

The Madan Mohon temple is located at Kóngba. The temple consists of Lord Krishna, Radha, Jagannath, Balabhadra, Subhadra, Ram Krishna, Gopaldeva, Vishnu, Chaitanya Mahaprabhu, Nityainanda. The idol of Lord Krishna was of metal and was brought from Mathura by two brothers named Bishnupur and Uttam from Mathura. The other idols are made of wood. It is said that the idol of Lord Krishna was accidentally discovered by Bishnupur while excavating earth at Mathura. The two brothers married Meitei women on their arrival and they were given the surname Mathurabashimayum by the Maharaja probably Bhagyachandra. They started worshipping the Krishna idols at the location where it stands today with the blessing of the Maharaja. The elder brother Bishnupur had one son named Thabal whereas the younger brother Uttam did not have any issue. When Imphal was bombarded at several places during the world war-II, the descendants of the Mathuramayum buried the idols under a bush in a place called Wareppa. All the family members of Mathuramayun died in the bombing except one small boy named Chura.

When the world war ended, nobody knew the whereabouts of the idol of Madan Mohon. A handsome boy used to appear and he acted strangely in and around Wareppa. When the local people followed him, he disappeared near a bush at Wareppa. People became suspicious. They dug out the bush and they found the idols of Lord Krishna. Immediately people recognized that the idol once belonged to the Mathurabashimayum family and the idol was returned to the boy. The boy Chura started worshipping the idol at a very young age. But he did it with all devotion and honesty. He bathed many times in a day to keep himself pure and clean for the service of Lord Krishna and he would go sprinkling Tulsi water on his way. So people fondly called him "Hangoi Chura" (Frog Chura).

People came to Madan Mohon temple to know their future. For this, they should dedicate to Lord Krishna eight or eighteen or 108 leaves of Tulsi (Ocimum sanctum) and request the Purohit to throw the Tulsi leaves three times to the head of Lord Krishna. If the Tulsi strikes the head, it means all success will come to the person. If it touches the ear, it means all happiness for the person. If it touches the eyes, it means some misfortune or bad days may come. If it touches the chest, then one may get gold and silver in plenty. If it touches the shoulder, then lots of troubles and responsibility may come. If it touches the legs and feet, then one may face death or extreme danger.

Presently, the temple is maintained by Mathurabashimayum Rajkumar, Mathurabashimayum Nandakishore and Mathurabashimayum Gourchandra. Each one will be in the service of God for six days in rotation. They organize Ratha Jatra, Jhulon, Jalakelli, Holi and Raas Lila every year.

SREE SREE RADHA KRISHNA MANIMANDIR OF ISKON

Sree Sree Radha Krishna Manimandir of ISKON is situated at Airport road, Imphal. (see plate- 255).

A.C. Bhaktivedanta Swami Prabhupada is the founder Acharya of the Hare Krishna movement. He founded ISKON (International Society for Krishna Consciousness) in New York, USA as a spiritual society in 1965 to propagate the message of the Bhagwad Gita. ISKON has got more than 200 temples in 70 countries. Bhaktisvarupa Damodara Swami (Dr. Thoudam Damudor Swami) was initiated by Srila Prabhupada and became his disciple in 1970. Damodara Swami was born in Toubul village on 9th December, 1937 (Thursday). In India there are about 40 ISKCON temples. Contemplating the traditions of the ancient Vaishnava tradition, its philosophy and practice, these spiritual temples have left a mark on all mankind. Visiting these temples proves to be a pleasant and revealing experience. ISKCON temples are dedicated to Lord Krishna and were built by the Hare-Rama Hare-Krishna cult followers. These complexes are elegantly built and there are few of the largest temple complexes in India. There are beautiful paintings of Russian artists on the different past times of Radha Krishna, Sita, Ram, Lakshman, Hanuman and Chaitanya Mahaprabhu.

Bhaktisvarupa Damodara Swami visited Manipur in August 1974 and met Longjam Kulabidhu Singh, AK. Mani and some members of the Gita Mandal. During those days, there were only three patron members of ISKON-Longjam Kulabidhu Singh, Sagolsem Ibochouba Singh and Sorokhaibam, Birmangol Singh. Bhaktiswarupa Damodara Swami started the ISKON movement in Manipur on 25th December, 1977 at Paona Bazar Thakurbari. On 29th January installation of Sri Sri Radha Krishna in the form of picture along with Sri Panchatatva and Guru Paramparas in the temple was made in a ceremony attended by a large gathering. On 31st January, 1978, a Nagar Sankirtana (Harinam Sankirtana) was performed in and around Imphal led by H.H. Bhaktisvarupa Damodara Swami. On 25th August, 1978, the ISKON temple was shifted to Airport Road. Four acres of land was donated Shrimati Longjam Ketuki Devi and Sri Longjam Kulabidhu Singh on 17th July, 1980. On 16 January, 1984, Brahmins from Tirupati performed Yajna for the installation ceremony. The foundation stone of the temple was laid on 22nd March, 1992. Sree Sree Radha Krishna Manimandir was inaugurated on 11 November, 2000. The floor covers an area of 11,230 sq. yard, double storied with three domes with a height of 55 feet. The architect was Mr. B. Roy Ghatak. Structural design was given by Dr. Ghosh Dastidar The temple is planned to look like a shining diamond when fully completed. Hence it is named Manimandir. Sri Ved Marwah, the Governor of Manipur and Sri W. Nipamacha Singh, Chief Minister of Manipur participated as honoured guests at the inaugural function. Three Brahmanas (Rajagurus) from Puri conducted the installation ceremony. 108 Brahmins from Manipur recited the whole of Srimad Bhagavatam and performed Yajnas (fire sacrifice) during the installation ceremony.216 children enacted the Maha Raas dance. Many national and international groups such as Ramayana artists from Bali, Indonesia participated at the ceremony. It was a month-long joyous festival.

The first Ratha yatra festival of the ISKON was organized in July, 2001. A special chariot was manufactured in Mumbai and it was transported to Manipur. Special programmes like Kirtan, Aarti, Pravachan and Prasadam are held every Sunday. ISKON has got more than 3000 life members. ISKON admits anyone who wants to know the science of God.

GOPINATH TEMPLE OF SANAKHYAHAL

The Gopinath Temple of Sanakhyahal is an old temple located in the Rajbari-I near the R.D.S School, Imphal. This temple was established around 1910. The idols consists of Gopinath (Krishna), Radha which Nara Singh used to worship at Brindabanchandra at Kangla when he was the Yuvaraj before 1891. Now the descendants of Nara Singh Maharaja worshipped it. The other idols consists of another set of Krishna, Radha, Jagannath, Balabhadra, Subhadra, Gourchandra, Nityainanda and Saligram. It is said that Nara Singh went to Vrindavan and brought Gopinath and Radha, which were made of metal. Nara Singh donated 35 Paris of land in honour of the temple. But the popularity of the temple is dwindling due to many factors including a long drawn court case among the descendants.

HIYANGTHANG LAIREMBI (KAMAKHYA) TEMPLE

Hiyangthang Lairembi is situated at Heibok Ching, about 10 km from Imphal towards Langthabal. (see plate-258) Thousands of people particularly young girls and boys used to come on the 3rd day of Durga Puja (Bor numit) for a prayer at this temple in the early morning. It is believed that "the Goddess will fulfill your wish if you ask for a blessing on this day at the right time." On other days, this temple is almost deserted. The Mandapa in front of the temple of Hiyangthang Leirembi is a matching structure to the beautiful and lofty temple structure. Both the temple and the Mandapa have provided architectural harmony with respect to the commanding site on the hillock overlooking the valley. The intricacy of the staircases to some distance, one sees the Mandapa only, and mistake it, to be the main temple. On reaching half way one finds the towering roofs of the main temple hovering above the Mandapa. The Mandapa hall is well maintained. The structure is raised on pillars and roof given concrete sheet covering. There are some paintings decorated on the walls of the hall depicting Lord Krishna's life story. These paintings are done by some Manipuri artist.

Heibok Ningthou was once a remarkable clan King who was expert in witchcraft and black magic. For a long time, he and his wife Hireima did not have any child. After some time, they had a very beautiful daughter called Irai Leima. She was a maiden of exceptional beauty. One day when she was fishing in the Liwa river, the Khuman King Kokpa, stricken by the beauty of Irai Leima approached her for marriage. Irai Leima replied that she would obey to her parent's wishes. The Khuman King consulted with his followers. It was decided that they would go to the Heibok Ningthou with all the presents in the form of

"Heijingpot". If the Heibok King agreed, he would marry Irai Leima and if he did not agree, he would bring Irai Leima by force. So Khuman Kokpa went to the house of Heibok King with many presents including cows and buffaloes. The Heibok Ningthou was taken by surprise. Seeing the arrogant attitude of Khuman King, he cursed that all his presents should be turned into stone. Immediately all the presents were turned into stone and all his followers had fled in fear. Khuman Kokpa came back dejected and full of remorse. One day, he drank the juice of the root of Tera (Bambax malabaricum) and he was fully intoxicated. Suddenly he decided to meet Iraileima. He came in his boat called "Hiyang". Seeing Khuman Kokpa, Iraileima fled towards Pakhra Ching. Khuman Kokpa pursued her. Heibok Ningthou saw Khuman Kokpa pursuing his daughter from a distance. Heibok Ningthou again cursed that his boat should be turned into stone and his oar should be grown as a tree. Immediately, whatever he had said happened. Being frustrated, Khuman Kokpa ran towards Heibok Ningthou with an intension to kill him. Again Heibok Ningthou cursed him to turn into stone. Khuman Kokpa was turned into a stone. Irai Leima saw all these happenings from a distance. She was afraid to return to her father. Heibok Ningthou called out his daughter with all his might but Iraileima never replied. She had ran away from her father. Irai Leima came out of the Lai Pakhra Ching, crossed the Liwa river and entered the house of Sarangthem Luwangba and remained hidden under the granary of Sarangthem Luwangba. When Sarangthem Luwangba had gone out for working in the paddy field along with his wife Thoidingjam Chanu Amurei, Irai Leima would come out and did all the household chores of the Sarangthem family. When Sarangthem Luwangba returned from work along with his wife, they were surprised how all these things happened. The same thing happened everyday. One day, he returned early and to his surprise, he saw one beautiful maiden doing the household chores and when he came nearer, she had disappeared below the granary. When he went under the granary, he could not find anything. He was quite surprised how this was possible. He invited all the clan members of Sarangthem Salai to discuss the matter. He narrated all what happened. They have searched everywhere. They have examined the spot where the maiden had disappeared. They could not find any clue.

In the mean time, Sarangthem Luwangba had a dream one day. In his dream Irai Leima appeared and told him "Oh father, from today onwards, I am merged to your clan. I am your daughter and immediately she disappeared".

They reported the matter to King Senbi Kyaamba (1467-1508 AD). Kyaamba sent Maibas and Maibis to see the spot. After examining the spot, the Maibas and Maibis reported "what you had seen was a goddess and appropriate arrangement and rituals should be performed to worship her". The King arranged all the necessary articles and the Maibis in their trance told the same thing which Sarangthem Luwangba had seen in his dream. After hearing all these things, King Kyaamba asked Luwangba to worship the goddess as his clan deity and every year, all his clan members should present vegetables, fruits and arrange a grand feast in honour of the deity. The day on which Sarangthem Luwnagba saw Irai Leima entering under the granary was the first Monday of Lamda and the day on which the Maibis and Maibas came was the first Tuesday of Lamda. Even today since the time of King Kyaamba, the Sarangthen Salais use to hold "Chaklong Katpa" (grand feast) every year in honour of the goddess and the goddess is known as "Hiyangthang Lairembi".

However, Hiyangthang Lairembi had been converted into Kamakhya (Durga) during the reign of Garib Niwaj. The third day of the Durga Puja festival is observed as Bornumit (Boon Day). This Bornumit is performed at the Hiyangthang Lairembi. Thousands of people will come and assemble from the early morning to seek boons and blessings from Hiyangthang lairembi at the Hiyangthang Lairembi Mandir. Elaborate arrangement is made to cater to the needs of thousands of people. But in fact, this has no relevance with the true story of Hiyangthang Lairembi. (Sarangthem Bormani, Meitei Ima Lairembi)

THONGNGAM MONDUM

The presiding deity of Thongngam Mondum is considered to be Shiva Mahadeva. However, people believed that Thongngam Mondum is the abode of "Leinung Mori Yotsungba". This "Leinung Mori Yotsungba" had been converted into Shiva Mahadeva during the time of Garib Niwaj. It is located at the Mondum ching. The temple is now managed by the Mondum Seva Marup. The deity is in the form of a huge stone of about 11 feet high and a hole (navel) in the middle. Originally it was around 3-4 feet high but Maharaja Bodhachandra excavated the earth around the Shiva idol to increase the height of the idol. People threw coins towards the navel. It is believed that those who can't get a son will get a son after having a prayer at the Thongam Mondum. Maharaja Bodhachandra was a great patron of Thongngam Modum.

LORD SANAMAHI TEMPLE, IMPHAL

The Lord Sanamahi temple is situated within the complex of the 1st battalion Manipur Rifles, Imphal. (see plate- 257 On 1st of Thawan, 1733

(Monday), Garib Niwaj worshipped Lainingthou Sanamahi and Leimarel Sidabi at Tollong Ingkhol (present 1st Manipur Rifles). It was patronized by King Kulachandra in 1891.

The structure is raised on an octagonal base, each component of which is 10′-5". The southern side has got flying steps. The facade carries a rectangular door with 7′ width. It is an octagonal structure with each component wall of 9′-4" breadth which meets the double cornice. The cornice below and above has got a series of slits arranged in a line over the octagonal structure. The roof structure is peculiar in pyramidal Gothic style, the arches incline at 45 degree to form a tapering octagonal structure which is truncated by Amalaka-Sila, on the top, in a form of a circular disc. It carries a pinnacle. A porch is also on the eastern side connecting the sanctum hall.

Internally the sanctum is octagonal. The structure is made of bricks. It is the only temple of Sanamahi religion in Manipur which was constructed particularly to enshrine the deity. The temple is also important for its architectural variety. The deity Lord Sanamahi is worshipped in the temple. However, the rituals are of typical Hindu style.

A weekly Puja known as 'Sagalchham' is performed on Tuesday, the annual festival is celebrated at the temple during 'Cheiraoba' the new year festival of Manipur and another festival celebrating during September at the temple is called 'Honjanungba'.

The decoration of deity and Puja system is based on Hindu style. The dress of the priest performing the rituals is indistinguishable from a Hindu priest. The Puja is performed by the priest daily in morning and evening at appropriate times of Ushakala and Sandhyakala.

IBUDHOU THANGJING TEMPLE OF MOIRANG

Ibudhou Thangjing Koirellai Lai is the biggest and most popular sylvan God in Manipur. The Temple is situated at Moirang Mayai Leikai (see plate-253). Another name of Thangjing is Koirellai. Ibudhou Thangjing guard the western boundary of Manipur and therefore. He faced towards the west and any one who prays or worships Ibudhou Thangjing, his wishes will be fulfilled and there will be peace and prosperity in the country.

Ibudhou Thangjing was worshipped for the first time by Iwang Puritlai Phang Phang Ponglel Hanba. Ibudhou Thangjing descended from Korou Awangba (heaven) to Malem (earth) and settled first at the foothill of Sareng Ching. He wished to start a new settlement at Kege and proceeded towards Kege along with his entourage on white tiger on Sunday in the month of

Sajibu through Ngangkha village. Thangjing ruled over Moirang for countless number of years. He then prepared for creation of Taibang (human world). Iwang Puritlai Phang Phang Ponglel Hanba was the last in the line of Lai (God) succession and the first in the line of Namu-pong (human)succession. He became the first human ningthou of Kege Moirang. In his time, the first and the only Maiba was Khoyam Moriphaobicha. Then a divine message was conveyed to Puritlai Phang Phang Ponglel Hanba. A strange event took place in his time. The young boys and girls did not smile. The children did not cry. The dogs did not bark and the cocks did not crow. The King's daughter Thangyai Leihoubi enquired about this unnatural phenomenon. The priest, Thingkol Miribacha after divination revealed that the King had forgotten to perform the rites and sacrifices to Ibudhou Thangjing. Immediately the rites were performed according to the instruction of Ibudhou Thangjing and thus normalcy was restored. The fifteen thoyas (Leikais) were asked to worship Ibudhou Thangjing. But only eight leikais were asked to assemble in front of Moirang Kangla Utra. Thus the Moirang Thangjing Lai Haraoba was started. The eight leikais were– Ngangkha leikai, Khoyol leikai, Nganglou leikai, Khambi leikai, Higa leikai, Okchin leikai, Chenglei leikai, Yaoshu leikai. The nine markets were–Khori keithel, Ngangkha keithel, Nongkhrangpokpi keithel, Aaun keithel, Okchil keithel, Higa keithel, Chenglei keithel, Yaosu keithel, Nganglou keithel (Sarangthem Bormani, Moirang Saion, 2003). The archaeological findings at Napachik, near Wangoo established the fact that in the second millennium B.C., Neolithic culture existed in this part of Moirang. The old chronicles like Moirang Ningthourol Lambuba, Moirang Ningthourol, folklore, oral traditions supported the view that Thangjing once ruled at Moirang in pre-historic times. Puritlai Phang Phang Ponglel Hanba married a Khuman girl named Mentomnu. His territory extended from Thangshoi in the east to Haoreng in the west.There are many legendary love stories like Khamba Thoibi, Henjunaha and Thongnang Lairoulembi, Khoyom Haoba and Yaithing Konu, Kadeng Thangjahanba and Tonu Laijinglembi, Uranaha Khongjomba and Pidongnu, Samba Naha Lamganba and Khamnu Yaiding Konu, Wanglen Pungdinghanba and Chakpa Yainu Fishaheibi, Akongjamba and Phaoibi, Nganba and Shangloulembi. It is believed that these plays were enacted by Ibudhou Thangjing as a part of the Saiyon mapan and Moirang Kangleirol. At the time of separation of Gods and human beings, the Gods gave Ningthoukhamba as the head of human beings three Maibas named Yangkhongjamba, Thonglen Haying Khongba and Kayaba. They were instructed how to perform Lai Haraoba ceremony. Since that time, the Lai Haraoba ceremony of Thangjing is being continued till today. The tradition of Maiba Hanba and Maibi Hanjabi is in existence since time immemorial. The Lai Haraoba ceremony is started from the Kalen Tritiya of every year. The Chaklong Katpa is performed on the 21 December of every year. Maibram Modhuchandra Singh is the present Maibahanba of Moirang Thangjing temple.. The temple is managed by the Lord Thangjing Seva Mandal chaired by Moirangthem Iboton Singh, Khadrakpa. Earlier, it was run by the Phamnaiba Cheirap of Moirang.

KONTHOUJAM LAIREMBI

The temple of Konthoujam Lairembi is one of the oldest temple of sylvan Gods located in beautiful surrounding with many big banyan trees. (see plate- 260, 261) All the ten banyan trees form a single banyan tree connected together. The banyan trees may be of at least 500 years old. The story of Konthoujam Lairembi runs like this :-

Haorok Konthoujam Aremba and his wife Huimu Leima were issueless for a long time. They prayed to God for giving them a son or a daughter. The penance of Haorok Konthou Aremba moved the God, who asked His daughter Chinglai Leima to incarnate as the daughter of Haorok Konthou Aremba.

In the mean time, King Soraren, (Some people called Salailen) who ruled in heaven with 1000 queens was without any issue. He was thinking to get married again in order to have a son or a daughter. In due course of time, Huimu Leima was pregnant. One day in a meeting of Gods and human beings where King Soraren was also present, Haorok Konthou Aremba declared that his wife was pregnant. King Soraren proposed to Haorok Konthou Aremba that "if the child to be born happens to be a son, he would be one of his bosom friends and if the child happens to be a daughter, she should be given to him as his queen". Haorok Konthou Aremba was embarrassed and not knowing what to reply he said "Yes". In due course of time, a daughter was born to Huimu Leima and she was named "Tampha Wangamloi Leisang Shaphabi". She grew up into a young maiden. She was a girl of exceptional beauty with extra ordinary qualities. One day, King Soraren arrived at the residence of the Haorok Konthou Aremba and reminded him of the promise he had made.

King Soraren was a powerful King of Gods and so Aremba had no power to confront him. He said "Oh King. I will abide by my promise. But I need to inform my daughter and consult with her. At the end of seven months, you can take her as your queen". Hearing that, King Soraren was very happy. At the end of seven months, King Soraren came back with the hope to take

Tamphal Wangamloi as his queen. Tampha Wangamloi exacted a promise from King Soraren that she would be head queen and nobody in her Konthoujam clan should suffer from disease or death. The King Soraren gladly promised to fulfill her wish. Thus Tampha Wangamloi was made the head queen of King Soraren. One day, Tampha Wangamloi requested King Soraren to give her the power of 1000 eyes and 1000 ears so that she could understand what was going on this earth. King Soraren replied that that was the power granted only to Gods and Goddesses and since she was the human being, she could not have the power. But King Soraren gave her the title of "Tampha Lairembi" or "Goddess Tampha." Since she had been married to God in the heaven, she was not allowed to go to earth and mix up with her family and friends. Only the dog which was given as a dowry by her mother Huimu Leima acted as a messenger between the Konthoujam family and Tampha Lairembi. In due course of time, a son was born to her.

In the mean time, the Haorokcham clan and Konthoujam clan jointly made a hunting expedition in which the dog which was used as a messenger died. The Konthoujam family was very unhappy. Huimu Leima cried over the death of the dog as if a son had died. She requested her Konthoujam clan to perform the funeral for the dog by cremating befitting the funeral of a member of the Konthoujam family. The Konthoujam clan had never experienced death or disease for a long time. So taking advantage of the death of the dog, they performed the funeral in a big way. Huimu Leima lamented over the loss of the dog. Tampha Lairembi heard the cries of her mother and saw the flames coming out from the funeral. She was worried if some calamity had happened to her Konthoujam clan. She asked her husband King Soraren the reason for the cry of her mother and the flame coming out of the funeral. King Soraren narrated the stories. But Tamphal Lairembi wanted to verify by going down to earth and meeting her family members. Her husband said there was no reason for worry. But she insisted on visiting her family. King Soraren arranged a golden ladder to reach the earth so that Tampha Lairembi could go down to earth and meet her family. But he warned her not to take any food or drinks while on earth otherwise the golden ladder would be withdrawn and she would not be allowed to return to heaven. Tampha Lairembi agreed. She came down to earth and met her family members. All the family members and her friends from far and near were excited to see her and they insisted that they should dine together to celebrate the occasion. Tampha Lairembi told the family members the terms and conditions imposed by her husband. She resisted the offer saying that if she would accept food and drinks, she would not be able to return to heaven. Her husband had 1000 eyes and 1000 ears and he somehow would come to know. At this, her friends suggested that she would lock seven layers of doors, seven layers of screen and nobody would come to know. Her mother strongly insisted that she should share food and drinks with her and her friends. Ultimately, unable to resist any further, she succumbed to pressure and she accepted the food and drinks. Immediately on taking the food, she heard a voice from heaven "Since you have accepted the food and drinks from earth, the golden ladder is withdrawn and you are not allowed to come back to heaven" Tampha Lairembi ran out and found that the golden ladder had been already withdrawn. She was very sad. She avoided taking food and drinks and she was reduced to skeleton. At this juncture, her mother-in-law Leimarel Langatombi came down and lived with her. This was a great consolation to her. Leimarel Langatombi said "your son in heaven was being looked after by 1000 queens. Everything was fine and you need not worry".

At this time, her son in heaven was only three months old. He started crying out of hunger. His father King Soraren gave him milk but he did no stop crying. He tried to console him but he would not stop crying. He called all his nobles and servants and asked them to help the child to stop crying. Thousands of Gods and Goddesses came forward to help but nobody could stop the child crying. Ultimately Chingkheirel Apamba came forward to try his luck. He sang hymes praising the child. The child stopped crying. King Soraren named his son as "Khoiriphaba". One day, Angoupalba Yaibirel Shidaba found Khoiriphaba crying near a tree. He brought the child to his home and asked his clan to look after the child. They looked after the child very carefully as a son of their own family.They named the child as "Puthiba". One day Khoiriphaba heard the conversation among the women "See how cute the child is. We loved him so much. His mother would have loved him many times we loved him. How much his mother would have suffered due to the loss of her child". Hearing the conversation, Khoiriphaba asked the women to tell him the whereabouts of his mother. But nobody could answer his question.. So Khoiriphaba decided to search for his mother. He descended to earth and came to Moirang near Khoiri Keithel. Night had already set in. Khoiriphaba did not know what to do. He started crying saying "Oh mother, Tampha Wangamloi Leisang Shaphabi, where can I find you". Moirang Thangjing and his queen Koirel Leima heard the cries of the child. They came out and saw the handsome boy. They asked him the names of his parents. Khoiriphaba mentioned the name of his mother. Then Moirang Thangjing knew that he was none other than the son of God King Soraren. So Khoiriphaba grew up under the care of Moirang Thangjing. In due course of time, Khoiriphaba made a lot of friends. He was about nine years old when he started wrestling, playing Mukna Kangjei, running race in competition with his friends. But he was always the champion. This had created a jealousy and enmity among his friends. One day one of his friends remarked "You do not know your parents. Our Ibudhou Thangjing picked up you from Khoiri Keithel. You belong to inferior Gods. You are not allowed to play with us from tomorrow". Khoiriphaba was very sad hearing the remark. He remained dejected for many days. Seeing his mood, Thangjing asked the reason for his sorrow. Khoiriphaba narrated the stories to Thangjing. Thangjing was very unhappy to hear the stories. He decided that the child should be sent to his mother without further delay. Then he called all the friends of Khoiriphaba to his place. All the friends, 27 in number came to Thangjing. Then Thangjing asked them to compete with Khoiriohaba in race, wrestling, Mukna Kangjei. Nobody volunteered to challenge him. Then Thangjing asked them "then why not tug of war. 27 of you could make a team and you would compete with Khoiriphaba alone in tug of war". Having confidence in the combined strength of 27 of them, all the 27 friends accepted the challenge. Thangjing put a condition, "if you win, you would be declared champion and if Khoiriphaba wins, then you have to send off Khoiriphaba to his mother at Haorok Konthoujam carrying Khoiriphaba in a palanquin". All the 27 friends accepted the challenge. But all the 27 friends were defeated again in the tug of war. On the next day, the 27 friends joined together and reported to Thangjing, who arranged for departure of Khoiriphaba. They brought Khoiriphaba in a palanquin towards Haorok Konthoujam to hand over Khoiriphaba to his mother. They came a long distance from Moirang. Then they came across a beautiful spot. On the journey,they could not resist the temptation of settling down in a beautiful village for a while. They proposed to Khoiriphaba to settle down for some time at that beautiful village. Khoiriphaba also agreed. They named the village as "Toubul". Some of the friends remained in waiting for them at a distance and this village was named as "Ngaikhong". After some time, all the friends left the place one after another and only Khoiriphaba was left alone. Khoiriohaba continued his journey towards Haorok Konthoujam for searching his mother. He came across a river where many women were found fishing using fishing net. Since morning, they could not catch a single fish. He walked up and down along the river bank. Seeing him helplessly walking up and down, one woman asked "Why are you walking up and down". Khoirphaba said "I want to cross the river but I do not know how to cross the river." Then one woman volunteered to take him on her back and helped him to cross the river. After putting Khoiriphaba on the other side of the river, the woman pull up her fishing net and it was full of fish of many varieties. This happened to the other women fishing at the spot as well. Then this village was named as "Kabow Wakching Kabok Khong". Khoiriphaba reached Haorok Konthoujam and started exploring each and every street with a view to find his mother. At this time, Tampha Lairembi saw her son Khoiriphaba in her dream in the shape of a 10 year old boy. She narrated about the dream to her mother-in-law Leimarel Langatombi. At this time, they heard the cries of a boy calling for his mother. Believing that it might be the voice of a village boy, they went to sleep. During day time,. Khoiriphaba remained hidden to avoid meeting with human beings. He appeared only at night crying for his mother. Tampha Lairembi and her mother-in-law heard the voice of the child again but this time, it was very near to their home. Her mother in law informed Tampha Lairembi that "It must be your son, we should go out and look for him". But Tampha Lairembi never believed that her son would come to her from heaven. At this time, many relatives from Konthoujam family also came and narrated the story of cry of a child for his mother. On the next evening, Khoiriphaba by chance happened to come to the courtyard, where his mother Tampha Lairembi was offering incense sticks for prayer. Seeing Tampha Lairembi he said "I could not breath any longer due to hunger. Please take me in for tonight. I will go back next morning. Please take me as your son". Tampha Lairembi asked "What is your name ? From where you come ? Where do you want to go ? What is the name of your parents?". Khoiriphaba said "My name is Khoiriphaba. Father Thangjing said I am the son of King Soraren and my mother is Haorok Konthoujam Tampha Wangamloi Leisang Shaphabi. I came to search for my mother. Tampha Lairembi at once embraced her son and started crying. All the family members shared food and drinks and spent the night happily together. King Soraren came to know about Khoiriphaba and Tampha Lairembi. So he came for a visit and spent days in the company of his wife and son. The visit became more frequent but he could not accept them to heaven. In due course of time, Khoiriphaba became full grown bachelor. He developed romantic relationship with Chinga Leima daughter of Irum Ningthou. He married Chinga Leima. Tampha Lairembi informed her husband King Soraren to accept and recognize the marriage. They brought and settle the newly wed couple at Haorok Kongthoujam. However, Chinga Leima became partially blind as she could not see any gold or silver or any hillock as she was accustomed to when she was living in her parental home. She insisted to her husband Khoiriphaba to build a home made of gold and silver on a hillock otherwise she preferred to go to her parental home. Khoiriphaba requested all the Gods and Goddesses to give him a hillock. But they declined to offer the hillock without permission from his father. However, King Soraren said that only Chingu Thangjing, Marjing, Koubru, Chingkheirel Apalba could provide the hillock for his son. Accordingly, all the four Gods produced many hillocks. Ultimately Khoiriphaba had chosen one hillock known as "Phoiching". Two golden houses were built there for the new couple. However, Khoiriphaba refused to go inside the house without his parents. All the Gods and Goddesses also insisted that the parents should stay in the house along with the new couple. So king Soraren, Tampha Lairembi, Khoiriphaba and Chinga Leima stayed at the new house. After some time, King Soraren left for heaven with a promise to come back again. After few years, Tampha Lairembi called King Soraren from heaven. King Soraren appeared before Tampha Lairembi and asked the reason for her calling. Tampha Leirembi said "You promised to come back. That is why I reminded you". King Soraren replied "Okay, let your clan Haorok Konthoujam erect a new temple, hoist the flag, offer new clothing, offer vegetables, fruits, beat the drum, play the Pena and do the invocation in my name. Let them chant my name, offer prayer and I would come down from heaven and do the divine sport of merry-making (Lai Haraoba) in presence of all members of the Haorokcham and Konthoujam clan. Then people would come to know that you are a Lairembi (Goddess) and then they should start worshipping you. I would grant you a boon that if they worship you as a Goddess, they would prosper in life, they would know no poverty, they would have a lot of children, they would live a long life". After some time, Haorokcham clan shifted their village to Haokha near Thoubal. The first settlers of Haokha was the Lisam Clan. At the time of Meidingu Thawanthaba, Haokhong Shinnaiba of Lisam Clan migrated from Moirang and settled at Haokha. They worshipped the God Soraren. Only recently (1973), the Lisam Clan had given the deity Soraren to the people in Haokha Soraren village so that the Lai Haraoba ceremony can be performed with the united efforts of the people. In olden days, the King of Manipur assigned to the Lisam Clan the making of "Li", a special earthen pot for drinking water for the King and also for feeding the new born child of the queen with milk from their "Li". The maximum concentration of Lisam clan is found in Haokha Soraren.

Chinga Leima started taking snakes, snails, leeches, eels as her food. One day, Khoiriphaba saw her sitting on the branch of a tree, eating snakes. Khoiriphaba brought her home and scolded her. Chinga Leima ran away. Khoiriphaba followed her from a distance. After following for a long distance, Khoiriphaba asked some women if they saw his wife Chinga Leima. Some women pointed towards the place where they have seen her. It was a market place. Khoiriphaba seized Chinga Leima in the middle of the market in presence of many people. There was a hot argument between them. People gathered around them to see what was happening. This market was named as "Langpok Keithel". Then Khoiriphaba cursed that this market should no longer be used as a market. To this day, this market was never used. Then they travelled together for a long distance and this place was named as "Lamsang". Then they spent the night at a place which was named as "Ningombam" and they stayed for some time at a place named "Lairenjam". The place where Khoiriphaba was bursting into anger was known as "Meitram". Then Tampha Lairembi and Soraren came in search of Khoiriphaba and Chinga Leima and they found them under a Kodom tree and therefore the name of the place was called "Kodompokpi". On their way back, they collected the dowry from Irum Ningthou and came back to Phoiching hillock and settled there. In due course of time, the power and strength of Khoiriphaba had increased tremendously so much so that the Phoiching hill started trembling. All the Gods, Goddesses and human beings alike became very much alarmed. Khoiriphaba was a God of immense strength. It is believed that if somebody worships and hears the story of Khoiriphaba, he would be free from all worries, miseries and conflicts in his life time.

KHAMLANGBA OF KAKCHING

Lainingthou Khamlangba is believed to have appeared from the teeth of Atingkok Kuru Sidaba. In one of his different incarnations, he became "Lainungmori Yotsungba Khunung Tektek Thangjaba". He married the princess of Mangang Ningthou, Marumbi Khoimom Lairemma Santhong Huimu Leima. He had a son named Amudon. He went on expeditions to the lands of Mayang and reached Takhel (Tripura) and married Lairemma Kalika. After some time, he came back to Manipur along with his wife Kalika and a number of servants. He stayed for some time at Khamlang Leirak, Uripok. He also stayed at Haobam Marak, Thanga Kambong, Awang Ngarian. He also married a girl from Sagolband. Then he came to Thoubal Haotabi Lamhang near Thoubal Tomjing. The group of Khamlangba while living at Uripok were known as Langsoi as they were iron –smiths and therefore the village where they stayed was known as Langsai. Langsoi is the pointed instrument made of either wood or iron which was used by the people of Khamlangba tribe for locating iron ore. (Dr.

Kh. Ratan Kumar, Lai Haraoba of Manipur, 2001). The occupation of Khamlangba was extraction of iron ores and manufacture of steel. He stayed for some time at Khuman Heiyel Loubuk and then came to Kheraching. One Nganba Tekcha Pamba Sora Laihat Thouba beheaded Irum Lai Tubi Kokling Lengba and there fore the name of the village was known as Kakching later known as Kakching Kullen and Kakching Wairi. Then some of the people had migrated and established another new village known as Kakching Khunou. Some people move northwards and established a new village known as Kakching Kameng. During the time of Samuroiba Ningthou, the temple of Khamlangba was shifted to Kakching Khullen. The Naorem clan also established another temple of Khamlangba at Kakching Wairi. The Mayanglambam Clan looked after the deity of Khamlangba at Kakching Khullen whereas the deity of Khamlangba at Kakching Wairi is looked after by Naorem clan.

People worship Khamlangba for peace and prosperity in the country, to be free from diseases and deaths and for driving away the evil spirits from the land. People still believed that Kahmalangba is a powerful sylvan God. (Wahengbam Lukhoi, Lai Haraoba, 2008)

SAMADHI OF MAHARAJA GAMBHEER SINGH

The Samadhi of Maharaja Gambheer Singh is located at Langthabal on the western side of the National Highway no-39 and is now in ruins. Gambheer Singh reigned as the king of Manipur during 1825 – 1834 and died due to heart ailments in his palace at Langthabal on 9th January, 1834. The memorial monument was erected on the cremation ground of the king. The monument is a very simple structure facing east having four walls with one opening in the east. The walls are 1.62 metres high and meet the curved eaves of the roof. The roof is dome shaped without ant decorative motif on the upper surface. (O. Ibochaoba Singh, Dr. P. Gunindra Singh Mutua Museum, Manipuri Forts and Monuments, Bulletin no. 5, March, 1997). Manipur is observing "Seven Years Devastation" every year but the Government and the people of Manipur tend to forget the King who saved us from "Seven Years Devastation

SAMADHI OF MAHARAJA NONGCHUP LAMGAINGAMBA (BHADRA SINGH)

The monument was erected on the cremation ground of Raja Nongchup Lamgaingamba (Bhadrasingh), who reigned as the king of Manipur in 1824 for only one year. The Samadhi is now in ruins and is standing on the right bank of the Nambool river inside the compound of the District and Session Court, Uripok, Imphal. The monument is constructed on a slightly raised platform, about 0.75 metres above the ground. The platform is made of bricks. The sanctum (oblong, 2.10 metres x 2.68 metres) rest on the platform with a projection in front facing east, which is the only access to the inner sanctum hall. The arch opening is constructed with wedged shaped bricks joined with lime and surki (brick powder). The walls, about 1.86 metres high do not have any decoration and meet the culvilinear eaves of the dome shaped roof. There is a crowning cap on the top of the roof. The end points of the eaves are slightly curved upward whereas the eaves are curved like a segment of a circle. The walls of the sanctum hall are plastered and no ventilation is provided in any side of the walls. (O. Ibochaoba Singh, Dr. P.Gunindra Singh Mutua Museum, Manipuri Forts and Monuments, Bulletin no. 5, March, 1997)

SAMADHI OF LUWANG NINGTHOU

The monuments was erected on the cremation ground of late Maisnam Gourshyam Singh, Luwang Ningthou, father of Maharani Kumudini, who died in 1848. The monument is located at the meeting point of the Liwa road and Heirangoithong road. This spot is still used as a cremation ground for the descendants of the Maisnam Gourshyam Singh.The monument consists of a square sanctum, which is interconnected with a low narrow porch in front. The projection in front accommodate the doorway and shared with the main structure identical to the finials. The walls of the sanctum are bricks. The four corners of the walls are provided with a pair of circular buttresses. From the top of the buttresses springs the curve cornice imitating the eaves of a thatched roof. The exterior walls of the sanctum are decorated with the floral motifs. The brick walls are plastered. Three small holes are provided on the western, eastern and southern walls to provide light to the sanctum hall. The roof of the sanctum hall is designed like a dome. The basal part of the dome forming the eaves of the roof are curved like a segment of a circle. The upper surface of the roof is decorated with floral motifs on the top of which there is a circular crown. Two Kalasa are placed on the top of the crown, one above the other and on the top of the Kalasa is fixed a Nilachakra. Internally, the sanctum is square in shape. The floor of the sanctum is not paved with stone or bricks but is of beaten earth. The inner walls of the sanctum hall rise vertically to a certain height, then started curving inward till they form a lancet arch. (O. Ibochaoba Singh, Dr. P. Gunindra Singh Mutua Museum, Manipuri Forts and Monuments, Bulletin no-5, March, 1997)

References

A. Chitraswor Sharma, "Meitei Nongaron", April, 1988.

Chander Sheikher Panchani "Manipur : Religion, Culture and Society", Konark Publishers Pvt. Ltd., New Delhi, 1987.

Kirankumar Mayanglambam, Iroisemba, Meitei Pu –wari , 1991.

L. Iboongohal Singh, N. Khelchandra Singh (adts), Cheitharol Kumbaba, Manipur Sahitya Parishad, Imphal, 1967.

Lai Hraoba,

Mayanglamabam Gourchandra "Meitrabakki Puyarida Kakching", People's Museum, Kakching, 2002.

Naorem Amuyaima, Pandit Achouba, "Shri Shri Jangannath Nirupon, Govinda Nirupon and Krishnachandra Nirupon", Kakching.

N. Khelchandra Singh, Sapam Bheigya, S. Rupoban Singh, Kangla, the Ancient capital of Manipur, 2006.

N. Khelchandra Singh,Ariba Manipuri Sahityagee Etihas, Imphal (1st publication).

O.K. Singh, Archaeology Researchers in Manipur, in Eastern Himalayas, Cosmo Publication, New Delhi.

O. Ibochaoba Singh, Dr. P. Gunindra Singh, Mutua Museum, Manipuri Temple Architecture, Bulletin No. 3, August, 1983.

O. Ibochaoba Singh, Dr. P. Gunindra Singh Mutua Museum, Manipuri Forts and Monuments, Bulletin no. 5, March, 1997.

T.C. Hodson "The Meitheis", B.R. Publishing Corporation, Delhi, Reptt, 1875.

P. Bharat Singh, The Sacred Jack Tree of Kaina, 2007.

Pangambam Bharat Singh IAS, Kangla, the national heritage of Manipur, 2008

R.K. Jhalajit Singh, A Short History of Manipur, O.K. Book Store and Publishers, Imphal, 1965.

Rajkumar Sanahal Singh, Manipuri Etihas, Imphal,1947.

Rajkumar Sanahal Guneshwar, Yaiskul "Manipur Govinda Nirupon", 1980.

Sarangthem Bormani, Meitei Ima Lairembi.

Sarangthem Bormani, Moirang Saion, 2003.

Wahengbam Lukhoi, Pandit Yaima, "Lai Haraoba", Manipur State Archives, Imphal, 2008.

W. Yumjao Singh "Report on the Archeological Studies in Manipur", Bulletin No. 1, Imphal, 1935.

Wahengbam Tomba, Meitei Ima Leirembi Taret ki hourakpa mingkgheirol, leipham amasung khufam, Lairikyengbam Awang Leikai 2006.

http://www.nriol.com/indiantourism/manipurtemple.asp

http://www.india-tours.com/destination/india/manipur/places-worship-manipur.html

http://travel.eindiamaps.com/travel-manipur/temples-in-manipur.html

Plate-240: Vishnu Temple at Bishnupur

Plate-241: Lord Krishna Temple at Brahmapur Leikai

Plate -242: Hanuman Temple at Mahabali

Plate -243: Govindajee Temple at Kangla

Plate-244: Brindabanchandra Temple at Kangla

Plate-245: Thangal General Temple

Plate -246: Lord Govindajee Temple

Plate -247: Gopinath Temple at Ningthoukhong

Plate -248: Abdeitya Temple at Bishnupur

Plate -249: Radha Madhav Temple of Ningthoukhong

Plate -250: Krishnachanda Temple at Kakching

Plate -251: Nara singh Temple at Kakching

Plate -252: Bijoy Govinda at Sagolband

Plate-253: Moirang Thangjing

Plate-254: Idols at Ramji Prabhu

Plate -255: Radha Krishna Manimandir of ISKON

Plate -256: Lord Nara Singh Temple of Naorem Leikai

Plate -257: Lord Sanamahi Temple

Plate-258: Hiyangthang Lairembi

Plate -259: Ramji Prabhu at Ningthem Pukhri Mapal

Plate -260: Konthoujam Lairembi

Plate -261: Gate to Konthoujam Lairembi

15

Historical Landmarks

CHRONOLOGY OF IMPORTANT HISTORICAL LANDMARKS

The chronology of impor'ant historical landmarks of Manipur is as follows :-

Table-46 Showing historical landamarks in Manipur

1405-1359 BC	Ningthou Kangba introduced Sagol Kangjei, Polo
33 A.D	Pakhangba's accession the Throne
154 A.D	Khuyoi Tompok ascended the Throne. PUNG was invented during his reign.
264 A.D	Taothing Mang ascended the Throne. He is regarded as one of the makers of Manipur.
568 A.D	Ura Konthouba issued coins for the first time .
1074 A.D	King Loiyumba ascended the Throne. Many social reforms took place during his reign.
1247 A.D	Puranthaba ascended the Throne. Chinese invaded Manipur during his reign but were defeated.
1467 A.D	Kyaamba ascended the Throne. He is noted for his Military and Administrative achievements.
1470 A.D	Kabow Valley and Chindwin were annexed to Manipur.
1533 A.D	King Kabomba defeated the Tripuris. Takhel Khong (canal) dug to commemorate the victory in 1534
1606 A.D	Arrival of Muslims during the time of Khagemba
1704 A.D	Arrival of Hinduism-King Charairongba was initiated into Vaishavism-Vaishnavism became state religion.

(Contd.)

(Contd. Table 46)

1709 A.D	Pamheiba (Garib Niwaj) ascended the Throne.
1736 A.D	Garib Niwaj's army crossed Ningthee river and captured Mayedu town on the banks of Yu River (presently in Myanmar).
1755 A.D	First Devastation (Khuntak Ahanba)
1762 A.D	The first alliance between Manipur & East India Company made.
1775 A.D	Wangkhei Echao-Worst recorded flood in Manipur.
1819 A.D	Seven Years' Devastation (1819-1826).
1826 A.D, February 1	Liberation of Manipur completed from Burmese rule under leadership of King Gambheer singh.
1826 A.D, February 24.	Treaty of Yandaboo signed.
1833 A.D	Jiribam was annexed to Manipur during Gambheer Singh's reign.
1834 A.D, January.	Kabow Valley transferred back to Burma.
1835 A.D	The Political Agency was established in 1835.
1885 A.D	Manipuris extended help to British Army in the Third Anglo-Burmese War leading to fall of Burma. First English School was established.
1890 A.D	Palace revolt broke out during Maharaja Surchandra's reign.
1891 A.D	The Anglo-Manipuri War of 1891
1891 A.D, April 23.	Khongjom War.
1891 A.D, April 27.	Manipur annexed into the British Empire.
1891 A.D, August 13.	Yubaraj Tikendrajit & General Thangal executed by the British at Pheida Pung
1894 A.D	Arrival of Christianity
1904 A.D	1st Nupi Lal (Women's War).
1907 A.D	Manipur State Durbar established.
1916 A.D	First Kuki Baptist Church established at Tujang Vaichong village.

(Contd.)

(Contd. Table 46)

1917 A.D	Kuki Uprising against the British started
1930 A.D.	Zeliangrong Movement started
1931 A.D, August.	Jadonang, a great Zeliangrong leader, was executed.
1932 A.D, October.	Rani , Gaidinliu was arrested
1939 A.D, December 12.	2nd Nupi Lal (Women's war)
1939 A.D	Movement for a Responsible Government started
1941 A.D	Maharaja Bodhchandra ascended the Throne.
1942 A.D.	Imphal was bombarded during Second World War
1944 A.D, April 14.	The Flag of Indian National Army (INA) first unfurled at Moirang.
1949 A.D, September 2.	Merger Agreement between the Govt of India and Manipur signed at Shillong
1957 A.D	Manipur became one of the Union territories of he Indian Union.Territorial Council replaces Advisory form of Govt.
1960	Panchayati Raj was introduced in Manipur .
1963 A.D	A Legislative Assembly established.. The All India Radio was inaugurated .
1963 A.D, December 19.	Status of Administrator raised from Chief Commissioner to Lt. Governor.
1967	President's rule was imposed for the first time in Manipur
1970 A.D	Construction of Loktak Project started.
1972 A.D, January 21.	Manipur became a fullfledged State .
1980	The Manipur University was established .
1983 A.D, May.	Commisioning of Loktak Project.
1987	TV Transmission Centre was opened .
1990 A.D	Manipur featured in the Railway map with introduction of Railway line at Jiribam.
1991 A.D, August 16.	Worst Air crash in the Manipur Area of Indian Airlines Boeing at Thangjing Hills.

(Contd.)

(Contd. Table 46)

1992 A.D, August 20.	Manipuri language included in the VIII Schedule to the Indian Constitution as a Major Indian language.
1992 A.D	The first sign of the outbreak of long standing communal clashes between the Naga & the Kuki tribes.
1993 A.D, May.	Communal clash between Meiteis & Meitei Pangans
1995	DDK, Imphal was opened .
1996	Okendrajit , (Pareihanba) , the last king of Manipur died
1997 A.D, July.	Ethnic clash between the Kuki & Paite tribes in Churachandpur district.
1997 A.D, August 4.	Largest procession in the history of Manipur to safeguard Manipur's territorial integrity.
2001A.D, June 18.	Mass protests against "Extension of Ceasefire between GoI-NSCN(IM) without territorial limits" which threatened the integrity of Manipur.
2004	Prime Minister Dr. Manamohon Singh handed over the Kangla Fort to Manipur people after occupation for about 113 years by the Assam Rifles .

Some of the important historical landmarks are described below :-

1. ARRIVAL OF MUSLIMS

The Manipuri Muslims are known as “Pangans” Some Meite is Pangans believed that the word “Pangan” is a derived from Bengal (Bangan = Pangan).

1.1. Antiquity theory

Some believed that the arrival of Muslims might have started in Manipur as early as 635/645 AD. R.K. Sanahal (1989:viii-xv) noted that Manipuri Muslim or Pangan clan, Aribam, had existed from king Naophangba’s time (428-518A.D.) and that the Manipuri King himself conferred the Aribam title on the Muslims. R. Brown (1874) noted that the Muslim in Manipur had been there “since a great antiquity”. Moirangthem Chandra Singh (Poireiton Khunthok) noted that “turban wearing Pangans” seemingly traced to Pang, a Tai tribe by conversion were found in Manipur. Some people says that the term “*Pangan*” is derived from “Pang” by adding the suffix “an” as early Pang ethnic (tribal) group was the first to embrace Islam.

Puyas such as 'Kanglei Langba Pakhangba', "Sakok Lamlen Ahanba", "Nongchup-haramlon" mentioned that a "Pangan Musalman guru" (saint) appeared in Manipur from the west during the reign of Naophangba (428-518 A.D.). However, these antiquity theories seems to be concocted because God revealed the Qur'an to Muhammed, God's final prophet through the angel Gabriel on many occasions between 610 A.D. and his death on Monday, 6th June, 632 A.D. It was almost impossible that the Islam religion reached Manipur during 428-518 A.D even before God revealed the Qur'an to prophet Muhammed.

1.2. Sufism theory

According to this theory, the Manipuri Muslims are the results of conversion from preaching by Sufis mainly of Chisti and Firdousee silsilas who proceeded onwards from Sylhet.

During the Naophangba period (428-518) "Musalman" saint (scholar) was henceforth recognized as "Pangan Musal-man guru" in subsequent puya literature handed down through generations of Meitei tradition of history preservation.(Farooque Ahmed Makakmayum). Since the Muslim preacher ('Musalman' is Persian terminology for 'Muslim') lived among the Pangs, he was addressed as "Pangan Musalman guru". Pang ethnic group is mentioned in the Poireiton Khunthok puya too as a Tai group. The Muslim saint was Amir Hamza who probably reached China and went back to Arabia where he died shortly after the battle of Uhud in 625 AD (The Sangai Express, 18 May 2006). But the word "Guru "is not used among the Muslims. This theory is also very unlikely for the reasons referred to above.

1.3. Muslimes arrived as prisoners of war

T.C. Hodson (1908) wrote: "The Pangan or Muhammedan settlers are distinct from the Meiteis, as is reasonable to expect, although it has been noted that many of the Muhamedan inhabitants of Sylhet and Cachar resemble the hill type. The Pangans are believed to have originated from Cachar as prisoners of war taken by Meiteis" (T.C. Hudson-1908).

In 1606, during the reign of King Khagemba (1597-1652), a large number of Muslims numbering upto 1000 from Sylhet entered Manipur to invade Manipur at the invitation of Prince Sanongba who revolted against his brother. They were captured including Sanongba by King Khagemba's force stationed at Toubul. During the battle, King Khagemba considered them harmless and also witnessed the skills and efficiency of the Muslims and asked them to stay on in Manipur. They were given free land and allowed to marry Meitei women and settle in Manipur. Khagemba's contemporary Cachari Kings were Pratap Narayan (1603-1610) and Bhimbal Narayan (1610-1636). It was only during the reign of Khagemba (1596-1651) that a large scale settlement of Muslims took place in Manipur. King Khagemba conferred the title of "Nongsamei" (Lion man) to Lairikyengbam Dhananjoy who fought bravely like a lion in the war and caused the invading Muslims to surrender. The royal chronicle and Puyas well documented this war.

1.4. Entourage theory

"The Mughal emperor sent three ambassadors to Manipur in 1662 A.D. and the King of Manipur also reciprocated. Thus gradually Manipur became more connected with India than with Burma" (R.M. Nath,1978,The Background of Assamese Culture, Guwahati, p. 90). This may have paved the way for more intimate relationships with Mughal India and as a result some more Muslims might have come to the Kingdom on an understanding of mutual development.

However, this theory is most unlikely. Both Mughals and Manipur in those days were in deep internal turmoil to send or receive ambassadors. There is no mention of such a thing in the royal chronicle.

Muhi ud-din Muhammad Aurangzeb Bahadur Alamgir I (Conqueror of the Universe) , more commonly known as Aurangzeb, the 6th Mughal Emperor ruled from 1658 to 1707. Aurangzeb was the third son of the fifth emperor Shah Jahan and Mumtaz Mahal. Shah Jahan followed the Mughal practice of assigning authority to his sons, and in 1634 made Aurangzeb Subahdar (governor) of the Deccan. He moved to Kirki, which, he renamed Aurangabad. In 1637, he married Rabia Durrani. In 1644, Aurangzeb's sister Jahanara Begum was accidentally burnt in Agra. This event precipitated a family crisis which had political consequences. Aurangzeb suffered his father's displeasure when he returned to Agra three weeks after the event, instead of immediately. Shah Jahan dismissed him to be the governor of the Deccan. In 1645, he was barred from attending the royal court for seven months. But later, Shah Jahan appointed him governor of Gujarat. He performed well and was rewarded. In 1647, Shah Jahan made him governor of Balkh and Badakhshan (present Afghanistan and Tajikistan), replacing Aurangzeb's ineffective brother Murad Baksh. These areas at the time were under attack from various forces and Aurangzeb's military skill proved successful. He was appointed governor of Multan and Sindh, and began a protracted military struggle against the Safavid army in an effort to capture the city of Kandahar. He failed, and fell again into his father's disfavour. In 1652, Aurangzeb was re-appointed governor of the Deccan. In an effort to extend the empire, Aurangzeb attacked the border kingdoms of Golconda (1657), and Bijapur (1658). Both times, Shah Jahan called off the attacks near the moment of Aurangzeb's triumph. In each case Dara Shikoh interceded and arranged a peaceful end to the attacks.

Shah Jahan fell ill in 1657, and was widely reported to have died. With this news, the struggle for the succession began. Aurangzeb's eldest brother, Dara Shikoh, was regarded as heir apparent. But Shah Jahan's second son Shah Shuja declared himself emperor in Bengal. Soon after, Shuja's youngest brother Murad Baksh, with secret promises of support from Aurangzeb, declared himself emperor in Gujarat. Aurangzeb, ostensibly in support of Murad, marched north from Aurangabad, gathering support from nobles and generals.

Following a series of victories, Aurangzeb declared that Dara had illegally usurped the throne. A series of bloody battles followed, with troops loyal to Aurangzeb battering Dara's armies at Samugarh. In a few months, Aurangzeb's forces surrounded Agra. Fearing for his life, Dara fled to Delhi, leaving Shah Jahan behind. The old emperor surrendered the Agra Fort to Aurangzeb's nobles, but Aurangzeb refused any meeting with his father, and declared that Dara was no longer a Muslim. In a sudden reversal, Murad went into exile in Arakan (present Myanmar) where he disappeared, and was presumed to be dead. Murad's former supporters, instead of fighting for Murad, defected to Aurangzeb. Meanwhile, Dara gathered his forces, and moved to the Punjab. The army sent against Shuja was trapped in the east, its generals Jai Singh and Diler Khan, submitted to Aurangzeb but allowed Dara's son Suleman to escape. Aurangzeb offered Shuja the governorship of Bengal. This move had the effect of isolating Dara and causing more troops to defect to Aurangzeb. Shuja, however, uncertain of Aurangzeb's sincerity, continued to battle his brother but his forces suffered a series of defeats at Aurangzeb's hands.With Shuja and Murad disposed off, and with his father Shah Jahan confined in Agra, Aurangzeb pursued Dara, chasing him across the north-western bounds of the empire. After a series of battles, defeats and retreats, Dara was betrayed by one of his generals, who arrested and bound him. In 1659, Aurangzeb arranged his formal coronation in Delhi. He had Dara openly marched in chains back to Delhi; when Dara finally arrived, Aurangzeb had Dara executed. Legends about the cruelty of this execution abound, including stories that Aurangzeb had Dara's severed head sent to the dying Shah Jahan. With his succession secured, Aurangzeb kept Shah Jahan under house arrest at the Agra Fort.

Many subjects rebelled against Aurangzeb's policies, among them his own șọn, Prince Akbar.

- In 1667, the Yusufzai Pashtuns revolted near Peshawar and were crushed.
- In 1669, the Jats around Mathura revolted and led to the formation of Bharatpur state after his death.
- In 1670, Chhatrapati Shivaji had opened the war against the Mughals. He opposed Aurangzeb with full strength and stopped him from entering the Deccan.
- In 1672, the Satnami, a sect concentrated in an area near Delhi, under the leadership of Bhirbhan and some Satnami. They took over the administration of Narnaul, and defeated Mughal forces in an advance on Delhi.

Thus there were a seris of problems in the Mughal empire.

Meidingu Khunjaoba, second son of Khagemba ascended the throne in 1652 at the age of 30 years. In the month of Lamda of 1653 when Khunjaoba went to Samjok along with his younger brother Tonaba for a war, Kuyong tribals invaded the kingdom. Khunjaoba's queen Takhembi prepared for a war in absence of her husband. Takhemba was a Thang-ta expert from her childhood. Sarangcha wa her Thang-ta master. When Tankhembi and Sarangcha were preparing for war, Sanakhombi, the wife of Khongjomba, younger brother of Khunjaoba also joined the war. They had a fierce battle with the Kuyog tribals. Ultimately, the Kuyong tribals ran away.

During Khunjaoba's reign, the Maram chief had not given the annual tribute. So in 1655, he sent his nephew, Kabomba (son of Tonaba) to Maram village to collect the tribute. But he was killed by the Maram Chief as a revenge of his father's murder by Meidingu Khagemba in 1645. On 3rd of Inga, 1666 (Thursday), queen Takhembi was divorced for alleged plotting a conspiracy against the king. Her five compatriots - Chirom Umma, Taram Keisungba, Pukchao, Chirom Thadoi, Sairem Keisang were all put to death. All their relatives revolted against the king. They entered Kangla on 27 Hiyanggei, 1666 and killed Khunjaoba, the king. This incident had led to a series of killings among the descendants and relatives of the king. All the descendants left Kangla and had gone to hiding at various places. Due to this chaotic condition, there was no king in Manipur for about one month till Paikhonba, son of Tonaba ascended the thron on 3rd Wakching, 1666 (FRiday)

Thus there was a deep turmoil in Manipur also.Hence the Entourage theory is a remote possibility.

Settlement of Manipuri Muslims

Early Muslim settlements have been recorded in the east of Imphal (R. Brown 1874). The entire land was under the control of King Those Muslims who entered Manipur during the Khagemba's time were given land as gifts from the King. and they were allowed to settle along the banks of rivers, where the land is very fertile and the transport during those days were through boat only. This date of settlement is recorded as 17th of Inga in Meitei Calendar year 1606 A.D.

Dress

A Meitei Muslim woman wears Phanek which is wrapped round the waist down to the foot. The upper body is covered with a blouse. Purdah system is observed by most of the elderly women. In some families, when a Muslim woman goes out of her house, she covers her entire body from the tip of her head to her feet. The dress of a Manipuri Muslim male is different from that of the Meitei male. A Muslim male wears pyjama, shirt or kurta and kisti cap. They wear a conical white cap on ceremonial occasions. They also like to wear long bottoned up coat or Achkan. They usually keep beard. (see plate-116)

Occupation

Agriculture is the main occupation of the Manipuri Muslims. In the earlier days, there were families, engaged in pottery, carpentry, masonry for generations. A number of them were also engaged as burglars and drummers attached to the Raja's army.

There was a Kaji appointed by the king to look after the affairs of the Muslims. During those days, there was no mosque. However, in the beginning of the 20th century, the Manipuri Muslims became self conscious. Many Manipuri Muslims were sent to Aligarh and other places in the Northern India for undergoing training as Maulavis. The first trained Maulavi returned to Manipur in 1910. They started Islamic revivalism in Manipur.

Their mother tongue is Manipuri. Urdu is also known to many Muslims.

Festivals

The Meitei Pangans observe two festivals in a year-Ramazan (Id-ul-Fitre) and Id –ul-Adha. They celebrate both the Ids with much prompt and show. Ramazan is a simple way of going on fast from day break to sunset to inculcate in himself discipline, the essence of sacrifice and purification of physiological and intestinal system. (see Chapter-13: Festivals). During Ramazan, they take the first meal before dawn and the next meal is taken after sunset. The routine of fast continues for a month. The Id is fixed on the new moon day when the moon is seen in the sky. On the last day, the fast is broken and in every house, the best food is prepared and the friends and relatives are invited. They meet each other in a happy and jubilant mood and embrace each other.

Muslim Influence in Manipur

Some people are of the opinion that Manipur's contacts with the Mughals traced to the time of Jahangir (1605–1622). Bengali migration in Manipur took place through Tripura. Tobacco plants and tobacco smoking spread in Manipur in 1610 from Bengal, which was a part of the Mughal empire. The first *hookah* (smoking pipe) imported was called *mangalphu* (Mughal pot). Chillies spread to Manipur through Mughal empire during the reign of Khagemba (1597–1652). Royal chronicles further records that two Mughal brick makers arrived in Manipur in 1671.

Role of Manipuri Muslims :

The Manipuri Muslims play an important role in the economic and social development of Manipur. They also played crucial roles in protecting and preserving the territorial integrity of Manipur. During the reign of Pamheiba in the 18th century Manipur was facing simultaneous attacks from Burma and Tripura. The combined attack was pushed back with the skills of Muslim soldiers. In the war of 1758 Manipur suffered massive losses at the hands of the Burmese, and many Muslims lost their lives. From 1819 to 1826, known as 'seven-year-devastation' in the history of Manipur, during the Burmese occupation of Manipur, Muslims had to run away to escape annihilation to parts of present-day Assam and Bangladesh, while some of them were carried away to Burma where their descendants still live. In 1891 Manipur was defeated by the British, many Muslims were killed in the battle and some were deported to Andamans.M.A Janab Khan mentioned that more than 30 Manipuri Muslims got injured during the Anglo-Manipuri War of 1891 of which three Muslims namely Miyamatullah, Sagei Ipham, son of Ijatullah of Kshetri Awang Leikai, Chaodonpa of Kiyamgei, Sher Shah Chibando Koot, Sagei Makak Mayum of Lilong Leihaokhong were killed in action whereas Chaobi Hyder, one of the sevem guards of the Chief Commissioner Mr. Quinton was arrested and transported to Andaman and Nicober Islands. (M.A. Janab Khan" Muslim

Fighters in the War of 1891, 100 Years (1891-1991: Manipur's Last war of Independence, DIPR, 1991.

Teachings of Allah

The word "Islam" means "Peace" and "Submission". In its secular sense, it means the establishment of peace. In the religious sense, Islam means submission to the will of God and obedience to His law. Islam derived from the Arabic root "Salema": peace, purity, submission and obedience. Islam dates back to the age of Adam and its message has been conveyed to man by God's Prophets and Messengers including Abrahim, Moses, Jesus and Muhammed. Islam's message has been restored and enforced in the last stage of the religious evolution by God's last Prophet and Messenger Muhammed. Muhammed. denounced idolatory. No picture or idol of Muhammed is therefore available. Eating of pork is forbidden. Money must never be lent on interest.

The word Allah in the Arabic language means God, or more accurately "The One and Only Eternal God, Creator of the Universe, Lord of all lords, King of all Kings, Most Compassionate, Most Merciful."

The Quran is the sacred book of the Muslims. Islam holds that the Quran was revealed to Muhammed by the angel Jibrîl (Gabriel) from 610 A.D. to his death in 632 A.D. The Quran was written down by Muhammed's companions while he was alive, although the prime method of transmission was oral. In 633 A.D, the written text was compiled, and in 653 A.D it was standardized, distributed in the Islamic empire and produced in large numbers. The present form of the Qur'an is regarded as God's revelation to Muhammed by Muslim believers. Academic scholars often consider it the original version authored or dictated by Muhammed. Muslim tradition agrees that it was fixed in writing shortly after Muhammed's death by order of Umar and Abu Bakr. The Qur'an itself expresses that it is the book of guidance from Allah, sent down to Muhammed (peace be upon him) through the angel Gabriel.Every word of it is the word of Allah. It was revealed over a period of 22 years in the Arabic language. It contains 114 Surahs (chapters) and over 6000 verses. Among the earliest meanings of the word, Quran imeans the "act of reciting".

The word Muslim means people who follow Islam. (Mu- people, Slim- Islam). In order to become a Muslim, one takes *Shahada,* which means bearing witness that: *There is no God but Allah and Muhammed is his final Prophet.* This declaration of faith, in essence, means that a Muslim believes that there is only one God, one Supreme Being, who has no partners or sons, who they call Allah, and that Muhammed Abdullah of Arabia, is the last and final Prophet.

Inherent in this declaration is the act of submission to the Supreme Being, the Creator of the Universe, who has the exclusive authority to prescribe a way of life which guarantees success in this life and the promise of paradise in the hereafter.

While Muslims are required to believe in all of God's scriptures, including the Torah and Gospels in their original form, they, however, are required to follow the divine instructions embodied in the Holy Quran, which they consider the final revelation from God. Muslims have seven cardinal articles of faith:

- belief in one God
- belief in God's Angels
- belief in all of God's prophets
- belief in all of God's scriptures
- belief in divine destiny
- belief in the day of judgement and,
- belief in the resurrection.

In essence, Muslims believe that God revealed religion in stages, at different times in the life and development of human beings and that Islam represents the final stage of guidance.

The faith of a Muslim is confirmed by five obligatory acts of worship:

- shahadah - belief in the oneness of God
- Salah- prayer five times a day
- Zakat-giving of alms to the poor
- *Sawm,* or fasting during the month of Ramazan, and
- Hajj- performing pilgrimage to Mecca at least once in a lifetime.

The five daily prayers

Muslims are commanded to perform salah five times a day. These prayers are obligatory on every Muslim above the age of puberty, with the exception being those who are mentally ill, too physically ill for it to be possible, menstruating, or experiencing post-partum bleeding.

Cleanliness and dress

When praying, the clothes that are worn and the place of prayer must be clean. Men and women are directed to cover their bodies (*aurah*) in reasonably loose-fitting garments. When in prayer, women must cover their heads. In accordance with tradition, many men choose to wear a kufi cap or other headcovering for prayer which is used also to secure the hair from covering the forehead. During 'sujud' the forehead should be in contact with the floor and not covered by hair.

Before conducting prayers, a Muslim has to perform a ritual ablution. The minor ablution is performed using water (*wudu*) or clean sand or dust (*tayammum*) when water is not available. In Sunni Islam, wudu' consists of washing the hands, mouth, nose, face, arms, forehead and hair, ears and feet three times each in that order.

Table-47 Showing names of prayers and prescribed time for Muslims

Name of prayer	*Prescribed time period (waqt)*
Fajr (رجف) (Dawn Prayer)	Dawn to sunrise
Dhuhr (رهظ) / Zuhr	An early after noon prayer until Asr
Asr (رصع)	Late afternoon prayer
Maghrib (برغم)	After sunset prayer
Isha'a (ءاشع)	Night prayer

In Islam, the ideology of brotherhood is very strong and is of high order. The Quran is the holy book of Muslims. The essence of Quran says that the day's solemn routine work of a Muslim starts with the payer to Almighty (Allah). The devotee starts his namaj (prayer) in the name of Allah with these utterances:

- Praise be to Allah, Lord of the world
- The beneficient, the merciful'
- Owner of the day of judgement
- Thee (alone) we worship, thee alone we ask for help
- Show us the straight path
- The path of those whom thou hast favoured
- Not, (the path of those whom earn thine anger nor of those who go astray)

Every Muslim is keen to go for pilgrimage to Mecca i.e. Haj. One should go for Haj after being free from liabilities of the family after marriage of his daughters and sons. After Haj, he must spend the rest of his life in religious pursuits. The idea of Haj is to inculcate botherhood through spiritual means. Islam is a natural religion with one central principle that God makes, upholds, governs and perfects all things. It has no caste or priest, requires no sacrifice or ceremonial ritual likely to distract the mind, or the thought of the God. "Abd and Rab" is the essence of the Teachings of Islam which determines Human position in Creation. Abd means one who has nothing originally his own but whatever he has he gets from his Rab (God), be it his life or its numerous constitutents (power and qualities), in fact his entire existence. Rab is the Supreme Being who creates and sustains his creation in entire existence, called "Rabbul Aalameen" (the Lord of all the worlds). Those who know "Rab" and accordingly to the point of realization, are called apostles and saints. (M.A. Haleen Eliasii, Muhammed Marmaduke Pickthall, The Holy Quraan, Adam Publishers & Distributors, New Delhi, 2005)

The Sunni Muslims consider life and character of Muhammed to be an ideal in Islam as Muhammed propounded it during his life time. Sunnah in Arabic means "well known path. They believed in following the path that Muhammed had shown.

The Prophet *Muhammed* was born at Macca on 22nd April, 571 A.D. His father Abdullah died at Madina while returning from Syria. The Prophet was brought up by his mother. On his mother's death, while yet a child, the Prophet passed into the care of his grand father Abdul Muttalib. Two years later, the grand father also died and the boy was brought up by his uncle Abu Talib. When the Prophet was thirty-five, he married Khadija, who bore him two sons and four daughters. The sons died in infancy. His younger daughter Fatima was married to his cousin Ali (the fourth Caliph), son of Abu Talib. His second daughter (Ruqayya) and on her death his third daughter (Ummi Kulsum) was married to Osman (the third Caliph). Fatima alone survived her father but died six month's after the Prophet's death.During his childhood, the Prophet often retired to a cave called Hira for meditation. In the fortieth year, he received his first wahi of message from God. The first to believe in his divine message was his wife Khadija followed by Waraqa (a blind scholar) and Abu Bakr his father in law and later the first Caliph. Next came his son-in-law, Osman (who later bacame the third Caliph). Omar (who became the second Caliph) was at first opposed to the Prophet but later joined the new faith. (M. Hidayatullah, Mulla Principles of Mahomedan Law, N.M. Tripathi Private Ltd. 1968). Eleven or thirteen women married to the Islamic prophet Muhammed. Muslims refer to them as Mothers of the Believers (Arabic: Ummu l-Mu'minîn.(http://en.wikipedia.org/wiki/Muhammad's_wives)

Islamic Funeral

Near death

At the time of near death when the soul starts to separate from the body, those around a dying Muslim should persuade him/her to mention the *Shahada* (There is no God but Allah).

After death

As soon as the soul leaves the body, people around the deceased should do the following:

- Close the deceased eyes
- Pray for his/her forgiveness
- Cover the whole body with a sheet or other cloth.
- Rush preparation of the body for burial
- Bury the deceased in the locality of his/her death
- Quickly settle all debts from his/her estate

Mourning

Mourning the deceased for three days is permitted. Uncovering the face of the deceased or kissing him is not forbidden. However, it is prohibited to express extreme emotion such as beating cheeks, tearing clothes, stamping feet, pulling the hair or express grief by wailing. It is acceptable to announce the death to increase the number of those praying for the deceased.

Washing the body

It is obligatory for Muslims to wash the body. Males should wash males and females should wash females. If the Muslim client cannot identify anyone to assist in this obligation, your local masjid probably will have a established committee who will perform this service.

The body must be washed three times and make sure that the water reaches all parts of the body

Use soap (make sure it contains no pork products)

Use perfume with water, if possible

Wash the woman's hair very well.

Comb the man's hair. Plait the woman's hair into three braids

Always start with the right side of the body and limbs.

There is a brief Islamic service and prayer reading at the masjid, and at the grave site.

2. ARRIVAL OF HINDUISM

Before the arrival of Hinduism, the valley people of Manipur (Meiteis) were practicing "Sanamahism". They worship Sanamahi as God. Hinduism came to Manipur in different stages. Manipur had witnessed the arrival of three distinct forms of Vaishnavism Viz, Nimbarka School (known as Nimandi), Ramananda School known as Ramanandi and lastly Chaitanya School (known popularly as Goudiya) one after the other.

King Kyaamba (1467-1508) installed an image of Vishnu which he received as a gift from Choupha Khek Khomba, the king of Pong. He requisitioned the services of Brahmins for the worship of Vishnu and Kirtana Songs were sung. The Brahmins had started pouring in from various parts of U.P., Assam, Bengal, Gujarat and Orissa from 15th Century A.D. onwards. The image of Vishnu was always with the successive Manipuri Kings who became incarnations of Vishnu. Vaishnavism made a steady development during the 16thand 17th Centuries. The Brahmin missionaries arrived in batches through the centuries upto 19th Century A.D.

King Charairongba (1697-1709) and his family were initiated first into Nimandi. Brahmins from Nabadwip, Krishnanagar, Kanchan Nagar of Bengal adorned the courts of Charairongba The Brahmins started arriving from this period and were given shelter and patronage by the Kings. In 1703 A.D. a Brahman preacher named Krishnacharya Das alias Rai Vanamali from Shweta Ganga, Puri arrived in Manipur. He was accompanied by his wife, Krishnamayi, two Shudras and a Brahmin named Balabhadra Brahmachari.On Wednesday, the 5th Sajibu (April), 1704, Krishnacharya formally initiated the King into Nirmandi cult of Vaisnavism. Under this cult, Shri Krishna is regarded as the full incarnation of Vishnu. Since Krishnacharya was the guru of the King, his descendants came to be known as the Guru Aribams or the family of the old Guru.

The **king Garib Niwaz** (1709–48) got himself initiated into Vaishnavism in Mera (Sept/Oct) in 1717 A.D. by appointing Gopal Das as his Guru. In 1724 A.D. the king exhumed the bones of his ancestors and had them cremated on the banks of the Chindwin (Ningthee river).It was from this time that cremation became the customary method of disposal of the dead. It was forbidden to keep unclean animals like pigs and hen in the house. Those who did not obey were sent to the rural areas. (Mrs. Parratt) The King took the sacred thread for the second occasion in 1729 A.D. on full moon day in the month of Wakching (Dec./Jan.). On Wednesday the Guru and the king bathed in the Lilong river. During 1728 A.D. Santi Das, a Hindu preacher from Sylhet, arrived in Manipur and started his mission to preach Ramanandi cult of Vaishnavism. Some subjects followed Santi Das but the king was not happy. Some people were also punished for following the new sect of Santi Das. However later on, the King himself became a follower of Santi Das.

In 1729 A.D., the King also worshipped Hanuman. A temple of Hanuman was built at the Mongba Umang (Mahabali) on the bank of Imphal River. A large image of Hanuman was installed in the temple.

On the 17th Mera (Sunday), 1732 all the sacred Puyas of Meteis written by Maichous (Scholars/Prophets/Sakei Pibas) were got collected and burnt down to ashes. This episode was known as "Puya Meithaba" (Burning of scriptures). (see plate-262).

In the year 1737 A.D. in the month of Hiyangei (Oct./Nov.) on the full moon day, on Thursday, Santi Das initiated the King along with 300 important persons into his religion. This way the king took thread for the third time. This event marked the beginning of Ramanandi cult in Manipur. The images of Rama with Sita, Lakshman, Bharat and Shatrughan were installed in the temples. During the time of King Garib Niwaz (1709-48), Vaishnavism became a state religion and it was practically forced on the people. At the instance of the King and his Brahmin Gurus, the people were forced to adopt the Bengali alphabets and Manipuri versions of the Indian epics, specially of Krittibasi Ramayana and Kashidasi Mahabharata appeared. The pilgrimage to the sacred place, Vrindaban was the greatest craving of the disciples and the Vaisnavites of Manipur. Shijaguru ongbi was the first who had the darshan of Radha-Krishna at the holy place, Vrindaban.

King Bhagyachandra or Jai Singh

After the death of Garib Niwaj the throne was occupied by three kings in rapid succession till 1759 A.D. When king Bhagyachandra or Jai Singh became the king, he and his subjects accepted the Chaitanya school of Vaishnavism and the King offered royal sanction to the sect. Rupa Paramananda was appointed Guru to the King. During this period, several Brahmins arrived in Manipur from different parts of India, such as Mathura, Vrindaban, Kanauj, Gujarat, Puri and Punjab. During the reign of King Bhagyachandra, the following remarakable events took place :-

1. He had seven images carved out of the jackfruit tree growing on the Kaina hill viz, Govinda, Biijoy Govinda, Anu Prabhu, Nityananda, Abdeitya, Madanmohon and Gopinath. The image of Govindajee was installed on 12th of Hiyangei (Friday), 1776 A.D. and a 5-day Ras Lila was enacted on 11th January, 1779 A.D. for the first time. The royal deity was named Govindajee.
2. The introduction of Manipuri Nata Sankirtana is the most remarkable gift of Bhagyachandra to Manipuri culture. What is distinctive of Nata Sankritana is the attempt at integration of the Tandava movements with the classical style of singing interspersed with folk elements and folk style of singing, giving a regional Manipuri touch to the entire presentation.

3. Raas Lila was the creation of Rajarshi Bhagyachandra. It was on record that Rajarshi Bhagyachandra entrusted a Guru, Kabo Khunbonga, to create the dance form based on Lai Haraoba movements and Guru did it in consultation with other experts and scholars. Thus the first Maha Raas based on the slokas of Bhagavatam was enacted at Langthabal Palace in 1779 A.D. as a part of the five day's performance. In the Nata Sankritana preceding the Raas Lila, Bhagyachandra played on pung (Mridanga) while his uncle, Ngoubram Shai was the leader of the vocal group. In the Maha Raas that followed young princess Bimbabati played the role of Radha while the chief Queen did the leading Sakhi (Makok Chingbi-Vrinda Sakhi) with other queens and members of royal family participating as Gopis. It would have been indeed an extraordinary spectacle for the devout audience, indeed a sight of the Gods to see.
4. The popular art of story telling (Wari-Leeba) was also introduced during the reign of King Bhagyachandra or Jai Singh, as a gift from the culture of Assam. Jayaram Sharma from Assam narrated the tenth chapter Bhagvatam for the first time. In course of time, this intensely dramatic art of narration took up the themes from Ramayana, Mahabharata and other puranas. Such is the great power exercised by the master story-tellers over the audience that they weep and laugh almost at the same time.
5. Bhagyachandra introduced also the art of Lairik Theeba-Haiba (narration followed by explanation) which assumed almost the form of Sankirtana. The recitation of the Bhagavatam and other allied texts like Chaitanya Charitamrita, Mahabharata, Lakshmana Digvijoy and other Vaishnava texts followed a pattern of raga singing in metrical cycle particular stanzas (mostly in payar chhanda), accompanied by another by way of interpreting the lines in appropriate rhythmical expressions. This is a duet performance in every mandap, following the traditional sequence of invocation, purva Raga and concluding with prayer.
6. Besides the bronze coins, gold and silver coins were also in circulation with such devout expressions like Sri Govinda Padasuman Madhukarasya (of the bee at the lotus feet of Govinda).
7. Various Lilas like Gostha, Udukhal and Goura Lila depicting the episodes of Radha–Krishna and Gouranga were introduced during the reign of Gambheer Singh, Nara Singh and Chandrakirti Singh (1834-44) (E. Nilakanta singh : Fragments of Manipuri culture, 1993).The Hindu belief

in trimanifestations of divinity: Brahman (the creator); Vishnu (the sustainer); and Shiva (the destroyer), is also the basis of Manipuri Hindus. Rama and Krishna are the principal incarnations of Vishnu.

The word Hindu is derived from the Sanskrit name for the river "Sindhu" as the religion flourished about 3000B.C in the Indus valley. In the Vaisnava sect, there are three paths to salvation :-

1. the path of Karma or actions
2. the path of Jnana or knowledge
3. the path of Bhakti or devotion

The union of individual with the Supreme Soul and thereby the attainment of "Moksa" or liberation is the core of Hindu Thought. The Karma Marg or path of action prescribes offering of sacrifices to the Gods and observance of domestic rites. Jnana Marg on attainament of knowledge for the sake of spiritual realization is one path. Bhakti Marg or the path of devotion to a personal form of God is based upon love and worship. The three paths are not mutually exclusive, they are endorsed by almost all the sects. The destiny of the liberated is to dwell in Vaikuntha enjoying the eternal bliss at the feet of Vishnu. Cow is venerated and is held as sacred animal by Hindus. Cow is the giver of Dharma, Artha, Kama and Moksha. She is the giver of milk and butter which are used in oblations. According to Puranas, Gods reside in every fibre of her being. Hindus believe in the trinity of God- Brahma (the creator), Bishnu (the preserver) and Shiva, (the destroyer). The concept of "Avatara" or descendants of God in human form is another important aspect of Hindu philosophy. Most of the Avataras are associated with Bishnu. The ten incarnations of Bishnu are

The ten avataras (incarnations) are 1. Matsyavatara (fish), 2. Koorma (tortoise), 3. Varaaha (boar), 4. Narasimha (the man lion), 5. Vaamana (the dwarf), 6. Parasurama (the angry man), 7. Rama (the perfect human), 8. Krishna (the divine statesman) of Mahabharata 9. Budha. The 10th avatar which is yet to appear is Kalki.

Chaitanya (1458-1513 A.D.) held that through love and devotion, song and dance, a state of ecstasy could be attained in which communion with God could be realized by the devotee. Love of God is the watchword of Chaitanya cult which exercised profound influence on the masses. Chaitanya is followed in Bengal, Bihar, Manipur etc.

In the Manipuri Hindus society, there is no caste system and there is no pratice of untouchability.

3. FIRST DEVASTATION (KHUNTAKAHANBA-1755-1759)

The first devastation of Manipur started from 1755 when Alaungpaya (1752-1760), the Burmese King invaded Manipur. The Burmese Kings had been harbouring grudges against the Manipur Kings for their repeated attacks to Burma during 1692 to 1738.

King Paikhomba (1666-1696) raided Samjok in 1692, took 15 prisoners and seized shields, swords, horses, muskets as trophies in addition to crops and buffaloes. During his time, elephants and horses were also bought from Kabow valley. The import of elephants from Burma continued as before and there was a matrimonial alliance between the king of Ava, Sane and Charai Rongba's daughter in 1704. But Chairai Rongba at the time of his death on 7th of Ingen, 1709 instigated his son Pamheima (Garib Niwaz) to invade Burma to avenge the neglect of his daughter by her husband, the King of Ava *(Awa mapung taakna panthengo")*. The opportunity came in 1717 when the messangers arrived from Ava with a fresh proposal for marrying the daughter of Garib Niwaz to the new Ava king, Taningganway. The Manipuri soldiers fell on the Burmese who came to receive the princess. 90 men and 110 women were captured alive, Burmese boats were destroyed with axes and sent them burning down the river Ningthee (Chindwin).The King of Ava sent a large expedition in revenge but it was ambushed in the swamps near Heirok. In 1718, there was a fierce battle in which 157 Burmese, 160 muskets and 10 horses were captured. The Manipuris looted and killed wantonly and carried away women and children to Manipur. The entire western bank of the Irrawadi river lay at the mercy of the Manipuris. Finally the King of Ava had to send all available troops to the troubled regions. But these troops lacked a supeme commander with an imaginative plan. In the midst of these raids, the King of Ava died in 1733 and was succeeded by his son Mahadhammaraza Dipadi. In 1735, the Manipuris attacked Myedu in Swebo district and carried off loot, cattle, a thousands of people. In 1737, the Manipuris killed two-thirds of the Burmese royal levey including the commander who was drunk and swept down to Tabayin in Swebo district, burning everything they met. In 1738, when the Burmese king Mahadhammaraza Dipadi garrisoned these places and Mingin in the upper Chindwin district, the Manipuris simply cantered past, camped at Thalunbyu west of Sagaing, burnt every house and monastery upto the walls of Ava and stormed the stockade built to protect the Kaunghmudaw pagoda., slaughtering the garrison cattle like a cattle in a pen and killing the commandant, a minister of the Hluttaw Council : the old door leaves of the Pagoda's eastern gateway show a gash made by the sword of

Garib Niwaj when he was forcing an entrance (G.E Harvey History of Burma, Frank Cass & Co. Ltd., London, 1967, page-208,). Mahadhammaraza Dipadi, King of Burma angered at his commanders' failure to repel the Manipuris used to expose him in the sun with a sword on their necks saying "If news of a failure like this comes to my golden ear again, I will chastise you with my sword". Neither he nor his predecessors since 1648 ever took the field in person. The Kingdom was doomed. In the mean time, the people, desperate and ashamed, longed for a new leader and the countryside is alive with rumours of a mighty man of valour who would rule over the people with god-given lances and demon-given swords. The King, Mahadhammaraza Dipadi took these rumours seriously, consulted astrologers and finally arrested one Maung Aung Zeya, a young man of 22 years, 5 feet 10 inches tall, handsome, son of the hunter chief of a village Moksobomyo at Shwebo having about 300 houses. His courteous and firm demeanor impressed the court, which accepted his denial of any interest in politics. When he came back home, he heard from his uncle, the Lord Mingyi that "Ava was bound to fall sooner or later". But when Ava fell, he was ready to fight for the country. He felled tody trees by the hundreds and made them into a stockade round his village, dug a moat, cleared the jungle outside to form glacis and rode out destroying ponds and filling in wells. Fortysix villages joined him and they raised few muskets. He burned all villages with the full consent of the village. and filled up all streams and wells. He cut down all tress and vegetations. Within an area of some ten miles from his village, the countryside became a desert with no place for shelter for any attacking army.

A group of Gwe Shans who were settled near Ava proclaimed their headman as the King of Burma joining hands with the Mons. The movement was suppressed by the Ava King but it proved that the Burmese King was without any prestige. But before the Mons could revolt, in 1740, the Burmese Governor of Pegu declared himself King of lower Burma. An expedition came down from Ava, executed him and appointed the Governor of Syriam to be the Governor of Pegu. However, the people offered the throne to a former royal official, Maung Aung Zeya, who ascended the throne taking the Mon title "Binnya Dala".

In the mean time, Garib Niwaz abdicated his throne in Manipur in 1748 in favour of his son, Chit Shai. As soon as Chit Sai ascended the throne, he expelled his father from the capital. In 1751, Garib Niwaz was exiled to Burma. Seeing the deteriorating condition of Burma, he came back. On his return journey, he was murdered by the henchmen of Chit Sai on the 26th of Poinu

(December), 1751. Chit Shai's evil actions had come to light in the beginning of 1752. He was forced to quit the throne in Kallen, 1752 by his brother Bharat Shai.

In 1752, Binnya Dala took Ava taking the Burmese King, Mahadhammaraza Dipadi prisoner and returned to Pegu However, there were two resistance movements:- the first led by a Burmese Commander and the second by the leader of the Gwe Shans who escaped when the movement was suppressed. Both the leaders declared themselves to be the King of Ava. The third potential force was Maung Aung Zeya. When the Mon troops came to his village to administer the oath of allegiance, they were met with withering fire from muskets. A stronger detachment was sent, which was also ambushed and wiped out even before they reached the ten miles of the artificial desert around Moksobo. The Mons calling for reinforcements from Pegu attacked again with a huge army. But Maung Aung Zeya defeated them. Changing the name of his village to Shwebo or "the place of Golden Commander", he proclaimed himself the King of all Burma taking the title of Alaungpaya or "the Great Lord who shall be a Budha one day".

In the mean time, Bharat Shai ascended the throne in Manipur in Kallen, 1752. but soon after, fearing an attack from Moirang, he fled to Burma) and took refuge with Alaungpaya, to whom he presented some princesses. Gour Shyam ascended the throne on 20th Hiyangei (Monday) 1753 He requested Alaungpaya to restore him to the throne. Alaungpaya called both Bharat Sai and Gourshyam but Gooursh yam failed to show up.

In 1755, Alaungpaya sent an expedition to "instill respect" into the Manipuris. The Manipuris found the Burmese on this occasion using firearms for the first time, their weapons like those of the Manipuris having previously been only swords, spears, bows and arrows. They fought a battle at Tamu where the Manipuris were defeated and they retreated to Kakching. Later on, a detachment of Manipuri troops headed by Bhagyachandra defeated the Burmese. (G.E Harvey History of Burma, Frank Cass & Co. Ltd., London, 1967, Page-228).

In the cold weather of 1758-59, Alaungpaya personally led an expedition against Manipur when Gour Shyam was the King of Manipur. Alaungpaya proceeded up to the Chindwin devastating the villages of Manipur to the west of Ningthee river. He crossed the hills by the Khambat route and entered the Manipur valley. At Pallel in the Imole Pass, they gave him battle. After a stubborn battle, the Manipuris fled. The King and all the people fled to the hills. Gourshyam took refuge in an isolated village on the eastern side of

Nongmaiching Hill. Later on, this place was known as "Maramba Pallen" now known as Moirang Puren. Alaungpaya entered Imphal only to find it empty for the inhabitants were hiding in the woods. He halted at Imphal for thirteen days, set up a stone inscription, took what loot there was, threw into the river two canons of a cubit caliber as they were too heavy to move and returned home leaving garrisons in permanent stockades at Tamu and Thaugdut. He massacred more than four thousands of his Manipuri prisoners because they stubbornly refused to march way into captivity. The incursions from Burma had succeeded in depopulating Manipur and stamping out Manipuri civilization completely. He had taken thousands of Manipuris. The Manipuris were famous for their skill in handicraft and the Burmese valued them highly, settling them in the capital in the riverine villages of Sagaing district and at Amarapura. They served as boatmen, as silversmiths, as silkworkers they introduced the *Acheik pattern.* They gave the Burmese army its best cavalry (the Cassey horse) and they supplied the bulk of the court astrologers, who at levees stood robed in white, intoning benedictions as the King took seat on the throne. The invasion of Alaungpaya is described as the "First Devastation" (G.E. Harvey History of Burma, Frank Cass & Co. Ltd., London, 1967, page-228). Alaungpaya died in 1760 at the age of 46.

Gourshyam abdicated his throne in 1759 in favour of his younger brother Jai Singh. Jai Singh ascended the throne on 7th of Sajubu (Thursday), 1759. However, he abdicated his throne in favour of his elder brother, Gourshyam due to murder of a Brahmin by the latter's servant at Tangkham village. He again ascended the throne on 29th Thawan, (Tuesday), 1763. Gourshyam died issueless in 1763.

4. SEVEN YEAR'S DEVASTATION (CHAHI TARET KHUNTAKPA)

Seven Year's devastation is the period from 1819 to 1826 in Manipur history when the Burmese invaded and occupied Manipur under the Burmese general Maha Bandula.and there was chaos and anarchy everywhere in Manipur. (see plate- 262)

This dark period in the history of Manipur was known as **"Chahi Taret Khuntakpa"** or Seven years Devastation.

In 1803, Chourajit Singh ascended the throne in Manipur.His brother Marjit conspired against him but he was defeated. He fled to Burma through Cachar and remained in Burma for six or seven years and in 1812, he succeeded in inducing the king of Ava, Bodawpaya (1782-1819) to take up his cause and to place him on the throne of Manipur for which he agreed to hand over the

Kabow valley to Ava and to acknowledge his dependence on the Burma King. Bodawpaya sent an expedition to Manipur to put Marjit Singh on the throne. Raja Chourajit Singh fled to Cachar with his brother Gambheer Singh and a few of his followers.

The Burmese then set Marjit Singh on the throne of Manipur. Marjit continued as king for five years (1813-1819) in undisturbed possession of Manipur. (G.E Harvey History of Burma, Frank Cass & Co. Ltd., London, 1967, page- 283). In 1818, he invaded the Cachar with a large force which penetrated the hills in three divisions. The eastern portion of Cachar was already overran by Marjit Singh. On hearing the news, his brother Chourajit Singh came to the rescue of Govindrachandra,, the king of Cachar. Marjit Singh made a quick retreat. At the commencement of the year 1823, Gambheer Singh had secured the possession of southern Cachar with the exception of Hailakandi, which was held by his brother Marjit.

In 1819, Bagidaw (1819-1837) became the king of Burma. Marjit failed to appear at Bagyidaw's coronation. Bagyidaw felt that Marjit had showed disloyalty to him by failing to appear at his coronation. Marjit Singh had to be rebuked for cutting teak timbers in the Kabow valley and for building a guilded palace which the Burmese allowed to no king but their own.

Thus the Burmese invaded Manipur to punish Marjit Singh in 1819 AD under the great Burmese general Maha Bandula. The Burmese occupied Manipur from 1819 to 1826. There was a battle at Kakching which was the scene of many former struggles between Burmese and Manipuris. Manipuris faced the invasion fiercely for seven days.The battle was terminated by the retreat of Marjit Singh. Majit Singh fled to Cachar and met his brothers Chouarjit Singh and Gambheer Singh. They re-entered Manipur in overwhelming strength. But they were defeated by the Burmese and the people fled to different places in the West. Most of the people from Manipur fled to Cachar and other neighbouring areas. The Burmese occupied and stayed in Manipur During this anarchy, Burmese destroyed Manipur badly. The palace was levelled to the ground.

Marjit Singh proceeded to drive out the king of Cachar, Govindachandra, who appealed to both the British and the Burmese to assist him to regain his kingdom. Then Govindachandra brought in the Burmese in 1824. The Burmese entered Assam and started atrocities. Refugees from Cachar fled into adjoining Jaintia. The British became alarmed that the trouble might spread to Bengal itself.Cachar and Jaintia, in spite of their smallness, were useful as buffer between Burma, Manipur and British Bengal. But both were overrun with refugees and the Burmese in pursuit. The British took swift action and declared both Cachar and Jaintia to be protectorates. The Burmese would not recognize this declaration as legal and continued to chase the rebel refugees. In Assam also, the Burmese continued to face resistance from rival claimants to the throne of Assam. In the mean time, crisis occurred in Arakan. In the mean time, the rival Manipuri princes in Cachar fell out over a polo pony. One of them applied to the English for help and so did the rightful Raja of Cachar. The new Governor General Lord Amherst started taking interest in the Burmese island of Shapuree in the Arakan Channel and also taking advantage of internal dissensions in Cachar. In 1823 the British Government opened communication with Gambheer Singh.

At the beginning of January 1824 the Officiating Magistrate at Sylhet, writing to the Governor General reported that 6,000 to 7,000 Burmese were assembled on the Manipur side, and were probably destined for Cachar. He further reported that two Burmese armies had actually invaded Cachar at the invitation of the Ex-Maharaja Govindchandra.

The Magistrate was directed to repel the Burmese by force. The Burmese Commander replied that they had received royal orders to reinstate Govindachandra on the throne of Cachar and to arrest the three Manipuri Chiefs-Chourajit Singh, Marjit Singh and Gumbheer Singh.

Before the formal declaration of war, there were clashes between the British and the Burmese forces at Tilain and Gambheer Singh was found to be of great help in capturing Tilain. By February, the British came to know Gambheer Singh as a bold, aspiring soldier and found in him an useful ally. In April, 1824, he was given to understand that if he could liberate Manipur from the Burmese, he would became the King of Manipur. Seeing the jealousy between Gambheer Singh and Chourajit, the British authorities decided to remove Chourajit from the scene and sent him to Nadia (West Bengal) on a monthly stipend of Rs.100. Marjit did not think it safe to remain in Cachar and went to Sylhet and spent the rest of his life there. Thus the stage was set for Gambheer Singh to advance to Manipur without any hindrance.

During this period, the male population in Manipur was reduced to a very low level, for majority of them were forcibly taken to Burma. Capt. R.B. Perberton (1835) said that Manipur was "doomed to the devastating visitation of Burmese armies which have nine or ten times swept the country from one extremity to the other with the apparent determination of extirpating a race whom they found it impossible permanently to subdue"

David Scott, in his memorandum to the Governor-General-in-charge, argued that the Manipuris could defend properly their country against the

Burmese with minimum help from the British India. "Of all the various tribes and nations of the eastern frontier", David Scott contended "the Manipuris were the only race from whom any effectual and valuable assistance could be expected, either offensively or defensively against the powerful nation like the Burmese." David Scott went to the extent of saying that they (Manipuris), being a gallant race, could be compared with the Rajputs of northern Hindustan, and they were sufficiently civilized and advanced in the art of Government. Having got these information, Brigadier General Shuldham suggested to Tucker, Commissioner of Sylhet that the increase of Manipur's levy was to be postponed for a time being. Thus, the Governor-General-in-Council at Fort William decided upon the detachment of a large body of regular force under the direct command of Brigadier-General Shuldham instead of sending Gambheer Singh's levy in advance and also postponed the granting of the amount of rupees one lakh to Gambheer Singh for meeting the expenses of increasing his infantry.

On 5 March,1824 the Governor General Lord Amherst made a formal proclamation of war. General Sir Edward Paget advised the Government of India to aim at the following objectives :

1. The expulsion of the Burmese from the territory they had recently annexed in Assam.
2. To dispatch an expedition by sea to subdue the maritime provinces of Ava and if possible, penetrate to the capital by the line of the Irrawaddi (Ayeyarwady) River.
3. to maintain a defensive attitude for the present on the Sylhet and Chittagong frontiers, merely strengthening the force there so as to prevent any further incursions from the Burmese force in Manipur and Arakan.

The war was started in the Brahmaputra, in Cachar and in Arakan. The Burmese were regarded as dangerous neighbours.

The British plan was to attack on three fronts: Assam {including Cachar}, Arakan {including the islands of Chanduba and Ramree} and the seaports of Rangoon Syriam Martaban, Tavoy and Mergui. Captain Canning was the chief adviser since he made three visits to the country.

Maha Bandula, the Burmese Commander-in–chief with headquarters in Assam decided on a two pronged attack, one from Assam and Manipur through Cachar and the other from Arakan, the two armies meeting in Bengal and together attacking Calcutta. Maha Bandula himself led the army from Arakan. Bandula used a combination of guerrilla tactics and frontal attacks. Burmese canons only fired balls whereas the British canons fired exploding shells.

On the Assam front, the British forces were superior in numbers and equipment and these factors, combined with what would now be called political warfare determined the campaign. On entering Assam territory a proclamation was made to exploit the unpopularity of the Burmese :

The proclaimation said :-

"It is well known to you that some years ago, the Burmese invaded your territory, and that they have since dethroned the Rajah, plundered the country, slaughtered Brahmins, and women and cows defiled your temples, and committed the most barbarous outrages of every kind so that vast numbers of your country men have been forced to seek refuge in our dominions where they have never ceased to implore our assistance. Our victorious army has crossed the boundary and we will drive the barbarians beyond the Burmakhood nor cease until we restore peace and security to your distracted country. Come forward therefore, without fear for the present or the future. You may rest assured that we will never consent to depart until we exclude our foe from Assam and re-establish in that country a Government adapted to your wants and calculated to promote the happiness of all classes".

The issue on this front was decided by the fall of Rangpur in January1825. Burmese sources explain that at this point the troops had been recalled to Rangoon, where the main battles of the war were fought. In any case, Cachar was evacuated by the Burmese leaving the Brahmaputra Valley under British control.

Thirty thousand souls were carried by the Burmese army from Assam alone. To cow the people, they were flayed alive, burnt in oil or driven in crowds into the village, prayer houses which were set on fire. Women, old as well as young were outraged with every circumstances of barbarity, sometimes bamboo cages were constructed to burn men, women and infants two hundred or so at a time and the more imaginative among the Burmese braves would add variations such as cutting pieces off the bodies of their lingering victims under whose eyes they would eat the raw flesh. Such being their energy, it is hardly surprising that the Burmese should, during the seven year's of their intervention in Assam have reduced the population by more than half. Even today, people are still speaking with a shudder of "*Manar Updrab*", the oppressions of the Burmese.

One Mahomed Ruffy recorded in June, 1826

"I am a native of the village Udarbund, in the country of Cachar. I have seen a prisoner of war in Ava. I was seized at my native village about twenty months ago. by a party of Burmese, belonging to the army. ...... About

six thousand prisoners including men, women and children were seized about the same time. We were chained two by two, got very little food, were made to carry heavy loads on the march. Women with infants at the breast and who on this account could not carry loads had the infants snatched from them, their heads chopped of before them and their bodies thrown into the rivers. I have witnessed murders of this description twelve or thirteen times myself. Old and sick persons who could not carry burdens were often killed by the Burmese soldiers and their loads, which consisted of plunders were divided among the other prisoners. (G.E. Harvey, History of Burma, Frank Cass & Co.Ltd., 1925, page- 298).

The Burmese said that these oppressions were committed out of set policy and the Burmese prided themselves on it so that foreigners should learn not to provoke them. Thus for sixty years, the Burmese would march into Manipur whenever the mood seized them, rounded up several thousand hapless people and reenact the same terrible scenes as before.

Sir Archibald Compbell had organized his forces in the Andaman Island.His idea was to occupy the maritime provinces of Ava and then to advance by the line of the Irrawaddy (Ayeyarwady) to the capital, Rangoon. On 11 May 1824 Sir Archibald Campbell with his fleet landed in Rangoon They found the whole town deserted.

The second attack on the Kemmendine stockade was successful on 11 June,1824 – and this gave Sir Archibald Campbell the command of the river immediately above Rangoon. The Burmese now withdrew their forces to Donabyu, fifty miles up the river. During the summer months Sir Archibald Campbell carried out several campaigns and captured some of the southern maritime possessions.The district of Tenasserim, comprising Tavoy and Mergui had long tracts of sea-coast, and potential supplies of cattle and grain. Tavoy was conquered easily on 8 september,1824. Mergui was occupied on 6 October 1824 and in November, Martaban was occupied.

The rainy season was now over and operations were again concentrated on Rangoon. The tactics of the Government in Ava now changed.The idea of Maha Bandula's leadership was to fight a pitched battle with the foreigners. They aimed at exterminating the invaders or taking them as captives to Ava.Everything was done in the way of supplies to equip Maha Bandula and his troops. His arrival in Ava, Captain Snodgrass described as "having acted as a spell in drawing forward the lately reluctant peasantry to range themselves under the banner of so popular a leader.

Maha Bandula's defeat in Kokine combined with the loss of nearly 200 of his war boats forced a reconsideration of his position. He did not again attempt offensive operations, but concentrated on defending his positions along the river. He established his headquarters at Danubyu on a raised part of the Delta, commanding the then main water route from Rangoon up country, at a point where the road from Rangoon to Bassein crossed the main Irrawaddy and continued along the high ground to Bassein.

The real attack on Danubyu began on 1 April, 1825.

On 1st April, 1825, Maha Bandula himself had been killed by a rocket or a mortar shell and with his death his army fell to pieces. There was nobody to take his place although it is related that his brother tried to assume command with indifferent success, his failure being rewarded by execution :

Sir Archibald Campbell left Danubyu on 3 April 1825 crossed the Irrawaddy and marched on to Prome, meeting little resistance.

On Manipur front, the British forces under Shuldham arrived at Bashkandi on 24 February, 1825. On 11 March, 1825, Shuldham reported that "the state of the road is such that it is quite impossible to send supplies on to the advance, either on camels, bullocks, elephants or men". The unusual rains also made the march much more hopeless. There remained Manipur Brigadier–General Shuldham, commanding Eastern frontier, abandoned his first attempt at transport and the beginning of the monsoon made it imposible.

Gambheer Singh and his 500 men then decided to take up the task which was considered impossible by Brigadier-General Shuldham. The British authorities supplied the arms for 500 troops for Gambheer Singh, who proceeded towards Manipur. It was denominated as the "Manipur Levy" and was paid, accounted and supplied with ammunition by the British Government. On 17th May,1825 Gambheer Singh entered Manipur from Sylhet with 500 Manipuri soldiers accompanied by Lt. Pemberton. They arrived at Bashkandi on 23 May, 1825 despite bad weather, inadequate supplies and innumerable hardships, they managed to reach the western limit of the valley of Manipur on 10 June, 1825. The Burmese forces had already evacuated the town of Imphal and encamped themselves at Andro, a place situated at the eastern side of Imphal. Gambheer Singh and his men occupied Imphal without much difficulty. Emboldened with these successes, Gambheer Singh further moved on to Andro but found it evacuated. The Manipuri forces did not meet any serious opposition from the Burmese army. This was so because the Burmese were hard-pressed on all sides. This is not to minimise the role of Gambheer Singh and his men towards the liberation of their country. Their training was not adequate and yet they accomplished what appeared to be impossible and what Brigadier-General Shuldham's regular force had not ventured to undertake. Lieutenant R.B. Pemberton who accompanied Gambheer Singh reported that the success of the campaign was due mainly to his (Gambheer) energy, perseverance and skill. At a time when there was a strong need to strengthen what had just been liberated, Gambheer Singh rushed back to Sylhet by the end of June, 1825 leaving behind 300 men and local armed volunteers to garrison Manipur. Gambheer Singh perhaps thought that the continuous retreat of Burmese forces might only be a tactical move and therefore needed a stronger and better equipped forces to face any fresh attack from Burma.

In 1825, this force under Gambheer Singh was increased to 2000 men, placed under the command of Captain Grant. Gambheer Singh resumed his second campaign on 18 December, 1825. During his six month's stay at Sylhet, Gambheer Singh could mobilize fresh reinforcements (1500 mushkets and requisite number of men). On arrival in Manipur, Gambheer Singh found that there were still 300 or 400 Burmese soldiers in the Kabow valley. After a few days, Gambheer Singh was again informed of the withdrawal of the Burmese soldiers from the valley to Tamu, a border town in Burma. The valley was left under the protection of 500 local people. Meanwhile, the Sumjok Raja mobilised about 200 men in and around Tamu to counter the Manipuri forces. It was here that the Manipuri whom Gambheer had sent early in January could hardly make any penetration into the enemy's camp.

On instructions from Bengal Sir Archibald Campbell wrote to the Burmese Ministers saying that he was authorized to start negotiation for peace. On 1 December, 1825 Sir Archibald Campbell made a combined naval and military attack on every possible part of the Burmese line.

Realising the seriousness of the situation, Gambheer Singh and Captain Grant lost no time to rush to the assistance of the advanced forces and joined them on 18 January 1826. On 19 January, 1826, the combined forces assaulted the Burmese positions, and though the latter made several spirited sorties to check the mounting attacks from Manipuri soldiers, they were resisted with greater spirit. By the night of 22 January, 1826, the Burmese began their retreat and completely evacuated the stockade.

Sir Archibald Campbell deputed Captain Lumsden and Havelook to the court of Ava with a conciliatory message to terminate the hostilities. The Burmese wanted a truce for twenty five days Sir Archibald Campbell agreed to twenty four hours.

A Burmese peace mission came to discuss terms with the British Commander but finding the demands too harsh, they returned to the capital. The British fought on until they reached Yandabo, only 50 miles from Ava. Another peace mission came from the King and this time, they had no other choice but to accept the British terms. This was the end of negotiations for the time being.

Treaty of Yandabo

The Treaty of Yandabo was signed on 24 February 1826.The war had lasted two years.

1. By this Treaty, the King of Ava would cede to the British territories of Arakan, Tenasserim, and Assam.
2. The Burmese would recognize Manipur, Cachar and Jaintia as British Territory.
3. With regard to Manipur, it is stipulated that should Gambheer Singh desire to return to that country, he shall be recognized by the King of Ava as Raja thereof
4. The Burmese would pay an indemnity of one million pounds sterling in four installments, the first installment to be paid immediately, the second installment within one hundred days from the signing of the treaty, the balance to be paid in annual installments within two years. Until the second installment was paid, the British army would not leave Ragoon.
5. The Burmese would receive a British resident representative at Ava and in turn the British would receive a Burmese resident representative at Calcutta.
6. The East India Company and the Burmese King would sign a commercial treaty in due course.
7. The British agreed to retire at once to Rangoon, and to quit the territories of Ava when the second installment of the fine was paid.

The cost of the war in lives and money to British was enormous. In all 40,000 troops were employed, and of these 15,000 died in Burma. The proportion of casualties in action was small; for example of the 3,586 British troops who landed in Rangoon on the first expedition, 3,115 were buried in Burma from wounds or disease, only 150 being killed in action. The war cost 13 million Pound Sterling of which 1 million was recovered from Burma by indemnity. (Dorothy Woodman" the making of Burma", The Cresset Press, London, 1962).

At the conclusion of the Yandabo Peace Treaty, after the end of Anglo-Burmese war in February 1826, Gambheer Singh was recognized as the Raja of Manipur.

The Government of Ava recognized the Independence of Manipur; desist from interference with Assam and Cachar; cede Arakan and its dependencies receive a British Resident at Amarapura ; pay 2 crores of rupees to pay for the war. Rangoon, Martaban and Tenasserim provinces being held in pledge by the British Government until the fine was discharged.

The liberation of Manipur from Burma was thus accomplished by Gambheer Singh and his men with the assistance of British. At the very outset, Lord Amherst, Governor General, made it clear that since Manipur had common boundary with Burma, the extension of British influence over the country would be viewed with jealousy and alarm by the court of Ava. He therefore argued that the question of extending British protection over Manipur be taken up only after receiving a detailed report from the man on the spot, David Scott.

Period of Reconstruction

According to article 2 of the treaty of Yandaboo concluded on 24 February, 1826, the King of Burma agreed to recognise Gambheer Singh as the King of Manipur. Obviously, the desire of the British officials in India was that Manipur should be treated as an independent kingdom, inhabited by a people with a deep-rooted antipathy to the Burmese.

Later, Grawford, the resident designate for Ava, reported that Burma considered Manipur as independent country and urged the British to treat her as such. The Burmese officials even expressed their desire that Gambheer Singh should not maintain European officials at his court. Though the question of the presence of foreign officials at Manipur was not settled the independent status of Manipur was recognised by Burma.

Gambheer Singh formally became King of Manipur in June, 1826 with a tiny population of 10,000 only. According to official account, many villages were destroyed and their inhabitants had been carried off as captives by the Burmese and those who had escaped had found asylum in Sylhet. Naturally, the task of reconstruction of the ruined country fell on Gambheer Singh. In bringing about stable condition and initiating constructive works, Gambheer Singh was assisted by his brother, Nar Singh. With the development of paddy fields covered by dense grass for cultivation, Manipur gradually regained the position of the pre-war period.

Gambheer Singh constructed the Palace of Manipur at Langthabal which was situated about 8 kilometres south from Imphal and the head-quarters of Manipur levy was also stationed there.

Soon after the conclusion of the treaty of Yandaboo, the supreme officials at Calcutta decided to discontinue the payment of Manipur levy. Yet, the supply of arms and ammunition was continued. Because, the local officials realised that the levy was indispensable to the security of North-Eastern frontier. They pointed out that the levy lightly equipped, might at the proper season, penetrate into Burma without any difficulty and might, if necessary, further advance on Ava by a direct march of fifteen days and strike at the very heart of the Burmese empire. Manipur was still considered as totally incompetent to defend itself against a Burmese invasion. Lord William Bentinck, in his minute, 25 March 1833, argued that if the British troops should be placed in it, adding thus: "... we can hardly doubt that the felling of security to the inhabitants of Manipur generally would be greatly increased by the permanent residence amongst them of such a body".

It was under these circumstances that two separate treaties were concluded with Manipur. By the treaty of 1833, the British government agreed to give to the Raja of Manipur the line of Jiri river and the western bend of the Barak river as a boundary. On the other hand, the Raja of Manipur agreed to the following conditions:

First, the Raja was to remove his Thana from Chandrapur to the eastern bank of the Jiri river.

Second, the Raja should not obstruct the trade between Manipur and Cachar and should not impose heavy duties on it.

Third, the Nagas were not to be prevented from selling or bartering ginger, cotton, pepper and every other article of the Banskandi and Udharban bazars.

Fourth, the Raja also agreed to maintain and repair the road passing through Khopum as and when the construction of the same had been finished.

Fifth, the Raja was under obligation to furnish a quota of Nagas to assist the construction of the road.

Sixth, in the event of war with the Burmese, the Raja should provide hill porters to assist in transporting the ammunition and baggage of British troops.

Seventh, in the event of anything happening on the eastern frontier of the British territoties, the Raja should readily assist the British government with his troops.

5. THE ANGLO-MANIPURI WAR OF 1891 (KHONGJOM WAR)

Manipur was an independent Kingdom on the eastern frontier of India bordering Burma, now called Myanmar. Its unbroken recorded history extends from 33 to 1891 A.D.

The kingdom of Manipur entered into three treaties with the British Government :

5.1. TREATY OF 1762

In 1762, King Bhagyachandra or Jai Singh concluded a treaty with the East India Company just 5 years after the Battle of Pallassey. The aim was to get military assistance from the Company against the Burmese. The Company sent armed troops to assist Manipur. But they could not advance beyond Cachar due to incessant rain and hilly terrain. The Court of Directors of the East India Company did not like the treaty and instructed Fort William not to proceed with the treaty. Manipur also found the Treaty expensive and unfruitful. Both parties therefore abandoned the Treaty.

5.2. TREATY OF YANDABO

By the treaty of Yandabo, 1826, concluded between the Burmese and the East India company, the Burmese monarch recognized the Independence of Manipur. In the time of Lord Amherst, the Burmese threatened the British district of Sylhet, then a part of Bengal. The Burmese had already overrun Manipur and Assam. Panic seized the population of Sylhet. Immediate action was called for. At this critical moment, Gambheer Singh, a son of Bheigyachandra made an alliance with East India Company. With an assistance of few hundred muskets from the Company, he easily drove out the Burmese from Manipur in June 1825. The company gave an additional aid of 1,500 muskets and he drove out the Burmese from the Kabow Valley, the land between the present Indo-Myanmar border and the Chindwin River. A wide zone of pace was thus established between British India and Myanmar. This was completed on 1st Feburary, 1826. The treaty of Yandabo was signed on 24 February 1826.

5.3. TREATY OF 1833

By the Treaty of 1833, concluded between the East India Company and Manipur, the Company ceded Jiribam in favour of Manipur. This was a rare instance of the English ceding territory to a foregn power.

In 1835, the Supreme Government of British India opened a Political Agency in Manipur. In the words of Lord William Bentinck, the then Governor General, "It was for the preservation of a friendly intercourse, and as the medium of communication with the Manipur Government, and, as occasion may require, with the Burmese Authorities on that frontier, and more specially to prevent border feuds and disturbances which might lead to hostilities between the Manipuris and the Burmese."

Manipur never accepted Subsidiary Alliance. It never paid tribute to the British prior to 1891 nor ceded any territory to them. There was no treaty guaranteeing British protection to Manipur, although Lord Dalhousie (1848-1856) attempted to keep Manipur firmly within British sphere of influence.

5.4. THE PALACE REVOLUTION -1891

On 21 September, 1890, there was the Palace Revolt, Angousana and Zillangamba, brothers of King Surchandra, revolted against the King. Surchandra took refuge in the residency of the Political Agent, Mr. Frank St.Clair Grimwood. He informed the Political Agent that he abdicated the throne and wished to go to Vrindaban. He along with his brothers and followers left Manipur in the evening of 23rd September at about 7.30 p.m.under an escort of 35 rifles of 44th Gurkha Light Infantry who saw the party safely to Cachar. On 3rd October, 1890, he reached Cachar and immediately he sent a telegram to Shillong saying that the Political Agent had misunderstood him and he had no intention of abdicationg the throne. On reaching Calcutta, Surchandra applied to the Viceroy on 14th November, 1890 to restore him to the throne.

Kulachandra (see plate-74) ascended the throne on 23 September, 1890 (Tuesday) at 3 p.m. according to Manipuri customs.

After much discussion and corrpondence, the Viceroy, Lord Landsdowne (see plate -78) (10 December 1988 to 11 October, 1894) took the following decisions as conveyed in their letter letter no. 360-E dated 21st February1891:-

1. That the Yubraj (Kulachandra) should be recognized as the Maharaja and that the Ex-Maharaja should not be restored.
2. That the Senapati (Tekendrajit) should be removed from Manipur.
3. The Chief Commissioner of Assam, Mr. J.W. Quinton should go to Manipur and announce the decision on the spot.

On the 7th March, 1891, Mr. J.W. Quinton left Golaghat for Manipur.with an escort of 400 men of the 42nd and 44th Gorkha Rifles under the command of Col. Charles MacDonald Skene. On the 22nd of March, 1891 the Chief Commissione arrived at Imphal. He was welcomed by Yubaraj Tikendrajit. Mr. Quinton planned to arrest Tikendrajit in the durbar at the Residency scheduled at midday on the following morning. The Maharaja and his three brothers Tikendrajit, Angou Sana, Zilangamba, together with several of the nobles had arrived at the appointed time at outer gate of the Residency compound. But they were asked to wait outside the gate since the translation of the decision of the Government of India into Manipuri was not yet completed. The waiting was for more than one hour. Later on, Tikendrajit left the gate complaining that he was feeling ill. All hope of arresting the Jubraj without incident had gone in vain. On 23rd March, 1891 at about 4.30 p.m, Mr. Grimwood along with Lt. Simpson (43rd Gurkha Rifles) came to the Durbar Hall and handed the King the Government of India's letter containing the decisions to recognize him as the King of Manipur but to deport his brother Tikendrajit outside Manipur. After consulting his advisors, the Maharaja responded that it was not in his power to surrender his brother and the Manipuri Durbar did not wish him to do so. Mr. Grimwood returned from the palace and announced that his mission had failed.

On the night of 23rd March, a Raas Lila was organized in honour of Mr. Quinton's visit. After the conclusion of the Raas Lila performance, the Chief Commissioner after consulting with Col Skene and Mr. Grimwood arrived at a decision to enforce the order of the Government of India. Tikendrajit's residence was inside the compound of the Kangla Fort. On the 24th of March 1891 at 3 A.M, British troops invaded and opened fire at the Palace Compound at 3.30 am of 24th March 1891. Guards of the Palace returned the fire and in the resulting battle, Lieutenant Brackenbury was mortally wounded, three Gurkha sepoys were killed and 14 Gurkha sepoys were wounded.

The British army entered the palace, and obtained possession of Tikendrajit's house. But when they occupy the house, Tikendrajit was not there. The British army committed atrocities on men, women and children. They killed women, boys and girls, male and female servants, desecreted the temple, stole the jewels of the idol. They burnt houses at Usham Leikai, Yambem Leikai, Saikhom Leikai. Then the full fire power of the Manipuri force was turned upon the Residency. Severe fighting continued for the whole day. Many British army personnel were killed. Mr. Quinton decided that the only alternative open to them was to seek a truce and parley with the Manipur Maharaja.

Mr. Quinton, the Chief Commissioner now realized that he had grossly underestimated the Manipuris, their weaponry, skill and firepower. He now wanted a truce. But Mr. Quinton accompanied by Mr. Grimwood and three other British officers entered the Palace compound without asking for or obtaining safe conduct from the Government of Manipur or even without giving prior notice. At this time, there was a violent mob shouting to punish the "Sahebs" for killing innocent civilians. (see plate-263) After an inconclusive talk in what is called a durbar, Grimwood (see Plate-86) was speared to death by Kajao Pukhramba Phingang. (see plate- 264). This heralded the onset of the Anglo-Manipuri war of 1891. Thangal General thought there was no use of continuing the negotiation with the British and thus the remaining British officers were eventually handed over to the public executioner.

1. Mr. J.W. Quinton, C.S.I I.E. Chief Commissioner of Assam. (see Plate-83)
2. Lt.Col. E. Med Skene, D.S.O. 42nd Gurkha Rifles. (see Plate-84)
3. W.H.Cossino, I.C.S. Assistant Secretary to the commission.
4. Lt. W.H. Simpson, 43rd Gurkha Rifles (see Plate-85)
5. and a Gurkha Bugler

The machinery of retribution was soon put in action. The British Government declared war against Manipur on 31st of March 1891. Within a fortnight, British forces mainly Gurkhas were converging on Manipur. By the first week of April, 1891, three columns converged at Manipur from Kohima, Cachar and Tamu. Each column consisted of 1000 soldiers. The Manipuris had sufficient quantities of arms and ammunation but not sufficient manpower as the population was small. This is where the British hit. The British sent troops in large numbers to 'over awe' Manipur. The most important battle of the war was fought at Khongjom, some 12 kilometers to the south of Thoubal.

5.5. THE KHONGJOM WAR

Maharaj Kulachandra made an appeal to the people to volunteer as soldiers in the fight against the British who had committed aggression against Manipur. Major Paona Brjabashi (see plate-75), Major Yengkhoiba (see plate-89), Wangkheirakpa and Maipak Sana proceeded to Thoubal with 700 soldiers and joined Yengkhoiba Major. After reaching Thoubal, Major Paona suggested that the main group would stay back at Thoubal as rear guard and the remaining would advance to Pallel. He wanted 400 men and one mountain gun. But Wangkheirakpa and Major Yengkhoiba refused to give him the mountain gun. Accordingly, Paona and Chongtha Miya proceeded to the front with 400 men. A small column of 30 men was sent to Kakching as an advance guard. There was an encounter between the advance party under

Wangkhei Meiraba Poila and British forces near Kakching. About 20 men including the Manipuri commnader were killed. Lt. Garnt's horse was shot dead and he narrowly escaped. Yaiskul Lakpa and his son Sengoisana died together along with three British army on 6th April, 1891. In the mean time, the British forces from Burma had arrived and were ready for the last battle.The Manipuri forces entrenched on the bank of the Khongjom river. There were only 1300 soldiers and they did not have the mountain gun. The British forces moved up to the Langathel hill overlooking the Manipuri fort. They had four mountain guns backed by Sikh and Gurkha infantry soldiers. On the 22nd April, the British artillery had bombarded the Manipuri fort. Paona had no mountain gun.He sent an urgent message to Wangkheirakpa at Thoubal, 7 miles away to send two mountain guns but no reply came from Thoubal. Paona therefore sent a message to the Maharaja to send the mountain gun. But on the suggestion of Thangal General, it was refused. Thangal pleaded that "the mountain gun was required to protect the palace.Moreover, Paona was just released from prison, who knew he might turn against the King." It is said that the Maharaja later on lamented and the mountain gun was actually sent from the palace but it was too late.

The mountain gun could not reach the Manipuri fort as it was already surrounded by the British forces. On 23rd April, 1891, having no other option, Paona decided to meet the inevitable to have a hand to hand fight with the British forces. (see plate-266) The British forces made a frontal attack on the Maniprui fort. The Manipuri forces were outnumbered. The fighting continued for the whole day. The Manipuris fought with determined efforts under the leadership of Paona Major. But ultimately, Paona Major was killed in action by Takhellambam Rashman Subedar from Cachar on 23rd April, 1891 (Thursday) along with 131 soldiers including Chinglensana. It is said that about 400 Manipuri heroes were killed in the Khongjom war. (see plates- 267-271) On the British side, Lt Garnt reported 2 men killed, 13 wounded includng himself and three other British Officers. Grant admitted that they fought as hard as they could and the Manipuris fought till the last.

The defeat of Manipur was partly due to some defects in the Manipuri Army. The Manipuri soldiers were using red jackets and white turbans as their uniform. This made them easy targets for the British. Many of the soldiers were volunteers, not regular army and therefore not properly trained and disciplined. Their marksmanship was poor. Most importantly who is the overall command of the Khongjom war was not identified. There was disagreement between Paona Brajabashi, Major Chongtha Mia, Wangkheirakpa and Major

Yengkhoiba. Major Paona could not use essential resources like mountain gun. Senapati Angousana stayed back at Lilong, not proceeding upto the war front. Why Maharaja Kulachandra or Bir Tikendrajit or Thangal General did not send the mountain gun in time to the war front or directly participate at the war is another weak point.

The result of the war was a foregone conclusion. The sun never set in the British Empire at that time. It was impossible to defeat the British at the end of the 19th Century or at the beginning of the 20th century. The three columns mentioned above met in the Manipur Palace on the 27th April and the Union Jack was hoisted. The Manipuris were never in doubt as to the result of the war. Their heroism lay in their readiness to lay down their lives in defence of freedom and march to the battle-field knowing fully well that they would not return again. The last words of Paona Brajabashi are inscribed in the Paona Memorial at Khongjom. (see plate- 266, 267). We come across such heroism in great poems and other good literature but not often in real life. Freedom–the Manipuris lost, but love of freedom–they retained.

Some of the heroes who sacrificed their lives at the Khongjom war-1891 are as follows :-

1. Paona Brajabashi
2. Wangkhei Meiraba Poila
3. Yaiskul Lakpa
4. Sengoisana
5. Chinglen Sana
6. Heirang Khongja
7. Khumbong Major
8. Loitongba Jamadar
9. Keisam Jamadar
10. Promce Chinglenkhomba
11. Thabal
12. Angangmacha and many others

Paona Brajabashi

Paona Brajabashi (see Plate- 75) was the son of Paonam Tulsiram (Tulla Singh) and Haobam Chanu Kunjeshwari, daughter of Major Haobam Binod Singh. Tulsiram was one of the sepoys in the Manipur levy in 1824. Paona was born on 20th December, 1833. He was living in the Haobam Leikai (present Babupara) From early childhood, he learnt the Thang–ta and war tactics from General Longjamba Loma Singh under instruction from Haobam Binoda Major.

At the age of 17 years, he went to Vrindaban in connection with the death ritual of his father Tulsiram. He also toured many places of U.P. and learnt Thang-ta from famous teachers /Gurus of that time.He returned to Manipur at the age of 23 years. He joined an expedition of Akam Hao along with General Longjamba Loma and Haobam Binoda Major. During the expedition, he saved the life of Chandrakirti Maharaj.After returning from the expedition, he was made Subedar and given one hectare of land. The Maharaja called him "Brajabashi" after learning that he spent quite a long time in Vrindaban. After some time, He married Hemomala daughter of Kabrambam Setu Senapati and Tomal Manjuri. Kabrambam Setu was made Senapati by Chandrakirti Maharaja on 16th October, 1852. At the age of 30 years, in 1863, he defeated one Punjabi martial art expert. After this incident, Maharaja Chandrakirti entrusted Paona Brajabnashi his sons Surchandra, Kulachandra, Tikendrajit, Angousana and Pakasana to teach Thang –ta. After some time, he shifted his house from Haobam Leikai to Keisamthong Laisom Leirak. In 1879, he went to Thibomei (Kohima) along with Surchandra, Thangal Major, Tikendrajit with an army of 2000 sepoys to subdue the Angami aggression where Mr. Damant was killed. The Angamese were defeated in the battle. In this expedition, Brajabashi saved the life of the Englishman when the latter was surrounded by the Nagas. The Englishman offered a present of one Paris of land to Brajabashi in recognition of his gallantry. He had four daughters namely Chaobihal, Thamchet, Numitlei, Dashumati and four sons namely Manik, Mantri, Ibochaoba and Tonsana. However, all other sons had died except the youngest Tonsana.

On the night of Monday of 23rd March, 1891, Mr. Quinton beseized the residence of Tikendrajit. A terrible fight ensued between the British soldiers and the Manipuri soldiers. When Brajabashi was at Keisamthong Laisom Leirak, he heard about the attack of the Manipur Palace by the British. Although unasked, he of his own accord at once set out for the palace and not caring for his own life returned the enemies fire. Within a few hours, most of the enemy soldiers fell dead and what once deemed a certain defeat suddenly turned into sweet victory.The king was so elated with triumphant joy and pride that at once, he took off his royal shirt and turban and gave them to Paona in recognition of his gallantry.

Paona Brajabashi was made Major on 17th April, 1891.He was sent to Thoubal to fight with the invading British troops by the King along with Chongtha Mia Major and 400 troops. The last day of the Anglo-Manipuri war was fought at Khongjom on 23rd April, 1891. Firing commenced at day break and continued till evening. At 5 p.m., the British beseized the camp at Khongjom.

Paona Brajabashi and his troops fought bravely.Paona Major, Khumbong Major, Loitongba Jamadar, Keisam Jamadar, Prince Chinglenkhomba and many others died in action.

The news of Paona's death at the Khongjom war reached his home at 9 p.m of 23rd April, 1891. His wife Hemomala and the four daughters, the youngest son Tonsana and son-inlaw Laisangbam Jhulon had a discussion on 24th April, 1891 and decided to go to Khongjom and bring back the dead body. They started for Khongjom on 25th April, 1891 avoiding all possible routes to avoid possible conflict with the invading British army. They reached Kakching and stayed there for the night. On the next day, they reached Khongjom. They found the dead body at the foot of Kheba Ching at the spot where the statue is now located. The dead body was already in a decomposed condition. They came back with the dead body along the Phunan hill range and reached Urup Arapti. He was cremated at the Yumkhaibam Hiden on 26th April, 1891 (Sunday) according to Hindu rites. His youngest son Tonsana Singh and his brother –in-law Jhulon planted two banyan trees at the site of cremation at Yumkhaibam Hiden (see plate-264). Every year, the Paonam family is observing the death anniversary of Paona Brajabashi on 26th April of every year since 1957.

It is time for the Government of Manipur to erect a memorial to this historical site where Paona Brajabashi was cremated.

Chinglen Sana Phunganai Sanglakpa

Chinglen Sana was the son of Pocha Sana, son of Singhajit, one of the sons of Maharaja Labyanachandra. He lived at Khwairamband (site of earlier civil hospital) near the Pologround. Their family was known as Kangjeibung Mapan Taba. He was appointed as Phunganai Sanglakpa (Officer in charge of institution of King's personnel).He married Moirangmayum Ningol Jhulon Khombi of Sagolband Moirangmayaum Leirak.When the British troops fled from the residency towards Cachar, Chinglen Sana pursued the retractors along the Cachar road. On 23rd April, 1891, he fought and resisted the advance of British column under the leadership of Paona Brajabashi.He died fighting with a sword in hand. His bravery and patriotism is still remembered by the people of Manipur. He left behind two sons–Sanajaoba and Pheira sana and three daughters–Mangolsana, Maipaksabna and Tharosana.

After the Khongjom War

Before the fall of the government, Kulachandra, Tikendrajit and other leaders left the Palace on 26 April, 1891 and went underground. After winning the Khongjom war, the British had an easy walk over on all fronts and marched to Imphal. Maharaja Kulachandra with 200 men fled to Chassad hills on his way to China. Meanwhile 22 guns and 26 boxes of dynamite and gun powder left behind at the palace were blown up through an accident. It was quite surprising that so much of arms and ammunition were not used in the battle against the British. Tikendrajit Singh and Thangal General went into hiding. Maharaja Kulachandra returned as the guide who promised to take him to China had betrayed him. He was arrested on 9th May, 1891. Thangal General surrendered. Tikendrajit was arrested (see plate- 79 and 81) in the evening of Saturday 23rd May, 1891.

On 27 April, 1891, Major Maxwell (see Plate-87) arrived and occupied the palace. The Raja's palace was looted before and the citadel was razed to the ground to make way for the permanent military camp. Captain Allen destroyed the Kangla sha in front of Kangla by artillery fire. The final act in this reversal of fortune was the public hanging of Tikendrajit and Thangal General. The execution of a prince upset Queen Victoria, who protested to Lansdowne suggesting that in general residents and political agents were overbearing.The viceroy was adamant on the matter. There were further reverberations of the Manipur affair in the House of Commons where the Government faced charges of perfidy for it was widely believed that the original durbar had been a device to abduct Tikendrajit. The allegations were strenuously denied both in London and in Calcutta. (Lawrence James, the Making of British India, RAJ, ABACUS, Page- 332)

Tikendrajit and Thangal General were charged with waging war against the Queen–Empress of India and abetment of the murder of British officers.They were sentenced to be hanged by the neck which had been confirmed by the Government of India and carried out. Yubraj Tikendrajit (32 years old) and Thangal General were hanged on 13th August, 1891 at Pheida Pung (Mapal Kangjeibung). Chirai Naga Alias Chirai Thangal was hanged on 13th October, 1891 at Central Jail, Imphal for murder of Mr. Melville, Superintendent of Telegraph Department. Kajao Pukhramba Phingang was hanged on 25th May, 1891 at Central Jail, Imphal for spearing to death Mr. Grimwood. Niranjan Subedar was hanged on 8th June, 1891 at Central Jail

The names of persons who were convicted by the British are given at page 144 under Chapter-4: Manipur Kingdom and Kings. The remaining 22 were transported for life to Port Blair, Andaman and Nicober (Kalapani). They undergo conviction at Ross Island and Viper Island. Ross Island is in the heart of Port Blair (10 minutes boat journey from the Phoenix Bay Jetty, Port

Blair), which housed the Government house, Troop Barracks, Cemetery, Church, Hospital, Press, Bakery. Dr. James Pattison Walker arrived at Port Blair aboard the East India Company steam frigate "Semiramis" on 10th March, 1858. He established the infamous and dreaded Penal Settlement with 200 convicts immediately after the First War of Independence, 1857 (Sepoy Mutiny). The infamous Cellular Jail completed in 1906 stood mute witness to the tortures meted out to the Freedom Fighters. Originally it consist of a seven pronged. pucca–coloured building with central tower acting as its fulcrum and a massive structure comprising honeycomb like corridors. Viper Island is a tiny, serene, beautiful island derives its name from the vessel "Viper" in which Lt. Archibald Blair came to the Island in 1789 with the purpose of establishing a penal settlement. This was the island where freedom fighters and dangerous convicts were put in fetters and were forced to work with their fetters on in this island. The ruins of the jail and gallows can be seen in this island.

5.6. TRIAL AND EXECUTION OF OF TIKENDRAJIT AND THANGAL GENERAL

Before the fall of the Government, the Maharaja, Tikendrajit and other leaders left the Palace on 26 April, 1891. They went underground. General Collet announced the occupation of Manipur by the British and ordered the people of Manipur to surrender all arms and ammunition to the British. The British Government issued a proclamation offering rewards for the capturing of the following persons:-

1.	Manipur Maharaja	Rs. 5000
2.	Tikendrajit	Rs. 5000
3.	Dolairoi Hanjaba	Rs. 2000
4.	Zilla Singh	Rs. 2000
5.	Thangal General	Rs. 2000

Niranjan subedar was arrested. Thangal General surrendered on 7th May, 1891. The Maharaja was captured on the 8th May 1891. Angousana and Zilla Singh captured.

Tikendrajit was arrested in the evening of Saturday 23rd May, 1891 (see Plate- 81) from the house of Thokchom Dewan of Singjamei Mathak after a severe struggle by Subedar Khelendra Singh from Cachar. The special court was formed under the presidency of Lt.Col. John Mitchell for the trial of the persons which commenced on 11th May, 1891. The trial of Thangal lasted from 22nd May to 28th May, 1891 and the judgement was announced on 1st

June, 1891. The trial of Tikendrajit lasted from 1st June to 10th June, 1891. The court found Tikendarjit, Kulachandra and Thangal General guilty and passed death sentences on all of them.

The Governor General confirmed the death sentence passed on Tikendarjit and Thangal General and commutted the death sentence of the Maharaja Kulachandra and Angou Sana into one of the transportation for life with forfeiture of property. The order was announced on 13th of August 1891.The two gallows were completed at Pheida Pung by mid-day on 13th August, 1981 and from early morning a crowd of Manipuris commenced to assemble and continued to increase till the time fixed for the execution when it must have aggregated over eight thousand persons, who kept up a wail of lament throughout the whole proceedings. On arrival at the gallows, the prisoners were again informed of the order of their execution and mounted the scaffold. Thangal was too weak to climb the scaffold. He was brought out by Yogendra Singh on his back. But the rope for hanging was found too short to reach his neck. Thangal was asked to raise his head so that the rope could be placed around his neck. Thangal refused to raise his head and burst out laughing. Ultimately, it was adjusted with the help of the officials. The drop fell and the death was instantaneous. The hanging took place at 5 p.m. After haging for one hour, the senior Surgeon A. Coleman examined the bodies and pronounced life to be extinct. Tikendarjit and Thangal General were hanged at the spot where the present Saheed Minar is standing. Tikendrajit was cremated at the Heecham Yaicham Pat at Janmasthan, Yaiskul. Kajao Pukhramba Phingang was hanged unto death for spearing Mr. Grimwood to death. (John Parratt, Saroj Parrat, 1992). Chirai Thangal Alias Chirai Naga was hanged on 13th October, 1891 for killing two Britishers including the Suprintendent of Telephone Department. Niranjan Subedar was hanged on 8th June, 1891 at the Central Jail.

6. ARRIVAL OF CHRISTIANITY

Christianity came to Manipur with the arrival of William Pettigrew in February, 1894. It was the long–cherished dream of the Political Agents in Manipur to convert the tribal population of Manipur to Christianity. The tribals in the hill areas had faith in their animistic rituals. They had a curiosity about a religion of a civilized world. They thought Hinduism was a religion of Brahmins and Pandits only or of those born in high classes.There was a vacuum in religious advancement. The British could recognize this and therefore their policy was to fill this vacuum by introducing Christianity with the idea of transforming the tribal way of life to the Christian way of life. Sir, James Johnstone disclosed this idea "I pointed out that the Nagas had no religion :that they were highly intelligent and capable of receiving civilization that with it they would want a religion and that we might just as well give them our own and make them in that way a source of strength, by thus attaching them to us". The British religious policy was very clear. Their objective was gradual conversion of the hill Nagas and Kukis into Christianity. Christianity was allowed to penetrate the hill areas but indirectly from Imphal. They knew that the princes were staunch Hindus and almost all people in the valley, which constituted the biggest section of the Manipur society had accepted Hinduism.They did not want to propagate Christianity in the valley.

The American Baptist mission in Burma made the first attempt to establish their mission station in Manipur in 1836. But because of the opposition both from the ruling princes of the state and the British Political Agent, no missionary was allowed to enter Manipur. In 1840, Rev. Jacob Tomlin, a former missionary of London Missionary Society in India suggested three places where the Welsh Calvinistic Methodist Foreign Mission Society, Liverpool, could send their missionaries and Manipur was one of them. The unsettled political situation in the state was the main factor which prevented the missionaries from entering it.

William Pettigrew

William Pettigrew came to Imphal on 6 February, 1894 after the Anglo-Manipur war of 1891. When he came to Imphal in 1894, he could speak Manipuri very well. Willam Pettigrew was born on 5 January, 1869 at Edinburgh, Scotland. He had an outstanding talent to learn any language very quickly. He was a member of the Church of England. He left England on 16 December, 1890. William Pettigrew arrived in Silchar, Cachar under the sponsorship of the Arthington Aboriginese Mission Society (named after Robert Arthington, a millionaire at Leeds,UK) in 1891. He learnt "Meiteilon" (Manipuri language). Initially, he was given permission to work in Imphal by the acting Political Agent, A. Porteous by establising a middle school at Imphal (Peettigrew School) on 6 February, 1894. In 1896 he translated the Gospel of St. John into Manipuri and distributed about 500 copies among the Manipuris in the valley. He also translated the Gospel of St. Mathew, St. Mark, the Epistles to the Romans and Corinthians under the sponsorship of the British and Foreign Bible Society.

He wrote some books for his school in the Meitei language. He wrote a Manipuri-English dictionary. He also translated Bible in Meiteilon for the convenience of the British officers and others. Some people lovingly described "Pettigew as a Meitei born in Scotland". During his stay at Imphal, he could convert one Angom Poran Singh, a local Meitei into Christianity and Pettigrew adopted him as his son. Thus a Meitei was the first Christian in Manipur. He shifted his headquarters from Imphal to Ukhrul to fulfil his evangelical objectives at the suggestion of Major Maxwell. In fact he was given an ultimatum by the Political Agent, Major Maxwell to stop his missionary work in Imphal and proceed to Ukhrul. During those days, the Tangkhuls of Ukhrul were strictly following animism. Pettigrew was allowed to work in Ukhrul among Tangkhuls. He opened the first school in the hill at Ukhrul on 10 February, 1897 with 24 boys. He learnt Tangkhul dialect and wrote two books for children in primary classes. Later on, he was joined by U.M. Fox in 1911. The Manipur Christian Association was formed in November, 1917. He also translated the Bible in Thadou and Kuki dialects in Roman script. Later on, with the permission of the Maharaja of Manipur, he changed his mission headquarters to Kangpokpi on 7 November, 1919. In 1926, he published the Tangkhul New Testament perhaps the first in a tribal language in Manipur. The American Baptist Mission declared the whole Manipur hills to be the exclusive mission field for Christian Missionary activities. On 5 February, 1910, Willam Roberts came to Senvon, the biggest Hmar village in Tipaimukh on the invitation of the village chief, Kamkholun. When Willaiam Robert started his activities, H.J. Higgins, the President of the Manipur Durbar sent a Manipuri Lambu with an order for William Roberts to leave Manipur. What had begun at Senvon in the teeth of opposition soon began to have its peripheral mission centres almost throughout North East India. Later on Roberts changed the name of mission into North East India General Mission in 1919.

Beginning of Conversion

When Pettigrew had just started his work, the Arthington Mission stopped supporting him. The American Baptist Mission took over the Manipur field from the Arthington Mission. Pettigrew started a school at Ukhrul. The villagers were angered because of his preaching and enforcement of strict discipline. It was considered to be an infringement on their age old customs and an attack upon their religion. In 1901, after five years of work, 12 boys attending the school were baptized. The Ukhrul Church, the first Christian Church in Manipur was set up. Later on some of his students took upon themselves the task of preaching.

Watkins W. Roberts and Christian mission in southern Manipur

Watkins W. Roberts, a young missionary from Wales, was responsible for the early conversion of Hmars in the Churachandpur district of Southern Manipur. Roberts soon recruited native workers among the new converts for the new Thado-Kuki Pioneer mission at Senvon. William Pettigrew visited Senvon in March 1912. Since only one missionary group was permitted to work in Manipur at that time, Roberts changed the name of his pioneer mission in to the North East Indian General Mission (NEIGM) in 1919. His group spread its areas of operation into the North Cachar Hills, Assam, Tamu, Burma and Tripura. [Lal Dena - Christian Proselytism 1894-1946 - in History of Modern Manipur 1826-1946, p 109, 1991].

Progress of Conversion

The progress of conversion up to 1921 was slow. The converts were mostly young men reading in the school. Afterwards larger groups started becoming Christians. Nearly half of the converts in the state were Tangkhuls alone. The rate of conversion picked up by 1921. So long the converts included individuals but groups and even whole villages came to the fold. The number of schools multiplied so did the converts. The students who came to Ukhrul accepted Christianity during their studies. When they went back to their villages they proclaimed the Gospel among their people. Churches were established in many villages. There were many occasions when the whole family, clan and the village accepted the new faith. The Tangkhul New Testament was published in 1926. The Tangkhuls actively took part in spreading the new faith. They persuaded the neighbouring tribes to become Christians.

The first Kuki Baptist Church was established at Tuyangvaichong village in 1916. Besides people, the village chief also accepted the new faith. The people of neighbouring villages also became Christians. The Kuki Chiefs exercised enormous power and if they accepted the new faith the whole village would accept the same. This paved the way for large scale conversion. When in a village some persons would be converted the adjoining Christians village would send a teacher to organize a Church. The spread of Christianity and establishment of many Churches necessitated the establishment of a mission headquarters. Kangpokpi for its central location and easy accessibility was selected for this purpose. On the completion of the building in 1919 Dr. Crozier moved to this new site. Rev. Pettigrew joined the headquarters in 1921. The missionaries set up a Middle English School, one orphanage, one Lepers asylum and a dispensary. The missionaries learnt the tribal language and communicated with the tribal in their language/dialect. Rev. Pettigrew spoke Tangkhul language and worked among Nagas. Dr. Crozier spoke Thadou-Kuki and worked mainly among the Thadous. The antagonism between the two major groups of tribes namely the Nagas and the Kukis led to the formation of separate associations. The Kukis formed an association of their own unit in 1943, known as the Kuki Christian Organisation to be known later as the Kuki Baptist Association (KBA), with its headquarters at Motbung. This became necessary due to the spread of Christianity among different tribes living in widely scattered areas. Every tribe in its village preferred setting up a Church. In 1954, the Kukis of the North East Manipur so far in association with the Tangkhuls formed a separate association of their own known as the North East Kuki Baptist Association Manipur.

Missionary work in Manipur Zeliangrong area started in 1919. K. Namrijinpou was the first convert among the Zeliangrong. He began preaching among his people. The Kuki Christians also preached among their Zeliangrong neighbours. A Church was organized and a school was opened in 1923 at Sempang, a new Christian village. Two more Churches were established at Sangrunpang and Taobam in 1924 and 1926 respectively. By 1930 there were eight Churches among the Zeliangrongs. After 1928 they were included within the North West Association with the Kukis of that area. In 1947 and 1948, the Kukis and the Zeliangrongs formed separate Associations. Systematic evangelistic work began in Mao area from 1923. Four Mao students studying in the Mission School at Kohima accepted Christianity first. Thus a beginning was made. The first Mao Church was established at Punanamei in 1927. The students enthusiastically were preaching the Gospel in the neighbouring villages and the response was encouraging. In 1930, the second Church was established at Pudunamei. There were cases of hostility and persecutions which slowed down the progress of conversion. The progress picked up by 1950 when there were 1000 Mao Christians and by 1955 their number reached 1411. In 1956 they formed their own association known as the Manipur North Naga Baptist Association.

The Gospel of Christ reached among the Vaipheis of eastern Manipur through the Kukis and the Tangkhuls. The Kuki-Chin tribes reside in the Churachandpur district in large number. The two Vaiphei young men studying in Aizawl accepted Christianity on March 17, 1910 and become the first converts among the Kuki-Chin tribes in Manipur. Rev. Roberts who was working at Aizawl found ample scope of spread of Christianity in Manipur. He set up a

Mission known as "The Chin Thadou Kuki Pioneer Mission". In 1924 he changed the name of the Mission to "The North East India General Mission." The progress of conversion was considerable as by 1931 there were 2478 Christians and by 1948, their number swelled to about 15000. This Mission pushed its work of conversion with full vigour. Churches were established among various Kuki tribes namely Paite, Vaiphei, Kuki, Hmar, Gangte, Zou, Simte etc. "The North East India General Mission is not affiliated with any denomination. They are Presbyterian form of baptism." This Mission celebrated its Golden Jubilee in 1960 and by then there were 26,678 Christians. From 1935 to 1960 there was rapid spread of Christianity. This period is marked by a new awakening. They repented for their past sins. Many families left their household gods and embraced the new faith. This revival made the growth of the Church very rapid. This naturally unnerved the non-believers who were still clinging to their old beliefs on spirits residing in different places. They felt that the preaching of the Gospel was an encroachment on their time-honoured customs and an attack upon the old religion.

During pre-independence days the foreign missionaries had the tacit support of the Political Agent. After all the missionaries were doing good work among the backward people. The Mission was the agency which was establishing schools and spreading not only Christianity but also education. The attitude of the Government was not hostile. But things changed after India became independent. Due to political reasons no new missionaries were allowed to come to Manipur and those already in this state as well as elsewhere found themselves in a peculiar predicament. There were indirect indications that they better leave the country which they did in course of time. "The missionaries left the state in early 1950s. The last missionary family to leave Manipur was Mr. J.S. Anderson, an American Baptist Missionary, stationed at Kangpokpi. He and his family left Manipur in 1954." They left their unfulfilled task to the native converts. Under the changed conditions the Church management fell on their shoulders. Christianity has spread throughout the state. There may be only a few villages where people are still animists. The old people are holding on to their old belief but they are not hostile to the new faith. One comes across a Church in almost every Christian village. The increase in the number of Churches after the 1950s is phenomenal. Most of the major tribes have set up associations for the management of Churches and associated activities. The tribals formed association of their own because they "preferred to hear the Gospel in their own language rather than in Metei-lon. In the associations, the majority tribes often dominate the minorities and the minorities felt they were being ignored. All the tribes had their own tribal consciousness and separate identities."

Most of the tribal converts of Manipur are Protestants. The Churches are self governing and have their Associations. Every three years gathering of these associations known as Convention is organized. The Manipur Baptist Convention (MBC) is the biggest Church organisation. Its administrative headquarters is at MBC Centre Church, Imphal. Each association is affiliated to the MBC directly. There has been maximum establishment of Churches among the Tangkhuls as more than 95 percent of the Tangkhuls are Christians. Besides religious services the Tangkhul Church also establishes schools, handicraft industry, dispensaries, orphanages, youth society, women's society etc. The Maring Naga Baptist Association (MNBA) is one of the affiliated Associations of the MBC. The administrative office of MNBA is at Machi village.

The Kukis are scattered in every part of the state. The Kuki Baptist Convention (KBC) adopts a kind of Presbyterian form of Church administration. The administrative office of the KBC is at D.M. College Road, Imphal. The KBC has constructed a Church building at New Lambulane Imphal. Other Churches are at: Chandel, Churachandpur, Kangpokpi, Tamei, Kangchup Chingkhong and Thinghat.

The Thadou Baptist Association (TBA) looks after Thadou Churches in the Sadar Hills district and Tamenglong district. The administrative centre of TBA is at Motbung. The Bible Society of India has published Bible in both the languages namely Kuki and Thadou. The Chhongthu Baptist Association is smaller than the Thadou Baptist Association in number. Its churches are very scattered.

The South East Manipur Baptist Association (SEMBA) is a multi-ethnic Association. There are six tribes within it namely the Anal, the Lamgang, the Chothe, the Tarao, the Moyon and the Monsang. These except the Lamgang are too small to form an Association for each tribe. The Lamgangs came out of SEMBA and formed the Lamgang Baptist Association with its administrative centre at Thamnapokpi. The Lamgang Baptist Association was recognised by the MBC in 1983. The other tribes followed suit and formed their own Associations namely the Anal Baptist Association, the Moyon Baptist Association, the Monsang Baptist Association and the Tarao to remain in SEMBA because of these two tribes being too small to form Association of their own. The Sadar Baptist Association was established in 1925. A very high percentage (95%) of the population of tribals in Sadar Hills are now Christians.

This Association has seven different tribal groups within it namely the Kukis, the Koms, the Koirengs, the Liangmeis, the Rongmeis, the Tangkhuls and even a few Meiteis. The administrative office of the Sadar Baptist Association is now at MBC Centre Church compound Imphal.

The MBC has relaxed its rules for recognition for associations and accordingly it is now possible even for small tribes to form association and get recognition. The Thangal Baptist Association was recognized by the MBC in 1985. The administrative office of the TNBA is at Yaikongpao. The Zeliangrong Baptist Association (ZBA) is a combination of four sub-tribes residing mainly in Tamenglong district such as Zemei, Liangmei, Ruongmei and the Puimei. The administrative head office of this Association is at Khongjaron near Tamenglong. The ZBA decided to upgrade itself to Zeliangrong Baptist Council (ZBCC) in 1985. This was followed by formation of Association for each tribe. The Rongmei Baptist Association Centre is at Langmei, the Zemei Naga Baptist Association has its Centre at Taosem and the Kabui (Inpui) Naga Baptist Association is at Haochang. The administrative office of the ZBA at Khongjaron is now the Centre of the ZBCC.

There is a slow progress of conversion to Christianity among the Marams. Majority of the Marams till today are animists. The Roman Catholic Church is actively working among them. "The Marams find it easy to become a Roman Catholic Christian because they could continue drinking even after becoming Christians, but to become a Baptist Christian, one has to abstain from drinking and live a pure life."

The Poumai Naga Baptist Association (PNBA) was recognised by the MBC in 1978. The administrative office of PNBA is at Purul Rosufu. The Kom-Hrem Baptist Church Association (KRBCA) is a combination of tribes such as the Aimol, the Chiru, the Koireng and the Kom. The Komhrem Baptist Churches are mostly in Tamenglong, Churachandpur, Chandel and Sadar Hills districts. The administrative office of the KRBC Churches is at Nungshai Chiru Village near Bishnupur. The Chins who migrated from Chin Hills of Burma to Tiddim area of Manipur after the World War II belonged to Baptist denomination when they were in Chin Hills. In the early 1960s they organized themselves in one Association called the Chin Baptist Association. Later on the MBC recognised it as one of the constituent bodies of the MBC. The Vaipheis of Sadar Hills and Ukhrul district organized themselves in one body, the Vaiphei Baptist Association (VBA) in 1976. This Association has its administrative office at New Lambulane, Imphal. The Gangte Baptist Association (GBA) was recognised by MBC in 1980. The administrative centre of GBA is at

Chiengkonpang, Churachandpur. There are some other Associations waiting to be recognised by the MBC.

Another Mission working among the tribes in Manipur is called the North East India General Mission (NEIGM). It is not connected with any church in India. "It functions entirely on its own, aided by funds collected from the Evangelical Congregational Churches in the United States of America". The NEIGM Church in Manipur was divided into different presbyteries according to the dialects. All the different presbyteries work together under the NEIGM. The headquarters of the NEIGM is at Churachandpur.The NEIGM has adopted a new name from 1986 known as Evangelical Congregational Church of India (ECCI).

The Presbyterian Church of North East India started working in Manipur from 1956. the Zou tribe joined the Presbyterian Church and one Presbytery was established in Manipur known as Manipur Gam Presbytery. The Vaipheis and Zous joined the Presbytery. Gradually some other tribes also joined. In 1968 the Vaipheis and the Kukis formed a new presbytery known as the Khuga Sadar Presbytery. Another presbytery was formed by the Zous of the eastern region known as the Manipur East Presbytery. The Kukis formed another presbytery in 1970 named Muollhangphei Presbytery.

There are Churches of other denominations and organisations. The important among these include the Indo-Burma Pioneer Mission (IBPM) which in 1930 adopted a new name called 'Independent Church'. Then, there is the Evangelical Luthern Church, established in 1979. The Roman Catholic Church (RCC) established a centre at Hundung near Ukhrul. The Roman Catholic Church usually accepts in its fold those who are excommunicated by the Baptist Church. It has established schools in many places. The important centres are Imphal, Churachandpur, Sugnu, Hundung, Tamenglong etc. Another Church organisation namely the Seventh Day Adventists (SDA) was brought to Manipur in 1951. The SDA accept the people excommunicated by the Baptist churches. The Mizos who migrated from Mizoram brought the Salvation Army Church (SAC) to Manipur in 1950s. Then there are the Fundamental Baptist Churches, Revival Church of God (RCG), Church of Christ, the Kuki Christian Church (KCC), the New Testament Baptist Churches Association, the Vanmi Devotees and the Zionist Association etc.

Social Life

Conversion to Christianity brought about a great change in social life among the tribal people. They learnt better ways of life and discarded the old customs. The dormitories or separate sleeping houses for boys and girls were no more necessary. According to their old custom, they used to bury the dead in front of the house. But now every Christian village has a cemetery outside the village. They are no more required to observe festivals and taboos. Now they observe Christian festivals-Christmas, Easter etc. They had different kinds of hair styles but now they cut their hair in western style. Earlier they had to marry within their clan and that too a particular relative for example daughter of maternal uncle and the like, whether they loved each other or not. But now this is no longer in vougue. The Church prohibits giving and receiving of bride price. The unmarried younger brother is not bound to marry the widow of his elder brother. The idea of superiority of one clan over the other does not prevail any more. Now all men are equal before the Lord.

"Christian impact is so great that all young people of today do not know the traditional customs, such as marriage, sacrifice, youth organisation and many others." The rice beer does not play the important part. Rather the Church officially prohibits the use of rice beer among the Christians.

Education

The tribal population do not have their own written script. Education was unknown to them. The missionaries for the first time introduced the Roman script. Rev. Pettigrew, Rev. W.R. Robert and Dr. Cronzier introduced the Roman script among the Tangkhuls, the Vaipheis and the Kukis respectively. In 1917 Rev. Robert with the help of Pastor Thangkai published through the effort of Rev. Pettigrew. Subsequently hymn books were published in the language of almost every tribe in Roman script. Of the 29 tribes, 17 have the whole New Testament in their language and 7 tribes namely Lushai (Mizo), Hmar, Paite, Thadou, Kuki, Tiddim Chin, Vaiphei and Tangkhul have the Holy Bible.

The missionaries were the pioneers in the spread of literacy in the hill areas of Manipur. The first primary school was established in Mao in 1893. "On 6th February 1894 Mr. Pettigrew began his work at Ukhrul among the Tangkhuls. In February 1897, 20 boys were enrolled in this school. The tribal people have progressed by leaps and bounds in the field of education after the first schools were set up by the missionaries in 1890s. At present, Bible has been translated into all dialects with Roman scripts. Presently, more than 90% of the hill tribals population are Christians. There are thousands of Churches spread all over the districts (see plate- 272)

Principles of Christianity

Jesus Christ, the founder of Christianity was a Jew. Jesus called himself "Son of God. Jesus preached that the man should have complete faith in God and establish the kingdom of God. The Kingdom of God means the authority of God is supreme in the universe. The first part of the Bible propounds that God is one, eternal, omnipotent and omniscient. The latter half of Bible propounds the notion that God constitute Father, Son and the Holy Spirit. The Bible is a collection of 73 writings. They are divided into two sections. The Old Testament has 46 writings and the New Testament consist of 27 writings. The Old Testament is based on Jewish sources and religious beliefs. The New testament includes personality, history and the preachings of Jesus Christ. (Rajendra Kumar Rajeev, World famous Religions –Doctrines and Sects, Family Books Pvt. Ltd, Putak Mahal, Delhi)

In 312 A.D, Emperor Constantine the Great started the process of Christianity as the State Religion. The Ten Commandments, or Decalogue, are a list of religious and moral imperatives that according to religious tradition, were written by God and given to Moses on the mountain referred to as "Mount Sinai" (Exodus 19:23) or "Mount Horeb" (Deuteronomy 5:2) in the form of two stone tablets. They feature prominently in Judaism and Christianity.

The phrase "Ten Commandments" generally refers to the very similar passages in Exodus 20:2–17 and Deuteronomy 5:6–21. Some distinguish between this "Ethical Decalogue" and a series of ten commandments in Exodus 34 that are labeled the "Ritual Decalogue".

Biblical Origins

The ten commandments were inscribed on what is called "tablets of stone", also referred to as "tablets of testimony" or "tablets of the Covenant", that God gave to Moses. Moses then gave them to the people of Israel in the third month after their Exodus from Egypt.

Table-48 Showing Ten Commandments

From Exodus 20:1-17

1. You shall have no other gods before me.
2. You shall not make for yourself an idol in the form of anything in heaven above or on the earth beneath or in the waters below. You shall not bow down to them or worship them; for I, the Lord your God, am a jealous God, punishing the children for the sin of the fathers to the

third and fourth generation of those who hate me, but showing love to a thousand {generations} of those who love me and keep my commandments.

3. You shall not misuse the name of the Lord your God, for the Lord will not hold anyone guiltless who misuses his name.
4. Remember the Sabbath day by keeping it holy. Six days you shall labour and do all your work, but the seventh day is a Sabbath to the Lord your God. On it you shall not do any work, neither you, nor your son or daughter, nor your manservant or maidservant, nor your animals, nor the alien within your gates. For in six days the Lord made the heavens and the earth, the sea, and all that is in them, but he rested on the seventh day. Therefore the Lord blessed the Sabbath day and made it holy.
5. Honor your father and your mother, so that you may live long in the land the Lord your God is giving you.
6. You shall not murder.
7. You shall not commit adultery.
8. You shall not steal.
9. You shall not give false testimony against your neighbor.
10. You shall not covet your neighbor's house. You shall not covet your neighbor's wife, or his manservant or maidservant, his ox or donkey, or anything that belongs to your neighbour.

7. FIRST NUPI LAL (FIRST WOMEN'S AGITATION -1904)

The following repressive measures of the British authorities caused a great resentment and dissatisfaction about the British rule among the people of Manipur.

1. The British authorities elected a minor boy of hardly 8 years of age to be the King of Manipur. The manner of selection was quite contrary to the wishes and expectation of the people. The people felt that the vacant throne would have to be filled up either by the ex-Maharaja Surchandra or his eldest son of 12 years of age. When the news of selection of the new king was announced, the people were very much disappointed
2. The Officer commanding of the field force issued an order disarming the whole population. The British authorities collected about 400 fire arms. The repressive measures of the British was regarded by the people as a great insult to them

3. The British Officers inflicted various oppressive measures against the people as a sort of punishment for the 1891 episode. Immediately after their occupation, they divided the Manipur standing army into four squads and used them for their work One squad was required to march to Khuzuma, 72 miles from Kohima to bring rations of 4000 mounds for the British troops at Imphal at free of cost.
4. The British authorities used the Manipuris as porters whenever they go on tour to different places of the state without any payment.
5. On 29th April, 1891 war, Major Maxwell was said to have abolished Slavery and Lallup system or forced labour but the British authorities used a large number of people as workers in the construction of Mao-Manipur road without any payment The British authorities proposed to acquire a sum of Rs. 250,000 from Manipur as a token of punishment for the 1891 war.
6. The British authorities proposed to impose a house tax of Rs. 2.00 per house in the valley and Rs 3.00 in the hills.
7. The British authorities decided that Manipur should bear half of the cost of the construction of the Mao–Manipur road and should meet the entire cost for maintenance of the bridle path until the cart road is completed.
8. The economic situation of the state and day to day livelihood of the common people was adversely affected by the Export and Import Policy of the British authorities, the so called "Free Trade Policy".

Under this policy, the British authorities exported thousands of mounds of rice free to Kohima as a resut of which the people of Manipur began to face the problem of scarcity of rice.

When the people were facing such hardship under the British administration, Sanatombi, daughter of ex-Maharaja Surchandra eloped to Major Maxwell by leaving her husband Nongmaithem Manikchand Singh. They traveled together on elephants in presence of huge crowd. After some time, she organized a Raas Lila in the Bunglow of Major Maxwell, which was criticized by the people for violating the norms and traditions of Raas Lila. People felt disgusted and were unhappy. Then after a few days, on Wednesday, the 6th July, 1904, the Khwairamband Keithel containing 28 sheds with seats for 300 market women was completely burnt down. The fire was so quick and it was evident that the fire started in several places at the same time.

In the midnight of 15th July 1904, the State Bungalow occupied by Captain Nuthall, tutor to Raja Churachand Singh and Mr. Dunlop, Assistant

Political Agent, Manipur was burnt down. The fire commenced from the roof of the verandah of the building. In this instance there was positive proof of incendiarism, as a bamboo with an oiled rag attached to it was discovered in the ruins. Police enquiries elicited no clue and the Political Agent and Superintendent of State offered a reward of Rs 500 to any person giving information which would lead to the conviction of the guilty persons.

Meanwhile, the Superintendent of State, Lt. Col. H. Maxwell revived the Lallup System in Imphal town for rebuilding the burnt house. A list showing the Chowkidar's beats in Imphal and a list giving the materials required for rebuilding the house were also enclosed. The Cheirap court was also requested to apportion the work among the several Leikais excepting no one. The Rajbari, foreigners, members of the Panchayat and Cheirap courts and state servants were exempted. The State engineer was instructed to take over the material collected and supervised the rebuilding operation. On the 27th Sept, 1904 some 300-400 Manipuris of Imphal came to the Residency and presented a petition to the Political Agent stating that the order came as a severe blow and it would give a cause to grief and suspicion. Lt. Col. H. Maxwell, the Superintendent of Manipur issued an order dated 28th September 1904. It reads: "I am unable to alter my decision. It is far easier for the people to bring to justice a criminal of this kind than the police and moreover the police have tried hard to detect the offenders.The inhabitants of Imphal have rural police (called Chowkidars) selected by themselves and these men have also failed to arrest the incendiary or incendiaries". "Unless the inhabitants of Imphal carry out the orders to rebuild the bungalow, a punitive police force will be posted in the town and the inhabitants will have to pay monthly the cost of the force". On hearing the result of the petition, the Rajkumars called a series of well attended meetings. He therefore issued a prohibitory order dated 30th Sept "prohibiting assemblies of more than 5 persons in one place for the purpose". But it was of no avail. Over 4000 men had collected by 3 p.m of 30th Sept and the meeting was held just 50 yards from the Sadar Bazar.

The shopkeepers were at once in a state of terror and expected every moment to have the bazar looted and they reported the matter to the Political Agent. He felt that the time had arrived to take measures for the safety of British subjects, and Europeans in Manipur to show the Manipuris that there was a limit to British patience.

He visited the officer commanding of the station and asked him for a force of Sepoys sufficient to overawe the unlawful assembly. He next went to the police lines and told off small guards to attend the houses of the European officers under the civil administration and at the quarter where most of the State employees (natives of India) resided.

He ordered 50 police sepoys to put on their uniform, armed themselves with sticks and proceed at once to the evening bazar. In the meantime the crowd had heard the alarm and assembly sound in the military lines close by, and commenced partly to disperse. As soon as the people saw the force marched in their direction, the movement was much accelerated. When they neared the place of the meeting the people were on the run. On the 30th Sept, 1904, the Political Agent was told by a prisoner and also by a police officer that "some people would attempt to break open and rescue the prisoners in the branch jails in the outskirts of Imphal." He therefore had taken the precaution of marching the prison population of the branch jail into the main jail.

On 5th October, 1904, the Political Agent found some three thousand women had got into the compound. And in a few minutes another two or three thousand arrived and all started shouting anti-government slogans at once. With his two chaprashis and much exertion he managed to silence them and get them seated. The women said that their husbands should not work at the bungalow and as they were the bread earner, the cost of any order he gave would fall on them. Fifteen policemen came to his assistance and shortly afterwards as the women were showing temper, he sent 30 more men and the large crowd remained in front of the Residency shouting and yelling. The political agent noted: "Of course their male relatives had sent them to put pressure on me". After two hours they managed to persuade the women to leave and in doing this Cheirap and Panchayat members offered him much assistance. He reports: "It was very difficult to know how to treat a mob of wild cats like this but I shall take care to disperse them next time before they became numerous".

He noted on 5th Oct 1904- "Arranged to apprehend the seven ringleaders simultaneously by civil police in plain clothes and all cantonment roads and others leading to civil quarter were closed. The Imphal Chaukidars who knew the police by sight were called in to the thana and kept there". Kala Sana, a descendent of Bhagyachandra Maharaja, the ringleader and six others were captured and six were quickly removed to the police thana, the seventh man was left behind as he had suddenly become ill. They were placed in the quarter-guard. The six Rajkumars were Kala Sana, Magazine Singh s/o Raja Nara Singh, Matan Singh, an adherent of Maharaja Surchandra, Chamu Sana, a descendant of the brother of Maharaja Bhagyachandra, Loitam Sana s/o Raja Devendra Singh and Thangokpa Sana s/o Raja Devendra Singh.

The State Engineer informed him that all bamboos required for the bungalow had been brought in that day and on 7th afternoon. The people said that they were cut two weeks ago but the Rajkumars issued orders not to carry them. The Political Agent wrote: "A very simple remedy was accidentally discovered to press back a mob of disorderly women and when applied the crowd at once dispersed. Since the 6th we have had no further trouble". His Excellency, the Viceroy Simla vide Telegram No 3388-EB dated 8th October 1904 informed His Majesty's Secretary of State, London which runs as follows: "On the 1st October the Chief Commissioner of Assam reported that the Manipuris had shown unrest for some time and had adopted a threatening attitude, ending in the assembly of 5000 men, without firearms, on the operance of a detachment of the regulars and police, the assembly dispersed. The disturbance had resulted from the action of the Political Agent. in Manipur in ordering the people to rebuild the Bungalow". The Political Agent in Manipur writes on 5th October that determination to resist authority is increasing and asks for one hundred military police from Kohima for this purpose. These are being sent by the Chief Commissioner of Assam. The trouble is evidently political and the outcome of opposition to the Raja.

On 7th October, 1904,the Cheirap and Panchayat members visited the Political Agent and reported that all trouble was at an end. A bazar with Muhammedan women sellers had been established in the police lines and towards evening many of the Leikais were carrying the bamboos to rebuild the burnt bungalow.

On 8th October,1904 the Cheirap and Panchayat members asked that no damage might be done to the town by the troops. His diary of this day records: "Ruling People all of one class and with a tendency to revolutions like Manipuris can only be undertaken by a strong force and our military garrison of under 450 men all told is too small."

The agitation was led by :-

1. Smt. Irengbam Ongbi Sanajaobi Devi of Naga Mapal, Lamabam Leikai
2. Smt. Leisangthem Kwathabi Devi of Thangmeiband
3. Smt. Irungbam Ningol Leimapokpam Ongbi Dhanbali Devi of Wangkhei Ningthem Pukhri Mapal
4. Smt. Laishram Ningol Juboti Devi of Naga Mapal etc.

In the beginning, the officials used police force against them.(see plate-274) A large number of women also got injured including dislocation of teeth. Facing this kind of situation, the British authorities decided to withdraw the order of reconstruction of the Bunglow. The Women's movement of 1904 was a great success and a great landmark in the history of Manipur (Usham Dhananjoy Singh, the Sangai Express, June 13th, 2006). Seven persons- Meghajit, Kalasana, Thangkokpa, Ngangba Lourung Purel, Sanajaoba, Loitomba, Mantrimayum Chamu were beaten severely on the charge of helping, supporting the Women's agitation. However, the Britishers had realized the might and unity of the Manipuri women for the first time. (N. Joykumar Singh, History of Modern Manipur edited by Lal Dena 1991)

8. KUKI UPRISING -1917-1919

The Kuki Uprising was described in history as Kuki Rebellion. The Kuki Uprising broke out on 7 March, 1917 and ends on 20 May 1919. The Kuki Uprising was the result of protest by the Kuki Chiefs against the Manipur Government's decision for recruitment of another 2000 Kuki labours for the first world war in Egypt.

Before the Kuki Uprising, the hill areas which forms about nine–tenth of the total area of Manipur state with practically no roads with jungle tracts passable only on foot was under the control of the Vice President of the Manipur Durbar. This office had no direct link with the hill people. The hill people only came in contact with "Lambus", who were peons or messengers of the Vice President. This was probably done by the British intentionally to fulfill their hidden agenda of converting the hill tribes into Christians.

Earlier, Raja Churachand had donated Rs. 134,000 as a war loan to the British authorities. In addition to this, the Raja had raised the Manipur Labour Corps with 2000 Nagas and Kukis and they were sent in May, 1917 much against their will to France for digging trenches, carrying loads and building base camps.

This time, the Raja Churachand proposed to recruit another labour corps comprising of mainly the Meiteies and Kukis to be commanded by himself for service in Egypt.The Kuki Chiefs strongly objected to this. Driven by the urgency of the matter, the Political Agent, Mr. J.C. Higgins proceeded to the hills to meet the Kuki Chiefs and sort out the matter. Even after a prolonged discussion, the Kuki Chiefs declined to give the labour force but offered to give money instead. Actually they paid Rs. 1500, three gongs and one mithun as salam. They said that it was a custom for the Kukis to bring the head of the dead men they killed. Frustrated with the outcome of the meeting, the Political Agent threatened the Kuki Chiefs either to give the labour force required or face punishment. On the other hand, Ngulkhup Haokip, Chief of Mombi village and Ngubul Haokip started the Kuki Uprising, 1917-1919.

Ngulkhup Haokip, sent around a message to all the Kuki villages that if they volunteered to send labour force, their villages would be burnt down and their women and children would be killed.

Mr. J.C. Higgins took it as a question of prestige and he proceeded to Mombi (Lonpi) (in Chandel district) along with Capt. Coote Ashwith and Lt. Halliday and 120 sepoys to punish the Kuki Chief on 17 October, 1917. He could not succeed with his mission, so he burnt down the Mombi village to the ground.

At this time, one Chingakham Sanachaoba Singh, who was considered to have possessed supernatural powers and who lived with his disciples at Kumbi spread a rumour that "the Kingdom of British is coming to an end now and wanted its people to be killed with them at the same time".

The Kuki Chiefs were determined even to risk their lives and properties than to give recruits for a labour corps. On 19 December 1917 the Government Forest Station at Ithai was burnt down by the Kukis and later the Ithai Police station near Sugnoo and Moirang Police station were attacked.

There was also a rumour that the Kukis might even attack Imphal about 22 December, 1917 and there was considerable anxiety and tension among the population in Imphal. At one stage, the Mr. Webster, Chief Secretary of East Bengal and Assam said "the trouble is our own making". Being seized of the gravity of the situation, the Chief Commissioner of Assam deputed Mr. Cosgrave to take charge of the Manipur as a Political Agent setting Mr. Higgins free to deal with the rebel Kukis.

The Government began to deploy Assam Rifles and Burma military police in the hills from 22 December, 1917. A detachment of 100 rifles from Kohima moved up the cart road to reinforce the Manipur garrison. Mr. Higgins started his expedition with 150 rifles immediately after Christmas. However, he suffered heavy losses at Ukha. Mr. Cosgrave along with his escort had to return for reinforcement after he was ambushed at Chakpi and he had to be received by a large force under Major Hackett. The Manipuri garrison had to be reinforced with double companies of Gurkhas from Kohima and Sadya. The Manipur garrison provided two columns of 160 rifles, the Naga Hills provided a third column and the Sadya provided a fourth coulmn. The Lushai Hills Battalion provided a strong outpost at Bungmual at the junction of the Lushai Hills, Chin Hills and Manipur state. The British authorities have to divert 800 Naga recruits who had been enrolled for service in France to the Kuki operations.

Mr. Higgins and Mr. Cosgrave moved with two Manipuri coulumns and destroy the Mombi village and other Kuki rebel villages after heavy fighting in January, 1918.

In early February, 1918, Mr. Hutton entered western Manipur hills with Naga Hills contingent to deal with the rebel Kuki villages. However, despite these oppressive measures, the situation was not improving. Mr. Cosgrave in his letter dated 21 Febraury, 1918 to the Government of Assam suggested use of aeroplanes for suppression of the Kuki rebels. A vigorous military campaign was launched with participation of Captain Mounterfierce of the Assam Rifles, Captain Coote, Mr. Higgins and Mr. Hutton. Maharaja Churachand himself went along with the President of the Durbar, Mr. Robert Henderson. The Kuki campaign was directed mainly against the British. The rebels also committed a series of brutal outrages against the surrounding villages for refusing to help the rebels or for providing help to the Brtish. In the next three months, 19 villages were raided with the loss of 193 lives and 26 persons missing. In October, 1918, 20 Kabui Naga villages were raided and burnt with loss of more than 85 lives in retallion against the latter's raid on Natjang Kuki village. The last and final operation was launched from November, 1918 under General Officer Commanding, Burma. Brigadier General Macquoid, D.N.O assisted by Mr. Higgins, ICS. By March, 1918, Pachei, the last of the leading Kuki Chiefs along with his followers were arrested. Mr. Ngulkh Chief of Mombi surrendered at Tamu. Mr. Ngulbul also surrendered. They were taken to the Imphal jail. In the trial that followed Mr. Khupkhotintong Haokip, Commander of the Kukis; Lhukhomang Haokip,Chief of Chassad and Mr. Chengjapao were sentenced to 20 years impronment and another 12 followers were given 15 years imprisonment Subsequently 12 Kuki leaders including Chengjapao Doungel, Lhukhomang Haokip Tintong Haokip were shifted to the cellular Jail of Andaman and Nicobar Island. During the campaign, 400 unlicensed guns were seized.

The Kuki Uprising had a far reaching impact on the administration and management of hill areas leading to reorganization of the hill administration. Mr.Cosgrave suggested to bring the hill administration under the absolute control of the Political Agent whereas the Chief Commissioner recommended placing it under the personal supervison of the Maharaja to be guided by the Political Agent. The Chief Commissioner, in his letter dated 19 April, 1919 to the Viceroy wrote "We must establish British sub-division officers at suitable places in the hills. These men, working under the President would reside in the areas all the year round, open up roads, administer simple justice, set up schools and hospitals and generally act as fathers to the hillmen and restore their confidence in the British Raj. The Viceroy in Council was inclined to accept the proposal. However, the finance department pointed out that the state revenue was not sufficient enough to meet the expenditure. They proposed certain financial concessions to the state - (a) the annual installment of Rs. 60,000 towards the liquidation of the loan of Rs. 250,000 granted to the state in 1917 might be reduced to Rs. 10,000 (b) the annual tribute of Rs. 50,000 payable by the Manipur Durbar might be reduced to Rs. 5000 for ten years (c) the state might be releived for the comtribution of Rs. 30,000 per annum towards maintenance of the Imphal- Mao road (d) there should be a separate budget for hill areas. With these financial concessions, it was hoped that the revenue generated will be utilized for the improvement in the administration of hill ares. Sir Nicholas Dodd Beaton Bell, Chief Commissioner of Assam accompanied by Captain H.R. Harington visited Manipur and declared the decision of the Governemnt of India regarding the financial concessions in the Manipur durbar.

The following changes were made in the administration of the hills areas :-

1. In 1919, C. Crimson, ICS, President of the Manipur State Durbar made a proposal to establish three subdivisions in the hills. Accordingly, in 1920 three new subdivisions–Churachandpur, named after the Maharaja Churachand, Ukhrul and Tamenglong were created. Each subdivision was placed under one European Subdivisonal officer (SDO) directly accountable to the President of the Durbar. Churachandpur was placed under B.C. Gasper, Tamenglong under W. Shaw. Considering the good communication, Mao, Maram, Mombi areas and the various hill tribes surrounding the valley were administered directly from Imphal under the President of the Durbar. Mr. L.L. Pater was appointed as the subdivisional officer of Ukhrul on 1 May, 1921. But the Tangkhul elders filed a petition against him for his immoral character with a girl of Ukhrul. Later a son and a girl was born to her. Mr. L.L. Pater was removed from his post on 31 March, 1922.
2. The President and the SDOs were vested with civil and judicial powers. The President had the power of a District Magistrate and the Sub divisional Officers had the power of a First Class Magistrate under the Indian Criminal Procedure Code of 1898. Appeals against the order of the SDO had to be made to the President and appeals against the order of the President had to be made to the Political Agent. (Lal Dena, History of Modern Manipur, 1991 –page- 126-134)

The portraits of the Kuki Chiefs who led the Kuki Uprising were displayed at the Queen Victoria Memorial Hall Calcutta and British Museum of U.K.

9. ZELIANGRONG MOVEMENT-1930-1949, (JADONANG-RANI GAIDILIU)

The Zeliangrong comprised of three tribes–Rongmei, Liangmei and Zemis.They inhabit mostly in the Tamenlong areas. The Zeliangrong people were deep rooted in their religious and social orthodoxy. There were many taboos and gennas which bound them.Christianity had already arrived in Tamengong and many tribal people had been converted into Chritianity. The British authtorities also imposed a house tax among the hill people including Tamenglong areas. All these measures had created dissatisfaction among the Zeliangrong people in Tamenglong area.

Jadonang

Jadonang, the Zeliangrong leader wanted to save their original religion from the onslaughts of the foreign religion.He also wanted to reform and revitalize the religion of his people. He even introduced some new elements in their religion. He was hardly 25 years of age when he started this movement. He was born in 1905 in Kambiron village, situated on the mountain range overlooking the Barak river. His father, Thiudai and mother Tabollu were simple farmers. Jadonang consulted his followers–mainly Gaidinliu of Nungkao, Lurungpu of Kukti, Takhennang of Cachar, Machunggong and Mudunneng of Kambiron, Namdichung of Gakoklong, Siphai of Bolongdai etc. about what needed to be done. They spread the rumour "the British Raj was coming to an end and the Kabui Raj was to be established in its place". They made a slogan "*Makam Meirui Gwang Tupuni*" meaning his people will become Kings. They made a secret plan for a revolt against the British. They trained the boys and girls as warriors and purchased arms and ammunitions. They learnt to send secret messages, count people in secrecy and call people in code words etc. The girls were taught to sing and dance with political themes. Jadonang was also influenced by Gandhiji's thoughts. When Gandhiji was supposed to visit Cachar in January,1927, Jadonang made a preparation to take 100 boys and 100 girls to present a dance with a song specially composed in praise of Gandhiji. By 1930, Jadonang's plan was well known to all the people in all the villages. He promised "a Naga heaven where there would be no wants–a land of plenty". He instructed the villagers to stop paying taxes rather they would pay tributes to the new kingdom and they would be ready to drive out the foreigners. However, it so happened that four traders from Imphal were murdered in March, 1930 in Kambiron village during the observance of "Dinei" when it was a taboo to admit outsiders into the village and people are forbidden to use fire during this genna day. At night the four traders lighted candles and were cooking their meals at the "parao". The local people took it as a violation of the "no fire genna in the night" and after a scuffle, the four traders were killed by a party led by one Lurungpu of Kukti village. Jadonang was not there on that particular day. He went to the house of one Lotthanang at Nugkao village. Jadonang on his return reprimanded the persons involved in the killing. Jadonang was preparing for a war by the end of 1931 and beginning of 1932. Sir Robert Reid, Governor of Assam wrote in 1931 "reports were received of a serious movement initiated by one Jadonang who set himself in Kambiron in Manipur as a Messiah King of Kabuis and Kacha Nagas". In the mean time, the murder of the four traders was made public. Lurungpu was arrested and he confessed to the crime after much torture. The Government decied to take action against Jadonang for intiating the anti-British movement. Investigations were commenced in February, 1931. Lam Subedar and two Lambus were sent to arrest Jadonang. When Jadonang and Gaidinliu with their followers were returning from a pilgrimage to Pubon (Bhubon cave), one police constable invited him at his house, it turned out to be a trap. Jadonang was arrested on 19 Febraury, 1931 at Cachar. Jadonang was imprisoned in Imphal jail. The report of the Assam Government dated 16 May, 1931 stated "Normal conditions now prevailed again and the idea of a Naga Raj has been dissipated. Jadonang, the instigator of all troubles is now under trial in the court of the Political Agent in Manipur". Meanwhile, repressive measures had been taken against the villages which supported the movement of Jadonang. On 13 June, 1931, Mr. Higgins, the Political Agent sentenced Jadonang to death by hanging. Thus Jadonang was hanged on Saturday, 29th August, 1931 at 6 A.M. on the bank of Nambul river behind the Imphal jail. He was a freedom fighter nibbed in the bud.

Rani Gaidinliu

After the death of Jadonang, Gaidinliu took up the leadership and continued the Jadonang movement as his trusted follower. Gaidinliu was born in Nungkao village on 26 January, 1915 (Thursday). She was the third daughter of the eight children of Lotthomang and Kalotlenliu. Gaidilniu was associated with Jadonang since the age of 13. Gaidinliu told the people "We are the free people, the white men should not rule over us. We will not pay house tax to the Government. We will not obey unjust laws like forced labour and compulsory porterage subscription". (see plate- 273)

She asked to people to preserve the traditional Naga culture. She asked the people to follow "the ARKA" (not impure) system of religion which was a reformed religion of her own people. She popularized the song composed by Jadonang and she used the name "Father of the Nation" in her political propaganda. The people donated money and a large number of young people volunteered for the fight against the British. The British Government became quite alarmed.The Assam Governor in Council ordered the operations against Gaidinliu under the direct control of J.P. Mills, Deputy Commissioner of Naga Hills using the military strength of the third and fourth Assam Rifles, to be assisted by the S.D.O of the North Cachar Hills and the Officer of Manipur. They organized searches for Gaidiliu everywhere. The photographs of Gaidinliu were distributed throughout the three districts of the Barak valley. Harvey, the President of the Manipur Durbar declared a reward of Rs. 200 for the arrest of Gaidinliu, which was subsequently raised to 520. It was further declared that there will be a remission of taxes for ten years to any village giving information about Gaidinliu. On 16 February, 1932, the Zeliangrong Nagas had an encounter with the Assam Rifles in North Cachar Hills In March, 1932, the Nagas again attacked the Assam Rifles outpost at Hangrum. In October, 1932, Gaidinliu moved eastward into Pulomi village and started construction of a wooden fortress, which was likely to accommodate about 4000 people after the pattern of the Assam Rifles barricade at Hangrum. The fortress was not yet ready. In the mean time, Captain Macdonald made a surprise attack on Pulomi village at dawn on 17 October, 1932. Gaidinliu and her followers could not make any resistance and Gaidinliu was arrested. Higgins, the Political Agent sentenced Gaidinliu to life imprisonment. All her followers were also arrested and imprisoned. Gaidinliu spent 14 years in British jails at Gauhati, one year at Shillong jail, six years at Aizawl jail, three years in Tura jail and four years in Meghalaya.She was ultimately released from Tura jail when India became independent in 1947. However, she was refused to return to Manipur and had to live at Yimrap, Mokokchung, Nagaland. Pandit Jawaharlal Nehru came to know of the revolutionary movement of Gaildinliu in 1937 when he visited Assam. He was shocked to learn that a young girl of 20 should suffer so much for the cause of her countrymen. In a press conference, he described Gaidinliu as the "Rani of the Nagas". Since that time, the tile of Rani has been appended to Gaidinliu – popularly and lovingly called "Rani

Gaidinliu" (Gangumei Kabui, History of Modern Manipur–edited by Lal Dena, page- 135)

10. SECOND NUPI LAL (SECOND WOMEN'S AGITATION -1939)

Nupilal-which means women's war in Manipuri- is one of the important movements in the history of Manipuri women. It sowed the new seeds of economic and political reforms for a new Manipur in the early 1940's. The Manipuri women were responsible for production, selling and marketing of food grains including paddy and rice. They managed the household economy and internal trade of food and clothing and they hold a free standard of living in the society. They were the most important buyers and sellers in the main market *Khwairamband Keithel* or Sanakeithel or Imphal Market. They control the market economy.

The Nupilal was started on 12th December, 1939 as an agitation by Manipuri women against the oppressive economic and administrative policies of the Manipur Maharaja and the Political Agent, Mr. Christopher Gimson of the British Government (1933-45) in Manipur, and later on, evolved into a movement for the constitutional and administrative reforms in Manipur.

The immediate causes of the Second Nupi Lal movement were:-

- extensive failure of agriculture of paddy crops due to excessive rain during July–August 1939
- damage to the paddy crops ready for harvesting in November, 1939 due to heavy rain and hailstorm
- mushroom growth of rice mills in Imphal
- heavy export of rice from Manipur to outside particularly to Kohima.
- increasing price of rice and scarcity of rice in Manipur resulting in famine like situation among the people.
- increasing monopoly of rice trade by some Marwari families
- introduction of motor lorries for quick transport of rice from Manipur resulting to rapid increase in the price of rice
- poor harvest of paddy due to outbreak of the World War II in 1939
- stockpiling of paddy and rice by the Marawaris.
- Severe shortage of rice consequent upon introduction of "Free Trade Policy".

The British authorities introduced a Free Trade Policy in Manipur. During 1897-98, they exported 25,230 mounds of rice, which increased to 36,436 mounds in 1898-99. From 1925, the Marwari Traders took over the monopoly of the export industry from the local traders. During 1925-26, they exported 155,014 mounds of rice from Manipur. They started using motor lorries for quick transport of rice from Manipur resulting to rapid increase in the price of rice. Before the motor lorries came to Manipur, most of the major transport of all kinds were by means of bullock, horse or handcarts and local people were able to control the exporting of rice easily. But since the introduction of the motor lorries and the increase of the Marwari Traders, the export policy started changing. The outflow of rice by motor lorries by then had increased substantially, much to unawareness of its limited stock, and hence the price of rice started soaring very high.

1. The export of rice was done under two different systems of tax
    1.1 Land Pass system. Under the Land Pass system, rice can be exported to the Kohima Civil Stations and the Assam Rifles posted in different areas in Assam.
    1.2 Cart System-Under the Cart system, free export of rice was allowed after paying Cart tax and the State could earn a lot of revenue. The mode of collection of revenue was done by an order of the office of the Political Agent. But in 1932, the order was revised and the responsibility of collection of revenue was given to a trading firm on payament of a fixed amount to the government on six minthly installments. This new system helped in the growth, expansion and consolidation of the Marawari business capital in Manipur. The quantum of rice export increased more than double –from 105,285 mounds in 1931-32 to 277,389 mounds in 1932-33. During 1938, the export of rice touched 372,174 mounds causing an economic dislocation affecting the normal day to day life of the people in Manipur.

At the same time, there was a huge quantity of rice at the hands of Marwari and the local women who were traders in rice and paddy were deprived of their means of livelihood.

As a result of these factors, there was a great shortage of foodgrains and the price of rice was increased from four annas per mound to Rs. two per mound and the rice was not avaibale at the market. In the mean time, the Marwari Traders set up rice mills, purchased a large quantity of paddy as much as they could, milled it and exported outside Manipur. All these factors led to immediate outbreak of the women's agitation.

According to the Administrative Reports of Manipur of December, 1939, one Aribam Chaobiton Devi from Terakeithel, Imphal organized a small group of four to five women from her own business circle and tried to stop the bullock carts selling paddy to the Marwari traders. They requested the authorities to stop the Marwari rice mills.

On 13th September, 1939; the State Durbar, in apprehension of the food shortage as rain still continued beyond the usual monsoon season, passed a resolution to ban rice export by denying any license for export to any individual (Lamyanba, 1973). However they had to still commit the export of rice to the Kohima Civil Station in Assam as per agreement to the supply for the battalions of British soldiers. But soon, the rice export was resumed following the Maharaja's order. This reopening of export of rice was directly responsible for creating additional shortage of rice and hence to the outbreak of *Nupi Lal* (Lal Dena, 1991).

As usual, on Dec 11, the women traders had arrived at the *Khwairamband Bazar* to do their business, but there was nobody to sell even a morsel of rice. Totally disappointed, they gathered and were all prepared for an agitation. Meanwhile there was another group of people campaigning against the price-rise of rice. These two groups combined together and started looking for Mayang traders to check if they were buying rice from any local people.

The actual outbreak of the movement occurred on December 12, 1939. On this day thousands of women from market gathered and asked the authority to close down all rice mills. They came to the Durbar (highest Manipuri appellate court, both in civil and criminals) at Imphal petitioning for the immediate ban on the export of rice from the state. While the Durbar was on session, they started shouting slogans: 'Stop the export of rice immediately,' 'Stop the running of rice mills,' etc. The authorities instead of convincing the women decided to take up some repressive measures against the women. While the Durbar Members fled through the back door, but Mr. Sharpe, the President of the Durbar could not escape and had to face the agitated women alone (*Lamyanba*, 1973). Meanwhile, the number of women going on rampage kept on increasing and all directing towards the Durbar Office. When the President told that the order of banning the rice-export couldn't be done without the order of the Maharaja who had gone to Nabadwip on pilgrimage, the women took him to the telegraph office and confined him there till there was a response from the Maharaja. Mr. T.A. Sharpe tried to convince the women for some hours. The women confined Mr. T.A. Sharpe, Major Cummins, the Civil Surgeon, Major Bullfield, Commndant of the 4th Assam Rifles along with some other officials of the Telegraph Office and refused to allow them to go for food.

Seeing the gravity of the situation, the Government started taking repressive measures. At about 2.30 p.m. of 12 December, 1939, a platoon of the Assam Rifles arrived with guns and fixed bayonets. Quite ignorant of the evil intention of the authorities and seeing the military personel coming from a far distance in drill, the women looked with wonder and appreciated the beauty of the military drill (see plate- 272, 273). The women came to know of their evil intention only when the Assam Rifles platoon approached them with bayonets. The women refused to leave in spite of repeated appeal. The women raised their moral by shouting slogans like "Manipur Mataki Jai". There was a clash between the unarmed women agitationists and the sepoys.

The Assam Rifles troops resorted to bayonet charge. About 30 women got injured of which 10 were admitted to hospital. Then a message came from the Maharaja on Dec. 14. But still the women insisted that the Maharaja's message did not give any clear indication of banning export of rice.

Then the women became aggressive and turned their attention toward mill owners. The mill owners had already given their written promise that they would not run their mill further. However, the mills continued to run. In turn, the agitators destroyed some of the mills for violating the agreement. They also decided to boycott the Keithel (bazaar). The boycott of the bazaar became a matter of concern to the authorities since the economy of the state would suffer if women refused to co-operate. The British authorities decided to use repressive measures against women leaders. (see plate- 275, 276). Accordingly, four of the important women leaders were arrested in January 1940 and put them in jail. However, women continued boycotting the bazaar. This agitation was organized without participation of any male member or with any male leadership. Even after this incident, the women used to sleep on the road in front of the lorries to stop the lorries and also to stop the mills.

Political activists like L.Kanhai and T.Ibotombi of Nikhil Manipur Mahasabha started to discuss the issues of the women's agitation. However they could not do much as most of the Members of Mahasabha were not able to do anything in the absence of Hijam Irabot who was away to Cachar by that time. When Irabot arrived on Dec.16th, the *Nupi Lal* entered a new phase as the women received the male support, which were in the dormant state till then. Irabot formed a new political party, Manipur Praja Samelani, as most of the members of Mahasabha did not agree to support the women's movement. Large public meetings were held with Irabot being the principal speaker. But on Jan. 9, 1940, he was arrested under section 124 of IPC on the grounds of inflammatory speeches (*Lamyanba*, 1973). After Irabot's arrest, his followers like Kanhai and others took up the cause of Nupi Lal and organised several meetings. Many people started following a sort of Civil Disobedience by refusing to pay feudal dues and taxes. Thus the movement initiated by the women received active support from their male counterparts at a later stage.

As the boycott of *Khwairamband Bazar*, which started since the outbreak of Nupi Lal, continued almost till the end of the summer of 1940, the economy of the state suffered badly. Facing the situation, the administrative authority tried all means to force or convince the women to attend the Bazar. Mr. Gimson, the political agent threatened the women that if they did not attend the market, he would allot the seat to anyone he liked. The women assured that if their demands are fulfilled, they would attend the market. The Government arrested five women leaders and imprisoned them for six months because of allged anti-government activities. After arrest of these women, the tempo died down gradually.

In August 1940, the Manipuri women filed a petition signed by Kumari, Rajani, Maipakpi, Sanatombi and Nganbi pointing out their main grievances as given below (Sanamani, 1976).

- The unfitness of the Durbar Members,
- The unfitness of the Police Member,
- The illegal action of the Inspector of Police,
- The illegal action of conviction of four women,
- The unexpected police assault on the Public on Jan 14, 1940 and
- The illegal action of Gulap Singh, *Amin.*

Thus, while the original demand of the women was confined to the banning of rice export, their later demands also included the changes of Durbar and Administrative set-up. Thus there is little doubt that *Nupi Lal* which started as a rice agitation against the policy of Maharaja and Marwari monopolies, later evolved into a movement of constitutional, political, and economic reforms in Manipur.

Mr. Robert Reid, the Governor of Assam was convinced that the cause of the Women's movement was the administrative lapse on the part of the Government. He asked the Maharaja of Manipur to make some considerable reforms in the administration of the state and make a determined effort to grapple the situation before it worsened. Mr. Robrt Reid wrote "the occasion for this was the economic grievances arising out of the rise in the prices of rice due to the excessive exports coupled with a genuine fear of a shortage means starvation, because it is impossible to import rice at a price which Manipur can pay. The heavy export in turn were the result of numerous rice mills which have sprang up in Manipur". Mr. C. Gimson linked the cause of the Women's agitation to the administrative lapses. The women's agitation therefore gave a profound impact on the administration of the state and on every aspect of the life of the Manipuris. It sowed the new seeds of economic and political reforms for a new Manipur in the early 1940s.

The agitation came to an end in 1942 when Imphal was bombarded by the Second World War. The 'Nupi Lal' was a great landmark in the history of Manipur. Although the movement was launched by the womenfolk, it broughtforth a constitution and administrative reforms in the region. The boycott of the market certainly convinced the state authorities that the women of Manipur could take up any form of agitation once they were fully convinced of their goal. This was apparent from how the colonial authorities during those days regarded the outbreak as the most important event of the year 1939. (N. Joykumar Singh, History of Modern Manipur edited by Lal Dena 1991)

Mach Leima (Manipuri Chanura Leishem Marup) has initiated to observe this today every year.

11. MOVEMENT FOR A RESPONSIBLE GOVERNMENT –see Chapter-4: Manipur Kingdom and Kings

12. MANIPUR AND WORLD WAR-II

The World War II started on 1st September, 1939 when a German force of 53 divisions supported by 1600 aircraft invaded Poland. During 12-31 January, 1942, the Japanese 15th Army's two reinforced divisions plus air support moved northwestward into Burma from neighbouring Thailand.

At the outbreak of World War II in South East Asia, 70,000 Indian troops were stationed in Malaya. After the start of the war, Japan's spectacular Malayan Campaign had brought under her control considerable of Indian Prisoners of War, notably nearly 55,000 after the fall of Singapore. The conditions of service within the British Indian Army as well as the conditions in Malaya had fed dissension among these troops. Many were used as forced labourers to build the infamous Thailand-Burma railway and the much romanticized "The Bridge over the River Kwai" More than 45,000 Indian and Malay soldiers were asked to shift their loyalties to the Japanese. Many refused and paid the price. From these troops, the First Indian National Army was formed under Mohan Singh Deb and received considerable Japanese aid and support. It was formally proclaimed in September 1942 and declared the subordinate military wing of the Indian Independence League in June that year. The unit was dissolved in December 1942 after apprehensions of Japanese motives with regards to the INA led to disagreements and distrust between Mohan Singh and INA leadership on one hand, and the leagues leadership, most notable Rash Behari Bose. The arrival of Subhas Chandra Bose in June 1943 saw the revival and reorganisation of the unit as the army of the Azad Hind Government that was formed in October 1943. Within days of its proclamation in October 1943, the Government had been accorded recognition by Germany, Fascist Italy, Croatia, Thailand, Ba Maw's Burmese government, and some other Axis-allied nations, as well as receiving felicitations and gifts from the government of neutral Ireland and Irish republicans. The Azad Hind government declared war on Britain and America in October 1943. In the early part of 1944, INA forces were in action along with the Japanese forces in an attaempt to enter India from Burma to achieve the "Freedom of India". In early 1945, the INA's troops were committed against the successful Allied Burma Campaign. The only way to enter India from Burma is through Manipur.

The war broke out in Manipur in 1942. The Japanese army attacked Imphal continuously, and the British and its Allies resisted fiercely. The first bombing of Imphal by the Japanese Tojo took place on Sunday, 10 May 1942 at various localities, namely, Khoyathong, Menjorkhul, Thangmeiband, Chingmeirong, Mantripukhri at Koirengei airstrip, etc. In the south, the Palel/Kakching airstrips were also bombarded. However, the British and their Indian engineers repaired the damages quickly every time. The bombing of Imphal and Manipur valley continued for almost two years. Imphal inhabitants had run away to different villages, which is still remembered as "Japan Lanchenba" or running away from the Japan war. The Japanese army took only two months to proceed from Singapore to Burma, and then the war had become deadlock at Imphal either side not being able to advance. Both the British and Japanese forces had fortified each side with a large number of soldiers and the best in their ranks. The Imphal situation was critical. Fierce fighting continued at the seige of Imphal. The Japanese attacked Kohima, 125 km to the north of Imphal with a small garrison of 3500 and without an airstrip, with their 15,000 strong soldiers via 'Hell's Gate' in order to cut off the Dimapur-Imphal road.

The Japanese quickly advanced to Burma, and their progress was unstoppable. At Myitkyina, the largest town in upper Burma, the Japanese had assembled a strong force with air-strips. Late in 1943, the Japanese command in Burma had been changed. A new headquarters, Burma Area Army was set up under Lieutenant-General Masakasu Kawabe. One of its subordinate formations was 15th Army, whose new commander was Lieutenant-

General Renya Mutaguchi. Mutaguchi had larger ambitions. He planned to exploit the capture of Imphal by advancing to the Brahmaputra River valley, thereby cutting the Allied supply lines to their front in northern Burma, and to the airfields supplying the Nationalist Chinese under Chiang Kai-shek over "The Himalayan Hump".

Mutaguchi's plan was supported by the Japanese Imperial Army HQ in Tokyo.

The only way to enter India from Burma was through Imphal. Therefore, the control of Imphal became the 'DO or DIE' for all sides.

Imphal was held by the Indian IV Corps. The British army and its Indian forces had strongly fortified the Imphal plain and Manipur valley. Airstrips were constructed at Tulihal, Imphal; at Koirengei, north of Imphal and at Palel / Kakching, 45 km south of Imphal at the Moreh-Tamu road. Mutaguchi planned to cut off and destroy the Allied units in their forward positions and then capture Imphal.

- The Japanese 33rd Division under Lieutenant-General Motoso Yanagida would destroy the Indian 17th Division at Tiddim, then attack Imphal from the south.
- Yamamoto Force, formed from units of the Japanese 33rd and 15th Divisions under Major-General Tsunoru Yamamoto, would destroy the Indian 20th Division at Tamu, then attack Imphal from the east.
- The Japanese 15th Division under Lieutenant-General Masafumi Yamauchi would envelop Imphal from the north.
- In a separate subsidiary operation, the Japanese 31st Division under Lieutenant-General Kotoku Sato would isolate Imphal by capturing Kohima, then exploit to Dimapur.

Also, the Japanese assumed that the British would be unable to use tanks on the steep jungle-covered hills around Imphal. For the sake of ease of movement and supply, the Japanese were leaving behind most of their field artillery, their chief anti-tank weapon. As a result, the Japanese troops would have very little protection against tanks if these were in fact used against them.

Even as the Japanese prepared to launch their attack, on March 5, 1944; the Allies launched the airborne phase of the second Chindit expedition. Japanese officers such as Major-General Noburo Tazoe, commanding the Japanese Army Air Force units in Burma, urged Mutaguchi to divert troops from his offensive to secure the Japanese rear areas against the Chindits. Mutaguchi dismissed these concerns, claiming that in a few weeks he would have occupied the air bases from which the Chindits were supplied.

Indian IV Corps in Imphal was commanded by Lieutenant-General Geoffrey Scoones. (IV Corps in turn was part of Fourteenth Army under Lieutenant-General William Slim.) When they received intelligence reports that a major Japanese offensive was impending, Slim and Scoones planned to withdraw into the Imphal plain and force the Japanese to fight with their logistics stretched beyond the limit. However, they misjudged the date on which the Japanese were to attack, and the strength they would use against some objectives. The Japanese launched their troops across the Chindwin River on March 8, 1944. Scoones only gave his forward divisions orders to withdraw to Imphal on March 13, 1944.

The Indian 20th Division under Major-General Douglas Gracey withdrew without difficulty, mainly because two of Yamamoto's battalions from the Japanese 15th Division were delayed at Indaw in northern Burma by the Chindits and were unable to intervene.

The Indian 17th Division under Major-General David Cowan was cut off by the Japanese 33rd Division. The Japanese 215 Regiment seized a supply dump at MS 109, twenty miles behind Cowan's leading outposts. The Japanese 214 Regiment seized Tongzang and a ridge named Tuitum Saddle across the only road, a few miles behind the Indian 17th Division's position.

At Tuitum Saddle, 214 Regiment were unable to dig in properly before they were hit by the Indian 48th Brigade on March 18. The Japanese suffered heavy casualties. Fighting around MS 109 was even more severe, but Cowan had taken steps to secure the most vulnerable point in the rear of his division, the bridge over the Manipur River. 17th Division crossed safely, demolishing the bridge behind them, and recovered the depot on March 25, 1944. They were forced to abandon large amounts of supplies, but removed most of the vehicles, food and ammunition. The Japanese were left only such items as clothing and blankets.

Scoones had nevertheless been forced to send the bulk of his only reserve, Indian 23rd Division under Major-General Ouvry Roberts, to the aid of 17th Division. The two divisions, now supplied by parachute drops from Allied aircraft, made their way back to the Imphal plain which they reached on April 4, 1944.

Meanwhile, Imphal had been left vulnerable to the Japanese 15th Division. The only force left covering the base, Indian 50 Parachute Brigade, was roughly handled at Sangshak by a regiment from the Japanese 31st Division on its way to Kohima. However, an earlier diversionary attack launched by Japanese 55th Division in Arakan had already failed. Slim was able to move the battle-hardened Indian 5th Division, including all its artillery and transport, by air from Arakan to the Central Front. The move was completed in only eleven days. Two of its brigades went to Imphal, and their leading troops were in action on April 3rd, 1944.

From the beginning of April,1944. the Japanese attacked the Imphal plain from several directions:

- 33rd Division attacked from the south at Bishnupur, where they cut a secondary track from Silchar into the plain. Yanagida, its commander, was already pessimistic and depressed by the failure to trap Indian 17th Division. He had also been rattled by a garbled radio message which suggested that one of his regiments had been destroyed at MS 109. He therefore advanced cautiously. By doing so, he might have lost a chance to gain success while the Indian 17th Infantry Division was resting after its retreat and Bishnupur was held only by Indian 32 Brigade (from 20th Division). Mutaguchi removed him from command.
- Yamamoto Force attacked the Shenam Saddle on the main road from Tamu into Imphal. The Shenam Saddle was ideal defensive terrain. Despite using heavy artillery and tanks, Yamamoto could not break through Indian 20th Division's well-sited defences. Detachments from two brigades of the Indian National Army (INA) fought on the Japanese side in this sector. The initial enthusiasm of most INA soldiers soon waned, and they deserted and straggled in increasing numbers.

Fierce fighting continued at the seige of Imphal. The Japanese attacked Kohima, 125 km to the north of Imphal with a small garrison of 3500 and without an airstrip, with their 15,000 strong soldiers via 'Hell's Gate' in order to cut off the Dimapur-Imphal road. This would obstruct the supply of ammunition, medicine, food, water, etc. from the upper Assam plains to Imphal. At the beginning of the battle, 5 April 1944, the garrison held all the hillocks which were in a commanding position above Kohima. But they were pushed back and the Japanese soldiers dug in the higher grounds. The fighting was so close that the district commissioner's garden was divided in the middle claiming alternately by the Japanese and the British, which later came to be known as 'no man's land'. They were not shooting at each other anymore but hand to hand bayonet charges were exchanged. Over 600 casualties were handled by Colonel Young D.S.O., a British doctor and his Indian staff. While Kohima was being attacked, Imphal valley was completely surrounded in all directions by the Japanese army at the hill tops with heavy artilleries. However, at that time, the Japanese had directed their aircrafts towards south in the

Arakan region where British forces are attacking. The propaganda from the British Government to the local people was that the Japanese were invading Manipur and India. Therefore, the INA under Subhash Chandra Bose along with the Japanese army did not receive much help and support they had expected from the natives.

15th Division encircled Imphal from the north. Its 60 Regiment captured a British supply dump at Kangpokpi on the main Imphal-Dimapur road, but once again, the depot had already been emptied of food and ammunition. 51 Regiment seized a vital hill, Nungshigum, which overlooked the main airstrip at Imphal. This was a major threat to IV Corps, and on April 13, Indian 5th Division counter-attacked, supported by massed artillery and the M3 Lee tanks of the 3rd Carabiniers. The Japanese regiment had no anti-tank weapons, and their troops occupying Nungshigum were driven from the hill with heavy casualties.

Manipuri war veterans narrated that two Japanese soldiers disguised themselves as local workers (the British employed a large number of local inhabitants as laborers and housekeepers) and stole an aircraft from the Palel airstrip. The INA used the airplane to drop leaflets narrating that the Japanese and the INA were in fact friends of India and that they were trying to free India from Britain. They had to show the picture of Netaji with Mahatama Gandhi. By that time Manipur already had a large number of followers of Gandhiji's Indian National Congress and they knew about Subash Chandra Bose's earlier role in the Congress Party. Finally, several locals joined INA, and underground movements started. The British army immediately collected all leaflets by offering large sums of money to those who were loyal and would bring it to them. Several members of the Manipur Mahasava and leaders from the hills and plains were rounded up at the Langthabal military camp. Thus, INA led by Netaji Subash Chandra Bose for the first time on 14 April 1944 hoisted the Indian tricolor flag at Moirang, 45 km south of Imphal at Tiddim road. (see plate- 277)

On June 11, 1944, 1st Lt. Walter Duch, Commanding Officer of the 10th Cargo Combat Squadron sent his aircraft to Imphal from Sylhet (235 km to the west of Imphal) on their first mission into combat. Those would be the first combat sorties flown by a Combat Cargo Unit. By that time it was clear that the locals were sympathetic towards the Japanese; so any strategic discussions were to be held in the absence of the local people. The fighting in the valley resulted in several loses. The 10th Squadron had one plane and crew listed as missing. Tokyo Rose - the female voice of Japan's radio propaganda campaign - broadcasted the news the next day and even listed the names of the dead crew members as well as the number of the air plane. The landing at Imphal airstrip was tricky. Although Japanese aircrafts were not a problem since they were fighting in the Arakans, ground firing was continuous from the hill tops. By then the strategies were no longer secret, the Royal Air Force (RAF) fighter aircrafts will circle the valley several times in order to confuse the Japanese artilleries, and the Cargo planes will land quickly on the airstrip below. The air campaign was successful. At last around noon of 22 June 1944 the 14th Army joined the troupe advancing down from Kohima at milestone 109 north of Imphal. By mid-July Ukhrul at the east, a Japanese stronghold between Imphal and Chindwin, was cleared adding to heavy casualties to the Japanese.

At Bishnupur, the Japanese 33rd Division held against the 17th Division (Black Cat) and the fighting was bitter with no side gaining any advantage. To root the Japanese, heaviest artillery was got together and bombarded the Japanese at Ningthoukhong Kha Khunou where the Japanese were at their strongest. It is said that not a single leaf was left on a tree after this action.

By early August 1944, Myitkyina was captured, and the Japanese were loosing at Imphal too. Monsoon was at its peak; heat, mosquitoes, shortage of food supply and ammunition caused a lack of enthusiasm and will power among the Japanese soldiers to proceed further. They were hungry, sick from malaria, and homesick fell upon them. The sick and retreating Japanese soldiers were provided help, food and shelter by local inhabitants of the hills and plains of Manipur. Despite the monsoon British and Allied forces decided to start an advance which could be largely supplied by air since the necessary technique had become highly developed and the RAF had command of the air. One line of progress would be Palel-Moreh/Tamu-Kalemyo and the other would be at Bishnupur-Moirang-Churachandpur-Tiddim.

After six weeks of Japanese seize, the Imphal plain was rescued. On 16 November 1944 the British moved to Moreh near Tamu but the advance was slow towards the Tiddim road because of mine fields laid by the retreating Japanese. Victory in Imphal was in fact the turning point of this war. The Japanese army for the first time was fighting a retreating war but not until many more lives were lost in both sides. After the conquest of the Imphal battle, Lord Mountbatten went to Sylhet and thanked the American Combat Cargo Groups personally. In December at Imphal in front of the Scottish, Gurkha and Punjab regiments General Slim was knighted by the viceroy along with three Corps Commanders, Christison, Scones and Stopford.

World War II ended after the atomic bomb 'Little Boy' was dropped from Enola Gay, the American B-29 Bomber, at Hiroshima on August 6, 1945, and another atom bomb (Fat Man) at Nagasaki three days later. In a true sense, the rescue of Imphal-Kohima could be described as the 'NORMANDY OF THE EAST'. Later after the war, World War II Memorial Cemetries were established both at Imphal and Kohima.

However, the most ignored were those innocent local people who died in this war. The forgotten Imphal-Kohima War will come to life every time you visit these War Cemetries. The burial sites are marked with bronze plaques recording their anguish and sacrifice: 'WHEN YOU GO HOME TELL THEM OF US AND SAY FOR YOUR TOMORROW WE GAVE OUR TODAY' depicts the war in an inscription at Kohima. At Bishnupur, south of Imphal, a Japanese War Memorial was also erected and another for the Indian National Army and Netaji Subash Chandra Bose at Moirang, 45 km to the south of Imphal at Tiddim Road.

The world war-II at Imphal was very costly to the Japanese. Here, 50,000 of the Japanese best soldiers lost their lives.

13. MANIPUR MERGER AGREEMENT : See Chapter-4, Manipur Kingdom.

References

Abdus Sattar, 1971, "In the Sylvan Shadows", Dacca.

Ahmed, Syed. 2002. 'Manipuris Outside Manipur'. *MRFD Bulletin.* Manipur Research Forum. Delhi: Vol. 2, issue 1.

Annual Administrative Report of Manipur, 1868–69, Selectionfrom the Records of the Government of India, Foreign Department, No. LXXVIII.

Atombapu Sarma of Manipur (1967): Religion and Cultural Integration of India

Brara, N. Bijaylakshmi.1998. *Politics, Society and Cosmology in India'sNortheast.* Delhi: Oxford University Press.

Brown, R.. 1873. *Statistical Account of Native State of Manipur and The Hill Territory Under Its Rule.* Calcutta: Office of the Superintendent of Government Printing, 1869.

Burma and Assam Frontier, Kuki Rising, 1917-1919, Resolution on the Late Kuki Rising Extract from the Proceedings of the ChiefCommissioner of Assam in the Political Department, No.8856 P. dated 27 September, 1920.

Burma and Assam Frontier, Kuki Rising, 1917-1919, L/PS/10/724, Orienta and India Office Collections (OIOC), British Library, London

Chaki–Sircar. Manjusri. 1984. *Feminism in Traditional Society: Women of Manipur Valley.* Ghaziabad: Shakti Books.

Chanda, Saswati and Alok Kumar Gupta. 2001. 'Trans Asian Movements and Cooperation in Transportation; An Initiative to Integrate the Asian Continent,' *Third Concept*. August. pp.15–20.

Chaube, S.K. 1999. *Hill Politics in Northeast India*. Delhi: Orient Longman.

Das & Purkayastha. 2002. *Annual Report*, 1999–2000, Ministry of Defence, Govt. of India.

Das, Gurudas. 2001. 'Trade between North Eastern Region and Bangladesh; Nature, Trends and Implications for Development Cooperation,' *Dialogue*. Vol. 2, no. 4. pp. 79–91.

Dena, Lal. 1999. 'The Kuki–Naga Conflict: Juxtaposed in the Colonial Context,' in Kailash Aggarwal (ed.). *Dynamics of Identity an Intergroup Relations in the Northeast India.* Shimla: IIAS. (ed.) 1991. *History of Modern Manipur (1826–194).* New Delhi:Orbit Publishers–Distributors.

Devi, Ksh. Bimola. 1998. 'Women in Social Movement in Manipur,' in M.N. Karna (ed). *Social Movement in Northeast India.* Delhi: Indian Publishing Company.

Don Moser and editors of Time-Life Books, *World War II: China-Burma-India*, (1978), Library of Congress no 77-93742.

Dr. Mohammed Ibrahim Elmasry c/o KW Islamic Association, P.O. Box 823, Waterloo.

Dr. M. Kirti Singh. "Religious Developments in Manipur in the 18th and 19th Centuries" 1982.

Dr. Saroj Nalini Parratt (1980) "Religions of Manipur".

Dr. Lal Dena "History of Modern Manipur" (1826-1946) -1990.

Dubey, S.M. (ed.) 1978. *Northeast India: A Sociological Study.* Delhi: Concept Publishing Company. 106.

Dun, E.W. 1886. reprinted in 1992. *Gazetteer of Manipur.* Delhi: Manas Publication.

Egreteau, Renaud. 2003. *Wooing the General: India's New Burma Policy.* Authors Press. Centre De Sciences Humaines.

E. Nilakanta Singh. "Aspects of Indian Culture" (1982).

Grimwood, Ethel. 1908. *My Three Years in Manipur.* London: St. Chaire.

Ghosh, G.K & S. Ghosh. 1997. *Women of Manipur.* Delhi: A.P.H. Publishing House.

Government of India. *Census of India*, 1954 Assam, Manipur and Tripura, Vol. XII, part II B.

Government of India. *Census of India*, 2001.

Government of India. *Census of India*, Vol. 3, Assam, part II, 1911, 1921, 1931.

Government of Manipur. 1999. *Statistical Handbook of Manipur*, Directorate of Economics & Statistics. Govt. of Manipur, Imphal.

Government of Manipur, *Administrative Reports of Manipur, 1906–07.*

Government of Manipur. *Administrative report of Manipur*, 1939–40.

Government of Manipur. *Tenth Plan Document* (2002–2007). Government of Manipur. Imphal.

Grierson, G.A. 1905., *Linguistic survey of India,* Vol. 3, part 3, Govt. Publication, Calcutta.

Hamilton, Francis. 1807. *An Account of Assam*, Calcutta.

Hodson, T.C. reprinted 1986. *The Meitheis.* Delhi: B.R. Publishing Corporation. reprinted 1996. *The Naga Tribes of Manipur.* New Delhi: Low Price Publications.

Horam, M., (ed.) 2000. *The Rising Manipur,* New Delhi: Manas Publication.

John G. Martin, "It Began at Imphal" The Combat Cargo Story - (1988).

Kshitimohan Sen. "Banglaar Sadhana (Bengali era 1352).

Kirti Chand Tensuba, "An Approach to the History of Meiteis and Thais" - (1993). "Nupi Lan, 1939" *Lamyar.ba*, vol. 5, no 51, December 1973.

Kabui, G.. 1991. *History of Manipur: Pre-Colonial,* Vol. 1. New Delhi. National Publishing House.

Louis Allen, *Burma: The longest War*, Dent Publishing, 1984, ISBN 0-460-02474-4 World War II: China-Burma-India, Bibliography, page 157 http://www.national-army-museum.ac.uk/pages/Second-war/far-east.html

No. 1 Squadron, Royal Indian Air Force, Imphal, Assam, 1944.

http://en.wikipedia.org/wiki/Battle_of_Imphal"

Categories: World War II operations and battles of the Southeast Asia Theatre

Several Internet Sources on World War II:

http://www.sweetbriar.demon.co.uk/burma2.htm

http://billwvb.simplenet.com/ComCar/comcarhome.htm

http://www.cbiinfo.com/stillwel.htm

http://www.cbiinfo.com/cbichron.htm etc.

http://en.wikipedia.org/wiki/Battle_of_Imphal"

www.positivemuslims.org.za

Maisnam, Dhaneswari. 2002. *Political Economy of Underdevelopment: An Enquiry About The Socio-Political Conditions in the State of Manipur.* New Delhi: M.Phil dissertation submitted to the CSSS. JNU.

Maitra, Ramtanu. 2003. 'Prospects brighten for Kunming Initiative,' *South Asia*, Feb. 12, @2003AsiaTimesOnlineCoLtd.

"Manipur Itihasta Nupi Lan" *Lamyanba,* Vol. 5, no. 52, January 1974.

Mohindro, N. 'Import Outweighs Export in Moreh Trade,' *Imphal Free Press.* Mrs. Parratt (Manipur Daily). Imphal: July 15, 1998.

N. Khelchandra Singh "Ariba Manipur Sahityaki Itihas,Manipuri » -1969: North East Sun, 1891, Oct.15-31, 1999: New Delhi.

Wink Caulthardt, 1891, "Races and Tribes of Indo-Chin Region", Dacca Oinam, Bhagat. 2003. 'Patterns of Ethnic Conflict in the Northeast: A Study on Manipur,' *Economic and Political Weekly,* May 24, 2003.

Ontario, CANADA N2J 4C2, "Islam, An Introduction". Undated.

Pemberton, R.B. 1835. *Report on the Eastern Frontier of British India.* Calcutta.

Ried, Robert. 1942. *History of Frontier Area Bordering Assam.* Shillong.

Richard M. Eaton, 1997, "The Rise of Islam and the Bengal Frontier 1204-1760", Delhi.

J.D. Anderson, 1913, "The Peoples of India", Delhi.

R.M. Nath, 1978, "The Background of Assamese Culture", Gauhati.

R.K. Sanhal Singh « Chingthangkhomba Maharah Ganga Chatpa (Manipuri-1972). Ed.

R.K. Jhalajit Singh "A Short History of Manipur -1965.

R.N. Dandekar. "Vaishnavism and Saivism A Fresh look" 1977.

Sashibhushan Das Gupta."Bharater Shakti-Sadhana Shakta Sahitya (Bengali era 1367).

Sachdeva, Gulshan. 2003. 'Fiscal Governance in the Northeast,' *Dialogue*, Vol. 5, no. 4, pp. 53–63, 2000. 'India Northeast: Rejuvenating a Conflict-riven Economy,' *Faultline*, vol. 6, pp.79–103.

Sayyid Abu Al-'Ala Maududi, Islam: Its Meaning and Message, in M. Tariq Quraishi (ed.), American Trust Publications, Indianapolis, Indiana, 1984, 12-14.

Sen, Sipra. 1992. *Tribes and Caste of Manipur*, Mittal Publication, New Delhi.

Sanajaoba, Naorem. (ed.) 1988. *Manipur: Past and Present.* New Delhi: Mittal Publication.

Singh, E. Bijoykumar. 1997. 'Indian Perspective of Economic Development of NE,' *Imphal Free Press.* Imphal: May 29. 1997. 'The Economy of Manipur in the Last Fifty Years,' *Imphal Free Press.* Imphal: August 21.

Singh, Khuraijam Bijoykumar. 2000. *Hinduism Among the Meiteis of Manipur: A Study of Continuity and Change.* New Delhi: M.Phil dissertation submitted to the CSSS. JNU.

Singh, M. Gojendra.1987. 'Brief History of Manipur', *Nehru and Manipur.* State level Committee. Imphal.

Singh, N. Joykumar. 1992. *Social Movement in Manipuir*, New Delhi: Mittal Publication.

Singh, N. Lokendro. 1998. *The Unquiet Valley.* New Delhi: Mittal Publications.

Singh, N. Mohendro. 1999. 'Development Experience of Manipur After 50 Years', *Imphal Free Press.* Imphal: December 14.

Singh, N. Tombi. 1972. *Manipur: A Study.* Delhi: Rajesh Printing Press.

Singh, R.K. Jhalajit. 1987. *A Short History of Manipur,* 2nd edition, Imphal.

Singh, Udai Bhanu 2003. 'Perspective on Myanmar–India Relations,' *Dialogue*, Vol. 5, No. 3. pp.112–23.

Singh, W. Ibohal. 1986. *The History of Manipur,* Imphal.

Sir William Slim, *Defeat Into Victory*, (1956).

Sir John Woodroffe. "The Serpent Power 1974".

Stone, Sir James. reprinted 1971. *My Experiences in Manipur and Naga Hills*. Delhi: Vivek Publishing House.

S.K. Chatterjee. Kirata-Jana-Kriti (1974): Sanamani Yambem. "Nupi Lan: Manipur Women's Agitation, 1939" *Economic and Political Weekly,* 21 February 1976, pp. 325-331.

Sir William Slim, *Defeat Into Victory*, (1956) Don Moser and editors of Time-Life Books, *World War II: China-Burma-India*, (1978), Library of Congress no 77-93742 Louis Allen, *Burma: The longest War*, Dent Publishing, 1984, ISBN 0-460-02474-4.

T.C. Hodson, 1908, "The Meitheis", Low Price Publication, Delhi.

Verghese. B.G 1996. *India's Northeast Resurgent; Ethnicity, Insurgency, Governance, Development*. Delhi: Konark. 2004.

Border Matters More Than Boundaries, From the Northeast.

Looking Out' *Man and Society*, Vol. 1, no. 1, ICSSR, North East Regional

Centre, Shillong: Meghalaya.

Yambem, Sanamani. 1976. 'Nupi Lan: Manipuri Women's Agitation, 1939,'

Economic and Political Weekly, Vol. XI, no. 8, Feb. 21.

Bullough, Vern; *Brenda Shelton, Sarah Slavin (1998). The Subordinated Sex: A History of Attitudes Toward Women. University of Georgia Press.* ISBN 978-0820323695.

Esposito, John *(1998). Islam: The Straight Path. Oxford University Press. ISBN 0-19-511233-4.* http://books.google.com/books?id=-05LGw AACAA J&dq=Islam:+The+Straight+Path.

Freyer Stowasser, Barbara (1996). Women in the Qur'an, Traditions, and Interpretation. Oxford University Press. ISBN 978-0195111484.

Guillaume, Alfred *(1955). The Life of Muhammad: A Translation of Ibn Ishaq's Sirat Rasul Allah. Oxford University Press. ISBN 0-1963-6033-1.*

Haykal, Muhammad Husayn *(1976). The Life of Muhammad.*

Khadduri, Majid *(1978). "Marriage in Islamic Law: The Modernist Viewpoints". American Journal of Comparative Law (The American Society of Comparative Law)* ***26*** *(2): pp. 213–218.* doi:10.2307/839669.

Lings, Martin *(1983). Muhammad: his life based on the earliest sources. Inner traditions international.*

al-Mubarakpuri, Safi ur Rahman *(1979). Ar-Raheeq Al-Makhtum. Muslim World League.*

Maududi, S. Abul A'la *(1967). The Meaning of the Qur 'an. Islamic publications ltd..* http://www.tafheem.net/main.html

Mernissi, Fatima *(originally published 1987 in French, 1991 english translation, Paperback 1993). The Veil and the Male Elite; A Feminist Interpretation of Women's Rights in Islam. Addison-Wesley (now Perseus Books).*

Nomani, Shibli *(1970). Sirat Al-Nabi. Pakistan Historical Society.*

Reeves, Minou *(2003). Muhammad in Europe: A Thousand Years of Western Myth-Making. NYU Press. ISBN 978-0814775646.*

Rodinson, Maxime *(1971). Muhammad. Allen Lane the Penguin Press.* http://books.google.com/books?id= LqR_mU0qpE4C& dq=muhammad +rodinson.

Vacca, V. "Sawda bint Zama ibn Qayyis ibn Abd Shams". in P.J. Bearman, Th. Bianquis, C.E. Bosworth, *E. van Donzel and W.P. Heinrichs. Encyclopaedia of Islam Online. Brill Academic Publishers. ISSN.*

Watt, William Montgomery *(1956). Muhammad at Medina. Clarendon Press. ISBN 0195772865.* http://books.google.com/books?id=qk0n AAAACA AJ&dq=muhammad+medina.

Watt, William Montgomery *(1974). Muhammad: Prophet and Statesman. Oxford University Press. ISBN 0198810784.* http://books.google.com/books?id=zLN2hNidLw4C&dq=muhammad+watt.

http://www.answering-christianity.com/wives.htm

http://en.wikipedia.org/wiki/Muhammad's_wives

Plate -262: Seven Years Devastation (Courtesy-RKCS)

Plate -263: People's angry reaction after the British attack Manipur Palace on24th March, 1891-Courtesy-RKCS

Plate -264: Mr. Grimwood speared to death by Kajao (March, 1891) Courtesy-RKCS

Plate -265: Anniversary of Puran Meithaba

Plate -266: Paona fighhting Khongjom War-1891
Courtesy-RKCS

Plate -267: Cremation Ground of Paona Major at Yumkhaibam Hiden

Plate -268: Paona Memorial at Khongjom

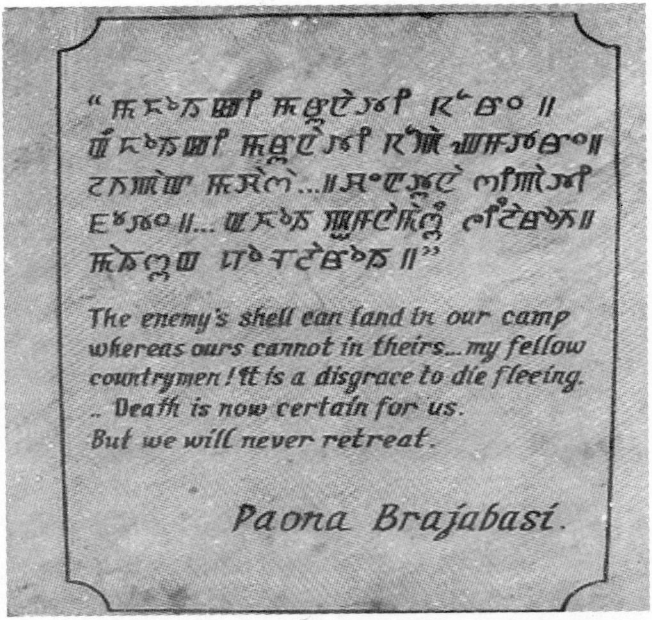

Plate -269: Last words of Major Paona Brajabashi

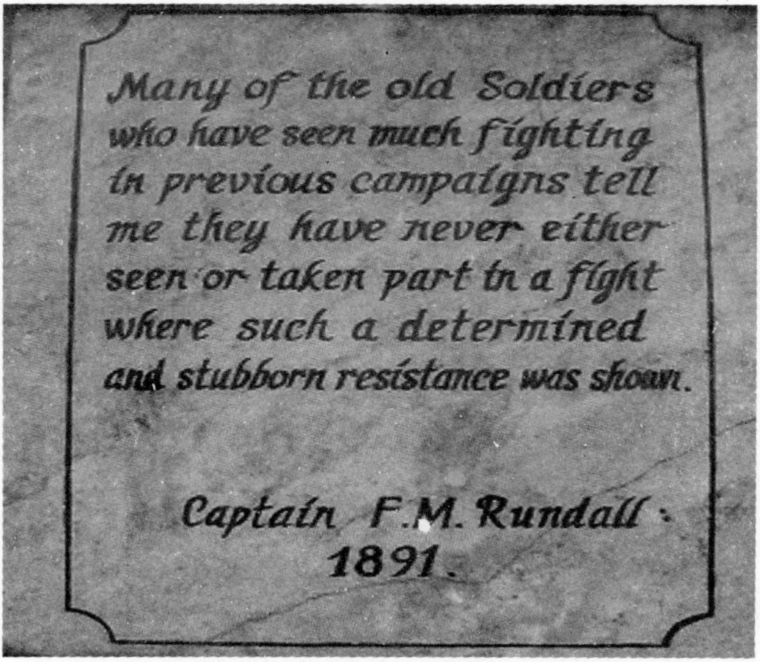

Plate -270: Last words of Capt Rundall on Khongjom War

Figure-271: Giving salute to Paona Major

Plate -272: St. Josesh Cathedral at Mantripukhri , Imphal

Plate -273: Rani Gaidinliu, 1932 (Courtesy- Thames and Hudson)

Plate -274: Scene of First Nupi Lal (1904)

Plates - 275, 276: Scene of Nupi Lal , 1939

Plates - 275, 276: Scene of Nupi Lal , 1939

Plate -277: Statue of Netaji Subash Chandra Bose at Moirang

16

Manipuri Dances

Legends say that discovery of Manipur is the result of the delight the God took in dancing. In fact, the Manipuri Dances has charmed the people all over the world.

Manipuri Dance (Meitei Jagoi) is one of the most beautiful dance styles of India. Manipuri Dance is one of the six classical dance styles of India, the others being *Bharata-natyam, Kathak, Kathakali, Kuchipudi,* and *Odissi*. Manipuri dance is purely religious and its aim is a spiritual experience. Dance is not only a medium of worship and enjoyment but also a door to attain divinity.The people of Manipur are well-known for their high cultural sense. They are very religious minded exclusively attached to Sree Krishna and Srimati Radhika. It is difficult to find Manipuri girl who cannot sing or dance. Not only girls but boys too excel in art and culture. Every Manipuri can dance without making extra effort and considerable time. Manipuri style of dance reflect the vibrant culture of the 31 different tribes of Manipur. A style peculiar to itself, its inspiration is purely religious. Witnessing the exquisite Manipuri dance - drama, in its original colourful settings, is simply an unforgettable experience.

These dances usually relates to :

1. Raas Lila : the love story of Radha and Krishna.
2. Gostha Lila
3. Khamba Thoibi Dance

4. Maibi Jagoi
5. Pung Cholom (Mridanga Dance),
6. Nupa Pala

Other Dance forms for the Tribal have been described in the relevant Chapters.

CLASSICAL MANIPURI DANCE FORMS

The world famous Manipuri Dance is very much distinct from other Indian Dance forms.The Manipuri Dance, whether folk, classical or modern, is devotional in nature. The dances of the Manipur have a high artistic and aesthetic value.

MANIPUR RAAS LILA

The Raas Lila, which is the epitome of classical Manipuri Dance expresses the sublime and transcendental love of Krishna and Radha and the Gopis' devotion to the Lord. It is usually performed in an enclosure in front of the temple throughout the night and watched with a deep sense of devotion by the devotees of Lord Krishna. The Raas Lila is a creation conceived by King Bhagyachandra of Manipur. In the Mandop (arena) attached to this temple, centering around the statue, with his own daughter, Bimbabati playing the role of Krishna's beloved Radha, the first 'Raas Lila' dance-drama was performed on 11th January, 1779 A.D; and it has now become the heritage of Meiteis who perform it yearly. Raas Lila performances are seasonal and varied. It is performed at the Mandop of the temple of Shree Shree Govindajee in Imphal on the nights of *Basanta Purnima, Sarada Purnima and Kartik Purnima* and then at the local temples later on. Raas Lila songs and dances depict the Lilas (Plays) of Lord Krishna as a child with the Gopis (milkmaids) of Vrindavan, and express their yearning for the union with the Lord.

The richness of the costumes gives lustre to the beauty of the art. The *Raas Lilas* are lyrical and have extremely graceful and sinuous movements coupled with light and soft steps, in which the heel practically never touches the ground. As to the composition, the performance is a combination of solo, duet and group dances. This highly stylised form of dance has sublimity, subtlety and grace. The movements are very grandeur and beautiful. The fixation of eyes is to the point of the tips of the fingers. It is fixed only at, not higher than forty five degree above, a distance of about three meters. The artist never looks at any person or audience as a mark of concentration to the Lord surrendering the outward world and illusions of Maya and also giving up all lust, greed, anger, envy, hatred and pride of the Gopis. The steps are very much acute and complex and never show outward feeling of lust and amorous play. Here lies the specific significance of the charms and beauties of the Manipuri Classical Dance, the Raas-Lila of Radha-Krishna in various episodes.

There is no restriction of the number of Gopis in the Raas-Dances. There is also no restriction of the duration of the performance. The Guru and Shutradhari should take as much time as they think it necessary for arousing the feelings of *rasa, raga, anuraga, bhava, bibhava,* etc. within the hearts of the Gopis as well as in the hearts of the audience. The Guru, the Shutradhari and the drum beaters together try to develop and depict the inner idea of the *gunnas* (the qualities of the Lord), the union of the individual selves with the only supreme power of love of Shri Krishna. Waiting for Shree Krishna, calling his name, decorating for this satisfaction are all the important steps sung by the Gopis shedding tears on the chicks.

When one sees the Raas-Lila of Manipur, he will be brought to a far off place in the heaven of Lord, the Creator as the style of the Choreograph, the distinction of the *mudras,* the suitability and beauty of the costumes, and the acuteness of the rhythms are supernatural.

There are different kinds of Raas-Lilas. They are:

1. Maha Raas-to be played on the full-moon day of Mera (October) based on Shrimad Bhagavata Panchyadhyaya.
2. Kunja Raas-to be played on the full-moon day of Hiyanggei (November) based on Brahma Beibarta Purana.
3. Vasanta Raas-to be played in the beginning from the full-moon day of Shajibu (April) to the full-moon of Kalen (May) based on Govinda Lila Amrita.
4. Nitya Raas-to be played on any auspicious day of ten months except Hiyanggei and Shajibu based on Govinda Lila Amrita.
5. Diba Raas-to be played in all months on any auspicious day, based on Govinda Lila Amrita.

While there is 'bhava' (emotion) of Radha's surrender to Krishna, in some, the other's have the theme of Radha-Krishna *"Shrinagar"*, and some depict the *"viyoga"* (separation) of Krishna. These are the themes of Geet Govinda Govindali Lamrita and other *Varnava* literacy works. Typical Raas Lila includes the following steps -

1. Krishna Abhisaar
2. Radha-Gupi Abhisar

3. Arrangement of Mondob
4. Rag-Alap of Gupis
5. Achouba Vangi Pareng
6. Krishna Nartan
7. Radha Nartan
8. Different kind of Dances of the Gupis

The Raas-Lila was performed in the field in its inceptions. Then, it comes to the Mandops. A young boy / girl plays the role of Krishna in the Raas Lila. (see plate- 278, 279, 280). This child seemed to be too young to dance. Surprisingly most of the dancers do not have a formal professional training.

The Maibas, Maibis, the King, the knights, the warriors, the ladies, the females, the girls, etc. are given special seats. But, now again stage performances within a limited, short period have been developed. Thus the technique of the production and presentation have been changed to a great extent. The Raas Lila dance makes a room for appreciating and drinking the nectar of the religious practices towards the truth, the good and the beauty with a complete surrender to the supreme Lord, Shree Krishna.

VASANTA RAAS

Vasant Raas was played on full moon (Purnima) night of Vasant (April – May) at the Royal palace. It has its origin in Brahma Vaivarta Purana and Padma Purana besides the Geet Govindam of poet Jayadeva. In tune with the exuberance of spring, the Gopis play Holi with Krishna. Krishna plays with the rival heroine Chandravali, which causes profound anger in Radha. Ultimately, Krishna had to bow down to Radha begging for her forgiveness. This theme is depicted with great imagination with the introduction of Padavali songs and appropriate dance movements. It takes at least four hours to have the full enactment of the Nritya-Natya called Vasanta Raas.

A Nata Sankirtana (see plate- 281) which starts with invocation to Krishna Chaitanya, must invariably precede any Raas Lila as the entire Lila is supposed to be conceived by Lord Chaitanya. When the *Nata Sankirtana* ends, the *Rasdhari* would play on the pung in *Raag macha,* to be followed by Sutra singing in *Lalit Raag.* Then there is invocations to the Guru and the *Vaishnavas* followed by description of the beauty of Vrindaban. Krishna (played normally by a young boy or girl of about 8 years) would get up from sleep and would go in abhisar in graceful dance movements to Vrindaban through songs in varied talas. He would reach the appointed place and play on the flute standing under the Kalpa tree, with flowers showering upon him from above. The Gopis led by Radha listen to the call of the flute and would start moving with songs and graceful body movements and the feet striking the talas. This is "Gopi Abhisar" when they move towards Krishna who warmly welcomes them with the words – "Listen to the women of Brajavindaban." The Gopis would sing in *Raag-vasant* about the beauty of Vrindaban and then play with the Lord in *talas-Tintal macha* and *Tanchap* in collaboration with the Sutradharis.

This would be followed by *"Bhangi Pareng Achouba"* of rare grace and beauty in movements accompanied by appropriate songs, describing the joy of the play between Krishna and the Gopis. An item of group dance by the Gopis follows, having the theme Roop Varnan led in singing by the Sutradhari normally in tala-Charitala. This is followed by. Krishna's dance steps, which would include a few somersaults also (called mala hunba). A group dance of the Gopis follows and then Radha would execute her graceful movements (see plate-276, 277). Holi khel-play with red powder (aaber) would follow and Krishna starts searching for Chandravali; the rival heroine and plays with her for a while which leads to Radha's profound anger (maan). Krishna, then seeks for Radha. After a frantic search, he would apologize to Radha with the help of the famous lines from *"Geet Govindam"*. Krishna shall literally bow down to her and beg forgiveness, which she grants of course. This is the stage of re-union initial and final reconciliation with the help of the Gopis who have no other interest than pleasing the lord and he is the divine shakti. Then another tala composition with songs- *"Khurumba Pareng"* of delicate movements shall follow. The Sutradharis and the Gopis would then sing a Yugal Prarthana and offer flowers to both. This is followed by prayers and Aarati with flame, when the entire audience shall stand up to join the collective prayer to Krishna and Radha. The Gopies would finally sing home coming *(griha-gaman)* and the Vasant Raas ends here.

CHARACTERISTIC FEATURES OF MANIPURI DANCE

1. The place where dance are held are sacred. It is considered to be a crime or sin to violate the rules. Anytime, anyplace is not good enough.
2. Dances are devotional or ritualistic rather than entertainment of the eyes. It is a Sadhan-Bhakti -kind of devotion to God for both the dancers and onlookers.
3. The dressing is so designed as to free them from any stimulus, excitement to the opposite sex. Dance is but the rhythmic expression of action and activities of life on the upper part of the body.

4. The artist never looks at any person or audience as a mark of concentration to the Lord surrendering the outward world and illusions of Maya and also giving up all lust, greed, anger, envy, hatred and pride of the dancers.
5. The steps of dancing are very much acute and complex and never show outward feeling of lust and amorous play.

TECHNIQUES OF MANIPURI DANCE

The technique of Manipuri dancing is based on an interesting principle of compensatory movement with the objective of achieving rounded movements and avoiding any jerks, sharp edges or straight lines. If the right hand is outstretched towards the right, for example, the body is tilted towards the left in order to offset the right side thrust. The movement towards the right has been balanced and subdued by one towards the left. This particularly contrasts with the technique of Bharata Natyam, in which, in the same example, the effort would generally be to emphasize the movement to the right. It is this aspect which imparts to Manipuri an undulating and soft appearance. This impression of softness actually hides a very tough regimen of body control.

Feet and Hand Movement

Similarly, the feet never strike the ground with a sound on impact, as this would interfere with the delicate flow of the body movements. The knees and ankles cushion the landing so that no sound ensues. Manipuri dancers do not even wear ankle bells, whose purpose is after all to accentuate the beats tapped out by the feet.

The Mudra's or Hand Movements in Manipuri dance are quite different from other classical dance forms.

RAAS MUSICAL INSTRUMENTS

Manipuri Dance is unique among the Classical Indian Dances in that the instrumentation is a central part of the dance, rather than as a side accompaniment. The main musical instrument in Manipuri dance is Kartal or cymbal. Another important instruments is the Dhulok or Pung (mridanga or drum). Dhaulok, Pung, Kartal, Manggang, and Sembung are the soul of Manipuri Sankritana music and Classical Manipuri Dance. It assumes an important ritual character, an indispensable part of all social and devotional ceremonies in Manipur, - the instrument itself becoming an object of veneration. Mandilla, used by the female performers, is similar to Kartal, but different in nature and smaller in size. The musical instrument which is Manipuri's own is Pena, a string instrument which is played by fiddling. The use of Baashis (flute) and Harmoniums are found in Manipuri Dance.

RAAS DANCE COSTUMES

The Raas Dance costumes and ornaments of Sri Radhika and the Gopis are colorful and beautiful. The female dancers wear a dress called "potloi". The Potloi (skirt the present day Raas dancers wear) is modeled on the one the Maharaja Bhagyachandra (1763-1798) saw in his dream. The costumes in Manipuri dance is very colorful, attractive and very richly bedecked. The lehenga is called "Kumin" with mirrors and zari work intricately woven into beautiful designs. It is layered with a transparent silk or "Pasuan". The choli is also embellished with zari, silk or gota embroidery. On the head, covering the face, they wear a transparent odhni, through which the expression and emotion on the face of the dancer can easily he seen. Gopies usually wear a red dress while Radha stands out in green attire. The male dancer, who is Krishna, wears a saffron (Gold coloured Muga/ Endi) dress.

Here is list of costumes and some terms related to the costumes and ornaments used in Manipuri Dance :-

- **Potloi** : Raas costume of Sri Radhika and the Gopis, designed by the Potllloi-setpa's who rent them for the performance at some rates.
- **Koknaam** : A gauze at overhead, embossed with silver Jari.
- **Meikhumbi**: A transparent and thin vail thrown over the head.
- **kumin:** An embroidered brightly colored silk skirt.
- **Pasuan:** A short flair of silver gauze over the kumin.
- **khaon:** Rectangular embroidered piece with belt.
- **koktumbi:** Cap covering the head with tapering end.
- **Thabret:** A griddle round the waist.
- **Khangoi:** Small rectangular belt over the Pasuan.
- **Leitreng**: Golden ring round the head.
- **Chura**: Made of peacock feathers, wired on top of head.
- **Pheijom:** Dhooti, a saffron dress (Gold coloured Muga/ Endi)
- **Khongjee** : Ornament for the foot.

THE EARLY PERIOD OF MANIPURI DANCE

A copper plate inscription credits King Khuiyoi Tompok (154-264 A.D) with introducing drums and cymbals into Manipuri dance. Maharaja Bhagyachandra (1759-1762 and 1763-1798 A.D.) codified the style, composed three of the five types of Raas Lilas, the Maha Raas, the Basanta Raas and the Kunja Raas, performed at the Sree Sree Govindajee Temple in Imphal during his reign and also the Achouba Bhangi Pareng dance. He designed an elaborate costume known as Kumil. The Govindasangeet Lila Vilasa, an important text detailing the fundamentals of the dance, is also attributed to him.

Maharaja Gambheer Singh (1825–1834 A.D) composed two parengs of the tandava type, the Goshtha Bhangi Pareng and the Goshtha Vrindaban Pareng. Maharaja Chandrakirti (1850-1886) a gifted drummer, composed at least 64 Pung choloms (drum dances) and two parengs of the Lasya type, the Vrindaban Bhangi Pareng and Khrumba Bhangi Pareng. The composition of the Nitya Ras is also attributed to him.

MANIPURI DANCE IN MODERN TIMES

This genre of dance became better known outside the region through the efforts of Rabindranath Tagore. The world poet was fascinated with the lovely and charming Manipuri Raas Lila at Machhimpur, a Bishnupriya Manipuri locality in the Sylhet District in Bangladesh in 1919. Rabindranath Tagore, the world poet, was a great patron of the Manipuri dance and culture. He immediately decided to open a new department of Manipuri Dance in his Shantiniketon University in Calcutta. He invited Guru Budhimantra Singh to Shantiniketan University. In 1926, Guru Naba Kumar joined the faculty to teach the Raas Lila. Other celebrated Gurus, Senarik Singh Rajkumar, Nileshwar Mukherji and Atomba Singh were also invited to teach there and assisted Tagore with the choreography of several of his dance-dramas. It was an epoch making event in the history of Manipuri Dance and within a decade in crossed its regional as well national arena and became a reputed international style. From 1919 to 1941, when the poet Tagore died, several Manipuri teachers served as faculty members at Shantiniketan, and gradually Manipuri dance became well known in Calcutta, then later Ahmedabad and other parts of India. He deserves a honorable place in the style and regarded as the "pioneer of Manipuri dance and culture". It was he who popularized the style with its high zenith among the people of the world. Guru Naba Kumar went to Ahmedabad to teach Manipuri dance in 1928. Soon, Guru Bipin Singh popularised it in Mumbai. Amongst his pupils, most well known are the Jhaveri sisters, Nayana, Suverna, Darshana and Ranjana.

In 1954, the Manipur Dance College of Imphal (renamed Jawaharlal Nehru Manipur Dance Academy in 1957) started with three great exponents of the genre in its faculty; Guru Amubi Singh, the principal, Guru Amudon Sharma and Guru Atomba Singh. Later Guru Bipin Singh became the principal of the Sri Sri Govindaji Nartanalaya (later renamed Manipur State Dance College) in Imphal: Kalavati Devi and M.K. Binodini Devi are the alumni of this institute. In 1972, Guru Bipin Singh, the Jhaveri sisters and Kalavati Devi founded Manipuri Nartanalaya in Mumbai, Kolkata and Imphal, and Rajkumar Singhajit Singh founded Manipuri Nrityashram in New Delhi.

The traditional Manipuri dance style embodies delicate, lyrical and graceful movements. The aim is to make rounded movements and avoid any jerks, sharp edges or straight lines. It is this which gives Manipuri dance its undulating and soft appearance. The feet movement is viewed as part of a composite movement of the whole body. The dancer puts his or her feet down, even during vigorous steps, with the front part touching the ground first. The ankle and knee joints are effectively used as shock absorbers. The dancer's feet are neither put down nor lifted up at the precise rhythmic points of the music but rather slightly earlier or later to express the same rhythmic points most effectively. The musical accompaniment for Manipuri dance comes from a percussion instrument called the Pung, a singer, small cymbals, a stringed instrument called the pena and wind instrument such as a flute. The drummers are always male artistes and, after learning to play the pung, students are trained to dance with it while drumming. This dance is known as Pung cholom. The lyrics used in Manipuri are usually from the classical poetry of Jayadeva, Vidyapati, Chandidas, Govindadas or Gyandas and may be in Sanskrit, Maithili, Brij Bhasha or others.

GOSHTHA LILA

The "Gushtha Lila" Dance also known as Sansenba is a group dance performed by a group of boys, wearing colorful dresses and ornaments dedicated to Lord Krishna. The theme of the dance that is described in the Mahabharata where Lord Krishna dances with his mates. The performers are generally young boys in the age group of four to five years. Stories detailing Krishna's childhood pranks are performed in *Goshta Lila*. The rendering of these stories combines divine inspiration with a lively spirit of fun. Sri Krishna's game, association with the pastoral boys, Yosoda's love for her son, The coming of sage Narada to the palace of Nanda and teaching Krishna and Balaram how to milk and graze the cattle are invariably shown. Then the Gopas go to tending cattle with the permission of their parents. When they start playing, two demons come to kill Krishna and Balaram by the order of Kamsa. The Roles of Nanda, Yosoda, Rohini, Narada and his disciples are performed by the elderly people. This play celebrates the story of Krishna through dance that is obviously derived from the older forms, but is more stylized, and altered considerably by the wearing colorful dresses like Pheijoms or Dhotis, Churas, Koknaams, Litrengs and Khobols. This highly stylised form of Dancing has sublimity, subtlety and grace.

KHAMBA THOIBI DANCE

Khamba Thoibi dance is a duet of male and female partners dedicated to Lord Thangjing of Moirang. (see plate- 282) This dance was once performed by Khamba and Thoibi, the hero and heroine of the Moirang in the Moirang Kangleiron. The dance tells the story of Khamba, a poor brave lad of Khuman clan who fell in love with Thoibi, a princess of Moirang. In 15th century AD, Khamba, a prince of the previously routed Khuman Royal family fell in love with Thoibi - a princess of the Moirang clan. The union have been to the political advantage of both Khumans and Moirangs; but the Moirang Chief resisted on purely personal grounds. The result was tragic for the young lovers.

This dance is a part and parcel of Moirang Lai-Haraoba. It is believed that the legendary hero-Khamba and heroin-Thoibi danced together before the Lord Thangjing, a celebrated deity of Moirang for peace and prosperity of the land.

The Khamba–Thoibi Dance, the "Maibi" dance (Priestess dance) and the "Leima Jagoi", form the "Lai Haraoba" dance. The "Lai Haraoba" dance, in many ways, is the fountainhead of the modern Manipuri dance form.

MAIBI DANCE

The Maibi dance is usually performed during the festival of Lai-Haraoba which is an annual ritual festival of the Meiteis (see plate-283). The Maibis, the priestesses considered to be spiritual mediums, trace through their dances the whole concept of cosmogony of the Meiteis and describe their way of life. Beginning with the process of creation, they show the construction of houses and various occupations of the people to sustain themselves. It is a kind of re-living of the way of life of the past. The Maibi holds such items as breath-taking ceremony of the God on the bank of a river, summoning its spirit in an earthen pot through nine threads and seven threads for God and Goddesses, dance of the Maibis holding the leaves of sacred plant called Langthrei between fingers.

PUNG CHOLOM

Pung Cholom may be in the form of the Mridanga dance or Dhumel or Drum dance. (see plate-284) Pung or Manipuri Mridanga is the heart and soul of Classical Manipuri dance. Without Pung or Manipuri Mridanga, no Manipuri Sankritana ceremony or no social and devotional ceremonies is possible. Pung Cholom is performed as an invocatory item preceding the Sankirtana and Raas Lila.The Pung Cholom is a vibrant Drum Dance, in which dancers play on the drum known as Pung while dancing with thrilling leaps and turns to a fast rhythm. It demands acrobatic abilities. There is the interplay of intricate rhythms and cross rhythms with varying markings of time from the slow to the quick with graceful and vigorous body movements leading to ecstatic heights. It is highly refined classical dance feature characterized by the modulation of sound from soft whisper to a thunderous climax. There is the interplay of intricate rhythms and cross rhythms with varying markings of time from the slow to the quick with graceful and vigorous body movements leading to encaustic heights. It is performed either as an integral part of Nat Sangkirtan (Pala Kirtana) or independently. As a part of Pala, it is performed by two players but as an independent dance at least 14 players follow the sequence of Pala Kirtana with about 40 complicated talas and Sanchars. The Maharajas in earlier days patronized this art. In fact many of the Maharajas are good Mridanga players.

NUPA PALA

Nupa Pala which is otherwise known as Kartal Cholom or Cymbal Dance is a characteristic of the Manipuri style of dance and music. The initial movements of this dance are soft and serene, gradually gathering momentum. It is a group performance of male partners, using cymbals and wearing snow white ball-shaped large turbans, who sing and dance to the accompaniment of Mridanga, an ancient classical drum "Pung" as it is called in Manipuri. The Nupa Pala acts as a prologue to the Raas Lila dances, besides an independent performance too, in connection with religious rites.

Sankeertan came as a logical development of *keertan*, the system of congregational singing brought to Manipur by missionaries from Bengal. It involved singing, dancing and chanting to the accompaniment of drums and cymbals. It did not take long for the Manipuri community to develop the *Sankeertan* into an art of dignity and great intensity. The dance can be performed solo or in a group. In *Kartal Cholom*, the dancers strike large metal cymbals adorned with trailing maroon tassels. The dance in this form is simpler than the *Pung Cholom*. Along with the dance, the cymbals are wielded and played gracefully.

FAMOUS MANIPURI DANCE GURUS

Most notably, King Bhagyachandra's daughter Bimbabati Devi (plate-64) was the first to perform the role of Radha, the heroine of the Raas Lila. Among Manipuri Dance Gurus (Reverend Teachers) Guru Maisnam Amubi Singh (plate-285) ranks top. He may be rightly called the "Father of Manipuri Dance and style". He was awarded with a number of the prestigious awards and titles. He has the past four decades with his disciplines. Guru Haobam Tomba Singh (Plate-286), Guru Takhel Changbam Amudon Sharma (Plate-288), Guru Singhajit Singh (Plate-292), Guru R.K. Priyogopalsana (Plate-287), Guru Bipin Singha (Plate-290), Guru Sagolsem Kalidamon, (Plate-291) Guru Brajabashimayum Thakurdon Sharma, Khaidem Lokeshwar Singh, Gurumayum Ibopishak Sharma, Guru R.K. Sanayaima Singh, Guru Sorokhaibam Naran Singh, Kongrailatpam Radhamohon Sharma, Ksh. Thouranishabi Devi are some of the famous Gurus. They are the Gurus who have spread the beauty of Manipuri dance all over the world and have been honoured both nationally-internationally on this subject and thus brought glories to the Manipuri community.

All of them have their dancing tours to England, America, Russia, Australia, Japan, Germany, Italy, France, Hongkong, Thailand, Bhutan, Srilanka etc. and earned great name and fame for their style. Among non-Manipuri dancers, the names of Preeti Patel, Savita Mehta, Sruuti Banerjee, Tamanna Rahman. In Bombay the famous performers and teachers are the Jhaveri Sisters - Nayana, Suverna, Darshana and Ranjana Jahveri.

The Javery sisters from Mumbai has contributed a great deal in the field of Manipuri dance and culture. They continue this tradition in their institution 'Manipuri Nartanalaya.

Some of the Gurus have got their Dance Colleges, institutions in Delhi, Mumbai, USA and other countries.

Some of the international performers of Manipuri dance are Guru Amubi, Guru Bipin Singh, his wife Kalabati Devi, Guru Singhajeet and his wife Charusheela, (see plate–283), Guru Surjaboro Sana, Guru Nileshwar Mukharjee from Bangladesh and Guru Senarik Rajkumar. The present noted Manipuri dancers of India and Bangladesh, as well as international fame are Hanjaba Guru Bipin Singha, Guru Chandrakanta Singha - Nartanachrya, Guru Nilmadhab Mukharjee, Guru Haricharan singha, Bibhaboti Devi, Kalabati Devi etc.

References

Ashim Kumar Singha/ Ksatrya, Sylhet, 2001.

Bidhan Sinha / Cultural Heritage of North-East India, 1999.

Dr M. Kirti Singh / Religious developments in Manipur in the 18th and 19th century, 1980.

Dr. Kirti Singh/ Religion and Culture of Manipur, 1st edn, Delhi, 1988.

Faubian Bowers / The Dances of India, NY 1st edition, 1953.

Gayotri Chatterjee / *Bharoter Nritokola.*

Goswami . O/History of Indian Music, Bombay 1961.

Kashiram Das -The Mahabharata of Vyasa, translated to Bengali by S. K. Das / A study of vedanta, C.U. 2nd edn, 1937.

Lila Rao / Manipuri dances.

Manipuri Rasleela Udyapan Parisad, Bangladesh / Suvenir, 1996.

N. Tomba Singha / Bhakti Rasa Numbumari, Imphal, 1st edn, 1969.

Nripendralal das / Sribhumi sylhete Rabindranath.

Projesh Banerjee / Dance of India.

Pandit Sena singha / Prachinadhunik Samkhipta Manipurer Itihas.

Pouri, 3rd issue, Sylhet, 1995.

Ragini Devi / Hindu Dances.

Raj Mohan Nath / The Background of Assamese Culture.

S. Kiranaswami / Musical Instruments of India.

Snigdha paul / Nritta-Norto-Natya.

Singha, Mahendra Kumar / Manipurer Prachin Itihas.

S. K. Das / A study of vedanta, C.U. 2nd edn, 1937.

Snigdha Paul / *Nritta-Norto-Natya* .

Sharma, Atombapu & Singh, Amubi / A Brief description of Manipuri dance, 1960.

Singha, Uttam Kumar/ Pouri, 3rd issue, 1995.

Swami Jyotirmayananda (1986). The Srimad Bhagavad Gita, translated in English by The Mahabharata of Vyasa, translated to Bengali by Kashiram Das.

S. K. Das / A study of vedanta, C.U. 2nd edn, 1937.

Tarun Kumar singha / Manipuri Nritya Probesika, 1968.

The Srimad Bhagavad Gita, translated in English by Swami Jyotirmayananda (1986).

The Mahabharata of Vyasa, translated to Bengali by Kashiram Das.

W. Ibohal Singh / The History of Manipur, Imphal 1986.

Zavhori, Darsana / Tala Sastras of Manipur.

Web sites :-

http://manipuri.20m.com/

http://manipurinfo.tripod.com/

http://www.mythinglinks.org/asia~india~dance.html

http://manipuri.20m.com/

http://manipuri.freehomepage.com

http://manipuri.org/, http://www.connectindia.com/manipuri.htm

http://www.mythinglinks.org/asia~india~dance.html

Complete Manipuri Dance Site in the web:

http://manipuri.20m.com/

http://manipuri.freehomepage.com

http://manipuri.org/

http://www.webindia123.com/dances/Manipuri/manipuri.htm

http://www.narthaki.com/manipuri/manipuri.htm

India Times: Manipuri - Mystery And Grace

http://www.connectindia.com/manipuri.htm

Plate -278: A popular Krishna Dancer

Plate-279: Krishna with Radha

Plate -280: Krishna with Gopis

Plate-281: Nata Sankirtana

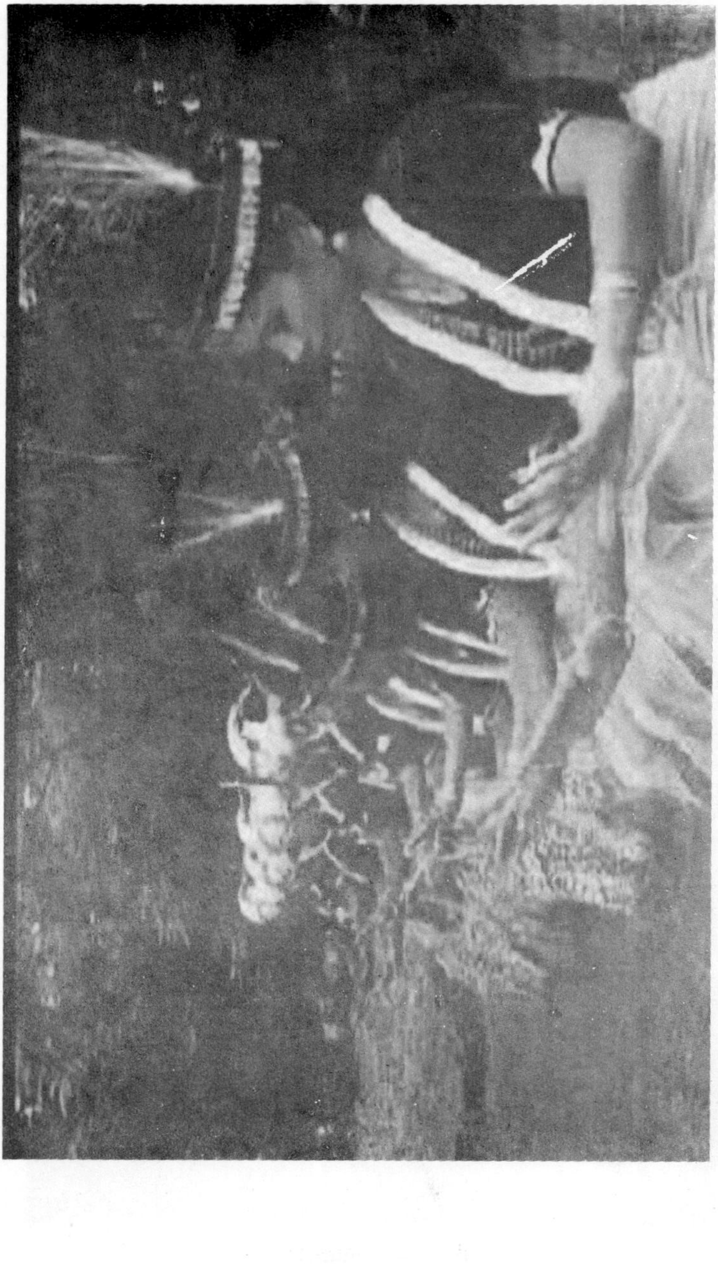

Plate -282 : Khamba Thoibi Dance

Plate - 283 : Maibi Jagoi

Plate - 284: Pung Cholom

Plate-285: Guru Maisnam Amubi Singh

Plate-286: Guru Haobam Tomba Singh

Plate- 287: Guru R.K. Priyogopalsana

Plate-288: Guru Takhel Changdram Amudon

Plate-289: Km. Savita Mehta (1921-2006)

Plate - 290: Guru Shri Bipin Singh, surrounded by his disciples

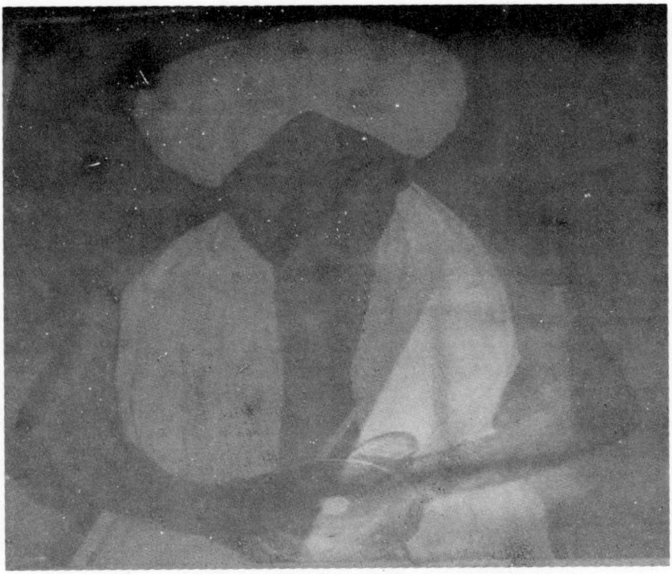

Plate- 291: Guru Sagolsem Kalidamon

Plate- 292: Guru Singhajit and his wife Charusheela,

ENCYCLOPAEDIA OF MANIPUR

ENCYCLOPAEDIA OF MANIPUR

(In 3 Volumes)

(Volume-3)

DR. KHOMDON SINGH LISAM

Encyclopaedia of Manipur

ISBN: 978-81-7835-864-2 (set)
ISBN : 978-81-7835-867-3 (Vol. 3)

Published in 2011 in India by
Kalpaz Publications
C-30, Satyawati Nagar,
Delhi-110052
E-mail: kalpaz@hotmail.com
Phone : 9212729499

Laser Type Setting by: Rudra Computer Graphics, Delhi
Printed at : Chawla Offset Printers, Delhi

Contents

17. Games and Sports in Manipur 816

• Beginning of Sports movement in Manipur • Sports Personalities of Manipur during Maharaja Churachand's Reign • Olympians from Manipur • Arjuna Award Winners • Other Sports Stars • Indigenous Games of Manipur • Mukna (Manipuri Wrestling) • Mukna Kangjei (Khong Kangjei) • Yubi Lakpi • Woolaobi • Hiyang Tannaba • Arambai Hunba • Kang Sanaba • Thang-Ta:

18. Sagol Kangjei (Polo) 846

• Sagol Kangjei (POLO) • Origin of Sagol Kangjei (Polo) in Manipur • Pana Sagol Kangjei • Manipur Sagol Kangjei during British Period • World's first Polo Club was established at Silchar in 1859 • Manipur Polo spread to other parts of British India • Manipur Polo Game spread to other parts of the World from 1868 • Manipur Polo Game spread to Malta in 1868 • Manipur Polo Game spread to England in 1869 • Manipur Polo Game spread to Argentina in 1873 : • Manipur Polo Game spread to Australia in 1876 • Manipur Polo Game spread to USA in 1876 • Manipur Polo Game spread to France in 1879 • Polo Players of Manipur during 19th Century • Languages of Polo Game • Chronology of development of Polo • History of Polo from other countries of the world

19. **Handlooms, Handicrafts and Textiles** 880

• Legends • Historical Background : • Modern Handloom and Handicrafts : • Handloom Population and Production • Textiles of the Meiteis • Design and embroidery used in Meitei Textiles • Textile of Nagas • Textile of Tangkhuls • Textile of Kabui Nagas • Textile of Hmars • Textile of Kukis • Textile of Paites • Pottery in Manipur • Cane and Bamboo works • Kouna Craft

20. **All Districts of Manipur** 909

• Imphal East District • Imphal West District • Thoubal district • Bishnupur Distrcit • Churachandpur District • Ukhrul District • Senapati District • Tamenglong District • Chandel District

21. **Indo-Myanmar Border Trade** 968

• Indo-Myanmar Border Trade • Present Status of Indo-Myanmar Trade Route through Moreh • Volume of Indo-Myanmar Trade • Volume of Trade through Moreh • Measures taken up by the Government of India / State Government • Potential areas of exports from Manipur to Myanmar • Potential areas of Import from Myanmar to Manipur • Tran-Asian Highways • Kunming Initiative

22. **Why Invest in the State?** 981

• Why Invest in the State? • Industrial Policy of Manipur • Package of Incentives • New Industrial Package for the North-East • Development of Industrial Infrastructure • Transport Subsidy • Fiscal Incentives • Relaxation of PMRY norms • Other Incentives • Procedure for release of assistance under the New Incentives. • Industrial Scenario of Manipur • Spinning Mill • Bamboo and paper industry • Silk and Tasar Industry • Industrial Corporations • Manipur Food Industries Corporation Ltd. • 200 TPD Cement Project in Manipur • Serpentinite and Idocrase Processing Industries • *Manipur Traditional Liquor Plant* • *Integrated pineapple Concentration Plant* • *Bamboo shoot Fermentation* • Medicinal plant Processing Industry. • Floriculture • Information Technology (IT) • Power Sector • Horticulture: •

Pottery • Business Opportunities • Agriculture • Tea • Yongchak • Medicinal Plants • Rice Flake (Chengpak) • Banking and Finance • Pineapple • Ginger • Manipur Traditional Liquor • Mushrooms: • Bamboo and Bamboo shoots • Rubber: • Identification of Feasible Industrial Projects in Manipur • Market Potential • Fruit Processing • Cane and Bamboo Production Project • Kouna Crafts Production Project • Orchids • Black scented rice • Proposed Projects

Appendix-1 : British Political Agents / Officers in Manipur
Appendix-2 : Instrument of Accession
Appendix-3 : Standstill Agreement
Appendix-4 : Govnors of Manipur
Appendix-5 : Chief Ministers of Manipur
Appendix-6 : Speakers of Manipur
Appendix-7 : Glossary
Appendix-8 : Index

Index 1113

Volume - 3

17

Games and Sports in Manipur

BEGINNING OF SPORTS MOVEMENT IN MANIPUR

Manipur is known as the land of sports. Considering the tiny size of the state, it has produced many Olympians, international and national level sports competitors.

Football is the most favourite and most popular game in Manipur. Football (Soccer) was first introduced in 1899 by Rev. William Pettigrew, the then teacher of the Johnston School. At the turn of the century, the Johnston School Football team was formed followed by a second one known as Maharaja team under the patronage of Maharaja Sir Churachand Singh. No organized tournaments were conducted prior to the First World War except frequent friendly matches among the Paltan Team, the Johnston School Team and the Maharaja Team. The Paltan Team was composed of some British Officers and Gurkha sepoys. The players of those days played bare footed. However, some of the players of the Paltan Team played with their boots on.

Sir Churachand Singh, KCSI, CBE (1891-1941), the Maharaja of Manipur was the founder patron of modern sports movement in Manipur. It was at his initiative that hockey, cricket, athletics, badminton, tennis, tennikoit etc.were introduced and popularised in Manipur. In1935 he sent a cricket team to Shillong and played matches against European Clubs there. He was also the founder president of the Assam Olympic Association. He sent a contingent of sports persons from Manipur at the First Olympic Games held at Jorhat in 1940. Manipur was the champion team winning most of the events including hockey. He groomed many promising sports persons under his personal supervision at the nicely maintained playground at his palace compound. He freely distributed sports goods to the schools and donated generously all types of sports equipment and materials not only in Manipur but also in Assam.

In 1920 Shri Phoni Mukerjee, a Bengali settled in Manipur, along with a few local youths formed the Manipur Town Club. It was under the banner of this club that organized tournaments mainly football and hockey at Kalimai ground (at present 1st Bn. Manipur Rifles ground). At his initiative, Manipur participated in the Bidhumukhi Knock-out Football Tournament at Lumding in Assam in 1933 and won it.

The entire expenses of the participation in the said tournament were borne by Maharaja Churachand Singh. Nine Cup, Jabar Memorial and Under Five Feet tournaments were some of the football competitions conducted by Manipur Town Club between 1935 to 1941. Manipur Town Club also ran "Yakairol Hockey Cup" donated by Dr. N. Leiren Singh regularly during the same period. Olympic movement in Manipur began with the formation of the Manipur Olympic Association in 1947 with Shri RK Madhurjit Singh and Shri N Binoy Singh as the founder President and Secretary respectively. In 1947, Manipur participated at the All Assam District Football Tournament at Shillong and won the team championship. Many ethnic groups including Meiteis, Tangkhuls, Kukis and Kabui represented the Manipur Team.

The Association conducted Olympic games regularly up to 1954. With the amalgamation of the Manipur Olympic Association and the Manipur Sports Association (Estd. 1948) under a new name, All Manipur Sports Association(AMSA), the later became the sole controlling body of all sporting activities in Manipur. The All Manipur Sports Association (AMSA) continued the annual Olympic game since 1955 under a new name of 'Manipur State Games'.

The Sports movement at the collegiate level began with the participation of the colleges of Manipur in the Guwahati University Annual Sports Festival since 1955. Outstanding sports persons from Manipur used to represent Guwahati University at the Inter-university tournaments until the foundation of the Manipur University in 1980. The Director of Education (U), Manipur successfully organized Annual Inter College Sports Festivals from 1988 to 1990 but discontinued since then. The Manipur University Sports Board is now confined to its activities mainly in organizing tournaments in a few selective disciplines with the help of the affiliated colleges of Manipur.

The pioneering works of Shri Indramani Singh in the field of body building, weight lifting, gymnastics, boxing etc. from around the year 1950 will ever be remembered by future generations. He also founded the Manipur Man Building Institute in 1953 with the help of other sports promoters - Shri L Manaobi Singh and Shri S Gambhir Singh and organized a sports extravaganza at Imphal in 1955, featuring Mr. and Miss Manipur contest in addition to most of the disciplines of modern Olympic games. A team of well-trained boxers from Calcutta was invited for an exhibition bout with the local boxers during the sports meet. The activities of the institute faded away mainly due to opposition from the AMSA, the then controlling body of sports and games in Manipur. A great landmark in the history of sports movement in Manipur is the rapid process of decentralization of sports administration breaking away one after another from the nucleus body, AMSA from the late seventies onwards and forming various State level Sports Associations affiliated to its corresponding apex federations at the national level. However, the AMSA still remains as the sole heir to all the assets and properties pertaining to it without its former sports activities. Manipur Women's Football Association formed in 1976 and affiliated to the Women's Football Federation of India is now under the aegis of the All Manipur Football Association since 1991 as per directive from the FIFA. The strong and sturdy women footballers from Manipur earned a big name by representing nine of its players at the 13th Bangkok Asiad Women's Football Team of India. Within a decade of its formation in 1976 the Manipur Hockey Association produced two Olympians-Shri P Nilakamal Singh (1984) and Shri Ksh Thoiba Singh (1988) and World Cup winner Shri L Tiken Singh (1986). In the women's front also Ksh Tinggongleima Chanu and W. Surjalata Devi were the silver medallist at the 13th Bangkok Asiad Women's Hockey Championship, 1998. The Manipur Olympic Association was again formed in 1976 and got affiliated to the Indian Olympic Association. Gradually State level sport associations affiliated to it began to swell in numbers. About 40 state level associations both in Olympics and non-Olympics events are now functioning in Manipur for the promotion of its respective disciplines. The Manipur Olympic Association in collaboration with the Government of Manipur organized the 5th National Games at Imphal in 1999. Other spectacular achievements of the sports persons of Manipur is their outstanding performances - both in the national and international level - in events like arm wrestling, Sepak Takraw, veteran athletics, trampoline. Tae-kwondo etc. Arjuna awardee from Manipur. Former Mr. India Shri N Maipak Singh participated in the Mr. Universe contest in Paris in 1972 and secured the 8th position in world ranking. Miss Kujarani Devi became a household name in India by her consistent performances in weight lifting for more than a decade in international competitions. She is also a recipient of the Rajiv Gandhi Khel Award of 1996. Ng. Dingko Singh won gold medal in boxing in the 13th Asian Games held in Bangkok.

In 2002, Manipur became the team champion of the Santosh Trophy (Football) by defeating Kerala in the final match. Regarding the Women's football, Manipur has no parallel. Out of 16 championship held so far in India, Manipur was the champion in 14 tournaments and secured second position in two tournaments.

Cricket was considered to be a dull game in Manipur and people started taking interest in Cricket only after seeing its daily coverage in the national TV network. Now-a-days young cricketers have utilized every available space in their surroundings as cricket grounds. Cricketers from Manipur will now be getting the much-awaited opportunity for exposure to big matches consequent upon the granting of associate membership of Manipur Cricket Association to the Board of Cricket Control in India in 1998. (Courtesy: S Lokeshwor Singh, Vice- President, Manipur Hockey Association)

SPORTS PERSONALITIES OF MANIPUR DURING MAHARAJA CHURACHAND'S REIGN

1. Kadachung (Cricket, also a good band player) from Keisamthong Kabui Khul
2. Abung (Cricket) from Keisamthong Kabui Khul
3. Khakhong (Cricket) from Keisamthong Kabui Khul
4. Azona (Cricket) from Keisamthong Kabui Khul
5. Thingom Thanil
6. Laishram Yaimabi Subedar
7. Gokul Singh, Jamadar
8. Maibam Iboton
9. Haobam Ibochouba
10. Akoijam Mani
11. Khomdram, Dhanachandra
12. Khaidem Kunjabi
13. Laishram Gourahari
14. Rajkumar Madhurjit Singh (Grandson of Bir Tikendrajit, Tennis)
15. Rajkumar Birchandra
16. Maharajkumar Lokendra (Tennis)

17. Huidrom Tombi Subedar (Meghachandra)
18. Purno and Khansa (Tennis)
19. Maibam, Samden
20. Maibam Tamra Singh
21. Laisram Gourahari
22. Maibam Iboton

(M.K. Binodini, Churachand Maharja gi Imung, 2008)

OLYMPIANS FROM MANIPUR

Since 1984, Manipur has been consistently a part of the Indian Olympic Team. The famous Olympians from Manipur are :

1. P. Nila Kamal. He was the first Olympian from Manipur. He represented India in the Olympic Games held at Los Angeles, 1984 as a goal keeper of the Indian Hockey Team (see plate- 302).
2. Ksh. Thoiba Singh : Thoiba represented Indian Hockey Team in the Olympic Games of 1988 held at Seoul,. South Korea. Thoiba was a forward hockey player.
3. Ngangom Dingko Singh -He represented India as a boxer at the Sydney Olympic in 2000. Dingko won the gold medal in the Bangkok Asian Games in 1998 in the bantamweight category. He is also Arjuna Award Winner (1998). The Government of Manipur named one street in honour of him.
4. Th. Sanamacha Chanu - Sanamacha represented India as a weight lifter. She won gold medals in the World Police Games in 1999 and the Asian Weightlifting Championship in Japan in 2000. In the 2002 Commonwealth Games in Manchester, England, Sanamacha won three gold medals. She got 6th position in the Sydney Olympic in 2000. She also represented India in the Athens Olympic Games in 2004. She is also Arjuna Award Winner (2000).
5. S. Suresh Singh – He represented India in Boxing at the Sydney Olympic in 2000.
6. L. Brojeshwori Devi-Borojeshwori represented India as a Judo player at the Sydney Olympic in 2000.
7. N. Kunjarani - Nameirakpam Kunjarani (see plate- 304) won bronze medals in the Asian Games in Beijing in 1990 and Hiroshima in 1994. She went on to win the gold medal in the Commonwealth Championships held at Nauru in 1995 in the 48-kilogram category. She represented India as a woman weight lifter in the Olympic Games at Athens in 2004 and secured fourth position. She also won Gold Medal for India in the

48 kg. category in the Melbourne Common Wealth Games in 2006. She is also first Arjuna Award Winner (1990). She was also awarded the prestigious "Rajiv Gandhi Khel Ratna Award" in 1996.

8. Laishram. Bombayla Devi represented India at the Beijing Olympics in archery in 2008.

9. Th. Tombi Devi represented India at the 2008 Beijing Olympics in Judo in 2008.

Three officials namely 1. Khoibi Salam Manager (2008, Beijing –Boxing) 2. Kh. Gunamani Singh, Coach (2008-Judo) and 3. Y. Budhachandra Singh observer, IOA (2008, Beijing) represented India at the Beijing Olympic 2008.

ARJUNA AWARD WINNERS

1. N. Kunjarani Devi (1990, Weight Lifting)
2. N. Dingko Singh (1998, Boxing)
3. Ksh. Tingongleima Chanu (2000 Hockey)
4. W. Surjalata (2003,Hockey)
5. Sanamacha Chanu (2000, Weight Lifting)
6. M.C. Merrycom(2003, Boxing) (see plate-305)-The boxing queen Mangte Chungneijang Merykom (aka Mary Kom or MC Merykom) won a silver medal at the AIBA World Women's Boxing Championship in USA in 2001 The next year she won the gold at the Second AIBA World Women's Senior Boxing Championship in Turkey in the 45-kg division. In 2003, she was honored with the Arjuna award. In November 2006 at the AIBA World Championships at Talkatora Indoor Stadium in New Delhi, she again won the gold in the 46-kg division.
7. Anita Chanu (2004, Judo)
8. Khumukcham Tombi (2007, Judo)

OTHER SPORTS STARS

Shri Sanayaima (won- the title of Champion of Champions title as Mr. India).

Oinam Bem Bem Devi (won- the title of Women Footballer of India, 2001).

Kumari Rameswari Devi (won the title of Best Sportspersons in the 31st National Game held in Punjab.

Waikhom Surjalata Devi lead the Indian Women Hockey Team as Captain in Commonwealth Games, Afro-Asian Games etc.

Tomba Singh was declared as "Best Footballer of the year" by the All India Football Federation.

Borun Yumnam won the Mr. India title at the 4th Senior National Body Building Championship in the 70 kg category.

Shyam Sharma the Mr. India title at the 4th Senior National Body Building Championship in the 90 kg category.

M.C. Merrycom won Gold Medal in the 46 kg category in the Women's Third World Boxing Championship held at Podolk, near Moscow in December, 2005 (see plate-305).

Yumnam Renubala Chanu won Gold Medal in 58 kg. category in the Women's Weightlifting event in the Melbourne Common Wealth Games in 2006

Laishram Monica Chanu won silver medal in the 69 kg category in the Women's Weightlifting event in the Melbourne Common Wealth Games in 2006 (see plate-306)

Imom Chanu, (Women's Hockey), Sangai Chanu Ibemhal, Deepmala Devi (Athletics- Walking Race), M. Suranjoy (Boxing) also participated at the Melbourne Common Wealth Games in 2006.

Thrice World Boxing Champion, MC Mary Kom and Gold Medalist L. Sarita on November 26th 2006.

Thokchom Nanao, World Boxing Champion, Gold Medalist, 2008 (see plate-307)

Kishan, Mr Asia Junior for 2007 (see plate-308)

Dr. Ngangbam Shantikumar, second at the 42nd Men's Senior Asian Body Building Championship held in Hong Kong from 16th to 21st July 2008. (see plate- 309)

Hmangte Parneichong Kom claimed 3 Gold Medals at The Youth Asian Weightlifting Championship at Amman, Jordan from Oct 28th to Oct 30th 2007 (see plate-311)

Kh. Pradeepkumar, Living With HIV(Brand Ambassador of MACS) bagged Bronze Medal 55 kgs category at the 9th Mr. India Inter-Sate Federation Cup Body Building Championship at Kerala from Jan 16-18 2009. (see plate-312)

L. Sarita Devi grabbed the "Best Boxer Award" in the 11th SRM-Federation Cup boxing Championship, held at Kattankulathur, Tamil Nadu on 14th July, 2007 (see plate-303, 313, 314)

Mayengbam Suranjoy won the Gold Medal at the Asian Boxing Champion -2009 held in China 7-13 June, 2009). (see plate-310).

After the successful hosting of the National Games at Imphal in 1999 and proper installation of the modern infrastructure at the Khuman Lampak Sports Complex, Imphal, the performance and the standard of Manipur sports in the national arena is considerably enhanced.

Table-49 Showing Manipur's Position in the National Games

Event	*Year*	*Venue*	*Manipur's Position*
1st National Games	1985	Delhi	14th Position
2nd National Games	1987	Kerala	14th Position
3rd National Games	1994	Maharastra	9th Position
4th National Games	1997	Karnataka	9th Position
5th National Games	1999	Imphal	1st Position
31st National Games	2001	Punjab	3rd Position
32nd National Games	2002	Hyderabad	4th Position
33rd National Games	2006	Assam	2nd Position

There are many famous footballers from Manipur like Renedy Singh, Gunabir Singh, Kiran Kongsai, James Singh and Tomba Singh who have made their mark on the national football scene. Tomba Singh was adjudged the AIFF's Player of the Year in 2003. Somatai Shaiza, or "Soso" was another famous footballer from this state. Among women hockey players Ksh Tinggongleima Chanu and W. Surjalata Devi were members of the silver medal winning team at the Bangkok Asian Games in 1998.

Manipur retained the Senior Women's National Football Championship title in 2007 beating Bengal. Manipur has totally dominated women's football in India. In the 33rd National Games in Guwahati, Assam in February 2007, Manipur came second in the final medals tally with 51 Gold medals ahead of other bigger states like Kerala, Punjab, Haryana, Uttar Pradesh, Karnataka, Madhya Pradesh, Tamil Nadu, Orissa etc.

In Manipur, Games and Sports are becoming an employment avenue for the young players. More than 500 sportspersons of Manipur are at present either employed outside the state or employed by various reputed clubs, institutions and agencies outside the state in various disciplines like Football, Hockey, Weight Lifting, Tae-Kwondo, Archery, Boxing, Gymnastics etc.

INDIGENOUS GAMES OF MANIPUR

The muscular race of Meitei is known for their games. The Mukna, Mukna Kangjei (Khong Kangjei), Sagol Kangjei (Polo), Yubi Lakpi, Woolaobi, Hiyang Tannaba, Arambai Hunba and Thang –Ta are some of the indigenous games of Manipur.

1. MUKNA (MANIPURI WRESTLING)

Mukna, generally regarded as one of the manliest of sports has been popular among the Manipuris from time immemorial. (see plate-293)

Mukna, is the Manipuri style of wrestling played between two male rivals for trial of physical strength and skills. The game is played between two rivals of the same physical built, weight and age. It has got fundamental rules and regulations. There are specific techniques such as Ningong (Hip throw) to left and right, Longkhrou (specific throw by twisting opponents calf) left and right, Khudong (throwing the opponent by raising him high), Khu–Theibi, Chepching, Kaplak Koibi, Heibongkabi, Ngakthi Chappa, Suptek, Chaokot etc. For each of the specific techniques (Lous), there are also counter Lous.

The person who never got defeated by his rival is known as *"Mukna Jatra"*. He is respected in the village and he will train other Mukna players. In the earlier days, Mukna competitions were controlled and organized by the *Pana Loisang* of the Ruler of the state and village organizations. There were four Panas-Ahallup, Naharup, Khabam and Laipham who control all fixtures and time for the games and State Meet in which final is invariably graced by the Ruler and presents the Title of Jatra (Champion) for the year along with reward of Thum Nama (a full bag of salt) and Ngabong Phi (clothe made of cotton), exemption of all state duties and Ningham Samjin dress (traditional head gear of Khamba). The game has two categories (1) Takhatnabi (League), (2) Naitom (Knockout). The young talents work and play all the year round with dedication for the title of 'Jatra' (Champion) of Mukna of Manipur. In olden days, this was one of the highly popular and prestigious game enjoying royal patronage

2. MUKNA KANGJEI (KHONG KANGJEI)

Manipuris play Mukna Kangjei, (see plate-294) a game which combines the arts of Mukna (like wrestling) and Kangjei (Cane Stick). The ball of the Mukna Kangjei is made of seasoned bamboo roots.

The origin of the game goes back well to animistic worship. People celebrate 'Lai Haraoba' (festival to please sylvan deities) and include this item to mark the end of the festival. Pandits believe that Meiḍingu Khagemba (1597-1652) patronised this game. In later generation, the game is organised in the villages. Presently, associations are formed in Panas with rules and regulations of Mukna Kangjei.

The game is played by two teams each consisting of seven players. All players hold a natural cane stick with root, gradually increasing the size of the root, to the length of about seven inches to play the ball made out of seasoned bamboo roots of approximately a diameter of four inches. The players put on Mukna Kisi Phijet (dress of cloth knot) to secure protection and holding each other. At present a short pant is added below Kisi (like cloth belt with knots).

The game starts by throwing the ball in front of the *Panjenbas* (leaders) of the two teams standing face to face to each other on the line. If possible they can pick up the ball and run. The process of running and obstructing each other to put the ball on the goal line of the ground is allowed. *Pun onba* (change of side) and end of the game is given by the command of the umpire. The rules for the game is known as *Kangjei lon.* It has improved a lot and was demonstrated during the Fifth; National Games 1999 at Imphal.

3. Sagol Kangjei- see Chapter -18 : Sagol Kangjei: Polo

4. YUBI LAKPI

Yubi (coconut) Lakpi (snatching). The game of Yubi Lakpi (coconut capturing) is a tough individual game. It looks like Rugby of the Americans. Before the start of the game, players rub their bodies with mustard oil and water to make slippery to catch. A coconut properly soaked with oil is placed in front of the Chief Guest of the function. (see plate-295, 296)

The players put on *kisi* (Langot) on an under pant properly tied in front. A senior Jatra is the umpire of the game to start and check fouls of the players. Before the start of the game, the coconut is placed in front of the seat of the Chief Guest. Each side has 7 players in a field that is about 45 metres x 18 metres in area. One end of the field has a rectangular box 4.5 x 3 metres, one side of which forms the central portion of the goal line. To score a goal a player has to approach the goal from the front with his oiled coconut and pass the goal line. The coconut serves the purpose of a ball and is offered to the King or the judges who sit just beyond the goal line. In ancient times the teams were not equally matched but the players, with the coconut had to tackle all the rest of the players. Official game is held on the occasion of the Holy Festival of Shree Govindajee at palace ground and with Royal presence. This game is closely organised for the religious Holy Festival of Manipur.

5. WOOLAOBI

Woolaobi is an outdoor game mainly played by young girls or young boys. Meitei mythology believe that Umang Lai Helloi Taret (Seven deities, seven sisters) play this game on the courtyard of the temple of Umang Lairembi. There is no fixed number of players. The participants may be divided into two groups : (1) Raiders (Attackers) and (2) Defenders (Avoiders). The attacker will say loudly and continuously "woo" without stopping his or her breath as long as he or she can continue and try to touch the avoiders. The avoider will run to escape from the attack of the raider. If a raider touches an Avoider, he is out. This process goes on till all avoiders are out or surrender. If a Raider fails to say "woo" or out of breadth before reaching the fixed station and touched by an Avoider, the Raider is out. Points are counted on the elimination of Raiders/Defenders.

Change of Side: If Raiders are tired they declare "Awa" and take rest for some time. Now time limit is decided for change. The game can be played in any place –in the open space –inside temples premises, in the courtyard or backyard. The young girls are very found of this game.

6. HIYANG TANNABA

Hiyang Tannaba (Boat Race/ Hi Yangba Tannaba) is a traditional Game of the Panas. (see plate-297). This is held during the month of November. According to Chengleirol chronicle, Hiyang Tannaba is believed to have started during the reign of Meidingu Naophongba (428-518A.D). A Chenglei King named Thangyi Tabung Khongdouba introduced the festival of "Hiyanglei Kumsaba" for the welfare of his community under the divine advice of Atiya Guru Sidaba. A chronicle named "Tharol Nongkhairol" mentioned of "Hiyanglei Kumsaba", which was performed every year in the month of Hiyangei. The "Hijin Hirao" chronicle mentioned that this festival was introduced by Luwang Ningthou Punsiba, who ruled in the seventh century A.D. at Yangla Heituppok, located at the Loijing Hill (Makubi Ching). The dress put up by the participants of the boat race comprised of "Thethang Chari Ningkham", "Punung Phiral Mangan Naiba", "Langla Singonthok Thouchum Khikloi Chin", "Sarik Ningthan gana Likha Meikoi Tomna "Historians and scholars are of the view that the present Hiyang dress might have been evolved from the one used during the "Hiyanglei Kumsaba" festival of the time of Chenglei King. During the time of Maharaja Khunjaoba, the second son of Khagemba. the Kangla Moat was dug out around the Palace to make it impregnable in the year of 1660 after he ascended the throne in 1652 and revived the festival of Hiyang Tannaba on a grand scale. In the traditional function two boats "Tanahi" (Race Boat) are detailed for leaders known as "Tengmai Leppa". In each boat forty Hiroys (Boatman) operate the boat. "Hiyang Hiren" (Main Boat) is meant for Vishnu Deva and Ningthou (The King) and follows the two race boats. Hiyang Hiren is regarded to be invested with spiritual powers and the game is associated with religious rites. The Meiteis believe that worship of the Hiyang Hiren will negate evil spirits. The rowers don traditional dresses and head gears. Each rival will have different colour. The boat which reaches the finishing line is the winner and all boatmen raise their oars (Nous) high in the air as a sign of reaching the finishing destination line first and thus the winner of the race is declared. The leader pays his respect to the deity Vishnu Dev and the King of Manipur.

7. ARAMBAI HUNBA

People of Manipur are very expert in and fond of riding horse specially those who are in the village near the breeding areas. Since the ponies are easily available, the young boys get the chance of riding ponies without saddle on horse back. Sometimes they ride horses using a rope in place of regular bridle throwing branches of small trees in place of Arambai. This practice helped the Manipur Arambai force as a martial art which was very much required during the advance and withdrawal of forces. This game was very popular as an indigenous game of the youth of Manipur. This game is displayed even now, during the festival "Kwak Jatra" after Durga Puja. The Manipuri Arambai forces played a big role in defeating the Burmese army during the time of Garib Niwaj. (see plate-299)

8. KANG SANABA

Kang is played by both Meitei males and females in Manipur. Manipuris believe Kang is a game played by Goddess "Panthoibi". "Kang" which is a flat and oblong instrument made of either ivory or lac. Normally each team has 7 partners. the game is also played as a mixed-doubles contest. In olden days 'Kang' was played during summer, starting from Cheiraoba (Manipur New Year) to Kang Chingba (Rath Yatra). Presently the game is played in several tournaments throughout the year. Manipuris religiously adhere to its time-frame as popular belief holds that if the game is played beyond its given limit, evil spirits invade the mind of players and spectators. It is also believed that Manipuris began to play this game well before Vaishnavism came to Manipur. It is an indoor game. It is played under a shed of building on a mud floor (court) smoothly leveled to suit the course of the 'Kang', the target on the court. It is well marked for the respective positions of the players of both sides to hit the target on the court. It has rules and regulations framed by the Kang Associations to suit the occasions of the games either for tournaments or friendly matches. The dignitaries of the Palace, even Maharani and Maharaja also participated at these social functions. Rules and regulations have been modified to suit the improved process of the game. It is a popular indoor game of the Meiteis. (see plate-300)

9. THANG-TA

Thang means sword, Ta means Spear. Thang –Ta means "the Sword and Spear". This is a traditional martial art of Manipur. The other name of Thang-Ta is "Huyen Lallong" (Art of warfare). (see plate-298, 301). In fact, this is the art and science of fighting a war. Three warriors-Paona Naol Singh (Paona Brajabashi), Ningthoukhongja Poila, Loukrakpam Sana Mityeng were great warriors and great masters of Thanga Ta. They have founded a distinct style of Thang Ta. Paona died fighting with the British at Khongjam during the Anglo-Manipuri war of 189. He faced the British canons with his sword. Nowadays, there is no war using swords and spear. So this has been converted into game or a performance show on the stage.

Lord Yehudi Menuhin said "We do need more martial arts training, wherever it is taught, it eliminates violence. That is so overlooked." In India, the Two Best known Martial Art Traditions—Thang Ta of Manipur and Kalaripayattu of Kerala, have survived through centuries and both have a strong spiritual basis with strict moral and ethical codes. They are meant for protection and defence and are opposed to viciousness, cruelty and violence. Thang-Ta is almost completely unknown today outside Manipur. Khilton Nongmaithem is one of the foremost exponents of Thang Ta, having studied Thang-Ta since the age of six years under traditional gurus who were responsible for rediscovering and propagating this nearly losing art. He has represented India in many international festivals throughout the USA, Sweden, Italy, Germany, China, and England. Both he and Henry Smith worked together in the Festival of Dance, Theatre and Martial Arts held in Calcutta in 1987, and also performed together in "Body, Breath and Blade" at the South Bank in London in 1995. Together they recently presented performances and workshops in the "Way of the Warrior" Festival held in London and Dusseldorf in 1998.

Thang-Ta integrates various weapons-the sword, spear, dagger, etc- with the internal practice of physical control through soft body movements coordinated with the rhythms of breathing. The aesthetic aspect of the martial arts of Manipur demand a great deal of balancing and body control. It makes a person physically and mentally so alert and well integrated that he becomes virtually impregnable.

The Thang-Ta techniques are very complicated and must be seen to be appreciated. Many western ladies used to cover their eyes, grasping for breath at the climax of the Thanga –ta presentation. The Master used to give warning to the performers "You may seriously injure your limbs by incorrect stepping if you loose temper".

The ethics of Thang Ta demands that one should not harm an enemy who is running away, who is hiding out of fear, who is crying out of fear and who has asked for protection. Violating any of this is considered a great sin.

For a warrior, every moment of his life is guided by certain rules. Eating, sleeping and even breathing are well regulated. Martial arts training, initially, is more physical in nature, but as one advances, it is more spiritual. The secrets of *yantra, mantra* and *tantra* are gradually revealed to the student. The warrior's main and only concern ought to be the protection of the land, people, king and the weak. This sense of selflessness cannot be better symbolised than the costume which he wears to war. It includes a sacred cloth usually worn by the dead, thus preparing him for the supreme most sacrifice.

"The most memorable performance with the sword involved in a blindfolded swordsman and a man lying on his back with five pieces of melon balanced on various parts of his body. A wedge of melon was placed on each knee, as well as in each hand, and a single wedge was precariously balanced between his chin and his chest, directly above the throat. The swordsman was blindfolded using a piece of cloth filled with sand, so that everyone could see that there was no way for him to peep through the cloth. After being blindfolded, the swordsman would begin a rhythmic chopping and prancing in place, while a third person took up a position directly opposite the swordsman. In the middle was the man lying with melon slices balanced on various parts of his body. Drumming and cymbals accompanied the whole act and the third man would begin chanting, in order to provide the blindfolded swordsman a directional cue.

Suddenly, the swordsman would surge forward, leaping and chopping in a very precise pattern. As he leaped over the man lying in his path, his sword deftly cut each piece of melon, including the piece directly over the man's throat. Every spectator was tense with expectation until the man lying on the ground would jump to his feet and the swordsman would rip off his blindfold. As people shouted their approval and clapped their hands, many would throw coins and currency notes into the stage in appreciation of this spectacle."

The heart of Thang-Ta is the "sword". There are literally hundreds of different sword drills for training the basic strokes and stepping patterns. Many are two person sets, but others may be practiced solo, at least initially. Thang Ta demands a great deal of self-discipline from its practitioners. It is feared that certain vices may even jeopardize those powers acquired through years of training, meditation and worship. Some types of food are also forbidden. The unarmed aspect of Thang-Ta is named "Sarit Sarat". Traditionally, it is taught after competence in weapons was gained. It uses footwork and handwork form the weapons forms, with a liberal dose of the native wrestling style (Mukna) thrown in.

The old traditional values emphasized in Yaahip, Chakcha, Phampham (literally Sleeping, Eating, Sitting) which are basic value based discipline systems of organizing the body and mind in order to reach perfection in totality of his life are most vigorously followed by the artist. The value emphasized in culture are thus to respect the elders in the family and in the community, to develop a spirit of sacrifice and love for the country, with the ability to give away ones life without rancour, not to hurt the enemy when he is running away or when he is naked, not to do whatever is against the moral order of the day.

Thengou : The First Steps of Creation

This movement pattern of the gods and goddesses is styled Thengou, a sacred ritualistic movement which the dancer with sword or spear executes on the symbolic head of lotus with thousand petals or the thousand-hooded top of Ananta Snake, called Pakhangba in Manipuri. It normally admits of nine kinds as below:

Akao Thengou, on account of vigorous thrusts.

Leiphal Thengou, owing to stamping by jumps.

Nongphal Thengou, stamping by turns.

Leicai Thengou, from stamping by feet jumping in or out.

Leitak Thengou, from carefully trading the ground.

Leinet Thengou, owing to stamping the earth by moving round and round.

Langkak Thengou, from touching the ground with shakes and care.

Akham Thengou, from a special type of movement which was danced by Kings in succession.

Leishit Thengou, on account of touching extensively the earth.

Akham Thengou, is supposed to bring great prosperity and peace to the land. Tradition says that this very Thengou was performed by Akham Mayon during the reign of King Khagemba of Manipur (1597-1652 A.D) by Apong Sarot-Khaiba and Thonglen Wangkheirakpa during the reign of King Garibaniwaz (1709-48 A.D); by Wangkhei Pandit Gopiram during the time of Rajarshri Bhagyachandra (1763-1798 A.D) Every performance of Thengou either with spear or sword must be accompanied by incantation of specific mantras.

According to legend, the Supreme Creator, Atiya Kuru Sidaba sitting levitated on his own breath, asked his son, Kuptreng (Sanamahi/ Asiba)) to fashion the universe. Completely baffled how to fabricate anything out of a void, he inquired of his father how to go about it. At this, the Atiya Kuru Sidaba opened his mouth and asked his son to look inside, where he saw the whole cosmos lying dormant, yet to manifest. He was also instructed to devise a dance named Thengou using the same configuration of nerves and veins inside his father as the model for the pattern of his movements on the ground, on which the universe would rest when it was created. Thus the first act of cosmology was dance, and Thengou was the first dance, made up of a combination of martial art movements.

It is a highly esoteric branch of Manipuri martial arts. Thengou, traditionally believed to have been originally performed by the Gods at the time of creation is a sacrosanct dance compositions, performed usually by holding either a sword and shield or a spear and shield. There are many variations based on one of the various sacred coiled snake motifs worshipped in Manipur. There are various forms of Thengous for bringing prosperity to the land or people, protecting the King, destroying the enemy, etc. They are performed on extremely rare occasions when a dire need concerning the well being of the country arises. The rituals involved are extremely elaborate. All the details including the auspicious moment, ceremonial offerings, purification rites, choice of place, kind of weapon, costume, movement, ground patterns and incantations, mentioned in the sacred texts are inviolable and thus scrupulously followed. It is believed that any mistake in its performance or its employment can bring untold misfortunes to the performer and his family, even to future generations. Thus only great masters with absolute proficiency, experience and pure minds perform Thengous. The Gurus, very reluctant to part with this knowledge, choose only those few disciples with proven integrity and maturity.

Thengou training is imparted in a secluded place, away from habitation or a sandy riverbank likely to be washed away in the next floods. For where Thengou is performed, the ground is imbued with such power that anyone desecrating it inadvertently may incur divine wrath. The training begins after sanctifying the land.

The weapons are also considered to have divine origin with symbolic significance. When Til Sidaba (a powerful god) decided to give up his body, different 'boxes' of his remains became various weapons. Swords, spears, etc., do take on varying forms resembling such boxes. Scholars have given elaborate interpretations on their significance and use. The weapon is not an ordinary object; it is energized and infused with a vital divine force and cannot be desecrated by employing it for any degrading pursuit.

Taa Khousarol (art of spear dance)

9 and 7 are sacred numbers to the Manipuris. As in the case of 9 Thengourols, the art of spear dance (Taa Khousarol) admits of 9 kinds and share the same myths and symbols with Thengourol. The only difference is that Taa Khousarol is a little more secular, agile, supplementary to Thengourol. The names of Khousarol are: Maram Nungshitpa, Maram Achouba, Maram Macha, Maram Nungjaoba, Kabui, Athou Chumthang, Athou Macha, Tangkhul, Athou Achouba and Thel. There are other types of Khousarol which are composed by various experts and handed down from generation to generation. They are used in Kwak-Jatra festival and Lai-Haraoba before large audience and in the open area. Every khousarol has fixed sequence and demands great skill and agility on the part of the performer. There are also solo or duet items done as a part of the ritual and prayer for prosperity. Unlike, Thengourol it is still in active form and practiced by the Gurus and priests. An analysis of the sequences of a particular Khousarol would reveal the different stages in the matter of hunting and catching the wild animals through artistic jumps and thrusts of spear.

Thangkairol (the art of sword fight)

Sword goes generally with spear and mastery of both the art was a must for every warrior worth the name in Manipur. Spear has many shapes and is used for specific purposes like guarding the King, hunting the tiger or elephant and for on horseback. Each type of spear has a name. Similarly different types and shapes of sword belong to specific clans, various ancestors and even deities, having distinctive names. Even the royal swords have specific names like Khoubomba of King Khagemba (1597-1652), Vajra Singh of King Gambheer (1825-34) and Chandrasen of Maharaja Chandrakirti (1834-1844).

Every warrior versed in spear has to enter the battle field with three types of spear viz. Hakthang Taa (attached to the body) Chaina Taa (fighting spear) and Taaron Taa (the additional spear) kept generally on the back. The shield has to be attached to it. The expert swordsman has to carry besides the Chungoi (Shield) three types of sword viz. Yetthang (right hand sword) Oithang (left hand one) and Tendong thang (additional sword) kept on the back and used like an arrow in times of emergency.

The art of sword fight, apart form its having various steps and movements in Manipuri names, has at the moment corresponding non – Manipuri terms like Yalak, Kalak, Shut, etc. and it is likely that this art has been influenced and enriched by a similar art of fencing in northern India. But it still preserves its distinctive art form and admits of specific steps and jumps and an expert swordsmen holding two swords could cover himself with the swords and protect himself against possible attacks from outside. Unfortunately, owing to incessant figh:s among princes of royal blood, there were times when this art was very much discouraged. During the British time, of course, there was a complete ban on the teaching of martial arts, thanks to their policy of subjugating a warrior race. But this old art is being revived again.

Martial Arts on the Stage

There has been a fashion of increasing popularity to present this art of sword and spear on the stage as performing arts, mostly in the form of decorative pieces or composed fights. But the way the performers take to this presentation in all seriousness clearly indicates that this is not just a dance form for enjoyment but movement full of surprises and excitement. Even though the contestants agree on some basic movements, there is considerable room for improvisation, which means that no two fights unlike the codified movements of dance are similar and each has a beauty and excitement of its own. It is indeed indicative of a proper training of some standard that some of the presentations in form of swoid fights, sword vs. spear fights, sword vs. axe fight, etc. have been raised to height of excellence and artistry, to the great delight of the spectators. Real fights cannot obviously be sponsored in the style of boxing or wrestling as the risks are immense. But these stage fights do not lack in the seriousness, agility and artistry of the real fight and hence the beauty of the presentation which sometimes eclipses the aesthetic performances.

Martial Arts: The Foundation for Classical Dances

Even though the classical dance forms of Manipuri claim affinity, sometimes with good reason, with the Natya Shastra and Abhinaya Darpana tradition, it has been increasingly proved that the steps, gaits and poses of sword and spear dances, provide the framework of some of the classical steps of Lai-Haraoba, Raas lila and Sankirtana movements, Chakra, Hastas of both hands which is a must for martial arts are used in Lai Haraoba and Raas Lila movements. The various poses of Pung Cholom and Pala Cholom of Nata Sankritana and of the Tandava movements of Lai Haraoba also display certain basic poses of sword fight and Thang –ta. Even the basic movements like Chali, Longlei and Uplei (bhrameri), Champra okpi and Lasing Kappi have been demonstrated as having some affinity with the steps and poses of martial arts.

References

Arambam Santoshkumar, President, "All Manipur Football Association", Football da

Jonathan Mark Kenoyer (1997): "Thangkairol; Manipur Sword Fighting of Eastern India", in PERSONAL GROWTH THROUGH MARTIAL ARTS, (edited by M.

Kiyoto and J. Lee) pp. 53-63.

Khilton Nongmaithem and Dainis Jirgensons (1998): Thang-Ta, The Martial Art of Manipur India, Journal of Asian Martial Arts, Vol. 7, no. 4, page 46-59].

Manipur, 2008, CADA Quarterly, Health for Future, Vol. 1, No. 1, Issue No.1

R.K. Madhurjit Singh

R. K. Singhajit Singh (1998): THE MARTIAL ARTS OF ASIA, Eliminating Violence - THE EYE, Vol. 5], [http://internetindia.com/theeye/vol5/martial.htm.

Shannaroisingee Numit -2003, Government of Manipur Department of Youth Affairs and Sports.

Shannaroisingee Numit -2004, Government of Manipur, Department of Youth Affairs and Sports, February, 25, 2004.

Shannaroisingee Numit -2006, Government of Manipur, Department of Youth Affairs and Sports, February, 25, 2006.

Shannaroisingee Numit -2008, Government of Manipur, Department of Youth Affairs and Sports, February, 25, 2008.

Stephan G. Voss: Japanese, European and Indian Sword Fighting; A comparative Study: in PERSONAL GROWTH THROUGH MARTIAL ARTS, (edited by M. Kiyoto and J. Lee) p. 75, 1997.]

[http://www.libertynet.org/solaris/Aikido/Events.html] He is also associated with NRITYA RANGAM (Manipuri Dance School) of Washington, D.C.

The Hula Sindamshang, Imphal (Khilton Nongmaithem) is the only Manipuri teaching Thang-Ta outside of Manipur."

Plate-293: Mukna

Plate -294: Kangjei

Plate-295: Yubi Lakpi

Plate-296: Yubi Lakpi

Plate -297 : Hiyang Tannaba

Plate -298: Thang –Ta

Plate -299: Arambai Hunba

Plate -300: Kang Sanaba

Plate -301: Women Thang –Ta

Plate-302: Nila Kamal, first Olympian receiving award from Prime Minster Narasingh Rao

Plate-303 Thrice World Boxing Champion MC Mary Kom & Gold Medalist L. Sarita on November 26th 2006.

Plate -304: N. Kunjarani , Weight Lifter Sydney Olympic, 2000

Plate -305: MC Mary Kom receiving prestigious CNN-IBN Indian Real Heroes award 2008

Plate -306: Laishram Monika, Silver Medalist in Common Wealth Games , Melbourne , 2006

Plate -307: Thokchom Nanao, World Boxing Champion, Gold Medalist being given a cheque of Rs. 50,000 by Bijoy Koijam MLA on 21st December 2008

Plate -308 Kishan , Mr Asia Junior for 2007 display his body on September 20, 2007.

Plates- 309 Dr. Ngangbam Shantikumar came second at the 42nd Men's Senior Asian Body Building Championship held in Hong Kong from 16th to 21st July 2008.

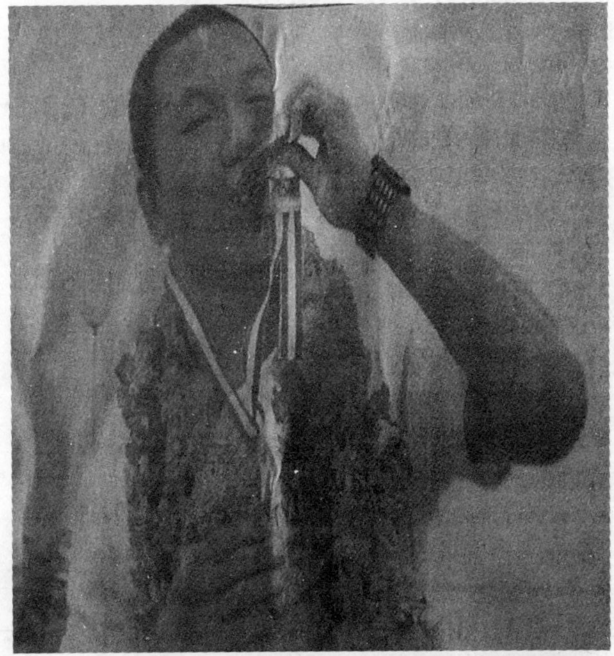

Plate-310 Mayengbam Suranjoy, Asian Boxing Champion - 2009 Held in China 7-13 June, 2009) received at the Imphal Airport on 19th June, 2009

Plate- 311 Hmangte Parneichong Kom who claimed 3 Gold Medals at The Youth Asian Weightlifting Championship at Amman, Jordan from Oct 28th to Oct 30th 2007

Plate-312: Kh. Pradeepkumar Living With HIV(Brand Ambassador of MACS) bagged Bronze Medal 55 Kgs category at the 9th Mr. India Inter-Sate Federation Cup Body Building Championship -at Kerala from Jan 16-18 2009.

Plate-313 L. Sarita Devi grabbed the "Best Boxer Award" in the 11th SRM-Federation Cup boxing championship, held at Kattankulathur, Tamil Nadu on 14th July, 2007.

Plate-314 L Sarita, Bronze Medalist at the 3rd Women's World Boxing Championship

18

Sagol Kangjei (Polo)

SAGOL KANGJEI (POLO)

Modern Polo (Manipuri Sagol Kangjei) is a gift of Manipur to the world. Sagol Kangjei was a favourite game of the kings and princes in Manipur. In ancient times. Manipuris played it as many as 100 on each side like a miniature battle under the patronage of the kings. Horses were used in the game of polo, and teams of riders tried to hit a wooden ball across the field with a long wooden mallet.

ORIGIN OF SAGOL KANGJEI (POLO) IN MANIPUR

The Manipuri chronicles (Puyas) traces the origin of Sagol Kangjei as early as 3100 BC. Loyalakpa, Oknarel, Namboolakpa, Yanggoi Ningthou, Thangjing, Wangbrel, Khoriphaba are the Chiefs among the players who first played the game during the days of the mythological age. Marjing, Khamlangba, Irumba, Ikoppa, Irongba, Nongshaba, Panthoiba are the sylvan Gods who played Sagol Kangjei.

According to "Kangjeiroi", an ancient treatise on Sagol Kangjei (Polo), King Kangba (1405-1359 B.C) introduced "Sagol Kang-jei" in its present form. Sagol means horse or pony, Kang-jei means Kangba's stick, Kangdroom for the round ball and Kangjeibung (Polo ground) means the polo field as evident from old Meitei script "Ningthou Kangbalon" by one Thongak Kurumba. The names Kangjei, Kangdrum, Kangjeibung were derived from the name "Kangba". He entrusted the making of Kangjei Kanghu (Polo stick) to one particular family clan which later on known as "Kanghujam".

Sagol Kangjei is associated with the God of the Chenglei tribe, Marjing, to whom the stick along with the ball are still offered in worship. The traditional Lai Haraoba festival of Manipur has a sequence dealing with the search of bride (Lai Nupi Thiba) on the part of Maibi (Priestess) with the Polo Stick in hand and mimicking the neighing of a horse. There are several books of Manipur like 'Thangmeirol' and 'Kangjeirol' (Art of Polo) which support the great antiquity of this game. The book Kangjeirol writes - "During a festival known as Ukrong Hongba, Kangba, (1405 B.C.) the King of Manipur showed a skill of dribbling a bamboo root club by his walking stick on the ground. He asked his subjects to play this game on horse back the next day. Accordingly, his subordinate officers along with common men, after having lunch thrown by the King, came out in new dress to the venue of the festival with their ponies and started playing the game as introduced by the King. The game was witnessed by the queen, Leima Tanu Sana sitting under a royal canopy amidst huge crowd. Deriving from the name of the king Kangba the game was known as Sagol Kangjei.

The Royal Chronicle of Manipur, *Cheitharol Kumbaba*, gives an account of a Polo match between the friends of Ngonda Lairen Pakhangba who ascended the throne of Manipur in 33 A.D. On that occasion he introduced his queen Laisana to the royal crowd as a proof of his marital fidelity to her.

The patronage and support of the Kings were the life-blood with which the game progressed over the centuries.

It was during the time of great King Khagemba (1597-1652) that the game had been transformed into a very active military game.

PANA SAGOL KANGJEI

According to Cheitharol Kumbaba, King Khagemba of Manipur introduced Pana Sagol Kangjei system in 1606 which are played between the four Panas of higher status and also between the two Panas of lesser status. The Panas of higher status were Laipham, Khabam, Ahallup and Naharup. Two Panas of lesser status were Hidakphanba and Potsangba.

Each team of the Pana (a social institution of Manipur) was given a particular colour of uniform for games.

Higher Status Panas:

1.	Laipham Pana	-	Red colour shirt
2.	Khabam Pana	-	Green colour shirt
3.	Ahallup Pana	-	White colour shirt
4.	Naharup Pana	-	Yellow colour shirt

Lesser Status Panas (Pana Khumei):

1. Hidak Phanba - Black colour shirt
2. Potsangba - Blue colour shirt

No Sagol Kangjei (Polo) game could be played between a Pana of higher status and a Pana of lower status. When the selected player's from Laipham Pana and Ahallup Pana made a combined team and played against the selected combined team of Khabam Pana and Naharup Pana, the Polo match was known as Chere-Kare. The fielding position of Sagol Kangjei is described below :-

Table-50 Showing fielding position of Manipur Sagol Kangjei

Sl. No.	*Team facing the South*	*Fielding position*	*Team facing the North*
1.	Marjing	Pan-ngakpa (Full back)	Thangjing
2.	Khamlangba	Pan-ngakchang (Half back)	Khoriphaba
3.	Irum Ningthou	Pallak Chang (Mid-fielder)	Wangbaren
4.	Ikop Ningthou	Langjei (Centre)	Yangoi Ningthou
5.	Irong Ningthou	Pallak Chang (Mid-fielder)	Mayokpha
6.	Nongshaba	Pangjeng Chang (No.2 forward)	Oknaren
7.	Panthoiba	Panjenba (No. 1 forward)	Loyarakpa

Height of Horses: The game can be played on ponies of any height. The average height of Manipuri ponies is 11 to 13 hands.

Size of the field: The dimensions of the rectangular playing field are 210 yards in length and 100 yards in width. But it can be played also on smaller fields according to local conditions.

Players: The number of players in a team will be seven.

Polo players wear *Pheijom* (Dhoti), may be cotton or silk, but the dhoti should be worn above the knee. The player should wear a *Kokyet* (Turban) on the head fixed by a chin strap known as *Khadangchet* and a traditional jacket with short sleeves. No shoe is used but to protect the ankles, the players use a piece of leather or thickly folded cloth known as *Khuning Khang* that is bandaged by a long narrow piece of cloth around the ankles. In between the knees and ankles players use Pads or thick leather as the guard of shins and calves known as *Khongyom* that is also fastened by straps. Colour of the shirt or jacket and chin strap or *Khadangchet* should be according to their respective Pana colour.

The *Huntre Hunba* or Referee will call out the mounted players in the midfield and ask them to line up. The *Huntre Hunba* will throw the ball upward as high as possible in the air shouting '*Huntre*' to indicate the start of the match and he has to come out quickly from the playing area. *Huntre Hunba* is done after every goal is scored.

There is a change of sides known as *Pallonba* when half of the stipulated goals have been scored by any team in traditional Manipuri Polo game. During the half time of the match, there is *Pot Lanba* meaning presentation of sweets, fruits, other eatables and flowers by the Polo fans, women folk and villagers to the dignitaries who witness the match and the Polo players.

Legend also has it that during the reign of King Charairongba in 1697 A.D, a team of 10 led by the King himself played a game against another team consisting of 100 players, with the smaller team winning the team.

The immense popularity of the game in Manipur through the ages is evident from the several polo grounds created all over Manipur valley. Every village has a polo ground, some having been constructed under the royal patronage. For instance, Cheitharol Kumbaba', the royal Chronicle of Manipur mentions- "On Monday, the second day of Hiyangei, a Pologround was constructed at Tenkai Kha".

When Chourjit was the King of Manipur (1803-1813), his brother Marjit revolted against him. In 1808, they decided to settle the issue of succession to the throne by a single combat in the Polo field located within the precinct of the palace. (see plate-315). Chourajit opted for sword and Marjit chose the spear. They fought on horse back fiercely. Marjit was defeated and fled to Ava.

MANIPUR SAGOL KANGJEI DURING BRITISH PERIOD

A British Political Agent (Mr. Gordon) was stationed at Imphal, the capital of Manipur from 1835. The British officers saw Sagol Kangjei (Manipuri Polo) as early as 1835 being played at Mapal Kanjeibung (Manipur Pologround) situated between the Sana Keithel and the British residency.

In the beginning of 1850s, the British saw the Manipuri princes Chourajit, Marjit, Gambheer Singh, Nara Singh practicing at one time the battle exercises on horse back with swinging of *Arambais* or at other times playing a strange game of "hockey on horse back" swinging a mallet and striking ball with equal gusto in the lush green plains of Cachar with their ever present retinues.

During 1853-54, Captain Robert Stewart, Assistant Deputy Commissioner of Cachar played Sagol Kangjei at Silchar, Cachar along with Manipuri princes. Lieutenant, John Shearer was excited to see the game for the first time in his life. He shouted "We must learn this game" when he witnessed the game at Silchar, Cachar. Today, he is considered as the father of British Polo. Somewhere about 1854 or a little later, the British and English planters in Cachar (Assam) learnt the Polo game from Manipuris. "During those days, there was no goal post. Carrying the ball upto the end of the boundary line was the Manipuri equivalent of a goal. On the western side was a stand for members of the Raja's family, most of whom were excellent players to witness the game.

Mapal Kangjeibung of Manipur was described by Sir James Johnston, the Political Agent of Manipur ((1877-1886) as "The famous polo ground, where the best Polo play in the world might be seen". Mapal Kangjieibung, was 225 yards long and 110 yards broad, and was covered with very fair turf.

WORLD'S FIRST POLO CLUB WAS ESTABLISHED AT SILCHAR IN 1859

In 1859 Stewart became the Deputy Commissioner and Lieutenant John Shearer joined as Assistant Deputy Commissioner. Captain Robert Stewart, and Lieutenant John Shearer enthusiastically took up the Manipuri Polo Game and they decided to start a polo club to play regular matches against the Manipuri players. In March, 1859, the world's first polo club outside Manipur was established at Silchar, Cachar by Captain Robert Stewart and Lt. John Shearer. The decision to establish the Silchar Polo Club was taken in a meeting and the founder members of the Silchar Polo Club were Captain Robert Stewart, Lt. John Shearer, James Davidson, Julius Sandermon, James Abemetly, Arthur Brownlow, Earnest Echardt, W. Walker and A. Stewart. Today, the oldest polo clubs outside India are the Malta Polo Club (1868), the All Ireland Polo Club in Dublin (1872), the Monmouth shire Polo Club in England (1872), and the Meadowbrook Polo Club in the United States (1877).

When Lord Curzon, the Viceroy of the British India visited Manipur, he wrote in the Viceroy's Note Book "There can be no doubt that the precedence belongs to Manipur." The popularity of Polo spread to the western countries like England, USA, Argentina, Australia, New Zealand from Manipur through other Indian cities like Calcutta, Jodhpur.

In 1861 polo was played in Dacca on the initiative of Captain Eustace Hill of Lahore Light Horse who saw the game being played on a trip to Cachar.

MANIPUR POLO SPREAD TO OTHER PARTS OF BRITISH INDIA

In 1862 polo was played in Calcutta and Calcutta Polo Club was formed in 1862. From Calcutta, the enthusiastic officers took it up to the principal cantonments of Northern India and Peshawar". By the end of the 19th century, there were some 175 polo clubs in India. Winston Churchill, who learned the game in 1895 when he was a young cavalry officer organized a polo club and purchased 25 horses from another regiment with the aim of winning India's prestigious inter-regional tournament. His team practiced every day in the blistering heat, and travelled up to 1,400 miles by train with its horses to play invitational matches. In 1899, Churchill's team won the inter-regional tournament.In My Early Life, he describes a game with the kinsmen of Sir Pratap Singh, the regent of Jodhpore: "Old Pratap, who loved polo next to war more than anything in the world, used to stop the game repeatedly and point out faults or possible improvements in our play and combination. 'Faster, faster, same like fly,' he would shout to increase the speed of the game. The Jodhpore polo ground rises in great clouds of red dust when a game is in progress. Winston Churchill advised parents "Don't give your son money," "As far as you can afford it, give him horses. No one ever came to grief — except honourable grief — through riding horses. No hour of life is lost that is spent in the saddle. Young men have often been ruined through owning horses, or through backing horses, but never through riding them; unless of course they break their necks, which, taken at a gallop, is a very good death to die."

In 1864, on invitation from Calcutta, the Silchar Polo Club raised a Manipuri polo team known as "The Band of Brothers" and Lt. John Shearer took them, with their ponies, to Calcutta by country boat. The team consisted of Toolsi Singh, Chowba Singh, Ammu Singh, Omah Singh, Tubal Singh, Aema Ba and Monga Pa. The Manipuri team easily defeated the Calcutta team. In 1875, Maharaja Chandrakirti sent two teams of Polo to Calcutta on the occasion of a visit to Calcutta by the Prince of Wales (later King Edward VII) during his visit to India (see plate-316) It was largely due to the tireless efforts of Lt. John Shearer that Sagol Kangjei (Manipuri Polo) got transformed into the popular game of modern polo of international fame.When Shearer retired as a Major General, he was rightly acknowledged as the father of English Polo.

MANIPUR POLO GAME SPREAD TO OTHER PARTS OF THE WORLD FROM 1868

From 1868, the Manipur Polo gained immense popularity and spread like Olympic Flame.

MANIPUR POLO GAME SPREAD TO MALTA IN 1868

In 1868, the Polo Game reached Malta and the game was played between soldiers and naval officers on their way home from India to England. In 1869, Edward Hartopp, of the 10th Hussars read an account of the game in "The Field Magazine" while stationed at Aldershot and, with fellow officers, organised the first game. Then known as "Hockey on Horseback," it was played on a hastily-rolled Hounslow Heath where a shortlist of about 10 rules was also hastily assembled.

MANIPUR POLO GAME SPREAD TO ENGLAND IN 1869

In 1869 the game was played in England between the 10th Hussars and the 9th lancers with eight on each side. The 10th Hussars won by three goals to two. This was the first European polo game. It raised the curiosity of the British society. Hurlingham started polo in 1874 and soon became the headquarters of the game. At that time, there were 8 riders in each team, the rules were almost non-existent and there were two periods of about 90 minutes each. The first polo club in England was Monmouth shire, founded in 1872 by Captain Francis "Tip" Herbert (1845- 1922), of the 7th Lancers, at his brother's estate at Clytha Park, near Abergavenny. Others, including Hurlingham, followed quickly.

MANIPUR POLO GAME SPREAD TO ARGENTINA IN 1873

In 1873, Thomas Taylor brought the first polo mallet to Argentinia. This piece, donated by Luis L. Lacey, is proudly kept and exhibited at the Venado Tuerto Polo Club.

In 1874, the club committee drew up the first code of rules, which reduced the number of players to five a side and included offside.

The first official match in Argentina took place on 3rd September 1875, played by Irishmen, estancia owners and English engineers at the Villanueva estancia in Ranchos, in the province of Buenos Aires. The game had been taken there by English and Irish engineers and ranchers.

In 1875, the "Hurlingham Polo Association" was founded which started a progressive officialization of the rules. It was not until 1883 that the number of players was reduced to five per team, then four But, it was John Watson (1856-1908), of the 13th Hussars, who formulated the first real rules of the game in India in the 1870s. He later formed the celebrated Freebooters team who won the first Westchester Cup match in 1886. He was a key player at the All Ireland Polo Club which was founded in 1872 by Horace Rochfort of Clogrenane, County Carlow.

In 1880, the first institution, Flores Polo Club, was founded in Argentina. Prominent players soon began to emerge: Sixto Martínez, his brother José, and Francisco Rodríguez. The sport continued to develop and subsequently new clubs appeared in different localities throughout Argentina. The pioneering institutions were Lomas Polo Club (1885), Belgrano Polo Club (1886) and the legendary Hurlingham Club (1886), which was to be the ruling institution of the game of polo for several years. In 1893 an open tournament was held for the first time between the Venado Tuerto, Media Luna and Cañada de Gómez, while towards 1895 the first delegation of Argentine polo players appeared in London, achieving an excellent and memorable performance. Since then Argentine Polo has maintained first place among international teams. Argentina dominates the professional sport, as its Polo team has been the uninterrupted world champion since 1949 and is today the source of most of the world's 10 goal (i.e., top-rated) players. It is also the source of the Raza Polo Argentino, the only purpose-bred Polo pony in general international demand.The Campeonato Argentino Abierto de Polo tournament is over 100 years old and still going strong, remains one of the most important polo competitions in the world. Today Argentina is considered as the Polo capital of the world. The best Polo ponies and the best players come from Argentina according to Polo Players Edition magazine. In Buenos Aires every December as many as 30,000 Polo fans attend the Argentine Open, the world's most prestigious tournament. In the land of the gaucho, boys growing up on estancias (estates) play polo as soon as they learn to ride; consequently, the majority of top-ranked players are Argentines, including 27-year-old Adolfo Cambiaso, the sport's tabloid-handsome superstar and current leading goal scorer on the World Polo Tour. The 1926 Open (Hurricanes vs. Argentina) had over 30,000 spectators. A single Polo match in the Westchester Cup Tournament was attended by more than 45,000 spectators and the Cup of the Americas in 1928 was viewed by over 100,000 dedicated Polo fans.

MANIPUR POLO GAME SPREAD TO AUSTRALIA IN 1876

In 1876, Lt Col Thomas St.Quintin, of the 10th Hussars, introduced the game to Australia. He is credited with being the Father of Australian Polo. Two of his brothers stayed on there as ranchers and helped the game to develop.

MANIPUR POLO GAME SPREAD TO USA IN 1876

In 1876, Polo was introduced to the USA by James Gordon Bennett Junior who had seen the game at Hurlingham during a visit to England. In

1876, one of the visitors to the Polo club in England was the publisher of the New York Herald, James Gordon Bennett (see Plate-329). Bennett was a famously eccentric man: it was Bennett who had sent Dr. Stanley on the famous expedition to find the lost explorer Dr. Livingston in 1871, and it was Bennett who returned from England in 1876, after viewing British polo, with a supply of sticks and balls. He dispatched New York's leading riding master, Harry Blasson, to Texas to purchase suitable Polo ponies.

In the spring of 1876, James Gordon Bennett hosted a special dinner party at his New York estate. His carefully selected guests were a dozen gentlemen who were members of the sporting set most likely to be attracted to the "new" game of Polo.A railcar loaded with Texas ranch horses was delivered by the meal's end, whereupon the gentlemen tried their hands at Polo. Immediately addicted, they embraced the sport and made it a part of their annual summer retreat in Newport, Rhode Island that summer. James Gordon Bennett formed club, and proceeded to establish playing fields for practices, near their summer 'cottages' on Bellevue Avenue. The Westchester Polo Club, based in Newport, became the first Polo club in the United States.

In 1876, in the United States, the first friendly games were played in Manhattan, at the Dickels Riding Academy. In the United States, the sport of Kings captured the enthusiasm of a future President of America. Theodore Roosevelt was bullish on the sport, founding the Oyster Bay Polo Club on Long Island, where he earned a 1-goal handicap in the late 1880s. Correspondence detailing Roosevelt's Polo adventures might very well have lead to his rough-and-tumble reputation. "At the very end while busily engaged in riding (an opponent) out, I got a tumble that knocked me senseless," Roosevelt wrote to a friend following a match in July, 1888. "I was all right in an hour and perfectly recovered in three or four days".

"Within the next 50 years of its introduction, Polo achieved extraordinary popularity in the United States. By the 1930's Polo was in the midst of a Golden Age Crowds in excess of 30,000 regularly attended international matches at Meadow Brook Polo Club (see Plate-328) on Long Island. The galloping game produced athletes who would doubtless have achieved greatness in any sport: Cecil Smith, the Texas cowboy, who held a perfect 10-goal rating for a still-record 25 years; Devereux Melbourne, instrumental in formulating modern styles of play; and Tommy Hitchcock, war hero, and the best of the best in international competition for two decades.

The game caught the imagination of the buccaneering class of the Gilded Age in America, and during the following years, other clubs were founded up and down the East Coast. The Polo game has undergone an unprecedented and remarkable expansion. At present, there are more than 225 member clubs with over 3,000 players.

In 1877, the Champion Cup was founded. The next change was the present scale of penalties for offside, foul riding or dangerous play. A short time after, the crooking of the adversary stick, unless in the act of hitting the ball, was forbidden. Then came the rule dividing the game into periods of ten minutes, with intervals of two minutes for changing ponies after each period, and five minutes at halftime. The height of ponies was fixed at I4~2, and a little later an official measurer was appointed, no pony being allowed to play unless registered at Hurling ham.

In 1877 the first series of outdoor Polo games took place in the United States at a Bronx racetrack. Informal games were being played in New York City and by 1877 at Jerome Park racetrack in Westchester County, N.Y., where the Westchester Polo Club was founded in this latter year.

In 1877, the first North American Polo club was formed, the Westchester Polo Club.

MANIPUR POLO GAME SPREAD TO FRANCE IN 1879

In 1879, in France, the first match was played in Dieppe: a French team, lead by the Duc de Guiche, played against a British team in 1880.

In 1881 the Meadow Brook Club was formed in Long Island, New.York., by such early outstanding players as Thomas Hitchcock, Sr., August Belmont, and Benjamin Nicoll. The size of the team was reduced to five and then, in 1881 in the United States and in 1883 in England, to four, the present number.

In 1886, the first international game, the "Westchester Cup", was played in Rhode Island Opposing Great Britain and the United States, it ended with the victory of the British Hurlingham Team. The popularity of Polo in America increased astonishingly through the first half of the 20th century. America's "golden age of Polo" came during the twenties and thirties: 80 polo clubs had sprung up around the U.S., and club members included such popular figures as Walt Disney, Clark Gable and Will Rogers.

In 1886, the Hurlingham Club of England was established, which introduced rules of polo game.

In 1988, the University of London Polo Club (ULPC) was formed in 1988 when students from University College London Riding Club entered a team in Peter Grace's Inter University Tournament. The following year, a University of London team was entered and the idea of forming an official club for members was mooted and a constitution was drawn up.

In 1888, handicaps were introduced by the USA and by England and India in 1910.The Handicap system appeared to help balance teams of different levers. New Zealand, South Africa, Australia and even Gibraltar and Malta soon followed.

In 1989, the Inter University Tournament of Polo was started in USA.

In 1890, the Polo Association (later the United States Polo Association/ USPA) was founded and standardized the rules. Polo spread throughout the country, although the game long remained one for the rich because of the expense of acquiring and maintaining a stable of polo ponies.

In 1990, the New Zealand Polo Association was formed, one year after Captain Savile (Aide-de-Camp to the Governor General) presented a trophy to be "played for annually by the Polo clubs in New Zealand". The Savile Cup is one of the oldest sporting trophies in New Zealand. still played for as the national club championship.

In 1890, the Polo Association (later the United States Polo Association/ USPA) was founded and standardized the rules. The Hurling ham handicap is revised during the winter, again in May, June and July, each handicap coming into force one month after the date of issue. The game grew faster, partly as the result of these rules.

On 22nd June, 1891, the Marquess of Ripon remarked during the House of Lords debate on Juvraj Tikendrajit's trial in England. "It (Manipur) is a small State, probably until these events took place very little known to your Lordships, unless, indeed, some of you may have heard of it as the birth place of the Game of Polo."

In 1910 a Polo handicap was established, based on the American system. This was modified in the English handicap by assigning to each player a handicap number as at golf. Polo has given rise to a new type of horse, an animal of 14 hands 2 in. with the power of a hunter, the courage of a race horse and the docility of a pony. At first the ponies were small, but now each pony must pass the Hurlingham official measurer and be entered on the register. The English Polo system of measurement is the fairest.

In 2000, a professional women's polo league, known as the United States Women's Polo Federation founded in USA. (see Plate- 331) The sixteen-team league plays across the country.

FAMOUS POLO PAYERS OF MANIPUR DURING 15TH CENTURY BC TO 19TH CENTURY

King Kangba, Khagemba, Chourajit, Marjit, Nara Singh, Yubaraj Tikendrajit (Koireng), Pakasana were established polo players of Manipur.

Other established Polo players were Toolsi Singh, Chowba Singh, Ammu Singh, Omah Singh, Tubal Singh, Aema Ba and Monga Pa.

LANGUAGES OF POLO GAME

The origins of Polo, its exotic ancestry and storied past have contributed to a heritage rich in colorful expression. Understanding that language adds yet another dimension to a fascinating sport.

- **Chukka:** This is the term used to describe the basic period of play. In Polo, each chukka is seven and a half minutes long and there are four chukkas in each match.
- **Foul:** This continues an infraction of the rules as laid down by the Polo Association. Most fouls govern safe riding and the concept of the line of the ball.
- **Goal:** A point is added to the score each time the ball travels between the goal post, whether hit in by attacker, defender or pony. The team's direction of play changes after each goal is scored.
- **Handicap:** The comparative rating of polo players awarded by the Polo Association, Handicaps are expressed in goals but do not describe the number of goals the player is expected to score, but rather the player's value to the team.
- **Hook:** One of the two defensive maneuvers allowed in the rules. In this case the mallet is used to block or interfere with another player's swing at the ball.
- **Line of the ball:** The imaginary line created by the ball as it travels across the field. The line of the ball may not be crossed or infringed except in exceptional circumstances. This is pivotal concept on which many fouls or infractions are based and is usually what the umpires are discussing after they have blown the whistle.
- **Mallet:** The stick used to hit the ball.
- **Near-side:** Is the left side of the horse.
- **Off-side:** Is the right side of the horse.
- **Out of bounds:** When the ball is hit out of bounds the clock continues to run and the ball is thrown in by the umpires at that spot.
- **Penalties:** Fouls result in the umpires awarding a shot at a goal (a penalty) to the offended team (the more severe the infringement, the closer to the goalmouth the penalty is awarded).
- **Puttees:** The leg wraps applied to the horse's lower legs for support and protection.

- **Referee:** The referee is off-field and has the final word in the case of a dispute between the two mounted umpires.
- **Ride-off:** A ride -off is used to break an opposing players concentration, move him off the line of the ball or spoil his shot.
- **Throw-in:** The game is started with a throw-in where the ball is literally thrown in between the line-up teams by the umpires.
- **Umpires:** These are on-field officials. Mounted on horses, umpires are usually active players responsible for enforcing the rules.

CHRONOLOGY OF DEVELOPMENT OF POLO

3100 year BC - Marjing, Thangjing, Wangbrel, Khoriphaba and the sylvan Gods played the game of Sagol Kangjei (Polo)

1405-1359 B.C According to "Kangjeiroi", an ancient treatise on Sagol Kangjei, King Kangba introduced "Sagol Kang-jei". Sagol means horse, Kang-jei means the stick and Kang-droom for the round ball as evident from old Meitei script "Ningthou Kangbalon" by one Thongak.The names Kangjei and Kangdrum were derived from the name "Kangba" who introduced the game.

600 BC. The first recorded game in Persia took place between the Turkomans and Persians (the Turkomans won). (see Plates-318-326).

33 A.D. The Royal Chronicle of Manipur, *Cheitharol Kumbaba*, gives an account of a Polo match between the friends of Ngonda Lairen Pakhangba, who ascended the throne of Manipur in 33 A.D

4th century AD. King Sapoor II of Persia learned to play, aged 7.

7th century AD. Polo spreads from China to Japan

1597-1652 : Khagemba, King of Manipur made it a very active military game. He also introduced the system of pana-wise match. There are 6 panas at the time of Khagemba- Ahallup, Naharup, Laipham, Khabam, Hidakphaba, Postsangba. The name of the competition was known as 'Pana Sagol-Kangjei'.

16th century AD. A polo ground (300 yards long and with goal posts 8 yards apart) was built at Ispahan, then the capital, by Shah Abbas the Great. The Moguls were largely responsible for taking the game from Persia to the east and by the 16th century the Emperor Babur had established it in India. Polo was revived in Japan by the 8th Shogun, Tokugawa Yoshimune (1684-1751) and was played until early 20th century. It was the favourite sport of the last Shogun who surrendered power to the Emperor in 1868.

1697 A.D. King Charai Rongba of Manipur played a team of 10 led himself against another team consisting of 100 players, with the smaller team winning the team.

1800- 27th of Hiyangei, (Saturday)-Labanya Chandra, king of Manipur died of head injuries during a Polo Game.

In March, 1859, the world's first Polo club was established at Silchar, Cachar by Captain Robert Stewart and Lt. John Shearer.

1861- Polo played for the first time in history in Dacca.

1862 - Polo played for the first time in history in Calcutta. Calcutta Polo Club, the oldest existing polo club, was founded.

In 1864, on invitation from Calcutta, the Silchar Polo Club raised a Manipuri polo team known as "The Band of Brothers" and Lt. John Shearer took them, with their ponies, to Calcutta by country boat. The team consisted of Toolsi Singh, Chowba Singh, Ammu Singh, Omah Singh, Tubal Singh, Aema Ba and Monga Pa. The Manipuri team easily defeated the Calcutta team.

In 1868, Polo Game reached Malta and the game was played between soldiers and naval officers stopping off there on their way home from India to England.

1868. Malta Polo Club founded. In 1869, Edward "Chicken" Hartopp, 10th Hussars, read an account of the game in The Field, while stationed at Aldershot, and, with brother officers, organised the first game - known then as "hockey on horseback"- on a hastily-rolled Hounslow Heath against The 9th Lancers. The 1st Life Guards and the Royal Horse Guards were quick to follow suit on grounds at Hounslow and in Richmond Park; and then on a small ground near Earl's Court known as Lillie Bridge.

1872. The first polo club in England was Monmouth shire, founded by Capt. Francis "Tip" Herbert (1845-1922), 7th Lancers, at his brother's seat, Clytha Park, near Abergavenny. All Ireland Polo Club was also founded in 1872 by Horace Rochfort of Clogrenane, Co. Carlow.

1873, Thomas Taylor brought the first Polo mallet to Argentinia. This piece, donated by Luis L. Lacey, is proudly kept and exhibited at the Venado Tuerto Polo Club.

1875. The first official match in Argentina took place on 3rd September, where the game had been taken by English and Irish engineers and ranchers.

1876. Lt. Col. Thomas St. Quintin, 10th Hussars, introduced the game to Australia - he was the "Father of Australian Polo" and two of his brothers stayed on there as ranchers and helped the game to develop.

1875 (30 August), the first local official game in Argentina was played by Irishmen, estancia owners and English engineers at the Villanueva estancia in Ranchos, in the province of Buenos Aires.

1875, the "Hurlingham Polo Association" was founded which started a progressive officialization of the rules.

1876, Lt Col Thomas St.Quintin, of the 10th Hussars, introduced the game to Australia.

1876, Polo was introduced to the USA by James Gordon Bennett Junior who had seen the game at Hurlingham during a visit to England. The first friendly games were played in Manhattan, at the Dickels Riding Academy.

1876- A match was also staged between the Calcutta Polo Club and the Manipuri team on the occasion of a visit to Calcutta by the Prince of Wales.

1877 The first series of outdoor Polo games took place in the United States at a Bronx racetrack. Informal games were being played in New York City

1877, The first North American polo club was formed, the Westchester Polo Club.

1879, The first official match in Argentina took place, where the sport of Polo was introduced by Irish ranchers at Shennan's Estancia.

1879, In France, the first match was played in Dieppe: a French team, lead by the Duc de Guiche, played against a British team in 1880.

1881 The Meadow Brook Club was formed in Long Island, New York, by such early outstanding players as Thomas Hitchcock, Sr., August Belmont, and Benjamin Nicoll.

1886, The first international game, the "Westchester Cup", was played in Rhode Island opposing Great Britain and the United States, it ended with the victory of the British Hurling ham Team.

1886, The Hurlingham Club of England was established, which introduced rules of Polo game. The size of the team was reduced to five in 1886,

1888, Handicaps were introduced by the USA and by England and India in 1910.The Handicap system appeared to help balance teams of different levers. New Zealand, South Africa, Australia and even Gibraltar and Malta soon followed.

1989, The Inter University Tournament of polo was started in USA.

1890, The Polo Association (later the United States Polo Association/ USPA) was founded and standardized the rules. Polo spread throughout the country, although the game long remained one for the rich because of the expense of the game.

1890, The New Zealand Polo Association was formed.

1895. The height for Polo ponies was raised from 14 hands to 14.2.

1910 – the Polo handicap was established, based on the American system. Handicaps were introduced in England and India.

1919. Height restriction on Polo ponies was abolished.

1988, The University of London Polo Club (ULPC) was formed.

2000, A professional women's polo league, known as the United States Women's Polo Federation founded in USA. The sixteen-team league plays across the country.

HISTORY OF POLO BY OTHER COUNTRIES OF THE WORLD :

Polo is known several local names in different countries such as - "Chaughan" (Persian), "Da-Kyu" (Japanese), "Khis-Kouhou" (Russian), "Djerid" (Turkish), and "Sagol Kangjei" (Manipuri/Indian). But the origin of the modern name Polo is perhaps derived from the Tibetan word "Pulu", which means a ball.

1. Greece

History tells that Alexander the Great, who conquered the Persian empire around 331 B.C., was an accomplished Polo player. His rival and later defeated enemy Darius of Persia sent him a mallet and a ball for him to practice before declaring war. Alexander answered: "I am the mallet and the ball is the world. Be alert". Some historians claimed that Polo existed from the reign of Alexander the Great in the 4th Century B.C. As Alexander and other conquerors swept across Asia, they carried the game with them to the new lands they conquered – eventually as far away as Japan and Mongolia.

2. Persia

Persian literature and art give us rich accounts (stories) of Polo. Many of the Persian manuscripts (books) that tell about Polo are beautifully illustrated with miniature paintings showing royalty and their best horsemen playing Polo. The 13th century poet Nizami weaves the love story of a King and his beautiful consort (mistress), around her ability in the Polo field. He describes matches between the King and his courtiers vs. his consort and her ladies-in-waiting. The wife of a 19th century Mughal Emperor was also skilled at Polo. So even women were Polo players. The women of the royal court could play Polo. It would not be a game for "common" people who couldn't afford a horse nor the time for sports. Polo was called "the sport of Kings".

The first recorded game took place in Persia in 600 BC, between the Turkomans and Persians (the Turkomans won). Emperor Cantacuzenus (ruled Byzantium 1341-1347) was one of the earliest recorded casualties of the sport. In the ancient city of Ispahan a Polo field was built in front of Ali Ghapu Palace by Shah Abbas the Great (ruled 1585-1628). Today, still used as a public park, it is the same size as a modern Polo field with its original stone goal posts in place.

In the 4th century A.D King Sapoor II of Persia learned to play Polo at the age of 7. In the 16th century AD a Polo ground (300 yards long and with goal posts 8 yards apart) was built at Ispahan, then the capital, by Shah Abbas the Great. The Moguls were largely responsible for taking the game from Persia to the east and by the 16th century the Emperor Babur had established it in India.

Firdausi (930-1020 A.D.), the most famous of Persia's poet-historian, gives a number of accounts of royal Polo tournaments in his 9th century epic, "Shahnamah". In the earliest account, Ferdausi, romanticizes an international match between Turanian force and the followers of Syavoush, a legendary Persian ruler from the earliest centuries of the Empire. The poet is eloquent in his praise of Syavoush's skills on the polo field. Firdausi also tells of Sapor-II Sassanid, King of the 4th Century A.D., who learned to play Polo when he was only seven years old. The greatest of Persian poets, Ferdausi, in his work "The Book of Kings" mentions Polo as the "National sport". Another 9th century historian, Dinvari, describes Polo and its general rules and gives some instructions to players including such advice as 'polo requires a great deal of exercise', 'if Polo stick breaks during a game it is a sign of inefficiency' and 'a player should strictly avoid using strong language and should be patient and temperate'. During the 10th century the Persian King Qabus also set down some general rules of Polo and especially mentioned the risks and dangers of the game.

The first references to the game in Persian literature date to 600 BC. But the best-known are contained in the 11th-century Rubaiyat of Omar Khayyam, who used polo as a metaphor for God's dominion over the apparent chaos of life:

Rubaiyat of Omar Khayyam.

The Ball no question makes of Ayes and Noes,
But Right or Left as strikes the player goes;
And He that toss'd thee down into the Field,
He knows about it all - He knows - He knows!

3. Iran

Some scholars believe that polo originated among the Iranian tribes sometime before Darius-I (521–485 BC) and his cavalry forged the first great Persian Empire in the 6th century B.C. Persian literature and art gave very good accounts of Polo in antiquity. Ferdoasi, the famed Iranian poet-historian, gives a number of accounts of royal Polo tournaments in his 9th century epic, Shahnamah (the Epic of Kings).

4. India

While the Persians and later the Mughals, knew the game as 'Chaughan', meaning mallet, variants of the game tested the horsemanship and courage of the participants under the name of 'Da-Kyu' in Japan, 'Khis - Kouhou' on the Russian steppes and 'Djerid' in Turkey.

In India, Polo was widely played in medieval times as is evidenced from the fact that Sultan Qutubuddin Aibak, founder of the Slave dynasty and builder of one of Delhi's most famous landmarks, the Qutub Minar, died of a fatal accident, impaled on the ornate horn of his own saddle after a fall on the Polo field in Lahore. However, it was Babar, the founder of the Mughal dynasty who established the popularity of Polo in India in the fifteenth century. The Emperor Akbar the Great was a patron of Polo which was regularly played at his court. He himself was described as an outstanding player in all branches of the game. He introduced a uniform set of rules for the game, and his vast Polo stables can still be seen near Agra.

Under the Mughals, Polo was the national sport of India until the end of sixteenth century. During the period that the house of Timur reigned supreme in Delhi, Polo enjoyed the patronage of Kings and nobles and was widely played in the provinces of the Empire and in the courts of the Rajput Kings.

However, the decline of the Mughal dynasty also heralded the decline of indigenous Polo in the country. In the unsettled times of the eighteenth century, when the imperial authority waned in the plains and peninsula of India, the sword ruled the land, and Polo all but vanished from the Indian scene.

The 13th century poet Nizami weaves the love story of the Sassanid King Khusru and his beautiful consort Shirin, around her ability on the Polo field, and describes matches between Khusru and his courtiers and Shirin and her ladies-in-waiting. Nurjahan, wife of the 17th century Mughal Emperor Jahangir, was also skilled at Polo.

5. China

Some believe that the Chinese were the first to try their hands at Polo. Polo was a popular royal pastime for many centuries in China, the Chinese probably having learned the game from the same Indian tribes who were taught by the Persians. The polo stick appeared on royal coats of arms in China and the game was part of the court life in the golden age of Chinese classical culture under Ming-Hung, the Radiant Emperor, who was an enthusiastic patron of equestrian activities. Less cultured, one might think, was the reaction of Emperor Tai Tsu in 910 A.D. who, according to one source, ordered all the other players beheaded after a favourite was killed in a match.

6. Northern Pakistan

The word *polo* is derived from "Pulu" -Balti for *ball.* Polo was played in Skardu (Baltistan), Ladakh, the Kargil area of India, and in a few places of Tibet and Nepal. The evidence of polo is found in a 4000-4500 year-old Balti story named Hilafoo Kaisaar". In northern Pakistan, where Polo is still played in its original form (free-style), a local variant is called "*Chogan*" (Chaughan)

"Let other people play at other things — the King of Games is still the Game of Kings"

This verse is inscribed on a stone tablet next to a Polo ground in Skardu, north of Kashmir, near the fabled silk route from China to the West. In one ancient sentence, it epitomises the feelings of many Polo players today. "The sport of Polo is without doubt the oldest ball game in the world."

From the sequence of events mentioned above, it is proved that modern Polo came to the Europe, America and Australia via Manipur, not from any other place. Sagol Kangjei (Polo) has been an indigenous game of Manipur as early as 3100 BC. Manipur was an isolated place full of difficult terrain and jungles where there was no possibility of learning this game from India or Chinese or Persia. What the rest of the world has learnt about Polo today is the Polo played in Manipur, not the polo played in Persia or anywhere else. This is evident after studying the history of modern polo. According to historical accounts, one British government official stationed in Manipur (then a princely state) during the late 19th century wrote an account of the sport, and thus its popularity spread. Therefore, the Guinness Book of Records in its 1991 edition (page 288) traces the origins of the game to Manipur, circa 3100 BC, where it was known as Sagol Kangjei.

References

Captain Younghusband, Polo in India, (nd.); J. Moray Brown, Polo (Vinton, 1896); T. Captain Younghusband, Tournament Polo (1897).

Captain de Lisle, Durham Light Infantry, Hints to Polo Players in India (1897);

Captain E. D. Miller, Modern Polo (19o~l).

Captain McCulloch, Manipuric and the Adjacent Tribes (1859). (T. F. D.)

David, Ceri (2008-11-23), "Going Polo", *Sunday Herald Sun*: Sunday magazine supplement (pp. 20-21).

Captain E. D. Miller, D.S.O., The Polo Players Guide and Almanack; The Polo Annual, ed. by L.V.L.

F. Dale, The Game of Polo (A. Constable & Co., 1897).

H.L. Fitzpatrick, Equestrian Polo, in.

Hurlingham Club, Rules of Polo, Register of Ponies; Polo and Riding Pony Society Stud Book (12 vols., 12 Hanover Square). Annuals: American Polo Association, 14~ J. Moray Brown, Riding and Polo, Badminton Library, revised and brought up to date by T. F. Dale (Longmans, 1899).

Liberty Street, New York; Indian Polo Association, Lucknow, N.P.

Major G. J. Younghusband, Tournament Polo (1904).

T. F. Dale Polo, Past and Present, Country Life; Walter Buckmaster, Hints on Polo Combination, Library of Sport (George Newnes Ltd., 1905; Vinton & Co., 1909).

Simmonds. Monthlies: Baileys Magazine (Vinton & Co.); The Polo Monthly (Craven House, Kingsway, London).

Polo in Persia: Firdousis Shahnama, translated as Le Livre des rois by J. Mohl, with notes and comm.; Sir Anthony Shirley, Travels in Persia (1569).

Polo in Constantinople: Cinnamus Joannes epitome rerum ab joanne et Alexio Commenis gest. (Bonn, 1836).

Polo in India: Ain-i-Akbari (1555); G. F. Vigne, Travels in Kashmir (Ladakh and Iskardo - 1842); Colonel Algernon Durand, The Making of a Frontier (1899).

Polo in Gilgit and Chitral: Polo in Baltistan. The Field (1888); Polo in Manipur,

Polo by Penina Meisels and Michael Cronan. Collins Publishers, San Francisco, 1992. ISBN 0-00-637796-3

http://www.argentinapolo.com/polohistory.htmlhttp://sportclubs.ucdavis.edu/horsepolo/history.htm

http://www.feliciawong.com/01Jaipur/AboutUs/History.shtml

http://www.sportpolo.com/History/default.htm

http://www.nickerstickers.com/horse/polopony.htm

Polo (2007). In Encyclopædia Britannica. Retrieved April 26, 2007, from Encyclopaedia Britannica Online". http://www.britannica.com/eb/article-5832/polo.

"Polo History". http://www.scottishpolo.com/history_game.html.

Naqsh-i Jahan Square in Isfahan is in fact a polo field which was built by king Abbas I in 17th century.

"Polo History". http://www.indiapolo.com/Polopedia/History/history.html.

Sir John Chardin, Voyage.f en Per,e (1686), ed. aug. denotes, &c. par L. Langles, 1811; Sir William Ouseley, Travels in Various Countries of the East, particularly Persia (1810).There are many allusions to polo in the poets, notably Nizami, Jami and Omar Khayyam.

Sarina Singh, Owen Bennett-Jones, Lindsay Brown, John Mock. *Pakistan & the Karakoram Highway*, Lonely Planet, 2004, ISBN 0864427093 p.55

Sports and Games of the 18th and 19th Centuries by Robert Crego. page 25. Published 2003. Greenwood Press. Sports & Recreation. 296 pages ISBN 0313316104

Sports and Games of the 18th and 19th Centuries by Robert Crego. Page 26 - 27. Published 2003. Greenwood Press. Sports & Recreation. 296 pages ISBN 0313316104 FIP

Spaldings Athletic Library (1904);

T. B. Drybrough, Polo (Vinton, 1898; revised, Longmans, 1906);

The Guinness Book of Records. 1991 edition (page 288)

World Cup VIII - 2007

http://www.tourismsouthasia.com/Pakistan/mountain_valleys/shandoor_polo_chitral.asp

http://www.youtube.com/watch?v=ZXm-PdF24Uo&feature=related

8o Campeonato Mundial de Polo: México 2008

www.telegraph.co.uk/news/worldnews/asia/china/3260092/Chinese-tycoon-Xia-Yang-inspired-by-Prince-Charles-to-restore-polo-to-Communist-China.html

http://www.ndhpolo.com/

http://www.britannica.com/EBchecked/topic/240505/Memo-Gracida

http://www.polomuseum.com/hof_inductees/inductees_year.htm

http://www.uspaproperties.com/historyofpolo.html

http://www.us-polo.org/history.htm

http://www.sportpolo.com/history/default.htm

http://www.lonympics.co.uk/historyofPolo.htm

http://www.thai-polo-club.com/history_of_polo.php

http://www.encyclopedia.com/doc/1O110-polo.html

http://www.polistas.co.uk/news/index.php?option=com_content
&view=article&id=54&Itemid=64

http://www.cais-soas.com/CAIS/Sport/polo.htm

http://www.games-1900http://en.wikipedia.org/wiki/Polo

Plate -315: King Chourajit and Yuvaraj Marjit-1808

Plate -316: Manipuri Polo Team at Calcutta -1875

Plate-317: Players of Manipur Polo at Inner Pologround, Manipur 1890

Plate-318: Ancient Persian Polo

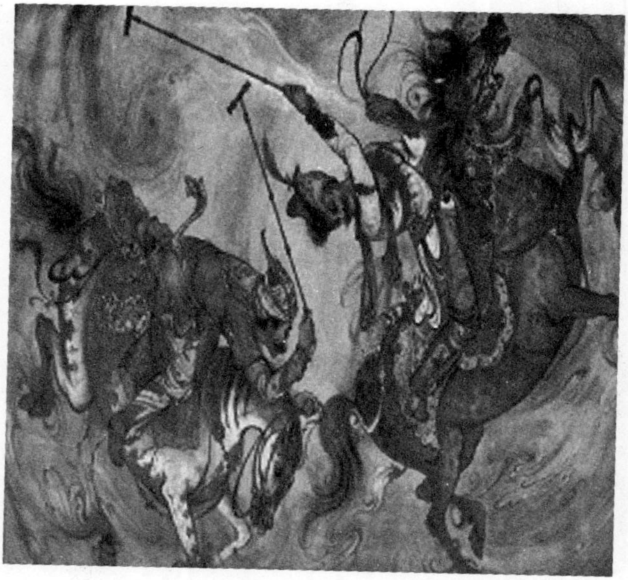

Plate-319: "Chogân" by Master Mahmmoud Farshchiyân

Plate-320:Chogan

Plate -321: Ancient painting of Polo

Plate -322: Tang Dynasty Chinese Courtiers-706 A.D.

Plate -323 Polo players China; Tang dynasty (618–907), 8th century Earthenware, traces of polychrome decoration Approx. 39.4 x 33 x 9.2 cm R.H. Norton Trust

Plate -324 A folio of Persian manuscript of Mathnavi of Guy-va Chogan (Khalnameh) by Tahmaseb Mirza

Plate -325: Attributed to the artist Sanvlah *Queen Humay Playing Polo with Her Slaves, from an illustrated Dara-nama* (The Tale of Darab) The British Library, Or. 4615, f.11v

Plate- 326: Terracotta- Female Player- 8th Century

Plate - 327: Rajput Princes playing Polo in medieval period

Plate -328: Polo at Meadowbrook-II 1938 –Howard W Frank

Plate -329: James Gordon Bennett introduced Polo in the United States in 1876

Plate-330: Polo played as a part of Olympic

Plate -331: Womens' Polo Team ,USA

Plates -332-333: Some of the Polo Games seen at the Mapal Kangjeibung, Imphal, Manipur, India

Plates -334: Some of the Polo Games seen at the Mapal Kangjeibung, Imphal, Manipur, India

Plates -335: Some of the Polo Games seen at the Mapal Kangjeibung, Imphal, Manipur, India

Plates -336:
Some of the Polo Games seen at the Mapal Kangjeibung, Imphal, Manipur, India

19

Handlooms, Handicrafts and Textiles

The Manipuri handlooms and handicrafts are renown all over the country. Manipur enjoys a distinct place amongst the Handloom zones in India. Handloom industry is the largest and the most common cottage industry in the State. From time immemorial handloom industry has been playing a vital role in the state economy. The traditional skill of handloom weaving was not only a status symbol for the Manipuri women-folk but it was also an indispensable aspect of the socio-economic life of Manipuri women. The handicraft of Manipur is artistic and reflects the creativity of Manipuri people.

LEGENDS

According to legend, Leimarel Sidabi introduced weaving as a part of creation of the universe. Chitnu Tamitnu, a goddess discovered the cotton and she also produced the yarn. When the threads are ready for weaving, she arranged the required equipments and constructed the "Sinnaishang" (work shed). It is also believed that the Goddess Panthoibi once saw a spider producing fine threads and making cobwebs and from it she found the idea of weaving and thus started weaving from materials obtained from membrane of bamboo and wood. According to Leithak Leikharol puya, two celestial heroes Ashiba and Konjin Tuthokpa were believed to have introduced the Meitei ways of dressing.

HISTORICAL BACKGROUND

The Meitei dress and culture were well advanced at the time of Nongda Lairen Pakhangba (33 A.D) when Chari Ningkham, Konkha Phurit, Samjin, Phiren Phurit and Lollei Kokyet were introduced for the King and Kumlang Phanek, Phiren Kanak, Kabrang Kanak Khawon Phurit and Luren Luhao were introduced for the Queen, Laisna. (Pakhangba Phambal and Kanglei Sanglen Puba Puya). Once while visiting his consort, Khuiyoi Tompok, son of Pakhangba killed his father at the instigation of Huitou Khaba Tou Suba, an enemy of Ningthouja Clan. Pakhangba appeared in the dream of his consort and advised her to weave royal dress taking the patterns on several parts of his body. Thus Khamen Chatpa, Ningkham Samjin, Khadangchet, Lamthang Khuthut, Ningthouphi and Leirum were introduced. Till today, Leirum is considered to be an essential item of bridal gifts.

It is believed that sericulture was introduced during the reign of Khuiyoi Tompok (154-264 A.D.). Nongmoinu Ahongbi, Queen of Khuiyoi Tompok gave birth to a daughter but the baby died after some time. The King and the Queen were very unhappy. After some time, they found silk worms appearing on the mulberry tree which sprang up on the grave of the deceased daughter. They believed that the worms were the incarnations of their daughter. They noticed that the worms were producing cocoons and out of the cocoons, they invented the art of making silk threads. They called the worms "Leima til" (a worm born out of the royal daughter). They entrusted the work of rearing the worms to some families at a village called "Leimapokpam" and "Leimaram". (Dr.K.Sobita Devi "Traditional Dress of the Meiteis", Bhubon Publishing House, Imphal, 1998)

During the reign of Meidingu Naothingkhong (663-763A.D), many dresses particularly coronation dresses were introduced such as "Phingang Pheijom", "Innaphi Langdom", "Phiren Phurit", "Konkha Phurit", "Pakloi", "Kokyet" as described in the Naothingkhong Phambal Kaba, Meitei Ariba Laining Laichat, Phambalon.

During the reign of Keiphaba Yanglou (969-984AD), embroidery work was introduced. Mayek Naibi (stripped phanek of females), Khoi Mayek, Khoijao, Khoi Akoibi, Hija Mayek were introduced. The Hija Mayek was named after the peculiar patterns of flowers found on the cross section of the timber cut for making "Hi (canoe) discovered by the Royal Chief Carpenter named Hijam Kondraba.

During the time of Meidingu Loiyumba (1074-1112 A.D), the weaving culture was highly flourished and Loiyumba allocated the weaving works of different patterns to different clans and Sageis – say Chakpram was responsible for production of Phiren, Thoudam for Phagang Phi, Ningthoujam for Chinphi, Khoisnam for Phimu Laphi, Wangpacham for Shammi Lanmi Phi, Shaphi Lanphi, Kongbam for Purum Phi, Lairenllakpam for Laiphi etc. Meidingu Loiyumba also introduced new designs of textiles like Urit Mahum, Makong Meiri and Muga Machu and Amuba were used. He even distributed the task of dyeing of different colours to different families and Sakeis.

Kwakpa Thawanthaba, son of Meidingu Thangbi Lanthaba (1302-1324) was considered to be the originator of Pheijom dress for male among the Meiteis. He married a Kamrup princes (Assam) named Chingulembi of Mleecha dynasty of Kamrup (Assam). He was influenced by the Pheijom culture when a group of people including the bodyguards came to Manipur at the time of marriage.

When Meidingu Kongyamba (1324-1335) defeated the Khuman King Lamyay Kaikhinba and the Khuman attire was absorbed in the Meitei culture.

When Kyaamba started worshipping Vishnu (1467-1508, the traditional dress like the Dhoti, Kurta, Innaphi (thin wrapper) were used. The production of silk yarn increased as a result of close contact with the Shans from the time of Meidingu Kyaamba.The Manipuri word "Kabrang" is derived from two words– "Kabow- Lang".

Khagemba (1597-1652) introduced the practice of giving special awards to the hill Chiefs, nobles and talented subjects in the form of special clothes. Thus "Mana Phi", Pari Phi", Wanphak Phurit" were introduced. Ningkham Phurit Lairen, Salai Kokyet, Ningkham Samjin, Lengkhang Phi, Kokyet Kangdrum, Phirangchi, Pana Phi were introduced.

Charairongba (1697-1709) introduced Pala Kokyet Achouba. During the time of Chandrakirti (1834-1844), Kokyet Phisang with Lamthang Khuthut Phijin in multicolour was produced. During the time of Bhagyachandra Maharaja (1763-1798), stitched shirt with woven patterns were introduced for the King, prince, princess and nobles. Maharaja Narsingha (1844-1850) introduced "Lushet Kokyet" and Churachand Maharaja (1891-1941) introduced' "Ajmeri Kokyet". (Dr. K. Sobita Devi "Traditional Dress of the Meities, Bhubon Publishing house, Imphal - 2008)

MODERN HANDLOOM AND HANDICRAFTS

Perhaps, the earliest attempt to bring the Manipuri handloom on modern lines was made by Mrs. Jolly, wife of Mr. E.M. Jolly. Chief Engineer of Manipur during the reign of Churachand Maharaja. She established an Arts and Crafts

Office at Imphal and did research on the various designs and patterns of Manipuri handicraft. She continued her work even after her husband left Manipur. (M.K. Binodini, Churachand Maharaj gi Imung, 2008)

In Manipur, every house possesses a loom (see plates -337, 338), and every Manipuri weave with a passion and style, unrivalled by any other state. Manipuri bed covers of Moirangfee and flower designs, silk and cotton sarees, scarves, blankets and shawls, in distinctive shades and designs make for an enchanting collection. A wide range of artistic handicrafts from bamboo, Peppier Mache, decorative ivory, dolls and jewellery make for prized souvenirs. These exquisite handlooms and handicrafts are sold at Khwairamband Keithel and Ima keithel, the largest exclusive women's market in India.

One of the special features of the industry is that women are the only weavers in Manipur.

HANDLOOM POPULATION AND PRODUCTION

According to the National handloom Census Reports 1988 there are about 2.71 lakh looms in Manipur. As per the National Handloom census reports 1996-97, there are 3.39 lakh weavers with 2.77 lakh different looms producing 86.40 lakh linear metres of handloom cloth per month.

In respect of Imphal, Thoubal and Bishnupur districts, the main handloom products are Cotton, Polyester cloths like Sarees, bed sheets, bed covers, curtain, towel (Bath towels, hand towels, face towels, etc), Table cloths, Fashion garments with intricate designs, cushion covers, pillow covers,

Table-51 Showing Handloom population and production in Manipur

Sl. No.	*District Name*	*No. of weaver*	*No. of loom*	*Consumption of yarn per month (in Kg.)*	*Production of cloth per month (in Metre)*
1.	Imphal	91820	68273	5, 01,936.10	44, 26,402.00
2.	Thoubal	37835	26586	1, 60,334.50	19, 33,600.00
3.	Bishnupur	53069	31420	1, 86,294.70	13, 25,974.00
4.	Churachandpur	39294	43847	56,502.10	3, 61,953.60
5.	Ukhrul	24233	22629	23,567.00	1, 98,933.50
6.	Tamenglong	35577	36918	1, 02,953.80	2, 29,434.30
7.	Senapati	44250	35443	12,763.80	92,901.12
8.	Chandel	13554	11639	26,204.70	71,615.00
	Total	339632	276755	10, 70,557.00	86, 40,814.00

(National Handloom Census Report - 1996-97)

Upholstery, Draperies, Scarves, Terry towels, dressing gown, Lashingphi (cotton tweed cloth) etc. and the five hill districts mainly produced Acrylic/ wool cloth like Tribal Shawl, Ladies' Lungies, Wall hanging and coverings, Upholstery, hanging bags, curtain, home furnishing etc.

Out of the total weavers 70% were working full time in the valley areas as against 30% in the hill areas. The incidence of low utilization of employment both in the hill and valley areas is due to lack of proper and efficient marketing mechanism. If proper marketing arrangement is made, the capacity utilization could be increased. In fact, if there is full utilization of the available manpower and equipment in the State, the production would be 115.20 lakh metre of handloom cloth per month.

Most of the weavers who are famous for their skill and intricate designing are from Wangkhei, Bamon Kampu, Kongba, Khongman, Utlou etc. in respect of fine silk items. Wangkhei Phi or Rani Phi is very popular (see plates–342, 343) The rest of the villages in the State produce all varieties of fabrics. Haophi (Tribal shawls) of various types, colours and designs are very common and popular. Tribal shawls with exotic designs and motifs are the products of five hill districts of the State. Fabrics and Shawls of Manipur are in great demand in the national and international market.

TEXTILES OF THE MEITEIS

According to Meitei folklores, it is the God of Handicrafts (Leisembi) who taught the Meiteis, the method of textile weaving as well as the mystique of the dance creation.

King Nongda Lairel Pakhangba (33 A.D) and the King Loiyumba (1074-1112) patronized the art of weaving. Weaving in Manipur is entirely the work of women. Weaving is a part of their domestic duties. Skills and proficiency in weaving is considered an essential qualification of womanhood. A Meitei girl is initiated with this art at a tender age, and throughout her life, she practices this art. Not only she supplies clothing to her family members but also make it a source of their income. Among the Meiteis, Kabuis, Thangkhuls and Kukis women, those who are practicing this craft are usually married women whereas, among the Paites and Hmars majority of the unmarried women practice weaving.

Cotton is not much grown in Manipur area. Whatever little is grown are neither enough nor of good quality. It is true that cotton is not grown much in Imphal proper but people in the hills grow part of their need in their Jhum fields, in between two crops. They purchase major part of their need of yarn either through the co- operatives or from the local shop. Those who produce cotton in their fields have to pass through different stages to make suitable yarn for weaving.

In order to produce proper yarn they pass through the following process:

- Ginning is the process of removing the seeds from the cotton.
- Guarding means cleaning the cotton by flicking method.
- Spinning is the process through which the cotton is wound round the wooden or iron spike.
- Winding is the process of transforming the yarn from wanks to bobbins.
- Twisting and Spinning
- Dyeing - the dying is done with indigenous dye stuff, mostly from barks and the common type of mordant.
- Sizing - Once the yarn is ready, they start weaving and finally the garments produced have to pass through the process of bleaching. Yarns are bleached to make them white or to prepare them for dying or printing.

DESIGN AND EMBROIDERY USED IN MEITEI TEXTILES

In Manipur, there are types of embroideries, which are specially made for warriors and to be presented by the King as a mark of distinction

Lanphi: War cloth, a special type of shawl embroidered by the women at home is used by the warriors at the time of going out for war.

Ningthouphi: Waistcoat, which is presented by the King to the warriors of the country.

Saijounba: Long coat, these were prepared with special embroideries for the very trusted courtiers of the King.

Phirananba: Small flags delicately embroidered and used by the warriors as plumes on their turbans.

Namthang-khut-hut: A design derived out of the head of Pakhangba on the wrapper. The cloth with this design taken from the belly of distinction. The clothe is meant to be used only by the ladies of the royal family.

Khamenchatpa: these designs are embroidered on the dhotis and are presented to the people of distinction.

Phirangji: a red coloured blanket presented to the persons of merit. The colour of the blanket is totally red and is believed to have been copied from the blood with the placenta.

*Moirangphi***,** is a temple design, this piece of cloth with peculiar design was invented by the princess Moirang Thoibi. This design is actually in red, green, black and blue colours and is woven in the borders of chaddars and sari.

Lashingphi is a very famous cloth. It is a light quilt. The usual shades are golden, orange, green, blue and red. This quilt replaces blankets during winters. The cotton wicks are artistically and adroitly arranged horizontally through the silky and striped bands of different fibre of the wrap. The different designs are named Likti design; Bottle design; Moibung design – attractive motifs; and Shamilan design with animal motifs.

Likli Design: Likli means bottle. This design is popularly known as the bottle design and is used on shoulder bags, bed covers etc. This design is evolved from the part of a loom.

Moibung design: this design is common on the bed-covers and has green, blue, maroon and chocolate shades.

Shamilanmi design: The Shamilanmi design (see plates- 344) is embroidered with motifs of horses, elephants and butterflies etc. shades of orange, green, blue and red are very common in these designed shawls. The shawls with this design are popularly known as the Naga chaddar as the Angami Nagas used the design.

Shamuphi (Elephant Clothe) : This is a special clothe depicting elephants and various other designs for presentation by the King to the Chiefs of hill tribes.

Leirum: This cloth thus woven is used by the Meities in ceremonial occasions. Among the Meities it is an essential item of presentation during the marriage.

Chum design: cloth designed after pattern is exclusively meant for a presentation to be made by the King to the people of high proficiency in dance and song, Pandits and heroes also receive this cloth as a recognition of their deep knowledge and heroism. This design is now woven not for the same purpose as in the beginning but on the ordinary door curtains, cushion cover and mats, etc. The shades commonly found are orange, brown, blue and chocolate.

Leirong design: It is a traditional floral design of Manipur and is said to be the mother design of all floral designs of Manipur. Among the Meities 'lei' means flower and 'rong' means design. This is a common design for the bed cover and tablecloths with several variations. The blue, green, orange and red are the common shades used for the design.

Bakey Design: The design was named after a Kuki woman who invented this design. This design was woven originally for skirts but now this design is practically found on any type of shawl and bed covers. The common shades are blue, green and maroon.

Kudam Manbi: Kudam means button. This design is known by several names. The most common one is, button design but the other popular one is known as Mitlaobi design or broad-eye design. The idea of this design is said to have originated from the patterns made of beads and cowries by the Kukis. (Dr. K. Sabita Devi - "Traditional Dress of the Meities", Bhubon Publishing House, Imphal, 1998, Mutua Bahadur; "Traditional Textiles of Manipur"; Matua Museum, Keisampat, Imphal, 1994)

TEXTILES OF NAGAS

Hodson (1911) has mentioned ten types of cloth patterns amongst Naga tribes.

- Pakhon phi, this is worn by men, the central portion is white and the borders are with black, blue and red lines:
- Leirum phi, red and white with black marks;
- Kairao phi, with red, black and blue strips;
- Lai phi is worn by women; it is with red and white stripes;
- Longkhum Kasum is worn by women; it is with red and white stripes.
- Sukham phi is a cloth with white ground with red and black border;
- Pordesum phi, the piece of cloth is with red, black, blue and white cross markings;
- Langoudesum phi, is woman's cloth with black and red stripes;
- Kasundesum phi is worn by women, it is with broad red and narrow black stripes;
- Melao phi is a waist cloth worn by Naga men, it is with blue and red strips.

TEXTILE OF TANGKHULS

Phangvai Kashan is used by female. It is a three-piece cloth separately woven and joined together. It is meant for rich ladies. These figures represent goddess Phangyai, the goddess of wealth. It is a python possessing a very long hair and whenever it enters into anybody's field, it is a good omen.

Changkham is a shawl and is used by both sexes as a wrapper. The bigger size is woven in three pieces. It has alternate black and red stripes in the middle. On the border, there are motifs of spear.

Seiyang Kashan is a three-piece woven cloth used by the female as Phanek (skirt).

Khankhan is used as a skirt for the females. It has red background with black and white stripes.

Kongla Kashan is a skirt with red, black and white stripes and the whole body is decorated with cross-signs.

Kashang Kashan is a skirt used by all females. The background of the skirt is red and has white stripes.

Khoram Phi is a wrapper used by both the sexes. The end border of Khoram Phi is decorated with different designs. scattered all over the body.

Thang-gang is an equivalent of Tangu Puon of Hmars, Paites. It is a special cloth to be used by the person who has proved his gallantry in war by killing enemies, and has a good house and has harvested a good amount of crop. They believe that, if a person wears this cloth without attaining such qualification, he is likely to be disfigured by the curse of god.

Phalengchi is a mill-made red blanket used to be presented by the Manipuri Raja to the Chief and his assistant. It is considered as highly prized possession. (see plates–351-353) (Mutua Bahadur "Tribal Hand Woven Fabrics of Manipur", Mutua Museum, Keisampat, Imphal, 2000)

TEXTILE OF KABUI NAGAS

Most of handloom products of Kabui Nagas are mostly ceremonial dance dresses.

Some of the products are :-

Pheishoi: Phei means cloth, shoi means skirt or lower garment for the ladies. This looks like a Phanek of the Meiteis but without border. Usually it is of black. Red and pink colour with a broad red border. Though this is a ceremonial dress but it is also used as daily dress.

Lejing Phel shoi: A skirt with grey base and red borders on two sides. The red border contains interlacing of various colours. The body has three white stripes flanked on two sides by a narrow black strap. Each white stripes contains three set of black and red arrow-shaped structures. The skirt is used both for daily use and for ceremonial occasions.

Langu Pheihoi: A skirt, used during ceremonial occasions only. The two borders are broad and of bright red colour. The red borders also have two white narrow stripes separated from one another. The border is often followed by narrow yellow and green straps. The rest of the body of the cloth is of black colour, containing three broad straps and are separated from one another. Throughout the length of the cloth, there are lines made of interlacing of yarns of various colours which extend from the middle of the red coloured side border to some portion of the black body which hang freely at this end.

Nai: This is a longoti type cloth used by the men folk for covering their private parts. But it is gradually going out of use.

Ranglan: This is a red coloured and stripped ceremonial lower garment for male, worn during the dance. It is made up of four pieces, which are joined together.

Song Nai: It is a dancing dress. The adolescent boys use it as lower garment during the dance. The Song Nai cloth is woven in two pieces and stitched together. At the two ends of the cloth there are flower petal design embroidered by tying cotton yarns and wool.

Phaingao: A ceremonial wrapper made of four pieces. The two side borders are red and boarder than the others. This is followed by narrow stripes of yellow, green and black respectively. The base of the cloth is white. The end borders are quite broad and have interlacing of different colours.

Philak: It is a kind of belt used by the boys and the girls during the ceremonial dances. It is white colour. This white coloured belt, side borders of which start with a narrow red stripe followed by yellow and green borders. Coloured tassel are tied in two free border ends of red and white threads.

Thiam Phai: This is a common black wrapper for daily use and is made of two pieces. It forms a part of the present to the parents of the bride, besides the bride price.

Kharam Phai: This is a common black wrapper having only white stripes near the border and is used mainly by the old people. This, like the Thiam Phai, is a present to the parents of the bride. (Matua Bahadur "Tribal Hand Woven Fabrics of Manipur", Matua Museum, Keisampat, Imphal, 2000)

TEXTILE OF HMARS

The Hmars weave many designs and some of the important ones are:

Thangsuo Puon: In Hmars language, Thangsuo Puon means famous cloth. It is a handloom cloth for the persons who earned the right to wear this by killing the maximum number of enemies in a war. Their wives are also allowed to use this cloth.

Puon Laisen: Puon Laisen is a red striped cloth. In Hmar language, it means cloth with middle in red colour, but the center has two black stripes. The cloth has several designs like Sakat Zang Zie, Disul, etc.

Hmarm: The loin cloth is used by the females, but gradually it is going out of use. It has only three designs, Varoul (means flocks of birds). This symbol represents the eye of the bird. Ngaruzie means bones of fish. The last one is Kokpuizik Zie looks like a plant intertwined.

Zakuolaisen: This is a blouse piece used mainly by the unmarried girls. Among the Hmars Zakuo means blouse, Lai means middle and Sen means red. Thus, it means a piece having a red stripe through the middle of the cloth. (Mutua Bahadur "Tribal Hand Woven Fabrics of Manipur", Mutua Museum, Keisampat, Imphal, 2000)

TEXTILE OF KUKIS

There are not many indigenous Kuki deigns on woven cloth. Only a few practice indigenous motifs.

Khamtang: The base of the cloth is black and the sides and end borders have yellow designs. It symbolizes the design marked on the upper side of python snake.

Thang Nang: It is again a simple black cloth having two designs at the end borders. One of the designs is known as Goshemjang, similar to a gourd musical instrument, the other is a diamond like design symbolizing the belly portion of the python.

Saipikhup: Saipi means elephant, khup means Knee. The design thus resembles elephant Knee. It is extensively used by the Thadous in Kampongarea.

Maijapem: This design resembles a fan made of bamboo and cane. In Kuki language Maijap means fan and Jem means colour.

Besides the above designs, the Kuki also weave some ordinary fabrics as the puonpaul. It is a quilt like cloth almost similar to the puon-ri of Hmar. They also weave a thick cloth, which is locally known as Deitang used for spreading. Absence of design is very much noticeable in Deitang. (Mutua Bahadur, "Tribal Hand Woven Fabrics of Manipur" Mutua Museum, Keisampat, Imphal, 2000)

TEXTILE OF PAITES

Paites like Kuki do not weave many indigenous designs in their cloth but whatever little designs are woven are indigenous and they attach distinctive value to the textiles.

Thangou Puon: The most important cloth among the Paites is Thangou Puon. There are some restrictions imposed on the use of this cloth. Unless a Paite kills his enemy either in inter-tribal feud or in general war, he is not entitled to wear a cloth with this design. The other alternative is to harvest the largest quantity of crop in the village and the Paites who actually performs this is allowed to wear the Thangou Puon.

Puon Dum: It is a National dress of Paites and is used at the time of condolence, official meetings, observance of National Day, etc. Puon Dum actually means a black cloth, but the cloth has only stripes of black along the white, yellow, red and green stripes.

Jawl Puon: Jawl in Paites language means friend and betrothed lover. The cloth is also named Shashengsin Puon meaning a cover cloth for a basket with meat carried by a married girl going for the first time to her husband's house. The girl either present this cloth to her husband or husband's married sister. The Jawl Puon has nine red stripes and eight black stripes alternately arranged running vertically throughout the length of the body. There are two rows of Shial Ltun design separated from each other and the end borders have motifs resembling the eyes of birds in yellow, pink, red and green colour.

Puon Pie: It is a type of quilt ; it is compulsory for every girl to bring one such cloth to her husband's house at the time of marriage.

Nikkiat: A loin cloth for women. It has gone almost out of use.

(see plate- 354) (Mutua Bahadur - 2000)

POTTERY IN MANIPUR

Pottery culture is very old in Manipur. Most of the pots are handmade and are of different colours (red, dark red and black). Pottery flourishes in Andro, Sekmai, Chairel, Thongjao, Nungbi and parts of Ukhrul and Senapati District. Chakpa women are good potters and they make different types of pots are made for ritualistic and ceremonial purposes. Pottery in Manipur is closely related with social, cultural and religious life. The art of pottery making in Manipur is practised by women without using wheel in a similar fashion as in the other northeastern states (see plate-340).

Myths about origin of pottery in Manipur

Once upon time, Manipur was surrounded by seven hillocks and the valley was full of water. Atiya Kuru Sidaba and Ima Leimarel Sidabi decided to create a world and thus descended from heaven. Atiya Kuru Sidaba drained out water. A voice from the heaven announced- "Dig out some clay and make a pitcher out of it and offer prayers for seven days then your wish will be fulfilled." After seven days of prayer, a male child of golden colour was found by the couple. The child was christened Sanamahi, he later shot down extra sun by his arrows and created various creatures dwelling on water, air and earth. Finally he created human being. Atiya Kuru Sidaba and Ima Leimarel

Sidabi disappeared after completing their task. Ima Leimarel Sidabi took several incarnations to carry out seven different tasks. `Panthoibi or Leima Leinaotabi, was among them, who created the first earthen-pot. Therefore, in the creation myth of Manipur, the earthen pot becomes the metaphor for the womb.

Common use of pottery

The pottery is used for ritualistic and domestic purpose.

Ritualistic-During childbirth, the placenta of the newly born child is cut-off and kept inside a small earthen pot (Chaphu). The Chaphu symbolises purity and sanctity.

Domestic-A variety of pottery like chaphu, uyan, pun are used for storing rice. Hentak chaphu is a container for keeping pounded fish mixture. Ishaiphu for containing water. Chini Chaphu is a small earthern pot with stalk containing sugar inside, especially made as toy for children. Chengphu is used to store rice. The Khum is a small pot used for taking out mixture from the big jars, also used as lid for small pots.

Technique of pottery-making

First the lump of clay is shaped into a slab. This slab is rolled to make a cylinder. A base is attached to it. Then it is put on a stool and log of wood so as to create a pot of desired shape. A thick soft wet cloth is wrapped around the open rim of cylinder to rotate it clock-wise and anti-clock wise alternately by holding it tightly by hand. By the end of this process the collar of pot gets ready. After the collar gets stiffened the pot is beaten with the wooden beater using stone anvil till it acquires the desired shape, size and thickness of wall.

Smoke stains are commonly found on almost all traditionally made and used terracotta pots of India. To some, it has ritualistic significance, some consider it auspicious yet some artist use it aesthetically to make a personal statement.

Firing of Pots

Baking of pots in open space is the practice among the potters of Manipur. But the Tangkhul potters fire in the forest where the fuel is available in plenty. A bed of either straw or dried leaves is made on ground. The Andro and Chairel spread dried cow- dung along with the straw to form a thick bed. The pots are then kept on the bed and covered by the dried leaves or straw or cow-dung. In this way three or four layers of pots are arranged alternatively with the pile straw or leaves in the form of a mould.

Colouring

Among the potters of Manipur valley, there is a belief that the pot or chaphu can not be used unless Kuhi, a liquid prepared out of the bark of tree (quircus sp) is sprinkled over it.

Places associated with pottery making in Manipur

According to colour schemes pottery in Manipur is divided into three categories. The black ware pottery, Grey ware pottery, Red ware pottery. The following places are associated with pottery.

1. Chairel and Thongojao village in Thoubal district (Red ware)
2. Andro village in Thoubal district,Chakpa tribe (Brick red with coat of blackish maroon colour)
3. Nungbi village in Ukhrul district, Tangkhul tribe (Glossy black in colour)
4. Oinam village in Senapati district, Poumai tribe (Dull black in colour)
5. Nongpok Sekmai village in Thoubal district (Red ochre colour)
6. Ningthemcha Karong village in Imphal west district, Meitei (Grey ware)
7. Leimaram village in Bishnupur district, Chakpa (pots for ritualistic occasion)

Financial Returns

In the past pottery was in great demand, each family needed them in rituals, festive occasions and also for day to day domestic use. However with the advent of metal utensils in 19th century, the pottery industry has declined. Unavailability of suitable clay, lack of expert potters, custom of producing pots only during season when there is less rain, the tedious work of firing are some of the factors causing hindrance to the tradition of pottery-making. As the financial returns of the production of Manipuri pottery is quite negligible and unless proper guidance and financial assistance are provided the pottery of Manipur is on the verge of extinction.

CANE AND BAMBOO WORKS

Use of cane and bamboo was mentioned in ancient manuscripts of pre-Christian era like Panthoibi Khonggul, Poreiton Khuntokpa, Thanga Chinggoirol and Yumsharol. Baskets were stored in Lups i.e. scaffolds suspended over the fire place for some time and then preserved to last for two generations. One can not imagine the cultural life the people living in the hills and valley of Manipur without bamboos and their products. It is believed that a family living in a house built without bamboo can never be a happy one. For the Meiteis, Bamboos are required from womb to tomb. In earlier time, the Maibis used to cut the umbilical cord of new born babies with wakthou made from Utang bamboo. Paya or fine bamboo splits made from Utang bamboo are used to tie a knot in building houses, in erecting fencing etc. Bamboos are also used in death rituals in many forms. (see plate- 339, 346)

Bamboo and cane are abundantly available in Manipur. Basketry has been a popular occupation for the people of Manipur. Various kinds of baskets of different shapes, sizes and designs are manufactured for domestic and ritualistic use. Heijing Kharai, Phiruk and Lukmai are exclusively meant for ceremonies such as wedding, birth and death rituals. For domestic purposes baskets like Likhai, Sangbai, Chengbon, Tabu, Phiruk, Meruk, Morah etc. are made. There are fishing equipments made of cane and bamboo. These are Longup, Lu, Tunggol etc. People of Maring tribe inhabiting the Chandel District are the main manufacturers of these types of baskets.

Over 130 species of bamboo are found in India and 44 varieties of bamboo are accounted for North Eastern States, of which Manipur has 15 varieties of bamboo and five varieties of cane. The natural bamboo forests of Manipur cover nearly 3,000 sq. km. and the bamboo production is around 2 lakh tonnes annually. Some of the varieties of bamboo found in Manipur have been described under Chapter-3: Geography, Fauna and Flora.

The cane available in Manipur is of three types :-

- Yairi *(Rubus idens)*
- Liren *(Rubus micus)*
- Leethit *(Rubus longunabuas)*

The following are some of the common items of cane and bamboo products:-

- Baskets like items for packaging, measuring, storing, carrying of goods, washing and fishing etc.
- Mats like items for ceiling, partition, fencing, sitting and walling etc.
- Fishing traps/tools
- Furniture like sofa sets, chairs, table, side tables, stool, *morah etc.*
- Walking stick.
- Umbrella handle.
- Trays.
- Decorative pieces like table lamp, wall hanging, ash tray, flower pot, flower and other models, etc.
- Caps/hats.
- Ply board (bamboo laminated).
- Tooth pick/Agarbati sticks.

- Musical instruments like flutes.
- Suit case.
- House construction materials like bamboo strips/slivers, rope, etc.

These items are in different designs according to the varying customs of different tribes of the State. The number of artisans engaged in cane and bamboo activity in Manipur is estimated at 1.50 lakhs approximately.

Trained Artisans in Cane and Bamboo trade

There are many trained master crafts and artisans in the state.The main objectives of the Bamboo and Cane Works are -

- To fulfill the needs of the state
- To explore possibility of export to other states and other countries
- To generate employment for the unemployed youth.
- To enhance income of the families of those youth.
- To create a sustainable business environment between the State and the rest of the country.
- To increase the revenue earnings of the State.

Marketing arrangements for selling the finished products as well as semi-processed raw materials may be taken up in many ways or through many channels as follows:-

- To sell direct to the customers at the production centre itself;
- To sell by opening Emporia/Sales out-lets at the main market places of the districts;
- To sell/supply to the State Handloom and Handicrafts Development Corporation/North Eastern Handloom and Handicrafts Development Corporation;
- To supply to handicrafts traders/exporters;
- To sell by participating Local/State/Regional/National Level Exhibitions/ Trade Fairs etc.;
- To supply to State Govt. Departments/Offices.

KOUNA CRAFT

Kouna, (*Scirpus lacustries*.Linn.) is a class of water-reed - a firm-stemmed water or marsh plant especially of genus - Phragmites. The plants grow wildly in the marshy land, ponds, canals, along the river and lake beaches. From time immemorial, these stalks, locally called Kouna, after drying are being used in making mats/mattresses by the people living mostly in the valley areas of the Manipur State. Kouna craft making mats/mattresses in different sizes, short and long is taken up by traditional artisans for economic earnings. The craft has now been taken up as a gainful economic activity by artisans/entrepreneurs in some areas in the State due to having high market demands. The plants are planted especially for economic utilization in the marshy paddy fields, canals, along the submerged river and lake shores. (see plate -347)

Table-52 Showing Kouna Growing Areas in Manipur

Kouna Growing Areas of Manipur		
1	Imphal West District	Konjeng Leikai
		Mayang Imphal.
2	Imphal East District	Thambal Khong.
		Kongba
		Singjamei Kshetrileikai.
		Khongman
3	Thoubal District	Khangabok.
		Nongpok Sekmai.
		Shikhong.
		Langmeithek.
		Ukhongshang.
		Chairel (East).
		Kakching.
4	Bishnupur District	Oinam.
		Keinou.
		Thinungei
		Phubala.
		Sunusiphai.
		Moirang.

Different materials made of Kouna are mats of different sizes, shapes and designs, It is really beautiful. One advantage of Kouna Fak is that it remains cool in spite of very hot weather.

The handloom and handicraft materials are available at the following places :-

- **Manipur Handlooms & Handicrafts Development Cooperation's Ltd.** (A Govt. of Manipur Undertaking, Paona Bazar, Ph. 221495)
- **Handloom House,** Manipur State Handloom Weaver's cooperative Society Ltd. Poana Bazar. Ph. 220340
- **Kangla Emporium,** Uripok. Ph. 222968
- **Eastern Handlooms & Handicrafts,** Poana Bazar.
- **Ima Market/Khwairamband Bazar.**

References

A.S. W Shimray "History of Tangkhul Nagas", Akansha Publishing House, New Delhi-110C59, 2001.

Dr. (Smt) K. Sobita Devi "Traditional Dress of the Meiteis", Bhubon Publishing House, Imphal, 1998

Dr. S.C. Joshi "Manipur : the Jewel of India", Akansha Publishing House, New Delhi-110059, 2002

Julian Jacobs "The Nagas : Hill People of North East India "Thames and Hudson, London, 1990

V.P. Sharma "The Hmars of Manipur : An anthropological Exploration ", Anmol Publications, 1992

Mutua Bahadur "Cane and Bamboo Crafts of Manipur", Mutua Museum, Keisampat, Imphal, 1994

Mutua Bahadur "Traditional Textiles of Manipur ", Mutua Museum, Keisampat, Imphal, 1994

Mutua Bahadur "Tribal Hand Woven Fabrics of Manipur ",Mutua Museum, Keisampat, Imphal, 2000

Mutua Bahadur, Ms. Y. Santabai, "Tribal Art of Manipur ", Mutua Museum, Keisampat, Imphal, 1996

T.C. Hudson "The Meitheis, Low Low Price Publications, Delhi-110052, 1908

T.C. Hudson "The Naga Tribes of Manipur ", Low Price Publications, Delhi-110052, 1911

Langsun D. Mate "The Mate Tribe of Manipur ", Omsons Publications, New Delhi, 2000

http://www.webindia123.com/craft/state/manipur/necklace.html

http://manipur.nic.in/handicrafts.html

http://www.mapsofindia.com/manipur/society-and-culture/handicrafts.html

http://investinmanipur.nic.in/handicraft.htm

http://www.indian-handicrafts-suppliers.com/traditional-handicrafts/manipur-handicrafts.htm

http://www.indian-handicrafts-suppliers.com/products/

http://www.indian-handicrafts-suppliers.com/traditional-handicrafts/manipur-handicrafts.htm

http://www.indian-handicrafts-suppliers.com/materials/

http://www.e-pao.net/epPageExtractor.asp?src=galleries. Handloom_ Handicrafts.html..

Plate -337: Traditional Weaving

Plate -338: Weaving a Modern Design

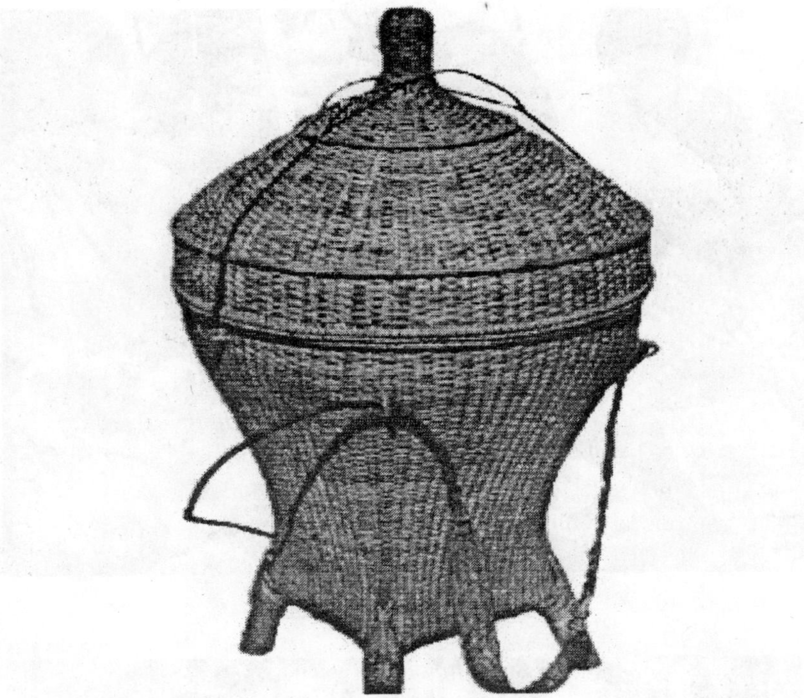

Plate-339: Tabu

Plate-340: Various Pots for sale

Plate -341: Potloi tuba

Plate -342: Rani Phi, Wang Khei

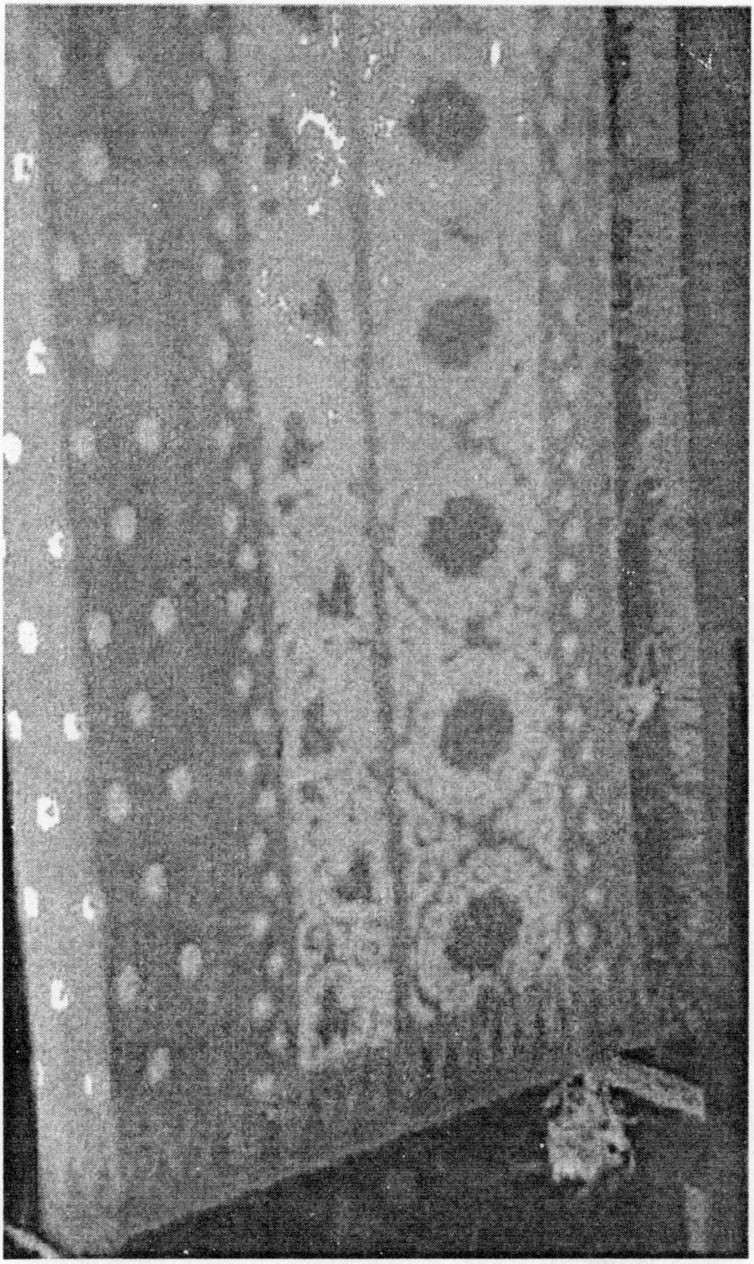

Plate -343 : Rani Phi, Wangkhei

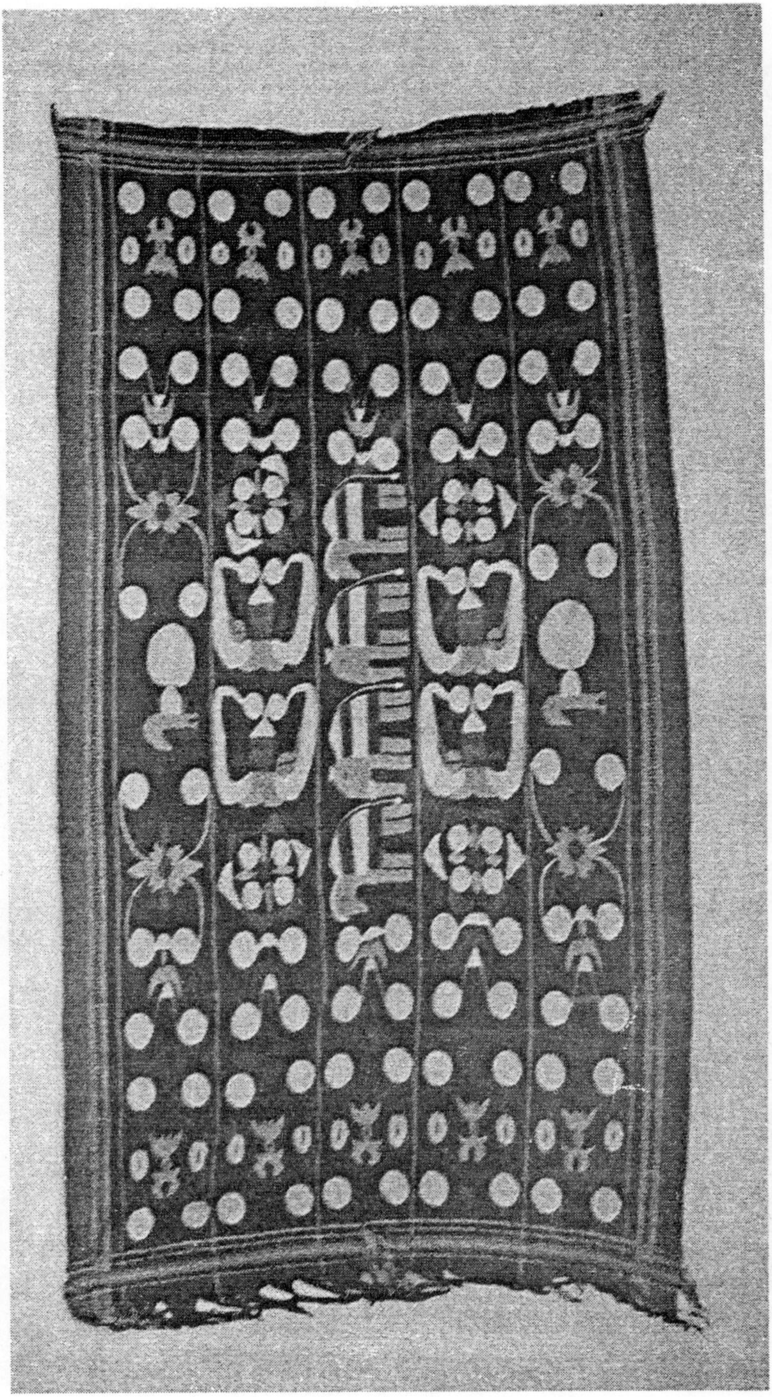

Plate -344: Shammi Lanmi Phi

Plate -345: Shentak Shenga

Plate-346 : Cane and Bamboo Works

Plate -:347: Kouna Works

Plate -348: Chothe Belt

Plate-349: Maram Shawl

Plate-350: Liangmei Shawl

Plate-351: Tangkhul Shawl

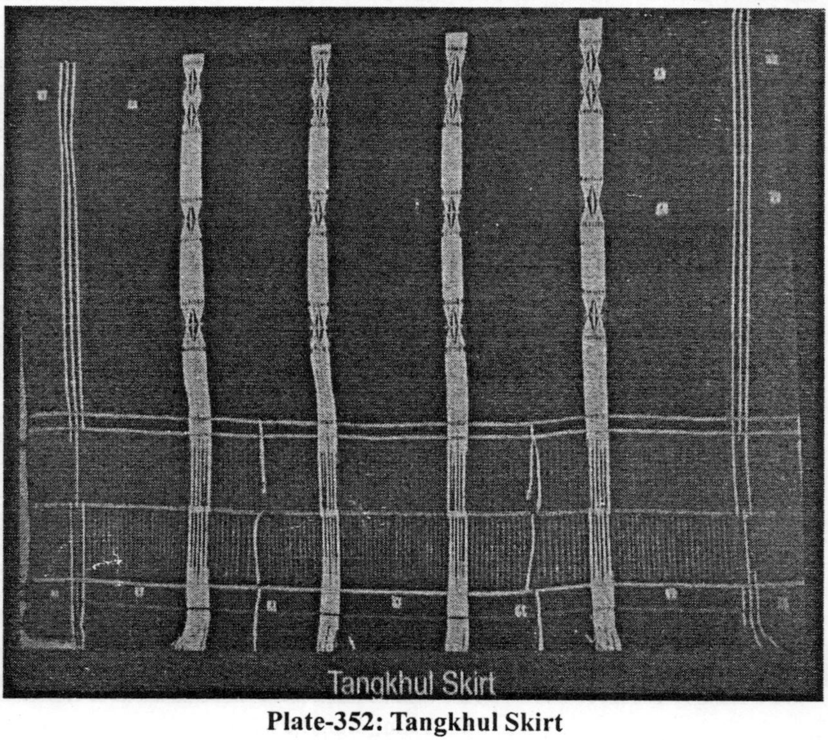

Plate-352: Tangkhul Skirt

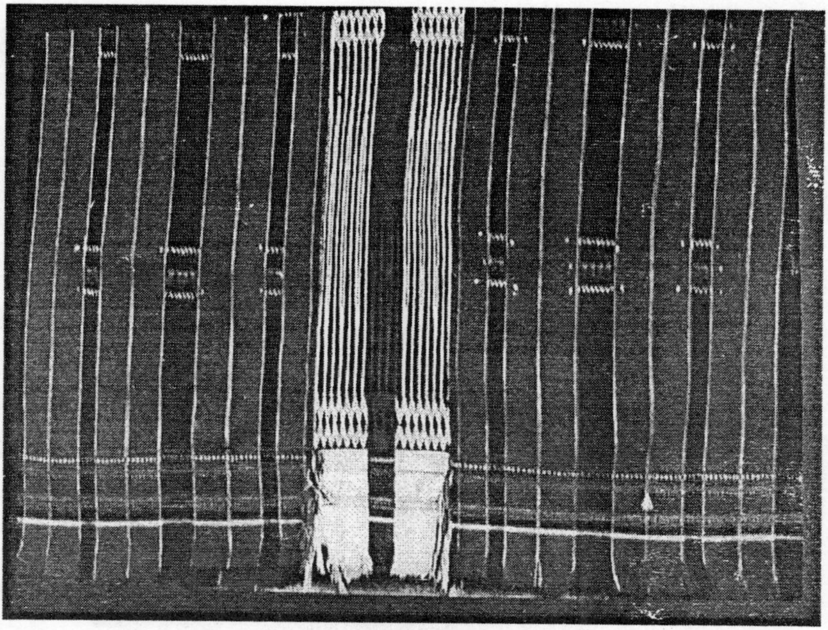

Plate-353: Tangkhuil Skirt

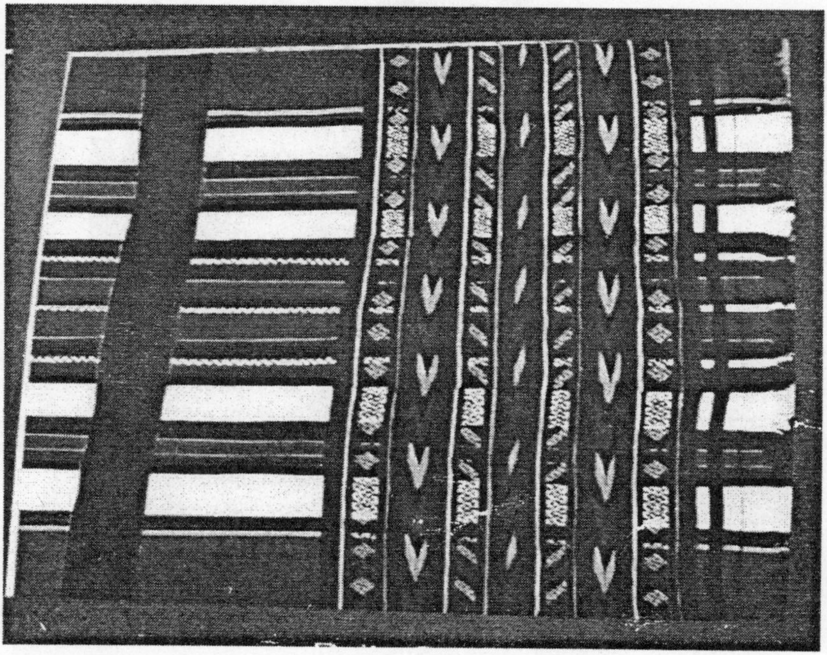

Plate -354: Paite Skirt

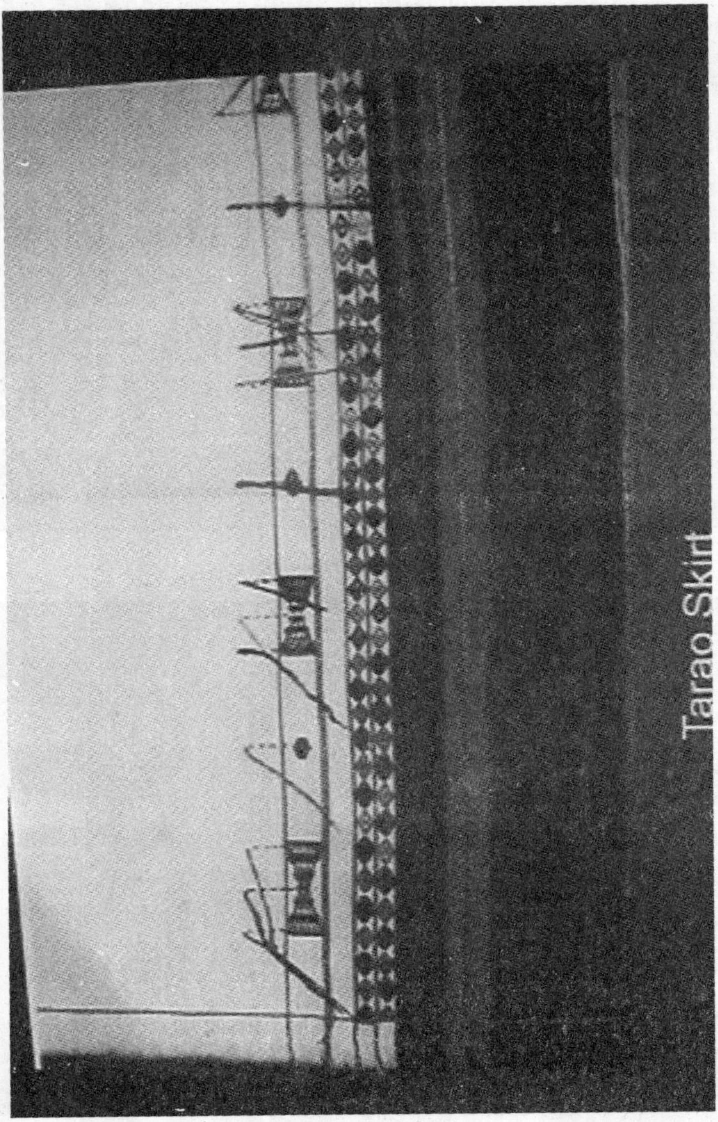

Tarao Skirt

20

All Districts of Manipur : Imphal East District

Imphal East District was established as a separate district on 18th June, 1997 with its head quarters at Porompat occupying the eastern part of valley plus Jiribam Subdivision. Imphal East district has an area of 469.44 sq. km, four subdivisions, 205 villages, 51864 households and 394876 populations. (Department of Statistics, Govt. of Manipur). The sex ratio is 992 and the literacy rate is 76.38%.

The District is situated at an altitude of 790 metres above the M.S. Level. The climate of the District is salubrious and monsoon is tropical. The minimum temperature goes down to 0.6 degree celsius in winter and 36 degree celsius in summer. The District is connected with National. Highway (NH) -39, N.H. 53 and N.H. 150. (see Map- plate -356)

Table-53 Showing Subdivision-wise villages, households, population

	District-wise villages -2001					
District	*Subdivision*	*Villages*	*Households*	*Male*	*Female*	*Total Population*
Imphal East	Jiribam	51	5812	19029	18799	37828
	Sawombung	67	12216	38495	35648	74143
	Porompat	52	21385	105754	107013	212767
	Keirao Bitra	35	12451	35093	35045	70138
	Subtotal-1	**204**	**51864**	**198371**	**196505**	**394876**

The population of District is 394876 according to 2001 census.

The total number of SDC Revenue Circles in the district is 9 (nine). There are 237 Revenue villages in the district. The total number of urban local bodies is 4 (four) comprising of two Municipalities and 2 (two) Nagar Panchayats. The two Municipalities are Imphal Municipal Council and Jiribam Municipal Council whereas the 2 (two) Nagar Panchayats are Andro Nagar Panchayat and Lamlai Nagar Panchayat.

There are three Community. Development (CD) Blocks in the district namely :- (1) Imphal East-I C.D. Block, Sawombung; (2) Imphal East-II C.D. Block, Keirao Bitra and (3) Jiribam C.D. Block. There are altogether 56 Gram Panchayats in the District. Block wise number of Gram Panchayats are as follows :

Table- 54

C.D.Block	*No. of Gram Panchayats*	*Population (1991 census)*
Imphal East-I C.D. Block, Sawombung	25	1,13,508
Imphal East-II C.D. Block, Keirao Bitra	25	1,13,059
Jiribam C.D. Block, Jiribam	6	28,077
TOTAL	56	2,54,644

There is a Zilla Parishad in the district comprising of 19 Zilla Parishad members.

The Assembly Constituencies are : Khundrakpam A.C., Heingang A.C., Khurai A.C., Kshetrigao A.C., Thongju A.C., Keirao A.C., Andro A.C., Lamlai A.C., Yaiskul A.C., Wangkhei A.C., Jiribam A.C.

Agriculture is the main occupation of the people in the district. In the district there are 27,000 hectares for cultivation of paddy of high yield variety and 4,100 hectares of land for improved local paddy field respectively. There are 450 hectares of land for cultivation of maize, 60 hectares for wheat and 350 hectares for potato in the district. The main food crops are paddy, potato and vegetables. Among the cash crops are sugar cane, maize, pulse, oil seed and other vegetables etc.

The total number of workers engaged in agriculture in the district was 42,473 as per 1991 census of which 28,661 were male and 13,812 were female. Spices like chilli, onion, ginger, turmeric and coriander of very good quality are grown in the district.

Table-55 Showing Area and Production of Important

Sl. No.	*Name of Crops*	*Area in Hectare*	*Production in MT*
A	Kharif crops		
1	Paddy (HYV)	27.00	80.14
2	Local paddy	4.10	5.44
3	Maize	0.45	0.80
4	Sugar cane	0.29	17.84
5	Kharif Pulse	0.22	0.26
B	Rabi crops		
1	Wheat	0.06	0.08
2	Pea and other pulses	1.53	1.09
3	Potato	0.35	1.52
4	Mustard and other Oilseed crops	0.60	1.22

Fauna and flora

The district has a rich and varied vegetation. The climatic conditions are suitable for a wide range of flowering and non-flowering trees and shrubs, Bamboos, Pipals and Kaubila are a common sight everywhere in the valley. Eucalyptus (Nasik), Amla, Parkia roxburgil (Tree bean/Yongchak), Arundo donax (Yengdhou) etc, are also very common. The hills are the homes of many valuable trees. A wide variety of medicinal plants are grown wild both in the hills and the plains. Carica papaya (Papaya), Citrus grandia (Pamelo), Mangifera indica (Mango), Prunus domestics (plum), Prumus persica (peach) Pyrus selerotine (pear), Psidium guavaya (guava), Famarindus indica (Tamarind) etc. are some of the important fruit bearing trees. A large variety of birds are also found in the district. Sparrow, swallow, owl, myna, pigeon, nightingale, king fisher, wood pecker, heron, kite etc are the common birds found in the district. The lakes and the marshy lands of the valley are the favourite habitat of a variety of rare migratory birds such as duck, storks, geese, snipe etc., arriving particularly in winter months from places as far as Siberia. The gradual decrease in the size of the habitats and the over-hunting and the netting have greatly reduced the number of such rare migratory birds visiting the district in recent years. Imphal East has got two swampy and marshy areas- Porompat and Akampat.

Rivers

The main rivers flowing in the Imphal East are the Imphal river, Iril river and Thoubal river.

Unique Handloom and Handicrafts

Wangkhei, Chingmeirong and Khurai areas are where handloom weaver co-operative societies are concentrated. Handloom products like Wangkhei Phi, Lashing Phi and Phanek and its different designs made by these weavers are in great demand both in Manipur and outside Manipur. This occupation provides employment to many women in the district. Cane and Bamboo works, Carpentry, Black smithy and Jewellery etc. are the important household industries among the male people in the district. The artisans in these trades are widely spread over the district. Smt Chungkham Rani Devi. of Wangkhei Lourembam Leikai, Imphal is a national awardee for her famous Wangkhei Phi, also known as Rani Phi after her name.

Horticulture

Horticulture products have been acquiring popularity with the people in the district. Fruits like pineapple, banana, lemon and papaya grow well in the district. Pineapple grows in plenty at the slope of Ngariyan Hill. There is considerable scope for increasing the area under different horticulture crops. The soil and climate favour for mass plantation of horticulture products in the district.

The following is the areas and production of horticulture crops in the district during 1998-99.

The District Industries Centre (DIC) Imphal East, Porompat was established on 31 October, 1997. The main objective for setting up of DIC is to provide gainful self employment opportunities to the educated unemployed youths in the small cottage industries, develop agro based and ancillary

Table-56 Showing areas and production under Horticulture

Sl. No.	*Crops*	*Area in Hectare*	*Annual production (M.T.)*
1.	Pineapple	650	3,700
2.	Banana	50	392
3.	Lemon	56	224
4.	Plum, Pear & Peach	30	180
5.	Papaya	230	1,150
6.	Mango	12	60
7.	Guava	30	138
8.	Others	250	397
	Total	1,358	6,646

industries, improve the skills of artisans and quality of their products, reduce the role of subsidies. The DIC envisages to function and lays down detailed guideline right from conducting techno-economic survey for preparing action plan.

Tourist Spots

The historical Manipur Palace is located here. Shree-Shree Govindajee Temple, a beautiful golden temple located in the palace compound is still shining here. The two war Cemeteries, maintained by British War Grave Commission might be attractive to the tourists. Besides, Hanuman Thakur Temple at Mahabali established during the time of Garib Niwaj is located here. Ramji Prabhu Temple established during the time of Garib Niwaj is also located here. Ningthem Pukhri excavated during the time of Garib Niwaj is also located here. In addition to this, there is a temple at Kaina, a holy place of the Hindu. There are two tourist homes in the district, one is at Kaina and another at Jiribam. In the district, the natural beauty of Poirou Pat rounded with the small hillock is beyond description. (see Chapter-12: Prominent Tourist Spots, see Chapter-14: Temples)

All India Radio

All India Radio,Imphal was commissioned on 15th August, 1963, (a) Primary service coverage area : 3000 sq. km, (b) Secondary coverage area : 4000 sq. km., (c) States/districts under coverage zone : With Medium Wave(MW) and Short Wave (SW), it covers the entire State of Manipur. Major languages are 1. Manipuri 2 Hmar 3. Paite 4. Kabui, 5. Thadou 6 Mao 7. Tangkhul, Minor languages are (Only songs)-Aimol, Gangte, Lamkang Mayon, Mizo, Liangmei, Maring, Zou, Chiru, Thangal, Anal, Maram, Monsang, Kom, Vaiphei, Chothe, Koireng, Simte.

Door Darshan Kendra (DDK), Imphal

The television station of DDK, Imphal is located at Porompat under Imphal East district.

IMPHAL WEST DISTRICT

The Imphal West District is the western portion of the Valley. Imphal West district has 519 sq. km. area, four subdivisions, 125 villages, 79078 households and 444382 populations. The 15-44 year population ratio is 47.51 %. The 15-48 year rural population (males) of Imphal West is 76,298 and 15-48 year urban population (males) of Imphal West as on 1st March, 2007 is 61148

Table-57 Showing Imphal West District Profile

1.	District Head quarter	Imphal
2.	Area	519 sq. kms.
3.	Population	4,39,532 (Census 2001)
4.	Male:	2,18,947
5.	Female:	2,20,585
6.	Subdivisions	3
7.	CD/TD Blocks	2
8.	Number of Towns	10
9.	Number of Inhabited villages	117
10.	Zilla Parishad	1
11.	Sex Ratio	1007 (per thousand males)
12.	Density of population	847 per sq. km.
13.	Literacy rate	80.61%
14.	Male Literacy	89.1%
15.	Female Literacy	72.24%
16.	Latitude	24.30° N to 25.00° N
17.	Longitude	93.45° E to 94.15° E
18.	Altitude	790 m above MSL
19.	Climate	Moderate
20.	Annual Rainfall	108.5 cm to 143.4 cm
21.	Temperature	20.4° C (average)
22.	National Highways	NH.No. 39 Indo-Burma/Myanmar Road, NH.No. 53 New Cachar Road

(Department of Statistics, Govt. of Manipur 2008). It is surrounded by Senapati District on the north, on the east by Imphal East and Thoubal districts, on the south by Thoubal and Bishnupur Districts, and on the west by Senapati and Bishnupur Districts. (See Map-Plate-357)

Important buildings and offices including the Governor's Bungalow, the Chief Minister's Bungalow, the Manipur Secretariat, the Legislative Assembly and most of the Government Departments are located in this district. The Kangla Fort, Shaheed Minar, Nupilal Memorial Complex, Manipur State Museum, Manipur Zoological Garden, War Cemeteries, the Central Library are also located here.

The Assembly constituencies in Imphal West are–Thangmeiband, Uripok, Sagolband, Keisamthong, Singjamei, Sekmai, Lamsang, Konthoujam, Patsoi, Langthaban, Naoria Pakhanglakpa, Wangoi, Mayang Imphal.

Demography

Population and some demographic indicators for this district are given in the tables below. The information furnished is based on All India Census - 2001.

Table-58 Showing demographic indicators of Imphal West

District	Subdivision	District-wise villages -2001 Villages	Households	Male	Female	Total Population
	Lamsang	48	10748	29032	28557	57589
	Patsoi	30	13019	35682	35433	71115
Imphal	Lamphelpat	12	34662	96823	98557	195380
West	Wangoi	35	20649	60244	60054	120298
	Subtotal-2	**134**	**79078**	**221781**	**222601**	**444382**

Climate

The district enjoys comfortable temperature throughout the year; not very hot in summer and not very cold in winter. Over all the climatic condition of the district is salubrious and monsoon tropical. The whole district is under the influence of the monsoons characterised by hot and humid rainy seasons during the summer, and cool and dry seasons during the winter. Temperature ranges from minimum of 0° C to maximum of 36°C. the average annual rainfall based on the meteorological data published for the years 1991-99 is 1259.5 mm. The district gets rainfall from the South-West monsoon.

Soil

The valley area of Imphal West district is fertile land and is mainly made up of alluvial soil of recent origin. The valley was once full of swamps and marshy lands, the important ones being Lamphelpat, Takyelpat, Sangaipat, Kakwapat, (pat means lake). The soil are mainly made up of shallow black, brown and alluvial soils which have been technically classified as *Udalfs-Ochrepts* and *Orchrepts-Aquepts-Fluvents.*

Rivers

Main rivers draining Imphal west plain are Imphal river, Nambool river and their tributaries. The Nambool river is made up of a number of small streams on its upper course. The course of the river is short and its outlet falls in Loktak Lake. This river passes through Imphal Municipality area dividing its area into almost two equal halves. This river serves as the main discharging drainage of Imphal Bazar area and its surroundings. During rainy season, swift flowing of water directed to it from its tributaries can't be contained in it. As a result, breach of its river banks causing water logging in the low lying area is of regular feature.

Road

Road Transport is used in all weather conditions throughout the year. Every part of the District is connected by a network of either Pucca or Kutcha roads. These roads may be classified into national highways, State highways, major district roads, other district and inter village roads. The Imphal-Dimapur Road (National Highway No. 39) and Imphal New Cachar Road (National Highway No. 53) are the two national highways which connect Imphal the capital of Manipur with neighbouring States of Assam and Nagaland.

Table-59 Showing Road Length(including Imphal East District)

Sl. No	*Item*	*Road Length (Km)*
1.	National Highway	109
2.	State Highways	183
3.	Other district Road	253
4.	Inter Village Roads	751
5.	Total Road Length	1481

All villages of the district are electrified. Installed capacity (State owned) is 6.88 MW, Electricity generated (State owned) is 0.40 MWH. There are 5(five) numbers of Diesel Power Houses in the District upto the year 1999-2000.

Imphal Khwairamband Keithei is the most important market for this district. Some important markets in the greater Imphal area are Singjamei Keithel, Kwak Keithel, Naoremthong Bazar, Tera Keithel, Kongba Keithel. It has two Municipalities viz. Imphal (part) and Nambol. Notified towns are Lamsang, Lilong (Imphal West part), Mayang Imphal, Samurou (part), Sekmai Bazar, Thongkhong Laxmi Bazar and Wangoi nd Lamjaotongba.

Economy

The result found from the 1991 Census is that 34% of the population are workers i.e. persons whose main activity is participation in any economically productive work by physical or mental activities.

According to 1991 Census, 41.78 of workers are in agricultural sectors and 58.22% are in non-agricultural sectors.

Handloom and handicrafts and other traditional cottage and small scale industries constitute the bulk of the industrial units. Important handloom products are bed sheets, pillow covers, shawls, scarfs, mosquito nets, curtains, phaneks (loincloth for women), chadars, etc. of various designs and colours.

Table-60 Showing Workers Statistics (1991Census)

Sl. No	*Item*	*Road Length (Km)*
1.	Total Main Workers	122,714
2.	Female Workers	46,266
3.	Male Workers	76,448
4.	Total Marginal Workers	7882
5.	Total Non-Workers	250,205
6.	Total Agricultural Workers	51278

Blacksmithy, Jewellery, cane and bamboo works, etc. are other important cottage industries. In the small scale sector, there are industries like carpentry and wooden furniture, saw mills, rice and flour mills, iron and steel works, repairing of cycles and automobiles, tailoring and embroidery, tyre retreating and vulcanising, etc. Among the large and medium industries are spinning Mill at Loitang Khunou and the Industrial Estate at Takyel for assembly of low cost bi-cycles and TV sets etc.

Tourist Spots

There are several tourist spots like the Kangla, Shaheed Minar, Nupilal Memorial, Cemeteries, Manipur State Museum, Zoological Garden etc. (see Chapter-12: Prominent Tourist Spots, see Chapter-14: Temples)

THOUBAL DISTRICT

The district came into existence in May, 1983 through a notification of the Government of Manipur under the Manipur Land Revenue and Land Reforms Act.1960. The district headquarters is at Thoubal. Thoubal district has got 514 sq. km. area, three subdivisions, 100 villages, 67681 households and 364140 populations (Department of Statistics, Govt. of Manipur). The sex ratio is 998 and the literacy rate is 67.90%. (see Map-Plate-358)

It lies between 23° 45' N and 24°45' N latitude and 93°45' E and 94°15' E longitude. It is bounded on the north by Imphal West district, on the east by Ukhrul and Chandel districts, on the south by Chandel and Churachandpur districts and on the west by the districts of Imphal West and Bishnupur. Its average elevation is not very much different from the rest of the Manipur Valley which is about 790 metres on an average above the M.S level. Although the district is a part of the valley, the area of the district is not entirely plain. Many rivers flow through the district and many lakes dot its surface. In fact, all important lakes of Manipur, with the exception of Loktak, are in this district.

Later on, on 25 November, 1983, Thoubal was bifurcated into Thoubal and Kakching sub-divisions, the latter comprising of Kakching and Waikhong

Tahsils with all their existing villages, the headquarters of Kakching sub-division being Kakching.

The district has two community development blocks one within each sub-division, each block coinciding with its respective sub-divisional areas minus the statutorily notified urban portion. It has nine main towns. namely, Lilong, Thoubal, Yairipok, Shikhong Sekmai, Wangjing, Heirok, Kakching, Kakching Khunou and Sugnu and a part of Samurou whose major portion is in the Imphal West District. Thoubal and Kakching are Municipalities.

Table-61 Showing demographic indicators of Thoubal district

	District-wise villages -2001					
District	*Subdivision*	*Villages*	*Households*	*Male*	*Female*	*Total population*
	Lilong	19	11912	36473	36178	72651
Thoubal	Thoubal	51	32521	86435	86200	172635
	Kaching	30	23248	59342	59512	118854
	Subtotal-3	**103**	**67681**	**182250**	**181890**	**364140**

The Assembly constituencies are –Lilong, Thoubal, Wangkhem, Heirok, Wangjing Tentha, Khangabok, Wabgai, Kakching, Hiyanglam, Sugnoo

Rivers

Imphal river, Thoubal river, Arong river, Wangjing river are the important rivers of Thoubal district. The Thoubal river originates in the hill ranges of Ukhrul and is an important tributary of the Imphal river. It passes through Yairipok and Thoubal before joining the Imphal at Irong near Mayang Imphal. The Imphal river rises in the hills of Senapati district and flows south. It forms the boundary of Thoubal district on its north and the west. During the dry seasons these rivers are quite shallow, during the rainy monsoon periods these rivers are very wild and frequent floods occur causing widespread damage to the paddy fields, property and life. These rivers were once good means of transport for valuable merchandise. Other rivers in the district are the Wangjing, the Arong and the Sekmai. These rivers originate in the hills of Ukhrul district. The Arong river flows through Khangabok and falls into Kharung Pat. The Wangjing river flows west through Heirok and Wangjing before joining the Loushi Pat. In earlier days, these rivers served as the routes for transportation of goods from one place to another. But nowadays, with the advent of cheap and faster means of road transport these rivers are no longer used for transport. But they are the sources of sand, pebbles and boulders which are used as building materials. Thus a large number of people depend on these rivers for their means of livelihood. They catch a variety of fishes (see Plate- 365)

Lakes

The south-western portion of the district is a low-land forming a part of the Loktak Lake region and this area has a number of shallow and rain fed lakes, the important ones being Kharung Pat, Ikop Pat, Pumlen Pat, Lousi Pat and Ngangou Pat. On the northern portion there is Waithou lake formed by the drainage waters sandwiched between Waithou hill on the west and the villages and paddy fields on the east. Due to constant siltation and reclamation of vast areas for agricultural purposes, the lakes are gradually shrinking in size and at present some of them are only in name. These lakes drain into the Imphal river. They provided very good fishing ground for a variety of fishes in the recent past.

Hills

Few hills and hiilocks are found in this district. Important ones are Mantak, Kwarok, Thongam Mondum–Punam. These hills are of low heights. The Punam hill has an elevation of 3310 feet above sea level. Geologically, Khekman range belongs to the Brail Series and Simsang formation. Constant deforestation have made these hills barren and unattractive. Local people and some NGOs are trying to make better use of these hills by planting pine apples.

Fauna and Flora

Various types of trees like Pipal, Kabulia (Oravila robusta), Khok (Albizzia Spp), Tera (Salimalia Malabarica), Sileima (Eugenia Pracox), Tairen (Cedrela toona) etc are found all over the district. Many types of Bamboos, plantain trees are common everywhere. The district supplies most of the Pine apple requirement of the state. Pears, Peach, Banana, Mangoes, Jack fruits, lemon, plum, guava, amla also thrive very well. Deer and jungle fowls are some of the wild animals found occasionally along the slopes of eastern hills adjoining the district. But the lakes in the district support many species of migratory birds such as partridge, snipe, duct, geese coming from far off Siberia. But the number of migratory birds is decreasing every year due to conversion of these lakes into agricultural lands.

Mineral Resources

There are some brine springs along the foothills on the eastern part of the district like Waikhong, Chandrakhong, Ningel and Sikhong. Water from the springs is boiled and salt is extracted by the simple method of evaporation. Salt is manufactured in the form of cakes of about 6-12 inches diameter. These salt cakes are considered to have good medicinal value. In olden days, women just after delivery used to take rice, dried fish and only this kind of salt. These salt cakes are used for ceremonial purposes also.

Thoubal district also have a number of places where red clay suitable for pottery is available mainly on the eastern side such as Waikhong, Nongpok Sekmai, Thongjao, Chairel etc. The people in these villages adopted pottery as their occupation and they produced pottery of good quality. Kakching was known for producing low grade Iron ore in olden days.

Agriculture

More than 70% of the people of Thoubal district depend on agriculture. Rice accounts for more than 90% of the total land area. The land is fertile and the yield per hectare is quite high. Kakching is known as the "granary" or "Rice Basket" of Manipur. Kakching, known as "granary of Manipur" produces more than 50% of the total rice export of this district. Double cropping is widely practiced in Kakching and surrounding areas. Even triple cropping is practiced in some areas. First paddy crop starting in February-March, second paddy crop in July or early August and the third crop of mustard seed, pulses etc in November. Apart from rice, sugarcane, oilseeds, maize, potatoes, pulses, chillies, vegetables are also grown in plenty. The district is the largest producer of sugarcane in Manipur. Sugarcane is cultivated in Thoubal, Wangjing, Kakching, Kakching Khunou, Wabgai. Maize is cultivated in Serou, Pallel, Kakching, Kakching Khunou. Vegetables such as cauliflower, cabbages, brinjal, peas, ground nuts, pumpkins are also cultivated in abundance.

Fishing

A large number of people in this district depend on fishing as full time occupation. Waithou Pat, Kharung Pat, Ikop Pat were once famous for supplying indigenous varieties of fish like Ngaton, Pengba, Tharak, Sareng, Ngaroi, Ngahou. These local varieties of fish were very tasty. But these types of fishes have now disappeared due to large scale use of pesticides and reclamation of the lakes. But now some private firms are coming up to rear these local; varieties of fishes. Still, the district is supplying the imported varieties of fishes like Rohu, Silver Carp, Mirror Carp, Grass Carp, Common Carp, Mirgle etc.

Industry

Industrially the district is backward. The Khansari Sugar Factory at Wangbal is the only medium sized industry set up in the district in 1973 with an installed capacity of 60 tones of sugar per day. Although the factory was initially intended to provide employment to about 200 persons, its actual production during the years since it has been commissioned was so much behind the targeted production that it is now running at huge loss for the last more than 10 years. This is due to mismanagement of the industry by the Government. The private sugarcane growers prefer to sell the sugarcane direct in the market instead of supplying it to the factory because of rampant corruption in the industry. It is high time for the State Government to open their eyes and try to privatize the Khansari Sugar Factory.

The most important industry from the point of view of employment potential and volume of out put is the handloom and handicraft industry. Bed sheets, *Chadars, Phaneks,* mosquito nets, bamboo baskets, mats and other caneworks, fishing nets, furniture, carpentry products, pottery articles, etc. are some of the notable products of this industry, Handloom industry is spread throughout the width and breadth of the district. To help the industry there is a proposal to set up Raw Material Bank to supply quality yarn to the weavers. Waikhong, Nongpok Sekmai, Thongjao and Chairel are important places where pottery articles are manufactured. Heirok and Khangabok are noted for bamboo baskets and harvesting mats (Yeina Phak in Meiteilon) made from *Arundo donax*, a variety of reed. Other industries are manufacture of salt from brine springs, manufacture of bricks, rice milling, repair of motor vehicles, manufacture of edible oils, production of cocoons and raw silk, etc. Salt is manufactured at Waikhong, Sikhong, Ningel and Chandrakhong; bricks at Kakching, Wangjing, Charangpat, Heirok and Khongjom; '*Soibum*', a product made from bamboo shoots is manufactured at Kakching. There are altogether 147 factories registered in the district under the Indian Factories Act upto March, 1987.

In order to uplift the industrial backwardness of the district the Government has taken in recent years a number of steps by way of providing grants, subsidies, hire purchase schemes, seed money, work sheds and training facilities to the promising industrial units.

Tourist Spots

Khongjom

It is in this district, at Khongjom, that the Paona Brajabashi and other heroes of Manipur sacrificed their lives while defending the independence and sovereignty of Manipur in the Anglo-Manipuri War of April, 1891. It is the place where last war of Manipur's independence was fought between the Manipuri and the British soldiers. It has got a memorial erected on a small hillock, Khongjom is well served by the National highway. An eight-bedded Tourist home has been functioning there since 1988. Khongjom is situated about 12 kms. to the south of Thoubal

Sugnu

Situated 74 kms. from Imphal, the place is an important trading centre on the south of the district. From this, a beautiful view of the Imphal river can be seen. It is on the Imphal - Sugnu State highway.

Waithou

The place is important for its scenic beauty. There is an inspection bungalow on the hill-side over looking the Waithou Lake. The place is noted for its tasteful pineapples. An exotic and delicious variety of local fish known as 'Ngaton' used to be available at this place abundantly till a few years back from now. It is on the National highway about 3 kms. from the district headquarters.

Kakching

It is the sub-divisional headquarters of Kakching sub-division and is a famous trading centre of a variety of vegetables, fishes and rice next to Thoubal, the biggest town in the district. The place is easily approachable from the National highway and is connected to the other State highways.

Thoubal

It is the district headquarter of Thoubal district and also the sub-divisional headquarters of Thoubal sub-division. Situated at a distance of 22 kms. from Imphal, the National highway No. 39 divides the town almost into halves from north to south length-wise. The Thoubal river flows through the centre of the town from east to west. It is the biggest town in the district and is one of the most important trading centre of the district. The town has all the infrastructures of a fast developing urban area.

Pallel

It is a place situated at the border of Thoubal and Chandel districts and is the meeting place of plain areas of Thoubal and the hill areas of Chandel. Indo-Myanmar road from Imphal to Moreh passes through it. With its hills and rivers the place has a beautiful landscape. Typical agricultural Products and nice handicrafts of the hilly people are regularly found in its daily market

BISHNUPUR DISTRICT

The Bishnupur district with its headquarters at Bishnupur (27 km from Imphal) was opened on 25 May, 1983. Stretching between 93.43^0 E and 93.53^0 E Longitudes and 24.18^0 N and 24.44^0 N Latitudes, it is bounded by Imphal West district on the north, by Churachandpur district on the south and Imphal West and Thoubal districts on the east. (see Map-Plate -359)

The Bishnupur district has 496 sq. km. area, three subdivisions, 55 villages, 35303 households and 208368 populations. The 15-44 years population ratio is 47.48%. The 15-48 rural population (males) as on 1st March, 2007 is 41328 and that of urban male population is 23116 (Department of Statistics, Govt. of Manipur). The sex ratio is 1004 and the literacy rate is 71.59%.

Table-62 Showing demographic indicators of Bishnupur district

District	*District-wise villages -2001*					
	Subdivision	*Villages*	*Households*	*Male*	*Female*	*Total population*
Bishnupur	Nambol	16	9501	26572	26999	53571
	Bishnupur	15	9170	27703	26658	54361
	Moirang	24	16632	50275	50161	100436
	Subtotal -4	**49**	**35303**	**104550**	**103818**	**208368**

There are three Sub-Divisions, viz (1) Bishnupur Sub-Division with its HQ at Bishnupur and (2) Moirang Sub-Division (opened on 12 December, 1983) with its HQ at Moirang and (3) Nambol Sub-Division with its HQ at Nambol. There are 6 (six) SDC Circles in the district. Nambol, Oinam and Bishnupur circles are situated within Bishnupur Sub-Division. Ningthoukhong, Moirang and Kumbi circles are situated within Moirang Sub-Division. The Meiteis constitute the largest population followed by the tribals and Meitei Pangan (Manipuri Muslims). Splinter number of Biharis and Marwaris are temporarily settled in the district mainly for business purposes.

As for the convenience of developmental activities of the rural areas there are two Community Development Blocks (C.D), namely (1) Bishnupur C.D. Block with its HQ at Bishnupur and (2) Moirang C.D Block with its HQ at Moirang Khunou. The Sub-Divisions are under the charge of one SDO each and the C.D Blocks are under the charge of one BDO each while the circles are under the charge of one SDC each.

There are 6 (Six) Assembly Constituencies, viz 1. Nambol A.C, 2. Oinam A.C, 3.Bishnupur A.C, 4. Moirang A.C, 5.Thanga A.C, and 6.Kumbi A.C.

The number of Gram Panchayats is 24 (12 G.P each in one block). As for the Local Self Government, there are 4 (four) Municipalities namely (1) Nambol, (2) Bishnupur, (3) Ningthoukhong and (4) Moirang.

The original name of Bishnupur was Lamangdong. There are five important temples in Bishnupur district

1. Vishnu Temple at Bishnupur
2. Gopinath at Ningthoukhong)
2. Abdeitya at Bishnupur
3. Radha Madhav Temple at Ningthoukhong
5. Ibudhou Thangjing at Moirang

(see Chapter-14: Temples)

The district profile is as follows :-

Table-63Showing Bishnupur District Profile

Location Altitude (Above MSL)	828.18 Metre
Area:-	
Total (1991 Census)	496.00 sq. km.
(a) Rural	458.98 sq. km
(b) Urban	37.02 sq. km
Population (1991 Census)	
(a) Total	1,80,773
(b) Male	91,125
(c) Female	89,648
(d) Rural	1,17,603
(e) Urban	63,170
Sex Ratio (Female per thousand males)	984
Density of Population per sq. km	364
Total Schedule Caste Population	2,333
% of S.C Population to total population	1.29 %
Total Scheduled Tribe population	9,575
% of S.T population to total population	5.30 %
Total no. of main workers	69,114

(Contd.)

(Contd. Table 63)

% of main workers to total population	38.23 %
Total no. of Marginal workers	11,078
% of Marginal workers to total population	6.13 %
Total Non-Workers	1,00,581
% of Non- workers to total population	55.64 %
No. of literates	82,063
No. of Female literates	30,538
No. of Male literates	51,525
Literacy Percentage	54.94 %
Male Literacy Percentage	68.59 %
Female Literacy Percentage	41.13 %
Municipalities	3 nos.
Small Town/NAC	4 nos.
Number of Village inhabited	45 nos.
Occupied Residential houses	27,299
Number of Households	29,726
Persons per occupied residential houses	7
Sub-Divisions	3
Community Development Blocks	2
Vidhan Sabha Seats	6
Gram Panchayats	24
Gram Panchayats members	128
Nyaya Panchayats	6
Hospitals (including PHCs, TB & Leprosy Hospital)	8
Beds available (Hospitals)	70
Dispensaries including Primary Health Centres	36
Reserved Forests	3.50 sq. km.
Protected Forests	0.10 sq. km.
Unclassed Forests	-
Total Reserved Forests and protected Forests	3.60 sq. km.
Total Forest Revenues	Rs. 1,03,054.00
Total length of Road	424.42 km.
Total Vehicles on road	121
Area and production of rice (1997-98)	17,72000
Area	Hectares
Production	40930 Tonnes.

Bishnupur Municipal Council

The Bishnupur Municipal Council is an urban local body. It was converted into a Council from Board under the Manipur Municipalities Act, 1994 (Act No. 43 of 1994) on 15th June, 1994. The spirit of the 74th. Constitutional (Amendment) Act is to devolve the power and functions listed in the 12th. Schedule to the Constitution to the urban local bodies.

The Moirang C.D. Block come into existence on 4th April, 1985 with its Head Quarters at Moirang Khunou about 1.5 km. from the Kumbi main road. It

Table-64 Showing names of Gram Panchayats in Bishnupur district

Sl. No.	*Name of Gram Panchayats*	*BPL Survey Population*
1.	Ngakhalawai	4085
2.	Tronglaobi	3297
3.	Torbung	3258
4.	Kwakta	5604
5.	Saiton	4105
6.	Moirangkhunou	5818
7.	Thanga	17144
8.	Thanga II	6292
9.	Kha-Thinugnggei	5851
10.	Wangoo	6724
11.	Wangoo Terakhong	4317
12.	Borayangbi	5706
	Total:-	62,187

was bifurcated from the erstwhile Bishnupur C.D. block. It has an area of 269 sq. km. with a population of 62, 187 (BPL Survey) inhabiting in 67 villages. The inhabitants are Meiteis, Muslims, Tribal, Bengali etc. These inhabitants mostly live on agriculture and fishing. The Loktak lake and Keibul Lamjao park are situated in this Block and the people of Thanga, Karang and villages in and around the Loktak lake live on fishing.

Tourist Spots

The special attractions are Keibul Lamjao, Loktak Lake, Phubala, INA Memorial, Moirang, Loukoi Pat Ecological park etc. (see Chapter- 12: Prominent Tourist Spots, Chapter-3 :Geography, Fauna and Flora)

Moirang

Located at 45 kms. from Imphal, Moirang is one of the main centres of early Meitei folk culture. Moirang is famous for the Khamba Thoiba legend. Moirang is also famous for the ancient temple of the pre-Hindu deity, Ibudhou Thangjing. Every year a ritual dance festival "Ibudhou Thangjing Lai Haraoba" is celebrated here in the month of May, where men and women, dressed in colourful traditional costumes sing and dance in honour of the Lord Thangjing at Moirang. The town also has a special place in the history of the Indian Freedom Struggle. It was at Moirang that the flag of the Indian National Army (INA) was first unfurled on April 14,1944. The INA Museum containing letters, photographs, badges of ranks and other memorabilia remind the visitors of the noble sacrifices made by the INA under the charismatic leadership of Netaji Subhash Chandra Bose. A statue of Netaji Subhash Chandra Bose is installed here. Moirang is also famous for its Loktak Lake and Keibul Lamjao National Park and Sangai. It has got an attractive spot known as Sendra.

Phuballa Resort

Phubala is a charming resort 40 km south from Imphal in Bishnupur district.It is situated on a little island on the western fringes of the Loktak lake. It is connected to the mainland by a low causeway. Boating and other water sports are being introduced here. There is also a tourist bungalow for tourist to stay.

Loukoipat Ecological Park

Under the Ecological Development plan of the Government of Manipur, the Management Committee was constituted of the District Level Officers and public leaders of Bishnupur for establishment and management of an Ecological park at Loukoipat, Bishnupur. Accordingly the Ecological park at Loukoipat , Bishnupur was established in the early part of 1992. Consequently, an amount of Rs. 1,84,070/- was provided in the early part of 1992 for construction of the following work as first phase :- (a) Main Gate, (b) Rock Garden, (c) Hawa Ghar, (d) Circular Path and (e) Japanese Pond.

CHURACHANDPUR DISTRICT

The Churachandpur district lies on the southwestern portion of the state, having 4570 sq. km. area, five subdivisions, 540 villages, 37626 households and 227905 populations. (Department of Statistics, Govt. of Manipur). The sex ratio is 993 and the literacy rate is 74.67%. Churachandpur is inhabited by about 15 hill tribes and another ten communities. (see Map-Plate -360)

Its location is 23°55' to 24°30' North and 92°59' to 93°50' East. The maximum temperature is 37°C while the minimum is 1°C. The highest rainfall is 3080 mm (Tinsong) and the lowest is 597 mm (Geljang). The maximum humidity is 100% and the minimum 61%. The beauty of the landscape is supplemented by the climate which is temperate and salubrious. The winter extending from November to February is cold, particularly in the hills but days are bright and sunny. The monsoon months stretch from May-June to September with heavy showers almost throughout the period. The spring and summer months are mildly pleasant despite high humidity. However, the low temperatures (ranging

Table-65 Showing demographic indicators of Churachandpur district

District	*District-wise villages -2001*					
	Subdivision	*Villages*	*Households*	*Male*	*Female*	*Total Population*
Churachandpur	Tipaimukh	40	4053	12965	12444	25409
	Thanlon	47	3518	11295	10762	22057
	Churachandpur	117	4716	14900	13480	28380
	North Churachandpur	280	21895	68093	64063	132156
	Singhat	56	3444	9979	9924	19903
	Subtotal-5	**546**	**37626**	**117232**	**110673**	**227905**

from 30°-35°C) prevents sultriness that is so common in eastern India. The climate imparts the people with considerable stamina and hardiness through the lack of rains during non- monsoon months and the consequent decline in water flow in the major rivers during that period makes the state a mono-crop economy.

According to the provisional data of 2001 census, the total population of the district is 2,27,905. The literacy rate in the district is quite high, the percentage being 64.38 (72.6% in male and 56.4% in female). The sex ratio is in favour of the female gender: 1034 per 1000 males With the improvement of the reach of medical facilities, the birth rate, death rate and the infant mortality rate have gone down.

Administrative Set up

The district is divided into 5 Revenue Sub-divisions, namely Churachandpur, Singngat, Thanlon, Parbung (Tipaimukh) and Henglep. There are 6 Tribal Development Blocks. The Revenue sub-Divisions are contiguous with the Tribal Development Blocks except for Churachandpur Sub-Division where there are two Blocks namely Churachandpur and Samulamlan. The Sub-Divisional Officer also functions as the Block Development Officer.

The district is inhabited by several tribes, mainly belonging to the Kuki-Chin-Mizo group. Each tribe has a distinct social order as well as community laws. Thadous, Hmars, Paites are the predominant groups. The system of hereditary chief ship as well as community ownership of village land is prevalent in the district. In case of hereditary chief ship, the chief is all-powerful as he controls not only the economy of the village through his ownership of the land but exercises social control over the households in the village. An overwhelming majority of the tribal population has been converted into Christianity. Christianity has not materially changed the social order but was the critical faith in bringing to an end the head-hunting wars and savagery that characterized early tribal societies. Education rapidly spread through English medium schools. In the last hundred years the society has undergone radical change from the past.

All tribal societies are patriarchal, but the women are not discriminated against. They play a significant role in agriculture and animal husbandry, besides being actively involved in weaving.

UKHRUL DISTRICT

Ukhrul is linked with Imphal, the state capital by a NH-150 about 84 Km. By ordinary passenger bus it takes about 3 hours. The Ukhrul district has got 4544 sq. km. area, five subdivisions, 198 villages, 23318 households and 140778 populations. (Department of Statistics, Govt. of Manipur 2008). The sex ratio is 920 and the literacy rate is 68.96%. Ukhrul is a land of colourful Tangkhuls. (see Map-Plate -361)

Ukhrul District is bounded by Myanmar in the East, Chandel District in the South, Imphal East and Senapati Districts in the West and Nagaland State in the North. The terrain of the district is hilly with a varying heights of 913 m to 3114 m (MSL). The climate of the district is of temperate nature with a minimum and maximum degrees of 3°C to 33°C. The average annual rainfall is

Table-66 Showing demographic indicators of Ukhrul district

		District-wise villages -2001				
District	*Subdivision*	*Villages*	*Households*	*Male*	*Female*	*Total Population*
Ukhrul	Ukhrul North	27	4342	12820	12331	25151
	Ukhrul Central	66	12837	42036	37155	79191
	Kamjong /Chassad	41	2211	6705	6232	12937
	Phungyar Phaisat	35	2259	6748	6545	13293
	Ukhrul South	29	1669	5156	5050	10206
	Subtotal – 6	**198**	**23318**	**73465**	**67313**	**140778**

1,763.7 mm (1991). The exact location of the district in the globe is 24 N-25.41 N and 94 E-94.47 E. The rainy season in the district is from May to beginning of October broadly but Winter is chilly.

The highest peak is the Khayang peak-3114 m (MSL), though the more popularly known peak is the Shirui Kashung Peak - 2,835 m (MSL). Ukhrul, the District HQ, is 2,020 m (MSL). Most of the major rivers originate from the crevices and slopes of this Shirui Peak.

The terrain of the district is rippled with small ranges and striped by few rivers. Somrah - Anggoching range, striped by Sanalok and Namba Lok; Shangshak - Phungyar range adjacent to which is the Shokvao - Mapithel - Kasom range striped by Tuyungbi and Taret Lok in the middle and Thoubal river in the West and Kachai - Hoomi - Tampak Ngashan (Mahadev) range, striped by the tributaries of Thoubal river n Eastern side and Iril River in the Western side.

Administrative set-up

Ukhrul District was first curved out as a Sub-Division in 1919. Later it was upgraded to a District in November, 1969. The District now has five Sub-Divisions which are co-terminus with the 5(five) Development Blocks. In addition to these administrative units the District has 4(four) Sub-Deputy Collectors Offices.

POLITY

The ancestors of the Tangkhuls follow a kind of hierarchy but democratic in practice. It is a combination of hierarchy and democracy, and hence, it can be termed as Hierarchical-Democracy or Democratic-Hierarchy. Thus, their ways of ruling and governance follow the principle of Federal Democracy. With the Chief of the Village at the head, there are the Clan Chiefs, who constitute the Hangva, the Village Authority. The collective wisdom of this Hangva governs the village administration. The decisions of the village authority is based on consensus unanimity. The pattern of sharing of power is federal in nature and apart from the central subjects the units/clans have their lists of subjects to regulate on their own. This is akin to the present division of subjects into the centre and the state lists of modern governments. There is also the wider administrative category at the regional level, though it has slightly less subjects but organized for serving common interests of the area. (see Chapter-10: Tangkhuls)

People

Tangkhul Nagas constitute the major bulk of the population. Others are some small percentage of Kukis, Nepalese and other Non-tribals. The Tangkhuls belong to the Mongolian race, fair in complexion, in facial appearance and stature.

Economy

Till about the middle of the 20th century, the business transactions of the people were on barter system and within the limit of the village only. There was not much commercial activity except selling of animals, salt, handloom materials, pottery products, wood and bamboo craft works, blacksmithy etc. The people could maintain and afford to meet their requirements for their day to day subsistence and livelihood. They were self-reliant and self-sufficient. But with the advent of modern civilization, they were suddenly exposed to capitalistic trend of fierce market competitions and urbanization. Their limited sources of income and resources could not meet both ends and sooner they were reduced to a people living below poverty line. They have yet to pick-up with the trends of modern economy. The main sources of income of the people can be broadly divided into 5 (five) divisions: Agriculture, Industries, Forest Wealth, Riverine wealth and animal husbandry (primitive method).

Religion

The Tangkhul Religion is a monotheistic religion with a little blend of animism and they worship with reverential owe the "Kazing Ngalei Kasa Akhava". This district is the birthplace of Christianity and Western education among the tribal in Manipur State, brought as early as 1896 by a Baptist Missionary, Rev. Pettigrew. Now, almost 99 % of the population have embraced Christianity. The main Christian sects are: Baptist Church, Catholic Church, Seventh Day Adventist Church, Church of Christ etc. (See Chapter-10: Tangkhuls)

Art and Culture

The life and art of the Tangkhul are attractive and captivating. Their different costumes and wears, utensils, architecture, monumental erections and memorial set-ups depict their dexterity in art, which also speak of their sense of beauty and finesse. Though there are common costumes and wears, both for male and female, there are also some costumes and wears exclusively meant for male and female.

Tourist spots: Important tourist spots are :-

1. Shirui Kashung (Shirui Peak), the floral garden of Shirui Lily.
2. Khankhui Cave
3. Hundung Mangva Cave.
4. Dilily Water Fall near Khayang Phungtha.
5. Azoa Jenephiu Magi Lake near Kachouphung.
6. Cold Water Fishery Project near zero point Phangrei, Shirui.
7. Saline Springs at Rajai, Marem, Maramphung, Kalhang, Luireishimphung.
8. Longpi Pottery at Longpi.
9. Khayang Peak
10. Chingjui Matza.
11. Phangrei Picnic Spot
12. Nillai Tea Estate on the way to Tolloi
13. MATA Industrial Complex, Lungpha.

Fauna and Flora

Ukhrul District is best introduced by its beautiful Shirui Lily, Lilium Mackleanae Sealy, grown only on the peak of Shirui Kashung, some 18 km. East of the district HQ. Ukhrul. Shirui Lily was declared the State Flower by the Government of Manipur on 21 March, 1989.

The District is gifted with rich flora and fauna. There are hundreds of varieties of trees, flowering plants, orchids of enumerable hues and kinds, Epiphetic ferns, varied species of plants and shrubs. Some of the known species of plants and trees are Alder (Alnus nepalensis), Prunus cirosirdes, Symingtonia, Acacia auriculifornis, Parkia javanica, Paraserrianthes falcotaria, Michelia oblanga, Cmilina arborea, pinus kerya, robinea psedudoacacia, besides various iris species, wild roses, red and white rhododendrons etc.

This tropical forest is also the habitat of many valued species of birds and animals. Many threatened species like, the tragopan blythii, pangolin (ant eater), salamander, tiger, porcupine, hooting monkey, leopard, big-small and medium size black bears, elephant, wild buffalo, wild boar, deer and stag, wild goat and many unidentified species are found in this region. Birds of various colours and sizes are also found here including some migratory birds. An area of 100 sq. km. around Shirui Peak has been declared as the National Park in 1998 by the Government of Manipur. Some of the important species of fish are; Golden Mhaseer (Tore Putitora) locally known as Ngara, Snow trout (schizothorax), locally known as Khainguila, Barilius guteltus, locally called

Ngapaila, Mastcembelus, locally known as Chipang, Botia species, locally known as Masengla, Naemecheilus species, locally known as Hangkorkhai, Chana species, locally known as Khaiva, Pontius species, locally known as Khaiwonla and khaipukla, Esomus species, locally known as Wonsangla, Gara species, cyprinio semiplotus, glyptothorax plailigopanoide, botisdorio, xenden cacila etc.

Kachai village is famous for lemon cultivation and production. Every year, there is Lemon festival to encourage and popularize lemon production in the district (see plates -366, 367)

Festivals.

The Tangkhul festivals are associated with the year-round seasonal agricultural activities. All these festivals associated with sacred religious rituals and there were strict codes of conduct for all these feasts. The major festivals are :

1. **Luira** - The seed sowing festival which falls around the months of January to March. This feast is celebrated with great fervour at Longpi and Hundung. Longpi, befitting their generosity, entertain their guests with lavish eats and drinks, whilst in Hundung one can see the maiden virgin dance performance.

2. **Yarra** - This is pre-cultivation festival and it falls around the months of April and May. Thought it celebrated by all, it is a youth festival.

3. **Mangkhap** – This is post-trans-plantation festival. This festival falls around the month of July. During this festival the people pray for luxurious growth of crops after thanksgiving prayer for the timely rain.

4. **Darreo** - This is a pre-harvest festival. Dharreo means the plucking of the new crop. On this day the first crops, fishes, live-stocks and other items are brought out for sale in the village market. It is fete day for the village. This day specially is observed in Hundung village.

5. **Chumpha** - This is a festival of thanksgiving for rich harvest, now gathered in the granary. The mother performs special offerings to the God of harvest and the keeper of the granary. While the mother performs her rituals all males are not allowed to enter the house, hence they stay outside the house for the night but with lavish supplies of eats and drinks. Because of the nature of its celebration, it is sometimes known as the Feast of the mother or the Feast of the granary. It falls around the months November and December.

6. **Longra khamang** -This festival is not general in nature but the family which had a rich harvest celebrates this festival inviting the group of the

son's or daughter's party who had worked in groups rotation-wise. This is a festival for giving special treatments to the sons and daughters.

7. **Thisham** - Thisham is a festival in commemoration of the dead. It is on this occasion that the Dance of the Dead is performed. This is the final rite performed by the family for the dead. It falls around the month of January.

Apart from these major festivals, there are some event-occasioned festivals like; Kashong Kahao Zakhalat, a sacred ritual for dispelling pests and germs; Maa Khungkashat, acknowledgement of the rich crop. Ears of corn are plucked and placed at a post set apart for this sacred ritual in the house; Mawonzai, a feast to invoke the graceful blessings of God to human labour; Khana Kasa, a purification and naming feast; Ming Kaphok, this is a title endowment feast; Chumsin Sa Kashai, this is the ordaining feast of the daughter-in-low to priestess-hood, thereby endowing her with all the rights and duties of a family mother. Prior to this, she is not allowed to enter into the granary; Shimsak Kasa, this is the royal or noble house construction feast; Maran-sak and Tarung Khangkasang, stone or tree trunks erection feast to display the wealth and power of the noble.

Food

Some special menu of the Tangkhuls are:

- Hancham : Known in Mietei Language as champhut, it is simple boiled vegetables without any spice.
- Khamui : Baked bread with special sticky rice. There are two methods of preparation; one is fried and the other is baked into cakes then wrap with panama or cardamom leaves and boiled.
- Vaitei : Ordinarily known as Khor, it is prepared with floured rice (sticky rice) made to ferment in a jar-filled water with floured sprouted-paddy grains.
- Paso : Prepared with sticky rice, processed same as (a) above, but without chaff.
- Chakhan : For those who don't relish the above drinks, simple fully boiled sticky rice with some soluble sweetening items are used.
- Chathur : Preparation, same as (iv) as also the materials, but let to cool and ferment. This is used as cold drink.
- Chicken Chatni : Simple boiled chicken mixed with chilli, ginger, native onion and spices

SENAPATI DISTRICT

The Senapati District was earlier known as Manipur North District which came into existence w.e.f 14 November 1969 with its headquarters at Karong. Later the district headquarter was shifted to Senapati on 13 December 1976. The District came to be known as Senapati District w.e.f. 15 July 1983. (see Plate- 362)

The Senapati district has got 3271sq. km. area, three subdivisions, 491villages, 25850 households and 156513 population. (Department of Statistics, Govt. of Manipur 2008). The geographical area is 3271.00 sq.km. The sex ratio is 928 and the literacy rate is 50.47%. Major Ethnic Communities are : Mao, Maram, Poumai, Zeliangrong, Thangal, Zemai, Liangmai, Roungmei, Tangkhul, Meitei, Kuki, Nepalese, Kipgen, Haokip, Gangte, Sitlou, Kom, Vaiphei, Chothe, Chiru, Maring

The Senapati District is located between 93.29° E and 94.15 ° East Longitude and 24.37 ° -25.37 ° North Latitude. The District is bounded on the south by Imphal West District, on the East by Ukhrul District, on the west by Tamenglong District and on the north by the state of Nagaland. The District is under humid subtropical climate. The soil is moderately fertile with clay loam soil with little patches of clay and loam. The temperature ranges from a minimum of 3.36°C to a maximum of 34.14°C. The annual rainfall ranges from 671 mm to 1454 mm. There are about 110 watersheds each of geographical size ranging from 2000 to 3000 hectares.

Table-67 Showing demographic indicators of Senapati district

		District-wise villages -2001				
District	*Subdivision*	*Villages*	*Households*	*Male*	*Female*	*Total population*
	Sadar Hills West	122	9568	30981	29964	60945
Senapati	Saitu Gamphazol	149	7202	23119	21011	44130
	Sadar Hills East	220	9080	26130	25308	51438
	Mao Maram					69131
	Paomata					27,065
	Purul					30,912
	Subtotal-7	**625**	**25850**	**80230**	**76283**	**283,621**

Roads

92 km of NH 39 passes through the District from the south end to the north end. Imphal- Tamenglong Road(IT road), Maram-Paren road, Tadubi-Tolloi-Ukhrul road, Maram-Ngari-Kachai road, Karong-Purul-Liyai road, Senapati-Khongdei-Phaibung road are other important roads in the district.

Administrative Set up

Senapati district has got six Assembly Constituencies- Saikul, Karong, Mao, Tadubi, Kangpokpi and Saitu, two district Councils-Manipur North Autonomous District Council, Senapati and Sadar Hills Autonomous District Council, Kangpokpi, six subdivisions- Tadubi, Paomata, Purul, Kangpokpi, Saikul and Saitu Gamphazol, four Development Blocks-Tadubi, Paomata, Saikul and Kangpokpi, four SDC Circles- Island, Kangchup, Willong and Phaibung. It has got five police stations - Senapati, Mao, Tadubi, Kangpokpi and Saitu Gamphazol,

Rivers

There are five rivers running through the district as shown below:-

Table-68 Showing sources and destinations of rivers in Senapati district

Sl. No.	*Name of the River*	*Aspect*	*Sources*	*Destination*	*Length (kms.)*
1.	Iril	South	Lakhamai of Purul Block	Imphal River	57.27
2.	Imphal	South	Maohing & Changoubung	Imphal River	38
3.	Barak	West	Karong-Mao area	Bramhaputra River	84.39
4.	Ithai	South	Selsi Thoubung area	Iril River	24.83
5.	Irang	South Western Block	Langka Chongjan area of Kangpokpi	Barak River	28.13

There are two Autonomous Hill District Councils-Manipur North Autonomous District Council, Senapati (MNADC), Sadar Hill Autonomous District Council with headquarters at Kangpokpi (SHADC)

Places to visit

Senapati : A new township and District Headquarters, Senapati is 62 km from Imphal. More than 30 government offices are located in the district headquarters. People of various ethnic communities are living in the town.

Maram Khullen : One of the biggest villages in the district, Maram Khullen is a very old and primitive village. It is an attractive destination for the anthropologist, research scholar and the like.

Yangkhullen : Yangkhullen is the largest Zemei village located 47 km from Maram Centre in Peren road. The primitive social and economic life is still prevailing in the village. It is situated amidst the steep cliff of beautiful landscape.

Mao : The last town of Manipur bordering Nagaland state, 107 km from Imphal and 28 km to Kohima, Mao is a very busy town. It is the granary of the surrounding villages and the gateway of the state. The Mao Inspection Bungalow built by the Royal Military Engineers in 1897 is a hundred year old. The cultural mosaic of Manipur is not complete without the colourful Mao Naga Dance.

Liyai : The village, 33 km from Tadubi towards the east is the home of various historical places like the stone monolith, the water pools, the Banyan tree, the male house and female house. The river Barak originates from the village.

Makhel : Makhel is the historical place of Naga dispersal and the legendary place of common origin of the Meiteis and Nagas. Makhel has the oldest pear tree memorial to the dispersal,. Makhel is a sacred place for many ethnic communities where they settled and migrated long back. There are historical monuments like 1. The sacred Banyan trees which are believed to have grown from the tomb of the Naga mother. 2. The farewell monolith. 3. The triomonolith (3 km south to Makhel). 4. The dispersal tree at Sajouba (2 km north to Makhel). 5. The hailstorm stone. 6. Village settlement stone. 7. The lucky stone etc.

Dzuko Valley : A most enchanting place, the valley can be reached by trekking from the border town of Mao. One can observe snowfall in winter and budding flowers of Dzuko lily in spring season. Dzukou valley with its pristine beauty blooms with a rare lily between May and July.

Purul : 19 km from Maram in NH 39, Purul is the home of indigenous games Toutou and wrestling. Toutou is played during New Year festival and wrestling is traditionally played on the eve of paddy transplantation festival which is known as Paoki falling in the first fortnight of May.

Agriculture:

The main crops are rice, maize, potato, cabbage and tomato. The predominant cropping pattern is mono cropping. The cultivation is partly

Jhuming, partly terraced and to some extent there is wetland cultivation. The paddy cultivation yield is one metric tone per hectare and four metric tone per hectare in Jhum fields and wetland respectively. The yield of maize is nearly 2 metric tone per hectare with High Yielding Variety seeds.

Table-69 Showing area of yield of various crops in Senapati district

Crop	*Area (in hectares)*	*Yields (in metric tone)*
Paddy	28,000	32.0
Maize	3,000	4.0
Wheat	100	0.3
Pulses	735	0.8
Pea	700	0.7
Mustard	2,000	1.0
Soyabean	100	0.1
Potato	1,200	6.0
Rice	24530	52880
Maize	2240	6400

Medicinal Plants.

Senapati district is very rich in medicinal plants. Some of the medicinal plants found in this district are given below :

Abrus precatorius Linn (local name - Chaning): A twining shrub. Scattered all over. Uses :- Seeds are Purgative, emetic, tonic, aphrodisiac- used in nervous disorders and cattle poisoning. roots possess glycyrrhizin and useful in coughs, colds and colic complaints. Paste of seeds is applied locally in sciatica, stiffness of shoulder joints and paralysis. Seeds are highly poisonous. Roots are used for treatment of Gonorrhoea, jaundice and Haemoglobinuric bile. Powdered seeds are said to disturb the uterine functions and prevent conception in women. The oil extracted from seeds is said to promote the growth of human hair.

Acacia Pruinescens Kurz: (local name - *Te-bam*) - A large woody climber armed with more or less recurved prickles Uses:- Plant is emetic, expectorant, and used as a substitute for senega; useful in bronchitis, pneumonia and asthma. Root is cathartic. Leaves are laxative, used in scabies and snake-bites. The herb may cause gastrointestinal irritation. Plant contains a cyanogenetic glucoside and alkaloid acalyphine. In Homeopathy, the herb is used against severe cough associated with bleeding from the lungs (haemoptysis) and insipient pthisis. Fresh juice of leaves is useful in case of croup.

Adiantum Aethiopicum Linn (local name - Mayur pambi, family - Adiantaceae)- A fern Uses :- Decoction of the fern is used by the South Africans as an abortificient ; also possess emetic and astringent properties. Infusion of fronds is used as emollient in cough and diseases of chest.

Adiantum Capillus-veneris Linn :(local name - Hansraj, family - Maidenhair fern) - A fern. Uses:- Plant is used as a pectoral, demulcent, expectorant and tonic. Boiled in wine it is given in case of hard tumours of spleen, liver and other viscera.

Adiantum Flabellulatum Linn : A fern - Rhizomes are used for cough and as an anthelminthic ; also used against grips.

Adiantum Incisum Forsk (local name - Mayur-pambi)-a fern- Used in hemicrania and diabetes.

Agrimonia Eupatoria Linn : (family – Rosaceae Agrimony)- A hairy herb with a perennial and woody rootstock. Uses:- Plant is used as an astringent, anti-helminthic, diuretic and tonic. Yields an essential oil which is active against Bacillus subtilis and Micrococcus pyogenes var. aureus. Vitamin K is also reported to be present.

Ainslisea Angustifolia (Compositae: Asteraceae)- A small herb. Common in the forest clearing. Uses:- Smashed leaves are applied to old wounds for healing.

Aporusa dioi Muell-Arg (family-Euphorbiaceae)- An evergreen tree. Uses :- Ethanolic extract of stem and leaves showed respiratory and cardiovascular activities.

Artemisia meritima Linn (local name - Leibakngou-manba, Compositae - Asteraceae family – Worm Seed)- A scandent shrub.- Leaf-extract is given in acute stomach pain. Smashed leaves are applied to abdomen and forehead as poultice in pains. Smashed shoots are thrown on water for trapping fishes.Flowers give the commercial Santonin for eradicating worms from stomach; leaf-infusion is used in intermittent fevers. Bark is antiseptic. Decoction is used as a febrifuge.

Bauhinia Tenuiflora Watt ex Clarke (local name - Chingthrao)- A large cirrhoses climber Uses:- Bark is used in diarrhoea.

Begonia palmata D.Don (local name- Banhang, family-Begoniaceae)- A small herb. Fairly common as an undergrowth in shaded regions of the forests.

Uses :- Plant-juice is poisonous to leeches and used to kill them when found in the nostrils of animals. Extract of succulent stalks is used for venereal diseases.

Cephalostachyam capitatum :Munro (Gramineae; Poaceae)-A bushy bamboo. Uses:- Infusion of leaves is given as tonic, also antihelminthic, stomachic and carminative.

Cirsium sinense C.B.Clarke- An erect herb. Uses:- Roots are used in flatulence : externally for ulcers and abscesses. Stems and leaves are antiscorbutic.

Clerodendrum Colebrookianu,Walp. (family - Verbenaceae)- A shrub with foetid smell. Uses :- Roots with bark is given in bronchitis and asthma. Leaf-juice is given to eradicate threadworms. Roots is used in asthma, cough and scrofulous affections. Leaves are vermifuge. Wood is tied around the neck against various ailments. The smell of the wood is believed to cure many diseases of the children.

Clerodedrum Colebrookianum :Walp. (family- Verbenaceae)- A shrub with foetid smell. Uses:- Leaves are used for rheumatic pains by the Khasis and Jaintias of Meghalaya.

Curcuma aromatia Salisb. (Local name – Lam-yaingang, Family-Wild Turmeric)- A rhizomatous, aromatic herb. Uses :- Rhizomes are tonic, carminative ; enter into composition used for bruises, contusions and sprains; also used in snake-bite.

Cynodon dactylon Pers : (Local name – Tingthou,Family-Gramineae:Poaceae Dhub Grass)- A perennial grass. Uses :- Extracted juice of the grass is applied to fresh cuts or injuries for stopping bleeding. Women suffering from excessive uterine bleeding are given fresh juice about 50cc along with sugar once daily for three days as remedy. Decoction of roots is given in dropsy and secondary syphilis, Plant juice is used in injuries, anasarca, hysteria, epilepsy and insanity ; also astringent in chronic diarrhoea and dysentery ; useful in catarrh of ophthalmia. Rhizome is used in genito- urinary troubles.

Daphne papyracea Wall.ex Steud. (family – Thymelaeaceae)- A shrub. Uses :- Plant is febrifuge, bitter and purgative. Sweet scented flowers are with antimicrobial activity. Roots are used as medicines for different diseases by the tribes of Eastern India.

Dicliptera roxburghiana Nees (Family–Acanthaceae) -A diffused herb with woody rootstock Uses:- Plant is used as a tonic.

Diospyros Lancaefolia :Roxb.(family – Ebenaceae)- A middle sized tree. Uses:- Infusion of leaves is prescribed for bath of anaemic children by the Bondos of Orissa.

Elatostema lineolatum :Wight (family–Urticaceae)- an undershrub. Uses:- Leaf-paste is applied to cuts by the Karbis of Assam.

Eleutherococcus cissifolius: (Family - araliaceae)-A small tree. Uses:- Leaves are used for stomach disorders.

Elsholtzia ciliate :(Thumb) Hyland-An aromatic herb.Uses:- Leaf-extract is prescribed in stomach disorders.

Equisetum arvense Linn (Family -Equisetaceae Field Horsetail)-Herb. Uses:- Source of Herba Equiseti, used as a diuretic ; has haemostatic properties, considered useful in dropsy, gravel and kidney affection. the ash of the plant is useful in acidity of the stomach and in dyspepsia.

Eucalyptus citriodora Hook. (Local name – Nasik Family – Myrtaceae Lemon Scented Eucalyptus)- A big tree. Uses :- Leaves are used as an ingredient for the preparation of an indigenous hair-lotion(Chinghi). Volatile oil vapour is antimicrobial.

Eupatorium birmanicum DC (local name- Langthrei, Compositae ; Asteraceae) - An undershrub. Uses:- leaf-juice is applied to the body in burning sensation. Leaf extract with milk is a remedy for leucorrhoea. The extract with honey is given in stomach ulcers.

Eupatorium cannabinum Linn (Family – Hemp Agrimony)-A herb Uses:- Plant is diuretic, antiscorbutic, cathartic, deobstruent,given in visceral obstructions, in swelling of leg, intermittent fevers, for fomenting sores, in influenza and as purgative.

Eupatorium odoratum Linn. (Local name – kambilei) -An undershrub. Uses:- Leaf-juice with salt is treated as poison ; fresh juice is given externally in Gonorrhoea. Plant is used as fish-poison.

Euphorbia hirta Linn. (Local Name – Pakhamba-maton) - A Trailing herb. Uses :- Plant is used in worm diseases of children. Plant-juice is given in dysentery, bowel complaints, cough and colic; plant decoction is used in bronchial affections and asthma. Latex is applied to warts. Plant is also used in diseases of genito-urinary tract.

Eurya japonica Thunb. (local name –Baunra, family – Theaceae)-A shrub. Uses:- Leaves are used as poultice on skin eruption.

Fleurya interrupta Gaudich. (Local name – Santhak, family Urticaceae)- an erect herb with stinging hair Uses:-Hair cause dermatitis ; leaf-paste is applied to carbuncle, root extract is diuretic.

Galinsoga parviflora Cav. (local name – Hameng shampakpi, Compositae – Asteraceae)-An erect herb. Uses:- Leaves with those of Ageratum conyzoides, Drymaria cordata and ginger are made into a paste and applied as a remedy for snake-bite by the khasis and Jaintias of Meghalaya.

Galium rotundilium Linn. (Rubiaceae)-A diffuse herb.Uses:- Plant is used for colic,sore throat and chest complaints.

Geranium nepalense Sweet (local name- Bhanda, Geraniaceae Nepal Geranium) - A perennial pubescent or softly hairy herb. Uses:- Plant is astringent,used in certain renal diseases. Roots contain a red colouring matter and are used for colouring medicinal oils.

Glochidion oblatum Hk.f. (Family –Euphorbiaceae)- A middle sized tree. Uses:- Extract of stem and root is given in dysentery.

Gossypyium arboretum Linn. (local name – Lashing, family – Malvaceae)- This cotton is grown in jhum cultivation. Uses :- Flowers are used in scabies and skin diseases. Seeds are used in hydrocele. Seeds are expectorant, demulcent and used for abortion. This is used in headache and considered nerve tonic. Leaf-juice is used in scorpion-sting and snake-bite. Roots are used in fever. Seeds are also used in gonorrhoea, gleet, cystitis and catarrh.

Grangea maderaspatana Poir. (local name – Leibungou, Compositae ; Asteraceae)- A herb,inflorescence yellow. Uses :- Decoction is used for giving bath in case of eczema and other skin diseases. Infusion of leaves is considered stoma chic, antispasmodic and deobstruent. Leaf-juice is used as instillation for earache.

Gynura cusimba (D.Don) Moore (local name – terapaibi, Compositae; Asteraceae)-A large succulent herb. Uses:- Juice expressed from the succulent stem and leaves is applied to fresh wounds for stopping bleeding and quick healing. Leaf-paste is applied to forehead to cure headache.

Hedera nepalensis Koch. (local name – Lablab, family – Araliaceae NEPAL IVY)- An evergreen woody climber Uses:- Fruits are stimulant, diaphoretic, cathartic; useful in febrile disorders. Berries and seeds contain glycoside a-hederin which is intensely haemolytic and acts as an irritant to the alimentary canal, causes vaso-constriction, lowers blood pressure and slows the heart. Leaf decoction destroys hair lice ; infusion of berry is used in rheumatism; gum is emmenagogue.

Festivals

Thounii : The new year cultural festival of Poumai Nagas is celebrated on 5 January to mark cultural resurgence, social interaction, family reunion.

Laonii : The sacred festival of Poumai Nagas is celebrated on completion of paddy transplantation which usually falls in the last fortnight of July. A festival of male sanctification, this is an occasion to interact and renew ties with brothers and sisters.

Chiithuni : The six day annual festival of Mao Nagas celebrated from 25th day of Chuthunikhro (Dec-Jan), meaning 'feast of dawn', is an occasion to rejuvenate the cultural heritage of the Mao Nagas.

Saleni : It is a customary festival of Mao Nagas, celebrated in the month of Salekhro (July) on completion of paddy transplantation. The whole men folk have to purify themselves by taking bath early in the morning in the pond.

Ponghi : The seven day customary festival of Maram Nagas is celebrated on 20th day of Ponghi-kii (July) on completion of paddy transplantation.

Kanghi : The seven day customary festival of Maram Nagas held in the month of Kanghi-kii (December). Wrestling is played during the festival in the Khullakpa's compound in stark naked to get shy away the devils so as to obviate misfortune and injury.

TAMENGLONG DISTRICT

Tamenglong district has got 4391 sq. km. area, 171 villages, 15130 households and 111499 populations. The 15-44 years population ratio is 46.94%. The 15-48 years rural population (males) as on 1st March, 2007 is 34485. (Department of Statistics, Govt. of Manipur 2008). The sex ratio is 922 and the literacy rate is 58.46%. The district is divided into four sub-divisions: Tamenglong, Tamei, Tousem and Nungba. (see Map-Plate-363).

Tamenglong is located along the western boundary of the state.Tamenglong is entirely composed of hills, ranges and narrow valleys. The hilltops and valley sides are dotted with small hamlets, located at strategic points. The land was believed to have been formed due to orogenic movement during cretaceous and Eocene period. The main rock formations are sandstone, shale, schist. Due to weak and fragile nature of rocks and high gradient of the hill slopes, landslide is a common phenomenon in the whole district in rainy season.

Tamenglong HQ can be reached through roadways. From Imphal (State Capital) three buses depart at 6.00 am weekdays (except Sunday) to reach Tamenglong in the same afternoon.

Tamenglong has got four subdivisions- Tamenglong, Tamei, Tousem, Nungba.

Tamenglong is inhabited by majority Zeliangrong Naga tribe (comprising of Rongmei, Liangmei, Zemei and Pumei) and Kukis, besides minority Hmars, Chirus and Khasis. Racially or physically and linguistically Zeliangrongs are Tibeto-Burman (Indo-Mongoloid) of Sino-Tibetan family of the Mongolian race. Based on history it is assumed that Mongoloid groups including Zeliangrong Nagas were inhabiting the upper course.

The Zeliangrong belongs to patriarchal social system. Each clan enjoys equal status. Clan exogamy is strictly observed. Cross-cousin marriage is most preferred but parallel cross-cousin is seldom practiced.

Besides following many other normal customs of a Naga-tribe, they also have some strange and fearful customs. Some of them are as below:

Nasitheimei or Nathitheimei

Should a woman die in childbirth the child is not permitted to live but buried with the dead mother.

Mandu (Bone money)

Mandu is the bone price of wife. Patrilineal relatives of the wife demand this. On the death of a wife, her father demands Mandu from the husband, or if he be dead, from the late husband's nearest relative. Mandu ensures that every care will be taken both of wife and offspring.

Marriage system

Besides normal marriage like by engagement or by elopement there are also other kinds of marriage.

- Noumang-mei-Nou-kao (Marriage by Service): With the agreement of both parties the boy stay at the girl's parents' house and stay for three to four years and live as husband and wife then finally return home.
- Chamemei: Here a girl is given in marriage even against her consent to a family to whom the girls parent are in debt or some obligations.

Table-70 Showing demographic indicators of Tamenglong district

District	Subdivision	*District-wise villages -2001* Villages	Households	Male	Female	Total Population
Tamenglong	Tamenglong West	53	2348	11034	10785	21819
	Tamenglong North	29	3007	11261	10646	21907
	Tamenglong	33	5522	19698	17338	37036
	Nungba	56	4253	16021	14716	30737
	Subtotal-8	**171**	**15130**	**58014**	**53485**	**111499**

- Naokakhaomei: In an accidental death of a man, the nearest next brother will look after the children and remarry the wife of his brother.

Tamenglong district of Manipur is blessed with a topography of irregular undulation. It has in its small area most of the awesome features that nature mould to a hilly terrain. Turbulent waters, roaring waterfall, pitching dark caves, enchanting lakes of the wilderness, rocks chiseled to wondrous form and yet the thick blanket of dense tropical forest most part of which are still virgin.

Fauna and Flora

Tamenglong District is blessed with virgin forests, exotic orchids, rare and endangered plants, and wildlife. The forest are the main source of timbers. Cane brakes are found in and around water bodies. The Sub-tropical forests are found on the highest altitudes. Varieties of orchids are found in this zone of forests. In the degraded forest areas the bamboo brakes are found in plenty.

Tamenglong district is rich in fauna and flora. Tamenglong is called "the land of hornbills". Great pied hornbill (Buceros bicornis homrai), and Indian pied hornbill are found here. (see plate – 375) The district is blessed with abundant bamboos, timbers, cane brakes, varieties of orchids. The forest are rich in wild life. Sambar deer, hog deer, Hoolock Gibbon, bear, fox, hyena, wild pig, wild dogs, slow loris, scrow, Leopard, Tigers are reported. Pheasants, peafowl, jungle fowls are important birds. Migratory herds of elephants are reported in winter months. Cobra, krait, viper, python are also found inside

Table-71 Showing Tamenglong District Profile

Geographical Area	4,391 sq kms.	
Population	111499	
Altitude (above MSL)	1260 m	
Latitude (HQ)	24.59 N	
Longitude (HQ)	93.30 E	
Humidity	76 (Min),	92 (Max)
Rainfall (HQ)	3135 mm.	
Temparature	31°C (Max)	4°C (Min)
Literacy	50.16 %	
Sub-Divisions	Tamenglong	
	Tamei	
	Tousem	
	Nungba	
Main Tribes (Inhabitants)	Zeliangrong Nagas	
	Kuki	
	Chiru	

large forests around Zeilad lake. Cranes, ducks and teal are also found in Zeilad lake. Varieties of exotic orchids are also available. Dendrobium vandal, Cymbidium, Cattleya, Lycaste, Phius tunkervels, Thunia alba, Paphiopedium are found in Barrack valley, Leimatak area and other places.

Festivals

Festivals and Dances of the Zeliangrong are closely linked up with religion, which is associated with their economic vocation and socio-cultural ethos. Festivals reflect different stages of agricultural activities, here talents, physical strength are expressed. Every month there is a festival. (see plates - 369, 370, 371)

The popular festivals are :- Gan-Ngai
Rih-Ngai (Chaga Ngai)
Gudui-Ngai
Banruhmei Orange festival- Tamenglong is famous for cultivation and production of oranges. Orange festival is held every year to encourage and popularize the orange production (see plates- 372, 373, 374)

Gan-Ngai

This festival is celebrated in the month of December-January after harvest for 5 (five) days. Blowing horn herald the festival, fresh fire is made with the ancient friction method and distributed in every household. Villagers, irrespective of age dressed in their best attire, keep up the dance and songs, intercepting only by short intervals of repose and break dedicated to feasting.

Rih-ngai: (Chaga Ngai)

Celebrate during January-February is this War festival which is exclusively for male. No stranger is allowed to enter the village. Men abstain from sexual intercourse and foods cooked by women are not taken. An interesting feature is Raangh-Kapmei or shooting at an effigy of a warrior with pointed bamboo splits. It is believed that one who hit the effigy on:

- the head, will be successful in war.
- the chest, will be successful in hunting.
- the abdomen, will be lucky in cultivation, etc.

Likewise there are altogether seven segments on the effigy, which they believed would reveal their fortune of the year.

Gudui-Ngai

Performed during the seed-sowing season in April. After completion of task like clearance of jungle for cultivation everyone will drink juice (dui) of ginger (Gu). Tug of war is performed between male and female as a symbolic representation of competition between God and Goddess for possessing the paddy. If the girls win it indicates a good harvest.

Banruhmei and Tarang

These are two feasts of merit performed by one who is bold, brave, philanthropist, generous and rich enough to feed the whole village. It is believed that if a man could perform both the feasts of merit during his lifetime, he is supposed to have accomplished his life's work.

During Banruhmei various songs and dances are performed observing strict forms. The entire villagers, irrespective of age, will participate the feast, which may last a few weeks. The wife of the host will perform a special dance with a rice beer cistern of gourd, pouring it out rhythmically.

Tarang (or Kaisumei) can be performed only by those who have performed Banruhmei, if he still can afford. Here the special house of merit called Tarang-kai is constructed.

Dances

The rich cultural heritage of the Zeliangrong is reflected in their varieties of art specially dances performed during their festivals. Dances are different in their steps, forms and seasons. Zeliangrong enjoy dancing throughout the day and the night.

Deep thudding of drums shake the ground underfoot & jar the body. Endless steps and forms under the moonlight and glares of the torches, dances of the night is quite an experience.

Zeiliangrong use a violin like musical instrument called Nrah to give accompany to songs.

Some of the popular dances of the Zeliangrong are as below:

Jaopa lam, Ri lam, Victory dance, War dance. Hansiangmai lam, Bamboo dance. Rangdai Lam, Dance of Hornbill. Mangrelim, Dance of Fly. Khuairuna lam, Bee's dance, Tariang lam, Spinning Dance, Ga lam, Crab dance, Maukana lam, Hawk dance, Makhom lam, Fertility dance.

Special Attractions

Along the river Barak there are seven waterfalls in series at close range.

The famous Tharon cave is located at about 27 kms from the district HQ. The map of the entire cave is engraved and painted on a stone at the main entrance. Archeological excavation of the cave shows affinities with Hobinian culture of North Vietnam. (see plate- 359)

The legendary Zeilad lake at Makoi (Atengba) is associated with a number of pythons, fishes and water birds. There are six other lakes nearby Guiphop Zei, Nrou Zei, Nap-sam Zei etc.

The Buning (N-piulong) meadow is located on the western side of the picturesque Tamei town. A number of well-groomed uneven small mounts, numerous glittering brooks studded the stretch. Come June the meadow is coloured with enchanting groud orchids and various wild lilies. Cry of Hoolock gibbon, howling of foxes, melodious chirping of birds altogether form Buning a big family of the wildlife evoking wonder and admiration of many who have witnessed the meadow.

CHANDEL DISTRICT

The Chandel District (earlier named Tengnoupal district) came into existence on 13 May 1974. It is a border district bordering Myanmar.

The Chandel district has got 3313 sq. km. area, four subdivisions, 351 villages, 12138 households and 118327 populations. The 15-44 years population ratio is 50.22%. The 15-48 years rural population (males) as on 1st March, 2007 is 31972 and that of urban population is 4628 (Department of Statistics, Govt. of Manipur 2008. It is a hill district with an area of 3,313 sq. km. The sex ratio is 986 and the literacy rate is 57.38%. (see Map-Plate -364)

The district headquarters is Chandel, which is about 64 km. away from Imphal. The National Highway No. 39 passes through this District. The District lies in the south-eastern part of Manipur. Its neighbours are Myanmar (erstwhile Burma) on the south, Ukhrul district on the east, Churachandpur district on the south and west, and Thoubal district on north.

The District is inhabited by several communities. It is sparsely inhabited by about 20 different tribes. They are scattered all over the district. Prominent tribes in the district are Anal, Lamkang, Kukis, Moyon, Monsang, Chothe, Thadou, Paite, and Maring etc. There are also other communities like Meiteis, and Muslims in small numbers as compared to the tribes. Non-Manipuris like Tamils, Bengalis, Punjabis, and Biharis are also settled in this district.

Table-72 Showing demographic indicators of Chandel district

District	Subdivision	Villages	Households	Male	Female	Total population
	District-wise villages -2001					
Chandel	Machi	58	3035	8728	8359	17087
	Tengnoupal	67	5735	16142	15620	31762
	Chandel	86	4904	13025	13251	26276
	Chakpikarong	140	7234	21846	21356	43202
	Subtotal-9	361	12138	59741	58586	118327

The Moreh town, the international trade centre of the state lies on the southernmost part of the District. When the Trans-Asian Super Highway comes into existence, Chandel district will be one of the gateways to the Asian countries.

Tengnoupal

It is about 20 km. from Chandel. The highest point on the Indo-Myanmar Road, from here one can have a fıll view of the valley of Manipur. When a visitor passed along the road, he will find himself above the clouds but in natural surroundings.

Moreh

This border town is located on the Indo-Myanmar Road, about 110 km. from Imphal. Being a commercial town it attracts a large number of people from neighbouring places. Moreh is only 5 km. from Tamu town, its Myanmar counterpart. Opening of the Border Trade turns Moreh into an important centre in the Northeast.

Forest

Table-73 Showing Area under Forest by Legal and Composition of Chandel District

Year	Reserved	Protected	Unclassed	Total
	Class of Forest (sq. km)			
1994-95	141.79	-	2461.81	2603.60
1995-96	141.79	-	2461.81	2603.60
1996-97	141.79	-	2461.81	2603.60
1997-98	141.86	-	3034.14	3176.00
1998-99	NA	NA	NA	NA

Transportation and Communication

Chandel district is connected by the National Highway No. 39 reaching up to Moreh. There are several buses plying from Imphal to Chandel daily. The State Highway No. 10 diverts from National Highway No. 39 at Pallel connecting the district head quarters.

1. To visit Chandel District HQ and Chandel block, one can catch Chandel buses at Keishampat Bus Parking (at Imphal) or catch any bus reaching Kakching and catch Chandel buses from Kakching or Kakching Lamkhai.
2. To visit Chakpikarong division (block), one can catch Chakpikarong buses at Keishampat Bus Parking (at Imphal) or catch any bus reaching Kakching and catch Chakpikarong buses from Kakching or Kakching Lamkhai.
3. To visit Tengnoupal division (block) or Moreh, one catch buses or Tata Sumos at Moreh Bus Parking at Kangla Park, at Imphal.
4. To visit Machi division (block), at present there is no bus service. Only trucks are carrying passengers between Machi and Kakching. So hiring of light vehicles is recommended to visit Machi.

Fauna and Flora

Like other hill districts of Manipur, Chandel also has varieties of flora and fauna. Various kinds of orchids, ornamental plants and even numerous plants are abundantly grown. Some of the medicinal plants available in Chandel are given below :-

Anisomeles indica (Thoiding Amuba : Manipuri): A strongly scented shrubby plant found in Pallel area, is used as an appetizer.

Anotis foetida (Khut-chappi : Manipuri): A small herb found in Sugnu and Pallel areas, its smashed roots are applied to fractured bone which acts as a poultice of plaster of Paris for setting and healing. The same is applied to boils.

Areca catechu (Supari : Manipuri) : A slender tall palm, cultivated in Moreh area. Paste of the nut after rubbing on the stone with water is applied to leucodermal patches.

Brucea javanica (Heining : Manipuri): A small deciduous tree found in Pallel, its fruits are used for diarrhoea, dysentery and malignant malaria. Poultice of leaves is applied in skin troubles. Roots are used in bowel complaints.

Crasscephalum crepidiodes (Terapaibi : Manipuri): A herb found in Moreh area, whose lotion of leaves is used as a mild stomachic.

The only ape found in India, the Hoolok Gibbon locally known as Yongmu, is also found in Chandel district. Similarly, the Slow Loris, the Stumped Tailed Macaque, the Pig Tailed Macaque are the other rare primates that occur in the forests. Sometimes rare nocturnal carnivores, the Clouded leopard and the Golden Cat are also sighted. The gigantic land animal, the elephant, makes seasonal migration into the Indo-Myanmar border areas. The Himalayan Black Bear is also found in Chandel. The rare and elusive Malayan Sun Bear is restricted to the Unique forests in the Indo-Myanmar border areas. Herds of Bison, as well as of Sambhar, can be seen during night in New Samtal area. Thai Pangolins can also sighted in the Indo-Myanmar border areas which falls under Chandel. Birds like Pheasant, Burmese peafowl and jungle fowls are also sighted in Chandel. The Yangoupokpi-Lokchao Wildlife Sanctuary, a protected area network in Manipur, is situated on the Indo-Myanmar border of Chandel. The sanctuary is the home of about 86 species of fishes, 6 species of amphibians, 29 species of mammalians.

Art and Culture

The following varieties of dances are popular :-

- **Paite Dance**

  Kinds: Dak Lam, Jangta Lam, Phit Lam, Ton Lam, and Silam Lam

- **Thadou Kuki Dance**
- **Tarao War Dance**

Each tribal group has their own distinct culture and tradition in their dance, music, dress, customary practices and pastimes. The folk dances of the ethnic tribes captivate the beholders with their exotic costumes and simple but graceful rhythm.

The Maring tribe are famous for their handicraft products. They are the main manufacturers of Likhai, Sangbai, Chengbon, Meruk (all containers), Morah (for sitting) and Long-up, Tengbol (for fishing), etc. which are made of cane and bamboo.

Every tribal group has distinct style of embroidery patterns on their dress.

Festivals

The following festivals are popular :-

1. Anal Festivals

- Ikam
- Inhla

- Philthabla (Hunting and fighting festival)
- Mikhemphan (Collection of money and food)
- Sungkhomlkhan (Fencing of village boundary with religious significance)

2. Thadou Festival

- Chon (A great festival of Thadous. Subdivided into Sha-ai, and Chai-lai).

3. Kuki Festival

- Chavan Kut (An important annual festival of Kuki tribes. Performed with great pomp and pageantry.)

4. Naga Festival

- Lui Ngai Ni (It is a Naga Seed Sowing Festival accompanied by various cultural activities and dances of Naga tribes.)

5. Monsang Festival

- Kum ether Borhin esha or Chanou Tangba (It is a Monsang custom festival for testing the newly harvested crops.)

6. Christmas

Christmas, the greatest festival of all the Christians, is observed for two days on 24th and 25th December. Prayers, reading of Gospels, singing of hymns, lectures on Jesus Christ, sports, and community feast etc., form the major part of the festival.

References

1. R. Gupta's Popular Manipur General Knowledge, Ramesh Publishing House, New Delhi, 2009
   http://manipur.nic.in/DistrictsinManipur.htm
   http://chandel.nic.in/
   http://senapati.nic.in/festival.htm
   http://senapati.nic.in/howtoreach.htm
   http://ukhrul.nic.in/ueconomy.htm

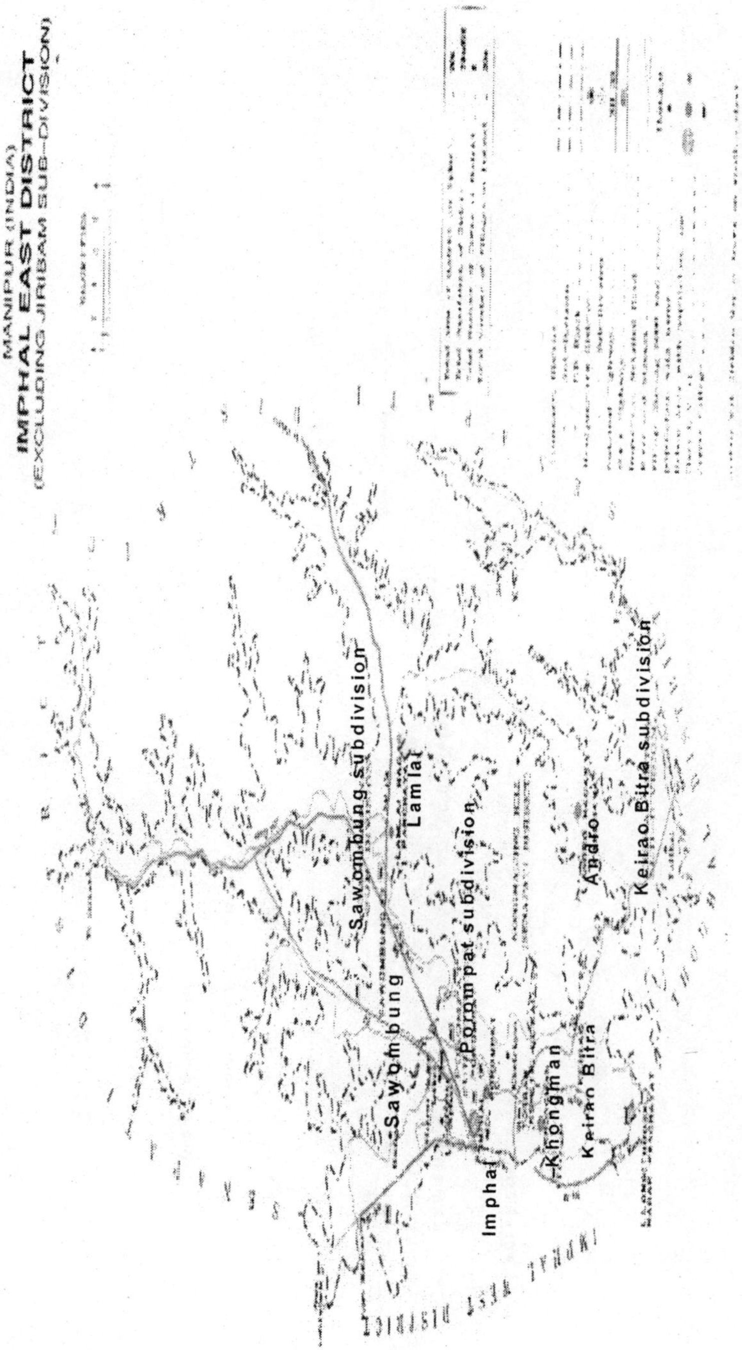
MANIPUR (INDIA)
IMPHAL EAST DISTRICT
(EXCLUDING JIRIBAM SUB-DIVISION)
Sawombung subdivision
Lamlai
Porompat subdivision
Andro
Keirao Bitra subdivision
Sawombung
Porompat
Khongman
Keirao Bitra
Imphal
IMPHAL WEST DISTRICT

Plate -356

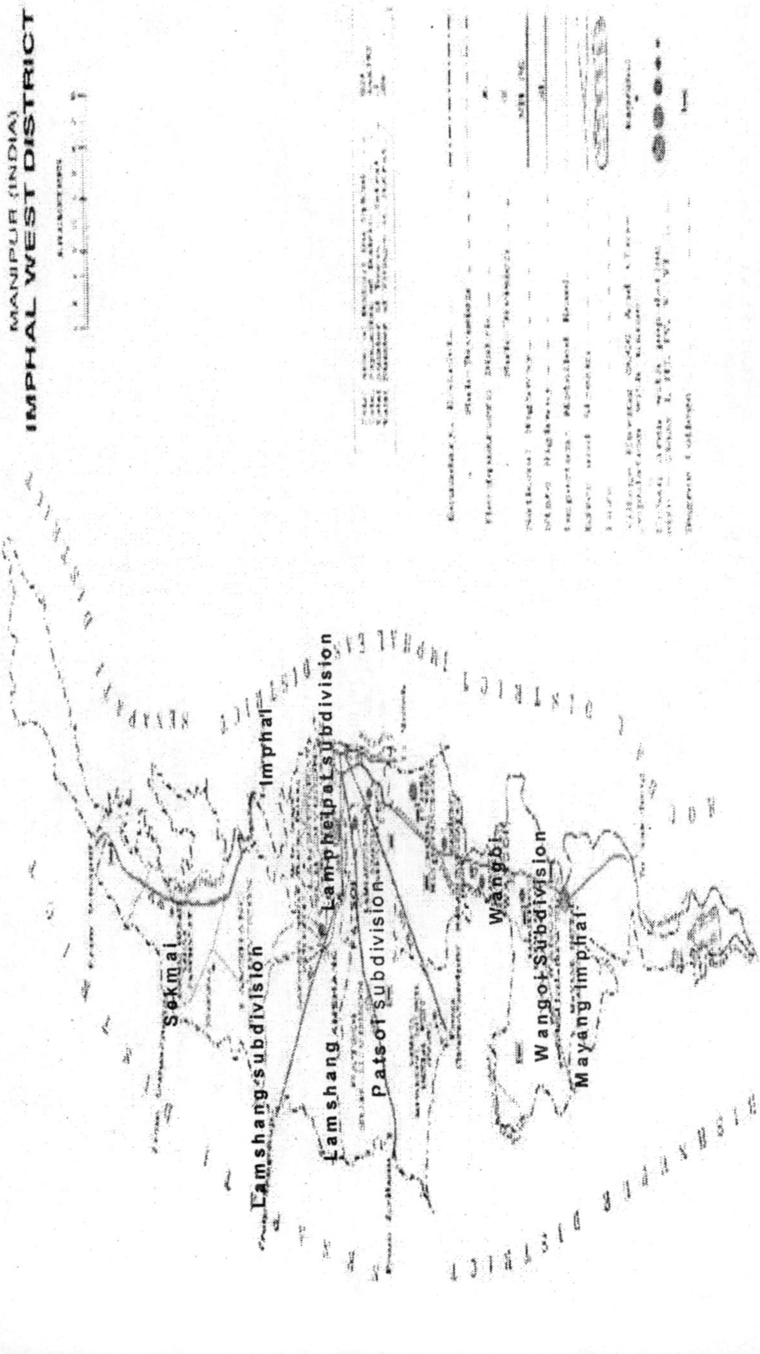
MANIPUR (INDIA)
IMPHAL WEST DISTRICT
Sekmai
Lamshang subdivision
Lamshang
Imphal
Lamphelpat subdivision
Patsoi subdivision
Wangoi
Wangoi Subdivision
Mayang Imphal

Plate -357

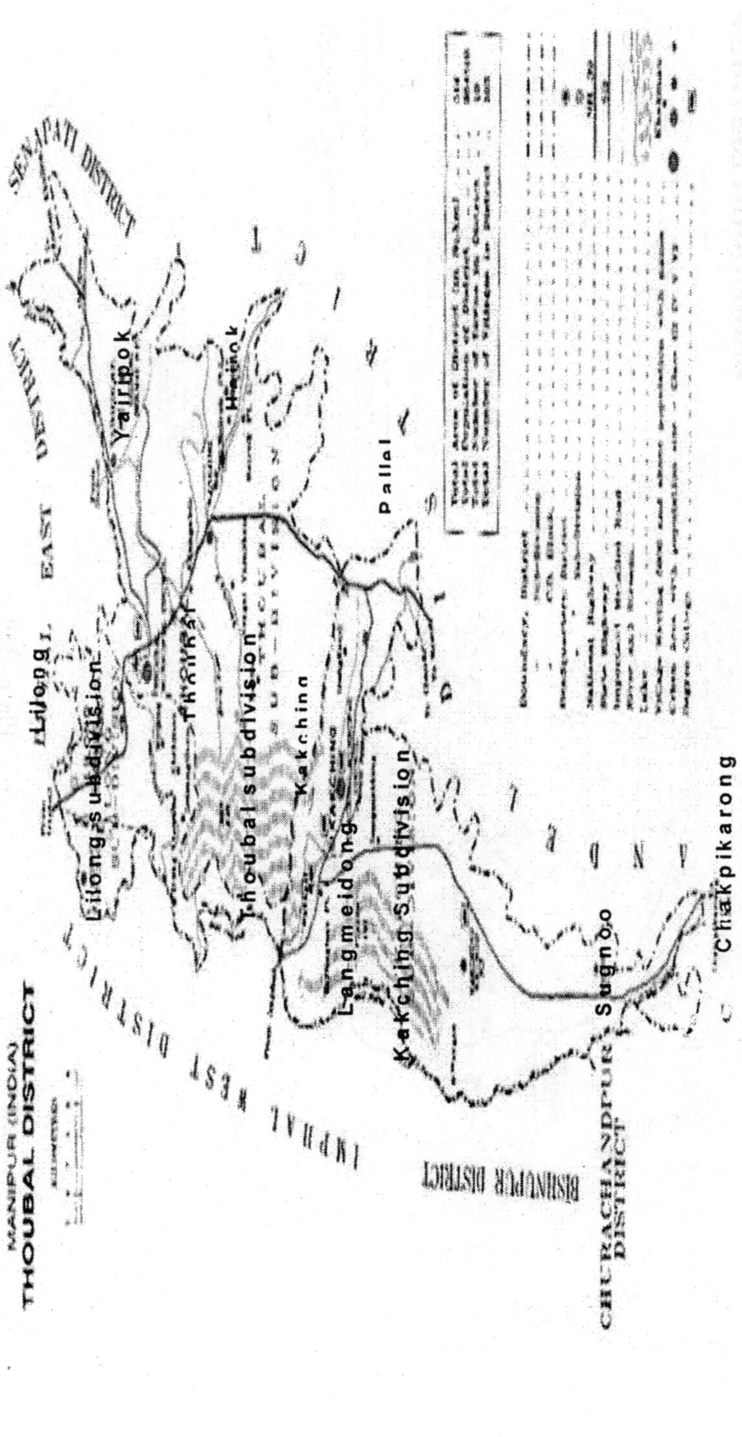
MANIPUR (INDIA)
THOUBAL DISTRICT
SENAPATI DISTRICT
IMPHAL EAST DISTRICT
IMPHAL WEST DISTRICT
BISHNUPUR DISTRICT
CHURACHANDPUR DISTRICT
Lilong
Lilong subdivision
Yairipok
Thoubal
Thoubal subdivision
Kakching
Pallel
Langmeidong
Kakching Subdivision
Sugnoo
Chakpikarong

Plate –358

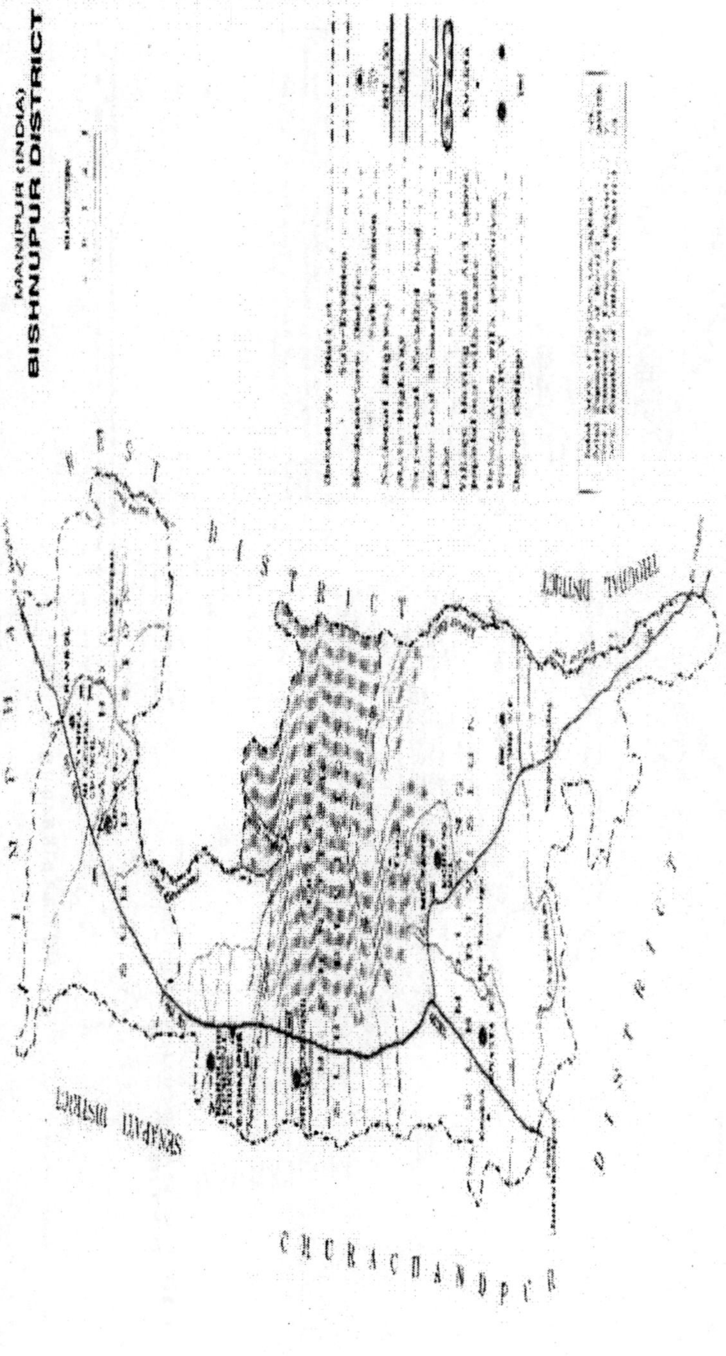

MANIPUR (INDIA)
BISHNUPUR DISTRICT
SENAPATI DISTRICT
THOUBAL DISTRICT
CHURACHANDPUR

Plate –359

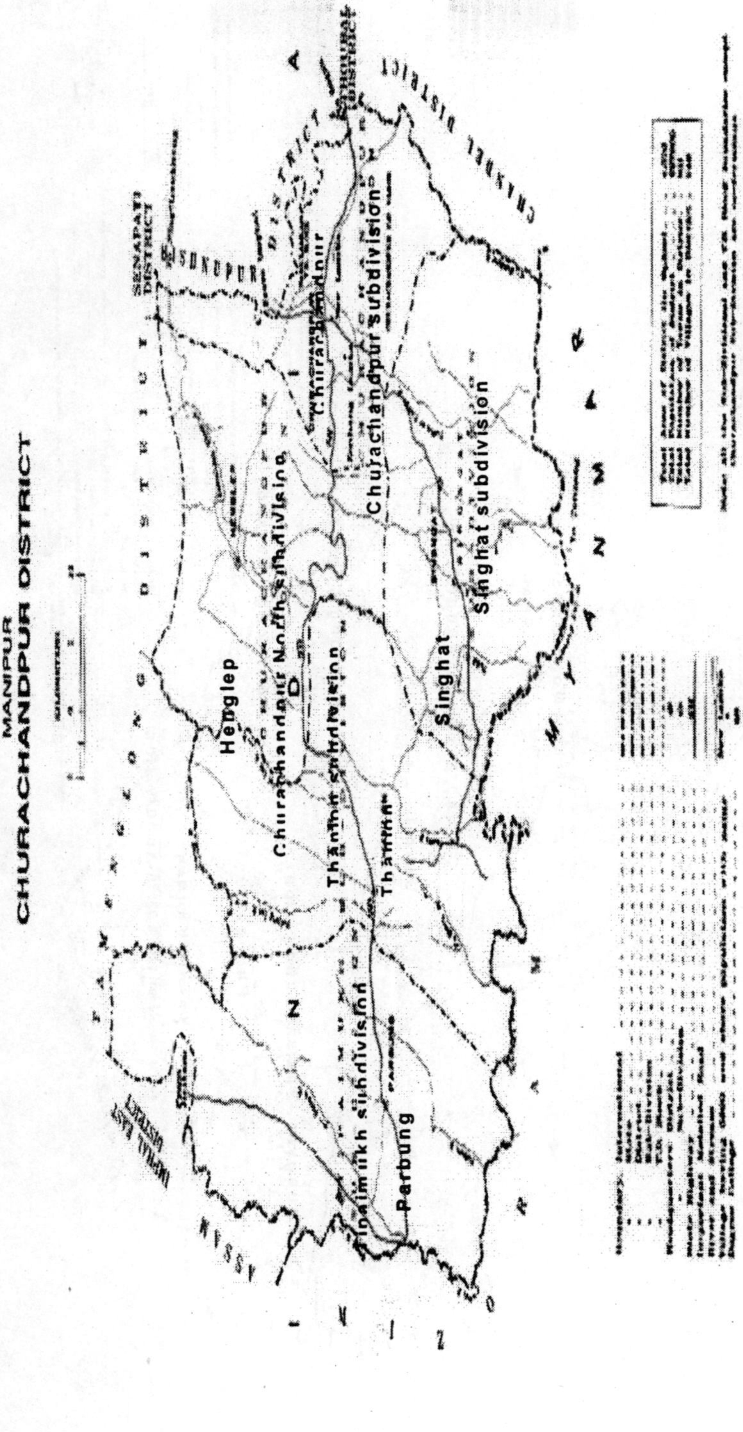
MANIPUR
CHURACHANDPUR DISTRICT
SENAPATI DISTRICT
CHANDEL DISTRICT
IMPHAL EAST DISTRICT
ASSAM
Henglep
Singhat
Singhat subdivision
Churachandpur subdivision
Parbung

Plate –360

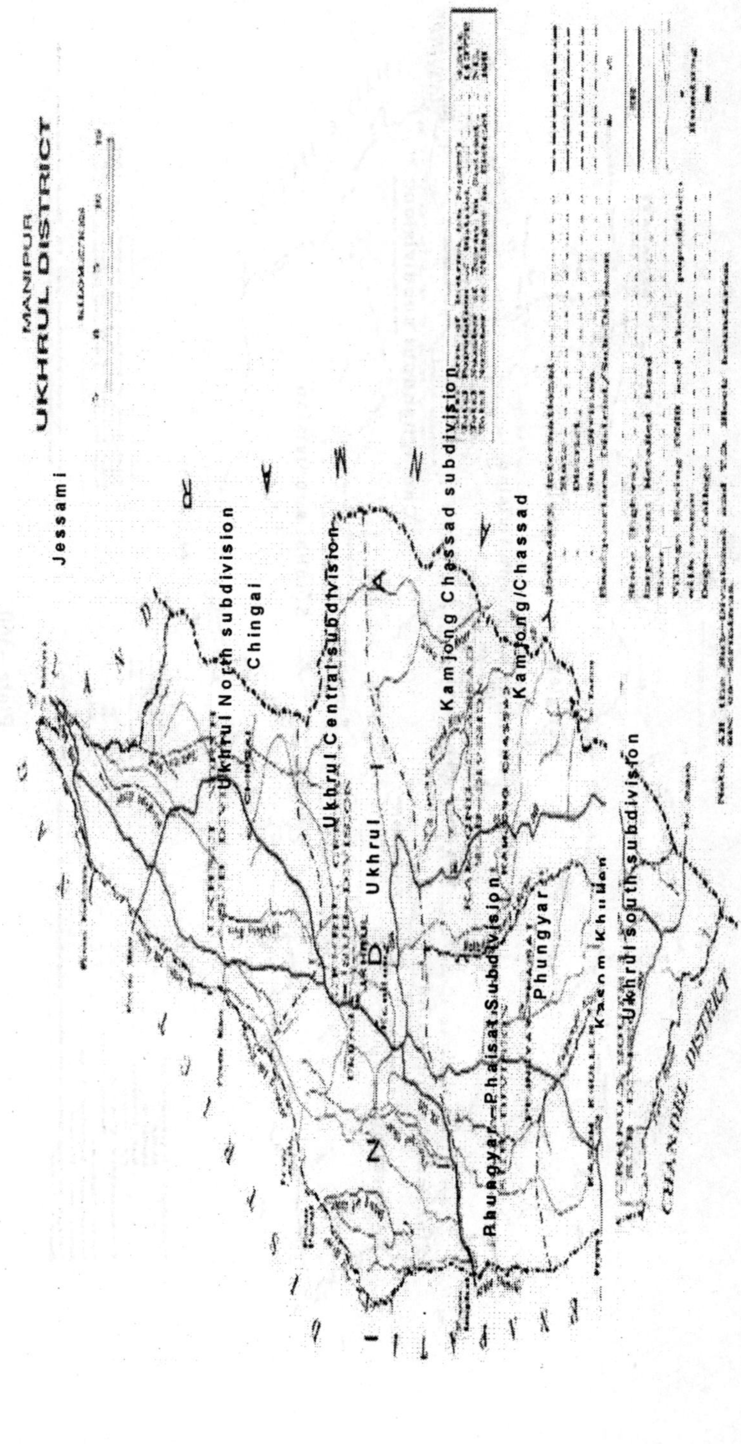
MANIPUR
UKHRUL DISTRICT
Jessami
Ukhrul North subdivision
Chingai
Ukhrul Central subdivision
Ukhrul
Kamjong Chassad subdivision
Kamjong/Chassad
Phungyar–Phaisat Subdivision
Phungyar
Kasom Khullen
Ukhrul south subdivision
CHANDEL DISTRICT

Plate –361

Map 36

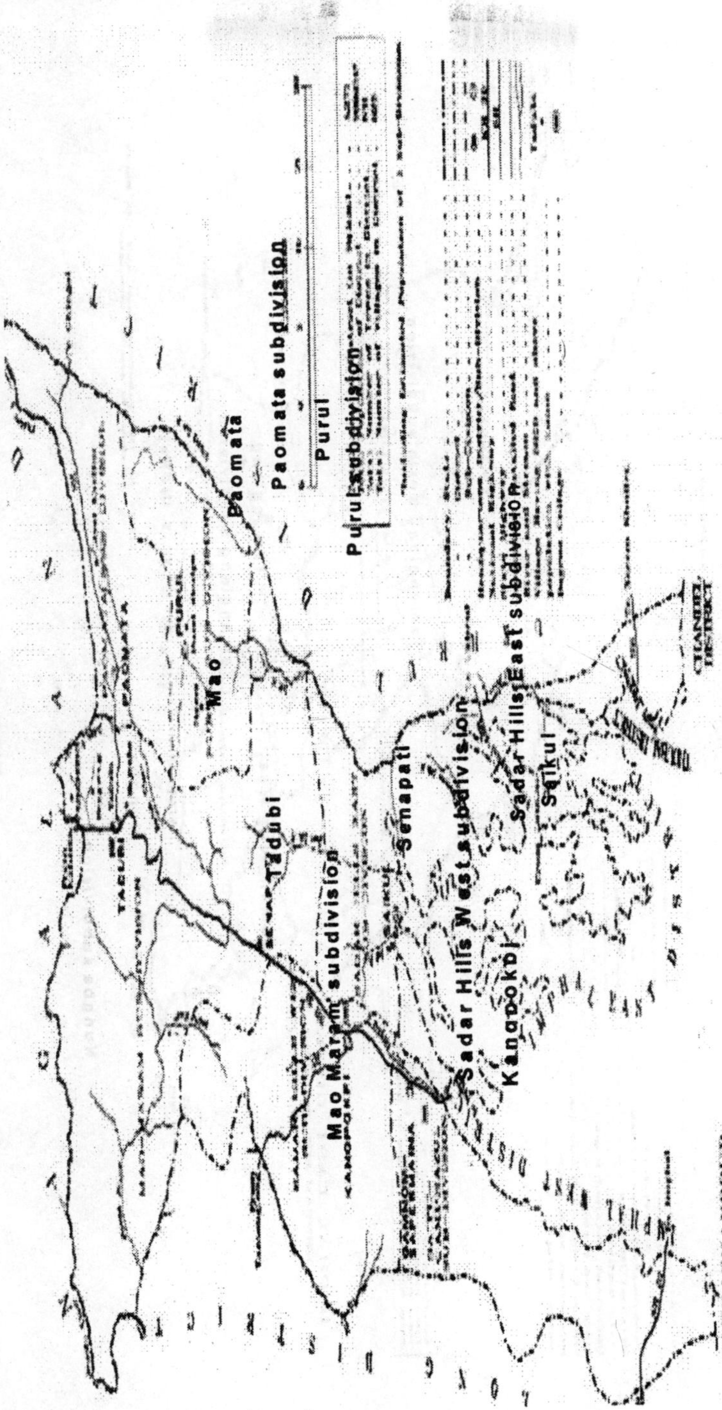

Plate –362

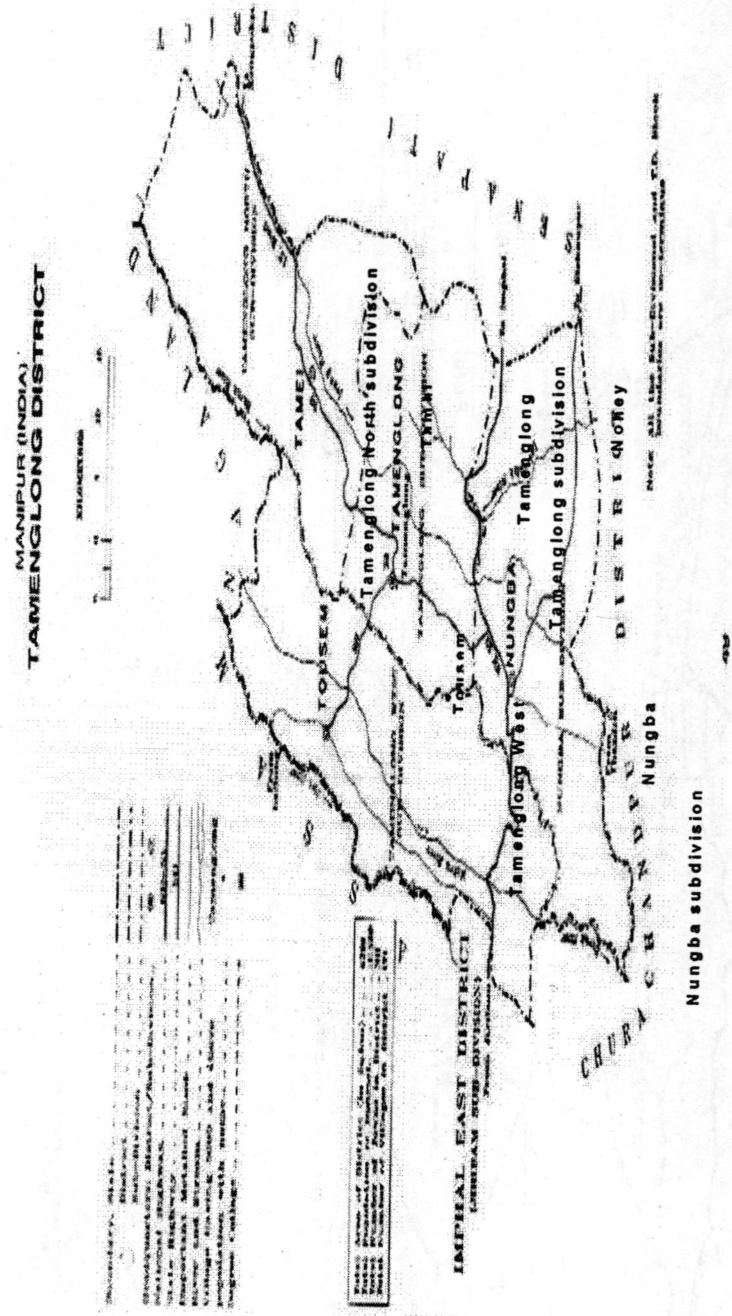
MANIPUR (INDIA)
TAMENGLONG DISTRICT
TAMEI
TOUSEM
TAMENGLONG
NUNGBA
Tamenglong North subdivision
Tamenglong
Tamenglong subdivision
Tousem
Tamenglong West
Nungba
Nungba subdivision
Noney
IMPHAL EAST DISTRICT
CHURACHANDPUR
DISTRICT

Plate –363

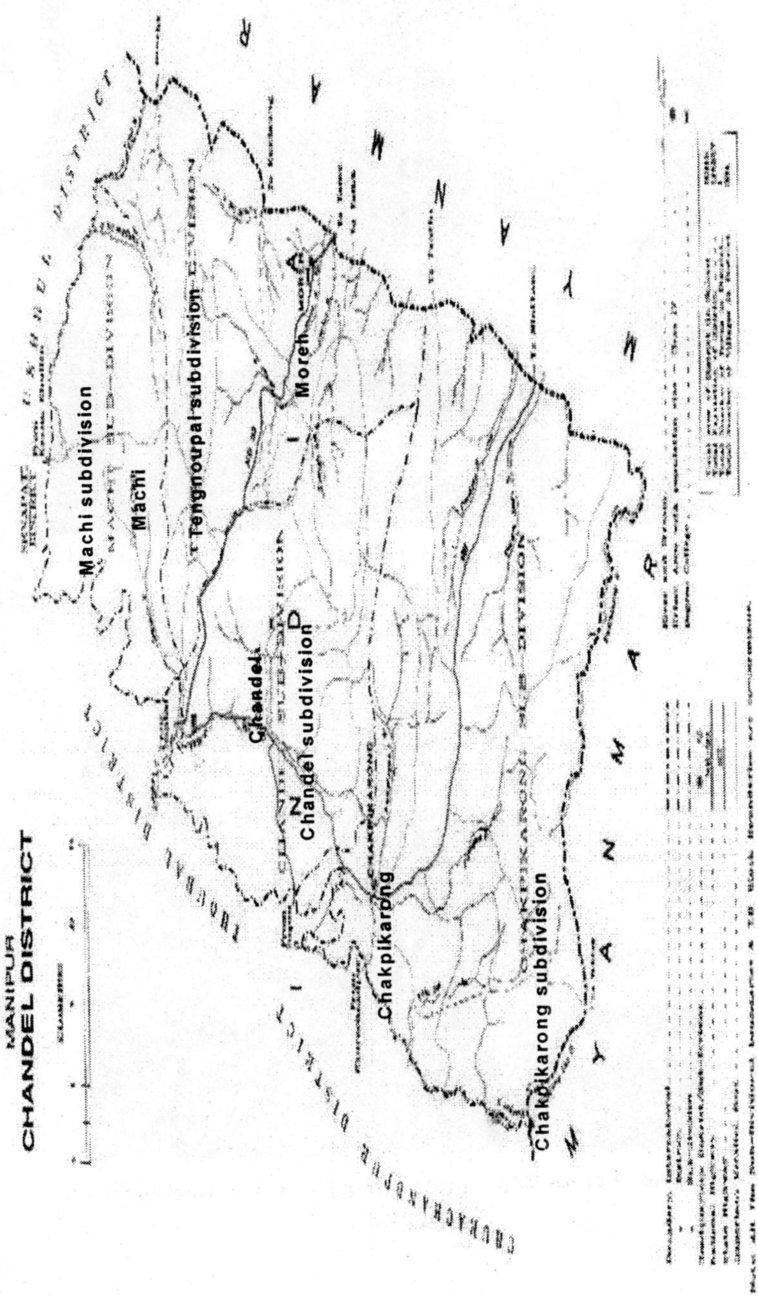
MANIPUR
CHANDEL DISTRICT
Machi subdivision
Machi
Tengnoupal subdivision
Moreh
Chandel
Chandel subdivision
Chakpikarong
Chakpikarong subdivision
Chakpikarong
M Y A N M A R

Plate -364

Plate -365: A big Ngaren fish at Yairipok, Thoubal

Plates -366 : Lemon Trees and Lemon festival in Kachai village, Ukhrul

Plates -367 : Lemon Trees and Lemon festival in Kachai village, Ukhrul

Plate -368: Tharon Cave

Plates -369 and 370: Dance Groups at Tamenglong

Plate -371:Festival mood Tamenglong

Plate -372: Orange Trees at Tamenglong

Plate -373: Governor inaugurating Orange festival

Plate -374: Orange Festival at Tamenglong

Plate -375:Hornbil, Tamenglong

21

Indo-myanmar Border Trade

Indo-Myanmar Border Trade is of immense importance for development of the border regions of the country. India shares about 1643 km border with Myanmar –Arunachal Pradesh (520 km), Manipur (398 km), Mizoram (510 km) and Nagaland (215 km) (Egreteau Renaud: 2003-49). The India-Myanmar bilateral trade has grown from $ 203.88 million in 1998-99 to $ 411.12 million in 2002-2003. India has emerged as the largest export market for Myanmar accounting to nearly one fourth of Myanmar's export. India absorbed 1.33 % of Myanmar's export in 1980-81, which was subsequently increased to 17.92% in 1990-91 and 23% by late 1990s. India's major export to Myanmar are agricultural products, primary and semi-finished iron and steel, pharmaceuticals. India's imports from Myanmar constituted hardly 0.54% in 1980-81, subsequently increased to 4.65% in 1997-98. India's import consists of pulses, beans, wood, wood products. By 2003, India became the fourth largest trading partner of Myanmar after Thailand, China and Singapore. Myanmar contributes about one third of India's requirement of pulses and one fifth of timber.

In order to expand trade, Myanmar has opened three border trade posts at Muse, Lwejel and Lizer; four posts along Myanmar-Thailand border at Tachilek, Myawaddy, Kawthaung and Myeik, two posts along Myanmar-Bangladesh border at Sittwe and Maungdaw and one post along Myanmar-India border at Tamu (Moreh on Indian side).

PRESENT STATUS OF INDO-MYANMAR TRADE ROUTE THROUGH MOREH

Trade is the engine of economic growth. The Indo-Myanmar Border Trade was inaugurated on 12th April, 1995 by Shri P. Chidambaram, the then Union Minister of State for Commerce, as a follow-up measure of the Trade Agreement signed between the two countries on the 21st January, 1994 in New Delhi and as a part of the India's "Look East" policy started in 1990 during the time of Prime Minister, Narashimha Rao. Moreh is the only Land Customs Station through which trade across land route from India to Myanmar takes place.

THE VOLUME OF INDO-MYANMAR TRADE DURING 1995-2000 WERE AS FOLLOWS

Table-74 Showing Myanmar: Volume of Border Trade (in Millions of US Dollar)

Year	*Export*	*Import*	*Volume of Trade*
1995-96	43.15	292.80	335.95
1996-97	58.40	298.72	357.12
1997-98	154.97	102.09	257.06
1998-99	146.30	153.97	300.27
1999-2000	196.40	147.99	344.39
Total	599.22	995.57	1594.79

Source:http://www.myanmar.com/ministry/commerce/bordertrade/FSborder trades.htm

THE VOLUME OF TRADE THROUGH MOREH DURING 1995-2002 WAS A S FOLLOWS :-

Table-75 Showing Year-wise volume of trade through Legal Route (Amount in Rupees)

Year	*Export*	*Import*	*Volume of Trade*
April, 1995 to March, 1996	10,45,27,782	5,38,99,029	15,84,26,811
April, 1996 to March, 1997	31,70,51,137	15,17,64,094	46,88,15,231
April, 1997 to March, 1998	22,44,72,930	35,08,34,823	57,53,07,753

(Contd.)

(Contd. Table 21)

Year	*Export*	*Import*	*Volume of Trade*
April, 1998 to March, 1999	5,06,09,710	3,74,39,616	8,80,49,326
April, 1999 to March, 2000	3,25,65,827	3,67,97,316	6,93,63,143
April, 2000 to March, 2001	5,29,17,530	19,38,523	5,48,56,053
April, 2001 to March, 2002	1,25,08,345	8,29,71,255	9,54,79,600

Source: Ministry of Commerce and Industry

There is a significant amount of illegal market as reflected by the customs seizure during 1999-2002.

Table-76 Showing Customs seizure during 1999-2002

Financial year	*Amount in Rupees*	*Main items seized*
1999-2000	3,56,59,603/-	VCD, Inverters, Battery, Precious stones, narcotic drugs (Amphetamine tabs, Ephedrine, Heroine Powder, etc.) Blanket, Cloth carpet, Myanmar currency, detergents, soap, readymade garments, shoes, chapples, edibles, etc.
2000-2001	4,02,21,474/	
2001-2002	4,01,32,944/-	

The opening of the Border Trade along the Tamu (Myanmar)-Moreh (Manipur) sector is quite significant as this would act as an economic bridge between industrially developed India and the booming economies of South East Asian countries.

The present volume of legal trade through Moreh-Tamu sector is only Rs. 7.38 crores of export–import against the Rs. 2818 crore volume of export-import between India and Myanmar. An unofficial record says that the volume of illegal trade at Moreh-Tamu sector is more than Rs. 1500 crores per annum whereas Rs. 500 cores at Champhai –Rih sector and Rs. 100 cores at Lungwa sector. Once these illegal trade is converted into legal with integrated composite check post system like the Wagha border between India and Pakistan or the Tachilek –Mae-Sai border between Myanmar-Thailand, this will certainly check the illegal trade and also improve the economy of Manipur.

Considering the volume of trade differences between legal and illegal (Customs Seizure), the State Government of Manipur proposes to tap the beneficial impact in both terms of social and economic development to the hinterland by enhancing regional economic co-operation within the framework of Indo-Asian Partnership.

MEASURES TAKEN UP BY THE GOVERNMENT OF INDIA / STATE GOVERNMENT

The following are the important measures which have been taken up :

1. Trade Centre providing facility to traders and entrepreneurs is being set up at Moreh and Imphal.
2. Improvement of Road, infrastructure under ASIDE Scheme.
3. Setting up of a Special Economic Zone.
4. Introduction of Inland Container Depot (ICD) and Warehousing Facility.

The setting up of Special Economic Zone at Moreh aims at

1. Exemption from Customs duty, Central Excise Duty, CST, etc.
2. Promotion of economic activities by curbing the illegal activities and capturing revenues.
3. Promotion of clusters of small scale units to create employment opportunity and develop export.
4. Creation of infrastructural facilities like communication including helicopter service, banking, post office, residential complex, power, water, etc.
5. Strengthening of Counselling-cum Grievances Redressal Cell and activating the State Level Export Promotion Committee (SLEPC) with the creation of Single Window Clearance.

The State Government is taking up necessary measures for development of the export-import. Institutional mechanism like up-gradation of the Industries Department, setting up of Counselling-cum-Grievance Committee, conducting general awareness programme, setting up of State level Export Committee which includes banks etc. has already been done.

Measures are also being taken up by creating infrastructure which will help in the setting-up and growth of industries directed towards export.

Setting up of an international standard bus station at Moreh is on card. Survey work is being taken up for Imphal-Mandalay road connectivity in connection with the Trans-Asian Highways project. The Government of Myanmar and the Government of India had taken up steps for starting tourist bus service between Imphal and Kalimyo with the objective of bringing the people of the two countries closer. Accordingly, the Government of India had also demanded a report from the State Tourism on the frequency and movement of the tourists from Manipur to Myanmar.

The Myanmar Passport Rules, 1948 contained a provision to the effect that indigenous nationals of those countries whose land borders are co-terminus with the border of Myanmar are exempt from Passport requirements, provided they were members of Hill Tribes inhabiting areas adjacent to the land border and did not proceed beyond 25 miles across the Land Border. This provision was modified in December, 1948 to allow continuous stay of tribal crossing over not exceeding 30 days.

The Government of India by a notification dated 26th September, 1950 exempted the indigenous tribal inhabiting areas within 25 miles of the Indo-Myanmar frontier from passport and Visa requirements provided any such national of the Union of Myanmar did not proceed beyond 25 miles (40 km) from the land border. Tribal from both sides enjoyed this exemption until June, 1968. However, the Government of India through a Notification unilaterally introduced a permit system to regulate their movement with a view to prevent entry of undesirable elements and checking of insurgent activity. This is a retrograde step.

POTENTIAL AREAS OF EXPORTS FROM MANIPUR TO MYANMAR

Myanmar offers opportunity for export of wide range of Indian products like Cars and Car spare parts, cycles and motor cycles, iron and steel products, drugs and pharmaceutical products, machinery and spare parts, fruits and vegetables, tea, rubber, medicinal plants and herbs,, silk, teak processing, power generation, cutting and polishing precious stones, stainless steel and aluminum utensils, cutting and polishing granites, polishing and milling pulses and oilseeds. The industries which have good prospects in the state of Manipur are Cars and Car spare parts, IT, cycle, cycle parts, motor cycles, cement, pulp, paper products, vanaspati, drugs, pharmaceuticals, steel, iron rods, spinning and weaving mills, plastic and plastic products, fruit processing, soap, toiletry products, rubber and rubber products, disposable syringes, hosiery and hosiery products, mineral based industrial products, TV sets etc.

POTENTIAL AREAS OF IMPORT FROM MYANMAR TO MANIPUR

At the same time, there is a strong demand for import of wood, timber (Teak, Khewu, Khanggra etc.),wood products, pulses, sugar etc. from

Myanmar. In addition, Manipur can import petrol diesel, essential commodities for day to day consumption from Myanmar instead of depending on National Highway No. 39.

It is a regional and global competition. Manipur will be left out of the sphere of influence if it is not prepared to meet the new demands and challenges. The State Government can play a pro-active role in shaping the orientation of the Look East Policy. The State Government can influence the Government of India to work out strategies to steer the course of events in the desired direction, which will be in the favour of Manipur. Moreh is like the mother cow who everybody milks but forgets to feed. Following the Supreme Court Order ban on transport of teak-wood via north eastern states, the Myanmar's economy in general and that of Manipur in particular is weakened a great deal. However movement of wood in the form of furniture and other finished products is allowed. Burmese teak is no. 1 in the world.

TRAN-ASIAN HIGHWAYS

The proposed railway line between Delhi to Hanoi (Vietnam) under the Greater Mekong Sub Regional Cooperation decided by the South East Asian countries foreign ministers at Phnom Penh, Cambodia on 20th June, 2003 will create more job opportunities, uplift socio-economic condition and also check the illegal cross border trade between India and Myanmar through Moreh. Recently the Government of India announced plans to invest nearly Rs. 850 crore over the next three years to develop infrastructure for growth of regional trade. Apart from the plans to increase road connectivity, a regular bus service between Imphal and Madalay and air cargo service between Imphal and Myanmar cities are also in the pipeline. Such investment for development of infrastructure will expand the connectivity between Manipur and South Asian Countries.

The proposed 1400 km long Trans Asian Highway connecting India-Myanmar-Thailand have been finalized by the respective Government of India, Myanmar and Thailand. Once these trade routes are opened up, then the volume of trade will increase manifold.

There is an ongoing project for construction of a trilateral highway from Moreh to Mae Soi in Thailand through Bagan in Myanmar. The progress of construction is being reviewed regularly by the foreign ministries of the three countries. Once this project is completed, it will further boost up the trade between India, Myanmar and Thailand which is also passing through Manipur (Dr.A. Rajmani Singh, India's Look East Policy and Manipur, "Manipur Today, Independence Day, 2008)

The National Highway No. 39 is the lifeline of Manipur. This road passes through Nagaland. Most of the essential commodities are brought from Assam and other states through Nagaland via the National Highway No. 39, which is 215 km highway running from Dimapur to Imphal. The problems of repeated blockade of National Highway No 39 can be immediately resolved once Manipuris are allowed to do day to day business with Tamu., which is hardly 110 km from Imphal.

The gate at Moreh –Tamu may be expanded to make it a four lane gate like the Wagha border between India and Pakistan or the Tachilek –Mae-Sai border between Myanmar-Thailand, to allow four vehicles to pass through at the same time. Facilities for checking passport and VISA may be opened up at Moreh as well as at Tamu. Foreign exchange facilities may be opened up both at Moreh as well as at Tamu. The Government may encourage private parties to open up at least three star and four star hotels in Moreh. There should be regular bus service between Imphal- Madalay – Kalimyo and upto Rangoon and also the Myanmar Government should be allowed to conduct regular bus service between Mandalay, Kalimyo and Imphal. Unless, there is a reciprocal agreement, the Myanmar Government may not be interested. The early history of Manipur shows that Manipur was having a trade and commercial relation with Burma (Myanmar) and also with China through Yunnan. The Manipuris strongly feel that if the eastern world is opened up through establishment of road, railway and air links, then there will be a faster development of Manipur and other north eastern states.

Manipur has got huge potential in sectors like automobile, IT, power, agro-based industries, food processing, horticulture, aquaculture, sericulture, floriculture, tourism, handloom and handicrafts, IT etc. A greater private sector involvement in the state economy will ensure local job creation and entrepreneurship development.

Kunming Initiative

The conference held at the Yunnan province of China on August 17, 1999 resolved to establish regional cooperation between China, India, Myanmar, and Bangladesh. The basic objective was to strengthen regional economic co-operation among contiguous regions of Eastern/North Eastern India, Bangladesh, China and Myanmar. The main thrust of the initiative was to improve the communications between the south-western region of China and the North Eastern Region of India by developing appropriate roads, railways, waterways and air links. There was an initiative to revive the ancient

Southern Silk Route between Assam and Yunnan, i.e. the Stilwell Road, or the Old Burma Road. The Stilwell Road stretches from Ledo in Assam to Myanmar, across the Phangsu Pass and joins Bhamo in Myanmar and then it extends to Yunnan province of China. The road covers a distance of 1668.8 km from Ledo to Kunming. However, the distance from Ledo to Kolkata is about 1704 km. This road is far shorter considering the present 70,000 km route someone has to travel around Hongkong and Singapore. The North Eastern states of India have unanimously demanded re-opening of the road to increase the volume of trade with Southeast Asian countries. If the Stilwell Road is reconstructed from Ledo in Assam to Mytkina in Myanmar, a mountainous 400 km stretch, this road can be extended to the Moreh–Tamu–Kalewa crossing on the Chindwin River. The Government of India had already constructed a road in 2001 connecting Tamu and Kalemyo, which can extend as far as Mandalay through the Border Roads Organization.

The Trans Asian Highway Project is a part of the Trans-Asian Movement (TAM). TAM is an initiative to integrate the countries of the Asian Continent through network of roadways and railways. Of the two priority routes identified as part of the Asian Highway, one passes through Iran, Pakistan, India and meets Nepal at Banbasa from which it re-enters India at Siliguri and further reaches Imphal via Bangladesh and then extends to Myanmar. Another part of this project is the regional and sub-regional routes. Here major corridors are identified, and they form a regional transport network that connects all significant regional ports, capital cities and major underserved areas with significant potentials for trade. One of the corridors identified, as high potential corridor, is the far North East India–Bangladesh. Another is the Guwahati–Shiliguri–Raiganj–Calcutta corridor. The corridor with high volume transport and trade flows is the Kathmandu–Birganj–Kolkata. As a part of this project, India has requested Myanmar for granting access to its territory through the Kaladan River to reach Akyab port in the Bay of Bengal. Though the river begins 50 km away from Aizwal, it covers a long stretch of nearly 150 km in Myanmar before meeting the Bay of Bengal at Akyab. It is opined that if the proposal is accepted India will be able to transport goods by river from Kolkata to Mizoram from where they can be further carried to other places through roadways. (Chanda, Saswati and Alok Kumar Gupta. 2001. 'Trans Asian Movements and Cooperation in Transportation; An Initiative to Integrate the Asian Continent,' Third Concept. August, 2001 pp.15–20).

Mizoram, which shares 720 km of border with Bangladesh and Myanmar could be linked to Akyab (now called Sittwe) in Myanmar, and if Bangladesh agrees, Agartala in Tripura could be connected to Chittagong. That will open up the entire North Eastern Region of India, making it the commercial outlet for the eastern trade (Maitra 2003). The second meeting of the Kunming Initiative, popularly called BCIM (Bangladesh, China, India, Myanmar), was held in New Delhi on 5-6,December, 2002. Talks were held on the development of regional infrastructure and trade, enhancement of tourism capacities, and improvement in mutual understanding between its members with the objective of implementing major economic projects based on long-term plans. The four partners sought to resolve and put aside their political problems so as to give more importance to trade. The initial measures were directed at improving the cross-border trade and the development of resources in the region.

The common people feel that this initiative will open a new vista of opportunities for the North East states. Geographically this region shares more international boundaries than with its internal mainland India. Opening up of the border will connect many of the border communities with their ethnic cousins living across the border. The people on both sides should have cultural affinities as well as commercial contacts. The Indo- Asian trade and economic cooperation through BCIM(Bangladesh, India, China and Myanmar), BIMSTEC (Bangladesh,-India-Myanmar –Sri Lanka –Thailand Economic Cooperation), ASEAN and ASEAN Regional Forum will uplift the socio-economic, cultural and political development of the region. In this way, Manipur will have close relationships with the South Asian markets.

The restriction of trade to 22 items may be relaxed and the list may be expanded to meet the demands of the people. Export items may include brand new cars, second hand cars, car spare parts motor cycles, motor cycle spare parts, bicycles, cycle parts, textiles, ready made clothing, leather goods, footwear, medicines, health beverages, plants and plant materials, horticulture products, handloom and handicraft items etc. Import items may include petrol, diesel, kerosene, essential commodity items of everyday use so that Manipur need not depend on National Highway no-39. Other import items should include timber (Teak, Khewu, Khanggra etc.).

Multiple checks posts may be abolished and one single check post should be authorized to check import-export. There are 53 check posts of various departments of the Government of Manipur and Nagaland from Moreh to Dimapur. The Indo-Myanmar trade is suffering from overregulation. The Government of India's strict insistence on the " Rule of Origin (ROO)" may be relaxed. The Supreme Court order banning the transport of teak timber via north eastern region may be vacated to encourage trade in this part of the country.

The State Government of Manipur may examine the feasibility of taking up the following measures :-

1. Ensure speedy completion of the Trans Asian Highway passing through Manipur and Moreh through timely release of fund, control of budget and proper monitoring.
2. Ensure speedy completion of the Rail link upto Imphal through proper monitoring with the Railway ministry.
3. Upgrade Imphal Airport into an international Airport with night landing facilities connecting with Mandalay, Yangon, Chiangmai, Bangkok, Singapore, Hongkong. All flights originating from Kolkata, Delhi, Chennai, Mumbai and Guwahati going to Bangkok, Singapore or Hong Kong may pass through Imphal Airport.
4. Bus services of international quality may be introduced between Imphal and Kalimyo, Imphal- Mandalay and back to begin with.
5. Establish Passport Office at Imphal for issuing passport and to deal with VISA formalities.
6. Foreign Exchange facilities may be opened at multiple places at Imphal and Moreh.
7. Credit Card system may be popularized in Manipur covering all important towns including Moreh.

References

Annual Administrative Report of Manipur, 1868–69, Selection from the Records of the Government of India, Foreign Department, No. LXXVIII.

Ahmed, Syed. 2002. 'Manipuris Outside Manipur'. MRFD Bulletin. Manipur Research Forum. Delhi: Vol. 2, issue 1.

Brara, N. Bijaylakshmi, 1998. Politics, Society and Cosmology in India's Northeast. Delhi: Oxford University Press.

Brown, R., 1873. Statistical Account of Native State of Manipur and The Hill Territory Under Its Rule. Calcutta: Office of the Superintendent of Government Printing.

Chaki–Sircar. Manjusri. 1984. Feminism in Traditional Society: Women of Manipur Valley. Ghaziabad: Shakti Books.

Chanda, Saswati and Alok Kumar Gupta. 2001. 'Trans Asian Movements and Cooperation in Transportation; An Initiative to Integrate the Asian Continent,' Third Concept. August. pp.15–20.

Chaube, S.K. 1999. Hill Politics in Northeast India. Delhi: Orient Longman.

Das & Purkayastha. 2002. Annual Report, 1999–2000, Ministry of Defence, Govt. of India.

Das, Gurudas. 2001. 'Trade between North Eastern Region and Bangladesh. Nature, Trends and Implications for Development Cooperation,' Dialogue. Vol. 2, no. 4. pp. 79–91.

Dena, Lal. 1999. 'The Kuki–Naga Conflict: Juxtaposed in the Colonial Context,' in Kailash Aggarwal (ed.). Dynamics of Identity an Intergroup Relations in the Northeast India. Shimla: IIAS.

_________. (ed.) 1991. History of Modern Manipur (1826–194). New Delhi: Orbit Publishers–Distributors.

Devi, Ksh. Bimola. 1998. 'Women in Social Movement in Manipur,' in M.N. Karna (ed). Social Movement in Northeast India. Delhi: Indian Publishing Company.

Dr. A. Rajmani Singh, India's Look East Policy and Manipur, "Manipur Today, Independence Day, 2008.

Dubey, S.M. (ed.) 1978. Northeast India: A Sociological Study. Delhi: Concept Publishing Company. 106.

Dun, E. W. 1886. reprinted in 1992. Gazetteer of Manipur. Delhi: Manas Publication.

Egreteau, Renaud. 2003. Wooing the General: India's New Burma Policy. Authors Press. Centre De Sciences Humaines. Delhi.

Grimwood, Ethel. 1908. My Three Years in Manipur. London: St. Chaire.

Ghosh, G.K & S. Ghosh. 1997. Women of Manipur. Delhi: A.P.H. Publishing House.

Government of India. Census of India, 1954 Assam, Manipur and Tripura, Vol. XII, part II B.

Government of India. Census of India, 2001.

Government of India. Census of India, Vol. 3, Assam, part II, 1911, 1921, 1931.

Government of Manipur. 1999. Statistical Handbook of Manipur, Directorate of Economics and Statistics. Govt. of Manipur, Imphal.

Government of Manipur, Administrative Reports of Manipur, 1906–07.

Government of Manipur. Administrative report of Manipur, 1939–40.

Government of Manipur. Tenth Plan Document (2002–2007). Government of Manipur. Imphal.

Gurudas Das, N. Bijoy Singh, C.J. Thomas "Indo-Myanmar Border Trade – Status, Problems and Potentials, Akansha Publishing House, New Delhi, 2005.

Singh, B.P, The problem of Change : A Study of North East India, New Delhi, Oxford University Press.

Sharma A and P.K. Mehta, 2002 "Exploring Indo-ASEAN Economic Partnership in Globalizing World, New Delhi, Bookwell.

Sunil Kumar, North East Federation on International Trade (NEFIT), 2004 "Potential of Expcrt from North East to South East Asia, ICSSR-NERC, Imphal, Nov. 8-9, 2004.

Das Gurudas" Trade between the North Eastern Region and Neighbouring Countries : Structures and Implications for Development, Akansa Publishing House, New Delhi, 2000.

Gaigongdin Panmei "Indo-Myanmar Border Trade" Souvenir : Seminar on Indo-Myanmar Border Trade, pp. 9-17, Department of Commerce and Industries, Manipur, October, 2004.

Grierson, G.A. 1905., Linguistic survey of India, vol. 3, part 3, Govt. Publication, Calcutta.

Hamilton, Francis. 1807. An Account of Assam, Calcutta.

Hodson,T.C. reprinted 1986. The Meitheis. Delhi: B.R. Publishing Corporation.

- reprinted 1996. The Naga Tribes of Manipur. New Delhi: Low Price Publications,

Horam, M., (ed.) 2000. The Rising Manipur, New Delhi: Manas Publication.

Kabui, G. 1991. History of Manipur: Pre-Colonial, Vol. 1. New Delhi. National Publishing House.

Maisnam, Dhaneswari. 2002. Political Economy of Underdevelopment: An Enquiry About The Socio-Political Conditions in the State of Manipur. New Delhi: M.Phil dissertation submitted to the CSSS. JNU.

Maitra, Ramtanu. 2003. 'Prospects brighten for Kunming Initiative,' South Asia, Feb. 12, @2003AsiaTimesOnlineCoLtd.

Mohindro, N. 'Import Outweighs Export in Moreh Trade,' Imphal Free Press (Manipur Daily). Imphal: July 15, 1998.

Oinam, Bhagat. 2003. 'Patterns of Ethnic Conflict in the Northeast: A Study on Manipur,' Economic and Political Weekly, May 24, 2003.

Pemberton, R.B. 1835. Report on the Eastern Frontier of British India. Calcutta.

Ried, Robert. 1942. History of Frontier Area Bordering Assam. Shillong.

Sachdeva, Gulshan. 2003. 'Fiscal Governance in the Northeast,' Dialogue, vol. 5, no. 4, pp. 53–63.,2000. 'India Northeast: Rejuvenating a Conflict-riven Economy,' Faultline, vol. 6, pp.79–103.

Sen, Sipra. 1992. Tribes and Caste of Manipur, Mittal Publication, New Delhi.

Sanajaoba, Naorem. (ed.) 1988. Manipur: Past and Presen. New Delhi: Mittal Publication.

Singh, E. Bijoykumar. 1997. 'Indian Perspective of Economic Development of NE,' Imphal Free Press. Imphal: May 29., 1997. 'The Economy of Manipur in the Last Fifty Years,' Imphal Free Press. Imphal: August 21.

Singh, Khuraijam Bijoykumar. 2000. Hinduism Among the Meiteis of Manipur: A Study of Continuity and Change. New Delhi: M.Phil dissertation submitted to the CSSS. JNU.

Singh, M. Gojendra.1987. 'Brief History of Manipur', Nehru and Manipur. State level Committee. Imphal.

Singh, N. Joykumar. 1992. Social Movement in Manipuir, New Delhi: Mittal Publication.

Singh, N. Lokendro. 1998. The Unquiet Valley. New Delhi: Mittal Publications.

Singh, N. Mohendro. 1999. 'Development Experience of Manipur After 50 Years', Imphal Free Press. Imphal: December 14.

Singh, N. Tombi. 1972. Manipur: A Study. Delhi: Rajesh Printing Press.

Singh, R.K. Jhalajit, 1987. A Short History of Manipur,2nd edition, Imphal.

Singh, Udai Bhanu 2003. 'Perspective on Myanmar–India Relations,' Dialogue, Volume 5 No. 3. pp.112–23.

Singh, W. Ibohal. 1986. The History of Manipur, Imphal.

Stone, Sir James. reprinted 1971. My Experiences in Manipur and Naga Hills. Delhi: Vivek Publishing House.

Thangjam Homen. 2004. 'Conflict and Its Impact on Women' a paper presented in a Seminar organized by Centre for Applied Sociology on 20th September 2004 at JNU. New Delhi.

Verghese. B.G. 1996. India's Northeast Resurgent; Ethnicity, Insurgency, Governance, Development. Delhi: Konark.

________, 2004. Border Matters More Than Boundaries, From the Northeast Looking Out' Man and Society, Vol. 1, no. 1, ICSSR, North East Regional Centre, Shillong: Meghalaya.

Yambem, Sanamani.1976.'Nupi Lan: Manipuri Women's Agitation, 1939,' Economic and Political Weekly, vol. XI, no. 8, Feb. 21.

http://www.fao.org/ag/agl/sw/wpnr/reports/y ta /z mm/mmtb28p.htm.

http://www.fao.org/ag/agl/sw/wpnr/reports/y ta /z mm/mmtb282p.htm.

http://www.fao.org/ag/agl/sw/wpnr/reports/y ta /z mm/mmtb311.htm.

22

Why Invest in The State?

Manipur lags in development far behind the national average. The availability of basic minimum services is very poor. The continuing gaps in infrastructural sectors have resulted in industrial backwardness of the state. Recognizing this position, the Prime Minister announced on 27 October, 1996 "New initiatives for the North Eastern Region" along with a Rs. 6100 crores special economic package including Rs. 703 crores for Manipur.

In pursuance of the "New Initiatives", the Government of India appointed a "High Level Commission" to critically examine the backlog in respect of the basic minimum services and the gaps in important sectors of infrastructure development in the region and suggest policies, programme and the requirement of funds to bridge such gaps and backlogs. The Commission has in its report entitled "Transforming the Northeast" (March, 1997), made an exhaustive 173 recommendations touching upon 27 areas for development. These, among others, include power, roads, civil aviation, railways, waterways, telecommunications, banking and financing, trade and transit, industry, etc. The report recommends a total of about Rs. 9,396 crores for the whole North Eastern region's requirement in respect of basic minimum services, of which Rs, 1,423 crores is for Manipur. It also makes room for an indicative requirement of Rs. 93,619 crores as total estimated investments in infrastructural sectors for the region as a whole, of which Manipur's share is Rs. 5,815 crores. That means, Manipur is going to receive hardly 6.21% of the estimated investment. This is a gross injustice. Manipur is supposed to receive at least Rs.13106 crores (around 14%) according to proportionate distribution of resources. We may submit this to the Government of India with proper justification.

The following sectorwise allocations were included in the report in respect of Manipur:

Table-77 Showing sector wise allocations of funds

Sl. No	*Sector*	*Allocation (in Crores)*
1.	Irrigation Sector	566
2.	Flood Control	45
3.	Railways	935
4.	Power Sector	3,740
5.	Transmission Sector	84
6.	Others	445
7.	Total	5,815

Shri Montek Singh Ahluwalia, the Deputy Chairman of the Planning Commission praised the state government for the rapid progress of development. The Planning Commission has given special attention to the infrastructure development including power, health services, road, and education in the state annual plans. Shri Okram Ibobi Singh, the Chief Minister of Manipur said that the state government was taking initiatives for expansion of area for horticulture, reducing deficit in production of food grains, raising per capita income to the national level and achieving the target of electrification of every village in Manipur by 2010-2011.

Further, the "High Level Commission" has recommended improvement of the National Highway No-39 (NH-39), the Imphal-Moreh sector in particular, to serve both as a commercial highway and as line of communication for construction of the Rs. 92 crores Tamu-Kalewa Highway sanctioned by Border Road Development Board, as Moreh could become a major nodal point for trade with the South East Asia along the proposed Trans-Asian Highway. In the banking and finance sector, the Commission has, inter alia, spelt out the need to consider industrial finance as part of priority sector lending. The recommendation on the industry sector recognises the need to establish export processing or special economic zones in the region to attract export oriented industries. The Government of Manipur is also vigorously pursuing to set up such an Export Processing Zone at Moreh.

The existing Indo-Myanmar Border Trade currently underway in the border towns of Moreh and Tamu has already paved the way for a full scale trade between India and Myanmar which would further extend to other adjacent countries like Thailand, Laos, South West China along the old Burma road and the proposed Trans-Asia Highway and railway. In this context, Manipur is the gateway to the International trade route connecting between Indian sub-continent including Nepal, Bhutan and Bangladesh. Resultantly, not only the production and trading units can flourish taking advantage of the expanding international trade but there is also good scope for investment in creating infrastructure facilities in the areas of road construction, power generation, developed industrial areas, water facilities, IT services, etc.

The climatic condition of the state is very much suitable for growing almost all kinds of agricultural and horticultural crops and taking up afforestation activities and as such, there is a great potential and prospects for large scale plantation of fruits and vegetables and setting up of agro-horticulture based industries particularly food processing industries. For instance, the agro-climatic condition is so suitable that potato can be harvested two times in a year.

There are more than four lakhs unemployed youths in the live register of the Employment Exchange. Of these, more than 2.5 lakhs are educated youths who are matriculates and above. There is therefore, adequate educated manpower for absorption to any economic/business venture in the State.

Manipur is unique in its craftsmanship. The artisans are adorned with innate qualities of craftsmanship. There are more than 1.5 lakh artisans in the trade of cane and bamboo alone.

In addition to the above mentioned strengths and opportunities, the State Government has fully taken note of the Central Govt.'s new economic policy initiatives in the post-1991 era to:

- Create a liberal investment environment for economic activity especially industrial activity.
- Minimise Government regulation and control.
- Move towards a supportive role, i.e. facilitation.
- Create internationally competitive basic infrastructure facilities.
- Extend preferential treatment to priority sectors of industrial activity through an incentive mechanism.
- Provide full freedom of industrial and commercial activity within clearly established and transparent parameter.

Keeping in view these new policy initiatives of the Government of India, the State Government have adopted the "Industrial Policy of Manipur, 1996". This policy among others seek to:

- create an integrated investor-friendly environment;
- bring about industry and trade supportive infrastructural establishments and other facility centres;
- maximise utilisation of various resources including raw materials and skills in the manufacturing sectors and accord priority to industrial investment;
- modernise technology and upgrade skill of the manufacturing units to improve the quality and thus competitiveness of the products;
- revive the sick industrial units;
- take positive steps to optimise the advantages offered by the recently opened Indo-Myanmar border trade through Moreh in Manipur; and,
- provide a comprehensive and attractive package of incentives to the industries.

(http://invest inmanipur.nic.in/why_invest.htm)

Industrial Policy of Manipur, 1996

The Manipur State Government has adopted the Industrial Policy of Manipur,1996 vide notification no. 58/8/94-IND dated 27th November, 1996 which is effective from 1st January, 1995. The main objectives of the policy are to ensure balanced economic growth through strategies which can offset the geographical disadavantages confronting the state and which can optimize its productive capacities and its vibrant human resource capital.The state will strive to catalyse the growth, reduce social disparity and poverty, create an environment conducive to investment; generate gainful employment especially for entrepreneurs and the educated unemployed.

Promotion of rapid industrialization is one of the important strategy, for which the state has taken up the following policy initiatives :-

- Create a liberal investor-friendly, investment environment for economic activity especially industrial activity
- Minimise Government regulation and control
- Maximise resource utilisation
- Move towards a supportive role i.e. facilitation
- Create internationally competitive basic infrastructure facilities
- Extend prefential treatment to priority sectors of industrial activity through an incentive mechanism

- Provide all freedom of industrial and commercial activity within clearly established and transparent parameters.

PACKAGE OF INCENTIVES

The package of incentives offered by the State Government over and above those provided by the Government of India are as follows:-

- Preferential allotment of land and subsidy on cost of land development.
- Provision for allotment of sheds to Small Scale Industry (SSI) Units and subsidise the monthly rent.
- Subsidies on Manpower Development.
- State Capital Investment Subsidy.
- State Transport Subsidy upto Siliguri and upto Patna on case to case basis by surface route.
- Interest Subsidy upto 7% on working capital and term loan taken from banks/financial institutions.
- Power subsidy on the tariff, drawal of power lines and purchase of diesel generating set.
- Subsidy for feasibility study and project report preparation.
- Subsidy for the cost of technical know-how obtained by Small Scale Industrial (SSI) units.
- Price preference of 20% in favour of SSI units.
- Reimbursement of Stamp duty and Registration fee for securing loans and other incentives from financial institutions.
- For purchase of testing equipment upto 25-30% of cost for improvement of the quality.
- State capital investments Subsidy for modernisation/ expansion/ diversification through purchase of plant and machinery

Manipur is well set to welcome investors as a major player in industrial development. The Government of Manipur is prepared to update the existing Industrial Policy to meet the requirements of private investors in the State.

NEW INDUSTRIAL PACKAGE FOR THE NORTH-EAST:

The Government of India has introduced a comprehensive new industrial policy for the North Eastern Region. It includes infrastructure support and both project and production related benefits that are meant for all industrial activities including those of small scale and agro and rural industries. The salient features of the policy are as follows:-

1. Development of Industrial Infrastructure.

• Government of India will provide entire expenditure on the establishment of Industrial Growth Centre. (Upto a ceiling of Rs. 15 crore as against Rs. 10 crore admissible earlier).

• Government of India would provide 80% of funds for Integrated Industrial Development Centres (IIDC's) as grant (as against 40% earlier) and balance 20% would be by SIDBI.

2. Transport Subsidy

The transport subsidy will be extended for a further period of seven years i.e. upto 31st March, 2007.

3. Fiscal Incentives

- The Industrial Growth Centres and IIDCs would be total tax free zone for the next 10 years. All industrial activity in these zones would be free from income tax, excise, for a period of 10 years from the commencement of production.
- Industries located in the growth centre would also be given capital investment subsidy at the rate 15% of their investment in plant and machinery, subject to a maximum ceiling of 30 lakhs.
- The commercial banks and the North East Development Financial Corporation (NEDFI) will have dedicated branches/counters to process application for term loans and working capital in these centres.
- An interest subsidy of 3% on the working capital loans would be provided for a period of ten years after the commencement of production.
- Similar benefits would also be extended to the new industrial units or their substantial expansion in other growth centres or IIDCs or industrial estates/parks/export promotion zones set up by the States in the NE region.

4. Relaxation of Prime Minister's Rozgar Yojna (PMRY) Norms

The PMRY would be expanded in scope to cover areas of horticulture, piggery, poultry, fishing, small tea gardens etc. so as to cover all economically viable activities. PMRY would have a family income ceiling of Rs. 40,000 per annum for its beneficiary along with his/her spouse and upper age limit will be relaxed to 40 years. Projects costing upto Rs. 2 lakhs in other than business sectors will be eligible for assistance. No collateral will be insisted for projects costing upto Rs. 1 lakh. Group financing upto Rs. 5 lakhs will be eligible.

Schemes will have subsidy component @ 15% with an upper ceiling of Rs. 15,000. The margin money may vary from 5% to 12.5% of the project costs to make the subsidy and margin contribution at 20% of the project cost.

5. **Other Incentives**

- A comprehensive insurance scheme for industrial units in the North East will be designed in consultation with General Insurance Corporation of India Ltd. and 100% premium for a period of 10 years would be subsidised by Central Government.
- A one time grant of Rs. 20 crore will be provided to the NEDFI by the Central Government through North Eastern Council (NEC) to fund techno-economic studies for industries and infrastructure best suited to this region.
- State Government may consider setting up of a "Debt Purchase Window" by the NEDFI which buys the debt of the manufacturing units particularly in respect of the supplies made to the Government Department so as to reduce the problem of blocking funds for these units.
- It may be considered to provide assistance for restructuring State PSUs from National Renewal Fund.

6. **Procedure for release of assistance under the New Incentives**

Currently central assistance for Transport subsidy is given on reimbursement basis. The expenditure is first incurred by States and then reimbursement claimed from Centre. Release under the growth centre scheme are made taking into consideration the physical and financial progress and release made by the State Governments. Inadequacy of funds with States delays the releases which affects the progress of implementation or puts the entrepreneurs to hardship. It has been decided that the transport subsidy budget would be released by a designated agency on the basis of the recommendation of the S.L.C. NEDFI would be designated as the nodal agency for release of transport subsidy.

INDUSTRIAL SCENARIO OF MANIPUR

The State Government participated in the industrialization campaign with the establishment of the *Manipur Spinning Mills Corporation Ltd.* in 1974 which started its commercial production in 1980. In order to facilitate growth of industries, the *Manipur Small Industries Corporation* was set up

Table-78 Showing Large and Medium Industries of Manipur

Sl.No.	*Name & Address*	*Year of Establishments*	*Product*	*Sector*
1.	Manipur Spinning Mills Corporation, Loitang Khunou, Manipur, P-27, Imphal West Dist. Manipur l	1973	Acrylic Yarn	State Govt.
2.	Khansari Sugar Mill, Thoubal Dist.	1973	Sugar	State Govt.
3.	Manipur Cycles Corporation, P.O.Takyel Industrial Estate, Nilo Singh Building, Kangchup Road, Imphal, Manipur	1985	Assembling Manufacturing Cycle	State Govt.
4.	Manipur Cement Limited, Hundung, C/O Directorate of Industries, Manipur.	1992	Cement	State Govt.
5.	Manipur Pulp & Allied, Dist. Imphal, Jiribum, Takyel Pat. Imphal, Manipur.	NA	Bamboo Chipping Product	State Govt.

(Contd.)

(Contd. Table 78)

Sl.No.	Name & Address	Year of Establishments	Product	Sector
6.	Manipur Vanaspati and Allied Industries Limited, Thangal Bazar, Imphal, Manipur	1988	Edible Ghee	State Govt.
7.	Manipur State Drugs and Pharmaceutical Limited, Imphal Dimapur Road, Nillkunthi, Imphal	1987	Pharmaceutical Product	State Govt.
8.	MAGFRUIT Limited Pharmaceutical Limited	NA	Fruit Processing Squash	State Govt.
9.	Manipur Electronics Development Corporation, Takyeal Industrial Estate, Imphal, Imphal West District.	1987	TV, Radio Assembling	State Govt.
10.	Peerless Steel Limited, Kanglatombi	NA	Rods	Private Sector
11.	Shree Manipur Flour Mills Limited, Mantripukhuri, Imphal, Imphal West District	1988	Wheat Flour	Private Sector
12.	K. B. Sons Private Limited, Lamsang, Imphal	NA	Brick Industries	Private Sector

in 1969 and it was further upgraded to *Manipur Industrial Development Corporation Ltd.* (MANIDCO) in 1987. *Manipur Handloom and Handicraft Development Corporation Ltd.* was set up in 1976 to directly help production and marketing of handloom and handicraft products. Subsequently, State sponsored undertakings like, *Manipur Electronics Development Corporation Ltd., Manipur Cements Ltd., Manipur State Drugs and Pharmaceuticals Ltd., Manipur Pulp and Allied Products Ltd. and Khandsari Sugar Factory* as a Govt. factory came up in the State. Regional/State branch offices of *Small Industries Service Institute, National Small Industries Corporation Ltd., Centre for Electronics Design and Technology* and *Central Institute of Plastic Engineering and Technology* were established to promote the growth of industries. District Industries Centres were set up in the districts in 1978-79 and decentralization of industrial growth in the rural areas began.

SPINNING MILL (MEDIUM SIZED)

Manipur is known for her spinning and weaving culture, especially silk and cotton. Earlier, every house of Manipur was related with cotton as well as silk culture. Every house of Manipur is having one loom i.e. loin loom or fly shuttle loom. Cultivation of cotton and oak tasar was common in the hills of Manipur.

The Manipur Spinning Mills Corporation Ltd. was established at Loitang Khunou. in 1972 and commissioned in the year 1974 for production of gray cotton yarn in hank form to cater to the needs of weavers of the State with a licensed capacity of 25,488 spindles. So far, 16,416 spindles only have been installed. Cotton is the main item of raw material for manufacture of yarn. The mill procured 2534 bales of cotton amounting to Rs. 257.37 lakhs, produced 358.44 M.T. of gray cotton yarn amounting to Rs. 329.74 lakhs and sold it along with 10.53 M.T. of waste cotton amounting to Rs. 3.22 lakhs during 2000-01. The sales turnover was Rs. 341.53 lakhs during 2000-01. No equity share capital was received from the Government of Manipur during 2000-01. There were 422 employees including 337 workers by the end of March 2001. The objective of the establishment of this mill was to provide yarn locally and make it available to the local weavers at a cheaper rate and also to give training facilities to them in weaving.

BAMBOO AND PAPER INDUSTRY

Bamboo is very important in the economic life of the state. It can replace three scarce resources viz. wood, metal, and oil. It is also a source of food, (viz. bamboo shoots and its leaves) both for man and animals. The main building materials, as well as agricultural and industrial materials are derived from bamboo. Bamboo can slow down the process of solid erosion. It maintains the ecological balance of the region too. Recently, a process has been discovered for distilling liquid diesel fuel from bamboo.

The state has vast resources of bamboo in the Tamenglong and Churachandpur districts of Manipur. In Manipur, there are many species of bamboo, viz., Longa, Utang, Khokwa, Saneibi, Maribob, Laiwa, Liwa, Watangkhoi, Nat, Unap, Vee, Wamu, Tenwa, Wak, Oonal, Mobiwa etc. Bamboo can grow easily in the valley areas as well as on the hill slopes of the state. Bamboo cultivation can check the problem of soil erosion in the hill areas of the state. Out of these species of bamboo, the Muli bamboo (Melacanna Bambusoides) is to make excellent paper. The bamboo forests cover an area of 3268 sq. km. in Manipur and the annual yield of bamboo is estimated at 14.40 lakh tons. The Barak Drainage area covers about 1500 sq kms of Bamboo forests. Jiribam has a vast bamboo forest comprising an area of about 387 sq. km. Bamboo has a number of uses and it is grown in every district of Manipur. Some variety of bamboo can be harvested every year. The quick grown varieties or early varieties of bamboo can be planted on the barren lands found both in hills and valley areas.

Thus establishing one bamboo-based (large-scale) industry in the state can also generate a huge revenue and great employment opportunity. It may have a long life span without any losses.

Another insulated paper mill of 25 tons per day capacity, based on the pine wood trees grown in the three districts of Senapati, Ukhrul, and Chandel district, is proposed to be set up at Karong of Manipur. In case of pine based paper mill, the life span will be very short and it will benefit only to a small section of people. It is also true that the paper is made not only from bamboo but it can also be made from water hyacinth (kabokang), paddy's straw, reeds, soft woods etc. which are found abundantly in the state. Moreover, the water of Loktak can be maintained in good condition by using its water hyacinth for paper production instead of spreading of Neochetina (an insect), to destroy scarce resources of water hyacinth.

SILK AND TASAR INDUSTRY

Manipur has got a tremendous potential for development of tasar culture as the oak shrubs (viz. 'Uyung' or 'Oak Tasar' and 'Sahi-kuhi' or Castanopsis indica) naturally grown in abundance in the foot hills of Manipur.

Earlier, only three branches of sericulture, viz. Mulberry, Muga and Eri were developed in some traditional pockets of the state, namely, Khurkhul, Leimaram, Phayeng and Thongjao etc. in a limited way.

There are four types of silkworms, which can be reared inside (internal) and outside (external) the rearing shed. (see Plate- 376) They are:

Outside the rearing shed:

- Tasar silkworm or Tasar leima (Uyung and Sahi kuhi/ Oak Tasar and (external) Castanopsis Indica)
- Muga silkworm or Muga leima (Nongnang kori and Tumitla/ Cinnamomum Ceceodephne)

Inside the Rearing shed

Eri silkworm or eri leima (kege/castor) (Internal) Mulberry silkworm or Kabrang Leima-Til (Kabrang Chak/Mulberry)

This silk worm rearing may benefit about 3,500 families in Manipur. In 1987, mulberry was planted in about 1000 hectares of land. For this purpose, about 50 lakhs of saplings (mulberry) were prepared and made for plantation. Another 40,000 hectares of land has been brought under systematic plantation of oak trees for rearing of oak tasar worms.

The rearing of silkworm (Tasar-Oak) was first established in 1973-74, Manipur is becoming a pioneer and best state of silk culture. The Sericulture Dept. of Manipur has its own sericulture research wing, which was established in the year 1984. Manipur has about 2 lakhs acres of Uyung (Oak Tasar, Botanically grouped under Quercusgenera plants, silk worm of tasar oak has three types:-

Uni.- voltin (Laid eggs once)

Bi -voltin (which laid eggs twice, and

Multi -voltin (which laid eggs more than twice)

The quality of tasar silk of Manipur is better in luster compared to tasar silk produced in other traditional states in India It is as good as that of tasar yarn of China which is the premier tasar silk producing country in the world. Thus, Manipur has the privilege of being the first state in India to produce oak tasar of unique quality in the country.

Traditional skilled artisans specially in silk, spinning and weaving are found concentrated in Thangmeiband and Chingmeirong areas extending upto adjoining villages like Heingang, Ahallup and Khabam villages. Skilled weavers specialised in weaving of cloth like delicate Lamthang khullak, Engineer fee,

Khudei Macha, Kokyet macha etc. are found concentrated in Wangkhei area near Ningthempukhri Mapal and some parts of Singjamet Chingamakha. Skilled loin-loom weavers producing items like Khwang phanek, Ngabong etc. are found in the areas of Imphal-East block and other parts of the state.

INDUSTRIALCORPORATIONS

There are ten State sponsored undertakings under the purview of the Department of Commerce and Industries, Manipur namely:

1. Manipur Handloom and Handicrafts Development Corporation Ltd.
2. Manipur Cements Ltd.
3. Manipur Spinning Mills Ltd.
4. Manipur Industrial Development Corporation Ltd.
5. Manipur Cycle Corporation Ltd.
6. Manipur Electronics Development Corporation Ltd.
7. Manipur Food Industries Corporation Ltd.
8. Manipur Pulp and Allied Products Ltd.
9. Manipur State Drugs and Pharmaceuticals Ltd. and
10. Manipur Vanaspati and Allied Industries Ltd.

All these undertakings have been facing financial problems and there was paucity of fund for maintenance. It means that they could not generate revenue. Many of these state-sponsored corporations are incurring heavy financial losses consecutively for the last more than 15 years. These corporation are not service –oriented organizations. These are profit oriented organizations. These should be run on business lines. Moreover, most of these corporation are suffering from mismanagement. Some of the examples are - Manipur Spinning Mills Ltd., Khansari Sugar Mill, Manipur Cements Ltd., Manipur Cycle Corporation Ltd, Maqnipur State Transport Corporation etc. In most cases, these corporation are headed by bureaucats, who run these corporation as Government Departments –not on business lines. The State Government can earn revenue to the tune of crores of Rupees just by closing these corporations.

It is high time that the state government take up timely and adequate measures for privatization of these corporations.

MANIPUR FOOD INDUSTRIES CORPORATION LTD.

The Manipur Food Industries Corporation Ltd. was commissioned in the year 1997 by changing the name from the erstwhile Manipur Sugar Mills Ltd. for development of viable food processing units in Manipur. The authorized share capital of the company is Rs. 7 crores. The company is going to establish a Food Processing Industrial Park near Mechanized Dye House Complex at Iroishemba, Imphal. The main objective for the establishment of Food Park is to provide basic infrastructural facilities such as land, building, cold storage, power, water supply and marketing facilities for the identified industrial units to be established by the selected entrepreneurs in the food park. The company will provide assistance and support services in the field of technical, financial, marketing, etc. to these units.

The project envisages to provide direct employment to 912 persons and indirect employment to more than 10,000 families at a project cost of Rs. 7.80 crores of which Rs. 4.00 crores will be financed by the Government of India. The Department of Food Processing, Government of India for the above project, has released a sum of Rs.1.60 crores.

200 TPD CEMENT PROJECT IN MANIPUR

The present annual demand of cement in Manipur is roughly 1.86 lakh tonnes. Viewing from the volume of demand of cement indicated above, it is highly prospective to put up new cement units in the State, at least a 200 TPD (Tonnes Per Day) plant. Considering the widespread availability of limestone and clay, setting up of a Cement Plant in Manipur will definitely have economic advantage instead of buying cement from outside. The product from such local units will also have a ready market in Myanmar through Moreh since the Indo-Myanmar border trade is now flourishing. Measuring the competitive advantage of export alone to Myanmar, Manipur thus has a distinct investment potential in cement industry.

A number of limestone occurrences have been located in Manipur. Of them, two clusters of limestone bodies - one at Phungyar and the other at Meiring in Ukhrul District. Limestone occurrence has been explored at Phungyar, Meiring, Mova, Kasom, Khangkhui, Lambui, Paovi, North Paorei, Shokpao, Yongphu, Shingda Marao, Shingkap, Shangsak, Koshu, Tongam, Mawai, Phalang, Nungou, Songphel, Sirarukhong, Huimin under Ukhrul district and also at Pallel, Mombi, Sajiktampak, Chakpikarong areas of Chandel district. The CaO content ranges from 37.3% to 50%. The Phungyar deposits have been estimated at 6.35 million tonne and the Meiring limestone will make up another reserve of about 5.76 million tonne. These reserves will be more than sufficient for a 200 TPD cement plant.The Phungyar deposit is composed of three limestone bands in a cluster located at about 5 km. from Phungyar Village, while the later is near Meiring Village about 8 km. from the Phungyar deposit. Both the villages are on a State highway the limestone deposits are nearby the respective villages. The Phungyar limestone have been explored in fair detail with drilling. Preliminary investigation has been carried out for the Meiring limestone and it is now being further explored with drilling. Both the deposits are of cement grade.

The Manipur Cements Ltd. was commissioned in 1988 to run and manage the 50 TPD Hundung Cement Factory and also to run other mineral based industries. The authorized share capital of the Company is Rs. 350 lakhs and the paid up share capital is Rs. 159.79 lakhs. The Company has a staff strength of 68 only. 98.35 M.T. of cement amounting to Rs. 3.34 lakhs was produced during 2000-01.

The project may be located at Yaingangpokpi, about 26 km. from Imphal on the Imphal-Ukhrul road and 82 km. from Phungyar limestone deposits, or somewhere nearer to Imphal, the State Capital and main marketing centre of the product. Yangangpokpi is an ideal place considering the availability of adequate power supply (3000 KVA), water supply (3.60 lakh litre per day) and good communication network.

SERPENTINITE AND IDOCRASE PROCESSING INDUSTRIES

Serpentinites are also commercially known as 'Green Marble'. It, like granite and marble, can be processed into monuments, tiles, slabs and other building blocks. It is considered that the serpentinites have a huge market potential, both as finished product and in raw forms, both within India and outside. Countries in the South-East Asia and the Middle East could be the important buyers. It can generate large scale employment and appreciable foreign exchange earnings. Serpentinites occur extensively in Chandel and Ukhrul Districts of Manipur within the Ophiolite Belt which spread over about 1600 sq. km. of area.

Idocrase has been found occurring in the host Serpentinites as pockets and lenses and also as floats. The massive green variety of Idocrase is also commercially called "Californite Jade" as misnomer. As recommended by the Gem Testing Laboratory, Jaipur of the Gem and Jewellery Export Promotion Council, the Idocrase may be cut and polished into any shape and cutting style which may be used as semi-precious jewellery items. The carving process may yield decorative items like ash-trays, pen stands, leaves, idols, or any other figure, bangles, etc. The processing industry is highly labour intensive with minimal infrastructure and fixed capital investment. Through extension of the Idocrase processing industry, Manipur can have a good potential for setting up gemstones cutting and polishing industry. Because, the traditional skill of high degree of excellence of the people, particularly women, of Manipur for dexterous handiwork is remarkable and it is the skill which matters most in the trade.

MANIPUR TRADITIONAL LIQUOR PLANT (DISTILLERY)

A high quality distilled liquor is produced in Manipur. Sekmai and Andro have been brewing liquor for centuries. The traditional liquor produced at Sekmai and Andro are well known for its good taste and good quality. The liquor is fairly comparable to other distlled alcohol available in any part of the world. Raw material is available in India and in Manipur. There is excellent market opportunity for the product.

Table 79 Showing Details of the Manipur Traditional Liquor Plant

1.	**Location : Sekmai, Manipur**	
2.	Nearest, Rail & Sea Connection	(1) Rail Jiribam, Manipur-240 Km & Dimapur, Nagaland- 200 Km (2) Road NH - 39 & 53 (3) Sea Kolkata
3.	Estimated Capital Cost of the Project	Rs. 1768.87 lakhs
4.	Capital Equipment	Un - polished rice storage unit, pre- mixing m/c, yeast preparation m/c, etc
5.	Raw materials	Rice
6.	Environment Impact	No adverse environmental impact as the project consists of waste treatment plant.
7.	Foreign Exchange Cost component	Nil
8.	Promoting Department	Department of Commerce & Industries, Govt. of Manipur
9.	Method of Selection of the private promoter	Through examination / evaluation by a selection committee after issuing adequate notice / publicity through print and electronics media.
12.	Policy Framework applicable to the project	State Industrial policy, Industrial Policy of NER & Government of India are applicable to the above project.

(Contd.)

(Contd. Table 79)

13.	Time-frame for selection & completion of selection of private Sector Sponsor /Developer	Within a period of 3 (three) months.
14.	Government Incentive packages applicable to the project	Capital investment, interest, power, transport subsidies, etc.
15.	Expected Return on investment	41%
16.	Recommended Debt Equity Ratio	2.43 : 1
17.	Expected source of Financing	(1) Promoter's contribution Rs. 395.00 lakhs (2) Govt. of India (subsidy) Rs.413.50 lakhs (3) Bank / FIs / Companies Rs. 960.37 lakhs
18.	Sovereign & Multilateral Guarantees	Promoter's collateral security & State Government guarantee.
19.	Feasibility Report	Available.
20.	Other General Information	Agro-Climatic conditions of the State is very much suitable for cultivation of paddy in large scale and processing technology of alcohol from rice is available. Technical manpower for Paddy cultivation and processing are available in the state. There shall be single window clearance whenever necessary for speedy implementation of the project. Logistic support shall be provided by the State Government whenever necessary.

INTEGRATED PINEAPPLE CONCENTRATION PLANT

The production of pineapple is 69432 MT in an area of 10000 Hectares during 2001-02. The proposed area under pineapple is 20,000 Hectares and

Table-80 Showing details of the Integrated pineapple Concentration Plant

1.	Location within State/Country	Thoubal, Manipur
2.	Nearest Rail, Road & Sea Connection	(1) Rail Jiribam, Manipur & Dimapur, Nagaland
		(2) Road NH- 39 & 53
		(3) Sea Kolkata

(Contd.)

(Contd. Table 80)

3.	Estimated Capital Cost of the project	Rs. 9005.00 lakhs
4.	Capital Equipment	Washing m/c, Juice extractor, steam boiler, aseptic packaging m/c. etc.
5.	Raw materials	Pineapple
6.	Environment Impact	The project is eco-friendly and consists of waste treatment plant. Hence, no adverse environmental impact.
7.	Foreign Exchange Cost component	Nil
8.	Promoting Department	Department of Commerce & Industries, Govt. of Manipur
9.	Method of Selection of the private promoter	Through examination/evaluation by a selection committee after issuing adequate notice/publicity through print and electronics media.
10.	Policy Framework applicable to the project	State Industrial Policy, Industrial Policy of NER & Government of India are applicable to the above project.
11.	Time-frame for the selection & completion of selection of private Sector Sponsor/Developer	Within a period of 3 (three) months.
12.	Government Incentive packages applicable to the project	Capital investment, interest, power, transport subsidies, etc.
13.	Expected Return on Investment	57%
14.	Recommended Debt Equity Ratio	1.67 : 1
15.	Expected source of Financing	1) Equity Rs. 300.00 lakhs
		2) Loan Rs. 500.00 lakhs
		3) Subsidy Rs. 105.00 lakhs
16.	Sovereign& Multilateral Guarantees	Promoter's collateral security & State Government guarantee.
17.	Feasibility Report	Preliminary report available.

(Contd.)

(Contd. Table 80)

18.	Other General Information	Agro-Climatic conditions of the State are very much suitable for cultivation of pineapple in large scale and processing technology is available in the Country. Technical manpower for Pineapple cultivation and processing are available in the state. There shall be single window clearance whenever necessary for speedy implementation of the project. Logistic support shall be provided by the State Government whenever necessary.

the expected yield of pineapple is 1,40,000 MT per annum. The plant requires about 90,000 MT of fresh and healthy pineapple.

***BAMBOO SHOOT FERMENTATION** (SEE PLATE- 368)*

Table-81 Showing details of the Bamboo shoot Fermentation project

1.	Location within State / Country	Tamenglong District
2.	Nearest Rail, Road & Sea Connection	(1) Rail Jiribam, Manipur
		(2) Road NH - 53
		(3) Sea Kolkata
3.	Estimated Capital Cost of the project	Rs. 100.00 lakhs
4.	Capital Equipment	Washing m/c, Fermenting m/c. etc.
5.	Raw materials	Bamboo.
6.	Environment Impact	The project is eco-friendly and consists of waste treatment plant. Hence, no adverse environmental impact.
7.	Foreign Exchange Cost component	Nil
8.	Promoting Department	Department of Commerce & Industries, Govt. of Manipur
9.	Method of Selection of the private promoter	Through examination / evaluation by a selection committee after issuing adequate notice / publicity through print and electronics media.
10.	Policy Framework applicable to the project	State Industrial Policy, Industrial Policy of NER & Government of India are applicable to the above project.
11.	Time-frame for selection & completion of selection of private Sector Sponsor / Developer	Within a period of 3 (three) months.

(Contd.)

(Contd. Table 81)

12.	Government Incentive packages applicable to the project	Capital investment, interest, power, transport subsidies, etc.
13.	Expected Return on Investment	30%
14.	Recommended Debt Equity Ratio	1 : 1
15.	Expected source of Financing	Private promoter & financial institutions.
16.	Sovereign & Multilateral Guarantees	Promoter's collateral security & State Government guarantee.
17	Feasibility Report	Available.
18.	Other General Information	(1) Raw material is abundantly available.
		(2) Improved technology is available.
		(3) Market and manpower readily available.

MEDICINAL PLANT PROCESSING INDUSTRY.

Table-82 Showing Medicinal plant Processing Industry.

1.	Location within State / Country	Thoubal, Manipur
2.	Nearest Rail, Road & Sea Connection	(1) Rail Jiribam, Manipur & Dimapur, Nagaland
		(2) Road NH- 39 & 53
		(3) Sea Kolkata
3.	Estimated Capital Cost of the project	Rs. 107.00 crores
4.	Capital Equipment	Equipment for cultivation and herbal preparation.
5.	Raw materials	Medicinal plants.
6.	Environment Impact	The project is eco-friendly and consists of waste treatment plant. Hence, no adverse environmental impact.
7.	Foreign Exchange Cost component	Nil
8.	Promoting Department	Department of Commerce & Industries, Govt. of Manipur
9.	Method of Selection of the private promoter	Through examination / evaluation by a selection committee after issuing adequate notice / publicity through print and electronics media.
10.	Policy Framework applicable to the project	State Industrial policy, Industrial policy of NER & Government of India are applicable to the above project.

(Contd.)

(Contd. Table 82)

11.	Time-frame for selection & completion of selection of private Sector Sponsor / Developer	Within a period of 3 (three) months.
12.	Government Incentive packages applicable to the project	Capital investment, interest, power, transport subsidies, etc.
13.	Expected Return on Investment	35%
14.	Recommended Debt Equity Ratio	2 : 1
15.	Expected source of Financing	Private promoter and financial institutions.
16.	Sovereign & Multilateral Guarantees	Promoter's collateral security & State Government guarantee.
17.	Feasibility Report	Preliminary report available.
18.	Other General Information	Manipur has 155 numbers of recognized tradable medicinal floras. The annual production value is estimated at Rs. 25.00 crores at present. There is good market demand and skilled manpower.

FLORICULTURE

Table-83 Showing details of the Floriculture project

1.	Location within State / Country	Senapati, Manipur	
2.	Nearest Rail, Road & Sea Connection	(1) Rail Jiribam, Manipur & Dimapur, Nagaland	
		(2) Road NH - 39 & 53	
		(3) Sea Kolkata	
3.	Estimated Capital Cost of the project	(1) GLADIOLUS	Rs. 23.05 lakhs
		(2) ANTHURIUM	Rs. 86.38 lakhs
		(3) DENDROBIUM	Rs. 98.03 lakhs
		(4)CARNATION	Rs. 78.46 lakhs
		Total	**Rs. 285.92 lakhs**
4.	Capital Equipment	Plantation racks, spraying m/c etc.	
5.	Raw materials	Gladiolus, Anthurium, Dendrobium, Carnation	
6.	Environment Impact	No adverse environmental impact.	
7.	Foreign Exchange Cost component	Nil	
8.	Promoting Department	Department of Agriculture / Horticulture, Govt. of Manipur	
9.	Method of Selection of the private promoter	Through examination /evaluation by a selection committee after issuing adequate notice / publicity through print and electronics media.	

(Contd.)

(Contd. Table 83)

10.	Policy Framework applicable to the project	State Industrial policy, Industrial policy of NER 7 Government of India are applicable to the above project.
11.	Time-frame for selection & completion of selection of private Sector Sponsor / Developer	Within a period of 3 (three) months.
12.	Government Incentive packages applicable to the project	As per norms.
13.	Expected Return on Investment	52%
14.	Recommended Debt Equity Ratio	3.38 : 1
15.	Expected source of Financing	(1) Equity Rs. 81.00 lakhs
		(2) Subsidy Rs. 50.00 lakhs
		(3) Loan Rs. 274.00 lakhs
16.	Sovereign & Multilateral Guarantees	1) Promoter's collateral security.
		2) State Government guarantee.
17.	Feasibility Report	Available
18.	Other General Information	Agro-Climatic conditions of the State are very much suitable for plantation of Gladiolus, Anthurium, Dendrobium & Carnation in large scale and horticulture technology is available. Technical manpower for Gladiolus, Anthurium, Dendrobium & Carnation planttion are available in the state. There shall be single window clearance whenever necessary for speedy implementation of the project. Logistic support shall be provided by the State Government whenever necessary.

INFORMATION TECHNOLOGY (IT)

Recognizing the vast potential of IT industry in the State, the Government of Manipur accords high priority to the Electronics and Information Technology sector as a major thrust area of development. A special package of incentives is provided to facilitate competitive growth of the sector.

Manipur has vibrant manpower potential ideally suited for electronics and IT based industries in view of the unpolluted and eco-friendly environment conditions and ever-growing qualitative work force. The Manipur Industrial Development Corporation Ltd. has been established as a public sector undertaking to fill up the gaps for development of electronics including information technology based industries in the State. The Centre for Electronics

Design and Technology of India (CEDTI) at Imphal caters to the entire North-East India. This Centre has been imparting training to all the prospective youth and officials of the State Government and other organizations from Manipur and the Region. The Government College of Technology at Imphal provides computer education up to the graduation level. A Masters course in computer applications is also imparted in the Manipur University. There are also a number of private institutions in the State providing IT education, like NIIT, APTECH, LCC etc. Computer education has been introduced in the school and college curriculums.

Community Information Centres with computers connected to the Internet via VSAT systems are being set up in every Block of the State and 33 nos. CICs will be operational shortly. Such centres not only act as a point from where the local public can avail of any kind of information, but also as training centre in the use of computers and the Internet. Work is underway to increase utility of these centres by incorporating Government to Citizen interfaces and Web content of local relevance.

The State Government of Manipur is at the final stage to adopt an IT Policy. Some of the objectives are :-

To set up the institutional framework to implement and monitor the policy.

To use E-Governance to upgrade the standard and quality of administration and to provide citizen-oriented, efficient and cost-effective government.

To promote investments and growth in IT industry, and encourage private sector initiative in IT related infrastructure and services, so as to increase the contribution of IT in the economic growth of the State.

To provide adequate infrastructure so that the IT sector can flourish.

To encourage percolation of IT literacy and education in the State.

To generate IT related employment opportunities for the educated youth.

Some IT areas where private participation is encouraged

- Setting up of an IT Park.
- Setting up of IT Enable Service Centres such as Call Centres etc.
- Development of a backbone network "Manipur State Wide Area Network" (MANNET) for voice, data and video transmission and dissemination.
- Issue of multi-function Electronic SMART cards to citizens.
- IT literacy programme in schools and colleges.

- To create infrastructure throughout the State for promotion of distance learning through IT.
- Setting up of Information Kiosks.
- Internet over Cable and other new technologies for internet penetration.

Telecom Infrastructure in Manipur

- Independent Satellite link with Delhi and Shillong
- Micro-wave link with Kohima and beyond
- 40 Digital Exchanges
- Internet C-II Net Working at Imphal with 810 connections to all District HQs.

POWER SECTOR

The Power supply of the State of Manipur depends upon the Central Sector Power Plants located in the North Eastern Region. The share of power for Manipur from the Central sector power plants including the shares from the unallocated share of power of the Central Projects is 141.15 MW when the plants are operated at their full capacity. The availability of power from the Central projects varies from month to month depending upon the hydro-power generation which are dependent on rainfall. At present, the availability of power from the Central Sector Power Plants during peak hours is 63.75 MW. The requirement of the State is 120 MW during peak hours. At present the State draws 83.75 MW by overdrawing 20 MW from the Central Projects. Availability of power from Central Sector Power Plants is shown below:-

Effective Availability(MW)Manipur's Share (MW)

Table-84 Showing available power supply in Manipur

Sl. No	*Source of Power Supply*	*Effective availability*	*Manipur's share*
1	Loktak H. E. Project	60	19.08
2	Kopili Hydro Electric Project	150	13.50
3	Doyang H. E. Project	18	1.73
4	Rangnadi H. E. Project	55	5.56
5	Assam Gas based Power Project (Kathalguri)	170	16.83
6	Agartala Gas Turbine Power Project (Ramchandranagar)	72	7.05
	Total	525	63.75

The peak power requirement of Manipur by the year, 2006-07 and 2011-12 as per the 16th Electric Power Survey of India are 252 MW and 406 MW respectively. The Region has many more ongoing projects. There will not be any shortage of power for the region as a whole and for the State of Manipur as well for another 10 years.

The State Power Department is currently engaged in taking necessary actions for generation of at least 1654.5 MW as below:-

Table-85 Showing projected availability of power supply in Manipur

1.	Loktak Down Stream HE Project	90.0	MW
2.	Irang HE Project	60.0	MW
3.	Tipaimukh H. E. Project	1500.0	MW
4.	Micro-Hydel projects at Leimakhong (Stage-III), Gelnel (Stage-I) and Tuipaki, Haipi, Maklang, Iring, Ijai and Tupul	4.5	MW
	Total	1654.5	MW

The State Power Department has completed construction of Heavy Fuel Based Power Project (6x6 MW) at Leimakhong. Trial run test of the six units has been done successfully in March and April, 2002. Commercial operation is being started shortly. Once the project is commercially operated the peak hour shortage of the State can be minimised.

There are seven 132/33 KV Sub-Stations with total capacity of 191.3 MVA to receive power from North Eastern Region Power Grid. These are located at Yurembam, Jiribam, Yaingangpokpi, Ningthoukhong, Kakching, Karong and Churachandpur. Altogether 35 Nos. of 33/11 KV Sub-Stations having a total capacity of 206.1 MVA are in operation for distribution.

Manipur is richly endowed with considerable Hydro Power Potential. The Loktak Hydro Electric Project (3x35 MW) commissioned in 1984 is so far the main source of power supply in the State. The present requirement of the State is 120 MW during peak hours, whereas the availability of power from the Central Sector Power plants is 63.75 MW and the State's Power Plants is 13 MW. The State Government's Heavy Fuel Based Power Projects (6x6 MW) at Leimakhong is now poised for commercial operation. There are seven 132/33 KV Sub-Stations with a total capacity of 191.9 MVA to receive power from the Regional Power Grid and thirty-five 33/11 KV Sub-Stations with a total capacity of 206 MVA for distribution.

The Demand of power

The peak power requirement of Manipur as per the 16th Electric Power Survey of India is as under:-

Table -86 Showing power requirement of Manipur by 2011-12

Particular	*Year* 2002-03	2003-04	2004-05	2005-06	2006-07	2011-12
Maximum Demand of Power (MW)	172	189	208	229	252	406

Potentials for growth

There are a large number of perennial streams and rivers in Manipur, which can be exploited for generating power through mini/small/major Hydel Projects. A total hydro potential of 1350 MW at 60% Load Factor has been estimated as of date.

The State of Manipur is currently engaged in taking up necessary action for generation of 1654.5 MW as below:-

Table- 87 Showing potential growth of power supply

1.	Loktak Downstream Hydro-Electric (H.E). Project	90.00	MW
2.	Tipaimukh H. E. Project	1500.00	MW
3.	Irang H. E. Project	60.00	MW
4.	Micro Hydel Project at Leimakhong (Stage-III), Genel (Stage-I) and Tuipaki, Haipi, Maklang, Iring, Ijai and Tupul	4.50	MW
	Total :	**1654.50**	**MW**

Loktak Down-Stream Hydro Electric Project (3x30 MW)

The project envisaged to utilise the tail race water of the upstream Loktak Hydro Electric Project which has been in continuous operation for the last 18 years with more than 120% efficiency. Availability of water for the new project is therefore assured. Techno-economic clerance of the project was given by Central Electricity Authority in Frebuary 1999 to implement it by National Hydro Electric Power Corporation (NHPC) at an estimated completed cost of Rs. 667.46 crores. The project site is located about 30 Kms. from National Highway No. 53 and about 90 Kms. from Imphal.

Tipaimukh Hydro-Electric (Multi-purpose) Project (6x250 MW)

Tipaimukh Hydro-Electric (Multi purpose) Project envisages construction of a 390 m long, 162.8 m high earthen core rock filled dam on the river Barak for generation of 1500 MW of power. The annual average energy generation has been estimated at 3821 million units. The project cost as estimated by the North-Eastern Electric Power Corporation is Rs. 5225.70 crore.

Irang Hydro Electric Project (60 MW)

The Irang river has perennial flow, which can be tapped for generation of power by construction of earth dam about 60 m high. The estimated cost of the project is about Rs. 352.00 crore.

Cluster of Micro Hydel Project in the State

The State has identified 17 feasible sites for investigation and implementation of Mini/Micro Hydel Projects with a total capacity of 44.95 MW.

Promotional and Fiscal Incentives

The State Government follows the guidelines and policy of Government of India for power generation programmes to be implemented by the Private Sector Units. Fiscal and Promotional incentives for participation by Private Sector Institution/Company in the generation and supply from generating stations are as follows:-

1. Wheeling and banking facilities for one year at nominal charges.
2. Permission for third party sale to any unit anywhere in the State.
3. Power purchase rate @ Rs.2.25 per unit (1994-95 based year) escalated @5%
4. Assurance of payment by the State Electricity Board/Electricity Department for Power Purchase by them.
5. Transport Subsidy
6. Tax holidays and
7. High priority on Hydro Power in the Generation Sector.

HORTICULTURE

Horticultural Resources

Manipur has vast potential for commercial plantation of fruits like pineapple, passion fruit, lemon, lime, orange, banana, amla, grapes, olive, etc.

Table -88 Showing area and horticultural resources in Manipur

Sl. No.	*Crops*	*1999-00*		*2000-01*		*2001-02*	
		Area '000 ha.	*Prodn '000 MT*	*Area '000 ha.*	*Prodn '000 MT*	*Area '000 ha.*	*Prodn '000 MT*
A.	**FRUITS**						
	Pineapple	10.00	68.97	10.02	69.14	10.08	69.43
	Banana	1.63	12.93	1.65	13.01	1.66	13.11
	Papaya	1.87	10.29	1.87	10.31	1.89	10.24
	Orange	0.90	3.68	0.93	3.70	0.94	3.76
	Mango	0.18	0.94	0.19	0.95	0.20	1.10
	Pear/peach	0.62	4.03	0.35	4.11	0.64	3.86
	Guava	0.71	2.41	0.72	2.46	0.73	2.48
	Lemon	1.10	5.07	1.13	5.14	1.13	5.17
	Jack fruits	0.29	1.14	0.29	1.16	0.30	1.20
	Others	7.27	8.67	7.30	8.67	7.30	8.81
B.	**VEGETABLES**						
	Cauliflower	1.00	10.00	1.01	10.10	1.01	10.10
	Cabbage	1.30	15.60	1.32	15.84	1.32	15.84
	Tomato	0.50	4.08	0.50	4.12	0.51	4.16
	Pea	1.00	5.76	1.01	5.81	1.01	5.82
	Radish	0.23	2.30	0.23	2.30	0.23	2.35
	Carrot	0.28	2.04	0.28	2.03	0.28	2.07
	French Bean	0.60	1.83	0.61	1.86	0.62	1.89
	Bhindi	0.70	2.31	0.71	2.34	0.72	2.38
	Brinjal	0.31	1.60	0.31	1.63	0.32	1.65
	Knol-khol	0.29	1.50	0.29	1.50	0.29	1.50
	Others	0.31	0.87	0.31	0.88	0.32	0.89
C.	**SPICES**						
	Chilli	7.01	22.78	7.01	22.78	7.03	23.06
	Ginger	1.10	11.00	1.10	11.00	1.11	11.14
	Onion	0.52	5.20	0.53	5.30	0.54	5.43
	Turmeric	0.31	3.72	0.32	3.78	0.32	3.78

The quality of the pineapple (Q-variety) so available in Manipur has distinctive taste and flavour. Out of the potential area of 2,77,000 hectares identified for plantation of fruits and vegetables, only 24,000 hectares are covered so far under different crops plantation. Vegetables like cauliflower, cabbage, tomato, etc. and spices like chilli, ginger, turmeric, etc. are in huge production.Area and production in respect of some of the fruits in the State are given below:

POTTERY

Manipur is a state embedded in deepest tradition of art and craft going back to a hoary antiquity. The tradition was further refined in the performing and martial arts so intimately that day to day life of the people was marked by an aesthetic consciousness even in the domain of crafts.

Pottery in Manipur is closely related with social, cultural and religious life. The art of pottery in Manipur is practised by women without using wheel in a similar fashion as in the other northeastern states.

Myths about origin of pottery in Manipur

Once upon time, Manipur was surrounded by seven hillocks and water every where. Seven suns burned day and night. Atiya Kuru Shidaba and Ima Leimaren Shidabi decided to create a world and descended from heaven. Atiya Kuru Shidaba drained out water through a hole with a trident. Once settled, they had a child to fulfill their wishes. A voice from the heaven announced- "Dig out some clay and make a pitcher out of it and offer prayers for seven days then your wish will be fulfilled". After seven days of prayer, a male child of golden colour was found by the couple. The child was christened Sanamahi, he later shot down six extra suns by his arrows and created various creatures dwelling on water, air and earth. Finally he created human being. Atiya Kuru Shidaba and Ima Leimaren Shidabi disappeared after completing their task. Ima Leimaren Shidabi took several incarnations to carry out seven different tasks.`Panthoibi or Leima Leinaotabi, was among them, who created the first earthen-pot. Therefore, in the creation myth of Manipur, the earthen pot becomes the metaphor for the womb.

Common use of pottery

The pottery is used for ritualistic and domestic purpose. Ritualistic- During childbirth, the placenta of the newly born child is cut-off and kept inside a small earthen pot (Chaphu). The Chaphu symbolises purity and sanctity.

Domestic- A variety of pottery like chapu, uyan pun is used for storing rice. Hentak chaphu is a container for keeping pounded fish mixture. Ishaiphu for containing water. Chini Chaphu is a small earthern pot with stalk containing sugar inside, especially made as toy for children. Chengphu t is used to store rice. The Khum is a small pot used for taking out mixture from the big jars, also used as lid for small pots.

Technique of pottery- making

First the lump of clay is shaped into a slab. This slab is rolled to make a cylinder. A base is attached to it. Then it is put on a stool and log of wood so as to create a pot of desired shape. A thick soft wet cloth is wrapped around the open rim of cylinder to rotate it clock-wise and anti-clock wise alternately by holding it tightly by hand. By the end of this process the collar of pot gets ready. After the collar gets stiffened the pot is beaten with the wooden beater using stone anvil till it acquires the desired shape, size and thickness of wall.

Smoke stains are commonly found on almost all traditionally made and used terracotta pots of India. To some it has ritualistic significance, some consider it auspicious yet some artist use it aesthetically to make a personal statement.

Firing of Pots

Baking of pots in open space is the practice among the potters of Manipur. But the Tangkhul potters fire in the forest where the fuel is available in plenty. A bed of either straw or dried leaves is made on ground. The Andro and Chairen spread dried cow- dung along with the straw to form a thick bed. The pots are then kept on the bed and covered by the dried leaves or straw or cow-dung. In this way three or four layers of pots are arranged alternatively with the pile straw or leaves in the form of a mould.

Colouring

Among the potters of the valley there is a belief that the pottery can not be used unless Kuhi a liquid prepared out of the bark of tree (quircus sp) is sprinkled over it.

Places associated with pottery making in Manipur:-

According to colour schemes pottery in Manipur is divided into three categories. The blackware pottery, greyware pottery, redware pottery.

1. Chairel and Thongojao village in Thoubal district (redware)
2. Andro village in Thoubal district, Chakpa tribe (brick red with coat of blackish maroon colour)
3. Nungbi village in Ukhrul district, Tangkhul tribe (glossy black in colour)
4. Oinam village in Senapati district, Poumai tribe (dull black in colour)

5. Nongpok Sekmai village in Thoubal district (red ochre colour)
6. Ningthemecha Karong village in Imphal West district, Meitei (greyware)
7. Leimaram village in Bishnupur district, Chakpa (pots for ritualistic occasion)

Financial Returns

In the past pottery was in great demand, each family needed them in rituals and festive occasion. With the advent of metal utensils in 19th century the pottery industry has declined. Unavailability of suitable clay, lack of expert potters, custom of producing pots only during season when there is less rain, the tedious work of firing Tangkhul and Oinam pottey are some of the factors causing hindrance to the tradition of pottery-making. As the financial returns of the production of Manipuri pottery is quite negligible and unless proper guidance and financial assistance are provided the pottery of Manipur is on the verge of extinction. (Shobita Devi).

BUSINESS OPPORTUNITIES

Agriculture

Agriculture is the mainstay of the State's economy. It engages 76% of the workers. The size of the cultivated area is, however, only 9.41% of the total geographical area of the State. Of this total cultivated area, 52% is confined to the valley. Therefore, half of the total valley area which accommodates 67% of the total population is occupied for agriculture purposes. The pressure on land in the valley is thus quite conspicuous.

Agriculture plays a vital role as it is the main backbone of the State economy till today. The agriculture is mainly dependent on monsoon however around 28.49% of area under cultivation is irrigated by canals. The main crop

Table-89 Showing varieties of Paddy available in Manipur

	Phourel		
	Phourel Amubi		
	Moirangphou		
	Taothabi		
	Huikap		
	Chakhao		
	Chakhao Poireiton		
	Tombung		

Table-90 Showing area and quantities of some agricultural products

Sl	Crops	1998-99 Area '000 ha.	1998-99 Production '000 MT	1999-2000 Area '000 ha.	1999-2000 Production '000 MT	2000-01 Area '000 ha.	2000-01 Production '000 MT
1.	Paddy	211.50	397.66	126.49	353.99	212.39	477.21
2.	Wheat	0.45	0.68	0.75	1.00	1.00	1.03
3.	Maize	16.50	29.60	13.84	24.88	16.50	33.16
4.	Pulses	16.37	13.10	21.50	14.87	22.20	16.45
5.	Oilseeds	15.11	9.26	20.33	13.90	22.75	15.21
6.	Potato	3.88	22.99	7.30	68.50	7.52	62.04
7.	Sugarcane	4.00	240.00	3.00	180.00	3.10	185.00

Source : Agriculture Department, Government of Manipur.

is paddy. Paddy is called "Phou" in Manipuri language. The scientific name is Oryza sativa Linn. The variety of paddy found in Manipur is of tall, high littering, fine grains, mostly photosynthetic, long duration type. The local species (Oryza sativa Linn Indica) are Moirangphou, Phoudum, Taothabi, Phouren, Phouren amubi, Kakching Phou, Huikap, Chakhao, Chakhao poireiton etc. Another wild variety (Oryza sativa Linn javanica) is also available – Murshi Laphou. Nowadays many hybrid varieties such as China paddy, China-1, China -1039, China -9888, KD etc are available. Double cropping is being practiced and is becoming popular. The state produces sizeable quantity of paddy, wheat, maize, pulses, oilseeds such as mustard, groundnut, soybeans, Sunflower, ginger, turmeric and fruits like pineapple, lime/lemon, banana, orange, papaya, plum and vegetables like, cauliflower, cabbage, tomato, pea, squash, carrot, pumpkin, etc. The existing area under fruits and vegetable crop is about 1.08% of the total geographical area and with such suitable agro-climatic conditions, the state still has lots of potential areas on the foot hills, mild hill slopes and along the river banks.

The existing area under cultivation of different crops in Manipur is 2,85,000 hectares as against the available potential area of 3,25,500 hectares. Rice, wheat, maize, oil seeds, potato and sugar cane etc. are the main cash crops in the state. Among these crops, cultivation of the paddy is the largest both in the plains and hills, and cover 82% of the total cultivated area. Besides the numerous varieties of local rice which are all unique in taste, two being highly specific to the state with distinctive scent and flavour are most preferred for pudding preparation *Chakhao-Poireiton (dark violet)* and *Chakhao (white)*.

Rice, wheat, maize, oil seeds, potato and sugarcane etc. are the main crops in the State. Among these crops, cultivation of paddy is the largest both in the plains and hills, and covers 82% of the total cultivated area. Among the variety of rice, there are two varieties of rice locally named as "Chakhao poireiton" having its natural colour (dark violet) and a distinct flavour and "Chakhao" having its natural white colour, scent and distinctive flavour. Next to paddy, maize is the second largest cultivated crop. It occupies about 40% of the gross cropped area and grown mainly in the hills.

Tea

Tea grows wild in Manipur since time immemorial. However, plantation of tea for commercial production has been started only from the year 1981-82 by Manipur Plantation Crops Corporation Limited in Jiribam.

The targeted project area of tea plantation is 425 hectares, out of which till the end of 1996 a substantive area of 260 hectares has already been covered. The yield of green tea leaf since inception upto 30th June, 1997 was 200 M.T. approximately. A target of 500 M.T. of green tea leaf is attempted during the current year. As there is no suitable alternative at present, green tea leaf are sold to the Jirighat Tea Estate, Cachar, Assam @ Rs. 5 Kg. (ex factory). The Corporation has collected a revenue of Rs. 10 lakhs upto the end of June, 1997. Considering the increasing trend of yield and productivity and also to arrest unremunerative income from sale of green tea leaf, a modern tea factory is being installed at Manipur Tea Estate, Jiribam. (see plates -379-380)

Tea is the most consumed beverage in the world, and thus greatly affecting the lives of many people in many countries. Tea was in Japan over 1,200 years ago, as well as in the holdings of the Mongolian and Ottoman Empires. The Portuguese navigators found tea in the 1500s and the Dutch capitalized on it as did the English. The Dutch colony of New Amsterdam (now New York in America), probably had tea prior to England. Tea reached the shores of England just after being introduced to Europe. The British truly institutionalized tea throughout its society and empire, as no other country did. Supposedly, Winston Churchill once said tea was more important than bullets. After the British East India Company was dissolved in 1833 tea became more widely popular, and the era of the clipper ships began.

Tea in many ways is the history of people. Tea goes back more than 5,000 years where it was first discovered in China. From China, tea has influenced the entire world as perhaps no other food agricultural product has. Now many countries produce tea, with the very best teas coming from China, India, Sri Lanka, Japan, Taiwan, with other countries producing some excellent teas, such as Kenya, Indonesia, et. al.

Tea plants (Camellia Sinensis) are hardy evergreen shrub grown in part shade to full shade. You can grow a tea plant easily in a greenhouse or on a porch even if you have to bring it in during the winter. Most tea varieties tolerate temperatures down to 20 degrees F. Tea plants prefer a wet humid summer and a cool, dry winter with no soil freezes.

*Tea Industry (*Medium Sized)

Formerly tea was not so popular among the local inhabitants of Manipur but it was grown in some pockets of the state (viz. Chanung area etc.). The climate and soil of the state are suitable to grow more tea on the hill sloes. Tea though is used as the Traditional Maiba (Physician) of Meetei used a common beverage as a medicinal herb. Tea and rubber were indigenous plants of the state. Tea was planted in an area of about 425 hectares at Tea Estate, Jiribam. Thousands of tea plants were planted there in the initial stage. There is a good hope for tea industry in the state. Not only the areas of Jiribam, but also the hill slopes of the state in other parts are suited for tea plantation. Since, tea is the most important of the beverage crops of the world and a portion of the world population drinks tea more than coffee or cocoa, Manipur has a better prospect for exporting tea if this industry is geared up. Manipur being a part of the monsoon region of Asia, is also having abundant cheap unskilled labourers, suitable amount of rainfall, varying from about 60^0 F to 75^0 F, with very little difference between winter and summer temperatures, specially in its hilly areas where tea plantation is being made. The prospect of tea industry in the state is very bright.

There are two main varieties of the tea plants. The small leaf variety, known as *Camellia Sinensis*, thrives in the cool, high mountain regions of central China and Japan. Camellia sinensis is the source of tea of commerce. The young processed leaves yield tea-the world's most important caffeine beverage. Tea plants are evergreen, medium sized shrub (4-6 ft) and can be grown outside. The broad leaf variety, known as *Camellia assamica,* grows best in the moist, tropical climates found in Northeast India and the Szechuan and Yunnan provinces of China. The plant produces dark green, shiny leaves and small, white blossoms.

According to an old Chinese saying, "superior tea comes from high mountains". The altitude and mountain mists help shield against too much sunlight and provide the proper temperature and humidity to allow the leaves to develop slowly and remain tender. The quality and taste of a particular tea is influenced by both the environment (soil, climate, and altitude) and the tea maker (who decides when and how the leaf is plucked and how it is processed). Most tea plants have a growth phase and a dormant period, usually during the winter. The leaves are plucked as the new tea shoots (or "flush") emerge. In hotter climates, the plants have several flushes and can be picked year-round. In cooler conditions at higher elevations, there is a distinct harvesting season. Leaves from the earlier flushes, usually in the spring, give the finest quality teas. There are four main types of tea preparations : green tea, black tea, oolong tea and white tea. All tea comes from the same plant. The specific variety of tea plant and the way the leaves are processed after harvesting determine the type of tea that is created.

Yongchak

Tree Bean (Parkia timoriana) or yongchak is one of the most common, popular item of food among the Manipuris. The tree bean, *Parkia. timoriana* (DC.) Merr. syn. *Parkia. roxburghii* G. Don belongs to the family Leguminosae and sub-family Mimosoideae. It is one of the most common multipurpose trees in Manipur having high commercial value, and is commonly grown in the backyard of houses, *jhums* and forests throughout Northeast India. It flowers during the months of September–October and the onset of fruiting starts from November onwards. The pod is available from November till April, and is consumed in all its developmental stages starting from the green, tender pods to the matured, black seeds, fresh or cleaned and sun-dried for future use during the off-season. The associating pungent smell in the seeds is due to the presence of thia-zolidine-4-carboxylic acid (TCA, thio-proline), a cyclic sulphur-containing amino acid.

Tree Bean produces long tender beans which are the most delicious vegetables of this region. It is taken in different forms of preparations, either fresh or cooked. According to the consumers' preference, the tree bean pods are consumed at different stages of maturity. The pod contains 15.6 to 18.0% Protein. This tree enjoys the status of a cash crop in Manipur. A tree bean when it starts bearing bean pods after 5-6 years of plantation, can fetch an income of Rs.10,000-20,000/-per annum at Farm Gate price.

It possess anti-carcinogenic properties and inhibits the formation of squamous cell carcinomas in the fore-stomach of rats. A number of workers have reported the biochemical and nutritional values of the plant, including various medicinal uses. During the months of June–July 2000, heavy infestation of caterpillars of *Cadra cautella* was observed on stored tree-bean seeds in properly sealed paper bags at Imphal, Manipur. These seeds were stored in April, after proper drying. Literature survey revealed few reports of pest infestation on *Parkia* spp. The pod-boring larvae of the pyralid moth, *Mussidia pectinicorella* Hamps. and torticid moth, *Argyroploce illepida* Btlr. infest the ripening seeds of *P. speciosa*, while *M. nigrivenella* Rago-not is a natural pest on *P. biglobosa*. (see plate -378)

Medicinal Plants

Low volume high value products being the only panacea for a profitable industry in the North Eastern Region, medicinal plants are befitting to this land locked region. Out of the medical plants grown in Manipur, 1200 species have been identified of which about 430 species are used as folk medicine, the rest remains as wastage in wilderness. (See Plates 382-396)

Table-91 Showing varieties of medicinal plants in Manipur

Sl No.	*Common Name*	*Technical Name*	*Manipuri name*
1.	Okra	Abelmoschus esculentus	Velundri
2.		Abrus Precatorius	Chang ning mei mubi
3.		Acacia farnesiana	Chigonglei
4.		Acanthospermum hispidum	Kabo Langthrei
5.		Acabnthus mollis	Krishna khubam
6.		Achyranthes aspera	Khujum Pere
7.		Acorus calamus	Ok-hidak
8.		Adenostemma lavenia	Lalukok
9.		Adenonthera pavonia	Rakta Chandon
10.		Adhatoda Vasica	Nongmangkha Angouba
11.		Adiantum capillus -veneris	Mayur Pambi
12.	Bael tree	Aegle marmelos	Hei Khagok
13.		Ageratum Conyzoides	Khongjai Napi
14.		Albizia Odoratissima	Uil
15.		Albizia Stipulata	Khok
16.		Allium aescalonicum	Meitei tilhou macha
17.		Allium cepa	Moroi tilhou
18.		Allum hookerii	Maroi Napakpi
19.		Allum odorum	Maroi Nakuppi
20.		Allum Sativa	Maroi Chanam
21.		Alocasia indica	Yendem
22.		Alocasia mecrorrhiza	Hongngoo
23.		Alepinia galanga	Kanghu
24.		Alpinia officinarum	Pulleimanbi
25.		Amaranthus spiranthus	Chengkruk tingkhang panbi
26.		Amaranthus viridian	Chengkruk
27.		Amonum subulatum	Illaichi achouba
28.		Ananas bracteatus	Lam kihom
29.	Pine apple	Anana comosus	Kihom
30.		Andrographis paniculata	Bhubati
31.		Anisomelus indica	Thoiding Angouba
32.		Aquilaria agalocha	Agor
33.		Aralia armata	Naosek manbi
34.		Ardisia colorata	Uthum
35.	Betel nut	Areca catechu	Kwa
36.		Agemone mexicana	Khomthokpi
37.		Artabotrys hexapetalus	Chini champra
38.	Jack tree	Artocarpus heterophyllus	Theibong
39.		Artocarpus lakoocha	Harikokthong
40.		Arundo donax	Yengthou
41.	Peacock flower	Asclepias curassavice	Krishna chura
42.		Asparagus filicinus	Nunggarei

(Contd.)

(Contd. Table 83)

Sl No.	*Common Name*	*Technical Name*	*Manipuri name*
43.		Auricularie delicate	Uchina
44.		Averrhoa carambola	Heinoujom
45.		Baccaurea apida	Moktok hei
46.		Becopa monnieri	Leibak kundo macha
47.		Bambousa nutans	Ootang waa
48.		Bambusa tulda	Waa
49.	Indian Spinach	Basella rubra	Urok sumban
50.	Bauhinia	Bauhinia purpura	Chingthrao angangba
51.	Mountain ebony	Bauhinia tenuiflora	Chingthrao angouba
52.	Bauhinia	Bauhinia vareigata	Chingthrao ngourunaba
53.		Benincasa hispida	Torbot
54.		Behula alnoides	Bhuja Patra
55.		Bidens pillosa	Hameng sampakpi
		Blumea balsamifera (Linn.) D.C	Langthrei
56.		Bixa orellana	Ureirom
57.		Bryonia grandis	Kwak thabi
58.		Cajanus cajan	Mairongbi
59.	Cane	Calamus floribundus	Lee
60.		Caloteopis gigontea	Angot
61.		Cannabis sativa Linn.	Ganja
62.		Cardiospermum halicacabun	Poklaobi
63.		Carica papaya	Awa thabi
64.		Carthamus tinchorius	Kushumlei
65.		Cassia laevegata	Thaonam Achouba
66.		Cassia tora	Thaonam
67.		Catharanthus roseus	Saheblei
68.		Cagrela toona	Tairen
69.		Celosia cristala	Haolei
70.		Celtis timorensis	Heikru
71.		Cinnanomum camphora	Karpur
72.		Cinnanomum tamala	Tejpata
73.		Cinnanomum zeylanicum	Ushingsha
74.		Cissus discolor	Kongouyen Achouba
75.		Citrus Latipes	Heiribob
76.		Citrus Limon	Champra
77.		Citrus maxima	Nobab
78.		Clenodendrum colebrookianum	Kuthab
79.	Clitoria	Clitoria ternatea	Aparajita
80.		Codonacenthus Pauciflorus	Nongpok Langthrei
81.		Coix Lacryma-jobi	Changning
82.		Coriandrum sativa	Phadigom
83.		Costus speciosus Sm.	Okchak-Khokki

(Contd.)

(Contd. Table 83)

Sl No.	Common Name	Technical Name	Manipuri name
84.		Crotalaria pallida	Lam hawaithrak
85.		Crotalaria spectabilis	U-hawaithrak
86.		Curcuma angustifolia	Yaipal
87.	Turmeric	Curcuma longa	Yaingang
88.		Cudrenia nepalensis	Saitingkhang
89.		Cycas pectinata	Yendang
90.		Cynodon dactylon	Tingthou
91.		Cyperus rotundus	Senbang Kokthum
92.		Dactyloctinium aegypticum	Pungphai
93.	Thorn apple-black	Datura streamonium	Sagoi hidak amuba
94.	Thorn apple	Datura suavelens	Sagoi hidak
95.		Dioscorea lata	Haa
96.		Dioscorea bulbifera	Lam haa
97.		Dioscorea pentaphylla	Haa angangba
98.		Eclipta alba	Uchi sumban
99.		Elsholtzia blanda	Lomba
100.		Entada scan dens	Kangkhil
101.		Eryngium foetidum	Awa Phadigom
102.		Erythrina indica	Kurao angangba
103.		Erythrina variegata	Kurao angouba
104.		Eucalyptus cicitriodora	Nasik
105.		Eupatorium bermonicum	Langthrei
106.		Eupatorium cannabinum	Langthrei manbi
107.		Euphorbia oncolata	Khomthokpi
108.		Euphoria longana	Nongang hei
109.		Euryale ferox	Thangjing
110.		Ficus benghalensis	Khongnagbot
111.		Ficus glovevata	Heibong
112.	Cluster fig	Ficus hispida	Ashi heibong
113.		Ficus rumphei	Khongnang
114.		Ficus religiosa Linn.	Sanakhongang
115.		Flacourtia Jangomas	Heitroi
116.		Foeniculum Vulgare	Pakhon
117.		Fragaria indica	Heirong Kak
118.		Galinsoga parviflora	Hameng Sampakpi
119.		Garcinia Xanthochymes	Heibong
120.		Gardenia Jasminoides	Kaboklei
121.	Cotton	Gossypium arboretum	Lashing Pambi
222.		Goniothalamus sesquipedalis	Leikham
123.		Gynura cusimbura	Tera paibi
124.		Hedychium coronarium	Takhellei angouba
125.		Hedychium marginatum	Takhellei angangba
126.		Hedychium spicatum	Takhellei Napu
127.	China Rose	Hibicus rosa-sinensis	Juba kusum

(Contd.)

(Contd. Table 83)

Sl No.	Common Name	Technical Name	Manipuri name
128.		Hibicus subderffa	Silot sougri
129.		Houyyuynia cordata	Tokningkhok
130.	Indian penntwort	Hydrocotyle asiatica	Peruk
131.		Ipinoea aquatica	Kolamni
132.		Ipinoea batatas	Manggra
133.		Iris bakeri	Kombirei
134.		Ixoya coccinea	Hameibon
135.		Jasminum multiflorum	Kundo macha
136.		Jasminum rex	Malika
137.		Jasminum sambac	Kundo
138.	Castor	Jatropha curcas	Awa kege
139.		Juglans regia	Heijuga
140.		Jussiaea repens	Ishing kundo
141.		Kaempferia rotunda Linn	Yai Thamna Manbi
142.	Srout leaf plant	Kalenchoe pinnata	Mana hidak
143.		Kaumpferia rotunda	Leibaklei
144.		Lagenaria siceraria	Khongdrum
145.		Lantana camara	Nongban lei
146.		Lemania australis	Nungsham
147.		Leucauna glauca	Chigonglei angouba
148.		Lonicera macrantha	Madhumati
149.	Tomato	Lycopersicon esculentum	Khamen ashinba
150.		Magnolia hodgsonii	U-thambal angangba
151.		Maleotus philippensis	Ureirom laba
152.		Matricaria capensis	Moirang langthrei
153.	Neem tree	Melia azedarach	Neem
154.		Melothria perpusilla	Lam thabi
155.		Mangifera indica	Linn. Heinou-
156.	Garden mint	Meha arvensis	Nungshi hidak
157.		Mereindra bengalensis	Kanghuman
158.		Mesua ferrea	Nageswar
159.		Michelia champaea	Leihao
160.		Michelia Montana	Leihao leisang
161.		Mimosa pudica	Lam ikaithabi
162.		Mimusops elengi	Bokul
162.		Mussaenda roxburghii	Hanurei
163.	Lotus	Nelumbo nucifera	Thambal
164.		Neomerica gracilis	Kombirei angangba
165.		Neptunia olevacia	Ishing Ikaithabi
166.	Oleander	Nurium indicum	Kabirei
167.		Nicotiana plumbaginifolia	Lam hidak mana
168.		Nyctanthus arbortritis	Singgarei
169.	Lily	Nymphaea nouchali	Tharo
170.		Nymphaea stellate	Thariktha
171.		Nymphorides indicum	Thariktha macha

(Contd.)

(Contd. Table 83)

Sl No.	*Common Name*	*Technical Name*	*Manipuri name*
172.		Ocimum basilicum	Naosek lei
173.		Ocimum gratissimum	Ram tulsi
174.	Sweet Basil	Ocimum sanctum	Tulsi
175.		Oenanthe Javanica	Komprek
176.		Oldenlandia diffusa	Lin marei
177.		Opuntia dillenii	Meipokpi
178.		Oxalis debilis	Ingkhol yensil
179.		Paederia foetida	Oinum
180.		Panax pseudo-ginseng	Ginseng
181.		Pandanus fertidus	Lam ketuki
182.		Pandanus odoratissimus	Ketuki
183.		Papaver Somniferrum	Kani Pambi
184.		Partcia roxburghii	Yongchak
185.	Passion Flower	Passiflora edulis	Radhika nachom
186.		Passiflora subpeltata	Kwak thabi
187.		Peristropho bicalyculata	Khuman langthrei
188.		Phlogacanthus thysiflorus	Nongmangkha
189.		Phyllanthus acidus	Kihori
190.	Emblic myrobalan	Phyllanthus emblica	Heikru
191.	Phyllantus	Phyllanthus simplex	Chakpa Heikru achouba
192.		Piper belle	Kwa mana
193.		Plantago erosa	Yempat
194.		Plectranthus ternifolius	Khoiju
195.	Pagoda tree-white	Plumeria acuminata	Khagi !eihao angouba
196.	Pagoda tree –red	Plumeria rubra	Khagi leihao angangba
197.		Pogostemon parviflorus	Sangbrei
198.		Polygonum	Phakpai
199.		Polygonum barbatum	Yelang
200.		Polygonum chinense	Angom yensil
201.		Primuda	Kengoi
202.	Guava	Psidium guajava	Pungton
203.		Psophocarpus tetragonolobus	Tengnoumanbi
204.	Promegranate	Penica granatum	Kaphoi
205.		Ranunculus sclevatus	Kakyel khujil
206.		Rhus semialata	Heimang
207.	Castor	Ricinus comnunis	Kege
208.		Rumex maritimus	Tarong khongchak
209.		Sccharum officinarum	Chungou
210.		Sagittaria sagittifolia	Koukha
211.	Sandal wood	Santalum album	Cha chandan
212.		Sapindus mukorossi Gaertn.	Kekru
213.		Saraceasoca	Ashoka tree

(Contd.)

(Contd. Table 83)

Sl No.	Common Name	Technical Name	Manipuri name
214.		Schizophyllum commune	Kanglayen
215.		Scutellaria discolor	Yennakhat
216.		Sisbania sesban	Chuchurangmei
217.		Solanum Xanthocarpum	Leipung khanga
218.		Spondias pinnata	Heining
219.		Stellaria media	Yerrum keirum
220.		Syzygium jambos Linn. (Alston).	Gulapjat
221.	Marigold	Tagetes erecta	Sanarei athonba
222.		Tamerindus indica	Mangge
223.		Terminalia arjuna	Kekru
224.		Terminalia arjuna	Mayokpha
225.	Teak	Tectona grandis	Chingsu
226.	Yellow oleander	Thevetia nevviifolia	Utonglei
227.		Toona ciliata M. Roem	Tairel
228.		Vanguirea Spinosa	Heibi
229.		Vitex negrendo	Urik shibi
230.		Wendilandia glabrata	Pheija
231.		Xylosma longifolia	Nong leisang
232.		Zanthxylum alatum Roxb	Mukthrubi
233.		Zanthoxylum rhetsa	Ngang
234.		Zingiber cassumunar	Tekhao yaikhu
235.	Garlic	Zingiber officinale	Shing
236.		Zizania latifolia	Ishing kambong
237.		Zizyphus mauritiana	Boroi

Rice Flake (Chengpak)

Preparation of Chengpak

Rice Flake popularly known as 'Chengpak' in Manipur and other state in the north-eastern region is a staple food of the people and is used in ritual ceremony. It is a wholesome food and has good nutritional value. Chengpak can be taken in different forms viz, raw, fried, soaked and it also can be taken by mixing together with milk, sugar and banana (known as Fola). The only raw material required is paddy. They can earn Rs. 200/- in a day and so their annual income is Rs. 72,000/-.

The equipments required for making the rice flake are:

- Rice flaking machine also known as the Pauda Machine
- Large Khang (a large frying pan)
- Oven (a large one)
- Large bucket, tub, etc.
- Cane basket, Yangkok (a large rounded and shallow cane basket used to make out the husk).

Process

The main steps are:

- drenching or dipping the paddy in order to take out the floated paddy husk.
- boiling the paddy for an hour and let it cool down.
- taking out the soaked paddy in heated khang.
- milling of dried paddy to flatten rice.
- cleaning with the help of yangkok.

Machinery

The only machinery required is the Chengpak making machine. Besides, khang and heating facility are required.

Kabok

Kabok is made from paddy and flatten rice. It is a staple food in north-eastern region. It is a low cost wholesome food and has good nutritional value. It can be taken in differnt forms with sesame, sugar and salt. It is used in ritual ceremony. They can earn Rs. 200/- (approx.) a day and so their annual income is Rs.72, 000/-

Types of Kabok

1. Kabok Akhingba or Sana Kabok (mixed with sugar)
2. Kabok Muri (mixed with salt)
3. Konok Kabok
4. Kabok Laloo
5. Thoiding Kabok
6. Kabok Kangsubi

Raw Materials

The only raw material required is paddy. Besides, flatten rice, sesame, sugar and salt.

Equipments Required

1. Oven (large and small)
2. Medium size earthen pots
3. Large Khang (a large frying pan)
4. Sand
5. Firewood

6. Cane Basket
7. A wire guage
8. Yangkok (a large rounded and shallow cane basket used to extract paddy husk).

Process

Main steps of Kabok Akhingba

1. frying the Chengpak Apoomba (not so beaten rice) to the earthen pots.
2. taking out the sand with the help of wire gauge.
3. mixing with the warm boiled sugar and making it in different shapes and sizes.

Main steps of Kabok Muri

1. mixing of the not so beaten rice with salt.
2. frying in the earthen pots.
3. extracting the sand with the help of wire guage.

Main steps of Konok Kabok

1. frying the paddy in the earthen pots.
2. extracting the sand with the help of the wire guage.
3. extracting the paddy husk with the help of Yangkok.
4. mixing with boiled sugar and make in different shapes and sizes.

Main steps of Laloo

1. grinding the Konok Kabok into powder.
2. mixing the grounded ones with the boiled sugar.
3. making in different shapes and sizes.

Main steps of Kabok Kangsubi

1. frying of the black sesame in a pan.
2. mixing the fried sesame with the boiled sugar.
3. making in different shapes and sizes.

Main steps of Thoiding Kabok are

1. taking out the not so fried kabok.
2. mixing with boiled sugar and fried sesame.

Machinery: The only machinery required is the Chengpak making machine or Pauda machine.

Baked gram

Baking of gram also known, as Hawai Angouba is one of the main sources of income of the Manipur State. Baking of gram consists of Soya bean, dry pea and grams, which is a staple food of the rural population. It is a low cost and has a good nutritional value. It is taken in different forms viz., mixing with mustard oil and grinding. So, their per capita income is Rs 84,000/ -approximately.

Materials Required are : Gram, Soya bean, Dried pea, sand, khang (a large, frying pan), cane basket, small wire gauge, firewood, mustard oil, oven, broom

Process

The main steps are: -

1. Making the fire with firewood
2. Heating the khang with sand with some drops of mustard oil in order to make a shining color of the gram
3. Frying the grains in the khang with the help of broom
4. Taking out the grain after baking

Agarbati (Dhup)

As branded agarbati is costly, the local people buy the local made agarbati which is made manually. Dhup making is one of the main sources of income of the rural population of the Manipur State. It is an essential item in ritual ceremony and is used in many households in everyday life. The local made agarbati is made of 'Mengkruk'(a scented crystal), charcoal, water and an imported scented brownish powder.

Materials Required

1. Powdered Mekruk
2. Scented Powder
3. Charcoal Powder
4. Water
5. Bamboo Chips

Process

The main steps are:-

1. Cutting the bamboo chips into fine sticks which is about 6 inches long.
2. Making a paste by mixing together with powdered Mekruk, charcoal powder and scented powder in the same amount.

3. Rolling of the fine stick with the paste.
4. Rolling with the scented powder.

Machinery : Sharp knife, a wooden frame or a small table, a plate, a grinder

Their per capita income is Rs. 30,000/-(apprx.)

BANKINGAND FINANCE

Finance is the key to investment and hence to the process of growth. In Manipur in 1999 only 86 branches are found operating, some "nominally" and some "effectively". 16 belongs to the State Bank of India and its Associates. 41 are branches of the nationalised banks, 29 are branches of the Regional Rural Banks. 51 are operating in rural areas. 14 are operating in semi-urban areas while 21 in the urban areas. The emerging irksome atmosphere of undesirable law and order prevailing in the rural and hill areas has largely occasioned the "sorry state of affairs" of gradual disappearance of banks. This is bad for the banks and worse for the economy.

The population per bank is fairly high. It is 28,384 in 1999 as against 8445 of Himachal Pradesh and All India Average of 15,070. Secondly, the Credit-Deposit Ratio is only 41.7% as against 68.5% in Andhra Pradesh and 93% in Tamil Nadu. In other words, the extent of credit-deployment for every unit of resource raised is fairly low. Thirdly, the per capita credit was only Rs.693 in Manipur as against Rs. 50,381 of Chandigarh and Rs.4,270 of kerala. What is possibly required at the programme of training on "Banking, Finance, Project Planning and Management".

Highlights of Banking in Manipur (1998-99)

1.	Number of bank branches	86
2.	Population per Bank	28,384
3.	Credit-Deposit Ratio (%)	41.7
4.	Per Capita Credit	Rs. 693
5.	Direct Finance to Farmers (up to 1998-99)	Rs. 19.09 crores
6.	Finance to Small Scale Units	Rs. 40.16 crores
7.	Recovery performance of the Manipur State Co-operative Bank (1998-99)	4%

PINEAPPLE

Pineapples are available for almost 8 months a year in Manipur. The present pineapple cultivated area is about 10,000 hectares with an annual yield of 70,000 MT. Both the two most-sought-after varieties of pineapple, viz. Kew (big size) and Queen (small size) are produced in commercial scale. packed toffee, whereas the Queen variety is most suitable for preparation of juice, pulp and squash. The 8-month availability of pineapples in Manipur makes the State highly advantageous for processing and export, the most striking specially being of the Kew variety for its tantalizing taste and flavour. There are huge demands of the products in and outside the Country. (see plate- 388, 399)

PASSION FRUIT

Passion fruit, both as fresh and in processed form like juice and concentrates, has excellent market world-wide because of its unique taste and flavour. Production of passion fruits is very limited in the world. Besides Equador, Brazil, Columbia, Australia, etc., India is one of the few producers of passion fruit in the world. Due to the specific agro-climatic condition required, the growth of passion fruit is limited even within India. The main growing region for passion fruits in India are Manipur, Mizoram, and Nagaland. (see plate-389)

In Manipur, passion fruit grows naturally. Large scale cultivation and farming has started recently. Both yellow and purple varieties are available in Manipur. Cultivation in large scales is now in the Senapati, Tamenglong, Chandel Churachandpur, Ukhrul, Thoubal and Bishnupur districts. The fruits can be harvested throughout the year depending upon the time of plantation. The APENDA has set up one model organic farming project for passion fruit at Mao of Senapati Districts by transferring the existing farm in about 10 hectares through one NGO, namely "Good Samaritan Social Service".

GINGER

Manipur produces large quantities of ginger suitable for processing of dry ginger, oil and oleoresin. A ready to serve drinks (RTS) general known as ginger lime - ginger and lime mixed (1:3) - has a good potential and demand in Manipur and the outside. (see plate-381)

MANIPUR TRADITIONAL LIQUOR

Manipur's traditional liquor generally called "Yu" is known for its quality comparable to any other best quality hard alcoholic drinks like Vodka. This local alcohol is manufactured by distillation of fermented rice in a traditional method with other ingredients mixed during the fermentation. There is a good scope for setting up distilleries for "Yu" and packaging them attractively for a wider outside market.

MUSHROOMS

A new thrust area is cultivation and processing of Mushroom. There is vast scope for commercial cultivation of mushrooms in the State which offers ideal weather conditions for mushroom cultivation throughout the year. Apart from the indigenous species, other suitable varieties of mushrooms for cultivation in the State are : *Agaricus bisporus* (Button mushrooms), *Agaricus bitorquis, Pleuratus flabellatus, Pleurutus Sajor-Caju, Pleuratus Ostreatus.* (see plate-26)

The State is having favourable climatic conditions for growing mushrooms. Wild varieties of mushrooms grow abundantly and some of such mushrooms are edible. Pleurotus and Agaricus mushroom varieties can be grown throughout the year in this State. Similarly other varieties such as, Auricularia Auricula (UCHINA), Schizphyllum commune (KANGLAYEN), Letimula edodes (THANGJIYEN), Volvariella SPP (CHARUYEN), etc. can also be cultivated. Substrate for cultivation of mushrooms are available locally except few chemicals that are to be procured from other states. Few varieties, which can be cultivated at normal conditions are given below:

	Varieties	*Season*
1.	Agaricus bisporus (Button Mushrooms)	December - March
2.	Agaricus bitorquis	February - April/August-October
3.	Pleurotus Flabellatus	April - July
4.	Pleurotus Sajor - Caju	August - November
5.	Pleurotus Ostreatus	December - March

BAMBOO AND BAMBOO SHOOTS:

Bamboo although not cultivated systematically, grow in wild abundantly along the low altitude hill areas where the rainfall is high. About 3,218 sq. kms. area are covered with bamboo forest mainly by Melocana bambusoides sp. (Moubi) in the reserved, protected and unclassed forest. The Forest Department, Government of Manipur has carried out survey of bamboo stock and growing stock of bamboo to determine the average yield per annum, as given below:

Table-92 Showing area and production of bamboos in Manipur

Sl. No	*Name of Block*	*Geographical area (sq. kms.)*	*Total Bamboo area (sq. kms.)*	*Qty. Of bamboo in lakh tonnes*	*Annual yield calculated on growing stick (in lakh tonnes)*
1.	Thanlon	1238.40	387.00	10.14	1.69
2.	Henglep	637.26	206.08	4.63	0.77
3.	Nungba	1465.44	278.14	13.89	2.28
4.	Tipaimukh	789.48	278.64	7.92	1.32
5.	Jiribam	309.60	36.12	0.70	0.12
6.	Tamenglong	1083.60	283.80	5.09	0.85
	Total:	5523.78	1470.28	42.37	7.03

Source : Forest Department, Government of Manipur.

The available resources of bamboo and bamboo shoots (see plate-377) are yet to be commercially utilised fully in Manipur. It is mainly consumed at present in the construction of houses, mat and baskets etc. About 20-30 MT of bamboo shoots are consumed annually for the production of canned bamboo shoots. Keeping in view the existing resources and its utilisation, there is still a good scope for commercial utilisation of bamboo in the following sectors:

Food Processing Sector

The average food value of bamboo shoot is given below:

Moisture	88.80 %
Protein	3.90 %
Fat	0.50%
Minerals	1.10%
Carbohydrates	5.70%
Calorific value	43.00 kcal.

With the high moisture content, Bamboo shoots can be processed into the following products:

(a) Canned Bamboo shoots:
   (i) In brine
   (ii) In curried vegetable
   (iii) In syrups
(b) Bamboo shoot candies
(c) Bamboo shoot chutney
(d) Bamboo shoot sweet pickles
(e) Fermented bamboo shoots (Locally named as Soibum and Soidon)
(f) Bamboo shoot powder

There is a good demand of the bamboo shoot products (orient food) in the local and export markets, specially, in countries namely Japan, Singapore, China, Thailand, Hongkong and U.K. etc. It is one of the prospective areas for investment.

RUBBER

Rubber Plantation under Forest Department, Manipur started in 1977-78 in Jiribam area covering about 938 Ha.

Potential Area: Jiribam area is, in fact, a non-traditional area for the Rubber plantation. However, due to prevalence of optimum climate, edaphic conditions required for successful growth of the rubber, Jiribam has got good potential for undertaking plantation of rubber in a large commercial scale. Besides, there is a good transport facility to connect the area with good markets of Rubber.

The outlying areas of Jiribam town are quite good potential areas for growing rubber trees. Plantations in a large scale can be taken up in areas on both the sides of Man Bahadur Road as far as Choudhurikhal. Special targets to utilise abandoned jhum areas in a productive manner by way of rubber plantation can be set and achieved. The higher the investment, the higher would be the financial returns.

Production: So far, a total of 15,000 nos. of Rubber trees were planted under tapping under half spiral alternate daily system (1/2 s d/2 system). All the mature areas were not put under tapping because of many factors such as non-availability of mature and tappable trees at regular spacing. The production of raw rubber is maximum during the dry season in Jiribam (Sep to January).

Scope for future cultivation: There is quite a good scope for cultivation of rubber in Jiribam area. In general, rubber trees can be put under tapping after 7 years of plantation and the financial returns would outpace the investment once tapping/production of raw rubber commences. As per Rubber Board Index expenditure norm, around Rs. 40,000/- per Ha. is the expenditure upto 7th Year of plantation and taking an average yield of 1000 kg of raw rubber per Hectare and market price (conservative figure) of Rs. 40/- per kg, the return would be to the tune of Rs. 40,000/- per Hectar. In other words, the investment made during the first 6-7 years may be said to have been recovered in the first year of tapping and production. Since rubber trees can be put under effective tapping for 25-30 years, the total return per Ha would be quite high.

Soil, Rainfall, etc.: Rubber trees required deep and well drained soil of lateritic type. It also requires humid, equable climate (21 to 35°C) and fairly well distributed annual rainfall of 200 cm for optimum growth.

Rubber Plantation in Jiribam was taken up by State Forest Department with the following objectives:

- to generate employment.
- to put abandoned jhum/degraded land under productive use.
- to demonstrate a viable alternative to shifting cultivation.
- to open avenue for new rubber based industrial ventures and,
- to earn revenue.

Rubber plantation related activities provided immense benefit to nearby people in particular to the people of Uchathol, Harinagar, Khasia, Jarolpokpi, Boiroikhal, Sabughat, Aglapur, etc. Even now also, quite a number of people from these areas are getting employment either in plantation works or in raw rubber production works. Besides, many abandoned jhum/degraded lands have been put under productive use and the viability of rubber plantation has been shown. With production of raw rubber, rubber-based industries can be set up to uplift the economy of the people.

Rubber plantation is also environment-friendly. With the nearby people fully aware of the economic benefits specially in the form of assured employment, there is a bright prospect of rubber plantation in Jiribam area. The only thing is that the people need to be involved in a committed manner. The economic lot of the people can be uplifted in a marked way by undertaking rubber plantation.

IDENTIFICATION OF FEASIBLE INDUSTRIAL PROJECTS IN MANIPUR

On the basis of the various agro-horticultural resources available in Manipur, the North Eastern Industrial consultants (NECON) had identified the following feasible Food Processing Industries based on the locally available raw materials:

Sl. No.	*Proposed project*	*Production Capacity*	*Estimated project cost*
1.	Fruits & vegetables Processing	80 MT/day	Rs. 405.00 lakhs
2.	Ginger dehydration and Oleoresin	33 MT/day	Rs. 750.00 lakhs
3.	Spices processing plant	5 MT/day	Rs. 284.00 lakhs
4.	Integrated Mushroom processing Plant	15 MT/day	Rs. 330.00 lakhs
5.	Lime Ginger (RTS) Plant	100 lakh bottles of 200 ml. per annum	Rs. 318.14 lakhs
6.	Agri Export Zone for Passion Fruit	2 MT/Hour	Rs. 2,784.00 lakhs
7.	Manipuri Traditional liquor Plant (Distillery)	9 lakhs lt./annum	Rs. 1,768.87 lakhs
8.	Integrated Pineapple Concentration Plant	50 MT/day	Rs. 9,005.00 lakhs
9.	Floriculture		Rs. 285.92 lakhs
10.	Custom Farming	1,000 Ha.	Rs. 377.00 lakhs
Total			Rs. 16,307.93 lakhs

Table-93

Showing production capacity of some industrial units

Sl. No	Processing Unit	Sector	Type	Capacity MT/annum	Type of products
1.	MAGFRUIT	Hort. & Soil Conservation, Govt of Manipur	SSI Unit	240	Canned fruits and vegetables, fruit syrups, pickles, jam jellies, RTS (Lime-ginger) cordials, squashes, candies, etc
2.	HEIRANG	Co-operative	-do-	240	-do-
3.	WAIFRU	N.G.O.	-do-	240	-do-
4.	RATNA FRUITS	PRIVATE	Cottage Scale	50	Squashes, jam
5.	LIKLA	-do-	-do-	50	Squashes, RTS, jam, jelly (Fruit based)
6.	SANA	-do-	-do-	50	Squashes, pickle, jelly, jam
7.	MANIFRU	-do-	-do-	50	-do-
8.	HILL FRUITS	-do-	-do-	50	Squashes, jam, etc.

MARKET POTENTIAL

The disadvantageous geographical situation and severity of the terrain have been standing in the way of industrial development and trade particularly of the Food Processing Industries which can thrive only through value addition and cost efficiency. It is high time to explore this untapped sector as processed fruits, vegetables, mushrooms, ginger, spices and rice etc. are having good demand in the local and export market. At present, many of such processed fruits and vegetables are imported to this State from other States and neighbouring countries through Myanmar. At the same time some of the units in this sector have been established and are being run successfully, catering to the local demand. This indicates existing potential available in this sector.

The most striking area is the production of pineapple (Kew-variety), having special taste and flavour. There has been demand of such pineapple products from MAGFRUIT by the C.I.S. countries. The MAGFRUIT had exported 168 MT of canned pineapple products to the erstwhile U.S.S.R. from the year 1983-84 to 1985-86. As the units are in the SSI and the cottage scale sectors, they are often in a disadvantageous condition for continuous tapping of such export markets. Moreover, these units are hardly kept in operation due to various constraints like inadequate working capital, non-availability of quality control system as well as inability to link up with the big marketing agencies in the cosmopolitan cities like Kolkata, Chennai, Delhi, Mumbai, etc. Once the sufficient production of such processed fruits and vegetables is made (with strict maintenance or quality, packaging and reasonable price), there is a big marketing potential not only in the local market, but also in major cities of our country and even export to the countries like Saudi Arabia, Kuwait, Dubai, Singapore, Nepal, Bangladesh, U.S.A., Germany, etc. Setting up of the identified projects based on modern technology and in the medium/large scale sector are most essential for the development of food processing industries in the State.

FRUIT PROCESSING

Temperate fruits like Peach, Pear and Apricots are lying ignored in the semi temperate zone in the North, North East and Eastern parts of the state for want of transport and market. Sub-tropical fruits like Pineapple, Orange, Lemon and Banana have the immediate potential for export. Production of these fruits are limited to the tune of 95,000-1,00,000 tones per annum. This industry is saturated at the level of domestic consumption due to lack of proper support. The only alternative to exploit these potentials is to provide special transport subsidy and assured market for the existing production units on the one hand and provide technology for production of juice concentrates, and Banana Butter on the other.

CANE AND BAMBOO PRODUCTION PROJECT (CBPP)

Manipur has 15 varieties of bamboo and 5 varieties of cane and some of these are widely exploited by traditional communities on selective basis. The bamboo forests cover of Manipur is nearly 3,000 sq. km. and the bamboo production is around 2 lakh tonnes annually. There is ample scope for cultivation and economic utilisation of cane and bamboo in many folds in the Manipur State to provide employment to the masses. New applications can open up the possible use of this rich genetic resource in a much wider manner than at any time in the past. Some of the varieties of bamboo found in Manipur are as follows :-

Sl. No.	*Local Name*	*Botanical name*
1.	Tenwa	Arundinaria callosa
2.	Watang khoi	Bambusa vulgaris
3.	Saneibi	Bambusa balcoa
4.	Khok	Bambusa khasiana
5.	Utang	Bambusa pallida
6.	Pokshang	Cepholostachyum
7.	Unan	Dendrocalamus strictus
8.	Uei	Dendrocalamus sericeous
9.	Longnga	Dendrocalamus flagellifer
10.	Meiribop	Dendrocalamus hamiltonii
11.	Moubi	Melocanna bambusoides
12.	Nat	Teinostachyum wightii

Cane and bamboo craft industry is covered under Handicrafts Industry within the ambits of encouragement/development plans of the office of the Development Commissioner (H/C), Ministry of Textiles, Government of India and also the Department of Commerce and Industries, Government of Manipur. Among the crafts/trades under Handicrafts Industry, cane and bamboo craft is the most wide-spread one throughout the State and becomes most employment generating and lively-hood earning craft because of availability of sufficient raw materials and local market demands including household consumption needs in addition to demands from outside the State including overseas.

The important cane and bamboo prducts in Manipur are as follows:-

1. Baskets like items for packaging, measuring, storing, carrying of goods, washing and fishing etc.
2. Mats like items for ceiling, partition, fencing, sitting and walling etc.
3. Fishing traps/tools
4. Furniture like side table, chairs, sofa sets, stool/mora etc.
5. Walking stick.
6. Umbrella handle.
7. Trays.
8. Decorative pieces like table lamp, wall hanging, ash tray, flower pot, flower and other models, etc.
9. Caps/hats.
10. Ply board(bamboo laminated)
11. Tooth pick/Agarbati sticks.
12. Musical instruments like flutes.
13. Suit case.
14. House construction materials like bamboo strips/slivers, rope, etc.

These items are in different designs according to the varying customs of different tribes of the State. The number of artisans engaged in cane and bamboo activity in Manipur is estimated at 1.50 lakhs approximately.

Trained Artisans in Cane and Bamboo trade.

There are many trained Artisans / Entrepreneurs in the Cane and Bamboo trade in the State. The number of trained artisans who passed out from the departmental training centres, Mobile training centres and other centres run by NGOs/ individual agencies as of 31st March, 2001 are as follows :-

Concept of the Cane and Bamboo Production Project

Taking advantage of the potentials for further development on cane and bamboo crafts due to having sufficient raw materials resources, skilled manpower resources, high market demand from within and outside the State and also keen interest from the Indian Chamber of Commerce(ICC), Confederation of Indian Industries (CII), NEDFI etc. for investment/buying of handicrafts products from the North East, the Government of Manipur take up the cane and bamboo project as a joint venture by setting up 10 units for Cane and Bamboo production in the State - one each at District Head Quarters

Table-94

Sl. No.	Name of District	Departmental training Centre	Deptt. Mobile Training Centres	NGO /Individual agencies	Total	Grand Total
1	Imphal East	57	98	30	128	185
2	Imphal West	-	412	64	476	476
3	Thoubal	90	32	-	32	122
4	Bishnupur	9	173	51	224	233
5	Senapati	-	1	36	37	37
6	Ukhrul	-	9	15	24	24
7	Churachandpur	64	16	42	58	122
8	Chandel	-	26	15	41	41
9	Tamenglong	-	-	-	-	-
	Total	**220**	**767**	**253**	**1020**	**1240**

and one at Block Head Quarters, Jiribam of Imphal East District, by acquiring improved type machinery.

Main objectives of the Cane and Bamboo Production Project are as follows:-

- Employment generation for unemployed youth.
- Enhancement of income to the families of those youth.
- Creation of business environment between the State and the rest of the country.
- Revenue earnings of the State.

The project consist of 10 units at the cost of Rs. 16.00 lakhs each and the total project cost was Rs. 160.00 lakhs, of which capital cost shall be Rs. 110.00 lakhs. The targets of Annual Sales/turnover shall be Rs. 208.00 lakhs for 1st year of operation, Rs. 234.00 lakhs for 2nd year and Rs. 260.00 lakhs for 3rd year and onwards. The project shall give employment to 800 persons directly. It will also create indirect employment to bamboo farmers/suppliers/traders/artisans/entrepreneurs who may use the machinery facilities of the units under the project.

The competitive advantage of the project over other cane and bamboo production units in the State shall be in terms of volume of production, quality and price because of the installation of improved type machinery.

The Implementation work of the Project shall be entrusted to either capable/deserving individuals or NGOs or Co-operative Societies as promoters. One such party for each units shall be selected by the State Government. Other funding agencies like the North Eastern Council (NEC), NEDFI CII and ICC will also participate.

The funding pattern of the project is proposed as below:-

• Promoter's contribution @ 12.5%	• Rs. 20.00 Lakh
• NEC's equity @25%	• Rs. 40.00 Lakh
• Investor's/NEDFI's equity@25%	• Rs. 40.00 Lakh
• Bank/NEDFI loan@ 37.5%	• Rs. 60.00 Lakh
Total	• **Rs. 160.00 Lakh**

State Government's role in the project shall be as under

- Arrangement for availability of land, if the promoters do not have sufficient land
- State Govt. guarantee, if necessary, in addition to the promoters' co-lateral security.

- Selection of capable/deserving private promoters by issuing Notice through printed media, TV/AIR for calling/inviting applications from individuals/NGOs/Co-operative Societies.
- Monitoring and Evaluation.
- Loan recovery
- Creation of security environment.
- Extension of Incentive packages as escort services.
- Any other assistance, wherever possible, for speedy and successful implementation of the project.

Under the UNDP assisted cane and bamboo project, integrated gene pool banks, tissue culture and plant multiplication nurseries will be set up by the Government of India at identified locations of Manipur. By supplying necessary inputs from these centres, cultivation of bamboo and cane of selected species according to the local needs will be taken up through the selected farmers. Procurement and supply of required quality and quantity of bamboo and cane materials may be made through contract suppliers from these farmers as well as local resources. This system will also create employment to the people.

Marketing arrangement

Marketing arrangements for selling the finished products as well as semi-processed raw materials may be taken up in many ways or through many channels as follows:-

- To sell direct at the production centre itself;
- To sell by opening Emporia/Sales out-lets at the main market places of the districts;
- To sell/supply to the State Handloom and Handicrafts Development
- Corporation/North Eastern Handloom and Handicrafts Development Corporation;
- To supply to handicrafts traders/exporters;
- To sell by participating Local/State/Regional/National Level Exhibitions/ Trade Fairs etc.;
- To supply to State Govt. Departments/Offices.

All the available media, trade fairs, web sites and e-commerce may be tapped to bring the benefits of a changed market place to the production unit.

KOUNA CRAFT PRODUCTION PROJECT (KCPP)

The Kauna industry

In Manipur, since time immemorial this plant is well adapted for making mats, cushions etc as a source of earning for rural landless farmers. This also confines in the domestic markets only. Reed Mat weaving once an ancient vocation, as an indispensable item of furnishing the household now attracts a huge foreign market where the state is lagging behind. Some farmers and entrepreneurs have started to participate in foreign market which, however, is very limited and cannot claim as a viable industry to compete with international market. There is a good scope for expansion of this market.

The Kouna, (*Scirpus lacustries*.Linn.) matting reed, a gregarious weed belonging to the Cypericeae is found at large in shallow lakes and marshy land of Manipur Valley where paddy cultivation are not suited at all. The plants grow wildly in the marshy land, ponds, canals, along the river and lake beaches. From time immemoral, these stalks, locally called Kouna, after drying have been being used in making mats/mattresses by the people living mostly in the valley areas of the Manipur State. Kouna craft making mats/mattresses in different sizes, short and long is taken up by traditional artisans for economic earnings. The craft has now been taken up as a gainful economic activity by artisans/entrepreneurs in some areas in the State due to having high market demands. The plants are planted especially for economic utilisation in the marshy paddy fields, canals, along the submerged river and lake shores.

Kouna growing areas in abundance are as under:

I. Imphal West District:
   (1) Konjeng Leikai
   (2) Mayang Imphal.

II. Imphal East District:
   (1) Thambal Khong.
   (2) Kongba
   (3) Singjamei Kshetrileikai.
   (4) Khongman.

III. Bishnupur District:
   (1) Oinam.
   (2) Keinou
   (3) Thinungei
   (4) Phubala.
   (5) Sunusiphai.
   (6) Moirang.

IV. Thoubal District
   (1) Khangabok
   (2) Nongpok Sekmai.
   (3) Shikhong.

(4) Langmeithek.
(5) Ukhongshang.
(6) Chairen (East).
(7) Kakching.

(a) Kouna craft concentration areas are as under:

I. Imphal West District
(1) Konjeng Leikai
(2) Keisamthong.
(3) Mayang Imphal Bengun.

II. Imphal East District
(1) Thambal Khong
(2) Kongba Nandeibam Leikai
(3) Singjamei Kshetrileika
(4) Khongman.

III. Bishnupur District
(1) Moirang.

IV. Thoubal District
(1) Khangabok.
(2) Shikhong.
(3) Langmeithek.
(4) Ukhongshang.
(5) Chairen (East)
(6) Kakching.

Kouna craft industry is also covered under handicrafts industries with encouragement from the Ministry of Textiles, Government of India and the Government of Manipur. Kouna products have not only local market demands but also demands from other Indian states and the foreign countries. These products are exported to countries like U.K., Netherland, German, France, UAE and Switzerland, etc. by traders/exporters/ NGOs. Some trading firms having business interest in Latin American countries have made inquires to the Department of Commerce and Industries, Manipur for kouna products especially for Cushion. The surging demands for kouna products surpass the current production in the State. As such, there is ample scope for large scale production of kouna items.

Some items of kouna products are :-

- Cushion of different sizes.
- Mat/Mattress of different sizes
- Stool (local name - Mora)

Concept of kouna craft production project:

The Government of Manipur is taking up a kouna craft production project as a joint venture with Indian Chamber of Commerce (ICC), Confederation of Indian Industries (CII), NEDFI etc. by setting up 10 units for kouna production in the following suitable identified areas :-

- Imphal East District – Kongba, Khongman, Nandeibam Leikai
- Imphal West – Konjeng Leikai, Mayang Imphal Bengun
- Thoubal District- Khangabok, Shikhong, Chairel (East)
- Bishnupur District- Moirang. Keinou. Phubala.

The main objectives of the kouna craft production project are as follows:-

- Employment Generation for unemployed youth.
- Enhancement of income to the families for those youth.
- Creation of business environment between the State and the rest of the country.
- Revenue earnings of the State.
- Foreign exchange earnings of the country.

The project shall consist of 10 units at the cost of Rs. 20.00 lakhs each and the total project cost shall be Rs. 200.00 lakhs, of which capital cost shall be Rs. 60.00 lakhs only. The expected annual sales/turnover shall be Rs. 288.00 lakhs for 1st year of operation, Rs. 324.00 lakhs for the 2nd year and Rs. 360.00 lakhs for the 3rd year and onwards. The project shall give employment to 560 persons under production programme and 500 persons under plantation programme.

For availability of sufficient and regular flow of supply of raw materials, large scale plantation programme needs to be taken up. Under this programme, 500 farmers from the suitable identified areas shall be selected and given loan @ Rs. 10,000/- per farmer for plantation of Kouna. They shall supply the raw materials (dry kouna) to the production units. 50 farmers shall tied up with each production unit which shall collect/recover the loan amount from the farmers by equal annual instalments for pay back to the investors. The farmers may adjust the loan instalments against their sales proceeds received from the production units.

Under plantation programme, the following villages around Loktak Lake and Ithai Barrage and other areas are identified:

I. **Bishnupur District**

1 Keinou

2 Thinungei

3 Phubala.

4 Sunusiphai.

5 Moirang

6 Ithai

7 Khordak

II. Thoubal District

1 Khangabok.

2 Nongpok Sekmai.

3 Chairen (East).

4 Mayang Imphal

5 Tera

6 Mondum.

The funding pattern of the project is as follows :-

Promoters' contribution @10%	Rs. 20.00 Lakhs
Investors/NEC/NEDFI's equity @ 20%	Rs. 40.00 Lakhs
Investors/Bank/NEDFI's loan @ 70%	Rs. 140.00 Lakhs
Total	**Rs. 200.00 Lakhs**

State Government's role in the project shall be as follows :-

- Arrangement for availability of land, if the promoters don not have sufficient land.
- State Government guarantee, if necessary, in addition to the promoter's collateral security.
- Selection of capable/deserving private promoters by issuing Notice through printed media, TV/AIR for calling/inviting applications from individuals/ NGOs/ Co-operative Societies.
- Monitoring and Evaluation
- Loan recovery.
- Creation of security environment.
- Extension of Incentive packages as escort services.
- Any other assistance, wherever possible, for speedy and successful implementation of the project.

Marketing arrangement

Marketing arrangements for selling the finished kouna products may be taken up in many ways or through many channels as follows:-

- To sell direct at the production centre itself;

- To sell by opening Emporia/Sales out-lets at the main market places of the districts;
- To sell / supply to the State Handloom and Handicrafts Development Corporation / North Eastern Handloom and Handicrafts Development Corporation;
- To supply to handicrafts traders/exporters;
- To sell by participating Local/State/Regional/National Level Exhibitions/ Trade Fairs etc.;
- To supply to State Govt. Departments/Offices.

Utilisation of agriculture waste

Rice Husk is one in Manipur which is wasted and disposed of in bulk by burning into ashes. The technology of converting this agriculture bye-products into a high-tech industry for producing Coarse Grain Rice Husk Board is the need of the hour.

Spices

Black Pepper is one which is still ignored but can be converted into a low volume high value Industry in Manipur. Manipur having varied agro-climatic condition, can grow tropical crops like Black Pepper in and along South Eastern, Southern plains bordering the Myanmar. For that matter Jiri and Moreh are the naturally located nodal areas to start with. Large Cardamom is another crop of high potential for it can be cultivated as an undergrowth along with *Alnus nepalensis* locally known as Pareng. Pareng is a unique non-leguminous tree which is endowed with a capacity of converting atmospheric nitrogen into nitrates by virtue of which the soil fertilities under the tree is never exhausted. Rather the fertility is enhanced by the leaf falls, the organic way. Pareng is a traditional forest in almost all the hill ranges of the state.

ORCHIDS

Nature has gifted Manipur with more than 600 varieties of Orchids. For all practical purposes, they are grouped into four types according to their flowering seasons. They are winter, spring, summer and autumn flowering orchids. YERUMLEI is one variety of choice that flowers long in winter. SAMJIREI and MAIBILEI are Spring flowering varieties of long duration. SAMJIREI ATHONBI and KHONGUPLEI are summer blooming varieties. KWAKLEI is one that blooms in autumn continuously for 3-4 months. They are popular and famous for their durability and beauty. (see plates – 32-44)

This is an area of prioritised towards a commercial production by tissue culture. The Consortium would facilitate technology transfer and awareness programme at the grassroots to abstain from misuse of this rare fortune.

Black scented rice

It is locally known as "Chak-hao-Amubi" in Manipur, meaning thereby Chak=Rice; Hao=delicacies, Amubi= Black; As the name indicates Chak-hao rice in Manipur is confined to serving as delicacy in local feast and festivities. It has high potential for export as it is liked by many South -East and East-Asian countries because of its attractive colour, glutinous and flavour.

Success in investing in Manipur will depend on four factors like: -

- Accurate estimation or at least feasible estimation of the Manipur's potential
- Proper Risk Assessment while investing in Manipur
- Proper understanding of the Indian and Manipur Financial System
- Careful strategic planning backed by thorough research on investment industry

Failure in investing in Manipur can depend on three factors like: -

- Underestimation of Manipur investment intricacies
- Overestimation of investment potential in Manipur
- Complexities and reservations of Indian and Manipur System

One point that investors should understand about investing in India is that India is an investment goldmine for long-term growth. While short term profits may be churned out from time to time but they are not of a penny's worth in the longer run.

PROPOSED PROJECTS

The following projects were proposed by the State Government as feasible projects for Manipur for the years 2009-2010.

But the State Government may like to initiate attracting investment to the tune of Rs. 10,000 -20,000 crores every year. Otheriwse, Manipur will not be able to overcome the deficiencies and the gap. It needs a meticulous planning and networking. The State Government should also consider closure or privatization of sick units, improving the overall managemenmt of the corporations on modern management lines, developing a long –term Industrial and Expoer-Import Policy, encouraging private investment, development of

Sl. No.	Proposed project	Production Capacity	Estimated project cost
1.	Fruits & vegetables Processing	80 MT/day	Rs. 405.00 lakhs
2.	Ginger dehydration and Oleoresin	33 MT/day	Rs. 750.00 lakhs
3.	Spices processing plant	5 MT/day	Rs. 284.00 lakhs
4.	Integrated Mushroom processing Plant	15 MT/day	Rs. 330.00 lakhs
5.	Lime Ginger(RTS) Plant	100 lakh bottles of 200 ml. per annum	Rs. 318.14 lakhs
6.	Agri Export Zone for Passion Fruit	2 MT/Hour	Rs. 2,784.00 lakhs
7.	Manipuri Traditional liquor Plant (Distillery)	9 lakhs lt./annum	Rs. 1,768.87 lakhs
8.	Integrated Pineapple Concentration Plant	50 MT/day	Rs. 9,005.00 lakhs
9.	Floriculture		Rs. 285.92 lakhs
10.	Custom Farming	1,000 Ha.	Rs. 377.00 lakhs
Total			Rs. 16,307.93 lakhs

human resources and capacity building, securing soft loans from international financial institutions like World Banks, speedy completion of the Rail Link, Trans-Asian Highway, development of infrastructure, opening of trade routes through South Asian Countries etc. This will transform the economy of Manipur and neighbouring states.

References

Administrative Staff college of India (2003) Study on 'Reorganization of Manipur.

Ashok K. Lahiri, Saumen Chattopadhyay, O.P. Bohra, E. Bijoy Kumar Singh, 'A Study of State Fiscal Reforms in Manipur, New Delhi; National Institute of Public Finance and Policy.

Basic Statistics of North Eastern Region (2003), Shillong: North Eastern Council.

Agro-Forestry based Farming System as an Alternative to Jhum' (1979), reprinted from the Seminar Proceeding on *Agro-Forestry, Organized by ICAR,* at Imphal, Manipur, May 16-17.

Ahluwalia, B.K. and Ahluwalia, Shashi (1984), *Social Change in* Manipur, New Delhi: Cultural Publishing House.

Ansari, S.A. (1991), Manipur: *Tribal Demography and Socio-economic Development*, Delhi: Daya Publishing House.

Basanta, N,(1998), *Socio-Economic Change in* Manipur *1891-1947*, Imphal: Wangkhai Angom Leikai.

Brown, R, *Statistical Account of Manipur*, 1873.

Burkill, I. H. (ed.), *A Dictionary of the Economic Products of the Malay Peninsula*, Ministry of Agriculture and Co-operatives, Kuala Lumpur, 1966, 2ndedn.

Centre for Monitoring Indian Economy, *Basic Statistic*, Vol. 2, Sept 1991, Mumbai.

Century Fund, New York, 1968.

Chandavarkar, A. (1994), 'Infrastructure Finance: Issues, Institutions and Policies', Policy Research Working paper 1374 The World Bank.

Census, 2001, Series 14, Manipur provisional Population Totals.

Davis, A.W. 'Annual Administration Report of the Manipur State for the Year 1907.

Draft Tenth Five Year Plan 2002-2007 and Annual Plan (2002-03)'.

Directorate of Information and Public Relations(DIPR) – Manipur – Commemoration of 50th Anniversary of India's Independence, 1997.

Department of Planning, Annual Plan -2008-2009 and 2009-2010.

Department of Industry, Annual Plan -2008-2009 and 2009-2010.

East India Human Development Report' (2004) *National Council of Applied Economic Research*, New Delhi: Oxford University Press.

Eichengreen, B. (1994), 'Financing Infrastructure in Developing countries: Lessons from the Railway Age Policy Research' Working Paper 1379, The World Bank.

Final Report TYPSA, Symond and Span, New Delhi.

Governme.it of India, PWD (2001), Institutional Development Strategy.

Government of Manipur, *Economic Review,* Department of Statistics, 1975-76.

Government of Manipur, *Statistical Handbook,* Department of Statistics, 1970.

Government of Manipur, *Statistical Abstract of Manipur,* Department of Statistics, 1967-68.

Gurudas Das, N. Bijoy Singh, C.J. Thomas "Indo-Myanmar Border Trade – Staus, Problems and Potentials, Akansa Publishing House, New Delhi-110059, 2005.

Hoeve, Jakarta, 1981.

Hopkins, H. C. F., *Kew Bull.*, 1994, 49.

Horam, M. (2000), *The Rising* Manipur *Including other North Eastern States*, New Delhi: Manas Publications.

Imperial Gazetteer of Manipur, 1909.

Joshua Thomas (ed) (2001), *Constraints in Development of* Manipur, New Delhi: Regency Publication.

J.B. Bhattacharjee (ed) (1994), *Studies in Economic History of North East India*, Delhi: Har Anand Publications.

J.C. Higgins, 'Administration Report Of the Manipur State for the Year 1909-1910'.

Kanjilal, U. N., Kanjilal, P. C. and Das, A., *Flora of Assam*, Avon, Delhi, 1982, vol. 2, p. 151.

Kalshoven, L. G. E., *The Pests of Crops in Indonesia* (revised and translated by van der Lann, P. A.), Ichtiar Baru-van .

Longvah, T. and Deosthale, Y.G., *Food Chem.*, 1998, 62, 477–481.

Manipur Sericulture Project in India (1997), Final Report submitted to the Mathew, T. (ed.) (1981), *North Eastern Hills Regions of India – Problems and Prospects of Development*. New Delhi: Agricole Publishing Academy.

Mishra, AK (1999), 'An Approximation of Soil Loss in Jhum in North Eastern Region of India', Barapani, Meghalaya, India; ICAR Research Complex for NEH Region, (Unpublished).

Maurice Dobb, *Studies in the development of Capitalism*, International Publication, New York, 1947.

Mohan, V. R. and Janardhanan, K., *Int. J. Food Sci. Nutr.*, 1993, 44, 47–53.

Myrdal Gunnar, *Asian Drama: An Enquiry into the Poverty of Nations*, Twentieth .

National Council of Applied Economic Research, *Economic Report*, 1961, New Delhi.

National Human Development Report (2001). Planning Commission (1963).

Overseas Economic Cooperation Fund', Japan. Imphal; SAPROF team, May.

Planning Department. (2003), Manipur Economic Survey. (1997, 2002), (Directorate of Rural Development and Panchayati Raj).

Planning Commission, Government of India.

Planning Department,Government of Manipur (1997-98), Ninth Five Year Plan and Annual Plan, Planning Department, Draft Annual Plan (2003-2004) Proposals (Write-Up) Vol.-1.

Planning Department April, 2003. Draft Tenth Five Year Plan (2002-07) and Annual Plan (2002-03).

Pakem, B. (1990), *Nationality, Ethnicity and Cultural Identity in North-East India,* New Delhi: Omsons Publications.

Power Sector: Diagnostic studies and Mid- Term recommendations' Centre for Infrastructure Management.

PWD (2001) Strategic Options Study (Final) TYPSA, Symonds and Span Consultants Pvt. Limited.

Robert,Thangjam, M. Damayanti, G. J. Sharma, *Department of Life Sciences, Manipur University, Imphal 795 003, India e-mail: maidam@ rediff mail.com.*

Regional transport Survey summary', The Technical Group for Transport Planning, New Delhi.

Quisumbing, E., Technical Bulletin, Dept. of Agriculture and Natural Resources, Manila, 1951, no. 16.

Report of the Committee on Land Tenure Systems in the North East (1989), New Delhi Planning Commission.

Ray and Alam, Forest Resources in Northeast India.

Ray, B. Datta and Alam K (2002), *Forest Resources in North East India*, Delhi: Omsons Publications.

Suvachittanont, W., Kurashima, Y., Esumi, H. and Tsuda, M., *Food Chem.*, 1996, 55, 359–363.

Sharma, B. D., Hore, D. K. and Salam, J. S., *Indian J. Plant Genet. Res.*, 1993, 6, 171–173.

Salam, J. S., Khuman, M. S. and Singh, M. P., *Curr. Sci.*, 1995, 68, 502.

Salam, J. S., *Agric. Sci. Digest*, 1996, 16, 189–191.

Statistical Handbook of Manipur (2002), *Directorate of Economics and Statistics,* Government of Manipur.

Shukla, S. P. (1997), 'Transforming the Northeast', High Level Commission Report to the Prime Minister, New Delhi.

Swaroop, V. (1994), 'The Public Finance of Infrastructure: Issues and Options',Policy Research Working Paper 1288, The World Bank.

Shimray, U. A. (2001), 'Ethnicity and Socio-Political Assertion: The Manipur Experience.' *Economic and Political Weekly*, 29 September.

Singh, B. (2001).

Singh, K. Roman kumar (1988), "Manipur: An Economic Interpretation (An employment oriented study)", in Singh, Sanajaoba (1988), Manipur *(Past and Present): The heritage and ordeals of civilisation*, Vol.1, History, Polity and Law", New Delhi: Mittar Publication.

Singh, N. Mohendro (2002), *Development Experience in* Manipur, Imphal: Institute of Development Studies.

Setamou, M., Schulthess, F., Gounou, S.Poehling, H. M. and Borgemeister, C., *Environ. Entomol.*, 2000, 29, 516–524.

Tahira, T., Tsuda, M., Wakabayashi, K., Nagao, M. and Sugimura, T., *Gann*, 1984, 75, 889–894.

Tahira, T., Ohgaki, H., Wakabayashi, K., Nagao, M. and Sugimura, T., *Food Chem. Toxicol.*, 1988, 26, 511–518.

Van der Goot, P., *Dierlijke vijanden van djengkol en peteh,* Meded, Algem. Proefst. Landb., 1940, no. 46.

White Paper on Manipur State Finance Department (As laid before the state legislature)' Imphal, July. (2002).

World Bank, *World Development Report*, 1986.

www.ncrwc.nic.in.

http://business.mapsofindia.com/investment-industry/investment-scenario.html.

http://www.censusindia.net.

http://www.censusindia.net/srs21.html.

http://www.indianeconomics.org/material/A-J+11.pdf.

http://www.prb.org/Template.cfm?Section=PRBandtemplate=/ContentManagement/ContentDisplay.cfmandContentID=9665.

http://manipur.nic.in.

http://manipur.nic.in/GOM.htm.

http://investinmanipur.nic.in.

Plate-376: Sericulture Cocoons

Plate -377:Bamboo shoots (Khongkhang village near Moreh)

Plate -378: Yongchak (Tree Bean)

Plate -379 : Tea Plantations in hill districts

Plate -380 : Tea Plantations in hill districts

Plate -381: Ginger

Plates -382 : Various medicinal plants grown in Manipur

Plates -383: Various medicinal plants grown in Manipur

Plates -384: Various medicinal plants grown in Manipur

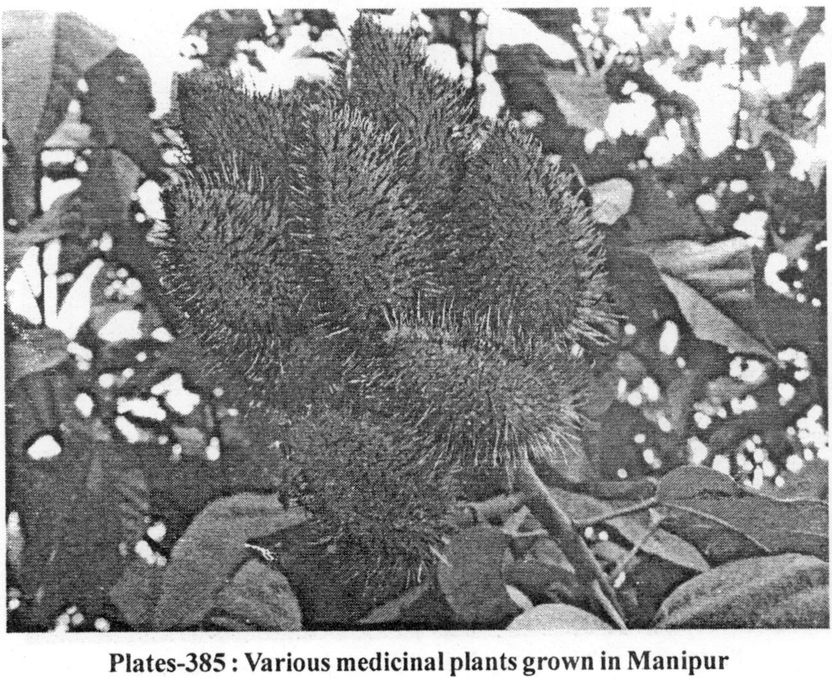

Plates-385 : Various medicinal plants grown in Manipur

Plates-386 : Various medicinal plants grown in Manipur

Plates-387 : Various medicinal plants grown in Manipur

Plates-388: Various medicinal plants grown in Manipur

Plates-389 : Various medicinal plants grown in Manipur

Plates-390: Various medicinal plants grown in Manipur

Plates-391: Various medicinal plants grown in Manipur

Plates-392: Various medicinal plants grown in Manipur

Plates-393: Various medicinal plants grown in Manipur

Plates -394 : Various medicinal plants grown in Manipur

Plates -395 : Various medicinal plants grown in Manipur

Plates -396: Various medicinal plants grown in Manipur

Plate -397: Pine apple cultivation

Plate -398: Passion fruits

Plate -399: People buying pine apples in Thoubal district

Appendix-1

British Political Agents/ Officers in Manipur

Sl.No	Name of the Political Agent	From	To Remarks
1.	Capt. George Gordon	1835	December, 1844
2.	Major. W. McCulloch	December, 1844	August, 1861
3.	Dr. Thomas Dillon	August, 1861	October, 1863
4.	Major . W. McCulloch	October, 1863	12 January, 1867
5.	Dr. R. Brown, FRCSE	13 January, 1867	April, 1871
6.	Major General W.F. Nuthall	April, 1871	May, 1872
7.	Col. Mowbray Thomas	May, 1872	July, 1873
8.	Dr. R. Brown, FRCSE	July, 1873	July, 1876
9.	D.H. Damant	July, 1876	1877
10.	Capt. E.I. Durand	1877	Oct. 1877
11.	Sir James Johnstone	October, 1877	March, 1886
12.	Major Trotter	1 April, 1886	31 July, 1886
13.	A.J. Primose	August, 1886	August, 1887
14.	F. St. Grimwood	August, 1887	February, 1889
15.	A.E. Heath	February, 1889	4 April, 1889
16.	F. St. Grimwood	19 May, 1889	24 March, 1891
17.	H. St. P. John Maxwell	13 September, 1891	22 December, 1892
18.	A. Porteous, ICS	22 December, 1892	2 July, 1894
19.	H. St. P. John Maxwell	2 July, 1894	18 December, 1896
20.	Capt. Henry Walter George Cole	19 December, 1896	3 July, 1897
21.	A. Porteous, ICS	4 July, 1887	3 June, 1898
22.	Capt. Henry Walter George Cole	4 June, 1898	1 July, 1898

(Contd.)

(Contd. Appendix-1)

Sl.No	Name of the Political Agent	From	To Remarks
23.	Major Albert. E. Woods	2 July, 1898	17 December, 1898
24.	H. St. P. John Maxwell	18 December, 1898	22 February, 1902
25.	Major Albert. E. Woods	23 February, 1902	6 December, 1902
26.	H.A. C. Colquhoun ICS	7 December, 1902	29 Jauary, 1903
27.	Major Albert. E. Woods	29 January, 1903	2 July, 1904
28.	H. St. P. John Maxwell	2 July, 1904	16 March, 1905
29.	Major J. Shakespeare	17 March, 1905	23 February, 1908
30.	A.W. Davies ICS	24 February, 1908	16 February, 1909
31.	Col. J. Shakespeare	17 February, 1909	19 March, 1914
32.	Lt. Col. Henry Walter George Cole, CSHA	20 May, 1914	27 May, 1917
33.	John Comyn Higgins, ICS	28 May, 1917	26 December, 1917
34.	William Alexander Cosgrave ICS	27 December, 1917	12 March, 1922
35.	Christopher Gimson ICS	15 March, 1922	23 November, 1922
36.	L.O. Clarke, ICS	24 November, 1922	5 April, 1924
37.	John Comyn Higgins, ICS	6 April, 1924	5 March, 1928
38.	C.G. Crawford ICS	12 March, 1928	23 November, 1928
39.	John Comyn Higgins, ICS	24 November, 1928	31 March, 1933
40.	Christopher Gimson,ICS	March, 1933	March, 1938
41.	Gerald Pakenham Stewart ICS	March, 1933	March, 1938
42.	Christopher Gimson ICS	December, 1938	December, 1946
43.	Gerald Pakenham Stewart ICS	December, 1946	14 October, 1947

Source- Pangambam Bharat Sigh, IAS, "Kangla, the National Heritage of Manipur", 2008.

Appendix-2
Instrument of Accession

Whereas the Indian Independence Act, 1947, provides that as from the fifteenth day of August, 1947, there shall be set up an independent Dominion known as INDIA, and that the Government of India Act, 1935, shall, with such omission, additions, adaptations and modifications as the Governor-General may by order specify, be applicable to the Dominion of India,

And whereas the Government of India Act, 1935, as so adapted, by the Governor General provides that an Indian State may accede to the Dominion of India by an Instrument of Accession executed by the Ruler thereof :

Now, therefore, I

Ruler of......................................, in the exercise of my Sovereignty in and over my said State do hereby execute this my Instrument of Accession; and

1. I hereby declare that I accede to the Dominion of India with the intent that the Governor-General of India, the Dominion Legislature, the Federal Court and any other Dominion authority established for the purposes of the Dominion shall, by virtue of this my Instrument of Accession but subject always to the terms thereof, and for the purposes only of the Dominion, exercise in relation to the State of——————————

——————————————————————————

(hereinafter referred to as "this State") such functions as may be vested in them by or under the Government of India Act, 1935, as in force in the Dominion of India, on the 15th Day of August 1947, (which Act as so in force is hereafter referred to as "the Act").

2. I hereby assume the obligation of ensuring that due effect is given to provisions of the Act within this State so far as they are applicable therein by virtue of this my Instrument of Accession.
3. I accept the matters specified in the scheduled hereto as the matters with respect to which the Dominion Legislature may make laws for this State.
4. I hereby declare that I accede to the Dominion of India on the assurance that if an agreement is made between the Governor-General and the Ruler of this State whereby any functions in relation to the administration in this State of any law of the Dominion Legislature shall be exercised by the Ruler of this State, then any such agreement shall be deemed to form part of this Instrument and shall be construed and have effect accordingly.
5. The terms of this my Instrument of Accession shall not be varied by any amendment of the Act or the Indian Independence Act, 1947, unless such amendment is accepted by me by Instrument supplementary to this Instrument.
6. Nothing in this Instrument shall empower the Dominion Legislature to make any law for this State authorising the compulsory acquisition of land for any purpose, but I hereby undertake that should the Dominion for the purpose of a Dominion law which applies in this State deem it necessary to acquire any land, I will at their request acquire the land at their expense, or, if the land belongs to me transfer it to them on such terms as may be agreed or, in default of agreement, determined by an arbitrator to be appointed by the Chief justice of India.
7. Nothing in this Instrument shall be deemed to commit in any way to acceptance of any future constitution of India or to fetter my discretion to enter into arrangement with the Government of India under any such future constitution.
8. Nothing in this Instrument affects the continuance of my Sovereignty in and over this State, or, save as provided by or under this Instrument, the exercise of any powers, authority and rights now enjoyed by me as Ruler of this State or the validity of any law at present in force in this State.
9. I hereby declare that I execute this Instrument on behalf of this State and that any reference in this Instrument to me or to the Ruler of the State is to be construed as including a reference to my heirs and successors.

Given under my hand this 26th day of October, nineteen hundred and forty-seven.

Acceptance of Accession by the Governor-General of India

I do hereby accept this Instrument of Accession.

Dated this ——————————————day of, nineteen hundred and forty-seven.

Governor-General of India.

SCHEDULE

The matters with Respect to which the Dominion Legislature may make Laws for this State,

A. Defence.

1. The naval, military and air forces of the Dominion and any other armed force raised or maintained by the Dominion any armed forces, including forces raised or maintained by an acceding State, which ate attached, to or operating with, any of the armed forces of the Dominion. 2. Naval military and air forces works administration of cantonment areas.
2. Arms, fire- arms; ammunitions;
3. Explosives.

B. External Affairs.

1. External affairs; the implementing of treaties and agreements with other countries; extradition including the surrender of criminals and accused persons to parts of this Majesty; dominions outside India.
2. Admission into and emigration and expulsion from, India including in relation, thereto the regulation of the movements in India of persons who are no, British subjects domiciled in India or subjects of any acceding State, pilgrimages to places beyond India.
3. Naturalization

C. Communications.

1. Posts and telegraphs including telephones, wireless, broadcasting and other like forms of communication.
2. Federal railways; the regulation of all railways other than minor railways in respect of safety, maximum and minimum rates and fare, station and service terminal charges, interchanges of traffic and the responsibility of railway administrations as carriers of goods and passengers; the

responsibility of the administrations of such railways as carriers of goods and passengers.

3. Maritime shipping and navigation including shipping and navigation on tidal waters; Admiralty jurisdiction.
4. Port quarantine.
5. Major ports, that is to say the declaration and delimitation of such ports, and the constitution and powers of Port Authorities therein.
6. Aircraft and air navigation; the provision of aerodromes; regulation and organization of air traffic and of aerodromes.
7. Lighthouses, including lightships beacons and other provisions for the safety of shipping and aircraft.
8. Carriage of passengers and goods by sea or by air.
9. Extensions to the powers and jurisdiction of members of the police force belonging to any unit to railway area outside that unit.

D. Ancillary.

1. Elections to the Dominion Legislature subject to the provisions of the Act and of any Order made there under.
2. Offences against laws with respect to any of the aforesaid matters.
3. Inquiries and statistics for the purposes of any of the aforesaid matters.
4. Jurisdiction and powers of all courts with respect to any of the aforesaid matters but, except with the consent of the Ruler of the acceding State, not so as to confer and jurisdiction or powers. upon any courts other than courts ordinarily exercising jurisdiction in or in relation to that.

Appendix-3

STANDSTILLAGREEMENT

Agreement between the State of .... and the Dominion of India

WHEREAS it is to the benefit and advantage of the Dominion of India as well as of the Indian States that existing agreements and administrative arrangements in the matters of common concern, should continue for the time being, between the dominion of India or any part there of and the Indian States;

Now therefore it is agreed between the .... State and the Dominion of India that :-

1. (1) Until new agreements in this behalf are made all agreements and administrative arrangement as to matters of common concern now existing between the Crown and any Indian State shall, in so far as may be appropriate, continue as between the Dominion of India or, as the case may be, the part thereof, and the State.

   (2) In particular, and without derogation from the generality of sub clause (1) of the clause the matters referred to above shall include the matters specified in the Schedule to this Agreement.

2. Any dispute arising out of this Agreement, or out of the agreements or arrangements hereby continued, shall unless any provision is made therein for arbitration by an authority other than the Governor – General

or Governor, be settled by arbitration according, as far as may be, to the procedure of the Indian Arbitration Act, 1899.

3. Nothing in this Agreement includes the exercise of any paramountcy functions.

....State

....

Secretary to the Government of India.

SCHEDULE

1. Air Communications.
2. Arms and equipment
3. Control of commodities.
4. Currency and coinage.
5. Customs.
6. Indian States Forces.
7. External Affairs
8. Extradition.
9. Import and Export Control.
10. Irrigation and Electric Power.
11. Motor Vehicles.
12. National Highways.
13. Opium.
14. Posts, Telegraphs and Telephones
15. Railways (including police and other arrangements in Railway lands).
16. Salt.
17. Central Excises, relief from double income – tax and other arrangements relating to taxation.
18. Wireless.

Appendix-4

Governors of Manipur

Name	*Start Year*	*End Year*
Gurubachand Jagat Singh	23 July, 2008	Till date
Shivinder Singh Siddhu	06 August, 2003	22 July, 2008
Shri Arvind Dave	13 June, 2003	5 August, 2004
Shri Ved Marwah	2 December, 1999	12 June, 2003
Shri O. N. Shrivastava	23 December, 1994	11 February, 1999
Lt. General V.K. Nayar PVSM	31 August, 1993	22 December, 1994
Shri K.V.Raghunath Reddy	20 March, 1993	30 August, 1993
Shri. Chintamani Panigrahi	10 July, 1989	19 March, 1993
General K.V. Krishna Rao	2 June, 1984	07 July, 1989
S.M.H. Burney	12 August, 1981	11 June, 1984
Shri L.P. Singh	21 September, 1973	11 August, 1981
Shri B.K Nehru	21 January, 1972	20 September, 1973

Appendix-5

Chief Ministers of Manipur

Name	*Start Year*	*End Year*
Okram Ibobi Singh	07 March, 2002	Till date
Radhabinod Koijam	15 February, 2001	01 June, 2001
Shri W. Nipamacha Singh	17 December, 1997	14 February, 2001
Shri Rishang Keishing	25 February, 1995	11 January, 1998
Shri Rishang Keishing	14 December, 1994	24/2/1995
Shri R. K. Dorendro Singh	9 April, 1992	30 January, 1993
Shri R.K. Ranbir Singh	23 February, 1990	7 January, 1992
Shri R.K. Jaichandra Singh	4 March, 1988	17 February, 1990
Shri Rishang Keishing	4 January, 1985	4 March,1988
Shri Rishang Keishing	19 June, 1981	4 January, 1985
Shri Rishang Keishing	27 November ,1980	28 February, 1981
Shri R.K. Dorendro Singh	14 January, 1980	26 November, 1980
Shri Yangmasho Saiza	29 June, 1977	14 November, 1979
Shri R.K. Dorendro Singh	23 July, 1975	23 July, 1977
Shri R.K. Dorendro Singh	6 December, 1974	23 July, 1975
Shri Yangmasho Shaiza	10 July, 1974	5 December, 1974
Md. Alimuddin	4 March,1974	8 July, 1974
Md. Alimuddin	23 March,1972	28 March, 1973
Shri M. Koireng Singh	19 February, 1968	25 October, 1967
Shri L. Thambou Singh	13 October, 1967	25 October, 1967
Shri M. Koireng Singh	20 March,1967	4 October, 1967
Shri M. Koireng Singh	1 July 1963	12 January, 1967
Shri M. K. Priyobarta Singh	14 August 1947	15 October, 1949
F.F Pearson	15 July, 1947	14 August 1947

Appendix-6

Speakers of Manipur

Speakers of Manipur			
Assembly	*Name of Speakers*	*Period*	
		From	*To*
I State Assembly (1948 - 49)	T.C. Tiankham	19 November, 1948	15 October, 1949
*I Territorial Council (1957 - 62)	1. H. Dwijamani Dev Sharma	September, 1957	October, 1958
	2. Sibo Larho	October, 1958	2 August, 1962
* I Territorial Assembly (1962-67)	1. M. Koireng Singh	3 August, 1962	21 July, 1963
	2. Kh. Ibetombi Singh	23 July, 1963	20 March, 1967
* II Territorial Assembly(1967 - 69)	1. S. Tombi Singh	21 March, 1967	24 October, 1967
	2. Sibo Larho	5 March, 1968	29 March, 1972
I Manipur Legislative Assembly (1972-73)	1. Dr. L.Chandramani Singh	30 March, 1972	8 March, 1974
II Manipur Legislative Assembly (1974-79)	1. R.K. Dorendra Singh	26 March, 1974	5 December, 1974
	2. Md. Alimuddin	16 December, 1974	4 September, 1975
	3. Dr. L. Chandramani Singh	18 September, 1975	21 October, 1978

(Contd.)

(Contd. Appendix - 6)

Speakers of Manipur			
Assembly	*Name of Speakers*	*Period*	
		From	*To*
	4. R.K.Ranbir Singh	12 January, 1979	18 February, 1980
III Manipur Legislative Assembly (1980-85)	1. Y. Yaima Singh	18 February, 1980	23 January, 1985
IV Manipur Legislative Assembly (1985-90)	1. W. Angou Singh	24 January, 1985	20 December, 1988
	2. Th. Devendra Singh	20 December, 1988	2 March, 1990
V Manipur Legislative Assembly (1990-95)	1. Dr. H. Borbabu Singh	2 March, 1990	9 January, 1995
	2. E. Biramani Singh	9 January, 1995	27 February, 1995
VI Manipur Legislative Assembly (1995-2000)	1. W. Nipamacha Singh	22 March, 1995	6 December, 1997
	2. K. Babudhon Singh	29 December, 1997	7 March, 2000
VII Manipur Legislative Assembly (2000-02)	1. Dr. S. Dhananjoy Singh	13 March, 2000	8 March, 2002
VIII Manipur Legislative Assembly (2002- 2007)	1. T.N.Haokip	12 March, 2002	7 December, 2005
	2. Dr. Md. Maniruddin Sheikh	9 December, 2005	15 March, 2007
IX Manipur Legislative Assembly (2002-)	Dr. S. Budhichandra Singh	16 March, 2007	Till date

Appendix-7

Glossary

Achouba	:	Big
Achou Ashang	:	People belonging to the aristocratic class
Aimol	:	An ethnic group of hill people
Amrita	:	A nectar to conquer death
Anal	:	An ethnic group of hill people
Angom	:	One of the Manipuri Clans
Anoubas	:	A new line of Brahmins who came into prominence during king Churachand's reign
Apanbi Ahal	:	2nd queen of the king
Apanbi Naha	:	4th queen of the king
Apokpa	:	Clan ancestor
Apokpa Khurumjaba	:	Worshipping of the Clan ancestor
Ava	:	Burma/ Myanmar
Ayekpa	:	Painter
Aribams	:	A line of old Brahmins who were first to get the status of royal priests during the reign of king Charairongba
Asuras	:	Demons
Baruni Kaba	:	Climbing the Baruni Hill
Brahmin	:	One belonging to the priest family who usually migrated from the west
Brahma Sabha	:	Council of Brahmins
Chak Chaba	:	Eating rice

Chakhum	:	Kitchen
Chamba	:	to wash
Chandan	:	Sandal paste on the forehead
Chaddar	:	A shawl or piece of cloth to wrap the upper portion of the body.
Chahi taba	:	Name given to the coming year
Chakpa Lai Haraoba	:	A festival of Umang Lais celebrated by the Lois communities of Manipur.
Cheiraoba	:	New year festival of Manipur.
Cheirap	:	Civil Court
Ching	:	Hill
Chingba	:	to contract
Chingmee	:	Hill men
Chiru	:	An ethnic group of hill people
Charnamrita	:	Flower water offered to the devotees of Hindu Temples
Dari	:	verandah
Dakshina	:	A token money given as apart of the ceremony
Dharma	:	Religion
Devta	:	The deity, God
Dolai	:	The palanquin
Durga	:	A Hindu Goddess
Durga Puja	:	Worshipping of Durga
Fajaba	:	Beautiful
Firoi	:	Death anniversary
Fukainaba	:	A process of diving the linage into further segments
Garot	:	Military Court
Gopi	:	Female co-dancer of Lord Krishna in Raas Lila
Gotra	:	Hindu Clan
Gouriya Dharma	:	A sect of Vaisnavism
Gurus	:	The reverend teachers of Hindu Religion
Hanba	:	Head of office
Hanjaba	:	Head of office
Hao	:	Tribal
Heloi	:	Nymph

Hidak Thakpa	:	Smoking tobacco
Houchongba	:	A ceremony of exchange of love and gifts between the valley people and hill people
Hiyanggei	:	Manipuri month (October-November)
Hidang	:	Assistant to the head of office
Higok Machu Phi	:	Blue coloured clothe
Hiyanggei	:	8th month of Manipuri Calendar
Haribola	:	Devotional shouting of the name Hari (Krishna)
He-Hori	:	Remembering Hari (Krishna) with devotional shouting
Id	:	Ramjan / festival of Muslims
Immung	:	Family, interior of the house
Immunglai	:	Household deity
Inn	:	Fishing net
Inga	:	3rd month (June-July) of Manipuri Calendar
Ingen	:	4th month of Manipuri Calendar
Imnaphi	:	A kind of shawl
Irai	:	Friday
Jati	:	Tribe
Kabui	:	An ethnic group of hill people
Kainaba	:	Divorce, to break away
Kalen	:	Manipuri month (April-May)
Kang	:	The Ratha Yatra festival
Kartal	:	Cymbal
Khubak Ishei	:	Singing and dancing devotional songs with clapping of hands
Kang Sanaba	:	A type of indoor game played by the Meiteis
Keinya Katpa	:	A kind of marriage without much ceremony
Khagi	:	China
Khainaba	:	Divorce
Khutnaiba	:	Artisan
Konheiba	:	Brass metal worker
Kokyet	:	Turban
Kshechri	:	A type of rice preparation mixed with pulses and turmeric (yellow rice)

Kurta	:	A type of shirt
Kuru	:	Equivalent of Guru
Lai	:	God or deity
Lai haraoba	:	Festival of Umang Lais or merry making of Gods
Lairembi	:	Goddess
Lamda	:	A Manipuri month (February-March)
Leikai	:	Locality
Linga	:	The phallus
Lei Chandan	:	Flower and sacred sandal paste give at religious ceremonies
Lakpas	:	Officer who work as communication agent
Lalup Kaba	:	A system of rendering free compulsory service to the king for ten days in every forty days
Lamboiba	:	Monk
Lamda	:	12th month of Manipuri Calendar
Lanba	:	Officer in charge
Langban	:	6th month of Manipuri Calendar
Leimakhubi Ahal	:	3rd queen of the king
Leimakhubi Naha	:	5 queen of the king
Leimarembi	:	Eldest queen / Maharani
Leipakpokpa	:	Tuesday
Loipot	:	Tribute to the king
Loipot Kaba	:	One who give tribute to the king
Loi thaba	:	to exile or to degrade as a punishment from the king
Loisang	:	Institute of local priests and priestess
Loo	:	A fishing trap
Luhongba	:	Marriage
Lukha thaba	:	Head taking
Lukhrabi	:	Widow
Lukhrabi macha	:	Child of a widow
Luton	:	Upper portion of the body
Maharaja	:	The great king
Maiba	:	Manipuri traditional priest
Maibi	:	Manipuri traditional priestess
Maibaism	:	practice relating to Maibas

Maibism	:	Practice relating to Maibis
Maichou	:	Scholar
Mandapa	:	Shed adjoining temples
Mantras	:	Incantations
Mani	:	Jewel
Mapu	:	Master/Owner
Mayaika	:	Middle room in Meitei house
Mayang	:	Outsider
Meiteis	:	The dominant tribe among the Manipuris
Mera	:	7th month of Manipuri Calendar
Mukna	:	Manipuri wrestling
Mukna kangjei	:	Manipuri hockey associated with wrestling
Marup	:	Friend or a voluntary organization/ Friendship
Mee	:	man
Meecham	:	Commoner
Meitei Laining	:	Meitei religion (Sanamahism)
Meitei Leipak	:	Manipur- land of Meiteis
Mera	:	Manipuri month (September-October)
Nahutpa	:	Ear piercing ceremony
Nganthak	:	Smoking pipe, held vertically with the help of palms and fingers of both hands while the smoke is sucked into the mouth Nongchup
Haram	:	People coming from the west
Nongchup Haram	:	People coming from the west
Nongpok Haram	:	People coming from the east
Ningthouja	:	one of the Manipuri Clans
Ningthoukaba	:	Monday
Nirvana	:	Release from the birth and death cycle
Nongsha	:	Lion
Nongmaijing	:	Sunday
Numit	:	Sun
Ojha	:	Teachers
Ougrichongba	:	Black magic of Manipur
Ougri	:	Ancient Song
Pagari	:	Turban
Pakhangba	:	Manipuri ruling king in 33 A.D

Pandit	:	Priest from the Brahmin class
Panthoibi	:	Name of the Goddess
Peepal	:	A kind of banyan tree worshipped by the Hindus
Phamnaiba	:	Noble
Phanek	:	Manipuri ankle length skirt for women
Pheijom	:	Loin cloth for Meitei males
Phungga Lairu	:	The Goddess of wealth dwelling at the Phungga
Phungga	:	Fire place in the Manipuri House
Poinu	:	9th month of Manipuri Calendar
Prasad	:	Offering distributed by the priest in the temple after completion of the ritual
Pung	:	Manipuri drum used in rituals and ceremonies and festivals.
Pung Cholom	:	A type of dance performed by the drummers
Purohit	:	Brahmin priest
Purohitism	:	Brahmin priestism
Pana	:	A division of the locality
Pandit	:	Literati
Pandit Louisang	:	Council of the Literati
Pari	:	One heactre of land
Paripuri	:	Geneaology
Paya	:	Split bamboo used to tie up something
Phairen	:	Manipuri month (January-February)
Phura	:	a small building to accommodate the deity
Piba	:	Head of a clan
Pibaren	:	Head of all Pibas
Pothang	:	A system of forced labour
Potyeng	:	Ceremonial gift
Puya	:	Od chronicle/manuscript
Sagei	:	Clan
Sajibu	:	First month of Manipuri Calendar
Salai	:	Clan
Sanamahi	:	Sanamahi religion
Sanasaba	:	Goldsmith
Saradha	:	Death ritual

Swasti Puja	:	Birth ritual performed on the sixth day of the birth of the child
Sidaba	:	One who never dies / God
Sumang	:	Courtyard
Takhel	:	Tripuri
Tekhao	:	Assam
Thangsaba	:	Blacksmith
Thiba	:	Ugly
Tulsi	:	Sacred Basil plant
Tulsibong	:	the spot where Tulsi is panted
Tuman Macha	:	A child of a woman by the union of her second husband
Sagolsen	:	Thursday
Saroi Khangba	:	Worship of evil spirit during the month of Lamda
Saren Chanba	:	A ritual
Saroi	:	Evil spirit'
Singlup	:	Firewood organization, an obligatory socially corporate organization
Tha	:	Moon
Turel	:	River
Radha Raman	:	Another name of Lord Krishna
Raja	:	King
Rajkumar	:	Somebody belonging to royal lineage
Salam	:	Salute
Sana	:	Gold/Princess
Sanakhwa	:	A respectful term to address the people of royal lineage
Sagol Kangjei	:	Polo
Shakti	:	Goddess of power
Rani	:	Queen
Maharani	:	The eldest queen
Rudraksha Mala	:	A type of necklace worn by saints and devotees made of Rudraksha nuts
Tantras	:	Techniques or know –how
Tilak	:	Mark of sandal paste on the forehead
Tirtha	:	A place of pilgrimage
Thabal Chongba	:	A type of Manipuri dance performed usually during Yaoshang festivals

Thangja	:	Saturday
Thawan	:	5th month of Manipuri Calendar
Udukhal Raas	:	A dance depicting the childhood of Lord Krishna
Umang Lai	:	Forest Gods, Sylvan Gods
Uningthou	:	A type of tree in Manipur good for timber
Utsab	:	A ritual feast
Wakching	:	10th month of Manipuri Calendar
Yai	:	Luck
Vasanta Raas	:	A form of Manipuri Raas Lila dance
Yaoshang	:	Holi festival of Manipur
Yek Thokpa	:	People belonging to the same clan who can not marry each other
Yek salai	:	Clan
Yumnak	:	Surnames, Maximal lineage
Yotsuba	:	Blacksmith
Yumchangba	:	Sacred genealogy of lineage
Yumsakeisa	:	Wednesday
Yumjao	:	The great house having five bed rooms, the original house of the Meiteis

Appendix-8

Index

Topic	*Page Number*	*Topic*	*Page Number*	*Topic*	*Page Number*
Abdeitya Temple of Lamangdong	410	Administration of Hill areas	157	Administration of villages	84
Agarbati	649	Anglo Burmese War – first	119	Anglo Burmese War - Third	134
Aimol	251	Airlines and destinations	7	Anal	252
Andro	376	Angami	252	Anglo Manipuri War –1891	141, 453
Animals	52	Angousana Singh Senapati	148	Apokpa Khurumba	210
Appendix,1-8	662	Archeological Findings	40	Arjuna Award Winners	508
Arambai Hunba	512	Arrival of Hinduism	439	Arrival of Muslims	430
Arrival of Christianity	462	All districts	552	Archival Sources	41
Art of sword fight	522	Account left by Europeans	39	Bamboo and Paper Industry	609
Ayangba	93	Bamboo Brakes of Manipur	65	Banking and Finance	642
Bamboo and Bamboo Shoots	644	Bamon / Purohitism	230	Barak river	47

(Contd.)

(Contd. Appendix-8)

Topic	*Page Number*	*Topic*	*Page Number*	*Topic*	*Page Number*
Bamboo Shoot Fermentation	616	Bengalis	202	Bhagyachandra	108
Bhadra Singh. Painter	133	Biblical origins	475	Bijoy Govinda Temple of Sagolband	412
Baruni	385	Biharis	200	Birds	52
Bharat shai	106	Bishnupur district	564	Black scented rice (Chakhao Amubi)	657
Bishnupriya	244	British Officers	662	Border dispute with Burma	132
Bodhchandra Singh	161	Boundaries of Manipur	44	Bus Services	10
Business opportunities	627	Cabinet Mission –Nagas	294	Cane Brakes of Manipur	66
Caves	48	Cane and Bamboo works	547	Cane and Bamboo Trade, trained artisans	548, 668
Cane and Bamboo production project	648	Cane and Bamboo production project, main objectives	650	Census Population	196
Chakpas	247	Cement Project	611	Chandrakirti Maharaja	125. 128

(Contd.)

(Contd. Appendix-8)

Topic	*Page Number*	*Topic*	*Page Number*	*Topic*	*Page Number*
Changes in the administrative structure during various kingships	83	Chandel district	587	Chahi taret Khuntakpa	117, 445
Chaobatol Singh Heigrujamba Subedar	153	Charairongba	99	Chawumba	216
Chauba Hida Machahal	150	Cheiraoba	382	Chengpak	638
Chinglen Sana Phunganai Sanglakpa	459	Chingthangkhomba	108	Chirai Naga alias Chirai Thangal	154
Chief Ministers of Manipur	671	Chiru	252	Chiithuni festival	588
Chit Shai	106	Cholera Epidemic	133, 158	Chourajit	116
Chorus Repertory Theatre	240	Chongtham Nilamani, Ava Purel	150	Chowkami Naga of Mayangkhang	153
Chongtha Mia Major	150	Christianity, arrival	468	Chronology of development of Polo	534
Christmas	392	Chothe Tribe	252	Chronology of Manipur Kings	77
Chumpha -festival of Tangkhul Naga	393, 579	Chronology of important historical landmarks	427	Churachandpur	380, 568

(Contd.)

(Contd. Appendix-8)

Topic	*Page Number*	*Topic*	*Page Number*	*Topic*	*Page Number*
Churachand Singh Maharaja	154	Coffee	637	City Distances	19
Climate of Manipur	44	Coins	35	Coronation of Govindajee	113
Classical Manipuri Dance Forms	494				
Construction of Imphal Cachar Road	126	Construction of Imphal-Mao Road	133	Conversion to Christians	469, 470
Copper Plates	33	Courier Services	16	Creation of Manipur	25
Creation of Galaxy	25	Creation of Clans and Yek Salai	26	Creation of Yumnak	215
Customs and Duties	6	Dance Gurus	502	Death Ritual of Meiteis	217
Debendra Singh	127	Design and embroidery of Meitei textiles	546	Dhaja Singh Mayengba	151
Different Names of Manipur	27	Dhana Singh Sagolsemba	152	Districts	558

(Contd.)

(Contd. Appendix-8)

Topic	*Page Number*	*Topic*	*Page Number*	*Topic*	*Page Number*
Durga Puja	386	Digendrajit, murder	158	Dhob	243
Entry Formalities	2	Different names of Manipur	27	Diwali	387
English Education	133	Excursions	21	Darreo festival	579
Famous Manipuri Dance Gurus	502	Facts about Manipur	17	Early Relations with Burma	92
Fauna and Flora	48	Feast of Merit	289, 346	Festivals of Christians	392
Festivals of Meiteis	382	Festivals of Kukis	397	Festivals of Manipur	382
Festivals of Muslims	399	Festivals of Tangkhuls	393	Festivals of Poumai Nagas	396
"First Devastation" (Khuntak Ahanba-1755-1759)	442	First Election of Manipur	177	Festivals of Zeliangrong Nagas	393
First Nupi Lan (Women's Agitation) -1904	476	First World War	158	Fishes of Manipur	53
Flowers	70	Forest	55	Floriculture	618
Food Industries Corporation	611	Fruits	75	Forms of address	219

(Contd.)

(Contd. Appendix-8)

Topic	Page Number	Topic	Page Number	Topic	Page Number
Gaan Ngai	401	Gaidinliu, Rani	478	Fruit Processing	648
Games and Sports in Manipur	505	Gangte	253	Gambheer Singh (Chinglen Nongdrenkhomba)	121
Geography, Fauna and Flora of Manipur	44	Ghuna Singh Ingujamba Jamadar	154	Garib Niwaj	100
Ginger	643	Gopinath Temple of Sanakhyahal	415	Ghuna Singh Khongdram	151
Gostha Lila	500	Government of India Act-1919	292	Gopinath Temple of Ningthoukhong	410
Government and Politics	203	Great Historical Gap	79	Gour Shyam	107
Govindajee-coronation	113	Guwho Naga of Mayangkhang	153	Government of India Act-1935	160, 293
Govindajee Temple of old Palace, Kangla	374, 403	Govindajee Temple of New Palace	405	Guna Singh, Khomdram	151
Glossary	674	Hotel facilities	11	Governors of Manipur	670

(Contd.)

(Contd. Appendix-8)

Topic	*Page Number*	*Topic*	*Page Number*	*Topic*	*Page Number*
Handloom population and production	538	Handloom and Handicrafts	536	Handloom and Handicrafts – historical background	536
Handloom, legends	536	Handloom and Handicrafts, modern	538		
Head Taking	289	Health Precautions	17	Hanuman Thakur Temple	403
Hill Ranges	45	Hinduism, arrival of	445	Heikru Hitongba	387
Historical Evidence	33	Historical Landmarks	427	History of Polo from other countries of the world	537
History of spread of Polo from Manipur	524-528	Historical Relevance	39	Hmar	356
Hmar, origin and migration	356	Hmar, Clans	356	Hmar, houses	357
Hmar, marriage	357	Hmar, family and inheritance 358		Hmar, traditional political system	358

(Contd.)

(Contd. Appendix-8)

Topic	*Page Number*	*Topic*	*Page Number*	*Topic*	*Page Number*
Hmar, Basung Sadar	358	Hmar, Thiempu	358	Hmar, Siehmang Upas (Councillors)	359
Hmar, Youth Dormitory (*Buonzawl)*	359	Hmar, Val Upsa	359	Hmar, Courtship :	360
Hmar, Religion	360	Hmar, Dances of	360	Hmar, Musical Instruments :	361
Hmar, Textiles	363	Hmar, Handicrafts of	364	Hmar, Decorative Arts :	366
Hiyangthang Lairembi Temple	415	Hirachandra	118	Hiyang Tanaba	512
How to reach Imphal	7	Horticulture	624	Hotel Facilities	11

(Contd.)

(Contd. Appendix-8)

Topic	*Page Number*	*Topic*	*Page Number*	*Topic*	*Page Number*
Identification of feasible industrial projects	655	How many Naga Tribes	279	Heecham Yaicham Pat	375
Ibudhou Thangjing Temple of Moirang	418	Important Kings /Maharajas of Manipur	89	Important Telephones	20
Imphal East district	552	Ima Keithel	373	Imphal City	368
Indo-Myanmar Border Trade	598	Imphal West	556	Imphal River	46
Indo-Myanmar Border Trade, potential areas of export from Manipur	592	Indo-Myanmar Trade route through Moreh	592	Indo-Myanmar Trade, volume	592
Indo-Myanmar Trade, volume through Moreh	593	Indo-Myanmar Trade, measures taken up by Govt. Of India and state govt.	594	Indo-Myanmar Trade, potential areas of export from Manipur	595

(Contd.)

(Contd. Appendix-8)

Topic	*Page Number*	*Topic*	*Page Number*	*Topic*	*Page Number*
Indo-Myanmar Trade, potential areas if import from Mynamar	595	Investment, Transport subsidy	606	Investment, fiscal incentives	606
Industrial Corporations	611	Indian Independence Act – 1947	172	Indigenous Games of Manipur	510
Industrial Policy of Manipur	604	Investment, package of incentives	605	Investment, new industrial package for the north-east:	605
Investment. Relaxation of Prime Minister's Rozgar Yojna (PMRY) norms	606	Industry, Spinning Mill	609	Industry, Bamboo and Paper	609
Industrial projects, feasible	646				
Industry, Market Potential	656	Industry, 200 TPD Cement Project	618	Industry, Serpentinite and Indocrase Processing	619

(Contd.)

(Contd. Appendix-8)

Topic	*Page Number*	*Topic*	*Page Number*	*Topic*	*Page Number*
Industry, Manipur Food Processing	618	Industry, Manipur Traditional Liquor	620	Industry, Pine Apple Concentration	621
Industrial Scenario in Manipur	607	INA Museum	377	Inner Line Permit	6
Information Technology (IT)	619	Instrument of Accession	175,664	Irabot's Struggle for a responsible government	167
Irang HE Project	630	ISKON Temple	422	Investiture Ceremony	156
Jadonang :	477	Jai Singh	108	Janmashtami	386
Jiribam, acquisition of	124	James Johnstone	130	Judiciary Relationship	87
Kabok	639	Kabui	274	Kacha Naga	255
Kaina	376	Kangba	89	Kang festival	385
Kangla Fort	369	Kang Chingba	385	Kang Sanaba	513
Kajao Pukhramba Phingang	148	Keibul Lamjao National Park	51, 378	Keiphaba	93

(Contd.)

(Contd. Appendix-8)

Topic	*Page Number*	*Topic*	*Page Number*	*Topic*	*Page Number*
Khagemba	97	Khamba Thoibi dance	500	Khamlangba of Kakching	424
Khomba	93	Kabow valley, loss of	122	Khongjom War	143, 456
Khonghampat Orchidarium	375	Khongjom	377	Khong Kangjei	517
				Khwairamband Keithel	373
Khongjom Parva	242	Khubak Ishei	243	Khuiyoi Tompok	92
Khullang ishei:	242	Khuntak Ahanba-1755-1759	448	Kingship	80
Kingdom , Kings	77			Kings of Manipur	89
Koirao Tribe	256	Koireng Tribe	257	Kouna Craft	549
Kouna Craft Production Project	652	Kouna Craft Production Project, concept	654	Kouna Craft Production Project, main objectives	654
Koikoi	90	Kohima Expedition	131	Kom	260

(Contd.)

(Contd. Appendix-8)

Topic	*Page Number*	*Topic*	*Page Number*	*Topic*	*Page Number*
Krishna Janmastami	386	Krishna Temple of Brahmapur Leikai	410	Krishna Chandra Temple of Kakching	408
Kuki Uprising -1917-1919	474	Konthoujam Lairembi	419	Kukis	127, 132, 349
Kukis, origin	349	Kukis, physical features	350	Kukis, dress and ornaments	350
Kukis, settlement	351	Kukis. Villages	351	Kukis, Houses	352
Kukis, family	352	Kukis, marriage	352	Kukis, divorce	352
Kukis-village administration	353	Kukis, Land and inheritance	354	Kukis, death ritual	354
Kukis, Som Inn	354	Kukis-musical instrument	354	Kukis, dances	354
Kukis, economic life	355	Kukis, games and sports	355	Kukis, food	354
Kut Festival	405	Kukis Bamboo Dance	398	Kumba Singh Laishraba	151
Kulachandra	137, 147	Kunming Initiative	597	Kyaamba	94
Labanya Chandra	115	Land Revenue	82	Leimapokpam Keirungba Temple	405
Lai Haraoba	389	Lai/Pawih	267	Lakes	47

(Contd.)

(Contd. Appendix-8)

Topic	*Page Number*	*Topic*	*Page Number*	*Topic*	*Page Number*
Lakpas	81	Langthabal	376	Lalupkaba	86
Laonii festival	404. 588	Language of Polo game	533	Lai Haraoba Ishei	234
Lamgang	260	Limestone	69	Lois	239
Loipotkaba	87	Loiyumba	93	Loktak Downstream HE Project	629
Log Drum	346	Lokendra Birjit, Wangkheirakpa	149	Longra Khamang	580
Loktak Pat (Lake) and Sendra Island	377	Loitongba	93	Lord Krishna Temple	402
Lord Sanamahi Temple	417	Lui-Ngai-Ni	393	Luira festival	579
Lugoon Thangba	216	Madan Mohan Temple of Kongba	413	Luwaang Punshiba	91
Maharaja Kulachandra Dhaja	137, 147	Maharaja Bodhchandra Singh	166	Maibas and Maibis	230
Manipuri Theatre	233	Manipuri Shumang Lila	231	Mangba Sengba Culture	163

(Contd.)

(Contd. Appendix-8)

Topic	*Page Number*	*Topic*	*Page Number*	*Topic*	*Page Number*
Maibi Dance	501	Maisnam Samu Singh	149	Mangkhap festival	579
Mandu (Bone money)	589	Manipuri Dances	494	Manipur and World War -II	483
Manipuri Cinema	234	Manipuri Folk Songs	235	Manipuri Common Words	221
Manipur Kingdom	76	Manipuri Dance, characteristic features	497	Manipuri Language	218
Manipuri Dance - Classical Forms	494	Manipur Traditional Liquor Plant	612	Manipuri Dance in modern times	499
Manipuri Raas Lila	494	Manipuri Dance Techniques	497	Manipuri Dance, early period	499
Making of Images	112	Manipuri Mayek and Scriptures	218	Manipur Merger Agreement	183
Manipur State Museum	374	Manipur Polo spread to England, 1869	523	Manipur Polo spread to British India	522
Manipur Polo spread to Malta	522	Manipur Polo spread to USA, 1876	524	Manipur Polo spread to Argentina, 1873	523
Manipur Polo spread to other parts of the world	522	Manipur Polo spread to France	525	Manipur Traditional Liquor	613

(Contd.)

(Contd. Appendix-8)

Topic	*Page Number*	*Topic*	*Page Number*	*Topic*	*Page Number*
Manipur Polo spread to Australia, 1876	524	Manipur food industries Corporation Ltd.	612	Market potential	647
Marketing arrangement	652				
Manipuri wrestling	516	Manipur Zoological Garden	375	Manipur Raas Lila	500
Manipuri Theatre	233	Martial Arts on stage	516	Manohar Sai	236
Maram	261	Marawaris	201	Martial Arts. foundation for classical dance	517
Maring	273	Marjit Singh	117	Mao	271
Mate Tribe	273	Medicinal Plants	584, 617,631	Medicinal Pant Processing Industry	617
Meitei Clans/ Salais /Yek	206	Meitei Birth Ritual	215	Meiteis	206
Meitei food	213	Meitei Dress and Ornamnets	212	Meitei Death Rituals	217
Meitei Lais	225	Meitei Singers	231	Meitei Folk Songs	235

(Contd.)

(Contd. Appendix-8)

Topic	*Page Number*	*Topic*	*Page Number*	*Topic*	*Page Number*
Meitei Literature	223	Meiteilon , Manipuri Language –Meitei Mayek	218	Meitei Houses	211
Meitei Marriage	214	Meitei Pangan (Manipuri Muslims)	196	Meitei Religion and animism	225
Meitei Rituals	214	Meitei Sagei and Yumnaks	206	Meitei Yumnak Creation	207
Mera Houchongba	388	Merger Agreement	183	Merger Agreement with other Princely states	181
Mineral; resources	68	Mizo	266	Military Service	82
Monsang	267	Moibung Ishei	236	Moirang	377
Movement of a responsible government	169	Moyon	267	Morung	286
Moreh	380	Monuments	433	Mukna	510
Mukna Kangjei	511	Mungyamba	96	Mushrooms	66, 643
Muslims, arrival of	438	Muslims, five daily prayers	442	Muslims, Islamic funeral	444
Murder of Digendrajit	164	Naa Hutpa	216	Naga Federal Government	298
Naga People's Convention	299	Naga National Movement	292	Naga Independence, declaration	295
Nagaland, Birth of	299	Naga Plebiscite –1951	296	Naga Shillong Accord	302

(Contd.)

(Contd. Appendix-8)

Topic	*Page Number*	*Topic*	*Page Number*	*Topic*	*Page Number*
Nagas- origin and migration	280	Naga Houses	283	Naga social life and village administration	284
Nagas- dress and ornaments	284	Naga Religion	283	Nagas handicrafts	285
Nagas-marriage	287	Nagas- child birth	287	Nagas- death rituals	288
Nagas- early relations with the British	289	Nagas- earlier Indo-Naga Peace Talks	300	Naga Peace Process-Manipur Factor	312
Naga Peace Process	307	Naga-Physical Features	281	Naga Tribes	279
Naga-head taking	281	Naga-Feast of Merit	289		
Names of people who were tried and punished for waging war against the queen empress	144	Nani Singh, Nepra Machahal	151	Naothingkhong	92
Nara Singh Temple of Kakching	409	Nara Singh Thakur Temple of Naorem Leikai	412	Nara Singh	127

(Contd.)

(Contd. Appendix-8)

Topic	*Page Number*	*Topic*	*Page Number*	*Topic*	*Page Number*
Nasitheimei or Nathitheimei	589	Nepalese	200	Nine Point Agreement of Nagas	294
Ningol Chakkouba	383	Ningthouba Singh	152	Ningthou Kangba	89
Ningthou. Sagei	218	Ningthou Khomba	93	Niranjan Subedar	149
Nityainanda Prabhu Temple of RIMS Road	413	Ningthouba Singh	152	NSCN	303
NSCN Demands-Weakness	314	Nongda Lairen Pakhangba	91	NSCN-K	305
NSCN Demands-Possible Solutions	321	NSCN-IM	303	Nupi Lal, second	485
Nupa Pala	502	Nupi Lal, first	470	Orchids	73, 657
Nupi Pala	236	Nupi Lal, second	479	Origin of Polo	520
Okendrajit Maharaja	191	Olympians from Manipur	507	Ougri	235
Origin of the name, Manipur	28	Origin of Meiteis	28	Palace Revolution	136, 454
Pakhangba	90	Paite	267	Pangka Dharma	161

(Contd.)

(Contd. Appendix-8)

Topic	*Page Number*	*Topic*	*Page Number*	*Topic*	*Page Number*
Paona Brajabashi	458	Pana Sagol Kangjei	519	Political Agents	662
Passion fruit	642	Paradhumba Singh Ashangba Khut	153	Peace Process, Nagas	307
Peace Process-, Nagas, Manipur factor	313	People of Manipur	195	Period of reconstruction	459
Pena Ishei	236	Piba	210	Pibaren	210
Pine Apple Concentration Plant	615	Phamnaiba	85	Phubala	378
Pine Apple	642	Pinus Casia Forest	57	Places of Interest	21
Poireiton Khunthokpa	90	Polo Players of Manipur during 19th Century	526	Polo, language of the game	527
Polo	518	Polo, history from other parts of the world	530	Population and People of Manipur	195
Polo, chronology of development	527	Pottery, common use	546,626	Pottery in Manipur	545, 625
Ponghi festival	588	Pottery, myths about origin	546,625	Pottery making , technique	546,626
Poumai Nagas	276	Pottery, firing	546,626	Pottery, places associated with	547,626

(Contd.)

(Contd. Appendix-8)

Topic	*Page Number*	*Topic*	*Page Number*	*Topic*	*Page Number*
Pottery , colouring	547, 626	Protected Area Permit	2	Proposed projects	657
Power sector	621	Purum	269	Pung Cholom	501
Punjabis	201	Raas Lila	113, 494	Political development of Manipur after India's Independence	176
Quinton	134	Raas Dance Costumes	498	Raas Musical Instruments	498
Radha Raman Temple of Langthabal	407	Radha Krishna Manimandir of ISKON	414	Radha Madhav Temple of Ningthoukhong	411
Ralte	260	Ramji Prabhu of Ningthem Pukhri Mapal	411	Ratha Yatra	385
Ralte	278	Rani Gaidinliu	478	Religious Relationship	88
Religion	204	Reptiles	52	Rice Flake	638
River, Iril	46	Rivalry between NSCN-IM and NSCN-K	306	Rivers	46
River, Nambool	46	Rubber	67, 645	Role of Manipuri Muslims	440
Sagei	216	Saheed Minar	373	Sacred Stones	230
Samadhi of Luwang Ningthou	425	Samadhi of Maharaja Gambheer Singh	424	Salhte /Soktes	278

(Contd.)

(Contd. Appendix-8)

Topic	Page Number	Topic	Page Number	Topic	Page Number
Sagol Kangjei/Polo	518	Sagol Kangjei, origin in Manipur	518	Samadhi of Maharaja Nongchup Lamgaingamba (Bhadra Singh)	425
Sagol Kangjei during British Period	521	Sanad	155	Sanamahi	225
Sanamahi Temple	425	Schedule Tribes	250	Second Nupi Lal-1939	485
Scheduled Castes	239, 250	Sekta Kei Mound	379	Sema	269
Second World War and Manipur	166, 489	Shirui Lily	72, 379	Senbi Kyaamba	94
Semi Evergreen Forests	60	Sepoy Mutiny	129	Service Relationship	85
Serpentinite and idocrase processing industries	613	Spices	656		
Senapati district	574	Shillong Accord	302	Signing of Standstill Agreement and Instrument of Accession	175
Seven Years devastation	445	Shirui Lily	72, 380	Shopping in Imphal	23

(Contd.)

(Contd. Appendix-8)

Topic	Page Number	Topic	Page Number	Topic	Page Number
Shumang Lila	239	Silk and Tasar Industry	610	Simon Commission -1929	292
Sikhs	196	Simte	270	Situation of Manipur immediately before independence	174
Singda	379	Situation of Manipur immediately before Merger Agreement	182	Signing of Merger Agreement	183
Situation of Princely states immediately before Independence	179	South Indians	201	Society and Conduct of Manipuris	203
Soil	55	Spinning Mill	615	Speakers of Manipur	672
Sports Stars of Manipur	508	Sports Personalities during Maharaja Churachand's reign	507	Sports movement in Manipur	505
Standstill Agreement	175, 668	Stone Inscriptions and Copper/Iron Plates	34	Spinning Mill	608
Surchandra Singh	135	Social Mores	211	Sub Alpine Forest	58
Taa Khousarol	516	Tamenglong	379, 582	Tangkhuls , origin	327, 329

(Contd.)

(Contd. Appendix-8)

Topic	*Page Number*	*Topic*	*Page Number*	*Topic*	*Page Number*
Tangkhul Awunga	336	Tangkhuls, Festivals	341	Tangkhuls and Meitei Ties	331
Tangkhuls, Migration	328	Tangkhuls, Musical Instruments	345	Tangkhuls, Swearing and Oath Taking	340
Tangkhuls, physical appearance	332	Tangkhuls, House	332	Tangkhuls, ornaments	333
Tangkhuls, Music and Dances	345	Tangkhuls, Art and Culture	346	Tangkhuls, Textiles and Clothes	346
Tangkhuls, tattooing	333	Tangkhuls, hair style (Coiffure)	333	Tangkhuls, weapons	334
Tangkhuls, Longshim	335	Tangkhuls. Ngalong	335	Tangkhuls, religion	335
Tangkhuls, Hangva	336	Tangkhuls, marriage	336	Tangkhuls, disposal of the dead	337

(Contd.)

(Contd. Appendix-8)

Topic	*Page Number*	*Topic*	*Page Number*	*Topic*	*Page Number*
Tangkhul War, Head Taking	339	Tangkhuls	327	Tarao	271
Tea Industry	628. 629	Teak Gurjan Forest	59	Telephone numbers	20
Teachings of Allah	441	Temples and monuments	401	Textiles of Hmars	544
Textiles of Kabui Nagas	543	Textiles of .Kukis	544	Textiles of Meiteis	539
Textiles of Meiteis, design and embroidery used	540	TDP Cement Project	612		
Textiles of Nagas	542	Thounii festival	588	Textiles of Paites	545
Textiles of Tangkhuls	542	Thadou	271	Thangal General	146
Thabal Chongba	384	Thaoba Singh Phanjao Jamadar	152	Thangal General Temple	374, 404
Thangjing Temple of Moirang	426	Thengou	514	Thangkairol	516
Thang Ta	513	Thongam Mondum	417	Thisam festival	580

(Contd.)

(Contd. Appendix-8)

Topic	Page Number	Topic	Page Number	Topic	Page Number
Tipaimukh HE Project	630	Thoubal district	559	Tikendrajit	145
Techniques of Manipuri Dance	503			Tonjao Singh Mongsataba Jamadar	153
Third Anglo – Burmese War	134	Totems	218	Tree Cults of ancient Manipur	229
Trial and execution of Tikendrajit and Thangal General	143, 461	Trans Asian Highways	596	Travel Agents	15
Treaty of Yandabo	121, 457	Tourist Information Centres	14	Trees of Manipur	60
Tourist Spots	368	Tree Bean Cultivation	68	Trilok Singh	151
Ukhrul	379, 570	Umang Lais	228		
Urakonthouba	92	Uru Singh Usurba	150	Uningthou	55
		Vasanta Raas	496	Vaiphei	272
Vishnu Temple	401	Waithou Lake	379	Vegetation	56

(Contd.)

(Contd. Appendix-8)

Topic	*Page Number*	*Topic*	*Page Number*	*Topic*	*Page Number*
Wari Liba	237	Watkin W. Roberts	464	War Cemetery	383
Wet hill forest	56	Wet Temperate Forest	58	Waterfalls	48
Why Invest in Manipur, package of incentives	611	Why Invest in Manipur, industrial scenario in Manipur	602	Why Invest in Manipur	609
Why should you visit Manipur	1	William Pettigrew	462	Wildlife-a rich natural heritage	49
Women's Agitation, first	476	Women's Agitation, second	485	Woolaobi	511
World War-II and Manipur	483	World's first Polo Club at Silchar -1859	521	Yaoshang	383
Yaithibi	242	Yarra festival	579	Yum Mangba	210
Yubi Lakpi	511	Yum Sanggaba	217	Yum Sengba	217
Yongchak	630	Zeliangrong	274	Zeliangrong Movement - 1930-1949	477
Zoological Garden	383	Zou	275	Zila Durbar at Cachar	130

Index

A

A'Chik Liberals Matgrik Army (ALMA), 460, 461
Abolition of
  Political Agent (office), 185
  Sanamahism, 334
  Slavery, 218
Aboriginal Tribes, 295
Abu Talik, m614
Adi Granth
  Dhana, 299
  Farid, 299
  Hymns, 299
  Kabir, 299
  Nam Dev, 299
  Pipa, 299
  Ramananda, 299
  Ravidas, 299
  Sadhna, 299
  Saini, 299
  Surdas, 299
Administration of
  Hill Area, 220
  Villages, 127
Administrative
  And Judiciary Functions, 528
  Structure, 126
Adultery
  Or Infertility base for Divorce, 528
  Punishable Among Kukis, 557
Aerobatic Activities, 804
African
  Slaves, 478
  Students, 474
Agartala, 166
Agartala Gas—, 1004
Agricultural Mainstay of Manipur, 1011
Ahluwalia, Montek Singh, 982
Ahom Kings, 127
Aimol, 378
AIR Imphal, 913
Akal Takht, 299
Akala, 139, 143
Akbar
  Hydari, Sir, Governor of Assam, 245, 253, 254, 447

The Great, 863
Akoijam Khemba—Labanga, 171
Alaungpaya, Burmese King, 720, 722, 723
Alexander the Great, 472
All
Districts of Manipur, 909
India Congress Committee, 237, 246, 247
Manipur Sports Association, (AMSA), 817, 818
White Commission, 445
Allen, Cap, 202
Allocation of Funds, 982
Amamba (Darkness), 32
Amarapura, Royal City, 191
Amarpura, King of Benares, 168
American
Baptist Church, 444
Baptist Mission, 745, 746, 749
Catholic Church, 476
Anal, 379
Backwardness, 750
Festivals, 951
Festivals, Ikam, 951
Festivals, Inhla, 951
Festivals, Mikhemphan, 952
Festivals, Philthabla, 952
Festivals, Sungkhomlkhan, 952
Ananta Shai, 163
Ancestor Worship, 334
Ancestral
Gods, 338
Property, 402
Ancient
Book and Chronicles, 42, 43
Monuments and Archaeological Sites and Remains Act, 1958, 656
Andaman and Nicobar Islands, 2, 212-214, 710, 728, 742
Cellular Jail, 762
Andro Nagar Panchayat, 910
Andro—Nungbi, 891
Angamese (Naga), 176, 380
Territories, 442
Angami Girls, 436
Angamis, 187, 439, 463, 487
Angao Singh of Kabo Leikai, 214
Anglo-Manipur War, 1891, 126, 200, 206, 295, 580, 658, 710, 734, 745
Angom, 39
Chanu, 230
Ningthou, 123
Poran Singh, 746
Angou Sana, 744
Angousana Senapati, Prince, 208
Animal Sacrifice, 333
Animism, 747
Animistic Rituals, 744
ANSAM, 482
Antiquity Theory, 705
ANVC, 470
Aos, 435, 439
Apokpa
Khuramjaba, 309, 313
Laipham (Shrine for Clan Ancestors), 312
Arab
Militia (Rape Camps), 474
Slave Trade, 477
Arabia, 705
Arabic, 36
Arakan, 725, 726, 775-778
Independent Arm, 470
Arambi Devi, 149
Arcade System, 662

Arjun Award Winners from Manipur, 821
Armistice Day, 451
Arms
  And Ammunitions, 732
  Procurement in Thailand, 459
Army
  Leaders, 144
  E Khulam, 144
  Haobam Aroy, 144
  Pala Koireng, 144
  Yumnam Kiyamba, 144
Art
  And Culture, 794, 931
  Of Pottery, 891
  Of Story Telling, 718
Arthington
  Aboriginese Mission Society, 745
  Mission, 746
Artifacts of Bamboo, 3
Artistic
  Designs, 659
  Handicrafts, 883
Arts and Crafts Offices, Imphal, 883
Arunachal Pradesh, 460, 465
Aryans, 40
ASEAN Regional Forum, 976
Ashiba and Konjin, 880
Ashoka, 301
Asian Highway-Iran-Pakistan-India-Nepal, 975, 982, 983
Asos, 463
Assam, 35, 36, 55, 56, 166, 173, 176, 181, 407, 448, 465
  And Arunachal Pradesh, 471
  And Bangladesh, 710
  And Cachar, 732
  Burma and Tripura, 747
  Disturbed Area Act, 1955, 450
  Gas—, 1004
  Olympic Association, 816
  Provincial Assembly, 233
  Rifles, 443, 467, 580, 761, 762, 766, 770
Assembly Constituencies, (AC), 910
Andro, 910
  Heingang, 910
  Jiribam, 910
  Keirao, 910
  Khundrakpam, 910
  Khurai, 910
  Kshetrigao, 910
  Lamlai, 910
  Thongju, 910
  Wangkhei, 910
  Yaiskul, 910
Atingkok, 32
Atiya
  Kuru (Guru), 32-35
  Kuru Sidaba, 361, 891
  Shidaba, 334, 335
Atomic Bomb, 779
Attack on Danubyu, 729
Aurangzeb, 706
  Governor Multan and Sindh, 706
  Policies, 708
Autonomous District Council, 471
Ava, 153, 154, 158, 168, 720-724, 728, 732, 733
  Harem, 154
Avataras, (Incarnations), 719
Award of
  CBE, 221
  KCSI, 221
Awunga, Chief of Tangkhul Village, 527, 542
Axis Allied Nations, 773

Azad Hind
Fauz (INA), 2
Hind Government Recognition, 773
Ba Maw's Burmese Government, 773
Croatia, 773
Fascist Italy, 773
Germany, 773
Thailand, 773

B

Bachelors Dormitory, 526, 559
Backward Tract, 444
Badawpaya, King of Ava, 168
Bagyidaw,
Bur King, 169, 170, 176
Coronation, 170
Baisakhi Amrit Sanskar, 298
Balabhadra,
Brahmachari, 716
Subhadra, Ram Krishna—Nityainanda, 671
Baladhan Tea Gardens, 442
Bamboo
And Bamboo Shoots, 1028
And Paper Industry, 990
Based Industries, 991
Brakes, 77
Forest, 991
Shoot Fermentation, 999
Bandula, Maharaja, Burmese Gen., 724, 726, 728, 729
Bangladesh, 460, 467, 469, 975
Bangladesh—Sri Lanka, 482
Bank Robberies, 460
Banking
And Finance, 1026
In Manipur, 1026
Baptist Church, 526
Activities in Manipur, 516
Missionaries, 931
Baptists, 399
Barak Drainage Area, 991
Barbarous Mountain Population, 444
Basket Making, 432
Battle of
Kakching, 149, 724
Thoubal, 172
Wangjing, 148
BCIM (Bangladesh, India, China, Myanmar), 976
Beijing
Leadership, 468
Raja, 184
Beiragya Dharma, 226, 227
Bell, Sir Nicholas Dodd Beaton, Chief Commissioner Assam, 763
Bengal, 36
Infantry, 190
Renaissance, 304
Bengali Migration in Manipur, 710
Bengalis, 303
Benoy Singh, 234
Bentinck, Lord William, Gov Gen, 176, 180, 733, 735
Bhadra Singh, Painter, 189
Bhadra Singh, Paintings, 189
Flowers, 189
Paintings,
Gour Leela, 189
Hiyang Tannaba, 189
Jhulon Leela, 189
Kaophaba, 189
Keiphaba, 189
Loikaba, 189

Nouka Bilasa, 189
Panch Tattvatas, 189
Radha Krishna, 189
Zila Durbar, 189
Bhagat Wani, 298
Bhagavad Gita, 672
Bhagavata Culture, 165
Bhagyachandra, 332
King, 583, 587, 667, 668, 670, 722
Maharaja, 44, 46, 758, 800, 805, 882
Bhakti Vedanta, AC Swami Prabhupada, 672
Bhamo, Principality, 137
Bharat Sai, 722
Bhartiya Janta Party, 306
Bhashkar, RK, Chairman Election Tribunal, 245
Bhirbhan, Satnami Leader, 708
Bhopal, 250
Bible
In Thadou and Kuki Dialect, 746
Sociey, 745
Society of India, 750
Biblical Organizations, 754
Bidhumukhi Knockout Football Tournament, 817
Bihari
Language-Magadhi, Bhojpuri, Maithili, 300
Muslims, 301
Biharis, 300
And Marwaris, 923
Bijoy Govinda, 163
Bilba, Silver Ring, 396
Bimbavati Devi d/o Bhagyachandra, 805
BIMSTEC, 976
Bir Tikendrajit Park, 584
Bir Tikendrajit, 584, 585
Bishnupriyas, 366-368
Culture, 369
Deities, 370
Dress and Ornaments, 370
Festivals, 369
Marriages, 369
Society, 369
Bishnupur (Lamangding), 656, 671, 917, 924
Municipal Council, 925
Profiles, 924, 925
Temples, 924
Bishnupur—Tiddim, 778
Black African Captives, 474
Bodhachandra, Son of Churachand, 222
Bodhchandra Singh, Maharaja, 231, 233, 237, 239, 242, 251-254, 256, 258-262, 521, 581, 676
Bogota, 235
Bolan Pet, 58
Boliver, 235
Bombing of Imphal by Japanese Tojo, 231, 232
Border
Commission, 189
Feuds, 180
Road Development Board, 982
Roads Organization (BRO), 975
Trade along with Tamu-Moreh Silcher Champhai Rite Border, 970
Trade Posts, 968
Lizer, 968
Mure, 968
Bordolo, Sir Gopinath, 449
Bose, Netaji Subhash Chandra, 2, 232, 233, 588, 589, 773, 777, 779, 926

Bose, Rash Behari, 773
Boundary Disputes, 189
Brahma
  Sabha, 226-228
  Samaj, 337
Brahmapur Leikei, 657
Brahmins in Manipur, UP, Assam, Gujarat, Orissa, 716
Brahmputra, 726
Branches of Sericulture, 992
  Mulberry—Muga, Eri, 992
Bride Price, 396, 397, 438, 528, 557
Brij bhasha, 802
Brinda Tulsi, 150
Brindabanchandra, 195
  Temple, 195, 582
Britain—Pakistan, 469
British
  Administration, 756
  Administrators, 444
  And Burmese Territory, 177
  And Indian Army Cemeteries, 23, 586
  And its Allies, 232
  And Japanese Soldiers, 3
  Army, 197, 232, 736
Baptist Church, 466
Bengal, 724
  Colonial Officers, 444
  Column, 200, 201, 741
  Commonwealth, 241
  Crown, 241, 466
  District of Sylhet, 734
  East India Company, 36, 154, 223, 1014
  Emigrants, 477
  Empire, 247
  Forces, 200, 580, 727, 729, 737
Government Awards for Capturing Persons, 743
Imperialism, 409
India, 223, 224, 234, 253, 726, 851
Indian Army, 772
Leaders, 241
Military Explorer, 429
Museum London, 51
Nationals, 467
Officers, 212, 213
Col Skene, 212
Cossin, 212
JW Quinton, 212
Lt Simpson, 212
Political Agent, 479, 745
Chronological Details, 1065-166
Political Officers, 181, 446
Power, 442
Puppet Gambheer Singh, 178
Raj, 247, 763, 764
Relations with Naga Tribes, 441
Religious Policy, 745
Rewards for Capturing Persons, 202
Dolai Hamjaba, 202
Manipur Maharaja, 202
Thangal, Gen., 202
Tikendrajit, 202
Zilengamba, 202
Role, 466, 467
Rule, 472, 755
Rule in India, 240, 242
Silcher Column, 200
Troops, 442
War Graves Commission in Manipur, 3, 913
USA, Pakistan, Bangladesh, China, 491

Brown Antlered Deer, 2, 62
Buddhism, 191, 301
    And Christianity, 473
Bunning Meadow, 948
Buranji of Ahoms, 36
Burial
    Cercmony, 397
    Of Dead Bodies, 135
    Sites, 779
Burma (modern Myanmar), 36, 147, 149, 153, 154, 158, 172, 179, 180, 190, 232, 238, 251, 295, 428, 460, 462, 469, 515, 574, 720, 723, 724, 732, 733, 745, 772, 773
    And Tripura, 710
    As Kabow, 36
    Communist Party, 234
    Military Police, 443, 761
    Pea Fouls, 65
Burma—Hainan, 63
Burmaj and Manipur, 522
Burman
    Envoy, 177
    Forces, 171, 172, 173, 188, 730
    Interim Govt., 238
Burmese, 35, 36
    Area Army, 773
    Army, 149, 174, 725
    As 'AVA', 36
    Camp of Nagas, 468
    Campaign, 148
    Communist, 233, 234
    Communist Party, 453
    Forces, 165, 725
    Governor of Pegu, 721
    Insurgents, Linkage With-, 469
    Invasion, 408, 580
    Mission (1702), 147
    Occupation of Manipur, 710
    Peace Mission, 731
    Troops, 173
Burney, Maj., 176, 177
Butler, Capt., 442

C

Cabinet Mission, 447, 467
Cachar, 35, 56, 57, 138, 142-144, 158, 161, 165, 166, 168, 169, 172, 173, 175, 182, 183, 186, 194, 200, 207, 233, 246, 251, 335, 442, 665, 724-727, 735, 741, 745, 764, 849, 850
    And Jaintia, 172
    And Manipur, 59
    And Sylhet, 59, 176
    And Tanu, 737
    And Tripure, 127
    Kings, 706
California Gold Rush, 478
Californite Jade, 995
Campbell, Sir Archibald, 728-730
Camps in Pakistan, 459
Cane and Bamboo Production Projects, 1035, 1036
Craft Industry, 1035
    Government Role, 1038
    Main Objectives, 1038
    Products in Manipur, 1036
Cane and Bamboo Works, 893-894, 912
    Trade, 895
    Trained Artisans in-, 895
Cane Brakes, 77
Capital Punishment, 132, 213
Capt. Cole, Political Agent, 221
Capt. Grant, 174, 176
Capt. Jenkins, 176

Caracas, 235
Card System, 768
Cash Economy, 410
Caste System, 472, 474, 480
Catholic Church, 525
Cattle Poisoning, 938
Caves, 60
- Hangkhui, 38, 516
- Khangkhui (Ukhrul)—Khukse (Churachandpur), 60
- Khuman, 659
- Lime, 591
- Mangang, 659
- Tharon, 38, 591, 948

Ceasefire
- Agreement, 454
- To Manipur, 487

Cellular Jail, 743
Cement Projects in Manipur, 994
Central
- Jail Imphal, 203
- Sector Power Plants, 1004

Centre for Electronic Design and Technology (CEDT), 990, 1003
Chahi Taret Khuntakpa, 582, 579
Chairai Rongba, 720
Chaitanya, 303, 719
- Mahaprabhu, 673
- Sect, 165

Chaitanyamarita, 332
Chak
- Age, 32

Chanaba (Community Feast), 318
- Divisions, Hayi, Haya, Khunung, Langba, 32

Chakpa (s), 143, 359
Chakpa Makhaongambi Princess, 147
Chaliha, BP, 466
Chandrakirti, CC Kouseswari Devi, Mother, 205
Chandrakirti, Maharaja, 132, 180-185, 188, 189, 191, 205-208, 314, 343, 344, 580, 582, 658, 740, 801, 882
- Attempts to Dethrone, 181, 183
- Death, 191
- Queens, 191
- Sent Polo Teams to Calcutta, 186

Changseu, 381
Chaoba Hida Machahal, 211
Chaoba, Mayanglambam, 665, 666
Chaobatol Singh, 214
Chaopha Khek Khoomba, Pong King, 655
Chaphu, 892
Charaikong, Maram Chief, 144
Charairongba, 579, 882
Chaughan (Polo) of the Mughals, 863
Chaurasi Khamba, 580
Check Post System, 970
Cheirap, 131, 132, 365
- Civil Court, 123
- Court, 757, 759
- Criminal Court, 219
- Ordinary Court, 187

Cheitharol Kumbaba, Royal Chronicle, 581, 658
Chen Baptist Association, (CBA), 751
Cheniu Artisans, 657
Chhongthu Baptist Association, 750
Chiang Kai-Shek, 774
Chidambaram, P, Fin Minister, 969
Chief
- Ministers of Manipur
  - Chronological Details, 1074
- Players of Polo, 846
- Loyalakpa—Khoriphaba, 846

Child Birth (Naga Women), 438

Chin
- Hills, 405, 408, 470, 761
- State of Burma, 295
- State of Mayanmar, 397

China, 143, 429, 468, 474, 518, 519, 552, 705, 742, 974
- And Burma, 36
- And Japan, 1015

China-Border with Arunachal Pradesh, 460
China—Taiwan, 1014
Chinese, 35, 36, 40
- AK Rifles, 460
- Invasion, 579
- Prisoners, 579
- Role, 468
- War Captures, 582

Ching Theng Khomba, 158, 159
- Sija Samjamani, Daughter, 158

Chinga Hills, 145
Chingakham Sanachaoba Singh, 761
Chinglen Sana, 741
Chingmeirong, 912
Chingthan Khomba, Maharaja, 403
Chingulembi of Mleecha, Kamrup Princess, 882
Chirai Naga, 215, 744
Chiru, 380
Chishi Swu, 459, 464
Chisti and Firdouse Silsilas, 705
Chit Shai, 721, 722
Chitnu Tamilnu, Goddess, 880
Cholera Epidemic, 189, 221
Chou En Lai, 468
Choupha Khek Khomba, King of Pong, 716
Chourajit Singh, 723, 724
Chowkami Naga of Mayangkhang, 215
Chowkop Chingjim, 171
Christian
- Conversion, 409
- Mission, 747
- Missionaries, 398, 466, 490, 479, 746
- Missionaries in Manipur, 515
- Thangal Society, 386

Christianity, Arrival of-, 744
Christians in Kerala, 474
Chungkham Rani Devi, Awardee of Wangkhe Phi, 912
Churachand Singh, (Sir), Maharaja, 126, 216, 219-222, 224, 225, 227-231, 233, 336, 344, 346, 576, 479, 521, 661, 663, 593, 762, 816, 817, 882
Churachand Singh, Raja, 756, 760
Churachand, Mayambunghal, Elder Brother of-, 227, 229
Churachandpur, 238
Churachandpur-Tiddien Route, 300
Churamani Singh, 211
Church
- Management, 749
- Of Christ, 399, 526
- Of England, 745
- Organization, 750

Churches at-, 750
Chandel, 750
Chingkhong, 750
Churachandpur, 750
- Kangchup, 750
- Kangpokpi, 750
- Tamei, 750
- Thighat, 750

Churchill, Winston, 851, 1014
CIA Arms, 467
CIS Countries, 1034

Civil
Administration, 758
And Criminal Courts, 187
Disobedience, 771
Disobedience Movement, 237, 244, 245, 252
War, 474
Clans, 35, 39, 378, 405, 557
And Marriages, 133
And Yek Salai, Creation of-, 33
Angom, 35, 310
Chenglei (Sarang leishangthem), 35
Exogamy, 944
Kanghujam, 134'
Khaba Ngangba, 35
Khuman, 35
Luwang, 25
Mangang, 35
Moirang, 35, 489
Ningthouja, 34, 659, 881
Pangan, Arabia, 704
Rajkumar, 185
Shanglakpam, 670
Sijagurumayum, 670
Songthu and Yeite, 387
System, 35, 134, 135
Classical
Dances Style of India, 794
Bharat Natyam, 794
Kathak, 794
Kathakali, 794
Kuchipudi, 794
Manipuri, 794
Odissi, 794
Manipuri Dances, 804
Poetry, 802
Chandidas, 802
Govindadas or Gyandas, 802
Jayadeva, 802
Vidyapal, 802
Clouded Leopard, 63
Coal Mines, 437
Coins of
Gambheer Singh, 47
King Ayangba, 44
King Bhagrachandra, 46
King Chitsai, 45
King Chourajit, 46
King Deva Najari Scripts, 44
King Jaising, 47
King Khagemba, 44
King Lairenba, 44
King Paikhumba, 44
King Ura Konthuba, 44
Coins, 44
Coleman, Sir Surgeon, 744
Colonial
America, 477
India, 477
Columbia, 235
University, 475
Columbus, Christopher, 478
Column Strength, 200
Combat Cargo Unit, 777
Communal
Award, 473
Violence, 241
Communication Structure, 396
Communist
Movement, 241
Party of China, 468
Party of India, 233, 238, 306
Communities, 398
Maring, 398
Tangkhul, 398
Thadou, 398

Community
- Development Blocks, 910, 924
- Bishnupur and Moirang, 924
- Information Centre (CICS), 1003
- Kabuis, 334
- Zeliangrong, 334

Computer Education, 1003
Confederation of Indian Industry, (CII), 1036, 1042
Congo Civil War, 475
Constituent Assembly, 248
Constitution Making Committee, 238
Constitutional Safeguard, 398
Construction of Kangla, Ashangbam Laiba, 578
Conversion, 515, 705, 746, 747
- Into Hinduism, 151
- To Christianity, 752

Coote, Capt., 762
Copper Plate at Kharam Pallel, 44
Copper/Iron Plates, 43
Coronation
- Dresses, 881
- Phingang pheijom—Phambalou, 881
- Of Shree Shree Govindjee, 164

Co-Sanguinary Marriage, 528
Cottage Industry (ies), 2, 407, 880
Counseling-Cum-Grievance Committee, 971
Counter-Insurgency Agencies, 461
Coupland, 446, 447
Courts of Justice, 118
Cremation- a Customary Method, 149
Cropping Pattern, 937
Cross-Cousin marriage, 528
Cultivation and Harvesting, 432
Cultures and Taboos, 384
Custom Seizure Items, 970
Customary Laws, 410
Customs and Deities, 7
Cymbel Dance, 804

D

Dacca, 175
Dacca Jail, 183
Dacca-Bangladesh-London-Pindi-Peking Channel, 467
Dalhouse, Lord, 735
Dalits, 474
Damodara Swamy, 672, 673
Dance,
- Kabiu Naga Dance, 2
- Khamba-Thoibi, 589
- Raas Lila, 2
- Tangkhul Naga Dance, 2

Dances in Chandel District, 951
- Paite Dance, 951
- Taraowar Dance, 951
- Thadou Dance, 951

Dances of Hmars, 566
- Chwng Dance, 566

Dar Lam, 568
- Hrang Lam, 568
- Lam Lam, 566
- Pheiphit Dance, 566
- Tinna Hla, 568

Dara Shikoh, 707
Dara's Son Suleman, 707
Darbar (Durbar), 126, 127
Darbu, 569
Darmang, 569
Das, Deshbandhu Chitranjan, 164
Dawi Gam (God of Junge), 396
Dawibawnu, Family Deity, 406

Daw-in, 396
Death
Ceremony, 405
Of Grimwood, Political Officer, 203, 206
Penalty, 151
Rituals, 226, 403, 439
Sentence, 744
Deb, Mohan Singh, Founder First Indian National Army, 772
Debendra Singh, Maharaja, 128
Declaration
Of Naga Independence, 1947, 448
On the Rights of Indigenous Peoples, 466
Defence of India Rule, 1944, 233
Degraded Classes, 130
Bishnupriyas, 130
Loi/Chakpa, 130
Ydithibi, 130
Deities Nara Singh—Chaitanya Mahaprobhu, 670
Desai, Morarji, former Indian PM, 458
Design and Embroidary in Meitei Textiles, 885
Details of Persons Tried for Waging War against Queen Empress, 204-205
Deve Gowda, HD, former Indian PM, 464
Devendra Singh, Raja, 182, 183, 758
Dewan of Manipur, 253
Dhaja Singh Mayengba, 212
Dhana Singh Sagolsemba, 213
Dharma Singh of Mayengbam Leikai, 212
Dharmi Sahitya in Bengal, 332
Digendrajit, 229, 230
Khureijan Tombimanba Sija, wife, 229
Dimapur Town, 7, 464
Dimasa National Volunteer (DNV), 461, 470
Dinachandra, 192, 193
Diplomatic and Trade Relations (Assam and Manipur), 36
Distances from Imphal from other Cities, 21
Distillery of Spirits, 130
District
Bishnupur, 59, 589, 914, 923, 927, 1042
Cachar, 72
Cachar, North Cachar and Aizwal, 561
Chandel (DC), 15, 398, 398, 402, 403, 405, 483, 488, 552, 948
And Churachandpur, 917
Art and Culture, 951
Border District Bordering Myanmar, 948
Flora and Fauna, 950
Transportation and Communication, 950
Chindwin, 149, 720
Churachandpur, 13, 68, 398, 405, 552, 923, 927, 948
And Chandel, 408
Darang, 212, 213
Ganjam, 261
Gulbarga, 474
Hoogly, 474
Industries Centre (DIC), 912, 913, 990
Naga Hills, 486
Sagaing, 723
Senapati, 43, 68, 396, 399, 401, 405, 483, 487, 519, 552, 914, 918

Ukhrul and Chandel, 991
Shwebo (Burma), 153
Sylhet, 477
Sylhet and Cachar, 296
Tamenglong, 15, 68, 407, 481, 483, 487, 591, 750, 751
Tangnoupal, 43
Thoubal, 914, 917, 918, 920, 923, 948, 1043
and Chandel, 923
and Bishnupur, 883
Tuensang, 429
Ukhrul, 15, 68, 83, 135, 403, 483, 488, 492, 515, 516, 591, 751, 918, 929, 930, 948, 994, 995
Ukhrul and Chandel, 917
Upper Chandwin, 153
Waikhong—Sikhong, 920
Divide and Rule, 482
Divine Right of Kings, 248
Divorce, 439
Domestic Deities, 338
Dongpi-dawi (Deity), 396
Dowry, 669
System, 528
Doyeng and Dhunsiri, 56
Dr. Thokchom Gobardhan Singh, First Manipur Doctor, 223
Dr.Rajendra Prasad, 241
Dragon God, 34
Dreams and Divinations, 532
Dress
And Diet, 138
Of Angamese, 434
Drum Dance, 804
Duliens/Dublians, (Hmar Sub Clan), 397
Durand, HM, 217
Durbar, 196-199, 206, 219, 220, 238, 762, 769, 771 see Darbar also
Durbar Hall, 213
Dutch Colony, 1014
Duty Free Personal Effects, 8
Dzuko Lily (flower), 937

E

East India Company, 734, 743
East Pakistan (Bangladesh), 452, 469
Eastern Nagaland (Myanmar), 462
Economic
Blockade, 471
Growth, 969
Policy, 131
Economy, 1026
Ecosystem, 63
Ecuador, 235
Ecuador—Australia, 1027
Educated Tribes of Manipur, 515
Education, 398, 407, 753
Eldi Deer, 2
Election Tribunal, 245
Emigrant Workers, 296
Emperor Constantine the Great, 754
Empire of Ava, 177
Endogamy, 557
England – Sri Lanka, 805
English Education in Manipur, 189
Enola Gay, 779
Entourage Theory, 706, 708
Essential Items, 232
Ethnic
Cleansing of Sudan, 474
Cleansing, 489
Communities, 936, 937
Groups, 39, 460

Insurgent Groups, 461
Tribes, 951
Ethnological Gallery, 585
Europe—Yemen, 472
Eustace, Hill, Capt., 850
Evangelical Congregational Churches (ECCI), 752
Event Occasional Festivals, 934
Keshong kahao Zakhalat, 934
Khanakasa, 934
Maa Khungkashat, 934
Maran-Sak, 934
Mawouzai, 934
Ming Kaphok, 934
Shim Sak Kasa, 934
Tarung Khanqkasang, 934
Evil Spirits, (Raikaphung), 526
Excavations, 51
Exchange Facilities, 8
Excluded Area, 446
Excommunication Exile, 132
Executed Officers Details, 199-200
Executions, 212, 213, 216, 744
Leisangthemba, 213
Wokramba, 213
Exhibits in Manipur State Museum, 585
Tribal Ornaments—Tribal Costumes, 585
Existence of Spirits (Chipee, ka-meo), 526
Exodus
Excerpts, 754, 755
From Egypt, 754
Exogamy, 528
Exploitation
Of Nagas or Kukis, 480
Of Nagas, 470
Export
Markets, 1034
Of Skins, 8
Processing Zone, 982

F

Factional Rivalry, 311
Facts About Manipur, 19-20
Fall of
Kohima, 188
Rangpur, 727
Singapore, 772
Famous Manipuri Dance Gurus, 805
Guru Bipur Singha, 805
Guru Haobam Tomba Singh, 805
Guru Maisnam Amubi Singh, 805
Guru RK Priyogopat Sana, 805
Guru Sagolsem Kalidamon—Guru Kongrailatpam Radhamohan Sharma, 805
Guru Singajit Singh, 805
Guru Takhel Changbam Amudon Sharma, 805
Fauna and Flora (FF), 55, 919, 932, 945
Feasts of Merit, 440, 441, 532, 541
Federal
Army, 453
Govt. of Nagaland, (FGN), 451-453, 454, 457, 468, 489
Female Dances, 800
Fertility, 440
Festival, 339, 403, 406, 933
Ahong Khongjingba, 150
Bedal, 388
Buren Limpeh, 398
Chalam Kei, 389
Chamar Sier, 389
Chaonlei, 389
Chathar Lei, 389

Chawng, 567
Cheiraoba, New Year Festival, 677
Chumpha, 933
Darreo, 933
Halangkar (Holi), 662
Heikru Hetongba, 163
Hiyangbi Kumsaba, 826
Kanghi, 395
Kangrai Mendai, 388
Kartika, 369
Khobol Seed Sowing Ceremony, 403
Kikhaiycu, 400
Koni, 389
Kwak Jatra, 669, 832
Lai Haraoba, 361, 832, 833, 847
Lamkir Lei, 389
Laoniis, 399
Leng Wai, 389
Longra Khameng, 933
Luira, 933
Mahares Purnima, 369
Maibi Dance, 2
Mangkhap, 933
Of Koni Tribes, 392
Palchoi, 388
Panchmi, 317
Phaguwa, 369
Ponghi 395
Raas Lila, 2
Rakakhori, 395
Rath Yatra, 150
Sepoyou, 400
Thadou, 952
Thangjing Lai Haraoba, 589
Thezinglap Chawn, 406
Thisham, 934
Yaosang, Great Festival of Meiteis, 165
Yarra, 933

Financial Operations, 460
First
Anglo-Burmese War, 173, 174
Census Operation in, 1881, 186
Devastation (Khuntakahanba), 720
Devastation of Manipur, 720
Kuki Baptist Church, 747
Nupilal (First Women Agitation), 755
Olympic Games, 816
Raas Lila, 164
World War in Egypt, 760
Fiscal Incentives, 1007
Fisheries, 60
Fishes, 921
Common Carp, 921
Grass Carp, 921
Mirgle Carp, 921
Mirror Carp, 921
Rohu, 921
Silver Carp, 921
Fishing in Imphal West District, 920
Five Finger Mountain, 517
Flag and Cap Satryagraha, 244
Floral Motifs, 657, 659
Flowers Varieties in Manipur, 82, 83
Folk Art of Tangkhuls, 41
Folklore and Legends, 428
Folktales and Legends, 518
Food Processing
Industrial Park, 994
Industries, 1034
Football, Popular Game of Manipur, 816
Foreign
Mission, 749
Nationals, 6

Foreigners (Protected Areas) Order, 1958, 3
Forest Survey of India, 68
Forest Types in Manipur, 69
Forfeiture of Property, 744
Formation of Bharatpur State, 708
Forts, 409
    Gotengkot, 409
    Hiengtam, 409
    William, 173, 726
Fossils of Cuttle Marine Fish, 39, 59
Fox, UM, 746
France, 221, 761, 1041
Franchise Sub-Committee, 245
Freedom Fighter, 743
FRRO (Foreigners Regional Registered Office), 3
Fruit Processing, 1034
Functional Groups, 129, 130
Funding Techno-Economic Studies, 987

G

Gallu-ai (Head Hunting), 406
Gambheer Singh, Maharaja, 44, 47, 171-176, 179, 180, 206, 314, 441, 585, 724, 726, 729-733, 801, 818
Gambheer Singh, Raja, 175-178
Gandhi and Nehru, 448
Gandhi Cap, 237, 244
Gandhi, Mahatma, 232, 245, 473, 764, 766, 777
Gandhi, Mrs. Indira, PM, 258, 455, 489, 585
Gandhi's (Mahatma)
    Indian National Congress, 232, 777
    Struggle for India's Freedom, 237
Gandhian Theory of Satyagraha, 261
Ganga, 166, 167
Gangte, 380
Gangte Baptist Association, (GPA), 751
Garbha Griha, 664
Garib Nawas, (King, Maharaja), 154, 155, 184, 367, 579, 581, 667, 669, 676, 721, 913
    Chit Shai, 155
Garo Hills, 460
Garot, Military Court, 123, 131
Gaudiya Vaishnavism, 165
Gem Testing Laboratory, 995
Genealogy, 309
German
    Forces, 232, 772
    Jews, 475
Germany, 221, 475, 1041
Ghose, Prafulla Chandra, Bengal Congress Leader, 246
Ghuna Singh Khongdram, 212
Girls Dormitory, 526
Gita Mandal, 673
Glossary of Manipuri-English Words, 1077-1084
Gokul Singh, 184
Gold and Silver Decorations, 144
Golden
    Cat, 951
    Triangle, 493
Gonvindajee Temple at Kangla, Rebuilt by Chandrakirti, 185
Gopis in Raas Dances, 796
Gordon, British Political Agent, 849
Gordon, Lt., 180
Govindchandra, Raja of Cachar, 172
Gorkha Rifles, 195
Goshtha
    Lila, 802

Vrindaban Pareng, 801
Gospel of
Christ, 748
St. John, 745
St. Mark, 745
St. Mathew, 745
Gostha Lila, 794
Gothic Style, 677
Gotras of Hinduism, 225
Atriys, 225
Bhardwaj, 225
Gautam, 225
Kashyap, 225
Shandilya, 225
Gournath Singh, Ahom Ruler, 166
Gourshyam, 722, 723
Government of
Balk and Badakhshan, 706
People's Republic of Nagaland (GPRN), 459, 462,
Governors of Manipur Chronological Details, 1073
Govindachandra, King of Cachar, 724, 725
Govindjee Temple, 165, 219, 220, 243, 244, 579, 587
Board, 663
Govt. of India Act,
1858, 223
1909, 223
1919, 223, 1919, 444
1935, 223, 249, 253, 257, 260, 1935, 446
Gowho Naga, 215
Gram Panchayat, 924
Gran Columbia, 235
Granary (ies), 433, 451
Granite and Marble, 995
Grant, Maj. Lt, 180, 202, 730
Grants of Land, 125
Grazing Grounds, 60
Great
Ang Clans, 434
June Uprising, 484
Greater
Bengal, 468
Mekong Sub-Regional Cooperation, 973
Mizoram As Autonomous Unit, 468
Nagaland or Nagalim, 471, 472, 459, 461, 485, 487, 488
Greek, 36
Green Marble, 995
Grimson, C, 771, 772
Grimwood, Frank Sir Clair, 735-737, 744
Political Agent, 305
Guerrilla Warfare, 171
Guna Singh, 211
Gurkha Sepoys, 816
Guru
Aribans, 146
Bhaskar, 163
Govind Singh, 297, 299
Granth Sahib, 297-299
Nanak Dev, 297, 298
Gurus, 801
Agomba Singh, 801
Amudon Sharma, 801
And Shutradhar, 796
Bipin Singh, 801, 802
Naba Kumar, 801
Nileshwar Mukherji, 801
Senarik Singh Rajkumar, 801

Guwahati University, 817
Gwe Shans, 721, 722

H

Habits and Manners, 138
Hackett, Maj., 761
Hainam Island, 517
Hajare, Chungkhau Lokhon, Sculpture, 665
Haling Groups, 361, 362
Hamrs,
 Dances, 566
 Musical Instruments, 568
Handicraft Industry, 750, 1035
Handicrafts, 3, 436, 583, 723, 880-908
Handicrafts of Hmars, 572
 Bemkhuong—Rel, 573
 Dawrawn, 572
 Kawngvar, 572
 Leider, 572
 Paikawing, 572
 Tlam, 572
 Handloom, 880-908
 Industry, 2, 880, 921
 Population, 883
 Products, 912
 Weavers Cooperative Societies, 912
 Zones in India, 880
Handloom and Handicrafts, 915
 Industry, 921
 Items, 976
Hangko
 Age, 32
 Divisions- Ko, Thoi, Poi, Tayo, 32
Hangva, 527, 528
Hanjok, 361, 362
Hanko and Chak, 32
Hanuman, 150
Hao City, 518, 519
Hao Religion, Monotheistic Religion, 526
Haobam Binoda, Maj, 739, 740
Haosas, Kuki Village Chief, 558
Hare Ram Hare Krishna Cult, 673
Hari Krishna Movement, 672
Hari, Lancelor, Lt. Gov. East Bengal and Assam, 220
Hazari/Pana Hazari, Military Officer, 124
Head
 Hunting, 432
 In Naga Hills, 429
 Wars, 486
 Taking, 430, 431, 437
Heads as War Trophy, 532
Health Precautions, 19
Heavy Artillery Manufacturing of-, 145
Heibok Ningthou, Clan King Expert in Witchcraft and Black Magic, 674, 675
Heibunglok Village, 398
Heisman Gopal, 229
Hentak Chaphu, 892
Heroes Who Sacrificed their Lives at Khongjom War, 739
 Paona Brajbasi—Angangmacha, 739
Higgins, HJ, Pres. Manipour Durbar, 746, 765, 766
Higgins, JC, 760-762
High Level Commission, 981, 982
High Yielding Variety Seeds, 938
Hija Mayek, 881
Hijam Irabot, 233, 234, 236, 238, 251, 770
 Struggle, 233

Hill
- Areas Administration, 763
- Districts of Senapati, Chandel, Tamenglong, Ukhrul, 488
- Ranges, 55, 56
- Tribes, 39, 228, 294, 760, 972

Hills, 919
- Kwawrok, 919
- Mantak, 919
- Of Churachandpur, 554
- Thoujam Mondum-Punam, 919

Himalayan
- Black Bear, 63
- Hump, 774
- Mountain Systems, 55

Hindu (s), 42
- Customs, 294
- God, Bishnu, 142
- Meiteis, 304, 308
- Monks, 147
- Sepoys, 184
- Vaishnavism, 294, 309

Hinduism, 38, 132, 225, 304, 359, 360, 335, 338, 479, 744, 745
- Arrivals, 715
- In Manipur, 314

Hiroshima, 779

History of Polo in Countries of World, 861
- China, 863
- Greece, 861
- India, 863
- Iran, 863
- Northern Pakistan, 864
- Persia, 861, 862

Hitler, 472

HIV/AIDS Prevention, 344
- Hiyang Tanaba (Boat Race), 670, 826
- Traditional Game of Panas, 826

Hluttaw Council, 153, 720

Hmar Clan, 562
- Ngurti—Sakum, 562

Hmar People's Convention (HPC), 461, 470

Hmars, 561
- Courtship, 566
- Decorative Arts, 573
- Handicrafts, 572
- In Churachandpur District, 747
- Language, 561
- Leaders, 564
- Marriage, 562
- Origin and Migration, 561
- Pot System, 564
- Religion, 566
- Settled in Tipaimukh and Churachandpur of Manipur, 561
- Textiles, 570, 889
- Thangsuo—Zakuolaisen, 890

Hobinian Culture of North Vietnam, 948

Hokishe Seema, 457

Holi, 672

Holy Places in Kangla Fort, 581
- Kangla Men Surung, 581
- Manglen, 581
- Nunggoibi, 581
- Nungjeng Pukhri (Pond), 581
- Site for Lord koubru, 581
- Site of Lord Wangbaren, 581

Hongkha Muja, 518

Hoolok Gibbon (Yongmu), 63, 951

Horticulture
- Crops, 912
- Resources, 1007

Hotels
- In Churachandpur, 13

In Tamenglong, 15
Housa, Chief, 396
House of Commons (UK), 742
Household Industries, 912
Houses of Kukis, (Malai Kuki Inn), 556
How to Reach Imphal, 8
Hsinbyushin, Burmese King, 158
Huntre Hunba, Referee, 849
Hutton, JH, Dy. Commissioner of Naga Hills of Assam, 445, 447
Hyderabad, 250
Hydro-Electric
Plant, 222
Projects, 1004
Doyang, 1004
Irang, 1007
Kopili, 1004
Loktak, 1004
Rangnadi, 1004
Tipaimukh, 1007

I

Idocrase Processing Industry, 995
Idols of-, 164
Bangshibadan at Khangabok, 164
Govindjee, 128
Gourangaprabhu at Keisampel, 164
Jagannath, Subhadra and Balabhadra, 662
Krishnachandra, 665
Lord Govindjee and Radha, 662
Madan Mohan, 672
Radha Govinda, 582
Radha Madhav, 668
Rama, 669
Sita and Hanuman, 667
Illegal Trade, 970
Ima Keithal (mothers market), 583, 584
Image of
Buddha in Black Marble, 178
Govindjee, 163, 164, 175, 670
Lord Govindjee, 661
Madanmohan, 164
Ram—Shatrughana, 717
Shree Anuprabhu, 164
Shree Nityainanda, 164
Shri Abdeitya Prabhu, 164
Vishnu, 716
Imkongliba Ao, 453
Immigrants, 40
Of Kukis, 182, 187
Imperial Japan, 474
Imphal, 2, 134, 176, 186, 232, 745, 746, 773
Airstrip, 778
And Chindwin, 778
And Mandlay, 973
And Myanmar, 973
By Bus, 10
By Train, 10
Cemetery, 586
City, Capital of Manipur, 576, 577, 587
East District (IED), 138, 909
Agriculture Main Occupation, 910
District Industries Centres, 912
Door Darshan Kendras, 913
Fauna And Flora, 911
Handlooms and Handicrafts, 912
HQs. Porompot, 909
Jiribhum Sub-Divisions, 909
Population, 910
Revenue Circles, 910
Rivers, 911

Imphal, 911
Iril, 911
Thoubal, 911
Tourist Spots, 913
Jail, 762, 765
Municipal Council, 910
To Nowgong, 441
West District (IWD), 913
Administrative Setup, 928, 930
Assembly Constituencies, 914, 924
Keisanthong, 914
Kouthoujam, 914
Lamsang, 914
Langtha Band, 914
Mayang Imphal, 914
Naoria Pakhang Lakpa, 914
Patsoi, 914
Sagol Band, 914
Sekmai, 914
Singjamei, 914
Thangmei Band, 914
Uripok, 914
Wangoi, 914
Economy, 915, 931
Main Towns, 918
Rivers, 915
Profile, 914
Imphal-Cachar Road, 181, 187
Imphal-Moreh Sector, 982
Independent Bengal, Conspiracy to Create- Comprising of-, 468
Assam, 468
Bhutan, 468
East Pakistan, 468
Manipur, 468
Nagaland, 468
Sikkim, 468
Tripura, 468
West Bengal, 468
Independent Kachin Land, 470
India or Pakistan, 247, 248
India's
Imports from Myanmar, 968
Look East Policy, 969, 973
Major Export in Myanmar, 968
Major Export in Myanmar, Agricultural Products, 968
Major Export in Myanmar, Primary and Semi-finished Iron and Steel, 968
Indian
Administration Service (IAS), 515
Airlines, 8, 9
Airlines, Flight Details, 10
Airlines, Flight Timings, 10
Armed Forces, 451
Army, 450
Civil Service, 127
Customs, 8
Dance Forms, 795
Freedom Struggle, 926
Hindu Society, 272
Independence Act, 1947, 239-241, 247, 251, 257, 448
Details, 240
Independence League, 772
IV Corps, 774
Missions, 3
National Army (INA), 2, 34, 232, 233, 237, 247, 589, 773, 776, 777, 779, 926, 927
Museum, (Moirang), 588, 926
National Congress, 237, 239, 252, 306
National Flag, 2, 233, 244

Olympic Association, 818
Penal Code, 184
Penal Code, 452, 770
Philosophy, 301
Prisoners of War, 772
Security Forces, 488
Slavery Act, 1843, 477
Slaves, 477
Troops, 451
Visa, 3
Indigenous
Fishes in Manipur, 65-67
Games of Manipur, 823-833
Kukna—Thang, 823-833
Indo-
Aryan Ethnic Groups, 300
Burma Pioneer Mission (IBPM), 752
Burma Road, 588
China Countries, 517
Myanmar
Border, 63, 951
Border Trade, (IMBT), 968-977, 983, 994
Road, 591, 949
Trade, 969, 976
Trade Route through Moreh, 969
Naga Issue, 466
Naga Peace Talk, 454
Indramani Singh, 818
Industrial
Backwardness, 921
Corporation Details, 993
Grown Centre, 986
Infrastructure Development, 986
Policy of Manipur, 1996, 984
Projects in Manipur, 1032
Industrialization, 984
Infiltration of Illegal Foreigners from-, 296
Nepal, Bangladesh, Burma, 296
Information Technology
Based Industry, 1002
Education, 1003
Enabled Services, 1003
Industry, 1002
Literacy Program, 1003
Park, 1003
Infrastructure
Development, 981, 982
Facilities, 994
Sectors, 981
Inherit, 396
Inheritance, 439
Among Hmars, 563
Among Kukis, 558
And Culture, 402
Laws, 439
Inner Line Permit, 7
Instrument of Accession, 241, 243, 249, 253, 259, 260
Text, 1067-1070
Insurgency, 460
Insurgent (s)
Groups, 461
Movements, 461
Of NSCN (IM), 459
Integrated
Industrial Development Centres (IIDC), 986
Pineapple Concentration Plant, 997
Inter-Clan Marriage, 405, 557
Interim Govt. of Manipur, 251
Internal Autonomy, 249
International
Film Festival of Wildlife in USA, 347

Performers of Manipuri Dance, 805
Guru Amuhi—Guru Senarik Rajkumar, 805
Trade Route, 983
Invasion of Ko-Lo-Feng, and I-Mau-Shun, 518
Investiture Ceremony, 218
Irabot Singh, 251
Irai Leima, 675
Ireland and Irish Republicans (neutrals), 773
Irengbam, 38
Iron Ores, 686
Iron Place of Maharaja Bhagyachandra, 44
Irrawady, 429
Isaak Muivah, Leadership, 465, 468
Isak Chishi Swu, 458
Ishori Devi, 231
Ishwori Devi, Maharani, 231, 242, 261
ISI, 460
ISKON (International Society for Krisnna Consciousness), 672, 673
Temples, 672, 673
Islamic
Codes, 297
Funerals, 714, 715
Issac Swu, 453
Ithai Barrage, 1042
Ivory, 8

J

Jack Fruit
Tree, 717
Images Carved out of -, 717
Trees, 161
Of Kaina, 1163, 164
Jadonang, Zeliangrong Leader, 764-766
Jadonang Followers, 764
Gaidinliu
Lurungpu of Kuki, 764
Ma Chunggong, 764
Mudunneng of Kembirin, 764
Namdichung of Gakoklong, 764
Siphai of Blongdai, 764
Takhennang of Cachar, 764
Jagannath, 671
Puri, 657
Subhadra Balabhadra, 662, 665
Jahanara Begum, Aurangzeb's Sister, 706
Jahangir, 36
Jai Singh, 314, 723
Jainism, 300
Jaintia, 725
Jaintia and Surma, 166
Jala Killi, 672
Jamir, SC, CM Nagaland, 464, 465, 485, 493
Japan, 2
Japanese
Army, 232, 772, 773, 777
Air Force, 774
Artilleries, 778
Malayan Campaign, 772
Occupation of Tangkhul Area, 516
Tojo, 773
War, 232
War Memorial, 779
Japhou Village, 398
Jatra or Jatrawali, 343
Jawl Puon, 891
Jaya Prakash Narayan, 466
Jehangir, Mughal Emperor, 710

Jenkin, Capt. 441
Jesus, 710
Jewelry Export Promotion Council, 995
Jews, 475
Jews and Romans, 475
Jhoomng Cultivation, 432
Jhulon, 672
Jhum (Shifting) Cultivation, 68, 497, 410, 564
    Culture, 558
Jhuming, 938
Jiribam, 734, 913, 991, 1030, 1031
    Municipal Council, 910
Jirighat, 59
Jirighat Tea Estate, Cachar (Assam), 1014
Johnston, Sir James, Political Agent, 576, 745, 582, 850
Johnston, Col. James, Political Agent Manipur, 56, 186-191
Joint Declaration, 464
Jubraj Tikendrajit, 205-207
Junagarh, 250

K

Kabo
Khari and Chapheng, 518
    Lei Kai, 149, 211
Kabok and Types, 1023
Kabui Exogamous Clans, 407
    Gangmei, 407
    Ganmei, 407
Kammei, 407
    Langmei, 407
Kabui
    Lila, 343
    Nagas, Textile, 888
    Textile, Pheishoi—Kharam Phai, 889
    Thangkhuls and Kukis Women, 884
Kabul, 476
Kacha Nagas, 383
    Traditional Beliefs, 384
Kachin
    Independent Army, (KIA), 458
    Legend, 517
    Rebels, 460
Kaina, 25, 667, 670, 671, 913
    Hill, 161
    Sacred Place of Hindus, 587
Kaito Sema, C-in-C, 453, 469
Kajao Pukhramba Phinganj (Hanged), 203
Kakching, 722, 737
    Granary of Manipur, 920
    Kameng, 686
Khullen, 686
    Wairi, 686
Kala
    Naga Hills, 183
    Sana, 758
Kalanaga and Tipaimukh, 59
Kaleum, Bur Commander, 171
Kali Temples, 147
Kalika Temple, 579
Kalyo Kengyu Area, 440
Kamakhya, 150
Kamkholun, Village Chief, 746
Kanching, 918
Kandhar, 706
Kang Chingba (Rathyatra), 827
Kang, Nagas Popular Game, 434
Kangjeiroi, Treatise on Polo, 846
Kangla
    Fort, 145, 658, 914, 917
    Ancient Manipur Palace, 578

British Attack on-, 197
Palace, 136
Ruins of Old Fortress, 23
Sha, 579, 580, 582, 742
Kangpokpi, 746, 747, 4749
Karam Manmohan Singh, First Manipur Producers, 346
Karen National Defence Organization, 469
Kargil Area, 864
Karong, Former HQs of Manipur, 935
Kawabe, Masakesu, Lt. Gen., 773
Kehovi Sema, 453
Keibul Lamjao
Deer Sanctuary, 4
National Park, Sangai, 23, 927
National Park in Loktak Lake, 2, 23
Kendat Province of Burma, 190
Kengtu gamba, Burmese Army Head, 149
Kevi Yalley, m458
Khagemba, Maharaja, 581, 882
Khagi, 143
Khalsa Panth, 299
Khamaran, 143
Khamba Thoibi Dance, 794
Khamlangba of Kakchinig, 685
Khangkhui Cave, 516
Khansari Sugar Factory at Wangbal, 921
Khaplang, SS, 458, 459, 462, 464, 496
Khasis, 175
Khaw Hausa, Traditional Chief, 406
Khemba Thoebi Dance, 803
Kho-Dawi (Village Deity), 396
Khojathong—Mantripukhri, 773
Khonghampat Orchidarium, 585
Orchid Yard, 23
Khongjom
Anglo-Manipur War, 588
Indo-Burma Road, 25
War, 201, 202, 670, 737-742
War Memorial, 4
Khousarol, Art of Spear Dance, 832
Khoutha, 381
Khrisanesa Angami, 453
Khuiyoi Tompok, 881
Khuman, King Kokpa, 674
Khumans, 39
Khumbet Raja, 140
Khumbng Chandramani and Nandalal, 167
Khunjaoba Mehar, 826
Khunthong Lakpas, 127
Khuong, 569
Khupkhotinlong Haokip, Kuki Commander, 762
Khurai, 912
Khusru, Sassanid King, 863
Khwai Lamabam Leikai, 164
Kinds of Raas Lila, 796
Diba Raas, 796
Kunja Raas, 796
Maha Raas, 796
Nitya Raas, 796
Vasanta Raas, 796
King
Angousana Brother, 735
Bagidaw, 724
Bhagyachandra (Jai Singh), Madhuchandra, Son, 166, 168
Bhagyachandra, (Jai Singh), 2, 36, 126, 155, 157-159, 161, 162, 165, 166, 168, 587, 717, 718
Creator of Raas Lila, 795
Queens, 167

Trial, 159
Bharat Shai, 155
Bhimbal Narayana, 706
Bodawpaya, Burmese King, 723
Bodhchandra, 669
Chalaamba, 143
Chandrakirti, 296, 443, 665, 666, 667
Charai Rongba, 146-148, 657, 716, 849, 858
Chit Shai, 155
Chourajit Singh, 167-169, 579, 668
Emperor George, 233
Gambheer Singh, 124
Garib Nawaz, 36, 45, 49, 126, 148-155, 364, 479, 657, 716, 717, 830
Gour Shyam, 155
Hirachandra, 170, 171
Forces, 172
Grandson of Bhagyachandra, 170
Kangba, 35, 134, 334, 335, 858
Khagemba, 36, 143-145, 296, 705, 706, 830, 832, 847
Khuiyuoi Tompok, 800
Khuman, 367
Knuiyoi Tompok, 137
Kyaamba, 126, 304, 666, 716
Labanya Chandra, 167, 170
Loiyumba, 126, 218, 310, 884
Luwan of Punshiba, 136
Madhuchandra, 167
Maramba, 40
Marjit Singh, 47, 170, 172
Meidingu Ayaangba, 138
Meidingu Loiyumba, 138
Meidingu Senbi Kyaamba, 139, 142, 143
Meidingu Yangtou, 138
Mindon, 191
Mungyamba, 143, 398, 579
Naothing Khong, 40, 137
Nara Singh, 658, 666
Ningthou Kangla, 133, 134, 139
Nongda Laireu Pakhaugba, 136, 884
Of Ahom Swarga Deve, 158
Of Ava, 720, 731
Of Kakching, 665
Of Manipur, 161, 167, 170, 171, 207, 217, 231
Of Mekhele, 49
Of Moirang, 148, 158
Of Nan-Chao, 518
Of Travancore, 248
Paikhomba, 720
Invaded Samjok, 720
Poireiton, Khunthokpa, 135
Pratap Narayana, 706
Senbi Kyaamba, 675, 676
Surchandra, 735
Swarga Deva Rajeshwar Singh, 158, 159
Thangbi Lanthaba, 40
Thangwai Ningthouba, 140
Thawanthaba of Ningthouja Meitei Dynasty, 519
Tongja Leela Pankhanba, 133
Migration of-, 133
Ura Konthouba, 137
Zillangemba Brother, 735
Kingdoms of Golkonda and Bijapur, 707
King-People Link Categories, 127
Judicial Relationship, 127
Religious Relationship, 127

Service Relationship, 127
Kings of Travancore and Hyderabad, 248
Kingship, 122-123
Kiratas of Vedic Literature, 37
Kitovi Zhgimomi, (Zhimomi), 462, 464
Kodin, 33
Kohima, 200, 206, 295
  And Mokokchung, 450
  Column, 200
  Expedition, 187, 188
Koi Koi, 134
Koirao, 385
  Festivals, 386
  Legends and Clans, 385
  Marriage and Inheritance, 386
  Society, 385
Koireng, 387
  Clans, 387
  Houses, Dress and Cultures, 388
  Origin and Legends, 390
  Physical Features, 387
  Status of Women, 387
Kom Hrem Baptist Church Association (KRBCA), 751
Kongpokpi Area, 58
Konyak, 437, 458, 459, 487
Kouna
  Main Objectives, 1042
  Products Items, 1041
  State Government Role, 1043
  Water Reed, 895
  Range, 58
Kouna Craft, 895
  Industry, 1039, 1041
  Production Projects (KCPP), 1039
Kouna Growing Areas, 1040-1042
  Bishnupur, 1040
  Imphal East District, 1040
  Imphal West District, 1040
  Thoubal, 1040
Krishna
  And Radha, 795
  Or Balaram, 802
  Temple, 579
Krishnamacharya Alias Rai Vanamali, 657
Krum Khou-Choubi, Queen, 135
Kukhato Sema, Federal PM, 468
Kukhato Shukhai Sema, 453, 455, 456
Kuki
  And Thadou, 750
  Baptist Association (KBA), 748, 750
  Chiefs, 747, 760-762, 764
  Chin Groups, 294
  Chin Tribals, 748
  Chin Tribes, 295
  Christian, 748
  Christian Church, (KCC), 752
  Christian Organization, 748
  Festivals, 952
  Chavan, 952
  Groups, 295
  National Organization, 488
  Rebellion, 760
  Rebels, 762
  Uprising in Manipur, 1917-1919, 409, 760-762
Kuki-Chin Linguistic Group, 409
Kuki-Chin-Mizo Group, 928
Kukis (khongjais), 182, 187, 221, 397, 480, 487, 488, 489, 552, 748, 750, 752, 753, 761
  And Hmars, 383, 552-574
  And Kabui, 817
  Dances, 560

Death Rituals, 559
Dress and Ornaments, 554
Economic Life, 560
Games and Sports, 560
Legend, 552, 553
Marriages, 557
Mongoloid Features, 554
Musical Instruments, 560
Nomadic Race Coming from Burma, 532
Nomadic Tribe, 555
Observes Exogamy, 557
Origin, 552
Physical Features, 554
Rebellion, 443
Refugees, 480
Textile, 890
Khamtaung—Maijapem, 890
Village, 480
Women, 554
Kulachandra Dhaja, Maharaja, 207
Kulachandra, Maharaja, 194, 201-203, 217, 585, 670, 735, 737, 738, 741, 742
Gen, 744
Kumba Singh Laishraba, 212
Kumlang Phanak, 881
Kunjarani Devi, Weight Lifting, 819
Kunming Province, 460
Kuptreng, 33, 34
Kurukshetra War, 368
Kwak-Jatra Festival, 832
Kyaamba, 56, 655, 565, 882
Kyaang, Shan Kingdom, 655

L

L Kanhai, 770, 771
Ladakh, 864
Lahore Light Horse, 850
Lai Haraoba, 2
Lai Regional Council, 398
Lai Tubi—, 686
Lai Yum Temple, 134
Lai, Semi-Nomadic Migratory Community, 398
Lainuras (Goddess), 34
Lairenjam Chanu Keiphaba, 138
Great Sinbe, 138
Master of Weaving and Embroidery, 138
Lairikyengbam Dhananjay, 706
Lakes, 59, 919
Guiphop Zei, 948
Heingang Pat, 60
Ishon Pat, 60
Kachouphung pat, 60
Kharung Pat, 60
Loktak, 2, 4, 23, 24, 58, 59, 63, 132, 138, 155, 579, 589, 590, 915, 919, 926
Loukoi Pat, 60
Lousi Pat, 60
Nap-Sam Zei, 948
Nrou Zei, 948
Sana Pat, 60
Utra Pat, 60
Waitheu, 4
Waithou, 591
Zeilad, (Associated with Pythons), 948
Legend, 948
Lakpas, 219
Communication Agent, 124
Lallup (War Organization), 218, 313
System, 126, 757
Lalupkaba, 129

Lamangdeng (Bishnupur), 655
Lamangdeng, Capt of King Kyaamba, 655
Lamlai Nagar Panchayat, 910
Lamphelpat, Shallow Lake, 576
Lamphi—Kudam Manbi, 885-887
Land
  And Mode of Inheritance, 558
  Pass System, 768
  Reform Act, 1960, 917
  Revenue, 126
Landsdowne, Lord, 735, 742
Langba Chak, 32
Langsoi, 665
Langthabal Camp, 777
Langthabal
  Hill, 163
  Military Camp, 233
Languages, 397
  Hmar, 397
  Kuki, 397
  Lushai, 397
  Paite, 397
Lanmass, Manipuri Soldier, 124
Lathaba Ceremony, 312
Latin American Countries, 235
Ledo in Assam, 975
Legal and Judiciary System, 187
Legends, 794, 880
Legends' About Naga Origin, 428
Leikais in Moirang, 589
Leima Taritnu, 134
Leimarel Sidabi, Introducer of Weaving, 880
Leimaren, God, 316, 407
Leirum, 881
Leisembi, (God of Handicrafts), 884
Lepers Asylum, 747
Lhota Nagas of Pangti, 442
Lhotas, 487
Liberation of Manipur from Burma, 732
Liengma, 439
Liling—Sugnoo Assembly Constituencies, 918
Lime Cave, 591
Limestones in-, 994
  Phungyar—Chandel District, 994
Linkages of NSCN-IM, 459
Literacy, 398, 405, 753
Liwa Sarei Village, 398
Liwachaning Village, 398
Localities, 231
  Nungyungbi—Koirengei Airstrip, 231
Locust, 136
Lois,
  Main Deities Worshiped, 360
  Origin, 359
  Physical Features, 360
  Religion, 360
  Rituals and Festivals, 360
  Settlement in Sakmai—Chairil, 359
Loithaba, Manufacturing Salt as Punishment, 132
Loktak Down-Stream Hydro-Electric Project, 1006
Loktak Lake, 58, 138, 579, 589, 590, 915, 926, 1042 see under lakes also
London Missionary Society, 745
Longjam Kulabidhi Singh, 673
Longjamba Loma Singh, Gen., 739
Longkhai, 434
Lord
  Amrest, Gov Gen., 172, 725, 726, 732, 734
  Buddha, 301

Curzon, Gov Gen., 219
Curzon, Viceroy of India, 850
Govindjee, 159. 163, 164, 166, 201, 582, 658
Irwin, 2
Krishna, 159, 165, 657, 663, 664, 671 672, 795-797, 802
Krishna and Radha, 668
Krishnachandra, 666
Landsdowne, 195
Mingyi, 721
Nara Singh Thakur, 670
Northbrook, Viceroy of India, 186, 207
Pakhangba, 580, 581
Shri Krishna, 303
Thangjing, 24, 589, 926
Loukoipat Ecological Park, 927
Lourung Putel, 200
Love Stones, 588
Luhongba (Marriage), 316
Luhupas, 515
Lunar Calendar, 49
Lushai (s), 184
Hills, 59, 246, 398, 761
People, 397
Lutherans, 399
Luwang Wamitkhu, 136

M

M Megha, 234
Machi Rule, 169
Machu Khul, 38
Madhuchandra, 184
Maduchandra, Mabiq, 171
Mafam-gi Manipur First Film, 346
Magadh, 300, 301
Magico-Religious Value, 339
Mahabharata, 37, 332, 368, 717
Mahadhammaraza, Dipali, Burmese King, 720, 721, 722
Maharaja
Bandula, Burman Commander,
Of Manipur, 186, 188, 262, 746, 816
Team, 816
Maharaja's State Council, 244, 245
Mahila Samelan, 236
Maibam Lekpa, Chief, 232
Maibas and Maibis, 341, 342
Maibi
Dance, 803
Jagoi, 795
Maichou Loisang, Council of Literati, 132
Main Christian Sects, 931
Baptist Church, 931
Catholic Church, 931
Church of Christ, 931
Seventh Day Adventure Church, 931
Maipak Sano, 200
Maithili, 802
Major Ethnic Communities of District Senapati, (MECDS), 935
Chiru, 935
Chothi, 935
Gangte, 935
Haokip, 935
Kipgen, 935
Kom, 935
Kuki, 935
Liangmai, 935
Mao, 935
Maram, 935
Maring, 935

Meitei, 935
Nepalese, 935
Poumai, 935
Roungmei, 935
Sitlore, 935
Tangkhuls, 935
Thangal, 935
Vaiphei, 935
Zeliangrong, 935
Zemai, 935
Major Hotels in Imphal, 13
Makokchung, 453
Malaya, 772
Malayan Sun Bear, 63
Malta Polo Club, 850, 859
Mamgalphu (Mughal Pot), 36
Manaobi Singh, 818
Mandlay, 153, 190, 191
Mandy, Bone Price of Wife, 944
Mangang Ningthou, 685
Mangba-Sengba Culture, 228, 479
Of Maharaja Churachand, 228
Mani, AK, 673
Manipur
A Little Paradise on Earth, 1
Administration of-, 220, 242
All Districts of-, 909-952
And Burma, 254
And Burma (Myanmar) Boundary, 521
And Sports, 816-833
And World War II, 772
Arambai Force, 826
As Kathis or Ponna, 35
Bamboo Varieties, 77
Baptist Convention (MBC), 750-752
Baptist Convention Centre, 750
Bengali Style of Dress, 304
Boundaries, 56
Bowl Shaped Lake, 33
British War Graves Commission in-, 3
Cavalry, 139
Cements, 990, 993, 995
Cemeteries, 3
Champion Santosh Trophy, 819
Christian Association, 746
Cinemas, 345, 346
Clans, 309
Climate, 55
Columns, 762
Conservation Sites in-, 62
Constitutional Assembly, 259, 260
Creation of-, 33
Dance College of Imphal, 801
Development Society, 583
Dresses and Ornaments, 316
Durbar (Darbar), 760
Economy, 970
Electronic Development Corp, 990
Ethnic Groups, 294
Famous Polo Players, 856
King Kangba—Pakasana, 856
Field Force, 212, 213, 215
Film Development Corporation, (MFDC), 346
Film Development Council, 346
Films Shown at International Film Festival, 346
Flower of Lofty Heights, 1
Foos, 318
Food Industries Corp., 993
Food Processing Sector, 1030
Friends Dramatic Union, 344
Garrison, 761

Green Paradise, 1
Handloom
And Handicrafts, 880
And Handicrafts Development Corp., 896, 990, 993
Industry, 2
Hills, 57
Hindu Temples in-, 655
Hindus, 324
Industrial
Backwardness, 981
Development Corp (MANIDCO), 990, 993, 1002
Scenario, 987
Infrastructure Sector, 981
International Border with Myanmar, 55, 56
International Trade Routes, 36
Jewel of India, 1
Kashmir on Earth (Nehru), 1
Kings Chronology, 118, 119
Known as Takhel, 36
Krishak Sabha, 237
Labor Corps, 221, 760
Land of Festivals, 2
Land of Jewels, 2
Land Revenue, 917
Language, 295, 301, 325, 341, 483
Legislative Assembly, 306
Magic Land, 1
Mahasabha, 233
Major Languages, 913
Hmar, 913
Kabui, 913
Manipuri, 913
Mao, 913
Paite, 913
Tangkhul, 913
Thudou, 913
Man Building Institutions, 818
Martial Art, 3, 831
Sarit Sarak, 3
Thang Ta, 3
Martyrs, 584, 585
Merger Agreement, 252, 257-260, 779
Museum, 51
Muslims (Pangans), 296, 704, 705, 710
Names, 36
Kangleipak, 36
Meitei Leibak, 36
Meitrabak, 36
Sanaleibak, 36
Nata Sankirtana, 717
North Autonomous District Council, 936
North Naga Baptist Association, 748
Occupation, 317
Olympic Association, 817, 818
Origin, 32-54
Palace, 23, 659, 661, 913
Part-C Status, 257
People of-, 1
People's Party (MPP), 306
Plantation Crops Corp., 1013, 1014
Polo Game, 851-853
Population by Religion, 306
Population of-, 295, 515
Princes, 849
Chourajit Singh, 849
Gambheer Singh, 849
Marjit Sing, 849
Nara Singh, 849
Pung Cholom, 2
Raas Lila, 2, 795, 801

Relations with Neighbourhood, 36
Revolution of 1891, 205
Rifles, 676
Rituals, 319
Birth, 321
Chawumba, 321
Death Rituals Ceremony, 323
Lugoon Thangba (Sacred Thread Ceremony), 322
Marriage, 319, 320
Waa Hutpa, 322
Yum Songgaba, 323
Sangai, 62
Seasons, 56
Second Town Liberated by INA, 2
Small Industries Corporation, 987
Society, 304, 324, 745
Spinning and Weaving Culture, 990
Spinning Mills, 987, 993
Sports Association, 817
State
Archives, 51, 213
Museum, 23, 914, 917
Assembly, 254, 483, 585
Communist Party, 237
Congress Party, 237, 244, 258
Congress, 245, 246, 251
Council, 239
Dance College, 802
Durbar, 239
Abolition of-, 224
Tourism Policy, 26
Switzerland of India (Lord Irwin), 2
Switzerland of the East, 1
Tangkhuls, 463
Tea Industry, 1014
Theatre, 344
Town Club, 817
Tradition of Nature Worship, 339
Traditional Liquor, 1027
Plant, 996
Unique in Craftsmanship, 983
University, 663, 1003
University Sports Board, 817
War of 1891, 305
War Veterans, 777
Wildlife in-, 61
Women, 229, 308, 312, 341
Social and Economic Life, 880
Women's Foot Association, 818
Zeliangrong Area, 748
Zoological Gardens (Park), 23, 585, 914
Manipuri
'Hindus' 149
Army, 149
As Khagi, 36
Calendar, 135
Chiefs, 725
Chourajit, 725
Gumbheer Sing, 725
Marjit, 725
Civilization, 723
Classical Dance, 795, 796
Community, 805
Custom, 194
Dance, List of Costumes and Ornaments, 800
Dances, 794-815
Purely Religious, 794
Forces (Troops), 174, 176
Handlooms, 882
Hindu Society, 719
Hindus, 719
Historical Landmarks Chronology, 701-752

Lambus, 220
Language, Common-Respectful
Words, 329
Poets, 332
Religious History, 658
Script, 326
Troops, 722
Women, 577, 771
Manjushri, 301
Manmohan Singh, PM, 580
Manufacturing
Of Silk, 130
Of Steel, 686
Salt, 130
Mao, 238, 392
Christian, 748
Naga Dance, 937
Maos, Poumeis, Marams and Thangals, 519
Maram, 393, 751
Maran Kesa, 541
Maratha States, 250
Marine Shells, 429
Maring, 395, 430
Naga Baptist Association (MNBA), 750
Tribes, 325
Marjit Singh, 167-169, 175, 184, 314, 580, 582, 723, 724
Markets of
Bukhara, 477
Rubber, 1031
Marriage
And Divorce, 402
By Agreement, 944
By Arrangements, 557
By Elopement, 944
By Mutual Love, 557
By Purchase, 557
By Service, 944
Co-Sanguinary, 528
Cross Cousin, 528, 944
Inter-Clan, 557
Systems, 944
Martial
Art Movement, 831
Art Training, 828
Arts, 826, 833
Law, 232
Marwaris, 301
Migrated from Rajasthan, 302
Marxism, 261
Revolutionary Theories, 251
Mass Rape by Indian Troops, 457
Masters of Thang-Ta, 828
Loukrakpam Sana Mityang, 828
Ningthoukhongja Poila, 828
Paona Naol Singh, 828
Matan Singh, 758
Mate
Girl, 396
Society, 396
Tribes, 396
Chningthat, 396
Haolim, 396
Langsun, 396
Sheilai, 396
Village, 396
Mautam, Famines, 410
Maxwell, Maj. Ch. Political Officer, 126, 212, 217, 742
Maxwell, William, Maj, 746, 756, 757
Mayangs, 368
Mayung Gurus, 479
McCulloch, Col., Political Agent, 182, 183

Medicinal Plants, 1046
In Senapati District-details, 938-940
Processing Industry, 1000
Varieties, 1017-1022
Meidingu
Charairongba, King, 665
Khunjaoba, Second Son of Khagemba, 708
Kongyamba, 882
Loiyumba, 881
Myaamba, 366
Naophongba, 826
Meiei Leipak or Meitrabak, 39
Mein Kampf, 472
Meiring, 994
Meitei
And Hundung Awunga, 521
And Tangkhuls, 40
Communities, 294, 295
Chakpas (Loi), 294
Animism, 333
Army, 149
Calandar, 709, 134
Clans/Yeks, 34
Community, 206, 515
Culture, 407, 882
Customs and Manners, 360
Dress, 881
Famous Authors, 332, 333
Folk Songs, 347
Folklore, 884
Girls, 225
Hindus, 296, 479
Houses, 315
Insurgents, 494
Jagoi (Manipuri Dances), 794
Language, 407, 746
Literature after World War II, 332
Marups, 294
Modern Literature, 332
Muslim Women, 709
Mythology, 825
Ornaments for Men Nagas, 435
Pangans, 709, 923
·Phanek Naibi, Manipur West Dress, 138
Phurup, 336, 337
Puya, 207
Religion, 145, 333, 360
Singers, 342
Singers, Sagolsem—Thanga Hshangbi, 342
Society, 40, 364, 367, 483
Women, 305
Meiteilon, Manipur Language, 745, 746
Meiteis, 308-358, 430
Meiteis Gotras, 150
Bhardwaj for Changlei, 150
Kashyap for Luwang, 150
Kaushik for Angoms, 150
Madhukalya for Khuman, 150
Moirang and Gautam for Phantek, 150
Sandilya for Ningthouja, 150
Social Status, 228
Meiteiten Speaking, 308
Memorial Stone at Kekrupat, 583
Menon, VP, 241, 248, 249, 257
Merger
Agreement, 250, 258-260
Agreement, Strength and Weaknesses, 259-260
Mexican Rule in California, 478
Michori, 219
Middle Eastern Slave Trade, 477
Migration (s), 34, 41, 405, 428

Mikir's and Rengma Hills, 443
Militant Outfits, 459
Military
    Expedition, 442
    Expedition to Ukhrul, 520
Mills, JP Commissioner of Naga Hills, 766
Mineral Resources, 920
Mingimala Bandlla, Gen. , 170
Ministry of Home Affairs, 3, 7, 465
Minor Languages of Manipur, 913
    Aimol, 913
    Anal, 913
    Chiru, 913
    Chothe, 913
    Gangte, 913
    Koireng, 913
    Kom, 913
    Lamkang Mayon, 913
    Liangmei, 913
    Maram, 913
    Maring, 913
    Mizo, 913
    Monsang, 913
    Simte, 913
    Thangl, 913
    Vaiphei, 913
    Zou, 913
Mission School Kohima, 748
Missionaries, 745
Mitchell, John, Lt. Col, 743
Mithun, 397, 410, 557, 559
Mizo, 397, 975
Mizoram, 55, 56, 58, 968
Mleecha Dynasty of Kamrup (Assam), 882
MLR and LR Act, 1960, 558
Modern
    Burma, 233
    Polo, 846
    Gift of Manipur, 846
Moglai, 35
Moguong, Shan King, 518
Mohan Singh of INA, 773
Mohendro Singh, 234
Moirang INA Memorial, 4
Moirang, 39, 59, 359, 722
    Puewn, 723
Moirang, Ancient Village, 24
Moiranghi, Traditional Meitei's Dress, 584
Moirongthem Gour Shyam, King, 665, 666
Mokokchung, 295, 442, 766
Moksha, 719
Mongba hanba Umang, 150
Mongolian
    And Ottoman Empires, 1014
    Ethnic Group, 37
Mongoloid
    Features, 554
    Rice, 294, 308
Mongoloids and Aryans, 297
Monogamy, 396, 528
Monotheism Religion, 931
Mons, 721, 722
Monsang Festivals, 952
Monsang Festivals, Chanou Tangba, 952
Monsang Pantha Village, 398
Monsang, 398
Moreh, 190, 592, 593, 949
    And Tamu, 983
Mortars, Explosives, 460
Moses, 710
Motbung, 748
Moulmein Sea Coast (Myanmar), 429

Mountbatten, Louis, 224, 240, 241, 247, 249, 778

Gen. Regiment, (33), 232

Plan, 240

Mounterfierce, Capt, 762

Moyon (Bujuur), 398

Baptist Association, 750

Moyon

Chiefs, 398

Khullen Village, 398

Mudras, 796

Muga Machu, 882

Mughal (s)

Ambassador to Manipur, 706

Brick Makers, 36

Dynasty, 863

Empire, 36

India, 476

Muhammad, 710

Muhammad—Inhabitants of Sylhet and Cachar, 705

Muhiuddin Muhammad Aurangzeb Bahadur Aurangzeb, 706, 707

Muivah, 459, 464, 471, 472, 481, 488, 496

Attempt to Assassinate-, 459

Thuigaleng, 459

Mukherjee, Phoni, 817

Mukna,

Jatra, 824

Manipuri Style of Wrestling, 823

MULTA (Muslims United Liberation Tigers of Assam), 461, 470

Multicheck Posts, 976

Mumtaz Mahal, 706

Mungya, 143

Murad Baksh, 707

Murder of Digendrajit, 229

Mushroom, 78

Musical Instruments, 568

Darkhuong, 568

Hnamut, 570

Pheiphit, 570

Raw Khuong, 570

Tingtong, 570

Muslim (s), 295-296

And Bishnupriya, 144

And Tribals, 297

Captives, 476

Cardinal Articles of Faith, 712

Five Daily Prayers, 712

From Uttar Pradesh-Bihar, 296

Influence in Manipur, 710

League, 240, 248

Mansabdars, 477

Pangans, (Muslims), 296

Princes, 248

Settlement in Manipur, 709

Dress, 709

Festivals, 709

Occupation, 709

Society, 297

Mutaguchi Plan, 774

Mutaguchi, Renya, Gen, 774, 776

Mutua Museum, 588

Myanmar, 83, 234, 459, 460, 461, 517, 518, 592, 593, 734, 1034

Arunachal Pradesh, 968

Export Market, 968

Indian Border, 968, 969

Passport Rules, 972

Thailand Border, 968

Myedu in Swsebo District, 720

Myitkyina, 778

Mysteries, 333

Mythology of Naga Origin, 434

N

N Rio, 471
Nabadwip, 164, 166, 167, 230
Nadia (West Bengal), 164
  District of West Bengal, 166
Naga
  Animists, 433
  Army, 149, 468
  Battle of 1879, 443
  Chiefs, 433, 444
  Chirai, 215
  Club in 1918, 467, 444
  Communities of Nagaland, 462
  Culture, 766
  Dress, 434, 436
  Festivals, 952
  Lin Ngai, 952
  Gowho, 215
  Groups of Manipur, 429, 433, 459, 469, 515
  Chiru, 429
  Kabui, 429
  Koireng, 429
  Mao, 429
  Maram, 429
  Mareng, 429
  Poumai, 429
  Tangkhul, 429
  Guerrillas, 468, 489
  Handicrafts, 436
  Hill Districts, 444, 447
  Hills, 7, 176, 188, 251, 429, 430, 442, 445, 447, 449, 450, 451, 466, 490, 493, 761, 762
  Home Guard (NHG), 453
  Hopo, 493
  Inhibited Areas in Burma, 462
  Insurgency (Khaplang), 461
  Insurgency, 469
  Insurgent, 468
  Insurgent Groups, 464
  Maternal Culture, 430
  Movement, 489
National Council (NNC), 251, 444, 457-450, 452, 453, 456-458, 466, 486, 489
  Leadership, 462
National Movement (NNM), 444, 467, 482, 485
Nationalism, 444
  Organization, 482
  Peace Mission, 454, 455
  Jaya Prakash Narayan, 456
  Michael Scott, 456
  Mr. Chaliha, BP, 456
  People's Convention (NPC), 453
  Political Leaders, 481
  Politicians in Bureaucracies, 481
  Poumai, 399
  Raids, 442
  Rebels, 467
  Rituals, 430
  Society of Nagaland, 434, 462, 485
  Students Federation of Nagai, 471
  Tribes, 206, 428-498, 444, 463, 493
  Tribes of Manipur, 295
  Underground
    Leaders, 485
    Men, 469
    Movement, 491
  Voluntary Plebiscite of 1951, 449
Nagais and Meiteis, 554
Nagaland, 7, 55, 56, 251, 766, 968
  Assembly, 488, 489

Baptist Church, 488
Baptist Church Council (NBCC), 462, 454
Birth of the State, 454
Board of Secondary Education, 463
Burmese Border, 467
For Christ, 444
Security Regulation, 1962, 453
State Congress Party, 485
Nagalim or People's Republic of Nagaland, 459, 471, 489
Nagar Panchayats, 910
Nagara Type of Temple, 661
Nagas, 176, 295, 397
And Kukis into Christianity, 745
And Mizos, 468
And Manipur, 519
And Meiteis, 429
Culture and Tradition, 428
Customs and Traditions, 429
Distinct Customs, Laws, Traditions or Social Life, 434
Kukis and Tibet-Burman Origin, 519
Not Snake Worshippers, 428
Occupation-Agriculture, 432
Of Mongoloid Race, 430
Of Nagaland, 429
Angami, 429
Ao, 429
Konyak, 429
Lhota, 429
Liangmai, 429
Rangma, 429
Sema, 429
Zemi, 429
Origin, 429
Origin and Migration, 429
Political and Communal Relationship with Ahom Armies, 428
Nagasaki, 779
Nani Singh, 212
Naoria Phuko, 336
Napachik Excavations, 39
Nara Singh, Maharaja, 181, 182, 192, 314, 562, 732, 580, 581, 582
Nara Singh, Raja, 758
Narasimha Rao, PV, former Indian PM, 464, 969
Narasingha, Maharaja, 882
Nata Sankirtan, 833
Movement, 833
Nathitheimei, 944
National
Awards, 346
Black Farmers Association, 479
Democratic Front of Bodo (NDFB), 470
Flag of Manipur, 242
Games Imphal, 818
Hydro-Electric Power Corporation (NHPC), 1006
Liberation Front of Tripura, (NLFT), 470, 1036, 1042, 1043
Parks, 63
Keibul Lamjao, 63, 64
Sankirtan, 804
School of Drama, 344, 345
Small Industries Corporation, 990
Socialist Council of Nagaland (NSCN), 450, 458, 491, 493, 494, 496
Birth, 458
Cadres, 488

Demand of Greater Nagaland, 485
Leaders, 496
Set UP, 459
Split, 458, 459
(IMuivah), 459, 460, 461, 462, 463-466, 470, 472, 480, 484, 488-491, 494, 497
Military Outfit, 462
(Khaplang), 461, 462, 463-465, 491, 493, 494
Socialist Women Organization of Nagalim (NSWON), 462
Nationalist Chinese, 774
Native
Americans, 478
Infantry Chittagong, 184
Navaratna Temple, 579
Nazi
Boycott of Jewish, 475
Germany, 475
NCP, 306
NECON (North Eastern Industrial Consultants), 1032
Nehru Manipuri Dance Academy, 801
Nehru, Pt. Jawahar Lal Nehru, PM, 1, 247, 258, 259, 766, 449, 450, 453, 454, 486
Nehu Rio, 463
Nemrangpuon (Shawl 5'x6'), 571
Neo Tibetans, 135
Neolithic
Man, 39
Tools, 39
Nepal, Bhutan and Bangladesh, 983
Nepalese, 300
Language, 300
Settled in Mao, Maram—Kangpokpi, 300
Settled in Tamei-Tamenglong, 300
Nervous Disorder, 938
Netherland, 1041
New
Economic Policy Initiatives, 983, 984
Granada, 235
Industrial Package for North East, 985
Initiatives, 981
Year Festival of Tangkhuls, 534
York Botanical Society, 592
Ng. Dingko Singh, Gold Medalist in Boxing, 819
Ngangbi Maharani, 219, 346
Ngariyan Hill, 912
Nikhil Hindu Manipuri Mahasabha, 224, 236, 237, 770
Nine Point Agreement, 447, 448, 449
Ningthem Pukhri, 913
Nirmandi Cult of Vaishnavism, 146, 716
Nobel Prize Winners, 304
Amartya Sen, 304
Mother Teresa, 304
Rabindranath Tagore, 304
Noklak Camp, 451
Nongda Lairen Pakhangba, 881
Nongmachingthiel, 723
Nongmaithem Manik Chand Singh, 756
Nongmoinu Ahongbi, Queen of Khuiyoi Tompok, 881
Non-Manipuri Dancers, 805
Preeti Patel—Tamanna Raman, 805
Normandy of the East, 779
North
Cachar, 442

Hills, 461, 747, 766
East
Council, (NEC), 987
Financial Corporation (NEDFC), 986, 987
Frontier Agency (NEFA), 488
Frontier, 732
India (NEI), 2, 64, 250, 407, 430, 432, 446, 467, 468, 469, 482, 746
India General Mission (NEIGM), 1919, 746, 747, 749, 752
Compound, 410
Insurgent Groups (PREPAK), 462
Kuki Baptist Association Manipur, 748
Region of India, 974, 981, 985, 1061
Reorganization Act, 1971, 488
West Association, 748
NPC (Nagaland People's Council), 465
NTPSL Thouba, 686
Nupa Pala, 795, 804
Nupi Lal, 771, 772
Nupi
Lals Revolt, 229
Shumang Lila, 343
Nupilal Memorial Complex, 914, 917
Nuptial, 236
Nuthal, Cap., 756
Nuthall, Maj Gen. WF, Political Agent, 190

O

O Ibobi Singh, CM Manipur, 580
Oak Tasar, 990
Oath Taking, 434
Och ai (Fishing), 406
Office of Yaiskullakpa, 144
Okendrajit, Maharaja, 262, 522, 581
Okram
Chaoba Singh, 670
Ibodi Singh, CM Manipur, 982
Old Palace Kangla, 658
Olympians from Manipur, 820-821
Olympic Games, 817, 818
Olympics, 816, 818
Ksh Thoiba Singh, 1988, 818
P Nilakumar Singh, 1984, 818
Omer, Second Caliph, 714
Orange Festival, 946
Orchid Species, 586
Orchids, 1044
Organizations, 234
Kabui Association, 234
Khul Union, 234
Kuki National Assembly, 234
Manipur Krishak Sabha, 234
Manipur Praja Sabha, 234
Meitei Marup, 234
Mizo Union, 234
Nongpok Apunba Marup, 234
Tangkhul Long, 234
Organize Military Services, 124
Origin of
Gun River, 404
Meiteis, 37
Aboriginal Settlers theory, 38
Hill Tribes Theory, 38
Hindu Descendant Theory, 37
Naga Origin Theory, 38, 40
Tartar Descendant Theory, 37
Tibeto Burman Origin Theory, 37
Orphanage, 747
Osman, Third Caliph, 714

Other Sports Stars from Manipur, 821-823

P

Pacha, Special Court for Women Cases, 187
Package Incentives by State Government, 985
Padmanabhiah, K, 464
Pagan, Burmese King, 518
Paina Brajbhasi, Maj., 588
Paites, 399, 408, 552
  Textile, 890
  Thangou Puon—Nikkiat, 891
Pakhangba, Deity, 659
Pakistan, 459, 460, 467, 469
Palace
  Revolt, 735
  Revolution (1891), 193, 735
Palaeolithic
  Man, 39
  Tools, 38
Pallel, 722
  Airstrip, 777
Pallel/Kakching Airstrip, 231, 232
Paltan Team, 816
Pamheiba or Garib Nawaz, Meitei King, 147, 148, 152, 153, 520, 710, 720 see under Gariba Nawaz
Pan German League, 475
Pana Hajari, Hd Office of Sepoys, 124
Pana Sagol Kangjei System, 847
Panas of
  Higher Status, 847
  Lower Status, 847, 848
  Meiteis, 129
  Ahallup, 129
  Khabam, 129
  Laipham, 129
  Naharup, 129
Panchai, 219
Pandit Moirangthem Chandra Singh, 126
Pangka
  Dharma, 225
  Sect, 227
Pangmi National Workers, 459
Panjao
  Napa Ching, 38
  Phallum Ching, 38
Panthoibi, Goddess, 827, 880
Paona
  Bazar, 583
  Brajabasi, Maj., 202, 737, 739-741
  Memorial, 739
PAP Conditions, 4
Paradhumba Singh, 215
Parental Property, 396
Part-C Territory, 261
Pass,
  Aimol, 159
  Chaukan, 135
  Imole, 722
  Phangsu, 975
Passion Fruit, 1027
Patel, Sardar Vallabhbhai, 247, 248, 249, 253
Peace Process, 482
Peasant Revolution, 234
Pegu, 721, 722
Pemberton, Cap. RB, 180, 725, 729, 730, 441
Pemberton, Lt., 176, 178
Pena Loisang, Institute of Musicians, 132

Penticostal, 399
People's United Liberation Front
(PULF), 461, 470
Peoples Comrade Party, 234
Persian, 36
Peru, 235
Pettigrew, William, 745-748, 753, 816, 931
Phamnaiba (Nobles), 128
Pheida Pung, 744
Phiza, AZ, 251, 405, 448, 449, 453, 458, 462, 466, 469, 485, 489
Phom, 463
Phou-Kouba Ceremonies, 318
Phuballa Resort, 590, 927
Phunal Hill, 163
Phunan, 38
Phungyar, 994
Piba, Structural Head of Sagai, 313
Pibren, Head of Pibas, 314
Pillai, GK, Secretary in the Ministry of Home Affairs, 465
Pine
Based Paper Mills, 991
Forests, 69
Ping Cholom, 833
Places Associated with Pottery, 893
Andro Village, 893
Chairel and Thongojai, 893
Leimarem Village, 893
Nong Pok Sekmai, 893
Nunglei Village, 893
Oinam Village, 893
Places
Of Interest in Manipur, 23
Open to Foreigners, 4
Places to Visit in Senaparti District, 936
Dzuko Valley, 937
Purul, 937
Liyai, 937
Makhel, 937
Mao, 937
Maram Khullen, 937
Yangkhullen, 937
Plain of Langthabal, 577
Planning Commission, 982
Plants Worship by Meiteis, 339
Plebiscite, 449
Poaching, 8
Poireiton Khunthokpa, 587, 604, 705
Poirou Pat, 913
Poland, 232, 772
Policies and Program, 981
Political
And Social Problems, 231
Controversies, 250, 251
Party, 234, 236, 238
Polo, 144, 148, 167
Game, 145
Gift of Manipur, 2
Ground, 577, 840
Teams, 186
Polygamy, 396, 477
Popular Dances of Zeliangrong, 947
Bamboo Dance, 947
Han Siangmai Lam, 947
Horn Bill Dances—Fertility Dances, 947
Jaopa Lam, 947
Rangdai Lam, 947
Ri Lam, 947
Victory Dance, 947
War Dance, 947
Popular Festivals of Tamenglong District, 946-947
Banruhmei, 946

Gan Ngai, 946
Gudin Ngai, 946
Rih-Ngai, 946
Port Blair, 208, 211, 212, 742, 743
Portuguese Navigation, 1014
Potential Areas of
Exports, 972
Imports, 972
Potlo (Skirt of Raas Lila), 800
Pottery
Culture, 891
In Manipur, 1009
Myths of Origin-, 1009
Places Associated with-, 1010
Techniques of Making, 1010
Making in Manipur, 893
Manufacturing Places, 921
Heirok, 921
Khangabok, 921
Nongpok Sekmai, 921
Thougjao, 921
Waikhong, 921
Poumai Naga, 399, 942
Baptist Association (PNBA), 751
Power Sector, 1004
Praja
Samelani, 236
Sangha Party, 236
Sangha, 236
Santi, Political Party, 247
Presbyterian Church of North East India, 752
Prime Minister Rozgar Yojna (PMRY), 986
Prince
Akbar, 708
Sanongba, 705
Zilongambo, 193
Princely
State of Manipur, 239
States, 223, 224, 248-250, 253, 254
Princes Bimbabati, 164, 165
Prisoners of War, 705
Priyobarta Singh, Maharaja, 252
Priyobarta Singh, MK, 253, CM Interim Govt., 241, 245, 246
Prominent Freedom Fighters, 304
Chitranjan Das—Rasbihari Bose, 304
Prominent Groups in Manipur, 294
Kuki-Chin, 294
Meiteis, 294
Nagas, 294
Prominent Tribes of District Chandel, (PTDC), 948
Anal, 948
Chothe, 948
Kukis, 948
Lamkang, 948
Maraing, 948
Monsang, 948
Moyon, 948
Paite, 948
Thadou, 948
Prophet Muhammad, 714
Abdulla Father, 714
Khadiya, Wife, 714
Protected Area Permit (PAP), 3, 7
Ptolemy, Greek Astronomer, 519
Ptolemy's Atlas, 36
Pung Cholam (Mridangam Dance), 795, 804, 805
Punjab, 302
Punjab Martial Art Expert from Lahore, 185

Puon
Dum, 891
Pie, 891
Puonlaisen, Dress of Hmar Women, 571
Purbanchal Pradesh, 246, 247, 251
Creation of-, 234
Purum, Old Kukis Tribe, 401
Purums Siblings, 401
Kheyang, 401
Makan, 401
Marrim, 401
Parpa, 401
Thao, 401
Puyas, 705
Kanglei Langba Pakhangba, 705
Sakok Lamlen Ahanba, 705

Q

Queen
Akoijam Chanu Apambi, 170
Haobam Chanu Liklai Pokpi, 182, 208
Kumudini, 181, 182, 665, 668
Laisra, 578
Linthoingambi, 139
Of Burma, 190
Quinton, Chaobi Hyder Guard of-, 710, 580, 710, 735
Quinton, Execution of-, 198
Quinton, JW, Chief Commissioner of Assam, 195-197, 205, 207, 208, 211-213
Quran, 710
Qutub Minar, 863
Qutubuddin Aibak Sultan, Founder Slave Dynasty, 863

R

Raas Lila, 163-166, 197, 219, 663, 665, 672, 718, 736, 756, 795-803, 805, 833
Love Story of Radha and Krishna, 794
Of Radha Krishna, 165, 661
Performance, 795
Raas Mandal Pukhri, 661, 164
Rabia Durrani, 706
Racial Discrimination, 474
Radha, 671
Radha Krishna, 673
Radha Raman (Lord Krishna), 663, 664
Rai Vanamali, Brahmin Preacher, 146, 716
Rainfed Lakes, 919
Ikop Pat, 919
Kharung Pat, 919
Louri Pat, 919
Ngangou Pat, 919
Pumlen Pat, 919
Raja
Churachand, 443
Girischandra, 164
Nara Singh, 217
Of Bodo Khimidi in Ganjam District, 261
Of Krishnanagar, 164
Of Manipur, 178, 732
Rammohun Roy, 474
Rajagopalachari, C, 248, 258
Rajarshri Bhagyachandra, 830
Creator Raas Lila, 718
Legend, 165, 166
Rajdhan Manik, King of Tripura, 166
Rajesh Pilot, 464

Rajkumar Kala Singh, 200
Rajmala of Tripuris, 36
Ram Tulsi, 150
Ramanandi Cult of Vaishnavism, 150
Ramaswamy, Aiyer, Sir CP, 248
Ramayan, 332, 717
Ramraj, Yubraj of Ramnagar, 231
Rani Gaidinbu, 408
    Of Nunskao, 764, 765, 766
Revolutionary Movement, 766
Rani Phi, 912
Rano Soriza, Phizo's Niece, 467
Rashi Devei, First Actress, 346
Rashtriya Janta Dal (RJD), 306
Ratan Thiyam, Padam Shri Awardee, 346
Rath Yatra, 672
    Or Kang Festival, 369
Raw Material Bank, 921
Rawal Amar Singh, 260, 261
Red Lands Rajbari, 256
Reed Mat Weaving, 1040
Reforms in Administration, 771
Refugees from Cachar, 172
Region of Kham, (Between Burma, Tibet and China), 135
Regional
    Economic Cooperation, 974
    Principalities, 118
Rural Banks, 1026
Reid, Robert, Governor of Assam, 771
Reign of
    Bhagyachandra, 520
    Chingkhong Poireiton, 35
    Gambheer Singh, Nara Singh, Chandrakiriti, 718
    Keiphaba Yanglou, 881
    Khagemba, 36, 521, 579
    Meidingu Naothingkhng, 881
    Naophangba, 578
    Nara Singh, 580
    Nongda Lairen Pakhangba, 578
Religious
    Persecution, 298
Rituals of Meiteis, 341
Rengcholams (Drums), 801
Rengmas
    Girls, 436
Rengmas Nagas, 438, 439
Republic of Colombia, 235
Resources of Bamboo, 1030
    In Yanglong and Churachandpur, 991
Restricted Area Permit, 7
Revivalist Movement of Sanamahism, 337, 338
Revolt of
    Mao Marias, 166
    Sana Borajaoba, 192
Rewal Amar Singh, Maj. Gen., 254
Rier Sekmai, 665
Rishang Keishing, 481, 483
Rites and Sacrifices, 532
Rituals and Ceremonies, 41
River
    Arong, 918
    Ayeyarwady, 153
    Barak, 58, 59, 166, 178, 186, 764, 936
    Brahmputra, 58, 59
    Cengba, 58
    Chandwin, 56, 58, 135, 141, 143, 149, 153, 234, 409, 517, 518, 562, 716, 975
    Dikhou, 36, 443
    Huang Heo, 517

Hung-Ho (China), 37
Imphal River, 33, 58, 163
Imphal, 576, 578, 657, 670, 716, 915, 918, 936
Irang, 58, 936
Iril, 58, 135, 136, 163, 576, 590, 936
Irrawady, 137, 148
Ithai, 936
Jiri, 58, 733
Leimatak, 58
Liwa, 674
Maklang, 134, 154
Makru, 58
Mekong, 562
Moo, 154
Moo and Chindwin, 140
Naga, 576
Nambool (Nambul), 58, 576, 765, 915
Nanmiya, 189
Ningthee or Khyendwen, 36
Ningthee, (Chindwin), 56, 58, 141, 405, 720
Salween Myanmar, 429, 562
Singda, 136
Thoubal, 58, 918, 930
Tizu, 431
Vijaya (Imphal River), 33
Wangjing, 918
Yangtze, 37, 517
Yulung, 561
Riyan, Unwritten Constitution of Tankgkhuls, 528
Road
Circuit, 4
Communication to Tamenglong, 408
Constructions, 138
Roberts, Ouvry, Indian Maj. Gen., 753, 775
Roberts, Watkins, W, 747
Role of
Manipur Muslims, 710
Pakistan and Bangladesh, 469
Roman, 36
Roman Catholic Church (RCC), 751, 752
Rope and Cane Products, 186
Ross Island, 742
Round Table Conference, 223
Royal
Air Force, 778
Airforce Planes, 232
Chronicle, 579
Rubber, 78
Crops, 78
Plantation, 78, 1030, 1031, 1032
Trees, 1032
Rudra Singh Yenkhoiba, 200
Ruins of the Uttra, 581
Rules and Regulations Imposed on Meiteis, 225
Rupa Parmananda, 717
Russel, Sir, Bertrand, 466, 467
Russia, 221

S

Sa-ai (Hunting), 406
Sacred
Banyan Trees, 937
Jack Tree of Kaina, 667, 670
Stones, 340
Thangapat Moat, 670
Sadar
Baptist Association, (SBA), 751

Hills, 750, 751
Hill Districts, 750, 751
Safavid Army, 706
Sagaing, Cap. 153
Sagei, 311-314, 360
Sagol Hamjaba, 200
Sagol Kangjei (Polo), 134, 825, 577, 846-864
Chronology of Development, 857-861
During British Period, 849
Explained, 846
Fielding Position, 848
Height of Horses, 848
Languages of-, 857
Origin in Manipur, 846
Size of Field, 848
Saiza Rano, 489
Sakhua, Traditional Religion, 410
Salam Tombi Singh—Laishram Achou, 239
Salieng, 381
Salt
Cakes, 920
Manufacturing Places, 921
Chandrakhong, 921
Ningel, 921
Sikhong, 921
Waikhong, 921
Springs, 144
Salvation Army Church (SAC), 752
Samadhi,
Luwang Ningthou, father of Maharaja Kumudini, 687
Maharaja Bodhchandra, 583
Maharaja Gambheer Singh, 686
Maharaja Nngchup Lamgaingamba (Bhadra Singh), 686
Samjok, 143, 148, 153, 518, 519, 708
Samjok Raja, 169
Samjok, Political, Social and Commercial Centre, 518
Samkirtan and Raas Lila, 804
Samlukhim, Head Gear, 571
Samu, Col, 198
Samugarh (Battle of), 707
Sana
Chappando, 185
Keithal, Biggest Market, 583
Keithel, Market Exclusively Managed by Women, 23
Ngamba, 200
Puya, Chronicle of Meitei Raja, 40
Yumjaotaba, 170-172
Sanafombi, 756
Sanamahi, 33, 34, 136, 145, 152, 294, 316, 334, 335, 338, 360, 369, 891
Faith, 335
God, 133
Martial Arts, 294
Martial Arts, Thang Ta, 294
Movement, 336, 337
Religion, 132, 334, 337
Temple, 579
Universal God of Meiteis, 145
Worshippers, 294
Yaithibi, 366
Sanamahism, 149, 715
Sanatombi and Ngambi, 771
Sangai, 2, 62
Sangai Handloom, 583
Sanglai—Chair, 397
Sangtam Nagas, 430
Sanjenthong Bridge, 51
Santi Das Gosai, 16, 367
Hindu Preacher, 150, 152

Sanyas Order, 226
Sapadrem, King of Cachar, 144
Sapam Lokhou, 587
Master Sculpture, 163
Sculpture, 671
Saradh Ceremony, 226, 227
Sati Burning, 153, 165
Satnami Seft, 708
Satyagraha Movement, 244
Leaders, 244
Saudi Arabia, 477
Saudi Arabia—Germany, 1034
Sawn Buk, Village Dormitory, 396
Scheduled Caste, 301
Category, 296
Scheduled Castes/Tribes, 377-397, 472
Scheduled Tribes, 480
In District Chandel, 378
In District Churachandpur, 377
In District Senapati, 378
In District Tamenglong, 378
In District Ukhrul, 378
Aimol, Anal—Kuki Tribe, 377
School,
Chaitanya, 715, 717
Nimbarka, 715
Ramananda, 715
Scott, Rev. Michael, 466, 467, 490, 491
Sculpture of Hanumanjee, 658
Seasonal Migration of Elephants, 63
Second
Nupi Lal, 767
Women's Agitation, 767
Sector, Electronic and IT Industry, 1002
Security
Forces, 455
Posts, 4556
Sekta Kei Mound, 38, 590
Self-Determination, 470
Semma Village, 431
Semu, 402, 403
Sena Puya, Royal Chronicle, 521
Senapati
And Sadar Hills Autonomous District Council, 936
Angousana, 739
District (Manipur North District), 935
Administrative Setup, 936
Rivers, 936
Senapati District Assembly
Constituencies, 936
Kangpokpi, 936
Karong, 936
Mao, 936
Sai Kul, 936
Saitu, 936
Tadubi, 936
Senapati District Festivals, 942
Chiithuni, 943
Kanghi, 943
Laonii, 942
Ponghi, 943
Saleri, 943
Thounii, 942
Senapati—Bishnupur Districts, 1027
Sendra, Islet, 23
Sendre Island, 589
Senvon, Biggest Hmar Village in Tipaimukh, 746
Sepak Takraw, Athelete, 818
Sepoy Mutiny, 1857, 223
And Manipur, 184
Sericulture, 881
Settlements in Nagaland, 407

Seven
Colour Flag, 337
Years Devastation, 580, 710, 723
Seventh Day Adventist Church, 526
Sexual Rights, 434
Sha Tanba, Hunting Ceremony, 361
Shah Jahan, 706, 707
Mughal Badshah, 476, 477
Shah Shuja, 476
Shahanama, 862, 863
Shaheed Minar, 584, 744, 914, 917
Shaiza, Yangmasho, 481, 483
Shan United Army, 470
Shangshak-Phungyar Range, 930
Shans, 36, 140, 141, 562, 882
Shans Burmese, 40
Shantineketan University, 801
Shapuree, Burmese Island, 725
Sharma,
Debashwar, Cong Whip, 245
Madhop Lalita, 236, 239
Robindro, First Actor, 346
Shifting Cultivation, 68
Shijaguru Ongbi, 717
Shillong Accord, 457, 458
Shir Govindjee Temple, 23
Shirui Hills of Manipur, 2
Shirui Lily, 2, 592
Shiva Mahadev, Presiding Deity of Thougngam Mondum, 676
Shivaji, Chhatrapati, 708
Shree
Govindjee, 587
Shree Govindjee, 661, 795
Shree Govindjee Temple, 584
Shri
Kirtidhwaja, 163
Krishna Brick Temple, 146
Shuja, 707
Shumang Lila, (Theatre of Musicians), 343, 344
Script Writers, 344
Shweta Ganga, Puri, 657, 716
Siam (Thailand), 232
Siamere-Chinese Linguistic Family, 37
Sibsagar, 36
Sidaba Mapu, Supreme God, 334, 335
SIDBI, 986
Sikh
Community, 240
Religion, 298
Sikhong Ninget Salt Spring, 665
Sikhs, 297, 298
Of Moreh, 299
Silcher, 206, 576, 745, 776
Column, 200
Constituency, 233
Jail, 233
Polo Club, 850, 851
Silk
And Tasar Industry, 991
Worms, 479
Silkwork and Types, 992
Silver Coins, 46, 47
Simoda, Japanese Soldier, 232
Simon Bolivar, 235
Simon Commission, 1929, 223, 445, 446, 467
Sinbee Leima, 133
Sing, LP, Governor of Assam, 457
Singu Miu, 158
Sinuing, 562
Sir Akbar Hydari's Tomb, 583
Sir Hydari Agreement, 448
Sita, Ram, Lakshman, Hanuman, 673
Skardu (Baluchistan), 864

Skene, Col, 736
Slash and Burn Method of Agriculture, 432, 558
Slavery, 382, 383, 470, 476-480
  And Christianity, 476
  From Greeks, 477
Slavery in,
  Chikim Society, 382
  Manipur, 217
  Mauritania, 477
  North America, 478
Slim, Gen., 778
Small Industries Service Institutions, 990
Smelting of Iron, 130
Smt. Amba Devi, 164
Social
  Contract, 397
  Order in Manipur Valley, 662
Socialist Republic in Manipur, 234, 251
Society –Literature, 308
Society
  Meitei, 364, 367
  Manipur, 304
  Thangal, 386
Soktes Villages, 401-403
Solo, Duet and Group Dances, 795
Somrah-Anggoching Range, 930
Somrath Hills, 521
Songbu (Chandel District), 38
Songshuiugreng, Land of Mais Settlement, 518
Songthu and Yeite Clans, 387
Sookampha and Samlongpha, 137
Soraren Achiba, Deity, 135
Sougaijam Somorendro, Opp. Leader, 246
Souk/Slaves, 382
South East
  And Middle East Countries, 995
  Asia, 2
  Asian
    Countris, 973
    Nations, 459
    Manipur Baptist Association (SEMBA), 750
Southern Silk Route, 975
Spain Forces, 235
Special
  Court Composition, 208
  Economic Zones, 982
  Economic Zone (ŚEZ), at Moreh, 971
Species of Bamboo, 991
  Longa—Mobiwa, 991
Sports Personalities of Manipur, 819
Sree Krishna and Srimati Radhika, 794
Sree Sree Radha Krishna Manimandir of ISKON, 672, 673
Sri Govindajee, God, 2
Sri Krishna, God, 2
SS Khaplang (NSCN-K), 459
Standstill Agreement, 242, 249, 251, 253 257, 259, 260
  Text, 1071-1072
State
  Administration, 229
  Bank of India, 8
  Economy, 880
  Of Mizoram, 398
Stewart, M Gerald, 242
Stewart, Robert, Commissioner of Cachar, 850
Stillwell Road, (Old Burma Road), 975
Stone Inscriptions, 43
Stone Inscriptions at
  Hao Chong, 44

Leisangkhong, 44
Maharaja Gambheer Singh, 44
Ngaprum Chingjeng, 43
Wangoi, 44
Stone Inscriptions of
Charairongba, 43
King Kyaamba, 43
Stone, Chaplon, PK, 462
Sub-Alpine Forests, 70
Sudan, 474
Sufism Theory, 705
Sumjok Raja, 730
Summer Olympics, 474
Sunni Muslims, 712
Surachandra, 217
And Tikendrajit, Sons of Chandrakirti, 188
Singh, Maharaja, 192-195, 201
Singh, Maharaja, Son of Chandrakirti, 192
Suspension of Operation Agreement, 454
Swaradha Ceremony, (Death Rituals), 316
Swaraj Kaushal, 464
Sylhet, 150, 166, 173, 174, 705, 732, 734
District in Bangladesh, 801
Light Infantry, 183
Or Cachar of Assam, 296
Sylvan Gods, 858
Sylvan Gods who Played Sagol Kangjei, 846
Ikoppa, 846
Irongba, 846
Isumba, 846
Khamlangba, 846
Marjing, 846
Nongshaba, 846
Panthoiba, 846
Syrian Christian, 474
System of Cheithaba, 142
Szechuan Province of China, 561

T

Tae-Kwondo, Arjun Awardee, 818
Tagore, Rabindranath, 801
Tai Group, 705
Tai Pong Pan (Manipur), 135
Tai-Pong-Pan, 35
Taiwanese Foreign Minister, 468
Takhal (Tripura), 685
Takhembi, Khunjaoba Queen, 708
Tamenglong, 238, 398, 591
District Profile, 945
Geographical Indicators, 944
Tamil Nadu, Kerala, Andhra Pradesh, 303
Tamu
Column, 200
Town (Burma), 174, 202, 949
Tangkhul
Dialect, 525, 746
Food, 934
Defined, 516
Folk Song, 518
Migration of-, 516
Naga Leader, 489
Of Ukhrul, 746
Origin, 518-521
Population, 516
Religion, 931
Rich Folklore, 518
Scripts, 41
Women, 430

Tangkhuls, 40, 41, 139, 295, 479, 487, 515-551, 930
And Meiteis Relationship, 521
Art and Culture, 540
Belief of Heaven and Hell, 526
Church, 750
Costume, 41, 42
Customs, 41, 528
Dialect, 525
Disposal of The Dead, 528, 529
Districts, 943
Sub-divisions, 943
Economy, 533
Festivals, 534
Chumphut Phanit, 535
Darrio, 535
Darshut Phanit, 535
Kathi Kasham, 537-539
Longra Khameng, 536
Luira Phanit, 534
Mang-Khap, 535
Thisham Phanit, 536
Yarra, 535
Folk, Folktales and Folksongs, 520, 521
Folksongs and Folklores, 540
Hair Style, 523
Hills, 522
Implements or Ornaments, 525
In Manipur, 462
Laa khanganui (Virgin Dance), 540
Language, 525
Marriages, 528
Music and Dances, 539
Musical Instruments, 539
Ollobii Kada, 539
Pena, 539
Saringda, 539
Tinglila, 539
Occupation, 523
Of Mongolian Race, 522
Ornaments, 519, 523
Poisoned Bows and Arrows, 525
Refined Customary Laws, 531
Religion or Hao Religion, 526
Saba, 41
Shawl—Changkhom, 519
Society, 528
Swearing and Oath Taking, 533
Tattooing, 523
Textile and Clothes, 541
War-Head Taking, 531
Warrior, 531
Weapons, 523
Women, 522
Zeliangrong Naga Tribe, 943
Tangpabela, 136
Tangsam, 382
Taningganway, Ava King, 720
Tanu Town, 592, 730
Taobaia, Smoke God, 34
Taoroinai, Snake God, 578
Taothabi, Rice Variety, 145
Tarao, Minor Community, 403
Tarpan Kalpa, 150
Tarpan Utshop, 192, 193
Tartar Hoho, 453
Tattooing, 440
Tax
Collection, 406
Free Land, 128
Tazoe, Maj. Gen, 774
Tea
Gardens, 437
Industry, 1014, 1015
Plantation Area in Manipur, 1014

Teak Gurjan Forests, 72
Techniques of Pottery, 892
Tekhao (Tripura), 147, 149
Telecom Infrastructure in Manipur, 1004
Temple,
  Shri Govindjee, 23
  Abdeitya, 667, 924
  Bijoy Govinda at Sabolband, 669
  Brindabanchandra, 195, 582
  Gopinath, 924
  Gopinath at Ningthoukhong, 667, 674
  Govindjee, 165, 219, 220, 243, 244, 579, 587
  Hanuman Thakur, 913
  IBudhou Thangjing, 677, 924
  Kalika, 579
  Kamakhya, 674
  Lai Yum, 134
  Leimapokpam Keirungba, 660, 661
  Lord Krishna, 579, 657
  Lord Krishnachandra of Kakching, 664, 665
  Lord Senamahi Temple, 676
  Madan Mohan of Kongba, 671, 672
  Mahakali, 658
  Nara Singh of Kakching, 666
  Navaratna, 579
  Nityeinanda Prabhu, 671
  Of Hanuman, 716
  Of Ibudhou Thengjing, 589
  Of Shree Govindjee, 582
  Of Thangal General, 584
  Radha Madhav, 668, 924
  Ramji Prabhu, 669, 913
  Sanamahi, 579
  Shri Hanuman Thakur, 657
  Shree Govindjee, 658, 661, 662, 663
  Shree Shree Govindjee, 584, 913
  Sir Richard, 185
  Thangla General, 659
  Vishnu Temple of Bishnupur, 655, 656
  Vishnu, 655, 924
Temples and Monuments, 655-700
Ten Years (10) Agreement, 448
Tengnoupal, Highest Point of Indo-Burma Road, 25, 949
Terrace Cultivation, 432
Textile, 880-908
Textile of
  Meiteis, 884
  Nagas, 887
  Phalengchi, 888
  Tangkhuls, 887
Th. Muivah, Gen. Secy. NNC, 458
Thabal, 671
Thado-Kuki Pioneer Mission, 747
Thadominbya, Shan King, 148
Thadou,
  Dialect, 404
  Marriage, 404
  Old Kuki Groups, 403
  Population, 404
Thadous Hmars Paites Group, 928
Thai-Cambodian Border, 460
Thailand, 460
Thailand, Laos, South West China, 983
Thamgal Tribesmen, 147
Thangal
  Baptist Association (TBA), 751
  Gen., 198, 199, 206, 207, 744, 580, 584, 742, 743

Trial, 585
Trial and Execution of-, 743
Thange Island, 132
Thangjaba Chakrapani, General, 153
Thangkairol, Art of Sword Fighting, 832
Thang-Ta, 185, 430, 739, 827
  Ethics, 828
  Techniques, 828
  Traditional Martial Art of Manipur, 827, 828
Thangwai Ningthou Kyaamba, 143
Thaoba Singh Phanjao Jamedar, 214
The Morung, Youth's Dormitory, 436, 437
Theatre Groups, 345
  Aryan Theatre, 345
  Chitrangda Natya Mandir, 345
  Marup Dramatic Union, 345
  Rup Mahal, 345
  Society Theatre, 345
Thendu, 438
Thendu Group, 434
Thengou Training, 831
Thengou, Sacred Ritualistic Movement, 830
Thibon Dynasty of Mandlay, 405
Thieks, 397
Thiempu (Priest), 565
Third
  Anglo-Burman War, (1885), 189
  Reich, 475
Thok Lila, 343
Thokchom Boro Singh, 234
Thongbam Yumjai, 226
Throne of Assam, 725
Tibet and Nepal, 864
Tibeto Burman, 397
  Languages, 37
  Mongoloid Ethnic Group, 40
  Races, 37
Tikendrajit Singh, 193-199, 202
  Cremation at Heicham yaichanu Pat at Janamsthan Yaiskail, 744
  Maharaja, 580, 582, 736, 742, 743
  Trial, 744
  Trial and Execution, 202, 203, 206, 743
Title of Manipuri Queens, 230
Tobacco, 144
  Plants, 36
Tomb of Naga Mother, 937
Tomgkuls, 748
Tomlin, Rev. Jacob, 745
Tonjao Singh Mangsataba, Jamedar, 214
Toother, May, 191
Top Chingtha, 145
Torah and Gospals, 712
Tourist,
  Baggage Re-Export Form (TBRE), 8
  Information Centres, 15
  Spots in Imphal West District, (IWD), 922
  Kakching, 922
  Khongjom, 922
  Pallel, 923
  Sugnu, 922
  Thoubal, 922
  Waithou, 922
Tourist Spots, 576-607, 932
  Govindajee Temple, 576
  Hanuman Temple, 576
  Kali Temple, 576
  Kangla Fort, 577-583
  Khwaramband Keithel, 576
  Manipur State Museum, 576
  Pologround, 576

Shaheed Minar, 576
Shirui Kashung—MATA Industrial Complex, 932
War Cemetery, 576
Towns and Business Centres, 302
Churachandpur, 302
Imphal, 302
Moreh, 302
TPD (200) Plant, 994
Trade
And Commerce, 118
Route Between Assam and Manipur, 176
Tradition of Ningthou, 314
Traditional
Craftsmen, 25
Laws and Customs, 434
Semantic Rituals, 294
Traditional Cloth of Vaiphei, 406
Khiangkawi, 406
Puandum, 406
Thansua, 406
Traditions of Wariliba and Lairik Thiba, 165
Trans-Asian
Highways, 973
Movement (ASM), 975
Transfer of
Kabow Valley to Burma, 178
Land, 558
Power, 247
Transport Subsidy, 986
Transportation of Life, 213, 214
Travel Insurance, 18
Treaty of
1762, 734
1833, 178, 734
1834, 178
Signatory of the Treaty, 180
Yandabo, 172, 174
Yandabo, (Details), 731, 734
Tree Cult, 339
Trees of Manipur Details, 74-76
Tribal
Chiefs, 220
Converts of Manipur, 750
Development Blocks, 928
Groups, 491, 566, 751, 951
Koirengs, 751
Koms, 751
Kukis, 751
Liangmeis, 751
Rongmeis, 751
Tangkhuls, 751
Language, 748
Leaders, 467
Population, 220, 744, 753
Shawls, 884
Textile and Basketry, 585
Tribes, 39, 294, 296, 428, 445, 753, 764, 1056
Anal, 750
Angamese, (Angamis), 188, 428, 445
Ao, 428
Bokul, 667
Chakpa, 135
Cheng Lei, 847
Clothe, 750
Hmar, 753
Katcha Nagas, 445
Kham, 135
Khamlangba, 665
Khu, 135
Kuki, 445, 753
Language, 750

Lhotas, 428, 445
Liangmei, 764
Lushai, 753
Maring, 325, 951
Mishmi, 562
Mizo, 397
Mon, 135
Naga, 135, 206
Nung, 135
Of Kukis, 749
Gangta, 749
Hmar, 749
Kuki, 749
Paite, 749
Vaiphei, 749
Zou and Simte, 749
Of Manipur (31 in number), 794
Of Tibeto-Burman, 517
Quiron-Naga, 147

Tribes of-, 429
Indonesia, 429
Myanmar, 429
Philippines, 429
Thailand, 429
Paite, 753
Poumai, 399
Ralte, 401
Rangmas, 445
Rongmei, 764
Salhte, 401
Sema, 401, 445
Simte, 401
Tangkhul, 753
Thadou, 753
Tiddim Chin, 753
Zemis, 764
Zou, 408, 409, 410, 752

Trilok Singh, 213

Tripple Cropping, 920

Tripura, 36, 138, 145, 246, 710
Tse Tung's Ideology, 459

Tucker, Commissioner of Sylhet, 726

Tuensang of NEFA, 449, 486

Tuisomjang Village, 396

Tuli Naga Regiment, 206

Tulis,
Army Regiments, 124
The Tulihan—Aya-Pural Tuli, 124

Tulsi Plant, 316

Tung-Pasian, God, 396

Turkomans and Persians, 858

Tusk Kukis, 1'47

Types of Worship, 145
Charat, 145
Karat, 145
Marat, 145

Typical Raas Lila Steps, 796, 797
Krishnadehisar, 796
Radha Gupi Abhisar—Radha Nartan, 797

U

U Aungsan, VP, Burmese Interim Govt., 233

U Nu, Burmese PM, 258, 450

UAE, 1041

UK, 1041

Ukhrul, 238, 479, 591, 592, 746
Church, 746
Home of Tangkhuls, 515

ULFA (United Liberation Front of Assam), 462, 470

Umang Lai (Population), 339
Moirang Thangjing—Yamjao Lairombi, 339

Umang Lai, (Forest Deity), 334, 335, 337, 338
God, 361
Haraoba, 41
Temple, 341
UN
Aided Projects, 3
Commission on Human Rights, 470
Declaration, 466
General Assembly, 466
Human Rights Organization, 460, 470
People's Organization (UNPO), 460
Working Group on Indigenous People (UNWGIP), 460, 470
Underground Movements, 232
Ungo Ching, 234
Unification
of All Naga Areas, 483
of Nagas, 464
Unilateral Cease Fire, 465
United
Liberation
Front (UNLF), 462
Front of the Seven Sisters (ULFSS), 461
Naga Council (UNC), 471, 482
States of America (US), 8, 235, 752
Army at Camp Upton in Yaphank, 451
Role, 467
USA—England, 828
Unlawful Activities (Prevention) Act, 1967, 457
Unqo Ching Hill Range, 143
Untouchability, 480
System, 472, 473
Ura Konthouba, 56
Urdu Singh Usurba, 211
Uttra, Ancestral Coronation Hill, 582

V

Vabbrubahan, 368
Vaiphei, 404, 405, 406, 752, 753
Baptist Association, (VPA), 751
Legend, 404
Society, 405
Traditional Religion, 406
Village, 406
Vaishnava Paths of Salvation, 719
Vaishnavism, 148, 150, 158, 165, 360, 363, 717, 827
As State Religion, 146
In Manipur, 479
Val Upasa, Chief of Buonzawl, 566
Valley
Assam, 446
Chindwin, 67, 429
Brahmputra River, 774
Hukawng, 37, 135
Indus, 719
Irrawady, 429
Kabow, 139, 141, 143, 168, 169, 174, 176-180, 182, 183, 234, 259, 562, 580, 655, 720, 724, 730, 734
Kangla, 576
Manipur, 37, 40, 58, 59, 134, 232, 245, 308, 576, 579, 591, 655, 662, 773, 774, 893
Varieties
of Fruits, 86
Orchids, 84-85

Ved Marwah, Governor of Assam, 673
Venezuela, 235
Venezuelan
  Revolutionary Army, 235
  War of Independence, 235
Vertebrates Faunas, 63
  Fishes—Common Otter, 63
Victory at Boyaca, 235
Vikramsila and Nalanda Universities, 301
  Ancient Indian Education Centres, 301
Village
  Administration, 384, 385, 402, 406, 558, 930
  Council, 384, 527
  Organization, 434
Viper Island, 742
Vishnu
  Temple, 655
  Worship, 656
Vivekananda, Swamy, 303
Vrindaban, 167, 168, 175, 194, 717, 735, 740, 795, 797, 798

W

Wagha Border, 970
Waikhong Salt Spring, 254
Waitheu Lake, 4
Wangmanao Silheika, 136
Wankhei, 912
Wanmkheirakpa, 200
War
  Cemeteries, 23, 586, 779, 913, 914
  Dances, 41
  Ta-Khonsaba, 41
  Tenkappa, 41
  Thang Hainaba, 41
  Tactics, 739
  Techniques, 294
Ward, Frank Kingdon, 83
Water
  Falls, 947
  Supply Plant, 222
Waterfalls, 60
  Barak Waterfalls—Khayang Waterfalls, 60
Watt, Sir George, 3
Weapons from Thailand, 465
Welsh
  Calvinistic Methodist Foreign Mission Society, 745
  Missionaries, 406
Western Sumi Totimi Hoho (WSTH), 462
Wet Temperate Forests, 69
Widow
  Marriage, 528
  Remarriage, 396, 557
Wildlife, 60
  (Protection) Act, 1972, 8
  Animal Skins, 8
  Species, 8
Wodaobi, Outdoor Game, 825
Wokha, 442
Women
  Agitation Leaders, 759
  In Head Hunting, 432
Women's
  Agitation, 760, 772
  Football Federation of India, 818
Market, 583, 584
Movement, 771
  Society, 750
Wongkhei—Utlou, 884

World
First Polo Club (Silcher), 850
Trade Towers, 491
War I, 221, 443, 444, 446, 816
War II, 2, 3, 24, 224, 232, 233, 447, 475, 516, 582, 671, 751, 772, 778, 779
War II and Manipur, 231
Wrestling, Common Game of Kukis, 560

Y

Yairipok and Thoubal, 918
Yaishkullapa, 165
Yaithibis, 294, 295, 363-366, 377, 479
Yamamoto Force, 774, 776
Yanagida, Motoso, Japanese Lt. Gen., 774, 776
Yandabo, 731-733
Peace Mission, 732
Yangoupokpi Lokchao Wildlife Sanctuary, 63
Yek Salai, 312
Yeks of Meiteis, 225
Yengkhoiba (Yenkhoiba), Maj., 201, 737, 739
Yenkhoiba Poile, 200
Yervada Jail, 473
Yimrap, 766
Yin and Shan Dynasties of China, 516
Yogendra Singh, 744
Yongchak, Popular Food among Manipuris, 1016
Youth Dormitory, 565
Yubi Lakpi, Coconut Capturing Game, 825
Yubraj Tikendrajit, 586
Yum
Changba Puya, Sacred Book, 133
Mangba (Birth-Death Pollution), 313
Mangba (Ritual Pollution), 311
Yumjao Ka Manga, Standard Meitei House, 315
Yumnaks, 309-312
Creation of-, 310
Yunnan Province of China, 137, 143, 468, 516, 517, 974, 975
Yuntung Shan, 562

Z

Zakulaisen, Women's Blouse, 571
Zasibito Nagi, 450
Zeliangrong, 497
Areas, 408
Baptist Association, 751
Community, 407
Groups, 407
Liangmei, 401
Rongmei, 401
Zemei, 401
Movement, 408, 764
Nagas, 766, 944
Patriarchal Social System, 944
Tribes, 943
Liangmei, 943
Pumei, 943
Rongmei, 943
Zemei, 943
Zemi Naga, 439
Zila
Durbar at Cachar, 186
Parishad, 910
Zilangamba, 196
Zingiang Province China, 517
Zionist Association, 752

Zo Ethnic Groups, 552
Zomi (s), 408-410, 552
Liberation Front, 470
Revolutionary Army (ZRA), 461, 470
Zou (s), 752
Agricultural Labour, 410
Community, 410
Conference, 410
Origin, 408